EUGENE O'NEILL

EUGENE O'NEILL

COMPLETE PLAYS
1932–1943

THE LIBRARY OF AMERICA

Volume arrangement, notes, and chronology copyright © 1988 by
Literary Classics of the United States, Inc., New York, N.Y.

Ah, Wilderness! © 1933, renewed 1960; *Days Without End* © 1934,
renewed 1961; *The Iceman Cometh* © 1946, renewed 1974. Published
by arrangement with Random House, Inc.

A Touch of the Poet © 1946, renewed 1973; *A Moon for the
Misbegotten* © 1945, renewed 1973. Published by arrangement
with PAC Holding S.A.

Long Day's Journey into Night © 1956, renewed 1984. Published by
arrangement with PAC Holding S.A. and Yale University.

Hughie © 1959, renewed 1987. Published by arrangement with
Yale University.

The text of *More Stately Mansions* is © 1988 and published by
arrangement with Oxford University Press.

The paper used in this publication meets the
minimum requirements of the American National Standard for
Information Sciences—Permanence of Paper for Printed
Library Materials, ANSI Z39.48—1984.

Distributed to the trade in the United States
and Canada by the Viking Press.

Library of Congress Catalog Card Number: 88-50687
For cataloging information, see end of *Notes* section.
ISBN 0-940450-50-X

―――――

First Printing
The Library of America—42

92042006

Manufactured in the United States of America

TRAVIS BOGARD
WROTE THE NOTES AND SELECTED
THE TEXTS FOR THIS VOLUME

Grateful acknowledgment is made to the National Endowment for the Humanities, the Ford Foundation, and the Andrew W. Mellon Foundation for their generous support of this series.

Contents

AH, WILDERNESS!

TO GEORGE JEAN NATHAN

who also, once upon a time, in peg-top trousers
went the pace that kills along the road to ruin

CHARACTERS

NAT MILLER, *owner of the* Evening Globe

ESSIE, *his wife*

ARTHUR

RICHARD

MILDRED *their children*

TOMMY

SID DAVIS, *Essie's brother*

LILY MILLER, *Nat's sister*

DAVID MCCOMBER

MURIEL MCCOMBER, *his daughter*

WINT SELBY, *a classmate of Arthur's at Yale*

BELLE

NORAH

BARTENDER

SALESMAN

SCENES

ACT ONE

Sitting-room of the Miller home in a large small-town in Connecticut—early morning, July 4th, 1906.

ACT TWO

Dining-room of the Miller home—evening of the same day.

ACT THREE
SCENE ONE

Back room of a bar in a small hotel—10 o'clock the same night.

SCENE TWO

Same as Act One—the sitting-room of the Miller home—a little after 11 o'clock the same night.

ACT FOUR
SCENE ONE

The Miller sitting-room again—about 1 o'clock the following afternoon.

SCENE TWO

A strip of beach along the harbor—about 9 o'clock that night.

SCENE THREE

Same as Scene One—the sitting-room—about 10 o'clock the same night.

Ah, Wilderness!

ACT ONE

SCENE —*Sitting-room of the Miller home in a large small-town in Connecticut —about 7.30 in the morning of July 4th, 1906.*

The room is fairly large, homely looking and cheerful in the morning sunlight, furnished with scrupulous medium-priced tastelessness of the period. Beneath the two windows at left, front, a sofa with silk and satin cushions stands against the wall. At rear of sofa, a bookcase with glass doors, filled with cheap sets, extends along the remaining length of wall. In the rear wall, left, is a double doorway with sliding doors and portières, leading into a dark, windowless, back parlor. At right of this doorway, another bookcase, this time a small, open one, crammed with boys' and girls' books and the best-selling novels of many past years —books the family really have read. To the right of this bookcase is the mate of the double doorway at its left, with sliding doors and portières, this one leading to a well-lighted front parlor. In the right wall, rear, a screen door opens on a porch. Farther forward in this wall are two windows, with a writing desk and a chair between them. At center is a big, round table with a green-shaded reading lamp, the cord of the lamp running up to one of five sockets in the chandelier above. Five chairs are grouped about the table —three rockers at left, right, and right rear of it, two armchairs at rear and left rear. A medium-priced, inoffensive rug covers most of the floor. The walls are papered white with a cheerful, ugly blue design.

Voices are heard in a conversational tone from the dining-room beyond the back parlor, where the family are just finishing breakfast. Then Mrs. Miller's voice, raised commandingly, "Tommy! Come back here and finish your milk!" *At the same moment Tommy appears in the doorway from the back parlor —a chubby, sun-burnt boy of eleven with dark eyes, blond hair wetted and plastered down in a part, and a shiny, good-natured face, a rim of milk visible about his lips. Bursting with bottled-up energy and a longing to get started on the Fourth, he nevertheless has hesitated obediently at his mother's call.*

TOMMY—(*calls back pleadingly*) Aw, I'm full, Ma. And I said excuse me and you said all right. (*His father's voice is heard*

5

speaking to his mother. Then she calls: "All right, Tommy," *and Tommy asks eagerly*) Can I go out now?

MOTHER'S VOICE—(*correctingly*) May I!

TOMMY—(*fidgeting, but obediently*) May I, Ma?

MOTHER'S VOICE—Yes. (*Tommy jumps for the screen door to the porch at right like a sprinter released by the starting shot.*)

FATHER'S VOICE—(*shouts after him*) But you set off your crackers away from the house, remember! (*But Tommy is already through the screen door, which he leaves open behind him.*)

(*A moment later the family appear from the back parlor, coming from the dining-room. First are Mildred and Arthur. Mildred is fifteen, tall and slender, with big, irregular features, resembling her father to the complete effacing of any pretense at prettiness. But her big, gray eyes are beautiful; she has vivacity and a fetching smile, and everyone thinks of her as an attractive girl. She is dressed in shirtwaist and skirt in the fashion of the period.*

(*Arthur, the eldest of the Miller children who are still living home, is nineteen. He is tall, heavy, barrel-chested and muscular, the type of football lineman of that period, with a square, stolid face, small blue eyes and thick sandy hair. His manner is solemnly collegiate. He is dressed in the latest college fashion of that day, which has receded a bit from the extreme of preceding years, but still runs to padded shoulders and pants half pegged at the top, and so small at their wide-cuffed bottoms that they cannot be taken off with shoes on.*)

MILDRED—(*as they appear—inquisitively*) Where are you going today, Art?

ARTHUR—(*with superior dignity*) That's my business. (*He ostentatiously takes from his pocket a tobacco pouch with a big Y and class numerals stamped on it, and a heavy bulldog briar pipe with silver Y and numerals, and starts filling the pipe.*)

MILDRED—(*teasingly*) Bet I know, just the same! Want me to tell you her initials? E. R.! (*She laughs. Arthur, pleased by this insinuation at his lady-killing activities, yet finds it beneath his dignity to reply. He goes to the table, lights his pipe and picks up the local morning paper, and slouches back into the armchair at left rear of table, beginning to whistle "Oh, Waltz Me Around Again, Willie" as he scans the headlines. Mildred sits on the sofa at left, front.*)

(*Meanwhile, their mother and their Aunt Lily, their father's sister, have appeared, following them from the back parlor. Mrs. Miller is around fifty, a short, stout woman with fading light-brown hair sprinkled with gray, who must have been decidedly pretty as a girl in a round-faced, cute, small-featured, wide-eyed fashion. She has big brown eyes, soft and maternal—a bustling, mother-of-a-family manner. She is dressed in shirtwaist and skirt.*

(*Lily Miller, her sister-in-law, is forty-two, tall, dark and thin. She conforms outwardly to the conventional type of old-maid school teacher, even to wearing glasses. But behind the glasses her gray eyes are gentle and tired, and her whole atmosphere is one of shy kindliness. Her voice presents the greatest contrast to her appearance—soft and full of sweetness. She, also, is dressed in a shirtwaist and skirt.*)

MRS. MILLER—(*as they appear*) Getting milk down him is like— (*Suddenly she is aware of the screen door standing half open.*) Goodness, look at that door he's left open! The house will be alive with flies! (*rushing out to shut it*) I've told him again and again—and that's all the good it does! It's just a waste of breath! (*She slams the door shut.*)

LILY—(*smiling*) Well, you can't expect a boy to remember to shut doors—on the Fourth of July. (*She goes diffidently to the straight-backed chair before the desk at right, front, leaving the comfortable chairs to the others.*)

MRS. MILLER—That's you all over, Lily—always making excuses for him. You'll have him spoiled to death in spite of me. (*She sinks in rocker at right of table.*) Phew, I'm hot, aren't you? This is going to be a scorcher. (*She picks up a magazine from the table and begins to rock, fanning herself.*)

(*Meanwhile, her husband and her brother have appeared from the back parlor, both smoking cigars. Nat Miller is in his late fifties, a tall, dark, spare man, a little stoop-shouldered, more than a little bald, dressed with an awkward attempt at sober respectability imposed upon an innate heedlessness of clothes. His long face has large, irregular, undistinguished features, but he has fine, shrewd, humorous gray eyes.*

(*Sid Davis, his brother-in-law, is forty-five, short and fat, bald-headed, with the Puckish face of a Peck's Bad Boy who has never grown up. He is dressed in what had once been a very natty loud light suit but is now a shapeless and faded nondescript in cut and color.*)

SID—(*as they appear*) Oh, I like the job first rate, Nat. Waterbury's a nifty old town with the lid off, when you get to know the ropes. I rang in a joke in one of my stories that tickled the folks there pink. Waterwagon—Waterbury—Waterloo!

MILLER—(*grinning*) Darn good!

SID—(*pleased*) I thought it was pretty fair myself. (*goes on a bit ruefully, as if oppressed by a secret sorrow*) Yes, you can see life in Waterbury, all right—that is, if you're looking for life in Waterbury!

MRS. MILLER—What's that about Waterbury, Sid?

SID—I was saying it's all right in its way—but there's no place like home. (*As if to punctuate this remark, there begins a series of bangs from just beyond the porch outside, as Tommy inaugurates his celebration by setting off a package of firecrackers. The assembled family jump in their chairs.*)

MRS. MILLER—That boy! (*She rushes to the screen door and out on the porch, calling*) Tommy! You mind what your Pa told you! You take your crackers out in the back yard, you hear me!

ARTHUR—(*frowning scornfully*) Fresh kid! He did it on purpose to scare us.

MILLER—(*grinning through his annoyance*) Darned youngster! He'll have the house afire before the day's out.

SID—(*grins and sings*)
"Dunno what ter call 'im
But he's mighty like a Rose—velt."
(*They all laugh.*)

LILY—Sid, you Crazy! (*Sid beams at her. Mrs. Miller comes back from the porch, still fuming.*)

MRS. MILLER—Well, I've made him go out back at last. Now we'll have a little peace. (*As if to contradict this, the bang of firecrackers and torpedoes begins from the rear of the house, left, and continues at intervals throughout the scene, not nearly so loud as the first explosion, but sufficiently emphatic to form a disturbing punctuation to the conversation.*)

MILLER—Well, what's on the tappee for all of you today? Sid, you're coming to the Sachem Club picnic with me, of course.

SID—(*a bit embarrassedly*) You bet. I mean I'd like to, Nat—that is, if—

MRS. MILLER—(*regarding her brother with smiling suspicion*) Hmm! I know what that Sachem Club picnic's always meant!

LILY—(*breaks in in a forced joking tone that conceals a deep earnestness*) No, not this time, Essie. Sid's a reformed character since he's been on the paper in Waterbury. At least, that's what he swore to me last night.

SID—(*avoiding her eyes, humiliated—joking it off*) Pure as the driven snow, that's me. They're running me for president of the W.C.T.U. (*They all laugh.*)

MRS. MILLER—Sid, you're a caution. You turn everything into a joke. But you be careful, you hear? We're going to have dinner in the evening tonight, you know—the best shore dinner you ever tasted and I don't want you coming home— well, not able to appreciate it.

LILY—Oh, I know he'll be careful today. Won't you, Sid?

SID—(*more embarrassed than ever—joking it off melodramatically*) Lily, I swear to you if any man offers me a drink, I'll kill him—that is, if he changes his mind! (*They all laugh except Lily, who bites her lip and stiffens.*)

MRS. MILLER—No use talking to him, Lily. You ought to know better by this time. We can only hope for the best.

MILLER—Now, you women stop picking on Sid. It's the Fourth of July and even a downtrodden newspaperman has a right to enjoy himself when he's on his holiday.

MRS. MILLER—I wasn't thinking only of Sid.

MILLER—(*with a wink at the others*) What, are you insinuating I ever—?

MRS. MILLER—Well, to do you justice, no, not what you'd really call— But I've known you to come back from this darned Sachem Club picnic— Well, I didn't need any little bird to whisper that you'd been some place besides to the well! (*She smiles good-naturedly. Miller chuckles.*)

SID—(*after a furtive glance at the stiff and silent Lily— changes the subject abruptly by turning to Arthur*) How are you spending the festive Fourth, Boola-Boola? (*Arthur stiffens dignifiedly.*)

MILDRED—(*teasingly*) I can tell you, if he won't.

MRS. MILLER—(*smiling*) Off to the Rands', I suppose.

ARTHUR—(*with dignity*) I and Bert Turner are taking Elsie and Ethel Rand canoeing. We're going to have a picnic lunch on Strawberry Island. And this evening I'm staying at the Rands' for dinner.

MILLER—You're accounted for, then. How about you, Mid?

MILDRED—I'm going to the beach to Anne Culver's.

ARTHUR—(*sarcastically*) Of course, there won't be any boys present! Johnny Dodd, for example?

MILDRED—(*giggles—then with a coquettish toss of her head*) Pooh! What do I care for him? He's not the only pebble on the beach.

MILLER—Stop your everlasting teasing, you two. How about you and Lily, Essie?

MRS. MILLER—I don't know. I haven't made any plans. Have you, Lily?

LILY—(*quietly*) No. Anything you want to do.

MRS. MILLER—Well, I thought we'd just sit around and rest and talk.

MILLER—You can gossip any day. This is the Fourth. Now, I've got a better suggestion than that. What do you say to an automobile ride? I'll get out the Buick and we'll drive around town and out to the lighthouse and back. Then Sid and I will let you off here, or anywhere you say, and we'll go on to the picnic.

MRS. MILLER—I'd love it. Wouldn't you, Lily?

LILY—It would be nice.

MILLER—Then, that's all settled.

SID—(*embarrassedly*) Lily, want to come with me to the fireworks display at the beach tonight?

MRS. MILLER—That's right, Sid. You take her out. Poor Lily never has any fun, always sitting home with me.

LILY—(*flustered and grateful*) I—I'd like to, Sid, thank you. (*Then an apprehensive look comes over her face.*) Only not if you come home—you know.

SID—(*again embarrassed and humiliated—again joking it off, solemnly*) Evil-minded, I'm afraid, Nat. I hate to say it of your sister. (*They all laugh. Even Lily cannot suppress a smile.*)

ARTHUR—(*with heavy jocularity*) Listen, Uncle Sid. Don't let me catch you and Aunt Lily spooning on a bench tonight—or it'll be my duty to call a cop! (*Sid and Lily both look painfully embarrassed at this, and the joke falls flat, except for Mildred who can't restrain a giggle at the thought of these two ancients spooning.*)

MRS. MILLER—(*rebukingly*) Arthur!

MILLER—(*dryly*) That'll do you. Your education in kicking a football around Yale seems to have blunted your sense of humor.

MRS. MILLER—(*suddenly—startledly*) But where's Richard? We're forgetting all about him. Why, where is that boy? I thought he came in with us from breakfast.

MILDRED—I'll bet he's off somewhere writing a poem to Muriel McComber, the silly! Or pretending to write one. I think he just copies—

ARTHUR—(*looking back toward the dining-room*) He's still in the dining-room, reading a book. (*turning back—scornfully*) Gosh, he's always reading now. It's not my idea of having a good time in vacation.

MILLER—(*caustically*) He read his school books, too, strange as that may seem to you. That's why he came out top of his class. I'm hoping before you leave New Haven they'll find time to teach you reading is a good habit.

MRS. MILLER—(*sharply*) That reminds me, Nat. I've been meaning to speak to you about those awful books Richard is reading. You've got to give him a good talking to— (*She gets up from her chair.*) I'll go up and get them right now. I found them where he'd hid them on the shelf in his wardrobe. You just wait till you see what— (*She bustles off, rear right, through the front parlor.*)

MILLER—(*plainly not relishing whatever is coming—to Sid, grumblingly*) Seems to me she might wait until the Fourth is over before bringing up— (*then with a grin*) I know there's nothing to it, anyway. When I think of the books I used to sneak off and read when I was a kid.

SID—Me, too. I suppose Dick is deep in Nick Carter or Old Cap Collier.

MILLER—No, he passed that period long ago. Poetry's his red meat nowadays, I think—love poetry—and socialism, too, I suspect, from some dire declarations he's made. (*then briskly*) Well, might as well get him on the carpet. (*He calls*)

Richard. (*no answer—louder*) Richard. (*no answer—then in a bellow*) Richard!

ARTHUR—(*shouting*) Hey, Dick, wake up! Pa's calling you.

RICHARD'S VOICE—(*from the dining-room*) All right. I'm coming.

MILLER—Darn him! When he gets his nose in a book, the house could fall down and he'd never—

(*Richard appears in the doorway from the back parlor, the book he has been reading in one hand, a finger marking his place. He looks a bit startled still, reluctantly called back to earth from another world.*

(*He is going on seventeen, just out of high school. In appearance he is a perfect blend of father and mother, so much so that each is convinced he is the image of the other. He has his mother's light-brown hair, his father's gray eyes; his features are neither large nor small; he is of medium height, neither fat nor thin. One would not call him a handsome boy; neither is he homely. But he is definitely different from both of his parents, too. There is something of extreme sensitiveness added—a restless, apprehensive, defiant, shy, dreamy, self-conscious intelligence about him. In manner he is alternately plain simple boy and a posey actor solemnly playing a role. He is dressed in prep. school reflection of the college style of Arthur.*)

RICHARD—Did you want me, Pa?

MILLER—I'd hoped I'd made that plain. Come and sit down a while. (*He points to the rocking chair at the right of table near his.*)

RICHARD—(*coming forward—seizing on the opportunity to play up his preoccupation—with apologetic superiority*) I didn't hear you, Pa. I was off in another world. (*Mildred slyly shoves her foot out so that he trips over it, almost falling. She laughs gleefully. So does Arthur.*)

ARTHUR—Good for you, Mid! That'll wake him up!

RICHARD—(*grins sheepishly—all boy now*) Darn you, Mid! I'll show you! (*He pushes her back on the sofa and tickles her with his free hand, still holding the book in the other. She shrieks.*)

ARTHUR—Give it to her, Dick!

MILLER—That's enough, now. No more roughhouse. You sit down here, Richard. (*Richard obediently takes the chair at right of table, opposite his father.*) What were you planning to do with yourself today? Going out to the beach with Mildred?

RICHARD—(*scornfully superior*) That silly skirt party! I should say not!

MILDRED—He's not coming because Muriel isn't. I'll bet he's got a date with her somewheres.

RICHARD—(*flushing bashfully*) You shut up! (*then to his father*) I thought I'd just stay home, Pa—this morning, anyway.

MILLER—Help Tommy set off firecrackers, eh?

RICHARD—(*drawing himself up—with dignity*) I should say not. (*then frowning portentously*) I don't believe in this silly celebrating the Fourth of July—all this lying talk about liberty—when there is no liberty!

MILLER—(*a twinkle in his eye*) Hmm.

RICHARD—(*getting warmed up*) The land of the free and the home of the brave! Home of the slave is what they ought to call it—the wage slave ground under the heel of the capitalist class, starving, crying for bread for his children, and all he gets is a stone! The Fourth of July is a stupid farce!

MILLER—(*putting a hand to his mouth to conceal a grin*) Hmm. Them are mighty strong words. You'd better not repeat such sentiments outside the bosom of the family or they'll have you in jail.

SID—And throw away the key.

RICHARD—(*darkly*) Let them put me in jail. But how about the freedom of speech in the Constitution, then? That must be a farce, too. (*Then he adds grimly*) No, you can celebrate your Fourth of July. I'll celebrate the day the people bring out the guillotine again and I see Pierpont Morgan being driven by in a tumbril! (*His father and Sid are greatly amused; Lily is shocked but, taking her cue from them, smiles. Mildred stares at him in puzzled wonderment, never having heard this particular line before. Only Arthur betrays the outraged reaction of a patriot.*)

ARTHUR—Aw say, you fresh kid, tie that bull outside! You ought to get a punch in the nose for talking that way on the Fourth!

MILLER—(*solemnly*) Son, if I didn't know it was you talking, I'd think we had Emma Goldman with us.

ARTHUR—Never mind, Pa. Wait till we get him down to Yale. We'll take that out of him!

RICHARD—(*with high scorn*) Oh, Yale! You think there's nothing in the world besides Yale. After all, what is Yale?

ARTHUR—You'll find out what!

SID—(*provocatively*) Don't let them scare you, Dick. Give 'em hell!

LILY—(*shocked*) Sid! You shouldn't swear before—

RICHARD—What do you think I am, Aunt Lily—a baby? I've heard worse than anything Uncle Sid says.

MILDRED—And said worse himself, I bet!

MILLER—(*with a comic air of resignation*) Well, Richard, I've always found I've had to listen to at least one stump speech every Fourth. I only hope getting your extra strong one right after breakfast will let me off for the rest of the day. (*They all laugh now, taking this as a cue.*)

RICHARD—(*somberly*) That's right, laugh! After you, the deluge, you think! But look out! Supposing it comes before? Why shouldn't the workers of the world unite and rise? They have nothing to lose but their chains! (*He recites threateningly*) "The days grow hot, O Babylon! 'Tis cool beneath thy willow trees!"

MILLER—Hmm. That's good. But where's the connection, exactly? Something from that book you're reading?

RICHARD—(*superior*) No. That's poetry. This is prose.

MILLER—I've heard there was a difference between 'em. What is the book?

RICHARD—(*importantly*) Carlyle's French Revolution.

MILLER—Hmm. So that's where you drove the tumbril from and piled poor old Pierpont in it. (*then seriously*) Glad you're reading it, Richard. It's a darn fine book.

RICHARD—(*with unflattering astonishment*) What, have you read it?

MILLER—Well, you see, even a newspaper owner can't get out of reading a book every now and again.

RICHARD—(*abashed*) I—I didn't mean—I know you— (*then enthusiastically*) Say, isn't it a great book, though—that part about Mirabeau—and about Marat and Robespierre—

MRS. MILLER—(*appears from the front parlor in a great state of flushed annoyance*) Never you mind Robespierre, young man! You tell me this minute where you've hidden those books! They were on the shelf in your wardrobe and now you've gone and hid them somewheres else. You go right up and bring them to your father! (*Richard, for a second, looks suddenly guilty and crushed. Then he bristles defensively.*)

MILLER—(*after a quick understanding glance at him*) Never mind his getting them now. We'll waste the whole morning over those darned books. And anyway, he has a right to keep his library to himself—that is, if they're not too— What books are they, Richard?

RICHARD—(*self-consciously*) Well—there's—

MRS. MILLER—I'll tell you, if he won't—and you give him a good talking to. (*then, after a glance at Richard, molli-fiedly*) Not that I blame Richard. There must be some boy he knows who's trying to show off as advanced and wicked, and he told him about—

RICHARD—No! I read about them myself, in the papers and in other books.

MRS. MILLER—Well, no matter how, there they were on his shelf. Two by that awful Oscar Wilde they put in jail for heaven knows what wickedness.

ARTHUR—(*suddenly—solemnly authoritative*) He commit-ted bigamy. (*then as Sid smothers a burst of ribald laughter*) What are you laughing at? I guess I ought to know. A fellow at college told me. His father was in England when this Wilde was pinched—and he said he remembered once his mother asked his father about it and he told her he'd committed bigamy.

MILLER—(*hiding a smile behind his hand*) Well then, that must be right, Arthur.

MRS. MILLER—I wouldn't put it past him, nor anything else. One book was called the Picture of something or other.

RICHARD—The Picture of Dorian Gray. It's one of the greatest novels ever written!

MRS. MILLER—Looked to me like cheap trash. And the second book was poetry. The Ballad of I forget what.

RICHARD—The Ballad of Reading Gaol, one of the great-est poems ever written. (*He pronounces it Reading Goal [as in goalpost].*)

MRS. MILLER—All about someone who murdered his wife

and got hung, as he richly deserved, as far as I could make out. And then there were two books by that Bernard Shaw—

RICHARD—The greatest playwright alive today!

MRS. MILLER—To hear him tell it, maybe! You know, Nat, the one who wrote a play about—well, never mind— that was so vile they wouldn't even let it play in New York!

MILLER—Hmm. I remember.

MRS. MILLER—One was a book of his plays and the other had a long title I couldn't make head or tail of, only it wasn't a play.

RICHARD—(*proudly*) The Quintessence of Ibsenism.

MILDRED—Phew! Good gracious, what a name! What does it mean, Dick? I'll bet he doesn't know.

RICHARD—(*outraged*) I do, too, know! It's about Ibsen, the greatest playwright since Shakespeare!

MRS. MILLER—Yes, there was a book of plays by that Ibsen there, too! And poems by Swin something—

RICHARD—Poems and Ballads by Swinburne, Ma. The greatest poet since Shelley! He tells the truth about real love!

MRS. MILLER—Love! Well, all I can say is, from reading here and there, that if he wasn't flung in jail along with Wilde, he should have been. Some of the things I simply couldn't read, they were so indecent— All about—well, I can't tell you before Lily and Mildred.

SID—(*with a wink at Richard—jokingly*) Remember, I'm next on that one, Dick. I feel the need of a little poetical education.

LILY—(*scandalized, but laughing*) Sid! Aren't you ashamed?

MRS. MILLER—This is no laughing matter. And then there was Kipling—but I suppose he's not so bad. And last there was a poem—a long one—the Rubay— What is it, Richard?

RICHARD—The Rubaiyat of Omar Khayyam. That's the best of all!

MILLER—Oh, I've read that, Essie—got a copy down at the office.

SID—(*enthusiastically*) So have I. It's a pippin!

LILY—(*with shy excitement*) I—I've read it, too—at the library. I like—some parts of it.

MRS. MILLER—(*scandalized*) Why, Lily!

MILLER—Everybody's reading that now, Essie—and it don't seem to do them any harm. There's fine things in it, seems to me—true things.

MRS. MILLER—(*a bit bewildered and uncertain now*) Why, Nat, I don't see how you— It looked terrible blasphemous— parts I read.

SID—Remember this one: (*he quotes rhetorically*) "Oh Thou, who didst with pitfall and gin beset the path I was to wander in—" Now, I've always noticed how beset my path was with gin—in the past, you understand! (*He casts a joking side glance at Lily. The others laugh. But Lily is in a melancholy dream and hasn't heard him.*)

MRS. MILLER—(*tartly, but evidently suppressing her usual smile where he is concerned*) You would pick out the ones with liquor in them!

LILY—(*suddenly—with a sad pathos, quotes awkwardly and shyly*) I like—because it's true:

> "The Moving Finger writes, and having writ,
> Moves on: nor all your Piety nor Wit
> Shall lure it back to cancel half a Line,
> Nor all your Tears wash out a Word of it."

MRS. MILLER—(*astonished, as are all the others*) Why, Lily, I never knew you to recite poetry before!

LILY—(*immediately guilty and apologetic*) I—it just stuck in my memory somehow.

RICHARD—(*looking at her as if he had never seen her before*) Good for you, Aunt Lily! (*then enthusiastically*) But that isn't the best. The best is:

> "A Book of Verses underneath the Bough,
> A Jug of Wine, A Loaf of Bread—and Thou
> Beside me singing in the Wilderness—"

ARTHUR—(*who, bored to death by all this poetry quoting, has wandered over to the window at rear of desk, right*) Hey! Look who's coming up the walk—Old Man McComber!

MILLER—(*irritably*) Dave? Now what in thunder does that damned old— Sid, I can see where we never are going to get to that picnic.

MRS. MILLER—(*vexatiously*) He'll know we're in this early, too. No use lying. (*then appalled by another thought*) That

Norah—she's that thick, she never can answer the front door right unless I tell her each time. Nat, you've got to talk to Dave. I'll have her show him in here. Lily, you run up the back stairs and get your things on. I'll be up in a second. Nat, you get rid of him the first second you can! Whatever can the old fool want— (*She and Lily hurry out through the back parlor.*)

ARTHUR—I'm going to beat it—just time to catch the eight-twenty trolley.

MILDRED—I've got to catch that, too. Wait till I get my hat, Art! (*She rushes into the back parlor.*)

ARTHUR—(*shouts after her*) I can't wait. You can catch up with me if you hurry. (*He turns at the back-parlor door—with a grin*) McComber may be coming to see if your intentions toward his daughter are dishonorable, Dick! You'd better beat it while your shoes are good! (*He disappears through the back-parlor door, laughing.*)

RICHARD—(*a bit shaken, but putting on a brave front*) Think I'm scared of him?

MILLER—(*gazing at him—frowning*) Can't imagine what— But it's to complain about something, I know that. I only wish I didn't have to be pleasant with the old buzzard—but he's about the most valuable advertiser I've got.

SID—(*sympathetically*) I know. But tell him to go to hell, anyway. He needs that ad more than you. (*The sound of the bell comes from the rear of the house, off left from back parlor.*)

MILLER—There he is. You clear out, Dick—but come right back as soon as he's gone, you hear? I'm not through with you, yet.

RICHARD—Yes, Pa.

MILLER—You better clear out, too, Sid. You know Dave doesn't approve jokes.

SID—And loves me like poison! Come on, Dick, we'll go out and help Tommy celebrate. (*He takes Richard's arm and they also disappear through the back-parlor door. Miller glances through the front parlor toward the front door, then calls in a tone of strained heartiness*)

MILLER—Hello, Dave. Come right in here. What good wind blows you around on this glorious Fourth?

(*A flat, brittle voice answers him: "Good morning," and a*

moment later David McComber appears in the doorway from the front parlor. He is a thin, dried-up little man with a head too large for his body perched on a scrawny neck, and a long solemn horse face with deep-set little black eyes, a blunt formless nose and a tiny slit of a mouth. He is about the same age as Miller but is entirely bald, and looks ten years older. He is dressed with a prim neatness in shiny old black clothes.)

MILLER—Here, sit down and make yourself comfortable. (*holding out the cigar box*) Have a cigar?

McCOMBER—(*sitting down in the chair at the right of table—acidly*) You're forgetting. I never smoke.

MILLER—(*forcing a laugh at himself*) That's so. So I was. Well, I'll smoke alone then. (*He bites off the end of the cigar viciously, as if he wished it were McComber's head, and sits down opposite him.*)

McCOMBER—You asked me what brings me here, so I'll come to the point at once. I regret to say it's something disagreeable—disgraceful would be nearer the truth—and it concerns your son, Richard!

MILLER—(*beginning to bristle—but calmly*) Oh, come now, Dave, I'm sure Richard hasn't—

McCOMBER—(*sharply*) And I'm positive he has. You're not accusing me of being a liar, I hope.

MILLER—No one said anything about liar. I only meant you're surely mistaken if you think—

McCOMBER—I'm not mistaken. I have proof of everything in his own handwriting!

MILLER—(*sharply*) Let's get down to brass tacks. Just what is it you're charging him with?

McCOMBER—With being dissolute and blasphemous—with deliberately attempting to corrupt the morals of my young daughter, Muriel.

MILLER—Then I'm afraid I will have to call you a liar, Dave!

McCOMBER—(*without taking offense—in the same flat, brittle voice*) I thought you'd get around to that, so I brought some of the proofs with me. I've a lot more of 'em at home. (*He takes a wallet from his inside coat pocket, selects five or six slips of paper, and holds them out to Miller.*) These are good samples of the rest. My wife discovered them in one of Muriel's bureau drawers hidden under the underwear. They're all in his handwriting, you can't deny it. Anyway, Muriel's confessed to me he wrote them. You read them and then say I'm a liar. (*Miller has taken the slips and is reading them frowningly. McComber talks on.*) Evidently you've been too busy to take the right care about Richard's bringing up or what he's allowed to read—though I can't see why his mother failed in her duty. But that's your misfortune, and none of my business. But Muriel is my business and I can't and I won't have her innocence exposed to the contamination of a young man whose mind, judging from his choice of reading matter, is as foul—

MILLER—(*making a tremendous effort to control his temper*) Why, you damned old fool! Can't you see Richard's only a fool kid who's just at the stage when he's out to rebel against all authority, and so he grabs at everything radical to read and wants to pass it on to his elders and his girl and boy friends to show off what a young hellion he is! Why, at heart you'd find Richard is just as innocent and as big a kid as Muriel is! (*He pushes the slips of paper across the table contemptuously.*) This stuff doesn't mean anything to me—that is, nothing of what you think it means. If you believe this would corrupt Muriel, then you must believe she's easily corrupted! But I'll bet you'd find she knows a lot more about life than you give her credit for—and can guess a stork didn't bring her down your chimney!

McCOMBER—Now you're insulting my daughter. I won't forget that.

MILLER—I'm not insulting her. I think Muriel is a darn nice girl. That's why I'm giving her credit for ordinary good sense. I'd say the same about my own Mildred, who's the same age.

McCOMBER—I know nothing about your Mildred except that she's known all over as a flirt. (*then more sharply*) Well, I knew you'd prove obstinate, but I certainly never dreamed you'd have the impudence, after reading those papers, to claim your son was innocent of all wrongdoing!

MILLER—And what did you dream I'd do?

McCOMBER—Do what it's your plain duty to do as a citizen to protect other people's children! Take and give him a hiding he'd remember to the last day of his life! You'd ought to do it for his sake, if you had any sense—unless you want him to end up in jail!

MILLER—(*his fists clenched, leans across the table*) Dave, I've stood all I can stand from you! You get out! And get out quick, if you don't want a kick in the rear to help you!

MCCOMBER—(*again in his flat, brittle voice, slowly getting to his feet*) You needn't lose your temper. I'm only demanding you do your duty by your own as I've already done by mine. I'm punishing Muriel. She's not to be allowed out of the house for a month and she's to be in bed every night by eight sharp. And yet she's blameless, compared to that—

MILLER—I said I'd had enough out of you, Dave! (*He makes a threatening movement.*)

MCCOMBER—You needn't lay hands on me. I'm going. But there's one thing more. (*He takes a letter from his wallet.*) Here's a letter from Muriel for your son. (*puts it on the table*) It makes clear, I think, how she's come to think about him, now that her eyes have been opened. I hope he heeds what's inside—for his own good and yours—because if I ever catch him hanging about my place again I'll have him arrested! And don't think I'm not going to make you regret the insults you've heaped on me. I'm taking the advertisement for my store out of your paper—and it won't go in again, I tell you, not unless you apologize in writing and promise to punish—

MILLER—I'll see you in hell first! As for your damned old ad, take it out and go to hell!

MCCOMBER—That's plain bluff. You know how badly you need it. So do I. (*He starts stiffly for the door.*)

MILLER—Here! Listen a minute! I'm just going to call *your* bluff and tell you that, whether you want to reconsider your decision or not, I'm going to refuse to print your damned ad after tomorrow! Put that in your pipe and smoke it! Furthermore, I'll start a campaign to encourage outside capital to open a dry-goods store in opposition to you that won't be the public swindle I can prove yours is!

MCCOMBER—(*a bit shaken by this threat—but in the same flat tone*) I'll sue you for libel.

MILLER—When I get through, there won't be a person in town will buy a dishrag in your place!

McCOMBER—(*more shaken, his eyes shifting about furtively*) That's all bluff. You wouldn't dare— (*Then finally he says uncertainly*) Well, good day. (*and turns and goes out. Nat stands looking after him. Slowly the anger drains from his face and leaves him looking a bit sick and disgusted. Sid appears from the back parlor. He is nursing a burn on his right hand, but his face is one broad grin of satisfaction.*)

SID—I burned my hand with one of Tommy's damned firecrackers and came in to get some vaseline. I was listening to the last of your scrap. Good for you, Nat! You sure gave him hell!

MILLER—(*dully*) Much good it'll do. He knows it was all talk.

SID—That's just what he don't know, Nat. The old skin-flint has a guilty conscience.

MILLER—Well, anyone who knows me knows I wouldn't use my paper for a dirty, spiteful trick like that—no matter what he did to me.

SID—Yes, everyone knows you're an old sucker, Nat, too decent for your own good. But McComber never saw you like this before. I tell you you scared the pants off him. (*He chuckles.*)

MILLER—(*still dejectedly*) I don't know what made me let go like that. The hell of skunks like McComber is that after being with them ten minutes you become as big skunks as they are.

SID—(*notices the slips of paper on the table*) What's this? Something he brought? (*He picks them up and starts to read.*)

MILLER—(*grimly*) Samples of the new freedom—from those books Essie found—that Richard's been passing on to Muriel to educate her. They're what started the rumpus. (*then frowning*) I've got to do something about that young anarchist or he'll be getting me, and himself, in a peck of trouble. (*then pathetically helpless*) But what can I do? Putting the curb bit on would make him worse. Then he'd have a harsh tyrant to defy. He'd love that, darn him!

SID—(*has been reading the slips, a broad grin on his face— suddenly he whistles*) Phew! This is a warm lulu for fair! (*He recites with a joking intensity*)

"My life is bitter with thy love; thine eyes
　　Blind me, thy tresses burn me, thy sharp sighs
　　Divide my flesh and spirit with soft sound—"
MILLER—(*with a grim smile*) Hmm. I missed that one.
That must be Mr. Swinburne's copy. I've never read him, but
I've heard something like that was the matter with him.

SID—Yes, it's labelled Swinburne—"Anactoria." Whatever
that is. But wait, watch and listen! The worst is yet to come!
(*He recites with added comic intensity*)
　　　　"That I could drink thy veins as wine, and eat
　　　　Thy breasts like honey, that from face to feet
　　　　Thy body were abolished and consumed,
　　　　And in my flesh thy very flesh entombed!"
MILLER—(*an irrepressible boyish grin coming to his face*) Hell
and hallelujah! Just picture old Dave digesting that for the
first time! Gosh, I'd give a lot to have seen his face! (*then a
trace of shocked reproof showing in his voice*) But it's no joking
matter. That stuff *is* warm—too damned warm, if you ask
me! I don't like this a damned bit, Sid. That's no kind of
thing to be sending a decent girl. (*more worriedly*) I thought
he was really stuck on her—as one gets stuck on a decent girl
at his age—all moonshine and holding hands and a kiss now
and again. But this looks—I wonder if he is hanging around
her to see what he can get? (*angrily*) By God, if that's true,
he deserves that licking McComber says it's my duty to give
him! I've got to draw the line somewhere!

SID—Yes, it won't do to have him getting any decent girl
in trouble.

MILLER—The only thing I can do is put it up to him
straight. (*with pride*) Richard'll stand up to his guns, no matter what. I've never known him to lie to me.

SID—(*at a noise from the back parlor, looks that way—in a
whisper*) Then now's your chance. I'll beat it and leave you
alone—see if the women folks are ready upstairs. We ought
to get started soon—if we're ever going to make that picnic.
(*He is halfway to the entrance to the front parlor as Richard enters from the back parlor, very evidently nervous about McComber's
call.*)

RICHARD—(*adopting a forced, innocent tone*) How's your
hand, Uncle Sid?

SID—All right, Dick, thanks—only hurts a little. (*He disappears. Miller watches his son frowningly. Richard gives him a quick side glance and grows more guiltily self-conscious.*)

RICHARD—(*forcing a snicker*) Gee, Pa, Uncle Sid's a bigger kid than Tommy is. He was throwing firecrackers in the air and catching them on the back of his hand and throwing 'em off again just before they went off—and one came and he wasn't quick enough, and it went off almost on top of—

MILLER—Never mind that. I've got something else to talk to you about besides firecrackers.

RICHARD—(*apprehensively*) What, Pa?

MILLER—(*suddenly puts both hands on his shoulders—quietly*) Look here, Son. I'm going to ask you a question, and I want an honest answer. I warn you beforehand if the answer is "yes" I'm going to punish you and punish you hard because you'll have done something no boy of mine ought to do. But you've never lied to me before, I know, and I don't believe, even to save yourself punishment, you'd lie to me now, would you?

RICHARD—(*impressed—with dignity*) I won't lie, Pa.

MILLER—Have you been trying to have something to do with Muriel—something you shouldn't—you know what I mean.

RICHARD—(*stares at him for a moment, as if he couldn't comprehend—then, as he does, a look of shocked indignation comes over his face*) No! What do you think I am, Pa? I never would! She's not that kind! Why, I—I love her! I'm going to marry her—after I get out of college! She's said she would! We're engaged!

MILLER—(*with great relief*) All right. That's all I wanted to know. We won't talk any more about it. (*He gives him an approving pat on the back.*)

RICHARD—I don't see how you could think— Did that old idiot McComber say that about me?

MILLER—(*joking now*) Shouldn't call your future father-in-law names, should you? 'Taint respectful. (*then after a glance at Richard's indignant face—points to the slips of paper on the table*) Well, you can't exactly blame old Dave, can you, when you read through that literature you wished on his innocent daughter?

RICHARD—(*sees the slips for the first time and is overcome by embarrassment, which he immediately tries to cover up with a superior carelessness*) Oh, so that's why. He found those, did he? I told her to be careful— Well, it'll do him good to read the truth about life for once and get rid of his old-fogy ideas.

MILLER—I'm afraid I've got to agree with him, though, that they're hardly fit reading for a young girl. (*then with subtle flattery*) They're all well enough, in their way, for you who're a man, but— Think it over, and see if you don't agree with me.

RICHARD—(*embarrassedly*) Aw, I only did it because I liked them—and I wanted her to face life as it is. She's so darned afraid of life—afraid of her Old Man—afraid of people saying this or that about her—afraid of being in love— afraid of everything. She's even afraid to let me kiss her. I thought, maybe, reading those things—they're beautiful, aren't they, Pa?— I thought they would give her the spunk to lead her own life, and not be—always thinking of being afraid.

MILLER—I see. Well, I'm afraid she's still afraid. (*He takes the letter from the table.*) Here's a letter from her he said to give you. (*Richard takes the letter from him uncertainly, his expression changing to one of apprehension. Miller adds with a kindly smile*) You better be prepared for a bit of a blow. But never mind. There's lots of other fish in the sea. (*Richard is not listening to him, but staring at the letter with a sort of fascinated dread. Miller looks into his son's face a second, then turns away, troubled and embarrassed.*) Darn it! I better go upstairs and get rigged out or I never will get to that picnic. (*He moves awkwardly and self-consciously off through the front parlor. Richard continues to stare at the letter for a moment—then girds up his courage and tears it open and begins to read swiftly. As he reads his face grows more and more wounded and tragic, until at the end his mouth draws down at the corners, as if he were about to break into tears. With an effort he forces them back and his face grows flushed with humiliation and wronged anger.*)

RICHARD—(*blurts out to himself*) The little coward! I hate her! She can't treat me like that! I'll show her! (*At the sound of voices from the front parlor, he quickly shoves the letter into the inside pocket of his coat and does his best to appear calm and*

*indifferent, even attempting to whistle "Waiting at the Church."
But the whistle peters out miserably as his mother, Lily and Sid
enter from the front parlor. They are dressed in all the elaborate
paraphernalia of motoring at that period—linen dusters, veils,
goggles, Sid in a snappy cap.)*

MRS. MILLER—Well, we're about ready to start at last, thank goodness! Let's hope no more callers are on the way. What did that McComber want, Richard, do you know? Sid couldn't tell us.

RICHARD—You can search me. Ask Pa.

MRS. MILLER—*(immediately sensing something "down" in his manner—going to him worriedly)* Why, whatever's the matter with you, Richard? You sound as if you'd lost your last friend! What is it?

RICHARD—*(desperately)* I—I don't feel so well—my stomach's sick.

MRS. MILLER—*(immediately all sympathy—smoothing his hair back from his forehead)* You poor boy! What a shame—on the Fourth, too, of all days! *(turning to the others)* Maybe I better stay home with him, if he's sick.

LILY—Yes, I'll stay, too.

RICHARD—*(more desperately)* No! You go, Ma! I'm not really sick. I'll be all right. You go. I want to be alone! *(Then, as a louder bang comes from in back as Tommy sets off a cannon cracker, he jumps to his feet.)* Darn Tommy and his darned firecrackers! You can't get any peace in this house with that darned kid around! Darn the Fourth of July, anyway! I wish we still belonged to England! *(He strides off in an indignant fury of misery through the front parlor.)*

MRS. MILLER—*(stares after him worriedly—then sighs philosophically)* Well, I guess he can't be so very sick—after that. *(She shakes her head.)* He's a queer boy. Sometimes I can't make head or tail of him.

MILLER—*(calls from the front door beyond the back parlor)* Come along, folks. Let's get started.

SID—We're coming, Nat. *(He and the two women move off through the front parlor.)*

(Curtain)

ACT TWO

SCENE—*Dining-room of the Miller home—a little after 6 o'clock in the evening of the same day.*

The room is much too small for the medium-priced, formidable dining-room set, especially now when all the leaves of the table are in. At left, toward rear, is a double doorway with sliding doors and portières leading into the back parlor. In the rear wall, left, is the door to the pantry. At the right of door is the china closet with its display of the family cut glass and fancy china. In the right wall are two windows looking out on a side lawn. In front of the windows is a heavy, ugly sideboard with three pieces of old silver on its top. In the left wall, extreme front, is a screen door opening on a side porch. A dark rug covers most of the floor. The table, with a chair at each end, left and right, three chairs on the far side, facing front, and two on the near side, their backs to front, takes up most of the available space. The walls are papered in a somber brown and dark-red design.

Mrs. Miller is supervising and helping the Second Girl, Norah, in the setting of the table. Norah is a clumsy, heavy-handed, heavy-footed, long-jawed, beamingly good-natured young Irish girl—a "greenhorn."

MRS. MILLER—I really think you better put on the lights, Norah. It's getting so cloudy out, and this pesky room is so dark, anyway.

NORAH—Yes, Mum. (*She stretches awkwardly over the table to reach the chandelier that is suspended from the middle of the ceiling and manages to turn one light on—scornfully*) Arrah, the contraption!

MRS. MILLER—(*worriedly*) Careful!

NORAH—Careful as can be, Mum. (*But in moving around to reach the next bulb she jars heavily against the table.*)

MRS. MILLER—There! I knew it! I do wish you'd watch—!

NORAH—(*a flustered appeal in her voice*) Arrah, what have I done wrong now?

MRS. MILLER—(*draws a deep breath—then sighs helplessly*) Oh, nothing. Never mind the rest of the lights. You might as well go out in the kitchen and wait until I ring.

27

NORAH—(*relieved and cheerful again*) Yes, Mum. (*She starts for the pantry.*)

MRS. MILLER—But there's one thing— (*Norah turns apprehensively.*) No, two things—things I've told you over and over, but you always forget. Don't pass the plates on the wrong side at dinner tonight, and do be careful not to let that pantry door slam behind you. Now you will try to remember, won't you?

NORAH—Yes, Mum. (*She goes into the pantry and shuts the door behind her with exaggerated care as Mrs. Miller watches her apprehensively. Mrs. Miller sighs and reaches up with difficulty and turns on another of the four lights in the chandelier. As she is doing so, Lily enters from the back parlor.*)

LILY—Here, let me do that, Essie. I'm taller. You'll only strain yourself. (*She quickly lights the other two bulbs.*)

MRS. MILLER—(*gratefully*) Thank you, Lily. It's a stretch for me, I'm getting so fat.

LILY—But where's Norah? Why didn't she—?

MRS. MILLER—(*exasperatedly*) Oh, that girl! Don't talk about her! She'll be the death of me! She's that thick, you honestly wouldn't believe it possible.

LILY—(*smiling*) Why, what did she do now?

MRS. MILLER—Oh, nothing. She means all right.

LILY—Anything else I can do, Essie?

MRS. MILLER—Well, she's got the table all wrong. We'll have to reset it. But you're always helping me. It isn't fair to ask you—in your vacation. You need your rest after teaching a pack of wild Indians of kids all year.

LILY—(*beginning to help with the table*) You know I love to help. It makes me feel I'm some use in this house instead of just sponging—

MRS. MILLER—(*indignantly*) Sponging! You pay, don't you?

LILY—Almost nothing. And you and Nat only take that little to make me feel better about living with you. (*forcing a smile*) I don't see how you stand me—having a cranky old maid around all the time.

MRS. MILLER—What nonsense you talk! As if Nat and I weren't only too tickled to death to have you! Lily Miller, I've no patience with you when you go on like that. We've been over this a thousand times before, and still you go on! Crazy, that's what it is! (*She changes the subject abruptly.*) What time's it getting to be?

LILY—(*looking at her watch*) Quarter past six.

MRS. MILLER—I do hope those men folks aren't going to be late for dinner. (*She sighs.*) But I suppose with that darned Sachem Club picnic it's more likely than not. (*Lily looks worried, and sighs. Mrs. Miller gives her a quick side glance.*) I see you've got your new dress on.

LILY—(*embarrassedly*) Yes, I thought—if Sid's taking me to the fireworks—I ought to spruce up a little.

MRS. MILLER—(*looking away*) Hmm. (*A pause—then she says with an effort to be casual*) You mustn't mind if Sid comes home feeling a bit—gay. I expect Nat to—and we'll have to listen to all those old stories of his about when he was a boy. You know what those picnics are, and Sid'd be running into all his old friends.

LILY—(*agitatedly*) I don't think he will—this time—not after his promise.

MRS. MILLER—(*avoiding looking at her*) I know. But men are weak. (*then quickly*) That was a good notion of Nat's, getting Sid the job on the Waterbury *Standard*. All he ever needed was to get away from the rut he was in here. He's the kind that's the victim of his friends. He's easily led—but there's no real harm in him, you know that. (*Lily keeps silent, her eyes downcast. Mrs. Miller goes on meaningly.*) He's making good money in Waterbury, too—thirty-five a week. He's in a better position to get married than he ever was.

LILY—(*stiffly*) Well, I hope he finds a woman who's willing—though after he's through with his betting on horse races, and dice, and playing Kelly pool, there won't be much left for a wife—even if there was nothing else he spent his money on.

MRS. MILLER—Oh, he'd give up all that—for the right woman. (*Suddenly she comes directly to the point.*) Lily, why don't you change your mind and marry Sid and reform him? You love him and always have—

LILY—(*stiffly*) I can't love a man who drinks.

MRS. MILLER—You can't fool me. I know darned well you love him. And he loves you and always has.

LILY—Never enough to stop drinking for. (*cutting off Mrs. Miller's reply*) No, it's no good in your talking, Essie. We've been over this a thousand times before and I'll always feel the same as long as Sid's the same. If he gave me proof he'd—but even then I don't believe I could. It's sixteen years since I broke off our engagement, but what made me break it off is as clear to me today as it was then. It was what he'd be liable to do now to anyone who married him—his taking up with bad women.

MRS. MILLER—(*protests half-heartedly*) But he's always sworn he got raked into that party and never had anything to do with those harlots.

LILY—Well, I don't believe him—didn't then and don't now. I do believe he didn't deliberately plan to, but— Oh, it's no good talking, Essie. What's done is done. But you know how much I like Sid—in spite of everything. I know he was just born to be what he is—irresponsible, never meaning to harm but harming in spite of himself. But don't talk to me about marrying him—because I never could.

MRS. MILLER—(*angrily*) He's a dumb fool—a stupid dumb fool, that's what he is!

LILY—(*quietly*) No. He's just Sid.

MRS. MILLER—It's a shame for you—a measly shame—you that would have made such a wonderful wife for any man—that ought to have your own home and children!

LILY—(*winces but puts her arm around her affectionately—gently*) Now don't you go feeling sorry for me. I won't have that. Here I am, thanks to your and Nat's kindness, with the best home in the world; and as for the children, I feel the same love for yours as if they were mine, and I didn't have the pain of bearing them. And then there are all the boys and girls I teach every year. I like to feel I'm a sort of second mother to them and helping them to grow up to be good men and women. So I don't feel such a useless old maid, after all.

MRS. MILLER—(*kisses her impulsively—her voice husky*) You're a good woman, Lily—too good for the rest of us. (*She turns away, wiping a tear furtively—then abruptly changing the subject*) Good gracious, if I'm not forgetting one of the most important things! I've got to warn that Tommy against giving me away to Nat about the fish. He knows, because I had to send him to market for it, and he's liable to burst out laughing —

LILY — Laughing about what?

MRS. MILLER — (*guiltily*) Well, I've never told you, because it seemed sort of a sneaking trick, but you know how Nat carries on about not being able to eat bluefish.

LILY — I know he says there's a certain oil in it that poisons him.

MRS. MILLER — (*chuckling*) Poisons him, nothing! He's been eating bluefish for years — only I tell him each time it's weakfish. We're having it tonight — and I've got to warn that young imp to keep his face straight.

LILY — (*laughing*) Aren't you ashamed, Essie!

MRS. MILLER — Not much, I'm not! I like bluefish! (*She laughs.*) Where is Tommy? In the sitting-room?

LILY — No, Richard's there alone. I think Tommy's out on the piazza with Mildred. (*Mrs. Miller bustles out through the back parlor. As soon as she is gone, the smile fades from Lily's lips. Her face grows sad and she again glances nervously at her watch. Richard appears from the back parlor, moving in an aimless way. His face wears a set expression of bitter gloom; he exudes tragedy. For Richard, after his first outburst of grief and humiliation, has begun to take a masochistic satisfaction in his great sorrow, especially in the concern which it arouses in the family circle. On seeing his aunt, he gives her a dark look and turns and is about to stalk back toward the sitting-room when she speaks to him pityingly.*) Feel any better, Richard?

RICHARD — (*somberly*) I'm all right, Aunt Lily. You mustn't worry about me.

LILY — (*going to him*) But I do worry about you. I hate to see you so upset.

RICHARD — It doesn't matter. Nothing matters.

LILY — (*puts her arm around him sympathetically*) You really mustn't let yourself take it so seriously. You know, something happens and things like that come up, and we think there's no hope —

RICHARD — Things like what come up?

LILY—What's happened between you and Muriel.

RICHARD—(*with disdain*) Oh, her! I wasn't even thinking about her. I was thinking about life.

LILY—But then—if we really, *really* love—why, then something else is bound to happen soon that changes everything again, and it's all as it was before the misunderstanding, and everything works out all right in the end. That's the way it is with life.

RICHARD—(*with a tragic sneer*) Life! Life is a joke! And everything comes out all wrong in the end!

LILY—(*a little shocked*) You mustn't talk that way. But I know you don't mean it.

RICHARD—I do too mean it! You can have your silly optimism, if you like Aunt Lily. But don't ask me to be so blind. I'm a pessimist! (*then with an air of cruel cynicism*) As for Muriel, that's all dead and past. I was only kidding her, anyway, just to have a little fun, and she took it seriously, like a fool. (*He forces a cruel smile to his lips.*) You know what they say about women and trolley cars, Aunt Lily: there's always another one along in a minute.

LILY—(*really shocked this time*) I don't like you when you say such horrible, cynical things. It isn't nice.

RICHARD—Nice! That's all you women think of! I'm proud to be a cynic. It's the only thing you can be when you really face life. I suppose you think I ought to be heartbroken about Muriel—a little coward that's afraid to say her soul's her own, and keeps tied to her father's apron strings! Well, not for mine! There's plenty of other fish in the sea! (*As he is finishing, his mother comes back through the back parlor.*)

MRS. MILLER—Why, hello. You here, Richard? Getting hungry, I suppose?

RICHARD—(*indignantly*) I'm not hungry a bit! That's all you think of, Ma—food!

MRS. MILLER—Well, I must say I've never noticed you to hang back at meal times. (*to Lily*) What's that he was saying about fish in the sea?

LILY—(*smiling*) He says he's through with Muriel now.

MRS. MILLER—(*tartly—giving her son a rebuking look*) She's through with him, he means! The idea of your sending a nice girl like her things out of those indecent books! (*Deeply offended, Richard disdains to reply but stalks woundedly to the screen door at left, front, and puts a hand on the knob.*) Where are you going?

RICHARD—(*quotes from "Candida" in a hollow voice*) "Out, then, into the night with me!" (*He stalks out, slamming the door behind him.*)

MRS. MILLER—(*calls*) Well, don't you go far, 'cause dinner'll be ready in a minute, and I'm not coming running after you! (*She turns to Lily with a chuckle.*) Goodness, that boy! He ought to be on the stage! (*She mimics*) "Out—into the night"—and it isn't even dark yet! He got that out of one of those books, I suppose. Do you know, I'm actually grateful to old Dave McComber for putting an end to his nonsense with Muriel. I never did approve of Richard getting so interested in girls. He's not old enough for such silliness. Why, seems to me it was only yesterday he was still a baby. (*She sighs—then matter-of-factly*) Well, nothing to do now till those men turn up. No use standing here like gawks. We might as well go in the sitting-room and be comfortable.

LILY—(*the nervous, worried note in her voice again*) Yes, we might as well. (*They go out through the back parlor. They have no sooner disappeared than the screen door is opened cautiously and Richard comes back in the room.*)

RICHARD—(*stands inside the door, looking after them—quotes bitterly*) "They do not know the secret in the poet's heart." (*He comes nearer the table and surveys it, especially the cut-glass dish containing olives, with contempt and mutters disdainfully*) Food! (*But the dish of olives seems to fascinate him and presently he has approached nearer, and stealthily lifts a couple and crams them into his mouth. He is just reaching out for more when the pantry door is opened slightly and Norah peers in.*)

NORAH—Mister Dick, you thief, lave them olives alone, or the missus'll be swearing it was me at them!

RICHARD—(*draws back his hand as if he had been stung—too flustered to be anything but guilty boy for a second*) I—I wasn't eating—

NORAH—Oho, no, of course not, divil fear you, you was only feeling their pulse! (*then warningly*) Mind what I'm saying now, or I'll have to tell on you to protect me good name!

(*She draws back into the pantry, closing the door. Richard stands, a prey to feelings of bitterest humiliation and seething revolt against everyone and everything. A low whistle comes from just outside the porch door. He starts. Then a masculine voice calls:* "Hey, Dick." *He goes over to the screen door grumpily—then as he recognizes the owner of the voice, his own as he answers becomes respectful and admiring.*)

RICHARD—Oh, hello, Wint. Come on in. (*He opens the door and Wint Selby enters and stands just inside the door. Selby is nineteen, a classmate of Arthur's at Yale. He is a typical, good-looking college boy of the period, not the athletic but the hell-raising sport type. He is tall, blond, dressed in extreme collegiate cut.*)

WINT—(*as he enters—warningly, in a low tone*) Keep it quiet, Kid. I don't want the folks to know I'm here. Tell Art I want to see him a second—on the Q.T.

RICHARD—Can't. He's up at the Rands'—won't be home before ten, anyway.

WINT—(*irritably*) Damn, I thought he'd be here for dinner. (*more irritably*) Hell, that gums the works for fair!

RICHARD—(*ingratiatingly*) What is it, Wint? Can't I help?

WINT—(*gives him an appraising glance*) I might tell you, if you can keep your face shut.

RICHARD—I can.

WINT—Well, I ran into a couple of swift babies from New Haven this after. and I dated them up for tonight, thinking I could catch Art. But now it's too late to get anyone else and I'll have to pass it up. I'm nearly broke and I can't afford to blow them both to drinks.

RICHARD—(*with shy eagerness*) I've got eleven dollars saved up. I could loan you some.

WINT—(*surveys him appreciatively*) Say, you're a good sport. (*then shaking his head*) Nix, Kid, I don't want to borrow your money. (*then getting an idea*) But say, have you got anything on for tonight?

RICHARD—No.

WINT—Want to come along with me? (*then quickly*) I'm not trying to lead you astray, understand. But it'll be a help if you would just sit around with Belle and feed her a few drinks while I'm off with Edith. (*He winks.*) See what I mean?

You don't have to do anything, not even take a glass of beer—unless you want to.

RICHARD—(*boastfully*) Aw, what do you think I am—a rube?

WINT—You mean you're game for anything that's doing?

RICHARD—Sure I am!

WINT—Ever been out with any girls—I mean, real swift ones that there's something doing with, not these dead Janes around here?

RICHARD—(*lies boldly*) Aw, what do you think? Sure I have!

WINT—Ever drink anything besides sodas?

RICHARD—Sure. Lots of times. Beer and sloe-gin fizz and—Manhattans.

WINT—(*impressed*) Hell, you know more than I thought. (*then considering*) Can you fix it so your folks won't get wise? I don't want your old man coming after me. You can get back by half-past ten or eleven, though, all right. Think you can cook up some lie to cover that? (*as Richard hesitates—encouraging him*) Ought to be easy—on the Fourth.

RICHARD—Sure. Don't worry about that.

WINT—But you've got to keep your face closed about this, you hear?—to Art and everybody else. I tell you straight, I wouldn't ask you to come if I wasn't in a hole—and if I didn't know you were coming down to Yale next year, and didn't think you're giving me the straight goods about having been around before. I don't want to lead you astray.

RICHARD—(*scornfully*) Aw, I told you that was silly.

WINT—Well, you be at the Pleasant Beach Hotel at half-past nine then. Come in the back room. And don't forget to grab some cloves to take the booze off your breath.

RICHARD—Aw, I know what to do.

WINT—See you later, then. (*He starts out and is just about to close the door when he thinks of something.*) And say, I'll say you're a Harvard freshman, and you back me up. They don't know a damn thing about Harvard. I don't want them thinking I'm travelling around with any high-school kid.

RICHARD—Sure. That's easy.

WINT—So long, then. You better beat it right after your

dinner while you've got a chance, and hang around until it's time. Watch your step, Kid.

RICHARD—So long. (*The door closes behind Wint. Richard stands for a moment, a look of bitter, defiant rebellion coming over his face, and mutters to himself*) I'll show her she can't treat me the way she's done! I'll show them all! (*Then the front door is heard slamming, and a moment later Tommy rushes in from the back parlor.*)

TOMMY—Where's Ma?

RICHARD—(*surlily*) In the sitting-room. Where did you think, Bonehead?

TOMMY—Pa and Uncle Sid are coming. Mid and I saw them from the front piazza. Gee, I'm glad. I'm awful hungry, ain't you? (*He rushes out through the back parlor, calling*) Ma! They're coming! Let's have dinner quick! (*A moment later Mrs. Miller appears from the back parlor accompanied by Tommy, who keeps insisting urgently*) Gee, but I'm awful hungry, Ma!

MRS. MILLER—I know. You always are. You've got a tape-worm, that's what I think.

TOMMY—Have we got lobsters, Ma? Gee, I love lobsters.

MRS. MILLER—Yes, we've got lobsters. And fish. You remember what I told you about that fish. (*He snickers.*) Now, do be quiet, Tommy! (*then with a teasing smile at Richard*) Well, I'm glad to see you've got back out of the night, Richard. (*He scowls and turns his back on her. Lily appears through the back parlor, nervous and apprehensive. As she does so, from the front yard Sid's voice is heard singing "Poor John!" Mrs. Miller shakes her head forebodingly—but, so great is the comic spell for her even in her brother's voice, a humorous smile hovers at the corners of her lips.*) Mmm! Mmm! Lily, I'm afraid—

LILY—(*bitterly*) Yes, I might have known. (*Mildred runs in through the back parlor. She is laughing to herself a bit shame-facedly. She rushes to her mother.*)

MILDRED—Ma, Uncle Sid's— (*She whispers in her ear.*)

MRS. MILLER—Never mind! You shouldn't notice such things—at your age! And don't you encourage him by laughing at his foolishness, you hear!

TOMMY—You needn't whisper, Mid. Think I don't know? Uncle Sid's soused again.

MRS. MILLER—(*shakes him by the arm indignantly*) You be quiet! Did I ever! You're getting too smart! (*gives him a push*) Go to your place and sit right down and not another word out of you!

TOMMY—(*aggrieved—rubbing his arm as he goes to his place*) Aw, Ma!

MRS. MILLER—And you sit down, Richard and Mildred. You better, too, Lily. We'll get him right in here and get some food in him. He'll be all right then. (*Richard, preserving the pose of the bitter, disillusioned pessimist, sits down in his place in the chair at right of the two whose backs face front. Mildred takes the other chair facing back, at his left. Tommy has already slid into the end chair at right of those at the rear of table facing front. Lily sits in the one of those at left, by the head of the table, leaving the middle one [Sid's] vacant. While they are doing this, the front screen door is heard slamming and Nat's and Sid's laughing voices, raised as they come in and for a moment after, then suddenly cautiously lowered. Mrs. Miller goes to the entrance to the back parlor and calls peremptorily*) You come right in here! Don't stop to wash up or anything. Dinner's coming right on the table.

MILLER'S VOICE—(*jovially*) All right, Essie. Here we are! Here we are!

MRS. MILLER—(*goes to pantry door, opens it and calls*) All right, Norah. You can bring in the soup. (*She comes back to the back-parlor entrance just as Miller enters. He isn't drunk by any means. He is just mellow and benignly ripened. His face is one large, smiling, happy beam of utter appreciation of life. All's right with the world, so satisfyingly right that he becomes sentimentally moved even to think of it.*)

MILLER—Here we are, Essie! Right on the dot! Here we are! (*He pulls her to him and gives her a smacking kiss on the ear as she jerks her head away. Mildred and Tommy giggle. Richard holds rigidly aloof and disdainful, his brooding gaze fixed on his plate. Lily forces a smile.*)

MRS. MILLER—(*pulling away—embarrassedly, almost blushing*) Don't, you Crazy! (*then recovering herself—tartly*) So I see, you're here! And if I didn't, you've told me four times already!

MILLER—(*beamingly*) Now, Essie, don't be critical. Don't be carpingly critical. Good news can stand repeating, can't it?

'Course it can! (*He slaps her jovially on her fat buttocks. Tommy and Mildred roar with glee. And Norah, who has just entered from the pantry with a huge tureen of soup in her hands, almost drops it as she explodes in a merry guffaw.*)

MRS. MILLER—(*scandalized*) Nat! Aren't you ashamed!

MILLER—Couldn't resist it! Just simply couldn't resist it! (*Norah, still standing with the soup tureen held out stiffly in front of her, again guffaws.*)

MRS. MILLER—(*turns on her with outraged indignation*) Norah! Bring that soup here this minute! (*She stalks with stiff dignity toward her place at the foot of the table, right.*)

NORAH—(*guiltily*) Yes, Mum. (*She brings the soup around the head of the table, passing Miller.*)

MILLER—(*jovially*) Why, hello, Norah!

MRS. MILLER—Nat! (*She sits down stiffly at the foot of the table.*)

NORAH—(*rebuking him familiarly*) Arrah now, don't be making me laugh and getting me into trouble!

MRS. MILLER—Norah!

NORAH—(*a bit resentfully*) Yes, Mum. Here I am. (*She sets the soup tureen down with a thud in front of Mrs. Miller and passes around the other side, squeezing with difficulty between the china closet and the backs of chairs at the rear of the table.*)

MRS. MILLER—Tommy! Stop spinning your napkin ring! How often have I got to tell you? Mildred! Sit up straight in your chair! Do you want to grow up a humpback? Richard! Take your elbows off the table!

MILLER—(*coming to his place at the head of the table, rubbing his hands together genially*) Well, well, well. Well, well, well. It's good to be home again. (*Norah exits into the pantry and lets the door slam with a bang behind her.*)

MRS. MILLER—(*jumps*) Oh! (*then exasperatedly*) Nat, I do wish you wouldn't encourage that stupid girl by talking to her, when I'm doing my best to train—

MILLER—(*beamingly*) All right, Essie. Your word is law! (*then laughingly*) We did have the darndest fun today! And Sid was the life of that picnic! You ought to have heard him! Honestly, he had that crowd just rolling on the ground and splitting their sides! He ought to be on the stage.

MRS. MILLER—(*as Norah comes back with a dish of sal-*

tines —begins ladling soup into the stack of plates before her) He ought to be at this table eating something to sober him up, that's what he ought to be! (*She calls*) Sid! You come right in here! (*then to Norah, handing her a soup plate*) Here, Norah. (*Norah begins passing soup.*) Sit down, Nat, for goodness sakes. Start eating, everybody. Don't wait for me. You know I've given up soup.

MILLER — (*sits down but bends forward to call to his wife in a confidential tone*) Essie — Sid's sort of embarrassed about coming — I mean I'm afraid he's a little bit — not too much, you understand — but he met such a lot of friends and — well, you know, don't be hard on him. Fourth of July is like Christmas — comes but once a year. Don't pretend to notice, eh? And don't you kids, you hear! And don't you, Lily. He's scared of you.

LILY — (*with stiff meekness*) Very well, Nat.

MILLER — (*beaming again — calls*) All right, Sid. The coast's clear. (*He begins to absorb his soup ravenously.*) Good soup, Essie! Good soup! (*A moment later Sid makes his entrance from the back parlor. He is in a condition that can best be described as blurry. His movements have a hazy uncertainty about them. His shiny fat face is one broad, blurred, Puckish, naughty-boy grin; his eyes have a blurred, wondering vagueness. As he enters he makes a solemnly intense effort to appear casual and dead, cold sober. He waves his hand aimlessly and speaks with a silly gravity.*)

SID — Good evening. (*They all answer "Good evening," their eyes on their plates. He makes his way vaguely toward his place, continuing his grave effort at conversation.*) Beautiful evening. I never remember seeing — more beautiful sunset. (*He bumps vaguely into Lily's chair as he attempts to pass behind her — immediately he is all grave politeness.*) Sorry — sorry, Lily — deeply sorry.

LILY — (*her eyes on her plate — stiffly*) It's all right.

SID — (*manages to get into his chair at last — mutters to himself*) Wha' was I sayin'? Oh, sunsets. But why butt in? Hasn't sun — perfect right to set? Mind y'r own business. (*He pauses thoughtfully, considering this — then looks around from face to face, fixing each with a vague, blurred, wondering look, as if some deep puzzle were confronting him. Then suddenly*

he grins mistily and nods with satisfaction.) And there you are!
Am I right?

MILLER—(*humoring him*) Right.

SID—Right! (*He is silent, studying his soup plate, as if it were
some strange enigma. Finally he looks up and regards his sister
and asks with wondering amazement*) Soup?

MRS. MILLER—Of course, it's soup. What did you think
it was? And you hurry up and eat it.

SID—(*again regards his soup with astonishment*) Well! (*then
suddenly*) Well, all right then! Soup be it! (*He picks up his spoon
and begins to eat, but after two tries in which he finds it difficult
to locate his mouth, he addresses the spoon plaintively.*) Spoon, is
this any way to treat a pal? (*then suddenly comically angry, putting the spoon down with a bang*) Down with spoons! (*He raises
his soup plate and declaims*) "We'll drink to the dead already,
and hurrah for the next who dies." (*bowing solemnly to right
and left*) Your good health, ladies *and* gents. (*He starts drinking the soup. Miller guffaws and Mildred and Tommy giggle.
Even Richard forgets his melancholy and snickers, and Mrs. Miller
conceals a smile. Only Lily remains stiff and silent.*)

MRS. MILLER—(*with forced severity*) Sid!

SID—(*peers at her muzzily, lowering the soup plate a little
from his lips*) Eh?

MRS. MILLER—Oh, nothing. Never mind.

SID—(*solemnly offended*) Are you—publicly rebuking me
before assembled—? Isn't soup liquid? Aren't liquids drunk?
(*then considering this to himself*) What if they are drunk? It's a
good man's failing. (*He again peers mistily about at the company.*) Am I right or wrong?

MRS. MILLER—Hurry up and finish your soup, and stop
talking nonsense!

SID—(*turning to her—again offendedly*) Oh, no, Essie, if I
ever so far forget myself as to drink a leg of lamb, then you
might have some—excuse for— Just think of waste effort
eating soup with spoons—fifty gruelling lifts per plate—bil-
lions of soup-eaters on globe—why, it's simply staggering!
(*then darkly to himself*) No more spoons for me! If I want
develop my biceps, I'll buy Sandow Exerciser! (*He drinks the
rest of his soup in a gulp and beams around at the company, suddenly all happiness again.*) Am I right, folks?

MILLER—(*who has been choking with laughter*) Haw, haw! You're right, Sid.

SID—(*peers at him blurredly and shakes his head sadly*) Poor old Nat! Always wrong—but heart of gold, heart of purest gold. And drunk again, I regret to note. Sister, my heart bleeds for you and your poor fatherless chicks!

MRS. MILLER—(*restraining a giggle—severely*) Sid! Do shut up for a minute! Pass me your soup plates, everybody. If we wait for that girl to take them, we'll be here all night. (*They all pass their plates, which Mrs. Miller stacks up and then puts on the side-board. As she is doing this, Norah appears from the pantry with a platter of broiled fish. She is just about to place these before Miller when Sid catches her eye mistily and rises to his feet, making her a deep, uncertain bow.*)

SID—(*raptly*) Ah, Sight for Sore Eyes, my beautiful Macushla, my star-eyed Mavourneen—

MRS. MILLER—Sid!

NORAH—(*immensely pleased—gives him an arch, flirtatious glance*) Ah sure, Mister Sid, it's you that have kissed the Blarney Stone, when you've a drop taken!

MRS. MILLER—(*outraged*) Norah! Put down that fish!

NORAH—(*flusteredly*) Yes, Mum. (*She attempts to put the fish down hastily before Miller, but her eyes are fixed nervously on Mrs. Miller and she gives Miller a nasty swipe on the side of the head with the edge of the dish.*)

MILLER—Ouch! (*The children, even Richard, explode into laughter.*)

NORAH—(*almost lets the dish fall*) Oh, glory be to God! Is it hurted you are?

MILLER—(*rubbing his head—good-naturedly*) No, no harm done. Only careful, Norah, careful.

NORAH—(*gratefully*) Yes, sorr. (*She thumps down the dish in front of him with a sigh of relief.*)

SID—(*who is still standing—with drunken gravity*) Careful, Mavourneen, careful! You might have hit him some place besides the head. Always aim at his head, remember—so as not to worry us. (*Again the children explode. Also Norah. Even Lily suddenly lets out an hysterical giggle and is furious with herself for doing so.*)

LILY—I'm so sorry, Nat. I didn't mean to laugh. (*turning*

on Sid furiously) Will you please sit down and stop making a fool of yourself! (*Sid gives her a hurt, mournful look and then sinks meekly down on his chair.*)

NORAH—(*grinning cheerfully, gives Lily a reassuring pat on the back*) Ah, Miss Lily, don't mind him. He's only under the influence. Sure, there's no harm in him at all.

MRS. MILLER—Norah! (*Norah exits hastily into the pantry, letting the door slam with a crash behind her. There is silence for a moment as Miller serves the fish and it is passed around. Norah comes back with the vegetables and disappears again, and these are dished out.*)

MILLER—(*is about to take his first bite—stops suddenly and asks his wife*) This isn't, by any chance, bluefish, is it, my dear?

MRS. MILLER—(*with a warning glance at Tommy*) Of course not. You know we never have bluefish, on account of you.

MILLER—(*addressing the table now with the gravity of a man confessing his strange peculiarities*) Yes, I regret to say, there's a certain peculiar oil in bluefish that invariably poisons me. (*At this, Tommy cannot stand it any more but explodes into laughter. Mrs. Miller, after a helpless glance at him, follows suit; then Lily goes off into uncontrollable, hysterical laughter, and Richard and Mildred are caught in the contagion. Miller looks around at them with a weak smile, his dignity now ruffled a bit.*) Well, I must say I don't see what's so darned funny about my being poisoned.

SID—(*peers around him—then with drunken cunning*) Aha! Nat, I suspect—plot! This fish looks blue to me—very blue—in fact despondent, desperate, and— (*He points his fork dramatically at Mrs. Miller.*) See how guilty she looks—a ver—veritable Lucretia Georgia! Can it be this woman has been slowly poisoning you all these years? And how well—you've stood it! What iron constitution! Even now, when you are invariably at death's door, I can't believe— (*Everyone goes off into uncontrollable laughter.*)

MILLER—(*grumpily*) Oh, give us a rest, you darned fool! A joke's a joke, but— (*He addresses his wife in a wounded tone.*) Is this true, Essie?

MRS. MILLER—(*wiping the tears from her eyes—defiantly*) Yes, it is true, if you must know, and you'd never have suspected it, if it weren't for that darned Tommy, and Sid poking his nose in. You've eaten bluefish for years and thrived on it and it's all nonsense about that peculiar oil.

MILLER—(*deeply offended*) Kindly allow me to know my own constitution! Now I think of it, I've felt upset afterwards every damned time we've had fish! (*He pushes his plate away from him with proud renunciation.*) I can't eat this.

MRS. MILLER—(*insultingly matter-of-fact*) Well, don't then. There's lots of lobster coming and you can fill up on that. (*Richard suddenly bursts out laughing again.*)

MILLER—(*turns to him caustically*) You seem in a merry mood, Richard. I thought you were the original of the Heart Bowed Down today.

SID—(*with mock condolence*) Never mind, Dick. Let them—scoff! What can they understand about girls whose hair sizz-chels, whose lips are fireworks, whose eyes are red-hot sparks—

MILDRED—(*laughing*) Is that what he wrote to Muriel? (*turning to her brother*) You silly goat, you!

RICHARD—(*surlily*) Aw, shut up, Mid. What do I care about her? I'll show all of you how much I care!

MRS. MILLER—Pass your plates as soon as you're through, everybody. I've rung for the lobster. And that's all. You don't get any dessert or tea after lobster, you know. (*Norah appears bearing a platter of cold boiled lobsters which she sets before Miller, and disappears.*)

TOMMY—Gee, I love lobster! (*Miller puts one on each plate, and they are passed around and everyone starts in pulling the cracked shells apart.*)

MILLER—(*feeling more cheerful after a couple of mouthfuls—determining to give the conversation another turn, says to his daughter*) Have a good time at the beach, Mildred?

MILDRED—Oh, fine, Pa, thanks. The water was wonderful and warm.

MILLER—Swim far?

MILDRED—Yes, for me. But that isn't so awful far.

MILLER—Well, you ought to be a good swimmer, if you take after me. I used to be a regular water rat when I was a boy. I'll have to go down to the beach with you one of these days—though I'd be rusty, not having been in in all these years. (*The reminiscent look comes into his eyes of one about to embark on an oft-told tale of childhood adventure.*) You know, speaking of swimming, I never go down to that beach but what it calls to mind the day I and Red Sisk went in swimming there and I saved his life. (*By this time the family are beginning to exchange amused, guilty glances. They all know what is coming.*)

SID—(*with a sly, blurry wink around*) Ha! Now we—have it again!

MILLER—(*turning on him*) Have what?

SID—Nothing—go on with your swimming—don't mind me.

MILLER—(*glares at him—but immediately is overcome by the reminiscent mood again*) Red Sisk—his father kept a blacksmith shop where the Union Market is now—we kids called him Red because he had the darndest reddest crop of hair—

SID—(*as if he were talking to his plate*) Remarkable!—the curious imagination—of little children.

MRS. MILLER—(*as she sees Miller about to explode—interposes tactfully*) Sid! Eat your lobster and shut up! Go on, Nat.

MILLER—(*gives Sid a withering look—then is off again*) Well, as I was saying, Red and I went swimming that day. Must have been—let me see—Red was fourteen, bigger and older than me, I was only twelve—forty-five years ago—wasn't a single house down there then—but there was a stake out where the whistling buoy is now, about a mile out. (*Tommy, who has been having difficulty restraining himself, lets out a stifled giggle. Miller bends a frowning gaze on him.*) One more sound out of you, young man, and you'll leave the table!

MRS. MILLER—(*quickly interposing, trying to stave off the story*) Do eat your lobster, Nat. You didn't have any fish, you know.

MILLER—(*not liking the reminder—pettishly*) Well, if I'm going to be interrupted every second anyway— (*He turns to his lobster and chews in silence for a moment.*)

MRS. MILLER—(*trying to switch the subject*) How's Anne's mother's rheumatism, Mildred?

MILDRED—Oh, she's much better, Ma. She was in wading today. She says salt water's the only thing that really helps her bunion.

MRS. MILLER—Mildred! Where are your manners? At the table's no place to speak of—

MILLER—(*fallen into the reminiscent obsession again*) Well, as I was saying, there was I and Red, and he dared me to race him out to the stake and back. Well, I didn't let anyone dare me in those days. I was a spunky kid. So I said all right and we started out. We swam and swam and were pretty evenly matched; though, as I've said, he was bigger and older than me, but finally I drew ahead. I was going along easy, with lots in reserve, not a bit tired, when suddenly I heard a sort of gasp from behind me—like this—"help." (*He imitates. Everyone's eyes are firmly fixed on their plates, except Sid's.*) And I turned and there was Red, his face all pinched and white, and he says weakly: "Help, Nat! I got a cramp in my leg!" Well, I don't mind telling you I got mighty scared. I didn't know what to do. Then suddenly I thought of the pile. If I could pull him to that, I could hang on to him till someone'd notice us. But the pile was still—well, I calculate it must have been two hundred feet away.

SID—Two hundred and fifty!

MILLER—(*in confusion*) What's that?

SID—Two hundred *and* fifty! I've taken down the distance every time you've saved Red's life for thirty years and the mean average to that pile is two hundred and fifty feet! (*There is a burst of laughter from around the table. Sid continues complainingly.*) Why didn't you let that Red drown, anyway, Nat? I never knew him but I know I'd never have liked him.

MILLER—(*really hurt, forces a feeble smile to his lips and pretends to be a good sport about it*) Well, guess you're right, Sid. Guess I have told that one too many times and bored everyone. But it's a good true story for kids because it illustrates the danger of being foolhardy in the water—

MRS. MILLER—(*sensing the hurt in his tone, comes to his rescue*) Of course it's a good story—and you tell it whenever you've a mind to. And you, Sid, if you were in any respon-

sible state, I'd give you a good piece of my mind for teasing
Nat like that.

MILLER—(*with a sad, self-pitying smile at his wife*) Getting
old, I guess, Mother—getting to repeat myself. Someone
ought to stop me.

MRS. MILLER—No such thing! You're as young as you
ever were. (*She turns on Sid again angrily.*) You eat your lobster and maybe it'll keep your mouth shut!

SID—(*after a few chews—irrepressibly*) Lobster! Did you
know, Tommy, your Uncle Sid is the man invented lobster?
Fact! One day—when I was building the Pyramids—took a
day off and just dashed off lobster. He was bigger 'n' older
than me and he had the darndest reddest crop of hair but I
dashed him off just the same! Am I right, Nat? (*then suddenly
in the tones of a side-show barker*) Ladies *and* Gents—

MRS. MILLER—Mercy sakes! Can't you shut up?

SID—In this cage you see the lobster. You will not believe
me, ladies *and* gents, but it's a fact that this interesting bi-
valve only makes love to his mate once in every thousand
years—but, dearie me, how he does enjoy it! (*The children
roar. Lily and Mrs. Miller laugh in spite of themselves—then look
embarrassed. Miller guffaws—then suddenly grows shocked.*)

MILLER—Careful, Sid, careful. Remember you're at home.

TOMMY—(*suddenly in a hoarse whisper to his mother, with an
awed glance of admiration at his uncle*) Ma! Look at him! He's
eating that claw, shells and all!

MRS. MILLER—(*horrified*) Sid, do you want to kill yourself? Take it away from him, Lily!

SID—(*with great dignity*) But I prefer the shells. All famous
epicures prefer the shells—to the less delicate, coarser meat.
It's the same with clams. Unless I eat the shells there is a
certain, peculiar oil that invariably poisons— Am I right,
Nat?

MILLER—(*good-naturedly*) You seem to be getting a lot of
fun kidding me. Go ahead, then. I don't mind.

MRS. MILLER—He better go right up to bed for a while,
that's what he better do.

SID—(*considering this owlishly*) Bed? Yes, maybe you're
right. (*He gets to his feet.*) I am not at all well—in very delicate condition—we are praying for a boy. Am I right, Nat?

Nat, I kept telling you all day I was in delicate condition and yet you kept forcing demon chowder on me, although you knew full well—even if you were full—that there is a certain, peculiar oil in chowder that invariably— (*They are again all laughing—Lily, hysterically.*)

MRS. MILLER—*Will* you get to bed, you idiot!

SID—(*mutters graciously*) Immediately—if not sooner. (*He turns to pass behind Lily, then stops, staring down at her.*) But wait. There is still a duty I must perform. No day is complete without it. Lily, answer once and for all, will you marry me?

LILY—(*with an hysterical giggle*) No, I won't—never!

SID—(*nodding his head*) Right! And perhaps it's all for the best. For how could I forget the pre—precepts taught me at mother's dying knee. "Sidney," she said, "never marry a woman who drinks! Lips that touch liquor shall never touch yours!" (*gazing at her mournfully*) Too bad! So fine a woman once—and now such a slave to rum! (*turning to Nat*) What can we do to save her, Nat? (*in a hoarse, confidential whisper*) Better put her in institution where she'll be removed from temptation! The mere smell of it seems to drive her frantic!

MRS. MILLER—(*struggling with her laughter*) You leave Lily alone, and go to bed!

SID—Right! (*He comes around behind Lily's chair and moves toward the entrance to the back parlor—then suddenly turns and says with a bow*) Good night, ladies—*and* gents. We will meet—bye and bye! (*He gives an imitation of a Salvation Army drum.*) Boom! Boom! Boom! Come and be saved, Brothers! (*He starts to sing the old Army hymn.*)

> "In the sweet
> Bye and bye
> We will meet on that beautiful shore."

(*He turns and marches solemnly out through the back parlor, singing*)

> "Work and pray
> While you may.
> We will meet in the sky bye and bye."

(*Miller and his wife and the children are all roaring with laughter. Lily giggles hysterically.*)

MILLER—(*subsiding at last*) Haw, haw. He's a case, if ever

there was one! Darned if you can help laughing at him—even when he's poking fun at you!

MRS. MILLER—Goodness, but he's a caution! Oh, my sides ache, I declare! I was trying so hard not to—but you can't help it, he's so silly! But I suppose we really shouldn't. It only encourages him. But, my lands—!

LILY—(*suddenly gets up from her chair and stands rigidly, her face working—jerkily*) That's just it—you shouldn't—even I laughed—it does encourage—that's been his downfall—everyone always laughing, everyone always saying what a card he is, what a case, what a caution, so funny—and he's gone on—and we're all responsible—making it easy for him—we're all to blame—and all we do is laugh!

MILLER—(*worriedly*) Now, Lily, now, you mustn't take on so. It isn't as serious as all that.

LILY—(*bitterly*) Maybe—it is—to me. Or was—once. (*then contritely*) I'm sorry, Nat. I'm sorry, Essie. I didn't mean to— I'm not feeling myself tonight. If you'll excuse me, I'll go in the front parlor and lie down on the sofa awhile.

MRS. MILLER—Of course, Lily. You do whatever you've a mind to. (*Lily goes out.*)

MILLER—(*frowning—a little shamefaced*) Hmm. I suppose she's right. Never knew Lily to come out with things that way before. Anything special happened, Essie?

MRS. MILLER—Nothing I know—except he'd promised to take her to the fireworks.

MILLER—That's so. Well, supposing I take her. I don't want her to feel disappointed.

MRS. MILLER—(*shaking her head*) Wild horses couldn't drag her there now.

MILLER—Hmm. I thought she'd got completely over her foolishness about him long ago.

MRS. MILLER—She never will.

MILLER—She'd better. He's got fired out of that Waterbury job—told me at the picnic after he'd got enough Dutch courage in him.

MRS. MILLER—Oh, dear! Isn't he the fool!

MILLER—I knew something was wrong when he came home. Well, I'll find a place for him on my paper again, of course. He always was the best news-getter this town ever had. But I'll tell him he's got to stop his damn nonsense.

MRS. MILLER—(*doubtfully*) Yes.

MILLER—Well, no use sitting here mourning over spilt milk. (*He gets up, and Richard, Mildred, Tommy and Mrs. Miller follow his example, the children quiet and a bit awed.*) You kids go out in the yard and try to keep quiet for a while, so's your Uncle Sid'll get to sleep and your Aunt Lily can rest.

TOMMY—(*mournfully*) Ain't we going to set off the sky rockets and Roman candles, Pa?

MILLER—Later, Son, later. It isn't dark enough for them yet anyway.

MILDRED—Come on, Tommy. I'll see he keeps quiet, Pa.

MILLER—That's a good girl. (*Mildred and Tommy go out through the screen door. Richard remains standing, sunk in bitter, gloomy thoughts. Miller glances at him—then irritably*) Well, Melancholy Dane, what are you doing?

RICHARD—(*darkly*) I'm going out—for a while. (*then suddenly*) Do you know what I think? It's Aunt Lily's fault, Uncle Sid's going to ruin. It's all because he loves her, and she keeps him dangling after her, and eggs him on and ruins his life—like all women love to ruin men's lives! I don't blame him for drinking himself to death! What does he care if he dies, after the way she's treated him! I'd do the same thing myself if I were in his boots!

MRS. MILLER—(*indignantly*) Richard! You stop that talk!

RICHARD—(*quotes bitterly*)

"Drink! for you know not whence you come nor why.

Drink! for you know not why you go nor where!"

MILLER—(*losing his temper—harshly*) Listen here, young man! I've had about all I can stand of your nonsense for one day! You're growing a lot too big for your size, seems to me! You keep that damn fool talk to yourself, you hear me—or you're going to regret it! Mind, now! (*He strides angrily away through the back parlor.*)

MRS. MILLER—(*still indignant*) Richard, I'm ashamed of you, that's what I am. (*She follows her husband. Richard stands for a second, bitter, humiliated, wronged, even his father turned enemy, his face growing more and more rebellious. Then he forces a scornful smile to his lips.*)

RICHARD—Aw, what the hell do I care? I'll show them! (*He turns and goes out the screen door.*)

(*Curtain*)

ACT THREE
Scene One

SCENE—*The back room of a bar in a small hotel—a small, dingy room, dimly lighted by two fly-specked globes in a fly-specked gilt chandelier suspended from the middle of the ceiling. At left, front, is the swinging door leading to the bar. At rear of door, against the wall, is a nickel-in-the-slot player-piano. In the rear wall, right, is a door leading to the "Family Entrance" and the stairway to the upstairs rooms. In the middle of the right wall is a window with closed shutters. Three tables with stained tops, four chairs around each table, are placed at center, front, at right, toward rear, and at rear, center. A brass cuspidor is on the floor by each table. The floor is unswept, littered with cigarette and cigar butts. The hideous saffron-colored wall-paper is blotched and spotted.*

It is about 10 o'clock the same night. Richard and Belle are discovered sitting at the table at center, Belle at left of it, Richard in the next chair at the middle of table, rear, facing front.

Belle is twenty, a rather pretty peroxide blonde, a typical college "tart" of the period, and of the cheaper variety, dressed with tawdry flashiness. But she is a fairly recent recruit to the ranks, and is still a bit remorseful behind her make-up and defiantly careless manner.

Belle has an empty gin-rickey glass before her, Richard a half-empty glass of beer. He looks horribly timid, embarrassed and guilty, but at the same time thrilled and proud of at last mingling with the pace that kills.

The player-piano is grinding out "Bedelia." The bartender, a stocky young Irishman with a foxily cunning, stupid face and a cynically wise grin, stands just inside the bar entrance, watching them over the swinging door.

BELLE—(*with an impatient glance at her escort—rattling the ice in her empty glass*) Drink up your beer, why don't you? It's getting flat.

RICHARD—(*embarrassedly*) I let it get that way on purpose. I like it better when it's flat. (*But he hastily gulps down the rest of his glass, as if it were some nasty-tasting medicine. The bartender chuckles audibly. Belle glances at him.*)

51

BELLE—(*nodding at the player-piano scornfully*) Say, George, is "Bedelia" the latest to hit this hick burg? Well, it's only a couple of years old! You'll catch up in time! Why don't you get a new roll for that old box?

BARTENDER—(*with a grin*) Complain to the boss, not me. We're not used to having Candy Kiddoes like you around— or maybe we'd get up to date.

BELLE—(*with a professionally arch grin at him*) Don't kid me, please. I can't bear it. (*Then she sings to the music from the piano, her eyes now on Richard*) "Bedelia, I'd like to feel yer." (*The bartender laughs. She smirks at Richard.*) Ever hear those words to it, Kid?

RICHARD—(*who has heard them but is shocked at hearing a girl say them—putting on a blasé air*) Sure, lots of times. That's old.

BELLE—(*edging her chair closer and putting a hand over one of his*) Then why don't you act as if you knew what they were all about?

RICHARD—(*terribly flustered*) Sure, I've heard that old parody lots of times. What do you think I am?

BELLE—I don't know, Kid. Honest to God, you've got me guessing.

BARTENDER—(*with a mocking chuckle*) He's a hot sport, can't you tell it? I never seen such a spender. My head's dizzy bringing you in drinks!

BELLE—(*laughs irritably—to Richard*) Don't let him kid you. You show him. Loosen up and buy another drink, what say?

RICHARD—(*humiliated—manfully*) Sure. Excuse me. I was thinking of something else. Have anything you like. (*He turns to the bartender who has entered from the bar.*) See what the lady will have—and have one on me yourself.

BARTENDER—(*coming to the table—with a wink at Belle*) That's talking! Didn't I say you were a sport? I'll take a cigar on you. (*to Belle*) What's yours, Kiddo—the same?

BELLE—Yes. And forget the house rules this time and re-member a rickey is supposed to have gin in it.

BARTENDER—(*grinning*) I'll try to—seeing it's you. (*then to Richard*) What's yours—another beer?

RICHARD—(*shyly*) A small one, please. I'm not thirsty.

BELLE — (*calculatedly taunting*) Say, honest, are things that slow up at Harvard? If they had you down at New Haven, they'd put you in a kindergarten! Don't be such a dead one! Filling up on beer will only make you sleepy. Have a man's drink!

RICHARD — (*shamefacedly*) All right. I was going to. Bring me a sloe-gin fizz.

BELLE — (*to bartender*) And make it a real one.

BARTENDER — (*with a wink*) I get you. Something that'll warm him up, eh? (*He goes into the bar, chuckling.*)

BELLE — (*looks around the room — irritably*) Christ, what a dump! (*Richard is startled and shocked by this curse and looks down at the table.*) If this isn't the deadest burg I ever struck! Bet they take the sidewalks in after nine o'clock! (*then turning on him*) Say, honestly, Kid, does your mother know you're out?

RICHARD — (*defensively*) Aw, cut it out, why don't you — trying to kid me!

BELLE — (*glances at him — then resolves on a new tack — patting his hand*) All right. I didn't mean to, Dearie. Please don't get sore at me.

RICHARD — I'm not sore.

BELLE — (*seductively*) You see, it's this way with me. I think you're one of the sweetest kids I've ever met — and I could like you such a lot if you'd give me half a chance — instead of acting so cold and indifferent.

RICHARD — I'm not cold and indifferent. (*then solemnly tragic*) It's only that I've got — a weight on my mind.

BELLE — (*impatiently*) Well, get it off your mind and give something else a chance to work. (*The bartender comes in, bringing the drinks.*)

BARTENDER — (*setting them down — with a wink at Belle*) This'll warm him for you. Forty cents, that is — with the cigar.

RICHARD — (*pulls out his roll and hands a dollar bill over — with exaggerated carelessness*) Keep the change. (*Belle emits a gasp and seems about to protest, then thinks better of it. The bartender cannot believe his luck for a moment — then pockets the bill hastily, as if afraid Richard will change his mind.*)

BARTENDER — (*respect in his voice*) Thank you, sir.

RICHARD—(*grandly*) Don't mention it.

BARTENDER—I hope you like the drink. I took special pains with it. (*The voice of the salesman, who has just come in the bar, calls* "Hey! Anybody here?" *and a coin is rapped on the bar.*) I'm coming. (*The bartender goes out.*)

BELLE—(*remonstrating gently, a new appreciation for her escort's possibilities in her voice*) You shouldn't be so generous, Dearie. Gets him in bad habits. A dime would have been plenty.

RICHARD—Ah, that's all right. I'm no tightwad.

BELLE—That's the talk I like to hear. (*With a quick look toward the bar, she stealthily pulls up her dress—to Richard's shocked fascination—and takes a package of cheap cigarettes from her stocking.*) Keep an eye out for that bartender, Kid, and tell me if you see him coming. Girls are only allowed to smoke upstairs in the rooms, he said.

RICHARD—(*embarrassedly*) All right. I'll watch.

BELLE—(*having lighted her cigarette and inhaled deeply, holds the package out to him*) Have a Sweet? You smoke, don't you?

RICHARD—(*taking one*) Sure! I've been smoking for the last two years—on the sly. But next year I'll be allowed—that is, pipes and cigars. (*He lights his cigarette with elaborate nonchalance, puffs, but does not inhale—then, watching her, with shocked concern*) Say, you oughtn't to inhale like that! Smoking's awful bad for girls, anyway, even if they don't—

BELLE—(*cynically amused*) Afraid it will stunt my growth? Gee, Kid, you are a scream! You'll grow up to be a minister yet! (*Richard looks shamefaced. She scans him impatiently—then holds up her drink.*) Well, here's how! Bottoms up, now! Show me you really know how to drink. It'll take that load off your mind. (*Richard follows her example and they both drink the whole contents of their glasses before setting them down.*) There! That's something like! Feel better?

RICHARD—(*proud of himself—with a shy smile*) You bet.

BELLE—Well, you'll feel still better in a minute—and then maybe you won't be so distant and unfriendly, eh?

RICHARD—I'm not.

BELLE—Yes, you are. I think you just don't like me.

RICHARD—(*more manfully*) I do too like you.

BELLE—How much? A lot?

RICHARD—Yes, a lot.

BELLE—Show me how much! (*then as he fidgets embarrassedly*) Want me to come sit on your lap?

RICHARD—Yes—I— (*She comes and sits on his lap. He looks desperately uncomfortable, but the gin is rising to his head and he feels proud of himself and devilish, too.*)

BELLE—Why don't you put your arm around me? (*He does so awkwardly.*) No, not that dead way. Hold me tight. You needn't be afraid of hurting me. I like to be held tight, don't you?

RICHARD—Sure I do.

BELLE—'Specially when it's by a nice handsome kid like you. (*ruffling his hair*) Gee, you've got pretty hair, do you know it? Honest, I'm awfully strong for you! Why can't you be about me? I'm not so awfully ugly, am I?

RICHARD—No, you're—you're pretty.

BELLE—You don't say it as if you meant it.

RICHARD—I do mean it—honest.

BELLE—Then why don't you kiss me? (*She bends down her lips toward his. He hesitates, then kisses her and at once shrinks back.*) Call that kissing? Here. (*She holds his head and fastens her lips on his and holds them there. He starts and struggles. She laughs.*) What's the matter, Honey Boy? Haven't you ever kissed like that before?

RICHARD—Sure. Lots of times.

BELLE—Then why did you jump as if I'd bitten you? (*squirming around on his lap*) Gee, I'm getting just crazy about you! What shall we do about it, eh? Tell me.

RICHARD—I—don't know. (*then boldly*) I—I'm crazy about you, too.

BELLE—(*kissing him again*) Just think of the wonderful time Edith and your friend, Wint, are having upstairs—while we sit down here like two dead ones. A room only costs two dollars. And, seeing I like you so much, I'd only take five dollars—from you. I'd do it for nothing—for you—only I've got to live and I owe my room rent in New Haven—and you know how it is. I get ten dollars from everyone else. Honest! (*She kisses him again, then gets up from his lap—briskly*) Come on. Go out and tell the bartender you want a room. And hurry. Honest, I'm so strong for you I can hardly wait to get you upstairs!

RICHARD—(*starts automatically for the door to the bar— then hesitates, a great struggle going on in his mind—timidity, disgust at the money element, shocked modesty, and the guilty thought of Muriel, fighting it out with the growing tipsiness that makes him want to be a hell of a fellow and go in for all forbidden fruit, and makes this tart a romantic, evil vampire in his eyes. Finally, he stops and mutters in confusion*) I can't.

BELLE—What, are you too bashful to ask for a room? Let me do it, then. (*She starts for the door.*)

RICHARD—(*desperately*) No—I don't want you to—I don't want to.

BELLE—(*surveying him, anger coming into her eyes*) Well, if you aren't the lousiest cheap skate!

RICHARD—I'm not a cheap skate!

BELLE—Keep me around here all night fooling with you when I might be out with some real live one—if there is such a thing in this burg!—and now you quit on me! Don't be such a piker! You've got five dollars! I seen it when you paid for the drinks, so don't hand me any lies!

RICHARD—I— Who said I hadn't? And I'm not a piker. If you need the five dollars so bad—for your room rent— you can have it without—I mean, I'll be glad to give— (*He has been fumbling in his pocket and pulls out his nine-dollar roll and holds out the five to her.*)

BELLE—(*hardly able to believe her eyes, almost snatches it from his hand—then laughs and immediately becomes sentimentally grateful*) Thanks, Kid. Gee—oh, thanks— Gee, forgive me for losing my temper and bawling you out, will you? Gee, you're a regular peach! You're the nicest kid I've ever met! (*She kisses him and he grins proudly, a hero to himself now on many counts.*) Gee, you're a peach! Thanks, again!

RICHARD—(*grandly—and quite tipsily*) It's—nothing— only too glad. (*then boldly*) Here—give me another kiss, and that'll pay me back.

BELLE—(*kissing him*) I'll give you a thousand, if you want 'em. Come on, let's sit down, and we'll have another drink— and this time I'll blow you just to show my appreciation. (*She calls*) Hey, George! Bring us another round—the same!

RICHARD—(*a remnant of caution coming to him*) I don't
know as I ought to—

BELLE—Oh, another won't hurt you. And I want to blow
you, see. (*They sit down in their former places.*)

RICHARD—(*boldly draws his chair closer and puts an arm
around her—tipsily*) I like you a lot—now I'm getting to
know you. You're a darned nice girl.

BELLE—Nice is good! Tell me another! Well, if I'm so nice,
why didn't you want to take me upstairs? That's what I don't
get.

RICHARD—(*lying boldly*) I did want to—only I— (*Then
he adds solemnly*) I've sworn off. (*The bartender enters with the
drinks.*)

BARTENDER—(*setting them on the table*) Here's your pleasure. (*then regarding Richard's arm about her waist*) Ho-ho,
we're coming on, I see. (*Richard grins at him muzzily.*)

BELLE—(*digs into her stocking and gives him a dollar*) Here.
This is mine. (*He gives her change and she tips him a dime, and
he goes out. She puts the five Richard had given her in her stocking
and picks up her glass.*) Here's how—and thanks again. (*She
sips.*)

RICHARD—(*boisterously*) Bottoms up! Bottoms up! (*He
drinks all of his down and sighs with exaggerated satisfaction.*)
Gee, that's good stuff, all right. (*hugging her*) Give me another kiss, Belle.

BELLE—(*kisses him*) What did you mean a minute ago
when you said you'd sworn off?

RICHARD—(*solemnly*) I took an oath I'd be faithful.

BELLE—(*cynically*) Till death do us part, eh? Who's the
girl?

RICHARD—(*shortly*) Never mind.

BELLE—(*bristling*) I'm not good enough to talk about her,
I suppose?

RICHARD—I didn't—mean that. You're all right. (*then
with tipsy gravity*) Only you oughtn't to lead this kind of life.
It isn't right—for a nice girl like you. Why don't you reform?

BELLE—(*sharply*) Nix on that line of talk! Can it, you hear!
You can do a lot with me for five dollars—but you can't reform me, see. Mind your own business, Kid, and don't butt
in where you're not wanted!

RICHARD—I—I didn't mean to hurt your feelings.

BELLE—I know you didn't mean. You're only like a lot of people who mean well, to hear them tell it. (*changing the subject*) So you're faithful to your one love, eh? (*with an ugly sneer*) And how about her? Bet you she's out with a guy under some bush this minute, giving him all he wants. Don't be a sucker, Kid! Even the little flies do it!

RICHARD—(*starting up in his chair—angrily*) Don't you say that! Don't you dare!

BELLE—(*unimpressed—with a cynical shrug of her shoulders*) All right. Have it your own way and be a sucker! It cuts no ice with me.

RICHARD—You don't know her or—

BELLE—And don't want to. Shut up about her, can't you? (*She stares before her bitterly. Richard subsides into scowling gloom. He is becoming perceptibly more intoxicated with each moment now. The bartender and the salesman appear just inside the swinging door. The bartender nods toward Belle, giving the salesman a wink. The salesman grins and comes into the room, carrying his highball in his hand. He is a stout, jowly-faced man in his late thirties, dressed with cheap nattiness, with the professional breeziness and jocular, kid-'em-along manner of his kind. Belle looks up as he enters and he and she exchange a glance of complete recognition. She knows his type by heart and he knows hers.*)

SALESMAN—(*passes by her to the table at right—grinning genially*) Good evening.

BELLE—Good evening.

SALESMAN—(*sitting down*) Hope I'm not butting in on your party—but my dogs were giving out standing at that bar.

BELLE—All right with me. (*giving Richard a rather contemptuous look*) I've got no party on.

SALESMAN—That sounds hopeful.

RICHARD—(*suddenly recites sentimentally*)

"But I wouldn't do such, 'cause I loved her too much,
    But I learned about women from her."

(*turns to scowl at the salesman—then to Belle*) Let's have 'nother drink!

BELLE—You've had enough. (*Richard subsides, muttering to himself.*)

SALESMAN—What is it—a child poet or a child actor?

BELLE—Don't know. Got me guessing.

SALESMAN—Well, if you could shake the cradle-robbing act, maybe we could do a little business.

BELLE—That's easy. I just pull my freight. (*She shakes Richard by the arm.*) Listen, Kid. Here's an old friend of mine, Mr. Smith of New Haven, just come in. I'm going over and sit at his table for a while, see. And you better go home.

RICHARD—(*blinking at her and scowling*) I'm never going home! I'll show them!

BELLE—Have it your own way—only let me up. (*She takes his arm from around her and goes to sit by the salesman. Richard stares after her offendedly.*)

RICHARD—Go on. What do I care what you do? (*He recites scornfully*) "For a woman's only a woman, but a good cigar's a smoke."

SALESMAN—(*as Belle sits beside him*) Well, what kind of beer will you have, Sister?

BELLE—Mine's a gin rickey.

SALESMAN—You've got extravagant tastes, I'm sorry to see.

RICHARD—(*begins to recite sepulchrally*)

> "Yet each man kills the thing he loves,
> By each let this be heard."

SALESMAN—(*grinning*) Say, this is rich! (*He calls encouragement.*) That's swell dope, young feller. Give us some more.

RICHARD—(*ignoring him—goes on more rhetorically*)

> "Some do it with a bitter look,
> Some with a flattering word,
> The coward does it with a kiss,
> The brave man with a sword!"

(*He stares at Belle gloomily and mutters tragically*) I did it with a kiss! I'm a coward.

SALESMAN—That's the old stuff, Kid. You've got something on the ball, all right, all right! Give us another—right over the old pan, now!

BELLE—(*with a laugh*) Get the hook!

RICHARD—(*glowering at her—tragically*)

> " 'Oho,' they cried, 'the world is wide,
> But fettered limbs go lame
> And once, or twice, to throw the dice
> Is a gentlemanly game,

But he does not win who plays with Sin
In the secret House of Shame!' "

BELLE—(*angrily*) Aw, can it! Give us a rest from that bunk!

SALESMAN—(*mockingly*) This gal of yours don't appreciate poetry. She's a lowbrow. But I'm the kid that eats it up. My middle name is Kelly and Sheets! Give us some more of the same! Do you know "The Lobster and the Wise Guy"? (*turns to Belle seriously*) No kidding, that's a peacherino. I heard a guy recite it at Poli's. Maybe this nut knows it. Do you, Kid? (*But Richard only glowers at him gloomily without answering.*)

BELLE—(*surveying Richard contemptuously*) He's copped a fine skinful—and gee, he's hardly had anything.

RICHARD—(*suddenly—with a dire emphasis*) "And then— at ten o'clock—Eilert Lovborg will come—with vine leaves in his hair!"

BELLE—And bats in his belfry, if he's you!

RICHARD—(*regards her bitterly—then starts to his feet belli-cosely—to the salesman*) I don't believe you ever knew her in New Haven at all! You just picked her up now! You leave her alone, you hear! You won't do anything to her—not while I'm here to protect her!

BELLE—(*laughing*) Oh, my God! Listen to it!

SALESMAN—Ssshh! This is a scream! Wait! (*He addresses Richard in tones of exaggerated melodrama.*) Curse you, Jack Dalton, if I won't unhand her, what then?

RICHARD—(*threateningly*) I'll give you a good punch in the snoot, that's what! (*He moves toward their table.*)

SALESMAN—(*with mock terror—screams in falsetto*) Help! Help! (*The bartender comes in irritably.*)

BARTENDER—Hey. Cut out the noise. What the hell's up with you?

RICHARD—(*tipsily*) He's too—damn fresh!

SALESMAN—(*with a wink*) He's going to murder me. (*then gets a bright idea for eliminating Richard—seriously to the bar-tender*) It's none of my business, Brother, but if I were in your boots I'd give this young souse the gate. He's under age; any fool can see that.

BARTENDER—(*guiltily*) He told me he was over eighteen.

SALESMAN—Yes, and I tell you I'm the Pope—but you don't have to believe me. If you're not looking for trouble, I'd advise you to get him started for some other gin mill and let them do the lying, if anything comes up.

BARTENDER—Hmm. (*He turns to Richard angrily and gives him a push.*) Come on, now. On your way! You'll start no trouble in here! Beat it now!

RICHARD—I will not beat it!

BARTENDER—Oho, won't you? (*He gives him another push that almost sends him sprawling.*)

BELLE—(*callously*) Give him the bum's rush! I'm sick of his bull! (*Richard turns furiously and tries to punch the bartender.*)

BARTENDER—(*avoids the punch*) Oho, you would, would you! (*He grabs Richard by the back of the neck and the seat of the pants and marches him ignominiously toward the swinging door.*)

RICHARD—Leggo of me, you dirty coward!

BARTENDER—Quiet now—or I'll pin a Mary Ann on your jaw that'll quiet you! (*He rushes him through the screen door and a moment later the outer doors are heard swinging back and forth.*)

SALESMAN—(*with a chuckle*) Hand it to me, Kid. How was that for a slick way of getting rid of him?

BELLE—(*suddenly sentimental*) Poor kid. I hope he makes home all right. I liked him—before he got soused.

SALESMAN—Who is he?

BELLE—The boy who's upstairs with my friend told me, but I didn't pay much attention. Name's Miller. His old man runs a paper in this one-horse burg, I think he said.

SALESMAN—(*with a whistle*) Phew! He must be Nat Miller's kid, then.

BARTENDER—(*coming back from the bar*) Well, he's on his way—with a good boot in the tail to help him!

SALESMAN—(*with a malicious chuckle*) Yes? Well, maybe that boot will cost you a job, Brother. Know Nat Miller who runs the *Globe*? That's his kid.

BARTENDER—(*his face falling*) The hell he is! Who said so?

SALESMAN—This baby doll. (*getting up*) Say, I'll go keep cases on him—see he gets on the trolley all right, anyway. Nat Miller's a good scout. (*He hurries out.*)

BARTENDER—(*viciously*) God damn the luck! If he ever finds out I served his kid, he'll run me out of town. (*He turns on Belle furiously.*) Why didn't you put me wise, you lousy tramp, you!

BELLE—Hey! I don't stand for that kind of talk—not from no hick beer-squirter like you, see!

BARTENDER—(*furiously*) You don't, don't you! Who was it but you told me to hand him dynamite in that fizz? (*He gives her chair a push that almost throws her to the floor.*) Beat it, you—and beat it quick—or I'll call Sullivan from the corner and have you run in for street-walking! (*He gives her a push that lands her against the family-entrance door.*) Get the hell out of here—and no long waits!

BELLE—(*opens the door and goes out—turns and calls back viciously*) I'll fix you for this, you thick Mick, if I have to go to jail for it. (*She goes out and slams the door.*)

BARTENDER—(*looks after her worriedly for a second—then shrugs his shoulders*) That's only her bull. (*then with a sigh as he returns to the bar*) Them lousy tramps is always getting this dump in Dutch!

(*Curtain*)

SCENE TWO

SCENE—*Same as Act One—Sitting-room of the Miller home—about 11 o'clock the same night.*

Miller is sitting in his favorite rocking-chair at left of table, front. He has discarded collar and tie, coat and shoes, and wears an old, worn, brown dressing-gown and disreputable-looking carpet slippers. He has his reading specs on and is running over items in a newspaper. But his mind is plainly preoccupied and worried, and he is not paying much attention to what he reads.

Mrs. Miller sits by the table at right, front. She also has on her specs. A sewing basket is on her lap and she is trying hard to keep her attention fixed on the doily she is doing. But, as in the case of her husband, but much more apparently, her mind is preoccupied, and she is obviously on tenterhooks of nervous uneasiness.

Lily is sitting in the armchair by the table at rear, facing right. She is pretending to read a novel, but her attention wanders, too, and her expression is sad, although now it has lost all its bitterness and become submissive and resigned again.

Mildred sits at the desk at right, front, writing two words over and over again, stopping each time to survey the result critically, biting her tongue, intensely concentrated on her work.

Tommy sits on the sofa at left, front. He has had a hard day and is terribly sleepy but will not acknowledge it. His eyes blink shut on him, his head begins to nod, but he isn't giving up, and every time he senses any of the family glancing in his direction, he goads himself into a bright-eyed wakefulness.

MILDRED — (*finally surveys the two words she has been writing and is satisfied with them*) There. (*She takes the paper over to her mother.*) Look, Ma. I've been practising a new way of writing my name. Don't look at the others, only the last one. Don't you think it's the real goods?

MRS. MILLER — (*pulled out of her preoccupation*) Don't talk that horrible slang. It's bad enough for boys, but for a young girl supposed to have manners — my goodness, when I was your age, if my mother'd ever heard me —

MILDRED — Well, don't you think it's nice, then?

MRS. MILLER — (*sinks back into preoccupation — scanning the paper — vaguely*) Yes, very nice, Mildred — very nice, indeed. (*hands the paper back mechanically*)

MILDRED — (*is a little piqued, but smiles*) Absent-minded! I don't believe you even saw it. (*She passes around the table to show her Aunt Lily. Miller gives an uneasy glance at his wife and then, as if afraid of meeting her eye, looks quickly back at his paper again.*)

MRS. MILLER — (*staring before her — sighs worriedly*) Oh, I do wish Richard would come home!

MILLER — There now, Essie. He'll be in any minute now. Don't you worry about him.

MRS. MILLER — But I do worry about him!

LILY — (*surveying Mildred's handiwork — smiling*) This is fine, Mildred. Your penmanship is improving wonderfully.

But don't you think that maybe you've got a little too many flourishes?

MILDRED—(*disappointedly*) But, Aunt Lily, that's just what I was practising hardest on.

MRS. MILLER—(*with another sigh*) What time is it now, Nat?

MILLER—(*adopting a joking tone*) I'm going to buy a clock for in here. You have me reaching for my watch every couple of minutes. (*He has pulled his watch out of his vest pocket—with forced carelessness*) Only a little past ten.

MRS. MILLER—Why, you said it was that an hour ago! Nat Miller, you're telling me a fib, so's not to worry me. You let me see that watch!

MILLER—(*guiltily*) Well, it's quarter to eleven—but that's not so late—when you remember it's Fourth of July.

MRS. MILLER—If you don't stop talking Fourth of July—! To hear you go on, you'd think that was an excuse for anything from murder to picking pockets!

MILDRED—(*has brought her paper around to her father and now shoves it under his nose*) Look, Pa.

MILLER—(*seizes on this interruption with relief*) Let's see. Hmm. Seems to me you've been inventing a new signature every week lately. What are you in training for—writing checks? You must be planning to catch a rich husband.

MILDRED—(*with an arch toss of her head*) No wedding bells for me! But how do you like it, Pa?

MILLER—It's overpowering—no other word for it, overpowering! You could put it on the Declaration of Independence and not feel ashamed.

MRS. MILLER—(*desolately, almost on the verge of tears*) It's all right for you to laugh and joke with Mildred! I'm the only one in this house seems to care— (*Her lips tremble.*)

MILDRED—(*a bit disgustedly*) Ah, Ma, Dick only sneaked off to the fireworks at the beach, you wait and see.

MRS. MILLER—Those fireworks were over long ago. If he had, he'd be home.

LILY—(*soothingly*) He probably couldn't get a seat, the trolleys are so jammed, and he had to walk home.

MILLER—(*seizing on this with relief*) Yes, I never thought of that, but I'll bet that's it.

MILDRED—Ah, don't let him worry you, Ma. He just wants to show off he's heart-broken about that silly Muriel—and get everyone fussing over him and wondering if he hasn't drowned himself or something.

MRS. MILLER—(*snappily*) You be quiet! The way you talk at times, I really believe you're that hard-hearted you haven't got a heart in you! (*with an accusing glance at her husband*) One thing I know, you don't get that from me! (*He meets her eye and avoids it guiltily. She sniffs and looks away from him around the room. Tommy, who is nodding and blinking, is afraid her eye is on him. He straightens alertly and speaks in a voice that, in spite of his effort, is dripping with drowsiness.*)

TOMMY—Let me see what you wrote, Mid.

MILDRED—(*cruelly mocking*) You? You're so sleepy you couldn't see it!

TOMMY—(*valiantly*) I am not sleepy!

MRS. MILLER—(*has fixed her eye on him*) My gracious, I was forgetting you were still up! You run up to bed this minute! It's hours past your bedtime!

TOMMY—But it's the Fourth of July. Ain't it, Pa?

MRS. MILLER—(*gives her husband an accusing stare*) There! You see what you've done? You might know he'd copy your excuses! (*then sharply to Tommy*) You heard what I said, Young Man!

TOMMY—Aw, Ma, can't I stay up a *little* longer?

MRS. MILLER—I said, no! You obey me and no more arguing about it!

TOMMY—(*drags himself to his feet*) Aw! I should think I could stay up till Dick—

MILLER—(*kindly but firmly*) You heard your ma say no more arguing. When she says git, you better git. (*Tommy accepts his fate resignedly and starts around kissing them all good night.*)

TOMMY—(*kissing her*) Good night, Aunt Lily.

LILY—Good night, Dear. Sleep well.

TOMMY—(*pecking at Mildred*) Good night, you.

MILDRED—Good night, you.

TOMMY—(*kissing him*) Good night, Pa.

MILLER—Good night, Son. Sleep tight.

TOMMY—(*kissing her*) Good night, Ma.

MRS. MILLER—Good night. Here! You look feverish. Let me feel of your head. No, you're all right. Hurry up, now. And don't forget your prayers.

(*Tommy goes slowly to the doorway—then turns suddenly, the discovery of another excuse lighting up his face.*)

TOMMY—Here's another thing, Ma. When I was up to the water closet last—

MRS. MILLER—(*sharply*) When you were *where*?

TOMMY—The bathroom.

MRS. MILLER—That's better.

TOMMY—Uncle Sid was snoring like a fog horn—and he's right next to my room. How can I ever get to sleep while he's— (*He is overcome by a jaw-cracking yawn.*)

MRS. MILLER—I guess you'd get to sleep all right if you were inside a fog horn. You run along now. (*Tommy gives up, grins sleepily, and moves off to bed. As soon as he is off her mind, all her former uneasiness comes back on Mrs. Miller tenfold. She sighs, moves restlessly, then finally asks*) What time is it now, Nat?

MILLER—Now, Essie, I just told you a minute ago.

MRS. MILLER—(*resentfully*) I don't see how you can take it so calm! Here it's midnight, you might say, and our Richard still out, and we don't even know where he is.

MILDRED—I hear someone on the piazza. Bet that's him now, Ma.

MRS. MILLER—(*her anxiety immediately turning to relieved anger*) You give him a good piece of your mind, Nat, you hear me! You're too easy with him, that's the whole trouble! The idea of him daring to stay out like this! (*The front door is heard being opened and shut, and someone whistling "Waltz Me Around Again, Willie."*)

MILDRED—No, that isn't Dick. It's Art.

MRS. MILLER—(*her face falling*) Oh. (*A moment later Arthur enters through the front parlor, whistling softly, half under his breath, looking complacently pleased with himself.*)

MILLER—(*surveys him over his glasses, not with enthusiasm— shortly*) So you're back, eh? We thought it was Richard.

ARTHUR—Is he still out? Where'd he go to?

MILLER—That's just what we'd like to know. You didn't run into him anywhere, did you?

ARTHUR—No. I've been at the Rands' ever since dinner. (*He sits down in the armchair at left of table, rear.*) I suppose he sneaked off to the beach to watch the fireworks.

MILLER—(*pretending an assurance he is far from feeling*) Of course. That's what we've been trying to tell your mother, but she insists on worrying her head off.

MRS. MILLER—But if he was going to the fireworks, why wouldn't he say so? He knew we'd let him.

ARTHUR—(*with calm wisdom*) That's easy, Ma. (*He grins superiorly.*) Didn't you hear him this morning showing off bawling out the Fourth like an anarchist? He wouldn't want to reneg on that to you—but he'd want to see the old fireworks just the same. (*He adds complacently*) I know. He's at the foolish age.

MILLER—(*stares at Arthur with ill-concealed astonishment, then grins*) Well, Arthur, by gosh, you make me feel as if I owed you an apology when you talk horse sense like that. (*He turns to his wife, greatly relieved.*) Arthur's hit the nail right on the head, I think, Essie. That was what I couldn't figure out—why he—but now it's clear as day.

MRS. MILLER—(*with a sigh*) Well, I hope you're right. But I wish he was home.

ARTHUR—(*takes out his pipe and fills and lights it with solemn gravity*) He oughtn't to be allowed out this late at his age. I wasn't, Fourth or no Fourth—if I remember.

MILLER—(*a twinkle in his eyes*) Don't tax your memory trying to recall those ancient days of your youth. (*Mildred laughs and Arthur looks sheepish. But he soon regains his aplomb.*)

ARTHUR—(*importantly*) We had a corking dinner at the Rands'. We had sweetbreads on toast.

MRS. MILLER—(*arising momentarily from her depression*) Just like the Rands to put on airs before you! I never could see anything to sweetbreads. Always taste like soap to me. And no real nourishment to them. I wouldn't have the pesky things on my table! (*Arthur again feels sat upon.*)

MILDRED—(*teasingly*) Did you kiss Elsie good night?

ARTHUR—Stop trying to be so darn funny all the time! You give me a pain in the ear!

MILDRED—And that's where she gives me a pain, the stuck-up thing!—thinks she's the whole cheese!

MILLER—(*irritably*) And it's where your everlasting wrangling gives me a pain, you two! Give us a rest! (*There is silence for a moment.*)

MRS. MILLER—(*sighs worriedly again*) I do wish that boy would get home!

MILLER—(*glances at her uneasily, peeks surreptitiously at his watch—then has an inspiration and turns to Arthur*) Arthur, what's this I hear about your having such a good singing voice? Rand was telling me he liked nothing better than to hear you sing—said you did every night you were up there. Why don't you ever give us folks at home here a treat?

ARTHUR—(*pleased, but still nursing wounded dignity*) I thought you'd only sit on me.

MRS. MILLER—(*perking up—proudly*) Arthur has a real nice voice. He practises when you're not at home. I didn't know you cared for singing, Nat.

MILLER—Well, I do—nothing better—and when I was a boy I had a fine voice myself and folks used to say I'd ought— (*then abruptly, mindful of his painful experience with reminiscence at dinner, looking about him guiltily*) Hmm. But don't hide your light under a bushel, Arthur. Why not give us a song or two now? You can play for him, can't you, Mildred?

MILDRED—(*with a toss of her head*) I can play as well as Elsie Rand, at least!

ARTHUR—(*ignoring her—clearing his throat importantly*) I've been singing a lot tonight. I don't know if my voice—

MILDRED—(*forgetting her grudge, grabs her brother's hand and tugs at it*) Come on. Don't play modest. You know you're just dying to show off. (*This puts Arthur off it at once. He snatches his hand away from her angrily.*)

ARTHUR—Let go of me, you! (*then with surly dignity*) I don't feel like singing tonight, Pa. I will some other time.

MILLER—You let him alone, Mildred! (*He winks at Arthur, indicating with his eyes and a nod of his head Mrs. Miller, who has again sunk into worried brooding. He makes it plain by this pantomime that he wants him to sing to distract his mother's mind.*)

ARTHUR—(*puts aside his pipe and gets up promptly*) Oh—sure, I'll do the best I can. (*He follows Mildred into the front parlor, where he switches on the lights.*)

MILLER—(*to his wife*) It won't keep Tommy awake. Nothing could. And Sid, he'd sleep through an earthquake. (*then suddenly, looking through the front parlor—grumpily*) Darn it, speak of the devil, here he comes. Well, he's had a good sleep and he'd ought to be sobered up. (*Lily gets up from her chair and looks around her huntedly, as if for a place to hide. Miller says soothingly*) Lily, you just sit down and read your book and don't pay any attention to him. (*She sits down again and bends over her book tensely. From the front parlor comes the tinkling of a piano as Mildred runs over the scales. In the midst of this, Sid enters through the front parlor. All the effervescence of his jag has worn off and he is now suffering from a bad case of hangover—nervous, sick, a prey to gloomy remorse and bitter feelings of self-loathing and self-pity. His eyes are bloodshot and puffed, his face bloated, the fringe of hair around his baldness tousled and tufty. He sidles into the room guiltily, his eyes shifting about, avoiding looking at anyone.*)

SID—(*forcing a sickly, twitching smile*) Hello.

MILLER—(*considerately casual*) Hello, Sid. Had a good nap? (*Then, as Sid swallows hard and is about to break into further speech, Mildred's voice comes from the front parlor,* "I haven't played that in ever so long, but I'll try," *and she starts an accompaniment. Miller motions Sid to be quiet.*) Ssshh! Arthur's going to sing for us. (*Sid flattens himself against the edge of the bookcase at center, rear, miserably self-conscious and ill-at-ease there but nervously afraid to move anywhere else. Arthur begins to sing. He has a fairly decent voice but his method is untrained sentimentality to a dripping degree. He sings that old sentimental favorite,* "Then You'll Remember Me." *The effect on his audience is instant. Miller gazes before him with a ruminating melancholy, his face seeming to become gently sorrowful and old. Mrs. Miller stares before her, her expression becoming more and more doleful. Lily forgets to pretend to read her book but looks over it, her face growing tragically sad. As for Sid, he is moved to his remorseful, guilt-stricken depths. His mouth pulls down at the corners and he seems about to cry. The song comes to an end. Miller starts, then claps his hands enthusiastically and calls*) Well done, Arthur—well done! Why, you've got a splendid voice! Give us some more! You liked that, didn't you, Essie?

MRS. MILLER—(*dolefully*) Yes—but it's sad—terrible sad.

SID—(*after swallowing hard, suddenly blurts out*) Nat and Essie—and Lily—I—I want to apologize—for coming home—the way I did—there's no excuse—but I didn't mean—

MILLER—(*sympathetically*) Of course, Sid. It's all forgotten.

MRS. MILLER—(*rousing herself—affectionately pitying*) Don't be a goose, Sid. We know how it is with picnics. You forget it. (*His face lights up a bit but his gaze shifts to Lily with a mute appeal, hoping for a word from her which is not forthcoming. Her eyes are fixed on her book, her body tense and rigid.*)

SID—(*finally blurts out desperately*) Lily—I'm sorry—about the fireworks. Can you—forgive me? (*But Lily remains implacably silent. A stricken look comes over Sid's face. In the front parlor Mildred is heard saying "But I only know the chorus"—and she starts another accompaniment.*)

MILLER—(*comes to Sid's rescue*) Ssshh! We're going to have another song. Sit down, Sid. (*Sid, hanging his head, flees to the farthest corner, left, front, and sits at the end of the sofa, facing front, hunched up, elbows on knees, face in hands, his round eyes childishly wounded and woe-begone. Arthur sings the popular "Dearie," playing up its sentimental values for all he is worth. The effect on his audience is that of the previous song, intensified—especially upon Sid. As he finishes, Miller again starts and applauds.*) Mighty fine, Arthur! You sang that darned well! Didn't he, Essie?

MRS. MILLER—(*dolefully*) Yes—but I wish he wouldn't sing such sad songs. (*then, her lips trembling*) Richard's always whistling that.

MILLER—(*hastily—calls*) Give us something cheery, next one, Arthur. You know, just for variety's sake.

SID—(*suddenly turns toward Lily—his voice choked with tears—in a passion of self-denunciation*) You're right, Lily!—right not to forgive me!—I'm no good and never will be!—I'm a no-good drunken bum!—you shouldn't even wipe your feet on me!—I'm a dirty, rotten drunk!—no good to myself or anybody else!—if I had any guts I'd kill myself, and good riddance!—but I haven't!—I'm yellow, too!—a yellow, drunken bum! (*He hides his face in his hands and begins to sob like a sick little boy. This is too much for Lily. All her bitter hurt and steely resolve to ignore and punish him vanish in a flash, swamped by a pitying love for him. She runs and puts her arm around him—even kisses him tenderly and impulsively on his bald head, and soothes him as if he were a little boy. Mrs. Miller, almost equally moved, has half risen to go to her brother, too, but Miller winks and shakes his head vigorously and motions her to sit down.*)

LILY—There! Don't cry, Sid! I can't bear it! Of course, I forgive you! Haven't I always forgiven you? I know you're not to blame— So don't, Sid!

SID—(*lifts a tearful, humbly grateful, pathetic face to her—but a face that the dawn of a cleansed conscience is already beginning to restore to its natural Puckish expression*) Do you really forgive me— I know I don't deserve it—can you really—?

LILY—(*gently*) I told you I did, Sid—and I do.

SID—(*kisses her hand humbly, like a big puppy licking it*) Thanks, Lily. I can't tell you— (*In the front parlor, Arthur begins to sing rollickingly "Waiting at the Church," and after the first line or two Mildred joins in. Sid's face lights up with appreciation and, automatically, he begins to tap one foot in time, still holding fast to Lily's hand. When they come to "sent around a note, this is what she wrote," he can no longer resist, but joins in a shaky bawl*) "Can't get away to marry you to-day, My wife won't let me!" (*As the song finishes, the two in the other room laugh. Miller and Sid laugh. Lily smiles at Sid's laughter. Only Mrs. Miller remains dolefully preoccupied, as if she hadn't heard.*)

MILLER—That's fine, Arthur and Mildred. That's darned good.

SID—(*turning to Lily enthusiastically*) You ought to hear Vesta Victoria sing that! Gosh, she's great! I heard her at Hammerstein's Victoria—you remember, that trip I made to New York.

LILY—(*her face suddenly tired and sad again—for her memory of certain aspects of that trip is the opposite from what he would like her to recall at this moment—gently disengaging her hand from his—with a hopeless sigh*) Yes, I remember, Sid. (*He is overcome momentarily by guilty confusion. She goes quietly and sits down in her chair again. In the front parlor, from now on, Mildred keeps starting to run over popular tunes but always gets stuck and turns to another.*)

MRS. MILLER—(*suddenly*) What time is it now, Nat? (*then without giving him a chance to answer*) Oh, I'm getting worried something dreadful, Nat! You don't know what might have happened to Richard! You read in the papers every day about boys getting run over by automobiles.

LILY—Oh, don't say that, Essie!

MILLER—(*sharply, to conceal his own reawakened apprehension*) Don't get to imagining things, now!

MRS. MILLER—Well, why couldn't it happen, with everyone that owns one out tonight, and lots of those driving, drunk? Or he might have gone down to the beach dock and fallen overboard! (*on the verge of hysteria*) Oh, I know something dreadful's happened! And you can sit there listening to songs and laughing as if— Why don't you do something? Why don't you go out and find him? (*She bursts into tears.*)

LILY—(*comes to her quickly and puts her arm around her*) Essie, you mustn't worry so! You'll make yourself sick! Richard's all right. I've got a feeling in my bones he's all right.

MILDRED—(*comes hurrying in from the front parlor*) What's the trouble? (*Arthur appears in the doorway beside her. She goes to her mother and also puts an arm around her.*) Ah, don't cry, Ma! Dick'll turn up in a minute or two, wait and see!

ARTHUR—Sure, he will!

MILLER—(*has gotten to his feet, frowning—soberly*) I was going out to look—if he wasn't back by twelve sharp. That'd be the time it'd take him to walk from the beach if he left after the last car. But I'll go now, if it'll ease your mind. I'll take the auto and drive out the beach road—and likely pick him up on the way. (*He has taken his collar and tie from where they hang from one corner of the bookcase at rear, center, and is starting to put them on.*) You better come with me, Arthur.

ARTHUR—Sure thing, Pa. (*Suddenly he listens and says*) Ssshh! There's someone on the piazza now—coming around to this door, too. That must be him. No one else would—

MRS. MILLER—Oh, thank God, thank God!

MILLER—(*with a sheepish smile*) Darn him! I've a notion to

give him hell for worrying us all like this. (*The screen door is pushed violently open and Richard lurches in and stands swaying a little, blinking his eyes in the light. His face is a pasty pallor, shining with perspiration, and his eyes are glassy. The knees of his trousers are dirty, one of them torn from the sprawl on the sidewalk he had taken, following the bartender's kick. They all gape at him, too paralyzed for a moment to say anything.*)

MRS. MILLER—Oh God, what's happened to him! He's gone crazy! Richard!

SID—(*the first to regain presence of mind—with a grin*) Crazy, nothing. He's only soused!

ARTHUR—He's drunk, that's what! (*then shocked and condemning*) You've got your nerve! You fresh kid! We'll take that out of you when we get you down to Yale!

RICHARD—(*with a wild gesture of defiance—maudlinly dramatic*)

> "Yesterday this Day's Madness did prepare
> Tomorrow's Silence, Triumph, or Despair.
> Drink! for—"

MILLER—(*his face grown stern and angry, takes a threatening step toward him*) Richard! How dare—!

MRS. MILLER—(*hysterically*) Don't you strike him, Nat! Don't you—!

SID—(*grabbing his arm*) Steady, Nat! Keep your temper! No good bawling him out now! He don't know what he's doing!

MILLER—(*controlling himself and looking a bit ashamed*) All right—you're right, Sid.

RICHARD—(*drunkenly glorying in the sensation he is creating—recites with dramatic emphasis*) "And then—I will come —with vine leaves in my hair!" (*He laughs with a double-dyed sardonicism.*)

MRS. MILLER—(*staring at him as if she couldn't believe her eyes*) Richard! You're intoxicated!—you bad, wicked boy, you!

RICHARD—(*forces a wicked leer to his lips and quotes with ponderous mockery*) "Fancy that, Hedda!" (*Then suddenly his whole expression changes, his pallor takes on a greenish, sea-sick tinge, his eyes seem to be turned inward uneasily—and, all pose*

gone, he calls to his mother appealingly, like a sick little boy) Ma!
I feel—rotten! (*Mrs. Miller gives a cry and starts to go to him,
but Sid steps in her way.*)

SID—You let me take care of him, Essie. I know this game
backwards.

MILLER—(*putting his arm around his wife*) Yes, you leave
him to Sid.

SID—(*his arm around Richard—leading him off through the
front parlor*) Come on, Old Sport! Upstairs we go! Your old
Uncle Sid'll fix you up. He's the kid that wrote the book!

MRS. MILLER—(*staring after them—still aghast*) Oh, it's
too terrible! Imagine our Richard! And did you hear him
talking about some Hedda? Oh, I know he's been with one
of those bad women, I know he has—my Richard! (*She hides
her face on Miller's shoulder and sobs heart-brokenly.*)

MILLER—(*a tired, harassed, deeply worried look on his face—
soothing her*) Now, now, you mustn't get to imagining such
things! You mustn't, Essie! (*Lily and Mildred and Arthur are
standing about awkwardly with awed, shocked faces.*)

(*Curtain*)

ACT FOUR
Scene One

Scene—*The same*—*Sitting-room of the Miller house*—*about 1 o'clock in the afternoon of the following day.*

As the curtain rises, the family, with the exception of Richard, are discovered coming in through the back parlor from dinner in the dining-room. Miller and his wife come first. His face is set in an expression of frowning severity. Mrs. Miller's face is drawn and worried. She has evidently had no rest yet from a sleepless, tearful night. Sid is himself again, his expression as innocent as if nothing had occurred the previous day that remotely concerned him. And, outside of eyes that are blood-shot and nerves that are shaky, he shows no after-effects except that he is terribly sleepy. Lily is gently sad and depressed. Arthur is self-consciously a virtuous young man against whom nothing can be said. Mildred and Tommy are subdued, covertly watching their father.

They file into the sitting-room in silence and then stand around uncertainly, as if each were afraid to be the first to sit down. The atmosphere is as stiltedly grave as if they were attending a funeral service. Their eyes keep fixed on the head of the house, who has gone to the window at right and is staring out frowningly, savagely chewing a toothpick.

Miller—(*finally—irritably*) Damn it, I'd ought to be back at the office putting in some good licks! I've a whole pile of things that have got to be done today!

Mrs. Miller—(*accusingly*) You don't mean to tell me you're going back without seeing him? It's your duty—!

Miller—(*exasperatedly*) 'Course I'm not! I wish you'd stop jumping to conclusions! What else did I come home for, I'd like to know? Do I usually come way back here for dinner on a busy day? I was only wishing this hadn't come up—just at this particular time. (*He ends up very lamely and is irritably conscious of the fact.*)

Tommy—(*who has been fidgeting restlessly—unable to bear the suspense a moment longer*) What is it Dick done? Why is everyone scared to tell me?

Miller—(*seizes this as an escape valve—turns and fixes his youngest son with a stern forbidding eye*) Young man, I've never

75

spanked you yet, but that don't mean I never will! Seems to me that you've been just itching for it lately! You keep your mouth shut till you're spoken to—or I warn you something's going to happen!

MRS. MILLER—Yes, Tommy, you keep still and don't bother your pa. (*then warningly to her husband*) Careful what you say, Nat. Little pitchers have big ears.

MILLER—(*peremptorily*) You kids skedaddle—all of you. Why are you always hanging around the house? Go out and play in the yard, or take a walk, and get some fresh air. (*Mildred takes Tommy's hand and leads him out through the front parlor. Arthur hangs back, as if the designation "kids" couldn't possibly apply to him. His father notices this—impatiently*) You, too, Arthur. (*Arthur goes out with a stiff, wounded dignity.*)

LILY—(*tactfully*) I think I'll go for a walk, too. (*She goes out through the front parlor. Sid makes a movement as if to follow her.*)

MILLER—I'd like you to stay, Sid—for a while, anyway.

SID—Sure. (*He sits down in the rocking-chair at right, rear, of table and immediately yawns.*) Gosh, I'm dead. Don't know what's the matter with me today. Can't seem to keep awake.

MILLER—(*with caustic sarcasm*) Maybe that demon chowder you drank at the picnic poisoned you! (*Sid looks sheepish and forces a grin. Then Miller turns to his wife with the air of one who determinedly faces the unpleasant.*) Where is Richard?

MRS. MILLER—(*flusteredly*) He's still in bed. I made him stay in bed to punish him—and I thought he ought to, anyway, after being so sick. But he says he feels all right.

SID—(*with another yawn*) 'Course he does. When you're young you can stand anything without it feazing you. Why, I remember when I could come down on the morning after, fresh as a daisy, and eat a breakfast of pork chops and fried onions and— (*He stops guiltily.*)

MILLER—(*bitingly*) I suppose that was before eating lobster shells had ruined your iron constitution!

MRS. MILLER—(*regards her brother severely*) If I was in your shoes, I'd keep still! (*then turning to her husband*)

Richard must be feeling better. He ate all the dinner I sent up, Norah says.

MILLER—I thought you weren't going to give him any dinner—to punish him.

MRS. MILLER—(*guiltily*) Well—in his weakened condition—I thought it best— (*then defensively*) But you needn't think I haven't punished him. I've given him pieces of my mind he won't forget in a hurry. And I've kept reminding him his real punishment was still to come—that you were coming home to dinner on purpose—and then he'd learn that you could be terrible stern when he did such awful things.

MILLER—(*stirs uncomfortably*) Hmm!

MRS. MILLER—And that's just what it's your duty to do—punish him good and hard! The idea of him daring— (*then hastily*) But you be careful how you go about it, Nat. Remember he's like you inside—too sensitive for his own good. And he never would have done it, I know, if it hadn't been for that darned little dunce, Muriel, and her numbskull father—and then all of us teasing him and hurting his feelings all day—and then you lost your temper and were so sharp with him right after dinner before he went out.

MILLER—(*resentfully*) I see this is going to work round to where it's all my fault!

MRS. MILLER—Now, I didn't say that, did I? Don't go losing your temper again. And here's another thing. You know as well as I, Richard would never have done such a thing alone. Why, he wouldn't know how! He must have been influenced and led by someone.

MILLER—Yes, I believe that. Did you worm out of him who it was? (*then angrily*) By God, I'll make whoever it was regret it!

MRS. MILLER—No, he wouldn't admit there was anyone. (*then triumphantly*) But there is one thing I did worm out of him—and I can tell you it relieved my mind more'n anything. You know, I was afraid he'd been with one of those bad women. Well, turns out there wasn't any Hedda. She was just out of those books he's been reading. He swears he's never known a Hedda in his life. And I believe him. Why, he seemed disgusted with me for having such a notion. (*then lamely*) So somehow—I can't kind of feel it's all as bad as I thought it was. (*then quickly and indignantly*) But it's bad enough, goodness knows—and you punish him good just the same. The idea of a boy of his age—! Shall I go up now and tell him to get dressed, you want to see him?

MILLER—(*helplessly—and irritably*) Yes! I can't waste all day listening to you!

MRS. MILLER—(*worriedly*) Now you keep your temper, Nat, remember! (*She goes out through the front parlor.*)

MILLER—Darn women, anyway! They always get you mixed up. Their minds simply don't know what logic is! (*Then he notices that Sid is dozing—sharply*) Sid!

SID—(*blinking—mechanically*) I'll take the same. (*then hurriedly*) What'd you say, Nat?

MILLER—(*caustically*) What I didn't say was what'll you have. (*irritably*) Do you want to be of some help, or don't you? Then keep awake and try and use your brains! This is a damned sight more serious than Essie has any idea! She thinks there weren't any girls mixed up with Richard's spree last night—but I happen to know there were! (*He takes a letter from his pocket.*) Here's a note a woman left with one of the boys downstairs at the office this morning—didn't ask to see me, just said give me this. He'd never seen her before— said she looked like a tart. (*He has opened the letter and reads*) "Your son got the booze he drank last night at the Pleasant Beach House. The bartender there knew he was under age but served him just the same. He thought it was a good joke to get him soused. If you have any guts you will run that bastard out of town." Well, what do you think of that? It's a woman's handwriting—not signed, of course.

SID—She's one of the babies, all right—judging from her elegant language.

MILLER—See if you recognize the handwriting.

SID—(*with a reproachful look*) Nat, I resent the implication that I correspond with all the tramps around this town. (*looking at the letter*) No, I don't know who this one could be. (*handing the letter back*) But I deduce that the lady had a run-in with the barkeep and wants revenge.

MILLER—(*grimly*) And I deduce that before that she must

have picked up Richard—or how would she know who he was?—and took him to this dive.

SID—Maybe. The Pleasant Beach House is nothing but a bed house— (*quickly*) At least, so I've been told.

MILLER—That's just the sort of damned fool thing he might do to spite Muriel, in the state of mind he was in— pick up some tart. And she'd try to get him drunk so—

SID—Yes, it might have happened like that—and it might not. How're we ever going to prove it? Everyone at the Pleasant Beach will lie their heads off.

MILLER—(*simply and proudly*) Richard won't lie.

SID—Well, don't blame him if he don't remember everything that happened last night. (*then sincerely concerned*) I hope you're wrong, Nat. That kind of baby is dangerous for a kid like Dick—in more ways than one. You know what I mean.

MILLER—(*frowningly*) Yep—and that's just what's got me worried. Damn it, I've got to have a straight talk with him— about women and all those things. I ought to have long ago.

SID—Yes. You ought.

MILLER—I've tried to a couple of times. I did it all right with Wilbur and Lawrence and Arthur, when it came time— but, hell, with Richard I always get sort of ashamed of myself and can't get started right. You feel, in spite of all his bold talk out of books, that he's so darned innocent inside.

SID—I know. I wouldn't like the job. (*then after a pause— curiously*) How were you figuring to punish him for his sins?

MILLER—(*frowning*) To be honest with you, Sid, I'm damned if I know. All depends on what I feel about what he feels when I first size him up—and then it'll be like shooting in the dark.

SID—If I didn't know you so well, I'd say don't be too hard on him. (*He smiles a little bitterly.*) If you remember, I was always getting punished—and see what a lot of good it did me!

MILLER—(*kindly*) Oh, there's lots worse than you around, so don't take to boasting. (*then, at a sound from the front parlor—with a sigh*) Well, here comes the Bad Man, I guess.

SID—(*getting up*) I'll beat it. (*But it is Mrs. Miller who appears in the doorway, looking guilty and defensive. Sid sits down again.*)

MRS. MILLER—I'm sorry, Nat—but he was sound asleep and I didn't have the heart to wake him. I waited for him to wake up but he didn't.

MILLER—(*concealing a relief of which he is ashamed—exasperatedly*) Well, I'll be double damned! If you're not the—

MRS. MILLER—(*defensively aggressive*) Now don't lose your temper at me, Nat Miller! You know as well as I do he needs all the sleep he can get today—after last night's ructions! Do you want him to be taken down sick? And what difference does it make to you, anyway? You can see him when you come home for supper, can't you? My goodness, I never saw you so savage-tempered! You'd think you couldn't bear waiting to punish him!

MILLER—(*outraged*) Well, I'll be eternally— (*Then suddenly he laughs.*) No use talking, you certainly take the cake! But you know darned well I told you I'm not coming home to supper tonight. I've got a date with Jack Lawson that may mean a lot of new advertising and it's important.

MRS. MILLER—Then you can see him when you do come home.

MILLER—(*covering his evident relief at this respite with a fuming manner*) All right! All right! I give up! I'm going back to the office. (*He starts for the front parlor.*) Bring a man all the way back here on a busy day and then you— No consideration— (*He disappears, and a moment later the front door is heard shutting behind him.*)

MRS. MILLER—Well! I never saw Nat so bad-tempered.

SID—(*with a chuckle*) Bad temper, nothing. He's so tickled to get out of it for a while he can't see straight!

MRS. MILLER—(*with a sniff*) I hope I know him better than you. (*then fussing about the room, setting this and that in place, while Sid yawns drowsily and blinks his eyes*) Sleeping like a baby—so innocent-looking. You'd think butter wouldn't melt in his mouth. It all goes to show you never can tell by appearances—not even when it's your own child. The idea!

SID—(*drowsily*) Oh, Dick's all right, Essie. Stop worrying.

MRS. MILLER—(*with a sniff*) Of course, you'd say that. I

suppose you'll have him out with you painting the town red the next thing! (*As she is talking, Richard appears in the doorway from the sitting-room. He shows no ill effects from his experience the night before. In fact, he looks surprisingly healthy. He is dressed in old clothes that look as if they had been hurriedly flung on. His expression is one of hang-dog guilt mingled with a defensive defiance.*)

RICHARD—(*with self-conscious unconcern, ignoring his mother*) Hello, Sid.

MRS. MILLER—(*whirls on him*) What are you doing here, Young Man? I thought you were asleep! Seems to me you woke up pretty quick—just after your pa left the house!

RICHARD—(*sulkily*) I wasn't asleep. I heard you in the room.

MRS. MILLER—(*outraged*) Do you mean to say you were deliberately deceiving—

RICHARD—I wasn't deceiving. You didn't ask if I was asleep.

MRS. MILLER—It amounts to the same thing and you know it! It isn't enough your wickedness last night, but now you have to take to lying!

RICHARD—I wasn't lying, Ma. If you'd asked if I was asleep I'd have said no.

MRS. MILLER—I've a good mind to send you straight back to bed and make you stay there!

RICHARD—Ah, what for, Ma? It was only giving me a headache, lying there.

MRS. MILLER—If you've got a headache, I guess you know it doesn't come from that! And imagine me standing there, and feeling sorry for you, like a fool—even having a run-in with your pa because— But you wait till he comes back tonight! If you don't catch it!

RICHARD—(*sulkily*) I don't care.

MRS. MILLER—You don't care? You talk as if you weren't sorry for what you did last night!

RICHARD—(*defiantly*) I'm not sorry.

MRS. MILLER—Richard! You ought to be ashamed! I'm beginning to think you're hardened in wickedness, that's what!

RICHARD—(*with bitter despondency*) I'm not sorry because

I don't care a darn what I did, or what's done to me, or anything about anything! I won't do it again—

MRS. MILLER—(*seizing on this to relent a bit*) Well, I'm glad to hear you say that, anyway!

RICHARD—But that's not because I think it was wicked or any such old-fogy moral notion, but because it wasn't any fun. It didn't make me happy and funny like it does Uncle Sid—

SID—(*drowsily*) What's that? Who's funny?

RICHARD—(*ignoring him*) It only made me sadder—and sick—so I don't see any sense in it.

MRS. MILLER—Now you're talking sense! That's a good boy.

RICHARD—But I'm not sorry I tried it once—curing the soul by means of the senses, as Oscar Wilde says. (*then with despairing pessimism*) But what does it matter what I do or don't do? Life is all a stupid farce! I'm through with it! (*with a sinister smile*) It's lucky there aren't any of General Gabler's pistols around—or you'd see if I'd stand it much longer!

MRS. MILLER—(*worriedly impressed by this threat—but pretending scorn*) I don't know anything about General Gabler— I suppose that's more of those darned books—but you're a silly gabbler yourself when you talk that way!

RICHARD—(*darkly*) That's how little you know about me.

MRS. MILLER—(*giving in to her worry*) I wish you wouldn't say those terrible things—about life and pistols! You don't want to worry me to death, do you?

RICHARD—(*reassuringly stoical now*) You needn't worry, Ma. It was only my despair talking. But I'm not a coward. I'll face—my fate.

MRS. MILLER—(*stands looking at him puzzledly—then gives it up with a sigh*) Well, all I can say is you're the queerest boy I ever did hear of! (*then solicitously, putting her hand on his forehead*) How's your headache? Do you want me to get you some Bromo Seltzer?

RICHARD—(*taken down—disgustedly*) No, I don't! Aw, Ma, you don't understand anything!

MRS. MILLER—Well, I understand this much: It's your liver, that's what! You'll take a good dose of salts tomorrow morning, and no nonsense about it! (*then suddenly*) My goodness, I wonder what time it's getting to be. I've got to go upstreet. (*She goes to the front-parlor doorway—then turns.*) You stay here, Richard, you hear? Remember you're not allowed out today—for a punishment. (*She hurries away. Richard sits in tragic gloom. Sid, without opening his eyes, speaks to him drowsily.*)

SID—Well, how's my fellow Rum Pot, as good old Dowie calls us? Got a head?

RICHARD—(*startled—sheepishly*) Aw, don't go dragging that up, Uncle Sid. I'm never going to be such a fool again, I tell you.

SID—(*with drowsy cynicism—not unmixed with bitterness at the end*) Seems to me I've heard someone say that before. Who could it have been, I wonder? Why, if it wasn't Sid Davis! Yes, sir, I've heard him say that very thing a thousand times, must be. But then he's always fooling; you can't take a word he says seriously; he's a card, that Sid is!

RICHARD—(*darkly*) I was desperate, Uncle—even if she wasn't worth it. I was wounded to the heart.

SID—I like to the quick better myself—more stylish. (*then sadly*) But you're right. Love is hell on a poor sucker. Don't I know it? (*Richard is disgusted and disdains to reply. Sid's chin sinks on his chest and he begins to breathe noisily, fast asleep. Richard glances at him with aversion. There is a sound of someone on the porch and the screen door is opened and Mildred enters. She smiles on seeing her uncle, then gives a start on seeing Richard.*)

MILDRED—Hello! Are you allowed up?

RICHARD—Of course, I'm allowed up.

MILDRED—(*comes and sits in her father's chair at right, front, of table*) How did Pa punish you?

RICHARD—He didn't. He went back to the office without seeing me.

MILDRED—Well, you'll catch it later. (*then rebukingly*) And you ought to. If you'd ever seen how awful you looked last night!

RICHARD—Ah, forget it, can't you?

MILDRED—Well, are you ever going to do it again, that's what I want to know.

RICHARD—What's that to you?

MILDRED—(*with suppressed excitement*) Well, if you don't solemnly swear you won't—then I won't give you something I've got for you.

RICHARD—Don't try to kid me. You haven't got anything.

MILDRED—I have, too.

RICHARD—What?

MILDRED—Wouldn't you like to know! I'll give you three guesses.

RICHARD—(*with disdainful dignity*) Don't bother me. I'm in no mood to play riddles with kids!

MILDRED—Oh, well, if you're going to get snippy! Anyway, you haven't promised yet.

RICHARD—(*a prey to keen curiosity now*) I promise. What is it?

MILDRED—What would you like best in the world?

RICHARD—I don't know. What?

MILDRED—And you pretend to be in love! If I told Muriel that!

RICHARD—(*breathlessly*) Is it—from her?

MILDRED—(*laughing*) Well, I guess it's a shame to keep you guessing. Yes. It is from her. I was walking past her place just now when I saw her waving from their parlor window, and I went up and she said give this to Dick, and she didn't have a chance to say anything else because her mother called her and said she wasn't allowed to have company. So I took it—and here it is. (*She gives him a letter folded many times into a tiny square. Richard opens it with a trembling eagerness and reads. Mildred watches him curiously—then sighs affectedly.*) Gee, it must be nice to be in love like you are—all with one person.

RICHARD—(*his eyes shining*) Gee, Mid, do you know what she says—that she didn't mean a word in that other letter. Her old man made her write it. And she loves me and only me and always will, no matter how they punish her!

MILDRED—My! I'd never think she had that much spunk.

RICHARD—Huh! You don't know her! Think I could fall in love with a girl that was afraid to say her soul's her own? I should say not! (*then more gleefully still*) And she's going to try and sneak out and meet me tonight. She says she thinks she can do it. (*then suddenly feeling this enthusiasm before*

Mildred is entirely the wrong note for a cynical pessimist —with an affected bitter laugh) Ha! I knew darned well she couldn't hold out—that she'd ask to see me again. (*He misquotes cynically*) "Women never know when the curtain has fallen. They always want another act."

MILDRED—Is that so, Smarty?

RICHARD—(*as if he were weighing the matter*) I don't know whether I'll consent to keep this date or not.

MILDRED—Well, I know! You're not allowed out, you silly! So you can't!

RICHARD—(*dropping all pretense—defiantly*) Can't I, though! You wait and see if I can't! I'll see her tonight if it's the last thing I ever do! I don't care how I'm punished after!

MILDRED—(*admiringly*) Goodness! I never thought you had such nerve!

RICHARD—You promise to keep your face shut, Mid— until after I've left—then you can tell Pa and Ma where I've gone—I mean, if they're worrying I'm off like last night.

MILDRED—All right. Only you've got to do something for me when I ask.

RICHARD—'Course I will. (*then excitedly*) And say, Mid! Right now's the best chance for me to get away—while everyone's out! Ma'll be coming back soon and she'll keep watching me like a cat— (*He starts for the back parlor.*) I'm going. I'll sneak out the back.

MILDRED—(*excitedly*) But what'll you do till nighttime? It's ages to wait.

RICHARD—What do I care how long I wait! (*intensely sincere now*) I'll think of her—and dream! I'd wait a million years and never mind it—for her! (*He gives his sister a superior scornful glance.*) The trouble with you is, you don't understand what love means! (*He disappears through the back parlor. Mildred looks after him admiringly. Sid puffs and begins to snore peacefully.*)

(*Curtain*)

SCENE TWO

SCENE—*A strip of beach along the harbor. At left, a bank of dark earth, running half-diagonally back along the beach, marking the line where the sand of the beach ends and fertile land begins. The top of the bank is grassy and the trailing boughs of willow trees extend out over it and over a part of the beach. At left, front, is a path leading up the bank, between the willows. On the beach, at center, front, a white, flat-bottomed rowboat is drawn up, its bow about touching the bank, the painter trailing up the bank, evidently made fast to the trunk of a willow. Halfway down the sky, at rear, left, the crescent of the new moon casts a soft, mysterious, caressing light over everything. The sand of the beach shimmers palely. The forward half (left of center) of the rowboat is in the deep shadow cast by the willow, the stern section is in moonlight. In the distance, the orchestra of a summer hotel can be heard very faintly at intervals.*

Richard is discovered sitting sideways on the gunwale of the rowboat near the stern. He is facing left, watching the path. He is in a great state of anxious expectancy, squirming about uncomfortably on the narrow gunwale, kicking at the sand restlessly, twirling his straw hat, with a bright-colored band in stripes, around on his finger.

RICHARD—(*thinking aloud*) Must be nearly nine. . . . I can hear the Town Hall clock strike, it's so still tonight . . . Gee, I'll bet Ma had a fit when she found out I'd sneaked out . . . I'll catch hell when I get back, but it'll be worth it . . . if only Muriel turns up . . . she didn't say for certain she could . . . gosh, I wish she'd come! . . . am I sure she wrote nine? . . . (*He puts the straw hat on the seat amidships and pulls the folded letter out of his pocket and peers at it in the moonlight.*) Yes, it's nine, all right. (*He starts to put the note back in his pocket, then stops and kisses it—then shoves it away hastily, sheepish, looking around him shamefacedly, as if afraid he were being observed.*) Aw, that's silly . . . no, it isn't either . . . not when you're really in love. . . . (*He jumps to his feet restlessly.*) Darn it, I wish she'd show up! . . . think of something else . . . that'll make the time pass quicker . . . where was I this time last night? . . . waiting outside the Pleasant Beach House . . . Belle . . . ah, forget her! . . . now, when Muriel's coming . . . that's a fine time to think of—! . . . but you hugged and kissed her . . . not until I was drunk, I didn't . . . and then it was all showing off . . . darned fool!

. . . and I didn't go upstairs with her . . . even if she was pretty . . . aw, she wasn't pretty . . . she was all painted up . . . she was just a whore . . . she was everything dirty . . . Muriel's a million times prettier anyway . . . Muriel and I will go upstairs . . . when we're married . . . but that will be beautiful . . . but I oughtn't even to think of that yet . . . it's not right . . . I'd never—now . . . and she'd never . . . she's a decent girl . . . I couldn't love her if she wasn't . . . but after we're married. . . . (*He gives a little shiver of passionate longing—then resolutely turns his mind away from these improper, almost desecrating thoughts.*) That damned barkeep kicking me . . . I'll bet you if I hadn't been drunk I'd have given him one good punch in the nose, even if he could have licked me after! . . . (*then with a shiver of shamefaced revulsion and self-disgust*) Aw, you deserved a kick in the pants . . . making such a darned slob of yourself . . . reciting the Ballad of Reading Gaol to those lowbrows! . . . you must have been a fine sight when you got home! . . . having to be put to bed and getting sick! . . . Phaw! . . . (*He squirms disgustedly.*) Think of something else, can't you? . . . recite something . . . see if you remember . . .

"Nay, let us walk from fire unto fire
From passionate pain to deadlier delight—
I am too young to live without desire,
Too young art thou to waste this summernight—"

. . . gee, that's a peach! . . . I'll have to memorize the rest and recite it to Muriel the next time. . . . I wish I could write poetry . . . about her and me. . . . (*He sighs and stares around him at the night.*) Gee, it's beautiful tonight . . . as if it was a special night . . . for me and Muriel. . . . Gee, I love tonight. . . . I love the sand, and the trees, and the grass, and the water and the sky, and the moon . . . it's all in me and I'm in it . . . God, it's so beautiful! (*He stands staring at the moon with a rapt face. From the distance the Town Hall clock begins to strike. This brings him back to earth with a start.*) There's nine now. . . . (*He peers at the path apprehensively.*) I don't see her . . . she must have got caught. . . . (*almost tearfully*) Gee, I hate to go home and catch hell . . . without having seen her! . . . (*then calling a manly cynicism to his aid*) Aw, who ever heard of a woman ever being on

time. . . . I ought to know enough about life by this time
not to expect . . . (*then with sudden excitement*) There she
comes now. . . . Gosh! (*He heaves a huge sigh of relief—then
recites dramatically to himself, his eyes on the approaching figure*)

"And lo my love, mine own soul's heart, more dear
Than mine own soul, more beautiful than God,
Who hath my being between the hands of her—"

(*then hastily*) Mustn't let her know I'm so tickled. . . . I
ought to be about that first letter, anyway . . . if women are
too sure of you, they treat you like slaves . . . let her suffer,
for a change. . . . (*He starts to stroll around with exaggerated
carelessness, turning his back on the path, hands in pockets, whistling with insouciance "Waiting at the Church."*

(*Muriel McComber enters from down the path, left front. She
is fifteen, going on sixteen. She is a pretty girl with a plump,
graceful little figure, fluffy, light-brown hair, big naïve wondering
dark eyes, a round, dimpled face, a melting drawly voice. Just now
she is in a great thrilled state of timid adventurousness. She hesitates in the shadow at the foot of the path, waiting for Richard to
see her; but he resolutely goes on whistling with back turned, and
she has to call him.*)

MURIEL—Oh, Dick.

RICHARD—(*turns around with an elaborate simulation of
being disturbed in the midst of profound meditation*) Oh, hello.
Is it nine already? Gosh, time passes—when you're thinking.

MURIEL—(*coming toward him as far as the edge of the
shadow—disappointedly*) I thought you'd be waiting right here
at the end of the path. I'll bet you'd forgotten I was even
coming.

RICHARD—(*strolling a little toward her but not too far—
carelessly*) No, I hadn't forgotten, honest. But I got to thinking about life.

MURIEL—You might think of me for a change, after all
the risk I've run to see you! (*hesitating timidly on the edge of
the shadow*) Dick! You come here to me. I'm afraid to go out
in that bright moonlight where anyone might see me.

RICHARD—(*coming toward her—scornfully*) Aw, there you
go again—always scared of life!

MURIEL—(*indignantly*) Dick Miller, I do think you've got
an awful nerve to say that after all the risks I've run making

this date and then sneaking out! You didn't take the trouble to sneak any letter to me, I notice!

RICHARD—No, because after your first letter, I thought everything was dead and past between us.

MURIEL—And I'll bet you didn't care one little bit! (*on the verge of humiliated tears*) Oh, I was a fool ever to come here! I've got a good notion to go right home and never speak to you again! (*She half turns back toward the path.*)

RICHARD—(*frightened—immediately becomes terribly sincere—grabbing her hand*) Aw, don't go, Muriel! Please! I didn't mean anything like that, honest I didn't! Gee, if you knew how broken-hearted I was by that first letter, and how darned happy your second letter made me—!

MURIEL—(*happily relieved—but appreciates she has the upper hand now and doesn't relent at once*) I don't believe you.

RICHARD—You ask Mid how happy I was. She can prove it.

MURIEL—She'd say anything you told her to. I don't care anything about what she'd say. It's you. You've got to swear to me—

RICHARD—I swear!

MURIEL—(*demurely*) Well then, all right, I'll believe you.

RICHARD—(*his eyes on her face lovingly—genuine adoration in his voice*) Gosh, you're pretty tonight, Muriel! It seems ages since we've been together! If you knew how I've suffered—!

MURIEL—I did, too.

RICHARD—(*unable to resist falling into his tragic literary pose for a moment*) The despair in my soul— (*He recites dramatically*) "Something was dead in each of us, And what was dead was Hope!" That was me! My hope of happiness was dead! (*then with sincere boyish fervor*) Gosh, Muriel, it sure is wonderful to be with you again! (*He puts a timid arm around her awkwardly.*)

MURIEL—(*shyly*) I'm glad—it makes you happy. I'm happy, too.

RICHARD—Can't I—won't you let me kiss you—now? Please! (*He bends his face toward hers.*)

MURIEL—(*ducking her head away—timidly*) No. You mustn't. Don't—

RICHARD—Aw, why can't I?

MURIEL—Because—I'm afraid.

RICHARD—(*discomfited—taking his arm from around her—a bit sulky and impatient with her*) Aw, that's what you always say! You're always so afraid! Aren't you ever going to let me?

MURIEL—I will—sometime.

RICHARD—When?

MURIEL—Soon, maybe.

RICHARD—Tonight, will you?

MURIEL—(*coyly*) I'll see.

RICHARD—Promise?

MURIEL—I promise—maybe.

RICHARD—All right. You remember you've promised. (*then coaxingly*) Aw, don't let's stand here. Come on out and we can sit down in the boat.

MURIEL—(*hesitantly*) It's so bright out there.

RICHARD—No one'll see. You know there's never anyone around here at night.

MURIEL—(*illogically*) I know there isn't. That's why I thought it would be the best place. But there might be someone.

RICHARD—(*taking her hand and tugging at it gently*) There isn't a soul. (*Muriel steps out a little and looks up and down fearfully. Richard goes on insistently.*) Aw, what's the use of a moon if you can't see it!

MURIEL—But it's only a new moon. That's not much to look at.

RICHARD—But I want to see you. I can't here in the shadow. I want to—drink in—all your beauty.

MURIEL—(*can't resist this*) Well, all right—only I can't stay only a few minutes. (*She lets him lead her toward the stern of the boat.*)

RICHARD—(*pleadingly*) Aw, you can stay a little while, can't you? Please! (*He helps her in and she settles herself in the stern seat of the boat, facing diagonally left front.*)

MURIEL—A little while. (*He sits beside her.*) But I've got to be home in bed again pretending to be asleep by ten o'clock. That's the time Pa and Ma come up to bed, as regular as clock work, and Ma always looks into my room.

RICHARD—But you'll have oodles of time to do that.

MURIEL—(*excitedly*) Dick, you have no idea what I went

through to get here tonight! My, but it was exciting! You know Pa's punishing me by sending me to bed at eight sharp, and I had to get all undressed and into bed 'cause at half-past he sends Ma up to make sure I've obeyed, and she came up, and I pretended to be asleep, and she went down again, and I got up and dressed in such a hurry—I must look a sight, don't I?

RICHARD—You do not! You look wonderful!

MURIEL—And then I sneaked down the back stairs. And the pesky old stairs squeaked, and my heart was in my mouth, I was so scared, and then I sneaked out through the back yard, keeping in the dark under the trees, and— My, but it was exciting! Dick, you don't realize how I've been punished for your sake. Pa's been so mean and nasty, I've almost hated him!

RICHARD—And you don't realize what I've been through for you—and what I'm in for—for sneaking out— (*then darkly*) And for what I did last night—what your letter made me do!

MURIEL—(*made terribly curious by his ominous tone*) What did my letter make you do?

RICHARD—(*beginning to glory in this*) It's too long a story—and let the dead past bury its dead. (*then with real feeling*) Only it isn't past, I can tell you! What I'll catch when Pa gets hold of me!

MURIEL—Tell me, Dick! Begin at the beginning and tell me!

RICHARD—(*tragically*) Well, after your old—your father left our place I caught holy hell from Pa.

MURIEL—Dick! You mustn't swear!

RICHARD—(*somberly*) Hell is the only word that can describe it. And on top of that, to torture me more, he gave me your letter. After I'd read that I didn't want to live any more. Life seemed like a tragic farce.

MURIEL—I'm so awful sorry, Dick—honest I am! But you might have known I'd never write that unless—

RICHARD—I thought your love for me was dead. I thought you'd never loved me, that you'd only been cruelly mocking me—to torture me!

MURIEL—Dick! I'd never! You know I'd never!

RICHARD—I wanted to die. I sat and brooded about death. Finally I made up my mind I'd kill myself.

MURIEL—(*excitedly*) Dick! You didn't!

RICHARD—I did, too! If there'd been one of Hedda Gabler's pistols around, you'd have seen if I wouldn't have done it beautifully! I thought, when I'm dead, she'll be sorry she ruined my life!

MURIEL—(*cuddling up a little to him*) If you ever had! I'd have died, too! Honest, I would!

RICHARD—But suicide is the act of a coward. That's what stopped me. (*then with a bitter change of tone*) And anyway, I thought to myself, she isn't worth it.

MURIEL—(*huffily*) That's a nice thing to say!

RICHARD—Well, if you meant what was in that letter, you wouldn't have been worth it, would you?

MURIEL—But I've told you Pa—

RICHARD—So I said to myself, I'm through with women; they're all alike!

MURIEL—I'm not.

RICHARD—And I thought, what difference does it make what I do now? I might as well forget her and lead the pace that kills, and drown my sorrows! You know I had eleven dollars saved up to buy you something for your birthday, but I thought, she's dead to me now and why shouldn't I throw it away? (*then hastily*) I've still got almost five left, Muriel, and I can get you something nice with that.

MURIEL—(*excitedly*) What do I care about your old presents? You tell me what you did!

RICHARD—(*darkly again*) After it was dark, I sneaked out and went to a low dive I know about.

MURIEL—Dick Miller, I don't believe you ever!

RICHARD—You ask them at the Pleasant Beach House if I didn't! They won't forget me in a hurry!

MURIEL—(*impressed and horrified*) You went there? Why, that's a terrible place! Pa says it ought to be closed by the police!

RICHARD—(*darkly*) I said it was a dive, didn't I? It's a "secret house of shame." And they let me into a secret room behind the barroom. There wasn't anyone there but a Princeton Senior I know—he belongs to Tiger Inn and he's

fullback on the football team—and he had two chorus
girls from New York with him, and they were all drinking
champagne.

MURIEL—(*disturbed by the entrance of the chorus girls*) Dick
Miller! I hope you didn't notice—

RICHARD—(*carelessly*) I had a highball by myself and then
I noticed one of the girls—the one that wasn't with the fullback—looking at me. She had strange-looking eyes. And
then she asked me if I wouldn't drink champagne with them
and come and sit with her.

MURIEL—She must have been a nice thing! (*then a bit falteringly*) And did—you?

RICHARD—(*with tragic bitterness*) Why shouldn't I, when
you'd told me in that letter you'd never see me again?

MURIEL—(*almost tearfully*) But you ought to have known
Pa made me—

RICHARD—I didn't know that then. (*then rubbing it in*)
Her name was Belle. She had yellow hair—the kind that
burns and stings you!

MURIEL—I'll bet it was dyed!

RICHARD—She kept smoking one cigarette after another—but that's nothing for a chorus girl.

MURIEL—(*indignantly*) She was low and bad, that's what
she was or she couldn't be a chorus girl, and her smoking
cigarettes proves it! (*then falteringly again*) And then what
happened?

RICHARD—(*carelessly*) Oh, we just kept drinking champagne—I bought a round—and then I had a fight with the
barkeep and knocked him down because he'd insulted her. He
was a great big thug but—

MURIEL—(*huffily*) I don't see how he could—insult that
kind! And why did you fight for her? Why didn't the Princeton fullback who'd brought them there? He must have been
bigger than you.

RICHARD—(*stopped for a moment—then quickly*) He was
too drunk by that time.

MURIEL—And were you drunk?

RICHARD—Only a little then. I was worse later. (*proudly*)
You ought to have seen me when I got home! I was on the
verge of delirium tremens!

MURIEL—I'm glad I didn't see you. You must have been awful. I hate people who get drunk. I'd have hated you!

RICHARD—Well, it was all your fault, wasn't it? If you hadn't written that letter—

MURIEL—But I've told you I didn't mean— (*then faltering but fascinated*) But what happened with that Belle— after—before you went home?

RICHARD—Oh, we kept drinking champagne and she said she'd fallen in love with me at first sight and she came and sat on my lap and kissed me.

MURIEL—(*stiffening*) Oh!

RICHARD—(*quickly, afraid he has gone too far*) But it was only all in fun, and then we just kept on drinking champagne, and finally I said good night and came home.

MURIEL—And did you kiss her?

RICHARD—No, I didn't.

MURIEL—(*distractedly*) You did, too! You're lying and you know it. You did, too! (*then tearfully*) And there I was right at that time lying in bed not able to sleep, wondering how I was ever going to see you again and crying my eyes out, while you—! (*She suddenly jumps to her feet in a tearful fury.*) I hate you! I wish you were dead! I'm going home this minute! I never want to lay eyes on you again! And this time I mean it! (*She tries to jump out of the boat but he holds her back. All the pose has dropped from him now and he is in a frightened state of contrition.*)

RICHARD—(*imploringly*) Muriel! Wait! Listen!

MURIEL—I don't want to listen! Let me go! If you don't I'll bite your hand!

RICHARD—I won't let you go! You've got to let me explain! I never—! Ouch! (*For Muriel has bitten his hand and it hurts, and, stung by the pain, he lets go instinctively, and she jumps quickly out of the boat and starts running toward the path. Richard calls after her with bitter despair and hurt*) All right! Go if you want to—if you haven't the decency to let me explain! I hate you, too! I'll go and see Belle!

MURIEL—(*seeing he isn't following her, stops at the foot of the path—defiantly*) Well, go and see her—if that's the kind of girl you like! What do I care? (*then as he only stares before him broodingly, sitting dejectedly in the stern of the boat, a pathetic figure of injured grief*) You can't explain! What can you explain? You owned up you kissed her!

RICHARD—I did not. I said she kissed me.

MURIEL—(*scornfully, but drifting back a step in his direction*) And I suppose you just sat and let yourself be kissed! Tell that to the Marines!

RICHARD—(*injuredly*) All right! If you're going to call me a liar every word I say—

MURIEL—(*drifting back another step*) I didn't call you a liar. I only meant—it sounds fishy. Don't you know it does?

RICHARD—I don't know anything. I only know I wish I was dead!

MURIEL—(*gently reproving*) You oughtn't to say that. It's wicked. (*then after a pause*) And I suppose you'll tell me you didn't fall in love with her?

RICHARD—(*scornfully*) I should say not! Fall in love with that kind of girl! What do you take me for?

MURIEL—(*practically*) How do you know what you did if you drank so much champagne?

RICHARD—I kept my head—with her. I'm not a sucker, no matter what you think!

MURIEL—(*drifting nearer*) Then you didn't—love her?

RICHARD—I hated her! She wasn't even pretty! And I had a fight with her before I left, she got so fresh. I told her I loved you and never could love anyone else, and for her to leave me alone.

MURIEL—But you said just now you were going to see her—

RICHARD—That was only bluff. I wouldn't—unless you left me. Then I wouldn't care what I did—any more than I did last night. (*then suddenly defiant*) And what if I did kiss her once or twice? I only did it to get back at you!

MURIEL—Dick!

RICHARD—You're a fine one to blame me—when it was all your fault! Why can't you be fair? Didn't I think you were out of my life forever? Hadn't you written me you were? Answer me that!

MURIEL—But I've told you a million times that Pa—

RICHARD—Why didn't you have more sense than to let him make you write it? Was it my fault you didn't?

MURIEL—It was your fault for being so stupid! You ought to have known he stood right over me and told me each word to write. If I'd refused, it would only have made everything worse. I had to pretend, so I'd get a chance to see you. Don't you see, Silly? And I had sand enough to sneak out to meet you tonight, didn't I? (*He doesn't answer. She moves nearer.*) Still I can see how you felt the way you did—and maybe I am to blame for that. So I'll forgive and forget, Dick—if you'll swear to me you didn't even think of loving that—

RICHARD—(*eagerly*) I didn't! I swear, Muriel. I couldn't. I love you!

MURIEL—Well, then—I still love you.

RICHARD—Then come back here, why don't you?

MURIEL—(*coyly*) It's getting late.

RICHARD—It's not near half-past yet.

MURIEL—(*comes back and sits down by him shyly*) All right—only I'll have to go soon, Dick. (*He puts his arm around her. She cuddles up close to him.*) I'm sorry—I hurt your hand.

RICHARD—That was nothing. It felt wonderful—even to have you bite!

MURIEL—(*impulsively takes his hand and kisses it*) There! That'll cure it. (*She is overcome by confusion at her boldness.*)

RICHARD—You shouldn't—waste that—on my hand. (*then tremblingly*) You said—you'd let me—

MURIEL—I said, maybe.

RICHARD—Please, Muriel. You know—I want it so!

MURIEL—Will it wash off—her kisses—make you forget you ever—for always?

RICHARD—I should say so! I'd never remember—anything but it—never want anything but it—ever again.

MURIEL—(*shyly lifting her lips*) Then—all right—Dick. (*He kisses her tremblingly and for a moment their lips remain together. Then she lets her head sink on his shoulder and sighs softly.*) The moon *is* beautiful, isn't it?

RICHARD—(*kissing her hair*) Not as beautiful as you! Nothing is! (*then after a pause*) Won't it be wonderful when we're married?

MURIEL—Yes—but it's so long to wait.

RICHARD—Perhaps I needn't go to Yale. Perhaps Pa will give me a job. Then I'd soon be making enough to—

MURIEL—You better do what your pa thinks best—and I'd like you to be at Yale. (*then patting his face*) Poor you! Do you think he'll punish you awful?

RICHARD—(*intensely*) I don't know and I don't care! Nothing would have kept me from seeing you tonight—not if I'd had to crawl over red-hot coals! (*then falling back on Swinburne—but with passionate sincerity*) You have my being between the hands of you! You are "my love, mine own soul's heart, more dear than mine own soul, more beautiful than God!"

MURIEL—(*shocked and delighted*) Ssshh! It's wrong to say that.

RICHARD—(*adoringly*) Gosh, but I love you! Gosh, I love you—Darling!

MURIEL—I love you, too—Sweetheart! (*They kiss. Then she lets her head sink on his shoulder again and they both sit in a rapt trance, staring at the moon. After a pause—dreamily*) Where'll we go on our honeymoon, Dick? To Niagara Falls?

RICHARD—(*scornfully*) That dump where all the silly fools go? I should say not! (*with passionate romanticism*) No, we'll go to some far-off wonderful place! (*He calls on Kipling to help him.*) Somewhere out on the Long Trail—the trail that is always new—on the road to Mandalay! We'll watch the dawn come up like thunder out of China!

MURIEL—(*hazily but happily*) That'll be wonderful, won't it?

(*Curtain*)

SCENE THREE

SCENE—*The sitting-room of the Miller house again—about 10 o'clock the same night. Miller is sitting in his rocker at left, front, of table, his wife in the rocker at right, front, of table. Moonlight shines through the screen door at right, rear. Only the green-shaded reading lamp is lit and by its light Miller, his specs on, is reading a book while his wife, sewing basket in lap, is working industriously on a doily. Mrs. Miller's face wears an expression of unworried content. Miller's face has also lost its look of harassed preoccupation, although he still is a prey to certain misgivings, when he allows himself to think of them. Several books are piled on the table by his elbow, the books that have been confiscated from Richard.*

MILLER—(*chuckles at something he reads—then closes the book and puts it on the table. Mrs. Miller looks up from her sewing.*) This Shaw's a comical cuss—even if his ideas are so crazy they oughtn't to allow them to be printed. And that Swinburne's got a fine swing to his poetry—if he'd only choose some other subjects besides loose women.

MRS. MILLER—(*smiling teasingly*) I can see where you're becoming corrupted by those books, too—pretending to read them out of duty to Richard, when your nose has been glued to the page!

MILLER—No, no—but I've got to be honest. There's something to them. That Rubaiyat of Omar Khayyam, now. I read that over again and liked it even better than I had before—parts of it, that is, where it isn't all about boozing.

MRS. MILLER—(*has been busy with her own thoughts during this last—with a deep sigh of relief*) My, but I'm glad Mildred told me where Richard went off to. I'd have worried my heart out if she hadn't. But now, it's all right.

MILLER—(*frowning a little*) I'd hardly go so far as to say that. Just because we know he's all right tonight doesn't mean last night is wiped out. He's still got to be punished for that.

MRS. MILLER—(*defensively*) Well, if you ask me, I think after the way I punished him all day, and the way I know he's punished himself, he's had about all he deserves. I've told you how sorry he was, and how he said he'd never touch liquor again. It didn't make him feel happy like Sid, but only sad and sick, so he didn't see anything in it for him.

MILLER—Well, if he's really got that view of it driven into his skull, I don't know but I'm glad it all happened. That'll protect him more than a thousand lectures—just horse sense about himself. (*then frowning again*) Still, I can't let him do such things and go scot-free. And then, besides, there's another side to it— (*He stops abruptly.*)

Mrs. Miller—(*uneasily*) What do you mean, another side?

Miller—(*hastily*) I mean, discipline. There's got to be some discipline in a family. I don't want him to get the idea he's got a stuffed shirt at the head of the table. No, he's got to be punished, if only to make the lesson stick in his mind, and I'm going to tell him he can't go to Yale, seeing he's so undependable.

Mrs. Miller—(*up in arms at once*) Not go to Yale! I guess he can go to Yale! Every man of your means in town is sending his boys to college! What would folks think of you? You let Wilbur go, and you'd have let Lawrence, only he didn't want to, and you're letting Arthur! If our other children can get the benefit of a college education, you're not going to pick on Richard—

Miller—Hush up, for God's sake! If you'd let me finish what I started to say! I said I'd *tell* him that now—bluff—then later on I'll change my mind, if he behaves himself.

Mrs. Miller—Oh well, if that's all— (*then defensively again*) But it's your duty to give him every benefit. He's got an exceptional brain, that boy has! He's proved it by the way he likes to read all those deep plays and books and poetry.

Miller—But I thought you— (*He stops, grinning helplessly.*)

Mrs. Miller—You thought I what?

Miller—Never mind.

Mrs. Miller—(*sniffs, but thinks it better to let this pass*) You mark my words, that boy's going to turn out to be a great lawyer, or a great doctor, or a great writer, or—

Miller—(*grinning*) You agree he's going to be great, anyway.

Mrs. Miller—Yes, I most certainly have a lot of faith in Richard.

Miller—Well, so have I, as far as that goes.

Mrs. Miller—(*after a pause—judicially*) And as for his being in love with Muriel, I don't see but what it might work out real well. Richard could do worse.

Miller—But I thought you had no use for her, thought she was stupid.

Mrs. Miller—Well, so I did, but if she's good for Richard

and he wants her— (*then inconsequentially*) Ma used to say you weren't overbright, but she changed her mind when she saw I didn't care if you were or not.

MILLER—(*not exactly pleased by this*) Well, I've been bright enough to—

MRS. MILLER—(*going on as if he had not spoken*) And Muriel's real cute-looking, I have to admit that. Takes after her mother. Alice Briggs was the prettiest girl before she married.

MILLER—Yes, and Muriel will get big as a house after she's married, the same as her mother did. That's the trouble. A man never can tell what he's letting himself in for— (*He stops, feeling his wife's eyes fixed on him with indignant suspicion.*)

MRS. MILLER—(*sharply*) I'm not too fat and don't you say it!

MILLER—Who was talking about you?

MRS. MILLER—And I'd rather have some flesh on my bones than be built like a string bean and bore a hole in a chair every time I sat down—like some people!

MILLER—(*ignoring the insult—flatteringly*) Why, no one'd ever call you fat, Essie. You're only plump, like a good figure ought to be.

MRS. MILLER—(*childishly pleased—gratefully giving tit for tat*) Well, you're not skinny, either—only slender—and I think you've been putting on weight lately, too. (*Having thus squared matters she takes up her sewing again. A pause. Then Miller asks incredulously*)

MILLER—You don't mean to tell me you're actually taking this Muriel crush of Richard's seriously, do you? I know it's a good thing to encourage right now but—pshaw, why, Richard'll probably forget all about her before he's away six months, and she'll have forgotten him.

MRS. MILLER—Don't be so cynical. (*then, after a pause, thoughtfully*) Well, anyway, he'll always have it to remember— no matter what happens after—and that's something.

MILLER—You bet that's something. (*then with a grin*) You surprise me at times with your deep wisdom.

MRS. MILLER—You don't give me credit for ever having common sense, that's why. (*She goes back to her sewing.*)

MILLER—(*after a pause*) Where'd you say Sid and Lily had gone off to?

MRS. MILLER—To the beach to listen to the band. (*She sighs sympathetically.*) Poor Lily! Sid'll never change, and she'll never marry him. But she seems to get some queer satisfaction out of fussing over him like a hen that's hatched a duck—though Lord knows I wouldn't in her shoes!

MILLER—Arthur's up with Elsie Rand, I suppose?

MRS. MILLER—Of course.

MILLER—Where's Mildred?

MRS. MILLER—Out walking with her latest. I've forgot who it is. I can't keep track of them. (*She smiles.*)

MILLER—(*smiling*) Then, from all reports, we seem to be completely surrounded by love!

MRS. MILLER—Well, we've had our share, haven't we? We don't have to begrudge it to our children. (*then has a sudden thought*) But I've done all this talking about Muriel and Richard and clean forgot how wild old McComber was against it. But he'll get over that, I suppose.

MILLER—(*with a chuckle*) He has already. I ran into him upstreet this afternoon and he was meek as pie. He backed water and said he guessed I was right. Richard had just copied stuff out of books, and kids would be kids, and so on. So I came off my high horse a bit—but not too far—and I guess all that won't bother anyone any more. (*then rubbing his hands together—with a boyish grin of pleasure*) And I told you about getting that business from Lawson, didn't I? It's been a good day, Essie—a darned good day! (*From the hall beyond the front parlor the sound of the front door being opened and shut is heard. Mrs. Miller leans forward to look, pushing her specs up.*)

MRS. MILLER—(*in a whisper*) It's Richard.

MILLER—(*immediately assuming an expression of becoming gravity*) Hmm. (*He takes off his spectacles and puts them back in their case and straightens himself in his chair. Richard comes slowly in from the front parlor. He walks like one in a trance, his eyes shining with a dreamy happiness, his spirit still too exalted to be conscious of his surroundings, or to remember the threatened punishment. He carries his straw hat dangling in his hand, quite unaware of its existence.*)

RICHARD—(*dreamily, like a ghost addressing fellow shades*) Hello.

MRS. MILLER—(*staring at him worriedly*) Hello, Richard.

MILLER—(*sizing him up shrewdly*) Hello, Son.

(*Richard moves past his mother and comes to the far corner, left front, where the light is dimmest, and sits down on the sofa, and stares before him, his hat dangling in his hand.*)

MRS. MILLER—(*with frightened suspicion now*) Goodness, he acts queer! Nat, you don't suppose he's been—?

MILLER—(*with a reassuring smile*) No. It's love, not liquor, this time.

MRS. MILLER—(*only partly reassured—sharply*) Richard! What's the matter with you? (*He comes to himself with a start. She goes on scoldingly.*) How many times have I told you to hang up your hat in the hall when you come in! (*He looks at his hat as if he were surprised at its existence. She gets up fussily and goes to him.*) Here. Give it to me. I'll hang it up for you this once. And what are you sitting over here in the dark for? Don't forget your father's been waiting to talk to you! (*She comes back to the table and he follows her, still half in a dream, and stands by his father's chair. Mrs. Miller starts for the hall with his hat.*)

MILLER—(*quietly but firmly now*) You better leave Richard and me alone for a while, Essie.

MRS. MILLER—(*turns to stare at him apprehensively*) Well— all right. I'll go sit on the piazza. Call me if you want me. (*then a bit pleadingly*) But you'll remember all I've said, Nat, won't you? (*Miller nods reassuringly. She disappears through the front parlor. Richard, keenly conscious of himself as the about-to-be-sentenced criminal by this time, looks guilty and a bit defiant, searches his father's expressionless face with uneasy side glances, and steels himself for what is coming.*)

MILLER—(*casually, indicating Mrs. Miller's rocker*) Sit down, Richard. (*Richard slumps awkwardly into the chair and sits in a self-conscious, unnatural position. Miller sizes him up keenly—then suddenly smiles and asks with quiet mockery*) Well, how are the vine leaves in your hair this evening?

RICHARD—(*totally unprepared for this approach—shame-facedly mutters*) I don't know, Pa.

MILLER—Turned out to be poison ivy, didn't they? (*then kindly*) But you needn't look so alarmed. I'm not going to read you any temperance lecture. That'd bore me more than it would you. And, in spite of your damn foolishness last night, I'm still giving you credit for having brains. So I'm pretty sure anything I could say to you you've already said to yourself.

RICHARD—(*his head down—humbly*) I know I was a darned fool.

MILLER—(*thinking it well to rub in this aspect—disgustedly*) You sure were—not only a fool but a downright, stupid, disgusting fool! (*Richard squirms, his head still lower.*) It was bad enough for you to let me and Arthur see you, but to appear like that before your mother and Mildred—! And I wonder if Muriel would think you were so fine if she ever saw you as you looked and acted then. I think she'd give you your walking papers for keeps. And you couldn't blame her. No nice girl wants to give her love to a stupid drunk!

RICHARD—(*writhing*) I know, Pa.

MILLER—(*after a pause—quietly*) All right. Then that settles—the booze end of it. (*He sizes Richard up searchingly—then suddenly speaks sharply.*) But there is another thing that's more serious. How about that tart you went to bed with at the Pleasant Beach House?

RICHARD—(*flabbergasted—stammers*) You know—? But I didn't! If they've told you about her down there, they must have told you I didn't! She wanted me to—but I wouldn't. I gave her the five dollars just so she'd let me out of it. Honest, Pa, I didn't! She made everything seem rotten and dirty—and—I didn't want to do a thing like that to Muriel—no matter how bad I thought she'd treated me—even after I felt drunk, I didn't. Honest!

MILLER—How'd you happen to meet this lady, anyway?

RICHARD—I can't tell that, Pa. I'd have to snitch on someone—and you wouldn't want me to do that.

MILLER—(*a bit taken aback*) No. I suppose I wouldn't. Hmm. Well, I believe you—and I guess that settles that. (*Then, after a quick, furtive glance at Richard, he nerves himself for the ordeal and begins with a shamefaced, self-conscious solemnity.*) But listen here, Richard, it's about time you and I had a serious talk about—hmm—certain matters pertaining to—and now that the subject's come up of its own accord, it's a good time—I mean, there's no use in procrastinating further—so, here goes. (*But it doesn't go smoothly and as he goes on he becomes more and more guiltily embarrassed and self-conscious and his expressions more stilted. Richard sedulously avoids even glancing at him, his own embarrassment made tenfold more painful by his father's.*) Richard, you have now come to the age when— Well, you're a fully developed man, in a way, and it's only natural for you to have certain desires of the flesh, to put it that way— I mean, pertaining to the opposite sex—certain natural feelings and temptations—that'll want to be gratified—and you'll want to gratify them. Hmm— well, human society being organized as it is, there's only one outlet for—unless you're a scoundrel and go around ruining decent girls—which you're not, of course. Well, there are a certain class of women—always have been and always will be as long as human nature is what it is— It's wrong, maybe, but what can you do about it? I mean, girls like that one you—girls there's something doing with—and lots of 'em are pretty, and it's human nature if you— But that doesn't mean to ever get mixed up with them seriously! You just have what you want and pay 'em and forget it. I know that sounds hard and unfeeling, but we're talking facts and— But don't think I'm encouraging you to— If you can stay away from 'em, all the better—but if—why—hmm— Here's what I'm driving at, Richard. They're apt to be whited sepulchres—I mean, your whole life might be ruined if—so, darn it, you've got to know how to— I mean, there are ways and means— (*Suddenly he can go no farther and winds up helplessly.*) But, hell, I suppose you boys talk all this over among yourselves and you know more about it than I do. I'll admit I'm no authority. I never had anything to do with such women, and it'll be a hell of a lot better for you if you never do!

RICHARD—(*without looking at him*) I'm never going to, Pa. (*then shocked indignation coming into his voice*) I don't see how you could think I could—now—when you know I love Muriel and am going to marry her. I'd die before I'd—!

MILLER—(*immensely relieved—enthusiastically*) That's the talk! By God, I'm proud of you when you talk like that! (*then hastily*) And now that's all of that. There's nothing more to say and we'll forget it, eh?

RICHARD—(*after a pause*) How are you going to punish me, Pa?

MILLER—I *was* sort of forgetting that, wasn't I? Well, I'd thought of telling you you couldn't go to Yale—

RICHARD—(*eagerly*) Don't I have to go? Gee, that's great! Muriel thought you'd want me to. I was telling her I'd rather you gave me a job on the paper because then she and I could get married sooner. (*then with a boyish grin*) Gee, Pa, you picked a lemon. That isn't any punishment. You'll have to do something besides that.

MILLER—(*grimly—but only half concealing an answering grin*) Then you'll go to Yale and you'll stay there till you graduate, that's the answer to that! Muriel's got good sense and you haven't! (*Richard accepts this philosophically.*) And now we're finished, you better call your mother. (*Richard opens the screen door and calls "Ma," and a moment later she comes in. She glances quickly from son to husband and immediately knows that all is well and tactfully refrains from all questions.*)

MRS. MILLER—My, it's a beautiful night. The moon's way down low—almost setting. (*She sits in her chair and sighs contentedly. Richard remains standing by the door, staring out at the moon, his face pale in the moonlight.*)

MILLER—(*with a nod at Richard, winking at his wife*) Yes, I don't believe I've hardly ever seen such a beautiful night— with such a wonderful moon. Have you, Richard?

RICHARD—(*turning to them—enthusiastically*) No! It was wonderful—down at the beach— (*He stops abruptly, smiling shyly.*)

MILLER—(*watching his son—after a pause—quietly*) I can only remember a few nights that were as beautiful as this— and they were long ago, when your mother and I were young and planning to get married.

RICHARD—(*stares at him wonderingly for a moment, then quickly from his father to his mother and back again, strangely, as if he'd never seen them before—then he looks almost disgusted and swallows as if an acrid taste had come into his mouth—but then suddenly his face is transfigured by a smile of shy understanding and sympathy. He speaks shyly.*) Yes, I'll bet those must have been wonderful nights, too. You sort of forget the moon was the same way back then—and everything.

MILLER—(*huskily*) You're all right, Richard. (*He gets up and blows his nose.*)

MRS. MILLER—(*fondly*) You're a good boy, Richard. (*Richard looks dreadfully shy and embarrassed at this. His father comes to his rescue.*)

MILLER—Better get to bed early tonight, Son, hadn't you?

RICHARD—I couldn't sleep. Can't I go out on the piazza and sit for a while—until the moon sets?

MILLER—All right. Then you better say good night now. I don't know about your mother, but I'm going to bed right away. I'm dead tired.

MRS. MILLER—So am I.

RICHARD—(*goes to her and kisses her*) Good night, Ma.

MRS. MILLER—Good night. Don't you stay up till all hours now.

RICHARD—(*comes to his father and stands awkwardly before him*) Good night, Pa.

MILLER—(*puts his arm around him and gives him a hug*) Good night, Richard. (*Richard turns impulsively and kisses him—then hurries out the screen door. Miller stares after him—then says huskily*) First time he's done that in years. I don't believe in kissing between fathers and sons after a certain age—seems mushy and silly—but that meant something! And I don't think we'll ever have to worry about his being safe—from himself—again. And I guess no matter what life will do to him, he can take care of it now. (*He sighs with satisfaction and, sitting down in his chair, begins to unlace his shoes.*) My darned feet are giving me fits!

MRS. MILLER—(*laughing*) Why do you bother unlacing your shoes now, you big goose—when we're going right up to bed?

MILLER—(*as if he hadn't thought of that before, stops*) Guess you're right. (*then getting to his feet—with a grin*) Mind if I don't say my prayers tonight, Essie? I'm certain God knows I'm too darned tired.

MRS. MILLER—Don't talk that way. It's real sinful. (*She gets up—then laughing fondly*) If that isn't you all over! Always looking for an excuse to— You're worse than Tommy! But all right. I suppose tonight you needn't. You've had a hard day. (*She puts her hand on the reading-lamp switch.*) I'm going to turn out the light. All ready?

MILLER—Yep. Let her go, Gallagher. (*She turns out the*

lamp. In the ensuing darkness the faint moonlight shines full in through the screen door. Walking together toward the front parlor they stand full in it for a moment, looking out. Miller puts his arm around her. He says in a low voice) There he is—like a statue of Love's Young Dream. (*Then he sighs and speaks with a gentle nostalgic melancholy.*) What's it that Rubaiyat says:

"Yet Ah, that Spring should vanish with the Rose!

That Youth's sweet-scented manuscript should close!"

(*then throwing off his melancholy, with a loving smile at her*) Well, Spring isn't everything, is it, Essie? There's a lot to be said for Autumn. That's got beauty, too. And Winter—if you're together.

MRS. MILLER—(*simply*) Yes, Nat. (*She kisses him and they move quietly out of the moonlight, back into the darkness of the front parlor.*)

(*Curtain*)

DAYS WITHOUT END

A Modern Miracle Play

To
CARLOTTA

CHARACTERS

(In the order in which they appear)

JOHN

LOVING

WILLIAM ELIOT

FATHER MATTHEW BAIRD

ELSA, *John Loving's wife*

MARGARET

LUCY HILLMAN

DR. HERBERT STILLWELL

NURSE

SCENES

Act One
PLOT FOR A NOVEL
Scene—John Loving's office in the offices of Eliot and
Company, New York City—an afternoon in
early Spring, 1932.

Act Two
PLOT FOR A NOVEL (CONTINUED)
Scene—Living-room of the Lovings' duplex apartment—
later the same afternoon.

Act Three
PLOT FOR A NOVEL (CONTINUED)
Scene One—The living-room again—evening of the
same day.
Scene Two—John Loving's study—later that night.

Act Four
THE END OF THE END
Scene One—The study and Elsa's bedroom—a little before
dawn of a day about a week later.
Scene Two—The interior of a church—a few minutes later.

Days Without End
ACT ONE
Plot for a Novel

SCENE—*John Loving's private office in the offices of Eliot and Company, New York City. On the left, a window. Before it, a chair, its back to the window, and a table. At rear of table, an armchair, facing front. A third chair is at right of table. In the rear wall, a door leading to the outer offices. At center of the room, toward right, another chair.*

It is afternoon of a cloudy day in Spring, 1932. The light from the window is chill and gray. At the rise of the curtain, this light is concentrated around the two figures seated at the table. As the action goes on, the light imperceptibly spreads until, at the close of the opening scene between John and Loving, it has penetrated to all parts of the room.

John is seated in the chair at left of desk. He is forty, of medium height. His face is handsome, with the rather heavy, conventional American type of good looks—a straight nose and a square jaw, a wide mouth that has an incongruous feminine sensitiveness, a broad forehead, blue eyes. He is dressed in a dark suit, white shirt and collar, a dark tie, black shoes and socks.

Loving sits in the armchair at rear of table. He is the same age, of the same height and figure, is dressed in every detail exactly the same. His hair is the same—dark, streaked with gray. In contrast to this similarity between the two, there is an equally strange dissimilarity. For Loving's face is a mask whose features reproduce exactly the features of John's face—the death mask of a John who has died with a sneer of scornful mockery on his lips. And this mocking scorn is repeated in the expression of the eyes which stare bleakly from behind the mask.

John nervously writes a few words on a pad—then stops abruptly and stares before him. Loving watches him.

LOVING—(*his voice singularly toneless and cold but at the same time insistent*) Surely, you don't need to make any more notes for the second part—your hero's manhood up to the time he (*a sneer comes into his voice*) at last finds love. I should think you could remember that—only too well.

JOHN—(*mechanically*) Yes.

LOVING—(*sneeringly*) As for the third part, I know you have the most vivid recollection of his terrible sin.

JOHN—Don't mock, damn you!

LOVING—So it's only in the last part that you will have to use your imagination. How are you going to end this interesting plot of yours? Given your hero's ridiculous conscience, what happens then?

JOHN—He has the courage to confess—and she forgives.

LOVING—The wish is father to that thought, eh? A pretty, sentimental ending—but a bit too pointed, don't you think? I'm afraid she might begin to wonder—

JOHN—(*apprehensively*) Yes. That's true.

LOVING—I advise you to make the last part so obviously fictitious that it will kill any suspicion which might be aroused by what has gone before.

JOHN—How can I end it, then?

LOVING—(*after a second's pause—in a voice he tries to make casual but which is indefinably sinister*) Why not have the wife die?

JOHN—(*starts—with a shudder*) Damn you! What makes you think of that?

LOVING—Why, nothing—except I thought you'd agreed that the further removed from present actuality you make your ending, the better it will be.

JOHN—Yes—but—

LOVING—(*mockingly*) I hope you don't suspect some hidden, sinister purpose behind my suggestion.

JOHN—I don't know. I feel— (*then as if desperately trying to shake off his thoughts*) No! I won't think of it!

LOVING—And I was thinking, too, that it would be interesting to work out your hero's answer to his problem, if his wife died, and imagine what he would do with his life then.

JOHN—No! Damn you, stop making me think—!

LOVING—Afraid to face your ghosts—even by proxy? Surely, even you can have that much courage!

JOHN—It is dangerous—to call things.

LOVING—Still superstitious? Well, I hope you realize I'm only trying to encourage you to make something of this plot of yours more significant—for your soul, shall I say?—than a cowardly trick!

JOHN—You know it's more than that. You know I'm doing it to try and explain to myself, as well as to her.

LOVING—(*sneeringly*) To excuse yourself to yourself, you mean! To lie and escape admitting the obvious natural reason for—

JOHN—You lie! I want to get at the real truth and understand what was behind—what evil spirit of hate possessed me to make me—

LOVING—(*contemptuously—but as he goes on a strange defiant note of exultance comes into his voice.*) So it's come back to that again, eh? Your old familiar nightmare! You poor, damned superstitious fool! I tell you again what I have always told you: There is nothing—nothing to hope for, nothing to fear—neither devils nor gods—nothing at all! (*There is a knock on the door at rear. John immediately pretends to be writing. At the same time his features automatically assume the meaninglessly affable expression which is the American business man's welcoming poker face. Loving sits motionlessly regarding him with scornful eyes.*)

JOHN—(*without looking up, calls*) Come in. (*The door in rear is half opened and William Eliot, John Loving's partner, looks in. He is about forty, stout, with a prematurely bald head, a round face, a humorous, good-natured mouth, small eyes behind horn-rimmed spectacles.*)

ELIOT—Hello, John. Busy?

JOHN—Foolish question, Bill.

ELIOT—(*His eyes pass over Loving without seeing him. He does not see him now or later. He sees and hears only John, even when Loving speaks. And it will be so with all the characters. They are quite unaware of Loving's existence, although at times one or another may subtly sense his presence. Eliot comes forward. He says jokingly*) You sound downhearted, John. Don't let our little depression get you. There's always the poorhouse. Quite cozy, too, they say. Peace for the weary—

LOVING—(*cuts in—mockingly*) There is much to be said for peace.

ELIOT—(*as if it were John who had spoken*) Yes, John, there sure is—these damned days. (*then giving John a glance of concern*) Look here. I think our troubles are getting your nerve. You've seemed worn ragged lately. Why not take a few days in the country?

JOHN—Nonsense! I'm fine. (*forcing a humorous tone*) What, besides the poorhouse, is on your mind, Bill?

ELIOT—Nothing but lunch. Ate too much again, damn it. What were you doping out when I came in? Got some new scheme for us?

JOHN—No.

LOVING—Merely trying to work out the answer to a puzzle—a human puzzle.

JOHN—(*hurriedly*) That is, I'm playing around with a plot for a novel that's come into my mind lately.

ELIOT—(*with amused surprise*) What? Good God, don't tell me the literary bug is biting you again? I thought you'd got that out of your system long ago when you got engaged to Elsa and decided to come in with me and make some money.

JOHN—Well, I thought I might as well do something with all this leisure. Oh, I'll probably never write it, but it's amusing to dope out.

ELIOT—Why shouldn't you write it? You certainly showed you could write in the old days—articles, anyway. (*then with a grin*) Why, I can remember when I couldn't pick up an advanced-thinker organ without running into a red-hot article of yours denouncing Capitalism or religion or something.

JOHN—(*smiling good-naturedly*) You always did have a mean memory, Bill.

ELIOT—(*laughs*) God, John, how you've changed! What hymns of hate you used to emit against poor old Christianity! Why, I remember one article where you actually tried to prove that no such figure as Christ had ever existed.

LOVING—(*his tone suddenly cold and hostile*) I still feel the same on that subject.

ELIOT—(*gives John a surprised glance*) Feel? Can't understand any one having feelings any more on such a dead issue as religion.

JOHN—(*confused*) Well, to tell the truth, I haven't given it a thought in years, but— (*then hurriedly*) But, for Pete's sake, let's not get started on religion.

ELIOT—(*changes the subject tactfully*) Tell me about this novel of yours, John. What's it all about?

JOHN—Nothing to tell yet. I haven't got it finally worked out.

LOVING—The most important part, that is—the end.

JOHN—(*in a joking tone*) But when I have, Bill, I'll be only too glad to get your esteemed criticism.

ELIOT—That's a promise, remember— (*then getting up*) Well, I suppose I better get back to my office. (*He starts for the door—then turns back.*) Oh, I knew there was something I'd forgotten to tell you. Lucy Hillman called up while you were out.

JOHN—(*carelessly*) Yes? What did she want?

ELIOT—Wanted you. Got my office by mistake. She'll call up later. It was important, she said to tell you.

JOHN—Her idea of important! Probably wants my advice on what to give Walter for a birthday present.

ELIOT—What the devil's got into Walter lately, anyway? Getting drunk as a pastime may have its points, but as an exclusive occupation— Not to mention all his affairs with women. How does Lucy stand it? But I hear she's going to pieces, too.

JOHN—I don't believe it. She isn't the kind to have affairs.

ELIOT—I don't mean that. I mean booze.

JOHN—Oh. Well, if it's true, you can hardly blame her.

ELIOT—There are children, aren't there? Why hasn't she the guts to divorce him?

JOHN—Don't ask me. We haven't seen much of Lucy, either, for a long time. (*He dismisses the subject by looking down at his pad, as if he wanted to start writing.*)

ELIOT—(*taking the hint*) Well, I'll move along.

JOHN—See you later, Bill. (*Eliot goes out, rear. After the door closes behind him John speaks tensely.*) Why did she phone? Important, she said. What can have happened?

LOVING—(*coldly*) Who knows? But you know very well she can't be trusted. You'd better be prepared for any stupid folly. And better get the end of your novel decided upon, so you can tell your plot—before it's too late.

JOHN—(*tensely*) Yes.

LOVING—(*the hidden sinister note again creeping into his*

coldly casual tone) There can be only one sensible, logical end for your hero, after he has lost his wife forever—that is, provided he loves her as much as he boasts to himself he does—and if he has any honor or courage left!

JOHN—(*gives a start—then bitterly*) Ah! I see now what you're driving at! And you talk of courage and honor! (*defiantly*) No! He must go on! He must find a faith—somewhere!

LOVING—(*an undercurrent of anger in his sneering*) Somewhere, eh? Now I wonder what hides behind that somewhere? Is it your old secret weakness—the cowardly yearning to go back—?

JOHN—(*defensively*) I don't know what you're thinking about.

LOVING—You lie! I know you! And I'll make you face it in the end of your story—face it and kill it, finally and forever! (*There is again a knock on the door and John's eyes go to his pad. This time Eliot comes in immediately, without waiting for an answer.*)

JOHN—Hello, Bill. What's up now?

ELIOT—(*comes forward, a twinkle in his eye*) John, there's a mysterious visitor outside demanding to see you.

JOHN—You mean—Lucy?

ELIOT—Lucy? No. This is a man. He ran into me before he got to Miss Sims and asked for you. (*grinning*) And as it's liable to be a bitter blow, I thought I better break the news in person.

JOHN—What's the joke? Who is it?

ELIOT—It's a priest.

JOHN—A priest?

LOVING—(*harshly*) I don't know any priests! Tell him to get out!

ELIOT—Now don't be disrespectful. He claims he's your uncle.

JOHN—My uncle? Did he give his name?

ELIOT—Yes. Father Baird. Said he'd just got in from the West.

JOHN—(*dumbfounded—forcing a smile*) Well, I'll be damned.

ELIOT—(*laughs*) My God, think of you having a priest for an uncle! That's too rich!

JOHN—I haven't seen him since I was a boy.

ELIOT—Why so scared? Afraid he's come to lecture you on your sins?

LOVING—(*angrily*) He may be a joke to you. He's not to me, damn him!

ELIOT—(*gives John a surprised, disapproving glance*) Oh, come, John. Not as bad as that, is it? He struck me as a nice old guy.

JOHN—(*hurriedly*) He is. I didn't mean that. I always liked him. He was very kind to me when I was a kid. He acted as my guardian for a while. But I wish he'd given me warning. (*then picking up the telephone*) Well, it's rotten to keep him cooling his heels. Hello. Send Father Baird in.

ELIOT—(*turning to the door*) I'll get out.

JOHN—No, as a favor, stay around until the ice is broken. (*He has gotten up and is going toward the door. Loving remains in his chair, his eyes fixed before him in a hostile stare, his body tensed defensively.*)

ELIOT—Sure. (*A knock comes on the door. John opens it and Father Matthew Baird enters. He is seventy, about John and Loving's height, erect, robust, with thick white hair, ruddy complexion. There is a clear resemblance to John and Loving in the general cast of his features and the color of his eyes. His appearance and personality radiate health and observant kindliness—also the confident authority of one who is accustomed to obedience and deference—and one gets immediately from him the sense of an unshakable inner calm and certainty, the peace of one whose goal in life is fixed by an end beyond life.*)

JOHN—(*constrained and at the same time affectionate*) Hello, Uncle! What in the world brings you—

FATHER BAIRD—(*clasping John's hand in a strong grip*) Jack! (*His manner is very much what it must have been when John was a boy and he was the guardian. Deeply moved, he puts his arm around John and gives him an affectionate hug.*) My dear Jack! This is— (*He sees Eliot and stops, a bit embarrassed.*)

JOHN—(*moved and embarrassed, getting away from*

arm) I want you to meet my partner—Bill Eliot—my uncle, Father Baird.

ELIOT—It's a great pleasure, Father.

FATHER BAIRD—(*shakes his hand—a formal, old-fashioned courtesy in his manner*) The pleasure is mine, Mr. Eliot. But I feel I've had the privilege of your acquaintance already through Jack's letters.

JOHN—Sit down, Uncle. (*He indicates the chair at right of desk. Father Baird sits down. John sits in his chair at left. Eliot stands by the chair at right, center.*)

ELIOT—Well, I'll leave you two alone and pretend to be busy. That's the hardest job we have now, Father—keeping up the pretense of work.

FATHER BAIRD—You have plenty of company, if that's any consolation. I get the same tale of woe from every one in our part of the country.

ELIOT—I'm afraid the company doesn't console a bit. They're all too darned whiney.

FATHER BAIRD—(*a twinkle coming into his eye*) Ah, who can blame you for whining when your omnipotent Golden Calf explodes into sawdust before your adoring eyes right at the height of his deification? It's tragic, no other word—unless the word be comic.

LOVING—(*his voice a mocking sneer*) And what salvation for us are you preaching? The Second Coming?

FATHER BAIRD—(*startled, turns to stare at John. Eliot also looks at him, surprised and disapproving of this taunt. Father Baird says quietly, without any sign of taking offense*) The First Coming is enough, Jack—for those who remember it. (*Then he turns to Eliot—in a joking tone*) If you knew how familiar that note sounds from him, Mr. Eliot. Here I've been feeling strange, looking at him and seeing what a big man of affairs he'd grown, and saying to myself, can this be my old Jack? And then he has to go and give himself away with a strain of his old bold whistling in the dark, and I see he's still only out of short pants a while, as I knew him last! (*He gives a comic sigh of relief.*) Thank you, Jack. I feel quite at home with you now.

ELIOT—(*immensely amused, especially at the expression of discomfiture on John's face—laughingly*) John, I begin to feel sorry for you. You've picked on some one out of your class.

FATHER BAIRD—(*with a wink at Eliot*) Did you hear him throw the word preaching in my face, Mr. Eliot—with a dirty sneer in his voice? There's injustice for you. If you knew what a burden he made my life for years with his preaching. Letter upon letter—each with a soap box inclosed, so to speak. The plague began right after I'd had to go West and leave him to his own devices. He was about to pass out of my guardianship and go to college with the bit of money his parents had left for him when he reached eighteen. So I had to let him go his own way. I'd learned it was no use fighting him, anyway. I'd done that and found it was a great satisfaction to him and only made him worse. And I had faith, if let alone, he'd come back to his senses in the end.

LOVING—(*sneeringly*) And how mistaken you were in that faith!

FATHER BAIRD—(*without turning—quietly*) No. The end isn't yet, Jack. (*He goes on to Eliot with a renewal of his humorously complaining tone.*) You wouldn't believe what a devil's advocate he was in those days, Mr. Eliot.

ELIOT—You needn't tell me, Father. I was his classmate. He organized an Atheists' Club—or tried to—and almost got fired for it.

FATHER BAIRD—Yes, I remember his writing to boast about that. Well, you can appreciate then what I went through, even if he didn't write you letters.

ELIOT—But he delivered harangues, Father, when he could get anybody to listen!

FATHER BAIRD—(*pityingly*) Ah, that must have been cruel, too. Mr. Eliot, I feel drawn to you. We've been through the same frightful trials.

JOHN—(*with a boyishly discomfited air*) I hope you're having a good time, you two.

FATHER BAIRD—(*ignoring him*) Not a moment's peace did he give me. I was the heathen to him and he was bound he'd convert me to something. First it was Atheism unadorned. Then it was Atheism wedded to Socialism. But Socialism proved too weak-kneed a mate, and the next I heard Atheism was living in free love with Anarchism, with a curse by

Nietzsche to bless the union. And then came the Bolshevik dawn, and he greeted that with unholy howls of glee and wrote me he'd found a congenial home at last in the bosom of Karl Marx. He was particularly delighted when he thought they'd abolished love and marriage, and he couldn't contain himself when the news came they'd turned naughty school-boys and were throwing spit-balls at Almighty God and had supplanted Him with the slave-owning State—the most grotesque god that ever came out of Asia!

ELIOT—(*chuckling*) I recognize all this, Father. I used to read his articles, as I was reminding him just before you came.

FATHER BAIRD—Don't I know them! Didn't he send me every one with blue pencil underlinings! But to get back to my story: Thinks I at this juncture, well, he's run away as far as he can get in that direction. Where will he hide himself next?

LOVING—(*stiffening in his chair—with angry resentment*) Run away? You talk as if I were afraid of something. Hide? Hide from what?

FATHER BAIRD—(*without turning—quietly*) Don't you know, Jack? Well, if you don't yet, you will some day. (*again to Eliot*) I knew Communism wouldn't hold him long—and it didn't. Soon his letters became full of pessimism, and disgust with all sociological nostrums. Then followed a long silence. And what do you think was his next hiding place? Religion, no less—but as far away as he could run from home—in the defeatist mysticism of the East. First it was China and Lao Tze that fascinated him, but afterwards he ran on to Buddha, and his letters for a time extolled passionless contemplation so passionately that I had a mental view of him regarding his navel frenziedly by the hour and making nothing of it! (*Eliot laughs and John chuckles sheepishly in spite of himself. Loving stares before him with a cold, angry disdain.*)

ELIOT—Gosh, I'm sorry I missed that! When was all this, Father?

FATHER BAIRD—In what I'd call his middle hide-and-go-seek period. But the next I knew, he was through with the East. It was not for the Western soul, he decided, and he was running through Greek philosophy and found a brief shelter in Pythagoras and numerology. Then came a letter which revealed him bogged down in evolutionary scientific truth again—a dyed-in-the-wool mechanist. That was the last I heard of his peregrinations—and, thank heaven, it was long ago. I enjoyed a long interval of peace from his missionary zeal, until finally he wrote me he was married. That letter was full of more ardent hymns of praise for a mere living woman than he'd ever written before about any of his great spiritual discoveries. And ever since then I've heard nothing but the praises of Elsa—in which I know I'll be ready to join after I've met her.

JOHN—(*his face lighting up*) You bet you will! We can agree on that, at least.

FATHER BAIRD—(*with a wink at Eliot*) He seems to be fixed in his last religion. I hope so. The only constant faith I've found in him before was his proud belief in himself as a bold Antichrist. (*He gives John a side glance, half smiling and half reproachful.*) Ah well, it's a rocky road, full of twists and blind alleys, isn't it, Jack—this running away from truth in order to find it? I mean, until the road finally turns back toward home.

LOVING—(*with harsh defiance*) You believe I—? (*then sneeringly*) But, of course, you would read that into it.

JOHN—(*bursts out irritably, as if he couldn't control his nerves*) But don't you think I'm about exhausted as a subject, Uncle? I do. (*He gets up nervously and moves around and stands behind Loving's chair, his hands on the back of the chair, his face directly above Loving's masked one.*)

ELIOT—(*gives the priest an amused smile*) Well, I'll get back to my office. (*Father Baird gets up and he shakes his hand heartily.*) I hope we'll meet again, Father. Are you here for long?

FATHER BAIRD—Only a few days, I'm afraid.

JOHN—(*coming around to them*) I'll fix up something with Elsa for the four of us, Bill—as soon as she's feeling stronger. We won't let him run away in a few days, now we've got him here.

ELIOT—Fine! See you again, then, Father. (*He goes toward the door.*)

FATHER BAIRD—I hope so, Mr. Eliot. Good day to you.

ELIOT—(*with the door open, turns back with a grin*) I feel it my duty, Father, to warn you that John's got writer's itch again. He's going to give us a novel. (*He laughs and closes the door behind him. John frowns and gives his uncle a quick uneasy glance.*)

JOHN—(*indicating the chair at right, center*) Take that chair, Uncle. It's more comfortable. (*He sits down in the chair at right of table where Father Baird had sat, while the priest sits in the one at right, center. Father Baird gives him a puzzled, concerned look, as if he were trying to figure something out. Then he speaks casually.*)

FATHER BAIRD—A novel? Is that right, Jack?

JOHN—(*without looking at him*) Thinking of it—to pass the time.

FATHER BAIRD—Then, judging from your letters, it ought to be a love story.

JOHN—It is—a love story.

LOVING—(*mockingly*) About God's love for us!

FATHER BAIRD—(*quietly rebuking*) Jack! (*A pause of silence. Father Baird gives John a quick glance again—then casually*) If you've any appointments, don't stand on ceremony; just shoo me out.

JOHN—(*turns to him shamefacedly*) Don't talk that way, Uncle. You know I wouldn't— (*with a natural, boyishly affectionate smile*) You know darned well how tickled I am to have you here.

FATHER BAIRD—I hope you're half as glad as I am to see you, Jack. (*He sighs.*) It has been a long time—too long.

JOHN—Yes. (*smiling*) But I'm still flabbergasted. I never dreamed you— Why didn't you wire me you were coming?

FATHER BAIRD—Oh, I thought I'd surprise you. (*He smiles.*) To tell you the truth, I confess I had a sneaking Sherlock Holmes desire to have a good look at you before you were expecting it.

JOHN—(*frowning—uneasily*) Why? Why should you?

FATHER BAIRD—Well, I suppose because, not having seen you, I'm afraid that to me you were still the boy I'd known, and I was still your suspicious guardian.

JOHN—(*relieved—with a boyish grin*) Oh! I see.

FATHER BAIRD—And now I have seen you, I still must admit that the gray in your hair is lost on me, and I can't get it out of my head you're the same old Jack.

JOHN—(*grinning with a boyish discomfiture*) Yes, and the devil of it is you make me feel that way, too. It's an unfair advantage, Uncle. (*Father Baird laughs and John joins in.*)

FATHER BAIRD—Well, I never took unfair advantage of you in the old days, did I?

JOHN—You certainly didn't. When I look back, I'm amazed you could have been so fair. (*quickly—changing the subject*) But you haven't told me yet how you happened to come East.

FATHER BAIRD—(*a bit evasively*) Oh, I decided a vacation was due me. And I've had a great longing for some time to see you again.

JOHN—I only wish I could have you stay with us, but there's no room. But you must have dinner with us to-night, and every night you're here, of course.

FATHER BAIRD—Yes, I'd like to see all of you I can. But there's this, Jack. You spoke to Mr. Eliot as if Elsa were ill.

JOHN—Oh, it's nothing serious. She's just getting over the flu, and still feels a bit low.

FATHER BAIRD—Then I'd better not come to-night.

JOHN—You better had or she'll never forgive you—or me!

FATHER BAIRD—Very well. I'm only too happy. (*A pause. He glances at John again with a curious puzzled fixity. John catches his eyes, is held by them for a moment, then looks away almost furtively.*)

JOHN—(*forcing a smile*) Is that the suspicious guardian look? I've forgotten.

FATHER BAIRD—(*as if to himself—slowly*) I feel— (*then suddenly*) There's something I want to tell you, Jack. (*A stern note comes into his voice.*) But first give me your word of honor there will be no cheap sneering.

JOHN—(*stares at him, taken aback—then quietly*) There won't be.

FATHER BAIRD—Well, it's often come to me in the past that I shouldn't have let you get so far from me, that I might be in part responsible for your continued estrangement from your Faith.

LOVING—(*with mocking scorn*) My faith?

JOHN—You know that's nonsense, Uncle.

LOVING—You have always nobly done your duty. You've

never let a letter pass without some pious reminder of my
fall—with the calm assurance that I would again see the light.
That never failed to make me laugh—your complacent assumption that like the Prodigal of His fairy tale, I—

FATHER BAIRD—(*sharply*) Jack! You promised!

JOHN—(*confusedly*) I know. I didn't mean— Go on with
what you started to tell me.

FATHER BAIRD—First answer me frankly one question.
Have you been greatly troubled in spirit by anything lately?

JOHN—(*startled*) I? Why do you ask that? Of course not.
(*then evasively*) Oh, well—yes, maybe, if you mean business
worries.

FATHER BAIRD—Nothing else?

JOHN—No. What could there be?

FATHER BAIRD—(*unconvinced—looking away*) The reason
I asked— You'll see in what I'm going to tell you. It happened one night while I was praying for you in my church,
as I have every day since I left you. A strange feeling of fear
took possession of me—a feeling you were unhappy, in some
great spiritual danger. I told myself it was foolish. I'd had a
letter from you only that day, reiterating how happy you
were. I tried to lose my dread in prayer—and my guilt. Yes,
I felt stricken with guilt, too—that I was to blame for whatever was happening to you. Then, as I prayed, suddenly as if
by some will outside me, my eyes were drawn to the Cross,
to the face of Our Blessed Lord. And it was like a miracle!
His face seemed alive as a living man's would be, but radiant
with eternal life, too, especially the sad, pitying eyes. But
there was a sternness in His eyes, too, an accusation against
me—a command about you! (*He breaks off and gives John a
quick glance, as if afraid of finding him sneering. Then, looking
away, he adds simply*) That's the real reason I decided to take
my vacation in the East, Jack.

JOHN—(*stares at him fascinatedly*) You saw—?

LOVING—(*in a bitter, sneering tone*) It could hardly have
been any concern for me you saw in His face—even if He
did exist or ever had existed!

FATHER BAIRD—(*sternly*) Jack! (*then, after a pause, quietly*)
Do you know Francis Thompson's poem—The Hound of
Heaven?

LOVING—I did once. Why?

FATHER BAIRD—(*quotes in a low voice but with deep feeling*)
"Ah, fondest, blindest, weakest,
I am He Whom thou seekest!
Thou dravest love from thee, who dravest Me."

LOVING—(*in what is close to a snarl of scorn*) Love!

JOHN—(*defensively*) I have love!

FATHER BAIRD—(*as if he hadn't heard*) Why do you run and hide from Him, as from an enemy? Take care. There comes a time in every man's life when he must have his God for friend, or he has no friend at all, not even himself. Who knows? Perhaps you are on the threshold of that time now.

JOHN—(*uneasily*) What do you mean?

FATHER BAIRD—I don't know. It's for you to know that. You say you have love?

JOHN—You know I have. Or, if you don't, you soon will after you've met Elsa.

FATHER BAIRD—I'm not doubting your love for her nor hers for you. It's exactly because I do not doubt. I am thinking that such love needs the hope and promise of eternity to fulfill itself—above all, to feel itself secure. Beyond the love for each other should be the love of God, in Whose Love yours may find the triumph over death.

LOVING—(*sneeringly*) Old superstition, born of fear! Beyond death there is nothing. That, at least, is certain—a certainty we should be thankful for. One life is boring enough. Do not condemn us to another. Let us rest in peace at last!

FATHER BAIRD—(*quietly*) Would you talk that way if Elsa should die?

JOHN—(*with a shudder*) For God's sake, don't speak about—

LOVING—Do you think I haven't imagined her death many times?

JOHN—The dread of it has haunted me ever since we were married.

FATHER BAIRD—Ah.

LOVING—You'll see that I face it—by proxy, at least—in my novel. (*a sneering taunt in his voice*) I think you'll be interested in this novel, Uncle.

FATHER BAIRD—(*staring at John, whose face is averted*) It's autobiographical, then?

JOHN—(*hastily*) No. Of course not. I only meant— Don't get that idea in your head, for Pete's sake. As I explained to Elsa, when I told her about the first part, it's really the story of a man I once knew.

LOVING—The first part will particularly interest you, Uncle. I am afraid you will be terribly shocked—especially in the light of your recent mystic vision!

FATHER BAIRD—I'm very curious to hear it, Jack. When will you tell me?

LOVING—(*defiantly*) Now!

JOHN—(*uneasily*) But no. I don't want to bore you.

FATHER BAIRD—You won't bore me.

JOHN—No— I—

LOVING—(*with harsh insistence*) The first part concerns my hero's boyhood here in New York, up to the age of fifteen.

JOHN—(*Under Loving's compulsion, he picks up the thread of the story.*) He was an only child. His father was a fine man. The boy adored him. And he adored his mother even more. She was a wonderful woman, a perfect type of our old beautiful ideal of wife and mother.

LOVING—(*sneeringly*) But there was one ridiculous weakness in her character, an absurd obsession with religion. In the father's, too. They were both devout Catholics. (*The priest gives a swift, reproachful look at John, seems about to protest, thinks better of it, and drops his eyes.*)

JOHN—(*quickly*) But not the ignorant, bigoted sort, please understand. No, their piety had a genuine, gentle, mystic quality to it. Their faith was the great comforting inspiration of their lives. And their God was One of Infinite Love—not a stern, self-righteous Being Who condemned sinners to torment, but a very human, lovable God Who became man for love of men and gave His life that they might be saved from themselves. And the boy had every reason to believe in such a Divinity of Love as the Creator of Life. His home atmosphere was one of love. Life *was* love for him then. And he was happy, happier than he ever afterward— (*He checks himself abruptly.*)

FATHER BAIRD—(*nods his head approvingly*) Yes.

JOHN—Later, at school, he learned of the God of Punishment, and he wondered. He couldn't reconcile Him with his parents' faith. So it didn't make much impression on him.

LOVING—(*bitterly*) Then! But afterward he had good reason to—

JOHN—But then he was too sure in his faith. He grew up as devout as his parents. He even dreamed of becoming a priest. He used to love to kneel in the church before the Cross.

LOVING—Oh, he was a remarkably superstitious young fool! (*His voice suddenly changes to hard bitterness.*) And then when he was fifteen, all these pious illusions of his were destroyed forever! Both his parents were killed!

JOHN—(*hurriedly*) That is, they died during a flu epidemic in which they contracted pneumonia—and he was left alone—without love. First, his father died. The boy had prayed with perfect faith that his father's life might be spared.

LOVING—But his father died! And the poor simpleton's naïve faith was a bit shaken, and a sinful doubt concerning the Divine Love assailed him!

JOHN—Then his mother, worn out by nursing his father and by her grief, was taken ill. And the horrible fear came to him that she might die, too.

LOVING—It drove the young idiot into a panic of superstitious remorse. He imagined her sickness was a terrible warning to him, a punishment for the doubt inspired in him by his father's death. (*with harsh bitterness*) His God of Love was beginning to show Himself as a God of Vengeance, you see!

JOHN—But he still trusted in His Love. Surely He would not take his mother from him, too.

LOVING—So the poor fool prayed and prayed and vowed his life to piety and good works! But he began to make a condition now—*if* his mother were spared to him!

JOHN—Finally he knew in his heart she was going to die. But even then he hoped and prayed for a miracle.

LOVING—He abased and humbled himself before the Cross—and, in reward for his sickening humiliation, saw that no miracle would happen.

JOHN—Something snapped in him then.

LOVING—(*His voice suddenly takes on a tone of bitter hatred.*) He saw his God as deaf and blind and merciless—a Deity Who returned hate for love and revenged Himself upon those who trusted Him!

JOHN—His mother died. And, in a frenzy of insane grief—

LOVING—No! In his awakened pride he cursed his God and denied Him, and, in revenge, promised his soul to the Devil—on his knees, when every one thought he was praying! (*He laughs with malignant bitterness.*)

JOHN—(*quickly—in a casual tone*) And that's the end of Part One, as I've outlined it.

FATHER BAIRD—(*horrified*) Jack! I can't believe that you—

JOHN—(*defensively*) I? What have I to do with it? You're forgetting I explained to you— Oh, I admit there are certain points of resemblance between some of his boyhood experiences and mine—his parents' death, for example. But that's only coincidence.

FATHER BAIRD—(*recovered now—staring at him—quietly*) I see.

JOHN—(*forcing a smile*) And please don't bring up those coincidences before Elsa, Uncle. She didn't notice them because I've never bored her with boyhood reminiscences. And I don't want her to get the wrong angle on my plot.

FATHER BAIRD—I'll remember, Jack. When will you tell me the rest of it?

JOHN—Oh, some time while you're here, maybe.

FATHER BAIRD—Why not to-night at your home?

JOHN—Well, I might—

LOVING—That is, if I can decide on my end before then!

JOHN—It would give me a chance to get your and Elsa's criticisms at the same time. She's been wanting to hear the rest of it, too.

FATHER BAIRD—(*regarding him—quietly*) Then, by all means. (*abruptly changing to a brisk casualness*) Well, I'll leave you and attend to some errand I have to do. (*He gets to his feet. He takes John's hand.*)

JOHN—Dinner is at seven-thirty. But come as long before

that as you like. I'll be home early. (*then with a genuine boyish affection*) I want to tell you again, Uncle, how grand it is to have you here—in spite of our arguments.

FATHER BAIRD—I'm not worried by our arguments. But I am about something about you that admits of no argument— to me.

JOHN—(*forcing a smile*) You're wasting worry. But what is it?

FATHER BAIRD—You've written me you were happy, and I believed you. But, now I see you, I don't believe you. You're not happy. Why? Perhaps if you had it out with me—

LOVING—(*mockingly*) Confess, eh?

JOHN—Don't be foolish, Uncle. I am happy, happier than I ever dreamed I could be. And, for heaven's sake, don't go telling Elsa I'm unhappy!

FATHER BAIRD—(*quietly*) Very well. We'll say no more about it. And now I'll be off. Good-bye until this evening, Jack.

JOHN—So long, Uncle. (*Father Baird goes out. John stands by the door, looking after him—then he comes slowly back and sits down in his chair and stares before him. Loving's eyes are fastened on him with a cold contempt.*)

LOVING—Damned old fool with his bedtime tales for second childhood about the love of God! And you—you're worse—with your hypocritical lies about your great happiness! (*The telephone on the table rings. John jumps nervously— then answers it in an apprehensive voice.*)

JOHN—Hello. Who? Tell her I'm out.

LOVING—You'd better find out what she wants.

JOHN—No, wait. I'll take it. (*then, his voice becoming guarded and pleasantly casual*) Hello, Lucy. Bill told me you'd called. What—? (*He listens—then anxiety creeping into his tone*) She phoned again? What about? Oh. I'm glad you called me. Yes, she has been wondering why she hasn't heard from you in so long. Yes, by all means, go. Yes, she's sure to be in this afternoon. Good-bye. (*He hangs up mechanically.*)

LOVING—(*sneeringly*) Your terrible sin begins to close in on you, eh? But then, it wasn't you, was it? It was some evil spirit that possessed you! (*He gives a mocking laugh—then*

stops abruptly and continues in his tone of cold, sinister insistence.)
But enough of that nonsense. Let's return to your plot. The
wife dies—of influenza that turns into pneumonia, let's say.

JOHN—(*starts violently—stammers*) What—God damn
you—what makes you choose that?

(*Curtain*)

ACT TWO

Plot for a Novel (Continued)

SCENE—*The living-room of the Lovings' duplex apartment. Venetian blinds soften the light from a big window at right. In front of this window is a table with a lamp. At left, front, an upholstered chair. At right of chair, a small table with a lamp. At right of table, in the center of the room, a sofa. In front of sofa, a low stand with cigarette box and ash trays. Toward right, another chair. In the left wall is a door leading to the dining-room. At rear of door, a writing desk. In the middle of the rear wall is a doorway leading to the hall.*

It is later the same afternoon.

Elsa enters from the hall at rear. She is thirty-five but looks much younger. She is beautiful with that Indian Summer renewal of physical charm which comes to a woman who loves and is loved, particularly to one who has not found that love until comparatively late in life. This beauty is a trifle dimmed now by traces of recent illness. Her face is drawn and she fights against a depressing lassitude. She wears a simple negligée.

As she comes in, she presses a button by the door and a buzzer is heard in the pantry. She comes forward and sits on the sofa. A moment later Margaret, the maid, appears from the dining-room at left. She is a middle-aged Irishwoman with a kindly face.

MARGARET—Yes, Madame?

ELSA—Hasn't the afternoon paper come yet, Margaret?

MARGARET—No, Madame, not yet. (*then with kindly reproof*) Didn't you take a nap like you promised you would?

ELSA—I couldn't get to sleep. But I do feel rested, so don't begin to scold me. (*She smiles and Margaret smiles back, a look of devoted affection lighting up her face.*)

MARGARET—You have to take care. The flu's a bad thing the way it leaves you weak after. And you're only out of your bed two days.

ELSA—Oh, I'm really quite well again. And I was too excited to sleep. I kept thinking of Mr. Loving's uncle. (*The telephone in the hall rings and Margaret goes toward the door in rear to answer it.*) Heavens, I hope that isn't he now. Mr.

133

Loving phoned me he told him to come early. But surely he wouldn't this early!

MARGARET—(*disappears in the hall. Her voice comes*) Just a moment and I'll see if she's in. (*She appears again in the doorway.*) It's Mrs. Hillman calling to see you, Madame.

ELSA—Oh, I'm glad. Tell her to come right up. (*Margaret disappears and is heard relaying this instruction. Then she appears in the hall outside the doorway, waiting to answer the door. Elsa speaks to her.*) I wish I didn't look so like a sick cat. Why is it every one decides to turn up when you look your worst?

MARGARET—Ah, you needn't worry, Madame. You look fine.

ELSA—Well, anyway, I don't mind Lucy. (*Nevertheless, she goes to the desk at left, rear, takes out a vanity case, powders her nose, etc. While she is doing this, Margaret moves to the entrance door in the hall and is heard admitting Mrs. Hillman and exchanging greetings with her, as she helps her off with her things. Elsa calls*) Hello, Stranger.

LUCY—(*calls back in a voice whose breeziness rings a bit strained*) That's right, sit on me the minute I set foot in your house! Well, I know I deserve it. (*Elsa goes to the doorway and meets her as she comes in, kissing her affectionately. Lucy Hillman is about the same age as Elsa. She is still an extremely attractive woman but, in contrast to Elsa, her age shows, in spite of a heavy make-up. There are wrinkles about her eyes, and her small, full, rather weak mouth is drawn down by sharp lines at the corners. She is dressed expensively in clothes a bit too youthful and extreme in style. She responds to Elsa's greeting with a nervous constraint.*) Hello, Elsa.

ELSA—You're a nice one! How long has it been—months! —not since before I went to Boston in February. (*She sits on the sofa and draws Lucy down beside her.*)

LUCY—I know. I'm in the dust at your feet.

ELSA—I've phoned you a dozen times, but you were always out. Or did you just tell them to say that? I've completely lost faith in you.

LUCY—But I was out, Elsa. How can you think—

ELSA—(*laughing—gives her a hug*) You're not taking me

seriously, are you? I know you'd hardly do that with me, after all these years.

LUCY—Of course, I wouldn't.

ELSA—But I did wonder a little at your sudden complete ignoring of our existence. So did John.

LUCY—(*hurriedly*) If you know all the stupid engagements that pile up—and all the idiotic parties Walter lets me in for. (*then changing the subject abruptly*) May I have a cigarette? (*She takes one from the box on the stand and lights it.*) Aren't you having one?

ELSA—Not now. (*She gives Lucy a puzzled glance. Lucy avoids her eyes, nervously flipping her cigarette over the ash tray. Elsa asks*) How are the kids?

LUCY—Oh, fine, thanks. At least, I think so, from the little I get to see of them nowadays. (*Bitterness has crept into this last. She again hurriedly changes the subject.*) But tell me all your news. What have you been doing with yourself?

ELSA—Oh, the same peaceful routine—going to a concert now and then, reading a lot, keeping house, taking care of John.

LUCY—The old perfect marriage that's been the wonder of us all, eh? (*again changing the subject*) What time does John usually get home? I don't want to run into him.

ELSA—Oh, not for an hour or so yet. (*smiling*) But why? What have you got against John?

LUCY—(*smiling with a strange wryness*) Nothing—except myself. (*then hurriedly*) I mean, look at me, I look like hell. I've had the damndest insomnia lately. And I'm vain enough not to crave any male viewing the wreckage until I've spruced up on a bath and cocktails.

ELSA—But that's silly. You look wonderful.

LUCY—(*dryly*) Thanks, liar! (*with a side glance of frank envy—unable to keep resentment out of her voice*) I especially don't care to be up for inspection beside you. The contrast is too glaring.

ELSA—But it's I who look like the devil, not you. I'm just getting over flu.

LUCY—Flu makes no never mind. It doesn't affect—what I mean. (*then with a hard flippant air*) Pardon me if I seem to indulge in the melancholy jitters. I'm becoming the damndest whiner and self-pitier. It's really too boring. (*She lights another cigarette. Her hands have a nervous tremor. Elsa watches her with a worried, affectionately pitying look.*)

ELSA—What is it, Lucy? Tell me.

LUCY—(*stiffening defensively*) What is what?

ELSA—I want to know what's troubling you. Now, there's no use denying it. I've known you too long. I felt it the moment you came in, that you were upset about something and trying to hide it.

LUCY—I don't know where you got that idea. (*defensively flippant*) Oh, really now, Elsa. Don't you go psychic on us!

ELSA—All right, then. Forgive my trying to pump you. But you got me into the bad habit yourself, you know, by always coming to me with your troubles. I only thought I might be able to help.

LUCY—You! (*She gives a hard little laugh.*)

ELSA—(*hurt*) You used to think I could.

LUCY—"Once, long ago—" (*then, suddenly with repentant shamefacedness*) Forgive me, Elsa. I'm rotten to be flip about that. You've been the most wonderful friend. And I'm such an ungrateful little slut!

ELSA—Lucy! You mustn't say that.

LUCY—(*hurries on with a simulation of frankness*) But honestly, you're mistaken this time. There's nothing wrong, except what seems to be wrong with every one, the stupid lives we lead—and, of course, the usual financial worries. So please don't bother your head about my troubles.

ELSA—All right, dear. (*then, after a slight pause—casually*) How is Walter these days?

LUCY—(*with a twisted smile*) I thought we weren't going to talk about my troubles! Oh, Walter is—Walter. You know him, Elsa. Why ask? But do you know any one, I wonder? Darned if I think you ever see what people really are. You somehow manage to live in some lost world where human beings are still decent and honorable. I don't see how you do it. If you'd always been a little innocent, protected from all ugly contacts— But, my God, your first marriage must have slapped your face with about every filthy thing a man can be—and that's plenty! Yet you sit here, calm and beautiful and unscarred—!

ELSA—(*quietly*) I have my share of scars. But the wounds are all healed—completely healed. John's love has done that for me.

LUCY—Yes—of course. (*Then, as if she couldn't control herself, she bursts out*) Oh, you and your John! You bring him up as the answer to everything.

ELSA—(*smiling*) Well, he is for me.

LUCY—Do you mean to tell me you're as much in love with him now as when you married him?

ELSA—Oh, much more so, for he's become my child and father now, as well as being a husband and—

LUCY—Lover. Say it. How incredibly Mid-Victorian you can be! Don't you know that's all we married ladies discuss nowadays? But you're lucky. Usually the men discussed aren't our husbands, and aren't even good lovers. But never say die. We keep on hoping and experimenting!

ELSA—(*repelled*) Don't talk in that disgusting way. I know you don't mean a word of it.

LUCY—(*stares at her resentfully for a second, then turns away, reaching for another cigarette—dryly*) Oh, you're quite sure of that, are you?

ELSA—(*gently*) Lucy, what is it has made you so bitter? I've noticed it growing on you for the past few years, but now it's completely got you. I—honestly, I hardly know you this time, you've changed so.

LUCY—(*hurriedly*) Oh, it's nothing that happened lately. You mustn't get that idea. (*then letting herself go—with increasing bitterness*) It's simply that I've grown sick of my life, sick of all the lying and faking of it, sick of marriage and motherhood, sick of myself! Particularly sick of myself because I endure the humiliation of Walter's open affairs with every damned floosie he meets! And I'm tired of pretending I don't mind, tired of really minding underneath, tired of pretending to myself I have to go on for the children's sakes, and that they make up to me for everything, which they don't at all!

ELSA—(*indignantly*) How can Walter be such a beast!

LUCY—(*with a look at Elsa that is almost vindictive*) Oh,

he's no worse than a lot of others. At least, he doesn't lie about it.

ELSA—But, for heaven's sake, why do you stand it? Why don't you leave him?

LUCY—Oh, don't be so superior and scornful, Elsa. I'll bet you wouldn't— (*She checks herself abruptly.*)

ELSA—What do you mean? You know very well I left my first husband the minute I found out—

LUCY—(*hurriedly*) I know. I didn't— Why don't I leave Walter? I guess because I'm too worn out to have the guts. And then I did try it once. The first time I knew he'd been unfaithful I did the correct thing and went home. I intended to tell Father I was through as Walter's wife. Only Father was away. Mother was there, and I broke down and told her. She took it quite philosophically—said I was a fool to expect too much, men were like that, even my father had— (*She gives a little shiver of aversion.*) That sort of squelched me. So I went back to Walter and he doesn't know to this day I ever left him.

ELSA—I'm so sorry, Lucy.

LUCY—(*returning to her air of hard cynicism*) No pity, please. After all, the situation has its compensations. He has tried nobly to be fair. He said I could have equal liberty to indulge any of my sexual whims.

ELSA—What a stupid fool!

LUCY—(*bitterly*) Oh, he didn't really mean it, you know. His vanity couldn't admit I'd ever feel the slightest desire outside of him. It was only a silly gesture he felt safe in making because he was so damned sure of me—because he knows, damn him, that in spite of all he's done to kill it there's still a cowardly slavish something in me, dating back to the happiness of our first married days, which still—loves him! (*She starts to break down, but fights this back and bursts out vindictively, a look of ugly satisfaction coming into her face*) But I warned him he'd humiliate me once too often—and he did!

ELSA—(*shocked*) You mean you—

LUCY—(*with a return of her flippant tone*) Yes, I went in for a little fleeting adultery. And I must say, as a love substitute or even a pleasurable diversion, it's greatly overrated. (*She gives a hard little laugh.*) How horribly shocked you look! Are you going to order me from your virtuous home?

ELSA—Lucy! Don't talk like that! It's only that I can't believe—none of this is really you. That's what makes it so— But please don't think I'm condemning you. You know how I love you, don't you?

LUCY—(*stares at her with a strange panic*) Don't, for God's sake! I don't want you to love me! I'd rather you hated me! (*But Elsa pulls her to her and she breaks down finally, sobbing, her face buried against Elsa's shoulder.*)

ELSA—There, there. You mustn't, dear. (*then as Lucy grows calmer—quietly*) Don't think I don't understand, because I do. I felt exactly the same when I found out about Ned Howell. Even though I'd stopped caring for him and our marriage had always been unhappy, my pride was so hurt I wanted to revenge myself and take the first man I met for a lover.

LUCY—(*looks up in amazement*) You went through that? I never dreamed—

ELSA—All that saved me from doing something stupid was the faith I had that somewhere the man was waiting whom I could really love. I felt I owed it to him and to my own self-respect not to deliberately disfigure myself out of wounded pride and spite.

LUCY—(*with sad bitterness*) You hit it when you say disfigure. That's how I've felt ever since. Cheap! Ugly! As if *I'd* deliberately disfigured *myself.* And not only myself—the man—and others I wouldn't hurt for anything in the world—if I was in my right mind. But I wasn't! You realize I wasn't, don't you, Elsa? You must! You above every one!

ELSA—I do, dear. Of course I do.

LUCY—I've got to tell you just how it came to happen— so you'll see. It was one of Walter's parties. You know the would-be Bohemian gang he likes to have. They were there in all their vulgarity, their poisonous, envious tongues wise-cracking at everything with any decent human dignity and worth. Oh, there were a few others there, too—our own people—this man was one of them. Walter was drunk, pawing over his latest female, and she got him to go home with her. Everybody watched me to see how I'd take it. I wanted to kill him and her, but I only laughed and had some more to drink. But I was in hell, I can tell you, and inside I kept swearing to myself that I'd show Walter— And I picked out this man—yes, deliberately! It was all deliberate and crazy! And I had to do all the seducing—because he's quite happy. I knew that, but I was crazy. His happiness filled me with rage—the thought that he made others happy. I wanted to take his happiness from him and kill it as mine had been killed!

ELSA—Lucy!

LUCY—(*with a hard laugh*) I told you I was in hell, didn't I? You can't live there without becoming like the rest of the crowd! (*hurrying on with her story*) I got him in my bedroom on some excuse. But he pushed me away, as if he were disgusted with himself and me. But I wouldn't let him go. And then came the strange part of it. Suddenly, I don't know how to explain it, you'll think I'm crazy, or being funny, but it was as if he were no longer there. It was another man, a stranger whose eyes were hateful and frightening. He seemed to look through me at some one else, and I seemed for a moment to be watching some hidden place in his mind where there was something as evil and revengeful as I was. It frightened and fascinated me—and called to me too; that's the hell of it! (*She forces a laugh.*) I suppose all this sounds too preposterous. Well, maybe it was the booze working. I'd had a lot. (*She reaches for a cigarette—returning to her hard flippancy*) And then followed my little dip into adultery.

ELSA—(*with a little shiver of repulsion*) Oh!

LUCY—But what a hideous bore this must be to you. Why did I have to tell you, I wonder. It was the last thing I ever wanted— (*turns on her in a flash of resentful vindictiveness*) It makes me out worse than you expected, eh? But suppose John were unfaithful to you—

ELSA—(*startled—frightenedly*) Don't! (*then indignantly*) Lucy! I won't have you say that, not even—

LUCY—I'm only asking you to suppose.

ELSA—I can't! I won't! And I won't let you! It's too—! (*then controlling herself—forcing a smile*) But I'm a bigger fool than you are to get angry. You simply don't know John, that's all. You don't know what an old-fashioned romantic idealist he is at heart about love and marriage. And I thank God he is! You'll laugh at me but I know he never had a single affair in his life before he met me.

Lucy—Oh, come on, Elsa. That's too much!

Elsa—Oh, please don't think I'm a naïve fool. I was as cynical about men in those days as you are now. I wouldn't have believed it of another man in the world, but with John I felt it was absolutely true to what I knew he was like inside him.

Lucy—You loved him and you wanted to believe.

Elsa—No. Even before I loved him, I felt that. It was what made me love him, more than anything else—the feeling that he would be mine, only mine, that I wouldn't have to share him even with the past. If you only could realize how much that meant to me—especially at that time, when I was still full of the disgust and hurt of my first marriage.

Lucy—Well, that's all very fine, but it's not proving to me how you can be so certain that never since then—

Elsa—(*proudly*) I know he loves me. I know he knows how much I love him. He knows what that would do to me. It would kill forever all my faith in life—all truth, all beauty, all love! I wouldn't want to live!

Lucy—You shouldn't let yourself be so completely at the mercy of any man—not even John.

Elsa—I'm not afraid. (*She smiles.*) The trouble with you is, you old cynic, you can't admit that our marriage is a real ideal marriage. But it is—and that's entirely John's work, not mine.

Lucy—His work?

Elsa—Yes. When I first met him I thought I was through with marriage for good. Even after I fell in love with him, I didn't want to marry. I was afraid of marriage. I proposed quite frankly that we should simply live together and each keep entire freedom of action. (*She laughs.*) Oh, I was quite ultra-modern about it! And it shocked John terribly, poor dear—in spite of all his old radical ideas. I'm sure it almost disillusioned him with me for life! He sternly scorned my offer. He argued with me. How he argued—like a missionary converting a heathen! He said he loathed the ordinary marriage as much as I did, but that the ideal in back of marriage was a beautiful one, and he knew we could realize that ideal.

LUCY—Ah, yes, the ideal! I heard a little talk about that once, too!

ELSA—He said no matter if every other marriage on earth were rotten and a lie, our love could make ours into a true sacrament—sacrament was the word he used—a sacrament of faith in which each of us would find the completest self-expression in making our union a beautiful thing. (*She smiles lovingly.*) You see, all this was what I had longed to hear the man I loved say about the spiritual depth of his love for me—what every woman dreams of hearing her lover say, I think.

LUCY—(*stirring uneasily—mechanically*) Yes. I know.

ELSA—And, of course, it blew my petty modern selfishness right out the window. I couldn't believe he meant it at first, but when I saw he did, that finished me. (*She smiles—then with quiet pride*) And I think we've lived up to that ideal ever since. I hope I have. I know he has. It was his creation, you see.

LUCY—Of course he has. Of course.

ELSA—And our marriage has meant for us, not slavery or boredom but freedom and harmony within ourselves—and happiness. So we must have both lived true to it. Happiness is proof, isn't it?

LUCY—(*deeply moved—without looking at Elsa, takes her hand and squeezes it—huskily*) Of course it is. Please forget the stupid rot I've said. I was only trying to get a rise out of you. We all know how wonderfully happy you and John are. Only remember, the world is full of spiteful liars who would do anything to wreck your happiness and drag you down to their level—what I was doing. So never listen— But of course you won't, will you? You have faith. (*She turns and kisses her impulsively.*) God bless you—and preserve your happiness!

ELSA—Thank you, Lucy. That's dear of you. (*then puzzledly*) But why should you be afraid that any one—

LUCY—(*jumps to her feet nervously*) Only my morbidness. I've been accused of so many rotten things I never did that I suppose I'm hipped on the subject. (*then abruptly*) Got to run now, Elsa—go home and get on my armor for another of Walter's parties. It's a gay life. The only hope is he'll be so broke before long no one will call on us but our forgotten friends. (*She gives a bitter little laugh and starts to go around the left of sofa—then, at a noise of a door opening in the hall— nervously*) Isn't that some one—?

ELSA—It must be John. (*She hurries around the right of sofa and back toward the doorway.*)

JOHN—(*calls from the hall*) Hello.

ELSA—(*going out, meets him as he appears in the hall just beyond the doorway—kissing him*) Hello, darling. You're early. I'm so glad.

JOHN—I thought, as I'd told Uncle to come early, I better— (*He kisses her.*) How do you feel, dear? You look much better.

ELSA—Oh, I'm fine, John. (*Lucy has remained standing by the left corner of the sofa, in a stiff, strained attitude, the expression on her face that of one caught in a corner, steeling herself for an ordeal. Elsa and John come in, their arms around each other. As they do so, Lucy recovers her poise and calls to him*)

LUCY—Hello, John.

JOHN—(*coming to her, his face wearing its most cordial, poker-faced smile*) Why, hello, Lucy. I thought I heard a familiar voice when I came in. (*They shake hands.*) A pleasant surprise. Been a long time since we've had this pleasure. (*Elsa has come forward behind him. The figure of the masked Loving appears in the doorway. During the next few speeches he moves silently to the corner of the long table before the window, right-front, and stands there, without looking at them, facing front, his eyes fixed in the same cold stare, the expression of his masked face seeming to be more than ever sneering and sinister.*)

LUCY—Now, don't you begin on that! Elsa has already given me hell.

ELSA—(*laughing*) And she's repented and been forgiven.

JOHN—Oh, that's all right, then.

LUCY—(*nervously*) I was just leaving. Sorry I've got to run, John.

ELSA—Oh, you can't, now. John will think he's driven you out.

LUCY—No, really, Elsa, I—

ELSA—You simply must keep John company for a few minutes. Because I've got to go to the kitchen. I trust Emmy on ordinary occasions, but when a long-lost uncle is coming to dinner, a little personal supervision is in order. (*She moves toward the dining-room at left.*)

LUCY—(*with a note of desperation*) Well—but I can't stay more than a second.

ELSA—I'll be back right away. (*She disappears through the dining-room door. The moment she is gone, John's cordial smile vanishes and his face takes on a tense, harried look. He is now standing behind the right end of sofa, Lucy behind the left end. In the pause while they wait for Elsa to get out of earshot, Loving moves silently over until he is standing just behind John but a step toward rear from him, facing half toward him, half toward front.*)

JOHN—(*lowering his voice—hurriedly*) I hope you've been careful and not said anything that—

LUCY—Might give you away? Of course, I didn't. And even if I were rotten enough to come right out and tell her, she'd never believe me, she has such a touching faith in you.

JOHN—(*wincing*) Don't!

LUCY—No. You're perfectly safe. There's only one thing I've got to warn you about. It's nothing, really, but—

JOHN—What?

LUCY—Walter has been telling people. He has to, you see, to keep up his pose of friendly understanding—

JOHN—But how does Walter know?

LUCY—Don't look so dismayed! He doesn't know—who it was. And you'd be the last one he'd ever suspect.

JOHN—How is it he knows about you?

LUCY—(*hesitates—then defiantly*) I told him.

JOHN—You told him? In God's name, why? But I know. You couldn't resist—watching him squirm!

LUCY—(*stung*) Exactly, John. Why do you suppose I ever did it, except for his benefit—if you want the truth.

JOHN—Good God, don't you think I know that? Do you imagine I ever thought it was anything but revenge on your part?

LUCY—And whom were you revenging yourself on, John?—now we're being frank.

LOVING—(*with sinister mockery*) Who knows? Perhaps on love. Perhaps, in my soul, I hate love!

LUCY—(*stares at John with frightened bewilderment*) John! Now you're like—that night!

JOHN—(*confusedly*) I? It wasn't I. (*angrily*) What do you mean by saying I was revenging myself? Why should I revenge myself on her?

LUCY—I don't know, John. That's a matter for your conscience. I've got enough on my own, thank you. I must say I resent your attitude, John. (*with a flippant sneer*) Hardly the lover-like tone, is it?

JOHN—(*with disgust*) Lover!

LUCY—Oh, I know. I feel the same way. But why hate me? Why not hate yourself?

JOHN—As if I didn't! Good God, if you knew! (*then bitterly*) And how long do you think you'll be able to resist telling Walter it was I, his old friend—so you can watch him squirm some more!

LUCY—John!

JOHN—And Walter will have to tell that to every one, too—to live up to his pose! And then—

LUCY—John! You know I wouldn't, even if I hated you as you seem to hate me. I wouldn't for Elsa's sake. Oh, I know you think I'm a rotten liar, but I love Elsa! (*then brokenly*) Oh, it's such a vile mess! What fools we were!

JOHN—(*dully*) Yes. (*bitterly again*) I'm sorry I can't trust you, Lucy. I can when you're yourself. But full of booze— I see what it will come to. I'll have to tell her myself to save her the humiliation of hearing it through dirty gossip!

LUCY—John! Oh, please don't be such a fool! Please!

JOHN—You think she couldn't forgive?

LUCY—I'm thinking of what it would do to her. Can't you see—?

JOHN—(*warningly, as he hears the pantry door opening*) Ssshh! (*quickly, raising his voice to a conversational tone*) Uncle is a grand old fellow. You'll have to meet him some time. You'd like him.

LUCY—I'm sure I would. (*then, as Elsa comes in from the dining-room*) Ah, here you are. Well, I've got to fly. (*She holds out her hand to John.*) Good-bye, John. Take care of Elsa.

JOHN—Good-bye, Lucy. (*Elsa puts an arm around her waist and they go back to the hall doorway.*)

ELSA—I'll get your things. (*They disappear in the hall. As soon as they have gone, John turns and, coming around the sofa, sits down on it and stares before him with hunted eyes. Loving moves until he is standing directly behind him. He bends over and whispers mockingly)*

LOVING—I warned you it was closing in! You had better make up your mind now to tell the rest of your novel to-night—while there is still time!

JOHN—(*tensely*) Yes. I must.

LOVING—But, first, it still remains to decide what is to be your hero's end. (*He gives a little jeering laugh.*) Strange, isn't it, what difficult problems your little dabble in fiction has brought up which demand a final answer! (*He laughs again—then turns to face the doorway as Elsa reënters the room. His eyes remain fixed on her as she comes forward. She comes quietly to the right end of the sofa. John does not notice her coming. Loving remains standing at right, rear, of John.*)

ELSA—A penny for your thoughts, John. (*He starts. She sits down beside him—with a smile*) Did I scare you?

JOHN—(*forcing a smile*) Don't know what's the matter with me. I seem to have the nervous jumps lately. (*then carelessly*) Glad to see Lucy again, were you?

ELSA—Yes—of course. Only she's changed so. Poor Lucy.

JOHN—Why poor? Oh, you mean on account of Walter's antics?

ELSA—Then you know?

JOHN—Who doesn't? He's been making as public an ass of himself as possible. But let's not talk about Walter. What did you think of the big event to-day: Uncle dropping out of the blue?

ELSA—It must have been a surprise for you. I'm dying to meet him. I'm so glad he could come to-night.

JOHN—Yes. So am I. (*As if his conversation had run dry, he falls into an uneasy silence. Elsa looks at him worriedly. Then she nestles up close to him.*)

ELSA—(*tenderly*) Still love me, do you?

JOHN—(*takes her in his arms and kisses her—with intense feeling*) You know I do! There's nothing in life I give a damn about except your love! You know that, don't you?

ELSA—Yes, dear.

JOHN—(*avoiding her eyes now*) And you'll always love me—no matter what an unworthy fool I am?

ELSA—Ssshh! You mustn't say things like that. It's not true. (*then smiling teasingly*) Well, if you love me so much, prove it by telling me.

JOHN—(*controlling a start*) Telling you what?

ELSA—Now, don't pretend. I know there's something that's been troubling you for weeks—ever since I came back from Boston.

JOHN—No, honestly, Elsa.

ELSA—Something you're keeping back because you're afraid of worrying me. So you might as well confess.

JOHN—(*forcing a smile*) Confess? And will you promise— to forgive?

ELSA—Forgive you for not wanting to worry me? Foolish one!

JOHN—(*hurriedly*) No, I was only joking. There's nothing.

ELSA—Now! But I think I can guess. It's about business, isn't it?

JOHN—(*grasps at this*) Well—yes, if you must know.

ELSA—And you were afraid that would upset me? Oh, John, you're such a child at times you ought to be spanked. You must think I've become a poor, helpless doll!

JOHN—No, but—

ELSA—Just because you've pampered me so terribly the past few years! But remember, we had barely enough to get along on when we were married—and I didn't appear so terribly unhappy then, did I? And no matter how poor we become, do you think it would ever really matter one bit to me as long as I had you?

JOHN—(*stammers miserably*) Sweetheart! You make me feel—so damned ashamed! God, I can't tell you!

ELSA—(*kissing him*) But, darling, it's nothing! And now promise me you'll forget it and not worry any more?

JOHN—Yes.

ELSA—Good! Let's talk of something else. Tell me, have you been doing anything more on the rest of your idea for a novel?

JOHN—Yes, I— I've got most of it thought out.

ELSA—(*encouragingly*) That's splendid. You just put your mind on that and forget your silly worries. But when am I going to hear it?

JOHN—Well, I told Uncle the first part and he was curious, too. So I threatened him I might give you both an outline of the rest to-night.

ELSA—Oh, that's fine. (*Then she laughs.*) And I'll confess it will be a great aid to me as a hostess. I'll probably feel a bit self-conscious, entertaining a strange priest-uncle for the first time.

JOHN—Oh, you won't be with him a minute before you'll feel he's an old friend.

ELSA—Well, that sounds encouraging. But you tell your story just the same. (*She gets up.*) It must be getting on. I'd better go up and start getting dressed. (*She goes around the left end of the sofa and back toward the hall door.*) Are you going up to your study for a while?

JOHN—Yes, in a minute. I want to do a little more work on my plot. The end isn't clearly worked out yet.

LOVING—That is, my hero's end!

ELSA—(*smiling at John encouragingly*) Then you get busy, by all means, so you'll have no excuse! (*She goes out. As soon as she is gone, John's expression changes and becomes tense and hunted again. Loving remains standing behind him, staring down at him with cold, scornful eyes. There is a pause of silence.*)

JOHN—(*suddenly—his face full of the bitterest, tortured self-loathing—aloud to himself*) You God-damned rotten swine!

LOVING—(*mockingly*) Yes, unfit to live. Quite unfit for life, I think. But there is always death to wash one's sins away—sleep, untroubled by Love's betraying dream! (*He gives a low, sinister laugh.*) Merely a consoling reminder—in case you've forgotten! (*John listens fascinatedly, as if to an inner voice. Then a look of terror comes into his face and he shudders.*)

JOHN—(*torturedly*) For God's sake! Leave me alone!

(*Curtain*)

ACT THREE
Plot for a Novel (Continued)
SCENE I

SCENE—*The living-room again. It is immediately after dinner. Father Baird is sitting in the chair at left, front, Elsa on the sofa, John beside her on her left, the masked Loving at right, rear, of John, in the chair by the end of the table before the window. John and Loving are in dinner clothes of identical cut. Elsa wears a white evening gown of extremely simple lines. Father Baird is the same as in Act One.*

Margaret is serving them the after-dinner coffee. She goes out through the dining-room door.

JOHN—(*puts an arm around Elsa's waist playfully*) Well, now you've got to know her, what do you think of her, Uncle? Weren't my letters right?

FATHER BAIRD—(*gallantly*) They were much too feeble. You didn't do her justice by half!

ELSA—Thank you, Father. It's so kind of you to say that.

JOHN—Ah! I told you that was one subject we'd agree on! (*then to Elsa in a tenderly chiding tone*) But I've got a bone to pick with you, my lady. You ate hardly any dinner, do you know it?

ELSA—Oh, but I did, dear.

JOHN—No, you only went through the motions. I was watching you. That's no way to get back your strength.

FATHER BAIRD—Yes, you need all the nourishment you can take when you're getting over the flu.

JOHN—(*worriedly—grasping her hand*) Sure you're warm enough? Want me to get you something to put over your shoulders?

ELSA—No, dear, thank you.

JOHN—Remember it's a rotten, chilly, rainy day out and even indoors you can't be too careful.

ELSA—Oh, but I'm quite all right now, John. Please don't worry about me.

JOHN—Well, don't let yourself get tired now, you hear? If you find yourself feeling at all worn-out, you just send Uncle and me off to my study. He'll understand. Won't you, Uncle?

149

FATHER BAIRD—Of course. I hope Elsa will feel I'm one of the family and treat me without ceremony.

ELSA—I do feel that, Father. (*then teasingly*) But do you know what I think is behind all this solicitude of John's? He's simply looking for an excuse to get out of telling us the rest of his novel. But we won't let him back out, will we?

FATHER BAIRD—Indeed we won't.

ELSA—The first part is so unusual and interesting. Don't you think so, Father?

FATHER BAIRD—(*quietly*) Yes. Tragic and revealing to me.

ELSA—You see, John, it's no use. We're simply going to insist.

LOVING—(*coldly mocking*) You're sure—you insist?

ELSA—Of course I do. So come on.

JOHN—(*nervously*) Well— (*He hesitates—gulps down the rest of his coffee.*)

ELSA—(*smiling*) I never saw you so flustered before, John. You'd think you were going to address an audience of literary critics.

JOHN—(*begins jerkily*) Well— But before I start, there's one thing I want to impress on you both again. My plot, up to the last part, which is wholly imaginary, is taken from life. It's the story of a man I once knew.

LOVING—(*mockingly*) Or thought I knew.

ELSA—May I be inquisitive? Did I ever know the man?

LOVING—(*a hostile, repellent note in his voice*) No. I can swear to that. You have never known him.

ELSA—(*taken aback, gives John a wondering look—then apologetically*) I'm sorry I butted in with a silly question. Go on, dear.

JOHN—(*nervously—forcing a laugh*) I— It's hard getting started. (*He turns and reaches for his coffee, forgetting he has drunk it—sets the cup down again abruptly and goes on hurriedly.*) Well, you will remember my first part ended when the boy's parents had died.

LOVING—And he had denied all his old superstitions!

JOHN—Well, as you can imagine, for a long while after their deaths, he went through a terrific inner conflict. He was seized by fits of terror, in which he felt he really had given his soul to some evil power. He would feel a tortured longing to pray and beg for forgiveness. It seemed to him that he had forsworn all love forever—and was cursed. At these times he wanted only to die. Once he even took his father's revolver—

LOVING—(*sneeringly*) But he was afraid to face death. He was still too religious-minded, you see, to accept the one beautiful, comforting truth of life: that death is final release, the warm, dark peace of annihilation.

FATHER BAIRD—(*quietly*) I cannot see the beauty and comfort.

LOVING—He often regretted afterwards he had not had the courage to die then. It would have saved him so much silly romantic pursuit of meaningless illusions.

ELSA—(*uneasily*) Oh, you mustn't talk that way, John. It sounds so bitter—and false—coming from you.

JOHN—(*confusedly*) I—I didn't— You forget I'm simply following what this man told me. (*hurrying on*) Well, finally, he came out of this period of black despair. He taught himself to take a rationalistic attitude. He read all sorts of scientific books. He ended up by becoming an atheist. But his experience had left an indelible scar on his spirit. There always remained something in him that felt itself damned by life, damned with distrust, cursed with the inability ever to reach a lasting belief in any faith, damned by a fear of the lie hiding behind the mask of truth.

FATHER BAIRD—Ah!

LOVING—(*sneeringly*) So romantic, you see—to think of himself as possessed by a damned soul!

JOHN—And in after years, even at the height of his rationalism, he never could explain away a horror of death—and a strange fascination it had for him. And coupled with this was a dread of life—as if he constantly sensed a malignant Spirit hiding behind life, waiting to catch men at its mercy, in their hour of secure happiness— Something that hated life!— Something that laughed with mocking scorn! (*He stares before him with a fascinated dread, as if he saw this Something before him. Then, suddenly, as if in reply, Loving gives a little mocking laugh, barely audible. John shudders. Elsa and Father Baird start and stare at John uneasily, but he is looking straight ahead and they turn away again.*)

LOVING—A credulous, religious-minded fool, as I've

pointed out! And he carried his credulity into the next period of his life, where he believed in one social or philosophical Ism after another, always on the trail of Truth! He was never courageous enough to face what he really knew was true, that there is no truth for men, that human life is unimportant and meaningless. No. He was always grasping at some absurd new faith to find an excuse for going on!

JOHN—(*proudly*) And he did go on! And he found his truth at last—in love, where he least expected he ever would find it. For he had always been afraid of love. And when he met the woman who afterwards became his wife and realized he was in love with her, it threw him into a panic of fear. He wanted to run away from her—but found he couldn't.

LOVING—(*scornfully*) So he weakly surrendered—and immediately began building a new superstition of love around her.

JOHN—He was happy again for the first time since his parents' death—to his bewildered joy.

LOVING—(*mockingly*) And secret fear!

ELSA—(*gives John a curious, uneasy glance*) Secret fear?

JOHN—Yes, he—he came to be afraid of his happiness. His love made him feel at the mercy of that mocking Something he dreaded. And the more peace and security he found in his wife's love, the more he was haunted by fits of horrible foreboding—the recurrent dread that she might die and he would be left alone again, without love. So great was the force of this obsession at times that he felt caught in a trap, desperate—

LOVING—And he often found himself regretting—

JOHN—(*hastily*) Against his will—

LOVING—(*inexorably*) That he had again let love put him at the mercy of life!

JOHN—(*hurriedly*) But, of course, he realized this was all morbid and ridiculous—for wasn't he happier than he had ever dreamed he could be again?

LOVING—(*with gloating mockery*) And so he deliberately destroyed that happiness!

ELSA—(*startledly*) Destroyed his happiness? How, John?

JOHN—(*turns to her, forcing a smile*) I'm afraid you will find this part of his story hard to believe, Elsa. This damned fool, who loved his wife more than anything else in life, was unfaithful to her. (*Father Baird starts and stares at him with a shocked expression.*)

ELSA — (*frightenedly*) It is — hard to believe. But this part is all the story of the man you knew, isn't it?

JOHN — Yes, of course, and you mustn't condemn him entirely until you've heard how it came to happen. (*He turns away from her again — jerkily*) His wife had gone away. It was the first time. He felt lost without her — fearful, disintegrated. His familiar dread seized him. He began imagining all sorts of catastrophes. Horrible pictures formed in his mind. She was run over by a car. Or she had caught pneumonia and lay dying. Every day these evil visions possessed him. He tried to escape them in work. He couldn't. (*He pauses for a second, nerving himself to go on. Then starts again.*) Then one night an old friend called — to drag him off to a party. He loathed such affairs usually, but this time he thought it would help him to escape himself for a while. So he went. He observed with disgust how his friend, who was drunk, was pawing over some woman right under the nose of his wife. He knew that this friend was continually having affairs of this sort and that his wife was aware of it. He had often wondered if she cared, and he was curious now to watch her reactions. And very soon he had an example of what her pride had to endure, for the husband went off openly with his lady. The man felt a great sympathy for her — and, as if she guessed his thought, she came to him, and he overdid himself in being kind. (*He gives a short bitter laugh.*) A great mistake! For she reacted to it in a way that at first shocked him but ended up in arousing his curiosity. He had known her for years. It wasn't like her. It fascinated him, in a way, that she should have become so corrupted. He became interested to see how far she would go with it — purely as an observer, he thought — the poor idiot! (*He laughs again. Father Baird has remained motionless, his eyes on the floor. Elsa's face is pale and set, her eyes have a bewildered, stricken look. John goes on.*) Remember, all this time he saw through her; he laughed to himself at her crude vamping; he felt he was only playing a game. Just as he knew she was playing a game; that it was no desire for him but hatred for her husband that inspired her. (*He gives a short contemptuous laugh again.*) Oh, he had it all analyzed quite correctly, considering the known elements. It was the unknown—

FATHER BAIRD—(*without raising his head*) Yes. (*He casts a quick glance at Elsa, then looks as quickly away. Her eyes are fastened on the floor now. Her face has frozen into a mask with the tense effort she is making not to give herself away.*)

JOHN—He had not the slightest desire for this woman. When she threw herself into his arms, he was repelled. He determined to end the game. He thought of his wife— (*He forces a laugh.*) But, as I've said, there was the unknown to reckon with. At the thought of his wife, suddenly it was as if something outside him, a hidden spirit of evil, took possession of him.

LOVING—(*coldly vindictive now*) That is, he saw clearly that this situation was the climax of a long death struggle between his wife and him. The woman with him counted only as a means. He saw that underneath all his hypocritical pretenses he really hated love. He wanted to deliver himself from its power and be free again. He wanted to kill it!

ELSA—(*with horrified pain*) Oh! (*trying to control herself*) I—I don't understand. He hated love? He wanted to kill it? But that's—too horrible!

JOHN—(*stammers confusedly*) No—I— Don't you see it wasn't he?

LOVING—But, I'm afraid, Elsa, that my hero's silly idea that he was possessed by a demon must strike you as an incredible superstitious excuse to lie out of his responsibility.

FATHER BAIRD—(*without lifting his eyes—quietly*) Quite credible to me, Jack. One may not give one's soul to a devil of hate—and remain forever scatheless.

LOVING—(*sneeringly*) As for the adultery itself, the truth is that this poor fool was making a great fuss about nothing— an act as meaningless as that of one fly with another, of equal importance to life!

ELSA—(*stares at John as if he had become a stranger—a look of sick repulsion coming over her face*) John! You're disgusting! (*She shrinks away from him to the end of the sofa near Father Baird.*)

JOHN—(*stammers confusedly*) But I—I didn't mean—forgive me. I only said that—as a joke—to get a rise out of Uncle.

FATHER BAIRD—(*gives a quick anxious look at Elsa—then quietly, an undercurrent of sternness in his voice*) I don't think it's a joke. But go on with your story, Jack.

JOHN—(*forcing himself to go on*) Well I—I know you can imagine the hell he went through from the moment he came to himself and realized the vileness he had been guilty of. He couldn't forgive himself—and that's what his whole being now cried out for—forgiveness!

FATHER BAIRD—(*quietly*) I can well believe that, Jack.

JOHN—He wanted to tell his wife and beg for forgiveness—but he was afraid of losing her love. (*He gives a quick glance at Elsa, as if to catch her reaction to this, but she is staring straight before her with a still, set face. He forces a smile and adopts a joking tone.*) And here's where I'd like to have your opinion, Elsa. The question doesn't come up in my story, as you'll see, but— Could his wife have forgiven him, do you think?

ELSA—(*starts—then tensely*) You want me to put myself in the wife's place?

JOHN—Yes. I want to see whether the man was a fool or not—in his fear.

ELSA—(*after a second's pause—tensely*) No. She could never forgive him.

JOHN—(*desperately*) But it wasn't he! Can't you see—

ELSA—No. I'm afraid—I can't see.

JOHN—(*dully now*) Yes. That's what I thought you'd say.

ELSA—But what does it matter what I think? You said the question of her forgiving doesn't come up in your novel.

LOVING—(*coldly*) Not while the wife is alive.

JOHN—(*dully*) He never tells her.

LOVING—She becomes seriously ill.

ELSA—(*with a start*) Oh.

LOVING—(*in a cold voice, as if he were pronouncing a death sentence*) Flu, which turns into pneumonia. And she dies.

ELSA—(*frightenedly now*) Dies?

LOVING—Yes. I need her death for my end. (*then in a sinister, jeering tone*) That is, to make my romantic hero come finally to a rational conclusion about his life!

ELSA—(*stares before her, not seeming to have heard this last—her eyes full of a strange, horrified fascination—as if she were talking aloud to herself*) So she dies.

FATHER BAIRD—(*after a worried glance at her—an undercurrent of warning in his quiet tone*) I think you've tired Elsa out with your sensational imaginings, Jack. I'd spare her, for the present, at least, the fog of gloom your novel is plunging into.

ELSA—(*grasps at this—tensely*) Yes, I'm afraid it has been too exciting— I really don't feel up to— During dinner I began to get a headache and it's splitting now.

JOHN—(*gets up—worriedly*) But why didn't you tell me? If I'd known that, I'd never have bored you with my damned plot.

ELSA—I—I think I'll lie down here on the sofa—and take some aspirin—and rest for a while. You can go with your uncle up to your study—and tell him the rest of your story there.

FATHER BAIRD—(*gets up*) An excellent idea. Come on, Jack, and give your poor wife a respite from the horrors of authorship. (*He goes to the doorway in rear.*)

JOHN—(*comes to Elsa. As he does so, Loving comes and stands behind her, at rear of sofa.*) I'm so darned sorry, Elsa, if I've—

ELSA—Oh, please! It's only a headache.

JOHN—You—you don't feel really sick, do you, dearest? (*He puts a hand to her forehead timidly.*)

ELSA—(*shrinks from his touch*) No, no, it's nothing.

LOVING—(*slowly, in his cold tone with its undercurrent of sinister hidden meaning*) You must be very careful, Elsa. Remember it's cold and raining out.

ELSA—(*staring before her strangely—repeats fascinatedly*) It's raining?

LOVING—Yes.

JOHN—(*stammers confusedly*) Yes, you—you must be careful, dearest.

FATHER BAIRD—(*from the doorway in rear—sharply*) Come along, Jack! (*John goes back to him and Loving follows John. Father Baird goes into the hall, turning left to go upstairs to the study. John stops in the doorway and looks back for a mo-*

*ment at Elsa frightenedly. Loving comes to his side and also stops
and looks at her, his eyes cold and remorseless in his mask of sinister
mockery. They stand there for a moment side by side. Then John
turns and disappears in the hall toward left, following Father
Baird. Loving remains, his gaze concentrated on the back of Elsa's
head with a cruel, implacable intensity. She is still staring before
her with the same strange fascinated dread. Then, as if in obedience to his will, she rises slowly to her feet and walks slowly and
woodenly back past him and disappears in the hall, turning right
toward the entrance door to the apartment. For a second Loving
remains looking after her. Then he turns and disappears in the
hall toward left, following Father Baird and John to the study.)*

(*Curtain*)

Scene II

Scene—*John Loving's study on the upper floor of the apartment. At left, front, is a door leading into Elsa's bedroom. Book-
cases extend along the rear and right walls. There is a door to the
upper hall at rear, right. A long table with a lamp is at center,
front. At left of table is a chair. In front of table a similar chair.
At right, front, is a chaise-longue, facing left.*

*Father Baird, John and Loving are discovered. The priest is sit-
ting on the chaise-longue, John in the chair at front of table, Loving in the chair at left of table. Father Baird sits in the same
attitude as he had in the previous scene, his eyes on the floor, his
expression sad and a bit stern. Loving's masked face stares at John,
his eyes cold and still. John is talking in a strained tone, monoto-
nously, insistently. It is as if he were determinedly talking to keep
himself from thinking.*

JOHN—I listen to people talking about this universal
breakdown we are in and I marvel at their stupid cowardice.
It is so obvious that they deliberately cheat themselves because their fear of change won't let them face the truth. They
don't want to understand what has happened to them. All
they want is to start the merry-go-round of blind greed all

over again. They no longer know what they want this country to be, what they want it to become, where they want it to go. It has lost all meaning for them except as a pig-wallow. And so their lives as citizens have no beginnings, no ends. They have lost the ideal of the Land of the Free. Freedom demands initiative, courage, the need to decide what life must mean to oneself. To them, that is terror. They explain away their spiritual cowardice by whining that the time for individualism is past, when it is their courage to possess their own souls which is dead—and stinking! No, they don't want to be free. Slavery means security—of a kind, the only kind they have courage for. It means they need not think. They have only to obey orders from owners who are, in turn, their slaves!

LOVING—(*breaks in—with bored scorn*) But I'm denouncing from my old soap box again. It's all silly twaddle, of course. Freedom was merely our romantic delusion. We know better now. We know we are all the slaves of meaningless chance—electricity or something, which whirls us—on to Hercules!

JOHN—(*with a proud assertiveness*) But, in spite of that, I say: Very well! On to Hercules! Let us face that! Once we have accepted it without evasion, we can begin to create new goals for ourselves, ends for our days! A new discipline for life will spring into being, a new will and power to live, a new ideal to measure the value of our lives by!

LOVING—(*mockingly*) What? Am I drooling on about my old social ideals again? Sorry to bore you, Uncle.

FATHER BAIRD—(*quietly, without looking up*) You are not boring me, Jack.

JOHN—(*an idealistic exaltation coming into his voice*) We need a new leader who will teach us that ideal, who by his life will exemplify it and make it a living truth for us—a man who will prove that man's fleeting life in time and space can be noble. We need, above all, to learn again to believe in the possibility of nobility of spirit in ourselves! A new savior must be born who will reveal to us how we can be saved from ourselves, so that we can be free of the past and inherit the future and not perish by it!

LOVING—(*mockingly*) Must sound like my old letters to

you, Uncle. It's more nonsense, of course. But there are times of stress and flight when one hides in any old empty barrel!

FATHER BAIRD—(*ignoring this—quietly*) You are forgetting that men have such a Savior, Jack. All they need is to remember Him.

JOHN—(*slowly*) Yes, perhaps if we could again have faith in—

LOVING—(*harshly*) No! We have passed beyond gods! There can be no going back!

FATHER BAIRD—Jack! Take care!

LOVING—(*mockingly again*) But, on the other hand, I'll grant you the pseudo-Nietzschean savior I just evoked out of my past is an equally futile ghost. Even if he came, we'd only send him to the insane asylum for teaching that we should have a nobler aim for our lives than getting all four feet in a trough of swill! (*He laughs sardonically.*) How could we consider such an unpatriotic idea as anything but insane, eh? (*There is a pause. Father Baird looks up and studies John's face searchingly, hopefully.*)

FATHER BAIRD—(*finally speaks quietly*) Jack, ever since we came upstairs, I've listened patiently while you've discussed every subject under the sun except the one I know is really on your mind.

JOHN—I don't know what you mean.

FATHER BAIRD—The end of your story.

JOHN—Oh, forget that. I'm sick of the damned thing—now, at any rate.

FATHER BAIRD—Sick of the damned thing, yes. That's why I feel it's important you tell it—now. This man's wife dies, you said. (*He stares fixedly at John now and adds slowly*) Of influenza which turns into pneumonia.

JOHN—(*uneasily*) Why do you stare like that?

FATHER BAIRD—(*dropping his eyes—quietly*) Go on with your story.

JOHN—(*hesitantly*) Well—I— You can imagine the anguish he feels after his wife's death—the guilt which tortures him a thousandfold now she is dead.

FATHER BAIRD—I can well imagine it, Jack.

LOVING—(*sneeringly*) And under the influence of his ridiculous guilty conscience, all the superstitions of his childhood, which he had prided himself his reason had killed, return to plague him. He feels at times an absurd impulse to pray. He fights this nonsense back. He analyzes it rationally. He sees it clearly as a throwback to boyhood experiences. But, in spite of himself, that cowardly something in him he despises as superstition seduces his reason with the old pathetic lie of survival after death. He begins to believe his wife is alive in some mythical hereafter!

JOHN—(*strangely*) He knows she knows of his sin now. He can hear her promising to forgive if he can only believe again in his old God of Love, and seek her through Him. She will be beside him in spirit in this life, and at his death she will be waiting. Death will not be an end but a new beginning, a reunion with her in which their love will go on forever within the eternal peace and love of God! (*His voice has taken on a note of intense longing.*)

FATHER BAIRD—Ah, then you do see, Jack! Thank God!

JOHN—(*as if he hadn't heard*) One night when he is hounded beyond endurance he rushes out—in the hope that if he walks himself into exhaustion he may be able to sleep for a while and forget. (*strangely, staring before him, as if he were visualizing the scene he is describing*) Without his knowing how he got there, he finds he has walked in a circle and is standing before the old church, not far from where he now lives, in which he used to pray as a boy.

LOVING—(*jeeringly*) And now we come to the great temptation scene, in which he finally confronts his ghosts! (*with harsh defiance*) The church challenges him—and he accepts the challenge and goes in!

JOHN—He finds himself kneeling at the foot of the Cross. And he feels he is forgiven, and the old comforting peace and security and joy steal back into his heart! (*He hesitates, as if reluctant to go on, as if this were the end.*)

FATHER BAIRD—(*deeply moved*) And that is your end? Thank God!

LOVING—(*jeeringly*) I'm afraid your rejoicing is a bit premature—for this cowardly giving in to his weakness is not the end! Even while he is kneeling, there is a mocking rational something in him that laughs with scorn—and at the last moment his will and pride revive in him again! He sees clearly by the light of reason the degradation of his pitiable surrender to old ghostly comforts—and he rejects them! (*His voice with surprising suddenness takes on a savage vindictive quality.*) He curses his God again as he had when a boy! He defies Him finally! He—!

FATHER BAIRD—(*sternly*) Jack! Take care!

JOHN—(*protests confusedly*) No—that's not right—I—

LOVING—(*strangely confused in his turn—hurriedly*) Pardon me, Uncle. Of course, that's wrong—afraid for a moment I let an author's craving for a dramatic moment run away with my sane judgment. Naturally, he could never be so stupid as to curse what he knew didn't exist!

JOHN—(*despondently*) No. He realizes he can never believe in his lost faith again. He walks out of the church—without love forever now—but daring to face his eternal loss and hopelessness, to accept it as his fate and go on with life.

LOVING—(*mockingly*) A very, very heroic end, as you see! But, unfortunately, absolutely meaningless!

FATHER BAIRD—Yes. Meaningless. I'm glad you see that.

JOHN—(*rousing a bit—defensively*) No—I take that back—it isn't meaningless. It is man's duty to life to go on!

LOVING—(*jeeringly*) The romantic idealist again speaks! On to Hercules! What an inspiring slogan! (*then a sinister note coming into his voice*) But there is still another end to my story—the one sensible happy end!

FATHER BAIRD—(*as if he hadn't heard this last*) Jack! Are you so blind you cannot see what your imagining his finding peace in the church reveals about the longing of your own soul—the salvation from yourself it holds out to you? Why, if you had any honesty with yourself, you would get down on your knees now and—

LOVING—Rot! How can you believe such childish superstition!

FATHER BAIRD—(*angrily*) Jack! I've endured all I can of your blasphemous insults to—

JOHN—(*confused—hurriedly*) I—I didn't mean—I'm sorry, Uncle. But it's only a story. Don't take it so seriously.

FATHER BAIRD—(*has immediately controlled himself—quietly*) Only a story, Jack? You're sure you still want me to believe that?

JOHN—(*defensively*) Why, what else could you believe? Do you think I—? (*then in an abrupt, angry tone*) But that's enough about the damned story. I don't want to talk any more about it! (*Father Baird stares at him but keeps silent. John starts to pace up and down with nervous restlessness—then stops abruptly.*) I—if you'll excuse me—I think I'll go down and see how Elsa is. (*He goes back toward the door. Loving follows him.*) I'll be right back.

FATHER BAIRD—(*quietly*) Of course, Jack. Don't bother about me. I'll take a look at your library. (*He gets up. John goes out. Loving turns for a moment to Father Baird, his eyes full of a mocking derision. Then he turns and follows John. Father Baird goes to the bookcase at right and runs his eyes over the titles of books. But he only does this mechanically. His mind is preoccupied, his expression sad and troubled. John's voice can be heard from below calling "Elsa." Father Baird starts and listens. Then from Elsa's bedroom John's voice is heard, as he looks for her there. He calls anxiously "Elsa"—then evidently hurries out again, closing the door behind him. Father Baird's face grows more worried. He goes to the doorway in rear and stands listening to a brief conversation from below. A moment later John comes in from rear. He is making a great effort to conceal a feeling of dread. He comes forward. Loving follows silently but stops and remains standing by the bookcase at left of doorway.*)

JOHN—She's—gone out.

FATHER BAIRD—Gone out? But it's still raining, isn't it?

JOHN—Pouring. I—I can't understand. It's a crazy thing for her to do when she's just getting over—

FATHER BAIRD—(*with an involuntary start*) Ah!

JOHN—What?

FATHER BAIRD—Nothing.

JOHN—(*frightenedly*) I can't imagine—

FATHER BAIRD—How long has she been gone?

JOHN—I don't know. Margaret says she heard some one go out right after we came upstairs.

FATHER BAIRD—(*with lowered voice to himself*) My fault, God forgive me. I had a feeling then I shouldn't leave her. (*John sinks down in the chair by the table and waits tensely—then suddenly he bursts out*)

JOHN—I never should have told her the story! I'm a God-damned fool.

FATHER BAIRD—(*sternly*) You would be more honest with yourself if you said a self-damned fool! (*hearing a sound from below*) There. Isn't that some one now? (*John stops for a second to listen, then hurries to the door in rear. Loving remains where he is, standing motionlessly by the bookcase.*)

JOHN—(*calls*) Is that you, Elsa?

ELSA—(*from downstairs—hurriedly*) Yes. Don't come down. I'm coming up. (*A moment later she appears in the hall-way.*)

JOHN—Darling! I've been so damned worried. (*He starts to take her in his arms.*)

ELSA—Please! (*She wards him off and steps past him into the study. She has taken off her coat and hat downstairs, but the lower part of her skirt and her stockings and shoes are soaking wet. Her face is pinched and drawn and pale, with flushed spots over the cheek bones, and her eyes are bright and hard. Father Baird stares at her searchingly, his face sad and pitying.*)

FATHER BAIRD—(*forcing a light tone—as she comes forward*) Well! You have given us a scare, my lady.

ELSA—(*tensely*) I'm sorry, Father.

FATHER BAIRD—Your husband was half out of his mind worrying what had happened to you. (*She sits in the chair in front of table. John stands at right of her. Loving has come up and stands by the right end of table, at right, rear, of John. His eyes are fixed on Elsa's face with an eager, sinister intentness.*)

JOHN—(*with increasing uneasiness*) Elsa! You look sick. Do you feel—?

FATHER BAIRD—I'll get her some whisky. And you make her go to bed at once. (*He goes out the door in rear.*)

JOHN—(*grabbing her hands*) Your hands are like ice!

ELSA—(*pulls them away from him—coldly, without looking at him*) It's chilly out.

JOHN—Look at your shoes! They're soaked!

ELSA—It doesn't matter, does it? (*A chill runs through her body.*)

JOHN—You've taken a chill. (*then forcing a tenderly bullying tone*) You'll go right to bed, that's what. And no nonsense about it, you hear!

ELSA—Are you trying the bossy tender husband on me, John? I'm afraid that's no longer effective.

JOHN—(*guiltily*) Why do you say that?

ELSA—Are you determined to act out this farce to the end?

JOHN—I—I don't know what you mean. What makes you look at me—as if you hated me?

ELSA—(*bitterly*) Hate you? No, I only hate myself for having been such a fool! (*then with a hard, mocking tone*) Shall I tell you where I went, and why? But perhaps I'd better put it in the form of a novel plot!

JOHN—I—I don't know what you're driving at.

ELSA—I went out because I thought I'd like to drop in on one of Lucy's parties. But it wasn't exciting—hardly any adultery going on— I had no opportunity—even if I'd been seized by any peculiar impulse of hatred and revenge on you. So I came home. (*She forces a hard, bitter laugh.*) There! Are you satisfied? It's all a lie, of course. I simply went for a walk. But so is your story about the novel a lie.

JOHN—(*stunned—stammers*) Elsa, I—

ELSA—For God's sake, John, don't lie to me any more or I— I know, I tell you! Lucy told me all about it this afternoon.

JOHN—She told you? The damned—

ELSA—Oh, she didn't tell me it was you. But she gave me all the sordid details and they were the same as those in your story. So it was you who told on yourself. Rather a joke on you, isn't it? (*She laughs bitterly.*)

JOHN—I— (*He blurts out miserably*) Yes—it's true.

ELSA—And it was a fine joke on me, her coming here. You would appreciate it, if you had seen how I sympathized with her, how I excused her to myself and pitied her. And all the while, she was pitying me! She was gloating! She's always envied us our happiness. Our happiness!

JOHN—(*writhing*) Don't!

ELSA—She must have been laughing at me for a fool, sneering to herself about my stupid faith in you. And you gave her that chance—you! You made our love a smutty joke for her and every one like her—you whom I loved so! And all the time I was loving you, you were only waiting for this chance to kill that love, you were hating me underneath, hating our happiness, hating the ideal of our marriage you had given me, which had become all the beauty and truth of life to me! (*She springs to her feet—distractedly*) Oh, I can't—I can't! (*She starts as if to run from the room.*)

JOHN—(*grabbing her—imploringly*) Elsa! For God's sake! Didn't my story explain? Can't you believe—it wasn't I? Can't you forgive?

ELSA—No! I can't forgive! How can I forgive—when all that time I loved you so, you were wishing in your heart that I would die!

JOHN—(*frantically*) Don't say that! It's mad! Elsa! Good God, how can you think—

ELSA—What else can I think? (*then wildly*) Oh, John, stop talking! What's the good of talk? I only know I hate life! It's dirty and insulting—and evil! I want my dream back—or I want to be dead with it! (*She is shaken again by a wave of uncontrollable chill, her teeth chatter—pitiably*) Oh, John, leave me alone! I'm cold, I'm sick. I feel crazy!

FATHER BAIRD—(*comes in through the doorway at rear—sharply*) Jack! Why haven't you got her to bed? Can't you see she's ill? Phone for your doctor. (*John goes out. Loving, his eyes remaining fixed on Elsa with the same strange look, backs out of the doorway after him.*)

FATHER BAIRD—(*coming to Elsa—with great compassion*) My dear child, I can't tell you how deeply—

ELSA—(*tensely*) Don't! I can't bear— (*She is shaken again by a chill.*)

FATHER BAIRD—(*worriedly, but trying to pretend to treat it lightly, reassuringly*) You've taken a bad chill. You were very foolhardy to— But a day or two in bed and you'll be fine again.

ELSA—(*strangely serious and bitterly mocking at the same time*) But that would spoil John's story, don't you think? That would be very inconsiderate after he's worked out such a convenient end for me.

FATHER BAIRD—Elsa! For the love of God, don't tell me you took his morbid nonsense seriously! Is that why you—?

ELSA—(*as if she hadn't heard him*) And when he reminded me it was raining, it all seemed to fit in so perfectly—like the will of God! (*She laughs with hysterical mockery, her eyes shining feverishly.*)

FATHER BAIRD—(*sternly—more to break her mood than because he takes her impiety seriously*) Elsa! Stop that mockery! It has no part in you!

ELSA—(*confusedly*) I'm sorry. I forgot you were— (*then suddenly hectic again*) But I've never had any God, you see— until I met John. (*She laughs hysterically—then suddenly forces control on herself and gets shakily to her feet.*) I'm sorry. I seem to be talking nonsense. My head has gone woolly. I— (*John enters from the hall at rear. As he comes forward, Loving appears in the doorway behind him.*)

JOHN—(*coming to Elsa*) Stillwell says for you to—

ELSA—(*distractedly*) No! (*then dully*) I'll go—to my room. (*She sways weakly. John starts toward her.*)

JOHN—Elsa! Sweetheart!

ELSA—No! (*By an effort of will, she overcomes her weakness and walks woodenly into her bedroom and closes the door behind her. John makes a movement as if to follow her.*)

FATHER BAIRD—(*sharply*) Leave her alone, Jack. (*John sinks down hopelessly on the chaise-longue. Loving stands behind him, his cold eyes fixed with a sinister intensity on the door through which Elsa has just disappeared. Father Baird makes a movement as if he were going to follow Elsa into her room. Then he stops. There is an expression of sorrowful foreboding on his face. He bows his head with a simple dignity and begins to pray silently.*)

LOVING—(*his eyes now on John—with a gloating mockery*) She seems to have taken her end in your story very seriously. Let's hope she doesn't carry that too far! You have enough on your conscience already—without murder! You couldn't live, I know, if—

JOHN—(*shuddering—clutches his head in both hands as if to crush out his thoughts*) For God's sake! (*His eyes turn to the priest. Then their gaze travels to a point in front of Father Baird, and slowly his expression changes to one of fearful, fascinated awe, as if he suddenly sensed a Presence there the priest is praying to. His lips part and words come haltingly, as if they were forced out of him, full of imploring fear.*) Thou wilt not—do that to me again—wilt Thou? Thou wilt not—take love from me again?

LOVING—(*jeeringly*) Is it your old demon you are praying

to for mercy? Then I hope you hear his laughter! (*then break-ing into a cold, vicious rage*) You cowardly fool! I tell you there is nothing—nothing!

JOHN—(*starts back to himself—stammers with a confused air of relief*) Yes—of course—what's the matter with me? There's nothing—nothing to fear!

(*Curtain*)

ACT FOUR

End of the End

SCENE I

SCENE—*The study is shown as in preceding scene, but this scene also reveals the interior of Elsa's bedroom at left of study.*

At right of bedroom, front, is the door between the two rooms. At rear of this door, in the middle of the wall, is a dressing table, mirror and chair. In the left wall, rear, is the door to the bathroom. Before this door is a screen. At left, front, is the bed, its head against the left wall. By the head of the bed is a small stand on which is a reading lamp with a piece of cloth thrown over it to dim its light. An upholstered chair is beside the foot of the bed. Another chair is by the head of the bed at rear. A chaise-longue is at right, front, of the room.

It is nearing daybreak of a day about a week later.

In the bedroom, Elsa lies in the bed, her eyes closed, her face pallid and wasted. John sits in the chair toward the foot of the bed, front. He looks on the verge of complete mental and physical collapse. His unshaven cheeks are sunken and sallow. His eyes, bloodshot from sleeplessness, stare from black hollows with a frozen anguish at Elsa's face.

Loving stands by the back of his chair, facing front. The sinister, mocking character of his mask is accentuated now, evilly intensified.

Father Baird is standing by the middle of the bed, at rear. His face also bears obvious traces of sleepless strain. He is conferring in whispers with Doctor Stillwell, who is standing at his right. Both are watching Elsa with anxious eyes. At rear of Stillwell on his right, a trained nurse is standing.

Stillwell is in his early fifties, tall, with a sharp, angular face and gray hair. The nurse is a plump woman in her late thirties.

For a moment after the curtain rises the whispered pantomime between Stillwell and the priest continues, the nurse watching and listening. Then Elsa stirs restlessly and moans. She speaks without opening her eyes, hardly above a whisper, in a tone of despairing bitterness.

ELSA—John! How could you? Our dream! (*She moans.*)

JOHN—(*in anguish*) Elsa! Forgive!

LOVING—(*in a cold, inexorable tone*) She will never forgive.

STILLWELL—(*frowning, makes a motion to John to be silent*) Ssshh! (*He whispers to Father Baird, his eyes on John. The priest nods and comes around the corner of the bed toward John. Stillwell sits in the chair by the head of the bed, rear, and feels Elsa's pulse. The nurse moves close behind him.*)

FATHER BAIRD—(*bends over John's chair and speaks in a low cautioning voice*) Jack. You must be quiet.

JOHN—(*His eyes are on Stillwell's face, desperately trying to read some answer there. He calls to him frightenedly*) Doctor! What is it? Is she—?

STILLWELL—Ssshh! (*He gives John a furious look and motions Father Baird to keep him quiet.*)

FATHER BAIRD—Jack! Don't you realize you're only harming her?

JOHN—(*confusedly repentant—in a low voice*) I'm sorry. I try not to, but— I know it's crazy, but I can't help being afraid—

LOVING—That my prophecy is coming true—her end in my story.

JOHN—(*with anguished appeal*) No! Elsa! Don't believe that! (*Elsa moans.*)

FATHER BAIRD—You see! You've disturbed her again! (*Stillwell gets up and, after exchanging a whispered word with the nurse, who nods and takes his place by the bedside, comes quickly around the end of the bed to John.*)

STILLWELL—What the devil is the matter with you? I thought you promised me if I let you stay in here you'd keep quiet.

JOHN—(*dazedly now—suddenly overcome by a wave of drowsiness he tries in vain to fight back*) I won't again. (*His head nods.*)

STILLWELL—(*gives him a searching look—to Father Baird*) We've got to get him out of here.

JOHN—(*rousing himself—desperately fighting back his drowsiness*) I won't sleep! God, how can I sleep when—!

STILLWELL—(*taking one arm and signaling Father Baird to take the other—sharply but in a voice just above a whisper*)

Loving, come into your study. I want to talk with you about your wife's condition.

JOHN—(*terrified*) Why? What do you mean? She isn't—?

STILLWELL—(*hastily, in a forced tone of reassurance*) No, no, no! What put that nonsense in your head? (*He flashes a signal to the priest and they both lift John to his feet.*) Come along, that's a good fellow. (*They lead John to the door to the study at right. Loving follows them silently, moving backward, his eyes fixed with sinister gloating intentness on Elsa's face. Father Baird opens the door and they pass through, Loving slipping after them. Father Baird closes the door. They lead John to the chaise-longue at right, front, of study, passing in front of the table. Loving keeps pace with them, passing to rear of table.*)

JOHN—(*starts to resist feebly*) Let me go! I mustn't leave her! I'm afraid! (*They get him seated on the chaise-longue, Loving taking up a position directly behind him on the other side of the chaise-longue.*) I feel there's something—

LOVING—(*with a gloating mockery*) A demon who laughs, hiding behind the end of my story! (*He gives a sinister laugh. Father Baird and even Stillwell, in spite of himself, are appalled by this laughter.*)

JOHN—(*starts to his feet—in anguish*) No!

FATHER BAIRD—Jack!

STILLWELL—(*recovering, angry at himself and furious with John—seizes him by the arm and forces him down on the chaise-longue again.*) Stop your damned nonsense! Get a grip on yourself! I've warned you you'd go to pieces like this if you kept on refusing to rest or take nourishment. But that's got to stop, do you hear me? You've got to get some sleep!

FATHER BAIRD—Yes, Jack. You must!

STILLWELL—You've been a disturbing factor from the first and I've been a fool to stand— But I've had enough! You'll stay out of her room—

JOHN—No!

STILLWELL—Don't you want her to get well? By God, from the way you've been acting—

JOHN—(*wildly*) For God's sake, don't say that!

STILLWELL—Can't you see you're no help to her in this condition? While if you'll sleep for a while—

JOHN—No! (*imploringly*) She's much better, isn't she? For God's sake, tell me you know she isn't going to— Tell me that and I'll do anything you ask!

LOVING—And don't lie, please! I want the truth!

STILLWELL—(*forcing an easy tone*) What's all this talk? She's resting quietly. There's no question of— (*then quickly*) And now I've satisfied you on that, lie down as you promised. (*John stares at him uncertainly for a moment—then obediently lies down.*) Close your eyes now. (*John closes his eyes. Loving stands by his head, staring down at his face. John almost immediately drops off into a drugged half-sleep, his breathing becomes heavy and exhausted. Stillwell nods to Father Baird with satisfaction—then moves quietly to the other side of the room, by the door to Elsa's bedroom, beckoning Father Baird to follow him. He speaks to him in a low voice.*) We'll have to keep an eye on him. He's headed straight for a complete collapse. But I think he'll sleep now, for a while, anyway. (*He opens the door to the bedroom, looks in and catches the eye of the nurse, who is still sitting in the chair by the head of the bed, watching Elsa. The nurse shakes her head, answering his question. He softly closes the door again.*)

FATHER BAIRD—No change, Doctor?

STILLWELL—No. But I'm not giving up hope! She still has a fighting chance! (*then in a tone of exasperated dejection*) If she'd only fight!

FATHER BAIRD—(*nods with sad understanding*) Yes. That's it.

STILLWELL—Damn it, she seems to want to die. (*then angrily*) And, by God, in spite of his apparent grief, I've suspected at times that underneath he wants—

LOVING—(*his eyes fixed on John's face, speaks in a cold implacable tone*) She is going to die.

JOHN—(*starts half-awake—mutters*) No! Elsa! Forgive! (*He sinks into drugged sleep again.*)

STILLWELL—You see. He keeps insisting to himself—

FATHER BAIRD—(*defensively*) That's a horrible charge for you to make, Doctor. Why, any one can see the poor boy is crazed with fear and grief.

STILLWELL—(*a bit ashamed*) Sorry. But there have been times when I've had the strongest sense of—well, as he said,

Something— (*then curtly, feeling this makes him appear silly*) Afraid I've allowed this case to get on my nerves. Don't usually go in for psychic nonsense.

FATHER BAIRD—Your feeling isn't nonsense, Doctor.

STILLWELL—She won't forgive him. That's her trouble as well as his. (*He sighs, giving way for a moment to his own physical weariness.*) A strange case. Too many undercurrents. The pneumonia has been more a means than a cause. (*with a trace of condescension*) More in your line. A little casting out of devils would have been of benefit—might still be.

FATHER BAIRD—Might still be. Yes.

STILLWELL—(*exasperatedly*) Damn it, I've seen many worse cases where the patient pulled through. If I could only get her will to live functioning again! If she'd forgive him and get that off her mind, I know she'd fight. (*He abruptly gets to his feet—curtly*) Well, talk won't help her, that's sure. I'll get back. (*He goes into the bedroom and closes the door silently behind him. Father Baird remains for a moment staring sadly at the floor. In the bedroom, Stillwell goes to the bedside. The nurse gets up and he speaks to her in a whisper, hears what she has to report, gives her some quick instructions. She goes to the bathroom. He sits in the chair by the bed and feels Elsa's pulse. The nurse comes back and hands him a hypodermic needle. He administers this in Elsa's arm. She moans and her body twitches for a second. He sits, watching her face worriedly, his fingers on her wrist. In the study, Father Baird starts to pace back and forth, frowning, his face tense, feeling desperately that he is facing inevitable tragedy, that he must do something to thwart it at once. He stops at the foot of the chaise-longue and stares down at the sleeping John. Then he prays*)

FATHER BAIRD—Dear Jesus, grant me the grace to bring Jack back to Thee. Make him see that Thou, alone, hast the words of Eternal Life, the power still to save—

LOVING—(*his eyes fixed on John's face in the same stare— speaks as if in answer to Father Baird's prayer*) Nothing can save her.

JOHN—(*shuddering in his sleep*) No!

LOVING—Her end in your story is coming true. It was a cunning method of murder!

FATHER BAIRD—(*horrified*) Jack!

JOHN—(*with a tortured cry that starts him awake*) No! It's

a lie! (*He stares around him at the air, as if he were trying to see some presence he feels there.*) Liar! Murderer! (*Suddenly he seems to see Father Baird for the first time—with a cry of appeal—brokenly*) Uncle! For God's sake, help me! I—I feel I'm going mad!

FATHER BAIRD—(*eagerly*) If you would only let me help you, Jack! If you would only be honest with yourself and admit the truth in your own soul now, for Elsa's sake—while there is still time.

JOHN—(*frightenedly*) Still time? What do you mean? Is she—worse?

FATHER BAIRD—No. You've only been sleeping a few minutes. There has been no change.

JOHN—Then why did you say—?

FATHER BAIRD—Because I have decided you must be told the truth now, the truth you already know in your heart.

JOHN—What—truth?

FATHER BAIRD—It is the crisis. Human science has done all it can to save her. Her life is in the hands of God now.

LOVING—There is no God!

FATHER BAIRD—(*sternly*) Do you dare say that—now!

JOHN—(*frightenedly*) No—I—I don't know what I'm saying— It isn't I—

FATHER BAIRD—(*recovering himself—quietly*) No. I know you couldn't blaspheme at such a time—not your true self.

LOVING—(*angrily*) It is my true self—my only self! And I see through your stupid trick—to use the fear of death to—

FATHER BAIRD—It's the hatred you once gave your soul to which speaks, not you! (*pleadingly*) I implore you to cast that evil from your soul! If you would only pray!

LOVING—(*fiercely*) No!

JOHN—(*stammers torturedly*) I—I don't know— I can't think!

FATHER BAIRD—(*intensely*) Pray with me, Jack. (*He sinks to his knees.*) Pray that Elsa's life may be spared to you! It is only God Who can open her heart to forgiveness and give her back the will to live! Pray for His forgiveness, and He will have compassion on you! Pray to Him Who is Love. Who is Infinite Tenderness and Pity!

JOHN—(*half-slipping to his knees—longingly*) Who is Love! If I could only believe again!

FATHER BAIRD—Pray for your lost faith and it will be given you!

LOVING—(*sneeringly*) You forget I once prayed to your God and His answer was hatred and death—and a mocking laughter!

JOHN—(*starts up from his half-kneeling position, under the influence of this memory*) Yes, I prayed then. No. It's no good, Uncle. I can't believe. (*then suddenly—with eagerness*) Let Him prove to me His Love exists! Then I will believe in Him again!

FATHER BAIRD—You may not bargain with your God, Jack. (*He gets wearily to his feet, his shoulders bowed, looking tragically old and beaten—then with a last appeal*) But I beseech you still! I warn you!—before it's too late!—look into your soul and force yourself to admit the truth you find there— the truth you have yourself revealed in your story where the man, who is you, goes to the church and, at the foot of the Cross is granted the grace of faith again!

LOVING—In a moment of stupid madness! But remember that is not the end!

FATHER BAIRD—(*ignoring this*) There is a fate in that story, Jack—the fate of the will of God made manifest to you through the secret longing of your own heart for faith! Take care! It has come true so far, and I am afraid if you persist in your mad denial of Him and your own soul, you will have willed for yourself the accursed end of that man—and for Elsa, death!

JOHN—(*terrified*) Stop! Stop talking damned nonsense! (*distractedly*) Leave me alone! I'm sick of your damned croaking! You're lying! Stillwell said there was no danger! She's asleep! She's getting better! (*then terrified again*) What made you say, a fate in my story—the will of God? Good God, that's—that's nonsense! I—(*he starts for the bedroom door*) I'm going back to her. There's Something—

FATHER BAIRD—(*tries to hold him back*) You can't go there now, Jack.

JOHN—(*pushing him roughly away*) Leave me alone! (*He opens the bedroom door and lurches in. Loving has come around*

*behind the table and slips in after him. Father Baird, recovering
from the push which has sent him back against the table, front,
comes quickly to the doorway.*

(*As John comes in, Stillwell turns from where he sits beside the
bedside, a look of intense anger and exasperation on his face. John,
as soon as he enters, falls under the atmosphere of the sick-room,
his wildness drops from him and he looks at Stillwell with pleading
eyes.*)

STILLWELL—(*giving up getting him out again as hopeless,
makes a gesture for him to be silent*) Ssshh! (*The nurse looks at
John with shocked rebuke. Stillwell motions John to sit down. He
does so meekly, sinking into the chair at right, center. Loving
stands behind the chair. Father Baird, after a look into the room
to see if his help is needed, exchanges a helpless glance with Stillwell, and then, turning back into the study but leaving the com-
municating door ajar, goes back as far as the table. There, after a
moment's pause, he bows his head and begins praying silently to
himself. In the bedroom, Stillwell turns back to his patient. There
is a pause of silent immobility in the room. John's eyes are fixed on
Elsa's face with a growing terror. Loving stares over his head with
cold, still eyes.*)

JOHN—(*in a low, tense voice—as if he were thinking aloud*)
A fate in my story—the will of God! Something— (*He
shudders.*)

LOVING—(*in the same low tone, but with a cold, driving intensity*) She will soon be dead.

JOHN—No!

LOVING—What will you do then? Love will be lost to you
forever. You will be alone again. There will remain only the
anguish of endless memories, endless regrets—a torturing remorse for murdered happiness!

JOHN—I know! For God's sake, don't make me think—

LOVING—(*coldly remorseless—sneeringly*) Do you think you
can choose your stupid end in your story now, when you
have to live it?—on to Hercules? But if you love her, how
can you desire to go on—with all that was Elsa rotting in her
grave behind you!

JOHN—(*torturedly*) No! I can't! I'll kill myself!

ELSA—(*suddenly moans frightenedly*) No, John! No!

LOVING—(*triumphantly*) Ah! At last you accept the true

end! At last you see the empty posing of your old ideal about man's duty to go on for Life's sake, your meaningless gesture of braving fate—a childish nose-thumbing at Nothingness at which Something laughs with a weary scorn! (*He gives a low, scornful laugh.*) Shorn of your boastful words, all it means is to go on like an animal in dumb obedience to the law of the blind stupidity of life that it must live at all costs! But where will you go—except to death? And why should you wait for an end you know when it is in your power to grasp that end—now!

ELSA—(*again moans frightenedly*) No, John—no!—please, John!

LOVING—Surely you cannot be afraid of death. Death is not the dying. Dying is life, its last revenge upon itself. But death is what the dead know, the warm, dark womb of Nothingness—the Dream in which you and Elsa may sleep as one forever, beyond fear of separation!

JOHN—(*longingly*) Elsa and I—forever beyond fear!

LOVING—Dust within dust to sleep!

JOHN—(*mechanically*) Dust within dust. (*then frightenedly questioning*) Dust? (*A shudder runs over him and he starts as if awakening from sleep.*) Fool! Can the dust love the dust? No! (*desperately*) O God, have pity! Show me the way!

LOVING—(*furiously—as if he felt himself temporarily beaten*) Coward!

JOHN—If I could only pray! If I could only believe again!

LOVING—You cannot!

JOHN—A fate in my story, Uncle said—the will of God!— I went to the church—a fate in the church— (*He suddenly gets to his feet as if impelled by some force outside him. He stares before him with obsessed eyes.*) Where I used to believe, where I used to pray!

LOVING—You insane fool! I tell you that's ended!

JOHN—If I could see the Cross again—

LOVING—(*with a shudder*) No! I don't want to see! I remember too well!—when Father and Mother—!

JOHN—Why are you so afraid of Him, if—

LOVING—(*shaken—then with fierce defiance*) Afraid? I who once cursed Him, who would again if— (*then hurriedly catching himself*) But what superstitious nonsense you make me remember. He doesn't exist!

JOHN—(*takes a step toward the door*) I am going!

LOVING—(*tries to bar his path*) No!

JOHN—(*without touching him, makes a motion of pushing him aside*) I am going. (*He goes through the door to the study, moving like one in a trance, his eyes fixed straight before him. Loving continues to try to bar his path, always without touching him. Father Baird looks up as they pass the table.*)

LOVING—(*in impotent rage*) No! You coward! (*John goes out the door in rear of study and Loving is forced out before him.*)

FATHER BAIRD—(*starting after him*) Jack! (*But he turns back in alarm as, in the bedroom, Elsa suddenly comes out of the half-coma she is in with a cry of terror and, in spite of Stillwell, springs up to a half-sitting position in bed, her staring eyes on the doorway to the study.*)

ELSA—John! (*then to Stillwell*) Oh, please! Look after him! He might— John! Come back! I'll forgive!

STILLWELL—(*soothingly*) There, don't be frightened. He's only gone to lie down for a while. He's very tired. (*Father Baird has come in from the study and is approaching the bed. Stillwell, with a significant look, calls on him for confirmation.*) Isn't that right, Father?

FATHER BAIRD—Yes, Elsa.

ELSA—(*relieved*) Oh. (*She smiles faintly.*) Poor John. I'm so sorry. Tell him he mustn't worry. I understand now. I love— I forgive. (*She sinks back and closes her eyes. Stillwell reaches for her wrist in alarm, but as he feels her pulse his expression changes to one of excited surprise.*)

FATHER BAIRD—(*misreading his look—in a frightened whisper*) Merciful God! She isn't—?

STILLWELL—No. She's asleep. (*then with suppressed excitement*) That's done it! She'll want to live now!

FATHER BAIRD—God be praised! (*Stillwell, his air curtly professional again turns and whispers some orders to the nurse.*)

(*Curtain*)

SCENE II

SCENE—*A section of the interior of an old church. A side wall runs diagonally back from left, front, two-thirds of the width of the stage, where it meets an end wall that extends back from right, front. The walls are old gray stone. In the middle of the side wall is a great cross, its base about five feet from the floor, with a life-size figure of Christ, an exceptionally fine piece of wood carving. In the middle of the end wall is an arched doorway. On either side of this door, but high up in the wall, their bases above the level of the top of the doorway, are two narrow, stained-glass windows.*

It is a few minutes after the close of the preceding scene. The church is dim and empty and still. The only light is the reflection of the dawn, which, stained by the color in the windows, falls on the wall on and around the Cross.

The outer doors beyond the arched doorway are suddenly pushed open with a crash and John and Loving appear in the doorway. Loving comes first, retreating backward before John whom he desperately, but always without touching him, endeavors to keep from entering the church. But John is the stronger now and, the same look of obsessed resolution in his eyes, he forces Loving back.

LOVING—(*as they enter—desperately, as if he were becoming exhausted by the struggle*) You fool! There is nothing here but hatred!

JOHN—No! There was love! (*His eyes fasten themselves on the Cross and he gives a cry of hope.*) The Cross!

LOVING—The symbol of hate and derision!

JOHN—No! Of love! (*Loving is forced back until the back of his head is against the foot of the Cross. John throws himself on his knees before it and raises his hands up to the figure of Christ in supplication.*) Mercy! Forgive!

LOVING—(*raging*) Fool! Grovel on your knees! It is useless! To pray, one must believe!

JOHN—I have come back to Thee!

LOVING—Words! There is nothing!

JOHN—Let me believe in Thy love again!

LOVING—You cannot believe!

JOHN—(*imploringly*) O God of Love, hear my prayer!

LOVING—There is no God! There is only death!

JOHN—(*more weakly now*) Have pity on me! Let Elsa live!

LOVING—There is no pity! There is only scorn!

JOHN—Hear me while there is still time! (*He waits, staring at the Cross with anguished eyes, his arms outstretched. There is a pause of silence.*)

LOVING—(*with triumphant mockery*) Silence! But behind it I hear mocking laughter!

JOHN—(*agonized*) No! (*He gives way, his head bowed, and sobs heartbrokenly—then stops suddenly, and looking up at the Cross again, speaks sobbingly in a strange humble tone of broken reproach.*) O Son of Man, I am Thou and Thou art I! Why hast Thou forsaken me? O Brother Who lived and loved and suffered and died with us, Who knoweth the tortured hearts of men, canst Thou not forgive—now—when I surrender all to Thee—when I have forgiven Thee—the love that Thou once took from me!

LOVING—(*with a cry of hatred*) No! Liar! I will never forgive!

JOHN—(*his eyes fixed on the face of the Crucified suddenly lighting up as if he now saw there the answer to his prayer—in a voice trembling with awakening hope and joy*) Ah! Thou hast heard me at last! Thou hast not forsaken me! Thou hast always loved me! I am forgiven! I can forgive myself—through Thee! I can believe!

LOVING—(*stumbles weakly from beneath the Cross*) No! I deny! (*He turns to face the Cross with a last defiance.*) I defy Thee! Thou canst not conquer me! I hate Thee! I curse Thee!

JOHN—No! I bless! I love!

LOVING—(*as if this were a mortal blow, seems to sag and collapse—with a choking cry*) No!

JOHN—(*with a laugh that is half sob*) Yes! I see now! At last I see! I have always loved! O Lord of Love, forgive Thy poor blind fool!

LOVING—No! (*His legs crumple under him, he slumps to his knees beside John, as if some invisible force crushed him down.*)

JOHN—(*his voice rising exultantly, his eyes on the face of the Crucified*) Thou art the Way—the Truth—the Resurrection and the Life, and he that believeth in Thy Love, his love shall never die!

LOVING—(*faintly, at last surrendering, addressing the Cross not without a final touch of pride in his humility*) Thou hast conquered, Lord. Thou art—the End. Forgive—the damned soul—of John Loving! (*He slumps forward to the floor and rolls over on his back, dead, his head beneath the foot of the Cross, his arms outflung so that his body forms another cross. John rises from his knees and stands with arms stretched up and out, so that he, too, is like cross. While this is happening the light of the dawn on the stained-glass windows swiftly rises to a brilliant intensity of crimson and green and gold, as if the sun had risen. The gray walls of the church, particularly the wall where the Cross is, and the face of the Christ shine with this radiance.*

(*John Loving—he, who had been only John—remains standing with his arms stretched up to the Cross, an expression of mystic exaltation on his face. The corpse of Loving lies at the foot of the Cross, like a cured cripple's testimonial offering in a shrine.*

(*Father Baird comes in hurriedly through the arched doorway. He stops on seeing John Loving, then comes quietly up beside him and stares searchingly into his face. At what he sees there he bows his head and his lips move in grateful prayer. John Loving is oblivious to his presence.*)

FATHER BAIRD—(*finally taps him gently on the shoulder*) Jack.

JOHN LOVING—(*still in his ecstatic mystic vision—strangely*) I am John Loving.

FATHER BAIRD—(*stares at him—gently*) It's all right now, Jack. Elsa will live.

JOHN LOVING—(*exaltedly*) I know! Love lives forever! Death is dead! Ssshh! Listen! Do you hear?

FATHER BAIRD—Hear what, Jack?

JOHN LOVING—Life laughs with God's love again! Life laughs with love!

(*Curtain*)

A TOUCH OF THE POET

CHARACTERS

MICKEY MALOY

JAMIE CREGAN

SARA MELODY

NORA MELODY

CORNELIUS MELODY

DEBORAH (*Mrs. Henry Harford*)

DAN ROCHE

PADDY O'DOWD

PATCH RILEY

NICHOLAS GADSBY

SCENES

ACT 1

Dining room of Melody's Tavern morning of
July 27, 1828

ACT 2

The same, later that morning

ACT 3

The same, that evening

ACT 4

The same, that night

A Touch of the Poet

ACT ONE

SCENE—*The dining room of Melody's Tavern, in a village a few miles from Boston. The tavern is over a hundred years old. It had once been prosperous, a breakfast stop for the stagecoach, but the stage line had been discontinued and for some years now the tavern has fallen upon neglected days.*

The dining room and barroom were once a single spacious room, low-ceilinged, with heavy oak beams and paneled walls—the tap-room of the tavern in its prosperous days, now divided into two rooms by a flimsy partition, the barroom being off left. The partition is painted to imitate the old paneled walls but this only makes it more of an eyesore.

At left front, two steps lead up to a closed door opening on a flight of stairs to the floor above. Farther back is the door to the bar. Between these doors hangs a large mirror. Beyond the bar door a small cabinet is fastened to the wall. At rear are four windows. Between the middle two is the street door. At right front is another door, open, giving on a hallway and the main stairway to the second floor, and leading to the kitchen. Farther front at right, there is a high schoolmaster's desk with a stool.

In the foreground are two tables. One, with four chairs, at left center; a larger one, seating six, at right center. At left and right, rear, are two more tables, identical with the ones at right center. All these tables are set with white tablecloths, etc., except the small ones in the foreground at left.

It is around nine in the morning of July 27, 1828. Sunlight shines in through the windows at rear.

Mickey Maloy sits at the table at left front, facing right. He is glancing through a newspaper. Maloy is twenty-six, with a sturdy physique and an amiable, cunning face, his mouth usually set in a half-leering grin.

Jamie Cregan peers around the half-open door to the bar. Seeing Maloy, he comes in. As obviously Irish as Maloy, he is middle-aged, tall, with a lantern-jawed face. There is a scar of a saber cut over one cheekbone. He is dressed neatly but in old, worn clothes. His eyes are bloodshot, his manner sickly, but he grins as he greets Maloy sardonically.

CREGAN—God bless all here—even the barkeep.

MALOY—(*with an answering grin*) Top o' the mornin'.

CREGAN—Top o' me head. (*He puts his hand to his head and groans.*) Be the saints, there's a blacksmith at work on it!

MALOY—Small wonder. You'd the divil's own load when you left at two this mornin'.

CREGAN—I must have. I don't remember leaving. (*He sits at right of table.*) Faix, you're takin' it aisy.

MALOY—There's no trade this time o' day.

CREGAN—It was a great temptation, when I saw no one in the bar, to make off with a bottle. A hair av the dog is what I need, but I've divil a penny in my pantaloons.

MALOY—Have one on the house. (*He goes to the cupboard and takes out a decanter of whiskey and a glass.*)

CREGAN—Thank you kindly. Sure, the good Samaritan was a crool haythen beside you.

MALOY—(*putting the decanter and glass before him*) It's the same you was drinking last night—his private dew. He keeps it here for emergencies when he don't want to go in the bar.

CREGAN—(*pours out a big drink*) Lave it to Con never to be caught dry. (*raising his glass*) Your health and inclinations—if they're virtuous! (*He drinks and sighs with relief.*) God bless you, Whiskey, it's you can rouse the dead! Con hasn't been down yet for his morning's morning?

MALOY—No. He won't be till later.

CREGAN—It's like a miracle, me meeting him again. I came to these parts looking for work. It's only by accident I heard talk of a Con Melody and come here to see was it him. Until last night, I'd not seen hide nor hair of him since the war with the French in Spain—after the battle of Salamanca in '12. I was a corporal in the Seventh Dragoons and he was major. (*proudly*) I got this cut from a saber at Talavera, bad luck to it!—serving under him. He was a captain then.

MALOY—So you told me last night.

CREGAN—(*with a quick glance at him*) Did I now? I must have said more than my prayers, with the lashings of whiskey in me.

MALOY—(*with a grin*) More than your prayers is the truth.

(*Cregan glances at him uneasily. Maloy pushes the decanter toward him.*) Take another taste.

CREGAN—I don't like sponging. Sure, my credit ought to be good in this shebeen! Ain't I his cousin?

MALOY—You're forgettin' what himself told you last night as he went up to bed. You could have all the whiskey you could pour down you, but not a penny's worth of credit. This house, he axed you to remember, only gives credit to gentlemen.

CREGAN—Divil mend him!

MALOY—(*with a chuckle*) You kept thinking about his insults after he'd gone out, getting madder and madder.

CREGAN—God pity him, that's like him. He hasn't changed much. (*He pours out a drink and gulps it down —with a cautious look at Maloy*) If I was mad at Con, and me blind drunk, I must have told you a power of lies.

MALOY—(*winks slyly*) Maybe they wasn't lies.

CREGAN—If I said any wrong of Con Melody—

MALOY—Arrah, are you afraid I'll gab what you said to him? I won't, you can take my oath.

CREGAN—(*his face clearing*) Tell me what I said and I'll tell you if it was lies.

MALOY—You said his father wasn't of the quality of Galway like he makes out, but a thievin' shebeen keeper who got rich by moneylendin' and squeezin' tenants and every manner of trick. And when he'd enough he married, and bought an estate with a pack of hounds and set up as one of the gentry. He'd hardly got settled when his wife died givin' birth to Con.

CREGAN—There's no lie there.

MALOY—You said none of the gentry would speak to auld Melody, but he had a tough hide and didn't heed them. He made up his mind he'd bring Con up a true gentleman, so he packed him off to Dublin to school, and after that to the College with sloos of money to prove himself the equal of any gentleman's son. But Con found, while there was plenty to drink on him and borrow money, there was few didn't sneer behind his back at his pretensions.

CREGAN—That's the truth, too. But Con wiped the sneer off their mugs when he called one av thim out and put a

bullet in his hip. That was his first duel. It gave his pride the
taste for revenge and after that he was always lookin' for an
excuse to challenge someone.

MALOY—He's done a power av boastin' about his duels,
but I thought he was lyin'.

CREGAN—There's no lie in it. It was that brought disgrace
on him in the end, right after he'd been promoted to major.
He got caught by a Spanish noble making love to his wife,
just after the battle of Salamanca, and there was a duel and
Con killed him. The scandal was hushed up but Con had to
resign from the army. If it wasn't for his fine record for bravery in battle, they'd have court-martialed him. (*then guiltily*)
But I'm sayin' more than my prayers again.

MALOY—It's no news about his women. You'd think, to
hear him when he's drunk, there wasn't one could resist him
in Portugal and Spain.

CREGAN—If you'd seen him then, you wouldn't wonder.
He was as strong as an ox, and on a thoroughbred horse, in
his uniform, there wasn't a handsomer man in the army. And
he had the chance he wanted in Portugal and Spain where a
British officer was welcome in the gentry's houses. At home,
the only women he'd known was whores. (*He adds hastily*)
Except Nora, I mean. (*lowering his voice*) Tell me, has he done
any rampagin' wid women here?

MALOY—He hasn't. The damned Yankee gentry won't let
him come near them, and he considers the few Irish around
here to be scum beneath his notice. But once in a while
there'll be some Yankee stops overnight wid his wife or
daughter and then you'd laugh to see Con, if he thinks she's
gentry, sidlin' up to her, playin' the great gentleman and
makin' compliments, and then boasting afterward he could
have them in bed if he'd had a chance at it, for all their modern Yankee airs.

CREGAN—And maybe he could. If you'd known him in
the auld days, you'd nivir doubt any boast he makes about
fightin' and women, and gamblin' or any kind av craziness.
There nivir was a madder divil.

MALOY—(*lowering his voice*) Speakin' av Nora, you nivir
mentioned her last night, but I know all about it without you
telling me. I used to have my room here, and there's nights

he's madder drunk than most when he throws it in her face he had to marry her because— Mind you, I'm not saying anything against poor Nora. A sweeter woman never lived. And I know you know all about it.

CREGAN—(*reluctantly*) I do. Wasn't I raised on his estate?

MALOY—He tells her it was the priests tricked him into marrying her. He hates priests.

CREGAN—He's a liar, then. He may like to blame it on them but it's little Con Melody cared what they said. Nothing ever made him do anything, except himself. He married her because he'd fallen in love with her, but he was ashamed of her in his pride at the same time because her folks were only ignorant peasants on his estate, as poor as poor. Nora was as pretty a girl as you'd find in a year's travel, and he'd come to be bitter lonely, with no woman's company but the whores was helpin' him ruin the estate. (*He shrugs his shoulders.*) Well, anyways, he married her and then went off to the war, and left her alone in the castle to have her child, and nivir saw her again till he was sent home from Spain. Then he raised what money he still was able, and took her and Sara here to America where no one would know him.

MALOY—(*thinking this over for a moment*) It's hard for me to believe he ever loved her. I've seen the way he treats her now. Well, thank you for telling me, and I take my oath I'll nivir breathe a word of it—for Nora's sake, not his.

CREGAN—(*grimly*) You'd better kape quiet for fear of him, too. If he's one-half the man he was, he could bate the lights out of the two av us.

MALOY—He's strong as a bull still for all the whiskey he's drunk. (*He pushes the bottle toward Cregan.*) Have another taste. (*Cregan pours out a drink.*) Drink hearty.

CREGAN—Long life. (*He drinks. Maloy puts the decanter and glass back on the cupboard. A girl's voice is heard from the hall at right. Cregan jumps up—hastily*) That's Sara, isn't it? I'll get out. She'll likely blame me for Con getting so drunk last night. I'll be back after Con is down. (*He goes out. Maloy starts to go in the bar, as if he too wanted to avoid Sara. Then he sits down defiantly.*)

MALOY—Be damned if I'll run from her. (*He takes up the paper as Sara Melody comes in from the hall at right.*)

(*Sara is twenty, an exceedingly pretty girl with a mass of black hair, fair skin with rosy cheeks, and beautiful, deep-blue eyes. There is a curious blending in her of what are commonly considered aristocratic and peasant characteristics. She has a fine forehead. Her nose is thin and straight. She has small ears set close to her well-shaped head, and a slender neck. Her mouth, on the other hand, has a touch of coarseness and sensuality and her jaw is too heavy. Her figure is strong and graceful, with full, firm breasts and hips, and a slender waist. But she has large feet and broad, ugly hands with stubby fingers. Her voice is soft and musical, but her speech has at times a self-conscious, stilted quality about it, due to her restraining a tendency to lapse into brogue. Her everyday working dress is of cheap material, but she wears it in a way that gives a pleasing effect of beauty unadorned.*)

SARA—(*with a glance at Maloy, sarcastically*) I'm sorry to interrupt you when you're so busy, but have you your bar book ready for me to look over?

MALOY—(*surlily*) I have. I put it on your desk.

SARA—Thank you. (*She turns her back on him, sits at the desk, takes a small account book from it, and begins checking figures.*)

MALOY—(*watches her over his paper*) If it's profits you're looking for, you won't find them—not with all the drinks himself's been treating to. (*She ignores this. He becomes resentful.*) You've got your airs of a grand lady this morning, I see. There's no talkin' to you since you've been playin' nurse to the young Yankee upstairs. (*She makes herself ignore this, too.*) Well, you've had your cap set for him ever since he came to live by the lake, and now's your chance, when he's here sick and too weak to defend himself.

SARA—(*turns on him—with quiet anger*) I warn you to mind your own business, Mickey, or I'll tell my father of your impudence. He'll teach you to keep your place, and God help you.

MALOY—(*doesn't believe this threat but is frightened by the possibility*) Arrah, don't try to scare me. I know you'd never carry tales to him. (*placatingly*) Can't you take a bit of teasing, Sara?

SARA—(*turns back to her figuring*) Leave Simon out of your teasing.

MALOY—Oho, he's Simon to you now, is he? Well, well. (*He gives her a cunning glance.*) Maybe, if you'd come down from your high horse, I could tell you some news.

SARA—You're worse than an old woman for gossip. I don't want to hear it.

MALOY—When you was upstairs at the back taking him his breakfast, there was a grand carriage with a nigger coachman stopped at the corner and a Yankee lady got out and came in here. I was sweeping and Nora was scrubbing the kitchen. (*Sara has turned to him, all attention now.*) She asked me what road would take her near the lake—

SARA—(*starts*) Ah.

MALOY—So I told her, but she didn't go. She kept looking around, and said she'd like a cup of tea, and where was the waitress. I knew she must be connected someway with Harford or why would she want to go to the lake, where no one's ever lived but him. She didn't want tea at all, but only an excuse to stay.

SARA—(*resentfully*) So she asked for the waitress, did she? I hope you told her I'm the owner's daughter, too.

MALOY—I did. I don't like Yankee airs any more than you. I was short with her. I said you was out for a walk, and the tavern wasn't open yet, anyway. So she went out and drove off.

SARA—(*worriedly now*) I hope you didn't insult her with your bad manners. What did she look like, Mickey?

MALOY—Pretty, if you like that kind. A pale, delicate wisp of a thing with big eyes.

SARA—That fits what he's said of his mother. How old was she?

MALOY—It's hard to tell, but she's too young for his mother, I'd swear. Around thirty, I'd say. Maybe it's his sister.

SARA—He hasn't a sister.

MALOY—(*grinning*) Then maybe she's an old sweetheart looking for you to scratch your eyes out.

SARA—He's never had a sweetheart.

MALOY—(*mockingly*) Is that what he tells you, and you believe him? Faix, you must be in love!

SARA—(*angrily*) Will you mind your own business? I'm not such a fool! (*worried again*) Maybe you ought to have told her he's here sick to save her the drive in the hot sun and the walk through the woods for nothing.

MALOY—Why would I tell her, when she never mentioned him?

SARA—Yes, it's her own fault. But— Well, there's no use thinking of it now—or bothering my head about her, anyway, whoever she was. (*She begins checking figures again. Her mother appears in the doorway at right.*)

(*Nora Melody is forty, but years of overwork and worry have made her look much older. She must have been as pretty as a girl as Sara is now. She still has the beautiful eyes her daughter has inherited. But she has become too worn out to take care of her appearance. Her black hair, streaked with gray, straggles in untidy wisps about her face. Her body is dumpy, with sagging breasts, and her old clothes are like a bag covering it, tied around the middle. Her red hands are knotted by rheumatism. Cracked working shoes, run down at the heel, are on her bare feet. Yet in spite of her slovenly appearance there is a spirit which shines through and makes her lovable, a simple sweetness and charm, something gentle and sad and, somehow, dauntless.*)

MALOY—(*jumps to his feet, his face lighting up with affection*) God bless you, Nora, you're the one I was waitin' to see. Will you keep an eye on the bar while I run to the store for a bit av 'baccy?

SARA—(*sharply*) Don't do it, Mother.

NORA—(*smiles—her voice is soft, with a rich brogue*) Why wouldn't I? "Don't do it, Mother."

MALOY—Thank you, Nora. (*He goes to the door at rear and opens it, burning for a parting shot at Sara.*) And the back o' my hand to you, your Ladyship! (*He goes out, closing the door.*)

SARA—You shouldn't encourage his laziness. He's always looking for excuses to shirk.

NORA—Ah, nivir mind, he's a good lad. (*She lowers herself painfully on the nearest chair at the rear of the table at center front.*) Bad cess to the rheumatism. It has me destroyed this mornin'.

SARA—(*still checking figures in the book—gives her mother an impatient but at the same time worried glance. Her habitual manner toward her is one of mingled love and pity and exasperation.*) I've told you a hundred times to see the doctor.

NORA—We've no money for doctors. They're bad luck, anyway. They bring death with them. (*A pause. Nora sighs.*) Your father will be down soon. I've some fine fresh eggs for his breakfast.

SARA—(*Her face becomes hard and bitter.*) He won't want them.

NORA—(*defensively*) You mean he'd a drop too much taken last night? Well, small blame to him, he hasn't seen Jamie since—

SARA—*Last* night? What night hasn't he?

NORA—Ah, don't be hard on him. (*a pause—worriedly*) Neilan sent round a note to me about his bill. He says we'll have to settle by the end of the week or we'll get no more groceries. (*with a sigh*) I can't blame him. How we'll manage, I dunno. There's the intrist on the mortgage due the first. But that I've saved, God be thanked.

SARA—(*exasperatedly*) If you'd only let me take charge of the money.

NORA—(*with a flare of spirit*) I won't. It'd mean you and himself would be at each other's throats from dawn to dark. It's bad enough between you as it is.

SARA—Why didn't you pay Neilan the end of last week? You told me you had the money put aside.

NORA—So I did. But Dickinson was tormentin' your father with his feed bill for the mare.

SARA—(*angrily*) I might have known! The mare comes first, if she takes the bread out of our mouths! The grand gentleman must have his thoroughbred to ride out in state!

NORA—(*defensively*) Where's the harm? She's his greatest pride. He'd be heartbroken if he had to sell her.

SARA—Oh yes, I know well he cares more for a horse than for us!

NORA—Don't be saying that. He has great love for you, even if you do be provokin' him all the time.

SARA—Great love for me! Arrah, God pity you, Mother!

NORA—(*sharply*) Don't put on the brogue, now. You know how he hates to hear you. And I do, too. There's no excuse not to cure yourself. Didn't he send you to school so you could talk like a gentleman's daughter?

SARA—(*resentfully, but more careful of her speech*) If he did, I wasn't there long.

NORA—It was you insisted on leavin'.

SARA—Because if he hadn't the pride or love for you not to live on your slaving your heart out, I had that pride and love!

NORA—(*tenderly*) I know, Acushla. I know.

SARA—(*with bitter scorn*) We can't afford a waitress, but he can afford to keep a thoroughbred mare to prance around on and show himself off! And he can afford a barkeep when, if he had any decency, he'd do his part and tend the bar himself.

NORA—(*indignantly*) Him, a gentleman, tend bar!

SARA—A gentleman! Och, Mother, it's all right for the two of us, out of our own pride, to pretend to the world we believe that lie, but it's crazy for you to pretend to me.

NORA—(*stubbornly*) It's no lie. He *is* a gentleman. Wasn't he born rich in a castle on a grand estate and educated in college, and wasn't he an officer in the Duke of Wellington's army—

SARA—All right, Mother. You can humor his craziness, but he'll never make me pretend to him I don't know the truth.

NORA—Don't talk as if you hated him. You ought to be shamed—

SARA—I do hate him for the way he treats you. I heard him again last night, raking up the past, and blaming his ruin on his having to marry you.

NORA—(*protests miserably*) It was the drink talkin', not him.

SARA—(*exasperated*) It's you ought to be ashamed, for not having more pride! You bear all his insults as meek as a lamb! You keep on slaving for him when it's that has made you old before your time! (*angrily*) You can't much longer, I tell you! He's getting worse. You'll have to leave him.

NORA—(*aroused*) I'll never! Howld your prate!

SARA—You'd leave him today, if you had any pride!

NORA—I've pride in my love for him! I've loved him since the day I set eyes on him, and I'll love him till the day I die! (*with a strange superior scorn*) It's little you know of love, and you never will, for there's the same divil of pride in you that's in him, and it'll kape you from ivir givin' all of yourself, and that's what love is.

SARA—I could give all of myself if I wanted to, but—

NORA—If! Wanted to! Faix, it proves how little of love you know when you prate about if's and want-to's. It's when you don't give a thought for all the if's and want-to's in the world! It's when, if all the fires of hell was between you, you'd walk in them gladly to be with him, and sing with joy at your own burnin', if only his kiss was on your mouth! That's love, and I'm proud I've known the great sorrow and joy of it!

SARA—(*cannot help being impressed—looks at her mother with wondering respect*) You're a strange woman, Mother. (*She kisses her impulsively.*) And a grand woman! (*defiant again, with an arrogant toss of her head*) I'll love—but I'll love where it'll gain me freedom and not put me in slavery for life.

NORA—There's no slavery in it when you love! (*Suddenly her exultant expression crumbles and she breaks down.*) For the love of God, don't take the pride of my love from me, Sara, for without it what am I at all but an ugly, fat woman gettin' old and sick!

SARA—(*puts her arm around her—soothingly*) Hush, Mother. Don't mind me. (*briskly, to distract her mother's mind*) I've got to finish the bar book. Mickey can't put two and two together without making five. (*She goes to the desk and begins checking figures again.*)

NORA—(*dries her eyes—after a pause she sighs worriedly*) I'm worried about your father. Father Flynn stopped me on the road yesterday and tould me I'd better warn him not to sneer at the Irish around here and call thim scum, or he'll get in trouble. Most of thim is in a rage at him because he's come out against Jackson and the Democrats and says he'll vote with the Yankees for Quincy Adams.

SARA—(*contemptuously*) Faith, they can't see a joke, then, for it's a great joke to hear him shout against mob rule, like one of the Yankee gentry, when you know what he came from. And after the way the Yanks swindled him when he came here, getting him to buy this inn by telling him a new coach line was going to stop here. (*She laughs with bitter scorn.*) Oh, he's the easiest fool ever came to America! It's that

I hold against him as much as anything, that when he came here the chance was before him to make himself all his lies pretended to be. He had education above most Yanks, and he had money enough to start him, and this is a country where you can rise as high as you like, and no one but the fools who envy you care what you rose from, once you've the money and the power goes with it. (*passionately*) Oh, if I was a man with the chance he had, there wouldn't be a dream I'd not make come true! (*She looks at her mother, who is staring at the floor dejectedly and hasn't been listening. She is exasperated for a second—then she smiles pityingly.*) You're a fine one to talk to, Mother. Wake up. What's worrying you now?

NORA—Father Flynn tould me again I'd be damned in hell for lettin' your father make a haythen of me and bring you up a haythen, too.

SARA—(*with an arrogant toss of her head*) Let Father Flynn mind his own business, and not frighten you with fairy tales about hell.

NORA—It's true, just the same.

SARA—True, me foot! You ought to tell the good Father we aren't the ignorant shanty scum he's used to dealing with. (*She changes the subject abruptly—closing Mickey's bar book*) There. That's done. (*She puts the book in the desk.*) I'll take a walk to the store and have a talk with Neilan. Maybe I can blarney him to let the bill go another month.

NORA—(*gratefully*) Oh, you can. Sure, you can charm a bird out of a tree when you want to. But I don't like you beggin' to a Yankee. It's all right for me but I know how you hate it.

SARA—(*puts her arms around her mother—tenderly*) I don't mind at all, if I can save you a bit of the worry that's killing you. (*She kisses her.*) I'll change to my Sunday dress so I can make a good impression.

NORA—(*with a teasing smile*) I'm thinkin' it isn't on Neilan alone you want to make an impression. You've changed to your Sunday best a lot lately.

SARA—(*coquettishly*) Aren't you the sly one! Well, maybe you're right.

NORA—How was he when you took him his breakfast?

SARA—Hungry, and that's a good sign. He had no fever

last night. Oh, he's on the road to recovery now, and it won't be long before he'll be back in his cabin by the lake.

NORA—I'll never get it clear in my head what he's been doing there the past year, living like a tramp or a tinker, and him a rich gentleman's son.

SARA—(*with a tender smile*) Oh, he isn't like his kind, or like anyone else at all. He's a born dreamer with a raft of great dreams, and he's very serious about them. I've told you before he wanted to get away from his father's business, where he worked for a year after he graduated from Harvard College, because he didn't like being in trade, even if it is a great company that trades with the whole world in its own ships.

NORA—(*approvingly*) That's the way a true gentleman would feel—

SARA—He wanted to prove his independence by living alone in the wilds, and build his own cabin, and do all the work, and support himself simply, and feel one with Nature, and think great thoughts about what life means, and write a book about how the world can be changed so people won't be greedy to own money and land and get the best of each other but will be content with little and live in peace and freedom together, and it will be like heaven on earth. (*She laughs fondly—and a bit derisively.*) I can't remember all of it. It seems crazy to me, when I think of what people are like. He hasn't written any of it yet, anyway—only the notes for it. (*She smiles coquettishly.*) All he's written the last few months are love poems.

NORA—That's since you began to take long walks by the lake. (*She smiles.*) It's you are the sly one.

SARA—(*laughing*) Well, why shouldn't I take walks on our own property? (*Her tone changes to a sneer.*) The land our great gentleman was swindled into buying when he came here with grand ideas of owning an American estate!—a bit of farm land no one would work any more, and the rest all wilderness! You couldn't give it away.

NORA—(*soothingly*) Hush, now. (*changing the subject*) Well, it's easy to tell young Master Harford has a touch av the poet in him—(*she adds before she thinks*) the same as your father.

SARA—(*scornfully*) God help you, Mother! Do you think Father's a poet because he shows off reciting Lord Byron?

NORA—(*with an uneasy glance at the door at left front*)
Whist, now. Himself will be down any moment. (*changing
the subject*) I can see the Harford lad is falling in love with
you.

SARA—(*Her face lights up triumphantly.*) Falling? He's
fallen head over heels. He's so timid, he hasn't told me yet,
but I'll get him to soon.

NORA—I know you're in love with him.

SARA—(*simply*) I am, Mother. (*She adds quickly*) But not
too much. I'll not let love make me any man's slave. I want
to love him just enough so I can marry him without cheating
him, or myself. (*determinedly*) For I'm going to marry him,
Mother. It's my chance to rise in the world and nothing will
keep me from it.

NORA—(*admiringly*) Musha, but you've boastful talk!
What about his fine Yankee family? His father'll likely cut him
off widout a penny if he marries a girl who's poor and Irish.

SARA—He may at first, but when I've proved what a good
wife I'll be— He can't keep Simon from marrying me. I
know that. Simon doesn't care what his father thinks. It's
only his mother I'm afraid of. I can tell she's had great influence over him. She must be a queer creature, from all he's
told me. She's very strange in her ways. She never goes out
at all but stays home in their mansion, reading books, or in
her garden. (*She pauses.*) Did you notice a carriage stop here
this morning, Mother?

NORA—(*preoccupied—uneasily*) Don't count your chickens
before they're hatched. Young Harford seems a dacent lad.
But maybe it's not marriage he's after.

SARA—(*angrily*) I won't have you wronging him, Mother.
He has no thought— (*bitterly*) I suppose you're bound to
suspect— (*She bites her words back, ashamed.*) Forgive me,
Mother. But it's wrong of you to think badly of Simon. (*She
smiles.*) You don't know him. Faith, if it came to seducing,
it'd be me that'd have to do it. He's that respectful you'd
think I was a holy image. It's only in his poems, and in the
diary he keeps— I had a peek in it one day I went to tidy
up the cabin for him. He's terribly ashamed of his sinful inclinations and the insult they are to my purity. (*She laughs
tenderly.*)

NORA—(*smiling, but a bit shocked*) Don't talk so bould. I don't know if it's right, you to be in his room so much, even if he is sick. There's a power av talk about the two av you already.

SARA—Let there be, for all I care! Or all Simon cares, either. When it comes to not letting others rule him, he's got a will of his own behind his gentleness. Just as behind his poetry and dreams I feel he has it in him to do anything he wants. So even if his father cuts him off, with me to help him we'll get on in the world. For I'm no fool, either.

NORA—Glory be to God, you have the fine opinion av yourself!

SARA—(*laughing*) Haven't I, though! (*then bitterly*) I've had need to have, to hold my head up, slaving as a waitress and chambermaid so my father can get drunk every night like a gentleman!

(*The door at left front is slowly opened and Cornelius Melody appears in the doorway above the two steps. He and Sara stare at each other. She stiffens into hostility and her mouth sets in scorn. For a second his eyes waver and he looks guilty. Then his face becomes expressionless. He descends the steps and bows — pleasantly*)

MELODY—Good morning, Sara.

SARA—(*curtly*) Good morning. (*then, ignoring him*) I'm going up and change my dress, Mother. (*She goes out right.*)

(*Cornelius Melody is forty-five, tall, broad-shouldered, deep-chested, and powerful, with long muscular arms, big feet, and large hairy hands. His heavy-boned body is still firm, erect, and soldierly. Beyond shaky nerves, it shows no effects of hard drinking. It has a bull-like, impervious strength, a tough peasant vitality. It is his face that reveals the ravages of dissipation — a ruined face, which was once extraordinarily handsome in a reckless, arrogant fashion. It is still handsome — the face of an embittered Byronic hero, with a finely chiseled nose over a domineering, sensual mouth set in disdain, pale, hollow-cheeked, framed by thick, curly iron-gray hair. There is a look of wrecked distinction about it, of brooding, humiliated pride. His bloodshot gray eyes have an insulting cold stare which anticipates insult. His manner is that of a polished gentleman. Too much so. He overdoes it and one soon feels that he is overplaying a role which has become more real than his real self to him. But in spite of this, there is something formidable and impressive about him. He is dressed with foppish elegance in old, expensive, finely tailored clothes of the style worn by English aristocracy in Peninsular War days.*)

MELODY—(*advancing into the room—bows formally to his wife*) Good morning, Nora. (*His tone condescends. It addresses a person of inferior station.*)

NORA—(*stumbles to her feet—timidly*) Good mornin', Con. I'll get your breakfast.

MELODY—No. Thank you. I want nothing now.

NORA—(*coming toward him*) You look pale. Are you sick, Con, darlin'?

MELODY—No.

NORA—(*puts a timid hand on his arm*) Come and sit down. (*He moves his arm away with instinctive revulsion and goes to the table at center front, and sits in the chair she had occupied. Nora hovers round him.*) I'll wet a cloth in cold water to put round your head.

MELODY—No! I desire nothing—except a little peace in which to read the news. (*He picks up the paper and holds it so it hides his face from her.*)

NORA—(*meekly*) I'll lave you in peace. (*She starts to go to the door at right but turns to stare at him worriedly again. Keeping the paper before his face with his left hand, he reaches out with his right and pours a glass of water from the carafe on the table. Although he cannot see his wife, he is nervously conscious of her. His hand trembles so violently that when he attempts to raise the glass to his lips the water sloshes over his hand and he sets the glass back on the table with a bang. He lowers the paper and explodes nervously*)

MELODY—For God's sake, stop your staring!

NORA—I—I was only thinkin' you'd feel better if you'd a bit av food in you.

MELODY—I told you once—! (*controlling his temper*) I am not hungry, Nora. (*He raises the paper again. She sighs, her hands fiddling with her apron. A pause.*)

NORA—(*dully*) Maybe it's a hair av the dog you're needin'.

MELODY—(*As if this were something he had been waiting to hear, his expression loses some of its nervous strain. But he replies virtuously*) No, damn the liquor. Upon my conscience, I've

about made up my mind I'll have no more of it. Besides, it's
a bit early in the day.

NORA—If it'll give you an appetite—

MELODY—To tell the truth, my stomach is out of sorts.
(*He licks his lips.*) Perhaps a drop wouldn't come amiss. (*Nora
gets the decanter and glass from the cupboard and sets them before
him. She stands gazing at him with a resigned sadness. Melody,
his eyes on the paper, is again acutely conscious of her. His nerves
cannot stand it. He throws his paper down and bursts out in bitter
anger*) Well? I know what you're thinking! Why haven't you
the courage to say it for once? By God, I'd have more respect
for you! I hate the damned meek of this earth! By the rock of
Cashel, I sometimes believe you have always deliberately encouraged me to— It's the one point of superiority you can
lay claim to, isn't it?

NORA—(*bewilderedly—on the verge of tears*) I don't— It's
only your comfort— I can't bear to see you—

MELODY—(*His expression changes and a look of real affection
comes into his eyes. He reaches out a shaking hand to pat her
shoulder with an odd, guilty tenderness. He says quietly and with
genuine contrition*) Forgive me, Nora. That was unpardonable. (*Her face lights up. Abruptly he is ashamed of being
ashamed. He looks away and grabs the decanter. Despite his
trembling hand he manages to pour a drink and get it to his
mouth and drain it. Then he sinks back in his chair and stares
at the table, waiting for the liquor to take effect. After a pause
he sighs with relief.*) I confess I needed that as medicine. I begin to feel more myself. (*He pours out another big drink and
this time his hand is steadier, and he downs it without much difficulty. He smacks his lips.*) By the Immortal, I may have sunk
to keeping an inn but at least I've a conscience in my trade.
I keep liquor a gentleman can drink. (*He starts looking over
the paper again—scowls at something—disdainfully, emphasiz-
ing his misquote of the line from Byron*) "There shall he rot—
Ambition's *dis*honored fool!" The paper is full of the latest
swindling lies of that idol of the riffraff, Andrew Jackson.
Contemptible, drunken scoundrel! But he will be the next
President, I predict, for all we others can do to prevent.
There is a cursed destiny in these decadent times. Every-
where the scum rises to the top. (*His eyes fasten on the date*

and suddenly he strikes the table with his fist.) Today is the 27th! By God, and I would have forgotten!

NORA—Forgot what?

MELODY—The anniversary of Talavera!

NORA—(*hastily*) Oh, ain't I stupid not to remember.

MELODY—(*bitterly*) I had forgotten myself and no wonder. It's a far cry from this dunghill on which I rot to that glorious day when the Duke of Wellington—Lord Wellesley, then—did me the honor before all the army to commend my bravery. (*He glances around the room with loathing.*) A far cry, indeed! It would be better to forget!

NORA—(*rallying him*) No, no, you mustn't. You've never missed celebratin' it and you won't today. I'll have a special dinner for you like I've always had.

MELODY—(*with a quick change of manner—eagerly*) Good, Nora. I'll invite Jamie Cregan. It's a stroke of fortune he is here. He served under me at Talavera, as you know. A brave soldier, if he isn't a gentleman. You can place him on my right hand. And we'll have Patch Riley to make music, and O'Dowd and Roche. If they are rabble, they're full of droll humor at times. But put them over there. (*He points to the table at left front.*) I may tolerate their presence out of charity, but I'll not sink to dining at the same table.

NORA—I'll get your uniform from the trunk, and you'll wear it for dinner like you've done each year.

MELODY—Yes, I must confess I still welcome an excuse to wear it. It makes me feel at least the ghost of the man I was then.

NORA—You're so handsome in it still, no woman could take her eyes off you.

MELODY—(*with a pleased smile*) I'm afraid you've blarney on your tongue this morning, Nora. (*then boastfully*) But it's true, in those days in Portugal and Spain— (*He stops a little shamefacedly, but Nora gives no sign of offense. He takes her hand and pats it gently—avoiding her eyes*) You have the kindest heart in the world, Nora. And I— (*His voice breaks.*)

NORA—(*instantly on the verge of grateful tears*) Ah, who wouldn't, Con darlin', when you— (*She brushes a hand across her eyes—hastily*) I'll go to the store and get something tasty.

(*Her face drops as she remembers.*) But, God help us, where's the money?

MELODY—(*stiffens—haughtily*) Money? Since when has my credit not been good?

NORA—(*hurriedly*) Don't fret, now. I'll manage. (*He returns to his newspaper, disdaining further interest in money matters.*)

MELODY—Ha. I see work on the railroad at Baltimore is progressing. (*lowering his paper*) By the Eternal, if I had not been a credulous gull and let the thieving Yankees swindle me of all I had when we came here, that's how I would invest my funds now. And I'd become rich. This country, with its immense territory cannot depend solely on creeping canal boats, as short-sighted fools would have us believe. We must have railroads. Then you will see how quickly America will become rich and great! (*His expression changes to one of bitter hatred.*) Great enough to crush England in the next war between them, which I know is inevitable! Would I could live to celebrate that victory! If I have one regret for the past— and there are few things in it that do not call for bitter regret—it is that I shed my blood for a country that thanked me with disgrace. But I will be avenged. This country—my country, now—will drive the English from the face of the earth their shameless perfidy has dishonored!

NORA—Glory be to God for that! And we'll free Ireland!

MELODY—(*contemptuously*) Ireland? What benefit would freedom be to her unless she could be freed from the Irish? (*then irritably*) But why do I discuss such things with you?

NORA—(*humbly*) I know. I'm ignorant.

MELODY—Yet I tried my best to educate you, after we came to America—until I saw it was hopeless.

NORA—You did, surely. And I tried, too, but—

MELODY—You won't even cure yourself of that damned peasant's brogue. And your daughter is becoming as bad.

NORA—She only puts on the brogue to tease you. She can speak as fine as any lady in the land if she wants.

MELODY—(*is not listening—sunk in bitter brooding*) But, in

God's name, who am I to reproach anyone with anything? Why don't you tell me to examine my own conduct?

NORA—You know I'd never.

MELODY—(*stares at her—again he is moved—quietly*) No. I know you would not, Nora. (*He looks away—after a pause*) I owe you an apology for what happened last night.

NORA—Don't think of it.

MELODY—(*with assumed casualness*) Faith, I'd a drink too many, talking over old times with Jamie Cregan.

NORA—I know.

MELODY—I am afraid I may have— The thought of old times— I become bitter. But you understand, it was the liquor talking, if I said anything to wound you.

NORA—I know it.

MELODY—(*deeply moved, puts his arm around her*) You're a sweet, kind woman, Nora—too kind. (*He kisses her.*)

NORA—(*with blissful happiness*) Ah, Con darlin', what do I care what you say when the black thoughts are on you? Sure, don't you know I love you?

MELODY—(*A sudden revulsion of feeling convulses his face. He bursts out with disgust, pushing her away from him*) For God's sake, why don't you wash your hair? It turns my stomach with its stink of onions and stew! (*He reaches for the decanter and shakingly pours a drink. Nora looks as if he had struck her.*)

NORA—(*dully*) I do be washin' it often to plaze you. But when you're standin' over the stove all day, you can't help—

MELODY—Forgive me, Nora. Forget I said that. My nerves are on edge. You'd better leave me alone.

NORA—(*her face brightening a little*) Will you ate your breakfast now? I've fine fresh eggs—

MELODY—(*grasping at this chance to get rid of her—impatiently*) Yes! In a while. Fifteen minutes, say. But leave me alone now. (*She goes out right. Melody drains his drink. Then he gets up and paces back and forth, his hands clasped behind him. The third drink begins to work and his face becomes arrogantly self-assured. He catches his reflection in the mirror on the wall at left and stops before it. He brushes a sleeve fastidiously, adjusts the set of his coat, and surveys himself.*) Thank God, I still bear the unmistakable stamp of an officer and a gentleman. And so I will remain to the end, in spite of all fate can do to crush my spirit! (*He squares his shoulders defiantly. He stares into his eyes in the glass and recites from Byron's "Childe Harold," as if it were an incantation by which he summons pride to justify his life to himself*)

"I have not loved the World, nor the World me;
I have not flattered its rank breath, nor bowed
To its idolatries a patient knee,
Nor coined my cheek to smiles,—nor cried aloud
In worship of an echo: in the crowd
They could not deem me one of such—I stood
Among them, but not of them . . ."

(*He pauses, then repeats*) "Among them, but not of them." By the Eternal, that expresses it! Thank God for you, Lord Byron—poet and nobleman who made of his disdain immortal music! (*Sara appears in the doorway at right. She has changed to her Sunday dress, a becoming blue that brings out the color of her eyes. She draws back for a moment—then stands watching him contemptuously. Melody senses her presence. He starts and turns quickly away from the mirror. For a second his expression is guilty and confused, but he immediately assumes an air of gentlemanly urbanity and bows to her.*) Ah, it's you, my dear. Are you going for a morning stroll? You've a beautiful day for it. It will bring fresh roses to your cheeks.

SARA—I don't know about roses, but it will bring a blush of shame to my cheeks. I have to beg Neilan to give us another month's credit, because you made Mother pay the feed bill for your fine thoroughbred mare! (*He gives no sign he hears this. She adds scathingly*) I hope you saw something in the mirror you could admire!

MELODY—(*in a light tone*) Faith, I suppose I must have looked a vain peacock, preening himself, but you can blame the bad light in my room. One cannot make a decent toilet in that dingy hole in the wall.

SARA—You have the best room in the house, that we ought to rent to guests.

MELODY—Oh, I've no complaints. I was merely explaining my seeming vanity.

SARA—Seeming!

MELODY—(*keeping his tone light*) Faith, Sara, you must have risen the wrong side of the bed this morning, but it takes two to make a quarrel and I don't feel quarrelsome. Quite the contrary. I was about to tell you how exceedingly charming and pretty you look, my dear.

SARA—(*with a mocking, awkward, servant's curtsy—in broad brogue*) Oh, thank ye, yer Honor.

MELODY—Every day you resemble your mother more, as she looked when I first knew her.

SARA—Musha, but it's you have the blarneyin' tongue, God forgive you!

MELODY—(*In spite of himself, this gets under his skin—angrily*) Be quiet! How dare you talk to me like a common, ignorant— You're my daughter, damn you. (*He controls himself and forces a laugh.*) A fair hit! You're a great tease, Sara. I shouldn't let you score so easily. Your mother warned me you only did it to provoke me. (*Unconsciously he reaches out for the decanter on the table—then pulls his hand back.*)

SARA—(*contemptuously—without brogue now*) Go on and drink. Surely you're not ashamed before me, after all these years.

MELODY—(*haughtily*) Ashamed? I don't understand you. A gentleman drinks as he pleases—provided he can hold his liquor as he should.

SARA—A gentleman!

MELODY—(*pleasantly again*) I hesitated because I had made a good resolve to be abstemious today. But if you insist— (*He pours a drink—a small one—his hand quite steady now.*) To your happiness, my dear. (*She stares at him scornfully. He goes on graciously.*) Will you do me the favor to sit down? I have wanted a quiet chat with you for some time. (*He holds out a chair for her at rear of the table at center.*)

SARA—(*eyes him suspiciously—then sits down*) What is it you want?

MELODY—(*with a playfully paternal manner*) Your happiness, my dear, and what I wish to discuss means happiness to you, unless I have grown blind. How is our patient, young Simon Harford, this morning?

SARA—(*curtly*) He's better.

MELODY—I am delighted to hear it. (*gallantly*) How

could he help but be with such a charming nurse? (*She stares at him coldly. He goes on.*) Let us be frank. Young Simon is in love with you. I can see that with half an eye—and, of course, you know it. And you return his love, I surmise.

SARA—Surmise whatever you please.

MELODY—Meaning you do love him? I am glad, Sara. (*He becomes sentimentally romantic.*) Requited love is the greatest blessing life can bestow on us poor mortals; and first love is the most blessed of all. As Lord Byron has it: (*He recites*)

>   "But sweeter still than this, than these, than all,
>   Is first and passionate Love—it stands alone,
>   Like Adam's recollection of his fall . . ."

SARA—(*interrupts him rudely*) Was it to listen to you recite Byron—?

MELODY—(*concealing discomfiture and resentment—pleasantly*) No. What I was leading up to is that you have my blessing, if that means anything to you. Young Harford is, I am convinced, an estimable youth. I have enjoyed my talks with him. It has been a privilege to be able to converse with a cultured gentleman again. True, he is a bit on the sober side for one so young, but by way of compensation, there is a romantic touch of the poet behind his Yankee phlegm.

SARA—It's fine you approve of him!

MELODY—In your interest I have had some enquiries made about his family.

SARA—(*angered—with taunting brogue*) Have you, indade? Musha, that's cute av you! Was it auld Patch Riley, the Piper, made them? Or was it Dan Roche or Paddy O'Dowd, or some other drunken sponge—

MELODY—(*as if he hadn't heard—condescendingly*) I find his people will pass muster.

SARA—Oh, do you? That's nice!

MELODY—Apparently, his father is a gentleman—that is, by Yankee standards, insofar as one in trade can lay claim to the title. But as I've become an American citizen myself, I suppose it would be downright snobbery to hold to old-world standards.

SARA—Yes, wouldn't it be!

MELODY—Though it is difficult at times for my pride to remember I am no longer the master of Melody Castle and

an estate of three thousand acres of as fine pasture and wood-
lands as you'd find in the whole United Kingdom, with my
stable of hunters, and—

SARA—(*bitterly*) Well, you've a beautiful thoroughbred
mare now, at least—to prove you're still a gentleman!

MELODY—(*stung into defiant anger*) Yes, I've the mare!
And by God, I'll keep her if I have to starve myself so she
may eat.

SARA—You mean, make Mother slave to keep her for you,
even if she has to starve!

MELODY—(*controls his anger—and ignores this*) But what
was I saying? Oh, yes, young Simon's family. His father will
pass muster, but it's through his mother, I believe, he comes
by his really good blood. My information is, she springs from
generations of well-bred gentlefolk.

SARA—It would be a great pride to her, I'm sure, to know
you found her suitable!

MELODY—I suppose I may expect the young man to request an interview with me as soon as he is up and about
again?

SARA—To declare his honorable intentions and ask you for
my hand, is that what you mean?

MELODY—Naturally. He is a man of honor. And there are
certain financial arrangements Simon's father or his legal representative will wish to discuss with me. The amount of your
settlement has to be agreed upon.

SARA—(*stares at him as if she could not believe her ears*) My
settlement! Simon's father! God pity you—!

MELODY—(*firmly*) Your settlement, certainly. You did not
think, I hope, that I would give you away without a penny
to your name as if you were some poverty-stricken peasant's
daughter? Please remember I have my own position to main-
tain. Of course, it is a bit difficult at present. I am temporarily
hard pressed. But perhaps a mortgage on the inn—

SARA—It's mortgaged to the hilt already, as you very well
know.

MELODY—If nothing else, I can always give my note at
hand for whatever amount—

SARA—You can give it, sure enough! But who'll take it?

MELODY—Between gentlemen, these matters can always be arranged.

SARA—God help you, it must be a wonderful thing to live in a fairy tale where only dreams are real to you. (*then sharply*) But you needn't waste your dreams worrying about my affairs. I'll thank you not to interfere. Attend to your drinking and leave me alone. (*He gives no indication that he has heard a word she has said. She stares at him and a look almost of fear comes into her eyes. She bursts out with a bitter exasperation in which there is a strong undercurrent of entreaty*) Father! Will you never let yourself wake up—not even now when you're sober, or nearly? Is it stark mad you've gone, so you can't tell any more what's dead and a lie, and what's the living truth?

MELODY—(*His face is convulsed by a spasm of pain as if something vital had been stabbed in him—with a cry of tortured appeal*) Sara! (*But instantly his pain is transformed into rage. He half rises from his chair threateningly.*) Be quiet, damn you! How dare you—! (*She shrinks away and rises to her feet. He forces control on himself and sinks back in his chair, his hands gripping the arms.*)

(*The street door at rear is flung open and Dan Roche, Paddy O'Dowd, and Patch Riley attempt to pile in together and get jammed for a moment in the doorway. They all have hangovers, and Roche is talking boisterously. Dan Roche is middle-aged, squat, bowlegged, with a potbelly and short arms lumpy with muscle. His face is flat with a big mouth, protruding ears, and red-rimmed little pig's eyes. He is dressed in dirty, patched clothes. Paddy O'Dowd is thin, round-shouldered, flat-chested, with a pimply complexion, bulgy eyes, and a droopy mouth. His manner is oily and fawning, that of a born sponger and parasite. His clothes are those of a cheap sport. Patch Riley is an old man with a thatch of dirty white hair. His washed-out blue eyes have a wandering, half-witted expression. His skinny body is clothed in rags and there is nothing under his tattered coat but his bare skin. His mouth is sunken in, toothless. He carries an Irish bagpipe under his arm.*)

ROCHE—(*His back is half turned as he harangues O'Dowd and Riley, and he does not see Melody and Sara.*) And I says, it's Andy Jackson will put you in your place, and all the slave-drivin' Yankee skinflints like you! Take your damned job, I says, and—

O'DOWD—(*warningly, his eyes on Melody*) Whist! Whist! Hold your prate! (*Roche whirls around to face Melody, and his aggressiveness oozes from him, changing to a hangdog apprehension. For Melody has sprung to his feet, his eyes blazing with an anger which is increased by the glance of contempt Sara casts from him to the three men. O'Dowd avoids Melody's eyes, busies himself in closing the door. Patch Riley stands gazing at Sara with a dreamy, admiring look, lost in a world of his own fancy, oblivious to what is going on.*)

ROCHE—(*placatingly*) Good mornin' to ye, Major.

O'DOWD—(*fawning*) Good mornin', yer Honor.

MELODY—How dare you come tramping in here in that manner! Have you mistaken this inn for the sort of dirty she-been you were used to in the old country where the pigs ran in and out the door?

O'DOWD—We ask pardon, yer Honor.

MELODY—(*to Roche—an impressive menace in his tone*) You, Paddy. Didn't I forbid you ever to mention that scoundrel Jackson's name in my house or I'd horsewhip the hide off your back? (*He takes a threatening step toward him.*) Perhaps you think I cannot carry out that threat.

ROCHE—(*backs away frightenedly*) No, no, Major. I forgot— Good mornin' to ye, Miss.

O'DOWD—Good mornin', Miss Sara. (*She ignores them. Patch Riley is still gazing at her with dreamy admiration, having heard nothing, his hat still on his head. O'Dowd officiously snatches it off for him—rebukingly*) Where's your wits, Patch? Didn't ye hear his Honor?

RILEY—(*unheeding—addresses Sara*) Sure it's you, God bless you, looks like a fairy princess as beautiful as a rose in the mornin' dew. I'll raise a tune for you. (*He starts to arrange his pipes.*)

SARA—(*curtly*) I want none of your tunes. (*Then, seeing the look of wondering hurt in the old man's eyes, she adds kindly*) That's sweet of you, Patch. I know you'd raise a beautiful tune, but I have to go out. (*Consoled, the old man smiles at her gratefully.*)

MELODY—Into the bar, all of you, where you belong! I

told you not to use this entrance! (*with disdainful tolerance*) I suppose it's a free drink you're after. Well, no one can say of me that I turned away anyone I knew thirsty from my door.

O'DOWD—Thank ye, yer Honor. Come along, Dan. (*He takes Riley's arm.*) Come on, Patch. (*The three go into the bar and O'Dowd closes the door behind them.*)

SARA—(*in derisive brogue*) Sure, it's well trained you've got the poor retainers on your American estate to respect the master! (*Then as he ignores her and casts a furtive glance at the door to the bar, running his tongue over his dry lips, she says acidly, with no trace of brogue*) Don't let me keep you from joining the gentlemen! (*She turns her back on him and goes out the street door at rear.*)

MELODY—(*His face is again convulsed by a spasm of pain— pleadingly*) Sara! (*Nora enters from the hall at right, carrying a tray with toast, eggs, bacon, and tea. She arranges his breakfast on the table at front center, bustling garrulously.*)

NORA—Have I kept you waitin'? The divil was in the toast. One lot burned black as a naygur when my back was turned. But the bacon is crisp, and the eggs not too soft, the way you like them. Come and sit down now. (*Melody does not seem to hear her. She looks at him worriedly.*) What's up with you, Con? Don't you hear me?

O'DOWD—(*pokes his head in the door from the bar*) Mickey won't believe you said we could have a drink, yer Honor, unless ye tell him.

MELODY—(*licking his lips*) I'm coming. (*He goes to the bar door.*)

NORA—Con! Have this in your stomach first! It'll all get cauld.

MELODY—(*without turning to her—in his condescendingly polite tone*) I find I am not the least hungry, Nora. I regret your having gone to so much trouble. (*He goes into the bar, closing the door behind him. Nora slumps on a chair at the rear of the table and stares at the breakfast with a pitiful helplessness. She begins to sob quietly.*)

(*Curtain*)

ACT TWO

SCENE—*Same as Act One. About half an hour has elapsed. The barroom door opens and Melody comes in. He has had two more drinks and still no breakfast, but this has had no outward effect except that his face is paler and his manner more disdainful. He turns to give orders to the spongers in the bar.*

MELODY—Remember what I say. None of your loud brawling. And you, Riley, keep your bagpipe silent, or out you go. I wish to be alone in quiet for a while with my memories. When Corporal Cregan returns, Mickey, send him in to me. He, at least, knows Talavera is not the name of a new brand of whiskey. (*He shuts the door contemptuously on Mickey's "Yes, Major" and the obedient murmur of the others. He sits at rear of the table at left front. At first, he poses to himself, striking an attitude—a Byronic hero, noble, embittered, disdainful, defying his tragic fate, brooding over past glories. But he has no audience and he cannot keep it up. His shoulders sag and he stares at the table top, hopelessness and defeat bringing a trace of real tragedy to his ruined, handsome face.*

(*The street door is opened and Sara enters. He does not hear the click of the latch, or notice her as she comes forward. Fresh from the humiliation of cajoling the storekeeper to extend more credit, her eyes are bitter. At sight of her father they become more so. She moves toward the door at right, determined to ignore him, but something unusual in his attitude strikes her and she stops to regard him searchingly. She starts to say something bitter—stops—finally, in spite of herself, she asks with a trace of genuine pity in her voice*)

SARA—What's wrong with you, Father? Are you really sick or is it just— (*He starts guiltily, ashamed of being caught in such a weak mood.*)

MELODY—(*gets to his feet politely and bows*) I beg your pardon, my dear. I did not hear you come in. (*with a deprecating smile*) Faith, I was far away in spirit, lost in memories of a glorious battle in Spain, nineteen years ago today.

SARA—(*Her face hardens.*) Oh. It's the anniversary of Talavera, is it? Well, I know what that means—a great day for the spongers and a bad day for this inn!

MELODY—(*coldly*) I don't understand you. Of course I shall honor the occasion.

SARA—You needn't tell me. I remember the other celebrations—and this year, now Jamie Cregan has appeared, you've an excuse to make it worse.

MELODY—Naturally, an old comrade in arms will be doubly welcome—

SARA—Well, I'll say this much. From the little I've seen of him, I'd rather have free whiskey go down his gullet than the others'. He's a relation, too.

MELODY—(*stiffly*) Merely a distant cousin. That has no bearing. It's because Corporal Cregan fought by my side—

SARA—I suppose you've given orders to poor Mother to cook a grand feast for you, as usual, and you'll wear your beautiful uniform, and I'll have the honor of waiting on table. Well, I'll do it just this once more for Mother's sake, or she'd have to, but it'll be the last time. (*She turns her back on him and goes to the door at right.*) You'll be pleased to learn your daughter had almost to beg on her knees to Neilan before he'd let us have another month's credit. He made it plain it was to Mother he gave it because he pities her for the husband she's got. But what do you care about that, as long as you and your fine thoroughbred mare can live in style! (*Melody is shaken for a second. He glances toward the bar as if he longed to return there to escape her. Then he gets hold of himself. His face becomes expressionless. He sits in the same chair and picks up the paper, ignoring her. She starts to go out just as her mother appears in the doorway. Nora is carrying a glass of milk.*)

NORA—Here's the milk the doctor ordered for the young gentleman. It's time for it, and I knew you'd be going upstairs.

SARA—(*takes the milk*) Thank you, Mother. (*She nods scornfully toward her father.*) I've just been telling him I begged another month's credit from Neilan, so he needn't worry.

NORA—Ah, thank God for that. Neilan's a kind man.

MELODY—(*explodes*) Damn his kindness! By the Eternal, if he'd refused, I'd have—! (*He controls himself, meeting Sara's contemptuous eyes. He goes on quietly, a bitter, sneering antagonism underneath.*) Don't let me detain you, my dear. Take his milk to our Yankee guest, as your mother suggests. Don't miss any chance to play the ministering angel. (*vindictively*) Faith, the poor young devil hasn't a chance to escape with you two scheming peasants laying snares to trap him!

SARA—That's a lie! And leave Mother out of your insults!

MELODY—And if all other tricks fail, there's always one last trick to get him through his honor!

SARA—(*tensely*) What trick do you mean? (*Nora grabs her arm.*)

NORA—Hould your prate, now! Why can't you leave him be? It's your fault, for provoking him.

SARA—(*quietly*) All right, Mother. I'll leave him to look in the mirror, like he loves to, and remember what he said, and be proud of himself. (*Melody winces. Sara goes out right.*)

MELODY—(*after a pause—shakenly*) I— She mistook my meaning— It's as you said. She goads me into losing my temper, and I say things—

NORA—(*sadly*) I know what made you say it. You think maybe she's like I was, and you can't help remembering my sin with you.

MELODY—(*guiltily vehement*) No! No! I tell you she mistook my meaning, and now you— (*then exasperatedly*) Damn your priests' prating about your sin! (*with a strange, scornful vanity*) To hear you tell it, you'd think it was you who seduced me! That's likely, isn't it?—remembering the man I was then!

NORA—I remember well. Sure, you was that handsome, no woman could resist you. And you are still.

MELODY—(*pleased*) None of your blarney, Nora. (*with Byronic gloom*) I am but a ghost haunting a ruin. (*then gallantly but without looking at her*) And how about you in those days? Weren't you the prettiest girl in all Ireland? (*scornfully*) And be damned to your lying, pious shame! You had no shame then, I remember. It was love and joy and glory in you and you were proud!

NORA—(*her eyes shining*) I'm still proud and will be to the day I die!

MELODY—(*gives her an approving look which turns to distaste at her appearance—looks away irritably*) Why do you bring up the past? I do not wish to discuss it.

NORA—(*after a pause—timidly*) All the same, you

shouldn't talk to Sara as if you thought she'd be up to anything to catch young Harford.

MELODY—I did not think that! She is my daughter—

NORA—She is surely. And he's a dacent lad. (*She smiles a
bit scornfully.*) Sure, from all she's told me, he's that shy he's
never dared even to kiss her hand!

MELODY—(*with more than a little contempt*) I can well believe it. When it comes to making love the Yankees are
clumsy, fish-blooded louts. They lack savoir-faire. They have
no romantic fire! They know nothing of women. (*He snorts
disdainfully.*) By the Eternal, when I was his age— (*then
quickly*) Not that I don't approve of young Harford, mind
you. He is a gentleman. When he asks me for Sara's hand I
will gladly give my consent, provided his father and I can
agree on the amount of her settlement.

NORA—(*hastily*) Ah, there's no need to think of that yet.
(*then lapsing into her own dream*) Yes, she'll be happy because
she loves him dearly, a lot more than she admits. And it'll
give her a chance to rise in the world. We'll see the day when
she'll live in a grand mansion, dressed in silks and satins, and
riding in a carriage with coachman and footman.

MELODY—I desire that as much as you do, Nora. I'm
done—finished—no future but the past. But my daughter
has the looks, the brains—ambition, youth— She can go far.
(*then sneeringly*) That is, if she can remember she's a gentlewoman and stop acting like a bogtrotting peasant wench! (*He
hears Sara returning downstairs.*) She's coming back. (*He gets
up—bitterly*) As the sight of me seems to irritate her, I'll go
in the bar a while. I've had my fill of her insults for one morning. (*He opens the bar door. There is a chorus of eager, thirsty
welcome from inside. He goes in, closing the door. Sara enters from
right. Her face is flushed and her eyes full of dreamy happiness.*)

NORA—(*rebukingly*) Himself went in the bar to be out of
reach of your tongue. A fine thing! Aren't you ashamed you
haven't enough feeling not to torment him, when you know
it's the anniversary—

SARA—All right, Mother. Let him take what joy he can
out of the day. I'll even help you get his uniform out of the
trunk in the attic and brush and clean it for you.

NORA—Ah, God bless you, that's the way— (*then, aston-*

ished at this unexpected docility) Glory be, but you've changed all of a sudden. What's happened to you?

SARA—I'm so happy now—I can't feel bitter against anyone. (*She hesitates—then shyly*) Simon kissed me. (*Having said this, she goes on triumphantly.*) He got his courage up at last, but it was me made him. I was freshening up his pillows and leaning over him, and he couldn't help it, if he was human. (*She laughs tenderly.*) And then you'd have laughed to see him. He near sank through the bed with shame at his boldness. He began apologizing as if he was afraid I'd be so insulted I'd never speak to him again.

NORA—(*teasingly*) And what did you do? I'll wager you wasn't as brazen as you pretend.

SARA—(*ruefully*) It's true, Mother. He made me as bashful as he was. I felt a great fool.

NORA—And was that all? Sure, kissing is easy. Didn't he ask you if you'd marry—?

SARA—No. (*quickly*) But it was my fault he didn't. He was trying to be brave enough. All he needed was a word of encouragement. But I stood there, dumb as a calf, and when I did speak it was to say I had to come and help you, and the end was I ran from the room, blushing as red as a beet— (*She comes to her mother. Nora puts her arms around her. Sara hides her face on her shoulder, on the verge of tears.*) Oh, Mother, ain't it crazy to be such a fool?

NORA—Well, when you're in love—

SARA—(*breaking away from her—angrily*) That's just it! I'm too much in love and I don't want to be! I won't let my heart rule my head and make a slave of me! (*Suddenly she smiles confidently.*) Ah well, he loves me as much, and more, I know that, and the next time I'll keep my wits. (*She laughs happily.*) You can consider it as good as done, Mother. I'm Mrs. Simon Harford, at your pleasure. (*She makes a sweeping bow.*)

NORA—(*smiling*) Arrah, none of your airs and graces with me! Help me, now, like you promised, and we'll get your father's uniform out of the trunk. It won't break your back in the attic, like it does me.

SARA—(*gaily puts her arm around her mother's waist*) Come along then.

NORA—(*as they go out right*) I disremember which trunk—

and you'll have to help me find the key. (*There is a pause. Then the bar door is opened and Melody enters again in the same manner as he did at the beginning of the act. There is the same sound of voices from the bar but this time Melody gives no parting orders but simply shuts the door behind him. He scowls with disgust.*)

MELODY—Cursed ignorant cattle. (*then with a real, lonely yearning*) I wish Jamie Cregan would come. (*bitterly*) Driven from pillar to post in my own home! Everywhere ignorance—or the scorn of my own daughter! (*then defiantly*) But by the Eternal God, no power on earth, nor in hell itself, can break me! (*His eyes are drawn irresistibly to the mirror. He moves in front of it, seeking the satisfying reassurance of his reflection there. What follows is an exact repetition of his scene before the mirror in Act One. There is the same squaring of his shoulders, arrogant lifting of his head, and then the favorite quote from Byron, recited aloud to his own image.*)

"I have not loved the World, nor the World me;
I have not flattered its rank breath, nor bowed
To its idolatries a patient knee,
Nor coined my cheek to smiles,—nor cried aloud
In the worship of an echo: in the crowd
They could not deem me one of such—I stood
Among them, but not of them . . ."

(*He stands staring in the mirror and does not hear the latch of the street door click. The door opens and Deborah [Mrs. Henry Harford], Simon's mother, enters, closing the door quietly behind her. Melody continues to be too absorbed to notice anything. For a moment, blinded by the sudden change from the bright glare of the street, she does not see him. When she does, she stares incredulously. Then she smiles with an amused and mocking relish.*

(*Deborah is forty-one, but looks to be no more than thirty. She is small, a little over five feet tall, with a fragile, youthful figure. One would never suspect that she is the middle-aged mother of two grown sons. Her face is beautiful—that is, it is beautiful from the standpoint of the artist with an eye for bone structure and unusual character. It is small, with high cheekbones, wedge-shaped, narrowing from a broad forehead to a square chin, framed by thick, wavy, red-brown hair. The nose is delicate and thin, a trifle aquiline. The mouth, with full lips and even, white teeth, is too large for her face. So are the long-lashed, green-flecked brown eyes, under heavy, angular brows. These would appear large in any face, but in hers they seem enormous and are made more startling by the pallor of her complexion. She has tiny, high-arched feet and thin, tapering hands. Her slender, fragile body is dressed in white with calculated simplicity. About her whole personality is a curious atmosphere of deliberate detachment, the studied aloofness of an ironically amused spectator. Something perversely assertive about it too, as if she consciously carried her originality to the point of whimsical eccentricity.)*

DEBORAH—I beg your pardon. (*Melody jumps and whirls around. For a moment his face has an absurdly startled, stupid look. He is shamed and humiliated and furious at being caught for the second time in one morning before the mirror. His revenge is to draw himself up haughtily and survey her insolently from head to toe. But at once, seeing she is attractive and a lady, his manner changes. Opportunity beckons and he is confident of himself, put upon his mettle. He bows, a gracious, gallant gentleman. There is seductive charm in his welcoming smile and in his voice.)*

MELODY—Good morning, Mademoiselle. It is an honor to welcome you to this unworthy inn. (*He draws out a chair at rear of the larger table in the foreground—bowing again*) If I may presume. You will find it comfortable here, away from the glare of the street.

DEBORAH—(*regards him for a second puzzledly. She is impressed in spite of herself by his bearing and distinguished, handsome face.*) Thank you. (*She comes forward. Melody makes a gallant show of holding her chair and helping her be seated. He takes in all her points with sensual appreciation. It is the same sort of pleasure a lover of horseflesh would have in the appearance of a thoroughbred horse. Meanwhile he speaks with caressing courtesy.*)

MELODY—Mademoiselle— (*He sees her wedding ring.*) Pray forgive me, I see it is Madame— Permit me to say again, how great an honor I will esteem it to be of any service. (*He manages, as he turns away, as if by accident to brush his hand against her shoulder. She is startled and caught off guard. She shrinks and looks up at him. Their eyes meet and at the nakedly physical appraisement she sees in his, a fascinated fear suddenly seizes her. But at once she is reassured as he shifts his gaze, satisfied by her reactions to his first attack, and hastens to apologize.*) I beg your pardon, Madame. I am afraid my manners have grown clumsy with disuse. It is not often a lady comes here now. This inn, like myself, has fallen upon unlucky days.

DEBORAH—(*curtly ignoring this*) I presume you are the innkeeper, Melody?

MELODY—(*a flash of anger in his eyes—arrogantly*) I am *Major* Cornelius Melody, one time of His Majesty's Seventh Dragoons, at your service. (*He bows with chill formality.*)

DEBORAH—(*is now an amused spectator again—apologetically.*) Oh. Then it is I who owe you an apology, Major Melody.

MELODY—(*encouraged—gallantly*) No, no, dear lady, the fault is mine. I should not have taken offense. (*with the air of one frankly admitting a praiseworthy weakness*) Faith, I may as well confess my besetting weakness is that of all gentlemen who have known better days. I have a pride unduly sensitive to any fancied slight.

DEBORAH—(*playing up to him now*) I assure you, sir, there was no intention on my part to slight you.

MELODY—(*His eyes again catch hers and hold them—his tone insinuatingly caressing*) You are as gracious as you are beautiful, Madame. (*Deborah's amusement is gone. She is again confused and, in spite of herself, frightened and fascinated. Melody proceeds with his attack, full of confidence now, the successful seducer of old. His voice takes on a calculated melancholy cadence. He becomes a romantic, tragic figure, appealing for a woman's understanding and loving compassion.*) I am a poor fool, Madame. I would be both wiser and happier if I could reconcile myself to being the proprietor of a tawdry tavern, if I could abjure pride and forget the past. Today of all days it is hard to forget, for it is the anniversary of the battle of Talavera. The most memorable day of my life, Madame. It was on that glorious field I had the honor to be commended for my bravery by the great Duke of Wellington, himself—Sir Arthur Wellesley, then. So I am sure you can find it in your heart to forgive— (*his tone more caressing*) One so beautiful must understand the hearts of men full well, since so many must have given their hearts to you. (*A coarse passion comes into his voice.*) Yes, I'll wager my all against a penny that even among the fish-blooded Yankees there's not a man whose heart doesn't catch flame from your beauty! (*He puts his hand over one of her hands on the table and stares into her eyes ardently.*) As mine does now!

DEBORAH—(*feeling herself borne down weakly by the sheer force of his physical strength, struggles to release her hand. She stammers, with an attempt at lightness*) Is this—what the Irish call blarney, sir?

MELODY—(*with a fierce, lustful sincerity*) No! I take my oath by the living God, I would charge a square of Napoleon's Old Guard singlehanded for one kiss of your lips. (*He bends lower, while his eyes hold hers. For a second it seems he will kiss her and she cannot help herself. Then abruptly the smell of whiskey on his breath brings her to herself, shaken with disgust and coldly angry. She snatches her hand from his and speaks with withering contempt.*)

DEBORAH—Pah! You reek of whiskey! You are drunk, sir! You are insolent and disgusting! I do not wonder your inn enjoys such meager patronage, if you regale all your guests of my sex with this absurd performance! (*Melody straightens up with a jerk, taking a step back as though he had been slapped in the face. Deborah rises to her feet, ignoring him disdainfully. At this moment Sara and her mother enter through the doorway at right. They take in the scene at a glance. Melody and Deborah do not notice their entrance.*)

NORA—(*half under her breath*) Oh, God help us!

SARA—(*guesses at once this must be the woman Mickey had told her about. She hurries toward them quickly, trying to hide her apprehension and anger and shame at what she knows must have happened.*) What is it, Father? What does the lady wish? (*Her arrival is a further blow for Melody, seething now in a fury of humiliated pride. Deborah turns to face Sara.*)

DEBORAH—(*coolly self-possessed—pleasantly*) I came here to see you, Miss Melody, hoping you might know the present whereabouts of my son, Simon. (*This is a bombshell for Melody.*)

MELODY—(*blurts out with no apology in his tone but angrily, as if she had intentionally made a fool of him*) You're his mother? In God's name, Madame, why didn't you say so!

DEBORAH—(*ignoring him—to Sara*) I've been out to his hermit's cabin, only to find the hermit flown.

SARA—(*stammers*) He's here, Mrs. Harford—upstairs in bed. He's been sick—

DEBORAH—Sick? You don't mean seriously?

SARA—(*recovering a little from her confusion*) Oh, he's over it now, or almost. It was only a spell of chills and fever he caught from the damp of the lake. I found him there shivering and shaking and made him come here where there's a doctor handy and someone to nurse him.

DEBORAH—(*pleasantly*) The someone being you, Miss Melody?

SARA—Yes, me and—my mother and I.

DEBORAH—(*graciously*) I am deeply grateful to you and your mother for your kindness.

NORA—(*who has remained in the background, now comes forward—with her sweet, friendly smile*) Och, don't be thankin' us, ma'am. Sure, your son is a gentle, fine lad, and we all have great fondness for him. He'd be welcome here if he never paid a penny— (*She stops embarrassedly, catching a disapproving glance from Sara. Deborah is repelled by Nora's slovenly appearance, but she feels her simple charm and gentleness, and returns her smile.*)

SARA—(*with embarrassed stiffness*) This is my mother, Mrs. Harford. (*Deborah inclines her head graciously. Nora instinctively bobs in a peasant's curtsy to one of the gentry. Melody, snubbed and seething, glares at her.*)

NORA—I'm pleased to make your acquaintance, ma'am.

MELODY—Nora! For the love of God, stop— (*Suddenly he is able to become the polished gentleman again—considerately and even a trifle condescendingly*) I am sure Mrs. Harford is waiting to be taken to her son. Am I not right, Madame? (*Deborah is so taken aback by his effrontery that for a moment she is speechless. She replies coldly, obviously doing so only because she does not wish to create further embarrassment.*)

DEBORAH—That is true, sir. (*She turns her back on him.*) If you will be so kind, Miss Melody. I've wasted so much of the morning and I have to return to the city. I have only time for a short visit—

SARA—Just come with me, Mrs. Harford. (*She goes to the door at right, and steps aside to let Deborah precede her.*) What a pleasant surprise this will be for Simon. He'd have written you he was sick, but he didn't want to worry you. (*She follows Deborah into the hall.*)

MELODY—Damned fool of a woman! If I'd known— No, be damned if I regret! Cursed Yankee upstart! (*with a sneer*) But she didn't fool me with her insulted airs! I've known too many women— (*in a rage*) "Absurd performance," was it? God damn her!

NORA—(*timidly*) Don't be cursing her and tormenting yourself. She seems a kind lady. She won't hold it against you, when she stops to think, knowing you didn't know who she is.

MELODY—(*tensely*) Be quiet!

NORA—Forget it now, do, for Sara's sake. Sure, you wouldn't want anything to come between her and the lad. (*He is silent. She goes on comfortingly.*) Go on up to your room now and you'll find something to take your mind off. Sara and I have your uniform brushed and laid out on the bed.

MELODY—(*harshly*) Put it back in the trunk! I don't want it to remind me— (*with humiliated rage again*) By the Eternal, I'll wager she believed what I told her of Talavera and the Great Duke honoring me was a drunken liar's boast!

NORA—No, she'd never, Con. She couldn't.

MELODY—(*seized by an idea*) Well, seeing would be believing, eh, my fine lady? Yes, by God, that will prove to her— (*He turns to Nora, his self-confidence partly restored.*) Thank you for reminding me of my duty to Sara. You are right. I do owe it to her interests to forget my anger and make a formal apology to Simon's mother for our little misunderstanding. (*He smiles condescendingly.*) Faith, as a gentleman, I should grant it is a pretty woman's privilege to be always right even when she is wrong. (*He goes to the door at extreme left front and opens it.*) If the lady should come back, kindly keep her here on some excuse until I return. (*This is a command. He disappears, closing the door behind him.*)

NORA—(*sighs*) Ah well, it's all right. He'll be on his best behavior now, and he'll feel proud again in his uniform. (*She sits at the end of center table right and relaxes wearily. A moment later Sara enters quickly from right and comes to her.*)

SARA—Where's Father?

NORA—I got him to go up and put on his uniform. It'll console him.

SARA—(*bitterly*) Console *him*? It's me ought to be consoled for having such a great fool for a father!

NORA—Hush now! How could he know who—?

SARA—(*with a sudden reversal of feeling—almost vindictively*) Yes, it serves her right. I suppose she thinks she's such a great lady anyone in America would pay her respect. Well, she knows better now. And she didn't act as insulted as she might. Maybe she liked it, for all her pretenses. (*again with an abrupt reversal of feeling*) Ah, how can I talk such craziness! Him and his drunken love-making! Well, he got put in his place, and aren't I glad! He won't forget in a hurry how she snubbed him, as if he was no better than dirt under her feet!

NORA—She didn't. She had the sense to see he'd been drinking and not to mind him.

SARA—(*dully*) Maybe. But isn't that bad enough? What woman would want her son to marry the daughter of a man like— (*She breaks down.*) Oh, Mother, I was feeling so happy and sure of Simon, and now— Why did she have to come today? If she'd waited till tomorrow, even, I'd have got him to ask me to marry him, and once he'd done that no power on earth could change him.

NORA—If he loves you no power can change him, anyway. (*proudly*) Don't I know! (*reassuringly*) She's his mother, and she loves him and she'll want him to be happy, and she'll see he loves you. What makes you think she'll try to change him?

SARA—Because she hates me, Mother—for one reason.

NORA—She doesn't. She couldn't.

SARA—She does. Oh, she acted as nice as nice, but she didn't fool me. She's the kind would be polite to the hangman, and her on the scaffold. (*She lowers her voice.*) It isn't just to pay Simon a visit she came. It's because Simon's father got a letter telling him about us, and he showed it to her.

NORA—Who did a dirty trick like that?

SARA—It wasn't signed, she said. I suppose someone around here that hates Father—and who doesn't?

NORA—Bad luck to the blackguard, whoever it was!

SARA—She said she'd come to warn Simon his father is

wild with anger and he's gone to see his lawyer— But that doesn't worry me. It's only her influence I'm afraid of.

NORA—How do you know about the letter?

SARA—(*avoiding her eyes*) I sneaked back to listen outside the door.

NORA—Shame on you! You should have more pride!

SARA—I was ashamed, Mother, after a moment or two, and I came away. (*then defiantly*) No, I'm not ashamed. I wanted to learn what tricks she might be up to, so I'll be able to fight them. I'm not ashamed at all. I'll do anything to keep him. (*lowering her voice*) She started talking the second she got in the door. She had only a few minutes because she has to be home before dinner so her husband won't suspect she came here. He's forbidden her to see Simon ever since Simon came out here to live.

NORA—Well, doesn't her coming against her husband's orders show she's on Simon's side?

SARA—Yes, but it doesn't show she wants him to marry me. (*impatiently*) Don't be so simple, Mother. Wouldn't she tell Simon that anyway, even if the truth was her husband sent her to do all she could to get him away from me?

NORA—Don't look for trouble before it comes. Wait and see, now. Maybe you'll find—

SARA—I'll find what I said, Mother—that she hates me. (*bitterly*) Even if she came here with good intentions, she wouldn't have them now, after our great gentleman has insulted her. Thank God, if he's putting on his uniform, he'll be hours before the mirror, and she'll be gone before he can make a fool of himself again. (*Nora starts to tell her the truth— then thinks better of it. Sara goes on, changing her tone.*) But I'd like her to see him in his uniform, at that, if he was sober. She'd find she couldn't look down on him— (*exasperatedly*) Och! I'm as crazy as he is. As if she hadn't the brains to see through him.

NORA—(*wearily*) Leave him be, for the love of God.

SARA—(*after a pause—defiantly*) Let her try whatever game she likes. I have brains too, she'll discover. (*then uneasily*) Only, like Simon's told me, I feel she's strange and queer behind her lady's airs, and it'll be hard to tell what she's really up to. (*They both hear a sound from upstairs.*) That's her, now.

She didn't waste much time. Well, I'm ready for her. Go in the kitchen, will you, Mother? I want to give her the chance to have it out with me alone. (*Nora gets up—then, remembering Melody's orders, glances toward the door at left front uneasily and hesitates. Sara says urgently*) Don't you hear me? Hurry, Mother! (*Nora sighs and goes out quickly, right. Sara sits at rear of the center table and waits, drawing herself up in an unconscious imitation of her father's grand manner. Deborah appears in the doorway at right. There is nothing in her expression to betray any emotion resulting from her interview with her son. She smiles pleasantly at Sara, who rises graciously from her chair.*)

DEBORAH—(*coming to her*) I am glad to find you here, Miss Melody. It gives me another opportunity to express my gratitude for your kindness to my son during his illness.

SARA—Thank you, Mrs. Harford. My mother and I have been only too happy to do all we could. (*She adds defiantly*) We are very fond of Simon.

DEBORAH—(*a glint of secret amusement in her eyes*) Yes, I feel you are. And he has told me how fond he is of you. (*Her manner becomes reflective. She speaks rapidly in a remote, detached way, lowering her voice unconsciously as if she were thinking aloud to herself.*) This is the first time I have seen Simon since he left home to seek self-emancipation at the breast of Nature. I find him not so greatly changed as I had been led to expect from his letters. Of course, it is some time since he has written. I had thought his implacably honest discovery that the poetry he hoped the pure freedom of Nature would inspire him to write is, after all, but a crude imitation of Lord Byron's would have more bitterly depressed his spirit. (*She smiles.*) But evidently he has found a new romantic dream by way of recompense. As I might have known he would. Simon is an inveterate dreamer—a weakness he inherited from me, I'm afraid, although I must admit the Harfords have been great dreamers, too, in their way. Even my husband has a dream—a conservative, material dream, naturally. I have just been reminding Simon that his father is rigidly unforgiving when his dream is flouted, and very practical in his methods of defending it. (*She smiles again.*) My warning was the mechanical gesture of a mother's duty, merely. I realized it would have no effect. He did not listen to what I said. For

that matter, neither did I. (*She laughs a little detached laugh,
as if she were secretly amused.*)

SARA—(*stares at her, unable to decide what is behind all this
and how she should react—with an undercurrent of resentment*)
I don't think Simon imitates Lord Byron. I hate Lord Byron's
poetry. And I know there's a true poet in Simon.

DEBORAH—(*vaguely surprised—speaks rapidly again*) Oh, in
feeling, of course. It is natural you should admire that in
him—now. But I warn you it is a quality difficult for a
woman to keep on admiring in a Harford, judging from what
I know of the family history. Simon's great-grandfather, Jonathan Harford, had it. He was killed at Bunker Hill, but I
suspect the War for Independence was merely a symbolic opportunity for him. His was a personal war, I am sure—for
pure freedom. Simon's grandfather, Evan Harford, had the
quality too. A fanatic in the cause of pure freedom, he became
scornful of our Revolution. It made too many compromises
with the ideal to free him. He went to France and became a
rabid Jacobin, a worshiper of Robespierre. He would have
liked to have gone to the guillotine with his incorruptible Re-
deemer, but he was too unimportant. They simply forgot to
kill him. He came home and lived in a little temple of Liberty
he had built in a corner of what is now my garden. It is still
there. I remember him well. A dry, gentle, cruel, indomitable,
futile old idealist who used frequently to wear his old uniform
of the French Republican National Guard. He died wearing
it. But the point is, you can have no idea what revengeful hate
the Harford pursuit of freedom imposed upon the women
who shared their lives. The three daughters-in-law of Jonathan, Evan's half-sisters, had to make a large, greedy fortune
out of privateering and the Northwest trade, and finally were
even driven to embrace the profits of the slave trade—as a
triumphant climax, you understand, of their long battle to
escape the enslavement of freedom by enslaving it. Evan's
wife, of course, was drawn into this conflict, and became their
tool and accomplice. They even attempted to own me, but I
managed to escape because there was so little of me in the
flesh that aged, greedy fingers could clutch. I am sorry they
are dead and cannot know you. They would approve of you,
I think. They would see that you are strong and ambitious

and determined to take what you want. They would have smiled like senile, hungry serpents and welcomed you into their coils. (*She laughs.*) Evil old witches! Detestable, but I could not help admiring them—pitying them, too—in the end. We had a bond in common. They idolized Napoleon. They used to say he was the only man they would ever have married. And I used to dream I was Josephine—even after my marriage, I'm afraid. The Sisters, as everyone called them, and all of the family accompanied my husband and me on our honeymoon—to Paris to witness the Emperor's coronation. (*She pauses, smiling at her memories.*)

SARA—(*against her will, has become a bit hypnotized by Deborah's rapid, low, musical flow of words, as she strains to grasp the implication for her. She speaks in a low, confidential tone herself, smiling naturally.*) I've always admired him too. It's one of the things I've held against my father, that he fought against him and not for him.

DEBORAH—(*starts, as if awakening—with a pleasant smile*) Well, Miss Melody, this is tiresome of me to stand here giving you a discourse on Harford family history. I don't know what you must think of me—but doubtless Simon has told you I am a bit eccentric at times. (*She glances at Sara's face— amusedly*) Ah, I can see he has. Then I am sure you will make allowances. I really do not know what inspired me—except perhaps, that I wish to be fair and warn you, too.

SARA—(*stiffens*) Warn me about what, Mrs. Harford?

DEBORAH—Why, that the Harfords never part with their dreams even when they deny them. They cannot. That is the family curse. For example, this book Simon plans to write to denounce the evil of greed and possessive ambition, and uphold the virtue of freeing oneself from the lust for power and saving our souls by being content with little. I cannot imagine you taking that seriously. (*She again flashes a glance at Sara.*) I see you do not. Neither do I. I do not even believe Simon will ever write this book on paper. But I warn you it is already written on his conscience and— (*She stops with a little disdaining laugh.*) I begin to resemble Cassandra with all my warnings. And I continue to stand here boring you with words. (*She holds out her hand graciously.*) Goodbye, Miss Melody.

SARA—(*takes her hand mechanically*) Goodbye, Mrs. Harford. (*Deborah starts for the door at rear. Sara follows her, her expression confused, suspicious, and at the same time hopeful. Suddenly she blurts out impulsively*) Mrs. Harford, I—

DEBORAH—(*turns on her, pleasantly*) Yes, Miss Melody? (*But her eyes have become blank and expressionless and discourage any attempt at further contact.*)

SARA—(*silenced—with stiff politeness*) Isn't there some sort of cooling drink I could get you before you go? You must be parched after walking from the road to Simon's cabin and back on this hot day.

DEBORAH—Nothing, thank you. (*then talking rapidly again in her strange detached way*) Yes, I did find my walk alone in the woods a strangely overpowering experience. Frightening—but intoxicating, too. Such a wild feeling of release and fresh enslavement. I have not ventured from my garden in many years. There, nature is tamed, constrained to obey and adorn. I had forgotten how compelling the brutal power of primitive, possessive nature can be—when suddenly one is attacked by it. (*She smiles.*) It has been a most confusing morning for a tired, middle-aged matron, but I flatter myself I have preserved a philosophic poise, or should I say, pose, as well as may be. Nevertheless, it will be a relief to return to my garden and books and meditations and listen indifferently again while the footsteps of life pass and recede along the street beyond the high wall. I shall never venture forth again to do my duty. It is a noble occupation, no doubt, for those who can presume they know what their duty to others is; but I— (*She laughs.*) Mercy, here I am chattering on again. (*She turns to the door.*) Cato will be provoked at me for keeping him waiting. I've already caused his beloved horses to be half-devoured by flies. Cato is our black coachman. He also is fond of Simon, although since Simon became emancipated he has embarrassed Cato acutely by shaking his hand whenever they meet. Cato was always a self-possessed free man even when he was a slave. It astonishes him that Simon has to prove that he—I mean Simon—is free. (*She smiles.*) Goodbye again, Miss Melody. This time I really am going. (*Sara opens the door for her. She walks past Sara into the street, turns left, and, passing before the two windows, disappears. Sara closes the*

*door and comes back slowly to the head of the table at center. She
stands thinking, her expression puzzled, apprehensive, and resentful. Nora appears in the doorway at right.*)

NORA—God forgive you, Sara, why did you let her go?
Your father told me—

SARA—I can't make her out, Mother. You'd think she
didn't care, but she does care. And she hates me. I could feel
it. But you can't tell— She's crazy, I think. She talked on and
on as if she couldn't stop—queer blather about Simon's
ancestors, and herself, and Napoleon, and Nature, and her
garden and freedom, and God knows what—but letting me
know all the time she had a meaning behind it, and was warning and threatening me. Oh, she may be daft in some ways,
but she's no fool. I know she didn't let Simon guess she'd
rather have him dead than married to me. Oh, no, I'm sure
she told him if he was sure he loved me and I meant his
happiness— But then she'd say he ought to wait and prove
he's sure—anything to give her time. She'd make him promise to wait. Yes, I'll wager that's what she's done!

NORA—(*who has been watching the door at left front, preoccupied by her own worry—frightenedly*) Your father'll be down
any second. I'm going out in the garden. (*She grabs Sara's
arm.*) Come along with me, and give him time to get over his
rage.

SARA—(*shakes off her hand—exasperatedly*) Leave me be,
Mother. I've enough to worry me without bothering about
him. I've got to plan the best way to act when I see Simon.
I've got to be as big a liar as she was. I'll have to pretend I
liked her and I'd respect whatever advice she gave him. I
mustn't let him see— But I won't go to him again today,
Mother. You can take up his meals and his milk, if you will.
Tell him I'm too busy. I want to get him anxious and afraid
maybe I'm mad at him for something, that maybe his mother
said something. If he once has the idea maybe he's lost me—
that ought to help, don't you think, Mother?

NORA—(*sees the door at left front begin to open—in a
whisper*) Oh, God help me! (*She turns in panicky flight and
disappears through the doorway, right.*)

(*The door at left front slowly opens—slowly because Melody,
hearing voices in the room and hoping Deborah is there, is delib-*

*erately making a dramatic entrance. And in spite of its obvious-
ness, it is effective. Wearing the brilliant scarlet full-dress uniform
of a major in one of Wellington's dragoon regiments, he looks extraordinarily handsome and distinguished—a startling, colorful,
romantic figure, possessing now a genuine quality he has not had
before, the quality of the formidably strong, disdainfully fearless
cavalry officer he really had been. The uniform has been preserved
with the greatest care. Each button is shining and the cloth is
spotless. Being in it has notably restored his self-confident arrogance. Also, he has done everything he can to freshen up his face
and hide any effect of his morning's drinks. When he discovers
Deborah is not in the room, he is mildly disappointed and, as always when he first confronts Sara alone, he seems to shrink back
guiltily within himself. Sara's face hardens and she gives no sign
of knowing he is there. He comes slowly around the table at left
front, until he stands at the end of the center table facing her. She
still refuses to notice him and he is forced to speak. He does so with
the air of one who condescends to be amused by his own foibles.)*

MELODY—I happened to go to my room and found you
and your mother had laid out my uniform so invitingly that
I could not resist the temptation to put it on at once instead
of waiting until evening.

SARA—*(turns on him. In spite of herself she is so struck by his
appearance that the contempt is forced back and she can only stammer a bit foolishly)* Yes, I—I see you did. *(There is a moment's
pause. She stares at him fascinatedly—then blurts out with impulsive admiration)* You look grand and handsome, Father.

MELODY—*(as pleased as a child)* Why, it is most kind of
you to say that, my dear Sara. *(preening himself)* I flatter myself I do not look too unworthy of the man I was when I
wore this uniform with honor.

SARA—*(an appeal forced out of her that is both pleading and
a bitter reproach)* Oh, Father, why can't you ever be the thing
you can seem to be? *(A sad scorn comes into her voice.)* The
man you were. I'm sorry I never knew that soldier. I think he
was the only man who wasn't just a dream.

MELODY—*(His face becomes a blank disguise—coldly)* I don't
understand you. *(A pause. He begins to talk in an arrogantly
amused tone.)* I suspect you are still holding against me my

unfortunate blunder with your future mother-in-law. I would not blame you if you did. (*He smiles.*) Faith, I did put my foot in it. (*He chuckles.*) The devil of it is, I can never get used to these Yankee ladies. I do them the honor of complimenting them with a bit of harmless flattery and, lo and behold, suddenly my lady acts as if I had insulted her. It must be their damned narrow Puritan background. They can't help seeing sin hiding under every bush, but this one need not have been alarmed. I never had an eye for skinny, pale snips of women— (*hastily*) But what I want to tell you is I am sorry it happened, Sara, and I will do my best, for the sake of your interests, to make honorable amends. I shall do the lady the honor of tendering her my humble apologies when she comes downstairs. (*with arrogant vanity*) I flatter myself she will be graciously pleased to make peace. She was not as outraged by half as her conscience made her pretend, if I am any judge of feminine frailty.

SARA—(*who has been staring at him with scorn until he says this last—impulsively, with a sneer of agreement*) I'll wager she wasn't for all her airs. (*then furious at herself and him*) Ah, will you stop telling me your mad dreams! (*controlling herself— coldly*) You'll have no chance to make bad worse by trying to fascinate her with your beautiful uniform. She's gone.

MELODY—(*stunned*) Gone? (*furiously*) You're lying, damn you!

SARA—I'm not. She left ten minutes ago, or more.

MELODY—(*before he thinks*) But I told your mother to keep her here until— (*He stops abruptly.*)

SARA—So that's why Mother is so frightened. Well, it was me let her go, so don't take out your rage on poor Mother.

MELODY—Rage? My dear Sara, all I feel is relief. Surely you can't believe I could have looked forward to humbling my pride, even though it would have furthered your interests.

SARA—Furthered my interests by giving her another reason to laugh up her sleeve at your pretenses? (*with angry scorn, lapsing into broad brogue*) Arrah, God pity you! (*She turns her back on him and goes off, right. Melody stands gripping the back of the chair at the foot of the table in his big, powerful hands in an effort to control himself. There is a crack as the chair back snaps in half. He stares at the fragments in his hands with stupid surprise. The door to the bar is shoved open and Mickey calls in.*)

MALOY—Here's Cregan back to see you, Major.

MELODY—(*startled, repeats stupidly*) Cregan? (*Then his face suddenly lights up with pathetic eagerness and his voice is full of welcoming warmth as he calls*) Jamie! My old comrade in arms! (*As Cregan enters, he grips his hand.*) By the Powers, I'm glad you're here, Jamie. (*Cregan is surprised and pleased by the warmth of his welcome. Melody draws him into the room.*) Come. Sit down. You'll join me in a drink, I know. (*He gets Cregan a glass from the cupboard. The decanter and Melody's glass are already on the table.*)

CREGAN—(*admiringly*) Be God, it's the old uniform, no less, and you look as fine a figure in it as ever you did in Spain. (*He sits at right of table at left front as Melody sits at rear.*)

MELODY—(*immensely pleased—deprecatingly*) Hardly, Jamie—but not a total ruin yet, I hope. I put it on in honor of the day. I see you've forgotten. For shame, you dog, not to remember Talavera.

CREGAN—(*excitedly*) Talavera, is it? Where I got my saber cut. Be the mortal, I remember it, and you've a right to celebrate. You was worth any ten men in the army that day! (*Melody has shoved the decanter toward him. He pours a drink.*)

MELODY—(*This compliment completely restores him to his arrogant self.*) Yes, I think I may say I did acquit myself with honor. (*patronizingly*) So, for that matter, did you. (*He pours a drink and raises his glass.*) To the day and your good health, Corporal Cregan.

CREGAN—(*enthusiastically*) To the day and yourself, God bless you, Con! (*He tries to touch brims with Melody's glass, but Melody holds his glass away and draws himself up haughtily.*)

MELODY—(*with cold rebuke*) I said, to the day and your good health, *Corporal Cregan.*

CREGAN—(*for a second is angry—then he grins and mutters admiringly*) Be God, it's you can bate the world and never let it change you! (*correcting his toast with emphasis*) To the day and yourself, *Major Melody.*

MELODY—(*touches his glass to Cregan's—graciously condescending*) Drink hearty, Corporal. (*They drink.*)

(*Curtain*)

ACT THREE

SCENE—*The same. The door to the bar is closed. It is around eight that evening and there are candles on the center table. Melody sits at the head of this table. In his brilliant uniform he presents more than ever an impressively colorful figure in the room, which appears smaller and dingier in the candlelight. Cregan is in the chair on his right. The other chairs at this table are unoccupied. Riley, O'Dowd, and Roche sit at the table at left front. Riley is at front, but his chair is turned sideways so he faces right. O'Dowd has the chair against the wall, facing right, with Roche across the table from him, his back to Melody. All five are drunk, Melody more so than any of them, but except for the glazed glitter in his eyes and his deathly pallor, his appearance does not betray him. He is holding his liquor like a gentleman.*

Cregan is the least drunk. O'Dowd and Roche are boisterous. The effect of the drink on Riley is merely to sink him deeper in dreams. He seems oblivious to his surroundings.

An empty and a half-empty bottle of port are on the table before Melody and Cregan, and their glasses are full. The three at the table have a decanter of whiskey.

Sara, wearing her working dress and an apron, is removing dishes and the remains of the dinner. Her face is set. She is determined to ignore them, but there is angry disgust in her eyes. Melody is arranging forks, knives, spoons, saltcellar, etc., in a plan of battle on the table before him. Cregan watches him. Patch Riley gives a few tuning-up quavers on his pipes.

MELODY—Here's the river Tagus. And here, Talavera. This would be the French position on a rise of ground with the plain between our lines and theirs. Here is our redoubt with the Fourth Division and the Guards. And here's our cavalry brigade in a valley toward our left, if you'll remember, Corporal Cregan.

CREGAN—(*excitedly*) Remember? Sure I see it as clear as yesterday!

RILEY—(*bursts into a rollicking song, accompanying himself on the pipes, his voice the quavering ghost of a tenor but still true—to the tune of "Baltiorum"*)

"She'd a pig and boneens,
 She'd a bed and a dresser,
 And a nate little room
 For the father confessor;
 With a cupboard and curtains, and something, I'm towld,
 That his riv'rance liked when the weather was cowld.
 And it's hurroo, hurroo! Biddy O'Rafferty!"

(*Roche and O'Dowd roar after him, beating time on the table with their glasses*—"Hurroo, hurroo! Biddy O'Rafferty!"—*and laugh drunkenly. Cregan, too, joins in this chorus. Melody frowns angrily at the interruption, but at the end he smiles with lordly condescension, pleased by the irreverence of the song.*)

O'DOWD—(*after a cunning glance at Melody's face to see what his reaction is—derisively*) Och, lave it to the priests, divil mend thim! Ain't it so, Major?

MELODY—Ay, damn them all! A song in the right spirit, Piper. Faith, I'll have you repeat it for my wife's benefit when she joins us. She still has a secret fondness for priests. And now, less noise, you blackguards. Corporal Cregan and I cannot hear each other with your brawling.

O'DOWD—(*smirkingly obedient*) Quiet it is, yer Honor. Be quiet, Patch. (*He gives the old man, who is lost in dreams, a shove that almost knocks him off his chair. Riley stares at him bewilderedly. O'Dowd and Roche guffaw.*)

MELODY—(*scowls at them, then turns to Cregan*) Where was I, Corporal? Oh, yes, we were waiting in the valley. We heard a trumpet from the French lines and saw them forming for the attack. An aide-de-camp galloped down the hill to us—

SARA—(*who has been watching him disdainfully, reaches out to take his plate—rudely in mocking brogue*) I'll have your plate, av ye plaze, Major, before your gallant dragoons charge over it and break it.

MELODY—(*holds his plate on the table with one hand so she cannot take it, and raises his glass of wine with the other—ignoring her*) Wet your lips, Corporal. Talavera was a devilish thirsty day, if you'll remember. (*He drinks.*)

CREGAN—(*glances uneasily at Sara*) It was that. (*He drinks.*)

MELODY—(*smacking his lips*) Good wine, Corporal. Thank God, I still have wine in my cellar fit for a gentleman.

SARA—(*angrily*) Are you going to let me take your plate?

MELODY—(*ignoring her*) No, I have no need to apologize for the wine. Nor for the dinner, for that matter. Nora is a good cook when she forgets her infernal parsimony and buys food that one can eat without disgust. But I do owe you an apology for the quality of the service. I have tried to teach the waitress not to snatch plates from the table as if she were feeding dogs in a kennel but she cannot learn. (*He takes his hand from the plate—to Sara*) There. Now let me see you take it properly. (*She stares at him for a moment, speechless with anger—then snatches the plate from in front of him.*)

CREGAN—(*hastily recalls Melody to the battlefield*) You were where the aide-de-camp galloped up to us, Major. It was then the French artillery opened on us. (*Sara goes out right, carrying a tray laden with plates.*)

MELODY—We charged the columns on our left—here— (*he marks the tablecloth*) that were pushing back the Guards. I'll never forget the blast of death from the French squares. And then their chasseurs and lancers were on us! By God, it's a miracle any of us came through!

CREGAN—You wasn't touched except you'd a bullet through your coat, but I had this token on my cheek to remember a French saber by.

MELODY—Brave days, those! By the Eternal, then one lived! Then one forgot! (*He stops—when he speaks again it is bitterly.*) Little did I dream then the disgrace that was to be my reward later on.

CREGAN—(*consolingly*) Ah well, that's the bad luck of things. You'd have been made a colonel soon, if you'd left the Spanish woman alone and not fought that duel.

MELODY—(*arrogantly threatening*) Are you presuming to question my conduct in that affair, Corporal Cregan?

CREGAN—(*hastily*) Sorra a bit! Don't mind me, now.

MELODY—(*stiffly*) I accept your apology. (*He drinks the rest of his wine, pours another glass, then stares moodily before him. Cregan drains his glass and refills it.*)

O'DOWD—(*peering past Roche to watch Melody, leans across to Roche—in a sneering whisper*) Ain't he the lunatic, sittin' like a play-actor in his red coat, lyin' about his battles with the French!

Roche—(*sullenly—but careful to keep his voice low*) He'd ought to be shamed he ivir wore the bloody red av England, God's curse on him!

O'Dowd—Don't be wishin' him harm, for it's thirsty we'd be without him. Drink long life to him, and may he always be as big a fool as he is this night! (*He sloshes whiskey from the decanter into both their glasses.*)

Roche—(*with a drunken leer*) Thrue for you! I'll toast him on that. (*He twists round to face Melody, holds up his glass and bawls*) To the grandest gintleman ivir come from the shores av Ireland! Long life to you, Major!

O'Dowd—Hurroo! Long life, yer Honor!

Riley—(*awakened from his dream, mechanically raises his glass*) And to all that belong to ye.

Melody—(*startled from his thoughts, becomes at once the condescending squire—smiling tolerantly*) I said, less noise, you dogs. All the same, I thank you for your toast. (*They drink. A pause. Abruptly Melody begins to recite from Byron. He reads the verse well, quietly, with a bitter eloquence.*)

"But midst the crowd, the hum, the shock of men,
    To hear, to see, to feel, and to possess,
    And roam along, the World's tired denizen,
    With none who bless us, none whom we can bless;
    Minions of Splendour shrinking from distress!
    None that, with kindred consciousness endued,
    If we were not, would seem to smile the less,
    Of all that flattered—followed—sought, and sued;
    This is to be alone— This, this is Solitude!"

(*He stops and glances from one face to another. Their expressions are all blank. He remarks with insulting derisiveness*) What? You do not understand, my lads? Well, all the better for you. So may you go on fooling yourselves that I am fooled in you. (*then with a quick change of mood, heartily*) Give us a hunting song, Patch. You've not forgotten "Modideroo," I'll be bound.

Riley—(*roused to interest immediately*) Does a duck forget wather? I'll show ye! (*He begins the preliminary quavers on his pipes.*)

O'Dowd—Modideroo!

Roche—Hurroo!

RILEY—(*accompanying himself, sings with wailing melancholy the first verse that comes to his mind of an old hunting song*)
> "And the fox set him down and looked about,
>   And many were feared to follow;
> 'Maybe I'm wrong,' says he, 'but I doubt
>   That you'll be as gay tomorrow.
> For loud as you cry, and high as you ride,
>   And little you feel my sorrow,
> I'll be free on the mountainside
>   While you'll lie low tomorrow.'
>   Oh, Modideroo, aroo, aroo!"

(*Melody, excited now, beats time on the table with his glass along with Cregan, Roche, and O'Dowd, and all bellow the refrain,* "Oh, Modideroo, aroo, aroo!")

MELODY—(*his eyes alight, forgetting himself, a strong lilt of brogue coming into his voice*) Ah, that brings it back clear as life! Melody Castle in the days that's gone! A wind from the south, and a sky gray with clouds—good weather for the hounds. A true Irish hunter under me that knows and loves me and would raise to a jump over hell if I gave the word! To hell with men, I say!—and women, too!—with their cowardly hearts rotten and stinking with lies and greed and treachery! Give me a horse to love and I'll cry quits to men! And then away, with the hounds in full cry, and after them! Off with divil a care for your neck, over ditches and streams and stone walls and fences, the fox doubling up the mountainside through the furze and the heather—! (*Sara has entered from right as he begins this longing invocation of old hunting days. She stands behind his chair, listening contemptuously. He suddenly feels her presence and turns his head. When he catches the sneer in her eyes, it is as if cold water were dashed in his face. He addresses her as if she were a servant.*) Well? What is it? What are you waiting for now?

SARA—(*roughly, with coarse brogue*) What would I be waitin' for but for you to get through with your blather about lovin' horses, and give me a chance to finish my work? Can't you—and the other gintlemen—finish gettin' drunk in the bar and lave me clear the tables? (*O'Dowd conceals a grin behind his hand; Roche stifles a malicious guffaw.*)

CREGAN—(*with an apprehensive glance at Melody, shakes his

head at her admonishingly) Now, Sara, be aisy. (*But Melody suppresses any angry reaction. He rises to his feet, a bit stiffly and carefully, and bows.*)

MELODY—(*coldly*) I beg your pardon if we have interfered with your duties. (*to O'Dowd and his companions*) Into the bar, you louts!

O'DOWD—The bar it is, sorr. Come, Dan. Wake up, Patch. (*He pokes the piper. He and Roche go into the bar, and Riley stumbles vaguely after them. Cregan waits for Melody.*)

MELODY—Go along, Corporal. I'll join you presently. I wish to speak to my daughter.

CREGAN—All right, Major. (*He again shakes his head at Sara, as if to say, don't provoke him. She ignores him. He goes into the bar, closing the door behind him. She stares at her father with angry disgust.*)

SARA—You're drunk. If you think I'm going to stay here and listen to—

MELODY—(*his face expressionless, draws out his chair at the head of the center table for her—politely*) Sit down, my dear.

SARA—I won't. I have no time. Poor Mother is half dead on her feet. I have to help her. There's a pile of dishes to wash after your grand anniversary feast! (*with bitter anger*) Thank God it's over, and it's the last time you'll ever take satisfaction in having me wait on table for drunken scum like O'Dowd and—

MELODY—(*quietly*) A daughter who takes satisfaction in letting even the scum see that she hates and despises her father! (*He shrugs his shoulders.*) But no matter. (*indicating the chair again*) Won't you sit down, my dear?

SARA—If you ever dared face the truth, you'd hate and despise yourself! (*passionately*) All I pray to God is that some-day when you're admiring yourself in the mirror something will make you see at last what you really are! That will be revenge in full for all you've done to Mother and me! (*She waits defiantly, as if expecting him to lose his temper and curse her. But Melody acts as if he had not heard her.*)

MELODY—(*his face expressionless, his manner insistently bland and polite*) Sit down, my dear. I will not detain you long, and I think you will find what I have to tell you of great interest. (*She searches his face, uneasy now, feeling a threat hidden behind his cold, quiet, gentlemanly tone. She sits down and he sits at rear of table, with an empty chair separating them.*)

SARA—You'd better think well before you speak, Father. I know the devil that's in you when you're quiet like this with your brain mad with drink.

MELODY—I don't understand you. All I wish is to relate something which happened this afternoon.

SARA—(*giving way to bitterness at her humiliation again—sneeringly*) When you went riding on your beautiful thoroughbred mare while Mother and I were sweating and suffocating in the heat of the kitchen to prepare your Lordship's banquet? Sure, I hope you didn't show off and jump your beauty over a fence into somebody's garden, like you've done before, and then have to pay damages to keep out of jail!

MELODY—(*roused by mention of his pet—disdainfully*) The damned Yankee yokels should feel flattered that she deigns to set her dainty hooves in their paltry gardens! She's a truer-born, well-bred lady than any of their women—than the one who paid us a visit this morning, for example.

SARA—Mrs. Harford was enough of a lady to put you in your place and make a fool of you.

MELODY—(*seemingly unmoved by this taunt—calmly*) You are very simple-minded, my dear, to let yourself be taken in by such an obvious bit of clever acting. Naturally, the lady was a bit discomposed when she heard you and your mother coming, after she had just allowed me to kiss her. She had to pretend—

SARA—(*eagerly*) She let you kiss her? (*then disgustedly*) It's a lie, but I don't doubt you've made yourself think it's the truth by now. (*angrily*) I'm going. I don't want to listen to the whiskey in you boasting of what never happened—as usual! (*She puts her hands on the table and starts to rise.*)

MELODY—(*with a quick movement pins hers down with one of his*) Wait! (*A look of vindictive cruelty comes into his eyes—quietly*) Why are you so jealous of the mare, I wonder? Is it because she has such slender ankles and dainty feet? (*He takes his hand away and stares at her hands—with disgust, commandingly*) Keep your thick wrists and ugly, peasant paws off the table in my presence, if you please! They turn my stomach! I advise you never to let Simon get a good look at them—

SARA—(*instinctively jerks her hands back under the table guiltily. She stammers*) You—you cruel devil! I knew you'd—

MELODY—(*for a second is ashamed and really contrite*) Forgive me, Sara. I didn't mean—the whiskey talking—as you said. (*He adds in a forced tone, a trace of mockery in it*) An absurd taunt, when you really have such pretty hands and feet, my dear. (*She jumps to her feet, so hurt and full of hatred her lips tremble and she cannot speak. He speaks quietly.*) Are you going? I was about to tell you of the talk I had this afternoon with young Harford. (*She stares at him in dismay. He goes on easily.*) It was after I returned from my ride. I cantered the mare by the river and she pulled up lame. So I dismounted and led her back to the barn. No one noticed my return and when I went upstairs it occurred to me I would not find again such an opportunity to have a frank chat with Harford—free from interruptions. (*He pauses, as if he expects her to be furious, but she remains tensely silent, determined not to let him know her reaction.*) I did not beat about the bush. I told him he must appreciate, as a gentleman, it was my duty as your father to demand he lay his cards on the table. I said he must realize that even before you began nursing him here and going alone to his bedroom, there was a deal of gossip about your visits to his cabin, and your walks in the woods with him. I put it to him that such an intimacy could not continue without gravely compromising your reputation.

SARA—(*stunned—weakly*) God forgive you! And what did he say?

MELODY—What could he say? He is a man of honor. He looked damn embarrassed and guilty for a moment, but when he found his tongue, he agreed with me most heartily. He said his mother had told him the same thing.

SARA—Oh, she did, did she? I suppose she did it to find out by watching him how far—

MELODY—(*coldly*) Well, why not? Naturally, it was her duty as his mother to discover all she could about you. She is a woman of the world. She would be bound to suspect that you might be his mistress.

SARA—(*tensely*) Oh, would she!

MELODY—But that's beside the point. The point is, my

bashful young gentleman finally blurted out that he wanted to marry you.

SARA—(*forgetting her anger—eagerly*) He told you that?

MELODY—Yes, and he said he had told his mother, and she had said all she wanted was his happiness but she felt in fairness to you and to himself—and I presume she also meant to both families concerned—he should test his love and yours by letting a decent interval of time elapse before your marriage. She mentioned a year, I believe.

SARA—(*angrily*) Ah! Didn't I guess that would be her trick!

MELODY—(*lifting his eyebrows—coldly*) Trick? In my opinion, the lady displayed more common sense and knowledge of the world than I thought she possessed. The reasons she gave him are sound and show a consideration for your good name which ought to inspire gratitude in you and not suspicion.

SARA—Arrah, don't tell me she's made a fool of you again! A lot of consideration she has for me!

MELODY—She pointed out to him that if you were the daughter of some family in their own little Yankee clique, there would be no question of a hasty marriage, and so he owed it to you—

SARA—I see. She's the clever one!

MELODY—Another reason was—and here your Simon stammered so embarrassedly I had trouble making him out—she warned him a sudden wedding would look damnably suspicious and start a lot of evil-minded gossip.

SARA—(*tensely*) Oh, she's clever, all right! But I'll beat her.

MELODY—I told him I agreed with his mother. It is obvious that were there a sudden wedding without a suitable period of betrothal, everyone would believe—

SARA—I don't care what they believe! Tell me this! Did she get him to promise her he'd wait? (*before he can answer—bitterly*) But of course she did! She'd never have left till she got that out of him!

MELODY—(*ignores this*) I told him I appreciated the honor he did me in asking for your hand, but he must understand that I could not commit myself until I had talked to his father and was assured the necessary financial arrangements could be concluded to our mutual satisfaction. There was the amount of settlement to be agreed upon, for instance.

SARA—That dream, again! God pity you! (*She laughs helplessly and a bit hysterically.*) And God help Simon. He must have thought you'd gone out of your mind! What did he say?

MELODY—He said nothing, naturally. He is well bred and he knows this is a matter he must leave to his father to discuss. There is also the equally important matter of how generous an allowance Henry Harford is willing to settle on his son. I did not mention this to Simon, of course, not wishing to embarrass him further with talk of money.

SARA—Thank God for that, at least! (*She giggles hysterically.*)

MELODY—(*quietly*) May I ask what you find so ridiculous in an old established custom? Simon is an elder son, the heir to his father's estate. No matter what their differences in the past may have been, now that Simon has decided to marry and settle down his father will wish to do the fair thing by him. He will realize, too, that although there is no more honorable calling than that of poet and philosopher, which his son has chosen to pursue, there is no decent living to be gained by its practice. So naturally he will settle an allowance on Simon, and I shall insist it be a generous one, befitting your position as my daughter. I will tolerate no niggardly trader's haggling on his part.

SARA—(*stares at him fascinatedly, on the edge of helpless, hysterical laughter*) I suppose it would never occur to you that old Harford might not think it an honor to have his son marry your daughter.

MELODY—(*calmly*) No, it would never occur to me—and if it should occur to him, I would damned soon disabuse his mind. Who is he but a money-grubbing trader? I would remind him that I was born in a castle and there was a time when I possessed wealth and position, and an estate compared to which any Yankee upstart's home in this country is but a hovel stuck in a cabbage patch. I would remind him that you, my daughter, were born in a castle!

SARA—(*impulsively, with a proud toss of her head*) Well, that's no more than the truth. (*then furious with herself and him*) Och, what crazy blather! (*She springs to her feet.*) I've had enough of your mad dreams!

MELODY—Wait! I haven't finished yet. (*He speaks quietly, but as he goes on there is an increasing vindictiveness in his tone.*) There was another reason why I told young Harford I could not make a final decision. I wished time to reflect on a further aspect of this proposed marriage. Well, I have been reflecting, watching you and examining your conduct, without prejudice, trying to be fair to you and make every possible allowance— (*He pauses.*) Well, to be brutally frank, my dear, all I can see in you is a common, greedy, scheming, cunning peasant girl, whose only thought is money and who has shamelessly thrown herself at a young man's head because his family happens to possess a little wealth and position.

SARA—(*trying to control herself*) I see your game, Father. I told you when you were drunk like this— But this time, I won't give you the satisfaction— (*Then she bursts out angrily*) It's a lie! I love Simon, or I'd never—

MELODY—(*as if she hadn't spoken*) So, I have about made up my mind to decline for you Simon Harford's request for your hand in marriage.

SARA—(*jeers angrily now*) Oh, you have, have you? As if I cared a damn what you—!

MELODY—As a gentleman, I feel I have a duty, in honor, to Simon. Such a marriage would be a tragic misalliance for him—and God knows I know the sordid tragedy of such a union.

SARA—It's Mother has had the tragedy!

MELODY—I hold young Harford in too high esteem. I cannot stand by and let him commit himself irrevocably to what could only bring him disgust and bitterness, and ruin to all his dreams.

SARA—So I'm not good enough for him, you've decided now?

MELODY—That is apparent from your every act. No one, no matter how charitably inclined, could mistake you for a lady. I have tried to make you one. It was an impossible task. God Himself cannot transform a sow's ear into a silk purse!

SARA—(*furiously*) Father!

MELODY—Young Harford needs to be saved from himself. I can understand his physical infatuation. You are pretty. So was your mother pretty once. But marriage is another matter. The man who would be the ideal husband for you, from a standpoint of conduct and character, is Mickey Maloy, my bartender, and I will be happy to give him my parental blessing—

SARA—Let you stop now, Father!

MELODY—You and he would be congenial. You can match tongues together. He's a healthy animal. He can give you a raft of peasant brats to squeal and fight with the pigs on the mud floor of your hovel.

SARA—It's the dirty hut in which your father was born and raised you're remembering, isn't it?

MELODY—(*stung to fury, glares at her with hatred. His voice quivers but is deadly quiet.*) Of course, if you trick Harford into getting you with child, I could not refuse my consent. (*Letting go, he bangs his fist on the table.*) No, by God, even then, when I remember my own experience, I'll be damned if I could with a good conscience advise him to marry you!

SARA—(*glaring back at him with hatred*) You drunken devil! (*She makes a threatening move toward him, raising her hand as if she were going to slap his face—then she controls herself and speaks with quiet, biting sarcasm.*) Consent or not, I want to thank you for your kind fatherly advice on how to trick Simon. I don't think I'll need it but if the worst comes to the worst I promise you I'll remember—

MELODY—(*coldly, his face expressionless*) I believe I have said all I wished to say to you. (*He gets up and bows stiffly.*) If you will excuse me, I shall join Corporal Cregan. (*He goes to the bar door. Sara turns and goes quietly out right, forgetting to clear the few remaining dishes on the center table. His back turned, he does not see her go. With his hand on the knob of the bar door, he hesitates. For a second he breaks—torturedly*) Sara! (*then quietly*) There are things I said which I regret—even now. I— I trust you will overlook— As your mother knows, it's the liquor talking, not— I must admit that, due to my celebrating the anniversary, my brain is a bit addled by whiskey—as you said. (*He waits, hoping for a word of forgiveness. Finally, he glances over his shoulder. As he discovers she is not there and has not heard him, for a second he crumbles, his soldierly erectness sags and his face falls. He looks sad and hopeless and bitter and old, his eyes wandering dully. But, as in the two preceding acts, the mirror attracts him, and as he moves from the bar door to stand before it he assumes his arrogant, Byronic pose again. He repeats in each detail his pantomime before the mirror. He speaks proudly.)* My-self to the bitter end! No weakening, so help me God! *(There is a knock on the street door but he does not hear it. He starts his familiar incantation quotes from Byron.)*

"I have not loved the World, nor the World me;
I have not flattered its rank breath, nor bowed
To its idolatries a patient knee . . ."

(The knock on the door is repeated more loudly. Melody starts guilt-ily and steps quickly away from the mirror. His embarrassment is transformed into resentful anger. He calls) Come in, damn you! Do you expect a lackey to open the door for you? *(The door opens and Nicholas Gadsby comes in. Gadsby is in his late forties, short, stout, with a big, bald head, round, florid face, and small, blue eyes. A rigidly conservative, best-family attorney, he is stiffly correct in dress and manner, dryly portentous in speech, and ex-tremely conscious of his professional authority and dignity. Now, however, he is venturing on unfamiliar ground and is by no means as sure of himself as his manner indicates. The unexpected vision of Melody in his uniform startles him and for a second he stands, as close to gaping as he can be, impressed by Melody's handsome distinction. Melody, in his turn, is surprised. He had not thought the intruder would be a gentleman. He unbends, although his tone is still a bit curt. He bows a bit stiffly, and Gadsby finds himself returning the bow.)* Your pardon, sir. When I called, I thought it was one of the damned riffraff mistaking the bar-room door. Pray be seated, sir. *(Gadsby comes forward and takes the chair at the head of the center table, glancing at the few dirty dishes on it with distaste. Melody says)* Your pardon again, sir. We have been feasting late, which accounts for the dis-array. I will summon a servant to inquire your pleasure.

GADSBY—*(beginning to recover his aplomb—shortly)* Thank you, but I want nothing, sir. I came here to seek a private interview with the proprietor of this tavern, by name, Mel-ody. *(He adds a bit hesitantly)* Are you, by any chance, he?

MELODY—*(stiffens arrogantly)* I am not, sir. But if you

wish to see Major Cornelius Melody, one time of His Majesty's Seventh Dragoons, who served with honor under the Duke of Wellington in Spain, I am he.

GADSBY—(*dryly*) Very well, sir. Major Melody, then.

MELODY—(*does not like his tone—insolently sarcastic*) And whom have I the *honor* of addressing? (*As Gadsby is about to reply, Sara enters from right, having remembered the dishes. Melody ignores her as he would a servant. Gadsby examines her carefully as she gathers up the dishes. She notices him staring at her and gives him a resentful, suspicious glance. She carries the dishes out, right, to the kitchen, but a moment later she can be seen just inside the hall at right, listening. Meanwhile, as soon as he thinks she has gone, Gadsby speaks.*)

GADSBY—(*with affected casualness*) A pretty young woman. Is she your daughter, sir? I seemed to detect a resemblance—

MELODY—(*angrily*) No! Do I look to you, sir, like a man who would permit his daughter to work as a waitress? Resemblance to me? You must be blind, sir. (*coldly*) I am still waiting for you to inform me who you are and why you should wish to see me.

GADSBY—(*hands him a card—extremely nettled by Melody's manner—curtly*) My card, sir.

MELODY—(*glances at the card*) Nicholas Gadsby. (*He flips it aside disdainfully.*) Attorney, eh? The devil take all your tribe, say I. I have small liking for your profession, sir, and I cannot imagine what business you can have with me. The damned thieves of the law did their worst to me many years ago in Ireland. I have little left to tempt you. So I do not see— (*Suddenly an idea comes to him. He stares at Gadsby, then goes on in a more friendly tone.*) That is, unless— Do you happen by any chance to represent the father of young Simon Harford?

GADSBY—(*indignant at Melody's insults to his profession—with a thinly veiled sneer*) Ah, then you were expecting— That makes things easier. We need not beat about the bush. I do represent Mr. Henry Harford, sir.

MELODY—(*thawing out, in his total misunderstanding of the situation*) Then accept my apologies, sir, for my animadversions against your profession. I am afraid I may be prejudiced. In the army, we used to say we suffered more casualties from your attacks at home than the French ever inflicted. (*He sits down on the chair on Gadsby's left, at rear of table—remarking with careless pride*) A word of explanation as to why you find me in uniform. It is the anniversary of the battle of Talavera, sir, and—

GADSBY—(*interrupts dryly*) Indeed, sir? But I must tell you my time is short. With your permission, we will proceed at once to the matter in hand.

MELODY—(*controlling his angry discomfiture—coldly*) I think I can hazard a guess as to what that matter is. You have come about the settlement?

GADSBY—(*misunderstanding him, replies in a tone almost openly contemptuous*) Exactly, sir. Mr. Harford was of the opinion, and I agreed with him, that a settlement would be foremost in your mind.

MELODY—(*scowls at his tone but, as he completely misunderstands Gadsby's meaning, he forces himself to bow politely*) It does me honor, sir, that Mr. Harford appreciates he is dealing with a gentleman and has the breeding to know how these matters are properly arranged. (*Gadsby stares at him, absolutely flabbergasted by what he considers a piece of the most shameless effrontery. Melody leans toward him confidentially.*) I will be frank with you, sir. The devil of it is, this comes at a difficult time for me. Temporary, of course, but I cannot deny I am pinched at the moment—devilishly pinched. But no matter. Where my only child's happiness is at stake, I am prepared to make every possible effort. I will sign a note of hand, no matter how ruinous the interest demanded by the scoundrelly moneylenders. By the way, what amount does Mr. Harford think proper? Anything in reason—

GADSBY—(*listening in utter confusion, finally gets the idea Melody is making him the butt of a joke—fuming*) I do not know what you are talking about, sir, unless you think to make a fool of me! If this is what is known as Irish wit—

MELODY—(*bewildered for a second—then in a threatening tone*) Take care, sir, and watch your words or I warn you you will repent them, no matter whom you represent! No damned pettifogging dog can insult me with impunity! (*As Gadsby draws back apprehensively, he adds with insulting disdain*) As for making a fool of you, sir, I would be the fool if I attempted to improve on God's handiwork!

GADSBY—(*ignoring the insults, forces a placating tone*) I wish no quarrel with you, sir. I cannot for the life of me see— I fear we are dealing at cross-purposes. Will you tell me plainly what you mean by your talk of settlement?

MELODY—Obviously, I mean the settlement I am prepared to make on my daughter. (*As Gadsby only looks more dumfounded, he continues sharply.*) Is not your purpose in coming here to arrange, on Mr. Harford's behalf, for the marriage of his son with my daughter?

GADSBY—Marriage? Good God, no! Nothing of the kind!

MELODY—(*dumfounded*) Then what have you come for?

GADSBY—(*feeling he has now the upper hand—sharply*) To inform you that Mr. Henry Harford is unalterably opposed to any further relationship between his son and your daughter, whatever the nature of that relationship in the past.

MELODY—(*leans forward threateningly*) By the Immortal, sir, if you dare insinuate—!

GADSBY—(*draws back again, but he is no coward and is determined to carry out his instructions*) I insinuate nothing, sir. I am here on Mr. Harford's behalf, to make you an offer. That is what I thought you were expecting when you mentioned a settlement. Mr. Harford is prepared to pay you the sum of three thousand dollars—provided, mark you, that you and your daughter sign an agreement I have drawn up which specifies that you relinquish all claims, of whatever nature. And also provided you agree to leave this part of the country at once with your family. Mr. Harford suggests it would be advisable that you go West—to Ohio, say.

MELODY—(*so overcome by a rising tide of savage, humiliated fury, he can only stammer hoarsely*) So Henry Harford does me the honor—to suggest that, does he?

GADSBY—(*watching him uneasily, attempts a reasonable, persuasive tone*) Surely you could not have spoken seriously when you talked of marriage. There is such a difference in station. The idea is preposterous. If you knew Mr. Harford, you would realize he would never countenance—

MELODY—(*His pent-up rage bursts out—smashing his fist on*

the table) Know him? By the Immortal God, I'll know him
soon! And he'll know me! (*He springs to his feet.*) But first,
you Yankee scum, I'll deal with you! (*He draws back his fist to
smash Gadsby in the face, but Sara has run from the door at right
and she grabs his arm. She is almost as furious as he is and there
are tears of humiliated pride in her eyes.*)

SARA—Father! Don't! He's only a paid lackey. Where is
your pride that you'd dirty your hands on the like of him?
(*While she is talking the door from the bar opens and Roche,
O'Dowd, and Cregan crowd into the room. Mickey stands in the
doorway. Nora follows Sara in from right.*)

ROCHE—(*with drunken enthusiasm*) It's a fight! For the
love of God, clout the damned Yankee, Major!

MELODY—(*controls himself—his voice shaking*) You are
right, Sara. It would be beneath me to touch such a vile lick-
spittle. But he won't get off scot-free. (*sharply, a commander
ordering his soldiers*) Here you, Roche and O'Dowd! Get hold
of him! (*They do so with enthusiasm and yank Gadsby from his
chair.*)

GADSBY—You drunken ruffians! Take your hands off me!

MELODY—(*addressing him—in his quiet, threatening tone
now*) You may tell the swindling trader, Harford, who em-
ploys you that he'll hear from me! (*to Roche and O'Dowd*)
Throw this thing out! Kick it down to the crossroads!

ROCHE—Hurroo! (*He and O'Dowd run Gadsby to the door
at rear. Cregan jumps ahead, grinning, and opens the door for
them.*)

GADSBY—(*struggling futilely as they rush him through the
door*) You scoundrels! Take your hands off me! Take— (*Melody looks after them. The two women watch him, Nora frightened,
Sara with a strange look of satisfied pride.*)

CREGAN—(*in the doorway, looking out—laughing*) Oh, it'd
do your heart good, Con, to see the way they're kicking his
butt down the street! (*He comes in and shuts the door.*)

MELODY—(*his rage welling again, as his mind dwells on his
humiliation—starting to pace up and down*) It's with his master
I have to deal, and, by the Powers, I'll deal with him! You'll
come with me, Jamie. I'll want you for a witness. He'll apologize to me—more than that, he'll come back here this very
night and apologize publicly to my daughter, or else he meets

me in the morning! By God, I'll face him at ten paces or across a handkerchief! I'll put a bullet through him, so help me, Christ!

NORA—(*breaks into a dirgelike wail*) God forgive you, Con, is it a duel again—murtherin' or gettin' murthered?

MELODY—Be quiet, woman! Go back to your kitchen! Go, do you hear me! (*Nora turns obediently toward the door at right, beginning to cry.*)

SARA—(*puts an arm around her mother. She is staring at Melody apprehensively now.*) There, Mother, don't worry. Father knows that's all foolishness. He's only talking. Go on now in the kitchen and sit down and rest, Mother. (*Nora goes out right. Sara closes the door after her and comes back.*)

MELODY—(*turns on her with bitter anger*) Only talking, am I? It's the first time in my life I ever heard anyone say Con Melody was a coward! It remains for my own daughter—!

SARA—(*placatingly*) I didn't say that, Father. But can't you see—you're not in Ireland in the old days now. The days of duels are long past and dead, in this part of America anyway. Harford will never fight you. He—

MELODY—He won't, won't he? By God, I'll make him! I'll take a whip. I'll drag him out of his house and lash him down the street for all his neighbors to see! He'll apologize, or he'll fight, or I'll brand him a craven before the world!

SARA—(*frightened now*) But you'll never be let see him! His servants will keep you out! He'll have the police arrest you, and it'll be in the papers about another drunken Mick raising a crazy row! (*She appeals to Cregan.*) Tell him I'm telling the truth, Jamie. You've still got some sober sense in you. Maybe he'll listen to you.

CREGAN—(*glances at Melody uneasily*) Maybe Sara's right, Major.

MELODY—When I want your opinion, I'll ask for it! (*sneeringly*) Of course, if you've become such a coward you're afraid to go with me—

CREGAN—(*stung*) Coward, is ut? I'll go, and be damned to you!

SARA—Jamie, you fool! Oh, it's like talking to crazy men! (*She grabs her father's arm—pleadingly*) Don't do it, Father, for the love of God! Have I ever asked you anything? Well, I ask you to heed me now! I'll beg you on my knees, if you like! Isn't it me you'd fight about, and haven't I a right to decide? You punished that lawyer for the insult. You had him thrown out of here like a tramp. Isn't that your answer to old Harford that insults him? It's for him to challenge you, if he dares, isn't it? Why can't you leave it at that and wait—

MELODY—(*shaking off her hand—angrily*) You talk like a scheming peasant! It's a question of my honor!

SARA—No! It's a question of my happiness, and I won't have your mad interfering—! (*desperately forcing herself to reason with him again*) Listen, Father! If you'll keep out of it, I'll show you how I'll make a fool of old Harford! Simon won't let anything his father does keep him from marrying me. His mother is the only one who might have the influence over him to come between us. She's only watching for a good excuse to turn Simon against marrying me, and if you go raising a drunken row at their house, and make a public scandal, shouting you want to murder his father, can't you see what a chance that will give her?

MELODY—(*raging*) That damned, insolent Yankee bitch! She's all the more reason. Marry, did you say? You dare to think there can be any question now of your marrying the son of a man who has insulted my honor—and yours?

SARA—(*defiantly*) Yes, I dare to think it! I love Simon and I'm going to marry him!

MELODY—And I say you're not! If he wasn't sick, I'd— But I'll get him out of here tomorrow! I forbid you ever to see him again! If you dare disobey me I'll—! (*beginning to lose all control of himself*) If you dare defy me—for the sake of the dirty money you think you can beg from his family, if you're his wife—!

SARA—(*fiercely*) You lie! (*then with quiet intensity*) Yes. I defy you or anyone who tries to come between us!

MELODY—You'd sell your pride as my daughter—! (*his face convulsed by fury*) You filthy peasant slut! You whore! I'll see you dead first—! By the living God, I'd kill you myself! (*He makes a threatening move toward her.*)

SARA—(*shrinks back frightenedly*) Father! (*Then she stands and faces him defiantly.*)

CREGAN—(*steps between them*) Con! In the name of God!

(*Melody's fit of insane fury leaves him. He stands panting for breath, shuddering with the effort to regain some sort of poise. Cregan speaks, his only thought to get him away from Sara.*) If we're going after old Harford, Major, we'd better go. That thief of a lawyer will warn him—

MELODY—(*seizing on this—hoarsely*) Yes, let's go. Let's go, Jamie. Come along, Corporal. A stirrup cup, and we'll be off. If the mare wasn't lame, I'd ride alone—but we can get a rig at the livery stable. Don't let me forget to stop at the barn for my whip. (*By the time he finishes speaking, he has himself in hand again and his ungovernable fury has gone. There is a look of cool, menacing vengefulness in his face. He turns toward the bar door.*)

SARA—(*helplessly*) Father! (*desperately, as a last, frantic threat*) You'll force me to go to Simon—and do what you said! (*If he hears this, he gives no sign of it. He strides into the bar. Cregan follows him, closing the door. Sara stares before her, the look of defiant desperation hardening on her face. The street door is flung open and O'Dowd and Roche pile in, laughing uproariously.*)

ROCHE—Hurroo!

O'DOWD—The army is back, Major, with the foe flying in retreat. (*He sees Melody is not there—to Sara*) Where's himself? (*Sara appears not to see or hear him.*)

ROCHE—(*after a quick glance at her*) Lave her be. He'll be in the bar. Come on. (*He goes to the bar.*)

O'DOWD—(*following him, speaks over his shoulder to Sara*) You should have seen the Yank! His coachman had to help him in his rig at the corner—and Roche gave the coachman a clout too, for good measure! (*He disappears, laughing, slamming the door behind him. Nora opens the door at right and looks in cautiously. Seeing Sara alone, she comes in.*)

NORA—Sara. (*She comes over to her.*) Sara. (*She takes hold of her arm—whispers uneasily*) Where's himself?

SARA—(*dully*) I couldn't stop him.

NORA—I could have told you you was wastin' breath. (*with a queer pride*) The divil himself couldn't kape Con Melody from a duel! (*then mournfully*) It's like the auld times come again, and the same worry and sorrow. Even in the days before ivir I'd spoke a word to him, or done more than make him a bow when he'd ride past on his hunter, I used to lie awake and pray for him when I'd hear he was fightin' a duel in the mornin'. (*She smiles a shy, gentle smile.*) I was in love with him even then. (*Sara starts to say something bitter but what she sees in her mother's face stops her. Nora goes on, with a feeble attempt at boastful confidence.*) But I'll not worry this time, and let you not, either. There wasn't a man in Galway was his equal with a pistol, and what chance will this auld stick av a Yankee have against him? (*There is a noise of boisterous farewells from the bar and the noise of an outer door shutting. Nora starts.*) That's him leavin'! (*Her mouth pulls down pitiably. She starts for the bar with a sob.*) Ah, Con darlin', don't—! (*She stops, shaking her head helplessly.*) But what's the good? (*She sinks on a chair with a weary sigh.*)

SARA—(*bitterly, aloud to herself more than to her mother*) No good. Let him go his way—and I'll go mine. (*tensely*) I won't let him destroy my life with his madness, after all the plans I've made and the dreams I've dreamed. I'll show him I can play at the game of gentleman's honor too! (*Nora has not listened. She is sunk in memories of old fears and her present worry about the duel. Sara hesitates—then, keeping her face turned away from her mother, touches her shoulder.*) I'm going upstairs to bed, Mother.

NORA—(*starts—then indignantly*) To bed, is it? You can think of sleepin' when he's—

SARA—I didn't say sleep, but I can lie down and try to rest. (*still avoiding looking at her mother*) I'm dead tired, Mother.

NORA—(*tenderly solicitous now, puts an arm around her*) You must be, darlin'. It's been the divil's own day for you, with all— (*with sudden remorse*) God forgive me, darlin'. I was forgettin' about you and the Harford lad. (*miserably*) Oh, God help us! (*suddenly with a flash of her strange, fierce pride in the power of love*) Never mind! If there's true love between you, you'll not let a duel or anything in the world kape you from each other, whatever the cost! Don't I know!

SARA—(*kisses her impulsively, then looks away again*) You're going to sit up and wait down here?

NORA—I am. I'd be destroyed with fear lying down in the

dark. Here, the noise of them in the bar kapes up my spirits, in a way.

SARA—Yes, you'd better stay here. Good night, Mother.

NORA—Good night, darlin'. (*Sara goes out at right, closing the door behind her.*)

(*Curtain*)

ACT FOUR

SCENE—*The same. It is around midnight. The room is in darkness except for one candle on the table, center. From the bar comes the sound of Patch Riley's pipes playing a reel and the stamp of dancing feet.*

Nora sits at the foot of the table at center. She is hunched up in an old shawl, her arms crossed over her breast, hugging herself as if she were cold. She looks on the verge of collapse from physical fatigue and hours of worry. She starts as the door from the bar is opened. It is Mickey. He closes the door behind him, shutting out an uproar of music and drunken voices. He has a decanter of whiskey and a glass in his hand. He has been drinking, but is not drunk.

NORA—(*eagerly*) There's news of himself?

MALOY—(*putting the decanter and glass on the table*) Sorra a bit. Don't be worryin' now. Sure, it's not so late yet.

NORA—(*dully*) It's aisy for you to say—

MALOY—I came in to see how you was, and bring you a taste to put heart in you. (*as she shakes her head*) Oh, I know you don't indulge, but I've known you once in a while, and you need it this night. (*as she again shakes her head—with kindly bullying*) Come now, don't be stubborn. I'm the doctor and I highly recommend a drop to drive out black thoughts and rheumatism.

NORA—Well—maybe—a taste, only.

MALOY—That's the talkin'. (*He pours a small drink and hands it to her.*) Drink hearty, now.

NORA—(*takes a sip, then puts the glass on the table and pushes it away listlessly*) I've no taste for anything. But I thank you for the thought. You're a kind lad, Mickey.

MALOY—Here's news to cheer you. The word has got round among the boys, and they've all come in to wait for Cregan and himself. (*with enthusiasm*) There'll be more money taken over the bar than any night since this shebeen started!

NORA—That's good.

MALOY—If they do hate Con Melody, he's Irish, and they

hate the Yanks worse. They're all hopin' he's bate the livin' lights out of Harford.

NORA—(*with belligerent spirit*) And so he has, I know that!

MALOY—(*grins*) That's the talk. I'm glad to see you roused from your worryin'. (*turning away*) I'd better get back. I left O'Dowd to tend bar and I'll wager he has three drinks stolen already. (*He hesitates.*) Sara's not been down?

NORA—No.

MALOY—(*resentfully*) It's a wonder she wouldn't have more thought for you than to lave you sit up alone.

NORA—(*stiffens defensively*) I made her go to bed. She was droppin' with tiredness and destroyed with worry. She must have fallen asleep, like the young can. None of your talk against Sara, now!

MALOY—(*starts an exasperated retort*) The divil take— (*He stops and grins at her with affection.*) There's no batin' you, Nora. Sure, it'd be the joy av me life to have a mother like you to fight for me—or, better still, a wife like you.

NORA—(*A sweet smile of pleased coquetry lights up her drawn face.*) Arrah, save your blarney for the young girls!

MALOY—The divil take young girls. You're worth a hundred av thim.

NORA—(*with a toss of her head*) Get along with you! (*Mickey grins with satisfaction at having cheered her up and goes in the bar, closing the door. As soon as he is gone, she sinks back into apprehensive brooding.*)

(*Sara appears silently in the doorway at right. She wears a faded old wrapper over her nightgown, slippers on her bare feet. Her hair is down over her shoulders, reaching to her waist. There is a change in her. All the bitterness and defiance have disappeared from her face. It looks gentle and calm and at the same time dreamily happy and exultant. She is much prettier than she has ever been before. She stands looking at her mother, and suddenly she becomes shy and uncertain—as if, now that she'd come this far, she had half a mind to retreat before her mother discovered her. But Nora senses her presence and looks up.*)

NORA—(*dully*) Ah, it's you, darlin'! (*then gratefully*) Praise be, you've come at last! I'm sick with worry and I've got to the place where I can't bear waitin' alone, listenin' to drunks

dancin' and celebratin'. (*Sara comes to her. Nora breaks. Tears
well from her eyes.*) It's cruel, it is! There's no heart or thought
for himself in divil a one av thim. (*She starts to sob. Sara hugs
her and kisses her cheek gently. But she doesn't speak. It is as if she
were afraid her voice would give her away. Nora stops sobbing. Her
mood changes to resentment and she speaks as if Sara had spoken.*)
Don't tell me not to worry. You're as bad as Mickey. The
Yankee didn't apologize or your father'd been back here long
since. It's a duel, that's certain, and he must have taken a
room in the city so he'll be near the ground. I hope he'll
sleep, but I'm feared he'll stay up drinkin', and at the dawn
he'll have had too much to shoot his best and maybe— (*then
defiantly self-reassuringly*) Arrah, I'm the fool! It's himself can
keep his head clear and his eyes sharp, no matter what he's
taken! (*pushing Sara away—with nervous peevishness*) Let go
of me. You've hardened not to care. I'd rather stay alone. (*She
grabs Sara's hand.*) No. Don't heed me. Sit down, darlin'.
(*Sara sits down on her left at rear of table. She pats her mother's
hand, but remains silent, her expression dreamily happy, as if she
heard Nora's words but they had no meaning for her. Nora goes
on worriedly again.*) But if he's staying in the city, why hasn't
he sent Jamie Cregan back for his duelin' pistols? I know he'd
nivir fight with any others. (*resentful now at Melody*) Or you'd
think he'd send Jamie or someone back with a word for me.
He knows well how tormented I'd be waiting. (*bitterly*) Arrah, don't talk like a loon! Has he ever cared for anyone except himself and his pride? Sure, he'd never stoop to think of
me, the grand gentleman in his red livery av bloody England!
His pride, indade! What is it but a lie? What's in his veins,
God pity him, but the blood of thievin' auld Ned Melody
who kept a dirty shebeen? (*then is horrified at herself as if she
had blasphemed*) No! I won't say it! I've nivir! It would break
his heart if he heard me! I'm the only one in the world he
knows nivir sneers at his dreams! (*working herself to rebellion
again*) All the same, I won't stay here the rist of the night
worryin' my heart out for a man who—it isn't only fear over
the duel. It's because I'm afraid it's God's punishment, all the
sorrow and trouble that's come on us, and I have the black
tormint in my mind that it's the fault of the mortal sin I did
with him unmarried, and the promise he made me make to

leave the Church that's kept me from ever confessin' to a priest. (*She pauses—dully*) Go to a doctor, you say, to cure the rheumatism. Sure, what's rheumatism but a pain in your body? I could bear ten of it. It's the pain of guilt in my soul. Can a doctor's medicine cure that? No, only a priest of Almighty God— (*with a roused rebellion again*) It would serve Con right if I took the chance now and broke my promise and woke up the priest to hear my confession and give me God's forgiveness that'd bring my soul peace and comfort so I wouldn't feel the three of us were damned. (*yearningly*) Oh, if I only had the courage! (*She rises suddenly from her chair— with brave defiance*) I'll do it, so I will! I'm going to the priest's, Sara. (*She starts for the street door—gets halfway to it and stops.*)

SARA—(*a strange, tenderly amused smile on her lips—teasingly*) Well, why don't you go, Mother?

NORA—(*defiantly*) Ain't I goin'? (*She takes a few more steps toward the door—stops again—she mutters beatenly*) God forgive me, I can't. What's the use pretendin'?

SARA—(*as before*) No use at all, Mother. I've found that out.

NORA—(*as if she hadn't heard, comes back slowly*) He'd feel I'd betrayed him and my word and my love for him—and for all his scorn, he knows my love is all he has in the world to comfort him. (*then spiritedly, with a proud toss of her head*) And it's my honor, too! It's not for his sake at all! Divil mend him, he always prates as if he had all the honor there is, but I've mine, too, as proud as his. (*She sits down in the same chair.*)

SARA—(*softly*) Yes, the honor of her love to a woman. I've learned about that too, Mother.

NORA—(*as if this were the first time she was really conscious of Sara speaking, and even now had not heard what she said— irritably*) So you've found your tongue, have you? Thank God. You're cold comfort, sitting silent like a statue, and me making talk to myself. (*regarding her as if she hadn't really seen her before—resentfully*) Musha but it's pleased and pretty you look, as if there wasn't a care in the world, while your poor father—

SARA—(*dreamily amused, as if this no longer had any impor-

tance or connection with her) I know it's no use telling you there won't be any duel, Mother, and it's crazy to give it a thought. You're living in Ireland long ago, like Father. But maybe you'll take Simon's word for it, if you won't mine. He said his father would be paralyzed with indignation just at the thought he'd ever fight a duel. It's against the law.

NORA—(*scornfully*) Och, who cares for the law? He must be a coward. (*She looks relieved.*) Well, if the young lad said that, maybe it's true.

SARA—Of course it's true, Mother.

NORA—Your father'd be satisfied with Harford's apology and that'd end it.

SARA—(*helplessly*) Oh, Mother! (*then quickly*) Yes, I'm sure it ended hours ago.

NORA—(*intent on her hope*) And you think what's keeping him out is he and Jamie would take a power av drinks to celebrate.

SARA—They'd drink, that's sure, whatever happened. (*She adds dreamily*) But that doesn't matter now at all.

NORA—(*stares at her—wonderingly*) You've a queer way of talking, as if you'd been asleep and was still half in a dream.

SARA—In a dream right enough, Mother, and it isn't half of me that's in it but all of me, body and soul. And it's a dream that's true, and always will be to the end of life, and I'll never wake from it.

NORA—Sure, what's come over you at all?

SARA—(*gets up impulsively and comes around in back of her mother's chair and slips to her knees and puts her arms about her—giving her a hug*) Joy. That's what's come over me. I'm happy, Mother. I'm happy because I know now Simon is mine, and no one can ever take him from me.

NORA—(*At first her only reaction is pleased satisfaction.*) God be thanked! It was a great sorrow tormentin' me that the duel would come between you. (*defiantly*) Honor or not, why should the children have their lives and their love destroyed!

SARA—I was a great fool to fear his mother could turn him against me, no matter what happened.

NORA—You've had a talk with the lad?

SARA—I have. That's where I've been.

NORA—You've been in his room ever since you went up?

SARA—Almost. After I'd got upstairs it took me a while to get up my courage.

NORA—(*rebukingly*) All this time—in the dead of the night!

SARA—(*teasingly*) I'm his nurse, aren't I? I've a right.

NORA—That's no excuse!

SARA—(*her face hardening*) Excuse? I had the best in the world. Would you have me do nothing to save my happiness and my chance in life, when I thought there was danger they'd be ruined forever? Don't you want me to have love and be happy, Mother?

NORA—(*melting*) I do, darlin'. I'd give my life— (*then rebuking again*) Were you the way you are, in only a nightgown and wrapper?

SARA—(*gaily*) I was—and Simon liked my costume, if you don't, although he turned red as a beet when I came in.

NORA—Small wonder he did! Shame on you!

SARA—He was trying to read a book of poetry, but he couldn't he was that worried hoping I'd come to say goodnight, and being frightened I wouldn't. (*She laughs tenderly.*) Oh, it was the cutest thing I've ever done, Mother, not to see him at all since his mother left. He kept waiting for me and when I didn't come, he got scared to death that his kissing me this morning had made me angry. So he was wild with joy to see me—

NORA—In your bare legs with only your nightgown and wrapper to cover your nakedness! Where's your modesty?

SARA—(*gaily teasing*) I had it with me, Mother, though I'd tried hard to leave it behind. I got as red as he was. (*She laughs.*) Oh, Mother, it's a great joke on me. Here I'd gone to his room with my mind made up to be as bold as any street woman and tempt him because I knew his honor would make him marry me right away if— (*She laughs.*) And then all I could do was stand and gape at him and blush!

NORA—Oh. (*rebukingly*) I'm glad you had the dacency to blush.

SARA—It was Simon spoke first, and once he started, all he'd been holding back came out. The waiting for me, and the fear he'd had made him forget all his shyness, and he said he loved me and asked me to marry him the first day we could. Without knowing how it happened, there I was with his arms around me and mine around him and his lips on my lips and it was heaven, Mother.

NORA—(*moved by the shining happiness in Sara's face*) God bless the two av you.

SARA—Then I was crying and telling him how afraid I'd been his mother hated me, Father's madness about the duel would give her a good chance to come between us; Simon said no one could ever come between us and his mother would never try to, now she knew he loved me, which was what she came over to find out. He said all she wanted was for him to be free to do as he pleased, and she only suggested he wait a year, she didn't make him promise. And Simon said I was foolish to think she would take the duel craziness serious. She'd only be amused at the joke it would be on his father, after he'd been so sure he could buy us off, if he had to call the police to save him.

NORA—(*aroused at the mention of police*) Call the police, is it? The coward!

SARA—(*goes on, unheedingly*) Simon was terribly angry at his father for that. And at Father too when I told how he threatened he'd kill me. But we didn't talk of it much. We had better things to discuss. (*She smiles tenderly.*)

NORA—(*belligerently*) A lot Con Melody cares for police, and him in a rage! Not the whole dirty force av thim will dare interfere with him!

SARA—(*goes on as if she hadn't heard*) And then Simon told me how scared he'd been I didn't love him and wouldn't marry him. I was so beautiful, he said, and he wasn't handsome at all. So I kissed him and told him he was the handsomest in the world, and he is. And he said he wasn't worthy because he had so little to offer, and was a failure at what he'd hoped he could be, a poet. So I kissed him and told him he was too a poet, and always would be, and it was what I loved most about him.

NORA—The police! Let one av thim lay his dirty hand on Con Melody, and he'll knock him senseless with one blow.

SARA—Then Simon said how poor he was, and he'd never accept a penny from his father, even if he offered it. And I told him never mind, that if we had to live in a hut, or sleep in the grass of a field without a roof to our heads, and work our hands to the bone, or starve itself, I'd be in heaven and sing with the joy of our love! (*She looks up at her mother.*) And I meant it, Mother! I meant every word of it from the bottom of my heart!

NORA—(*answers vaguely from her preoccupation with the police—patting Sara's hair mechanically*) Av course you did, darlin'.

SARA—But he kissed me and said it wouldn't be as bad as that, he'd been thinking and he'd had an offer from an old college friend who'd inherited a cotton mill and who wants Simon to be equal partners if he'll take complete charge of it. It's only a small mill and that's what tempts Simon. He said maybe I couldn't believe it but he knows from his experience working for his father he has the ability for trade, though he hates it, and he could easily make a living for us from this mill—just enough to be comfortable, and he'd have time over to write his book, and keep his wisdom, and never let himself become a slave to the greed for more than enough that is the curse of mankind. Then he said he was afraid maybe I'd think it was weakness in him, not wisdom, and could I be happy with enough and no more. So I kissed him and said all I wanted in life was his love, and whatever meant happiness to him would be my only ambition. (*She looks up at her mother again—exultantly*) And I meant it, Mother! With all my heart and soul!

NORA—(*as before, patting her hair*) I know, darlin'.

SARA—Isn't that a joke on me, with all my crazy dreams of riches and a grand estate and me a haughty lady riding around in a carriage with coachman and footman! (*She laughs at herself.*) Wasn't I the fool to think that had any meaning at all when you're in love? You were right, Mother. I knew nothing of love, or the pride a woman can take in giving everything—the pride in her own love! I was only an ignorant, silly girl boasting, but I'm a woman now, Mother, and I know.

NORA—(*as before, mechanically*) I'm sure you do, darlin'. (*She mutters fumingly to herself*) Let the police try it! He'll whip them back to their kennels, the dirty curs!

SARA—(*lost in her happiness*) And then we put out the light and talked about how soon we'd get married, and how happy we'd be the rest of our lives together, and we'd have children—and he forgot whatever shyness was left in the dark and said he meant all the bold things he'd written in the poems I'd seen. And I confessed that I was up to every scheme to get him, because I loved him so much there wasn't anything I wouldn't do to make sure he was mine. And all the time we were kissing each other, wild with happiness. And— (*She stops abruptly and looks down guiltily.*)

NORA—(*as before*) Yes, darlin', I know.

SARA—(*guiltily, keeping her eyes down*) You—know, Mother?

NORA—(*abruptly comes out of her preoccupation, startled and uneasy*) I know what? What are you sayin'? Look up at me! (*She pulls Sara's head back so she can look down in her face— falteringly*) I can see— You let him! You wicked, sinful girl!

SARA—(*defiantly and proudly*) There was no letting about it, only love making the two of us!

NORA—(*helplessly resigned already but feeling it her duty to rebuke*) Ain't you ashamed to boast—?

SARA—No! There was no shame in it! (*proudly*) Ashamed? You know I'm not! Haven't you told me of the pride in your love? Were you ashamed?

NORA—(*weakly*) I was. I was dead with shame.

SARA—You were not! You were proud like me!

NORA—But it's a mortal sin. God will punish you—

SARA—Let Him! If He'd say to me, for every time you kiss Simon you'll have a thousand years in hell, I wouldn't care, I'd wear out my lips kissing him!

NORA—(*frightenedly*) Whist, now! He might hear you.

SARA—Wouldn't you have said the same—?

NORA—(*distractedly*) Will you stop! Don't torment me with your sinful questions! I won't answer you!

SARA—(*hugging her*) All right. Forgive me, Mother. (*a pause—smilingly*) It was Simon who felt guilty and repentant. If he'd had his way, he'd be out of bed now, and the two of us would be walking around in the night, trying to wake up someone who could marry us. But I was so drunk with love, I'd lost all thought or care about marriage. I'd got to the place where all you know or care is that you belong to love, and you can't call your soul your own any more, let alone your body, and you're proud you've given them to love. (*She pauses—then teasing lovingly*) Sure, I've always known you're the sweetest woman in the world, Mother, but I never suspected you were a wise woman too, until I knew tonight the truth of what you said this morning, that a woman can forgive whatever the man she loves could do and still love him, because it was through him she found the love in herself; that, in one way, he doesn't count at all, because it's love, your own love, you love in him, and to keep that your pride will do anything. (*She smiles with a self-mocking happiness.*) It's love's slaves we are, Mother, not men's—and wouldn't it shame their boasting and vanity if we ever let them know our secret? (*She laughs—then suddenly looks guilty.*) But I'm talking great nonsense. I'm glad Simon can't hear me. (*She pauses. Nora is worrying and hasn't listened. Sara goes on.*) Yes, I can even understand now—a little anyway—how you can still love Father and be proud of it, in spite of what he is.

NORA—(*at the mention of Melody, comes out of her brooding*) Hush, now! (*miserably*) God help us, Sara, why doesn't he come, what's happened to him?

SARA—(*gets to her feet exasperatedly*) Don't be a fool, Mother. (*bitterly*) Nothing's happened except he's made a public disgrace of himself, for Simon's mother to sneer at. If she wanted revenge on him, I'm sure she's had her fill of it. Well, I don't care. He deserves it. I warned him and I begged him, and got called a peasant slut and a whore for my pains. All I hope now is that whatever happened wakes him from his lies and mad dreams so he'll have to face the truth of himself in that mirror. (*sneeringly*) But there's devil a chance he'll ever let that happen. Instead, he'll come home as drunk as two lords, boasting of his glorious victory over old Harford, whatever the truth is! (*But Nora isn't listening. She has heard the click of the latch on the street door at rear.*)

NORA—(*excitedly*) Look, Sara! (*The door is opened slowly and Jamie Cregan sticks his head in cautiously to peer around the room. His face is battered, nose red and swollen, lips cut and puffed, and one eye so blackened it is almost closed. Nora's first reaction is a cry of relief.*) Praise be to the Saints, you're back, Jamie!

CREGAN—(*puts a finger to his lips—cautioningly*) Whist!

NORA—(*frightenedly*) Jamie! Where's himself?

CREGAN—(*sharply*) Whist, I'm telling you! (*in a whisper*) I've got him in a rig outside, but I had to make sure no one was here. Lock the bar door, Sara, and I'll bring him in. (*She goes and turns the key in the door, her expression contemptuous. Cregan then disappears, leaving the street door half open.*)

NORA—Did you see Jamie's face? They've been fightin' terrible. Oh, I'm afraid, Sara.

SARA—Afraid of what? It's only what I told you to expect. A crazy row—and now he's paralyzed drunk. (*Cregan appears in the doorway at rear. He is half leading, half supporting Melody. The latter moves haltingly and woodenly. But his movements do not seem those of drunkenness. It is more as if a sudden shock or stroke had shattered his coordination and left him in a stupor. His scarlet uniform is filthy and torn and pulled awry. The pallor of his face is ghastly. He has a cut over his left eye, a blue swelling on his left cheekbone, and his lips are cut and bloody. From a big raw bruise on his forehead, near the temple, trickles of dried blood run down to his jaw. Both his hands are swollen, with skinned knuckles, as are Cregan's. His eyes are empty and lifeless. He stares at his wife and daughter as if he did not recognize them.*)

NORA—(*rushes and puts her arm around him*) Con, darlin'! Are you hurted bad? (*He pushes her away without looking at her. He walks dazedly to his chair at the head of the center table. Nora follows him, breaking into lamentation.*) Con, don't you know me? Oh, God help us, look at his head!

SARA—Be quiet, Mother. Do you want them in the bar to know he's come home—the way he is. (*She gives her father a look of disgust.*)

CREGAN—Ay, that's it, Sara. We've got to rouse him first. His pride'd nivir forgive us if we let thim see him dead bate like this. (*There is a pause. They stare at him and he stares sightlessly at the table top. Nora stands close by his side, behind the table, on his right, Sara behind her on her right, Cregan at right of Sara.*)

SARA—He's drunk, isn't that all it is, Jamie?

CREGAN—(*sharply*) He's not. He's not taken a drop since we left here. It's the clouts on the head he got, that's what ails him. A taste of whiskey would bring him back, if he'd only take it, but he won't.

SARA—(*gives her father a puzzled, uneasy glance*) He won't?

NORA—(*gets the decanter and a glass and hands them to Cregan*) Here. Try and make him.

CREGAN—(*pours out a big drink and puts it before Melody—coaxingly*) Drink this now, Major, and you'll be right as rain! (*Melody does not seem to notice. His expression remains blank and dead. Cregan scratches his head puzzledly.*) He won't. That's the way he's been all the way back when I tried to persuade him. (*then irritably*) Well, if he won't, I will, be your leave. I'm needin' it bad. (*He downs the whiskey, and pours out another—to Nora and Sara*) It's the divil's own rampage we've had.

SARA—(*quietly contemptuous, but still with the look of puzzled uneasiness at her father*) From your looks it must have been.

CREGAN—(*indignantly*) You're takin' it cool enough, and you seein' the marks av the batin' we got! (*He downs his second drink—boastfully*) But if we're marked, there's others is marked worse and some av thim is police!

NORA—God be praised! The dirty cowards!

SARA—Be quiet, Mother. Tell us what happened, Jamie.

CREGAN—Faix, what didn't happen? Be the rock av Cashel, I've nivir engaged in a livelier shindy! We had no trouble findin' where Harford lived. It's a grand mansion, with a big walled garden behind it, and we wint to the front door. A flunky in livery answered wid two others behind. A big black naygur one was. That pig av a lawyer must have warned Harford to expect us. Con spoke wid the airs av a lord. "Kindly inform your master," he says, "that Major Cornelius Melody, late of His Majesty's Seventh Dragoons, respectfully requests a word with him." Well, the flunky put an insolent sneer on him. "Mr. Harford won't see you," he says. I could see Con's rage risin' but he kept polite. "Tell him," he says, "if he knows what's good for him he'll see me. For if he don't, I'll come in and see him." "Ye will, will ye?" says the flunky, "I'll have you know Mr. Harford don't allow drunken Micks to come here disturbing him. The police have been informed," he says, "and you'll be arrested if you make trouble." Then he started to shut the door. "Anyway, you've come to the wrong door," he says, "the place for the loiks av you is the servants' entrance."

NORA—(*angrily*) Och, the impident divil!

SARA—(*In spite of herself her temper has been rising. She looks at Melody with angry scorn.*) You let Harford's servants insult you! (*then quickly*) But it serves you right! I knew what would happen! I warned you!

CREGAN—Let thim be damned! Kape your mouth shut, and lave me tell it, and you'll see if we let them! When he'd said that, the flunky tried to slam the door in our faces, but Con was too quick. He pushed it back on him and lept in the hall, roarin' mad, and hit the flunky a cut with his whip across his ugly mug that set him screaming like a stuck pig!

NORA—(*enthusiastically*) Good for you, Con darlin'!

SARA—(*humiliatedly*) Mother! Don't! (*to Melody with biting scorn*) The famous duelist—in a drunken brawl with butlers and coachmen! (*But he is staring sightlessly at the table top as if he didn't see her or know her.*)

CREGAN—(*angrily, pouring himself another drink*) Shut your mouth, Sara, and don't be trying to plague him. You're wastin' breath anyway, the way he is. He doesn't know you or hear you. And don't put on lady's airs about fighting when you're the whole cause of it.

SARA—(*angrily*) It's a lie! You know I tried to stop—

CREGAN—(*gulps down his drink, ignoring this, and turns to Nora—enthusiastically*) Wait till you hear, Nora! (*He plunges into the midst of battle again.*) The naygur hit me a clout that had my head dizzy. He'd have had me down only Con broke the butt av the whip over his black skull and knocked him to his knees. Then the third man punched Con and I gave him a kick where it'd do him least good, and he rolled on the floor, grabbin' his guts. The naygur was in again and grabbed me, but Con came at him and knocked him down. Be the mortal, we had the three av thim licked, and we'd have dragged auld Harford from his burrow and tanned his Yankee hide if the police hadn't come!

NORA—(*furiously*) Arrah, the dirthy cowards! Always takin' sides with the rich Yanks against the poor Irish!

SARA—(*more and more humiliated and angry and torn by*

conflicting emotions—pleadingly) Mother! Can't you keep still?

CREGAN—Four av thim wid clubs came behind us. They grabbed us before we knew it and dragged us into the street. Con broke away and hit the one that held him, and I gave one a knee in his belly. And then, glory be, there was a fight! Oh, it'd done your heart good to see himself! He was worth two men, lettin' out right and left, roarin' wid rage and cursin' like a trooper—

MELODY—(*without looking up or any change in his dazed expression, suddenly speaks in a jeering mumble to himself*) Bravely done, Major Melody! The Commander of the Forces honors your exceptional gallantry! Like the glorious field of Talavera! Like the charge on the French square! Cursing like a drunken, foul-mouthed son of a thieving shebeen keeper who sprang from the filth of a peasant hovel, with pigs on the floor—with that pale Yankee bitch watching from a window, sneering with disgust!

NORA—(*frightenedly*) God preserve us, it's crazed he is!

SARA—(*stares at him startled and wondering. For a second there is angry pity in her eyes. She makes an impulsive move toward him.*) Father! (*then her face hardening*) He isn't crazed, Mother. He's come to his senses for once in his life! (*to Melody*) So she was sneering, was she? I don't blame her! I'm glad you've been taught a lesson! (*then vindictively*) But I've taught her one, too. She'll soon sneer from the wrong side of her mouth!

CREGAN—(*angrily*) Will you shut your gab, Sara! Lave him be and don't heed him. It's the same crazy blather he's talked every once in a while since they brought him to—about the Harford woman—and speakin' av the pigs and his father one minute, and his pride and honor and his mare the next. (*He takes up the story again.*) Well, anyways, they was too much for us, the four av thim wid clubs. The last thing I saw before I was knocked senseless was three av thim clubbing Con. But, be the Powers, we wint down fightin' to the last for the glory av auld Ireland!

MELODY—(*in a jeering mutter to himself*) Like a rum-soaked trooper, brawling before a brothel on a Saturday night, puking in the gutter!

SARA—(*strickenly*) Don't, Father!

CREGAN—(*indignantly to Melody*) We wasn't in condition. If we had been—but they knocked us senseless and rode us to the station and locked us up. And we'd be there yet if Harford hadn't made thim turn us loose, for he's rich and has influence. Small thanks to him! He was afraid the row would get in the paper and put shame on him. (*Melody laughs crazily and springs to his feet. He sways dizzily, clutching his head—then goes toward the door at left front.*)

NORA—Con! Where are you goin'? (*She starts after him and grabs his arm. He shakes her hand off roughly as if he did not recognize her.*)

CREGAN—He don't know you. Don't cross him now, Nora. Sure, he's only goin' upstairs to bed. (*wheedlingly*) You know what's best for you, don't you, Major? (*Melody feels his way gropingly through the door and disappears, leaving it open.*)

SARA—(*uneasy, but consoling her mother*) Jamie's right, Mother. If he'll fall asleep, that's the best thing— (*Abruptly she is terrified.*) Oh God, maybe he'll take revenge on Simon— (*She rushes to the door and stands listening—with relief*) No, he's gone to his room. (*She comes back—a bit ashamed*) I'm a fool. He'd never harm a sick man, no matter— (*She takes her mother's arm—gently*) Don't stand there, Mother. Sit down. You're tired enough—

NORA—(*frightenedly*) I've never heard him talk like that in all the years—with that crazy dead look in his eyes. Oh, I'm afeered, Sara. Lave go of me. I've got to make sure he's gone to bed. (*She goes quickly to the door and disappears. Sara makes a move to follow her.*)

CREGAN—(*roughly*) Stay here, unless you're a fool, Sara. He might come to all av a sudden and give you a hell av a thrashin'. Troth, you deserve one. You're to blame for what's happened. Wasn't he fightin' to revenge the insults to you? (*He sprawls on a chair at rear of the table at center.*)

SARA—(*sitting down at rear of the small table at left front—angrily*) I'll thank you to mind your own business, Jamie Cregan. Just because you're a relation—

CREGAN—(*harshly*) Och, to hell with your airs! (*He pours out a drink and downs it. He is becoming drunk again.*)

SARA—I can revenge my own insults, and I have! I've beaten the Harfords—and he's only made a fool of himself for her to sneer at. But I've beaten her and I'll sneer last! (*She pauses, a hard, triumphant smile on her lips. It fades. She gives a little bewildered laugh.*) God forgive me, what a way to think of— I must be crazy, too.

CREGAN—(*drunkenly*) Ah, don't be talkin'! Didn't the two of us lick them all! And Con's all right. He's all right, I'm sayin'! It's only the club on the head makes him quare a while. I've seen it often before. Ay, and felt it meself. I remember at a fair in the auld country I was clouted with the butt av a whip and I didn't remember a thing for hours, but they told me after I never stopped gabbin' but went around tellin' every stranger all my secrets. (*He pauses. Sara hasn't listened. He goes on uneasily.*) All the same, it's no fun listening to his mad blather about the pale bitch, as he calls her, like she was a ghost, haunting and scorning him. And his gab about his beautiful thoroughbred mare is madder still, raving what a grand, beautiful lady she is, with her slender ankles and dainty feet, sobbin' and beggin' her forgiveness and talkin' of dishonor and death— (*He shrinks superstitiously— then angrily, reaching for the decanter*) Och, be damned to this night! (*Before he can pour a drink, Nora comes hurrying in from the door at left front.*)

NORA—(*breathless and frightened*) He's come down! He pushed me away like he didn't see me. He's gone out to the barn. Go after him, Jamie.

CREGAN—(*drunkenly*) I won't. He's all right. Lave him alone.

SARA—(*jeeringly*) Sure, he's only gone to pay a call on his sweetheart, the mare, Mother, and hasn't he slept in her stall many a time when he was dead drunk, and she never even kicked him?

NORA—(*distractedly*) Will you shut up, the two av you! I heard him openin' the closet in his room where he keeps his auld set of duelin' pistols, and he was carryin' the box when he came down—

CREGAN—(*scrambles hastily to his feet*) Oh, the lunatic!

NORA—He'll ride the mare back to Harford's! He'll murther someone! For the love av God, stop him, Jamie!

CREGAN—(*drunkenly belligerent*) Be Christ, I'll stop him for you, Nora, pistols or no pistols! (*He walks a bit unsteadily out the door at left front.*)

SARA—(*stands tensely—bursts out with a strange triumphant pride*) Then he's not beaten! (*Suddenly she is overcome by a bitter, tortured revulsion of feeling.*) Merciful God, what am I thinking? As if he hadn't done enough to destroy— (*distractedly*) Oh, the mad fool! I wish he was— (*From the yard, off left front, there is the muffled crack of a pistol shot hardly perceptible above the noise in the barroom. But Sara and Nora both hear it and stand frozen with horror. Sara babbles hysterically*) I didn't mean it, Mother! I didn't!

NORA—(*numb with fright—mumbles stupidly*) A shot!

SARA—You know I didn't mean it, Mother!

NORA—A shot! God help us, he's kilt Jamie!

SARA—(*stammers*) No—not Jamie— (*wildly*) Oh, I can't bear waiting! I've got to know— (*She rushes to the door at left front—then stops frightenedly.*) I'm afraid to know! I'm afraid—

NORA—(*mutters stupidly*) Not Jamie? Then who else? (*She begins to tremble—in a horrified whisper*) Sara! You think— Oh, God have mercy!

SARA—Will you hush, Mother! I'm trying to hear— (*She retreats quickly into the room and backs around the table at left front until she is beside her mother.*) Someone's at the yard door. It'll be Jamie coming to tell us—

NORA—It's a lie! He'd nivir! He'd nivir! (*They stand paralyzed by terror, clinging to each other, staring at the open door. There is a moment's pause in which the sound of drunken roistering in the bar seems louder. Then Melody appears in the doorway with Cregan behind him. Cregan has him by the shoulder and pushes him roughly into the room, like a bouncer handling a drunk. Cregan is shaken by the experience he has just been through and his reaction is to make him drunkenly angry at Melody. In his free hand is a dueling pistol. Melody's face is like gray wax. His body is limp, his feet drag, his eyes seem to have no sight. He appears completely possessed by a paralyzing stupor.*)

SARA—(*impulsively*) Father! Oh, thank God! (*She takes one step toward him—then her expression begins to harden.*)

NORA—(*sobs with relief*) Oh, praise God you're alive! Sara

and me was dead with fear— (*She goes toward them.*) Con! Con, darlin'!

CREGAN—(*dumps Melody down on the nearest chair at left of the small table—roughly, his voice trembling*) Let you sit still now, Con Melody, and behave like a gintleman! (*to Nora*) Here he is for ye, Nora, and you're welcome, bad luck to him! (*He moves back as Nora comes and puts her arms around Melody and hugs him tenderly.*)

NORA—Oh, Con, Con, I was so afeered for you! (*He does not seem to hear or see her, but she goes on crooning to him comfortingly as if he were a sick child.*)

CREGAN—He was in the stable. He'd this pistol in his hand, with the mate to it on the floor beside the mare. (*He shudders and puts the pistol on the table shakenly.*) It's mad he's grown entirely! Let you take care av him now, his wife and daughter! I've had enough. I'm no damned keeper av lunatics! (*He turns toward the barroom.*)

SARA—Wait, Jamie. We heard a shot. What was it?

CREGAN—(*angrily*) Ask him, not me! (*then with bewildered horror*) He kilt the poor mare, the mad fool! (*Sara stares at him in stunned amazement.*) I found him on the floor with her head in his lap, and her dead. He was sobbing like a soul in hell— (*He shudders.*) Let me get away from the sight of him where there's men in their right senses laughing and singing! (*He unlocks the barroom door.*) And don't be afraid, Sara, that I'll tell the boys a word av this. I'll talk of our fight in the city only, because it's all I want to remember. (*He jerks open the door and goes in the bar, slamming the door quickly behind him. A roar of welcome is heard as the crowd greets his arrival. Sara locks the door again. She comes back to the center table, staring at Melody, an hysterical, sneering grin making her lips quiver and twitch.*)

SARA—What a fool I was to be afraid! I might know you'd never do it as long as a drink of whiskey was left in the world! So it was the mare you shot? (*She bursts into uncontrollable, hysterical laughter. It penetrates Melody's stupor and he stiffens rigidly on his chair, but his eyes remain fixed on the table top.*)

NORA—Sara! Stop! For the love av God, how can you laugh—!

SARA—I can't—help it, Mother. Didn't you hear—Jamie? It was the mare he shot! (*She gives way to laughter again.*)

NORA—(*distractedly*) Stop it, I'm sayin'! (*Sara puts her hand over her mouth to shut off the sound of her laughing, but her shoulders still shake. Nora sinks on the chair at rear of the table. She mutters dazedly*) Kilt his beautiful mare? He must be mad entirely.

MELODY—(*suddenly speaks, without looking up, in the broadest brogue, his voice coarse and harsh*) Lave Sara laugh. Sure, who could blame her? I'm roarin' meself inside me. It's the damnedest joke a man ivir played on himself since time began. (*They stare at him. Sara's laughter stops. She is startled and repelled by his brogue. Then she stares at him suspiciously, her face hardening.*)

SARA—What joke? Do you think murdering the poor mare a good joke? (*Melody stiffens for a second, but that is all. He doesn't look up or reply.*)

NORA—(*frightened*) Look at the dead face on him, Sara. He's like a corpse. (*She reaches out and touches one of his hands on the table top with a furtive tenderness—pleadingly*) Con, darlin'. Don't!

MELODY—(*looks up at her. His expression changes so that his face loses all its remaining distinction and appears vulgar and common, with a loose, leering grin on his swollen lips.*) Let you not worry, Allanah. Sure, I'm no corpse, and with a few drinks in me, I'll soon be lively enough to suit you.

NORA—(*miserably confused*) Will you listen to him, Sara—puttin' on the brogue to torment us.

SARA—(*growing more uneasy but sneering*) Pay no heed to him, Mother. He's play-acting to amuse himself. If he's that cruel and shameless after what he's done—

NORA—(*defensively*) No, it's the blow on the head he got fightin' the police.

MELODY—(*vulgarly*) The blow, me foot! That's Jamie Cregan's blather. Sure, it'd take more than a few clubs on the head to darken my wits long. Me brains, if I have any, is clear as a bell. And I'm not puttin' on brogue to tormint you, me darlint. Nor play-actin', Sara. That was the Major's game. It's quare, surely, for the two av ye to object when I talk in me natural tongue, and yours, and don't put on airs loike the late lamented auld liar and lunatic, Major Cornelius Melody, av His Majesty's Seventh Dragoons, used to do.

NORA—God save us, Sara, will you listen!

MELODY—But he's dead now, and his last bit av lyin' pride is murthered and stinkin'. (*He pats Nora's hand with what seems to be genuine comforting affection.*) So let you be aisy, darlint. He'll nivir again hurt you with his sneers, and his pretindin' he's a gintleman, blatherin' about pride and honor, and his boastin' av duels in the days that's gone, and his showin' off before the Yankees, and thim laughin' at him, prancing around drunk on his beautiful thoroughbred mare— (*He gulps as if he were choking back a sob.*) For she's dead, too, poor baste.

SARA—(*This is becoming unbearable for her—tensely*) Why —why did you kill her?

MELODY—Why did the Major, you mean! Be Christ, you're stupider than I thought you, if you can't see that. Wasn't she the livin' reminder, so to spake, av all his lyin' boasts and dreams? He meant to kill her first wid one pistol, and then himself wid the other. But faix, he saw the shot that killed her had finished him, too. There wasn't much pride left in the auld lunatic, anyway, and seeing her die made an end av him. So he didn't bother shooting himself, because it'd be a mad thing to waste a good bullet on a corpse! (*He laughs coarsely.*)

SARA—(*tensely*) Father! Stop it!

MELODY—Didn't I tell you there was a great joke in it? Well, that's the joke. (*He begins to laugh again but he chokes on a stifled sob. Suddenly his face loses the coarse, leering, brutal expression and is full of anguished grief. He speaks without brogue, not to them but aloud to himself.*) Blessed Christ, the look in her eyes by the lantern light with life ebbing out of them— wondering and sad, but still trustful, not reproaching me— with no fear in them—proud, understanding pride—loving me—she saw I was dying with her. She understood! She forgave me! (*He starts to sob but wrenches himself out of it and speaks in broad, jeering brogue.*) Begorra, if that wasn't the mad Major's ghost speakin'! But be damned to him, he won't haunt me long, if I know it! I intind to live at my ease from now on and not let the dead bother me, but enjoy life in my

proper station as auld Nick Melody's son. I'll bury his
Major's damned red livery av bloody England deep in
the ground and he can haunt its grave if he likes, and boast
to the lonely night av Talavera and the ladies of Spain and
fightin' the French! (*with a leer*) Troth, I think the boys is
right when they say he stole the uniform and he nivir fought
under Wellington at all. He was a terrible liar, as I remember him.

NORA—Con, darlin', don't be grievin' about the mare.
Sure, you can get another. I'll manage—

SARA—Mother! Hush! (*to Melody, furiously*) Father, will
you stop this mad game you're playing—?

MELODY—(*roughly*) Game, is it? You'll find it's no game.
It was the Major played a game all his life, the crazy auld
loon, and cheated only himself. But I'll be content to stay
meself in the proper station I was born to, from this day on.
(*with a cunning leer at Sara*) And it's meself feels it me duty
to give you a bit av fatherly advice, Sara darlint, while my
mind is on it. I know you've great ambition, so remember it's
to hell wid honor if ye want to rise in this world. Remember
the blood in your veins and be your grandfather's true de-
scendent. There was an able man for you! Be Jaysus, he nivir
felt anything beneath him that could gain him something, and
for lyin' tricks to swindle the bloody fools of gintry, there
wasn't his match in Ireland, and he ended up wid a grand
estate, and a castle, and a pile av gold in the bank.

SARA—(*distractedly*) Oh, I hate you!

NORA—Sara!

MELODY—(*goes on as if he hadn't heard*) I know he'd advise that to give you a first step up, darlint, you must make
the young Yankee gintleman have you in his bed, and afther
he's had you, weep great tears and appeal to his honor to
marry you and save yours. Be God, he'll nivir resist that, if I
know him, for he's a young fool, full av dacency and dreams,
and looney, too, wid a touch av the poet in him. Oh, it'll be
aisy for you—

SARA—(*goaded beyond bearing*) I'll make you stop your
dirty brogue and your play-acting! (*She leans toward him and
speaks with taunting vindictiveness, in broad brogue herself.*)
Thank you kindly but I've already taken your wise advice,

Father. I made him have me in his bed, while you was out drunk fightin' the police!

NORA—(*frightenedly*) Sara! Hault your brazen tongue!

MELODY—(*His body stiffens on his chair and the coarse leer vanishes from his face. It becomes his old face. His eyes fix on her in a threatening stare. He speaks slowly, with difficulty keeping his words in brogue.*) Did you now, God bless you! I might have known you'd not take any chance that the auld loon av a Major, going out to revenge an insult to you, would spoil your schemes. (*He forces a horrible grin.*) Be the living God, it's me should be proud this night that one av the Yankee gintry has stooped to be seduced by my slut av a daughter! (*Still keeping his eyes fixed on hers, he begins to rise from his chair, his right hand groping along the table top until it clutches the dueling pistol. He aims it at Sara's heart, like an automaton, his eyes as cold, deadly, and merciless as they must have been in his duels of long ago. Sara is terrified but she stands unflinchingly.*)

NORA—(*horror-stricken, lunges from her chair and grabs his arm*) Con! For the love av God! Would you be murthering Sara? (*A dazed look comes over his face. He grows limp and sinks back on his chair and lets the pistol slide from his fingers on the table. He draws a shuddering breath—then laughs hoarsely.*)

MELODY—(*with a coarse leer*) Murtherin' Sara, is it? Are ye daft, Nora? Sure, all I want is to congratulate her!

SARA—(*hopelessly*) Oh! (*She sinks down on her chair at rear of the center table and covers her face with her hands.*)

NORA—(*with pitifully well-meant reassurance*) It's all right, Con. The young lad wants to marry her as soon as can be, she told me, and he did before.

MELODY—Musha, but that's kind of him! Be God, we ought to be proud av our daughter, Nora. Lave it to her to get what she wants by hook or crook. And won't we be proud watchin' her rise in the world till she's a grand lady!

NORA—(*simply*) We will, surely.

SARA—Mother!

MELODY—She'll have some trouble, rootin' out his dreams. He's set in his proud, noble ways, but she'll find the right trick! I'd lay a pound, if I had one, to a shilling she'll see the day when she'll wear fine silks and drive in a carriage wid a naygur coachman behind spankin' thoroughbreds, her nose in the air; and she'll live in a Yankee mansion, as big as a castle, on a grand estate av stately woodland and soft green meadows and a lake. (*with a leering chuckle*) Be the Saints, I'll start her on her way by making her a wedding present av the Major's place where he let her young gintleman build his cabin—the land the Yankees swindled him into buyin' for his American estate, the mad fool! (*He glances at the dueling pistol—jeeringly*) Speakin' av the departed, may his soul roast in hell, what am I doin' wid his pistol? Be God, I don't need pistols. Me fists, or a club if it's handy, is enough. Didn't me and Jamie lick a whole regiment av police this night?

NORA—(*stoutly*) You did, and if there wasn't so many av thim—

MELODY—(*turns to her—grinningly*) That's the talk, darlint! Sure, there's divil a more loyal wife in the whole world—(*he pauses, staring at her—then suddenly kisses her on the lips, roughly but with a strange real tenderness*) and I love you.

NORA—(*with amazed, unthinking joy*) Oh, Con!

MELODY—(*grinning again*) I've meant to tell you often, only the Major, damn him, had me under his proud thumb. (*He pulls her over and kisses her hair.*)

NORA—Is it kissin' my hair—!

MELODY—I am. Why wouldn't I? You have beautiful hair, God bless you! And don't remember what the Major used to tell you. The gintleman's sneers he put on is buried with him. I'll be a real husband to you, and help ye run this shebeen, instead of being a sponge. I'll fire Mickey and tend the bar myself, like my father's son ought to.

NORA—You'll not! I'll nivir let you!

MELODY—(*leering cunningly*) Well, I offered, remember. It's you refused. Sure, I'm not in love with work, I'll confess, and maybe you're right not to trust me too near the whiskey. (*He licks his lips.*) Be Jaysus, that reminds me. I've not had a taste for hours. I'm dyin' av thirst.

NORA—(*starts to rise*) I'll get you—

MELODY—(*pushes her back on her chair*) Ye'll not. I want company and singin' and dancin' and great laughter. I'll join the boys in the bar and help Cousin Jamie celebrate our wonderful shindy wid the police. (*He gets up. His old soldierly bearing is gone. He slouches and his movements are shambling and clumsy, his big hairy hands dangling at his sides. In his torn, disheveled, dirt-stained uniform, he looks like a loutish, grinning clown.*)

NORA—You ought to go to bed, Con darlin', with your head hurted.

MELODY—Me head? Faix, it was nivir so clear while the Major lived to tormint me, makin' me tell mad lies to excuse his divilments. (*He grins.*) And I ain't tired a bit. I'm fresh as a man new born. So I'll say goodnight to you, darlint. (*He bends and kisses her. Sara has lifted her tear-stained face from her hands and is staring at him with a strange, anguished look of desperation. He leers at her.*) And you go to bed, too, Sara. Troth, you deserve a long, dreamless slape after all you've accomplished this day.

SARA—Please! Oh, Father, I can't bear— Won't you be yourself again?

MELODY—(*threatening her good-humoredly*) Let you kape your mouth closed, ye slut, and not talk like you was ashamed of me, your father. I'm not the Major who was too much of a gintleman to lay hand on you. Faix, I'll give you a box on the ear that'll teach you respect, if ye kape on trying to raise the dead! (*She stares at him, sick and desperate. He starts toward the bar door.*)

SARA—(*springs to her feet*) Father! Don't go in with those drunken scum! Don't let them hear and see you! You can drink all you like here. Jamie will come and keep you company. He'll laugh and sing and help you celebrate Talavera—

MELODY—(*roughly*) To hell wid Talavera! (*His eyes are fastened on the mirror. He leers into it.*) Be Jaysus, if it ain't the mirror the auld loon was always admirin' his mug in while he spouted Byron to pretend himself was a lord wid a touch av the poet— (*He strikes a pose which is a vulgar burlesque of his old before-the-mirror one and recites in mocking brogue*)

"I have not loved the World, nor the World me;
I have not flatthered uts rank breath, nor bowed
To uts idolatries a pashunt knee,
Nor coined me cheek to smiles,—nor cried aloud
In worship av an echo: in the crowd
They couldn't deem me one av such—I stood
Among thim, but not av thim . . ."

(*He guffaws contemptuously.*) Be Christ, if he wasn't the joke av the world, the Major. He should have been a clown in a circus. God rest his soul in the flames av tormint! (*roughly*) But to hell wid the dead. (*The noise in the bar rises to an uproar of laughter as if Jamie had just made some climactic point in his story. Melody looks away from the mirror to the bar door.*) Be God, *I'm* alive and in the crowd they *can* deem me one av such! I'll be among thim and av thim, too—and make up for the lonely dog's life the Major led me. (*He goes to the bar door.*)

SARA—(*starts toward him—beseechingly*) Father! Don't put this final shame on yourself. You're not drunk now. There's no excuse you can give yourself. You'll be as dead to yourself after, as if you'd shot yourself along with the mare!

MELODY—(*leering—with a wink at Nora*) Listen to her, Nora, reproachin' me because I'm not drunk. Troth, that's a condition soon mended. (*He puts his hand on the knob of the door.*)

SARA—Father!

NORA—(*has given way to such complete physical exhaustion, she hardly hears, much less comprehends what is said—dully*) Lave him alone, Sara. It's best.

MELODY—(*as another roar is heard from the bar*) I'm missin' a lot av fun. Be God, I've a bit of news to tell the boys that'll make them roar the house down. The Major's passin' to his eternal rest has set me free to jine the Democrats, and I'll vote for Andy Jackson, the friend av the common men like me, God bless him! (*He grins with anticipation.*) Wait till the boys hear that! (*He starts to turn the knob.*)

SARA—(*rushes to him and grabs his arm*) No! I won't let you! It's my pride, too! (*She stammers*) Listen! Forgive me, Father! I know it's my fault—always sneering and insulting you—but I only meant the lies in it. The truth—Talavera— the Duke praising your bravery—an officer in his army— even the ladies in Spain—deep down that's been my pride, too—that I was your daughter. So don't— I'll do anything you ask— I'll even tell Simon—that after his father's insult to you—I'm too proud to marry a Yankee coward's son!

MELODY—(*has been visibly crumbling as he listens until he appears to have no character left in which to hide and defend himself. He cries wildly and despairingly, as if he saw his last hope of escape suddenly cut off*) Sara! For the love of God, stop—let me go—!

NORA—(*dully*) Lave your poor father be. It's best. (*In a flash Melody recovers and is the leering peasant again.*)

SARA—(*with bitter hopelessness*) Oh, Mother! Why couldn't you be still!

MELODY—(*roughly*) Why can't you, ye mean. I warned ye what ye'd get if ye kept on interferin' and tryin' to raise the dead. (*He cuffs her on the side of the head. It is more of a playful push than a blow, but it knocks her off balance back to the end of the table at center.*)

NORA—(*aroused—bewilderedly*) God forgive you, Con! (*angrily*) Don't you be hittin' Sara now. I've put up with a lot but I won't—

MELODY—(*with rough good nature*) Shut up, darlint. I won't have to again. (*He grins leeringly at Sara.*) That'll teach you, me proud Sara! I know you won't try raisin' the dead any more. And let me hear no more gab out of you about not marryin' the young lad upstairs. Be Jaysus, haven't ye any honor? Ye seduced him and ye'll make an honest gentleman av him if I have to march ye both by the scruff av the neck to the nearest church. (*He chuckles—then leeringly*) And now with your permission, ladies both, I'll join me good friends in the bar. (*He opens the door and passes into the bar, closing the door behind him. There is a roar of welcoming drunken shouts, pounding of glasses on bar and tables, then quiet as if he had raised a hand for silence, followed by his voice greeting them and ordering drinks, and other roars of acclaim mingled with the music of Riley's pipes. Sara remains standing by the side of the center table, her shoulders bowed, her head hanging, staring at the floor.*)

NORA—(*overcome by physical exhaustion again, sighs*) Don't mind his giving you a slap. He's still quare in his head. But he'll sing and laugh and drink a power av whiskey and slape sound after, and tomorrow he'll be himself again—maybe.

SARA—(*dully—aloud to herself rather than to her mother*) No. He'll never be. He's beaten at last and he wants to stay beaten. Well, I did my best. Though why I did, I don't know. I must have his crazy pride in me. (*She lifts her head, her face hardening—bitterly*) I mean, the late Major Melody's pride. I mean, I did have it. Now it's dead—thank God—and I'll make a better wife for Simon. (*There is a sudden lull in the noise from the bar, as if someone had called for silence—then Melody's voice is plainly heard in the silence as he shouts a toast:* "Here's to our next President, Andy Jackson! Hurroo for Auld Hickory, God bless him!" *There is a drunken chorus of answering* "hurroos" *that shakes the walls.*)

NORA—Glory be to God, cheerin' for Andy Jackson! Did you hear him, Sara?

SARA—(*her face hard*) I heard someone. But it wasn't anyone I ever knew or want to know.

NORA—(*as if she hadn't heard*) Ah well, that's good. They won't all be hatin' him now. (*She pauses—her tired, worn face becomes suddenly shy and tender.*) Did you hear him tellin' me he loved me, Sara? Did you see him kiss me on the mouth— and then kiss my hair? (*She gives a little, soft laugh.*) Sure, he must have gone mad altogether!

SARA—(*stares at her mother. Her face softens.*) No, Mother, I know he meant it. He'll keep on meaning it, too, Mother. He'll be free to, now. (*She smiles strangely.*) Maybe I deserved the slap for interfering.

NORA—(*preoccupied with her own thoughts*) And if he wants to kape on makin' game of everyone, puttin' on the brogue and actin' like one av thim in there— (*She nods toward the bar.*) Well, why shouldn't he if it brings him peace and company in his loneliness? God pity him, he's had to live all his life alone in the hell av pride. (*proudly*) And I'll play any game he likes and give him love in it. Haven't I always? (*She smiles.*) Sure, I have no pride at all—except that.

SARA—(*stares at her—moved*) You're a strange, noble woman, Mother. I'll try and be like you. (*She comes over and hugs her—then she smiles tenderly.*) I'll wager Simon never heard the shot or anything. He was sleeping like a baby when I left him. A cannon wouldn't wake him. (*In the bar, Riley starts playing a reel on his pipes and there is the stamp of dancing feet. For a moment Sara's face becomes hard and bitter again. She tries to be mocking.*) Faith, Patch Riley don't know it but he's playing a requiem for the dead. (*Her voice trembles.*) May the hero of Talavera rest in peace! (*She breaks down and sobs, hiding her face on her mother's shoulder—*

bewilderedly) But why should I cry, Mother? Why do I mourn for him?

NORA—(*at once forgetting her own exhaustion, is all tender, loving help and comfort*) Don't, darlin', don't. You're destroyed with tiredness, that's all. Come on to bed, now, and I'll help you undress and tuck you in. (*trying to rouse her—in a teasing tone*) Shame on you to cry when you have love. What would the young lad think of you?

(*Curtain*)

MORE STATELY MANSIONS

CHARACTERS

JAMIE CREGAN

MICKEY MALOY

NORA MELODY

SARA (*Mrs. Simon Harford*), *her daughter*

SIMON HARFORD, *Sara's husband*

JOEL HARFORD, *his brother*

DEBORAH (*Mrs. Henry Harford*), *mother of Simon and Joel*

ETHAN

WOLFE

JONATHAN } *children of Simon and Sara Harford*

OWEN (HONEY)

NICHOLAS GADSBY, *an attorney*

CATO, *the Harfords' coachman*

SCENES

ACT ONE

SCENE ONE: Dining room of Melody's Tavern, an Inn in a Massachusetts village near a city—night in October 1832.

SCENE TWO: A cabin on the shore of a small lake near the village—the following afternoon.

ACT TWO

SCENE ONE: Deborah's garden, Henry Harford's home in the city—a night in summer, 1836.

SCENE TWO: Sitting-room of Sara Harford's home in a neighboring textile mill town—the following night.

ACT THREE

SCENE ONE: Simon Harford's office at Harford, Inc. in the city—a morning in Fall of 1840.

SCENE TWO: Deborah's garden, the Harford home in the city—afternoon of the same day.

SCENE THREE: The parlor of the Harford home—night of the same day.

ACT FOUR

SCENE ONE: Simon Harford's office again—morning in summer 1841.

SCENE TWO: Deborah's garden—evening of the same night.

EPILOGUE: Same as Act One, Scene Two, the cabin on the lake—afternoon in Spring, 1842.

More Stately Mansions

ACT ONE
Scene One

Scene—*The dining room of Melody's Tavern, an Inn in a Massachusetts village near a city. The Tavern is over a hundred years old. It had once been a prosperous haven for travellers, a breakfast stop for the stagecoach, but the stage line had been discontinued years ago and the Inn fallen upon lean, unprosperous days.*

The dining room, and what is now the barroom, had once been a single spacious room, low-ceilinged, with heavy oak beams and panelled walls. It is now divided into two rooms by a pine partition, the barroom being the section off left. The partition is painted in a poor imitation of the panelled walls, which only makes it stand out more as an eyesore.

The appearance of the dining room gives evidence of a poverty-stricken neglect. Nothing in it has been repaired or freshened in years. The tablecloths are dirty and stained. On the partition at left, front, is a cracked mirror, hanging askew. Farther back, near the door leading to the Bar, a cupboard is fixed to the partition. In the rear wall, center, is the door leading to the street with two windows on either side of it. In the right wall, toward front, is a door to a little hallway off the kitchen, where the stairs to the upper floor are. At extreme front, right, is a high schoolmaster's desk with a stool.

Four tables are placed around the room, one at left, front, one at rear, to the left of the street entrance, one at right in back of the door to the hall, and the fourth at center, front. The two which are at left, front, and at right are square with four chairs. The other two are larger with three chairs to each long side and a chair at each end. It is night of a day in Fall, 1832. The room is lighted by three cheap lamps in brackets, one to each wall, and a candle on the table at center, front.

Jamie Cregan is discovered sitting in the chair at front of the table at left front. He is fifty-two but drunkenness has aged him and he looks in his sixties. An obviously Irish peasant type, he is tall and emaciated. His face is long, hollow-cheeked and lantern-jawed with small dark eyes, a wide, loose-lipped mouth, a twisted broken pug nose. There is the scar of a saber-slash over one cheek-bone. His ragged hair is a dirty white. He is dressed in old black clothes that are worn threadbare. A drunkard, there yet remains in him something likable, a fundamental decency, the dim flicker of an old soldier's courage and devil-may-care spirit. He sits slumped forward in his chair, sober now, in a stupor of melancholy, staring before him. A decanter of whiskey, three-quarters full, and several empty glasses are on the table in front of him.

For a moment after the rise of the curtain, there is silence. Then from the floor above comes the sound of voices and the rising and falling wail of an Irish keen for the dead. Cregan stirs and mutters to himself resentfully.

CREGAN—Ah, keen with your mouths and pretend, but there's divil a one in the world but miself and Nora cares in their hearts he's gone. (*He slumps into brooding dejection again. The door from the Bar is opened and Mickey Maloy, the barkeep, comes in. Maloy is as typically the Irish peasant as Cregan. He is thirty-four with a sturdy physique beginning to run into fat. He has a healthy, honest, common, fresh-complected face with curly dark hair and small blue eyes, twinkling with an amiable cunning. His mouth is set in the half-leering grin of a bartender's would-be, worldly-wise cynicism. He glances at Cregan with a look of mingled liking and contempt for his weakness.*)

MALOY—(*automatically appraising the decanter—grinning*) Glory be, it's three-quarters full yet! Are ye sick, Jamie? (*Cregan gives no sign of having heard the jibe. Mickey sits in the chair opposite him.*) I've been takin' stock of what liquor's left. There's enough for Nora to kape on. With me to help her— (*grudgingly*) and you too, if you'd stay sober—she'll have a livin' from this place. (*He pauses, then goes on resentfully.*) We'd have no cause to worry for Nora if it wasn't for the debts himself run up in the days he was playin' the grand gentleman.

CREGAN—(*starts from his stupor and pounds his fist on the table angrily*) Let you close your big mouth—and him dead upstairs! I'll not hear a word against him!

MALOY—(*unimpressed—contemptuously*) To hell wid you. (*Cregan relapses into dejection again. Maloy glances at him with a grudging sympathy.*) But I know how ye feel, Jamie, and I'm glad for him there's one to mourn him widout lyin'! (*From upstairs there comes again the wail of the keen. Maloy glances up.*) Well, it's a beautiful wake Nora's givin' him, anyways, and a grand funeral tomorrow. (*He gives Cregan a nudge.*) Let you rouse yourself, Jamie, and not sit there half dead. Come on, have a taste wid me like Con Melody'd want you to if he was alive here. You know he'd only laugh at you and call you a liar for pretendin' grief at his death.

CREGAN—(*with a change of mood—resentfully*) He would, damn him! He couldn't believe there was decency in anyone. (*He pours out a big drink from the decanter which Mickey has shoved toward him.*)

MALOY—(*pours a small drink for himself*) Because there was none in him. (*raising his glass*) Here's health. (*They drink.*)

CREGAN—(*melancholy again*) Poor auld Con. The dew don't taste the same, an' him not here.

MALOY—(*sardonically*) He's needin' a drink bad where he is now.

CREGAN—(*with a shudder*) Don't say it.

MALOY—(*smacking his lips judiciously*) The dew tastes right to me. It's his private stock and he knew whiskey, if it did kill him.

CREGAN—(*somberly*) It wasn't the dhrink killed him.

MALOY—(*grins*) You'll be tellin' me next it was something he ate.

CREGAN—(*angrily*) Yerrah, don't make fool's jokes an' Con Melody a corpse! It wasn't whiskey killed him, I'm sayin'. He was strong as a bull an' his guts was made of iron. He could have drunk a keg a day an' lived for twenty years yet if the pride and spirit wasn't killed inside him ivir since the night he tried to challenge that Yankee coward, Harford, to a duel, and him and me got bate by the police and arrested. And then his own daughter turnin' traitor and marryin' Harford's son. That put the final shame on him! He's been a walkin' corpse ivir since, drinkin' to forget an' waitin' for death, while he'd be talkin' in brogue wid all the bog-trotters came in, tellin' stories an roarin' songs, an' dancin' jigs, pretendin' he had no edication an' was no bhetter 'an they were.

MALOY—(*stubbornly*) He wasn't better. It was in the days

before that happened, when he used to lie about bein' a gintleman, an' his father only a Galway shebeen-keeper, that he was pretendin'.

CREGAN—(*harshly*) Arrah, don't talk! Didn't he go to the College in Ireland, and hadn't he his own estate till he ruined himself! Wasn't he as fine an Officer as you'd find in Wellington's Army when he was a Major of Dragoons in Spain and I served under him? To hell wid what his fader was! He raised Con to be a gentleman, and Con Melody was a gentleman! (*He adds, making the sign of the cross*) May God rest his soul in peace.

MALOY—(*crosses himself automatically*) Amen. I'll say no more. It's bad luck to spake ill of the dead, anyways. (*He pauses.*) Will Sara come for the funeral, d'you think?

CREGAN—(*viciously*) God's curse on her if she don't! Nora wrote her when himself was bad took, and she's had plenty of time.

MALOY—I doubt she'll come. She hated him. You know as well as me there's nivir been a word between them in the four years since she married. And, anyways, she was always stuck up and givin' herself airs. I'll wager by this she's so high and mighty she'd feel shame to visit her poor Irish relations even for her father's funeral.

CREGAN—(*fiercely*) Poor relations, is it? Her own mother! (*The door from the hall at right is opened and Nora Melody appears.*)

MALOY—(*warningly*) Whist!

(*Nora walks slowly toward them. She is forty-five, a typical Irish peasant woman with a shapeless, heavy figure. She must have been extremely pretty as a girl—she still has beautiful eyes—but drudgery has worn her down, constant weariness of body and spirit has made her too tired to care about her appearance, so that, even now dressed in her best black mourning, she appears older and more unattractive than she really is. She has a round head with thinning grey hair, almost white, arranged with a half-hearted attempt at neatness. Her face is broad with high cheekbones, the complexion a blotchy pallor. Everything about her body appears swollen—her neck, her nose, her lips, her sagging breasts, her legs, feet, ankles, and wrists, her hands with fingers knotted by rheumatism. Yet despite her appearance, there is a spirit in her that*) *shines through her grief and exhaustion, some will behind the body's wreckage that is not broken, something kindly and gentle and unselfish, an essential humble fineness of character, a charm.)*

NORA—(*as she comes to them—complaining but without bitterness*) Faix, it's a great help you are, Mickey, sittin' here takin' your ease.

MALOY—(*gets to his feet guiltily*) I've been makin' a list av the stock—

NORA—(*wearily*) Arrah, who cares now? Go up to the wake, that's a good lad, and see people have what they're wantin', an' lave me a chance to rest. My legs are broken under me. (*She sits down exhaustedly in Mickey's place at the table.*)

MALOY—I'll go, surely. But be damned if I'll ask what they're havin'! They'll drink ye out of house an' home wid any encouragement. (*He goes to the door at right and goes out, grumbling to himself. Nora sags in her chair with a weary sigh. Cregan relapses into his mood of depression, staring before him. Nora glances at him.*)

NORA—You've nivir been up to the wake at all, Jamie.

CREGAN—(*dully*) I don't want to look on him dead. (*with bitterness*) An' I don't want to see the crowd av thim pretendin' sorrow to his corpse, who hated and mocked him livin'.

NORA—(*gently reproachful*) You're bitter. (*He doesn't reply. She looks at him with understanding sympathy—gently*) You're missin' himself, Jamie?

CREGAN—I am, Nora.

NORA—(*pats his hand consolingly*) He's grateful for your sorrow, I know. You were the one friend he had in the world.

CREGAN—(*bitterly*) I'm thinkin' now I was maybe only a drunken sponge who helped him kill himself.

NORA—Don't think it. Sure, you know as well as me, it was the broken heart of his pride murthered him, not dhrink. Think only of what good you did him. It was only wid you he'd forgit once in a while and let himself remember what he used to be. An' wid me. (*her voice breaking*) I'm missin' him, too, Jamie. (*She sobs softly.*)

CREGAN—(*pats her shoulder gently*) Don't cry. We'd ought to be glad for his sake. He's where he longed to be now in the peace of death. (*changing the subject abruptly to distract her mind*) Sara'd ought to come soon, don't you think?

NORA—(*has stopped crying—dully*) Yes—if she'll come.

CREGAN—(*without conviction*) Av course she'll come.

NORA—I don't know. What do I know of her now? It's four years since I've laid eyes on her. I've only her letters, an' what are letters? It's aisy to remember to write to hide you're forgettin'. An' Sara had great pride in her, her father's own pride, and great ambition to raise herself in the world, and maybe she's grown shamed of me.

CREGAN—God curse her, thin!

NORA—(*immediately reacting defensively*) Let you not curse my Sara, Jamie Cregan! But it's my fault. I should be shamed to talk wrong of her, an' her so sweet in every letter, beggin' me kindly to visit her, an' her husban', too, God bless him, an' I nivir had the dacency to go, even when her children was born, but always was afeered to lave Con alone. An' she always asked if I needed money.

CREGAN—She nivir sent any.

NORA—If she didn't, it was because she knew I'd send it right back to her. So don't you be sayin'—

CREGAN—(*sullenly*) I'll say divil a word. (*a pause*) What'll you do, Nora, now himself is gone?

NORA—(*dully*) Kape on here. What else? It'll pay better now himself is gone. I'll kape on until all his debts is paid. (*She sighs wearily.*) It'll take a long time.

CREGAN—Arrah, why don't you let them whistle for their money, like he did. (*admiringly*) It's little Con Melody ivir let debts bother him! (*then with a change of tone*) All the same I know, if he didn't, that the men he owed would have kicked him out in the gutter, if they hadn't liked and trusted you.

NORA—(*simply*) I never let Con know that. (*proudly*) True for you. They trusted me. And I'll pay every penny. I've my pride, too.

CREGAN—Ye have. You're a good woman, Nora, an' the rist av us are dirt under your feet.

NORA—(*with a touching, charming, pathetic little smile of pleased coquetry that lights up her face*) It's you have the blarneyin' tongue, Jamie.

CREGAN—(*with an answering grin*) I have not. I'm a great

one for telling the truth, ye mean. (*with a change of tone*) Maybe Sara'll pay off his debts for you.

NORA—(*defensively*) She'll not, then! Do you think I'd ask her?

CREGAN—Why not? She's his daughter. She's a right—

NORA—Well, I've no right. She has her husband an' three young children to think of, an' another comin'. An' if I would take her money, what she's got is her husband's not hers. (*with scornful pride*) Do you think I'd let a Harford pay for Con Melody? Even if I had no pride, I'd be afeered to. Con would rise from his grave to curse me!

CREGAN—(*with grim appreciation*) Aye, divil a doubt, he would! His rage'd bring him back from the flames of hell! (*then hastily*) I'm jokin'. Don't heed me, Nora. (*Someone tries the handle on the bolted street door at rear. Then there is a knock.*)

NORA—(*wearily*) Go tell them it's the side door for the wake. (*Cregan goes and unbolts the door—then backs away as Sara with her husband, Simon Harford, behind her, step into the room.*)

(*Sara is twenty-five, exceedingly pretty in a typically Irish fashion, with a mass of black hair, a fair skin with rosy cheeks, and her mother's beautiful deep-blue eyes. There is a curious blending in her appearance of what are commonly considered to be aristocratic and peasant characteristics. She has a fine thoughtful forehead. Her eyes are not only beautiful but intelligent. Her nose is straight and finely modeled. She has small ears set close to her head, a well-shaped head on a slender neck. Her mouth, on the other hand, has a touch of coarse sensuality about its thick, tight lips, and her jaw is a little too long and heavy for the rest of her face, with a quality about it of masculine obstinacy and determination. Her body is concealed by the loose dress of mourning black she wears but, in spite of it, her pregnancy, now six months along, is apparent. One gets the impression of a strong body, full breasted, full of health and vitality, and retaining its grace despite her condition. Its bad points are thick ankles, large feet, and big hands, broad and strong with thick, stubby fingers. Her voice is low and musical. She has rid her speech of brogue, except in moments of extreme emotion.*

(*Simon Harford is twenty-six but the poise of his bearing makes him appear much more mature. He is tall and loose-jointed with a wiry strength of limb. A long Yankee face, with Indian resemblances, swarthy-complected, with a big straight nose, a wide sensitive mouth, a fine forehead, large ears, thick brown hair, light brown eyes, set wide apart, their expression sharply observant, and shrewd but in their depths ruminating and contemplative. A personality that impresses one incongruously as both practical and impractical. He speaks quietly, in a deep voice with a slight drawl. He is dressed in black. He is carrying in his arms the youngest of his three sons, Jonathan, just a year old.*

(At first sight of Sara and Simon as they enter the room, the impression one gets of their relationship, one feels that here is as loving and contented a marriage as one could find.)

SARA—*(as she enters—to Cregan with genuine warmth)* Jamie! *(She holds out her hand.)*

CREGAN—*(takes it coldly, bitter resentment in his voice)* Better late than never.

SARA—*(hurt and resentful)* I came as soon as—

NORA—*(has jumped to her feet—with a happy cry)* Sara, darlin'—

SARA—*(rushing to meet her)* Mother! *(They meet at left rear of the table at front and embrace and kiss. Meanwhile, Simon Harford stands just inside the door, smiling a bit embarrassedly. He turns to Cregan, who is closing the door, meaning to greet him pleasantly, but Cregan avoids his eye and leaves him standing there while he goes and sits sulkily in the chair at front of the table at left, rear.)*

NORA—*(weeping with joyous relief)* You've come, God bless you! *(She cries sobbingly but triumphantly over Sara's shoulder.)* Didn't I tell you she'd come, Jamie Cregan!

SARA—*(soothingly)* Of course I've come. There now, Mother dear, don't cry. You're making me cry, too. *(She breaks away from her mother's embrace, smiling and brushing tears from her eyes.)* And here's Simon waiting to greet you, Mother.

SIMON—*(comes toward them, smiling at Nora with a genuine affection)* It's good to see you again, Mother.

NORA—*(aware of him for the first time is embarrassed and instinctively bobs him an awkward curtsy—respectfully)* Good evening to you, Sor. *(then a smile of humble gratitude and*

pleasure as she diffidently takes the free hand he holds out to her)
Mother, did you call me? That is kind of you. (*then forgetting
everything as her eyes fall on the baby*) Glory be, you've brought
the baby.

SARA—I had to, Mother. The other two are old enough to
leave with the servant. But he's too little yet.

NORA—(*officiously maternal*) Arrah, ain't he as welcome as
the flowers in May, the darlin'. Here! Give him to me, Sor.
(*rebukingly to Sara*) Did you make your poor husband carry
him, you lazy girl?

SARA—(*laughingly*) No, Simon just took him outside the
door. But he likes to, anyway. (*then solicitously as Nora
cuddles the baby in her arms*) Careful, Mother. Don't wake
him.

NORA—Teach your grandmother! If I didn't know how to
carry babies, where would you be? (*then to Simon, mindful of
her duty as hostess*) Take a chair, Sor. Sit down Sara Darlin'.
(*She sits at right of the small table at left, front. Sara in the chair
at left end of the long table at front, center. Simon in the first
chair at the same table to right, rear, of Sara. Nora croons over
the baby.*) Wake you, would I, Acushla? It's little she knows.
My, haven't you a fine handsome face! You're the image of
your grandfather— (*She stops abruptly.*)

SARA—(*sharply resentful*) He's not! There's not the slightest
resemblance— (*She stops abruptly, too.*)

NORA—(*half to herself, her eyes sad and haunted*) Never
mind, never mind. He's gone now. (*She forces her attention on
the baby and talks hurriedly.*) What's your name, Darlin'? Your
mother wrote me. Let me see can I remember. The first was
Ethan. That's a quare Yankee name you'd not forget. The
next was Wolfe Tone. That's a grand Irish hero's name you
can't forget nather. And yours is—wait now—another
Yankee name—ah!—Jonathan, that's it.

SARA—(*maternally tender now*) And the one that's coming,
if it's a boy, we're going to call Owen Roe.

NORA—(*solicitously*) Ah, I was forgettin' you're— How are
you feelin', Darlin'?

SARA—(*embarrassed, with a glance at Simon*) As fine as can
be, Mother. I'm so healthy it never has bothered me at all.
(*changing the subject abruptly*) It was Simon's idea, the Irish

names. He likes the sound of them. It's the poet in him. (*Simon starts and gives her a strange suspicious glance.*) Only he wanted to call them all Irish, but I wouldn't let him, it wasn't fair. (*She laughs.*) So we agreed to divide, and I'd choose the American ones, and he could—

CREGAN—(*breaks in jeeringly*) So it was your husband had to shame you to give Irish names to your children, was it? (*They all start, having forgotten his presence.*)

SARA—(*stung*) Mother! I'll not stand Jamie insulting—

SIMON—(*quietly admonishing*) Sara. (*She glances at him and bites her lip.*)

NORA—(*angrily*) Jamie! Hush your blather! (*Cregan subsides sullenly. She turns to Simon apologetically.*) Don't mind him, Sor. (*From upstairs, at the wake, comes the sound of a wailing keen of sorrow. Sara starts and her face hardens. Nora's face grows dully grief-stricken. She mutters miserably*) We're all forgettin' him. (*She looks at Sara appealingly.*) Sara. You'll want to come up and see him now.

SARA—(*stiffening—coldly*) If you want me to, Mother.

NORA—(*sadly reproachful*) If *I* want?

SIMON—(*quietly*) Of course, Sara wishes to pay her last respects to her father.

SARA—(*again glances at him—then quietly*) Yes, I do, Mother.

NORA—(*relieved—quickly, as if afraid Sara may change her mind*) Then come now. (*She and Sara rise.*) We'll leave the baby in the back room I've fixed for you. He won't hear the noise there to wake him. (*She goes to the door at right. Sara starts to follow, her face set to face an ordeal. As she passes Simon he takes her hand and pats it reassuringly. For a moment she looks down into his eyes. Then her face softens with love and she bends over and kisses him impulsively.*)

NORA—Are you comin', Sara?

SARA—(*all hostility gone from her voice*) Yes, Mother. (*She goes quickly over and follows her mother off, right. A pause. Simon stares before him abstractedly. Cregan, from his chair at left, rear, regards him, frowning. He has been watching everything and is having a struggle with himself. He begins to feel liking and respect for Simon and he bitterly resents feeling this. Finally he gets up and comes to the table at left, front, ignoring Simon, and defiantly*

pours himself a big drink. Simon gets up and approaches him smil-
ingly with outstretched hand.)

SIMON—How are you, Mr. Cregan? I guess you've forgotten me. I met you here once with Major Melody.

CREGAN—(*placated in spite of himself, takes his hand—a bit*
stiffly) I hadn't forgotten but I was thinkin' maybe you had.
(*then punctiliously polite*) Will ye sit down and drink wid me,
Mr. Harford?

SIMON—With pleasure, Mr. Cregan. (*They sit down, Cre-*
gan at left—Simon at right of table. Simon pours a small drink
and raises his glass.) Your good health, Sir.

CREGAN—Drink hearty. (*Suddenly a fierce look of suspicious*
distrust comes over his face—harshly) Wait! I've a better toast
for you! To Ireland and the Irish and hell roast the soul of
any damned Yank that wud kape thim down!

SIMON—(*gravely*) Amen to that, Mr. Cregan. And may
they gain what they have longed for and fought for so long—
liberty! (*He touches his glass to Cregan's and drinks. For a mo-*
ment Cregan stares at him in comical confusion, then he gulps his
own drink hastily.)

CREGAN—(*wiping the back of his hand across his mouth—*
abashed and respectful) Thank ye, Sor. (*then in a burst of honest*
admiration) You're a man, divil a less, and Sara has a right to
be proud she's your wife.

SIMON—(*embarrassed in his turn*) Oh no, it's I who should
be proud to be her husband.

CREGAN—(*flatly*) I don't agree with you. (*He hesitates,*
staring at Simon uncertainly—then impulsively and appealingly,
lowering his voice and speaking rapidly) Listen, Sor. I've somethin' to say to you, before Nora comes. She's a grand woman!
(*as Simon is about to assent*) Oh, I know you know that or I'd
not be talkin'. An' she's had hell's own life wid Con. Nora
deserves peace in the days that's left her, if ivir a woman did.
An' now he's gone, she's her chance. But there's his debts.
It's her honor to pay them, but it'll take years of more slaving— (*Again there is a wailing keen from the room above and*
suddenly his expression changes to a guilty self-contempt and he
stares at the ceiling with a haunted, frightened look and mutters
to himself) Did you hear me, Con? It's a black traitor I am to
your pride—beggin' from a Harford! (*He turns on Simon*

fiercely threatening.) You'll forget what I've said, d'ye hear? I'm dead drunk! It's the whiskey talkin'! (*then as he hears a sound from the hall—imploringly*) Whist! Here's someone. For the love av God, don't let on to Nora I told ye or she'd nivir spake to me again! (*then quickly changing his tone as Sara enters from the hall at right*) It's a pleasure to drink wid ye, Mr. Harford. Will ye have another taste?

SIMON—(*playing up to him*) Not now, thank you, Mr. Cregan. (*Sara comes to them. She is white and shaken, her eyes have a stricken look, and her lips are trembling. Simon rises and puts his arm around her protectingly. She clings to him.*)

SARA—(*in a trembling voice*) You shouldn't have made me go, Simon. I'd forgotten him—almost. Now he's alive again—lying there in his Major's uniform I remember so well, with the old sneer I hated on his lips! (*She shudders. Simon pats her shoulder but can find nothing to say. She goes on.*) I couldn't stay. I can't bear the sight of death. It's the first time I've seen it and I hate it! It's life with you I love. I don't want to think it can ever end. (*She stares before her strangely.*) He was lying there with the old sneer—like death mocking at life!

SIMON—(*soothingly*) Don't think of it. It's over now.

SARA—(*controlling herself*) Yes, I know, I won't. (*forcing a smile*) You and Jamie seem to have gotten friendly all of a sudden. Don't you think I've got the best husband a woman could have, Jamie?

CREGAN—He's a man—if he is a Harford. (*Sara resents this but sees that Simon is smiling and she smiles too. Cregan goes on hesitantly.*) Askin' your pardon, Sor—but, av ye plaze, all them above at the wake will be gossipin' you're here, an' they'll take it bad if you don't go up—

SARA—(*angrily*) Let them think what they please!

SIMON—(*ignoring her—to Cregan*) I'll go right away. (*He turns.*)

SARA—(*clings to his arm*) No! I don't want death seeing you. We—we're so happy now. It'll bring bad luck.

SIMON—(*smiles teasingly and pats her cheek*) Now, now. Remember what you promised me about your superstitions.

SARA—That I'd forget all but the good luck ones. (*She forces a smile.*) I'll try again, Simon. (*She kisses him.*) Go up then—only don't stay long. (*Simon goes out right. Sara's eyes follow him. Then she sits in the first chair at left rear of the long table at center, her expression again strained and fearful. Cregan pours another drink and downs it, regarding her frowningly. Then he gets up and takes the chair on her right, at the end of the table.*)

CREGAN—(*with thinly veiled hostility*) You've changed, Sara.

SARA—(*resenting his tone*) Have I? (*then resolved not to quarrel, forcing a smile*) Well, I hope it's for the better—for Simon's sake.

CREGAN—(*sneeringly*) You've made yourself a fine, high-toned, Yankee woman, God pity you! It's great shame you must feel to have to come here an' associate wid us poor Irish.

SARA—(*stung*) Jamie! You know that's a lie! You know it was Father I was always ashamed of and he's dead now.

CREGAN—(*bitterly*) Thank God, you're saying.

SARA—You know I was ashamed of him just because he was such a crazy snob himself, with all his lies and pretenses of being a gentleman, and his being ashamed of my poor mother.

CREGAN—(*grimly*) He had none of his auld lies and pretenses wid him the past years since you married an' broke his heart.

SARA—Are you trying to blame me—?

CREGAN—He pretended to be one av us, instead. He never spoke except in a brogue you could cut with a knife, like an ignorant bog-trotter had just landed—except when he was too drunk to watch himself.

SARA—(*with a shrinking movement*) I know. Mother wrote me. (*suddenly deeply moved in spite of herself*) Poor Father! God forgive him. He never knew what he was himself. He never lived in life, but only in a bad dream. (*then with an abrupt change to disdainful scorn*) You don't have to tell me, Jamie. Didn't I see him, before I left, own up life had beaten him and lose the last speck of pride?

CREGAN—An' you scorned him for it, and still do, even while you say it was his lyin' pride shamed you! Faix, you're his daughter still, as you always was! You're like him, inside you, as he was at his worst!

SARA—It's a lie! (*controlling her temper—quietly*) You've

been drinking or you wouldn't be so unfair to me. I haven't changed, Jamie, not in the way you suspect.

CREGAN—We'll soon see. Tell me this, are you goin' to help your mother now in her troubles?

SARA—What do you think me? Of course, I'll help her! Don't I love her more than anyone in the world, except Simon and the children!

CREGAN—(*eagerly*) That's the talk! Then you'll give your word to pay off his debts?

SARA—(*stiffening*) His debts?

CREGAN—(*misunderstanding*) Faix, ye didn't think he'd ivir paid them, did ye? He didn't change that much, divil a fear. He owed ivry one in creation—two thousand or more, it must come to. But I know how well your husband's bin doin' in his business. It'd be aisy for you to—

SARA—Would it, indeed! Do you think I'd ever ask Simon to give the money we've slaved to save to pay the debts of his drunken squandering? Two thousand! And just when we're planning to buy out Simon's partner—and us with children to bring up and educate! Do you think I'm a fool?

CREGAN—(*his anger rising*) It's for your mother's sake. They might take the roof from over her head.

SARA—A fine roof! Let them! It'll be a good thing to free her from it. She's been a slave to this drunkard's roost too long. And I'll look after her, never fear, and see she wants for nothing.

CREGAN—Ye think Nora'd take charity from you? It's plain you've forgot the woman your mother is. (*losing his temper*) You've become a Yankee miser wid no honor ye wouldn't sell for gold! (*furiously*) God's curse on your soul, an' your mother's curse—!

SARA—(*with a cry of superstitious fear*) No! Don't! (*then flying into a rage herself and lapsing unconsciously into peasant brogue*) Hold your gab! Is it the likes of a drunken fool like you, who's sponged on my father for whiskey since the time you came to America, just because you're his cousin—is it you has the impudence to be talkin' to me about honor?

CREGAN—(*delighted at having broken her control—bitingly*) Someone has to—seein' you haven't any. (*with a grin of vindictive pleasure*) I'm glad to hear ye talk in your natural brogue an' forget the grand lady. Faix, there may be some red blood in ye yet beneath your airs!

SARA—Shut your mouth or I'll— (*She rises and seems about to strike him. Cregan chuckles. She controls herself—quietly*) I am sorry I lost my temper, Jamie. I ought to know better than to mind you.

CREGAN—(*enraged again*) Arrah, to hell wid your lady's airs! I'd rather have your insults! (*He stops abruptly as Nora appears in the doorway at right—getting to his feet, sullenly*) Here's herself. I'll be goin' up to the wake. (*He passes Nora as she comes in and goes out right. Nora sits wearily in the first chair at rear of the center table, right.*)

NORA—(*dully*) Was Jamie quarreling wid you? Don't heed him.

SARA—I don't, Mother. (*She sits in the chair at her mother's right.*)

NORA—(*sadly*) He's wild wid loneliness, missin' your father. (*A pause. Nora's face lights up.*) Mr. Harford came up to the wake.

SARA—(*annoyed*) Don't say Mr. Harford. You must call him Simon.

NORA—(*humbly*) It sounds too familiar, and him such a gentleman.

SARA—Nonsense, Mother! I don't like you to play humble with him—as though you were a servant. He doesn't like it either.

[. . . . .]

NORA—(*resentfully*) Why wouldn't I?

SARA—Because it's crazy. To give up life for a living death! I'd rather kill myself!

NORA—Don't be sneerin' just because your father, God forgive him, brought you up a haythen. (*stubbornly*) I would do it—and I will!

SARA—(*with a mocking smile*) There's no worse thing you could do if you want to make Father turn over in his grave.

NORA—(*triumphantly*) He'll not, then! I've been waitin' to tell you. He came back to the Faith before he died.

SARA—(*startled*) He never did! I don't believe you!

NORA—It's God's truth, Sara! Afther the doctor said he

was dyin' I begged him. He wouldn't answer for a long time, until I said, "Con, if you've ivir felt one bit av love for me, you'll do this for me now!" an' I cried my heart out. Then he opened his eyes an' there was a quare smile in them, an' he spoke, forgettin' to put on the brogue. "Yes," he says, "I still owe you that last bit of pride to pay for your love, don't I? An' I'm a gentleman about debts of honor, at least. So call in your priest." An' I did, an' he died with the rites av the Church. So ye needn't talk av his turnin' over in his grave.

SARA—(*her face hard—with intense bitterness*) No. I needn't. There's not that much pride left in him now. Even his spirit is dead.

NORA—(*resentful and a bit frightened*) Why do you make that bitter talk, God forgive you? Ain't you glad his soul's found peace, at last?

SARA—Not the peace of death while he was still alive. Oh, I know he died long ago—the spirit in him. But maybe I hoped, in spite of hating him, that he'd kept that last pride! Maybe I admired that one thing in him—his defiance of a God he denied but really believed in! (*She gives a bitter little laugh.*) Well, I know now why he died with that sneer on his lips. It was at himself!

NORA—(*protesting pitifully*) It's no sneer at all! It's the smile av his soul at peace! (*She breaks down and sobs.*) Don't take that from me, Sara!

SARA—(*moved and ashamed—patting her shoulder*) There Mother, don't. I—forgive me— (*changing the subject*) When will you go in the Convent?

NORA—(*sadly*) God knows. Tomorrow if I could. But there's a pile av debts to be paid first. I want no dishonor on his name, an' I'd feel it was cheatin' to go in the Convent widout a clear conscience. (*then hastily*) But nivir mind that. You've your own troubles. And it's nothin' at all.

SARA—(*hesitates—then blurts out*) I can ask Simon—

NORA—(*stiffening—proudly*) You'll not! You'll be kind enough to mind your own business av you plaze!

SARA—(*relieved and hating herself for being relieved*) But we'd be only too happy—

NORA—(*gently*) I know, Darlin'—an' God bless you. But

I'd nivir be able to look myself in the face if I held you back when you're just startin' in life.

SARA—But we could afford—

NORA—(*roughly*) No, I'm sayin'! To the divil wid me! My life is done! All I ask for myself is a bit av peace before the end. But I'm askin' more for you! I want you to rise in the world, an' own the things your father once owned an' you was born to—wealth an' a grand estate an' you ridin' in your carriage like a Duchess wid coachman an' footman, an' a raft av servants bowin' an' scrapin'.

SARA—(*her face lighting up—with a determined confidence*) I'll have all of that, Mother, I take my oath to you.

NORA—(*enthusiastically*) So ye will, Darlin'! I know it! An' won't I be proud, watchin' you rise, an' boastin' to the world! Even in the Convent, I'll be prayin' the Blessed Virgin to help you! (*guiltily*) God forgive me, maybe I shouldn't say that. (*reassuring herself*) Ah, I know Almighty God will find it enough if I give up all worldly thoughts for myself an' He'll forgive my pride in you! (*dismissing this eagerly*) Tell me now—how is the business doin'? You haven't written in a long while.

SARA—(*eagerly—unconsciously lapsing a little into brogue*) It's doing fine, Mother. We've just finished building an addition to the mill and the cottons we're weaving are as good or better than any foreign ones. By we I mean Matthew, too, but it'll soon be only us, because Simon is buying him out.

NORA—(*proudly*) So he's buyin' out his partner, is he? The last you wrote, you didn't know if you could persuade him.

SARA—(*with a smile*) I had a hard time, he's that stubborn. I had to plead with him it was for my sake and the children's. He's so afraid of getting in too deep. And it's so silly because after I get his mind made up, there's no stopping him. (*with a proud toss of her head*) And don't think it's just a wife, blind with love, boastin'. It's common talk of our town he's the ablest young merchant in the trade and has a great future before him.

NORA—(*admiringly*) Ah, ain't that grand, now! You'd nivir think it to meet him—I mean, he's so quiet and gentle.

SARA—(*with a laugh*) Let you be a man meetin' him in

business, and tryin' to get the best of him, you'd find him different. (*practically*) Of course, it doesn't do to boast yet. We're only on the first step. It's only a small mill that you wouldn't notice at all compared to the big ones. But business is leapin' up and once we have Matthew out of it—he wants to travel in Europe and he's only too anxious to sell at a bargain—we'll have all the profits for ourselves.

NORA—(*teasing admiringly*) Musha, you have grand business talk! To hear you, you'd think it was you was his partner, no less!

SARA—So I am! I'm no fool, Mother. I've got brains for more than just sleepin' with the man I love an' havin' his children an' keepin' his house. Ask Simon. He talks over everything with me. I've made him. At first, he was all for never sayin' a word about business at home, and treatin' me like a stuffed bird in a glass case he had to protect from the world, but I soon got him over that. Now he depends on me, an' I'll say for myself I've never advised him wrong. (*She smiles.*) The only foolish thing he ever did he did without askin' me. He had someone buy the old farm here for him where he used to live in the cabin by the lake.

NORA—Did he, now? I heard tell it was sold. Ivery one was wonderin' who was the fool— (*hastily*) I mane, they say divil a one has ivir made it pay.

SARA—(*frowning*) I know. It was foolish. But he was that shamed when I found out—like a little boy caught stealing jam—that I couldn't scold. And he had all kinds of excuses that it was a wise notion because, if the worst happened, it'd be easy to fix up the old farmhouse on it, and you could at least raise a living from it, and we'd always have it to fall back on. Then when I laughed at him and said that was no fear it'd ever come to that, he owned up he'd really bought it for sentiment because it was there we first loved each other.

NORA—(*guiltily embarrassed*) Arrah, don't think av that now. Wasn't you married right after? God forgave you the sin.

SARA—(*proudly defensive*) I've never asked His forgiveness. I'm proud of it. (*changing the subject abruptly*) So, of course, when he told me that, I forgave him. And maybe it'll come in useful in the end. There's over two hundred acres, and he bought it for a song, and the little lake on it is beautiful, and there's grand woods that would make a fine park. With a mansion built on the hill by the lake, where his old cabin was, you couldn't find a better gentleman's estate.

NORA—(*with admiring teasing*) Glory be, but you're sure av havin' your way!

SARA—(*determinedly*) I am, Mother, for this is America not poverty-stricken Ireland where you're a slave! Here you're free to take what you want, if you've the power in yourself. (*A pause—her expression suddenly becomes uneasily thoughtful.*) I think Simon had other reasons for buying the farm he didn't tell me—maybe that he didn't tell even himself. He has queer lonely spells at times when I feel he's in a dream world far away from me.

NORA—Yes, he's a touch av the poet, God pity him—like your father. (*A wailing keen comes from the floor above. Nora's face becomes sorrow-ridden. She shivers, and makes the sign of the cross.*)

SARA—(*her thoughts made more uneasy by this disturbance— irritably*) Why do you let them keen, Mother? It's old ignorant superstition. It belongs back in Ireland, not here! (*Then, as her mother doesn't hear her, she goes on uneasily.*) Sometimes I feel he's thinking that if it wasn't for me and the children he'd be living alone back in his cabin by the lake writing poetry like he used to, or else writing the book he was planning, to show people how to change the Government and all the laws so there'd be no more poor people, nor anyone getting the best of the next one, and there'd be no rich but everyone would have enough. (*She finishes scornfully.*) He doesn't talk about that anymore, thank God! I've laughed it out of him! I've told him you can make new laws but you can't make new men and women to fit them, so what's the use of dreaming? I've said, even if he could make it come true, it would be a coward's heaven he'd have, for where is the glory of life if it's not a battle where you prove your strength to rise to the top and let nothing stop you! (*She says this last with exultance. Then she smiles fondly.*) But I'm a fool to take his dreams seriously. Sure, when he's himself, there's no one takes more joy in getting ahead. If you'd see his pride sometimes when he comes home to tell me of some scheme he's accomplished. (*She laughs.*) Oh, he's a queer mixture. (*then intensely*) And I love him, every bit of him! I love him more than ever any woman loved a man, I think. I'd give my last drop of blood to make him happy! And he is happy! (*Again there is the wailing keen from the wake above. Nora gets to her feet, wearily.*)

NORA—(*dully*) I'd better go up to the wake. They'll think it wrong I'm staying away from him so long. (*She hesitates— feeling she must make some comment on what Sara has said, which she has only half heard.*) I wouldn't worry over Simon bein' happy. Sure, you've only to see the love in his face when he looks at you. (*then inconsequently*) Does he ever hear from his people?

SARA—(*resentfully*) From his father? No fear. He won't ever let Simon's name be spoken in their home. But Simon's mother writes him letters. Not often, though. I'll say this for her, she's never tried to interfere. (*then cynically*) Maybe it's because Simon's father never gives her the chance. (*then honestly*) No, that's not fair. I ought to feel grateful to her. It was the two thousand dollars she sent Simon after we were married gave us our start. (*resentfully*) Not but what we didn't pay her back every penny as soon as we'd saved it. I made Simon do that, for all his saying she wanted it to be a gift and we'd hurt her feelings. (*with a toss of her head*) I have my feelings, too. I'm accepting no gifts from her.

NORA—(*has not been listening to this at all—dully*) I'll go up to him now. (*She starts for the door at right as Simon enters it. He smiles at her and she forces a smile in return and goes out. He comes over and sits beside Sara, giving her a pat on the cheek as she smiles up at him.*)

SARA—How's the baby?

SIMON—Sound asleep. (*He hesitates—then making up his mind—uncomfortably*) Listen, Sara. There's one thing we ought to talk over and decide right away—for your mother's sake.

SARA—(*stiffens, glancing at him suspiciously*) What's that?

SIMON—(*quietly*) About your father's debts.

SARA—(*angrily*) How do you know? Was Jimmie Cregan begging to you?

SIMON—(*placatingly*) Now don't blame him.

SARA—(*angrily*) Ah, if that drunken fool would only mind his own business!

SIMON—(*quietly*) It's your business, isn't it? And we're partners, aren't we? So it's my business, too. Please don't feel bitter toward Cregan. He may have his faults. Who hasn't? (*smiling*) Perhaps even you and I have some. (*She glances at him with quick guilty suspicion.*) But he is a good friend to your mother.

SARA—(*sneeringly*) As long as she has free whiskey for him to sponge!

SIMON—(*frowns—a bit sharply*) Sara! That's not— (*He controls himself and pats her hand—gently*) I hate to hear you sneering and full of bitterness. That isn't you, you know.

SARA—(*clasps his hand—humbly*) No. It isn't the me who loves you. I know that, Simon. (*resentfully*) It's coming here does it to me. It brings back the past. It makes Father live again. Ah, why can't he be dead, and not have his ghost walk in my heart with the sneer on his lips?

SIMON—(*repelled*) Sara! (*then more gently—slowly*) One must forgive the dead, for their sakes, but even more for our own.

SARA—(*squeezing his hand*) Oh, I know!

SIMON—(*persuasively*) Try and forget him. It's of your mother we must think now. She has had a hard life. How hard you know better than anyone.

SARA—(*sadly*) I do. Poor Mother! Not an hour of joy or peace did he give her since the day she married him, but only slavery. (*then hurriedly—and guiltily*) But the debts come to two thousand dollars. That's a pile of money, Simon. No matter how much we wanted to, we couldn't afford right now—

SIMON—(*easily*) Oh, I think we can. You're forgetting what we've put aside to buy out Matthew. We can use part of that.

SARA—(*tensely*) And not buy him out, after all our plans? (*angrily*) No! I won't have it!

SIMON—(*sharply*) Sara!

SARA—(*hastily*) I mean it means so much to your future that you'd never forgive yourself!

SIMON—(*quietly*) What about your mother's future? Could we forgive ourselves if we deliberately ignored that?

SARA—(*hurriedly*) And anyway, it's no use talking, because I've already talked to her. I said I'd ask you to pay his debts for her.

SIMON—(*his face lighting up*) Ah, I knew you—

SARA—(*an undercurrent of triumph in her voice*) And she told me to mind my business for my pains! She was mad and insulted. So you might as well put it from your mind. (*with incongruous pride*) My mother may be an ignorant, simple woman but she's a proud woman, too. If you think she'd ever let a Harford pay Father's debts, you're badly mistaken.

SIMON—(*quietly*) I know your mother's pride and I admire her for it. (*then with a smile—calculating*) But I think we can get around her, if we go about it shrewdly. In the first place, before we let her know, I'll look up all the creditors and pay them. Then we'll face her with an accomplished fact. She will resent it, of course, but I've been figuring out a way to put it to her so that she'll be reconciled—that it's a sin for her to put her duty to God off just because of pride and that if she waited she might not live to enter a Convent. I can even see the Priest and persuade him to talk to her. I'll ask her, too, if it's fair of her to keep on the feud with my father against me, and if it isn't time, now your father's dead, to forgive and forget, for her grandchildren's sake, who have both Melody and Harford blood in them. I'll—

SARA—(*with a helpless sigh—exasperatedly*) Arrah, you needn't go on! (*her manner changing—with a trembling tender smile*) Don't I know better than any, without your boasting, that you're a sly one to look into a woman's heart and see her weakness and get your own way. (*proudly*) And don't I love you for it, and for being kind and sweet and good, and putting shame on me for a greedy selfish pig. (*She raises his hand impulsively and kisses it.*)

SIMON—(*tenderly*) Don't say that! You're the dearest, most precious— (*He hugs her to him.*)

SARA—(*stubbornly*) I'm not! I'm a fool always dreaming of wealth and power and pride, even while I know in my heart that doesn't matter at all, that your love is my only wealth— to have you and the children. (*pitifully*) But I can't help

dreaming, Darling. I've known what you haven't—poverty—
and the lies and dirt and hurt of it that spits on your pride
while you try to sneer and hold your head high!

SIMON—(*soothingly*) I know, Dear.

SARA—You don't. You couldn't. (*pleadingly*) But please
know, Simon Darling, that for all the greed in me, I was only
fooling myself. My conscience—and my honor, for I have
honor, too—would never have rested easy until we paid the
debts for Mother. (*She laughs.*) So thank you kindly, Sir, for
beating me and saving me having to beat myself. (*She kisses
him.*)

SIMON—(*teasing tenderly*) Maybe I guessed that. (*He
laughs.*) You can't fool me.

SARA—(*teasing, with a note of taunting coming in*) No. And
you can't fool me. Don't I guess that, besides all your goodness of heart, you're glad of the excuse not to buy out your
partner, because you're afraid of the whole weight of the business on your shoulders.

SIMON—(*starts—sharply*) What makes you say that! It's
not true. I should think I'd already given you ample proof.
If I'm afraid it's not for that reason, as you well know. (*bitterly*) But, do you know, I wonder? Will you ever understand—?

SARA—(*alarmed now*) Darling, I was only teasing. (*pulling
him to her—with rough possessive tenderness*) Come here to me.
Don't push away, now! Don't you know I wouldn't hurt you
for the world?

SIMON—(*giving in—but stiffly*) I don't like that kind of
teasing. (*She kisses him. He relaxes against her body. His face
softens. Finally he forces a laugh.*) Forgive me, I'm a fool. (*then
almost boastfully*) To show you how wrong you are, I've already figured out how we can pay your father's creditors, and
still buy out Matthew's interest.

SARA—(*eagerly*) Ah, don't I always tell you you've the
brains to beat the world!

SIMON—I'll simply get him to take my note for the
difference.

SARA—(*uncertainly*) I don't like notes. My father always—

SIMON—(*tauntingly*) Who is being afraid, now? (*then eagerly*) But you needn't be. With the profits from the business,

as I intend to reorganize it, I can pay him in no time, and then—

SARA—(*gloatingly*) Oh, then I know you'll make the money come flying in! (*She suddenly looks guilty and forces a laugh.*) There I go with my greedy dreaming again. But it's because when we were married it was such a hurt to my pride that I knew your family and their friends thought you'd lowered yourself through me. I swore then I'd help you rise till you were bigger than your father or any of them.

SIMON—(*his face hardening*) It would be a satisfaction to me, too, to prove to Father, in the only terms he can understand—

SARA—(*aggressively*) And to your mother.

SIMON—(*his expression changing—in a tone that is tinged with self-contempt*) Mother? I hardly think my achievement on that plane could impress her greatly.

SARA—Why not, I'd like to know?

SIMON—(*frowns and shrugs his shoulders*) Well, her point of view is a bit different from yours—ours, I should say.— (*He is interrupted by a knock on the door at rear.*)

SARA—(*irritably*) Someone for the wake, I suppose. I'll go. (*She goes and unbolts the door—then starts back with a surprised gasp as she sees a tall, black, powerfully-built negro in a coachman's uniform standing before the door.*) What do you want?

CATO—(*removes his hat—with polite dignity*) Mister Simon Harford, Ma'am. Is he heah?

SIMON—(*astonished*) Why hello, Cato. (*He goes back to meet him.*) It's all right, Sara. Let him come in. (*She steps aside and Cato enters. He is about fifty-five with whitening, crinkly hair. Simon, smiling with genuine pleasure, holds out his hand. Cato takes it embarrassedly.*) It's good to see you again, Cato.

CATO—(*grinning*) Thank you, Mister Simon. I'm happy to see you. (*They come forward. Sara follows them, her expression uneasy and suspicious.*)

SIMON—This is my wife, Cato. She's often heard me speak of you. (*Cato bows respectfully. Sara forces a smile.*)

SARA—Yes, indeed, Cato. He's never forgotten how good you were to him when he was a boy.

SIMON—Oh, Cato and I are old friends, aren't we, Cato?

CATO—(*grins embarrassedly*) Thank you, Suh. Thank you,

Ma'am. Your mother sent me, Suh. I'se got a letter she tol' me give in your hands and only your hands. (*Sara stiffens resentfully. Cato takes a letter from his inside pocket and hands it to Simon.*) She say wait til you read it and you tell me de answer and I tell her.

SIMON — (*opens the letter. It is only a few lines. As he reads his face lights up.*) Tell her my answer is, of course I'll meet her there.

CATO — Yes, Suh. I'll tell her. Now I better git back quick. She tell me sneak out and sneak in so nobody see and tell yo father. (*He bows to Sara.*) Good night, Ma'am. Good night, Suh. (*He hesitates — then blurts out*) Effin you don't mind, I'se wishin' you happiness!

SIMON — Thank you, Cato. Good night.

SARA — (*touched, her face softening*) Thank you, Cato. Good night. (*Cato makes a hurried sidling-backwards exit through the door at rear, closing it behind him. Sara sits in the chair at right end of the table at center, front, her face again stiff and resentful. Simon stands with the letter in his hands, sunk in a smiling reverie. Then his eyes fall on Sara and he starts as if awakening.*)

SIMON — Here's Mother's letter, if you'd care to read it.

SARA — (*stiffly*) No. It was meant for you alone.

SIMON — Nonsense. I'll read it to you. It's only a note. (*He reads*) "I have your letter telling me you are coming up for your father-in-law's funeral and it occurs to me that we might take this opportunity to see each other again, if only for a moment. If you agree, and if Sara will consent to a brief leave-of-absence for you —"

SARA — Why shouldn't I consent? Does she think I'm afraid?

SIMON — (*resentful in his turn*) Don't be silly. She's only joking. (*He goes on reading*) "— let us meet at your old cabin tomorrow afternoon at three o'clock. I hope you can come. I am most curious to see how much you've changed, and I promise you will discover me to have changed, too, though not by evidence of the ravages of time on my poor face, I trust." (*Then he laughs.*) Hello. Here's a joke on her. I didn't notice before, but she's signed it "Deborah." She must have been in such a hurry —

SARA — It seems a strange letter to me.

SIMON—(*impatiently*) I've always told you you can't judge anything she does by ordinary standards. (*He smiles.*) She takes a childish pride in being fancifully willful and eccentric. You surely saw that, the one time you met her, even though you only talked with her a moment.

SARA—I saw it, yes. And I guessed beneath it she was a woman with a will of iron to get her own way.

SIMON—(*laughs*) Iron and Mother! That's funny, Sara. Quicksilver would describe her better.

SARA—Maybe. But she promises you she's changed.

SIMON—(*smiling*) She couldn't change if she tried. From her letters of the past year or so, I'd say she had simply become more herself, if that were possible.

SARA—Maybe. (*She hesitates—then slowly*) I wish you wouldn't go, Simon.

SIMON—(*astonished*) Not go? When she asks me to? When we haven't seen each other in four years? Surely you wouldn't want me to hurt her like that? (*then shortly*) Anyway, I've already said I would go.

SARA—You could send a note by Jamie. You could lie and make an excuse.

SIMON—(*sharply*) Sara! (*He stares at her frowningly.*) I can't understand— (*His face softens and he puts his arm around her.*) Here, here. This won't do. What has come over you?

SARA—(*doggedly*) Why does she want you to meet her at your old cabin?

SIMON—(*cajolingly*) Because it's out of the way and she won't be seen going there. She can't take any chance that Father might find out, you know. And I suppose it naturally suggested itself. I wrote her I had bought the property, so she knows she won't be trespassing.

SARA—(*resentfully*) It's mine. You put it in my name. I hope you told her that. (*with sudden agitation*) Oh, I know I'm stupid, Simon, but I can't help suspecting she hates me in her heart and would like nothing better than a chance to come between us.

SIMON—(*stares at her—then laughs teasingly but with a note of taunting*) Ah, who's the one who is afraid now? (*then with increasing sharpness*) You have absolutely no justification for talking of Mother like that. It's not only absurd, it's ungrateful. She favored our marriage. It was her money that helped us. And now you want me to lie out of seeing her! I don't know what to think of you, Sara, when you act like this!

SARA—(*frightened*) Please don't think badly, Simon. I know it's crazy. Maybe it's being pregnant makes me nervous and afraid of everything.

SIMON—(*immediately shamefaced*) I, —I'm sorry, Dear. (*He kisses her with awkward tenderness.*)

SARA—It's because I love you so much, and I never can believe my good luck in having you. I'm always afraid of something happening.

SIMON—(*hushing her—tenderly*) Foolish One! As if anything could— (*He kisses her.*)

SARA—(*presses him to her with a fierce possessiveness and kisses him. Then she pushes him back and jumps to her feet with a happy laugh.*) There! The craziness is all gone. Of course, you must see your mother. She's been good to us, and I'll never stop being grateful, and you're to give her my best respect and love. (*then bullying him lovingly*) And now, quick with you, and go to bed. I want you to have a good rest so you'll look healthy and handsome and she'll see how well I take care of you. (*She pulls his arm and he gets to his feet smilingly.*) Go on. Get along with you. (*She urges him toward the door at right.*) I'll be in as soon as I've had another word with Mother. But mind you're fast asleep by then!

SIMON—(*laughingly*) Oh, I'll mind. Don't I always obey like a devoted slave? (*He goes out.*)

SARA—(*looks after him, smiling fondly, then sits down, sighing. She stares before her, deep in thought. Her expression suddenly becomes uneasy, suspicious, and calculating.*) She's still got her hold on him. She's up to some trick. (*with smouldering anger*) Well, I'll fool her! I'll go there and hide. I can easy get the key from his pocket— (*then guiltily*) What would he think of me? But he won't ever know. (*scornfully*) Ah, the divil take honor! It's something men made up for themselves! As if she'd ever let honor stand in her way!

(*Curtain*)

Scene Two

Scene—*A log cabin by a lake in the woods about two miles from the village. It is just before three in the afternoon of the following day.*

The cabin is ten feet by fifteen, made of logs with a roof of warped, hand-hewn shingles. It is placed in a small clearing, overgrown with rank, matted grass. The front of the cabin, with a door at center, and a small window at left of door, faces front, overlooking the lake. Another window is in the wall facing right. At the left side is a stone chimney. Close by the left and rear of the cabin is the wood—oak, pine, birch, and maple trees. The foliage is at the full of brilliant Autumn color, purple and red and gold mingled with the deep green of the conifers.

The cabin gives evidence of having been abandoned for years. The mortar between the stones of the chimney has crumbled and fallen out in spots. The moss stuffing between the logs hangs here and there in straggly strips. The windows have boards nailed across them. A weather-beaten bench stands against the wall at left of the door. It is home-made, heavily constructed, and is still sturdy.

The clearing is partly in sunlight, partly shadowed by the woods.

As the curtain rises Sara appears by the corner of the cabin, right, having come by a short-cut trail from off rear, right, along the shore of the lake. She has evidently hurried for she is breathless and panting. She looks around the clearing furtively. Her expression is a mixture of defiant resentment and guilt. She wears the same mourning of Scene One. She hastily unlocks the door and changes the key to the inside. Leaving the door ajar, she comes stealthily to the edge of the woods at left, front, and peers up a path which leads from the clearing into the woods. She starts and darts back to the door, enters the cabin and closes the door noiselessly behind her and locks herself in. For a moment there is silence. Then Simon's mother, Deborah Harford, steps into the clearing from the path, at left, front.

Deborah is forty-five but looks much younger. She is small, not over five feet tall, with the slender, immature figure of a young girl. One cannot believe, looking at her, that she has ever borne children. There is something about her perversely virginal. Her face is small, heart-shaped, olive-complected, astonishingly youthful, with only the first tracing of wrinkles about the eyes and

*mouth, a foreshadowing of sagging flesh under the chin, and of
scrawniness in the neck. It is framed by a mass of wavy white hair,
which by contrast with the youthfulness of her face, gives her the
appearance of a girl wearing a becoming wig at a costume ball.
Her nose is dainty and delicate above a full-lipped mouth, too
large and strong for her face, showing big, even white teeth when
she smiles. Her forehead is high and a trifle bulging, with sunken
temples. Her eyes are so large they look enormous in her small face.
Beautiful eyes, black, deep-set, beneath pronounced brows that
meet above her nose. Her hands are small with thin, strong, tapering fingers, and she has tiny feet. She is dressed daintily and
expensively, with extreme care and good taste, entirely in white.
Her habitual well-bred manner is one of mercurial whimsicality —
a provocative unconventional frankness of speech. But one senses
that underlying this now is a nervous tension and restlessness, an
insecurity, a brooding discontent and disdain.*

DEBORAH — (*looks around the clearing — bitterly*) And I
hoped he would be here, eagerly awaiting me! (*She forces a
self-mocking smile.*) What can you expect, Deborah? At your
age, a woman must become resigned to wait upon every
man's pleasure, even her son's. (*She picks her way daintily
through the long grass toward the bench, answering herself resentfully.*) Age? I am only forty-five. I am still beautiful. You harp
on age as though I were a withered old hag! (*mocking again*)
Oh, not yet, Deborah! But now that the great change is upon
you, it would be wise, I think, to discipline your mind to
accept this fate of inevitable decay with equanimity. (*She gives
a little shiver of repulsion — determinedly*) No! I will not think
of it! I still have years before me. (*She breaks a leaf off the
branch fastidiously and sits down — sneeringly*) And what will
you do with these years, Deborah? Dream them away as you
have all the other years since Simon deserted you? Live in the
false life of books, in histories of the past? Continue your
present silly obsession with scandalous French Eighteenth
Century memoirs? Dream yourself back until you live in them
an imaginative life more real than reality, until you become
not the respectable, if a trifle mad, wife of the well known
merchant, but a noble adventuress of Louis's Court, and your
little walled garden, the garden of Versailles, your pathetic

summerhouse a Temple of Love the King has built as an assignation place where he keeps passionate tryst with you, his
mistress, the unscrupulous courtesan, forsooth, greedy for
lust and power! (*She laughs softly with sneering self-mockery—
tauntingly*) Really, Deborah, this latest day dream is the most
absurd of all the many ridiculous fantasies in which you have
hidden from yourself! I begin to believe that truly you must
be more than a little mad! You had better take care! One day
you may lose yourself so deeply in that romantic evil, you will
not find your way back. (*answering herself with defiant bravado*) Well, let that happen! I would welcome losing myself!
(*abruptly—angry*) But you distort and exaggerate, as you always do! You know I do not take it seriously. I am lonely and
bored! I am disgusted with watching my revolting body decay. Anything to forget myself. Besides, there is a perfectly
rational explanation. I have seriously taken up the study of
Eighteenth Century France to occupy my mind. I have always
admired the Bourbons—perhaps because Father's stupid adoration of Napoleon prejudiced me against Napoleon, I suppose, and made me want to love his enemies. (*impatiently*)
No, no, don't be absurd! That has nothing to do with it. I
admire the manners and customs of that period, that is all. I
would like to have lived then when life was free and charming
and fastidious, not vulgar and ignoble and greedy as it is in
this country today. (*She stops abruptly—exasperatedly*) But
how stupid! These insane interminable dialogues with self!
(*with a sudden tense desperation*) I must find someone outside
myself in whom I can confide, and so escape myself. If I only
had a close woman friend, someone strong and healthy and
sane, who dares to love and live life greedily instead of reading and dreaming about it! What a mistake it was to warn off
friendship from my life like a prying trespasser! (*answering
herself mockingly*) Quite true, Deborah, but don't tell me you
hope to make Simon into such a friend—a man and your
son. (*argumentatively*) Well, that is not so absurd as it appears.
He always had a sensitive, feminine streak in him. He used to
sense so much intuitively, to understand without my putting
into words, and I hope he still— (*then derisively*) You forget he
has changed, as you know from his letters. You are thinking

of the Simon that was, your Simon, not the contented husband of that vulgar Irish biddy, who evidently has found
such a comfortable haven in her arms! (*with bitter sadness*) Yes,
it is hopeless. What am I doing here? Why did I come? And
he keeps me waiting. Perhaps he is not coming. Perhaps she
would not permit him— (*in a burst of anger*) Am I to sit all
afternoon and wait upon his pleasure? (*springing to her feet*)
No! I will go! (*controlling herself—in a forced reasonable tone*)
Nonsense, he told Cato to tell me he would come. He would
never break his word to me, not even for her. I know, from
his letters, he still loves me. (*She sits down again.*) I must stop
my ridiculous, suspicious worrying. He is not late. It is I who
am early. I have only to be patient—keep my mind off bitter
thoughts—stop thinking—wile away the time—with any
dream, no matter how absurd, if it serves the purpose of comforting me until he comes—shut my eyes and forget—not
open them until he comes— (*She relaxes, her head back, her
eyes shut. A pause. Then she dreams aloud to herself.*) The Palace
at Versailles—I wear a gown of crimson satin and gold, em-
broidered in pearls—Louis gives me his arm, while all the
Court watches enviously—the men, old loves that my ambition has used and discarded, or others who desire to be my
lovers but dare not hope—the women who hate me for my
wit and beauty, who envy me my greater knowledge of love
and of men's hearts—my superior talents for unscrupulous
intrigue in the struggle for power and possession—I walk
with the King in the gardens—the moonlight sobbing in the
fountains—he whispers tenderly: "My Throne it is your
heart, Beloved, and my fair kingdom your beauty, and so of
all Sovereigns of the earth I am most blessed"—he kisses me
on the lips—as I lead him into the little Temple of Love he
built for me— (*There is a sound from up the path at left,
through the woods, front. She starts quickly and opens her eyes as
Simon comes into the clearing.*)

SIMON—(*his face lighting up*) Mother! (*He strides toward
her.*)

DEBORAH—(*rising—still half in her dream—in a tone of
arrogant displeasure*) You have been pleased to keep me waiting, Monsieur.

SIMON—(*disconcerted—then decides she is joking and laughs*) Not I, Madame! I'm on the dot. It's you who are early. (*He kisses her.*) Mother, it's so good to—

DEBORAH—(*her arrogance gone—clinging to him, almost hysterically*) Oh, yes! Yes! Dear Simon! (*She begins to sob.*)

SIMON—(*moved*) Don't! (*tenderly chiding*) Here, here! You crying! I can't believe it. I don't remember ever seeing you cry.

DEBORAH—(*stops as suddenly as she had begun—pulling away from him*) No. And it is a poor time to begin. Tears may become a woman while she's young. When she grows old they are merely disgusting. (*She dabs her eyes with her handkerchief.*)

SIMON—(*gives her another puzzled look*) Oh, come now. (*smiling*) You're only fishing for compliments, Mother. You're as young and pretty as ever.

DEBORAH—(*pleased—coquettishly*) You are gallant, Sir. My mirror tells me a crueler story. Do you mean to say you don't see all the wrinkles? Be truthful, now.

SIMON—I can see a few, just beginning. But for your age it is amazing—

DEBORAH—(*flashes him a resentful glance*) It is true, I am well preserved. (*abruptly*) But how foolish of us to waste precious moments discussing an old woman's vanity. (*She puts her hands on his shoulders.*) Here. Turn about is fair play. Let me examine you. (*She stares into his face critically.*) Yes. You have changed. And quite as I had expected. You are getting your father's successful merchant look.

SIMON—(*frowns and turns away from her*) I hope not! (*changing the subject*) Sit down, Mother. (*She does so. He stands examining the cabin.*) I shall have to send someone out here to repair things. I wish I could do it myself. (*He passes his hands over the logs lovingly.*) What labor it cost me to build this without help. Yet I was never happier. (*He tries the door—searches his pocket.*) Funny, I could have sworn I had the key. But perhaps it is better. It would only make me melancholy.

DEBORAH—(*casts a sharp appraising glance at his face*) Yes, it is always sad to contemplate the corpse of a dream.

SIMON—(*answers before he thinks*) Yes. (*then defensively*) Unless you have found a finer dream.

DEBORAH—Oh, I know. Love is worth any sacrifice. I told you that, if you will remember. How is Sara?

SIMON—Well—and happy.

DEBORAH—You are as much in love?

SIMON—More. I cannot imagine a marriage happier than ours.

DEBORAH—I am glad. But, of course, I knew. You have protested in every letter how happy you were. (*He flashes a suspicious look at her. She goes on casually.*) And the children? Sara expects another before long, I believe you wrote.

SIMON—Yes.

DEBORAH—All this child-bearing. It must be a strain. Is she pretty still?

SIMON—More beautiful than ever.

DEBORAH—There speaks the devoted husband! I was wondering if you would bring her with you today.

SIMON—(*surprised*) You said nothing in your note about bringing her. I thought you wanted to see me alone.

DEBORAH—I did. But perhaps I see now it might have been as well— (*quickly*) I had begun to think perhaps Sara might not permit you to come—

SIMON—(*frowning*) Permit me? You talk as though I were a slave.

DEBORAH—Well, one is, isn't one, when one is in love? Or so I have read in the poets.

SIMON—(*smiling*) Oh, to love I am a willing slave. But what made you think Sara—?

DEBORAH—Well, a woman's love is jealously possessive— or so I have read—and she knows how close you and I used to be in the old happy days. You were happy in those days with me, weren't you, before you graduated from Harvard and had to leave me and find your own life in the world?

SIMON—(*moved*) Of course I was, Mother—never more happy.

DEBORAH—(*tenderly*) I am glad you still remember, Dear. (*She pats his hand.*)

SIMON—And I am grateful for all you did afterwards— your approval of our marriage, your generosity in helping us financially to make a start.

DEBORAH—It was Sara, wasn't it, who insisted on your paying back as a loan what I had meant as a gift?

SIMON—(*uncomfortably*) Yes, she didn't understand— She is very sensitive and proud— (*hurriedly*) But she is as grateful to you as I am. She will never forget your kindness.

DEBORAH—(*with a trace of disdain*) I am grateful for her appreciation. (*changing the subject abruptly*) Tell me, do you ever think now of the book you were so eager to write when you resigned in disgust from your father's business and came out here to live alone—the one inspired by the social philosophy of Jean Jacques Rousseau—your Utopian plan for a new society where there would be no rich nor poor, where all would be content with enough and live in perfect amity without envy or greed. You never mentioned it in your letters. Have you abandoned the idea entirely?

SIMON—(*reluctantly*) For the present. I have so little time now. (*defensively*) Oh, I think of it often and some day I'll write it.

DEBORAH—I see.

SIMON—(*suspiciously*) What made you ask about that now, Mother?

DEBORAH—(*carelessly*) Nothing. This place reminded me, I suppose. And you really should write it. The times are ripe for such a book, in these days when our republic is sinking into a corrupt decline. With four years more of Mr. Jackson in power—and even your father admits he is sure of re-election—the precedent will be irrevocably set. We shall be governed by the ignorant greedy mob for all future time. (*She laughs with malicious amusement.*) Your poor father! He wishes Massachusetts would secede from the Union. One has but to mention the name of Jackson to give him violent dyspepsia.

SIMON—(*grinning*) I can imagine. (*then scornfully*) It's ridiculous snobbery for him to sneer at the common people. He should remember his grandfather was only a Welsh immigrant farmer. Not that I hold any brief for Andrew Jackson. His spoils system is a disgrace to the spirit of true Democracy. (*He shrugs his shoulders.*) But it is also an inevitable development of our system of government. That system was wrong from the beginning. It confused freedom with separation from England, and then mistook the right to vote for Liberty. To be truly free, we must start all over again. In a free society there must be no private property to tempt men's greed into enslaving one another. We must protect man from his stupid possessive instincts until he can be educated to outgrow them spiritually. But at the same time, we must never forget that the least government, the best government. We must renounce the idea of great centralized governments, and divide society into small, self-governing communities where all property is owned in common for the common good. In my book I will prove this can easily be done if only men—

DEBORAH—(*cynically*) Ah, yes, if only men—and women—were not men and women!

SIMON—(*frowns, then smiles*) Now you're as cynical as Sara. (*She stiffens.*) That is her objection, too. (*then with embarrassment*) But I'm afraid I'm boring you with my perfect society.

DEBORAH—No. I'm only too happy to discover the old idealistic dreamer still exists in you.

SIMON—(*self-consciously*) I haven't spoken of such matters in so long— (*He forces a laugh.*) Your influence, Mother! You were always such a sympathetic audience.

DEBORAH—(*quietly*) I still am. But are you, I wonder?

SIMON—(*preoccupied, ignores her question, and goes on doggedly as if he had to finish expressing his ideas*) I still believe with Rousseau, as firmly as ever, that at bottom human nature is good and unselfish. It is what we are pleased to call civilization that has corrupted it. We must return to Nature and simplicity and then we'll find that the People—those whom Father sneers at as the greedy Mob—are as genuinely noble and honorable as the false aristocracy of our present society pretends to be!

DEBORAH—(*bitingly*) No doubt. However, I would still be nauseated by their thick ankles, and ugly hands and dirty finger nails, were they ever so noble-hearted! (*She suddenly cries with a desperate exasperation*) Good Heavens, did I come here to discuss politics, and the natural rights of man—I, who pray the Second Flood may come and rid the world of this stupid race of men and wash the earth clean! (*She gets to her feet—with curt arrogance*) It is getting late, I must go.

SIMON—Go? You've just come! (*pleadingly*) Mother! Please! Forgive me if I've bored you. But it was you who brought it up. (*coaxingly*) Come. Sit down, Mother. (*She sits down again.*) You haven't told me a word about yourself yet.

DEBORAH—(*bitterly*) I am afraid, though you might listen kindly, you could not hear me, Simon.

SIMON—(*gently reproachful*) I used to hear, didn't I?

DEBORAH—(*bitterly*) Once long ago. In another life. Before we had both changed.

SIMON—I haven't changed—not in my love for you. (*sadly*) It hurts that you can believe that of me, Mother.

DEBORAH—(*bitterly*) Oh, I no longer know what to believe about anything or anyone!

SIMON—Not even about me?

DEBORAH—Not even about myself.

SIMON—(*regards her worriedly—gently*) What has happened, Mother? (*frowning*) Is it anything Father has done?

DEBORAH—(*astonished*) Good Heavens, no! (*She bursts into genuinely amused laughter.*) My dear boy, what an absurd idea! It is easy to see you have forgotten your old home. Your father is much too worried about what President Jackson will do or say next, and what effect it will have on imports and exports, to bother with me, even if I would permit him to.

SIMON—Is it anything Joel—?

DEBORAH—Worse and worse! If you could see your brother now! He is head of the bookkeeping department, which is about as high as his ability can ever take him, to your father's disgust.

SIMON—(*with satisfaction*) I knew Joel had no ability. Father must be disappointed.

DEBORAH—Joel has become a confirmed ledger-worm. I think he tried once to find me listed on the profit side of the ledger. Not finding me there, he concluded he must merely be imagining that I existed. (*Simon laughs.*) I invited him to visit me in my garden not long ago—

SIMON—(*with a boyish scowl—jealously*) Why? What could you want with him?

DEBORAH—(*with a sharp interested look at him*) Anyone for company! You don't know how lonely I have grown since you— Poor Joel! He looked as astounded as if a nun had

asked him to her bedroom. And when he came—with the air,
I might say, of a correct gentleman who pays a duty call on a
woman of whom he disapproves—he determinedly recited
impeccable platitudes and stared the flowers out of countenance for half an hour, and then fled! You would have
laughed to see him.

SIMON—(*resentfully*) Yes, he must have been out of place.

DEBORAH—(*smiles with satisfaction at his tone*) He was indeed. So you need not be jealous, Dear. I remembered you
and all our old happy days there. (*She pauses—then slowly*)
No, I have not changed because of anything Joel— Hardly!

SIMON—(*gently*) Then what is it, Mother?

DEBORAH—Why, nothing has happened, Dear, except
time and change.

SIMON—You seem so lonely.

DEBORAH—(*patting his hand*) I am glad you know that.
Now I feel less lonely.

SIMON—It's hard to believe that about you. You were
always so independent of others, so free and self-sufficient.
All you ever needed was the solitude of your garden, or your
room—your books and your dreams.

DEBORAH—(*bitterly*) Yes, that was my arrogant mistake,
presuming myself superior to life. But a time comes when,
suddenly, all that security in solitude appears as weakness and
cowardice, a craven running away, and hiding from life. You
become restless, and discontent gnaws at your heart while
you cast longing eyes beyond the garden wall at life which
passes by so horribly unaware that you are still alive!

SIMON—How can you say Life has passed you by,
Mother? That's foolish. You—

DEBORAH—(*unheeding*) While you are still beautiful and
life still woos you, it is such a fine gesture of disdainful pride,
so satisfying to one's arrogance, to jilt it. But when the
change comes and the tables are turned and an indifferent life
jilts you—it is a repulsive humiliation to feel yourself a condemned slave to revengeful Time, to cringe while he lashes
your face with wrinkles, or stamps your body into shapeless-
ness, or smears it with tallow-fat with his malicious fingers!
(*anticipating his protest*) Oh, I realize I am hardly as bad as
that yet. But I will be, for I constantly sense in the seconds

and minutes and hours flowing through me, the malignant
hatred of life against those who have disdained it! But the
body is least important. It is the soul, staring into the mirror
of itself, knowing it is too late, that it is rejected and forever
alone—seeing the skull of Death leer over its shoulder in the
glass like a roué in a brothel ogling some life-sick old trull!

SIMON—(*shrinking with repulsion*) Mother! That's—that's
too morbid!

DEBORAH—(*seeing his shocked face, gives a little mocking
laugh*) Poor Simon, I warned you I had changed. Have I
shocked you dreadfully? Mothers should never have such
thoughts, should they? Not even while dreaming to themselves? (*She laughs again.*) Forgive me. I am afraid my mind
has been corrupted by reading so many French Eighteenth
Century Memoirs of late. I believe I wrote you that I had
started studying history. But perhaps you did not take it seriously. I was always studying something, wasn't I? The time
I have wasted hiding in my mind!

SIMON—(*rebukingly*) Don't tell me you regret— (*abruptly*)
You didn't write me it was that kind of history.

DEBORAH—(*smiles at him teasingly*) No doubt I was
ashamed to confess. But I find the French Eighteenth Century the most instructive and congenial period in modern
history for me.

SIMON—(*abruptly changing the subject*) What of your old
passion for Hindu Philosophy? Don't tell me you have given
that up!

DEBORAH—Yes. Long ago. Or, to be exact, a year ago.
This past year of change has seemed so long! It happened I
awoke one day from my dream of self-renunciation, and indifference to the opposites, to find Life sneaking out my door
renouncing me, taking the indifferent opposites along with
him. From that moment the Sacred Books became for me
merely a rubbish of lifeless words. And Brahma nothing at all
but a foreign name for Death. (*She smiles bitterly—self-mocking*) As I have said, it is pleasant to your superior disdain to
renounce life, but an intolerable insult when life renounces
you. As for my excursions into Oriental wisdom, I see it now
as the flight of one who, bored at home, blames the surroundings, and sails for far lands, only to find a welcoming

figure waiting there to greet one—oneself! (*She smiles bitterly*.) And straightaway the exotic palms turn into old familiar elms or maples, the houses are the same old houses, the gardens the same gardens, and the natives only one's old neighbors with fewer clothes and a darker sunburn—(*Simon chuckles amusedly*)—and one is as bewilderedly at home and not at home as ever! (*She pauses—then shrugging her shoulders*) I should have known I could have no enduring faith in any other-life religion. Being a Minister's daughter killed that in me. My father's life and his beyond-life expectations were too absurdly incongruous. (*She smiles mischievously*.) Poor man, how dreadfully embarrassed he would have been if Christ had ever called on him, especially if he came to the front door, with all the neighbors peering spitefully from behind curtains, hoping this Jacobin tramp would turn out to be a poor relation whose existence Father had concealed from them.

SIMON—(*laughs*) Poor Grandfather! You're always so hard on him.

DEBORAH—(*with gloating malice*) He was so proud of having sprung from an aristocratic old family. And yet he did try so hard to identify himself with Christ. But there was no point of resemblance except his poverty, and he was ashamed of that. And he couldn't help bearing God a grudge because He never kept His promise and let the meek devour the earth. Father's real idol was Napoleon. *He* didn't wait on promises, *he* wasn't meek, *he* took the earth! Father worshipped him. He used even to have the newspaper *Moniteur* sent him from France—his one extravagance—and gloat over each new victory. (*She sneers spitefully*.) Poor man! If you could imagine anyone less like Napoleon! Except in bodily stature. Poor Father was plump and insignificant.

SIMON—I wish I remembered him. He must have been a strange character.

DEBORAH—Extremely commonplace, you mean. Don't you recognize the symptoms? He was one of the great mob of greedy meek. He was Everyman. (*then with a sudden exasperation*) Great Heavens, why do I recall him? And what a stupid conversation! Politics, first and now, religion and family gossip about the dead! It was silly of me to come! (*She makes a move to rise but Simon catches her arm*.)

SIMON—(*soothingly*) Now, Mother! It isn't stupid to me. If you knew how delighted I am to sit and hear you talk again. It's like old times! It brings back all the happiness of the past—the hours together in your garden, as far back as I can remember.

DEBORAH—(*moved—pats his hand*) I am happy you have not forgotten, Dear.

SIMON—(*smiling musingly*) Are you still as incorrigible a dreamer as ever, Mother? (*She stiffens and gives him a suspicious, defensive look.*) I can remember times—I must have been very little, then—when you would sink into a dream, your eyes open but no longer seeing me. I would speak to you but you wouldn't hear me. You were far off somewhere. Then I'd be frightened—

DEBORAH—(*relieved, smiling tenderly*) That was silly, Dear. I was probably dreaming about you, of how, when you grew up, you and I—

SIMON—(*again with a musing smile*) Are you still as accomplished an actress as you used to be?

DEBORAH—(*starts—forcing a laugh*) Why, what a thing to say, Simon!

SIMON—Oh, I meant it admiringly, Mother. I was remembering—I must have been very little then, too—how you used to act out each part when you'd read me fairy stories. One moment you'd be the good fairy, or the good queen, or the poor abused little Princess— That was wonderful. But the next moment you'd be the evil Queen, or the bad fairy or the wicked witch, and I'd be all gooseflesh with terror! (*He chuckles.*)

DEBORAH—(*gives him a strange glance—almost tauntingly*) You were extremely sensitive and imaginative—as a child.

SIMON—(*frowning*) The trouble was, your acting confused my mind about you. Sometimes I got bewildered trying to keep you distinct and separate from the part you played.

DEBORAH—(*strangely*) Yes, I have experienced that bewilderment, too—when trying to reconcile my opposites.

SIMON—(*suddenly looks at her—smilingly*) What role do you play nowadays, Mother?

DEBORAH—(*stiffens, avoiding his eyes and forcing a laugh*) I? What nonsense, Dear. You forget I have no audience now.

SIMON—(*teasingly*) Oh, you were always your own audience, too. I felt that. So tell me—

DEBORAH—No, I assure you I've foresworn dream dramas. I'm too painfully conscious of reality these days, and its banality is too grotesquely in contrast—

SIMON—Now, don't tell me you've given up imagination and resigned yourself to the dull humdrum of being merely Mrs. Harford. I won't believe it. You couldn't if you tried. I'm sure you still fly from that deadly boredom into a secret life of your own—or at least, into the life in books—

DEBORAH—(*gives him a quick searching glance—with feigned carelessness*) Oh, if that's what you mean, yes. I'll confess there are times now when I become so bored with myself that I do try to escape into Eighteenth Century France. Life was so much more romantic and exciting for a woman then, don't you think? As the Memoirs depict it, anyway, and as I recreate it from them in my imagination. (*more decidely*) Yes, if I had had the choice, I would have chosen to live then. In fact, there are moments when I become so absorbed in the life of that period that I lose all sense of the present and feel that I did live then, that I am living there again. (*forcing a careless smile*) Perhaps my study of Eastern wisdom left me with a desire to believe in reincarnation. Sometimes I feel— (*forcing a careless laugh*) But that is very silly, of course.

SIMON—Why is it silly? Who knows? Anyway, about the life in books, I know I have often felt it more real to me than reality. (*He adds with an undercurrent of resentment*) Or I used to in the old days when I had time for books. Especially the poetry you would read aloud to me. (*He smiles musingly.*) Remember Byron, Mother, and your favorite Childe Harold stanza? (*He recites*)

> I have not loved the World, nor the World me;
> I have not flattered its rank breath, nor bowed
> To its idolatries a patient knee
> Nor coined my cheek to smiles,—nor cried aloud
> In worship of an echo: in the crowd
> They could not deem me one of such—I stood
> Among them, but not of them—

(*He breaks off—tenderly*) Do you remember, Mother?

DEBORAH—I do now. I forgot Byron after you had gone. I remember now, too, the stanza that begins: "But quiet to quick bosoms is a hell." And then, in the following one: "—all unquiet things which stir too strongly the soul's secret springs." (*She forces a smile.*) I fear loneliness is making me into a most unquiet thing. (*then with a laugh*) Your memories of the past encourage me to carry confession further and admit I do still have the childish habit of daydreaming and acting romantic roles in my mind to wile away the time.

SIMON—(*grows teasing*) I knew it. I know you.

DEBORAH—(*lightly*) You did, but do you? You forget time has changed me. (*still lightly, but with an undercurrent of taunting*) And you. You are a contented husband and father now, a successful merchant, so like your father! (*Simon frowns with annoyance.*) I greatly fear you would be horribly shocked if I should tell you the nature of the part I play in my Eighteenth Century past!

SIMON—(*grins*) I'll chance it, Mother. Remember your old wicked witches led me always to be prepared for the worst!

DEBORAH—(*playfully but a growing undercurrent of compulsive, deadly seriousness as she goes on*) Oh, I warn you this is more wicked than any witch. She was a creature of pure fantasy, a fairy tale. But this is real life, even though it be past—and perhaps Time is but another of our illusions, and what was is forever identical with what is, beneath the deceiving, changing masks we wear.

SIMON—(*a bit impatiently*) Well, out with the terrible secret, Mother. I promise not to be too horrified. Are you an evil Queen of France who never was?

DEBORAH—(*suddenly seems to lose herself—arrogantly*) No. I could be if it were my whim, but I prefer to be the secret power behind the Throne—a greedy adventuress who has risen from the gutter to nobility by her wit and charm, by the sale of her beauty, by her talent for marvelous intrigue—who uses love but loves only herself, who is entirely ruthless and lets nothing stand in the way of the final goal of power she has set for herself, to become the favorite of the King and make him, through his passion for her, her slave! (*She ends up on a note of strange, passionate exultance.*)

SIMON—(*startled and repelled—sharply rebuking*) Mother! (*She starts dazedly. He goes on quickly with a curt resentful contempt.*) No, I am not shocked. It is too damned idiotic! (*She gives a shrinking, cowering movement as though he had struck her in the face. Suddenly the absurdity strikes his sense of humor and he grins.*) No, that's a lie. You really did shock me for a second, Mother. Stunned me, even! (*He chuckles.*) But now I have a picture in my mind of you sitting in your walled-in garden, dressed all in white, so sedulously protected and aloof from all life's sordidness, so delicate and fastidious and spiritually remote—and yet in your dreams playing make-believe with romantic iniquity out of scandalous French memoirs! (*He laughs almost derisively.*)

DEBORAH—(*stung to fury, a flash of bitter hatred in her eyes, drawing herself up with fierce, threatening arrogance*) You dare to laugh at me, Monsieur! Take care—! (*Then as he stares at her in petrified amazement, she controls herself and forces an hysterical laugh.*) There! You see! I can still be a convincing actress if I wish! Poor Simon, if you could see your horrified face! Don't you see this is all a joke, that I made up that nonsense on the spur of the moment just to tease you?

SIMON—(*relieved, grins sheepishly*) You did fool me. For a moment I thought you were serious—

DEBORAH—Serious! My dear boy, I hope you don't think your poor mother has gone quite insane! (*abruptly*) But let's forget my stupid joke and return to common sense in the little time left us. I must go. Tell me, how is your business progressing these days? Judging from your letters, you must be making a great success of it.

SIMON—(*reluctantly*) Oh, only in a very modest way as yet, Mother.

DEBORAH—You hope to do even better? I am sure you will—with Sara to inspire you.

SIMON—Yes, it is all for her. Everything I have is in her name.

DEBORAH—(*gives him a searching look—smiling curiously*) I see.

SIMON—See what? I owe it to her—

DEBORAH—Of course you do. (*She smiles.*) But I didn't

mean that. My thought was fanciful—that perhaps thus you contrived to hide from yourself.

SIMON—(*resentfully*) You are right to call that fanciful.

DEBORAH—(*teasingly*) And I think you're playing modest with me about your success. Why, in one of your letters, you boasted that the town considered you the most talented of its young merchants.

SIMON—I wasn't boasting, Mother. Good Heavens, what is there to boast about? It requires no high order of talent to be a successful tradesman—merely a cunning acquisitiveness. I meant my boasting humorously. I thought it would make you laugh.

DEBORAH—Oh, I did laugh then. Now I see there is nothing incongruous about it. After all, you are your father's son. It is natural you should have inherited his ability. You are so like him now, in many ways, it's astonishing.

SIMON—(*irritated*) Oh, nonsense, Mother.

DEBORAH—It's true. It struck me the minute I saw you. And do you know, although he never permits himself to speak of you, I am sure he keeps informed of all you do, and is quite proud of you.

SIMON—(*coldly*) I can dispense with his approval.

DEBORAH—What a strange boy you are! One would think you were ashamed of your success.

SIMON—Why should I be ashamed?

DEBORAH—Why, indeed? Unless you regret your lost poet's dream of a perfect society.

SIMON—I haven't lost it! And it isn't just a dream. I can prove—

DEBORAH—(*carelessly*) Oh, I know. Your book. But you said you had given that up.

SIMON—I said I had had no time lately—

DEBORAH—Four years is a long "lately." But why should you be ashamed of that? You must learn to laugh at your dreams if you hope ever to be happy.

SIMON—(*defensively*) I am happy now!

DEBORAH—We all pass through a callow period when our vanity prompts us to believe we may become poets or philosophers or saviours of mankind—when we dream of spiritual beauty and a greedless world. But we soon discover the world we must live in (is greedily practical and could bitterly resent being saved from its gross appetite, but we must eat or be eaten, and an ounce of flesh is worth a ton of spirit.

SIMON—(*repelled*) I never thought I'd ever hear you—

DEBORAH—I am trying to drive the nonsense from your head, for your own peace of mind, and Sara's. You must forget what you once wanted to be and face yourself as you are, and not be ashamed.

SIMON—I am not ashamed! Why do you keep insisting?— (*then suddenly giving in—moodily*) Well perhaps, now and then, I do feel a little guilty.

DEBORAH—Ah!

SIMON—But I remind myself that what I am doing is merely a means. The end is Sara's happiness. And that justifies any means!

DEBORAH—I've found the means always becomes the end —and the end is always oneself.

SIMON—I propose to retire as soon as we have enough. I'll write my book then.

DEBORAH—You have agreed with Sara how much is enough?

SIMON—(*hesitates—then lies*) Yes, of course. (*A pause. He frowns and goes on moodily.*) I'll admit I do get deathly sick of the daily grind of the counting house—the interminable haggling and figuring and calculation of profits, the scheming to outwit the other man, the fear that he may outwit you—a life where Mammon is God, and money the sole measure of worth! It is not the career I would have chosen. I would have lived here in freedom with Nature, and earned just enough to support myself, and kept my dreams, and written my book. (*somberly*) Yes, sometimes I feel spiritually degraded, and a traitor to myself. I would confess that only to you, Mother.

DEBORAH—Ah.

SIMON—(*hastily*) But when I come home and see Sara's happiness and hold her in my arms, then my discontent seems mean and selfish and a petty vanity.

DEBORAH—(*fights back an expression of repulsion*) Yes. Of course. (*then calculatingly*) The danger is that your discontent will grow and grow with your success until— But, good heavens, I sound like Cassandra! Forgive me! And now I really must go, Simon. (*She gets up and they come to the path front at left. Suddenly she says, strangely*) No, you go first.

SIMON—But why don't we walk together as far as the road?

DEBORAH—(*with strange arrogant petulance*) No! That would be meaningless. Please obey me. It is my whim to send you away. (*then forcing a joking tone*) Goodness, how alarmed you look! You have forgotten me, I think. Can't I be whimsical, as of old, if it please me?

SIMON—(*puzzled but smiling*) Of course you can.

DEBORAH—(*kissing him*) Goodbye, Dear. Write me frankly of your discontents. There should be no secrets between us. I shall be, as ever, your Mother Confessor. (*Then she gives him a little push.*) Now go!

SIMON—(*hesitates—moved*) I— Goodbye, Mother. (*He turns reluctantly.*)

DEBORAH—(*suddenly overcome by contrition and a tender love*) Wait!(*She embraces him again.*) My dear son! Forgive me for trying to poison your happiness. Forget all I have said! Have no regrets! Love is worth everything! Be happy! (*She kisses him—then pushes him away down the path—sharply commanding*) No! Don't speak! Go! (*She turns away. Simon stares at her for a moment, deeply moved—then turns and disappears down the path. Deborah turns back to look after him—with a wry smile*) I honestly meant to take back the poison—but I fear it served only to inject it more surely into his soul. (*then self-mockingly*) Bosh, Deborah! You overestimate your powers for intrigue! You confuse life with stupid dreams. He will forget in her arms. (*her face hardening*) Besides, it is ended. I have dismissed that Irish biddy's husband from my life forever. I shall never see him again. (*Then she smiles to herself with a perverse pride.*) At least I have proven to my own satisfaction, how easy it would be to steal happiness from her, if it were my whim, and I were given the opportunity.

(*As she says this last the cabin door is silently unlocked and opened and Sara comes out. She stands outside the door for a moment hesitantly. Then, her face set and determined, she advances noiselessly until she stands a few paces from the oblivious Deborah. She takes her in from head to foot with a searching glance, her*

*eyes narrowing. But there is no hatred or anger visible in her
expression. If she feels any, she has forced it back beneath the surface, and there is a certain calm dignity and strength of character in her face and whole attitude. Whatever the battle with her
passions has been, she has fought it out inside the cabin.*)

SARA — (*speaks quietly in a polite, carefully considered and ar-
ticulated English*) I beg your pardon, Mrs. Harford. (*Deborah
gives a frightened gasp, whirling to face her. For a moment the
two stare at each other, Sara steady and calm, Deborah recovering
from her surprise, her face hardening into a haughtily-questioning
mask. Sara makes her a little bow. A hint of a mocking smile on
her lips.*) I am happy to meet you again and to know you at
last Mrs. Harford. I feel I do know you now, you see, because
I was in the cabin all the while since you came.

DEBORAH — (*with a flash of arrogant fury*) You dared to
listen!

SARA — (*quietly*) I did. I came on purpose to listen. I suspected you were up to some trick. I wanted to know what it
was so I could guard against it. (*a trace of contempt creeping
into her voice*) Though after all I've heard, I know now I was
a fool to be afraid of you.

DEBORAH — (*stammers guiltily*) So you heard— (*then with
biting contempt*) You have the effrontery to boast of it! You
have so little shame! You are so ignorant of all honor!

SARA — (*her face beginning to flush — but still quietly*) I am,
yes.

DEBORAH — Well, I expected you to be low and unscrupulous, considering your origin, but I never thought you'd
boast of it!

SARA — (*stung — her inward anger beginning to show, and
with it her brogue, but still keeping her voice quiet*) I have my
honor and it's a true woman's honor that you don't know
but you'd give your soul to know! To have love and hold it
against the world, no matter how! That's my honor! (*gradually losing her control and lapsing more and more into brogue*)
As for what you're after saying about my origin—don't put
on your fine lady's airs and graces with me! Do you think
you'll fool me after what I've heard? (*with a savage, jeering
scorn, advancing a threatening step*) God pity you for a fool,
then! (*Deborah in spite of herself, shrinks back. Sara gloats trium-*

phantly) Ah, you shrink away, don't you? You're afraid! I'm too strong for you! Life is too strong for you! But it's not too strong for me! I'll take what I want from it and make it mine! (*mockingly*) And aren't you envyin' me that strength now in your heart, for all your pretendin'? Aren't you thinkin' that if you could have my strength to love life, and your brains for schemin' and dreamin' of power, you'd make yourself Queen of the world! Oh, I know you now! I know you well! You to put on the airs of a Duchess wid me! You to talk of honor when in your dream what are you but a greedy, contrivin' whore! (*Deborah shrinks back cowering still farther. Sara goes on more quietly but with a derisive taunting.*) But it's only in a dream! You've the wish for life but you haven't the strength except to run and hide in fear of it, sittin' lonely in your garden, hearin' age creep up on you, and beyond the wall the steps of Life growin' fainter down the street, like the beat of your heart, as he strolls away forgettin' you, whistlin' a love tune to himself, dreaming of another woman!

DEBORAH—(*stammers*) That's a lie! (*She sways weakly as though she were about to faint—exhaustedly*) I—I feel a little faint—I— (*She starts weakly for the bench.*)

SARA—(*with an abrupt change to her quiet polite manner, takes her arm*) Let me help you, Mrs. Harford. (*She leads Deborah to the bench.*) You must rest a while. It's a long walk back to the road.

DEBORAH—(*sinks down on it—quietly*) Thank you.

SARA—(*stands looking down at her*) I ask your pardon for losing my temper, Mrs. Harford. I'd promised myself I would not. But the things you said—

DEBORAH—(*quietly*) I know. Please forgive me.

SARA—I came out of the cabin because there's a lot of things I want to say to you. (*defiantly*) And I'm going to say them. (*She pauses but Deborah remains silent. She stares at her and suddenly a look of pity comes over her face. She speaks gently.*) But before that I want to tell you how sorry I was when Simon laughed. (*Deborah gives a little shrinking shudder.*) I was listening. I could feel it coming. I waited, praying he wouldn't. When he did, it was like a knife in me, too. (*Deborah raises her eyes for a second to stare at her with an instinctive grateful wonder. Sara goes on.*) I want to apologize for him.

He didn't know. How can a man know about the truth of the lies in a woman's dreams?

DEBORAH—(*lifts her eyes to stare at her wonderingly again—with a faint smile*) I thought you were a fool. I am afraid I am beginning to like you, Sara.

SARA—(*embarrassedly—forcing a joking tone*) Oh, don't try to fool me with blarney. You hate me worse than poison, that's the truth. And I hate you. (*then with resentment and now and then a trace of brogue but quietly*) I want to say I'm glad I listened. I've told you I was afraid you were up to some trick. And you were. Oh, I saw through your reminding him about that crazy book of his, although I didn't blame you for trying to get back at him after he'd laughed. You wanted to put doubt and disgust for himself in his mind, and make him blame me for a greedy fool who'd made him a slave and killed his fine poet's dream. (*She laughs scornfully.*) It's you who are the fool. It's little you know Simon, if you are his mother. Sure, what man doesn't complain of his work, and pretend he's a slave, but if ever you saw him when he comes home to me, so proud and happy because he's beat someone on a sale, laughing and boasting to me, you wouldn't hope you could use his old dream of a book that'll change the world to dissatisfy him. I know what he really likes—the world as it is—and I'm not worried by what he thinks he ought to like. (*She pauses. Deborah sits in silence, her eyes on the ground, as though she didn't hear or was completely indifferent. Sara goes on more resentfully.*) But what I wanted to say is, you don't know me. I may have a greed in me. I've had good reason to have. There's nothing like hunger to make you greedy. But the thing you don't know is that there's great love in me too, great enough to destroy all the greed in the world. If I thought it meant his happiness, I'd live here in this hut, or in a ditch with him, and steal praties from the farmers to feed him, and beg pennies with my children, on the road, to buy pen and ink and paper for his book, and still I'd laugh with the joy of love! (*She pauses again. Deborah remains silent. She goes on.*) I heard you, when he said he'd retire to write his book when we had enough, sneer to him that I'd never have enough. It's little you know me, if you think I want him all his life to dirty his hands with trade, when all I'm dreaming of is to make him retire, a landed gentleman the minute we've enough, and to bring my children up as gentlemen. You sneered at my origin. You think in your Yankee pride and ignorance, because my father ruined himself with drink and gambling in Ireland, that the dirty Inn he came down to own here, is all I've known. But I was born on a great estate that was my father's, in a grand mansion like a Castle, with sloos of servants, and stables, and beautiful hunters. My father was a gentleman, and an officer, who served with honor in Spain under the great Duke of Wellington. (*abruptly with exasperated self-scorn*) Arrah, what am I sayin'? Am I boastin' of him? (*with a sudden return to her quiet correct manner*) I beg your pardon, Mrs. Harford, for boring you with talk of my father. The truth is, I am not proud I am his daughter. He was a drunken fool, full of lying pretensions— (*hastily, with stubborn defiance*) But what I've said is true all the same!

DEBORAH—(*without raising her eyes—smiling strangely*) Did I think you were strong and unscrupulous? But you are also very weak and honorable, I'm afraid. (*She laughs softly.*)

SARA—(*stares at her uneasily—then defiantly*) You'd better not think I'm weak, or have any honor but one. I'll tell you something to prove it. You'll remember the night your husband sent his lawyer to buy off my father from any claims I had on Simon, and my father got mad with rage at the insult and went to challenge him to a duel. I was afraid there'd be a row you'd use as an excuse to keep Simon from marrying me, but I knew Simon would feel bound to me in honor if— So I came out here in the night to make him take me. (*She smiles tenderly.*) I found I didn't need to. He loved me so much, nothing could take him from me. And then I felt guilty and confessed how bad I'd been. And then we— But it was for love only. (*abruptly defiant again*) But I would have done it for the other reason if I'd had to!

DEBORAH—(*raises her eyes to stare at her with hate—scornfully*) You need not convince me you are capable of any vileness to get what you want. (*Then she drops her eyes—with a strange little mocking laugh*) You are boasting, Sara. Oh, I don't doubt you would have. That's your strength. But afterwards your weak honor would have made you confess to him—perhaps even tell him he need not marry you, anyway.

SARA—(*taken aback—blurts out*) Yes, I told him that before—

DEBORAH—(*laughs*) I am beginning to know you, Sara.

SARA—(*again stares at her uneasily—resentfully threatening*) I don't care what you know. I've only this left to say to you. Stay in your dreams and leave me and mine alone. Simon is mine now. (*then politely*) I must go. Simon will be wondering where I have gone. I promise you I won't confess that. I'll bid you goodbye now, Mrs. Harford.

DEBORAH—(*looks up—coldly*) Goodbye. I promise you, in turn, I never intend to see your husband again, or even write to him. (*with arrogant disdain*) Do you presume to think I would touch anything of yours?

SARA—(*contemptuously*) No. You know I wouldn't let you. (*She smiles mockingly and goes off right, rear, to the short cut along the lake.*)

DEBORAH—(*her face full of bitter hatred*) Vulgar, common slut! Boastful fool! If I wished—if I had the opportunity— (*sneeringly*) And now her honor will make her remind him constantly of his book, when he wants to forget— (*She laughs spitefully.*) I could not have contrived it better! (*abruptly*) No. It is ended. Forgotten. Dead. It is cheap and mean and sordid. Like life. I will not let it touch me. (*She frowns as if desperately concentrating her mind. Gradually her tension relaxes and her eyes become dreamy and she stares before her unseeingly. Finally she murmurs happily to herself*) The Palace at Versailles—the King and I walk in the moonlit gardens—"My Throne it is your heart, Beloved, and my fair Kingdom your beauty"— (*A faint smile of arrogant satisfaction forms on her lips. Then abruptly she starts awake and springs to her feet, furious at herself.*) No! I have done with that insane romantic vaporing! I will never dream again! Never! Not if I have to pluck my idiot brain from my skull! I will face change and loneliness, and Time and Death and make myself resigned! (*A bitter ironical smile comes to her lips.*) After all, what else can you do now, Deborah? You would always hear his laughter.

(*Curtain*)

ACT TWO

Scene One

SCENE—*A corner of the garden of Deborah Harford's home in the city on a warm moonlight night in June, 1836.*

The corner is formed by a brick enclosing wall, eight feet high, at rear and right. This wall borders a neighboring property at rear, a quiet street lined with elms at right. At center is an octagonal summerhouse, its walls and pointed roof entirely covered by ivy. At left and right of the summerhouse are shrubs with a line of Italian cypresses behind them along the wall. The shrubs, of various sizes, are all clipped into geometrical shapes, cones, cubes, cylinders, spheres, pyramids, etc. They give the place a curious, artificial atmosphere. It is like a fantastic toy garden magnified, in which nature is arrogantly restricted and arbitrarily distorted to form an appropriate setting for a perversely whimsical personality.

In the side of the summerhouse facing front is a narrow arched door, painted a Chinese lacquer red. The floor is raised from the ground and three steps lead up to the door. In front of these steps is lawn, with two small stone benches, facing right-front, and left-front, on the edge of a narrow brick-paved walk which surrounds a little oval pool. From this pool two paths lead directly right and left, the left one passing behind a spherical shrub at left-front to the house. The right one leads to an arched door, painted green, in the wall at right, opening on the street. There is a wrought iron lantern hanging from a bracket in the wall above the door, in which a little lamp burns brightly. There is a sound of men's voices from down the path off left, and a moment later Nicholas Gadsby, the Harford lawyer, appears accompanied by Deborah's younger son, Joel. Gadsby is a short, tubby man of fifty-six, with a head almost completely bald, a round red face, and shrewd little grey eyes. Every inch the type of conservative, best-family legal advisor, he is gravely self-important and pretentious in manner and speech, extremely conscious of the respect due his professional dignity. He is dressed with a fastidious propriety in mourning black.

Joel Harford is twenty-nine, tall and thin, with a slight stoop in his carriage. His face is pale and handsome. Judged by its separate features, each of which has an aristocratic distinction, it should possess distinction. But it remains the face of a methodical mediocrity, who within his narrow limits is not without determi-

338

nation, and a rigid integrity, but lacks all self-confidence or am-
bition beyond these limits. His whole character has something
aridly prim and puritanical about it. He has brown hair, cold
light blue eyes, a pointed chin, an obstinate mouth. His voice is
dry. A voice prematurely old. His mourning suit is well tailored.
They stop as they come to the pool. Gadsby stares around him,
looking for someone. His manner is shocked and indignant, and
at the same time pathetically confused, as though he'd just been
confronted by a fact which he knows to be true but which is so
outrageous he cannot bring himself to accept it.

GADSBY—(*trying to conceal his shattered poise behind a fussy,*
impatient air) Well? She isn't here. I didn't think she would
be. Under the circumstances. At this time of night. But you
insisted—

JOEL—(*dryly, indicating the summerhouse*) You will find her
hiding in there, I think.

GADSBY—(*stares at the summerhouse—with a sort of bewil-*
dered offended dismay) In there? God bless me. I cannot believe—? I know how eccentric your mother— But at such a
time, one would think—

JOEL—(*dryly*) You have not seen her for some time. She
has grown increasingly eccentric. And since the night Father
died she has appeared— Well, to be frank, deliberately deranged is the only way I could truthfully describe—

GADSBY—(*appalled*) Deranged? (*rebukingly*) Come, come,
Joel. Naturally, the shock—her grief.

JOEL—(*coldly*) No. Whatever the cause be, it is not grief.

GADSBY—(*shocked*) Come, come. A shocking statement
for you to make. I refuse to— (*then bewilderedly*) You said
"deliberately."

JOEL—I have felt it was deliberate. You may judge for
yourself.

GADSBY—(*with defensive asperity*) Ridiculous. I have
known your mother since before you were born. Eccentric,
yes. Deliberately and provokingly unconventional. Childishly
self-willed. Irresponsibly whimsical and fanciful. But always a
well-bred, distinguished gentlewoman, a charming hostess,
witty and gay—and beautiful.

JOEL—(*stiffens resentfully*) I have never considered her

beautiful. And I think even you will not think her beautiful now. (*with thinly concealed relish*) She looks her full age now, and more. (*then guiltily, with abrupt cold reproof*) But you are forgetting the business which brings us here.

GADSBY—(*guiltily*) Yes, of course. We must see your mother at once. (*then explosively*) By heaven, I wish I could forget. Joel! I still cannot believe that your father could—

JOEL—(*interrupts sharply*) It would be better if you were the one to call her out. I have never been welcome here.

GADSBY—(*turns to the summerhouse and calls*) Deborah! (*There is no answer. He goes to the foot of the steps—fussily impatient, more sharply*) Deborah! This is Nicholas! I must see you at once. A matter of the gravest importance has come up. (*He pauses, then turns to Joel uneasily.*) God bless me, Joel, you don't think anything can have happened to her? (*But even as he is speaking the door is slowly opened outwards and Deborah appears. Her back is to the door as though she had groped backwards in the darkness, her hand behind her feeling for the knob, keeping her face turned toward something from which she retreats. As the door opens her body, pressed against it, turns as it turns until it faces toward left, front, as the door is two-thirds open. But she keeps her head turned so that she is still looking back over her shoulder into the dark interior. Gadsby takes a step back, regarding her bewilderedly. Joel stares at her with a cold emotionlessness. Suddenly a little shudder runs over her; she gives a smothered gasp and wrenches her eyes from the darkness inside and pushes the door back against the house, wide open, and faces front. As he sees her face, Gadsby cannot restrain a startled exclamation of shocked alarm and even backs frightenedly away from her a step or two. For there is a shocking transformation in her appearance. Where she had always before looked astonishingly youthful for her age, she now seems much older than her forty-nine years. Her olive complexion has turned a displeasing swarthy. The dry skin is stretched tightly over the bones and has the lifeless sheen of a shed snakeskin. Her black eyes are sunk in deep hollows beneath their heavy brows and have an unhealthy feverish glitter. They appear more enormous than ever in her small oval face. There are deep lines from her nose and the corners of her mouth, between her eyes and across her forehead. Her lips appear contracted and shrunken over her still perfect set of big, even teeth. There are hollows under her cheek-*

bones and in her slender neck. The skin sags under her chin. There is the quality of a death's head about her face, of a skull beginning to emerge from its mask of flesh. Where her figure had been slender it is now thin, but it is still graceful in all its movements, and by contrast with her face, youthful. She is dressed all in white.)

DEBORAH—(*staring at Gadsby but with eyes that are still fixed inward, frightenedly and fascinatedly, something in her own mind—in a low voice that has lost its old musical quality and become flat and brittle*) I am glad you came, Nicholas, I must never go in there again! (*She gives a little shudder.*)

GADSBY—(*trying to recover from his shocked surprise at the change in her*) There is something in there that frightens you, Deborah?

DEBORAH—(*strangely, as if talking to herself*) Something? Outside me? No, nothing is there but I. My mind. The past, Dreams. My life, I suppose you might call it, since I have never lived except in mind. A very frightening prison it becomes at last, full of ghosts and corpses. Yes, in the end, and I have reached the end, the longing for a moment's unthinking peace, a second's unquestioning acceptance of oneself, become so terrible that I would do anything, give anything, to escape! (*Her voice has become lower and tenser.*) That is what frightened me. After you called. Oh, not before. Before, I was so longingly fascinated, I had forgotten fear. The temptation to escape. Open the door. Step boldly across the threshold. (*bitterly*) And, after all, good God, why should I be frightened? What have I to lose except myself as I am here.

GADSBY—God bless me, Deborah, you cannot mean—

DEBORAH—Death? Oh, no. There is a better way—a way by which we still may live. As one has always wished to live. As the woman one has always desired to be. One has only to concentrate one's mind enough, and one's pride to choose of one's own free will, and one can cheat life, and death, of oneself. It would be so easy for me! Like pushing open a door in the mind and then passing through with the freedom of one's lifelong desire! (*tensely her eyes glowing*) I tell you, before you called, I saw that door, as real as the door I have just opened, and I was reaching out my hand to— (*then with a frightened shudder*) No, I am glad you called. Because I am not sure that one completely forgets then. If I were, I would have gone.

(*abruptly shaking off this thought—trying to force a natural tone but still strangely*) No, do not fear, Nicholas, that I will outrage your sense of propriety by suicide. I assure you Henry's dying completely disillusioned me with death.

GADSBY—(*partly regaining his fussy self-importance—rebukingly*) That is hardly a befitting attitude— (*then solicitously*) It is very bad for you to come out here to brood over Henry's death.

DEBORAH—(*strangely*) Brood? No. But I have tried to make it real to myself—to examine it as a fact. I have said to myself: "Why can't you face the new fact, Deborah? Your husband is dead. He was buried this morning. These are facts." "Oh, I know. But I can't comprehend them as facts yet." "Why not, Deborah. You surely should be experienced in facing facts by this time." "Yes, God knows I should. I have lived with reality many years now. That afternoon at the cabin with Simon seems a lifetime ago, and he is more dead to me than Henry. I have kept the oath I made to myself then. Have not allowed myself to dream. Have not hidden from my life. Have made myself accept it as it is. Made myself a decently resigned old woman, saying to myself: 'So is so, and you must not hope it could be more.' Made myself each morning and night confront myself in the mirror and bow a well-mannered bow to age and ugliness. Greet them as my life-end guests. As elderly suitors for my body, roués in their bored withered hearts, their smiles insinuating the desire of Death. Not charming company, but a hostess must honor even unwelcome guests." So all day for years I have lived with them. And every night they have lain abed with me. (*smiling strangely with a bitter satisfaction*) Oh, yes, indeed! I have disciplined my will to be possessed by facts—like a whore in a brothel!

GADSBY—(*shocked*) Deborah!

DEBORAH—(*goes on as if she hadn't heard*) I have deliberately gone out of my way to solicit even the meanest, most sordid facts, to prove how thoroughly I was resigned to reality. Joel will remember one night at supper when I actually asked my husband: "How is trade these days? Tell me. I feel a deep interest. Has President Jackson's feud with the Bank of the United States had an adverse effect on your exports and imports?" A silence that shrank back, stamping on its own toes. In his eyes and Joel's a wondering alarm. Has this alien woman gone completely insane? No, she is merely being fantastical again. Deborah has always been fantastical. (*She gives a little mocking laugh.*)

JOEL—(*coldly hostile*) That is what you are being now, Mother. And we have no time to listen—

GADSBY—(*who has been staring at Deborah fascinatedly, bewilderedly uncomprehending but disturbed because he senses her despair, now attempts to regain a brisk, professional air, clearing his throat importantly*) Humph. Yes, Deborah. We must—

DEBORAH—(*ignoring this—with the same strange inward stare, and the air of talking aloud to herself*) And now Henry is dead. Gone from life forever. I am free. Can't you understand that? (*She shakes her head slowly.*) No. His death will not live in me. It is meaningless. Perhaps I am too dead myself— And yet I witnessed his dying. The dutiful wife sat by his bedside. He seemed not to suffer but to be impatient and exasperated. As though he had an important appointment with God to discuss terms for the export of his soul, and Life was needlessly delaying him. And then came nothing. An expiring into nothing. And that was death. Is that why it cannot live for me? Did I think death would be something in itself—a beginning, not just the end of life? What did I expect? What was I hoping? For Death to open the door and enter the room, visible to me, the good King of Life come at last to escort one into his palace of peace, a lover keeping a life-long promised tryst? (*She smiles with a taunting self-mockery.*) I regret to see living as a mistress of facts has not entirely killed your fanciful imagination, Deborah! You and your lover-Kings! Had you, perchance, personified your own death in your whimsical imagination, and fallen in love with it? Then Henry's extinction should richly disillusion you! Oh, it has. There was nothing at all but a meaningless ceasing to breathe, and I suppose that is only logical and reasonable. If Life had meaning then we might properly expect its end to have as much significance as—as the period at the close of a simple sentence, say. But it has no meaning and the sentence, worn out by futile groping within its own stupid obscurities, stammers haltingly to an unintelligible end—and that is all. Like an aimless improvisation on a far-off, out-of-tune piano that tinkles into silence. And death is no more than a muddy well into which I and a dead cat are cast aside indifferently! (*Suddenly she presses both hands to her temples with an agonized, distracted gesture—tensely*) Ah, good God, can I never stop this everlasting thinking and questioning, this sneering and jeering and spitting at my own heart—a helpless slave to a mind that runs on and on like a mad perpetual motion machine I cannot stop? (*wildly*) Ah, and you wonder I was tempted to open that door and escape! I tell you I am still tempted—that I will not endure being the tortured captive of my mind much longer—whatever the cost of release—

GADSBY—(*alarmed and bewildered*) Deborah. I beg of you, compose yourself. This—this is most unsuitable conduct— even when I consider the natural shock of grief. I cannot condone—such—such lack of decent control—

DEBORAH—(*stares at him—a sudden transformation comes over her as she forces her obsession back and becomes her usual self again. She smiles at him—an amused, derisive smile.*) Your rebuke is well taken, Nicholas. I fear I was boring you as surely as I was myself. (*dryly*) May I ask to what I owe the honor of your visit, Gentlemen? It is a rare pleasure indeed to see you in my garden, Joel.

JOEL—(*stiffly*) I assure you, Mother, I would never intrude unless circumstances—

GADSBY—(*interrupts worriedly, his mind now occupied with the matter at hand*) The circumstances are these, Deborah: In going over Henry's private papers, we made the astounding discovery— (*He interrupts himself—indignantly*) Upon my soul, I could not credit the evidence of my own eyes! I knew Henry since we were boys together. I would have sworn he would be the last man on earth to indulge in such outrageous folly!

DEBORAH—(*astonished and interested*) Outrageous folly? No, that does not sound like Henry, Nicholas. (*coolly*) I think we could discuss this mystery more calmly if we sat down. (*She sits on the step of the summerhouse. Gadsby and Joel on the stone benches by the pool, at left-front and right-front of her, respectively. She notices the look of disapproval Joel gives her white dress.*) I see you disapprove of my changing back to my accustomed white, Joel. Please remember, although I detest mourning and think it ridiculous, I did wear it at the funeral before the world. That is all your father would consider my duty. Never that I should play the hypocrite to myself.

GADSBY—(*frowns rebukingly*) Now, now. It is no time— (*overcome with indignation again*) I tell you, Deborah, this is incredible!

DEBORAH—What is "this"?

JOEL—(*coldly*) We found two letters in Father's strong-box, one addressed to Mr. Gadsby, the other to me. They were written some weeks ago. He had a premonition he might die suddenly. The letters are practically identical. They—

GADSBY—(*feels it incumbent on him to take over now—in his best family-lawyer manner*) I must warn you, Deborah, to be prepared for a dreadful surprise. (*He pauses. She stares at him calmly. He is thrown off stride by her lack of reaction and becomes even more portentous.*) These letters are confessions that Henry had been secretly gambling in Western lands.

DEBORAH—(*incredulously*) Gambling? Henry?

GADSBY—(*nods solemnly*) Yes, Deborah. Unbelievable!

JOEL—(*coldly*) As a result, Mother, the Company stands on the brink of bankruptcy.

GADSBY—It appears he had overreached his resources during the past few years. Sunk too much capital in new ships. Borrowed too freely, and then yielded to the temptation to regain a sound position by making a quick profit in Western lands. He lost, of course. What could an honorable, conservative merchant like Henry know of such wild speculation? (*giving way more and more to indignation and rabid political partisanship*) And what a time he chose to expand the activities of his Company. With his reputation for shrewdness and caution! When the country is in turmoil, with uncertainty the only certainty, thanks to that idol of the scum, that criminal lunatic in the White House! And, even with Jackson's passing, there will be no relief from this damnable demogoguery! It seems tragically probable his jackal, Van Buren, will succeed him!

DEBORAH—(*cuttingly but with an amused twinkle in her eye*) An excellent Whig electioneering speech, Nicholas. But wasted on a poor widow who has no vote. And hardly in the spirit so soon after a funeral, do you think, although I know Henry would agree with every word.

GADSBY—(*crushed*) I—forgive me. I—er—I am greatly upset—and I blame conditions for Henry's folly.

DEBORAH—(*staring before her strangely*) It would appear I have spent my life with a stranger. If I had guessed he had folly hidden in his heart and a gambler's daring— Who knows? (*She shrugs her shoulders with a bitter little smile.*) Too late, Deborah.

JOEL—(*stares at her with chilly disapproval*) I said, Mother, that the Company is faced with ruin. That is what we came to discuss with you.

DEBORAH—(*looks at him with distaste*) Discuss with me? You know I haven't the slightest knowledge of trade.

JOEL—I know you have never taken the slightest interest. But now you must.

DEBORAH—(*arrogantly*) Must?

GADSBY—(*interposing*) What Joel means, Deborah, is that in his letters Henry suggests certain steps should be taken which, if they can be successfully negotiated, may save the firm.

DEBORAH—(*indifferently*) Then you have only to take the steps, Nicholas.

GADSBY—They can be taken only with your consent, since Henry's will bequeaths the Company jointly to you and Joel. I may add that Joel has given his consent.

JOEL—(*stiffly*) I consider it my duty to Father's memory. What he proposes is the one possible way to preserve the honor of his name. For that I am willing to make any sacrifice of my personal feelings.

DEBORAH—(*stares at him exasperatedly*) If you only knew, Joel, how many times I wish to pinch you to discover if you're stuffed!

JOEL—I have long realized I bore you, Mother. You will doubtless find Simon more congenial.

DEBORAH—(*stiffens startledly—in a flash her face becomes as hard and cold as Joel's*) Pray, what has your brother to do with this?

GADSBY—If you will permit me to explain, Deborah. Simon has everything to do with it.

DEBORAH—(*tensely*) He shall have nothing to do with anything that concerns me. You know his father's attitude regarding him. It was in obedience to what I knew would be my husband's wish that I did not inform Simon of his death, nor invite him to the funeral. I forbid you to bring his name into this discussion. I have forgotten him. (*Joel regards her with a cold surprise. Gadsby is astonished and taken aback.*)

GADSBY—I did not realize you felt so bitterly toward Simon.

DEBORAH—I do not feel bitter. I feel nothing.

GADSBY—I had thought, and Henry must have thought, or he would never—

DEBORAH—I never let Henry know my thoughts. Simon is dead to me. And I will not have him resurrected. That is final.

GADSBY—(*with a trace of asperity*) It cannot be final, Deborah. If you will pardon my saying so, it is no time for personal feelings. It is a time to consider what you owe, in honor, to your husband's good name.

DEBORAH—I cannot believe Henry would ever—

GADSBY—(*with dignity*) I trust you are not doubting my word, Deborah. If you will only let me explain—

DEBORAH—Very well. I will listen. But I warn you—

GADSBY—No, I cannot accept that. You must keep an open mind for the sake of the Company, and—

DEBORAH—I care nothing for the Company!

JOEL—(*coldly resentful*) You forget what you owe it, then—your home, the comforts you have enjoyed, the privacy you cherish, the aloofness from life you pride yourself upon! I think you have not yet faced what has happened as it will affect your own future, Mother. You will have to sell this home. You will have nothing. What will you do? Go and beg Simon and his wife to let you live on charity with them?

DEBORAH—(*passionately*) I would rather beg in the gutter!

JOEL—Of course, you may always have a home with me. But on a bookkeeper's wage—

DEBORAH—(*scornfully*) Can you possibly imagine—?

JOEL—(*coldly*) No. So I advise you to listen to Mr. Gadsby, as he requests, with an open mind.

GADSBY—Joel is right, Deborah. Your position is—er—

precarious, unless— (*plunging into his subject*) What Henry suggests is this: (*He hesitates a bit—uncomfortably*) He realized that Joel has not had the requisite executive experience to take control under such difficult circumstances.

JOEL—(*emotionlessly*) I am not grateful to you for sparing my feelings, Mr. Gadsby. It is my practice to face the truth about myself. Father knew I have not the ability to be head of the Company under any circumstances. In my narrow sphere, no man could serve the Company more faithfully. But, beyond that, I am worthless to it.

DEBORAH—(*stares at him wonderingly—slowly*) There are times when I almost respect you, Joel. (*He gives no sign of having heard her.*)

GADSBY—(*clears his throat embarrassedly*) Humm. (*then briskly*) Henry appears to have had complete confidence in Simon's ability, in spite of his disapproval of his personal conduct. He seems to have carefully followed Simon's career.

JOEL—He did. He obtained constant, confidential reports on the condition of my brother's business. I know that because the reports were made through me. Father did not wish to appear in the matter.

DEBORAH—(*with a sincerely pitying glance*) Poor Joel, your father never had time to spare for others' feelings.

JOEL—(*seems to become more frozen—icily*) I dislike pity, Mother.

GADSBY—(*embarrassedly again*) Henry's suggestion is that you and Joel approach Simon—

DEBORAH—(*flaring up again*) I? Go begging to Simon? Never, I tell you! I did that once— (*abruptly stops, as Joel fixes a cold inquisitive stare on her*)

GADSBY—(*testily*) If you will let me continue, you will see Henry did not suggest you ask Simon for favors. What he recommended is a straight business deal which involves no personal obligations whatever, which will be equally to Simon's advantage and yours. He knew that Simon's business is still a small local affair. Nothing to compare to the Harford Company, which is known and respected wherever our trade is carried. To be its head is to be a leading figure in commerce—as Simon, who once worked under his father and knows the business, will be the first to appreciate.

DEBORAH—(*tensely*) So I am to ask Simon to accept the leadership of the Company, is that it?

GADSBY—Yes. A controlling interest. That is only just if he saves it from ruin. And Henry believed he has the means to save it. According to him, the condition of Simon's business is astonishingly sound from a cash standpoint. He has been shrewd enough to anticipate conditions, and foresee the ruin which is gathering around us. He has been putting all his profit into specie. Of course, from such a small business, it is no tremendous sum, but—

JOEL—It is enough. Specie has become rare and highly prized. A payment in specie here and there will restore confidence.

GADSBY—Henry appreciated, too, that many people here in the city have kept an eye on Simon's success. Because he was Henry Harford's son. The announcement that Simon will assume control will have a very salutary effect. There will be no inclination to grow uneasy and take to prying into conditions—which would be fatal just now. It will be taken for granted the Company is as sound as ever. Henry had learned, too, that Simon had been made a very favorable offer to sell his mill. So there should be no difficulty on that score. (*He hesitates—then uncomfortably*) Humm— Of course, Henry foresaw that there might be difficult personal aspects. He knew that Simon still feels a resentment—

DEBORAH—If we are facing facts, let us face them. Simon hated him.

GADSBY—But Henry evidently believed that you and Simon still felt a mutual affection, and that you could persuade—

JOEL—(*coldly*) Simon will not wish you to be ruined, Mother.

DEBORAH—(*tensely*) So I am cast in the role of chief beggar! (*controlling herself—dryly*) Henry must have lost his shrewdness in more ways than one. He fails to consider the one person who can laugh at his calculations, and who will take great pleasure in doing so—Simon's wife! It is she who controls his affairs. He does nothing without consulting her, and if you think she will ever consent— Oh no, you will find she has never forgiven Henry for humiliating her pride, and this will be a glorious opportunity to revenge herself! And you will discover everything Simon possesses is in her name.

GADSBY—Henry knew that. He—er—evidently relied on your tact and diplomacy, Deborah, to convince her how advantageous for her own future it would be—

DEBORAH—I? She hates me like poison!

GADSBY—I am sure, if you wished, you could easily win her confidence. A woman of her type would be no match for you, with your intelligence and charm.

DEBORAH—(*suddenly struck by a thought—with a strange, almost eager, little laugh*) My talent for intrigue? Yes, this could be the opportunity— (*then with a start—violently*) No! That has no meaning now! It is dead and forgotten!

GADSBY—(*stares at her puzzledly—then in his lawyer's tone*) One further thing Henry suggested, to make his proposal as equitable as possible for Simon and his—er—family. He thought, as they would have to sell their present home and come to the city, and as this home, which he bequeaths to you Deborah, is much too large for you and Joel, that—

DEBORAH—(*tensely*) That I should invite that vulgar Irish biddy and her brats to live with me! (*again suddenly struck by her thought, with almost a gloating smile*) Yes, that would be a greater opportunity than I had ever hoped— (*then resisting more violently than before—furiously*) No! How dare you insult me like this! How dare you make such a shameless proposal!

JOEL—(*with cold bitterness*) It is Father who proposes it, Mother. You owe it to him to do all in your power—

DEBORAH—(*stares at him—bitterly*) And I hoped I had at last escaped the dunning of wifely duty! (*with a strange desperate anguish*) For the love of God, hasn't his death even that meaning?

JOEL—(*coldly relentless*) We are waiting for your consent, Mother.

DEBORAH—(*bitterly hostile*) What an implacable bill-collector you would make, Joel! (*violently*) No, I will not have it! What have I to do with the Company? Let it be ruined! Do you think I fear poverty? What have I ever cared for things outside me? And I have experienced poverty before and did not let it touch me—the most degrading form, that of a minister's household, where one must pretend one welcomes it as a mark of kinship with God! (*desperately*) No! He is dead! All my debt to him is paid! I refuse—!

GADSBY—(*embarrassed—clears his throat*) Humm! As your attorney, Deborah, I strongly advise you to consent.

DEBORAH—(*violently, rising to her feet*) No! I tell you I swore to myself years ago I would never involve myself in such a low intrigue! And I still desired life then. Do you think you can tempt me now when I am an ugly resigned old woman whose life is only in the mind? You are wasting your time, Gentlemen. (*She makes a gesture of arrogant dismissal.*) You will kindly leave me in peace.

JOEL—(*with cold condemnation*) How long are you going to keep us waiting here on your perverse whims? I have always disliked this garden. (*He stares around him with dislike.*) Nothing is natural, not even Nature.

GADSBY—(*staring around him in turn—as if fighting against her influence*) Yes, Deborah. The atmosphere is hardly conducive to—common sense, shall I say. (*then strangely and haltingly as if the influence took hold on him, staring at her*) My dear Deborah. Why should you talk of being old? Ridiculous! You, ugly? You are beautiful! (*Instinctively her face lights up with an eager grateful smile.*) Why, you could be the most wooed widow in the city! I myself would jump at the chance— (*Deborah gives a soft, gratified little laugh. He goes on hastily.*) Not that there ever was a chance. I know that. Besides, this is hardly the time to speak of— You will forgive me, Joel. Your father always permitted me a little harmless gallantry. He knew your mother could never take a short, fat man seriously. Nor could any other woman. Of course, there was Napoleon. But I admit I am no Napoleon, although at times I have dreamed— (*abruptly wrenching his eyes from hers—grumbles irritably to himself*) Humph! What rubbishy thoughts for a man of my years and profession. Her eyes always did make a fool of me. (*reacts to an extreme professional portentousness*) I must protest against your acting so childishly, Deborah. You know there is one honorable course to take. As a woman of breeding and honor, you have no possible choice.

DEBORAH—(*staring before her—with an undercurrent of tense eagerness*) Yes, I suppose it is my duty to see it only in that light. And then there is no choice, is there? It is fate!

(*with a strange urgency*) But you must bear witness, Nicholas, that I fought against this opportunity, that I did not desire it and did all in my power to reject it—that it is destiny—my duty as an honorable woman—and there is no way I could possibly avoid—

JOEL—(*coldly impatient*) You consent?

DEBORAH—(*slowly—as if forcing the words out in spite of herself*) Yes. I consent. (*She suddenly gives a little shiver of dread—strangely*) Ah! I feel tempted to live in life again—and I am afraid!

JOEL—(*coldly matter-of-fact now*) It's settled, then. We will go and see Simon tomorrow. I shall arrange for places in the stage the first thing in the morning. (*He bows with cold courtesy to his mother.*) Good night, Mother. I am going in the house. There is much to do. (*to Gadsby*) Are you coming, Sir?

GADSBY—Yes, Joel. (*He starts to go with Joel—then stops, after a glance at Deborah.*) Go on. I'll follow in a moment. (*Joel goes. Deborah is staring before her, oblivious. Gadsby looks at her with a pitying, if uncomprehending, sympathy. He coughs embarrassedly—attempting a joking tone*) Upon my soul, Deborah, I—er—I cannot see what there is to be apprehensive about in your consenting to the one sensible course.

DEBORAH—(*strangely*) I am afraid of myself, Nicholas.

GADSBY—(*puts on a kindly bullying tone*) Stuff and nonsense! You have done too much brooding alone. It has made you morbid. You should welcome this opportunity to escape—

DEBORAH—I am afraid I do, Nicholas.

GADSBY—It will distract your mind and give you a new, healthy interest in life.

DEBORAH—(*with a bitter intense yearning*) Ah, if it only could be a new interest, Nicholas, and not an old one risen from my dead. With what joy I would welcome it, then! With what humble gratitude would I give thankfulness to God for the undreamed of miracle! (*passionately*) Oh, if you knew how I have prayed for resurrection from the death in myself!

GADSBY—(*worriedly uncertain and pitying*) I—I do not understand you.

DEBORAH—(*forcing a smile—contemptuous and at the same

time affectionate) No, that is why I can safely tell you all my secrets, Nicholas.

GADSBY—(*offended but determined to finish speaking his mind*) I *do* understand this, Deborah. It is not good to detach oneself as completely from the common life as you have done. But now you have a chance to start anew. It depends entirely on your own attitude whether this shall mean the opportunity for a new life of human warmth and companionship and family affection. I remember how devoted you once were to Simon.

DEBORAH—(*stiffening*) I am afraid I could only pretend ever to forgive Simon.

GADSBY—(*ignoring this—hurrying on*) You may even find you can like his wife, when you know her. Forgetting prejudice, you must admit she has been an estimable wife and mother. She must have her good points, if you will see them. She is evidently no fool, and it is not fair to blame her for her origin. (*hastily, with an uneasy glance at her*) Oh, I expect you to storm at me for pleading her case, but we must try to be just.

DEBORAH—(*to his amazement—calmly*) I will not storm. I could find it much easier to forgive her. I understand her feeling toward me. In her place, I would feel the same. (*She smiles wryly.*) There. You see how just I am.

GADSBY—(*astonished—eagerly*) I do, indeed! Why then, there is no obstacle. But I was thinking most of your grandchildren—the opportunity they present to you. You can have no feeling against them, nor blame them in any way for the past. Your blood is in them. They are yours in part. Children in this garden would clear the stifling atmosphere. A little childish laughter and simple joy in being alive. After all, you have given it the aspect of a child's toy garden, made lifesize. They would feel at home here. But I am thinking of it from the standpoint of your future happiness, Deborah. Do you see—?

DEBORAH—(*slowly with a simple sincerity*) Yes. I do see, Nicholas, like an amazing revelation—a miraculous hope that would never have occurred to me if you hadn't— It could be the chance for a new life—escape from the death within myself, from my mind's torturing treadmill of futility. Resign myself to be a grandmother! That could be a resignation in which I might find a purpose in living and a meaning outside myself. (*She stares at Gadsby wonderingly—mockingly but with affection*) You astonish me, Nicholas. I have heard of wisdom from babes, but who could dream of it from a bachelor. (*teasingly*) I really believe you are trying to make a good woman of me, Nicholas! (*then quickly, seeing he is hurt*) No. Forgive my teasing. I am truly grateful. (*intensely*) If you could know how grateful! And I swear to you I will try. It will not be easy. You do not know how bitterly Sara suspects me. Or how well she understands—what I was. It will be difficult to convince her of my good motives and persuade her to trust me with her children. I shall have to show her I no longer want Simon. (*her face hardening*) But that should be easy because I do not. He ceased to be my son four years ago. She is welcome to her husband. (*with more and more of vitality in her tone*) In a way it will be a great challenge to my talent for successful intrigue. I shall have to be very cunning. Her weakness is she is sentimentally honorable and proud and full of pity. I must be very meek and humble. (*suddenly, angry at herself*) No! I talk as if I were planning to pretend and play a part! But I *am* meek now! I *am* humble! I am willing to beg her on my knees to give me this chance to be reborn! I can love her for it if she does! Because if she can trust me, I can learn to trust myself again! I can make her love me and her children love me! I can find love again! (*She smiles exultantly.*) Oh, I may surprise myself, I think, with my undreamed-of talents as a good woman! Already at the mere prospect of escape, I feel a rebirth stirring in me! I feel free! (*She laughs with a strange self-conscious embarrassment and shyness.*)

GADSBY—(*with an approving, benevolent smile*) Good! Excellent! I am delighted you—

DEBORAH—(*with an abrupt change to a strange hectic air of bravado*) And to prove my escape—as a symbol— Watch and bear witness, Nicholas!— I will cast out my devil, the old Deborah—drag her from her sneering place in my mind and heart—(*she makes a movement with her arms and hands of pulling something out of her head and heart and pushing it from her*) and push her back where she belongs—in there—in perpetual darkness— (*She advances up the steps—with a final push*)

"Depart from me, ye cursed!" (*She grabs the doorknob, shutting the door.*) And shut the door! Lock it! (*She does so.*) There! (*suddenly in a burst of triumphant, vindictive hatred*) Now question, and sneer and laugh at your dreams, and sleep with ugliness, and deny yourself, until at last you fall in love with madness, and you implore it to possess you, and scream in silence, and beat on the walls until you die of starvation. That won't take long, now you no longer have me to devour, Cannibal!

GADSBY—(*uneasy*) Come, come, Deborah. This is all most unseemly!

DEBORAH—(*turns to him—with the same strange air, but quietly now*) It is done! She is dead to me. (*then her face lighting up—tensely*) Shhhh! Do you hear, Nicholas?

GADSBY—(*startled and bewildered*) Hear what?

DEBORAH—The footsteps beyond the wall. They have stopped receding. I think Life remembers he had forgotten me and is turning back. (*Suddenly she is conscious of the expression on Gadsby's face and she bursts into natural teasing laughter.*) Heavens, Nicholas! What an alarmed face! Did you think it was a burglar I heard?

GADSBY—(*relieved—huffily, his dignity ruffled*) God bless me! Who could know what to think? Life, indeed! What fantastic rubbish, Deborah!

(*Curtain*)

SCENE TWO

SCENE—*Sitting-room of Sara Harford's home in a textile mill town about forty miles from the city. The following night. The room is small, a typical room of the period, furnished without noticeable good or bad taste. The atmosphere is one of comfort and a moderate prosperity.*

At front, to the left of center, is a table with a lamp and three chairs grouped around it. In the middle of the left wall is a closed door leading into Simon's study. In the left corner, rear, is a sofa, facing right-front. The doorway to the entrance hall, and the stairs to the second floor, is in the middle of the rear wall. At right of this doorway is a cabinet with a lamp. There are two windows in the right wall, looking out on the front garden and the street. Between the windows is a desk with a chair. At right-front is a big arm chair. A rug covers most of the floor.

As the curtain rises, from the hall at rear the sound of small boys' arguing voices is heard coming down the stair well from the floor above. Then Sara's voice trying to quiet them and, for the moment, succeeding. In this pause, the door from the study at left is opened and Simon enters. Physically, he appears to have changed no more than one would normally expect. His spare frame has put on ten pounds or so but it still has the same general effect of loose-jointed, big-boned leanness. His large-featured Yankee face looks his thirty-one years. But there is a noticeable change in the impression his personality projects—a quality of nervous tension, the mental strain of a man who has been working too hard and put unrelieved pressure on himself. As he comes into the room, he is frowning, his eyes preoccupied. He comes to the table and stands staring down at it preoccupiedly. He is startled from his thoughts by a hubbub from the floor above, a chorus of boys' excited voices, the sound of scuffling coming through the ceiling, followed by a resounding thump and a chorus of laughter. Simon's expression changes. His face lights up. He smiles and chuckles to himself. Then Sara's voice is heard in a commanding tone, and the uproar subsides obediently. Simon sits in the chair at left front of table. He picks up two folded newspapers from the table, puts one paper aside, starts to open the other, hesitates, then determinedly opens it. His eyes fix on one story. As he reads it, his face becomes hard and bitter. He hears Sara coming down the stairs in the hall and at once represses his thoughts and looks back toward the doorway at rear smilingly.

Sara enters at rear. She is flushed, her hair disarranged on one side, her eyes laughing and fondly maternal. She exudes an atmosphere of self-confident loving happiness and contentment. She is much better looking than she had been in her pregnancy. Her figure is buxom, but beautifully-proportioned with full breasts, still firm and solid in spite of having nursed four children, and a slender waist.

SIMON—Well! What's been going on up there? I thought the ceiling was coming down.

SARA—(*comes forward laughingly*) We had a pillow fight.
They were so full of high spirits I thought I'd better let them
take it out or they'd never settle down to sleep. If you'd seen
Honey! He stood on his bed and aimed a great blow at Ethan
and missed and came tumbling off to the floor. I was frightened he'd hurt himself, but not a bit. He sat there laughing
to kill himself, and we all had to laugh, too. (*She laughs —
then suddenly shamefaced*) But what a way for me—and you
in your study trying to write. Simon, I'm sorry, Darling. (*She
kisses him impulsively.*)

SIMON—(*gives her a little hug*) Nothing to be sorry about.
I couldn't get interested in it tonight, anyway. (*He looks away
from her. She sits in the chair at right, front, giving him a quick
questioning look, trying to read his thoughts.*)

SARA—(*notices the paper in his hand for the first time —too
casually*) What paper is it you've been reading?

SIMON—Garrison's *Liberator*. (*teasingly but with a resentment underneath*) I know you don't approve.

SARA—(*protestingly*) No, now. I never said that, Simon. I
want the poor black niggers set free just as much as you
—if they can find a way to do it that won't ruin the country. (*as she sees his smile*) Oh, I know. You think I'm thinking
only of us. Well, maybe I am. If you don't look after yourself no one else will. And you are a cotton mill owner who
depends on the Southern planters. There's many here envy
your success and would play you a mean trick if they could,
like telling the planters you were Abolition so they'd black-
list you or—

SIMON—(*frowning*) I'm not in the habit of advertising my
opinions, am I? They're nobody's business but my own.

SARA—(*with satisfaction*) I know, and that's all I ask you
to remember. (*She looks at him quizzically and smiles with
fond amusement.*) It's lucky you don't make speeches about
your opinions or you'd have the whole world bewildered. As
far as I can make out you're a Massachusetts Whig and a
South Carolina Democrat, too. You're for Webster and high
tariff—

SIMON—(*cynically*) To protect our cotton goods. You approve of that, surely.

SARA—At the same time you were for Calhoun, who hates

high tariff, when he wanted Nullification of the Union. I
don't approve of that, Simon. I'm all with President Jackson
there, that Union must be preserved at any price.

SIMON—(*sharply*) I see State rights as a symbol of the individual's right to freedom. (*then quickly*) But why talk of that
now. The issue has been settled by a compromise, for the
time being.

SARA—I know it's settled. (*then teasingly*) And you're Abolition, too, and that's not Whig nor Democrat. (*She laughs.*)
You're a queer man when it comes to politics. You'd better
leave them to me. I'm for the party that protects our interests—as long as it protects them and not one minute longer.
That's simple enough, isn't it? (*She laughs.*)

SIMON—I'm quite willing to leave them to you. You know
very well I am not really interested, that my one true belief is
that the whole system is fundamentally rotten, lock, stock and
barrel, and— (*He stops abruptly and self-consciously—curtly*)
But this argument is ridiculous. I was only teasing you about
the *Liberator*. I was reading the newspaper.

SARA—(*uneasily*) Oh, I meant to hide it. I didn't want you
to see—

SIMON—(*his face hardening*) Why? I knew Father had died.
The report of his funeral means nothing. It seems to have
been an eminent occasion. Daniel Webster and every Whig
notable in the city was there. That would have pleased Father.

SARA—(*resentfully*) I can't understand your mother not inviting you to the funeral. (*bitterly*) Unless she thought I
wouldn't let you go without me, and she didn't want her
poor Irish relations shaming her before the notables!

SIMON—(*mollifyingly*) Now, now. Don't let your mind return to that old bitterness. I think it was simply that she
knew Father wouldn't have wished me to come and pretend
grief for public opinion's sake. He had his virtues and the
foremost was his hatred of hypocrisy in any form. (*then with
growing bitterness*) As for her having Joel write me he was
dead instead of writing me herself, you know I've never had
a letter from her since I saw her that time at my cabin, although I kept writing her until it was all too plain she had
no further interest— (*He hesitates—then slowly*) I've never
told this—it seemed too ridiculous—but I'm afraid I must

have done something then to offend her, which she's never forgiven, although I can't imagine what. Except one thing, which is too childish— But then, she is childish. She was telling me of some silly flight of her imagination and my sense of humor got the better of my tact, and I couldn't help laughing—

SARA—I know. You shouldn't have laughed, Simon.

SIMON—(*staring at her*) You know?

SARA—(*quickly*) I know you shouldn't have laughed, whatever it was. There's a time when women have to admit to themselves that age and death are real, and they get touchy about their dreams. (*abruptly*) But I think the reason she hasn't written you is because she's a wise woman and knows it'd do no good for her to interfere—

SIMON—I'd hardly call the letters she once wrote me interfering.

SARA—She was always reminding you about your book.

SIMON—(*stares at her—smilingly*) You objected to that? But for the last couple of years, who has been encouraging me to write it?

SARA—I have. But that's different. That was so you'd have anything you wish from life to keep you content. And, anyway, I have a right— (*She grasps his hand and presses it— tenderly possessive*) Because I love you, and you're mine, and your happiness is my happiness.

SIMON—(*moved*) I know, Dear. And my one happiness is to give you happiness. (*A pause. He goes on jokingly but with a resentment underneath.*) Why, often I had forgotten all about the darned thing, or I'd want to forget, but you would remind me and send me into my study to work on it like a regular slave-driver!

SARA—(*laughingly*) Oh, I'm not as bad as that, Darling. I'd only speak of it when I'd see you had one of your black lonely fits on, and I'd be afraid you were regretting—

SIMON—(*frowning*) Regretting what? That's silly, Sara. That's all in your mind. If you'd seen what was really in mine, you'd have discovered it was something to do with the mill that made me preoccupied. (*then jokingly as before*) But I've had a dark suspicion for some time about the secret motive behind your persistence in encouraging me to write the book.

I think you calculated very cunningly the best way to convince me it was nonsense was to make me attempt it and then prove to myself—

SARA—(*guiltily*) No.

SIMON—You were sure the absurdity of it was bound to strike me finally. There I was at night in my study trying to convince myself of the possibility of a greedless Utopia, while all day in my office I was really getting the greatest satisfaction and sense of self-fulfillment and pride out of beating my competitors in the race for power and wealth and possessions! (*He laughs, bitterly amused.*) It was too absurd. I couldn't go on forever cheating myself like that, refusing to face myself as I really am. So I made a final decision tonight to forget the book. (*sharply*) Final, do you hear, Sara? Remember that and don't ever mention the damned thing again.

SARA—(*unable to keep a certain triumph from her voice*) You're giving it up forever?

SIMON—Yes, to prove that, and wipe the slate clean, I threw all I've done in the fireplace and burned it. Not that there was much beyond notes. I've destroyed so many beginnings at different times. And I can confess to you now that many nights when you thought I was writing, I was simply sitting there with my mind a blank, bored— (*He hesitates— then blurts out*) Yes, why not admit it frankly—bored to death with the idea of it! (*He suddenly casts a quick glance at her face, as if regretting this admission—in a forced joking tone*) You don't have to look so triumphant, Sara.

SARA—(*guiltily*) I'm not. I— (*then bluntly*) No, I won't lie. I am glad you have found it out for yourself. You know I've never believed your dream would work, with men and women what they are.

SIMON—(*smiling a bit bitterly*) With us as we are, for example? (*quickly*) But you're quite right. My old romantic obsession with Rousseau's fake conception of the inner nature of man was a stupid mistake. Rousseau, as I see him now, was a weak, moral, sentimentalist—a coward who had neither the courage nor ability to live in a world of facts and accept the obvious truth about man—which is that man is compounded of one-tenth spirit to nine-tenths hog— (*quickly*) No. Rousseau was simply hiding from himself in a superior, idealistic dream. (*sneeringly*) As Mother has always done, in a different way. You were right to blame her, Sara. She did have a weakening influence on me when I was young, encouraging me to live in dreams and take a superior scornful attitude about the world of fact and life as it is. It was really her influence that made me first conceive the idea of my book. I can see that now—her haughty disdain for Father because he was naturally absorbed in his business. (*He laughs scornfully.*) And yet all the time she owed everything to his business—the comfort she loved, the protected privacy, her fanciful walled-in garden, the material security which gave her the chance to remain aloof and scornful! It's too idiotic and stupid when you consider it! (*then frowning*) But why think of that now? Except I thank God I freed myself in time, and then met and loved you, who are so simply and courageously and passionately conscious of life as it is, and love it and are healthily eager and happy to be alive and get all you can from it, and don't have to hide from yourself in dreams of what might be in impossible other worlds! (*abruptly*) But I don't know why I'm doing all this talking. All I wanted to tell you was my final decision about the book.

SARA—I'll remember, Darling, and I'll never mention it again. I'm only too happy—

SIMON—(*ignoring this—preoccupiedly*) No, all you have to do to see how sentimentally naive Rousseau's conception was, is to study history—or merely read your daily newspaper and see what man is doing with himself. After all, his deeds constitute the true revelation of his nature. What he desires is what he is. (*with a bitter enthusiasm*) There's the book that ought to be written—a frank study of the true nature of man as he really is and not as he pretends to himself to be—a courageous facing of the truth about him—and in the end, a daring assertion that what he is, no matter how it shocks our sentimental moral and religious delusions about him, is good because it is true, and should, in a world of facts, become the foundation of a new morality which would destroy all our present hypocritical pretences and virtuous lies about ourselves. (*He laughs.*) By God, it's a fascinating idea. I've half a mind to try it!

SARA—(*who has been listening uneasily—protesting resent-*

fully) Ah now, don't start thinking of another book and getting one of your lonely fits of discontent! What have you to complain of in life? Haven't you love and me and the children? Isn't that enough?

SIMON—(*protests guiltily*) Of course it's enough! I would be an ungrateful fool if— And I'm not discontented or complaining. Don't you see that this new book would show that it was nonsense to complain about oneself or be ashamed of oneself? (*quickly—forcing a laugh*) But you're taking me too seriously, Sara. I was merely amusing myself playing with the idea. I have no intention whatever—

SARA—(*relieved, smiling now, maternally amused*) If it isn't just like you to start dreaming a new dream the moment after you've woke up from the old! It's the touch of the poet in you!

SIMON—(*resentfully*) Nonsense! Don't be sentimental, Sara. There never was any poet in me. And I'm through with all idiotic ideas of becoming an author. I couldn't spare the time, for one thing, even if I wanted. (*with more and more of a business-like air*) It's a difficult period for trade this country is in now. I've got to concentrate all my brains and energy on our business affairs. (*frowning*) Conditions are becoming worse every day. (*with a flash of vindictive anger*) That mad fool, Jackson! What does he know of business—an ignorant, mob-rousing, slave-dealing plantation owner! The cowardly tariff compromise he accepted coupled with his insane banking policy are ruining the country!

SARA—Well, he can't ruin us. We've got fifty thousand dollars, the most of it in gold English guineas. The hard times won't touch that.

SIMON—(*with satisfaction*) No. They will make it more valuable.

SARA—(*proudly*) And didn't you have the brains to see the hard times coming before anyone, and guard us against them. I'm so proud of you, Darling!

SIMON—(*pleased*) Well, yes, I did, if I do say it myself. Though I deserve no credit except for ordinary horse sense. Any fool should have seen the crash was bound to come. But they didn't. My competitors kept on expanding while I was cutting operations down. And now it's too late. They're caught, poor devils. (*He smiles with satisfaction.*) Yes, we'll weather the storm, Sara. And when the time comes we will be in a position to take advantage of others' lack of foresight. There will be splendid bargains in bankrupt mill property to be picked up right here in town. That will be our opportunity to expand and profit by the inevitable upturn which must follow the period of stagnation. (*enthusiastically*) And you can bet we will not be blind to our opportunity, will we?

SARA—(*proudly*) *You* won't, I know. It's all your brains.

SIMON—(*lovingly, patting her hand*) No, no. There is no you, nor I. There is only we. (*then enthusiastically*) Yes, there are great opportunities ahead of us. It won't take long for us to get the hundred thousand we have set as our goal. Or more.

SARA—No. That's enough. We promised ourselves—

SIMON—(*smiling*) But wouldn't two hundred thousand, say, be better than one?

SARA—(*smiling*) Maybe, but—

SIMON—It would give you a fine country estate and greater security for the future.

SARA—Give us, you mean. It's for you. I don't want you slaving in trade all your life. I want you to retire a landed gentleman and live at your ease. (*then calculatingly*) Of course, the more you've got to retire on, the safer you'd feel. But I don't want you to take risks and get in too deep.

SIMON—You used to laugh at me for saying that. (*He smiles teasingly—with a note of taunting*) Who is being afraid now? (*then earnestly*) You don't realize what extraordinary opportunities there will be, Sara. In shipping, for example, there are many firms, from the rumors I hear, on the verge of bankruptcy already. Later on I know we could buy up one for comparatively nothing.

SARA—(*uneasily*) No, stick to your own trade, Simon, whatever you do.

SIMON—But it is one of my trades. Don't forget I had my first business training with my father's Company.

SARA—(*with a trace of vindictive hope*) You don't think maybe his Company is in trouble?

SIMON—(*frowning*) No, of course not. Father was much too cautious and shrewd. He took no chances even in the best times. And I'm sure he had everything arranged for the future, so that in case of his death, all Joel would have to do would be to carry on a traditional ritual of conservative policy—small risks and moderate profits—and be a Harford figurehead, while the real work is done by the competent subordinates Father has trained. (*He sneers.*) That is about all Joel is good for, as Father knew. (*then impatiently*) But all that is nothing to me. What I was going to say is that we can't dismiss the shipping trade as something that doesn't concern us. Properly considered, it is a part of our business—or it ought to be. Our cotton is brought to us on ships, isn't it? If we owned our own shipping company, managed as economically and efficiently as I know I could manage it, it would be of tremendous advantage to our mills—

SARA—(*uneasily*) Oh, I see, Darling. It's only that I have a feeling that railroads are bad luck. (*bitterly scornful, lapsing into brogue*) My father, God pity him, was always prating about the great future for the country there was in them, and how he considered them the proper investment for a patriotic gentleman—and him without a dollar to his name! I can hear him now telling my mother— (*Her face suddenly grows sad— scornfully*) Poor Mother! She didn't live long in her Convent to enjoy the rest she'd prayed for. She'd no more than got her wish when she had to die. (*She sighs.*) Ah well, she died at peace, anyway! (*with scorn*) Though it's not the peace of giving up life for a living death I'd ever want for myself. (*then conscience-strickenly to Simon*) But what am I doing, reminding you of death now. Forgive me, Darling.

SIMON—(*intent on his own calculating thought, has not been listening—vaguely*) Forgive what? (*then excitedly*) I tell you, Sara, the more I think of it, the more opportunities I foresee. Take banking. Banks are beginning to fail right and left already, and before long I prophesy that some of the strongest and most desirable ones will be so weakened that you could buy control—

SARA—(*laughingly*) Stop! You have my head spinning! If you keep on, you'll be dreaming yourself the King of America before you know it!

SIMON—(*starts and grins sheepishly*) I was getting a bit beyond myself, wasn't I? (*then with a strange self-compulsive insistence*) Still, if we had that two hundred thousand in specie now, no dream would be too impossible.

SARA—(*scolding him as though he were a small boy*) Now, now, you're too greedy. And you mustn't do so much planning and scheming, when it's getting near bed time, or you'll never settle down to sleep. You haven't been sleeping well lately, and I won't have you getting excited and making yourself so tired and nervous.

SIMON—(*leans back in his chair, suddenly conscious of weariness*) Yes, I am tired. But I'll sleep soundly again now I've put that damned book out of my mind. (*He closes his eyes. Sara looks at him with tender maternal worry. He opens his eyes to stare before him.*) What a damned fool a man can make of himself by clinging to the irresponsible, sentimental dreams of his youth long after he has outgrown them and experience has proven how stupidly impractical they are! Keep on deliberately denying what he knows himself to be in fact, and encourage a continual conflict in his mind, so that he lives split into opposites and divided against himself! All in the name of Freedom! As if Freedom could ever exist in Reality! As if at the end of every dream of liberty one did not find the slave, oneself, to whom oneself, the Master, is enslaved! (*He chuckles bitterly.*)

SARA—(*uneasily*) Ah now, Darling, don't start that black loneliness—

SIMON—(*throws off his mood—with a relieved laugh*) Oh, I'm not. That's finished and done with. I promise not to bewilder you with opposites ever again. (*jokingly*) I'll be all high tariff and Whig and Daniel Webster and pro-Union from now on. (*tenderly*) Above all, pro our union, forever one and indivisible, Sara!

SARA—(*moved—pats his hand*) Darling! That's my only politics in life, too!

(*They are interrupted by the sound of the knocker on the front door, coming from the hall at rear. They look surprised. Sara starts to get up but Simon is before her.*)

SIMON—I'll go. Now who the devil— (*He goes out, rear, frowning irritably. Sara sits listening. From the hall Simon's voice is heard exclaiming with startled astonishment—*"Mother!" *and Deborah's voice* "Simon." *Sara springs to her feet and stands tensely defensive, her expression frightened for a second, then hardening into hostility. Deborah's voice again. Then Simon's and Joel's in cold formal greeting to each other. A moment later Deborah and Simon appear in the doorway at rear with Joel behind them. Deborah wears deep mourning. It becomes her, giving her a quality of delicate, fragile sorrow. Outwardly she is all disciplined composure, the gracious well-bred gentlewoman, with just the correct touch of quiet resignation in her bearing which goes with her widow's black. But one senses an inner tense excitement. At sight of her, Sara instantly puts on her most ladylike manner as if responding in kind to a challenge.*)

DEBORAH—(*comes forward with a gracious smile, holding out her hand—simply*) I am glad to see you again, Sara. I hope you remember me from our one meeting just before you and Simon were married.

SARA—(*takes her hand, smiling in return—a bit stiltedly*) I do. It is a great pleasure, Mrs. Harford.

SIMON—(*indicating Joel—coldly*) This is my brother, Joel, Sara. (*Joel makes her a formal bow, his face cold and expressionless, but remains silent. Sara, following his lead, acknowledges the introduction in silence, then turns to Deborah.*)

SARA—Won't you sit down? (*She indicates the chair in which she had been sitting. Deborah takes it.*) You sit there by your mother, Simon. (*She goes to the armchair at right, front. Simon sits in his old place at left, front, of table. Joel takes the chair at rear of table.*)

SIMON—(*confused by this unexpected visit—forcing a smile, his tone almost resentful*) This *is* a surprise, Mother. When—?

DEBORAH—We arrived on the stage about an hour ago and went to the hotel to make ourselves presentable.

SIMON—The hotel? You must stay with us. We have a room for you, if not for Joel—

JOEL—(*coldly*) I should stay at the hotel in any case.

DEBORAH—No, no. I would not dream of imposing on Sara's hospitality.

SARA—(*smiles cordially*) I insist with Simon, Mrs. Harford. (*She goes on in a tone that becomes, in spite of herself, defiantly bragging.*) We've a fine room always ready. We've had Southern planters as our guests, and they seemed well pleased, although they're gentlemen who are used to great mansions on their estates— (*Abruptly she is ashamed of her bragging and adds lamely*) We should feel very offended if you refused us, Mrs. Harford.

DEBORAH—Why then, since you are kind enough to put it that way, Sara, I accept your hospitality with pleasure. It is the more grateful because it will give me an opportunity of knowing your children. I know when I see them I shall be not only resigned but happy to be an old grandmother. (*For a moment she looks into Sara's eyes with a strange, almost pleading earnestness.*)

SARA—(*stares back suspicious and puzzled for a moment— then she softens*) I'm sure you'll like them. No one could help— (*She smiles.*) But, of course, they're mine and I'd be bound to think that.

JOEL—(*in his cold emotionless voice*) If you will pardon me, Mother, I think the sooner we make clear the business that brought us here, the better. We must obtain Simon's decision tonight so I can return on the first stage tomorrow.

DEBORAH—(*quickly*) And Sara's decision. I suggest Simon take you to his study. You can explain your mission there, and leave me to tell Sara—why I am here. I want her to know that while our reasons for being here have an obvious connection, they are really not the same reasons at all. (*She stares at Sara again with the same earnest, almost pleading, look. Sara reacts as before, at first suspiciously, then puzzledly relenting.*)

SIMON—(*frowns—resentfully*) You always take a childish delight in playing the mysterious, Mother. (*turning to his brother—curtly*) My decision on what?

DEBORAH—Certain last wishes of your father's, and a bargain he proposes. (*She smiles.*) I need not warn you to scrutinize it closely or you may get the worst of it.

JOEL—(*coldly rebuking*) Mother!

SIMON—(*stares at her and then smiles—dryly*) I naturally would, Mother. But thank you for the warning.

DEBORAH—It was your father's wish that you decide this matter solely on its merits as a business opportunity—as though the party of the other part were a stranger. That is my wish, too. I want that clearly understood because Joel is a sentimentalist and will doubtless urge all sorts of fanciful family obligations. You will kindly disregard any nonsense of that kind.

JOEL—(*with cold anger*) Mother! I protest!

SIMON—(*his face hardening*) I flatter myself I do not need to be reminded by Joel or anyone of my just obligation.

JOEL—(*coldly*) I shall urge no such obligations on Simon, Mother. I am too well aware he is indifferent to them. Besides, there is no question of obligations. (*He turns to Simon.*) Father's proposal is immensely to your advantage.

SIMON—(*dryly—getting to his feet*) In your opinion. Perhaps not in mine. We shall see. (*He starts for the study door at the left, Joel following.*)

SARA—(*uneasy—warningly*) Simon, remember—

SIMON—(*turns back reassuringly*) Don't worry. You know I will make no decision without your consent. (*He turns and opens the study door and bows curtly to Joel to precede him. They go inside and shut the door. There is a pause of silence in which Deborah and Sara stare at each other. Deborah again with the strange earnest, almost pleading, look. Sara suspicious, puzzled, yet impressed by the change she senses in Deborah in spite of herself.*)

DEBORAH—(*simply*) It is a long time since our meeting at the cabin. I am sure you notice how greatly I have changed since then.

SARA—(*uneasily*) I do. On the outside, I mean. In your looks. (*then with a cruel revengeful satisfaction*) You look an old woman now. (*tauntingly*) But I suppose you still dream you're the King of France's sweetheart, God pity you!

DEBORAH—(*winces in spite of herself—then with a quiet smile*) You wish to test me? I cannot blame you for being suspicious. Yes, I look an old woman now, Sara. Well, why not? I am an old woman inside me. And I have not dreamed that dream since that day. Can you believe that, Sara?

SARA—(*stares at her—then nods slowly*) I believe you. You couldn't, remembering how he'd laughed. (*then impatiently*) But it's no business of mine. And it isn't telling me why you're here or what you want of me.

DEBORAH—(*hesitates—then quietly with a deep pleading sincerity*) I came to beg charity from you, Sara.

SARA—(*stares at her, not able to believe her ears*) You! To beg charity from me! (*then with harsh suspicion*) Ah, what trick are you up to now?

DEBORAH—No. Can't you feel how I have changed, Sara? Please do! That old Deborah you knew and justly suspected is dead. There is no trick now, Sara. It is the truth that I have come to beg—

SARA—(*staring at her believes—then cannot restrain a burst of gloating triumph lapsing into broad brogue*) You, the great lady Harford! Glory be to God, if my father could have lived to see this day.

DEBORAH—(*ignores this—with the same pleading sincerity*) I came to beg you for the chance to live in life again, to begin a new second life in which I will welcome reality and not fly from it, in which I will forget as one long dead the old vain selfish greedy fool and coward you knew who hid from herself in ridiculous romantic dreams. Forget, too, the self who succeeded her, whom you have not known, who resigned herself to death-in-life and fell in love with Death, and even with insanity. (*She shudders—then pleadingly again*) There is only one possible chance for me to live again, Sara, and only you can give it to me.

SARA—(*moved*) Ah, you poor woman! (*then hastily wary*) No. I'll see. I'd have to know more. I'm buying no pig in a poke, thank you! (*then jeering, not unkindly*) Are you sure you could live if you had the chance? You're a timid dreamy creature and you're not strong like me. (*boastfully*) I'll love life with my last dying groan!

DEBORAH—With your help, I would not be afraid. (*pleadingly again*) I want the chance to be unselfish, to live in others' lives for their sake and not my sake. I want to make myself an unselfish mother and grandmother, to learn how to live for others' happiness, to earn their love by giving and not taking! (*She smiles at Sara—a trembling smile pleading for belief.*) I want even to become a loving mother-in-law who can rejoice in your happiness as my son's wife and his happiness as your husband.

SARA—(*moved—impulsively with a strange, almost servile, humble gratitude*) Ah, that's good and kind of you, Madam. (*then abruptly hostile—contemptuously*) If you're not lying to play me some trick!

DEBORAH—(*ignoring this—pleadingly*) I feel now what I felt that day at the cabin, even when I hated you, that you and I are not natural enemies in our hearts—that in a way we complement each other and each has something the other lacks and needs—

SARA—(*resentfully*) If you imagine I have any need for your great lady's airs and graces, you're badly mistaken, Mrs. Harford!

DEBORAH—(*continuing as if she hadn't heard*) I feel now what I felt then, that if we gave each other the chance, we could be close friends and allies and even grow to love each other.

SARA—(*moved*) Are you begging me for—? (*then with a strange derisive satisfaction*) Indeed and you've changed entirely, when you can lower yourself from the high pride of yourself in your dreams to— (*She stops abruptly and stares at her warily—grudgingly*) Maybe I could like you. I know I don't hate you any more. I'm too sure of Simon now. I know nothing you could do— And if I could trust you—

DEBORAH—(*earnestly*) You can, I swear to you! Don't you feel you can trust me now?

SARA—(*moved but warily*) I do—now. But you'd have to prove—

DEBORAH—All I ask is a chance to prove it, Sara. (*persuasively*) After all, you won't be risking anything. You would know if I tried to deceive you, and you could always make Simon get rid of me again.

SARA—(*grimly*) I could. I'm glad you know that. And I would. I hope you know that, too!

DEBORAH—I do know it, and I would be the last to blame you. (*pleadingly*) What I'm begging for above all, Sara, is the chance to find a new life—and unselfish love—through the lives of my grandchildren. I want to become a good, loving grandmother. If you knew how horribly alone I have been for so long, Sara, sitting in my garden with an empty dreamless mind, with only the hope of death for company—a garden where Spring is but the beginning of Winter. It and I need to be reminded that Life is not the long dying of death but the happy greedy laughter of children! (*She pauses—then adds quietly*) Will you give me that chance, Sara?

SARA—(*moved*) It's true you have nothing in life, poor woman, and how could I be so cruel and hard hearted as to turn you away, when I'm so rich and you so poverty-stricken.

DEBORAH—Then you will! Oh, thank you, Sara. I am more grateful than you can know! It means the difference between life and death to me!

SARA—(*uneasy, as if already regretting her consent*) I'm only doing it because it was through the money you loaned us when we were married we got our start, and we owe it to you in honor— I've never liked being in debt to you, but now we'll be square and even. (*then suddenly suspicious*) Wait! What has this got to do with the business his brother is telling Simon? You haven't explained what that business is yet.

DEBORAH—(*smilingly evasive*) I'd rather not, Sara, if you don't mind. I know nothing of business, and, anyway, I want you to decide from what Simon tells you about it, purely on its merits as a business opportunity. You will be able to do this without being influenced by your old suspicion of my motives now that you see how I have changed and you know that my only real interest is the chance for a new life, which you can give me whether you and Simon decline his father's offer or not.

SARA—But what is the offer? You can tell me that.

DEBORAH—(*carelessly*) Why, all I understand about it is that my husband realized that Joel hasn't the ability to be the head of a big company, while Simon has proved he has the ability. So my husband suggested that in case of his death Joel and I should offer Simon a controlling interest if he would assume direction of the Company's affairs.

SARA—(*her eyes gleaming triumphantly*) My husband to be head of the Harford Company? Ah, if my father—! (*She stops abruptly—then frowning*) But I don't see— If Simon's father wanted that, why didn't he have it in his will?

DEBORAH—(*with a mocking smile*) No, no, my husband was much too proud a man for that. He could not publicly admit he had been wrong in disinheriting Simon, or that he needed his help. Not even for the sake of the Company which was his one beloved. (*bitterly*) He preferred to bequeath to me the humiliation of begging— (*hastily*) Of course, you understand, Sara, it is a bargain my husband suggested. He was not the man to give anything for nothing. The Company, I believe, is at present in need of cash, and he knew you—

SARA—(*her face hardening*) Ah, so that's it! The gold we've slaved to save! (*curtly*) No, thank you, Mrs. Harford. My husband has his own business, and it's enough. We don't want the Harford Company.

DEBORAH—(*shrugs her shoulders indifferently*) Well, that's for you and Simon to decide. I appreciate your viewpoint and I won't blame you if you refuse. But please don't make any decision from what I say. Wait until Simon tells you all the facts. He will know if there is any advantage for you in the offer. Oh, there's another thing I was forgetting. My husband proposed that, in fairness to you, since you would necessarily have to make your home in the city, I make over to you, as part of the bargain, a one-half interest in my house and garden, so that you could live there by right of ownership and not feel under any obligation—

SARA—(*her eyes gleaming again*) The Harford mansion! I know it's one of the finest in the city.

DEBORAH—Yes, it is really a very beautiful and valuable property, Sara. And I need not tell you how delighted I would be. I will be so horribly lost living there alone. In fact I want to double my husband's offer, and deed the whole property over to you so that it will be entirely yours, and you will have the sole management of it. All I ask in return is that you allow me to live there with you—and my grandchildren. (*She adds laughingly*) Oh, I admit this is shameless bribery on my part, Sara, but I am so alone, and it would mean so much to me—

SARA—(*touched and greedy*) I think it's very generous of you, Mrs. Harford. (*then warily*) But, of course, it depends on what Simon—

DEBORAH—Oh, certainly, but I hope he will find the business part of it advantageous. And now, let us not talk of business anymore. I really know so little— (*eagerly*) Could I see my grandchildren now? Oh, I know they must be asleep. All I wish is a peek at them, so I can begin feeling myself an actual, living, breathing grandmother! (*She laughs gaily.*)

SARA—(*smiling—touched*) Indeed you can. Their grandmother has the right. (*She runs from her chair and Deborah gets up, too.*) Only I better go up alone first and make sure they're asleep. If one of them was awake and saw you he'd be so excited and full of questions—

DEBORAH—(*smiling*) Oh, I know. I remember Simon— (*She stops abruptly, her expression suddenly bitterly resentful.*)

SARA—I'll be right back, Mrs. Harford.

DEBORAH—(*throws off her mood—smilingly*) I would be grateful if you could call me Deborah from now on.

SARA—(*with instinctive humility*) No, that's too familiar— (*then hating herself for this—assertively*) All right, I will, Deborah. (*She goes out, rear.*)

DEBORAH—(*stares after her—as if in spite of herself, an expression of triumphant gloating forces itself on her face, and she smiles jeeringly*) At least old age has not impaired your talent for acting, Deborah! (*then savagely*) No! You lie! You know you lie! I meant every word sincerely! What if I did misrepresent the business aspect of it? That is nothing to me! That concerns Simon! I only use it! The real issue for me is between Sara and me, and that is decided! And I am grateful to her! I already feel an affection for her! I will make myself love her! She has been kind and generous and understanding! She has given me life again! I feel freed from myself, eager to live! I— (*She stops abruptly and sits down again as the door from the study is opened and Simon enters with Joel. Joel's expression is one of cold, bitter humiliation. Simon is repressing a feeling of gloating satisfaction and excited calculation. He comes and puts a protecting, possessive hand on his mother's shoulder.*)

SIMON—(*gently*) Poor Mother. I'm so sorry. (*She gives a quick bitter look up at his face and moves her shoulder away from his hand. He goes on comfortingly.*) But never mind. You mustn't worry anymore. (*in an almost bragging tone*) I think, without flattering myself, I can promise I'll soon win back for you all his stupid folly has lost.

JOEL—(*with cold anger*) It is cowardly to insult the dead.

SIMON—(*stung—turns on him—bitingly*) Is it an insult to state a fact? He did act like a fool, as Mother will agree—

DEBORAH—(*coldly*) I agree with Joel that the dead are, after all, the dead. (*Simon stares at her in resentful surprise. She adds curtly*) Am I to understand you accept your father's proposal?

SIMON—(*resentfully*) Of course. Did you think I would refuse to save you from being ruined and left a pauper?

DEBORAH—(*sharply*) No, no! We will have none of such consideration, if you please. I told you it is my wish, as it was your father's, that there be no hypocritical family sentiment in this bargain.

SIMON—(*taken back and hurt*) Hypocritical, Mother?

DEBORAH—Yes, hypocritical. You hated him and you certainly owe him no obligation. As for you and me, we have not even corresponded in years. We have forgotten each other. Our old relationship of mother and son died, from perfectly natural causes, long ago. In the meanwhile, we have both changed completely in character—

SIMON—(*bitterly*) Yes, I begin to see how completely you have changed!

DEBORAH—(*indifferently*) Good, I am glad you do. And I see as clearly the transformation in you. Well, then? Are we to pretend we are what we were, or are we to be sensible and frankly admit the obvious truth that we are now strangers? Admit it without resentment as the inevitable result of time and circumstance. I believe it is very important for us to do that, Simon—here and now—to free each other from the sentimental duty to remember a past each of us has forgotten. I think it is extremely necessary, now that conditions beyond our control, have brought us together again, that we start our new relationship on a foundation of lasting fact so it may have the chance to develop into a pact between friends who can rejoice in each other's successful freedom. (*She pauses— then adds with a little taunting smile*) Anyway, I warn you frankly that, even if I tried, I could never play the role of a slavish loving mother convincingly again.

SIMON—(*bitterly*) I am glad you admit it was just a role.

DEBORAH—(*ignoring this*) So now you ought to appreciate why I must insist you consider your father's and my proposal purely and simply as a business deal. Accept, if it strikes you as a profitable opportunity. If not, decline it. And no more sentimental maundering about poverty. Why should the Company's ruin necessarily condemn me to rags. I have no doubt you would offer me a home with you. If not, Joel has—

SIMON—Naturally, Mother, I would welcome you—

DEBORAH—Well, then, no need, is there, to have pathetic visions of my begging in the gutter? Besides, I could—or so Nicholas Gadsby assures me—always marry well again.

JOEL—(*repelled—coldly*) I consider it grossly improper of you, Mother, with Father scarcely cold in his grave, to—

SIMON—(*repelled—coldly*) I agree with you, for once, Joel. It is revolting, Mother! (*then with a sneer*) And I would not take Gadsby's flattery too seriously. It is not so easy to catch a rich husband—even for a young and beautiful woman.

DEBORAH—(*smiling*) That jeer might have hurt my vanity once, Simon, but now I am a grandmother, I am long past the desire to possess husbands. (*She laughs.*) Besides, you'll admit I can always have Nicholas, and he is quite well off.

JOEL—(*rebukingly*) Mother! This ill-timed levity is—

DEBORAH—Inconsequential—to you, I know. (*She turns to Simon with a return of her cold curtness.*) Well, I hope you are thoroughly convinced now that whatever is arranged must be on a strictly business basis so there can be no possibility of any future misunderstanding about sentimental obligations. I refuse to be indebted—to you—for anything.

SIMON—(*stares at her—then brusquely*) Very well, Mother. (*He sits at the table—Joel behind it—curtly*) As I have told Joel, I will accept Father's proposal only on one condition. If you cannot agree to it, there is no more to be said.

DEBORAH—(*coldly*) And what is the condition?

JOEL—(*with cold anger*) It is preposterous, Mother—an insult to my father's memory!

SIMON—(*ignoring him*) There can be no question of my giving up my prosperous business here to take up his bankrupt one. That is absurd. Father, in his blind vanity, grossly overestimated the prestige of his name. I have never needed that prestige. I do not need it now. I have never been his son. I have always been myself. My condition is that I absorb his Company in mine. His Company must cease to exist. There must be only my Company.

JOEL—(*angrily*) You see, Mother! Father would rather have faced ruin a thousand times—

DEBORAH—(*dryly*) But unfortunately he left me to face it.
(*She stares at Simon—with a strange smile*) I see, Simon, what
an opportunity this is for you to realize a life-long ambition.
(*then briskly*) I accept your condition.

JOEL—I protest, Mother! You have let him beat you down
like a swindling horse-trader! He sees the tremendous advantage for him in Father's offer. He would accept it uncondi-
tionally if you—

DEBORAH—(*cuttingly*) Your protest is voted but kindly remember mine is the final decision. (*with a smile*) I want your
brother to drive the hardest bargain he can, to be unscrupulous and merciless—

SIMON—(*dryly*) Naturally you could expect no mercy in a
strictly business deal, Mother. (*then matter-of-factly*) Then the
matter is settled—provided, of course, Sara consents, and you
may take that for granted.

DEBORAH—Yes, I have talked with Sara and I think you
will have no trouble convincing her.

SIMON—(*with resentful curtness*) I know that, Mother. Sara
does as I advise in these matters.

JOEL—(*gets to his feet—stiffly to Simon*) I bid you good
night. I shall go to the city by the morning stage and have
the announcement made that you are assuming control of the
Company.

SIMON—(*curtly giving orders*) Yes, see to that if you please.
The sooner it is known the better. You never can tell in these
days when creditors may grow uneasy, and suspicious.

JOEL—(*stiffly*) Before I go. I wish to protest again, in
Father's name, against what I consider the dishonor of your
conduct and of my mother's. You will, of course, wish me to
resign from my position.

SIMON—(*indifferently*) No. You are an excellent head
bookkeeper, I know. So why should I? And I shall see that
you are given an interest in my Company, commensurate,
under the circumstances, with the interest you were left in
Father's Company.

JOEL—(*stiffly*) I shall engage an attorney to protect that
interest.

SIMON—(*impatiently*) Attorney or no attorney, I could

easily swindle you out of it, if I liked. But you are too helpless a foe. (*He nods curtly in dismissal.*) Good night.

JOEL—(*stiffly*) I will keep my position only because I feel it my duty to Father's memory to do all I can—for I warn you that, whatever you do, the Company will always be my father's Company in my eyes.

SIMON—(*irritably*) I do not care a tinker's damn what it is in your eyes. (*Joel stares at him, is about to say something more, then bows stiffly to Simon, ignoring his mother, and stalks out the door at rear. Simon frowns exasperatedly after him—then suddenly chuckles with amusement, with a change of manner towards Deborah of their one-time intimate sharing of a joke.*) God, he'll never change, will he, Mother? He isn't a man. He's a stuffed moral attitude!

DEBORAH—(*unconsciously falling into the mood of their old affectionate intimacy—laughing maliciously*) Yes, haven't I always said Joel is God's most successful effort in taxidermy! (*They laugh amusedly together—then stop abruptly and stare at each other. Deborah defensively, Simon resentfully.*)

SIMON—I must confess, Mother, after all your explanation, I still do not see why you should suddenly take such an antagonistic attitude toward me as you have. (*hopefully*) Or was that simply for Joel's benefit?

DEBORAH—(*lightly*) Good heavens, no! Is Joel important? No, it was for your benefit—and mine.

SIMON—One would think I had in some way deeply offended you. Whereas, if either of us has cause to feel injured, it is I! For some time after we last met, I kept writing you and you never deigned to answer.

DEBORAH—Because at that last meeting I realized that our old relationship was quite dead, and there was no good keeping up a pretense for sentiment's sake. You are wrong to think my present feeling is one of antagonism. I have no reason to feel that. No, my feeling is one of indifference. (*Simon looks hurt and startled. She goes on quietly.*) I will be quite frank, Simon. If I had heard of your death— Oh, of course, I would have tried to be dutiful and recapture sentimental, fond motherly memories of what used to be between us, but I am afraid I would have been as indifferent to your death as you have changed to be, as I would be to the death of a stranger, which is what you really are to me now.

SIMON—(*woundedly*) Mother!

DEBORAH—No, no, please, let us face the truth. You would have felt the same if I had died.

SIMON—No!

DEBORAH—Yes. Why deny it? That is what Time does to us all. We forget and pass on. It is perfectly natural—and necessary. You have your life of a husband to live. You have your children. One can only think of so much. One must forget and eliminate the past. Why not admit that?

SIMON—(*coldly—his face hard*) Very well. I do admit it.

DEBORAH—Good! There the past is finally buried, and we can start again and learn to become friends. I want to be the friend of Sara's husband, Simon. I want to be proud of what you are, of what you will do to recoup the Harford fortune, of the great success in your chosen career I see before you. I am determined to live with a world that exists, Simon, and accept it as good because it is, and all else is not. I have forgotten my old silly presumptuous cowardly disdain for material success. I hope to live to see you become a Napoleon of finance.

SIMON—(*stares at her—bursts out with contemptuous disgust*) It is no lie that you have changed—incredibly! (*then abruptly and eagerly*) But what you say is true. Finance is only one medium for ambition in the country today, through which one can conquer the power where possession alone gives you the liberty to be free! (*He smiles.*) It is a strange coincidence that you should come tonight and say these things. Just before you came I had torn up and burned what I had done on that absurd book—set myself free of the past—

DEBORAH—(*quietly*) I congratulate you. You are wise. It was meaningless except as an obstacle in your way—a sentimental memory of a dead self. (*Sara enters from the rear. They turn to her. She looks disturbed for a second at finding them close together, then comes forward smilingly.*)

SARA—I'm sorry to keep you waiting so long, Deborah, but our talking here had wakened Jonathan and I had to get him back to sleep. (*glancing from one to the other—with a trace of suspicion*) What are you talking about? Where's Simon's brother?

DEBORAH—(*gaily*) Simon was talking over this business— for the last time, I hope.

SIMON—Joel just left. I'm sending him to the city by the first stage to announce that we are taking over Father's Company and making it a part of our business. (*with a gloating grin at her*) Do you understand, Sara? His Company ceases to exist. We absorb it. There will be only one Company.

SARA—(*her eyes lighting up with a vindictive triumph*) Ah, leave it to you! If my father had only lived to see— (*then with sudden dismay*) Then you decided it all—without waiting to ask me!

SIMON—Because I was sure of your consent and I knew Mother had talked to you.

SARA—But she didn't—

DEBORAH—No, Simon, you know I haven't the knowledge to explain all the business details.

SARA—She was begging me—

DEBORAH—Yes, I begged Sara to forget all the bitterness in the past, now your father is dead, and allow me to become her friend. And she promised she would try.

SARA—Yes, I did. But—

SIMON—(*with a strange, resentful air—almost sneeringly*) It is strange to think of you two as friends.

DEBORAH—(*with a little smile*) He doesn't believe we can be, Sara.

SARA—(*defensively*) Why can't we, I'd like to know? I've always felt grateful to her for giving us our start in life.

DEBORAH—Yes, we will prove it to him, won't we? We won't let him discourage us.

SIMON—(*frowning—irritably*) Discourage you? What a stupid thing to say, Mother! You know very well nothing would please me more.

DEBORAH—(*laughingly*) There, Sara. Now we have your husband's blessing.

SIMON—(*changing the subject abruptly—to Sara*) To get back to business: I didn't wait for your consent because I knew you couldn't possibly refuse such a good bargain. (*then almost as if he were showing off his authority before his mother*)

And after all, you know from experience you can trust my judgement.

SARA—(*uneasily again*) I do know, yes. But—

SIMON—(*enthusiastically now*) I tell you, Sara, this is the luckiest kind of coincidence—an extraordinary opportunity for us—exactly the chance for expansion and growth we were hoping for. (*with a sly glance at his mother—chuckling complacently*) And a finer bargain than I would have dreamed possible, thanks to Mother. I was going to be merciful and generous, but she insisted I consider it nothing but a business deal, and drive the hardest bargain I could. So I did, and I don't mind confessing in her presence, now the deal is completed, that we will be getting something for practically nothing.

DEBORAH—(*laughing*) And so am I. I had nothing and I am getting Sara's friendship and a chance to make a new start in life as a good grandmother. (*She turns to Sara—eagerly*) But all this talk of business is meaningless to me. What is important— May I go up and see my grandchildren now, Sara?

SIMON—(*frowning—curtly*) No, they're asleep. You'd only wake them.

SARA—(*defending her*) All she wants is to peek at them from the door. Isn't it, Deborah?

DEBORAH—Yes. To meet myself as a grandmother by seeing them in the flesh. And you can trust me not to wake them, Simon. (*smilingly*) You forget I've had experience. Many a time I looked in at you and never disturbed you.

SARA—(*smiling at him maternally—teasingly*) Oh, him. It's hard to get him to sleep but once he drops off you could fire a cannon and he'd never budge.

DEBORAH—Yes, that's the way he used to be when he was little. (*She laughs.*) I can see you have made him your eldest son, as well as your husband, Sara.

SARA—(*laughingly*) Oh, he's been that from the day we married. (*teasingly*) Only don't let him hear you, Deborah. I'd offend his dignity.

DEBORAH—Well, I hope you notice I am not one bit jealous of you taking my place, Sara—now.

SARA—(*stares at her*) Yes, I do notice. I feel it.

DEBORAH—I'm so glad you do, Sara, because now there can never be any misunderstanding on that score. And I know you won't be jealous if I can make your children love me. I do want them to love me.

SARA—Ah, don't think that of me. I'm not that selfish and greedy. I'll be only too happy— Don't I know how lonely and lost you must have been all those years without love to live for. (*She takes Deborah's arm—gently*) Come along now and see the children. (*They start back, ignoring Simon, who has listened frowningly, feeling completely out of it, his face hardening with resentment.*)

SIMON—(*sharply*) Wait! (*as they turn back—injuredly*) You might at least wait until I have finished explaining about the bargain I drove, Sara.

SARA—(*humoring him*) Of course, Darling. (*to Deborah, teasingly*) That's the way he is now. Once he gets his mind set on business the devil himself couldn't stop him.

DEBORAH—(*seriously*) Well, I'm sure he owes his great success to that power for concentration, and that it will lead him on to greater and greater achievement. So it's really an admirable quality. (*Simon stares at her suspiciously but she appears absolutely sincere.*)

SARA—Oh, I know, and I'm so proud of him, Deborah.

SIMON—So proud you can't even listen while I tell you—

SARA—(*placatingly*) Ah now, don't get angry at me. Darling, can't you take a little teasing without— (*then resentfully herself*) Much good it will do me to listen now after you went ahead and agreed without consulting me at all!

SIMON—(*harshly*) You know very well my asking your consent has never been anything but a formality. What do you really know of business? It is I alone who have the right—

SARA—(*suddenly frightened and hurt*) Simon! You've never said that before! You—

SIMON—(*guiltily*) I'm sorry, Sara. No, and I wouldn't say it now if you'd give me a chance to ask your consent. It isn't too late for you to refuse. Nothing is signed yet. I can still back out, if you wish.

SARA—After you've given your word? (*proudly*) I hope Deborah knows I've too much honor for that!

DEBORAH—(*jokingly*) But can't you see, Sara, all he wants is to prove to you how clever he has been for your sake, and have you say you're proud of him.

SARA—(*smiling*) Oh, he knows that. I'm all the time telling him how proud I am, and making him vain and spoiling him! (*She laughs fondly.*) So go on now and tell me, Darling.

SIMON—(*made self-conscious and ill at ease—awkwardly*) What I wanted to say is— (*Suddenly he stares at his mother—sneeringly*) You a doting old grandmother, Mother? You will forgive me if I cannot picture that transformation! You've never cared about children, except as toys to play with in your garden and beguile your boredom—unless my memory is all wrong!

DEBORAH—(*undisturbed—smiling*) Yes, that is true, more's the pity. But that was an old dead me who was afraid of life. I am not that now. (*to Sara*) He doesn't want to believe that I have changed, Sara.

SIMON—(*sneeringly*) Oh, I'm open to proof. But it will take a lot of proving, Mother.

SARA—(*resentful at him—rebukingly*) Ah now, you shouldn't sneer at your mother like that. It's not kind. You ought to help her and take her word. What do you know of women? But I tell you I feel it in her no matter how she's lied to herself in the past, she's not lying to herself now. (*She glances at Deborah affectionately—smiling*) I'd still feel that, even if I knew she thought she was lying and wanted to lie.

DEBORAH—(*gives her a strange grateful look*) Thank you, Sara. I am absolutely sure now we can become great friends.

SARA—(*to Simon*) And I'm certain it's going to mean content for her, Simon, if you'll not interfere. (*arrogantly with a touch of brogue*) Sure, do you think I'm that stupid she could fool me? I know the fancy she has for the children already without a sight of them, and once she's seen them she can't help loving them. (*proudly*) Who could? And won't it be a great help for them to grow up fine gentlemen to have a grandmother who's a great lady— (*She stops abruptly—guilty and humiliated.*) Never mind. What is it you were going to say about the bargain, Simon? (*without waiting for him to answer*) Maybe you don't know or you couldn't act so unfriendly toward her, that your mother, as part of the bargain, is going to deed over her fine mansion and land in the city to us. She'll only live there as our guest and I'll have the whole management and be the mistress.

SIMON — (*his face hardening*) I will not consent to that.

SARA — (*defiantly*) But I have consented, and it's only fair you leave me to decide about our home, which is my business, if you want me to agree with what you've decided about the Company.

SIMON — I told Joel I did not want even the one-half interest in Mother's home that Father suggested she offer me. We will rent a house first, and later buy our own home. We need be under no obligation to Mother—

DEBORAH — (*sharply*) I told you there could be no question of obligations. I made the offer to Sara as part of my bargain with her — (*smilingly*) and, to be frank, I think I am getting all the best of it. I will still have all the privileges of my home and none of the responsibilities of actual ownership. And I will have Sara and my grandchildren for company. No, if there is any obligation, I am obliged to Sara.

SARA — (*smilingly*) No, Deborah, it's a great bargain for us, too. (*to Simon, a bit impatiently*) Can't you see, Simon, that we'll be getting a fine mansion for nothing at all, with a beautiful, spacious garden for the children to play in.

DEBORAH — (*staring at him with a strange mocking little smile — jokingly*) Really, Sara, your husband's attitude is most unflattering. You would think I was some wicked old witch, the way he dreads the thought, living in the same house with me!

SIMON — (*resentfully*) Don't be silly, Mother. I—

DEBORAH — (*as before*) He seems to feel so antagonistic to me because I didn't answer a few letters. But I know you appreciate my reasons for that, Sara.

SARA — I do, and I'm grateful you had the fairness and good sense not to—

SIMON — (*bitterly*) So it is I who am antagonistic, Mother? Well, perhaps I am — now — with good reason — but if I am, whose wish was it—? (*then abruptly with cold curtness, shrugging his shoulders — to Sara*) But, as you said, Sara, our home should be your business, and I am willing to abide by your decision. It is really a matter of indifference to me what house

I live in. I shall have to concentrate all my attention on reorganizing my Company and for a long time to come I can see I shall have to do practically all my living at my office. (*becoming more and more enthusiastic—eagerly*) You can't realize what an opportunity this is for me, Sara, and what a tremendous bargain I have got! Father became panic-stricken, the coward, the minute he found himself out of his conservative depth. He greatly exaggerated the danger. It will be easy for me—

DEBORAH—(*turning to Sara—gaily*) Let's leave our Napoleon to his ambitious destiny and go up to the children, Sara.

SARA—(*teasingly*) Yes, let's. He'll be owning the whole world in his mind before you know it. (*They turn towards the door at rear, laughingly.*)

SIMON—(*resentful—coldly*) Wait. Although I have agreed to let you decide where we shall make our home, Sara, I would like to utter a word of warning—in Mother's presence, so that everything may be open and above board. (*sneeringly*) You will forgive me if I do not possess the entire confidence in this sudden friendship between you you both appear to have. Oh, I do not doubt you think you feel it now, but it will be a difficult matter when two such opposites as you are have to live together in the same home day after day, with continual friction and conflict of character developing.

SARA—(*resentfully*) You've no right to expect the worst. And if it should happen, we can always change it one way or another, can't we?

DEBORAH—(*gaily*) Yes, you can always dispossess me. You will have the legal right to, you know. But I am sure I will never give you just cause. You trust me not to, don't you, Sara?

SARA—Yes, I do.

DEBORAH—(*smiling, with a strange undercurrent*) I promise to leave you entirely alone, Simon. So you need not worry. As for you thinking Sara and me as hostile opposites, that, I believe, is something which exists only in your mind, because you persist in remembering the dead me who was your mother. But Sara, at heart, sees how I have changed, and that she and I can have much in common, now.

SARA—(*stubbornly*) Yes, I do, Simon.

SIMON—(*resentfully*) All right then. I have nothing more

to say. But don't forget I warned you. And remember I have the right to expect a peaceful atmosphere in my home. I will have too many important things on my mind to be distracted by domestic dissensions. So please don't come to me—

DEBORAH—(*gaily—but with a strange undercurrent*) I hereby take a solemn oath never to come to you.

SARA—(*staring at him—puzzled and resentful*) What's come over you, Darling? It is not like you to act so grudging and stubborn— I can't see—

DEBORAH—(*as before*) Yes, one would actually think you resented us becoming friendly, Simon. (*to Sara—teasingly*) Men are such vain little boys, Sara. I have an idea he would prefer us to be jealous enemies and fight a duel to the death—

SIMON—(*forcing a laugh*) What a fantastic idea, Mother! And you think you have changed! (*He comes to them—protesting*) You know very well, and Sara knows, it has always been my dearest hope that circumstances would someday present you and Sara with the opportunity really to know each other. I was sure when that happened, you could not help loving each other, and I am delighted that, at last, my hope has been realized. I made the objection I did only because I wanted to convince myself you were sure of each other's good faith. My experience in business has made me over-cautious about contracts entered into in haste, perhaps. But now I admit myself entirely convinced. I congratulate you—and myself on my good fortune. I needed only your reconciliation to complete my happiness and give me absolute confidence in the future. (*He kisses them. Sara's face lights up happily. Deborah's remains teasingly mocking.*)

(*Curtain*)

ACT THREE
Scene One

Scene—*Simon's private office in the offices of Simon Harford, Inc. in the city four years later. It is an early morning in the late summer, 1840.*

The room is small, well-proportioned, panelled in dark wood. The furniture is old, heavy and conservative. A dark rug is on the floor of polished oak boards. On the walls are pictures of Washington, Hamilton, Daniel Webster, and, incongruously, John C. Calhoun.

In the left wall are two windows looking out on the street. Between the windows is a chair, facing right. Before the chair, a large table with drawers which serves as Simon's desk, with another chair on the other side of it, facing his. In the rear wall right, is a door leading into the hall. At left of this door, a tall cabinet stands against the wall. At right, front, is a door leading into the bookkeeper's office. Farther back against the wall, is a high desk with a tall stool in front of it. At front, right, is another chair facing left.

As the curtain rises, Simon enters at rear and comes to his table. He has changed greatly in the four years and looks older than the thirty-five he is. His body has put on twenty pounds or more of solid flesh, mostly around his chest and shoulders and arms, which gives him a formidably powerful appearance. On the other hand, his face has become thinner, more heavily lined and angular. There are patches of grey over his temples. His expression is that of one habitually tense, with a mind disciplined to function efficiently at a high pitch while suppressing all manifestation of nerves. His manner is curtly dictatorial. He speaks rapidly and incisively. He is dressed conservatively in dark clothes, obviously expensive.

SIMON—(*before sitting down, picks up an engagement pad from the table and glances at it*) Nothing of importance—except the railroad directors—that isn't important now—a signing of papers—it is finished—it is mine. (*He tosses the pad on the desk and sits down—stares at the table top a moment.*) Mustn't forget Sara's engagement—it is time I did something to take her away from Mother's influence—make her my old Sara again— (*then frowning*) Bah!—better leave well enough

alone—I really don't want her here interfering in my business—in which she takes no more interest, anyway—as little
as Mother— (*then dismissing it*) Well, let's hope she's early
before the others begin trooping in— (*He picks up the morning mail stacked on his desk and at once becomes concentrated on
going through it. The manner in which he does this is characteristic. He goes from one letter to the next with astonishing rapidity,
seeming to take in the contents of each at a glance and make an
instant decision, setting it on the table at his right, or dropping it
in the waste basket.*

(*The door from the bookkeeper's office at right is opened and Joel
Harford enters, closing the door quietly behind him. He stops to
glance at his brother, then comes and stands in front of his desk.
Joel looks older. The stoop in his shoulders is more pronounced, with
a suggestion of weariness and resignation now beneath the uncom-
promising rigidity of his habitual poise. He stands waiting, staring
at Simon with his customary cold disapproval. Simon deliberately
ignores Joel's presence—or attempts to, but it immediately gets on
his nerves, and at last he exclaims exasperatedly, stopping his work
with a nervous jerk.*)

SIMON—Well? Don't stare like a frozen codfish! Is this
another of your periodical duty-to-the-Company protests
against my management? If so, I don't care to listen.

JOEL—(*stiffly*) As a stockholder, it is my right—

SIMON—(*contemptuously*) Your right has no power, so you
have no right. But relieve your conscience, if you must. Only
be quick. I have no time— (*tensely explosive again*) Damn
you! You have the stupid effrontery to criticize my leadership
in the face of all I've accomplished in four years! I have five
mills now, all running profitably, instead of one. I have transformed what was Father's bankrupt business into a marine
division of my Company which is a model of its kind. I
have—

JOEL—(*interrupts coldly*) I do not minimize what you have
done in that respect. What I object to is your reckless use of
credit which continually leaves the Company in a fundamentally unsound position. You pay off debts only in order to
borrow more largely. You go on gambling—

SIMON—Don't be a frightened old woman! (*arrogantly*) It
is not gambling when I know the dice are loaded in my favor

by my ability to turn any possible contingency into a fresh opportunity.

JOEL—You think only of further expansion. That is bad enough when you restrict it to your proper sphere, but when you adventure into new fields— (*stiffly*) I refer now to the deal for the railroad you are to conclude this morning. I am unalterably opposed to this folly. You know nothing of railroading.

SIMON—Neither do most of those engaged in it. (*arrogantly*) But unlike them I *will* know all there is to know. Anything I choose to make mine, I make mine!

JOEL—Finally, I want to warn you again against the growing unscrupulousness of your methods, the ruthlessness with which you take advantage of others' misfortunes. You are making the Company feared and hated.

SIMON—(*curtly*) Good! I want it to be feared. As for others, I do to them as they would do to me—if they could! I ask no quarter. Why should they? (*contemptuously*) What a sentimental ass you are, Joel! You would like to apply to business the ethics men and women pretend to observe toward one another in their private lives. That is as stupid as trying to play poker by the rules for chess. The game of Commerce has its own ethics, and they are more frank and honest—and so, more honorable!—truer to the greedy reality of life than our hypocritical personal ones. The only moral law here is that to win is good and to lose is evil. The strong are rewarded, the weak are punished. That is the sole justice which functions in fact. All else is an idealistic lie about things as they are not and never were—and can never be, men—and women—being what they are. A lie that I would be stupid to permit to get in my way, or in my Company's way.

JOEL—(*coldly*) I am thinking of my father's Company, not of you. But I realize I am wasting words. (*He turns toward the door to right.*) I will go back to my work.

SIMON—(*with nervous exasperation*) Yes, for God's sake! Now your duty to your conscience is done, get out! (*Then as Joel goes toward the door, suddenly his whole expression and manner change and he speaks in a strange conciliating tone.*) Wait. Sit down a while. (*He indicates the chair at right of his desk. As Joel stares in cold surprise without making any move toward the chair, he bursts out angrily*) I said sit down! Either you obey me or you look for another job! Don't think because you happen to be my brother, you can presume—! (*Joel's face betrays no emotion. He comes back and sits down stiffly in the chair. Simon's manner abruptly becomes strangely placating.*) I'm sorry, Joel. Didn't mean to fly out at you like that. It has been a strain getting this affair of the railroad settled. My nerves are on edge. (*He pauses. Joel sits staring at him. He goes on and gradually his eyes drop from Joel to his desk, and more and more it seems he is talking to himself.*) It's the usual reaction. I concentrate all my mind and energy to get a thing done. I live with it, think of nothing else, eat with it, take it to bed with me, sleep with it, dream of it—and then suddenly one day it is accomplished—finished, dead!—and I become empty, exhausted, but at the same time restless and aimless and lonely, as if I had lost my meaning to myself—facing the secret that success is its own failure. (*with a wry smile*) A vacation would be in order at such times—relaxation, complete change. But where? How? A voyage to France, say. With Sara. A second honeymoon. But Sara would not leave the children, and to take the children along would mean it would be their vacation with their mother, not mine with my wife. It would be no change for me. I have enough of that atmosphere at home. (*He pauses—then with a sneer*) Perhaps Sara would even insist on taking Mother with us. She might feel lonely without her. They have grown to be such loving friends, drawn to each other by their devotion to the children! (*forcing a joking tone*) I assure you, I am left entirely out of it now—in the lonely cold, so to speak. Sometimes, I feel a stranger in my own house. That is Mother's doing, of course. She imagines she has been very subtle, that I have not seen— Whereas the truth is, I have had too many important Company affairs on my mind to bother. But I promised myself that as soon as I had time, I would put a stop to her greedy scheming, and now the railroad deal is completed— (*He smiles strangely.*) That may be the change in activity I need. I have neglected my interests in my home too long, unwisely entrusted them to others to protect—a sure way to be swindled (*He pauses— then strangely*) If you ever fall in love, Joel, take my advice and do not marry. Keep love your mistress with no right of ownership except what she earns day by day, what she can make you pay for possession. Love should be a deal forever incomplete, never finally settled, with each party continually raising the bids but neither ever concluding a final sale. (*He laughs mockingly at Joel's coldly disapproving face.*) Yes, my advice to you would be to shun marriage and keep a whore instead!

JOEL—(*with cold disgust*) Such ideas are on a par with your conception of honor in business dealings. (*rebukingly*) I cannot see why you wish to discuss such matters with me.

SIMON—(*as if surprised at himself*) No, for that matter, neither can I—except that my mind is empty and restless, and I can trust you to listen without hearing much. (*again with a conciliating manner*) I wanted to ask you: Why is it you never come to visit Mother? I am sure she would like—

JOEL—(*dryly*) You know she has as little desire to see me as I have to see her.

SIMON—(*strangely*) You should come, if only out of curiosity. You would be astounded at the way she has transformed herself (*sneeringly*) into a doting old grandmother. I think you would not know her now, any more than I know her. But the grandmother phase of her transformation is not the strangest. Although difficult to believe of Mother, it is at least understandable as the whim of a lonely old woman. It is her affection for Sara that is most incredible. I never thought that would last a month before they became enemies again. But it has become even more harmonious and intimate— seemingly. I have watched its development with the greatest curiosity. I think they both knew I was watching, and were determined to prove— Mother, at any rate. The strangest thing has been to notice how she has gradually taken what she needed of Sara into herself. Physically she has steadily grown younger and stronger and fleshier. She looks more like the mother of my children now than their grandmother. Or so she appears to me. That is why I would like you to see her. I want an outside observer to verify my perception of her. I know my suspicions cannot be mere fantasies of my mind, and yet I would like to be sure.

JOEL—(*stiffly*) If Mother ever requests me to visit her, I will do so, as is my duty as her son. Otherwise, I will not.

SIMON—(*ignoring this*) It is as though she had slowly taken possession of Sara in order to make of my wife a second self through which she could live again—to use Sara as a strong sanctuary in which she could hide from her old cowardly self, so terrified by life. (*with a strange grim smirk*) Or, in another aspect, trick Sara into being an accessory in the murder of that old self, which was once my mother. And so leave me motherless. Which at the same time by becoming Sara, leave me wifeless, for naturally I could not regard— (*He stops abruptly—then goes on with an increasing brooding strangeness.*) It has been difficult to see clearly what she was doing, to discern which of many greedy purposes was her main purpose, what the final achievement is she is working and scheming toward. I have been very confused as I have observed the two of them, and yet I have had flashes of revelation, too. Sometimes the two have appeared to lose their separate identities in my mind's eye. Have seemed, through the subtle power of Mother's fantastic will, to merge and become one woman—a woman in Mother's image, but not her as I have ever known her. No, a strange woman, like a figure of woman in the abstract, spirit of Woman made flesh and flesh of her made spirit, mother and wife in one—to whom I was never anything more than a necessary adjunct of a means to motherhood—a son in one case, a husband in the other—but now no longer needed since the mother by becoming the wife has my four sons to substitute for me, and the wife having them, no longer needs a husband to use in begetting—and so I am left alone, an unwanted son, a discarded lover, an outcast without meaning or function in my own home but pleasantly tolerated in memory of old service and as a domestic slave whose greed can be used to bring in money to support Woman! (*with a calculating vindictive calculation*) Yes, that is what Mother flatters herself she has accomplished. But she doesn't realize there are fundamental weaknesses in her plan, that the past is never dead as long as we live because all we are is the past. She is going to discover, beginning today, and Sara, too, that whenever I wish, I take back what belongs to me, no matter— (*He checks himself with a sudden wary glance at Joel's expressionless face.*) But all these fanciful speculations are nonsense, of course, which you mustn't take seriously—the reaction of my mind, left restless and purposeless after the strain of successfully completing the railroad deal.

JOEL—(*gets up from his chair—coldly*) I have not listened. I have no interest whatsoever in your private affairs. And I know you were simply using me to talk aloud to yourself. If you have done, may I go back to my work.

SIMON—(*explodes with tense exasperation*) Yes. Take your idiotic conscience to hell out of here. I will direct the Company as I choose! And until I ask for your advice, which will be never, kindly keep your mouth shut! (*Joel turns and goes into the bookkeeper's office at right, closing the door behind him. Simon looks after him—with angry self-contempt*) By God, when I begin making a spiritual confidant of him, I should begin, also, to doubt my own sanity! (*Then he relaxes and falls to brooding again.*) But no. Even that dull fool realized I was really addressing myself—because I have no one but myself—because I have been left alone—driven out of all lives but my own— Mother has seen to that—by God, I was right to ask Sara to come here this morning!—it's high time I began to take back what is mine! (*He fights down his anger—with brooding bitterness again*) Yes, Mother has been clever and subtle—left me with no life but this one which she always despised—this daily grind of slavery to an unscrupulous greed for power— the ambition to be a Napoleon among traders!—I, who once dreamed—! (*abruptly with self-exasperation*) Rubbish!—no hypocritical pretenses, if you please— You have no right— Your old dream was childish idealism—a stupid boy's misconception of man's true nature—which is that of a hog, as your experience with him, and with yourself, has already demonstrated—the possession of power is the only freedom, and your pretended disgust with it is a lie—why, only a week ago you were so completely absorbed in the winning of the railroad you did not give a damn for anything else in the world! You were as passionately enthralled as a lecher gaining a new mistress, as happy as a gambler who risks everything he possesses on the turn of a card— (*with a strange satisfied chuckle*) Except, of course, I had stacked the cards beforehand so I could not lose! (*matter-of-factly*) No, you must allow for your present state of mind—the reaction of emptiness after

success—you've always felt it— But never so strongly before—there is a finality in this—as if some long patient tension had snapped—as if I'd reached the end of a blind alley
in my mind where I no longer have the power to discipline
my will to keep myself united—another self rebels—
secedes—as if at last I must become two selves from now
on—division and confusion—a war—a duel to the death—
(*He adds with revengeful bitterness*) Well, let those who are responsible for the challenge beware, for I will make it their
duel, too! I have learned only too well in my life here the
strategy of dividing in order to conquer—of creating strife
and rivalry, and waiting until the two opponents are exhausted destroying each other—then I step in and take advantage of their weakness to possess them both. (*He smiles
with a gloating revengefulness.*) Yes, Mother and Sara! Henceforth, I must insist you both sit in this game and take up the
two opposing hands you have dealt me and play them with
all your greed!—I must demand that each of you henceforth
takes upon herself her full responsibility for what I have become, to its last final implication! (*abruptly—impatient*) Bah!
What rubbishy fantasies!—As if I really desired two damned
possessive women prying and interfering in my private business!—and I talk as though I had conceived some elaborate
plan of compaign against their alliance—if I have, it is hidden
in my mind—I do not yet see clearly—all I know is that on
an impulse I asked Sara to come here—some confused feeling
that if I get her alone away from Mother's influence, I would
desire her again—it is a long time since I have slept with
her—but at home her body has become repugnant, her
beauty ugly—and, anyway, she is too preoccupied being the
children's mother to have any love to spare—that, also, is
part of Mother's scheme to dispossess me— (*irritably*) Rot!
For God's sake, forget your idiotic suspicions of her! That
silly old woman's senile mind is too occupied with pretending
contentment as a doting grandmother, to engage in such
elaborate conspiracy—although she is undoubtedly responsible for much of the indifference—but to return to Sara,
hadn't I better think out more exactly how I shall attack?—
no, wait until you feel her out and see how much of the old
greedy Sara still lies behind her present self of contented, sat-

isfied mother—the ambitious Sara who used to long to own
an Irish-castle-in-Spain, gentleman's estate!—who was willing to use any means or to pay any price—even her beautiful
body—to get what she wanted—as when, that night at the
cabin before we were married, she made me take her body so
I'd be bound in honor to marry her, and then use me as a
first step in her rising in the world!—as unscrupulous and
ruthless as a whore selling herself!—if that hadn't happened,
I might never have married her—the long engagement
Mother advised might have opened my eyes to that common
greedy nature hidden behind her beauty—the lust masquer-
ading as love!—if I possessed the insight into woman's true
nature I have now I would have swindled her into giving
herself by promising marriage—and then having had all I
wanted of her, deserted her—it would have served her right
to be beaten at her own game—I would have forgotten her
and returned to Mother, waiting for me in her garden— (*bitterly*) But she wasn't waiting for you, you fool!—she had
driven you out before you knew Sara—she wanted to be rid
of you, so she could be free—she was through with you—
she no longer wanted or needed your love—she was just as
ruthless and unscrupulous about discarding you as Sara was
in taking you—your happiness didn't count—yes, again it is
a case of Mother being really responsible—I would never
have fallen in love with Sara if—and her responsibility began
a long time before that, too—I had not felt any really serene
happiness in her garden since I was a little boy—she made it
plain that I possessed no right to be with her, that I was
merely permitted to remain there to amuse her, a toy that her
whim tired of and ruthlessly discarded!—that nonsense about
her summerhouse—that was her way of showing me—and
she took pains to point it out to me by implication that day
she deliberately made up the fairy tale about the exiled Prince
and the magic door— Yes, I never knew peace or faith in life
again from that day— (*angry at himself*) Damnation!—what
a sentimental ass, to be digging back in the past to boyhood
memories—the pastime of weaklings with no present or future!— (*bitterly*) Nevertheless, it does trace the responsibility—and guilt—to the source—and indicates the line poetic
justice should pursue to recompense and punish— In the case

of Sara, too—Mother's is the spiritual greed, but the material lust is Sara's— Mother did not drive me to a career in the slave markets of trade where in buying one sells oneself—or sit me at a table in the gambling dive of commerce—she read Byron aloud, and despised business—it was Sara's lust, dreaming of Irish castles in Spain and a landed lady's estate, that has made me a cotton good's Napoleon!—who drove me to make her proud of me at any price— (*He pauses—then with an air of bitter satisfaction*) I begin to see in part the plan of the campaign I must start when she comes—she must be forced, gradually, of course, to take over her full responsibility—to share the burden and the cost—to pay back what is mine—all that I still desire from her, at least! (*He sits staring before him, frowningly concentrated, his expression becoming coldly ruthless and calculating.*)

(*The door from the hall at rear is opened and Sara enters. She has not changed much in appearance in the five years. Has grown a little more matronly, perhaps, but seems no older. Is still exceedingly pretty, strong and healthy, with the same firm pronouncedly female figure. But she is dressed much better, with discriminating taste and style now, and expensively. In her personality, however, one is at once conscious of a decided change in quality, from her old positive, eagerly-grasping aliveness to a more passive, satisfied contentedness. Her manner has taken on a lot of Deborah's self-assured poise, and her way of speaking copies Deborah, although the rhythm of Irish speech still underlies it. She stands looking at Simon but he is oblivious of her presence. Sara smiles assuredly, a smile that has lost its old passionate tenderness and become maternal, complacent in possessiveness—a smile that takes its proprietorship for granted. Smiling with growing amusement, she tip-toes forward until she stands by his table.*)

SARA—You might ask me to sit down, Simon. (*He jumps startledly in his chair.*)

SIMON—(*his frayed nerves exploding angrily—as if he did not recognize her*) God damn it, what do you mean by sneaking—! (*then confusedly*) Oh, it's you. I didn't—

SARA—(*taken aback but forcing a smile*) Well! That's a nice greeting, I must say, after you begged me to come.

SIMON—I apologize, Sara. For a moment, I didn't recognize who it was. (*He springs to his feet—with a forced cordiality, indicating the chair across the table*) Sit down, do. (*She sits in it and he sits down again.*)

SARA—I had no idea you'd gotten so nervous. You haven't seemed to be at home.

SIMON—(*affecting carelessness*) Perhaps I control myself better there. Or perhaps, on the other hand, you have been too occupied with family affairs to notice!

SARA—(*smiling*) If that isn't like you, to put the blame on me, when it's you who come home every night with your head so full of business you might as well be on the moon for all the attention you pay your mother or me. (*with a trace of bitterness*) Or the children. (*abruptly changing the subject—with a forced interest*) Speaking of business, tell me about the Company. You've been doing wonders with it, I know. You never mention it anymore to us at home, but everyone tells me you're becoming the young Napoleon of trade here in the city.

SIMON—(*pleased but at the same time scornful*) The most flattering comparison the mind of woman can imagine! If men and women had ever admired Christ one-tenth as much as they admire that greedy adventurer, what a success Christianity might have been! (*He laughs sneeringly—then abruptly with a proud boastful air*) Here's a bit of news about my success you haven't heard yet, Sara. I've got the railroad now. You remember I promised myself I would. Well, it's mine!

SARA—(*with forced enthusiasm*) Isn't that fine! I congratulate you, Simon.

SIMON—(*with a preening satisfaction*) I have a final meeting with the directors this morning. Merely a formality. They've already agreed to my terms. Not easy terms for them to accept, I might add! They are left without a vestige of real power. I become absolute master. But they had no choice. They were on the verge of bankruptcy. I did not strike until I knew they were divided among themselves and weakened by dissension and jealousy and conflicting purposes—which I had secretly encouraged, by the way, to hasten the end. (*enthusiastically*) Wait till you see what I do with the road in a couple of years! I have learned from their mistakes. I'll make no mistakes!

SARA—(*her enthusiasm more forced*) I'm sure you won't.

SIMON—(*noticing her tone—deflated, and for a second boy-ishly hurt*) You're not very enthusiastic.

SARA—(*hastily*) Oh, I am. (*forcing a smile*) Maybe my feelings are a little hurt. You used to say "us" and "ours" and now everything with you is "I" and "mine."

SIMON—(*stares at her sharply—as if he saw with satisfaction some calculation verified*) Ah, you feel that?

SARA—(*hastily and defensively*) No. It's selfish of me to talk like that. God knows I've more than enough to content me with a beautiful mansion for my home, and as happy a life as a woman could wish with Deborah and my children, without grudging you what is yours.

SIMON—(*dryly*) Yes, one should never complain of the price one must pay for what one wants from life—or thinks one wants.

SARA—(*a bit defiantly*) I know what I want, and I have it.

SIMON—(*ignoring this*) For example, I might complain with equal reason that you used to speak of our home and our children, while now—

SARA—(*in her turn stares at him sharply*) Ah! You feel that, do you?

SIMON—(*carelessly*) No, I said I might. But I have too many important affairs on my mind to give much thought to—

SARA—(*trying to conceal her disappointment*) I'm glad you're frank about it. After all, it's only natural. You can't give your mind to everything. (*bitterly*) And we've seen for a long time, Deborah and I, that you care more for the Company than anything else in life.

SIMON—(*ignoring this last—carelessly but with a taunting undercurrent*) Anyway, I must confess I cannot believe your possessive adjectives are more than a boast. I always have the feeling at home that, although Mother has relinquished all outward show of ownership and authority, she has managed to keep in possession.

SARA—(*resentfully*) Well, you're wrong. I have the only say about everything, and she's happy to let me have it.

SIMON—(*smiling*) Yes, Mother has always had a subtle talent for contriving it so that others must desire what she desires—and then generously giving them their way!

SARA—She hasn't with me. I'm not such a fool—

SIMON—Not when you're on your guard. But you're so kind and sentimental you never suspect—

SARA—There's nothing to suspect! No woman could be a truer friend than she's been to me! She's more like a sister, or my own mother, than a mother-in-law. And she's been such a good grandmother to the children—even if she does spoil them.

SIMON—(*gives her a calculating glance*) Yes, she is spoiling them. There's no doubt about that.

SARA—(*defensively*) If she does, it's only because she's still a child in her heart, herself, a great part of her, and like one of them. And there's no harm. I can always correct any bad ways she gets them into.

SIMON—(*watching her*) Of course, there's no harm done— if you're sure you haven't let it go too far.

SARA—(*angrily*) I haven't! I can take care of my children, thank you, without any advice— (*accusingly*) Is that your reason for inviting me here—to try and make trouble between your mother and me?

SIMON—(*curtly*) Don't be ridiculous! I'm delighted at the friendship which has developed between you. The more so, because I never dared hope—

SARA—(*almost tauntingly*) We know you didn't. Well, we fooled you!

SIMON—Make trouble? Don't you think I appreciate peace and harmony in my home, if only for selfish reasons.

SARA—You should.

SIMON—Do you imagine I'd prefer to have you at each other's throats?

SARA—No. That'd be crazy. (*then reproachfully*) While we're talking of this, Simon, I want to say something I've meant to for a long time. I know you've kept a secret grudge against her in your heart. But isn't it about time you stopped being so childish, and forgave—

SIMON—(*sharply*) Don't be stupid. There's nothing to forgive. What makes you say I harbor a grudge? Do we ever quarrel? Am I not always pleasant with her?

SARA—Yes, as you'd be to an acquaintance in the street!

SIMON—(*impatiently*) But what's the use of pretending we

have anything in common anymore, when we haven't. Just because she happened to bear me into the world! This absurd sentimental sense of obligation between parents and children! Obligation for what? Almost any fool of a woman can have a son, and every fool of a man has had a mother! It's no great achievement on either side, and all the hypocritical values we set on the relationship are stupidity.

SARA—(*angrily*) That's not true! I've my four sons and I know the love I feel for them, and the love they feel for me!

SIMON—(*ignoring this*) And don't tell me Mother minds my indifference. She has learned not to need me.

SARA—(*with a trace of vindictive satisfaction*) That's true enough. She doesn't miss you now she has the children.

SIMON—(*bitterly*) Yes. As you have.

SARA—(*stares at him defiantly*) As I have, yes. (*then with a strange eagerness—teasingly*) Don't tell me you're jealous of the children—with me?

SIMON—(*curtly resentful*) I have had too many important matters on my mind to bother about your children. That's your business.

SARA—(*bitterly*) No, I know you never give them a thought— (*then forcing a smile—placatingly*) But I hope you didn't ask me here—for the first time in Heaven knows how long—just to quarrel with me. (*She gets up and comes around the table to him.*) I know I didn't come for that. (*She puts a hand on his shoulder.*)

SIMON—(*moved*) Forgive me. I'm tired. Worn out and nervy. This railroad deal has been a strain.

SARA—(*looks down at him worriedly*) I know, Simon. You haven't looked well for a long time—not like yourself at all.

SIMON—(*bitterly*) Then you do notice once in a while.

SARA—(*ignoring his tone—smilingly*) Did you think you're the only one can notice anything? Your mother has seen it, too. She pays some attention to you even if you don't to her.

SIMON—(*coldly*) Indeed? And what was it you both noticed?

SARA—(*pauses—then slowly*) That you've been changing in some queer way inside you. Sometimes at night when you sit in the parlor with us, all of a sudden, it's like a stranger staring at us. It's a frightening feeling, Simon. I think I began to notice it around the time you started sleeping in your own room away from me—

SIMON—(*stares at her calculatingly—then with a deliberately provocative coarse sensuality*) Ah, that's it, eh? Your body felt swindled and it made you suspicious, I suppose, that I might have found another woman's body that is more beautiful and desirable to mine than yours? You probably think I must be secretly keeping some beautiful mistress who has stolen your place in bed! (*He smiles tauntingly.*)

SARA—(*startled and repelled*) Simon! You know such a nasty thought would never enter my head! It's the last thing I'd ever suspect! And I don't see how it could come into your mind— (*She gives him a look of suspicion, all the jealousy of her passionately possessive nature beginning to flare up.*) Unless you've had the thought yourself—

SIMON—(*his face lighting up with satisfaction—provocatively*) No, no. I was only joking.

SARA—(*jealously angry—forgetting all ladylike poise*) I don't believe you! You must have had the wish— (*With a sudden fierce passion she grabs his head and turns his face up to hers.*) Look at me! If I thought you wanted another woman—!

SIMON—(*puts his arm around her and hugs her to him, his face triumphantly gratified—teasingly*) Well, what would you do?

SARA—I'll kill her, that's what I'd do! And you, too! (*then miserably frightened*) Simon! You don't deny it! Tell me—!

SIMON—(*provocatively unconvincing, hugging her again*) No, no. Of course I would never—

SARA—You don't say that as if you meant it! (*struggling to free herself*) Let me go! I don't want you hugging me—when maybe you're wishing it was another— (*Furious at the thought, she grabs his shoulders and shakes him fiercely.*) Tell me the truth, I'm saying! Is that the real reason you began sleeping alone—that you'd found someone prettier, and grown tired of me? Is it to confess that you had me come here? Are you going to ask me to set you free to be hers? (*savagely*) If you are, you can hold your prate! I'll see her in hell first! If any woman thinks she can take you, she'll find I'll fight to the death! I'd tear her to pieces, first! And you! And myself! I'd do anything! (*She sits down on the arm of his chair and hugs him to her with passionate possessiveness.*) You're mine till death, and beyond death, and I'll never let you go, do you hear! (*She kisses him passionately on the lips.*)

SIMON—(*his face happy now with confident possession and aroused desire*) So you really are jealous?

SARA—(*fiercely*) Of course I'm jealous! Am I flesh and blood? Don't I love you more than all the world?

SIMON—Do you? I thought the children—

SARA—(*almost contemptuously*) Ah, the children! (*hastily*) Not that I don't love them with all my heart. But they're not my lover and husband! You come first!

SIMON—Do I? I shouldn't say from your actions for a long time—

SARA—My actions! Are you trying to say I'm to blame? Why, there's nights when you stare as if you were wondering who I was and what was my business there. You sit with us deep in your thoughts, as if I was dead. Or you converse with us so pleasant and polite, like a gentleman guest come in to spend the evening.

SIMON—Perhaps I do feel like a dispossessed intruder. You know I never approved of our living with Mother.

SARA—(*impatiently*) Ah, don't blame her. She's as sweet as can be to us. (*then going on*) And behind all your pleasant talk to us, you mean something else, and when you're thinking, it isn't about business deals alone you're scheming . . . (*confusedly*) I don't know how to say it, Darling, but it's as though the minute you came home I felt everything begin to change until nothing is what it seems to be, and we all get suspicious of each other.

SIMON—(*stares at her fixedly*) What? Even you and Mother?

SARA—(*reluctantly*) Yes. (*hastily*) No, I meant it might if we weren't careful. It's like a spell that tries to come between us. (*defiantly*) But we don't let it.

SIMON—(*ignoring this last*) Ah. That is strange. I thought you had both entirely forgotten your old jealous animosity, that you lived in a perfect harmonious unity of interests and desires now. Why, sometimes as I watch you I become so intensely conscious of your unity that you appear as one woman to me. I cannot distinguish my wife from— It is a bewildering confusion in which I myself seem to lose my separateness, to dissolve, to have no life except within— (*with strange bitter intensity*) Suffocating! Devouring! I have to fight it with all my will! (*catching himself and hastily forcing a casual tone*) But that's absurd nonsense, of course—a fanciful flight of imagination. My mind has been under such a strain lately, it's gotten out of control.

SARA—(*strangely*) Is that when you stare at us as though you hated us? (*then forcing a smile*) That's a queer crazy notion for you to have, Simon—that you can't tell your own wife from—her. (*with strange resentment*) But I think I know the kind of feeling that you mean. I've felt myself at times that she'd like me to have no wish but her wish, and no life that wasn't ruled by her life.

SIMON—(*watching her*) Yes, Mother has always been extremely greedy for others' lives. You have to be constantly on guard—

SARA—(*defiantly*) But she knows I'm too strong— (*abruptly shamefaced*) Ah, what am I saying! It's mean and wrong of me to suspect her. It's only that she's been so lonely all her life, poor woman. I won't hear a word against her! (*accusingly with rising jealous anger*) And don't think I don't see you've changed the subject to her so you wouldn't have to answer me about having a mistress. (*She suddenly breaks—miserably*) Tell me you haven't, Simon! I couldn't bear— (*She starts to sob.*)

SIMON—(*springs up and hugs her to him—passionately*) Of course I haven't, Sweetheart! What a mad idea! Here! Look at me! (*He lifts her face to his.*) I swear on my honor—!

SARA—(*relieved—joyously*) Oh, Darling. I know I'm foolish—but I love you so! (*She kisses him and he responds, hugging her with a passionate desire. She breaks away, stirred and happy, but modestly embarrassed—with a soft laugh*) We mustn't. Supposing someone came in. It's a long time since you've kissed me—like that—Darling.

SIMON—A long time since you've given me the chance!

SARA—(*teasing tenderly*) I like that! When I've been hoping every night! You'll say next it was I that wanted you to sleep alone. (*sadly*) You don't know how you hurt me when you did that, Simon. I tried to believe your excuse that you didn't want to keep me awake when you couldn't sleep because your mind kept making plans for the Company. But I couldn't help fearing the real reason was you didn't want me.

SIMON—(*passionately*) You know I want you now, don't you?

SARA—(*desirously but embarrassed*) Oh, here—now—yes—But at home—

SIMON—Yes, at home everything changes, as you said.

SARA—You're different—here. Here, you're my old Simon. It's like old times.

SIMON—That's why I asked you to come. Because I want to be your old Simon and want you again. Because I want you to want me as you used to. But at home there is always Mother coming between us.

SARA—(*frowns*) Yes, it's true you feel her always there, watching— (*Simon gives her a sharp calculating glance. She adds hastily, defensive and guilty*) But you mustn't blame her. She doesn't mean to interfere. She can't help being there. And I'm sure she doesn't bother her head about what we do. You only imagine that, Darling, because you think of her as the kind of woman she used to be. The trouble is you've paid so little attention to her for years you haven't noticed the change in her. You don't know the nice, kind contented old grandmother she is now.

SIMON—(*sneeringly*) Mother was always an accomplished actress. (*then quickly and calculatingly, pretending to give in*) Well, perhaps you're right. I must admit she seems sincere in her affection for your children.

SARA—(*eagerly*) Oh, she is, Simon! She loves them dearly and they love her.

SIMON—From their talk, they must spend a great deal of their time in her garden.

SARA—(*Resentment shows in her face.*) Yes, they do. But now they'll be away at school a lot of the day. (*then defensively*) It's good for them to be with her. She's a great lady and her influence helps train them to grow up gentlemen.

SIMON—Well, of course, if you don't mind—

SARA—(*defensively*) Why should I mind?

SIMON—I'd say there can be such a thing as too much of her influence for their good. You see, I remember my experience with her maternal possessiveness. If I hadn't got away from her, before it was too late, she'd have made me entirely dependent upon her for life—a tenth-rate poet—a day-dreaming romantic fool, wasting my days lazily lolling in her garden, without the ambition or courage to be free, contentedly enslaved to her fantastic whims!— (*He checks himself—hurriedly*) So you can understand why I am worried about her influence over our children. After all, they are my sons, too, Dear, and although you don't give me credit for it, I do have their futures constantly in mind.

SARA—(*gratefully*) I'm so happy to know you think of them. It hurt me to feel you didn't—because they're you and me together—our love—you in me— (*She hugs him to her and kisses him—then pushes back from him bashfully.*) I ought to be ashamed. I don't know what makes me so brazen. (*hastily*) About her and the children. I'd never mention it if you hadn't, that I don't think it's good her reading poetry at them all the time, especially Byron. I hate him because I remember my father, reciting it to himself before the mirror and putting on the airs of a lord, or a Napoleon, and him sponging on my mother for life, without a dollar to his name!

SIMON—(*frowning*) Yes, Mother is very romantic. She used to read Byron to me. (*He recites sneeringly*) "This makes the madmen who have made men mad by their contagion— all unquiet things which stir too strongly the soul's secret springs, and are themselves the fools to those they fool."

SARA—(*tenderly proud*) Ah, it's different when you recite it! I love it! (*She hugs him.*) You're a big boy still with the old touch of the poet in you, and I love you for it!

SIMON—(*frowns—curtly*) Nonsense. That is dead in me. (*boastfully*) You forget I am the president of a railroad, too, now—or soon will be. (*He smiles at her.*) The railroad I promised you.

SARA—(*happily*) That does sound like my old Simon. I'd like to feel again that what is yours is mine, too.

SIMON—(*hugging her*) Then you can begin thinking of yourself as my partner again from this moment on. (*with strange boyish enthusiasm*) I have our new partnership all planned, Sara. Wait till you hear. (*then quickly and calculat-*

ingly) But first, let's get this matter of Mother and the children settled. I agree that it's bad to have her muddling their brains with romantic dreams. We want them trained to live with reality so when the time comes they will be capable of serving our Company as we decided long ago they could best serve it—Ethan as manager of our marine division, Wolfe to direct the banking branch which we will own before long, Jonathan as our railroad executive, and Honey our representative in politics.

SARA—(*smiling happily*) Ah, you have great dreams for them, haven't you? And I thought you'd forgotten— Forgive me, Darling.

SIMON—(*smiling*) No, I have never forgotten our plans for their lives. And I am confident they will have the brains and ability, provided we don't permit Mother to poison their minds with nonsense.

SARA—(*resentfully now*) She's always telling them stuff about how they must do what they want, and be free.

SIMON—(*sneeringly*) Good God, does she still harp on that stupid dream? As if man born of woman could hope to be free. The freer he is of outside things, the more abject slave he becomes to himself! (*sharply*) It's our duty to the children to put a stop to her interfering before it's too late, Sara.

SARA—Yes. (*hesitantly*) I could ask her not to— (*then guiltily*) No, I'd be ashamed. It would be like breaking my part of a bargain I'd made in honor to trust her.

SIMON—(*dryly*) It was no part of the bargain, was it, that she should steal your children and make them her children?

SARA—(*defensively*) Ah now, that's going too far. She's never tried— (*resentfully*) Anyway, they know who their mother is and who they love best.

SIMON—(*dryly provocative*) Do they? I have the idea they are becoming as confused between you as I. (*quickly*) I mean as I am at home. Here, you yourself, my wife, my partner— my mistress, too, I hope. (*He hugs her desirously.*)

SARA—(*responding passionately*) Yes, let me be that above all, Darling! Don't ever dream of loving another!

SIMON—(*abruptly with a strange, brisk business-like tone*) We've allowed things to get in a confused muddle at home.

I've been too preoccupied with the Company's affairs, and you've been too busy housekeeping for Mother and acting as nurse girl while she's left free to play she's their mother to them.

SARA—(*with a flash of resentful anger*) Ah, I'd like to see her try—! I'm glad you had me come here today. I feel different here with you. I begin to see a lot of things I've been blind to. I begin to remember times when I've made myself not suspect her! Maybe I have been too trusting taking her at her word as I would my own mother that's gone. Maybe I've given in to her too much, and let her put her thoughts in my mind until I mistook them for my thoughts, and was obeying her without knowing it, and letting her make a slave of me. (*stung at the thought—threateningly*) But she'll not make a fool of me anymore!

SIMON—It's very true that Mother works in peculiar ways to steal what she desires. You must bear in mind that she has never been quite normal. She's always been different from all other women, whimsical and perversely fanciful, not to be judged by normal standards. My father always considered her entirely irresponsible. Even her best friends have put her down as more than a little queer ever since she was a girl. Yes, we might as well be frank, Sara. There is an unbalanced imaginative streak in her that one must continually guard against.

SARA—(*uneasily*) You mean she's insane? (*reacting against this*) Ah no, that's crazy, Simon. I won't let you say such wicked things. The poor woman!

SIMON—(*sharply*) I didn't say insane. Of course, she's not insane. I meant she has no sense of the right to freedom of others. (*then with a smile*) I don't see why you should be so indignant. I know in the old days you suspected her of being a little crazy.

SARA—(*guiltily defensive*) Maybe I did—the way she was. And didn't she tell me herself she'd got to the point where she didn't dare go in that summerhouse of hers for fear she'd never come out again. That's crazy, isn't it?

SIMON—(*strangely*) Who knows? It all depends— Do you know if she ever goes in the summerhouse now?

SARA—No. She always keeps it locked. The children used

to plague her to open it but she never would. (*uneasily*) Why do you ask?

SIMON—(*evasively*) Well, it shows she's not as changed within herself as she pretends, doesn't it? (*again in a brisk, business-like tone*) Then you agree. The children must be forbidden to go to her garden or her rooms in future. She can see quite enough of them, when you and I are present. And you stay away from her garden, too.

SARA—I hardly ever go. I've always had a feeling she didn't want me there.

SIMON—(*briskly*) Then you'll give orders to the children.

SARA—Yes. (*then guiltily*) But who will tell her?

SIMON—Why you, of course.

SARA—It'll break her heart. She's been so good— I promised her— When I think of how sweet she's been to me— I hate hurting her.

SIMON—(*avoiding her eyes—calculatingly, with feigned reluctance*) Well, I suppose I could tell her, if you want to be spared.

SARA—(*relieved—eagerly*) Would you? But promise me you won't be cruel to her, Simon. If you'll put yourself out to be kind, and make up with her, she won't feel so lonely at losing the children.

SIMON—(*concealing his satisfaction—matter-of-factly*) Don't be foolish, Dear. You can rely on me to treat Mother considerately, if only for selfish reasons. I want peace in my home. I know her erratic unstable mind, and that a sudden shock to her vanity might have dangerous consequences. So I shall call on my memories of the past and humor her as I would a fanciful child. I'll drop in at her garden on my way home this evening. (*with a strange happy satisfied air*) There. That puts Mother in her place—back where she belongs. Let's forget her now and think only of us. (*He gives her a loving, possessive hug.*) As we did in the old days.

SARA—(*happily*) I'm only too glad to, Darling. Tell me the plans you've made for our new partnership.

SIMON—Just what I want to do. I have grown very lonely, Sara. Achievement no longer means what it once did because I have no one to share it. In the old days what made it significant was that it was for you. I knew it was what you desired from me and it was my delight to give you your desire, and prove I had not failed you and that your love could justly be proud of me.

SARA—(*protesting a bit guiltily*) And do you think I'm not still proud? But I am, Darling.

SIMON—Here, now, alone with me again, you mean? Yes, I can believe that. And I want to propose to you that we should start our old life together again.

SARA—I want that as much as you, Darling. If you knew how unhappy and ugly I've felt since you started sleeping alone—and even before that when you'd lie beside me as if I wasn't there.

SIMON—I never felt we were alone—there, in Mother's house. That's why I had you come here. I want to ask you to help me create a new life of opportunity and ambition and boundless desire for our love, distinct and separate from our life as husband and wife at home—a life completely free from the influence of Mother and the children, in which we can be lovers again. (*He presses her to him passionately.*)

SARA—(*sensually aroused—kissing his hair*) Darling! You know I'd love nothing better! I'll do whatever you want.

SIMON—Good! I knew Mother couldn't have entirely destroyed in you my old Sara who desired so passionately to take what she wanted from life, no matter what the cost.

SARA—(*resentfully*) Destroyed me? She knows better than to try! And don't talk as though I'd ever stopped wanting you. It's you who got so all you wanted was the Company. You even took it to bed with you in your thoughts. It wouldn't let you sleep.

SIMON—(*ignoring this, goes on with a smile at her of a strange, perverse, insinuating lechery*) I want the old Sara, whose beautiful body was so greedily hungry for lust and possession, whose will was as devoid of scruple, as ruthlessly determined to devour and live as the spirit of life itself! (*He hugs her.*) The Sara who came to my cabin on that night long ago, before we were married, with her mind made up to use her beautiful body to keep anyone from taking what she regarded as hers, to make sure of a husband—

SARA—(*guiltily*) Ah, don't say— (*reproachfully*) You'd never have known I had that in mind if my honor and my love hadn't confessed it to you! And you were proud I wanted you that much! You loved me for it! So you shouldn't remember it against me.

SIMON—(*passionately*) Against you? How can you think that? I tell you I desired her more than anything in life! And now I desire her to come back more than anything in life! She was the inspiration for my career. I owe her all my success. She is the cause of the Company, the spirit of its ambition! Now I need her again to inspire me and it! I want her to come back to me here, as she came to me that night, willing to gamble with the highest possible stake, all she has, to win by any possible means, to sell her dearly.

SARA—(*half pleased and flattered and half guiltily defensive*) Ah, don't talk of it that way—as if I was some low street girl who came that night to sell herself. I was bound I'd have you because I loved you so much. (*flusteredly*) But I don't want you to remember it. I never think of it but I'm ashamed I could have been so bold and brazen. (*then proudly*) But, all the same, I'm always proud of it, too.

SIMON—(*amorously playful*) Well then, I know you will be willing to become your old true self again for me. It is she I need and want to possess me now, and be as bold and brazen about it as of old—and as beautiful and as desirable! I must confess, Sweetheart, that I have become as bored with the meek, contented, passionless, ambitionless, commonplace woman, the virtuous good wife and mother that Mother's influence has made you at home, as you must be yourself in your secret heart.

SARA—(*impulsively*) Yes. That's true when—

SIMON—Ha! I knew it! (*He hugs her.*) But for the old passionate greedy Sara, I would give all I possess again.

SARA—(*teasingly—but with a strange undercurrent of boastfulness*) Well, look out then. I could be her, for I love you just as much now. But, maybe, you'd better let her sleep. She might be bolder than ever and want more! (*She kisses him—then suddenly embarrassed and shy, pushes back from him.*) But what a way for me to act! Here in your office, of all places! (*then strangely*) But it's strange, I feel in a way it's being here with you makes me feel—there's a queer thing in the air here that makes you—and I'd stayed at home so long I'd forgotten— (*confusedly*) But I don't know what I mean— (*She hugs him passionately again.*) Except I love you now with all of me and all my strength, and there's no one else in the world, and I'm yours and you're mine, and I don't care how shameless I am! (*She kisses him.*)

SIMON—Sweetheart! That fits in exactly with my plans for our future here. I hoped you would feel as you do. You ought, because the Company is you. Your nature is its nature. It derived its life from your life. You are its mother. It was born of you—just as my life in it was born of you, and is your life which you must claim for your own again.

SARA—(*moved but at the same time puzzled*) Darling! But you're taking it too deep for me and getting me confused. Tell me plainly what your plan is.

SIMON—(*with a brisk, business-like air now*) This: The children will be away most of the day at school from now on. You'll be free. Well, I want you to work with me here in the Company as my secretary and secret partner.

SARA—(*amazed and joyous—her face lighting up eagerly*) Darling! Do you really mean—?

SIMON—Then you'll do it?

SARA—(*excitedly*) Will I? It's too good to be true! It's what I always used to want, don't you know that? Even in the old days, before we lived with your mother, I felt shut out from this part of your life, with you away from me in it all day. (*She kisses him.*) Oh, you make me so happy, Darling, when you prove you want me that much!

SIMON—(*teasing with a suggestive lecherous air*) Wait! There's a condition. Nothing for nothing, is the rule here, you know. You'll have to pay for this opportunity.

SARA—(*smiling*) Stop teasing now and tell me. I'll do anything you want.

SIMON—(*teasing as before*) What! Do you mean to tell me a virtuous wife and mother like you will agree to become my mistress?

SARA—(*shocked, embarrassed, and at the same time amused and curiously fascinated and delighted*) So— Then I'm the mistress you were wishing for! Well, God be thanked, you weren't dreaming of any other!

SIMON—(*teasing as before*) No, you are the one. I don't

know of anyone else who would be more desirable. And I can make you a most favorable offer.

SARA—(*protestingly, but curiously pleased*) To hear you you'd think I was a wicked fancy woman you were offering to buy. That's a nice way to talk to a decent wife! (*teasingly*) But let's hear your offer. Maybe it's not enough. I value myself highly, I'll have you know!

SIMON—(*teasingly as before*) I'll agree to pay with all my worldly goods. You can get the whole Company from me for your own—that is, of course, piece by piece, as you earn it! I put no limit whatever on the wages you may demand for your love.

SARA—(*greedily*) The whole Company to be mine! (*forcing a joking tone*) Well, I'm flattered you set so high a price on me. It proves I still must be beautiful to you, for you to want me that much. (*She kisses him suddenly with passionate gratitude.*) Oh, Darling, and I was so afraid I'd become ugly to you and you were sick of me.

SIMON—Then you will take the place?

SARA—You know I will. (*She hides her face on his shoulder shamefacedly—then suddenly lifts it and bursts out*) But don't be talking of wages. Aren't I always yours just for the taking for love of you!

SIMON—(*smiling playfully*) No, no! Forget that! I have no rights whatever except what you choose to sell me. This is a new secret life for us, remember, which concerns the Company's life, since it will be lived here in it. So it must be strictly a business partnership, a deal for profit on both our parts. A double life of amorous intrigue for each of us, too, if it pleases our fancy to think of it that way. You will be revenging yourself on your husband who has grown bored with his virtuous wife, by selling yourself to a lover. And I think the husband will be keeping a beautiful mistress to take my wife's place. (*He laughs with an undercurrent of taunting.*) Come, confess now, doesn't this prospect of a sinful double life with me give something in you a proud feeling of new life and freedom.

SARA—(*fascinatedly*) Yes. (*then hugging him, with a little lustful, tender laugh*) Aren't you the big boy, still making up games! But I'll play any game with you you like, as being as

you think I'm beautiful and you want me. (*She laughs again —
this time with a touch of warm boldness.*) And it will be fun
playing I'm a wicked, lustful, wanton creature and making
you a slave to my pleasure and beauty. (*with a strange undercurrent of gloating contempt*) All the same, I think you're a fool
to let me cheat you into buying what you own already! (*Suddenly shocked at herself she stops guiltily and stares at him bewilderedly.*) God forgive me, what makes me talk like— Darling,
you know I don't mean— (*jokingly but resentfully and suspiciously, too*) I think it's your teasing. You're leading me on to
talk before I think— (*confusedly*) No, I don't mean to say
that, either.

SIMON— (*teasingly*) Well, we needn't go into the meaning
of what you mean now, Beautiful Mistress. I am sure that will
all become clear to you as you go on. It's enough now to
know you've agreed and that's all settled. I am glad it was so
simple. I was afraid you might raise objections.

SARA— (*tenderly now*) Objections? When you want me and
I want you?

SIMON—Well, Mother won't approve of my taking you
away, as well as the children.

SARA— (*resentfully*) It's none of her business.

SIMON— (*with a strange gloating air*) Poor Mother. She
will be very lonely again. I think she will welcome visits even
from me in her garden. (*quickly*) All I'm afraid of now, Sara,
is that when you get home with her she will make you change
your mind.

SARA— (*resentfully*) Make me? I'd like to see her. She
knows better. She knows who's the stronger. But don't make
me think of her now. (*She kisses him.*) All I want to think of
now is that you want me again.

SIMON— (*hugs her—passionately*) I do! I have never wanted
you so much! No, not even in the days before we were married! Your body is beautiful, Sweetheart!

SARA— (*kisses him passionately*) Darling! (*Then she breaks
away—with a soft happy laugh*) Aren't we the shameless ones!
(*then suddenly staring at him uneasily and sadly*) But I wish—
even if you're still joking—you wouldn't talk as if my body
was all I meant to you. Love is more than—

SIMON— (*ignores this—slowly*) Yes, you will have to learn

to be shameless here. That is to say, to free yourself from false shame and be what you are. In your new life and work, in order to be successful, you will have to deal daily with the greedy fact of life as it really lives and devours itself, and forget all the sentimental lies and moral hypocrisies with which its ugliness is hidden. You will have to strip life naked, and face it. And accept it as truth. And strip yourself naked and accept yourself as you are in the greedy mind and flesh. Then you can go on—successfully—with a clear vision—without false scruples—on to demand and take what you want—as I have done! (*then in a more matter-of-fact tone*) But you will discover all this for yourself. You will be successful. You have this natural talent. And I know you will find the game I play here in the Company as fascinating a gamble as I find it. (*strangely now—as if he were talking aloud to himself*) A fascinating game. Resembling love, I think a woman will find. A game of secret cunning stratagems, in which only the fools who are fated to lose reveal their true aims or motives—even to themselves. You have to become a gambler where face is a mask. But one grows lonely and haunted. One finally gets a sense of confusion in the meaning of the game, so that one's winnings have the semblance of losses. The adversary across the table in whose eyes one can read no betraying emotion beyond an identical lust—this familiar stranger to whom with a trustful smile one passes the cards one has marked, or the dice one has loaded, at the moment he accepts them trustfully becomes oneself.

SARA—(*protests uneasily*) Now, Darling, please don't be mixing everything up in my mind. I don't know what you mean by that queer talk of marked cards and loaded dice.

SIMON—(*smiling but with a threat underneath*) Oh, you will someday. I promise you you will. (*then as she stares at him uneasily—abruptly briskly business-like*) Well, I think we've settled everything. (*He glances at his watch.*) I'll have to ask you to go now. The railroad directors will be here in a few minutes. You will start your work here tomorrow morning.

SARA—(*has gotten off the arm of his chair—jokingly bobs him a curtsy*) Yes, Sir. At your service. But you haven't told me my secretary duties yet. Remember I've no experience. You'll have to train me.

SIMON—(*curtly now*) I will. By my example. You'll learn quicker that way. At first, all I wish you to do is sit and watch how I deal with everything. As though you were an understudy learning to play my part. As you learn, I will let you act in my stead now and then until finally you will find yourself capable of taking my place—if ever the need arises.

SARA—(*excitedly*) Me! Oh Simon, it sounds too grand!

SIMON—In your spare time, when I am away, I want you to draw plans for the country estate with the great mansion you used to dream about where we are going to retire when we have enough. (*She looks startled and embarrassed. He smiles strangely.*) What's the matter? Is it that the idea of my ever retiring hasn't occurred to you for a long time? I was just to go on and on—while you remained contentedly at home with Mother and your children?

SARA—(*guiltily defensive*) I thought that was what you wanted. (*hurriedly and a bit confusedly*) But I never forgot my dream of the estate, never fear! How could I forget I was born on my father's great estate, in a castle, with a great park and stables and— (*hastily*) But I haven't felt I ought to want— I have your mother's house, as beautiful a mansion as there is in the city, and I was content. I mean, I felt I oughtn't to be greedy for more.

SIMON—Well, from now on, remember you cannot want too much! No price is too high for me to pay my mistress for her love, eh? (*He pats her cheek playfully.*)

SARA—(*repelled—pulling away*) Darling, I wish you wouldn't talk as if love—

SIMON—(*ignoring this*) You shall have your estate. Of course, it wouldn't do to withdraw that much capital from the Company now. There is so much to be accomplished before the Company can be free and independent and self-sufficient. But as soon as we have enough. Meanwhile, if you get it actually planned to the last detail, then you will have everything all ready when the time comes.

SARA—(*excitedly and greedily now*) Yes! Oh, that will be fun! And I've got every bit of it clear in my mind—or I used to have—

SIMON—You can afford to make bigger, more ambitious

plans now, in view of the Company's progress since you last dreamed of it.

SARA—(*greedily*) Oh, I can always dream bigger dreams, and I'll be only too delighted to make plans— (*then checking herself, guiltily*) Well, I'd better go now, and not be in your way. (*She kisses him—tenderly*) Goodbye, my Darling! You've made me so happy. You're the sweetest dearest husband— (*then with shy passion*) No, I'm forgetting. It's love again now, isn't it! And I'm your wicked, evil mistress! (*She laughs devilishly.*) And don't you forget I'm your mistress, now, and start wanting some other woman! (*She kisses him again— then breaks from his arms and opens the door.*)

SIMON—Wait! Mother will be curious about your visit here but don't tell her anything. Leave that to me. I can make the meaning clearer to her I think.

SARA—(*pityingly but at same time scornfully*) Ah, poor woman. I'm not anxious to tell her— (*then with a sudden, maliciously gloating smile*) She'll be so suspicious, trying to lead me on to tell, and yet pretending to herself to be too high and mighty a lady to lower her pride to ask me! Well, it'll do her good! She's gotten to think she owns me! (*She stops abruptly, guilty and ashamed.*) Ah, I ought to be ashamed! What makes me feel like that here? (*She looks around the office almost frightenedly—then hastily*) I'll go now. (*She goes out and closes the door.*)

SIMON—(*looks after her and smiles strangely—ironically*) Well, that half of my responsibility sharing scheme is launched successfully—Sara is not very clever at bargains— too trustful of promises—not a good judge of real values— or prices—but she will learn by experience—I will see to it she learns—in a year she will not know herself. (*He walks back to his desk.*) Yes, that part of it will work itself out according to plan. (*He suddenly frowns resentfully—impatient*) Plan?—what plan?—you'd think this was some intricate intrigue you were starting, whereas it is very simple—you want Sara—all right, you take her, and that's all there is to it—as for Mother, she has interfered and carried on an intrigue to isolate you—she must be taught to confine her activities to their proper sphere—to remain back where she belongs—very well, put her in her place this afternoon—

and that will settle her half of it. (*He sits down at his desk—with a strange smile of anticipation*) But it won't be so easy to deceive her—she peers suspiciously behind face values—she knows the real price is always concealed—I shall have to force her mind back into the past where her ambitions belong—where I once belonged with her— (*He pauses. His expression becomes relaxed and dreamy. His voice sinks to a low nostalgic musing tone, hardly above a whisper.*) It will be pleasant to find myself in her garden again after all these years—it will be a relief to leave this damned slave pen and talk with someone whose mind is not crucified on this insane wheel—whose greed, at least, is of the spirit—I remember it used to be so restful in her garden—life existed only as a rumor of War beyond a high wall, a distant, drowsy din, a muffled squelching of feet in a trough—far-off, dim, unreal, divorced and separate, with no sense of a confusing union— (*He stops. A pause. There is a knock on the door at right. At once Simon becomes the formidable, ruthless head of the Company. He calls curtly*) Come in. (*Joel enters.*)

JOEL—The directors are in the outer office. I thought I should pay them the courtesy of announcing them myself, considering their importance.

SIMON—(*acidly*) They have no importance. They had it when they had power. But I took it from them. So now they have none. They are ruined and worthless. They have nothing! And your courtesy is meaningless and a cruel joke which mocks at their plight. If I was one of them, I would knock you down. (*sharply*) Tell them to come in. (*Joel stares at him—then goes out.*)

(*Curtain*)

SCENE TWO

SCENE—*Same as Scene One of Act Two, the corner of the Harford garden with the octagonal Chinese summerhouse. Late afternoon sunlight from beyond the wall at right, falls on the pointed roof and the upper part of the arched lacquer-red door and ivy covered walls of the summerhouse. The shrubs, clipped as*

*before in arbitrary geometrical designs, and the trees along the
brick wall at rear glow in different shades of green. The wall at
right casts a long shadow. The lawn is a bright green, setting off
the deeper green of shrubbery and trees. The water in the small
oval pool before the summerhouse is still another shade of green.
The garden has the same appearance as before of everything
being meticulously tended and trimmed. This effect is a morbid
oppressive one of artificiality, and perverse childish fantasy, of nature distorted and humiliated by a deliberately mocking, petulant
arrogance.*

*Deborah is sitting on the steps leading up to the summerhouse
door, dressed all in white. She appears greatly changed from the
previous Act. Where she had seemed a prematurely-old, middle-
aged woman then, she now has the look of a surprisingly youthful
grandmother. Actually, she appears much younger now at fifty-
three than she had then at forty-nine. Her body and face have
filled out a little. There is something of repose and contentment in
her expression, something of an inner security and harmony. But
her beautiful dark eyes and her smile still retain their old imaginative, ironical aloofness and detachment.*

*Her four grandchildren, the sons of Simon and Sara, are
grouped about the pool in front of her. Ethan, the eldest, in his
twelfth year, is sitting on the stone bench at rear of pool on her
right. Wolfe Tone, a year younger, is sprawled on his back on the
narrow coping of the pool at front, his folded hands supporting his
head, staring up at the sky. Jonathan, a year and a half younger
than Wolfe, and Owen Roe ("Honey"), the youngest, who is
seven and a half, are sitting sideways, facing each other, on the
stone bench on Deborah's left, playing a game of casino with the
bench as table.*

*Ethan is tall and heavily built for his age, broad-shouldered and
muscular. His face is strong, broad, good-looking in a rugged,
rough-hewn mould. There is a resemblance to Deborah about his
forehead and deep-set dark eyes. He has his mother's straight black
hair, and obstinate, passionate mouth. But his nose and chin and
swarthy complexion are his father's. His manner is groping and
awkwardly self-conscious, but stubbornly, almost sullenly, determined.*

*Wolfe is an opposite type, of medium height for his age, slender
and wiry. His face is handsome and aristocratic, pale, with light*

*brown hair and hazel eyes. The resemblance to Sara's father, Cor-
nelius Melody, is marked and there is also much that reveals Deborah in his face and expression. Added to this is a cold immobility
about the cut of his features as a whole that immediately brings to
mind his uncle, Joel Harford. He does not resemble his father or
his mother. His manner is politely pleasant and compliant, but it
is the distant amiability of indifference.*

*Jonathan is undersized with a big head too large for his body.
He is also thin but one gets no impression of frailty or weakness
from him but of an exhaustless energy. The general facial resemblance to his father is so striking one does not notice any other. His
hair is brown, his complexion swarthy, his eyes grey-blue. His manner is quick, self-assured, observant and shrewd. "Honey" takes
after his mother's side of the family. He is an obvious Irish type
with a clear skin, rosy and white complexion, blue eyes and curly
black hair. A chubby, roly-poly youngster. He is lazy, laughing
and good tempered, full of health and animal spirits, his eyes
bright with a sly humor, his smile infectious and charmingly
ingratiating.*

*From all four boys one gets the impression of an underlying nat-
ural boyishness—a feeling that each is in one way or another too
old for his years.*

*Deborah is reading aloud from Byron's "Childe Harold." Ethan
listens with absorbed interest, his eyes fixed on her face. Wolfe stares
at the sky, his expression emotionless. One cannot tell whether he
is listening or not. Jonathan's and Honey's attention appears to be
wholly concentrated on their game.*

DEBORAH—(*reads—and one feels that for the moment she
has forgotten her audience and is reading aloud to herself*)

But Quiet to quick bosoms is a Hell,
And there hath been thy bane; there is a fire
And motion of the Soul which will not dwell
In its own narrow being, but aspire
Beyond the fitting medium of desire;
And, but once kindled, quenchless evermore,
Preys upon high adventure, nor can tire
Of aught but rest; a fever at the core,
Fatal to him who bears, to all who ever bore.

This makes the madmen who have made men mad
By their contagion; Conquerors and Kings,
Founders of Sects and Systems, to whom add
Sophists, Bards, Statesmen, all unquiet things
Which stir too strongly the soul's secret springs,
And are themselves the fools to those they fool;
Envied, yet how unenviable! What stings
Are theirs! One breast laid open were a school
Which would unteach Mankind the lust to shine or rule:

Their breath is agitation, and their life
A storm whereon they ride, to sink at last,
And yet so nursed and bigoted to strife,
That should their days surviving perils past,
Melt to calm twilight, they feel overcast
With sorrow and supineness, and so die;
Even as a flame unfed, which runs to waste
With its own flickering, or a sword laid by,
Which eats into itself, and rusts ingloriously.

(*She stops and stares before her.*)

ETHAN—(*starts from his concentrated attention—with an affectionate, understanding smile*) You were reading that to yourself, too, weren't you, Grandmother?

DEBORAH—(*starts—then smiles affectionately*) Perhaps, Ethan. There is a lesson in it—a warning for each of us—such as—(*with a strange note of self-mockery*) well, to be suitably grateful for a calm twilight, for example. But, of course, that is not the lesson youth should learn from it.

ETHAN—(*scowling*) I hate lessons. I don't see any lesson in it.

WOLFE—(*speaks up quietly without moving*) I do.

DEBORAH—(*stares at him—strangely*) Yes. I'm afraid you may, Wolfe. But perhaps it's the wrong lesson. (*Wolfe stirs uneasily but continues staring at the sky.*)

ETHAN—(*jealously*) Oh, him! He sees everything, to hear him tell it!

DEBORAH—(*smiling*) I think he does see too much.

ETHAN—He only pretends to, so he can pretend he's too good for anything, and doesn't want what he knows he can't get.

JONATHAN—(*without looking up from the cards—grinning*) That's right, Ethan.

DEBORAH—Another country heard from! I didn't know you were listening, Jonathan.

JONATHAN—(*self-assuredly*) Oh, I can mind the game and keep track of what's going on at the same time. And win, too. (*He plays a card.*) There. Big casino. That beats you, Honey.

HONEY—(*grins with ungrudging admiration*) You always beat me. But you can't beat Wolfe.

JONATHAN—I would if he wasn't so darned lucky. I play better. It's just his luck.

WOLFE—It is not. It's because I don't care whether I win or not. You only like winning. That's why you make mistakes.

DEBORAH—(*smiling*) A profound observation, Wolfe. You will grow up to be a philosopher, I think.

WOLFE—(*distrustfully*) What's a philosopher? (*then with a quick indifference*) I don't care what I grow up to be.

JONATHAN—I'm going to own a railroad. Father wants me to.

HONEY—I'm going to be a gentleman and 'lected President of America, like Mother wants me.

DEBORAH—(*smiling*) I'm afraid you can't be both nowadays, Honey.

HONEY—(*For a moment his grin vanishes and he gives her a scornful, defiant look.*) Mother says I can. (*smiling again, to Jonathan*) Come on. Let's play 'nother. This time I'll show you.

ETHAN—(*jealously*) Aw, don't talk to those crazy kids, Grandmother. Read some poetry.

JONATHAN—(*dealing—jeeringly*) We know what Ethan's going to do—to hear him talk big! He won't do what Father and Mother want! Oh, no!

HONEY—(*joins in jeeringly*) He won't go to Harvard! He won't be a gentleman!

ETHAN—(*with sullen doggedness*) Well, I won't. Wait and see.

JONATHAN—He's going to run away to sea and be a sailor!

ETHAN—I will, too.

WOLFE—(*indifferently*) Well, why don't you, then? Who cares what you do?

ETHAN—(*turns to glance at him*) Shut up, you! Mother and Father care. And Grandmother.

DEBORAH—(*gently*) Indeed I do care, Ethan.

WOLFE—(*goes on indifferently*) Why anyone with sense would want to be a sailor working like a nigger slave—

JONATHAN—They don't get hardly any pay either. Ethan 'll never get rich.

WOLFE—(*ignoring this*) On a dirty, smelly ship—

ETHAN—(*stung—angrily*) That's a lie! Ships aren't dirty. They're the prettiest things in the world! And I love the sea! (*more angrily, stares at his feet threateningly*) You take that back or I'll—

DEBORAH—Now, now. Giving Wolfe a bloody nose wouldn't convince him that ships and the sea are beautiful, would it?

WOLFE—(*calmly*) He won't hit me. He knows he can lick me, and Ethan's not a coward.

ETHAN—(*abashed*) No. 'Course I won't. Only don't you say—

WOLFE—(*indifferently*) All right. Ships are beautiful then. Who cares?

ETHAN—(*glares at him again—then sits down, abruptly changing the subject*) Please read some more, Grandmother— that part about the ocean. That shows how Lord Byron loved the sea.

WOLFE—Who cares about him? Except I'd like to have been born a lord.

DEBORAH—(*smiling—assuredly*) Yes, that would entitle you to any amount of disdainful indifference, wouldn't it? (*then to Ethan*) You must know that part by heart, Ethan.

ETHAN—I do. But it's better when you read it, Mother— (*hastily—embarrassed*) 'Scuse me, I mean, Grandmother.

DEBORAH—(*gives him a tender look*) You needn't apologize. I like you to call me Mother.

WOLFE—(*turns his head to stare at her—enviously*) You like it when I get mixed up, too. Why do you?

DEBORAH—(*starts, forcing a smile*) Why, I suppose because I'm so fond of your mother I'd like to be her. And, of course, because I love you, too. (*He stares, then turns abruptly to gaze up at the sky again. Deborah begins to read.*)

There is a pleasure in the pathless woods,
There is a rapture on the lonely shore,
There is society, where none intrudes,
By the deep Sea, and music in its roar:
I love not Man the less, but Nature more,
From these our interviews, in which I steal
From all I may be, or have been before,
To mingle with the Universe, and feel
What I can ne'er express—yet cannot all conceal.

Roll on, thou deep and dark blue Ocean—roll!
Ten thousand fleets sweep over thee in vain;
Man marks the earth with ruin—his control
Stops with the shore;—upon the watery plain
The wrecks are all thy deed, nor doth remain
A shadow of man's ravage, save his own,
When, for a moment, like a drop of rain,
He sinks into thy depths with bubbling groan—
Without a grave—unknelled, uncoffined, and unknown.

JONATHAN—(*suddenly speaks without looking up from his game*) Sinks with bubbling groan—no better than a drop of rain—unknown. That'll be you if you don't watch out, Ethan. (*He adds with a curt, contemptuous, practical finality that recalls his father*) And that's foolishness.

HONEY—(*echoing him*) Yes, Ethan's a fool.

ETHAN—(*who had been listening with dreamy intensity—recoiling*) Shut up, you! (*to Deborah—eagerly*) Now skip to the one that begins: "And I have loved thee, Ocean."

WOLFE—(*interrupts impatiently*) No! That's enough for Ethan, Grandmother. He's had his share. Read my part—the one you say you used to like so much, and don't anymore. (*As she hesitates, strangely reluctant, he turns his head to stare at her—insistently*) Go on. Why don't you ever want to read that?

DEBORAH—(*starts—evasively*) Why, no particular reason, except that I no longer believe it. And it hardly strikes the right note of inspiration for a future banker. But if you insist— (*She recites without looking at the book, a note of personal arrogance growing more marked in her voice as she goes on, staring straight before her.*)

I have not loved the World, nor the World me;
I have not flattered its rank breath, nor bowed
To its idolatries a patient knee,
Nor coined my cheek to smiles,—nor cried aloud
In worship of an echo: in the crowd
They could not deem me one of such—I stood
Among them, but not of them—in a shroud
Of thoughts which were not their thoughts, and still could,
Had I not filed my mind, which thus itself subdued.

I have not loved the World, nor the World me,—
But let us part fair foes; I do believe,
Though I have found them not, that there may be
Words which are things,—hopes which will not deceive,
And Virtues which are merciful, nor weave
Snares for the failing: I would also deem
O'er others' griefs that some sincerely grieve—
That two, or one, are almost what they seem,—
That Goodness is no name—and Happiness no dream.

WOLFE—(*staring at her—strangely*) And you don't agree with that anymore?

DEBORAH—(*starts—forcing a smile, carelessly*) No, it is much too bitter and disdainful a dream for a contented grandmother.

WOLFE—(*stares at her—curiously*) You spoke it then as if you still meant it.

DEBORAH—(*forcing a joking manner*) Oh, I'm an accomplished actress, as your father could tell you. (*He stares at her—then turns his head to look up at the sky again. Honey gives a sly, laughing chuckle over something in the card game.*)

WOLFE—(*without looking*) Watch out, Jonathan. Honey's cheating. I can tell by his laugh.

JONATHAN—(*half turns his head to reply—as he does so Honey transfers cards from his pocket to his hand. Jonathan says laughingly*) Don't I know! He can't help giving himself away. But he's always so tickled with himself he never sees that as soon as he starts cheating I cheat back to show I can win at that game, too. (*He turns back to the game—suddenly he grabs Honey's hand.*) Hey! That's too much! Look, Wolfe! Look! Ethan! See what he's up to now! He's been putting extra cards in his hand! (*He laughs—to Honey*) You ninny! Don't you think I'd notice you have too many cards? How'd you expect—?

HONEY—(*choking with merriment*) But that makes it funnier if I did fool you! (*He laughs unrestrainedly, a merry entirely shameless and droll guffaw. Looking at him the others, Deborah included, cannot help joining in.*)

ETHAN—(*disgusted with himself for laughing—scowls*) It's all right to laugh but if Mother knew, wouldn't she take you over her knee! You know she's always telling us about honor.

HONEY—(*still chuckling—confidently*) She won't know.

DEBORAH—No, we promised we'd never tell on each other, didn't we?

HONEY—And I did it playing with her the other night, anyway, and she couldn't help laughing.

DEBORAH—(*smiles at him*) Well, Honey, all I can say is, if you hope to be President you'll have to learn to be more skillful. (*She laughs—then stops suddenly, listening to something beyond the wall at right.*) There's your father coming home.

WOLFE—(*staring at her wonderingly*) You can always tell his walk from anyone's, can't you?

DEBORAH—(*smiling—with a sneer beneath*) That's easy now, Wolfe. He walks with the proud tread of a conquering Napoleon. (*Suddenly, listening, her expression changes to one of alarmed surprise and she stares at the door in the wall with dread—tensely*) He has stopped— (*For a moment there is a tense silence in which the boys, conscious of the change in her, regard her puzzledly. Then there is a sharp rap of the knocker on the door and Deborah quivers frightenedly.*)

JONATHAN—(*starts for the door*) I'll let him in—

DEBORAH—(*in a panic*) No! (*Then she stammers confusedly*) I must be mistaken. It cannot—be your father. He has never dared— I mean, he would never come unless I invited him, and I would never—

WOLFE—(*staring at her*) What are you so frightened about, Grandmother?

DEBORAH—(*fighting to control herself*) I'm superstitious. I'm afraid—like your mother. I don't like strangers attempting to intrude— (*then with swift urgency*) Run to the house and get your mother, Ethan! Tell her she should come here at once! (*But, as he starts to obey, frowning and puzzled, there is a louder knock on the door and Simon's voice calls sharply:* "It's I, Mother. Open the door!" *Again Deborah's expression changes completely. All fear vanishes from her face; she seems in a flash to become arrogantly self-confident. A little smile of gloating scorn comes to her lips and she murmurs softly*) Well, it is not I who wish— (*with abrupt impatience*) Well, Jonathan? Don't you hear your father? Open the door. (*He stares at her puzzledly— then goes and opens the door. Simon comes in and Jonathan closes the door after him. Simon approaches his mother, giving a quick glance around, his face set in a coldly pleasant smile.*)

SIMON—Good evening, Mother.

DEBORAH—(*coldly pleasant in her tone*) This is an unexpected pleasure, Simon.

SIMON—Evidently. Such whispering I heard, cooling my heels before the sacred portals. I trust I have not intruded on any secret conspiracy.

DEBORAH—(*startled—stares at him*) Conspiracy? (*coldly pleasant again*) Naturally we were surprised. We could not believe our good fortune.

SIMON—(*turning to his sons*) You boys go to the house. I have to talk to your grandmother.

DEBORAH—(*uneasily*) I would like them to remain in the garden, if you don't mind.

SIMON—(*coldly domineering*) As it happens, I do mind, Mother. (*For a moment, angered, she stares at him defiantly. Then she shrugs her shoulders with assumed indifference and looks away. He turns to the boys who are standing hesitantly, glancing puzzledly from his face to hers—sharply*) You heard what I said. (*They start, reply obediently,* "Yes, Father," *and hurry off down the path at right. He turns back to Deborah—curtly*) I happen to know their mother is waiting for this chance to see them alone. (*She gives him a quick suspicious glance. He bows with dry formality.*) If I may sit down, Mother?

DEBORAH—(*coldly*) Of course. This is your property. Pray do so. (*She sits on the steps again.*)

SIMON—Sara's property. (*He sits on the stone bench on her left.*)

DEBORAH—(*with a trace of mockery*) But what is hers is yours. Or so I felt you thought.

SIMON—(*pleasantly*) Yes, that is quite true. (*He pauses, glancing around the garden. She glances quickly at him again, her expression set in indifference, but her eyes suspicious and curious. He remarks casually*) Sara has probably told you of her visit to my office this morning.

DEBORAH—No.

SIMON—(*wondering*) She hasn't?

DEBORAH—No. I am not curious. She told me before she left you had asked her to come there.

SIMON—(*feigning surprise*) That I had asked her? (*She glances at him sharply. He goes on carelessly.*) Well, it is of no importance who asked whom, I suppose. You say she has not mentioned our interview in any way?

DEBORAH—(*with forced indifference*) No. I imagine it concerned property of yours—her name and papers you wished her to sign. She knows I would not be interested in that.

SIMON—Her purpose in coming had nothing to do with papers. Although, of course, it did concern property. (*He adds with a sneering smile*) You know Sara.

DEBORAH—(*as if caught off guard, starts to sneer herself*) Yes, you may be sure I— (*She catches herself and looks at him defensively.*)

SIMON—As you'll see, Sara suspects—and with good reason, I think—that she is being secretly swindled of what is rightfully hers.

DEBORAH—(*startled—with feigned indifference*) I cannot believe Sara imagines that. What is the nature of the plot you claim she suspects, if I may ask? (*She sneers*) Not that her husband is defrauding of his love, I trust?

SIMON—(*smilingly*) As a matter of fact, that was one of the matters she wished to discuss with me.

DEBORAH—Indeed? It is silly of her to wish to keep what she no longer needs.

SIMON—(*ignoring this*) Not that she holds me responsible for her loss. She very shrewdly suspects whose hidden influence is really to blame.

DEBORAH—(*stares at him—then coldly scornful*) I am not interested in all this mysterious insinuation. I do not believe Sara ever—

SIMON—(*interrupts as if he hadn't heard*) I was very glad she came. It gave me a chance to talk over with her a new arrangement at the office I have been contemplating for some time. I had to obtain her consent—which she was only too willing to give, as it turned out. I find it advisable, from many standpoints, to add a private confidential secretary to my employ.

DEBORAH—(*scornfully*) And you had to have Sara's consent for that?

SIMON—(*smilingly*) You will understand why when I tell you the one person who possesses the qualifications I desire is a very young and beautiful woman.

DEBORAH—(*starts—her first instinctive reaction one of vindictive satisfaction and gloating pity*) Ah! Poor Sara! So this is what your great romantic love comes to in the end! I always knew— (*Abruptly and guiltily her reaction changes to one of overstressed moral indignation.*) How dare you mention such filth to your mother! Have you become so utterly coarse and debased, so lost to all sense of decency, that you feel no shame but actually boast you are deliberately planning to dishonor yourself and disgrace your family? (*then with disdain*) But I don't know why I should be surprised. After all, this is an inevitable step in the corruption of your character that I have had to watch for years, until I could hardly recognize my son in the unscrupulous greedy trader, whose soul was dead, whose one dream was material gain! Now, after this final degradation, I cannot recognize my son in you at all! He is dead and you are a repulsive stranger I will not allow myself to know!

SIMON—(*has been watching her with a gloating satisfaction—mockingly*) Yet if I am not mistaken, Mother, you were not altogether displeased to see Sara's husband become so worthy, in your mind, of being her husband.

DEBORAH—It's a lie! That you can have such a vile suspicion proves to what depths your mind—!

SIMON—May I point out that you have been jumping too eagerly to conclusions, Mother. I have not said my secretary was to be anything more intimate than my secretary. (*Deborah looks guilty and discomfited. He adds with a mocking smile*) I am afraid the good grandmother you have become has not entirely forgotten the French Eighteenth Century Memoirs in which she once lived, or such an improper suspicion could never enter her mind.

DEBORAH—(*stares at him strickenly—pleadingly*) Simon! It is not kind to make me remember— (*with dread*) Oh, why did you come here? What—?

SIMON—(*ignoring this*) And I don't see how you can think Sara would ever consent—unless you secretly believe her true nature is so greedy that she would sell anything if offered the right price.

DEBORAH—(*stares at him fascinatedly—with a strange eagerness*) So that's it! You offered— (*with a strange taunting laugh*) Then you have been made a fool of. She has swindled you by selling rights to property she no longer needs or wants!

SIMON—Ah! And you think it was you who brought that about?

DEBORAH—(*distractedly*) No! No! How dare you think I could concern myself with your low greeds! (*violently*) And I will not think such ignoble things about Sara's motives! I will not have you put such thoughts in my mind about a woman to whom I owe an eternal debt of gratitude, who is the sweetest, kindest, most generous-hearted—

SIMON—I am sorry to have to disillusion you, Mother, but I think you will discover before our interview is over that Sara has not been as blind as you hoped, nor as unsuspectingly trustful as you imagined. (*Deborah starts and stares at him uneasily. He goes on in a pleasant matter-of-fact tone like one disinterestedly stating facts.*) You made the mistake of underestimating your adversary. Your vanity made you overconfident in your superior subtlety of mind. It does not do to hold one's enemy in the battle for supremacy in too much contempt—

DEBORAH—I will not have you talk as though Sara and I were engaged in some fantastic duel—as though our home were a battleground! It is insane of you. I bitterly resent your intruding here without my consent and attempting to create suspicion and jealousy between Sara and me. You cannot! We have reached too deep an understanding. We have built up too close a friendship through our mutual love for the children! Through love of them we have learned to love each other! I trust her and I know she trusts me! It would take more than your obviously malicious insinuations to shake my faith in her!

SIMON—(*coldly domineering*) We will deal with the facts, if you please, Mother, not with sentimental posing.

DEBORAH—(*staring at him with a fascinated dread—stammers*) Simon! Why are you saying such things? What are you trying to do? I feel behind this— I know this is some insane plot to revenge yourself on me!

SIMON—(*with a cold smile*) Plots and intrigues! You must be still dreaming of eighteenth-century romance, Mother! Revenge on you? That is a mad idea, Mother, coming from you who have seemingly grown so sane. Revenge for what? As far as I remember, there was never a serious quarrel between us—merely a difference in philosophical outlook between you whose true nature is to hide from life in dreams and I whose inner compulsion is to deal solely in reality and the facts of things. I thought even that trifling quarrel of the past had vanished in indifference and been forgotten long ago.

DEBORAH—I have forgotten it. But I know you—

SIMON—(*as if she hadn't spoken*) I know I have forgotten it. (*Suddenly his tone changes to a bitter smouldering resentment.*) Revenge for what, I ask you? It was I who long ago, after I graduated from Harvard, decided of my own free will it was high time I began to live in my own life and not in your life! I then freed myself from your influence, which would have kept me always a tenth-rate versifier, scribbling imitations of Byron's romantic doggerel, wasting my mind humoring your fantastic whims and playing roles of childish make-believe here in your garden with you, lost in dreams, while love escaped and life passed down the street beyond the wall, forgetful we were hidden here. (*He pauses, staring around the garden. His tone has taken a strange quality of nostalgic yearning. He murmurs as if to himself*) It is so restful here. I had forgotten how restful it was. (*Deborah stares at him. Her expression has lost its bitter resentment, has suddenly lighted up with a gloating, triumphant perception.*)

DEBORAH—(*with a little smile—carelessly*) So you have

never forgotten that old quarrel? As you say, it was childish of us. I remember now I used to be of the opinion it was I who made you leave, who forced you out into your own life. So that I might be free.

SIMON—(*curtly*) Yes, you consoled your pride with that lie. But the truth was, if I had wished, I could have remained here with you forever. You are honest enough to confess that now, I hope?

DEBORAH—(*still watching him—smilingly*) Yes, if you wish. I appreciate that a Napoleon of affairs must believe implicitly in his own star. (*She laughs softly—teasingly*) You are still such a strange greedy boy, do you know it, Dear?

SIMON—(*again glancing around the garden—with again the tone of nostalgic yearning*) Yes, I had forgotten the quiet and the peace here. Nothing has changed. The past is the present. (*Suddenly he turns on her—harshly accusing*) You are the only jarring discordant note. Because you are not the same. You are a stranger here. This garden of your old self disowns the doting old granny you have made yourself pretend to be.

DEBORAH—(*Watching him, her eyes gleam with a secret gloating—quietly*) I do not feel alien here. Perhaps it is you whom my garden disowns, in hurt pride, because you long ago disowned it.

SIMON—(*with sullen boyish boastfulness*) Yes, I did. I'm glad you admit it. (*then justifying himself—placatingly*) Well, it could hardly expect me to stay buried alive forever.

DEBORAH—(*quietly, her eyes gleaming*) No, I suppose not. (*She pauses, probing under a casual tone.*) I am sorry you do not believe in my sincerity as a good grandmother.

SIMON—(*sneering resentfully*) Oh, you were always able to play a part so convincingly that you fooled even yourself!

DEBORAH—(*with a soft teasing laugh*) Don't tell me you are jealous of your children, too!

SIMON—(*curtly*) Too? I don't know what you mean. Jealous? Don't be absurd, Mother. Beyond observing your obvious campaign to obtain control of the children, and pitying Sara for what I mistakenly thought was her blind trustfulness, I have regarded the matter as none of my business.

DEBORAH—(*starts to protest angrily—checks herself and*

changes the subject—quietly casual) Speaking of business, how are the Company's affairs these days? I am sure you must be becoming richer and more powerful all the time.

SIMON—(*in a boastful tone*) Yes, I am, Mother. I concluded a deal today which adds a railroad to the Company's properties.

DEBORAH—(*flatteringly but with underlying sarcasm*) How splendid! My congratulations, Dear.

SIMON—(*pleased*) Thank you, Mother. (*then in his brisk, business-like tone*) Oh, it's nothing in itself. But it has significance as another step forward. It's an added link in the chain in which my ships bring cotton to my mills to be made into my cloth and shipped on my railroad. (*frowning impatiently*) But there is a lot to be done before the chain is completed.

DEBORAH—(*with a little mocking smile*) Yes, I perceive it is not enough.

SIMON—(*deadly serious*) Far from it. The next step must be to acquire my own bank. Then I can control and manipulate all the Company's financing.

DEBORAH—I see. And you will want your own stores here in the city to sell your goods.

SIMON—Yes. I have that in mind.

DEBORAH—And at the other end of your chain you should possess plantations in the South and own your own nigger slaves, imported in your own slave ships.

SIMON—(*staring before him, tense and concentrated, his expression hard and ruthless—eagerly*) Yes. Of course. I had not considered that but it is obviously the logical final step at that end. (*She stares at him and gives a little uneasy shrinking movement. He turns to her with an affectionate teasing smile.*) You are wonderfully shrewd and farsighted, Mother, for a beautiful lady who has always affected superior disdain for greedy traders like my father and me.

DEBORAH—(*impulsively—with a trace of seductive coquetry*) You find me still a little beautiful? I fear you are merely flattering a poor ugly old woman.

SIMON—(*ignores this*) I am glad to find you changed in that one respect, Mother. You now have the courage to face some of the things that have reality. You don't have to cower behind romantic idealisms from every ugliness of truth. (*He stares at her strangely.*) The ugliness of life you would learn, if you possessed it as long as I have now, can become identical with beauty.

DEBORAH—(*uneasily*) I do not understand you.

SIMON—(*strangely*) Well, as I admitted to you, I do not understand all the implications of the duel of duality myself—not yet—but I will in the end, I promise you! (*She looks away from him, as frightened as if this were a threat. He speaks casually.*) Yes, I am glad you appreciate what I am achieving through the Company. I see now that behind your old pose of lofty spiritual contempt, you were proud of Father's ability in trade. I will make you prouder of me than you ever were of him, Mother.

DEBORAH—(*her eyes gleaming again—softly*) Ah. But I am already, Dear.

SIMON—(*boastfully*) He had scruples. I have none. He disguised his greed with Sabbath potions of God-fearing unction at the First Congregationalist Church. Else he had feared to swallow it. I fear no God but myself! I will conquer every obstacle. I will let nothing stand between me and my goal!

DEBORAH—(*uneasily again*) What goal, Simon?

SIMON—(*turns to her in surprise*) But I thought you saw that, Mother. My goal is to make the Company entirely self-sufficient. It must not be dependent upon anything outside itself for anything. It must need nothing but what it contains within itself. It must attain the all-embracing security of complete self-possession—the might which is the sole right not to be a slave! Do you see?

DEBORAH—(*strangely moved*) I see, Dear—that you have gone very far away from me—and become lost in yourself and very lonely.

SIMON—(*vaguely*) Lost? Oh no, don't imagine I have lost. I always win. My destiny is victory at any cost, by any means. (*abruptly boyishly boastful again*) Wait and see, Mother! I'll prove to you I can lead the Company to glorious, final triumph—complete independence and freedom within itself! (*He pauses and looks around the garden, then he sighs wearily—strangely*) But sometimes lately, Mother, alone in my office, I have felt so weary of the game—of watching suspiciously each card I led to myself from across the table—even though I had marked them all—watching my winnings pile up and becoming confused with losses—feeling my swindler's victorious gloating die into boredom and discontent—the flame of ambition smoulder into a chill dismay—as though that opponent within had spat an extinguishing poison of disdain—

DEBORAH—(*strangely, tenderly sympathetic*) Oh, I know! I know, Dear! I used to know so well! (*tensely*) I tell you I had once reached a point where I had grown so lost, I had not even a dream left I could dream without screaming scornful laughter at myself. I would sit locked in the summerhouse here, so no one could come between and protect me from myself, in the dark, squatting on folded legs in mockery of mystic meditation—sit there for hours in wisdom-ridiculing contemplation of myself, and spit in my mind, and spit in my heart, like a village idiot in a country store spitting at the belly of a stove—cursing the day I was born, the day I indifferently conceived, the day I bore— (*with a terrible intensity*) Until I swear to you, I felt I could by just one tiny further wish, one little effort more of will, push open the door to madness where I could at least believe in a dream again! And how I longed for that final escape! (*She suddenly turns and stares at him with hatred.*) Ah! And you wonder why I hate you! (*abruptly overcome by a panic of dread, starting to her feet*) Simon! What are you trying to do! Leave me alone! Leave the past in its forgotten grave! (*trying to control herself and be indifferent*) But that is foolish. You are simply being childishly morbid and silly. Frankly, I am bored with listening to your nonsense. I will go in the house now. Sara must be wondering what is keeping me, now the sun is setting. (*She starts for the path off left. As she does so, Simon, without looking at her begins to speak again in his tone of nostalgic yearning. As he speaks she stops, makes herself go on, stops again, tries to go on, finally stops and turns to stare at him.*)

SIMON—Then I began to remember lately—and long for this garden—and you, as you used to be and are no longer—and I as I was then before I became a wife's husband and a children's father and a Company's President—that old harmonious union in the spirit of you and me—here in the freedom of a dream—hiding from the slave market of life—in this safe haven, where we could repose our souls in fantasy, in happy masquerades and fairy tales and the sustaining bravadoes of romantic verse—evade, escape, forget, rest in peace! (*He sighs wearily.*) I regret I have lost that paradise in which you were the good, kind, beloved, beautiful Queen. I have become so weary of what they call life beyond the wall, Mother.

DEBORAH—(*moved and fascinated, takes a step toward him— tenderly*) I see you have, my son. (*then diffidently but at the same time putting forth all her charm coquettishly and playfully*) But perhaps—who knows?—your loss is not irrevocable, Dear. We—you and I—in partnership in a new company of the spirit, might reorganize your bankruptcy—if I may put it in terms you understand. (*She smiles teasingly.*)

SIMON—(*with a passionate eagerness*) Yes! (*He grabs her hand.*)

DEBORAH—(*as if the touch of his hand alarmed her—shrinks back, turning away from him—guiltily stammers*) No! I swore to her—I would never interfere. I cannot! Unless you offer me more proof I cannot believe she has been guilty of the treachery to me that would set me free to welcome this opportunity— (*with sudden fierce passion*) Ah! If she only would be guilty I could be myself! I could be free to dream again! (*horrified at herself*) No! I am content. I have all I desire. (*She turns to Simon—resentfully and derisively*) My dear boy, your childish fancies are ridiculous. Do be sensible. We do not really wish such nonsense. And if we did, it would be impossible, we have both changed so much. (*carelessly taunting*) But, if you care to drop in here once in a while on your return from work I know the children would be pleased to see you. You could boast to them of your heroic exploits as the Company's victorious little Napoleon.

SIMON—(*stiffens, stares at her with hatred for a second—then coldly, in a curt business-like tone*) I'm glad you mentioned the children. It reminds me of my real purpose in coming here. I must inform you that Sara and I have decided you are having a very bad influence on our children—

DEBORAH—(*startled—resentful and uneasy*) That is ridiculous. Why, I have been at pains not to influence them at all! I teach them to rely on themselves, to own their own lives

and be what they want to be, to have the courage to preserve
their independence and freedom!

SIMON—I remember only too well your ideal of freedom
for others, Mother—that they must not be the slave of anyone but you!

DEBORAH—(*with a strange eagerness*) You say Sara decided—? (*guiltily*) No! I won't believe you!

SIMON—Sara decided that henceforth the children must be
forbidden to see you except in the house when either she or
I are present to protect them.

DEBORAH—(*strickenly—with increasing desperateness*) You
mean they are to be taken from me? I am to be left entirely
alone again—with no life but the memory of the past— Ah!
You can't be so cruel! I have made myself love them! I have
created a new life in which I am resigned to age and ugliness
and death out of that unselfish devotion to them and to their
mother— (*abruptly, her face hardening with an eager hatred*)
And you say Sara decided this? (*desperately*) No! I won't
believe—

SIMON—(*curtly*) I would hardly lie about something you
can confirm as soon as you see her.

DEBORAH—(*fighting a battle within herself—eagerly*) No,
that would be too stupid. It must be true.

SIMON—You'll find she is giving them their orders in the
house right now.

DEBORAH—(*with an almost joyous vindictiveness*) Ah, if she
has betrayed me and broken all her pledges! That releases me!
I am under no further obligation! I owe her nothing but—
(*fighting herself again but more weakly*) No! I still cannot believe! I know her too well! I know she loves and trusts me!
She would never suspect me—

SIMON—(*curtly*) Nonsense, Mother. You know there is
nothing strange about her being jealous of your stealing her
children. You used to be jealous of her—

DEBORAH—(*arrogantly*) I? Jealous of that common, vulgar
biddy? (*then eagerly—with a vindictive satisfaction*) So she is
jealous of me? Well, perhaps she has cause to be!

SIMON—Naturally, she is afraid—

DEBORAH—(*gratified*) So she is afraid of me? (*with a
vindictive laugh*) But her fear is too late. I already have Ethan

and Wolfe. They can never forget me! The other two still have
too much of her in them— (*again fighting herself desperately*)
But I know it wasn't Sara who decided this! It was you! But
you never think of the children. It must have been she! Yes,
yes! You are right! I have been a fool! I should have known!
And I *have* known deep down inside me! I have never entirely
trusted her! I have always suspected her of hypocrisy! I have
resented her interference and possessiveness. I have hated the
intolerable debt of daily gratitude! (*then brokenly*) But how
could she do this to me! She knows how much the children
have meant to me! She knows without them, I shall be lost
again!

SIMON—(*pleasantly, almost teasingly*) Come now, Mother.
Let's have done with posing. You are not really as exercised
by the loss of the children as you pretend. I think that you
are honestly relieved, and feel liberated from an irksome duty
that was becoming a bore.

DEBORAH—(*fiercely*) No! I love— (*abruptly with eagerness
again*) Well, perhaps you are right, Dear.

SIMON—You were never intended for the job of Sara's un-
paid nursemaid. Nor for the role of doting grandmother. You
are still too young and beautiful—

DEBORAH—(*flattered*) No, I know I am not. But I love
your thinking so, Dear. (*with a wry, bitter smile*) You are deceived by that false, fleeting Indian summer glow, the mocking presage of impending winter.

SIMON—(*as if he hadn't heard*) I will confess now, Mother,
I have watched with anxiety the corrupting effect of the hypocritical life you have been leading on your character—the
gradual loss of your former aristocratic distinction, your old
fanciful charm, the quality you once had of being unique and
unlike all other women. I have seen you fall completely under
Sara's influence and become merely a female, common, vulgar, a greedy home-owner, dreamless and contented!

DEBORAH—(*angrily*) You are talking nonsense! I have told
you it is I who have influenced her! Deliberately! As part of
my scheme! (*hastily*) No! What made me say that? I had no
scheme. I simply wished—

SIMON—I have watched her dispossess you from yourself
and take possession. (*with a resentful intensity*) By God, there

have been times when, as I watched you together in the house at night, she would seem to steal all identity from you and absorb you! Until there was but one woman—her!

DEBORAH—(*with a strange exultant satisfaction*) Ah, you felt that, did you? That we were one, united against— That is what I wished to do! (*gloatingly*) Poor boy, I can appreciate how frightened— (*then angrily*) But you are blind or you would have seen it was I who took possession of her in order to— (*She checks herself—hastily*) But, as you say, it is very confusing. One cannot see clearly what or why— (*frightenedly*) And I do not care to see. Why do you put such morbid nonsense in my mind? Besides, it does not matter now that you have shown me clearly, Dear, I do not need her to take back what is mine. I mean, naturally, after the treacherous way she has betrayed my trust in her, there can be no question of any further friendship between us. Although, of course, I shall go on pretending. I will not give her the satisfaction of letting her see how she has hurt— And, anyway, I know I have won and I am already revenged.

SIMON—(*staring before him—strangely*) Yes, Mother, I rely on you to help me keep her in her rightful place hereafter.

DEBORAH—(*regards him calculatingly—then with a caressingly gentle air*) And my place? What place do you intend me to have now, Dear?

SIMON—(*with a queer, hesitating embarrassment*) Why, here in your garden, of course, as always in the past.

DEBORAH—(*softly insinuating*) Alone? I was not always alone in the past, if you will remember. (*She pats his hair with maternal tenderness as if he were a boy—with a teasing laugh*) What? Have you no hope to offer your poor lonely mother?

SIMON—(*awkwardly stiff and formal to cover his strange embarrassment*) I do not wish you to be too lonely, Mother. I will be happy to consider any suggestion you—

DEBORAH—(*with a teasing laugh, ruffling his hair playfully*) Ah! I see! Still Napoleon! Still so proud! It must be I! I must know my new place and beg! Very well. I will play your humble slave, Sire. Will you deign to visit me here and comfort my exile?

SIMON—(*stiffly*) I wish you would not speak so fancifully, Mother. Please remember we are dealing with reality now and not with romantic dreams. (*then eagerly under his awkward formality*) In reply to your request, I shall be delighted to drop in and keep you company here for a while each afternoon on my way home.

DEBORAH—(*gloatingly tender*) Good! Now that is off your mind, Dear. You have won that victory and can rest on your laurels for a while. (*She laughs and kisses him playfully on the forehead, and sits on the steps again. A pause. He looks round the garden and she regards him with an amused motherly smile.*)

SIMON—(*again with the yearning note*) Yes, it is very restful here. A little rest here each day will restore the soul. (*He sees the volume of Byron on the steps. He picks it up—with a forced casual air*) What's this? Ay, Byron. Sara bitterly resents your poisoning her children's minds with such romantic rubbish. She wants them to be inspired by practical ideals. Her dread is that any of them should resemble her father and shame her pride. I have had to be so careful never to shame her pride. (*He examines the volume—with pleased boyish surprise*) I thought this looked familiar. It is the same, isn't it, Mother— the one I gave you for your birthday long ago. (*turning over the pages*) Yes, here's the inscription. "To my beloved Mother." (*to her, with a boyish, grateful smile*) This makes me happy, Mother. I thought, of course, you must have burned this— (*abruptly with a taunting, challenging air*) I mean after I decided to leave you and begin my own life.

DEBORAH—(*smiles amusedly—softly*) Oh, I agree now it was you who left me and not I who sent you away. And I did want to burn your gift, I was so furious with you, but I could not.

SIMON—(*satisfied, turning over the pages—eagerly*) Yes, here are the parts I marked, and the parts you marked, and the parts we marked together. (*again in his tone of yearning nostalgia*) Do you remember, Mother, we would be sitting here just as we are now, and I'd ask you to read aloud to me—

DEBORAH—(*softly*) I remember, Dear, as clearly as if it were yesterday. Or, even, as though it were now.

SIMON—(*intent on the book*) Remember this? We both marked it. (*He reads*)

> . . . there is a fire
> And motion of the Soul which will not dwell
> In its own narrow being, but aspire
> Beyond the fitting medium of desire;

(*He stops and stares around the garden—strangely*) It is a long time since I have thought of the soul. Out there in the gutters called streets beyond the wall it appears to me a weak sentimental supposition, a superstitious superfluity—but here in this garden— (*He checks himself as he meets her eyes staring at him with a tender gloating fixity. He reads again.*) "And, but once kindled, quenchless evermore." (*He pauses, giving the pause a tense significance—thoughtfully*) "Evermore." Yes, it is, I think, the most cowardly and convenient of all man's evasions, that he forgets the present is merely the last moment of the past, and the delusion of his hope he calls the future is but the past returning to demand payment of its debt.

DEBORAH—(*uneasily, with a little shiver*) I do not like that thought, Dear.

SIMON—(*does not seem to hear her—reads again*)

> Preys upon high adventure, nor can tire
> Of aught but rest;

(*He smiles at her—teasingly*) I have observed for some time how tired you were with rest, Mother. (*He reads again.*)

> . . . a fever at the core
> Fatal to him who bears, to all who ever bore

(*He smiles.*) Well, there is no zest in living unless one preys upon high adventure by gambling with danger. I have discovered that as leader of the Company. As for it being fatal, that's a coward's thought, eh, Mother? Remember what Frederick the Great said to his Grenadiers who hesitated to be slaughtered for his greed and glory: "You damned stupid blackguards, do you want to live forever?" (*He laughs.*)

DEBORAH—(*forcing a laugh*) Yes, so stupid of them, wasn't it?

SIMON—(*turns the pages—with a return to boyish enthusiasm*) Ah! This was our favorite. I don't have to look at the book. I still know it by heart. I could never forget— I'll bet you can guess what it is, Mother.

DEBORAH—(*smiling fondly—teasingly*) Why, how excited

you are, Dear. What a romantic boy you still are at heart! Yes,
I'm sure I can guess— (*She recites—with growing arrogance*)

      I have not loved the World, nor the World me;

      I have not flattered its rank breath,—

SIMON—(*breaks in and takes it up, taking on her tone of
arrogant disdain*)

      . . . nor bowed

      To its idolatries a patient knee,

      Nor coined my cheek to smiles,—

DEBORAH—(*with a scornful hauteur*)

      . . . nor cried aloud

      In worship of an echo:

SIMON—

      . . . in the crowd

      They could not deem me one of such—

DEBORAH—

      . . . I stood

      Among them but not of them—

(*He joins in here and they both finish together.*)

      . . . in a shroud

      Of thoughts which were not their thoughts,—

(*They stop abruptly and stare at each other—then they both burst
out laughing merrily, and Deborah claps her hands.*)

SIMON—I remember so well now, Mother!

DEBORAH—Yes, that was just as it used to be, wasn't it?
(*From the house off left Sara's voice is heard calling in a tone of
repressed uneasiness:* "Simon, are you in the garden?" *The two
both start resentfully. Deborah gives him a hostile contemptuous
look.*) She wants her husband. You had better go.

SIMON—(*angrily, as if aloud to himself*) God, can I never
know a moment's freedom! (*He calls curtly, almost insultingly*)
I am here with Mother. What do you want now? (*Sara's voice
answers with an attempt at carelessness, but betraying hurt and
anxiety at his tone:* "Nothing, Darling. I simply wanted to be
sure." *A door is heard closing. Simon says with a chuckle*) She
wants to be sure. I thought she sounded a little uneasy, didn't
you, Mother?

DEBORAH—(*with a malicious smile*) Yes, now you mention
it—even a little frightened perhaps.

SIMON—(*frowning—with his curt authoritative air*) Never

mind, Mother, I will not permit such an intrusion on our privacy to occur again. I have already ordered her never to come here. (*then eagerly insistent*) Now let's forget her existence. We had a moment ago. We were back in the past before she lived in us.

DEBORAH—(*tenderly*) I am only too happy, Dear. (*She takes his hand—with a seductive playfulness*) Take my hand so you will not get lost.

SIMON—(*kisses her hand with a shy boyish impulsiveness*) Oh, don't be afraid, I will never leave you again, Mother. (*He pauses—still holding her hand, staring before him with a tender, reminiscent smile*) Do you know what had come into my mind as we laughed together? A memory that goes back long before our Byron days, when I was still at the fairy tale age, and you would read them aloud to me, here. Or, what I liked better, you would make up your own tales. They seemed so much more real than the book ones I couldn't help believing in them.

DEBORAH—(*uneasily, forcing a laugh*) Good Heavens, you are going far back! I had forgotten—

SIMON—(*insistently*) You can't have forgotten the one I just remembered. It was your favorite. And mine. It comes back so clearly. I can see you sitting there, as you are now, dressed all in white, so beautiful and so unreal, more like a character in your story than a flesh and blood mother, so familiar and yet so strange, so near and yet so far away— (*He suddenly stares at her—a bitter accusation in his voice*) You always took such care to preserve your pose of remaining disdainfully aloof from life! One would have thought you were afraid that even your own child was a greedy interloper who was plotting to steal you from your dreams!

DEBORAH—(*uneasily and guiltily—forcing a laugh*) Why, what a mean suspicious thought for you to have had about your poor mother, Dear!

SIMON—(*as if he hadn't heard this last—staring before him into the past again*) You would be sitting there before the summerhouse like a sentry guarding the door. (*Again he turns on her resentfully.*) Why did you make that silly rule that no one was ever allowed to go in the summerhouse but you? You wouldn't even permit me— Why did you make such a mysterious hocus pocus about it? (*He glances at the summer-house contemptuously.*) After all, it's ordinary enough. There are similar ones in many gardens. The way you acted gave the impression it was some secret temple of which you were high priestess! (*He laughs sneeringly.*) No one would have cared a damn about going in there, anyway!

DEBORAH—(*with a strange, taunting smile*) Oh, but you know that isn't true, Dear. You used to plead and beg by the hour—

SIMON—Only because you made such a mystery of it. Naturally, that made me curious.

DEBORAH—Yes, you were a dreadfully inquisitive, prying little boy, always asking questions— You would never learn to mind your own business.

SIMON—Well, when you forbid a boy to go anywhere, without giving him any sensible reason—

DEBORAH—(*a bit sharply, as if he were still the boy*) But I did. I explained over and over again that I felt all the rooms in the house, even my bedroom, were your father's property. And this garden I shared with you. I naturally desired one place, no matter how tiny, that would be mine alone, where I could be free to dream and possess my own soul and mind. It's just that you stubbornly refused to believe that. You were such a vain little boy. (*teasingly*) You didn't want to admit I could live, even for a moment, without you, did you, Dear? (*then abruptly*) But you have no cause to complain now. I have not opened the door for years and I will never again set foot in it. As you may guess from what I told you of my last experience alone in there. (*She gives a little shudder.*)

SIMON—(*stares at her with a strange fixity*) You mean when you laughed and spat in your heart until you longed to open any door of escape?

DEBORAH—(*with a shiver—hurriedly*) Yes, yes! Why do you remember that so well? Let us change the subject, if you please.

SIMON—(*insistently*) Why haven't you had it torn down, and not let it remain as a constant reminder.

DEBORAH—(*defensively*) Because its outside reminds me of nothing. It is part of the garden. It belongs here, that is all. I do not notice it. (*pleadingly*) I asked you to talk of something else, Dear. You were starting to remember a fairy tale.

SIMON—(*eagerly*) Yes, I want to tell you, Mother. But the strange part is that there is a connection with the summerhouse.

DEBORAH—(*startled*) Ah! Then I do not care to hear—

SIMON—Oh, not in your story. The connection was in my imagination, because of the silly mystery you made of the damned place, I suppose. (*He begins to tell the story, staring before him as if he visualized it.*) The story was this, Mother. I'll tell it without attempting to reproduce the fantastic romanticism with which you delighted to embellish your dreams. There was once upon a time, long ago in the past, a young King of a happy and peaceful land, who through the evil magic of a beautiful enchantress had been dispossessed of his realm, and banished to wander over the world, a homeless, unhappy outcast. Now the enchantress, it appeared, had in a last moment of remorse, when he was being sent into exile, revealed to him that there was a way in which he might regain his lost kingdom. He must search the world for a certain magic door.

DEBORAH—(*with a start*) Ah.

SIMON—She told him there was no special characteristic to mark this door from other doors. It might be any door, but if he wished to find it with all his heart, he would recognize it when he came to it, and know that on the other side was his lost kingdom. And so he set forth and searched for many years, and after enduring bitter trials, and numberless disappointments, he at last found himself before a door and the wish in his heart told him his quest was ended. But just as he was about to open it, confident that he had but to cross the threshold to re-enter his kingdom, where all had been happiness and beauty and love and peace, he heard the voice of the enchantress speaking from the other side, for she was there awaiting his coming. She called to him mockingly: "Wait. Before you open I must warn you to remember how evil I can be, and that it is probable I maliciously lied and gave you a false hope. If you dare to open the door you may discover this is no longer your old happy realm but has been changed by me into a barren desert, where it is always night, haunted by terrible ghosts, and ruled over by a hideous old witch, who wishes to destroy your claim to her realm, and the moment you cross the threshold she will tear you to pieces and devour you."

DEBORAH—(*with a little shudder—forcing a laugh*) Oh, come now, Dear. I am sure I never— It is you who are adding silly embellishments of fantastic evil. I remember the story as an ironically humorous tale.

SIMON—(*goes on as if she had not interrupted*) "So you had better be sure of your courage," the enchantress called warningly, "and remember that as long as you stay where you are you will run no risk of anything worse than your present unhappy exile befalling you." Then he heard her laugh. And that was all. She did not speak again, although he knew she remained there, and would always remain, waiting to see if he would dare open the door. (*with a strange bitterness*) But he never did, you said. He could not make up his mind. He felt she was lying to test his courage. Yet, at the same time, he felt she was not lying, and he was afraid. He wanted to turn his back on the door and go far away, but it held him in a spell and he could never leave it. So he remained for the rest of his life standing before the door, and became a beggar, whining for alms from all who passed by, until at last he died. (*He turns to stare at her—forcing a smile, resentfully*) That, I suppose, constitutes the humorous irony you remembered?

DEBORAH—(*laughingly, a strange gloating in her face and an undercurrent of taunting satisfaction in her voice*) Yes, I remember that ending now, and I must confess I still think it shows an amusing insight into the self-betraying timidities that exist in most of us. (*teasingly*) I remember how resentful you were at the ending. You used to insist I imagine a new ending in which the wicked enchantress had reformed and become a good fairy and opened the door and welcomed him home and they were both happy ever after. (*She laughs.*)

SIMON—And you would laugh at me. (*He stares at her— with a strange challenging look*) I would still like to discover if you could possibly imagine a happy ending to that tale.

DEBORAH—(*uneasily, meeting his stare*) Why? (*then hastily turning away and forcing a laugh*) But what silly nonsense,

Simon. What a child you are! Fairy tales, indeed! What a preoccupation for a Napoleon of facts!

SIMON—(*smiles pleasantly*) Yes, absurd, I admit. It must be the atmosphere of this garden. But the point I was getting at is that I was very impressionable then and your story was very real to me and I connected it with real things. The door of the tale became identified in my mind with the door there (*he looks at the summerhouse door*) to your forbidden summer-house. I used to boast to myself that if I were the King I would not be afraid, I would gamble recklessly on the chance— (*Suddenly, moved by a strange urgency, he springs to his feet and goes past her up the steps to the door—harshly*) Let's have done with the mystery right now! (*He seizes the knob.*)

DEBORAH—(*starts to her feet in a panic of dread and grabs his other arm*) No, Simon! No! (*Then her panic is strangely transformed into an outraged, arrogant fury—glaring at him with hatred and repulsion, in a quivering passion, commandingly*) Come away! Obey me this instant! How dare you! Have you lost all decency? Will your vulgar greed leave me nothing I can call my own? Is no solitude sacred to you?

SIMON—(*overcome by this outburst, moves back down the steps obediently like a cowed boy*) I'm sorry, Mother. I—I didn't think you'd mind now—

DEBORAH—(*relieved and a bit guilty*) I can't help minding. Forgive me for losing my temper, Dear. I don't know what I said—or what I meant— The truth is I have become super-stitious—remembering the last time I was in there—and I was afraid—and lost.

SIMON—(*has recovered his poise as she has weakened—curtly*) That is damned nonsense, Mother. There's nothing there, of course.

DEBORAH—(*with a little shiver*) You think not? But I re-member I am there.

SIMON—Rot! That's insanity, Mother.

DEBORAH—(*slowly—with dread*) Yes, I know that is what it is. (*hurriedly*) I suppose it's very ridiculous. There is noth-ing in there but dark and dust and spider webs—and the silence of dead dreams.

SIMON—(*smiling*) Well, anyway, it would not be a happy ending, would it, for me to go in alone? No, someday, I will give you the courage to open the door yourself and we will go together. (*He takes her hand, gently—pretending to joke but with an underlying seriousness*) I think I could be absolutely sure then that the beautiful evil enchantress had reformed and become a good fairy and my happy kingdom of peace was here. Surely, you couldn't forbid me that happy dream, Mother?

DEBORAH— (*fascinatedly*)   No— perhaps,   together— I might not be afraid—there may come a time when I might even welcome—now that she is conspiring to take life from me again— (*with a strange gloating smile*) Yes, she would have only herself to blame if— (*then with a shiver of dread*) No! I don't know what I mean! (*turning on him with forced scorn*) You are being absurd, Simon. It is grotesque for a grown man to act so childishly. I forbid you ever to mention this subject again. It is only on that condition I can agree to welcome you in my garden, you have the same rights here you had in the past but no more. (*pleadingly*) Surely that is enough for your happiness, Dear.

SIMON— (*with a mocking gallantry, kissing her hand*) Your wish my law, Madame. I shall be, as in the past, a slave to your every whim.

DEBORAH— (*abruptly changing to a gay, seductive coquetry*) That is as should be, Monsieur. (*laughingly*) I am happy to see that vulgar peasant slut has not made you forget all the old gallantry and gracious manners I taught you, Dear. (*From the house off left comes Sara's voice, and now the uneasiness and suspicion in it are obvious behind the casual words. She calls:* "Simon, are you still in the garden?")

SIMON— (*starts—calls out angrily*) Yes! Of course, I'm here! Why? What do you want of me now? (*A pause. Then Sara's voice comes, hurt and a little forlorn:* "Nothing, Darling. It's getting near supper time, that's all." *Her voice suddenly takes on a resentful commanding tone:* "It's time you came in, do you hear me?")

DEBORAH— (*staring at him—with a bitter, jealous derisiveness*) Your slut commands you now, it seems! As the weak slave of her every greedy whim you had better obey! (*Then as, stung, he starts to make an angry reply, Deborah anticipates him and calls with an undertone of gloating mockery*) Don't worry, Sara. I'll bring him back to you. (*A pause. Then Sara calls back, uneasily with a forced carelessness:* "Oh, you needn't bother, Deborah. His hunger would drive him here soon anyway." *A door is heard closing as she goes back in the house. Deborah gives a malicious laugh.*) A little forced in its self-confidence, that last, didn't you think, Dear? More than a little frightened! (*She gets up. He also rises. She speaks with a cruel eagerness.*) Let us go in now, Dear—together. I am eager to see her. I want to see how frightened she is. (*She takes his arm—tenderly*) Oh, I am so happy—so very happy, Dear!—to have my son again!

SIMON—(*tenderly*) Not half so happy as I am to have my mother again! (*They start to go off, left. Abruptly he stops—in a tone of warning advice made more effective by a provocative hint of taunting behind it*) I want to warn you again, Mother, not to underestimate your enemy. It is all very well to be confident of your possessive power, which I would be the last to deny. But remember she is strong, too. She can match your superiority of mind and spirit with her overpowering physical greed for things as they are, your dreams with her facts, your evasions with her eager acceptances. Where you are sickly and over-refined and timidly superstitious, she is healthy and would break down any door that stood between her and ownership. So take care that the moment you see her you do not surrender to her influence again and let her cunning trick you into confusing what is yours with what is hers and identifying your self with her self. You must jealously defend your separate, unique individuality, your right to freedom, or— And I know you do not want her laughing at you up her sleeve anymore, as she has been doing.

DEBORAH—(*has been listening with growing anger—blurts out*) Laughing at me! The stupid vulgar fool! If she only knew! And you are equally stupid or you could not say such idiotic things! (*arrogantly boastful*) I tell you it is I who have been laughing in my mind at her! It is I who have made a ridiculous trusting gull of her! Swindled her with lies into feeling affection and friendship so I could steal her children. How simple and blind you are, Simon, despite all your experience in marking cards and loading dice to play successfully the game of dispossession! Who made her feel that she was I, and whose will was it that made her no longer need you but banish you into lonely exile in your separate room? I tell you I have secretly intrigued from the first day you came here, schemed and deceived and hypocritically played the doting grandmother. To what end? (*She smiles gloatingly.*) Why, you should see that clearly, at least. You are here, are you not?— my son who can never wish again to leave his mother! (*She laughs with a coquettish taunting and taps his cheek playfully.*) It is singular that such a conquering Napoleon cannot recognize a complete victory and a crushing defeat when he sees them!

SIMON—(*stares at her with a curious, objectively appraising look—then with a satisfied objectively approving nod*) Yes, make yourself believe that, Mother, and you can safely defy her. After all, there is a great deal of truth in that aspect of it, as I have suspected. Your truth, of course. Not Sara's. Nor mine. And not even the whole of your truth. But you and I can wait to discover what that is later on. (*He smiles with pleasant casualness.*) Just now I think we had better go in to supper.

DEBORAH—(*pulling away, stares at him with a puzzled frightened dread*) Simon! What—? (*then conquering her fear and suddenly gloating takes his arm again—eagerly*) Yes! Let us go in. I can't wait to tell her you are going to be with me each evening, that you are now my own dear son again!

SIMON—(*sharply commanding*) No! Not until I give you permission to speak. I will choose the most effective time. (*coldly and curtly*) You will kindly not forget, Mother, all this reorganization of my home is my affair and must be carried out exactly as I have calculated. You had better not interfere if you expect me ever to keep you company. (*brusquely*) Come. It is getting late. (*She is again looking at him with bewildered dread, has shrunk back, taking her hand from his arm. But he ignores this and grasps her arm and makes her walk off beside him up the path to the house.*)

(*Curtain*)

SCENE THREE

SCENE—*Parlor of the Harford mansion—a high-ceilinged, finely-proportioned room such as one finds in the Massachusetts*

*houses designed by Bulfinch or McIntire and built in the late 1790s.
The walls and ceiling are white. A rug covers most of the floor of
waxed dark wood. A crystal chandelier hangs from the middle of
the ceiling at center, toward front. At extreme left-front a small
table against the wall, facing right, then a door leading to the
entrance hall, another chair, and farther back, a table. In the
middle of the rear wall is the door to Simon's study. On either side
of it, a chair facing front. Against the right wall, toward rear,
another table. Farther forward, a high window looking out on the
street, then a chair, and finally, at right-front, a fireplace. At left,
rear of the fireplace, is a long sofa with a small table and reading
lamp by its left end. Toward front, at left, is an oval table with
another lamp. A chair is by right rear of this table, facing right-
front. Another chair is at left-front of this table, facing directly
front. It is around nine o'clock at night of the same day.*

*Sara, Simon, and Deborah are discovered—Sara in the chair
at left-front of the table, Simon across the table from her in the
chair at rear-right of it, Deborah on the left end of the sofa by the
lamp. Sara is pretending to work on a piece of needle-point but she
is obviously preoccupied with her thoughts. Deborah has a book in
her hands but she stares over it, as preoccupied as Sara. Simon also
holds a book and keeps his eyes fixed on it but his eyes do not move
and his mind is very evidently elsewhere. All have changed their
clothes. The two women wear semi-formal evening gowns, Deborah's all white, Sara's a blue that matches the color of her eyes.
Simon is dressed in black.*

*For a moment after the curtain rises there is an atmosphere of
tense quiet in the room, an eavesdropping silence that waits, holding its breath and straining its ears. Then, as though the meaning
of the silence were becoming audible, their thoughts are heard.*

SARA—(*thinking*) Thank God, there's a moment's peace
where I can think—ever since they came in, the three of us
conversing so pleasant—as if nothing had happened—she's a
good one at hiding her feelings—you'd think, taking the children away meant nothing to her—maybe it doesn't—maybe,
like he claims, she was only pretending—no, I know she
loved them—it's her great-lady pride won't give me the satisfaction to know she's hurt—and there's something more behind it—I thought they'd never come in—I heard them

laughing once—and when they came in she looked as gay as
you please—something about him, too—sly—like there was
a secret between them— I was a fool to let him go to her
crazy garden— (*vindictively*) Well, I know he hasn't told her
yet I'm going to work with him— I'll tell her the mistress
part of it—let her try to smile when she knows that! (*impatiently with a side glance at Simon*) Why doesn't he tell her and
get it over—if he doesn't soon, I will!—

DEBORAH—(*thinking*) In the garden, at the end, I was so
sure of him—but he changed when he saw her—something
in his eyes of her old physical power over him—a reflection
of her common, vulgar prettiness—a change in her, too—I
felt her warm greedy femaleness deliberately exuding lust in a
brazen enticement—she was not half as frightened as I
hoped—still, she was uneasy—she couldn't hide her suspicion—and when he tells her he is coming to my garden every
evening she will realize her crude animalism is of no avail
now—that he is my son again— (*impatiently, with a side
glance at Simon*) Why does he wait?—does he shrink from
hurting her?—well, remembering her base betrayal of my
trust, I will not shrink!

SARA—(*reassuring herself—thinking*) Ah, I'm a fool to
waste a thought on her—hasn't he kept his word about the
children?—and don't I remember at the office how much he
wanted me—even the part of him that belongs to the Company will be mine now—all of him—and my children, too,
will be all mine!—there'll be no more sharing with her—this
is my home!—she'll be no better than a strange guest, living
on charity—let her keep to her garden where she'll harm no
one but herself—let her dream herself into a madhouse, if she
likes, as long as she leaves me and mine alone!—it'd serve her
right for her lies and meanness, trying to steal my children
when I trusted her!—

DEBORAH—(*thinking—self-reassuringly and then gloatingly*)
She is only pretending to work on her needle-point—thinking—yes, quite as frightened in her thoughts, I think, as Simon and I had hoped—it's merely my imagination that reads
desire for her in his eyes—I remember how tender he became
in the garden—how loving—how much he needed me—
my beloved son!—never to be taken from me again—every

evening in the garden I will encourage him to live with me in the past before he knew her—before he ever thought of women—to be my little boy again—I will bind him to me so he can never reject me and escape again—she will become no more than the empty name of wife, a housekeeper, a mother of children, our Irish biddy nurse girl and servant!—

SIMON—(*staring at his book—thinks with gloating satisfaction as though his mind guessed their thoughts*) I have good reason to congratulate myself, I think—all goes in accord with my plan—everything moves back into its proper place— they are divided and separate again—they do not sit together on the sofa as has been their wont—I am where I belong between them—there will be no further confusion in my mind—no devouring merging of identities—no more losing myself in their confusion—henceforth all is distinct and clearly defined—two women—opposites—whose only relation derives from the relationship of each to me—whose lives have meaning and purpose only in so far as they live within my living—henceforth this is my home and I own my own mind again!—I am a free slave-owner! (*He smiles to himself gloatingly and begins to read. As if their minds had partly sensed the tenor of his thought, the two women turn to stare at him with a stirring of suspicion and resentment. They both look quickly away.*)

SARA—(*thinking*) He isn't reading—just pretending to— smiling to himself—sly—

DEBORAH—(*her thoughts in the same key as Sara's*) What is he thinking, I wonder?—of the Company and this secretary-mistress he boasted?—I hate that smug, lustful, greedy trader's smile of his!—

SARA—(*thinking resentfully*) I know that smile—when he's managed a foxy deal for the Company and cheated someone—he spoke at the office as though he was driving a bargain for a mistress—I hope he doesn't think he'll cheat me— I was a fool to let him see I wanted him so much!—

DEBORAH—(*thinking resentfully*) It was unwise to agree so soon to his pleading—I remember, even when he was little, he realized how his begging made me weak, and he used it to get his own way—well, he will discover again, if he has forgotten, that I have ways of getting my way, too!

SARA—(*thinks self-reassuringly and a bit contemptuously*) Ah, I mustn't be uneasy—didn't he show he wanted me as much as I want him?—or maybe more, if I'd tried—so why should I worry my mind?—I'll attend to my needle-point and not let these foolish thoughts disturb me— (*She begins to work determinedly.*)

DEBORAH—(*thinks self-reassuringly*) This is senseless and stupid!—to make myself uneasy and resentful—after he's proved so conclusively—it's unfair to him—I'll be sensible and read my book— (*She begins to read determinedly. There is a pause of silence. It is Simon who stops attempting to distract his mind first. His eyes cease reading and stare at the book pre-occupiedly.*)

SIMON—(*thinking*) Yes, I think I can foresee every move of my present campaign here—not even Napoleon planning Austerlitz—Good God, what an insane comparison!—Mother's romantic influence!—nevertheless, I can prophesy exactly every possible development in this battle—but will this one victory insure a peace of perpetual conquest?—who knows? —the immediate future is all I can foretell clearly—my plan doesn't go beyond—I don't even know yet what I wish the final outcome to be, or what is the exact nature of the final peace I want to impose— (*with forced self-reassurance*) Bah! I will cross those bridges when I come to them—sufficient for the day that I control the game now and can have it played as I wish—make them think that each may win—deal the marked cards to give each in turn the semblance of winning so each may mistake losses for gains— (*frowning again— uneasily*) But it means I must always remain in the game my-self—be as careful and watchful now outside the office as in it—never relax my vigilance—there is always the danger of failure—bankruptcy and ruin—alliance of devouring ene-mies—an unceasing duel to the death with life!— (*He makes an unconscious shrinking movement of dread—determinedly self-scornful*) Bah! What nonsense! You would think I saw myself as the victor's spoils—when it is I who will be the victor— (*He tries to read again but at once gives up the attempt.*) I can-not concentrate on this damned book—I read a paragraph and do not remember the sense or find any meaning—

DEBORAH—(*has ceased reading and is staring over her book—*

thinking resentfully) I cannot read—my eyes follow words but that is all—I feel a restless dread—I cannot help remembering the past—he has awakened so much I had hoped was dead—it is a dangerous price to pay—

SARA—(*has stopped sewing—thinks irritably*) It's no good!—I can't put my mind on sewing—I feel something is staring over my shoulder—watching my thoughts pushing and crowding in my brain like a lot of mad sheep something has frightened, and I'm not able to stop them—it's strange here tonight—it's not the house it's been—not home at all—there's no peace— (*Unconsciously she sighs regretfully.*) It's so changed from the contented way we've been here nights for so long—she and I would be sitting together on the sofa laughing and telling each other about the children—he'd sit alone, thinking out schemes for his Company—minding his own business and not bothering us—

DEBORAH—(*with a little shudder*) Yes, a frightening price to demand of me—to release the forgotten Deborah who was his mother from the tomb of the past—how silly he acted about the summerhouse—a grown man—nothing is sacred or secret to him—how tense the quiet is in this house to-night—as though a bomb were concealed in the room with a fuse slowly sputtering toward—and the silence waits—holding its breath—hands clapped over its ear—a strange haunted house—so changed from what it was last night—and every night for years—she would sit here by my side—we would laugh together, thinking of the children—I had forgotten him sitting alone there—he might have been a million miles away—he was buried in the past—I did not need him—

SIMON—(*thinking—uneasily*) Perhaps I should have waited—until I had determined the true nature of the final conquest I desire more clearly—I am more cautious with my campaigns for the Company—I calculate first exactly what I want to win—am sure the game is worth the candle—the unceasing vigilance it will demand of me is going to prove an added strain—it begins already—my home is becoming a battlefield—so different from other nights—there was peace here, of a kind—at least an atmosphere in which I could be indifferent to their existence and concentrate on my ambitions for the Company—a man's work in a man's world of fact and reality— (*irritably*) What made their petty sentimental women's world of lies and trivial greeds assume such a false importance?—why did I have to meddle in their contemptible ambitions and let them involve me in a domestic squabble about the ownership of children?—I, the leader of a great Company, a figure of first importance in the life of a great city, a man men fear and envy—

SARA—(*regretfully*) Much as I ought to hate her now for the sneak he showed her to be, I can't help wishing he'd never told me—he's a fool to think she could ever have taken my children—I can keep what's mine from the devil himself—it may be weak of me but I wish I could have kept on thinking she was my friend and trusting her—feeling proud of having helped her—

DEBORAH—(*regretfully*) Much as I detest her treachery, I find something in me wishing he had not unmasked her—is there any one of us whose soul, stripped naked, is not ugly with meanness?—life is at best a polite pretending not to see one another—a game in which we tacitly agree to make believe we are not what we are—a covenant not to watch one's friends too clearly, for the sake of friendship—and I have grown to lean upon her health and strength—as one leans against a tree, deep rooted in the common earth—and what if she had taken the children?—if she had done it herself, I would have understood her jealousy—I have been a loving mother, too—I would have forgiven her, remembering my own greed—

SARA—(*as though responding to Deborah's thought, gives Simon a resentful look*) If only he hadn't interfered—why did he take the sudden notion to start minding our business?—

SIMON—(*frowning—thinks self-exasperatedly*) What stupid impulse drove me to start taking a hand in their measly woman's game—now, of all times, when I've just assumed the added responsibility of the railroad!—what the devil possessed me to ask Sara to come to the office?—now I won't have a separate man's life free of woman even there!

SARA—(*thinking resentfully*) If I hadn't gone to his office —I had a feeling I shouldn't—that he was up to some scheme—

SIMON—(*thinking*) What bosh to tell her I needed a secretary!—she'll only be in my way—and I'll have no privacy—she'll pry greedily into everything—

SARA—(*thinking*) As if I hadn't enough to do taking care of my home and my children without his making me slave for his Company! (*scornfully*) Is he that weak he can't even manage his own man's business without my—?

SIMON—(*thinking*) My ridiculous proposal to make her my mistress!—if I wanted one I could buy girls by the dozen—young and pretty—fresh and not yet possessed—not a body I already own—which possession has made worthless to me—if she hopes she can ever again make me the greedy slave to it I once was— (*He turns to stare at her with a vindictive hostility.*)

SARA—(*thinking—not noticing he is looking at her*) If he thinks his asking me to be his mistress pleased me—treating his wife as if she was a whore he'd pick up on the street and ask her price—and he ought to know I was through wanting him—content he'd left me free to sleep by myself in peace—I was a fool to let him hug and kiss me like he did at the office and make me remember—make me like a beast in heat that's a slave to her need and can't help herself—but I'll show him it will be the other way round this time, and I'll be the one to keep free! (*She turns to stare at him with revengeful hostility then, as they meet each other's eyes, each turns away guiltily. Forcing a casual tone—speaks to him.*) Yes, Simon? You were going to speak to me?

SIMON—(*in a like casual tone*) I? No. I thought you—

SARA—No.

SIMON—I was preoccupied with my thoughts.

SARA—So was I.

SIMON—(*a taunt coming into his tone*) I was thinking of Mother, as it happens.

SARA—(*casually*) That's strange. So was I. (*Neither of them looks at her. A pause.*)

DEBORAH—(*thinking—resentfully*) He lied—he said that to hurt her—much as I ought to hate her, I pity her when I see him deliberately trying to humiliate—and if he was thinking of me, it is against my wishes—just as his coming to my garden this afternoon—forcing his way in—one would think a man of his birth and breeding would have more delicacy—would not desire to come where he knows he is unwelcome—

SIMON—(*thinking—resentfully*) By that lie I've put Mother back in my mind—what impelled me to visit her garden again—mysterious summerhouse—all that insane nonsense—Good God, I'll be playing with toys next, and begging her to tell me a fairy tale!—so damned weak of me to offer to visit her each evening—I have no time to waste humoring her senile whims and pretending to take her crazy dreams of romance seriously— (*He stares at her with vindictive hostility.*)

DEBORAH—(*thinking with bitter hostility*) His proposal to visit me each evening—as if he were doing me a favor, forsooth!—I do not want him intruding on my life—I never even wanted him to be conceived—I was glad to be rid of him when he was born—he had made my beauty grotesquely ugly by his presence, bloated and misshapen, disgusting to myself—and then the compulsion to love him after he was born—like a fate forced on me from without, in spite of myself, not of my own will, making me helpless and weak—love like an enslaving curse laid on my heart—my life made dependent on another's living, my happiness at the mercy of another's selfish whims— (*She turns to stare at him with vindictive hostility. Then, as each meets the other's eyes, each turns away guiltily.*)

SIMON—(*speaks to her forcing a casual tone*) Yes, Mother? You wanted to speak to me?

DEBORAH—(*echoing his tone*) No, Simon. I thought you—

SIMON—No. (*then with a taunt in his tone*) I was not thinking of you, but of Sara.

DEBORAH—(*carelessly*) That is strange, I was thinking of her, too. (*Neither of them look at her. A pause.*)

SARA—(*thinking—resentfully*) He lied to her—it's little thought he ever gives me anymore except when his lust wants something—he said that to hurt her—he's sneering at her—poor woman!—I find it hard to hate her—there's too much pity in my heart—she can't read her book—she's too upset—she's thinking how she'll miss the children—alone all day—I won't be here to keep her company—he'll have me at the office—alone in the past, where she'll have nothing but her old mad dreams to turn to for comfort—he'll have her in an asylum in the end, if he's not careful!—it's a terrible thing he can hate his own mother so!—I didn't even hate my father that much—and if I did hate him, it was on account of my poor mother—the way he sneered at her—Simon sneers at his mother—and Deborah has been like a mother to me—I was proud of having a second mother who's a great lady of a fine Yankee family, who doesn't talk in ignorant brogue like my poor mother did, and is too proud to let love for any man make a fool and a slave of her—who has always kept herself free and independent— (*bewilderedly*) Ah, what makes me remember the past and get the dead mixed up with the living in my mind—like he said he's confused Deborah and me in his mind—his mind, that's just it—it's he that brings confusion to us!

DEBORAH—(*thinking bitterly*) This is all his doing—the malicious plot of a greedy, evil, morbidly jealous child—I know he has lied to me—that he drove her to betray my trust—she would never of her own will—she had begun to look upon me as a second mother—to come to me for advice—to look up to me—and I was happy to regard her as my daughter—because in her affectionate trust I felt safe from myself—because her strength and health and acceptance of life gave me a faith in my own living—a support—and now he dares to take that security away from me!—to offer me in exchange an insane confusion—ghosts from the past to haunt me—with the insolence of one doing a favor or bearing a gift!—

SARA—(*thinking*) Why do I let him?—I'm not helpless—I'm not a thought he moves around in his mind to suit his pleasure—I ought to go to her now and talk with her truthfully—get her to be truthful with me—I'll forgive her if she'll forgive me—and between us we can soon put an end to his tricks!—

DEBORAH—(*thinking*) What fools we are to allow him to do this to us!—if she'd sit with me here as on other nights, we'd understand and forgive each other—with her strength and health beside me, I can defend myself against his greedy dreams—I have only to call her over— (*They both speak to each other simultaneously*—"Sara" "Deborah." *They bend forward so they can see each other past him and they smile at each other with a relieved understanding. Deborah speaks with a strange gentleness.*) Yes, Daughter. I ought to have known you guessed my thoughts.

SARA—(*getting up—with a gentle smile*) Maybe I did Mother—and I hope you guessed mine. May I come and sit with you?

DEBORAH—I was going to ask you to. Of course you may, Dear. (*Sara goes around the table and passes behind Simon, ignoring him, and goes to the sofa. Deborah pats the sofa on her left, smiling an affectionate welcome.*) This is your place, you know, beside me.

SARA—(*bends impulsively and gives her a daughterly kiss on the cheek*) I know, Mother. (*She sits down, close beside her, so their arms touch.*)

SIMON—(*who has been pretending to read—with contemptuous relief*) Ah, so they have decided to forget and forgive—well, I confess I feel relieved—this hate was becoming a living presence in the room—and in my mind—I felt hopelessly involved in it—through my own fault, too—I was stupid to meddle—but now we will be back where we were on other nights and my mind is free to mind its own business— (*A sudden sly malicious look comes to his face.*) Meanwhile, keeping an eye on them to make sure this sentimental reunion is not too successful—but each is lying and acting, of course—playing the hypocrite in the hope of gaining some advantage—it will be amusing to watch—

SARA—(*turns to Deborah with impulsive frankness*) I want to beg your forgiveness, Mother—about the children. It was mean of me to let myself be made jealous, and not to trust you.

DEBORAH—(*takes her hand—gently*) I understand. One cannot help being jealous. It is part of the curse of love.

SARA—(*with a quick resentful look at Simon*) Yes, you do feel cursed by it when it's too greedy.

DEBORAH—(*patting Sara's hand*) Thank goodness, we've understood each other and what might have developed into a stupid quarrel is all forgotten now, isn't it?

SARA—Yes, and I'm happy to be here beside you again, feeling your trust and friendship—

DEBORAH—(*presses her hand and keeps it in hers*) And I'm so happy to have you back, Dear. I had begun to feel so weak and at the mercy of the past.

SARA—(*gently*) Ah now, don't think of what's past. (*with bullying affection*) Shame on you and you with four handsome grandchildren to love, and everything in life to live for.

DEBORAH—(*eagerly*) Then I may have the children back?

SARA—Indeed you may! And remember I wasn't really the one who took them away from you. (*She casts a resentful look at Simon.*)

DEBORAH—(*deeply moved*) You are so kind and generous, Dear! I hate myself for having permitted my mind to be tempted— (*She gives Simon a bitter hostile look.*) But that's over. We have beaten him. (*A pause. The two women sit with clasped hands, staring defiantly at Simon.*)

SIMON—(*moves restlessly, his eyes fixed on the book—thinking with a forced, uneasy derision*) Is it possible, after all that has happened between us today, that they actually hope to re-establish their selfish, greedy union—which denied me and shut me out and left me alone— (*bitterly vindictive*) Then I'll soon prove to them— Mother forgets I haven't told Sara yet about my plan to visit her every evening from now on—and Sara forgets Mother doesn't know yet she is to be the mistress I—I have hesitated to tell them so far because—because what?—because I know that then the die will be cast irrevocably, and there can be no possible turning back?—because something in me is afraid?— (*forcing a self-scornful tone*) afraid?—nonsense!—it is for them to be afraid—but I wish I could see the exact nature of the final plan I desire more clearly before I—

SARA—(*as if influenced by his thought, gives him a quick resentful look—slowly*) All the same, Deborah, I know how unhappy you felt, sitting alone here. I was miserable myself over there with him between us.

DEBORAH—(*glancing at Simon resentfully—lowering her voice to a whisper*) Yes. That's just it, Sara. We must never again allow him to come between—

SARA—(*in a whisper*) Ah! It was he who made me believe you were trying to steal my children's love from me. (*They bend closer to each other until their heads are about touching, and all during the following scene talk in whispers, their eyes fixed on Simon.*)

DEBORAH—I am sure he did. Just as he tried to make me believe you had gone to his office with the deliberate purpose of betraying me.

SARA—(*stares at Simon with bitter hostility*) So that's what he told you, is it? It's a lie. It was all his scheming. He asked me to come there.

DEBORAH—Yes, I see that clearly now.

SARA—I wonder what mad trick he's up to. Why can't he leave us in peace? What more can he want of us? Haven't we given him all of our time he's any right to? (*bitterly*) But men are the devil's own children! They're never content. They must always grab for more.

DEBORAH—(*bitterly*) It's true. You bear them and hope you are free, but it's only the beginning of a new slavery, for they start with their first cry to accuse you and complain of their fate like weaklings and demand your life as if it were their right to possess you!

SARA—It's seeing us content with our children without him. He can't bear the thought—

DEBORAH—(*beginning to smile with vindictive satisfaction*) Yes, he was always a greedy jealous boy. That's where we may have him at our mercy, I think, Sara. His jealousy drives him to need us. But we already have four sons—

SARA—(*beginning to smile, too*) And so we don't have to need him. (*She laughs softly and jeeringly and Deborah laughs with her. Simon stirs uneasily and his eyes cease to follow the lines and stare at the page.*)

DEBORAH—Yes, the more I consider it, Sara, the more confident I feel that it is really he who is helpless and lonely and lost—who begs for love and is completely at our mercy!

SARA—(*threateningly*) Then let him look out how he plays scheming tricks to destroy our peace! We might lose patience with his greediness and he'd find himself driven out in the night without—to sleep in his office with his Company for a mistress!

SIMON—(*his eyes staring on his book now—thinking with a tense dread*) I still feel hatred like a living presence in this room—stronger—drawing closer—surrounding—threatening—me— (*fighting himself*) But that's absurd—they hate each other now— (*frightenedly*) But it seems to have gotten very cold in this room—nonsense!—you know it is an extremely warm night—but it has become dark in here and the room is unfamiliar—nonsense!—it's the same old parlor in the house where you were born and the lamps burn brightly—but surely it cannot be my imagination that Mother and Sara have vanished—as on so many nights before—Mother took her hand and led her back—as if she opened a door into the past in whose darkness they vanished to reappear as one woman—a woman recalling Mother as I knew her long ago—but not her—a stranger woman—unreal, a ghost inhumanely removed from living, beautiful and coldly remote and arrogant and proud—with eyes deliberately blind—with a smile deliberately amused by its own indifference—because she no longer wants me—has taken all she needed—I have served my purpose—she has ruthlessly got rid of me—she is free—and I am left lost in myself, with nothing! (*He has dropped the book in his lap and straightened himself tensely, gripping the arms of his chair, staring before him frightenedly. As his thoughts have progressed, the expressions on the two women's faces have mirrored his description as though, subconsciously, their mood was created by his mind. They become proudly arrogant and coldly indifferent to him. He goes on thinking with increasing dread.*) But it is different now—that is what she was on other nights—her nature has changed—not indifferent now—she stares at me with hate—she is revengeful and evil—a cannibal witch whose greed will devour! (*Their expressions have changed to revengeful gloating cruelty and they stare at him with hate. He starts forward in his chair as if he were about to fly in horror from the room.*)

DEBORAH—(*smiling gloatingly*) See, Sara, he is not even pretending to read now. He is thinking. He must have heard what we were whispering; he looks so uneasy and defeated.

SARA—(*smiling gloatingly*) As scared as if he saw a ghost!

DEBORAH—(*her tone becoming contemptuously pitying*) So like a little boy who is lost.

SARA—(*contemptuously pitying*) Yes, that's like him. There's so much of that weakness in him. Maybe that's what I've loved most in him.

DEBORAH—Because it makes him need you so terribly! Oh, I know! I know so well! I remember— (*Her expression softens to a condescending maternal tenderness.*) Perhaps we are being too hard on him. After all, what he has tried to do has been so obviously childish and futile.

SARA—It's because he's jealous, and that proves how much he loves us.

DEBORAH—Yes, I think instead of being angry, we should merely be amused, as we would be at the mischief of a bad sulky boy.

SARA—(*smilingly—complacently maternal*) And forgive him if he promises not to do it again.

DEBORAH—(*smiling like Sara*) He won't, I know, as soon as he is compelled to realize he can't gain anything by being wicked—except to be severely punished. (*She speaks to Simon with an amused, teasing smile.*) Wake up, Dear! (*He starts and turns to stare at them bewilderedly.*) Why do you stare as if we were strangers?

SARA—(*teasingly*) It's like he always is lately. His mind is so full of grand schemes for the Company we might as well be in another world! (*laughingly*) You might be more polite to your ladies, Darling.

SIMON—(*as if suddenly emerging from a spell—with an impulsive grateful relief*) Ah! Thank God, each of you is here again! (*He checks himself abruptly and looks away from them hastily and hurries on in a confused, evasive, explanatory tone.*) I beg your pardon. I had forgotten you were here. I was thinking of the Company's affairs. I must have dozed off and dreamed—

DEBORAH—(*turns to Sara—with gloating amusement*) He must have dreamed we no longer loved him. (*She smiles at Simon with a tender, scornful pity.*) My poor boy! Do tell us what you dreamed. (*He ignores her. She laughs teasingly.*) He won't do it, Sara. He was always stubbornly secretive about his dreams, even as a little boy. And so greedily inquisitive about mine. That was the unfair part. He thought I had no right to have any secrets from him. (*She calls teasingly*) Simon. Why don't you answer me? What was it you dreamed just now that made you so afraid? (*He doesn't seem to hear. She laughs softly.*) No, it's no good, Sara. He is pretending to be quite oblivious to our existence again, to be too deeply absorbed in his great schemes of manly ambition, inspired by the career of Napoleon! But we know he is very uneasy now, not sure of himself at all, wondering what we will decide to do about him.

SARA—(*with a little laugh*) Yes, he has a guilty conscience and he knows he ought to be punished.

SIMON—(*as if he hadn't heard them, but confusedly apologetic and almost humbly placating and apprehensive, avoiding their eyes*) I—I am afraid I interrupted a private discussion between you. I remember now you were whispering together. Pray continue. I am interested in this book and you need not mind my presence. You can dismiss me from your minds entirely—for the present. I will even regard it as a favor if you do, because, to be truthful, your thinking of me intrudes on my thoughts and confuses me—at a time when it is imperative I concentrate my mind on defining the exact nature of the final goal of my ambition, precisely what peace I desire to impose after—

SARA—(*contemptuously*) Ah, he's off at the head of his Company again, Deborah, prancing on a great white thoroughbred Arab stallion around and around his mind, like old Boney himself! (*with a strange boastfulness*) But don't forget, Darling, I'm my father's daughter and wasn't he an officer and a gentleman who helped the Duke drive old Boney out of Spain, and took all he'd gained from him!

DEBORAH—(*smiling teasingly*) Yes, I agree with you that whatever plans he makes now concern us in making our plans. If he didn't want us to mind him, he shouldn't have minded our business, should he? (*She laughs softly, teasing and Sara laughs with her. Simon ignores them, staring at his book, pretending to read but his eyes are motionless. Deborah goes on.*) But, of course, if by not mind he means not take too seriously, we agree, don't we? We mustn't mind him. We must make allowances and not judge him too harshly. He has always been a romantic boy in whose backward imagination everything became confused—real life with fairy tales—facts with poetic fancies—common summerhouses with enchanted palaces—and heaven knows what other incredible, presumptuous nonsense! Everyone who ever knew him in the old days considered him a queer, erratic boy, subject to spells in which he was irresponsible and impracticable—a little crazy, to be frank. His own father never thought him strictly dependable. Even I have been afraid at times he has inherited a stupid folly of grandeur hallucination—from my father, who, as I have confessed to you, Sara, was a weak minister who in dreams confused Napoleon with himself and with God. (*Her tone has become strange, and bitterly sneering, and she stares before her, smiling with a taunting scorn. Abruptly she checks herself and turns to Sara with a change to a tone of growing, condescending pity.*) So we must be fair and not punish his naughtiness too severely, poor boy.

SARA—(*with condescending pity*) Ah no, we know he loves us and means no harm, poor darling.

DEBORAH—(*a threat in her tone now*) But we better make it clear to him right now we will not tolerate any more of his malicious meddling in our affairs. (*She turns to Simon.*) Listen, Simon. When you interrupted us we were discussing your stupid attempt to ruin the peace and harmony of your home and destroy with your morbid jealousy the trust and loving friendship that exists between your wife and mother—

SARA—(*bitterly*) Yes, wouldn't it divert him from worrying about the Company to have us fight a duel to the death to see which of us he'd deign to give his love to!

DEBORAH—(*coldly*) Unfortunately, Simon, while you may be extremely successful in swindling men at their childish gambling for material possessions, you are far too transparent to cheat us with your obviously marked cards and clumsily loaded dice when you venture to play for the possession of love.

SARA—Yes, we're more than a match for you there. So you'd better stop right now, for your own good.

DEBORAH—(*smiles at him now, cajolingly affectionate*) But we have agreed to forgive you, Dear—just because you are such a silly jealous boy.

SARA—Because you've proved, Darling, how dearly you love us.

DEBORAH—And because, now that we know how much you need our love, we cannot blame you for feeling bitter because we let the children take your place so completely. We admit that was very wrong of us. But, you see, Dear, we had misunderstood your seeming preoccupation with the Company's affairs. You should have told us you couldn't be happy without our love. We were completely taken in by your pretending. (*to Sara—tenderly mocking*) He appeared to be so free; didn't he, Sara?

SARA—(*smiles teasingly*) He did. As independent as you please!

DEBORAH—(*teasingly penitent*) We are sorry, Dear. We humbly beg your forgiveness.

SARA—(*with the same air*) We promise it won't happen again, Darling. We'll never let you out of our love again.

DEBORAH—You will be our first born and best beloved again. (*teasing with a coquettish, enticing air*) So now won't you forget and make up with us, Dear? (*Simon continues to stare at the book as if he did not hear them.*)

SARA—(*cajolingly*) Come over here and sit with us now, that's a good lad. You look so lost over there alone. (*She moves over and pats the sofa between her and Deborah—enticingly*) Look, you can sit here and have love all around you. What man could ask more of life? (*mockingly*) You'll be between us, as you've been trying to be.

DEBORAH—(*laughingly*) Yes, I do not think there is any danger in that now, Sara. (*She pats the sofa invitingly.*) Come, Dear. (*He does not seem to hear. Deborah laughs softly.*) What? Still so vain and stubborn? (*to Sara*) Well, since the mountain is too proud to come to Mahomet— (*She takes Sara's hand and they rise to their feet. Their arms around each other's waists, they advance on Simon with mocking, enticing smiles. They are like two mothers who, confident of their charm, take a possessive gratification in teasing a young, bashful son. But there is something more behind this—the calculating coquetry of two prostitutes trying to entice a man.*) We must humor his manly pride, Sara. Anything to keep peace in our home! (*She laughs.*)

SARA—(*laughingly*) Yes. Anything to give him his way, as long as it's our way! (*They have come to Simon who stares as if he did not notice their approach, and yet instinctively shrinks back in his chair. They group together in back of him, Deborah at left-rear and Sara at right-rear of his chair. They bend over, each with an arm about the other, until their faces touch the side of his head. Their other arms go around him so that their hands touch on his chest.*)

DEBORAH—(*teasing tenderly*) Now don't shrink back into yourself, Dear. Why are you so afraid?

SARA—(*teasing tenderly*) We're not going to eat you, Darling, if you are that sweet. (*Their arms hug him, tenderly possessive.*)

SIMON—(*tensely, his eyes in a fixed stare on the page of his book thinking with a mingling of fascinated dread and an anguished yearning*) I cannot keep them separate—they will not remain divided—they unite in spite of me—they are too strong here in their home—the stronghold of woman, the possessor of children—it is a mistake in strategy to attack them here—they unite against the invader—they hate as one— (*more confusedly*) But I must remember they only seem to become one—it is due to the confusion of my thoughts—it exists only in my mind—an hallucination, a dream, not a fact of reality—but I feel her arms around me—they are real—and she is good now, not evil—she loves me—she does not hate me because she loves me, as she always did before—I need not fear her revenge—that she is waiting for an opportunity to get rid of me—no, I can trust her now at last—she is mine and so I can surrender and be hers, as I have always desired— (*He relaxes with a dreamy smile of content in their arms and murmurs drowsily in gentle wonder*) Why, I see clearly now that this is the final conquest and peace I must have had in mind when I planned my campaign—and I have won the deciding victory over them already! (*He gives a strange chuckle of satisfaction, and closes his eyes.*)

DEBORAH—(*smiles, maternally gloating and tenderly possessive*) You see, Sara. There was no cause for us to be afraid. (*with a strange contemptuous arrogance*) I can always, whenever I wish, make him my little boy again. (*She kisses him on the cheek.*) Can't I, Dear?

SARA—(*gives her a quick resentful jealous look*) I wasn't the one who was afraid. Don't I know whenever I want, I can make him my lover again, who'd give anything he has for me! (*She kisses his other cheek.*) Can't I, Darling? (*She and Deborah suddenly turn and stare at each other with defiant, jealous enmity over his head, pulling their hands away so they no longer touch on his chest, but each still holds him. Simon starts and stiffens in his chair.*)

DEBORAH—(*fighting with herself*) Sara—forgive me—I didn't mean—it's what he did in the garden made me forget— (*pleadingly*) But we mustn't let ourselves forget, Sara. We must remember what he has tried to do! We must keep united and defend the peace of our home as one woman or—

SARA—(*penitently*) I know—I shouldn't have said—it's what he did to me at the office—but I won't forget again. (*Their hands touch around Simon again but now he strains forward against them.*)

SIMON—(*thinking bitterly*) Fool! To allow myself to be swindled by that mad dream again! Your final victory and peace, eh? Are you insane? She loves none but herself, I tell you! She is greedy and evil! Trust her and you will only find yourself again driven out beyond a wall, with nothing, with the door slammed shut forever behind you, and the sound of her mocking arrogant laughter—left alone to marry the first unscrupulous schemer with a beautiful body you meet who wishes to sell herself and fulfill her greedy ambition to own a slave and use him to acquire children and wealth and a nouveau-riche estate!—No! (*He jerks forward to his feet from their arms. They each give a frightened pleading cry. He turns to stare from one to the other for a moment in a dazed awakening confusion—stammering*) Ah! You are both there. I thought—I beg your pardon—I must have dozed off again and dreamed— (*then with increasing hostility and derision*) But no, it couldn't have been all a dream, for I remember your coming over to me. I remember watching you with amusement and saying to myself: What damned hypocrites they are! By God, if I didn't know each of them so well I would be swindled into believing in their sincerity! Each has learned tricks of deceit from the other! Mother has made Sara almost as convincing an actress as she is, while she has stolen from Sara a false appearance of honest frankness which lends a common natural air to her romantic artificiality! (*then curtly and rudely*) Well, now that the little farce is

over, if you will permit me to sit down and return where
you belong— (*The two women's faces grow cold and hostile and
defiant. But they are also full of dread.*)

DEBORAH—(*ignoring him, takes Sara's hand*) Come, Sara.
(*They pass behind him to sit on the sofa side by side, as before,
clasping each other's hand. They stare at Simon defiantly and apprehensively. He sits in his chair and stares at his book again,
pretending to ignore them.*)

SIMON—(*thinking uneasily*) I feel their hate again—there
is no doubt now it is against me—it was a stupid blunder to
attack them openly in the woman's home where they have
made themselves so strong—my attack has only served to
unite them— (*calculatingly*) But one learns by one's mistakes—in future, I shall wait until I have each alone—at the
office—the garden—at night here, I shall remain apart—lock
myself in my study, if need be, for greater safety—safety?—
what nonsense!—what have I to fear?—it is I who deal the
cards and control the game—who cannot lose— (*calculating
more confidently and gloatingly now*) Yes, if I am not here they
must turn upon each other—they cannot keep up this pretense—which is all for my benefit— (*He gives them a quick
glance—then, as his eyes meet their hostility, he hastily brings
them back to his work—uneasily*) How they stare—their hatred
for me is obvious now—I shall be glad to be alone in my
study—I can think of something more important than this
damned, petty domestic war—I almost regret now I ever
should have considered it important enough to make its confusion a decisive issue— (*He suddenly looks up but avoids their
eyes—with a forced angry resentment*) For God's sake, why do
you stare like that? Have you no business of your own to
mind, or no thought of your own to think? (*He snaps his book
shut and springs to his feet—angrily to conceal his apprehension*)
Can I never have a moment's privacy in my own home in
which I can think clearly? I work like a slave all day to stuff
your insatiable maws with luxury and wealth and gross security for the rearing of children! Is it too much to ask in return
that I be permitted a little peace of mind at night here, and
not have my thoughts constantly invaded and distracted?
(*with an attempt at assertive dictatorial authority that rings hollow*) You force me to remind you of a fact you have chosen

to ignore, that I am the man of this household and the master. I will not tolerate any more of your interference! If you persist in it, I will be compelled to force either one or the other of you to leave my home—and my life!—forever! That is my final warning! (*He turns toward the door at left, avoiding their eyes. His domineering tone becomes even less convincing.*) I'm going to my study. Hereafter, I shall spend my evenings there alone, and you may do as you please. Tear this house apart, destroy it, devour each other in your jealous rage and hatred, if you must, until only one of you survives! After all, that would be one solution of— But leave me alone! I will not let you involve me and attempt to tear me in half between you! It will be useless for you to try to hound me in my study, for I shall lock myself in! (*He strides to the study door and opens it—then turns, avoiding their eyes, and murmurs in strange, confused, weakly apologetic tones*) I—I beg your pardon for being rude—I am worn out—have worked too hard on this railroad deal—and now I have it, I seem to have nothing—in victory I feel defeated—the winnings seem like disguised losses—that naturally confuses my mind— (*He pauses. Suddenly he has the beaten quality of one begging for pity. But they remain staring as one at him, their eyes hard and unforgiving. He stammers appealingly*) You—you know how much I love each of you—it is only when you unite to dispossess me that you compel me to defend my right to what is mine—all I ask is that each of you keep your proper place in my mind—do not trespass or infringe on the other's property— (*Abruptly his tone becomes slyly taunting.*) But I am forgetting I arranged all that today. I will leave you now to inform each other of the secret you are each so cunningly concealing. I think, when you have, the issue will be quite clear and free of confusion. (*He smiles sneeringly but is afraid to meet their eyes. He turns quickly, goes in his study, and locks the door. They stare at the door. There is a moment's silence.*)

DEBORAH—(*slowly, hardly above a whisper, but with a taunting, threatening scorn in her tone*) He has locked the door. (*She smiles faintly.*) I have a suspicion, Sara, that our big jealous boy has become very frightened and wishes now he hadn't been so wicked—now, when it's too late.

SARA—(*smiling faintly*) I have the same suspicion myself, Deborah.

DEBORAH—(*uneasily*) Too late for him, I mean. We have seen through him. We know what he is trying to do. We know what he really is now, in his heart. How vindictive and evil—and mad! I do not recognize him now as the son I gave life to—and once loved. And I am sure you do not recognize in this strange evil man, embittered and hateful—

SARA—(*bitterly*) No, he's not the man I loved and gave myself to. I never would have—to this man.

DEBORAH—(*urgent and a little desperate*) But we mustn't let him make it too late for us—to continue to be as we have been to each other. We have proved now that as long as we constantly remember that this is something his mind is trying to do to our minds—to make them as evil and vindictive—and mad!—as his—to poison them with his hatred—we can successfully defend our home from ruin and remain united in trust and friendship and love, and keep him outside us where he is powerless, and in the end force him to surrender and submit rather than have us drive him from his home! Promise me you will never forget this, Sara. I swear to you I will not!

SARA—And I swear to you, Deborah! I know it's all the poison in his mind trying to make our minds the slave of his, so he can own us body and soul. Do you think I could ever hate you the way I did when you came in with him from the garden, if he hadn't poisoned my mind with the past at his office?

DEBORAH—(*slowly*) Yes, he is very clever at poisoning with the past. (*She shudders—then urgently*) But we have sworn to each other! We will remember it is he and not us!

SARA—Yes!

DEBORAH—(*hesitates uneasily—then trying desperately to be confidently matter-of-fact, and forcing a smile*) Then I think we can now safely tell each other what the arrangements he spoke of are. As far as I am concerned, I was hiding mine from you only because he said he wished to tell you and made me promise I wouldn't.

SARA—He did the same with me. (*with a sudden underlying*

hostility) I was only too eager to let you know. (*then guiltily*) I mean—

DEBORAH—(*stiffening*) Yes, I can imagine you were. But I think not any more eager than I was— (*She checks herself. In silence, the two women fight together within themselves to conquer this hostility. Then Deborah says gently*) Tell me your secret, Daughter. Whatever it is, I will remember it is his doing, and I will understand.

SARA—(*gratefully*) Thank you, Mother. And I'll understand when you tell me— (*She blurts out hastily with an undercurrent of guilty defiance*) It's nothing much. He got me to agree to work with him at his office from now on. I'm to start tomorrow—

DEBORAH—(*her expression startled and unable to conceal an uprush of jealous hate*) Ah! Then you are the woman he boasted he was living with as a— (*Instinctively she withdraws her hand from Sara's.*)

SARA—(*bitterly*) You said you'd understand!

DEBORAH—(*contritely—grabbing her hand again*) I will! I do!

SARA—(*hurriedly and guiltily evasive*) I'm to be his secretary and a secret partner. He seemed so nervous and tired out and distracted, and he asked me wouldn't I please help him with his work and share— It's something I always used to want to do. I used to feel I was shut out of that part of his life. (*appealingly*) You can understand that, Deborah?

DEBORAH—(*sneeringly*) I can. I know only too well how greedy— (*fighting this back—guiltily*) I mean, it is your right. Of course I understand, Sara.

SARA—(*reacting to the sneer—defensively*) It's my right, surely. I'm glad you admit that. (*A gloating boast comes into her tone.*) He said he was so lonely. He said he missed me so much and wouldn't I let him have a life just with me again away from home. He said I was still so beautiful to him and how much he wanted me, and I knew he was telling the truth, so I was only too happy to give my consent.

DEBORAH—(*angrily*) Ah! (*She again jerks her hand away.*)

SARA—(*guiltily*) I'm sorry. I didn't mean to boast. (*She reaches for Deborah's hand again.*) But that isn't all of it. Wait till you hear the rest and you won't be angry. I could feel the change in him as he is now in his office—that he's grown so greedy and unscrupulous and used to having his own way as head of the Company, that if I refused him, he'd only buy another woman to take my place and I'd lose him. (*pleadingly*) So you see he had the power to make me consent. You can understand that, can't you? You're a woman, too.

DEBORAH—(*tensely*) I am making myself understand. Besides, this has nothing to do with me. It is entirely your business.

SARA—(*bitterly*) Yes, business. That's the way he talked. You'd think he was making a deal for his Company. If you think I liked him insulting his wife and acting as if I was a street whore he'd picked up and was asking her price—

DEBORAH—(*tensely*) Why should I think of it, Sara? It's entirely your affair. (*She pauses—then strangely with an increasingly bitter vindictiveness*) But—you appealed to me as a woman, didn't you? You mean forget he is anything to me. I can. I have forgotten him several times before in my life. Completely as if he had never been born. That is what he has never forgiven. If I were in your place I would hate him, and I would revenge myself by becoming what he wished me to be! I would become it so ruthlessly that, in the end, he would feel cursed by having what he wanted! I would make him pay for me until I had taken everything he possessed! I would make all his power my power! Until I had stripped him bare and utterly ruined him! Until I had made him a weak slave with no ambition left but his greed for me! And when he had no more to pay me, I would drive him out of my life to beg outside my door! And I would laugh at him and never permit him to return—! (*She stops abruptly—guiltily*) But it is really none of my business, Sara. I do not mean to interfere between husband and wife or presume to advise you. (*confusedly*) I—I don't see how I can have such vile, disgusting dreams—unless he is still thinking of us in his study, his mind still deliberately willing to poison mine. (*with a flash of renewed vindictiveness*) And as a woman I still say it would be poetic justice if you destroyed him by giving him his desire! And as a woman, my pride will glory in your revenge— (*then hastily and guiltily*) I hope you understand, Sara, and do not think I am a cruel, evil mother.

SARA—(*with a vindictive smile—strangely*) I understand well enough. If you think there isn't a woman in me who felt exactly like that the moment I guessed what he was up to, you don't know me! And he doesn't! But he'll find out— (*then guiltily*) I don't know how I can think such wickedness—except it's what you said that he's still poisoning us. (*abruptly changing the subject*) But now tell me what he made you agree to that you've been hiding. I'll understand, whatever it is, that he did it.

DEBORAH—(*with a strange vengeful gleam in her eye*) Yes, we have been forgetting my part of it, haven't we? Well, it's merely this, Sara, that he begged me to give him a life alone with me again away from his office and his home.

SARA—(*stares at her suspiciously*) What do you mean? (*Instinctively she starts to pull her hand away from Deborah.*)

DEBORAH—(*with a trace of mockery*) Now, now. You promised to understand. (*Sara controls herself. Deborah goes on matter-of-factly.*) He begged me to let him keep me company in my garden every evening from now on. (*Sara stiffens with hostility and then fights it back.*) And, as I know how lonely I would be in the future without the children—

SARA—(*eagerly*) But I've told you you'll have them back. You asked me if you could.

DEBORAH—(*with a taunt underlying her cool persuasive tone*) Yes, but I had forgotten then— No, Sara, you are very generous and I am most grateful, but I really will not need them, now that I have my own son again.

SARA—(*gives way to a flash of jealous, uneasy anger*) Ah, and so that's what it is! I knew I shouldn't have let him go to you! I've always known if you were ever given the chance—! (*She jerks her hand from Deborah's.*)

DEBORAH—(*pleading now frightenedly, grabbing Sara's hand*) Sara! You promised to remember! But it's my fault. I'm afraid I sounded as if I were taunting you. Forgive me. I really didn't mean— The truth is—I didn't want him in my garden ever again. I hated him for forcing his way in. But then he lied and made me hate you. He tricked me into remembering the past with him. He made himself appear like a little boy again, so forlorn and confused and lost in himself—needing my love so terribly! So I couldn't help but consent. Surely, as a mother, you can understand that, Sara!

SARA—(*has controlled herself—tensely*) I do, Deborah. I've sons of my own and I know how I'll long to have them back after they've left me.

DEBORAH—(*with a sort of taunting satisfaction*) Then you have no objection, Sara?

SARA—(*defensively*) Why should I? You're his mother. You've a right. And I'll have my own sons all to myself now. I'll have him all day at the office. No, you're entirely welcome. (*with a strange bitter vindictiveness*) And when I think of the way he swindled me into letting him go to your garden—and of all he's done today to make us hate each other—I tell you, as woman to woman, I hate him so much that if I was in your place I'd give him his wish, and I'd let him go back and back into the past until he gets so lost in his dreams he'd be no more a man at all, but a timid little boy hiding from life behind my skirts! Or, better still, no more than a nursing baby with no life or hunger of his own outside me! And I'd dandle him on my lap and laugh at his mad cries for liberty! (*then abruptly ashamed and uneasy*) But those are evil thoughts he's putting in my mind. I'd never think them myself.

DEBORAH—(*with a strange bold manner*) There is no need to be ashamed before me, Sara. I admit that has occurred to my mind, too—in the garden when I hated him for intruding— After all, if he will insist on trespassing in the past—! (*She gives a soft, gloating little laugh.*) Yes, I do not think we have anything to fear, Sara. Between us we can soon force him to realize how foolish he was to destroy the peace and harmony of our house. In a very short time, he will feel torn apart and driven quite insane between us, and he will beg us on his knees to restore that peace and not punish his wickedness anymore, but forgive him and take him back into our home again!

SARA—(*vindictively*) And won't I laugh to see him beg!

DEBORAH—We will both laugh. (*They laugh softly together.*) And this, I think, will be his last rebellion. He has fought for liberty before and was beaten. He must be very tired. After this defeat, I believe, he will scream with fear if anyone ever mentions the word freedom. (*then urgently*) But we must keep on understanding each other! We must never forget our purposes are identical. We must trust each other and remain united in spirit, friends and allies, and never let him make us hate each other! Let us swear that again, Sara!

SARA—I swear I won't!

DEBORAH—And I swear! (*She smiles contentedly and pats Sara's hand.*) That's settled, then. Now I think we can safely forget him and be as we have been on so many other nights—simple and contented and at peace with each other and with life.

SARA—(*smiling*) I'd like nothing better, and it's a help to have him out of the room so we don't have to wonder what he's thinking to himself. (*with a change of tone to that of the doting mother*) Tell me about the children when they were with you in the garden, like you always do.

DEBORAH—(*smiling fondly*) Of course I will. (*Then she pauses, trying to remember—finally she admits guiltily*) I can't seem to—I'm afraid I have entirely forgotten, Sara.

SARA—(*piqued—resentfully*) You've always remembered before.

DEBORAH—(*reproachfully*) Now! I know I have, but— A lot of things have happened since then to disturb my mind.

SARA—(*contrite in her turn*) Ah, don't I know. (*then uneasily*) And they're still happening. Even if he is locked in his study. I can still feel his thoughts reaching out—

DEBORAH—(*with a little shiver of dread*) Yes, I, too— (*There is a pause during which they both stare straight before them. The expression of each changes swiftly, mirroring what is entering their minds, and becomes sly and evasive and gloatingly calculating. Their clasped hands, without their being aware of it, let go and draw apart. Then each sneaks a suspicious, probing glance at the other. Their eyes meet and at once each looks away and forces a hypocritically affectionate, disarming smile. Deborah speaks quickly and lightly.*) How quiet we are. What are you thinking, Daughter?

SARA—(*quickly and lightly*) Of how foolish men can be, Mother, never content with what we give them, but always wanting more.

DEBORAH—(*lightly*) Yes, they never grow up. They remain greedy little boys demanding the moon.

SARA—(*getting up from the sofa*) I'll get my sewing, to keep myself occupied, and come back to you.

DEBORAH—Yes, do. And I will read my book. (*Sara goes slowly toward her old chair at left-front of table. Deborah's eyes remain fixed on her and abruptly her expression changes to one of arrogant disdainful repulsion and hatred and she thinks*) You vile degraded slut!—as if I could ever believe your lies again!—as if you needed encouragement from me to become the vulgar grasping harlot you were born to be!—but I am glad I encouraged you because that is the one sure way to make him loathe the sight of you—in the end he will know you for what you are and you will so disgust him that he will drive you out of his life into the gutter where you belong!—you are too stupid to see this—but I see!—and I will see to it he sees!

SARA—(*having come to the chair, fiddles around unnecessarily gathering up her sewing things, keeping her back turned to Deborah while she thinks*) She must think I'm the greatest fool was ever born if she hopes I'd ever trust her again—as if he'd waste his time in her garden every evening humoring her crazy airs and graces if she hadn't begged him to!—but let her look out, what tricks she'll be up to to take him from me—I'll keep what's mine from her if I have to drive her into the asylum itself! (*A pause. She stands motionless, her back to Deborah. Both their expressions change to a triumphant possessive tenderness.*)

DEBORAH—(*thinking*) Then my beloved son will have no one but me!

SARA—(*thinking*) Then my Darling will have only me! (*She turns, making her face smilingly expressionless and goes back toward the sofa.*)

(*Curtain*)

ACT FOUR
SCENE ONE

SCENE—*Same as Scene One of Act Three—Simon's private office. Changes have been made in its appearance. A sofa has been added to the furniture. Placed at front, center, it is too large for the room, too garishly expensive and luxurious, its blatant latest-stylishness in vulgar contrast to the sober, respectable, conservatism of the old office of Simon's father. It offends the eye at once, as an alien presence. It has the quality of a painted loud-mouthed bawd who has forced her way in and defied anyone to put her out.*

Other changes are a mirror in an ornate gilt frame hanging over Sara's high desk at right, rear, and tacked on the right wall beside her desk is a large architect's drawing in perspective of a pretentious, nouveau-riche country estate on the shore of a small private lake with a beach in the foreground and a wharf with small pleasure craft moored to it. A road leads back from the wharf up an elaborately terraced hill to an immense mansion, a conglomerate of various styles of architecture, as if additions had been added at different times to an original structure conceived on the model of a medieval, turreted castle. At rear, on one side of this edifice, are imposing stables. Surrounding these buildings on three sides are woods that have been cleared and made into a park.

It is an early morning in midsummer of the following year, 1841.

Sara is discovered seated on the high stool before her desk, working with a ruler and drafting instruments on a plan. A marked change is noticeable in her appearance. Her body has grown strikingly voluptuous, and provocatively female. She is dressed extravagantly in flamboyant clothes, designed with the purpose of accentuating her large breasts, her slender waist, her heavy rounded thighs and buttocks, and revealing them as nakedly as the fashion will permit. Her face has a bloated, flushed, dissipated, unhealthy look with dark shadows under her eyes. There is something feverishly nervous and morbidly excited about it. Its prettiness has been coarsened and vulgarized. Her mouth seems larger, its full lips redder, its stubborn character become repellently sensual, ruthlessly cruel and greedy. Her eyes have hardened, grown cunning and calculating and unscrupulous. There is a stray suggestion in her face now of a hardened prostitute, particularly in its defiant defensive quality, that of one constantly anticipating attack by a brazen assertiveness which concedes a sense of guilt. Her manner varies between an almost masculine curt abruptness and brutal frankness, plainly an imitation and distortion of Simon's professional manner, and a calculating feminine seductiveness which constantly draws attention to her body.

The door from the bookkeeper's room at right, is opened noiselessly, and Joel Harford enters, closing the door behind him. He is the same in appearance, retains the cold emotionless mask of his handsome face. But there is a startling change in his manner which now seems weak, insecure and furtive, as though he were thrown off balance by some emotion he tries to repress, which fascinates and at the same time humiliates him. For a moment he stands glancing about the room vaguely, his gaze avoiding Sara. She is conscious of his presence but ignores him. Finally his eyes fasten on her and, seeing she is apparently absorbed in her work, he stares up and down the curves of her body with a sly, greedy desire.

SARA—(*suddenly explodes angrily in a snapping of nerves, slamming her rule on the desk and turning on him, her voice stridently domineering as though she were rebuking a servant*) Don't stand there gawking! What do you want? Speak up! (*But before he can do so she goes on more angrily.*) How dare you come in here without knocking? You know Simon's orders! And I've ordered you! You better remember, if you want to keep your job! (*then controlling her anger—curtly*) Well? What is it?

JOEL—(*has cringed for a second, then immediately has regained his cold poise*) Mr. Tenard, the banker, is in the outer office. I thought, considering his position, I had better announce him myself.

SARA—(*with gloating scorn*) His position, is it? His position now is under Simon's feet, and my feet, as he very well knows!

JOEL—He states he had a letter from you making an appointment with Simon.

SARA—That's true. I wrote him at Simon's dictation. What Simon wants of him I can't see. We've taken his bank from him. He's stripped bare. (*then with a cunning greedy smile*) But he must have something we want, or Simon wouldn't waste time on him. (*curtly*) Well, you see Simon's not here yet. Tell Tenard to wait.

JOEL — (*making no move to go — emotionlessly*) My brother seems to be late every day now.

SARA — (*betraying an inner uneasiness by forcing a too-careless tone*) Ah, he's taken to paying your old mother a morning visit in her garden as well as in the evening. She's failing rapidly in her mind, poor woman, growing childish and living altogether in her dreams. Simon thinks he ought to humor her all he can so she won't take leave of her senses altogether. (*abruptly, forcing a laugh*) And what if he is late? He knows, the way he's trained me, I can take care of anything here as well as he could.

JOEL — (*with an undercurrent of spite*) As long as you don't mind his keeping *you* waiting.

SARA — (*stares at him — defensively*) Just what do you mean by that?

JOEL — (*betraying an inner jealous excitability, his eyes unconsciously fixed on the sofa — sneeringly*) I — I am not unaware why you are so insistent about my knocking before I — intrude.

SARA — (*watching him, her face lighting up with a cunning satisfaction — her expression very like a prostitute's now as she smiles seductively and mockingly*) So that's what's bothering you! Well, that's my business.

JOEL — (*his eyes fixed fascinatedly on her now*) Your business! Yes, I quite realize you are — what you are.

SARA — (*plainly enjoying this, moves her body seductively — teasingly*) And what am I, Joel Darlin'?

JOEL — (*trying to take his eyes from her*) I — I am fully aware of the means you have used in the past year to get my brother to sign over his interests one by one to you.

SARA — You don't think my love is worth it?

JOEL — (*stammers*) I would not use the word love —

SARA — (*teasingly*) Why wouldn't you? You're a sentimental fool, I'm afraid, Joel. What else is love, I'm asking you? (*Suddenly she looks guilty and repelled — hastily*) No! That's Simon's idea, not mine!

JOEL — I suppose you pride yourself you have cunningly swindled him? (*He laughs gratingly.*) But it's the other way round. It's you who have been swindled!

SARA—(*angrily*) That's a lie! (*scornfully*) You fool, you! Do you think, after all he's taught me, I haven't learned to get all I'm worth to him?

JOEL—(*ignoring this—sneeringly*) All this imposing edifice of power and greed he has built so unscrupulously—which you have him to put in your name—what is it in fact but a house of cards? You know he has been gambling more and more recklessly in the past year. It was bad enough before you came here, but since he started playing Napoleon to show off his genius to you, he has abandoned all caution! Debt has been piled upon debt! If you had to pay the debts on the properties he has made over to you tomorrow—there would be nothing left! His position, and yours, depends entirely upon the myth he has created of his invincibility, his uncanny luck, that his touch turns everything to gold! But once let the slightest doubt arise, and his enemies see his true position—and their opportunity to revenge themselves—and strip you of everything you possess.

SARA—(*with forced defiance*) Let them try! They couldn't! He'll always beat the world! (*then abruptly—frightened and shaken*) Oh, I know, Joel! Sometimes, I go mad worrying! But I can't stop him. And when he's with me, I think what he thinks. I can't help it!

JOEL—(*ignores this—with a strange air of being fascinated by the danger*) I tell you there is danger every second. It would take only a rumor. A whisper spoken in the right ear. This banker who is waiting. How he must hate Simon. If he had the slightest inkling—

SARA—(*fascinatedly*) I know. (*then frightenedly*) Joel! You sound as though you'd like— (*imploringly*) You wouldn't—!

JOEL—(*jerking himself back to his pose—coldly*) I? You insult my life-long loyalty to the Company. Do you believe everyone is like you and Simon, devoid of all probity and honor? (*then with almost a smirk*) Besides, you forget I still own an interest—which is not yet for sale, although I might consider— (*hastily*) I'm merely pointing out that you had been swindled. (*sneeringly*) But you would realize it if you spent more time examining the true value of his gifts and less on designing your impossible Irish-Castle-in-Spain! (*He indicates the plan on the wall scornfully.*)

SARA—(*furiously*) Impossible, is it? We'll see! That's one debt I'll make him pay—the debt the Harfords owe my father's daughter! (*abruptly changing to a scornful curt tone*) I'm a fool to listen to your silly gab. I ought to know you well enough by this to laugh at you, the way Simon does, for an old stick-in-the-mud always prophesying ruin and—! (*harshly*) Get back to your work! You're wasting my time and I'm sick of you! (*She turns back to her desk.*)

JOEL—(*stands staring at her, then moves mechanically to the door at right and is about to open it when suddenly he turns— angrily*) I do protest! I own an interest; it is my right. I pro- test against you and my brother turning this office—my father's office—into a brothel room for your lust! Everyone is getting to know—to smirk and whisper! It is becoming an open scandal—a filthy public disgrace! I— (*He stammers to a halt—his eyes fixed on her in helpless fascination. She has turned to him and again there is the look of a smiling prostitute about her face.*)

SARA—(*smiling and moving her body seductively—teasingly*) Now, Joel, Darlin', you shouldn't look at me like that, and me your brother's wife. (*She laughs provokingly.*)

JOEL—(*fighting with himself—stammers*) I do not under- stand you. I do not see why you should laugh—like a com- mon street woman. My brother's wife should have more modesty. I was only looking at your new dress and admiring it. Simon buys you a new dress every week now. Is that part of the bargain? You should not let his greed turn his wife into a low woman whose beauty is for sale! I protest! (*He swallows as if he were strangling and tears his eyes from her teasing gloat- ing ones—he stammers*) No, no! I do not mean— I ask your pardon for saying such things. It is not like me at all. The truth is I have changed in the past year. I do not recognize myself. I disgust myself. It is the atmosphere of disgusting greed here which has become so vilely intensified since you came. I no longer recognize this as my father's office—or myself as my father's son. Something has happened to make me greedy, too. So please forgive and overlook—

SARA—(*her prostitute air gone—pitying and frightened*) Oh, don't I know? Haven't I changed, too, so I don't know my- self. Don't I disgust myself, at times. But it's not me. It's

Simon. It's what he wants. I've got to be what he wants. He makes me want to be what he wants! (*controlling herself—simply*) I forgive you, Joel. And please forgive me.

JOEL—(*gently*) I? Of course, Sara. And thank you for your kindness and understanding. (*dully*) I'll go back to my work now. (*He turns to the door but again, with his hand on the knob his eyes fix on her body and grow greedy and he stammers*) I only wish to say—I've quite decided to sell my interest in the business—that is, to you, if you would care to consider— (*He stops— Again the prostitute leer has been called back to her face. She laughs teasingly. He wrenches open the door and flings himself into the bookkeeper's room, slamming the door behind him.*)

SARA—(*looks after him, smiling to herself with a cheap vanity*) Who'd think it of him? So stuck-up and full of don't-touch-me airs! One of the high and mighty Yankee Harfords! And now I've got him under my feet, begging! He'd pay all he's got! I could strip him bare—and cheat him in the bargain—pretend when I'd really give him nothing! (*She chuckles.*) The fools of men! It's too easy for us to cheat them! They want to be cheated so they can cheat themselves! (*She stares in the mirror at herself admiringly—coquettishly in brogue*) Who'd have dreamed it Sara Melody—you in your beauty to have such power over bright and mighty men! By the Eternal, as my father used to swear, I think you could take what you wanted from any one of them! And if he is a poor slave of a bookkeeper, he's a handsome man, and he owns an interest— (*She suddenly shivers with repulsion and tears her eyes from the mirror strickenly—in a guilty whisper*) God forgive me! Me, to have such thoughts! Like a dirty whore smiling at men in the street and showing her leg! What's happened to me. A year ago and I'd never have dreamed such a thought, not even in sleep, but now it seems natural—to be a part of me— (*She stares around her frightenedly.*) It's being here so long, working as his whore, with no life except in his greed—with my children running wild at home as if they had no mother—while I sit here like a miser counting gold, making plans for the grand estate I'll have, or dreaming of my mills and my ships on the sea and my railroad that he's paid me for using my body like a dirty whore's—he's made me think that life means selling yourself, and pride is to get the highest price you can, and that love is lust—it's only lust he wants—and he's made me feel it's all I want and if I didn't have that hold on him, I'd lose him!—she'd take him back with her entirely— (*then with angry defiance*) She'll never! He may forget me when he's with her but once I've got him here, I've only to kiss him and he forgets she's alive! And what if I was having thoughts about Joel? It was only what every woman thinks at times in her heart—was any one of us ever content with one man?—who didn't feel she was worth more—that she'd been swindled by marriage—who didn't want every man to want her to prove her worth to herself, who didn't feel, if she was free, she could get more for herself— (*vindictively*) Let him look out how he comes here late and keeps me waiting his pleasure, like a slave, or I'll show him I can have what I want without him, and get my price for it, too. (*She laughs spitefully—then suddenly tears her eyes from the mirror and shrinks into herself with horrified disgust.*) Ah, you dirty whore, you! Oh, God help me! I must be going daft—as daft as that mad old witch in her garden. (*then with increasing anger*) And who wouldn't be daft, going home every night to that hell with her? Never a moment's peace—hating her and feeling her hate me—watching every move she makes and knowing she's watching me—knowing it's a duel to the death between us—if she'd only leave me alone!—if she'd only be content with what's hers and not try to steal what's mine!—but she's bound she'll get him away from me, and make him drive me out in the street— (*with threatening hatred*) But by God, he can't! And I won't stand much more from her!—She's driving me too far—a little more and my hate will have no pity left! I know her weakness and her fear of going crazy— I'll drive her into the asylum where she belongs, the mad old fool! She's making this life too small for the two of us! One of us must go—and by the Powers it won't be me! (*then hastily*) But let's pray I won't need to, and I can get rid of her the way we planned. Now Simon has the bank I'll make him stop wanting more and let the profit add up. I'll pay off the debts, and we'll sell out and I'll build the estate and I'll pay her a pension to stay alone in her garden. (*trying to reassure herself*) Yes, it won't take long—I'll soon be rid of her. (*then distractedly*) If he'll only let me!—If I'll only let myself not want more and more! (*She jumps from her stool and paces around in a nervous panic.*) Why doesn't he come?—I can't bear life without him with me!—What makes him so late?—That mad old witch keeps him dreaming in her garden to make him late on purpose to torment me! (*in a fury*) And he knows it! He lets her do it!—Well, I won't wait, my fine Simon! Not alone! I've stood enough from you! I'll call in Joel to keep me company!—I'll change entirely to the whore you want me to be, and we'll see how you like that! (*She is moving towards the bookkeeper's room when the door from the rear is opened and Simon comes in. He has changed greatly, grown terribly thin, his countenance is ravaged and pale and haggard, his eyes deep sunken. There is, however, a strange expression of peace and relaxation on his face as he enters, a look of bemused dreaminess in his eyes.*)

SARA—(*with a cry of hypocritical happy relief, rushes and throws her arms around him and hugs him passionately*) Oh, Darling! I love you so! (*Then her tension snapping, she bursts into sobs and hides her face against his shoulder.*)

SIMON—(*looks startled and bewildered as if only half awakened from a dream—pats her shoulder mechanically—vaguely*) There, there. (*He stares around him, thinking and frowning, as though not quite realizing yet where he is or how he got there.*)

SARA—(*stops crying instantly at the tone of his voice—jerks back, holding him by the shoulders, and stares into his face—frightened and pleading*) Simon! You sound—! (*forcing a joking tone*) For the love of heaven, don't you know where you are or who I am?

SIMON—(*trying to force himself from his day dream—vaguely placating*) Of course, Sara. Don't be silly. (*Then he relapses and smiles with a bemused pleasure and speaks dreamily.*) Do you know, this morning, talking with Mother, I suddenly remembered something I had never remembered before. Nothing important. Just an incident in her garden long ago. The astonishing thing is that she says I wasn't more than a year old at the time. And yet it appeared as clear as if it were yesterday—or was happening again this very morning. Nothing important, as I've said. Childish and meaningless. But it gave me a feeling of power and happiness to be able to recall the past so distinctly.

SARA—(*stares at him—frightened and resentful*) Simon! Wake up! You're here with me! (*She kisses him fiercely.*) Come back to me! To hell with her crazy dreams! I love you! I'm your wife and you're mine! (*She kisses him again.*) Can't you feel how I love you? Tell me you love me.

SIMON—(*with a start, awakes completely. His expression changes and becomes tense with desire and he presses her body to his and kisses her passionately.*) Sweetheart! You know I want you more than life!

SARA—(*with a sudden revulsion of feeling, pushes back from him—desperately*) No! Please! I want love— (*then forcing a laugh*) But you'll be making fun of me for being a sentimental fool! (*She throws herself in his arms again—passionately*) Oh, I don't care what I am as long as I have you!

SIMON—(*passionately*) My dear beautiful mistress! (*He tries to take her to the couch.*)

SARA—(*breaks away from him. The common prostitute calculating look is back in her face now. She laughs tantalizingly.*) Oh, no, you don't! You've a lot of business to attend to. I'll have no laziness. You've got to earn me, you know! You wouldn't want me if I gave myself for nothing, and let you cheat me! Not you! I know you. You'd think I was a stupid fool not to have learned more from your teaching and example, and your doing your best to train me.

SIMON—(*laughs with amused admiration*) You've been a very apt pupil. You'll soon give your master cards and spades. (*teasing derisively*) What do you want me to pay you this time, Beautiful, Insatiable One? You have about all I possess already.

SARA—(*greedily*) Well, there's the bank we've just smashed and got control of.

SIMON—(*laughingly*) Oh, so that's it! I might have known. In fact, I anticipated and have had the papers drawn. But, of course, I won't sign them until after—

SARA—(*mockingly*) Aren't you the cautious one! Are you afraid I'd cheat you? But how do I know you mightn't refuse to sign after—?

SIMON—(*laughingly*) Oh, I might like to, but you know I haven't the power anymore. You've taken that from me, too! Your beauty has become more desirable to me than a thousand banks stuffed with gold! (*He tries to draw her to him—passionately*) Darling One! Haven't you learned by this time that my greatest happiness is to prove to you—and to myself—how much you are worth to me? (*He tries to kiss her.*)

SARA—(*evading his embrace—coquettishly*) No, I said. Later. (*She kisses him tantalizingly.*) But here's a kiss to bind the bargain.

SIMON—But I have to run down to the mill today. As you know there's been some discontent about our lowering wages and the hands are sending a deputation to ask me to reconsider.

SARA—(*her face hardening—commandingly*) You put your foot down on that! Fire them! There's plenty to take their place, and starving will teach them a lesson.

SIMON—I agree with you. The Company needs every penny of profit from the mill it can possibly extort. (*then smiling*) But about our bargain. You said later, but I can't get back until late afternoon just in time for my evening visit with Mother. So—

SARA—(*harshly domineering*) So you'll forget her and only remember me!

SIMON—(*struggling to resist—strangely the musing, dreamy expression showing in his face*) But I remember I promised her—

SARA—(*harshly*) You'll forget her, I'm saying! (*then moving her body with coarse suggestiveness—with a prostitute's calculating seductive air*) Isn't having me worth that to you? If it isn't, I'll have to find some other man who values me higher.

SIMON—(*hungrily*) No, no! Anything you ask!

SARA—(*triumphantly, almost sneeringly*) That's better! (*then resentfully and going on with an increasing show of jealous, bitter anger*) And that reminds me, I've a bone to pick with you. You were late again this morning on account of seeing her. I had to sit here alone—waiting and worrying— You let her keep you to make me wait. She did it on purpose to spite me! Ah, don't make excuses for her. Don't I know the hatred and jealousy and the designing greed behind her acting and pretending and her airs and graces of a great lady! It's you she makes a fool of, leading you back to her in the past before you were mine, twisting you around the fingers of her

dreams, till you're as mad as she is! But she doesn't fool me!
I see through her greedy scheming. And I warn you she'd
better watch herself or I'll get to the end of my pity!

SIMON—(*His expression has changed during her speech to one
of gloating satisfaction. He smiles teasingly.*) What? Don't tell
me you're becoming jealous again, Sara?

SARA—(*with forced scorn*) Jealous of that ugly old witch,
who's old enough to be my mother!

SIMON—(*smiling*) Then you mustn't act as if you were. To
hear you one would think you feared my poor little old
mother as a beautiful dangerous rival.

SARA—(*sneeringly*) Her! A skinny wizened hag no man
would look at twice!

SIMON—(*curtly—in command now*) Very well, then. Why
do you talk nonsense? (*sharply matter-of-fact*) We've had this
out many times before, Sara. I've explained until I'm tired
that I think it advisable, for our own sakes if not for hers, to
humor her in any way I can, even if it involves my wasting
valuable time—and, if you like, playing the fool myself. You
appear to cherish the absurd idea that it is a fascinating happiness for me to sit in a garden with a woman, whose mind
is far gone in second childhood, and be forced to watch her
greedy spirit, starved by her life-long fear of life, groping in
the past and clutching at the dead. (*dryly*) I assure you I can
think of many more enjoyable activities— (*He stares at her
desirously—with a smile*) Such as being here with you in my
arms, Beloved One.

SARA—(*gratefully*) Darling!

SIMON—(*with a return to his matter-of-fact tone, shrugging
his shoulders*) But, after all, I must not complain. Sometimes
she amuses me. Sometimes it is restful in her garden. You do
not begrudge me a little rest, I hope. Anyway, she is my
mother. I owe her some consideration. And someone has to
humor her and keep her from being too much alone in her
fantastic mind, or we would have a lunatic on our hands.

SARA—I've told you before I'm willing to have her have
the children for company again, instead of you, and you
ought to make her agree—

SIMON—(*curtly and resentfully*) Nonsense. I would never
permit— She does not want your children now that she

has— (*abruptly changing the subject—pleasantly*) But I'll admit, you have reason to complain of me for being late. I have no right to cheat you of time that belongs to you and the Company. I promise in future I'll remember not to humor her into leading my mind so far back that I forget— (*hastily again, going to his desk with his most alert authoritive executive air*) Well, I'll make up for lost time. Tenard is here, isn't he? (*She nods.*) You can tell Joel to have him sent in.

SARA—(*her manner that of an efficient obedient secretary*) Yes, Sir. (*She opens the door at right, sticks her head in and speaks to Joel—then comes back to the desk opposite Simon and waits for orders.*)

SIMON—(*looks at his watch*) I'll have time to dispose of him before I catch my train. You can go back to work on your plans for the estate. (*She turns back toward the desk at right, rear. He glances at the plans—flatteringly, with an undercurrent of mockery*) By the way, my congratulations on the additions you have made since I last examined it.

SARA—(*pleased*) I'm glad you like them.

SIMON—Now that you'll soon possess a bank, too, you can afford to add still more. (*He smiles—teasingly*) I am sure in your dreams you have already thought of more.

SARA—(*with a greedy little laugh*) Oh, trust me, I can always think of more! (*She stares at the plan—with a strange dreaminess and exultance*) I'll make it the grandest, most beautiful mansion that ever a woman's dream conceived as a house for his pride and her love for her husband! Ah, won't it be a beautiful life, when I can sit back at my ease there, in the castle of my dreams, in my own house, without a care in the world, with long nights of deep sleep, not turning and twisting in nightmares like I do now, with never a debt, knowing the banks are crammed with my gold, watching my sons grow up handsome rich gentlemen, having my husband and my lover always by me and all of him mine with no will or thought or dream in his heart or brain but the great need to love me!

SIMON—(*stares at her back—quietly with a mocking irony tinged with a bitter, tragic sadness*) There is a poem by Doctor Holmes you should read sometime—for added inspiration. (*He quotes from "The Chambered Nautilus."*)

Build thee more stately mansions, O my soul,
As the swift seasons roll!
Leave thy low-vaulted past!
Let each new temple, nobler than the last,
Shut thee from heaven with a dome more vast,
Till thou at length are free,
Leaving thine outgrown shell—

(*He pauses—then his gaze turned inward, he murmurs aloud to himself, as Sara continues to stare with fascinated, dreamy longing at the plan, not paying any attention to him.*) You must have that engraved over the entrance. And Mother should put it over the magic door to her summerhouse. And I, on the ceiling of this Company's offices—in letters of gold! (*He sneers self-mockingly—then slowly with a sinister determination*) But I will be soon! Oh very soon, now! Either by one way or the other—rid forever of either one or the other—thanks to either Sara or Mother! (*He starts guiltily and speaks with a hastily-assumed casualness to Sara.*) I am glad to see, Sara, that you have very properly ignored my stupid muddle-mindedness in remembering childish verses here. I should save such nonsense for my dutiful honoring of my poor old mother.

SARA—(*oblivious to him, staring at her plan, her tone becoming more and more coarsely greedy*) Stables full of thoroughbred hunters and fast trotters! Me the great lady, full of airs and graces, riding in my carriage with coachman and footman, through the castle park, or out past the lodge down the road to the city, with the crowds on the street staring, their hearts eaten with envy, and the shopkeepers bowing and scraping, and me gazing down my nose at them, and at the whole pack of the meek, weak, timid, poor poverty-stricken beggars of life! (*vengefully*) No one will ever dare sneer at my origin then, or my poverty! By the Eternal God, I'll spit in their faces and laugh when they thank me kindly for the favor! (*She chuckles viciously—then abruptly her expression changes to one of guilty shame and she exclaims confusedly*) No! I don't mean it! God forgive me, what makes me say such evil, spiteful things? They're not in my dream at all! All I want is a safe home for our love—and peace!

SIMON—(*rebukingly gently but firmly*) Now, now! No

backsliding into cowardly sentimental remorse, Beautiful Mistress. Remember what I've impressed on you so often in the past year. This office is no garden of dreams. It is a battlefield of reality, where you must face the fact of yourself as you are—and not as you dream you ought to be—where one eats or is eaten. It is silly to be ashamed of the undesirable fact that the humiliation of the conquered is part of the conqueror's pride in victory.

SARA—(*has turned to stare at him fascinatedly—murmurs mechanically*) Yes, I suppose—but— (*There is a knock on the door at rear. At once her attitude becomes that of the efficient secretary.*) That must be Tenard, Sir. Shall I let him in?

SIMON—(*A strange, calculating gloating comes into his face.*) No. I've just had an idea, Sara. Let Tenard wait outside the door for awhile like the ruined beggar he is. It will put him in a more uneasy, receptive frame of mind. (*He gets up from his chair.*) Come and sit in my place. I want you to handle Tenard, while I watch. You have learned a great deal in the last year. I am immensely proud of your rapid progress.

SARA—(*uncertainly*) I'm glad, Simon.

SIMON—Now I'd like to see you put your knowledge into practice. Prove that, no matter what happened to me, you are fully competent to direct the destiny of this Company to a befitting conclusion.

SARA—(*uneasily*) What could happen to you?

SIMON—(*shrugs his shoulders—carelessly*) Who knows? All men are mortal. There is always death.

SARA—(*frightenedly*) Don't say it, Darling.

SIMON—(*in same tone*) Or sickness, accident. Who knows? Life is a gamble and Fate a master sharper where stacked cards and loaded dice can cheat the cleverest swindler.

SARA—(*frightenedly*) Don't talk like that.

SIMON—Or I might simply go away—for a long, much-needed rest.

SARA—(*flaring up—with frightened jealous anger*) Ah, I know who put that in your mind! And I know she'd stop at nothing now to get you away with her! Not even if she had to drive you as mad as she is!

SIMON—Nonsense! Your jealousy is becoming an insane obsession. What has that poor childish old woman got to do with it? All I meant was I might sometime want to leave you in charge. You've bought the Company, anyway, so—

SARA—(*frightenedly*) You'd leave me—? (*then coarsely self-confident, with her prostitute's seductive smile*) I'd like to see you try to want to! Don't you know I've bought you, too? (*There is another knock on the door but neither heeds it.*)

SIMON—(*stares at her body—struggling with himself—stammers yearningly*) Yes, I know—and it's my greatest happiness to belong to you—to escape myself and be lost in you—I'll pay anything!

SARA—(*laughs softly—triumphantly seductive and coarse*) That's my Simon! That's the way I like you to talk—about life and love—and not about death, or madness like trying to leave me.

SIMON—(*starts toward her—lustfully*) Beloved! (*There is another knock on the door, sharp and impatient. It penetrates and breaks the spell. Simon tears his eyes from her and at once his manner becomes curtly business-like—dryly*) I think our friend is now sufficiently fearful and humiliated. Sit here, Sara. I am confident you can soon show him his place.

SARA—(*comes to the desk—smiling gloatingly*) Yes, under my feet, isn't it? (*She laughs softly and sits down in Simon's chair.*) But I don't even know why you had him come, Simon. We've ruined him. He has nothing left we want, has he?

SIMON—Yes. A few years of his life. He's past his prime but he's a capable banker and can still be useful to us. Not as he is now, of course. He is too full of old-fashioned ethics and honor. We know that because it made him so open to attack and so easy to ruin. But he can be made to forget all that and become an obedient servant, if you can discover his weakness and then use it without scruple. You will find a couple of notes I made on the pad about his present circumstances. The rest I leave in your capable hands, My Beautiful. Just bear in mind that the end you desire always justifies any means and don't get life confused with sentiment, as you used to. (*He laughs, moving away from her to her desk, at right, rear.*) Pretend to yourself he is I begging for your favors and you cannot fail to swindle him successfully and get what you want. (*There is another, banging knock on the door. He calls curtly*) Come in!

(*The door is opened and Benjamin Tenard enters. He is a tall, robust, full-chested man in his sixties with a fine-looking Roman face, his clothes expensively conservative. He has the look of success, of financial prosperity still stamped on him from long habit. It is this facade which makes the sense one immediately gets that he is a broken man inside, insecure, bewildered and frightened, all the more pityingly acute. His face as he enters is flushed with humiliated pride.*)

TENARD—(*begins to protest insultedly to Simon*) See here, Harford! You made an appointment with me, not I with you! Yet I am allowed to cool my heels in your outer office and then stand outside your door knocking and knocking like someone—!

SARA—(*breaks in in a pleasantly indifferent tone without any hint of apology*) Sorry to have kept you waiting, Mr. Tenard. It was necessary. (*He turns to stare at her in surprised confusion not having noticed her at first.*)

TENARD—I—I beg your pardon, Mrs. Harford. I did not see—

SARA—(*nodding at the chair opposite her*) Won't you sit down?

TENARD—(*uncertainly, glancing at Simon*) Thank you.

SIMON—(*smiling with cold pleasantness*) It's all right. Your appointment is really with my wife. She has full authority to act for me. So if you will pardon me, I have some important work to do here. (*He nods at the plans on Sara's desk, turns his back on Tenard, sits down, and during the scene between them pretends to be concentrated on the plans. Tenard comes and sits in the chair opposite Sara.*)

SARA—(*after a quick glance at the pad—smiling coolly—as she goes on, her tone and manner become more and more an exact mimicry of Simon's executive manner*) I presume you wonder why I wished to see you, Mr. Tenard. Just as I was wondering why you ever consented to come—under the circumstances.

TENARD—(*humiliated and guilty*) You mean because your husband is responsible for ruining me?

SARA—(*smiling coldly*) Simon does nothing without my consent, Mr. Tenard. I thought that was the cheapest way to take possession of your bank.

TENARD—(*unable to keep hate and a look of horror entirely*

from a glance at her) Yes, I have heard rumors that you advise him. I could not believe a woman— (*then almost frightenedly as if he is afraid he is prejudicing her against him—avoiding her eye and forcing a smile*) I bear no grudge. All is fair in war. I realize that. Perhaps, I considered the methods used not quite ethical—(*with increasing suppressed bitterness*)—not to say ruthless and unscrupulous. There are some who would describe them in even stronger terms.

SARA—(*curtly*) I am not interested in moral attitudes. You owned something I desired. You were too weak to hold it. I was strong enough to take it. I am good because I am strong. You are evil because you are weak. Those are the facts.

TENARD—(*gives way for a second to outraged indignation*) An infamous credo, Madam! (*then hastily, almost cringingly*) I—I beg your pardon. You may be right. New times, new customs—and methods. (*forcing a laugh*) I suppose I am too old a dog to learn new tricks of a changed era.

SARA—(*smiling coldly*) I hope not—for your sake, Mr. Tenard.

TENARD—(*stares at her stupidly*) Eh? I don't believe I understand— (*hastily forcing a good-natured, good-loser air*) But, as I said, I have no hard feelings. That's why I consented to come here—to show you I bear no grudges.

SARA—(*not smiling now—her face hardening into a ruthless mercilessness*) Let us be frank and not waste my time. I know your true reason for coming. You are ruined. You have had to sell everything. You haven't a dollar. But you have an old mother, a wife, a widowed daughter with two children, all of whom depend upon you for support. You have applied to various banks for a position. None of them want you. You are too old. The evil reputation of recent failure prejudices them against you. One or two have offered you a minor clerk's job—out of contemptuous pity, like a penny of charity tossed to a beggar.

TENARD—(*with humiliated anger*) Yes, damn them! But I—

SARA—(*goes on as if he had not interrupted*) Which your pride refused. Moreover, the wage would have been insufficient to support your family except in a shameful poverty to which they are unaccustomed. You were afraid that, suffering the humiliation of such poverty, your mother, your wife, your daughter, would begin to blame you and to feel a resentful contempt for your weakness.

TENARD—(*staring at her fascinatedly—blurts out in anguish*) And hide it! That would be the worst! To feel them hiding it—out of pity.

SARA—But there was one last desperate hope. You heard I had not yet chosen anyone to manage your old bank for me. You came here hoping against hope that the reason I had sent for you— (*She pauses—then smiles with cold pleasantry.*) I am pleased to tell you that is the reason. Mr. Tenard, I do offer you that position.

TENARD—(*the strain snapping, gives way pathetically and brokenly to relief and gratitude*) I—I don't know how to thank you— I apologize for having misjudged you— (*hastily*) Of course, I accept the position gladly.

SARA—(*coldly*) Wait. There are conditions. But before I state them, let me say that any sentiment of gratitude on your part is uncalled for. I am not doing this for your sake or your family's. What happens to you and yours is naturally a matter of entire indifference to me. I am solely concerned with what is mine, or what I wish to make mine.

TENARD—(*uneasily—forcing a smile*) You are—brutally frank, at least, Mrs. Harford. (*with growing apprehension*) What are your conditions?

SARA—(*smiling pleasantly*) I warn you your pride will probably be impelled to reject them. At first. But I ask you to bear in mind that pride is a virtue only in the strong. In the weak it is a stupid presumption. (*her face and voice hardening*) The conditions are that you agree to obey every order mechanically, instantly, unquestioningly, as though you were the meanest worker at the looms in my mills, or a common sailor in my ships, or a brakeman on my railroad.

TENARD—(*humiliated but forcing a reasonable tone*) You can rely on me, I have been the head of a business myself. I know the desirability of prompt obedience.

SARA—I can offer you a salary that will enable you very moderate comfort for your family, and so continue to purchase in part, at least, their former love and respect.

TENARD—(*stammers confusedly*) I—I thank you—

SARA — I am saying these things because, in order to avoid all future misunderstanding, I want you to face the cost of my offer before you accept.

TENARD — (*in a panic to get this ordeal over and run away*) I understand. But you need not— I have no choice, I accept.

SARA — (*cruelly insistent*) There is still the matter of your old-fashioned ideals of honor in business dealings to consider. I hope you appreciate from your recent experience with my methods that, as my employee, you will have to forget all such scruples. You will be required to conduct my bank business with the entire ruthlessness as to the means used of a general in battle. The end I desire to accomplish must justify any and every means to you. Where it is necessary, you must faithfully do things which may appear to your old conceptions of honor like plain swindling and theft. Are you willing to become a conscious thief and swindler in your own eyes?

TENARD — (*at last insulted beyond all prudent submission— stammering with outrage*) I— You must be mad, Madam— You dare— But I cannot answer a woman— I know it must be your husband who— A woman would never— (*He springs to his feet and turns on Simon in a fury.*) Damn you, Sir! You blackguard, do you think I have sunk to your level? I'll see you in hell first! I'd rather be a dog! I'd rather starve in the gutter. (*He strides to the door at rear.*) That's my answer to your infamous offer, Sir. (*Simon has not turned, gives no sign of hearing him. Tenard grabs the handle of the door.*)

SARA — (*suddenly bursts out in a strange rage as if he had touched something deep in her and infuriated her—lapsing into broad brogue, forgetting all her office attitudes—glaring at Tenard with savage denunciation*) Arrah, God's curse on you for a man! You and your pride and honor! You're pretending to love your women and children and you're willing to drag them down with you to suffer the bitter shame of poverty, and starve in the gutter, too!

TENARD — (*stares at her torturedly*) It's a lie! They would never wish me— (*Then all at once he seems to collapse inside. He nods his head in a numbed acquiescence, forcing a vacant smile.*) Yes, I suppose, entirely selfish—no time to remember self. Thank you, Madam, for reminding me of my duty. I wish to say I see your point about policy of bank—only practical viewpoint—business is business— (*He forces a choked chuckle.*) Must remember the old adage—sticks and stones—and poverty—break—but names don't hurt. Let who will cry thief! I accept the position, Madam—and thank you again—for your—charity! (*He wrenches open the door and flings himself into the hall, slamming the door. Simon gets off his stool and comes to Sara with a smile of approval.*)

SIMON—Well done! You disposed of him as well as I could. I'm proud of you.

SARA—(*Her expression is changing. There is a look of dawning horror in her eyes. She forces a smile—mechanically*) I'm glad you're proud. But it was you—what you wanted me—

SIMON—Oh, no. Don't play modest now. (*He pats her cheek—playfully*) That last touch finished him, and that was all your own. I had calculated he would leave, indignant and insulted, but be forced to come back after he'd faced his women again. But your method was far cleverer. (*He pats her shoulder.*)

SARA—(*staring before her—mechanically*) Yes, I didn't leave him one last shred of his pride, did I? (*She suddenly breaks— with a sob*) Oh, the poor man! God forgive me! (*Abruptly she turns on Simon—with rising bitter anger*) It wasn't I! It was you! You— Ah, don't I know what you're trying to do, make a cruel greedy whore of me, so you can go back and sneer with her at what a low, common slut I am in my heart! (*re-vengefully*) But I won't let you! I'll go to Tenard! He'll be crazy to revenge himself now! I've only to give him a hint of the true condition of the Company to turn him loose to de-stroy you! And then where would you be, you and your Company? You strutting with pride, playing you're a little Na-poleon! You'd not have a penny! And I'd be free to take my children and go to the old farm and live like a decent, honest woman working in the earth! (*She suddenly collapses, sobbing, hiding her face in her hands.*) I can't go on with this! I won't!

SIMON—(*who has listened, watching her with an impatient frown—pats her shoulder perfunctorily—curtly*) Come now, Sara. I know you've just been under a severe strain. But that's no excuse to talk so absurdly. (*He sits down opposite her— curtly*) That nonsense about your ruining the Company. Don't you realize it's your Company now?

SARA—I realize you've swindled me, paying me with things loaded down with debts, if that's what you mean.

SIMON—(*smiling*) Ah, now you begin to talk like yourself again. (*rebukingly*) Such nonsense, Sara! As if you were a woman who would deliberately ruin herself for the sake of anything. And there are your children to be considered. You would hardly ruin them.

SARA—(*shakenly*) No.

SIMON—(*scornfully*) You go to that old farm, where there's only my old cabin and a ruin of a farm house. A farm that hasn't been cultivated since God knows when. You would have to work like a slave for a bare living, with your pride tortured by the shame of poverty! (*He laughs.*) Don't tell me you can imagine yourself contented living in a potato patch with your bare feet in the earth like a common peasant!

SARA—(*with a shiver of repulsion*) No. I'd hate to sink to that after all my high dreams.

SIMON—Exactly. So don't talk silly. As for your fears about the Company, you sound like Joel playing Jeremiah. (*jokingly*) You are not complaining about the way I manage your properties, I hope. Haven't I reorganized your railroad in two years so that now it is one of the best run small roads in the country?

SARA—Yes. But the debt—?

SIMON—I'm amazed to hear you worrying about debts. It's unworthy of your father's daughter. He never let debts bother him.

SARA—(*suddenly smiling, with a proud toss of her head— boastfully*) True for you! He let them whistle for their money and be damned! (*then hastily and guiltily*) But I'm not like him. I—

SIMON—(*with a strange tense excitement*) Of course, you are right in thinking there is constant danger—that a whisper, a hint of the truth, a rumor started among the many defeated enemies who have such good reason to envy and hate you!

SARA—(*defensively*) Reason to hate me?

SIMON—(*smiling*) Well, do you imagine Tenard loves you, for example?

SARA—(*confusedly*) But it was you—

SIMON—(*ignoring this, goes on tensely*) There's no question about the danger. It's like walking a tight rope over an abyss where one false step—

SARA—(*frightenedly*) Oh, I know! It's driving me crazy! I can't sleep, worrying!

SIMON—But you mustn't look down, for then you grow confused and the temptation seizes you to hurl yourself—Don't you think I know by long experience how that impulse fascinates you, how terrible the longing is to make an end of suspense and gain forgetfulness and peace at any cost—the passionate yearning to destroy oneself and be free!

SARA—(*frightenedly*) Darling! Don't think of it! Don't make me think—

SIMON—I know only too well how tempted you are to whisper and start the rumor of the truth among your enemies—

SARA—No! I'd never! I was only talking!

SIMON—To throw the burden of responsibility and guilt off one's shoulders, to release oneself from the cursed treadmill of greed! Not to have to go on! To be able to be still, or to turn back to rest! (*He is staring before him with a fascinated yearning.*)

SARA—(*frightened, grasping his arm*) Darling! Please don't stare like that! It makes you look so—strange and crazed—you frighten me!

SIMON—(*controls himself—with a smile*) Oh, come now, there's nothing crazy about using your enemies' revenge to give you your heart's desire! That seems to me a very cunning, Machiavellian scheme—as ironically amusing as the end of one of Mother's old, fantastic fairy tales. Except, of course, this would be a happy end.

SARA—(*flaring up angrily*) Ah, I know it's her puts all this craziness in your head. Wouldn't she laugh with joy to see me ruin myself and lose all I have in the world! But I'll never let her drive me to that! So don't you talk to me of the temptation, when you know I was only joking when I said—

SIMON—I? I was only warning you against it. You must not be weak. You must be courageously and ruthlessly what you are! You must go on to more and more!

SARA—(*protests miserably*) No. I don't want to. I've

enough. (*pleadingly*) Oh, Simon Darling, won't you stop and be content now you've got the bank? Won't you let the profit add up, and not make more debts to buy more, but pay off what you owe? And as soon as the debts are paid and we're safe, we'll pension off your mother, and give her the house to live alone in, where she'll have no one to hurt but herself, and I'll build my estate and have a home of my own for my husband and my children—(*she presses against him with a calculating, wheedling seductiveness*) and best of all, for my lover I'm madly in love with.

SIMON—(*ignoring this last—curtly*) No. You know you cannot do that now. Not unless you wish to ruin yourself. It would be fatal for you to withdraw from the Company the large amount of capital needed to build such a large estate. The battle for this bank has strained your resources to the breaking point. A dollar in cash is worth a hundred to you now. No, you can't stop now. You must go on.

SARA—(*distractedly*) No! I won't! I can't! I've come to the end!

SIMON—(*as if she hadn't spoken*) You must keep your eyes fixed on the final goal of your ambition. Force yourself not to look down. Keep your whole mind and will concentrated on what must still be accomplished before your Company can be out of danger, safe and absolutely self-contained, not dependent on anything outside itself for anything, needing nothing but itself. Until that is done, how can you enjoy any true security or freedom within yourself—or any peace or happiness. Surely you must see that clearly, Sara?

SARA—(*pitifully confused*) I—I don't know—I know I want peace and happiness in your love.

SIMON—(*goes on in the same tone*) You still have to have stores to retail your cotton goods. Your own plantations worked by your own nigger slaves. Your own slave ships and your own slave dealers in Africa. That will complete the chain on the end. You see how that will protect you, don't you?

SARA—(*impressed in spite of herself and beginning to be greedily fascinated*) Yes, I do see. I'm not such a fool about business after all your training. And, of course, I'd like to feel absolutely safe, and that no one had a chance with what was mine. (*then tensely desperate*) But Darling—I'm so worried—

SIMON—(*goes on the same*) On this end, the stores are the last possible link— (*then with a strange laugh*) Of course, it would be the crowning achievement if I could conceive a scheme by which the public could be compelled to buy your cotton goods and only yours—so you would own your own consumer slaves, too. That would complete the circle with a vengeance! You would have life under your feet then, wouldn't you? Beautiful Greedy One—just as you have me! (*He laughs, his eyes glowing with desire, and hugs her.*)

SARA—(*her face lighting up with a responsive passion— laughingly*) Yes, I'd like that. I'd be satisfied then. So see that you find a way to do it! (*then with proud admiration*) And leave it to you, I'll wager you will! There's no stopping you, once you want anything! Haven't I always said you've the strength and the power to take anything from life your heart wished for!

SIMON—(*teasingly, hugging her*) With such an insatiable mistress to inspire me, how could I dare be weak? It is your heart which has done the wishing, and I could not respect myself unless you were proud of me.

SARA—(*passionately*) And I am proud! I've the grandest strongest lover that was ever owned by a woman! (*She kisses him ardently.*) Darling!

SIMON—(*passionately*) Sweetheart! (*then with an abrupt return to his strange, obsessed excitement*) So don't let me hear any more of your timid worry about danger. What if there is danger? It lends spice to life! What if it is a tremendous gamble, with the cards stacked by the fate within you, and the dice loaded? Your father's daughter should be proud to be a born gambler and love the risk for its own sake! I'll bet he would have found his greatest happiness in staking his soul with the devil against the world on the turn of a card!

SARA—(*excitedly, with a proud toss of her head*) Wouldn't he, though! Didn't he ruin himself gambling, the estate and all he possessed in life, and never blinked an eye or lost the sneer on his lips! He was a great gentleman! And he'd keep that same sneer if he played the devil, for he'd know if the devil won he'd gain only what he owned already, and he'd be laughing up his sleeve how he'd cheated him! (*She laughs with gloating amusement.*)

SIMON—(*stares at her—with a strange smile*) Yes, I have come to know that same exultant laughter at myself. (*abruptly, with a complete change to a curt business-like matter-of-fact tone*) Well, that's settled. You will go on. (*He glances at his watch.*) And now I'll have to go and catch my train. (*He starts for the door. She gets in his way.*)

SARA—(*seductively*) Leaving me without a kiss? When I'm making myself all you want me to be? (*She suddenly embraces him with a passionate possessiveness.*) Never mind! Be cruel to me! Be anything you like! I'm dirt under your feet and proud to be! For there's no price in life too great to pay to keep you mine! If it's a whore you love me to be, then I am it, body and soul, as long as you're mine! (*She kisses him fiercely.*) I love you so, Darling! I want you! I can't bear you to leave me now! But you'll come back here, won't you? I'll be waiting and longing—

SIMON—(*kisses her passionately*) Yes! I swear to you! Nothing could keep me from—

SARA—(*with uneasiness—pleadingly now*) You won't forget me like you did this morning, and go to keep your engagement to visit her? You'll remember you promised me you'd forget her and let her wait.

SIMON—(*vindictively*) Of course! Let the cowardly old witch wait until Domesday! It will serve her right to be alone in the twilight she dreads so with her idiotic superstitious terror of the haunted summerhouse! I am sick and tired of beseeching her to have the courage— (*He stops abruptly and his expression changes to bitter, angry resentment—harshly accusing*) What are you trying to do, eh? I had forgotten her! Why do you make me remember? Damnation, can't I be free of her even here in your arms? Why do you think I pay such an outlandish price to keep a mistress? You seem compelled to remind me, to put her back in me! That is the one kind of swindling I refuse to tolerate from you! What trick are you up to? Have you made a secret bargain with her to play one another's game? She never lets me forget you long in her garden. She pretends to be jealous of you, just as you pretend— But, by God, though you may hate each other, I know you hate me more and have determined to drive me out and get rid of me! But you had better not go on with your plot, because I warn you—it will be I who— (*He checks himself, his eyes gleaming with a wild threat.*)

SARA—(*staring at him—in a panic of dread*) Simon! Don't look like that! What's happened to you? (*suddenly resentful and angry herself*) God pity you for a fool! Have you lost your senses, to say such crazy blather! Bargain with her, is it? Play her game for her? When I hate her like hell itself! When my one wish about her is to drive her away forever where she can never come back to steal what's mine—

SIMON—(*staring at her—with a cold calculating sneer*) So you boast here behind her back, but with her you're afraid of her!

SARA—It's a lie! I, afraid of a poor old—

SIMON—(*tauntingly*) Do you think I've stopped watching you together in the house at night. You're afraid she might prove to be the stronger if it came to a final decision. So you still pretend to be her friend. (*slowly*) I will believe your boasting, Sara, when you prove you want me to be yours enough that you have the courage to— (*in a burst of strange deadly hatred*) Are you going to let her come between us forever? Can't you rid our life of that damned greedy evil witch?

SARA—(*stares at him with dread—but with a fascinated eagerness too—in a whisper*) You mean you want me to—

SIMON—(*with a change to a lover's playful teasing—pats her cheek*) I want you to do anything in life your heart desires to make me yours. You should know that by this time, Beloved. God knows I have paid you enough to prove it to you! (*He laughs and kisses her.*) I must catch my train. Goodbye until this afternoon. (*He goes out, rear. She stands looking after him, the same expression of horrified eagerness on her face.*)

(*Curtain*)

SCENE TWO

SCENE—*Same as Scene Two of Act Three—the corner of Deborah's garden with the summerhouse. It is around nine o'clock the same night. There is a full moon but clouds keep passing across it so that the light in the garden is a dim, pallid, ghostly grey, in which all objects are indistinct and their outlines merge into one another, with intermittent brief periods of moonlight so clear one could read by it, in which the geometrical form of each shrub and its black shadow are sharply defined and separate. Their alternating lights are like intense brooding moods of the garden itself, and under the spell of either it has more compellingly than ever before the atmosphere of a perversely magnified child's toy garden, unnatural and repellently distorted and artificial.*

Deborah is discovered pacing back and forth along the path between the pool in front of the summerhouse and the door to the street in the wall at right. Her manner is pitifully distraught, nervous, tense, frightened and desperate. One feels she is fighting back complete nervous collapse, wild hysterical tears. Yet at the same time she is a prey to a passionate anger and her eyes smoulder with a bitter, jealous fury and hatred. A great physical change is noticeable in her. Her small, immature, girlish figure has grown so terribly emaciated that she gives the impression of being bodiless, a little, skinny, witch-like, old woman, an evil godmother conjured to life from the page of a fairy tale, whom strong sunlight would dissolve, or a breath of reality disperse into thin air. Her small, delicate, oval face is haggard with innumerable wrinkles, and so pale it seems bloodless and corpse-like, a mask of death, the great dark eyes staring from black holes. She is dressed in white, as ever, but with pathetically obvious touches of calculating, coquettish feminine adornment. Her beautiful white hair is piled up on her head in curls so that it resembles an Eighteenth Century mode. Her withered lips are rouged and there is a beauty-spot on each rouged cheek. There is a pitiful aspect about her of an old portrait of a bygone age come back to haunt the scene of long-past assignation.

DEBORAH — (*distractedly*) God, how long have I waited like this—hours!—hours since supper even—watching, their prying eyes sneering—mocking, snickering under their breath, exchanging smiles—but frightened, too—she has told them to beware of me, I am a little crazy—then after supper out here again—waiting again—waiting, waiting!— why do I?—what makes me make myself?—why don't I go in the house?—hide in my room and lock the door—why do I stay here and hope?—Oh, how can he be so cruel?!—how can he do this to me? (*She suddenly stops and listens tensely—eagerly*) There—footsteps—someone coming up the street! It must be he at last! (*She rushes over and pulls open the door in the wall at right and looks out in the street—then closes it again—dully*) No one— (*bitterly*) Except Life, perhaps, who walks away again now—again forgetful I am still alive— (*She turns away from the door.*) How many times now have I run to open the door, hoping each time— (*flaring into sudden anger*) How dare he humiliate me like this! a common, vulgar, money-grubbing trader like his father!—I made his father respect my pride— I humiliated him— You had better beware, Simon!—if you think I will bear your insults without retaliating!— (*then trying pitifully to reassure herself*) No, no, I must not blame him—he has been detained at the mill by something unforseen— (*with angry scorn*) Ah, how can you make excuses—lie to yourself when you know the truth—he deliberately forgot you—he is even now lying in the arms of that slut, laughing with her to think of the pitiable spectacle you make waiting in vain! (*in a fury*) Ah, if I were sure of that. I would have no more scruples!—I would make him go in the summerhouse instead of protecting him from his insane desire—that would revenge me for all his insults! (*As she is speaking the moon comes from behind a cloud and shines clearly on the summerhouse door. She stops and stares at it fascinatedly—then turns away hastily with a shiver of dread.*) No!—I could not—he is my beloved son who has returned to me—and he will come here soon—he loves me—he would never deliberately wound—he knows how lonely I am—that his visits here are all of happiness and peace that is left me—all that remains to me of life—if he took them from me, I!— But he will explain it is not his fault, he was unavoidably detained— But if he had been detained at the mills—that does not explain why she has not returned home either—he must be with her!— (*distractedly*) Ah, how can I blind myself—as if I did not know she has turned his office into a brothel bedroom—she is vile and unscrupulous—she uses her one superiority—her body—plays upon the only feeling he has for her—makes herself a whore to keep her hold on him!—anything to keep him from me!—but he shall not!—I can be unscrupulous, too—he thinks I will always be afraid—the

fool!—she doesn't realize I have but to take his hand, as he
wishes, and lead him from her life forever!— (*She has again
stopped by the summerhouse and is staring fascinatedly at the door.
Then again she tears her eyes away with a shudder—desperately*)
Oh, why can't she leave me alone!—why does she force me
to hate her so terribly—I am afraid of what her hate is making me become—I know so well the scheme she has in mind
to get rid of me—to drive me insane—she deliberately goads
me!—tempts me—it is horrible to be compelled to constantly resist—it exhausts my mind, my will— (*She shudders—then with a sudden change to a scornful gloating*) What a
stupid animal—can't she see that in the end her hate will give
me the courage I need—that something in me hopes that she
will succeed—but, of course, she hopes I would go alone—
(*She laughs sneeringly.*) Oh no, my dear Sara, I would take
what is mine with me! (*Her eyes are fixed on the summerhouse
door again. The moon passes behind a cloud and the light grows
dim. She turns away frightenedly.*) No! I could not!—I could
not—and there is no need—I have beaten her already—I
have taken him from her—as I always knew I could if she
gave me the opportunity— (*She laughs with arrogant scorn.*)
What a fool she is to imagine she could match me in intrigue—I who have spent years of my life dreaming of the
power I might wield—I have been too subtle for her—I have
used even her strength against her—encouraged him to make
a whore of her—to feel himself devoured and enslaved—until now he sees her as the filthy slut she is—his one desire is
to escape her—soon she will disgust him so, he will drive her
out of my house into the gutter with her brats—meanwhile,
I have led him back, step by step, into memory, into the past,
where he longs to be—where he is my child again—my
baby—where my life is his only life—where he is safe beyond
her grasping claws! (*Her face has taken on a soft, dreamy ecstatic
look—exultantly*) My beloved son and I—one again—happily
ever after—safely hidden from life in our old dreams! (*Her
eyes fasten on the summerhouse door—abruptly frightened—she
turns away to stare about the garden uneasily.*) If he would only
come!—I am afraid alone in this garden at night—slowly as
night descends it becomes strange—somber and threatening
—it seems to be evil—it becomes Nature again—a Nature

my arrogant whim had distorted into ridiculous artificial forms—an enslaved Nature, ground under, thwarted and sneered at—in the day it pretended to be humbly resigned—but as dark comes it strains at its chains like a black slave and longs for revenge and freedom—I feel the bitter, poisoned hatred of each amusingly humiliated shrub. (*She shivers.*) And something in my nature responds—pities—hates—would help it escape—to possess me—within its evil embrace I would forget fear and pity—I would have no mercy for those who sneer and deride— (*She pauses—then with increasing bitterness and suspicion*) Why do I lie and tell myself it is I who have led Simon back into the past, when I know it is he who has forced me to carry out his evil scheme of revenge— (*protesting frightenedly*) No!—how can I have such a mad suspicion—I should be glad—it proves how he loves me—how much he needs my love— (*suspiciously again—sneering at herself*) Love? You know he is incapable of love—love is a passion of the soul—that greedy trader lost his soul long ago when he left me—now he is as soulless as his father—lust is the only passion he feels now—no, do not let him deceive you into believing it is love for you that impels him—what is it, then?—hate?—the hate for me she has put in his mind?—a conspiracy with her to drive me from his life—to imprison me here alone—driving me back farther and farther within myself—until he finally tricks me into unlocking the door, taking his hand—and at the last moment he will snatch his hand away, push me inside alone with that mad woman I locked in there—to be possessed by her again—never to come out— (*The moon again comes from behind a cloud and shines on the summerhouse. She gives a dreadful little laugh.*) And then, of course, it would be so simple to have me locked up in an asylum— (*furiously*) Yes!—I see through your scheme, Simon!—I can see you now, lying in her arms, laughing as you gloat together! But take care! I am not some stupid merchant you swindle!—I am not impressed by your ridiculous posing as a little Napoleon!—nor am I that poor dull-witted peasant you cheat and make a whore of—you will find I will outwit you—I will be the one to snatch away my hand and leave you alone in there with that old mad Deborah who will have no scruple—and you beat the walls, screaming for escape at any cost! (*She suddenly stops, trembling with horror at herself, and presses her hands to her head torturedly.*) Oh, God have mercy,—I must stop thinking—if I go on like this, there will be no need for anyone outside me to—I will drive myself in there! (*She paces back and forth distractedly, glancing with dread around the garden.*) This garden has become horrible. I am afraid of myself here— Oh, if my son would only come!—he is not coming!—why don't I go in the house?—no, I must wait!—he promised me—he has been detained—I must be patient—find some way to pass the time—not think of horrible impossible things—I am still mistress of my mind—I can still dream, if it pleases me— I remember when I waited for him at the cabin that afternoon, I passed the time pleasantly in dreaming—and when I opened my eyes he was there— (*determinedly*) I can do that again. I will! (*She sits on the stone bench at right-rear of the pool, closing her eyes, her face grows tense as she concentrates her will, deliberately hypnotizing herself into a trance. A pause. Then she relaxes slowly and murmurs dreamily*) The gardens at Malmaison—the summerhouse—the Emperor— (*Her dream becomes disturbed and puzzled and uneasy but she only half awakes.*) No—I do not wish this—it is not the same—not Versailles and the King—the Emperor Napoleon?—how strange—I had thought I hated him—Father's silly confusing him with God—and Simon pretending he is like— I always wanted to live in a time before he lived—and now I see that was very cowardly of me—to deny him—so silly to run and hide like a little bashful girl— (*sinking happily into dreams*) The Emperor kisses me— "My Throne, it is your heart, Dear Love, and I—"

(*While she is saying this last, Sara slinks in noiselessly along the path from the house on the left. She looks worn out and dissipated, with dark circles under her eyes, her hair dishevelled, her dress wrinkled and awry, like a prostitute the morning after a debauch. She stands regarding Deborah with a cruel mocking leer of satisfaction.*)

SARA—(*to herself*) Ah, I knew what my keeping him away would do to her! She's like I hoped she'd be! I'll have only to goad and taunt and make game of her now to drive her over the edge where she'll never find the way back! And it's what Simon wants, too, to be rid of her. It's what he asked me to do!

DEBORAH—(*in her dream, her face lighting up with love*) At last you have come, Sire. My poor heart was terrified you had forgotten I was waiting.

SARA—(*In spite of herself, her eyes grow pitying.*) No. God forgive me. The poor creature! I couldn't—not yet—not unless it's the only way to save him from her madness.

DEBORAH—(*laughs softly and seductively, rising to her feet*) Yes, give me your hand and let us go within, Sire, where we will be hidden from the ugliness of life—in our Temple of Love where there is only Beauty and forgetfulness! (*She holds out her hand and clasps that of her royal dream lover and turns towards the door and slowly begins to ascend the steps.*)

SARA—(*with a gloating eagerness*) She's going to do it herself! I won't need to! I've only to let her alone! And that's what Simon wants.

DEBORAH—I have the key here, Sire. I have worn it lately over my heart. (*She reaches down inside her bodice and pulls out a key on a cord around her neck—hesitates frightenedly—then unlocks but does not open the door.*)

SARA—(*eagerly but at the same time frightenedly*) She's unlocked it! Nothing will stop her now! I've only to mind my own business. Why did I come here? I don't like seeing it, when I could prevent her. But it's what Simon wants—and I want!

DEBORAH—(*with a little shiver, holding back, forcing a little smile*) I—I confess I am a little frightened, Sire. So foolish of me—but— (*pleadingly*) Oh, swear to me again you would not deceive me—that it is love and forgetfulness!

SARA—(*struggling with herself*) She's frightened! She knows even in her dream! Ah, though I hate her more than hell, I pity her now! But why should I? It's little pity she'd have for me if she saw her chance—

DEBORAH—(*forcing a determined, exalting tone*) But even if it were hell, it will be heaven to me with your love! (*She puts her hand on the knob.*)

SARA—(*fiercely*) Yes, go to hell and be damned to you and leave Simon alone to me! (*Then just as Deborah is turning the knob she springs toward her.*) Stop! Let go of that door, you damned old fool! (*Deborah starts and half-awakens with a bewildered cry, pulling her hand from the door, and stands dazed and trembling. Sara reaches her side. She is angry at herself for interfering now and takes it out on Deborah, grabbing her by the shoulders and shaking her roughly.*) Wake up from your mad dreams, I'm saying! I've no patience to humor your daftness.

DEBORAH—(*whimpering with pain and fright like a child*) Let go! You are hurting me! It isn't fair! You are so much stronger! Simon! Make her let me alone! (*Sara has let go of her. Deborah stares at her fully awake now. She makes a shaken attempt to draw herself up with her old arrogance.*) You! How dare you touch me!

SARA—(*shamefacedly*) I'm sorry if I hurt you, but I had to wake you—

DEBORAH—(*with vindictive fury now*) Oh, I'd like to have you beaten! Lashed till the blood ran down your fat white shoulders!

SARA—(*bitterly resentful*) Divil a doubt you would! And that's the thanks I get for stopping you!

DEBORAH—How dare you come here!

SARA—(*angrily*) To hell with your airs and graces! Whose property is it, I'd like to know? You're the one who has no right here!

DEBORAH—Oh!

SARA—But the only reason I came was because I took pity on you, knowing you'd be kept waiting out here all night, like an old fool, if I didn't tell he'd come home with me and forgotten all about you.

DEBORAH—Then—it is true. He did go back to the office, instead of— He went back to you! You made him, with your filthy—

SARA—(*tauntingly*) Made him? You don't know the strength of his love for me! I couldn't have kept him from me, if I'd wanted!

DEBORAH—You came here to tell me—so you could gloat! You vulgar common slut!

SARA—(*goadingly*) And I've more to tell you. He's paid the last visit here he'll ever pay you. He swore to me on his honor, lying in my arms, he never wanted to see you again, he was sick of wasting time humoring your craziness!

DEBORAH—(*in a fury of jealous hatred, making a threatening movement toward her*) You lie! He would never— He will come! Oh, you despicable filthy harlot!

SARA—He'll never come here again, I'm telling you! So don't be dreaming and hoping! (*then angrily*) A filthy harlot, am I? Well, I'm what he loves me to be! And it's not for you to call names, my high and mighty lady, or to give yourself airs. What were you in your crazy dreams just now—what have you always prided yourself you could be if you had the courage—but the greatest whore in the world!

DEBORAH—(*shrinking back to the foot of the steps as if she'd been struck—guiltily*) No, no! Only in a silly fancy—to amuse my mind—to wile away the time— How dare you insult me by thinking I could ever really wish— It's because you have the vile disgusting mind of a common street woman. You judge everyone by yourself.

SARA—(*roughly scornful*) Arrah, don't be talking! You don't fool me! (*jeering derisively*) I'll say this for you you have grand tastes! It used to be King Louis of France, no less, you had for your man! But now it's the Emperor Napoleon, God pity you! My, but aren't you the fickle, greedy one! You've never enough! (*She laughs with coarse cruelty.*)

DEBORAH—(*shrinking back up the steps as Sara keeps coming nearer to her—distractedly*) Don't! Don't! Oh, how dare you laugh!

SARA—(*with cruel mocking insistence*) It'll be the Czar of Russia next! Aren't you the beautiful evil woman with all the kings and rulers of the earth, that are or ever was, down on their knees at your feet!

DEBORAH—(*shrinking back to the top step—stammers distractedly*) Don't! Don't! Let me alone!

SARA—(*following her*) Begging you to let them sleep with you! (*with savage contempt*) When out of your mad dreams you're only a poor little wizened old woman no common man on the street would turn to look at, and who, in the days when the men did want you, didn't have the blood or the strength to want them but ran and hid in her garden.

DEBORAH—(*with a pitiful, stammering, hysterical laugh*)

Yes! So ridiculous, isn't it? So pitiful and disgusting and horrible! (*distractedly*) Don't! Don't remind me! Don't make me
see! (*wildly*) I can't endure myself! I won't! I'll be free at any
cost! I— (*She turns and grabs the knob of the door.*)

SARA—(*instinctively makes a grab for her and pulls her
away—covering her guilty fear with a rough anger*) Come away
from that!

DEBORAH—(*struggling*) No! Let me go!

SARA—(*angrily*) You will, will you? (*She picks Deborah up
in her strong arms, as if she weighed nothing, sets her down before
the bench at right and forces her down on it—angrily*) Sit there
and be quiet now! I've had enough of your tricks! If you
think you'll make me have your madness on my conscience,
you're mistaken! (*Deborah crumples up and falls sideways face
down on the bench and bursts into hysterical sobbing. Sara speaks
with a grim satisfaction.*) Ah, thank God, you can cry. Maybe
that will bring some sense back in your head, and you won't
be calling names that make me lose my temper and force me
to do things to you I don't want to do except as a last resort
if you keep on. (*Her tone becomes more and more persuasive as
Deborah's crying gradually spends itself.*) But I don't think you'll
want to keep on now. Not after what happened today—him
keeping you waiting here and making an old fool of you! And
I've told you the truth, he swore he'd never come to you
again. It was part of the price I made him pay for me when
he came back from the mills. Well, do you mean to tell me,
in the face of that, you'll go begging him to visit you? You've
got more pride in you than that, I hope. And anyway, it
would do you no good. He'd only refuse you. He'd laugh at
you again. He's mine now, I tell you! He's paid me everything he has. He has nothing left but me. He has no life
except in my love. And I love him more than ever woman
loved a man! I'm mother, wife, and mistress in one. He
doesn't need you. You're out in the cold. You're beaten. (*Deborah is still now and listening tensely but she does not raise her
head. Sara goes on almost wheedlingly.*) Listen to me. The real
reason I came here was to have a sensible talk with you, and
ask you to face the truth that I've won and you're beaten.
You're finished and well you know it! Well you know a moment ago I could have driven you in there where the only

door out leads to an asylum! I didn't because I hoped you'd be sensible and not make me do it! I hoped you'd admit you were beaten and give up. (*almost pleadingly*) Won't you own up now that it's no good going on with your mad schemes? If you'll swear to stop, I'll stop too and make peace with you. And I'll give in on my side to make it fair with you. I'll give the children back to you to keep you company and stand between you and your dreams, and you'll be as contented as you were before. And I won't hate you. You know I don't like your forcing me to hate you, don't you? (*She pauses. Deborah remains still. Sara's anger rises.*) Well? Haven't you a tongue in your head? It's you, not me, ought to beg for peace! I've made you a decent offer, and it's your last chance.

DEBORAH—(*abruptly straightens up and stares at her with hard revengeful eyes—with a mocking smile*) You are even more stupid than I thought. Don't you know your begging for peace is a confession of how insecure you are in your fancied victory? I am convinced now that you realize that any time I choose I can take Simon away with me!

SARA—(*frightenedly*) You mean, into madness, with you? (*savagely*) I swear by Almighty God I'll murder you if you try that.

DEBORAH—(*coldly disdainful*) And get your children's mother hanged?

SARA—(*taken aback*) I'll do it a way no one will discover!

DEBORAH—(*coldly contemptuous*) Simon would know. Do you think your husband would love a wife who had murdered his mother?

SARA—You think he wouldn't? I tell you, he'd thank me for it! If you knew how he hated you now for trying to make him hate me! He begged me today to get rid of you, so he and I could be free!

DEBORAH—(*shakenly*) You lie! He loves me! It's you he hates! You have become vile and disgusting to him! He loathes your foul flesh, your filthy, insatiable greeds! He has implored me to drive you out of life into the gutter from which you sprang! Or if that takes too long, he has hinted I might find some subtle way that might never be suspected, to poison you!

SARA—(*shakenly*) Ah, it's the evil liar you are! He loves

me! He'd never! But I know it's in your mind and I'll take good care what I eat or drink from now on!

DEBORAH — (*suddenly gives way to a horrified realization*) Sara! Oh, no! For God's sake, how can you think I—? (*then her face hardening again—defiantly*) I refuse your offer of peace. I do not trust you. How could I trust you? I trusted you once. Besides, even if your begging for peace did not clearly reveal to me how weak you are, your stopping me from opening the door would. You could really have won then but you did not have strength. You are weakly sentimental and pitiful. You cannot be ruthless. You are feeble with guilty scruples. You will always defeat yourself at the last. (*scornfully*) You fool! Do you think, in your place, I would ever have stopped you? I would have laughed with joy! I could watch you lashed to death, with the blood running down your gross white back, and never raise a finger to save you! (*arrogantly*) Pah! What a fool I have been! It is you who are doomed by your weakness to inevitable defeat. I am the stronger as I always knew I would be, if given the opportunity.

SARA — (*angrily*) So that's your answer, is it? That's what you think? That's my thanks for— (*vindictively*) You old lunatic, you'll see if I have any pity on you the next time!

DEBORAH — (*haughtily—as if addressing a servant*) I see no reason for prolonging this tiresome interview. You have no business in this garden. Will you be good enough to return to the house where you belong and attend to your children. I know my son is waiting for an opportunity to see me alone.

SARA — (*angrily, turning toward the path off left*) I'll go, and be damned to you! I've come to the end of pity! (*with cruel vindictiveness*) He's waiting hoping to hear I've found you locked inside there and we can get the asylum to take you away!

DEBORAH — (*her will beginning to crumple under this attack—distractedly*) Oh, no! You are lying! Not my beloved son! He couldn't!

SARA — (*jeering savagely*) I'll be sorry to disappoint him but I'll promise him you're near the end and it won't be long before we're free! (*She starts to go.*)

DEBORAH — (*with a pitiful frightened cry*) Sara! No! (*She*

runs to her wildly and grabs her arm—stammering with terror)
Don't go! Don't leave me alone, here! I—I'm afraid! Please
stay! I—I'll do anything you ask! I'll admit you've won! I'll
make peace! I'll promise anything you want! Only—don't
leave me here! I need your strength or I'll— (*She throws her
arms around Sara and begins to sob hysterically.*) Oh, how can
you be so cruel to me?

SARA—(*has stared at her at first suspiciously and resentfully—
then gloating triumphantly but moved in spite of herself—finally,
as Deborah weeps, she is overcome by pity and soothes her as she
would a child*) There, there now. Don't be frightened. I'm
here. I'm strong enough for the two of us. And it's all over
now. We won't destroy each other anymore. You'll have the
children back. You'll be happy and contented. You know I
didn't want to be cruel to you.

DEBORAH—(*brokenly*) I know. And you know I didn't.

SARA—(*gently*) Come in the house with me now. You
must go to bed and rest. It's a wonder if you haven't caught
your death already, chilled by the night and the dew.

DEBORAH—(*exhaustedly—with humble affectionate gratitude*) You are so generous and kind and warm. I know that
in my heart so well. How could I have forgotten? How could
I have longed so horribly for your death—the one friend I
have ever possessed, the one person who has ever understood
my pride. I am really so humbly grateful, and yet— How
could I be so vile and evil?

SARA—(*soothingly*) Ah well, wasn't I just wishing you
locked up in an asylum? I'm worse than you. But it's over
now. We've made peace. We'll forget. (*urging her*) Let's go in
the house now. You're trembling. You've taken a chill. Come.

DEBORAH—You are so thoughtful and good. (*Sara begins
to lead her off left. Abruptly she stops—with dread*) No. We're
forgetting he is there, Sara. We must wait. We can't face him
yet. We would be too weak. We must stay here together,
trusting each other, until we get back our old strength to defy
him as one woman. The strength his evil jealous greed has
corrupted and destroyed! (*desperately*) Yes, it is he! He! Not
us! We have been driven to this!

SARA—(*resentfully*) Ah, don't I know how he's driven
me!

DEBORAH—(*her desperation angry*) He! He! He! Only he! We saw that so clearly when he first started to goad us into this duel to the death! We swore to each other that we would constantly bear in mind it was he, not us. In him, not in us! We saw our danger if we ever let him make us forget that.

SARA—I know! But, in a few days he'd made us forget! He made us deceive each other and hate and scheme—

DEBORAH—Yes! Devote our lives to destroying each other! In meek obedience to his whim! Oh, what weak fools we have been! How could we be so blind and stupid!

SARA—Because we loved him so much! And didn't he know that, the sly schemer, and use it to have his own way!

DEBORAH—We could have defeated him so easily! We would have been so much stronger! He would have had no more strength than a little boy or a baby! We could have kept him absolutely dependent on us, with no life except within our life.

SARA—And he'd have been happy and content, not destroyed with hunger and mad with greed like he is now.

DEBORAH—Yes! He would have been supremely happy and utterly contented with nothing but our love. But no! It wasn't enough! He had to play the great self-liberator, the conquering Napoleon, of others, with his women, too.

SARA—(*with resentful contempt*) Arrah, he's like all the greedy fools of men, never knowing when they're well off.

DEBORAH—If we had carried out our determination to remain united we could so easily have curbed his insane rebellion against happiness. He would have had to beg us to restore our peace to him. But instead we let him revive a dead hate of the past to start us clawing and tearing at each other's hearts like two mad female animals he had thrown in a pit to fight for his love—while he stands apart and watches and sneers and laughs with greedy pride and goads each on in turn to murder the other!

SARA—(*with bitter anger*) And when only one is left living, he knows she'll be so weakened by the long duel he can easily make a slave of her who'll never have strength to claim her body or soul her own again! (*While she is talking, unnoticed by them both, Simon appears behind them, entering from the path at left. He does not make his presence known but stands staring at*

*them. He is in a state of terrific tension, and there is a wild look
in his eyes, cunning, calculating and threatening and at the same
time baffled and panic-stricken.*)

DEBORAH—Yes, that is what he is trying to accomplish, of
course—use one to rid him of the other.

SARA—Or both to be rid of both! (*She laughs bitterly.*) Ah,
wouldn't he strut and puff out his chest before the mirror
then, boasting what a great little independent man he was, if
he were free of the two of us!

DEBORAH—(*sneering bitterly*) Yes, he would be finally convinced then he was a reincarnation of Napoleon! Yes, I hadn't
thought of it before but now I see that must be his most
ambitious dream. (*Her face hardens cruelly.*) It would serve
him right if we turned the tables on him, Sara. We could have
the strength now as we are united again as one woman.

SARA—(*fascinatedly*) You mean, throw him in the pit—to
fight it out with himself?

DEBORAH—For our love—while we watched with gratified womanly pride and laughed and goaded him on!

SARA—(*eagerly—but with hesitant dread, too*) Until—

DEBORAH—Yes, Sara. Until at last we're finally rid of him.
(*with tense hatred and longing*) Oh God, think of how simply
contented we could be alone together with our children—
grandmother and mother, mother and daughter, sister and
sister, one woman and another, with the way so clear before
us, the purpose and meaning of life so happily implicit, the
feeling of living life so deeply sure of itself, not needing
thought, beyond all torturing doubt and sneers and question,
the passive "yes" of self-possession welcoming the peaceful procession of demanding days! (*She pauses—then a bit
guiltily*) I hope you do not think it evil of me that I can find
it in myself to wish he were not here.

SARA—(*fascinatedly*) No—there have been times at the
office when I—

DEBORAH—He has taught us that whatever is in oneself is
good—that whatever one desires is good, that the one evil is
to deny oneself. (*tensely*) Again, it is not us but what he has
made us be! So on his head—

SIMON—(*speaks with a tense quiet casualness*) You are mistaken, Mother. (*They both whirl on him with startled gasps of*

terror and cling to one another defensively. Then as he advances, they shrink back to the edge of the bench at the right rear of pool, keeping the pool between them and him. He goes on with the same tense brittle quiet.) You are hiding from yourself again, Mother. And Sara seems to have caught the cowardly habit from you. It is stupid of you to blame me. It is not on my head but in your hearts. I have merely insisted that you both be what you are—that what you are is good because it is fact and reality—that the true nature of man and woman, to which we have hitherto given the bad name of evil because we were afraid of it, is, in a world of facts dominated by our greed for power and possession, good because it is true. And what is evil, because it is a lie, is the deliberate evasive sentimental misunderstanding of man as he is, proclaimed by the fool, Jean Jacques Rousseau—the stupid theory that he is naturally what we call virtuous and good. Instead of being what he is, a hog. It is that idealistic fallacy which is responsible for all the confusion in our minds, the conflicts within the self, and for all the confusion in our relationships with one another, within the family particularly, for the blundering of our desires which are disciplined to covet what they don't want and be afraid to crave what they wish for in truth. (*He smiles a thin tense smile.*) In a nutshell, if you will pardon the seeming paradox, all one needs to re-member is that good is evil, and evil, good. (*As they have lis-tened, the faces of the two women have hardened into a deadly enmity.*)

DEBORAH—(*tensely and threateningly*) Do you hear, Sara. We must not forget.

SARA—(*in the same tone*) No, we owe it to him to be what he wants.

SIMON—(*his tense quiet beginning to snap*) But I did not come out here to discuss my meditations on the true nature of man. (*He pauses—then the strain breaking, his voice trem-bling, he blurts out in violent accusation*) I—I was trying to concentrate my thoughts on the final solution of the problem. I have been forced to the conclusion lately that in the end, if the conflicting selves within a man are too evenly matched—if neither is strong enough to destroy the other before the man himself, of which they are halves, is exhausted by their

struggle and in danger of being torn apart between them—
then that man is forced at last, in self-defense, to choose one
or the other—

DEBORAH—(*starts—staring at him uneasily*) To choose,
Simon?

SARA—(*echoing her*) To choose, Simon?

SIMON—To throw all his remaining strength to one and
help it to destroy the other. That appears to me now to be
the one possible way he can end the conflict and save his
sanity before it is too late.

DEBORAH—(*beginning to be cruelly gloating now*) You hear
what he's confessing, Sara?

SARA—(*echoing her tone*) That we've been too strong for
him, and he's near the end.

SIMON—(*as if he hadn't heard*) Before my mind is torn and
clawed to death between them and devoured!

DEBORAH—(*gloatingly*) Yes, he is much nearer the end
than I had thought.

SARA—(*in same tone*) Yes, we've only to wait and we'll
soon be free of him. (*She chuckles.*) Well, I should have known
he hadn't much strength left to go on with! If you knew how
I've beaten him at the office! I've stripped him clean, Deborah! I got the bank from him today. He's ruined and finished!
He's nothing left to offer me! And if he hopes, after all he's
taught me, that he can cheat me into giving something for
nothing, he's a bigger fool even than I think him! (*She
laughs.*)

DEBORAH—(*smiles gloatingly*) Oh, I have guessed, Sara. I
have been with you in spirit and been proud of you in my
imagination! I have helped you all I could by urging him to
encourage your greed. (*then almost boastfully*) But I should
have guessed how near the end he is through my own experience with him, Sara. If you could see how I have led him
farther and farther away, back into the past, until now all I
have to do is say one word, or even have the thought in silence, and our great man-conquering Napoleon becomes a
stubborn, nagging, begging little boy whose only purpose or
ambition in life is to possess the happy ending of an old silly
fairy tale! (*She laughs and Sara joins in her laughter.*)

SARA—(*staring at Simon—mockingly*) Well, well, you're a

great one for teaching us that everyone is for sale and it should be a woman's pride to get the highest price she can, but I'm thinking in the end it will be us who have taught you about high prices!

DEBORAH—(*mockingly*) Yes, I am sure he will have learned that a woman's pride costs more than he could ever afford to pay without going bankrupt.

SARA—(*scornfully resentful*) So he'll choose, will he, the great man? Like a master picking which of two slaves he'd like to own! But suppose they don't choose to let him choose?

DEBORAH—(*echoing her tone*) Yes, it would be very stupid of them, when all they have to do is to wait together and stand apart and watch while he destroys himself and sets them free. Encourage him to do so, even. Goad him on with their laughter. (*She laughs softly and Sara laughs with her.*)

SIMON—(*with an abrupt change to his matter-of-fact tone*) I don't know what you're talking about, Mother. I attempt to explain an abstract problem of the nature of man, and you and Sara begin talking as if you, personally, were directly concerned in it! (*He chuckles dryly.*) An amusing example of the insatiable ambition of female possessiveness, don't you think? (*curtly*) Never mind. It is my fault for being such a fool as to discuss it with you. I know the one problem that interests you. (*He becomes angrily excited.*) God knows I could hardly be unaware of it tonight! I heard you from my study quarreling out here, clawing and tearing at each other like two drunken drabs fighting over a dollar bill! God, it becomes disgusting! You might at least have the decency to confine your revolting greedy brawls to the house! Do you want to create a public scandal, screaming where all the neighbors can hear, cursing and threatening to murder each other!

DEBORAH—(*quietly*) We were not screaming. You could not possibly have heard us in your study. I am afraid what you heard were the voices of your own mind. You were dreaming your old dream of liberty for men, perhaps, and listening to your hopes.

SIMON—(*with angry excitement*) That's a lie! I heard you as clearly as if I were here! I could not concentrate my thoughts on the final solution of the problem, listening to your screaming hatred! It seemed there would never be a moment's peace in my life again—that you would go on with your horrible duel, clawing and tearing each other, until my mind would be ripped apart! (*He checks himself uneasily— quickly, trying to adopt a tone of confident scorn*) I heard you, I tell you. So don't attempt to evade your guilt by saying I imagined it. Are you trying to insinuate I am going insane? Ridiculous! You will find you were talking louder than you realized. Hatred seldom remembers to keep its voice decently lowered. And then when you finally did become quiet, there was no peace— It was the stillness that follows a shriek of terror, waiting to become aware— I was afraid one of you had killed the other. I thought when I came here I would find only one—

DEBORAH—(*staring at him—cannot control a shrinking shudder*) We know—you have been hoping—

SARA—(*with a shudder*) Ah, God forgive me!

SIMON—(*wildly*) Well, I might have been hoping. Suppose I was? Do you think I can endure living with your murderous duel forever—always between you—a defenseless object for your hatred of each other—rent in twain by your tearing greedy claws? No! I tell you there comes a point where the tortured mind will pay any price for peace! (*He suddenly breaks and sinks on the bench at left of pool, his head clutched convulsively in his hands—brokenly*) Why can't you stop? Why won't you make peace between you? I will do anything you wish! Is there no love or pity left in your hearts? Can't you see you are driving me insane? (*He begins to sob exhaustedly— the two women sit together, as one, on the other bench, staring at him. Their first reaction is one of victory. But there is no satisfaction or triumph. They are exhausted and without feeling.*)

DEBORAH—(*dully*) We have won, Sara.

SARA—(*dully*) Yes, Deborah. He admits he's beaten. (*They stare at him. He remains still, his head in his hands. Suddenly, their faces, as one face, are convulsed by pitying, forgiving maternal love.*)

DEBORAH—Our poor boy! How could we be so cruel!

SARA—Our poor darling! How could we feel as we were feeling about you! (*Then, as one, they spring to their feet and go to him, separating, one coming round one side of the pool,*) *the other round the other. They kneel at each side of him, putting an arm around him, hastening to tenderly console and comfort him.*)

DEBORAH—There, there! Our beloved son!

SARA—Our husband! Our lover!

DEBORAH—You mustn't cry, Dear. You break our hearts when you cry.

SARA—There's nothing need frighten you now. We've forgiven you.

DEBORAH—We love you again.

SARA—You'll be hidden safe and sound in our love, where no one can hurt you.

DEBORAH—Yes, it's so silly of you to be frightened, Dear. Couldn't you see as soon as we came here we had made peace between us?

SARA—And now you're at peace in our peace, don't you feel that, Darling?

SIMON—(*raises his head, a confused, dreamy wondering peace in his face—dazedly*) Yes. It is very restful here. I am very grateful to you for life. (*He turns to Sara.*) I love you, my mother. (*He turns to Deborah.*) I love you, my— (*He stops guiltily—then springs from their arms to his feet, stammering distractedly*) No, no! I could not live in such confusion! (*Keeping his back to them, as they remain kneeling, he adds with a sneering mockery*) As for this peace of yours, if you think I can be taken in by such an obvious sham— (*The two women spring to their feet. Both cry as one with anguished despair:* "Simon! Don't!" *and each grabs one of his arms and clings to it. Simon trembles with his effort to control himself. He speaks with a hurried acquiescence.*) I ask your pardon. My mind is still extremely confused. It is such an unexpected shock—to find Sara here where she never intrudes—and then to hear of your confusing reconcilement— But it was very evil of me to doubt and sneer—particularly as I love you both so deeply and it is my dearest wish for my women to live in harmony and I may enjoy love and peace in my home!

SARA—(*with happy relief*) Darling! (*She hugs his arm.*)

DEBORAH—Dear! (*then teasingly*) And here's the kiss you cheated me of a moment ago. (*She kisses his cheek.*)

SIMON—(*smiles pleasantly*) Thank you, Mother. (*then with*

a too-pleasant, natural affectionate air) Well, all is forgotten and forgiven then, and I start a new happy life within your united love, is that it?

DEBORAH—(*gaily tender*) Oh yes, Dear! And we will make you so happy! Won't we, Sara?

SARA—(*gaily tender*) Indeed we will! He won't know himself!

SIMON—(*pleasantly*) I am sure I will not. Let us sit down and rest for a moment together then, shall we, in this garden so hidden from the ugliness of reality, where it is always so restful— (*Then, as they are about to sit, he suddenly exclaims*) Ah, what a fool I am. I had entirely forgotten the object of my coming here. It had nothing to do with your quarrel, which, as you say, must have been merely my imagination. I came to remind you, Sara, it's the children's bedtime and they are waiting for your goodnight kiss. They were a bit hurt, I might add. It isn't like their mother to forget.

SARA—(*guilty—rebuking herself*) Ah, the poor darlings. Bad cess to me, how could I forget—

SIMON—(*with a calculating insistence*) You'd better take a good look at Honey. Unless I'm mistaken, he's getting a cold. It seemed to me he was a bit feverish.

SARA—(*worriedly*) Ah, the poor lamb, and me out here gabbing— (*She starts off the path at left, then hesitates.*) You're coming in?

DEBORAH—(*quickly*) Yes, of course—

SIMON—(*quickly*) Yes, it's too damp and chilly. We'll go in, Mother. But you better run ahead, Sara, and see Honey.

SARA—(*worriedly*) Ah, I hope he's not going to be sick. I'll— (*She hurries off, left. Simon turns and stares at his mother.*)

SIMON—(*with a sneering chuckle*) Well, you must admit I got rid of her very successfully, Mother.

DEBORAH—(*staring at him—smiles gloatingly*) Yes, I felt that was what you were doing. She is such a stupid, trustful— (*then tensely*) No! You are making me say that! I—

SIMON—(*ignoring this*) She will be occupied fussing over Honey and getting them all to bed. She will not notice we have remained out here.

DEBORAH—(*stiffening—coldly*) I am not remaining here.

SIMON—(*ignoring this*) It will give us an opportunity to be alone.

DEBORAH—(*tensely*) I do not wish to be alone with you. I am going in and help her with the children. I am going in! At once! (*She takes a step towards left, stiffly, as if by a determined effort of will staring at him with a fascinated uneasiness. He reaches out and takes one of her hands and she stops, trembling, rooted to the spot. She stammers*) You—you may do as you please. It is not my affair—(*her tone becomes taunting*) if you choose to stay out here alone in the darkness—and make an idiot of yourself—dreaming childish make-believe—like a silly little boy—you, a grown man!—if you could only see yourself!—what a ridiculous comic figure!—a Napoleon who believes in fairy tales and marches to Moscow in search of a magic door—the Emperor whose greatest ambition is to invade and capture a summerhouse in his mother's garden and conquer spider webs and the dirt and mould of old dreams and the forgotten ghost of an absurdly vain and selfish and cowardly woman who longed to escape— (*She forces a sneering laugh.*) But I—I am sick and tired of humoring you, as one would a half-witted child. I am finished with your romantic nonsense. I have talked it over sensibly with your wife and she agrees with me that my permitting you to come here was a great mistake. It has benefitted neither of us. It only encourages you in your most cowardly weakness of character—your ignoble fear of a man's responsibilities in life—your streak of sickly-mindedness and unbalanced fantasy. And, for my part, your visits have bored me to exhaustion! Furthermore, my grandchildren will keep me company again now, and I shall have no time to spare for you. (*with a sneering smile*) Of course, perhaps they might consent to humor you by letting you take part in their games, but I think it would be bad for you to encourage your morbid childishness. No, on second thought, I will not permit that either. I forbid you to ever come to this garden again! Do you hear me, Simon?

SIMON—(*frowning—with a touch of impatience*) I have heard you talking, yes. But I know you were not really addressing me, but attempting to cheat your own mind. So I paid no attention—

DEBORAH—(*uneasily*) Ah. (*tensely*) Will you kindly let go my hand? I wish to go in and join Sara.

SIMON—(*quietly*) You know you do not, Mother. What has your rare and fastidious, dreaming poet's soul in common with that mating and begetting female animal who is all material greed?

DEBORAH—(*stares at him, her eyes lighting up with satisfaction*) Ah! You see what she really is at least, do you? Haven't I always told you she was nothing more than a common, vulgar— (*abruptly*) No, no! She is a finer woman than I! She is sweet and generous and kind! Why do I let you twist my mind! And you—it is despicable of you to speak like that about a woman who has been such a good wife to you and who loves you so deeply and unselfishly.

SIMON—(*sneeringly*) You are speaking of my mistress, I think. But I owe her nothing. She made me pay two-fold the value of every pound of flesh—

DEBORAH—(*disdainfully*) What did you expect? She is a natural born— (*then catching herself—jeeringly*) It serves you right! I am very glad she— I told her to make you realize, in the only terms you could understand, what a woman's love is worth!

SIMON—(*taunting in his turn*) Oh, I am not grudging her her price. She is very beautiful. No one could have a more desirable mistress!

DEBORAH—(*tensely—tugging to pull her hand away*) Let me go! You have become gross and filthy! The touch of your hand disgusts me! (*with an abrupt change of tone—sneering jealously*) And you are a blind, besotted fool to call her beautiful! She has youth and health and a certain peasant prettiness, but that is all. She has thick ankles and fat hips and rough dish-washing hands. She— (*violently*) No! You cannot make me think ill of her and enviously criticize her beauty—

SIMON—You are quite right about her repellent fleshiness. I have been so conscious of it lately I have almost screamed with repulsion each time I touched her.

DEBORAH—(*her eyes lighting up with vindictive triumph*) Ah, so at last— Oh, I knew it in the end— (*fighting with herself*) No! How dare you disdain the wife who loves you, as if she were a low prostitute you had bought and then grown tired of and were planning to discard—

SIMON—Yes, I have grown tired of her. I have had enough of her. All I want now is to get rid of her forever.

DEBORAH—(*eagerly*) Simon! Do you really mean— (*struggling with herself again*) No! You are lying to save your face! You do not fool me! It is she who is tired of you. Good heavens, what woman wouldn't be disgusted with the greedy, soulless trader in the slave market of life you have become— the vulgar tasteless lustful owner of goods—the cotton mill Napoleon! It is Sara who has had enough and now is planning to get rid of you! Planning with me! I shall help to find the most effective means—I shall advise her never to go to your office again. Why should she waste her youth and beauty now you have nothing left to offer her! (*vindictively*) We will give you the freedom you used to dream about! We will laugh when we find you begging on the street of every woman who passes a little pitying love to save your soul from starvation! And finally, the solitary soul you used to be so proud of in yourself as a mark of unique, superior distinction will come cringing and whining and pleading to our door and implore us to open and take you back in to our love again—at any price! (*She laughs jeeringly—then with an abrupt change to a strange remorseful pity*) No—forgive me—I do not mean to be cruel and laugh— But you— (*then eagerly*) Simon! Is it true you are really planning to get rid of her now? (*savagely*) Ah! Haven't I prophesied to your office that the time would come when you would feel so devoured and degraded and enslaved by vice that you would loathe her and drive her out in the gutter where she belongs!

SIMON—No. Driving her out in the streets to ply her trade is not the way to escape her, Mother. She would stand before the door soliciting—begging for love. It would be her revenge to never allow me to forget the past. She would still live in my life, greedily possessing it.

DEBORAH—(*furiously*) Ah! What a contemptible confession of weakness and cowardice! Have you no pride nor shame that you can admit yourself such a weak, will-less slave?

SIMON—She would still be beautiful and desirable.

DEBORAH—A base slave to a vulgar common trollop! And you call yourself my son!

SIMON—I cannot tell you how sick I am of being a fool who keeps a whore in luxury and power and watches helplessly while she swindles and ruins him. But what can I do when her beauty arouses my desire? (*tensely*) Oh, if you knew how desperately I long to escape her and become again only your son!

DEBORAH—(*deeply moved—stammers*) I—I know. Dear—I know that must be true because—I have longed so desperately myself— (*then abruptly with a distracted suspicion and resentment*) Oh, how can you lie like that? How can you be such a hypocrite? Do you think I can believe—you have any feeling for me whatever—except scorn and hatred—when you deliberately kept me waiting here hour after hour—deliberately ignored and humiliated—spat in the face of my pride—my love—while you lay in the arms of that low slut and laughed with her to think of me here listening to each footstep on the street, thinking each time—excusing you, and lying to myself—hoping against hope, like a swindled, defrauded fool! (*She glares at him with hatred.*) Ah, how I hated you! How I cursed the night you were conceived, the morning you were born! How I prayed that you would die and set me free from the intolerable degrading slavery— (*She stops, appalled—stammers*) No! I don't mean—I couldn't mean— (*brokenly*) Forgive me—but— Oh Simon, how could you be so horrible and cruel to me! (*then ashamed of her abjectness—her pride forcing a pitiful attempt at a belittling tone*) But how ridiculously emotional and dramatic I sound! So absurd! I fear there must be a great deal of truth in the accusation you always make that I am always acting an unreal part! The truth is I did not much mind your not coming. I was annoyed. Naturally, I do not like absent-minded people who forget appointments. But I was also very glad to be alone for a change, and be relieved of the strain of humoring your fantastic childish whims and morbid yearning with the past. I was free to be myself. It was a pleasure to sit here in my own mind and dream— (*She checks herself—sharply*) I would like to go in the house now and join Sara. Will you kindly let go of my hand?

SIMON—(*staring into her eyes—slowly and compellingly*) I wish you to sit here beside me, Mother, and let me explain—

DEBORAH—(*stares back fascinatedly—with confused eagerness*) Yes, I knew you'd explain when you came. I kept telling myself, he will explain and I will see it was not his fault and forgive him. (*She sits on the bench beside him as if his will drove her down.*)

SIMON—(*quietly*) I realize how hurt you must have been, but I thought you would understand it was not I. It was she who insisted I must deliberately forget and return to her instead.

DEBORAH—(*tensely*) I know! I knew that must be true! I know my Simon would never— (*then bitterly*) But that doesn't excuse you! You deliberately consented!

SIMON—(*with tense quiet*) What could I do? She is so beautiful and she demanded it as part of her price. And you must remember that there with her, my life lives in her life, and hers in mine, and I am her Simon, not yours. So how could I wish to remember you?

DEBORAH—(*tensely—making a futile movement to rise*) And you think that excuses— I will not listen!

SIMON—(*ignoring this*) Just as here with you now, as always in the past before she intruded, my life lies in your life, and yours in mine, and I am your Simon and my one longing is to forget she is alive.

DEBORAH—(*immediately eagerly tender*) Yes, Dear, I want you to forget.

SIMON—(*goes on in the same tone of tense quiet*) You know her true nature well enough to realize it was she who made me laugh with her in her arms to think of you waiting here like an old fool—

DEBORAH—(*in a deadly fury*) Yes! I could hear her! The infamous harlot! And to think I just let her deceive me into making peace! But there will be no peace as long as we both remain alive! I will make her pay! Oh, how terribly I hate her! How terribly I wish that she would die! That someone would murder— (*She stops frightenedly.*)

SIMON—(*in same tone of tense quiet*) I am glad you see there is no possibility of getting rid of her as long as she is alive. (*He pauses.*) If she were dead, of course— (*insin-*

uatingly) If someone stumbled and fell against her when she was starting to descend the steep front stairs, it would be obviously an accident if—

DEBORAH—(*in a shuddering whisper*) Simon!

SIMON—Yes, I agree that is too uncertain.

DEBORAH—(*stammers in confused horror*) Agree? But I never—!

SIMON—Poison would be certain. And no one would ever suspect anything but natural illness in an eminent, wealthy family like ours.

DEBORAH—Simon! Good God in heaven, have you gone mad?

SIMON—(*with a cold impatience*) No. Quite the contrary. I am being extremely sane. I am alive as it is behind our hypocritical pretences and our weak sentimental moral evasions of our natural selves. I am facing the truth. I am dealing with the facts of things as they are. I am not frightened by the bad names we have called certain acts, which in themselves, are perfectly natural and logical—the killing of one's enemies, for example. Our whole cowardly moral code about murder is but another example of the stupid insane impulsion of man's petty vanity to swindle himself into believing human lives are valuable, and related to some God-inspired meaning. But the obvious fact is that their lives are without any meaning whatever—that human life is a silly disappointment, a liar's promise, a perpetual in bankruptcy for debts we never contracted, a daily appointment with peace and happiness in which we wait day after day, hoping against hope, listening to each footstep, and when finally the bride or the bridegroom cometh, we discover we are kissing Death.

DEBORAH—No! Stop!

SIMON—Or, obsessed by a fairy tale, we spend our lives searching for a magic door and a lost kingdom of peace from which we have been dispossessed by a greedy swindler.

DEBORAH—(*suddenly taunting*) Ah, if you are going to start harping on that childish nonsense—

SIMON—And when we find it we stand and beg before it. But the door is never opened. And at last we die and the starving scavenger hogs of life devour our carrion! (*with sudden strange fury*) No, by God, it shall not happen to me! What has been taken from me, I take back!

DEBORAH—(*terrified*) Simon! Don't look like that! You frighten me!

SIMON—(*quietly again*) So, let us not be sentimental and vain about the value of others' lives to us, Mother. Or of our own lives to ourselves. Regarded sensibly, we should all have clauses in our wills expressing gratitude to, and suitably rewarding anyone who should murder us. The murderer, I think, possesses the true quality of mercy. (*He chuckles sardonically.*) So, although I know how you have always, at any cost, escaped confronting facts—

DEBORAH—(*with strange scorn*) You are a fool! As if I did not once think exactly as you have been thinking. I used to sit alone in there in disdainful self-contemplation (*she looks at the summerhouse*) and make my mind face every fact until my thoughts beat with broken bleeding hands at the walls of my brain and I longed to escape by any door— (*stops abruptly— staring frightenedly at the door*) But I do not wish to remember that dead woman!

SIMON—(*as if she hadn't spoken*) You must at least admit it—your right in self-defense to kill the enemy who plots to destroy. Surely you cannot be blind to the fact that Sara's jealous hatred has reached a pitch now where she will use any means whatsoever to get rid of you.

DEBORAH—(*eagerly*) Yes! I know! (*struggling with herself*) No! It's a lie! She would never—

SIMON—And you must acknowledge that in your mind you have murdered her countless times. So I cannot see why the thought should make you shudder now.

DEBORAH—(*confusedly*) Yes, I confess I have dreamed— But those were dreams. Now it becomes real—when you put it in my mind. It begins to live in my will. It is born. It begins to me, to direct itself toward a consummation, like a destiny! (*struggling with herself*) No! I will not let you put it in my mind! (*with wild desperation*) But you have! It is there now! It will go on! I cannot stop it! And one day soon I will be hating her young body and her pretty face, and I will follow her to the top of the stairs—! Or I will remember the gardener keeps arsenic in the cellar for killing vermin—! (*deliberately jumping to her feet*) No! I couldn't—I couldn't! It is your thought, not mine! How can you think your mother— You are horrible! How could I have borne such a cruel, evil monster into the world! You terrify me! You are insane! I am afraid to be alone with you! (*pulling at her hand*) Let me go! I will call Sara! (*She calls*) Sara! Sara!

SIMON—(*keeps hold of her hand—quietly*) She cannot hear. She is too busy devouring her children. (*He pulls her gently back—quietly*) Come. Sit down, Mother. What have you and I to do with her—except to plan together how we may be free of her? (*persuasively*) I am sorry if I frightened you by forcing you to confront your desire to murder her.

DEBORAH—(*weakly letting herself be pulled down beside him*) No! Not my wish! Yours!

SIMON—I did it to make you realize what must inevitably happen soon. That the hate between you has reached a crisis—that one life cannot longer contain you both without being torn apart and destroyed! (*He suddenly bursts out with a terrible intensity*) I tell you I have reached the end of the tether! I cannot go on! One of you must cease to live in me! It is you or she! Can't you see I am trying to make clear to you that I have chosen you?

DEBORAH—(*her face lighting up with a passionate joy*) You mean—you really mean— Oh, I know! I knew in the end I could not fail! Oh, my son! My beloved son! (*then frightened*) But not murder— You must not murder—promise me you will not—

SIMON—No. There is another way for us to be free.

DEBORAH—Ah! Oh, I will do anything, if you will not compel me to murder! What—?

SIMON—We will leave her here. We will go together so far away from the reality that not even the memory of her can follow to haunt my mind. We will go back where she never existed. You have only to open that door— (*His eyes fasten on the summerhouse door with a fascinated longing.*)

DEBORAH—(*stares at it with dread and longing herself— forcing a belittling tone*) Now, Dear, you mustn't start harping on that fantastic childish nonsense again!

SIMON—(*ignoring this—gets to his feet—holding her hand,*

his eyes on the door—eagerly) But we must hurry, Mother. She will come back before long. She will try to keep me within her greed. She will open her arms to me. She is very beautiful. She will make me believe her lust is love.

DEBORAH—(*her face hardening—gets to her feet*) No! I am willing to pay any price to save you from her, and if this is the one possible way, so be it! (*She takes a step toward the door—then her eyes fixed on it, she recoils, shuddering, stammers*) No! Wait!

SIMON—(*his eyes on the door—fascinated*) I have waited ever since I was a little boy. All my life since then I have stood outside that door in my mind, begging you to let me re-enter that lost life of peace and trustful faith and happiness! I cannot wait any longer, Mother. And you cannot wait. You must choose between me and yourself. You once chose yourself and drove me out, and that has happened since then. Now you must either choose to repudiate that old choice, and give me back the faith you stole from me, or I will choose her!

DEBORAH—No!

SIMON—I will choose her! And then there will be no choice left to you but to run and hide within yourself in there again, and dream yourself into the madhouse to escape yourself!

DEBORAH—(*horrified*) Simon! For God's sake, how can you say such things to your mother who loves you more than life! As if you wished—

SIMON—I wish to be free, Mother!

DEBORAH—(*anguished*) Oh! You can admit that to me!

SIMON—Free of one of my two selves, of one of the enemies within my mind, before their duel for possession destroys it. I have no longer any choice but to choose. Either you and all the life of dreams, in which love is spirit, of which you are the living symbol in my mind—or her and all the world of reality in which flesh is fact, and love is the body's lust. To belong wholly to either is my one possible escape now. (*He adds grimly*) Or would you prefer I should go insane—and so be rid of me again?

DEBORAH—(*shuddering*) No! Oh, how can you say—! You must be insane already or you wouldn't—

SIMON—I am waiting, Mother—for you to open that

door, and give me back what was mine—my kingdom of the spirit's faith in life and love that your greed for yourself dispossessed me from!

DEBORAH—(*bitterly*) So it was all my doing, was it? You have changed your tune! You have always boasted your love of liberty and the natural rights of man left of its own free will! (*She sneers tauntingly.*)

SIMON—You are speaking of something my pride was forced to choose long after I had been driven out in spirit. Naturally, to keep my self-respect—to go on living at all—I had to pretend I had found more worthy objects for my dreams—and, to the outside world to which you exiled me, a more unselfish object for my love, someone who would be mine, and not I, hers!

DEBORAH—(*her eyes gleaming with satisfaction—tauntingly*) And how Sara has turned the tables and cheated you, poor boy! How common prettiness has but to smile and pretend desire for your desire and you begin begging on your knees! (*She laughs.*) I must warn you to take care, Dear. Your pride is making the most humiliating confessions for a Napoleon among men! Why, I begin to think now you were to have no life at all that did not hide within a woman's life— that you have never loved liberty at all but hated and dreaded it! (*She laughs mockingly.*)

SIMON—(*coldly*) You are compelling me to choose her. (*He lets go her hand.*) Very well. I shall go to her. Do not attempt to follow me in the house. I shall lock you out as you once did me. You will stay here alone until you do what you must do to escape. I have no doubt you will find happiness in a foolish dream as a King's courtesan! And I shall be free to be Sara's—body and soul. Goodbye, Mother. (*He turns to go.*)

DEBORAH—(*grabs his hand—pleading frantically*) No! For God's sake, don't leave me alone here! I will do anything you ask! (*She leads him a step towards the door—then falters again and begins to argue desperately as if she were trying to convince a child.*) But—it is all so silly and childish—so absurd and perverse—and revolting—for you, a grown man—a great man of worldly affairs—to remember—to make into a literal fact—an old fairy story—a passing fantasy of my brain—I made up in an idle moment to amuse you and make you laugh.

SIMON—(*with bitter hatred*) You know that is a lie, Mother! To make me realize you hated your love for me because it possessed you and you wanted to be free! To hurt me, to taunt me, to laugh at my love, to force me from you back into myself! That's why you told it!

DEBORAH—(*weakly*) No! How can you think I could be so cruel to my beloved little boy? (*then defensively*) But even if what you accuse me of is true, surely I had a right to own my own life!

SIMON—(*ignoring this*) You know I knew who you meant by the evil enchantress and that I was the exiled Prince!

DEBORAH—(*defensively*) You are being ridiculous. That was your old selfish demand that I might not even dream of myself without including you! (*trying to argue again—desperately*) But surely you see how idiotic it is to connect the door and that silly tale, which has no existence except in your fanciful imagination, with the actual wooden door of a common old summerhouse—the one we see so clearly in the moonlight now! Why that—that really is insane, Simon.

SIMON—(*tensely*) I know very well it is a wooden door to an actual summerhouse—in the reality outside us— But I know, too, as you know, that in the deeper reality inside us, it has the meaning our minds have given it.

DEBORAH—Your mind has given it one meaning, but in mine it has an opposite—you think it is the door to some fantastic dream of Heaven, but I remember the hell—

SIMON—(*ignoring this—obsessedly*) It exists in our minds as a symbol of our destiny, a door through which you drove me out of your love when you became evil and greedy for a false freedom. Surely you see that is what you meant in your symbolic fairy tale?

DEBORAH—No! No! It was merely a humorous fantasy— a capricious whim! I meant nothing!

SIMON—(*in same tone*) The actual door there is a necessary concrete symbol. Your opening it and leading me inside will be the necessary physical act by which your mind wills to take me back into your love, to repudiate your treachery in driving me out of your heart, to deny the evil ruthless woman your dreams of freedom made you and become again your old true self, the mother who loved me alone, whom alone I loved! (*He smiles at her with a sudden awkward tenderness.*) So you see it is all perfectly rational and logical in my mind, and there is nothing insane about it, Mother. The kingdom of peace and happiness in your story is love. You dispossessed yourself when you dispossessed me. Since then we have both been condemned to an insatiable, unscrupulous greed for substitutes to fill the emptiness, the loss of love we had left within us. (*He stares obsessedly at the door again.*) But you have only to open that door, Mother—which is really a door in your own mind—

DEBORAH—(*with a shudder*) I know!—and I know only too well the escape it leads to!

SIMON—(*pats her hand—tenderly persuasive, but his eyes are fixed on the door*) Forget those silly fears, Mother. They came after. We have gone back before they existed, or the woman who dreamed them existed. Just as we are now back in a life before Sara existed in me and I in her. We have got rid of her.

DEBORAH—(*eagerly*) Yes! I will pay anything to do that to her!

SIMON—We are back here in your garden on the day you told me that story. (*He pauses—then turns on her with a bitter vindictive condemnation.*) You knew I knew what you meant me to know! I have never forgotten the anguished sense of being suddenly betrayed, of being wounded and deserted and left alone in a life in which there was no security or faith or love but only danger and suspicion and devouring greed! (*harshly*) By God, I hated you then! I wished you dead! I wished I had never been born!

DEBORAH—(*with an obviously fake air of contrition thinly masking a strange, cruel satisfaction*) Did you, Dear? I am sorry if I hurt you. It is true I hoped you would guess what I meant. You were such a stubborn greedy little boy, so inquisitive and pryishly possessive. I could feel your grasping fingers groping toward every secret, private corner of my soul. I had come to the point when I even preferred Joel because I was utterly indifferent to him, where at times I hated you and wished you had never been born. So I had to do something to warn you, and I thought a fairy tale would be the most tactful way— (*Abruptly her expression changes to one of horror for herself—distractedly*) No! I never meant—! You put it in my mind! It's insane of you to make me confess such horrible things! And how can you admit you hated your mother and wished her dead!

SIMON—(*contritely stammers*) I— Forgive me, Mother!— I did only because you— (*then passionately*) All I ask is that you go back and change that—change the ending—open the door and take me back—and all that has happened since, which you began that day, will be out of memory, forgotten! There will be only love and faith and trust in life—the old greedless security and content with what we have! There will be only you and I! There will be peace and happiness to the end of our days! Can't you believe me, Mother? I tell you I know!

DEBORAH—(*shakingly—staring at the door fascinatedly*) Oh, if I could, Dear! If I only could believe, how willingly I would go! If you knew how I have loved you, how desperately I have longed to have you back, to take you from her, to know you were mine alone, to be nothing but your mother, to live and forget myself, to live solely in your life, to make any sacrifice of self with happiness, exultantly in self-fulfillment, to dream no dream except to love you more and more! (*passionately*) Yes! I think I believe now—believe that if the mind wills anything with enough intensity of love it can force life to its desire, create a heaven, if need be, out of hell! (*with a strange triumphant laugh*) Yes, taking you with me, I would have no fear of insanity, for all is fair in love, and love would make it sane.

SIMON—(*strangely*) Yes, we need not concern ourselves with the bad names men have given to things they fear or do not understand. (*He laughs harshly.*) Good God, if the reality of hoggish greed and dog eat dog and lust devour love is sane, then what man of honorable mind would not prefer to be considered lunatic! (*with sudden urgency*) Come, Mother! Let us leave this vile sty of lust and hatred and the wish to murder! Let us escape back into peace—while there is still time!

DEBORAH—(*with forced eagerness, mounts the first step*) Yes, let us hurry, Dear—before I can think— (*then she stops— desperately*) But I must warn you—I could never forgive myself if I did not warn you once more of the danger—

SIMON—(*scornfully proud*) Danger? Don't you know Sara has made me a greedy gambler who loves danger and the greatest possible risk? What do I care if the fate in there has stacked the cards and loaded the dice? I promise you I will outswindle it and steal our happiness and love from under its nose! (*boastfully*) What I want I have the power to take, and will always take! You forget they do not call me a Napoleon of trade without my having proven my right to the title!

DEBORAH—(*hangs back resentfully now—almost jeeringly*) You had better not boast of your power to enslave, for I warn you you may bitterly regret your daring if you find it is, in truth, the evil enchantress of my fairy tale who waits there to enslave you in her arms! If I remember the mad woman I locked in there, she must have chosen madness long ago, because she was entirely ruthless and unscrupulous, a daring courtesan who takes what she wants by any means she can, even madness. She will not recognize you as her son! She never had a child. Her pride would have made her kill herself before she would ever have shared herself, or seen her beauty grow bloated and misshapen, with an alien's possession! Her arrogance would never put her life in bondage to another's life, or create another she would be forced to love as she loved herself! She has loved herself alone! She has remained free! You will be no more than another man to her—that is, no more than a slave to her every whim and caprice—like the King before she discarded him to make a fool of Napoleon whom her poor weakling of a father confused with God and himself! (*She stops abruptly—guiltily confused—and stammers stupidly*) I—please do not mind me—I do not think I know what I was saying—

SIMON—(*has turned on her sneeringly*) I should hope not! You remember how I had to laugh at you the time you boasted to me of that preposterous romantic evil dream about yourself! You, my poor little, old mother! (*He gives a taunting, sneering chuckle.*)

DEBORAH — (*stung — with furious hatred*) How dare you—! (*then with a sudden change to an ominous gentleness*) But I see. You are so cunning to get your own way by any means, aren't you, Dear—like Napoleon? You were clever enough to see that while love might make me hesitate, for your sake, hate would give me the necessary courage to be quite ruthless in thinking only of winning a final victory over her. (*She laughs softly, turns abruptly and goes up the remaining steps — tenderly*) Come, Dear. Mother is only too glad to do anything you ask her to now.

SIMON — (*strangely*) We will go far back before that laughter existed, Mother. You will not know you ever heard it, then, or that I ever laughed. There will be peace and unity. We shall have gone back beyond separations. We shall be one again. (*suddenly in a panic*) But hurry, Mother! Hurry! I hear someone coming! It must be she! But I will run away from her now and hide in my mind back there in our past together. She will be a stranger!

DEBORAH — (*begins to assume an air of a cruel ruthless gratification*) Let her come! It will add strength to my hatred! And it will be a pleasure to have her witness my final victory! Now I have decided, I am stronger than she ever dared to be! (*She moves so that she stands protectingly before Simon, her right hand on the knob of the door. Sara comes hurrying in from the left. She is in a panic of apprehensive dread. When she sees them both still outside the summerhouse, this changes to rage against Deborah.*)

SARA — (*to Deborah*) You liar! You thief! You black-hearted traitor! I should have known better than to leave you— But God be praised I'm back in time!

DEBORAH — (*jeering quietly*) Yes. You are just in time—to bid us farewell!

SARA — (*frightened — forcing a commanding tone*) Simon! Come here to me away from that door! Do you want to lose what little wits you've left, playing her crazy games with her? (*But Simon appears not to have heard her, or to have noticed her coming. He keeps behind his mother turned sideways to Sara, his eyes fixed fascinatedly on the door.*)

DEBORAH — (*addressing him over her shoulder, her eyes on*

Sara) My love, you no longer remember this woman, do you? You will not permit a vulgar, common slut to intrude and delay our departure.

SIMON—(*starts and turns his head to stare at Sara without recognition over his mother's shoulder. His face has a strange, mad, trance-like look. He murmurs obediently*) No, Mother. (*He addresses Sara with a sharp arrogance.*) Who are you? What do you want? How dare you trespass here and start making a disgusting scene? Do you think my mother's garden is the parlor of a brothel?

SARA—(*shrinks as if she'd been struck—strickenly*) Simon! Don't speak like—

SIMON—By what right do you presume to call me by my first name? I do not know you. (*strangely*) It is true you remind me of a mistress I once bought to amuse myself observing her greedy attempt to swindle me of myself. But it was I who swindled her by paying her with counterfeit appearances. Then when her lust began to bore me, I deserted her and went off with another woman, an old lover in my childhood. (*He adds hastily*) Whom I loved with a great pure love, a spiritual love of the mind and the soul, rare and beautiful, her ethereal passion, a love belonging to fantasy and dreams!

SARA—(*tremblingly*) Simon! It is mad you are!

SIMON—(*disdainfully—as if he were addressing a servant*) Begone! Before I summon the police! (*pointing to the door in wall at right*) That door leads to the street where you belong. Go back and ply your trade there. Your body defiles the pure atmosphere of my mother's garden.

SARA—(*pitifully*) Darling! It's I! Your Sara!

DEBORAH—(*gloating—haughtily*) You have my son's orders! (*then to Simon*) But I think, Dear, it might be simpler for us to leave her now.

SIMON—(*eagerly*) Yes, Mother. Let us go!

DEBORAH—(*exultantly*) Yes! I can now! I am as strong as I ever wished to be in any dream! I will take what my whim desires from life, and laugh at the cost! (*She laughs and with an abrupt movement jerks open the door behind her so it stands back against the wall. Simon gives a gasping eager cry and leans forward, staring into the darkness inside. But Deborah does not turn to it but remains confronting Sara.*)

SARA—(*wildly*) No! (*rushes up and grabs Deborah's skirt and falls on her knees before her*) For the love of God have pity, Deborah!

DEBORAH—(*starts*) Pity? (*then angrily*) Would you remind me of pity now, you scheming slut?

SARA—(*pleadingly*) Remember I had pity on you!

DEBORAH—You lie! I will not remember! I have forgotten pity. (*She kicks at Sara viciously.*) How dare you hold me! Let me free!

SARA—(*pleadingly*) I'm asking your pity for him, not for me! You love him! You can't do this!

DEBORAH—(*scornful*) You weak sentimental fool! Love is proud, not pitiful! It takes what it desires! (*hastily*) You dare to speak of pity! You, the harlot whose greed is devouring him and driving him insane! It's because I love him that I must save him from your destroying lust! So let go! (*She kicks her skirt from Sara's hand and half turns to the door, grabbing Simon's arm.*) Come, Dear! Quick! Let us go where we cannot hear her lies about love and pity!

SIMON—(*with a crazy eagerness*) Yes! The door is open! I feel our old peace and happiness waiting to welcome us! Take my hand, Mother!

SARA—(*wildly, grabbing Deborah's skirt again*) No! Wait! Listen! Deborah! I give up! I admit I'm beaten now! I'll pay you any price you ask, if only—

DEBORAH—(*triumphantly*) Ah! So you admit— I always knew that in the end— (*then with arrogant disdain*) You have the impertinence to believe there is anything you possess that I could be so low as to desire? You flatter yourself!

SIMON—(*turns his head a little from staring inside the summerhouse—dazedly and uneasily*) Sara? Sara? Who? Who are you talking to, Mother? What is she trying to make me remember? How could I? This is long before any other woman. There is only your love. I do not need her. Make her leave us alone, Mother!—so we can go back to peace.

DEBORAH—(*cruelly scornful and at the same time uneasy*) Yes, I will not listen to her pleading lies! We will go—

SARA—(*in anguish*) Simon! Darling! It's her madness in there! It's the asylum!

DEBORAH—(*shakenly—fighting back fiercely*) You lie! Our

minds will compel it to be our dream! Our love can make a heaven even in hell if we are together—if we are one again! (*She half turns to Simon but keeps her eyes averted from the door-way.*) Do not listen to this low, vulgar harlot, Dear! What could she know of the transfiguring power of the mind, or the miraculous power of the spirit, she whose soul is a pound of greedy flesh! (*She reaches out her hand which he clasps eagerly.*) Here is my hand, Dear! Come! (*She tries to [ ] determinedly—to rush in with her eyes shut, leading him.*)

SARA—(*distractedly—throws herself forward and flings her arms around Deborah's legs—pleading wildly*) For the love of God! For the love of your son, Deborah! You can't! And don't you see there's no need now! You can have him back without— I'm telling you I'll give him up to you! I'll go away! I'll leave him to you! I'll never trouble you again! You'll be rid of me! And that's all you've wanted, isn't it? So, for the love of God, stop—!

DEBORAH—(*stares at her, her face lighting up eagerly, but unable to believe her ears*) You really mean—you will give up—go away—never again intrude or trespass—on what is mine?

SARA—I will—for love of him—to save him. You can have him all to yourself again. I know I can trust your love for him, once I'm out of the way, to protect him from himself—and from your own mad dreams. And I know, when he has only you to love, he'll forget me, and he won't be destroyed and torn between us within himself.

DEBORAH—(*eagerly*) Yes! I swear to you I will protect and make him contented and at peace with life. (*complacently*) After all, I am his mother, and I would give my life for him. (*relaxing with a smile of triumph*) Ah! (*then immediately with suspicious anger*) You're lying! This is all another of your cunning tricks! Do you still think I trust you?

SARA—(*dully*) No, Deborah. I'm beyond tricks now. I'm finished.

DEBORAH—(*smiles down at her with contemptuous gloating*) You must be utterly beaten, then—more beaten than I ever hoped you could be! Evidently, I gave you credit for more strength and pride than you possess! (*sneeringly*) But I think I see! You've swindled him out of everything he owns, except

what you find you cannot steal—what is mine—himself! So
now, having got all you can, he's useless to you and you'll
discard him like the unscrupulous slut you are, and go soliciting a new victim! Is that it? (*She sneers insultingly. A strange
angry hostility is creeping into her attitude as if, now she had won
a complete victory, she was beginning to feel it was a defeat.*)

SARA—(*dully*) No. I'll sign all that over to you. I don't
want it. All I'll keep is the old farm, so I'll have a home for my
children, and can make a living with them. I'll take them
there tomorrow. (*She gets to her feet slowly and exhaustedly.*)

SIMON—(*who has remained tense and motionless, staring fascinatedly into the darkness inside the summerhouse—in a boyish
uneasy whisper, tugging at her hand*) Why are you waiting,
Mother? We mustn't wait—or it may be too late! You will
get afraid again. (*But neither woman seems to hear him.*)

DEBORAH—(*sneering more insultingly*) You are welcome to
the farm. I am glad you at last realize what you are and where
you belong. A stupid peasant tilling the soil, her bare feet in
the earth, her gross body stinking of sweat, a dumb brainless,
begetting female animal with her dirty brats around her!
(*jeeringly*) But what becomes of your grand estate, and the
ridiculous Irish dream castle in Spain?

SARA—(*resignedly—without resentment*) That was foolishness. I'm done with that, too.

DEBORAH—(*sneeringly*) What virtuous Christian resignation! How shamelessly abject and humble you are!

SARA—(*quietly*) If I'm humbled, it's by myself and my
love, not by you. (*with a flash of pride*) And I'm proud of that.
For, if I'll never rise to owning a grand estate now, I've risen
in life now in the only way that counts, above myself, which
is more than you'll ever do! I can wish him happiness without
me, and mean it! Yes, and I can even wish you to be happy
so you can make him happy, and mean that, too!

DEBORAH—(*for an instant moved in spite of herself—stammers gratefully*) I—thank you, Sara—you are generous and
fine— (*then in a burst of sneering hostility*) You lie! You cannot
fool me! This is all cheap acting, and the role of sacrificed,
unselfish love is absolutely fake to your true nature! (*jeeringly*) The truth is what I have always known! You are incapable of love! I alone really love him because I would rather

see him dead—or kill him myself!—than give him up to another woman!

SARA—(*quietly*) You don't believe that. You know no woman could love a man more than when she gives him up to save him!

DEBORAH—(*with strange repressed fury*) I know—I begin to see your scheme—the trick behind—with your superior self-sacrificial airs—you want to show me you—to make me feel vile and contemptible—

SARA—(*quietly and exhaustedly*) No. I've told you I'm beyond scheming. I'm too—dead. (*dully*) I'll leave you now, Deborah. I'll get the children up now and take them to a hotel where he can't find us. You keep him out here until I'm gone. That's the best way, to get it over and done now. You can explain in any way you think it best for you and him. But make it strong that I'm sick of him, and I'm getting another man and I never want to see him again. Give him a good excuse to give himself to forget me. That's all he needs to bring him peace with you alone. (*then giving Simon a worried look*) And look out you bring him back to his senses right away now. It isn't good for him to stay long—so far away in the past as you've taken him. (*She turns to go off left—brokenly, without looking at him*) God bless you, Simon, Darling, for all the joy and love you gave me, and give you peace and happiness!

SIMON—(*with a sort of bewildered anguish*) Mother! Someone is calling me! I'll have to go! I cannot remain back here much longer! Hurry, Mother! Hurry!

SARA—Goodbye, Deborah. (*She starts to walk away.*)

DEBORAH—(*stammers weakly*) No—Sara— (*then fiercely*) Goodbye and good riddance! Get out! Go! Leave me alone! I hate the sight of you! (*then brokenly*) No, Sara—forgive—wait—I want to say—my gratitude—want to tell you—you are beautiful and fine—so much more beautiful—fine—than I— (*then bursting into a jealous fury, glaring at her with hatred*) Ah, God damn you. You low, scheming trollop! Do you think I don't see through you? All this hypocritical sentimental posing! Your false self-sacrificial airs! You the noble loving woman! I am the evil one who desires her son's life! Whose greed does not scruple to use any means—base and

utterly ignoble—cruel and insatiable. You dare insult me so!
—humiliate and put me to shame before my son!—my beloved son— You dare to boast before him you love him more
than I, his mother, who, ever since the day I bore him, would
gladly give my life for his happiness! As if a low lustful creature like you could even imagine the depth of the love I have
for him, let alone feel it! And yet you have the vulgar effrontery to pretend— (*in a fresh burst of savage passion*) You liar!
But I'll prove to you who is the final victor between us, who
is the one who loves him most! (*She turns to face the darkness
within the doorway.*)

SIMON—(*with an eager cry*) Mother! At last! Hurry! She is
coming to take me!

SARA—(*frightenedly*) Simon!

DEBORAH—(*pulls her hand violently from his*) No! Alone!

SIMON—(*despairingly—grabbing at her hand*) Mother!

DEBORAH—(*flings his hand away—with a strange boastful
arrogance*) Alone, I said! As I have always been. As my pride
and disdain have always willed I be!—hating the vile sordid
ugliness of life—choosing to keep my spirit pure and untouched and unpossessed!—my soul my own!—at any
cost—at any sacrifice— (*looking at him now with repulsion*) Go
away! Do not dare to touch me! What are you to me! I am
my own! Ah, how could I have ever been so weak as to allow
you to intrude on my dream and involve me in a filthy sordid
intrigue with a greedy, money-grabbing merchant and his
peasant slut of a wife! I, if I had been born in a nobler time,
could have had the love of a King or an Emperor! (*to Simon
with hatred*) You—get back to the greasy arms of your wife
where you belong! (*With extraordinary strength she gives him
a push in the chest that drives him off balance and sends him
spinning down the steps to fall heavily and lie still by the stone
bench at left of pool.*)

SARA—(*flings herself on her knees beside him and raises his
head*) Simon! (*He stirs and moans feebly.*)

DEBORAH—(*turns and stops on the threshold, confronting the
darkness—with a self-contemptuous laugh*) To think you were
afraid, Deborah! Why, what is waiting to welcome you is
merely your last disdain! (*She goes in quietly and shuts the
door.*)

SARA—(*oblivious to her going*) Darling! Are you hurt bad?
(*She feels his body.*) I can't find anything broken—but I heard
his head hit—

SIMON—(*suddenly raises his head and stares at the door and
mutters stupidly the unhappy end of the fairy story*) So the Prince
waited before the door and begged for love from all who
passed by. (*He falls back in her arms in a faint.*)

SARA—(*frightenedly*) Simon! Merciful God! Speak to me,
Darling! (*In a panic she puts her hand over his heart—relieved*)
No, he's only fainted. (*She chafes his wrists.*) Maybe it's best.
He'd be trying to get in there. (*She stops rubbing his wrists
and turns to stare at the summerhouse—in an awed horrified
whisper*) God help me, she's done it. (*with admiration*) Ah,
it's a great noble lady you couldn't help proving yourself in
the end, and it's you that beat me, for your pride paid a
price for love my pride would never dare to pay! (*She shudders—then with growing intensity*) But I swear to you now,
Deborah, I'll try to keep up my end of the bargain and pay
back all I can. I see now the part my greed and my father's
crazy dreams in me had in leading Simon away from himself
until he lost his way and began destroying all that was best
in him! To make me proud of him! (*brokenly*) Ah, forgive
me, Darling! But I'll give my life now to setting you free to
be again the man you were when I first met you—the man I
loved best!—the dreamer with a touch of the poet in his
soul, and the heart of a boy! (*with a strange almost masochistic
satisfaction*) Don't I know, Darling, the longing in your heart
that I'd smash the Company into smithereens to prove my
love for you and set you free from the greed of it! Well, by
the Eternal, I'll smash it so there'll be nothing left to tempt
me! It's easy. It needs only a whisper of the true condition
to Tenard, pretending I'm a fool woman who takes him into
her confidence, now he's in the Company. (*with a gloating
smile*) I can hear the revenge in his heart laughing, rushing
out to tell all our enemies and combine with them to pounce
down and ruin us! Well, they can't take the old farm anyway, and we'll live there, and the boys will work with me,
and you'll never have to lift your hand again, but you can
spend your days in your old cabin where you first were
mine, and write poetry again of your love for me, and plan

your book that will save the world and free men from the curse of greed in them! (*She pauses guiltily.*) God forgive me, I'm happy at the mere thought of it, and it's no price at all I'll be paying to match yours, Deborah, if I'm happy! (*then with an abrupt change to practical calculation*) That reminds me, before I start the whisper, I'll get all the Company's cash from the banks and put it in her name, along with this house, with Joel to take care of it, so she'll have enough and plenty to keep her here, with her garden, and the comfort and riches and luxury that's due the great Princess on her grand estate she'll be on in her dream till the day she dies! (*While she has been saying this last, the door of the summerhouse has slowly opened and Deborah has appeared. She now stands on the top of the steps. Her eyes have a still, fixed, sightless, trance-like look, but her face is proud, self-assured, arrogant and happy, and she looks beautiful and serene, and many years younger.*)

DEBORAH—(*in a tone of haughty command*) Be quiet! Who is talking? How dare you come here? Who are you?

SARA—(*starts and stares at her—in an awed whisper*) Ah, God pity her, the poor woman!

DEBORAH—(*coming down the steps— As she does so, Sara gets to her feet, letting Simon's head rest back on the grass.*) Answer me! (*A look of recognition comes over her face—with a regal gracious condescension*) Ah, you are the Irish kitchen maid, are you not? I remember you—

SARA—(*An impulse of angry insult flashes in her eyes—but immediately she controls this, whispering pityingly to herself*) Poor creature! She's hidden herself in her dream forever!

DEBORAH—(*approaching her, erect and arrogant and grace-ful, her head held high*) What are you doing in the Palace grounds at this hour, poor peasant? Do you not know there is a terrible punishment for trespassing in my domain?

SARA—(*humoring her—bobs her an awkward servant-girl curtsy and speaks humbly*) I know I have no right here, My Lady. If you'll be kind enough to forgive me, I'll never intrude again.

DEBORAH—This garden is the Emperor's gift to me. He is very jealous of my privacy. (*then with a cautious backward glance at the summerhouse*) Sush, we must not wake him. (*with a soft gloating little laugh*) But he sleeps soundly. My love is

too great for him. It devours him. In my arms, he is so
weak—so like a little boy, the Great Napoleon! So small,
compared to my great love! He will give me the world, and
still it will be too little! (*then suddenly—sharply and suspiciously*)
Why are you silent? Do you dare to doubt me?

SARA—(*humbly*) Indeed I don't, Your Majesty.

DEBORAH—(*reassured and pleasant*) I am not Majesty, my
poor woman. Of course, if it were my whim— He would
gladly divorce his wife, who is a stupid, common woman,
quite unworthy. But I tell him marriage is a trader's bargain.
It corrupts love which shall be always beautiful and free. (*then
with a condescending kindliness*) But you would not understand
that. You have not told me why you are here, poor peasant.
You came to keep an assignation with your lover, I suppose.
Doubtless some groom from my stables. You peasants are
such animals. But never mind. I am disposed tonight to be
lenient toward all lovers, for love's sake. I forgive you.

SARA—(*with another curtsy*) Thank you, My Lady. (*then
impulsively*) I wanted to ask you to forgive me, Deborah.

DEBORAH—(*wonderingly*) Deborah? Who is Deborah?
(*Her eyes fall on Simon. She starts—then indifferently*) Who is
that lying at your feet? Your lover? Is he dead? Did you murder him for love of him? Oh, do not be afraid. I understand
everything a woman's love could possibly compel her to desire. I know she can even kill herself to prove her love, so
proud can she be of it.

SARA—(*quietly*) I am sure you know that, My Lady. (*She
stares at Deborah and suddenly her face is convulsed with a look
of horrified suspicion and she grabs her by the arm and stammers*)
For the love of God, Deborah, tell me you're not just pretending now—for love of him, to save him and set him free!
That would be too great a price— I couldn't let you—!

DEBORAH—(*trembles and seems about to collapse—avoiding
Sara's eyes, falteringly*) I—I do not understand you— You
must not—! (*Suddenly she is the arrogant grand dame again—
with haughty anger—snatching Sara's hand off her arm*) You
forget yourself. Do not presume to touch me. Your presence
wearies me. I must go back to the Emperor. See that you take
your lover away at once and never return here.

SARA—(*stammers*) Yes, My Lady. (*confusedly to herself*) No, no—I'm a fool. She's really gone forever in her dream! But— Tell me this, are you happy now? Ah,—My Lady?

DEBORAH—(*smiles condescendingly*) You are impertinent. But I forgive it, because I *am* happy. And I wish you may be happy with your lover, too. (*haughtily*) But now farewell, good woman. (*She holds out her hand arrogantly.*) You may kneel and kiss my hand.

SARA—(*A flash of insulted pride comes to her eyes and for a second she seems about to retreat angrily—then impulsively she kneels and kisses her hand.*) Thank you for your great kindness, My Lady. (*Deborah turns from her to ascend the steps. Sara adds huskily*) And God bless you.

DEBORAH—(*ascending the steps, looks back, with a smile of gracious understanding amusement*) Why, thank you, good woman. I think that I may say that he has blessed me. (*She goes in the summerhouse and closes the door behind her.*)

SARA—(*stares after her—miserably*) I wonder—I wonder— Oh, God help me, I'll never be sure of the truth of it now! (*Simon groans and stirs and looks up at her.*)

SIMON—(*murmurs stupidly*) Mother. Hurry. Let us go. Peace and happiness.

SARA—(*at once forgetting everything but him*) Yes, Darling. We'll go. Come on. Raise yourself. (*She bends and puts her arm around his shoulder to help him.*) That's it.

SIMON—(*dazedly—like a little boy*) I fell and hit my head, Mother. It hurts.

SARA—I'll bathe it for you when we get in the house. Come along now. (*She turns him into the path leading off left and urges him along it.*)

SIMON—(*dazedly*) Yes, Mother.

SARA—(*with a fierce, passionate possessive tenderness*) Yes, I'll be your mother, too, now, and your peace and happiness and all you'll ever need in life! (*They disappear off left.*)

(*Curtain*)

EPILOGUE

SCENE—*Same as Act One, Scene Two, Simon's old cabin by the lake on the farm. It is a late afternoon of a fine day in early June of the following year, 1842.*

There is a great change in the cabin and little clearing from the abandoned, neglected appearance it had in the first act scene of *1832*. The grass, a fresh green, has been cut and the paths across it from the woods at left to the door of the cabin, and from the door down to the shore of the lake, off right, are clearly defined. The windows of the cabin are washed and clean, with their frames a newly painted white. The chinks in the logs have been caulked, the chimney patched up with fresh mortar. The bench against the wall of the cabin has been painted green.

Sara's and Simon's youngest son, Owen Roe "Honey" Harford, is discovered, squatting on his heels on the grass before the bench, playing a game with a jackknife, flipping it from his fingers to make it stick in the ground. He wears only an old shirt and a pair of short pants. Both are dirty. So are his sunburned, freckled face, his hands and bare legs and feet. He is going on nine and a half now, is big for his age, stout and healthy. His face is typically Irish with blue eyes, dark curly hair, and he has a marked resemblance to his mother. His expression is happy and good-natured. He has a charming ingratiating grin and a sparkle of sly, droll humor in his inquisitive eyes. As he plays he sings softly Thomas Moore's "Believe me if all those endearing young charms." He has a fine voice, clear and pure.

His brother, Jonathan, next to him in age, a year and a half older, comes in from the path at left. Although older he is smaller than Honey, undersized, thin and wiry, with a large head out of proportion with his body. His face is long, with a big nose, and sharp intelligent grey eyes, and straight mouse-colored hair. He is dressed much the same as Honey but his clothes are clean, as are his face and hands and legs. He gives one the impression of being older than his years, full of a tense nervous vitality, but remarkably self-disciplined and sure of his own capabilities. Between these two younger brothers the relationship is one of close affection with Jonathan the leader, a bit bullyingly superior and condescending, and Honey an admiring satellite, but not so admiring he does not poke constant fun at him.

JONATHAN—(*stops just inside the clearing and attracts his brother's attention*) Ssstt! (*Honey looks up. Jonathan beckons and Honey goes to him without stopping his song. Jonathan asks in a low voice*) Is he still there?

HONEY—What d'you think? I'd have gone after him, wouldn't I if he'd left. (*He starts singing again.*)

JONATHAN—(*scornfully*) He could sneak out and you'd be too lazy to catch him. (*scowling*) Shut up that music, can't you?

HONEY—(*derisively*) Now? I sing good. You're jealous because you can't keep a tune! Anyway, Father likes it. Once when I stopped he called out to keep on. (*He glances back at the cabin.*) I think he's asleep now. I peeked in the window and he's lying down.

JONATHAN—(*anxiously*) Did he know you all right? I mean, really know he was your father?

HONEY—(*eagerly*) Sure! He talked like he used to—before he got sick. And the way he was talking to himself he remembers this place, and when he used to live here, and everything.

JONATHAN—(*relieved*) That's fine. Gosh, I hope he'll be all right now, for keeps! (*with a trace of bitterness*) It's been no fun having him out of his head for so long, acting like a kid, and us having to pretend to him he was our brother.

HONEY—Yes. It's been crazy. (*then guiltily—loyally*) But he couldn't help it. It was brain fever. Mother says brain fever always does that to people.

JONATHAN—(*guiltily*) Who's blaming him? He's my father, too. (*abruptly changing the subject*) Mother just got back from the funeral. Ethan told her how Father seemed to wake up all of a sudden and knew all of us in the potato field this morning, and asked for her, and how we'd lied and told him she'd gone to the city shopping. She burst out and started to cry she was so happy. She sent me down to tell you to keep him here. She'll be down as soon as she's changed her clothes. She doesn't want him to see her in mourning. She doesn't want him to know Granny's dead yet.

HONEY—I'm glad Granny's dead. Aren't you? She was a crazy old fool. I got to hate her.

JONATHAN—(*frowning*) So did I. But we ought to forget that now.

HONEY—(*stubbornly*) I won't. She hated Mother. I don't see why Mother had to go to her funeral, or why she never let us say a word against her.

JONATHAN—(*sharply*) That's Mother's business. (*then practically*) Anyway, what's the use of thinking about it now.

HONEY—(*grinning*) I won't anymore. (*in brogue*) The divil take her! (*He turns away, carefree, and begins to sing again—then stops abruptly, looking around him.*) Let's go for a swim, as soon as Mother comes. Gosh, I like it out here. I don't mind being poor, do you?

JONATHAN—(*scornfully*) You like it? Yes, you do! When you don't have to work!

HONEY—Well, who wants to be a farmer? You don't. Neither does Ethan. Nor Wolfe either, even if he pretends not to care.

JONATHAN—(*seriously*) No, I don't want to be a farmer. And I won't be any longer than I have to. There's no money in farming. You can't get ahead. (*determinedly*) And I'm going to get ahead.

HONEY—I'm going to own an hotel and run a livery stable. I love horses. And renting rooms and hiring out carriages, that's easy.

JONATHAN—(*scornfully*) Something easy! That's what you always want!

HONEY—(*grins*) Sure! I'll get mine! (*then after a glance up the path*) Here comes Mother. (*He dashes over and sits on the bench as if he were dutifully keeping guard. A moment later Sara enters. She wears a cheap calico working dress and is barefooted. Her fair complexion is tanned and her fine figure is strong, firm and healthy. She looks younger and at the same time older. Younger in that her face is no longer haggard, lined and tense. Older because of the look of resigned sadness in her eyes and the streaks of white in her black hair. Just now, however, her face is lighted up by an excited hope that is afraid that it is too good to be true.*)

SARA—(*in a whisper to Jonathan as she enters*) He's in the cabin?

JONATHAN—(*nods*) He's asleep.

HONEY—(*comes over toward her—virtuously*) I never stopped keeping guard over him one moment, Mother.

SARA—(*mechanically*) That's a good boy. (*then a bit dis-*

appointedly) Asleep, is he? I'd best let him sleep then. He's so weak. I was hoping he'd— It's hard to wait, wondering if he'll know me.

HONEY—Can I go swimming now—me and Jonathan?

SARA—(*welcoming his interruption, surveys him critically*) You can. But you'll go up to the house first and get soap to take with you, and you'll use it! Look at you! You can get more dirt on you in an hour than two pigs could in a week! Look at your clothes, too! And to think I ever dreamed of making you a gentleman! (*She gives him an affectionate pat and push.*) Get along with you. Go up to the field first, and you and Johnny help Ethan and Wolfe finish the row they're doing. Tell them they can stop work after that and come swimming. We all have a right to take a bit of a holiday and give thanks to God, if your father is getting well— (*She gives a longing look toward the cabin, but uneasy, afraid her hope may not be true. The two boys start eagerly off left. Suddenly she has a thought—guiltily*) Wait. Did you remember, like I asked you, to say a prayer for your grandmother's soul at the time of the funeral? (*They hang their heads and avoid her eyes. She says sadly*) I see you didn't. (*to herself*) Poor woman! I was the only one really to mourn her. I kept my distance at the cemetery, with my veil on my face so none would know me. Ah, if she ever knew in her dreams what I've suffered, with him all mixed up and lost in his mind, calling me Mother, as if I was her, and forgetting he'd ever had a wife, she'd feel she was the one who'd won in the end after all.

HONEY—(*fidgeting impatiently*) Can we go now, Mother?

SARA—(*starts—then sharply*) You can't till you've said the prayer. You had no right to forget. Get down on your knees, now! (*as they hesitate sheepishly—peremptorily*) You hear me! (*They flop down self-consciously. She goes on argumentively.*) Just because we have no faith in it doesn't mean it mightn't be true. No one knows. And it does no harm. It's a mark of respect. Say a prayer now. (*The two boys exchange looks. They feel silly and giggly.*)

JONATHAN—We've forgotten. What'll we say, Mother? (*She starts and hesitates, looking confused.*)

HONEY—(*with an impish grin*) You don't remember any either, Mother.

SARA—(*hastily*) Say God rest her in peace, and that'll do.

JONATHAN AND HONEY—(*burst out in mechanical chorus*) God rest her in peace.

(*They bound to their feet with relief that the absurd business is over. As they do so the door from the cabin is opened and Simon appears. He is terribly emaciated, pale and hollow-eyed, as though he had passed through a long and devouring fever. His eyes have a groping and bewildered stare. His clothes, the same as he wore in Act Four, are clean and well kept, but wrinkled now as though he had slept in them. He stands in the doorway, fixing his eyes on Sara, clinging weakly to the door frame for support. The boys see him at once and start. Sara guesses from their faces and whirls around. She tries to speak but is terrified to risk it, and only her lips move soundlessly.*)

SIMON—(*with a great gasp of relief and longing*) Sara! (*He takes a weak, faltering step toward her.*)

SARA—(*with a happy cry*) Simon! (*She rushes to him.*) Darling! Oh, thank God you know me! (*She throws her arms around him and hugs him to her. The two boys give them an embarrassed, and yet happy look and then dart away up the path.*)

SIMON—(*stammers brokenly*) My love! I was so afraid I had lost you!

SARA—(*tenderly—with a trembling smile*) Lost me, is it? You couldn't. I'd never let you—not in this life—nor in death, neither! But you know I love you! (*protestingly*) Sit down. Here like we used when we first knew love—me on the bench and you on the grass with your head on my lap. (*She sits on the bench and he obeys mechanically, sitting on the grass, his arms around her hungrily and clingingly, his head on her lap. She goes on in a blissful, tender, emotional croon.*) There now. Don't talk for a while. Just rest and be happy, Darling.

SIMON—(*lets himself relax for a second, closing his eyes*) Yes, Sweetheart. (*Then he jerks awake—pleading almost hysterically*) No! You must tell me. At once! I want to know! I've been lying in there trying to remember—how I got here—why?—when?—what happened?

SARA—(*bullying him soothingly*) Now, now. Be quiet, and I'll tell you. There's nothing to be worried about. You've been sick with brain fever you got from working too hard and worrying too much about the Company—and I brought you here to get well. And now you are well, Darling.

SIMON—(*dazedly*) Brain fever? Yes—that would explain—(*frightenedly*) But—

SARA—(*pulling his head back*) Sush now, I tell you. Everything is all right. All the doctors said it was the most natural thing for you to lose your memory for a while. It's the way the sickness takes everyone that gets it.

SIMON—(*beginning to be relieved*) Is it? (*forcing a smile*) Well, I've come out all right, haven't I? (*pleading again*) But please tell me everything, Sara. I feel, so strange—as if part of me were lost—or had died. (*He shudders.*) It's a horrible feeling.

SARA—Sush, be quiet and I'll tell you every bit of it. (*Then she hesitates and casts a worried look at him—calculatingly*) But maybe it would be simpler if you told me first the last thing you remember.

SIMON—(*with frowning concentration*) The last? I have one clear memory. It came to me when I was lying in the cabin. The last thing I can remember was one day at the office I had an appointment with the directors of the bankrupt railroad to sign a final agreement forcing them out and taking it over. (*A look of bitter self-disgust comes to his face.*) Damned hog and fool that I was!

SARA—(*with a deep breath of relief*) So that's the last you remember! (*then quickly*) Ah, don't be blamin' yourself, Darlin'. That was all my fault. I was always egging you on. I was never content. Nothing would do me but you must become a Napoleon of business. It was me was the greedy fool, Darlin'. With my dream I got from my father's boasting lies that I ought to rise above myself and own a great estate. But that's dead and gone and I'm cured of it, so don't worry.

SIMON—(*obviously comforted by this—protests weakly*) No, you're not to blame. I had the same greedy streak in me. (*then almost accusingly*) But it was true you were the inspiration. I was so afraid you couldn't be proud of me unless I kept on—

SARA—Ah, don't talk. I'm prouder of you now you're all mine again than ever I've been since the day I first met you. (*She kisses him tenderly.*) But now tell me what else you remember of that day.

SIMON—(*frowning*) I remember you came in. I was surprised because you hadn't been there for a long time.

SARA—(*stares at him*) Ah.

SIMON—(*forcing a smile*) You had seemed to become entirely wrapped up in the children and to have forgotten me. I confess I felt a bit jealous. So what was my delight to have you tell me you felt guilty for neglecting me, and lonely, too, and you wanted us to be again as close as we were in the old days, and you asked if I'd give you the job of my confidential secretary.

SARA—(*gives him a strange look—slowly*) Ah, you remember I asked you that, do you?

SIMON—(*with a smile*) Yes, I remember it distinctly, and how happy it made me.

SARA—(*forcing a laugh*) Well, God be praised. You're well again when you can remember that so clearly.

SIMON—(*uneasily again*) But—I can't remember a thing after that. How long ago was that Sara?

SARA—(*hesitating apprehensively*) Well, maybe longer than you'd think. Only bear in mind it's only natural, the doctors say, that with brain fever you forget not only the time you're sick but a long time before it—sometimes years. (*She hesitates—then blurts out*) That day at the office was five years ago.

SIMON—(*frightenedly*) Five years! Good God!

SARA—(*hastily*) Now, now! Don't be worried! I'm telling you the truth when I say there's nothing in those years you'd miss remembering if you knew.

SIMON—(*excitedly*) I must know everything, Sara. All that happened!

SARA—(*with an evasive teasing tone*) You're a great one for asking to know everything and have all, aren't you? But my memory's not that good. I've forgotten a lot since I brought you here on the farm to get well—here where the spell of the sun and the earth is in me and life is clear and simple. And right now with you in your right senses and me in mine, it's hard to remember it ever happened, except as a dream in my mind, a nightmare. (*As he stirs uneasily, she forces a joking tone.*) But what I remember clear as day is the one important thing, that you and I kept as much in love as ever, and more than ever! You're glad to hear that, I hope.

SIMON—(*smiling tenderly*) I know that without remembering, Dear. Nothing could ever change that.

SARA—No, it couldn't. And nothing ever will. Another thing worth remembering is that your sons grew into the fine lads they are now, that you can be proud of.

SIMON—I am, Sara. I was so proud of them today in the field when I first—awakened from my nightmare—and saw them. (*then excitedly*) But what else? Tell me! The Company? Do I have to go back?

SARA—(*with a certain savage satisfaction and at the same time bitterness*) Ah, don't let the damned old Company bother you. It went bankrupt and the creditors stripped us clean. We've not a thing in the world except this farm. We're as poor as Job's turkey. You're free as you always wanted to be in your heart. We're back where we started with only our love for riches! (*hastily*) And it's more than enough! It's the greatest treasure in the world!

SIMON—(*stares before him—with a dreamy exultance*) Yes, it is, Sara. Love! Freedom from greed! This is a happy awakening for me, Sara. I confess I always hoped something would turn up to release me from the soul-destroying compulsion to keep on enslaving myself with more and more power and possessions.

SARA—(*smiling tenderly—but with an undercurrent of pitying scorn for his weakness*) Don't I know it? I could almost hear your heart dreaming it at times.

SIMON—That's why I gambled as I did. But my cursed luck kept me winning when I wanted to lose. Many a time I was tempted to deliberately ruin the Company. But I was afraid you would think me a coward and never forgive me.

SARA—(*roughly tender*) Then get that idea out of your head right now. Don't have it in our new life that's beginning. It shows how little you know me. If you'd read my heart, as I'd read yours, you'd seen I wanted to be free as much as you.

SIMON—(*gratefully—kissing her hand*) Sweetheart! Forgive me! What a fool I was! If I'd known—

SARA—(*proudly*) And I proved it! It was I who smashed it! Oh, it couldn't have gone on long after you took sick. But I didn't wait. I used old Tenard to do it for me. You'd have laughed to see the crafty way I fooled him. I'd learned a lot about men from you, working in your office, and watching the fools come in and try to hide their greed and fear and the price tag of their souls hanging in their eyes!

SIMON—(*bewilderedly*) Tenard? The banker? What had he to do?

SARA—You took his bank from him.

SIMON—I? But what did I want with his bank? Good God, wasn't I burdened enough already?

SARA—You wanted to give it to me because I wanted it. You don't know how greedy I get. Haven't I told you I egged you on? I alone was to blame. You did everything for love of me.

SIMON—(*eagerly*) Yes, now that you've said it yourself, that is the real truth of it, Sara.

SARA—(*a bit mockingly*) It is. It's the best excuse in the world for you. So forgive yourself, do you hear? And I'll make up to you by doing everything I can for the rest of life to keep you free and happy.

SIMON—Oh, I know I'll be happy now, Sara. I never really wanted to leave here, you know. It was a great mistake your insisting I go into business. Because I was bound to fail in the end. It really isn't in me to succeed. It's a damned sordid hog's game.

SARA—I know, Darling. You're a gentleman and a poet at heart, and a lost child in a world of strangers. I'll never ask you to succeed again. With the boys helping me you'll have a living here, at least, and you needn't ever lift your hand. You can be in your dream of a world free of greed where men are good, and write the books you planned here in the old days. And maybe write a poem of your love for me once in a while, as you used. And there will be a song of happiness in my heart, knowing you're happy, even when I'm digging praties in the field, with my bare feet in the earth like a poor ignorant bog-trotter. (*She starts—then adds proudly*) I mean, like the common woman I am, and my mother was, whose one pride is love.

SIMON—(*pats her hand tenderly*) You're the finest woman on earth. (*then weakly, even reluctantly assertive*) But don't think I will spend all my time on my back writing poetry. I can do my share of work in the fields. Of course, I'm too weak now. But later I'll be strong—

SARA—(*bullying him*) You won't. You've done enough. You'll do as I say! You're mine, now!

SIMON—(*gratefully—resting his head on her breast*) Yes, yours, Sweetheart. Everything in and of me yours! That is my heart's whole desire now! (*again weakly assertive*) But don't think I'll let you and the boys support me. I'll at least do enough work on the farm to earn—

SARA—Oh, an hour now and again, for the exercise, like a gentleman's hobby. I'll let you do that. But it will be a long time before you're strong enough. So rest now and don't think of it, but be at peace. (*She cuddles his head against her. He closes his eyes.*)

SIMON—(*vaguely and drowsily*) I seem to remember I tried to find relaxation from the grinding daily slavery to the Company by engaging my mind in some study of the duality of man's nature. Did I, Sara, or is that just a dream?

SARA—(*uneasily*) Just a dream, Darling. You were too worried about business to have time. Anyway, you've got too much sense to waste thought trying to solve the old puzzle of life that there's no answer to, except an answer of death that's no comfort except to those who have lost love.

SIMON—(*vaguely*) No, it's silly. There's no duality in me, I know. At least, not now.

SARA—(*after a pause—unwillingly as though her conscience forced her to speak*) There's something you haven't asked me— about your mother.

SIMON—(*vaguely and drowsily—and indifferently*) That's true, I had forgotten. But I think the reason is I have a feeling that Mother is dead. She is, isn't she?

SARA—(*blurts out*) Yes. She's dead.

SIMON—(*indifferently*) I think I can picture what the rest of her life was without your telling me. I remember what a doting, contented old grandmother she had become. I imagine she grew more and more wrapped up in the children, and more at peace with herself, and was quite happy and reconciled to life—and to death—by the time she died. Isn't that true?

SARA—(*tensely*) Yes. That's what happened to her. Exactly.

SIMON—(*indifferently*) I'm glad. All that Mother ever needed was some unselfish interest that would take her away from her childish day-dreaming and give her the courage to live in reality. It was fortunate for her you were generous enough to give her the opportunity by sharing the children with her and becoming her close friend—I remember how grateful she was to you. I hope she remained so to the end.

SARA—(*tensely*) I—I'm grateful to her.

SIMON—(*drowsily*) I remember it was such a pleasure to me to find you two get on together so well. I had been afraid— But why speak of that now, when it all worked out so happily. (*Sara smiles a twisted bitter smile over his head.*) I was glad for her own sake, particularly. Your friendship meant so much to her. Poor Mother, she was always such a lonely, isolated woman.

SARA—She was, and she was proud to be, no matter what it cost her. She was a great lady.

SIMON—(*as if something in her voice frightened him—uneasily*) She— Mother *was* happy when she died, wasn't she? Wasn't she, Sara?

SARA—(*tensely*) No woman could be happier. She had all the love her heart dreamed of. (*then hastily*) But don't think of the dead, Darling. It's bad luck with our new life starting. Think only of me, and my love for you, and that you're safe and at peace in it, at last!

SIMON—(*drowsily smiling*) I am only too glad to, Sweetheart. That's all—I ever want to remember. (*a pause—more drowsily*) I feel so sleepy. Your breast is so soft and warm— forgive if I— (*He falls asleep.*)

SARA—(*stares down at his face with a fierce, brooding tenderness—then speaks to herself with a strange intermixture of maternal admiration and pride, and a bitter resentment*) Ah, sleep, my Darlin'. Sleep on my breast. It's yours like the heart beating inside it! Rest in peace. You're home at last where you've always wanted to be. I'm your mother now, too. You've everything you need from life in me! (*She chuckles to herself bitterly and admiring.*) But ain't you the craftiest, greediest man that ever walked the earth, God forgive you, to keep on and never let anybody beat you, not even yourself, but make life give you your own stubborn way in the end! But don't think I'm complaining, for your way is my way! Yes, I've made even that mine, now! (*She laughs softly with a strange gaiety. The four boys enter from the path at left, on their way to the lake, led by Ethan and Wolfe. The two latter look the same as in Act Three, Scene Two, except that Ethan is taller and heavier, and Wolfe taller and still slender. As their eyes fall on their father and mother, they are all embarrassed, look away, and quicken their pace to hurry past them down the path to the lake off right. Sara speaks.*) SuSSH! Quiet now. He's asleep. (*They disappear off right. Her eyes follow them. She speaks aloud to herself dreamily, her thoughts with her sons now—proudly*) Fine boys, each of them! No woman on earth has finer sons! Strong in body and with brains, too! Each with a stubborn will of his own! Leave it to them to take what they want from life, once they're men! This little scrub of a farm won't hold them long! Ethan, now, he'll own his fleet of ships! And Wolfe will have his banks! And Johnny his railroads! And Honey be in the White House before he stops, maybe! And each of them will have wealth and power and a grand estate— (*She stops abruptly and guiltily—self-defiantly*) No! To hell with your mad dreams, Sara Melody! That's dead and done! You'll keep your hands off them if you have to cut them off to do it! You'll let them be what they want to be, if it's a tramp in rags without a penny, with no estate but a ditch by the road, so long as they're happy! You'll leave them free, do you hear, and yourself free of them! (*She looks down at Simon's sleeping face on her breast—with a brooding, possessive, tender smile*) After all, one slave is enough for any woman to be owned by! Isn't it true, my Darling? (*She laughs with a gloating, loving, proud, self-mockery—then bends and kisses him softly so as not to awaken him.*)

(*Curtain*)

THE ICEMAN COMETH

CHARACTERS

HARRY HOPE, *proprietor of a saloon and rooming house**

ED MOSHER, *Hope's brother-in-law, one-time circus man**

PAT MCGLOIN, *one-time Police Lieutenant**

WILLIE OBAN, *a Harvard Law School alumnus**

JOE MOTT, *one-time proprietor of a Negro gambling house*

PIET WETJOEN ("THE GENERAL"), *one-time leader of a Boer commando**

CECIL LEWIS ("THE CAPTAIN"), *one-time Captain of British infantry**

JAMES CAMERON ("JIMMY TOMORROW"), *one-time Boer War correspondent**

HUGO KALMAR, *one-time editor of Anarchist periodicals*

LARRY SLADE, *one-time Syndicalist-Anarchist**

ROCKY PIOGGI, *night bartender**

DON PARRITT*

PEARL*
MARGIE* } *street walkers*
CORA

CHUCK MORELLO, *day bartender**

THEODORE HICKMAN (HICKEY), *a hardware salesman*

MORAN

LIEB

*Roomers at Harry Hope's.

SCENES

ACT ONE

Scene—Back room and a section of the bar at Harry Hope's—early morning in summer, 1912.

ACT TWO

Scene—Back room, around midnight of the same day.

ACT THREE

Scene—Bar and a section of the back room—morning of the following day.

ACT FOUR

Scene—Same as Act One. Back room and a section of the bar—around 1:30 A.M. of the next day.

Harry Hope's is a Raines-Law hotel of the period, a cheap ginmill of the five-cent whiskey, last-resort variety situated on the downtown West Side of New York. The building, owned by Hope, is a narrow five-story structure of the tenement type, the second floor a flat occupied by the proprietor. The renting of rooms on the upper floors, under the Raines-Law loopholes, makes the establishment legally a hotel and gives it the privilege of serving liquor in the back room of the bar after closing hours and on Sundays, provided a meal is served with the booze, thus making a back room legally a hotel restaurant. This food provision was generally circumvented by putting a property sandwich in the middle of each table, an old desiccated ruin of dust-laden bread and mummified ham or cheese which only the drunkest yokel from the sticks ever regarded as anything but a noisome table decoration. But at Harry Hope's, Hope being a former minor Tammanyite and still possessing friends, this food technicality is ignored as irrelevant, except during the fleeting alarms of reform agitation. Even Hope's back room is not a separate room, but simply the rear of the barroom divided from the bar by drawing a dirty black curtain across the room.

The Iceman Cometh

ACT ONE

SCENE—*The back room and a section of the bar of Harry Hope's saloon on an early morning in summer, 1912. The right wall of the back room is a dirty black curtain which separates it from the bar. At rear, this curtain is drawn back from the wall so the bartender can get in and out. The back room is crammed with round tables and chairs placed so close together that it is a difficult squeeze to pass between them. In the middle of the rear wall is a door opening on a hallway. In the left corner, built out into the room, is the toilet with a sign "This is it" on the door. Against the middle of the left wall is a nickel-in-the-slot phonograph. Two windows, so glazed with grime one cannot see through them, are in the left wall, looking out on a backyard. The walls and ceiling once were white, but it was a long time ago, and they are now so splotched, peeled, stained and dusty that their color can best be described as dirty. The floor, with iron spittoons placed here and there, is covered with sawdust. Lighting comes from single wall brackets, two at left and two at rear.*

There are three rows of tables, from front to back. Three are in the front line. The one at left-front has four chairs; the one at center-front, four; the one at right-front, five. At rear of, and half between, front tables one and two is a table of the second row with five chairs. A table, similarly placed at rear of front tables two and three, also has five chairs. The third row of tables, four chairs to one and six to the other, is against the rear wall on either side of the door.

At right of this dividing curtain is a section of the barroom, with the end of the bar seen at rear, a door to the hall at left of it. At front is a table with four chairs. Light comes from the street windows off right, the gray subdued light of early morning in a narrow street. In the back room, Larry Slade and Hugo Kalmar are at the table at left-front, Hugo in a chair facing right, Larry at rear of table facing front, with an empty chair between them. A fourth chair is at right of table, facing left. Hugo is a small man in his late fifties. He has a head much too big for his body, a high forehead, crinkly long black hair streaked with gray, a square face with a pug nose, a walrus mustache, black eyes which peer

near-sightedly from behind thick-lensed spectacles, tiny hands and
feet. He is dressed in threadbare black clothes and his white shirt
is frayed at collar and cuffs, but everything about him is fastidiously clean. Even his flowing Windsor tie is neatly tied. There is a
foreign atmosphere about him, the stamp of an alien radical, a
strong resemblance to the type Anarchist as portrayed, bomb in
hand, in newspaper cartoons. He is asleep now, bent forward in
his chair, his arms folded on the table, his head resting sideways
on his arms.

   Larry Slade is sixty. He is tall, raw-boned, with coarse straight
white hair, worn long and raggedly cut. He has a gaunt Irish face
with a big nose, high cheekbones, a lantern jaw with a week's
stubble of beard, a mystic's meditative pale-blue eyes with a gleam
of sharp sardonic humor in them. As slovenly as Hugo is neat, his
clothes are dirty and much slept in. His gray flannel shirt, open at
the neck, has the appearance of having never been washed. From
the way he methodically scratches himself with his long-fingered,
hairy hands, he is lousy and reconciled to being so. He is the only
occupant of the room who is not asleep. He stares in front of him,
an expression of tired tolerance giving his face the quality of a
pitying but weary old priest's.

   All four chairs at the middle table, front, are occupied. Joe Mott
sits at left-front of the table, facing front. Behind him, facing
right-front, is Piet Wetjoen ("The General"). At center of the
table, rear, James Cameron ("Jimmy Tomorrow") sits facing front.
At right of table, opposite Joe, is Cecil Lewis ("The Captain").

   Joe Mott is a Negro, about fifty years old, brown-skinned, stocky,
wearing a light suit that had once been flashily sporty but is now
about to fall apart. His pointed tan buttoned shoes, faded pink
shirt and bright tie belong to the same vintage. Still, he manages
to preserve an atmosphere of nattiness and there is nothing dirty
about his appearance. His face is only mildly negroid in type. The
nose is thin and his lips are not noticeably thick. His hair is crinkly
and he is beginning to get bald. A scar from a knife slash runs
from his left cheekbone to jaw. His face would be hard and tough
if it were not for its good nature and lazy humor. He is asleep, his
nodding head supported by his left hand.

   Piet Wetjoen, the Boer, is in his fifties, a huge man with a bald
head and a long grizzled beard. He is slovenly dressed in a dirty
shapeless patched suit, spotted by food. A Dutch farmer type, his

*once great muscular strength has been debauched into flaccid tal-
low. But despite his blubbery mouth and sodden bloodshot blue eyes,
there is still a suggestion of old authority lurking in him like a
memory of the drowned. He is hunched forward, both elbows on
the table, his hands on each side of his head for support.*

*James Cameron ("Jimmy Tomorrow") is about the same size
and age as Hugo, a small man. Like Hugo, he wears threadbare
black, and everything about him is clean. But the resemblance
ceases there. Jimmy has a face like an old well-bred, gentle bloodhound's, with folds of flesh hanging from each side of his mouth,
and big brown friendly guileless eyes, more bloodshot than any
bloodhound's ever were. He has mouse-colored thinning hair, a
little bulbous nose, buck teeth in a small rabbit mouth. But his
forehead is fine, his eyes are intelligent and there once was a competent ability in him. His speech is educated, with the ghost of a
Scotch rhythm in it. His manners are those of a gentleman. There
is a quality about him of a prim, Victorian old maid, and at the
same time of a likable, affectionate boy who has never grown up.
He sleeps, chin on chest, hands folded in his lap.*

*Cecil Lewis ("The Captain") is as obviously English as Yorkshire
pudding and just as obviously the former army officer. He is going
on sixty. His hair and military mustache are white, his eyes bright
blue, his complexion that of a turkey. His lean figure is still erect
and square-shouldered. He is stripped to the waist, his coat, shirt,
undershirt, collar and tie crushed up into a pillow on the table in
front of him, his head sideways on this pillow, facing front, his
arms dangling toward the floor. On his lower left shoulder is the
big ragged scar of an old wound.*

*At the table at right, front, Harry Hope, the proprietor, sits in
the middle, facing front, with Pat McGloin on his right and Ed
Mosher on his left, the other two chairs being unoccupied.*

*Both McGloin and Mosher are big paunchy men. McGloin has
his old occupation of policeman stamped all over him. He is in his
fifties, sandy-haired, bullet-headed, jowly, with protruding ears
and little round eyes. His face must once have been brutal and
greedy, but time and whiskey have melted it down into a good-
humored, parasite's characterlessness. He wears old clothes and is
slovenly. He is slumped sideways on his chair, his head drooping
jerkily toward one shoulder.*

Ed Mosher is going on sixty. He has a round kewpie's face—

a kewpie who is an unshaven habitual drunkard. He looks like an enlarged, elderly, bald edition of the village fat boy—a sly fat boy, congenitally indolent, a practical joker, a born grafter and con merchant. But amusing and essentially harmless, even in his most enterprising days, because always too lazy to carry crookedness beyond petty swindling. The influence of his old circus career is apparent in his get-up. His worn clothes are flashy; he wears phony rings and a heavy brass watch-chain (not connected to a watch). Like McGloin, he is slovenly. His head is thrown back, his big mouth open.

Harry Hope is sixty, white-haired, so thin the description "bag of bones" was made for him. He has the face of an old family horse, prone to tantrums, with balkiness always smoldering in its wall eyes, waiting for any excuse to shy and pretend to take the bit in its teeth. Hope is one of those men whom everyone likes on sight, a softhearted slob, without malice, feeling superior to no one, a sinner among sinners, a born easy mark for every appeal. He attempts to hide his defenselessness behind a testy truculent manner, but this has never fooled anyone. He is a little deaf, but not half as deaf as he sometimes pretends. His sight is failing but is not as bad as he complains it is. He wears five-and-ten-cent-store spectacles which are so out of alignment that one eye at times peers half over one glass while the other eye looks half under the other. He has badly fitting store teeth, which click like castanets when he begins to fume. He is dressed in an old coat from one suit and pants from another.

In a chair facing right at the table in the second line, between the first two tables, front, sits Willie Oban, his head on his left arm outstretched along the table edge. He is in his late thirties, of average height, thin. His haggard, dissipated face has a small nose, a pointed chin, blue eyes with colorless lashes and brows. His blond hair, badly in need of a cut, clings in a limp part to his skull. His eyelids flutter continually as if any light were too strong for his eyes. The clothes he wears belong on a scarecrow. They seem constructed of an inferior grade of dirty blotting paper. His shoes are even more disreputable, wrecks of imitation leather, one laced with twine, the other with a bit of wire. He has no socks, and his bare feet show through holes in the soles, with his big toes sticking out of the uppers. He keeps muttering and twitching in his sleep.

As the curtain rises, Rocky, the night bartender, comes from the bar through the curtain and stands looking over the back room. He is a Neapolitan-American in his late twenties, squat and muscular, with a flat, swarthy face and beady eyes. The sleeves of his collarless shirt are rolled up on his thick, powerful arms and he wears a soiled apron. A tough guy but sentimental, in his way, and good-natured. He signals to Larry with a cautious "Sstt" and motions him to see if Hope is asleep. Larry rises from his chair to look at Hope and nods to Rocky. Rocky goes back in the bar but immediately returns with a bottle of bar whiskey and a glass. He squeezes between the tables to Larry.

ROCKY—(*in a low voice out of the side of his mouth*) Make it fast. (*Larry pours a drink and gulps it down. Rocky takes the bottle and puts it on the table where Willie Oban is.*) Don't want de Boss to get wise when he's got one of his tightwad buns on. (*He chuckles with an amused glance at Hope.*) Jees, ain't de old bastard a riot when he starts dat bull about turnin' over a new leaf? "Not a damned drink on de house," he tells me, "and all dese bums got to pay up deir room rent. Beginnin' tomorrow," he says. Jees, yuh'd tink he meant it! (*He sits down in the chair at Larry's left.*)

LARRY—(*grinning*) I'll be glad to pay up—tomorrow. And I know my fellow inmates will promise the same. They've all a touching credulity concerning tomorrows. (*a half-drunken mockery in his eyes*) It'll be a great day for them, tomorrow—the Feast of All Fools, with brass bands playing! Their ships will come in, loaded to the gunwales with cancelled regrets and promises fulfilled and clean slates and new leases!

ROCKY—(*cynically*) Yeah, and a ton of hop!

LARRY—(*leans toward him, a comical intensity in his low voice*) Don't mock the faith! Have you no respect for religion, you unregenerate Wop? What's it matter if the truth is that their favoring breeze has the stink of nickel whiskey on its breath, and their sea is a growler of lager and ale, and their ships are long since looted and scuttled and sunk on the bottom? To hell with the truth! As the history of the world proves, the truth has no bearing on anything. It's irrelevant and immaterial, as the lawyers say. The lie of a pipe dream is what gives life to the whole misbegotten mad lot of us, drunk or sober. And that's enough philosophic wisdom to give you for one drink of rot-gut.

ROCKY—(*grins kiddingly*) De old Foolosopher, like Hickey calls yuh, ain't yuh? I s'pose you don't fall for no pipe dream?

LARRY—(*a bit stiffly*) I don't, no. Mine are all dead and buried behind me. What's before me is the comforting fact that death is a fine long sleep, and I'm damned tired, and it can't come too soon for me.

ROCKY—Yeah, just hangin' around hopin' you'll croak, ain't yuh? Well, I'm bettin' you'll have a good long wait. Jees, somebody'll have to take an axe to croak you!

LARRY—(*grins*) Yes, it's my bad luck to be cursed with an iron constitution that even Harry's booze can't corrode.

ROCKY—De old anarchist wise guy dat knows all de answers! Dat's you, huh?

LARRY—(*frowns*) Forget the anarchist part of it. I'm through with the Movement long since. I saw men didn't want to be saved from themselves, for that would mean they'd have to give up greed, and they'll never pay that price for liberty. So I said to the world, God bless all here, and may the best man win and die of gluttony! And I took a seat in the grandstand of philosophical detachment to fall asleep observing the cannibals do their death dance. (*He chuckles at his own fancy—reaches over and shakes Hugo's shoulder.*) Ain't I telling him the truth, Comrade Hugo?

ROCKY—Aw, fer Chris' sake, don't get dat bughouse bum started!

HUGO—(*raises his head and peers at Rocky blearily through his thick spectacles—in a guttural declamatory tone*) Capitalist swine! Bourgeois stool pigeons! Have the slaves no right to sleep even? (*Then he grins at Rocky and his manner changes to a giggling, wheedling playfulness, as though he were talking to a child.*) Hello, leedle Rocky! Leedle monkey-face! Vere is your leedle slave girls? (*with an abrupt change to a bullying tone*) Don't be a fool! Loan me a dollar! Damned bourgeois Wop! The great Malatesta is my good friend! Buy me a trink! (*He seems to run down, and is overcome by drowsiness. His head sinks to the table again and he is at once fast asleep.*)

Rocky—He's out again. (*more exasperated than angry*) He's lucky no one don't take his cracks serious or he'd wake up every mornin' in a hospital.

Larry—(*regarding Hugo with pity*) No. No one takes him seriously. That's his epitaph. Not even the comrades any more. If I've been through with the Movement long since, it's been through with him, and, thanks to whiskey, he's the only one doesn't know it.

Rocky—I've let him get by wid too much. He's goin' to pull dat slave-girl stuff on me once too often. (*His manner changes to defensive argument.*) Hell, yuh'd tink I wuz a pimp or somethin'. Everybody knows me knows I ain't. A pimp don't hold no job. I'm a bartender. Dem tarts, Margie and Poil, dey're just a side line to pick up some extra dough. Strictly business, like dey was fighters and I was deir manager, see? I fix the cops for dem so's dey can hustle widout gettin' pinched. Hell, dey'd be on de Island most of de time if it wasn't fer me. And I don't beat dem up like a pimp would. I treat dem fine. Dey like me. We're pals, see? What if I do take deir dough? Dey'd on'y trow it away. Tarts can't hang on to dough. But I'm a bartender and I work hard for my livin' in dis dump. You know dat, Larry.

Larry—(*with inner sardonic amusement—flatteringly*) A shrewd business man, who doesn't miss any opportunity to get on in the world. That's what I'd call you.

Rocky—(*pleased*) Sure ting. Dat's me. Grab another ball, Larry. (*Larry pours a drink from the bottle on Willie's table and gulps it down. Rocky glances around the room.*) Yuh'd never tink all dese bums had a good bed upstairs to go to. Scared if dey hit the hay dey wouldn't be here when Hickey showed up, and dey'd miss a coupla drinks. Dat's what kept you up too, ain't it?

Larry—It is. But not so much the hope of booze, if you can believe that. I've got the blues and Hickey's a great one to make a joke of everything and cheer you up.

Rocky—Yeah, some kidder! Remember how he woiks up dat gag about his wife, when he's cockeyed, cryin' over her picture and den springin' it on yuh all of a sudden dat he left her in de hay wid de iceman? (*He laughs.*) I wonder what's happened to him. Yuh could set your watch by his periodicals before dis. Always got here a coupla days before Harry's birthday party, and now he's on'y got till tonight to make it. I hope he shows soon. Dis dump is like de morgue wid all dese bums passed out. (*Willie Oban jerks and twitches in his sleep and begins to mumble. They watch him.*)

WILLIE—(*blurts from his dream*) It's a lie! (*miserably*) Papa! Papa!

LARRY—Poor devil. (*then angry with himself*) But to hell with pity! It does no good. I'm through with it!

ROCKY—Dreamin' about his old man. From what de old-timers say, de old gent sure made a pile of dough in de bucket-shop game before de cops got him. (*He considers Willie frowningly.*) Jees, I've seen him bad before but never dis bad. Look at dat get-up. Been playin' de old reliever game. Sold his suit and shoes at Solly's two days ago. Solly give him two bucks and a bum outfit. Yesterday he sells de bum one back to Solly for four bits and gets dese rags to put on. Now he's through. Dat's Solly's final edition he wouldn't take back for nuttin'. Willie sure is on de bottom. I ain't never seen no one so bad, except Hickey on de end of a coupla his bats.

LARRY—(*sardonically*) It's a great game, the pursuit of happiness.

ROCKY—Harry don't know what to do about him. He called up his old lady's lawyer like he always does when Willie gets licked. Yuh remember dey used to send down a private dick to give him the rush to a cure, but de lawyer tells Harry nix, de old lady's off of Willie for keeps dis time and he can go to hell.

LARRY—(*watches Willie, who is shaking in his sleep like an old dog*) There's the consolation that he hasn't far to go! (*As if replying to this, Willie comes to a crisis of jerks and moans. Larry adds in a comically intense, crazy whisper*) Be God, he's knocking on the door right now!

WILLIE—(*suddenly yells in his nightmare*) It's a God-damned lie! (*He begins to sob.*) Oh, Papa! Jesus! (*All the occupants of the room stir on their chairs but none of them wakes up except Hope.*)

ROCKY—(*grabs his shoulder and shakes him*) Hey, you! Nix! Cut out de noise! (*Willie opens his eyes to stare around him with a bewildered horror.*)

HOPE — (*opens one eye to peer over his spectacles — drowsily*) Who's that yelling?

ROCKY — Willie, Boss. De Brooklyn boys is after him.

HOPE — (*querulously*) Well, why don't you give the poor feller a drink and keep him quiet? Bejees, can't I get a wink of sleep in my own back room?

ROCKY — (*indignantly to Larry*) Listen to that blind-eyed, deef old bastard, will yuh? He give me strict orders not to let Willie hang up no more drinks, no matter—

HOPE — (*mechanically puts a hand to his ear in the gesture of deafness*) What's that? I can't hear you. (*then drowsily irascible*) You're a cockeyed liar. Never refused a drink to anyone needed it bad in my life! Told you to use your judgment. Ought to know better. You're too busy thinking up ways to cheat me. Oh, I ain't as blind as you think. I can still see a cash register, bejees!

ROCKY — (*grins at him affectionately now — flatteringly*) Sure, Boss. Swell chance of foolin' you!

HOPE — I'm wise to you and your sidekick, Chuck. Bejees, you're burglars, not barkeeps! Blind-eyed, deef old bastard, am I? Oh, I heard you! Heard you often when you didn't think. You and Chuck laughing behind my back, telling people you throw the money up in the air and whatever sticks to the ceiling is my share! A fine couple of crooks! You'd steal the pennies off your dead mother's eyes!

ROCKY — (*winks at Larry*) Aw, Harry, me and Chuck was on'y kiddin'.

HOPE — (*more drowsily*) I'll fire both of you. Bejees, if you think you can play me for an easy mark, you've come to the wrong house. No one ever played Harry Hope for a sucker!

ROCKY — (*to Larry*) No one but everybody.

HOPE — (*his eyes shut again — mutters*) Least you could do—keep things quiet— (*He falls asleep.*)

WILLIE — (*pleadingly*) Give me a drink, Rocky. Harry said it was all right. God, I need a drink.

ROCKY — Den grab it. It's right under your nose.

WILLIE — (*avidly*) Thanks. (*He takes the bottle with both twitching hands and tilts it to his lips and gulps down the whiskey in big swallows.*)

ROCKY—(*sharply*) When! When! (*He grabs the bottle.*) I
didn't say, take a bath! (*showing the bottle to Larry—indignantly*) Jees, look! He's killed a half pint or more! (*He turns
on Willie angrily, but Willie has closed his eyes and is sitting
quietly, shuddering, waiting for the effect.*)

LARRY—(*with a pitying glance*) Leave him be, the poor
devil. A half pint of that dynamite in one swig will fix him
for a while—if it doesn't kill him.

ROCKY—(*shrugs his shoulders and sits down again*) Aw right
by me. It ain't my booze. (*Behind him, in the chair at left of
the middle table, Joe Mott, the Negro, has been waking up.*)

JOE—(*his eyes blinking sleepily*) Whose booze? Gimme
some. I don't care whose. Where's Hickey? Ain't he come yet?
What time's it, Rocky?

ROCKY—Gettin' near time to open up. Time you begun to
sweep up in de bar.

JOE—(*lazily*) Never mind de time. If Hickey ain't come,
it's time Joe goes to sleep again. I was dreamin' Hickey come
in de door, crackin' one of dem drummer's jokes, wavin' a
big bankroll and we was all goin' be drunk for two weeks.
Wake up and no luck. (*Suddenly his eyes open wide.*) Wait a
minute, dough. I got idea. Say, Larry, how 'bout dat young
guy, Parritt, came to look you up last night and rented a
room? Where's he at?

LARRY—Up in his room, asleep. No hope in him, anyway,
Joe. He's broke.

JOE—Dat what he told you? Me and Rocky knows different. Had a roll when he paid you his room rent, didn't he,
Rocky? I seen it.

ROCKY—Yeah. He flashed it like he forgot and den tried
to hide it quick.

LARRY—(*surprised and resentful*) He did, did he?

ROCKY—Yeah, I figgered he don't belong, but he said he
was a friend of yours.

LARRY—He's a liar. I wouldn't know him if he hadn't told
me who he was. His mother and I were friends years ago on
the Coast. (*He hesitates—then lowering his voice*) You've read
in the papers about that bombing on the Coast when several
people got killed? Well, the one woman they pinched, Rosa
Parritt, is his mother. They'll be coming up for trial soon, and

there's no chance for them. She'll get life, I think. I'm telling you this so you'll know why if Don acts a bit queer, and not jump on him. He must be hard hit. He's her only kid.

ROCKY—(*nods—then thoughtfully*) Why ain't he out dere stickin' by her?

LARRY—(*frowns*) Don't ask questions. Maybe there's a good reason.

ROCKY—(*stares at him—understandingly*) Sure. I get it. (*then wonderingly*) But den what kind of a sap is he to hang on to his right name?

LARRY—(*irritably*) I'm telling you I don't know anything and I don't want to know. To hell with the Movement and all connected with it! I'm out of it, and everything else, and damned glad to be.

ROCKY—(*shrugs his shoulders—indifferently*) Well, don't tink I'm interested in dis Parritt guy. He's nuttin' to me.

JOE—Me neider. If dere's one ting more'n anudder I cares nuttin' about, it's de sucker game you and Hugo call de Movement. (*He chuckles—reminiscently*) Reminds me of damn fool argument me and Mose Porter has de udder night. He's drunk and I'm drunker. He says, "Socialist and Anarchist, we ought to shoot dem dead. Dey's all no-good sons of bitches." I says, "Hold on, you talk 's if Anarchists and Socialists was de same." "Dey is," he says. "Dey's both no-good bastards." "No, dey ain't," I says. "I'll explain the difference. De Anarchist he never works. He drinks but he never buys, and if he do ever get a nickel, he blows it in on bombs, and he wouldn't give you nothin'. So go ahead and shoot him. But de Socialist, sometimes, he's got a job, and if he gets ten bucks, he's bound by his religion to split fifty-fifty wid you. You say—how about my cut, Comrade? And you gets de five. So you don't shoot no Socialists while I'm around. Dat is, not if dey got anything. Of course, if dey's broke, den dey's no-good bastards, too." (*He laughs, immensely tickled.*)

LARRY—(*grins with sardonic appreciation*) Be God, Joe, you've got all the beauty of human nature and the practical wisdom of the world in that little parable.

ROCKY—(*winks at Joe*) Sure, Larry ain't de on'y wise guy in dis dump, hey, Joe? (*At a sound from the hall he turns as Don Parritt appears in the doorway. Rocky speaks to Larry out of the side of his mouth.*) Here's your guy. (*Parritt comes forward. He is eighteen, tall and broad-shouldered but thin, gangling and awkward. His face is good-looking, with blond curly hair and large regular features, but his personality is unpleasant. There is a shifting defiance and ingratiation in his light-blue eyes and an irritating aggressiveness in his manner. His clothes and shoes are new, comparatively expensive, sporty in style. He looks as though he belonged in a pool room patronized by would-be sports. He glances around defensively, sees Larry and comes forward.*)

PARRITT—Hello, Larry. (*He nods to Rocky and Joe.*) Hello. (*They nod and size him up with expressionless eyes.*)

LARRY—(*without cordiality*) What's up? I thought you'd be asleep.

PARRITT—Couldn't make it. I got sick of lying awake. Thought I might as well see if you were around.

LARRY—(*indicates the chair on the right of table*) Sit down and join the bums then. (*Parritt sits down. Larry adds meaningfully*) The rules of the house are that drinks may be served at all hours.

PARRITT—(*forcing a smile*) I get you. But, hell, I'm just about broke. (*He catches Rocky's and Joe's contemptuous glances—quickly*) Oh, I know you guys saw— You think I've got a roll. Well, you're all wrong. I'll show you. (*He takes a small wad of dollar bills from his pocket.*) It's all ones. And I've got to live on it till I get a job. (*then with defensive truculence*) You think I fixed up a phony, don't you? Why the hell would I? Where would I get a real roll? You don't get rich doing what I've been doing. Ask Larry. You're lucky in the Movement if you have enough to eat. (*Larry regards him puzzledly.*)

ROCKY—(*coldly*) What's de song and dance about? We ain't said nuttin'.

PARRITT—(*lamely—placating them now*) Why, I was just putting you right. But I don't want you to think I'm a tightwad. I'll buy a drink if you want one.

JOE—(*cheering up*) If? Man, when I don't want a drink, you call de morgue, tell dem come take Joe's body away, 'cause he's sure enuf dead. Gimme de bottle quick, Rocky, before he changes his mind! (*Rocky passes him the bottle and glass. He pours a brimful drink and tosses it down his throat, and hands the bottle and glass to Larry.*)

ROCKY—I'll take a cigar when I go in de bar. What're you havin'?

PARRITT—Nothing. I'm on the wagon. What's the damage? (*He holds out a dollar bill.*)

ROCKY—Fifteen cents. (*He makes change from his pocket.*)

PARRITT—Must be some booze!

LARRY—It's cyanide cut with carbolic acid to give it a mellow flavor. Here's luck! (*He drinks.*)

ROCKY—Guess I'll get back in de bar and catch a coupla winks before opening-up time. (*He squeezes through the tables and disappears, right-rear, behind the curtain. In the section of bar at right, he comes forward and sits at the table and slumps back, closing his eyes and yawning.*)

JOE—(*stares calculatingly at Parritt and then looks away—aloud to himself, philosophically*) One-drink guy. Dat well done run dry. No hope till Harry's birthday party. 'Less Hickey shows up. (*He turns to Larry.*) If Hickey comes, Larry, you wake me up if you has to bat me wid a chair. (*He settles himself and immediately falls asleep.*)

PARRITT—Who's Hickey?

LARRY—A hardware drummer. An old friend of Harry Hope's and all the gang. He's a grand guy. He comes here twice a year regularly on a periodical drunk and blows in all his money.

PARRITT—(*with a disparaging glance around*) Must be hard up for a place to hang out.

LARRY—It has its points for him. He never runs into anyone he knows in his business here.

PARRITT—(*lowering his voice*) Yes, that's what I want, too. I've got to stay under cover, Larry, like I told you last night.

LARRY—You did a lot of hinting. You didn't tell me anything.

PARRITT—You can guess, can't you? (*He changes the subject abruptly.*) I've been in some dumps on the Coast, but this is the limit. What kind of joint is it, anyway?

LARRY—(*with a sardonic grin*) What is it? It's the No Chance Saloon. It's Bedrock Bar, The End of the Line Café, The Bottom of the Sea Rathskeller! Don't you notice the beautiful calm in the atmosphere? That's because it's the last harbor. No one here has to worry about where they're going next, because there is no farther they can go. It's a great comfort to them. Although even here they keep up the appearances of life with a few harmless pipe dreams about their yesterdays and tomorrows, as you'll see for yourself if you're here long.

PARRITT—(*stares at him curiously*) What's your pipe dream, Larry?

LARRY—(*hiding resentment*) Oh, I'm the exception. I haven't any left, thank God. (*shortly*) Don't complain about this place. You couldn't find a better for lying low.

PARRITT—I'm glad of that, Larry. I don't feel any too damned good. I was knocked off my base by that business on the Coast, and since then it's been no fun dodging around the country, thinking every guy you see might be a dick.

LARRY—(*sympathetically now*) No, it wouldn't be. But you're safe here. The cops ignore this dump. They think it's as harmless as a graveyard. (*He grins sardonically.*) And, be God, they're right.

PARRITT—It's been lonely as hell. (*impulsively*) Christ, Larry, I was glad to find you. I kept saying to myself, "If I can only find Larry. He's the one guy in the world who can understand—" (*He hesitates, staring at Larry with a strange appeal.*)

LARRY—(*watching him puzzledly*) Understand what?

PARRITT—(*hastily*) Why, all I've been through. (*looking away*) Oh, I know you're thinking, This guy has a hell of a nerve. I haven't seen him since he was a kid. I'd forgotten he was alive. But I've never forgotten you, Larry. You were the only friend of Mother's who ever paid attention to me, or knew I was alive. All the others were too busy with the Movement. Even Mother. And I had no Old Man. You used to take me on your knee and tell me stories and crack jokes and make me laugh. You'd ask me questions and take what I said seriously. I guess I got to feel in the years you lived with us that you'd taken the place of my Old Man. (*embarrassedly*) But, hell, that sounds like a lot of mush. I suppose you don't remember a damned thing about it.

LARRY—(*moved in spite of himself*) I remember well. You were a serious lonely little shaver. (*then resenting being moved, changes the subject*) How is it they didn't pick you up when they got your mother and the rest?

PARRITT—(*in a lowered voice but eagerly, as if he wanted this chance to tell about it*) I wasn't around, and as soon as I heard the news I went under cover. You've noticed my glad rags. I was staked to them—as a disguise, sort of. I hung around pool rooms and gambling joints and hooker shops, where they'd never look for a Wobblie, pretending I was a sport. Anyway, they'd grabbed everyone important, so I suppose they didn't think of me until afterward.

LARRY—The papers say the cops got them all dead to rights, that the Burns dicks knew every move before it was made, and someone inside the Movement must have sold out and tipped them off.

PARRITT—(*turns to look Larry in the eyes—slowly*) Yes, I guess that must be true, Larry. It hasn't come out who it was. It may never come out. I suppose whoever it was made a bargain with the Burns men to keep him out of it. They won't need his evidence.

LARRY—(*tensely*) By God, I hate to believe it of any of the crowd, if I am through long since with any connection with them. I know they're damned fools, most of them, as stupidly greedy for power as the worst capitalist they attack, but I'd swear there couldn't be a yellow stool pigeon among them.

PARRITT—Sure. I'd have sworn that, too, Larry.

LARRY—I hope his soul rots in hell, whoever it is!

PARRITT—Yes, so do I.

LARRY—(*after a pause—shortly*) How did you locate me? I hoped I'd found a place of retirement here where no one in the Movement would ever come to disturb my peace.

PARRITT—I found out through Mother.

LARRY—I asked her not to tell anyone.

PARRITT—She didn't tell me, but she'd kept all your letters and I found where she'd hidden them in the flat. I sneaked up there one night after she was arrested.

LARRY—I'd never have thought she was a woman who'd keep letters.

PARRITT—No, I wouldn't, either. There's nothing soft or sentimental about Mother.

LARRY—I never answered her last letters. I haven't written her in a couple of years—or anyone else. I've gotten beyond the desire to communicate with the world—or, what's more to the point, let it bother me any more with its greedy madness.

PARRITT—It's funny Mother kept in touch with you so long. When she's finished with anyone, she's finished. She's always been proud of that. And you know how she feels about the Movement. Like a revivalist preacher about religion. Anyone who loses faith in it is more than dead to her; he's a Judas who ought to be boiled in oil. Yet she seemed to forgive you.

LARRY—(*sardonically*) She didn't, don't worry. She wrote to denounce me and try to bring the sinner to repentance and a belief in the One True Faith again.

PARRITT—What made you leave the Movement, Larry? Was it on account of Mother?

LARRY—(*starts*) Don't be a damned fool! What the hell put that in your head?

PARRITT—Why, nothing—except I remember what a fight you had with her before you left.

LARRY—(*resentfully*) Well, if you do, I don't. That was eleven years ago. You were only seven. If we did quarrel, it was because I told her I'd become convinced the Movement was only a beautiful pipe dream.

PARRITT—(*with a strange smile*) I don't remember it that way.

LARRY—Then you can blame your imagination—and forget it. (*He changes the subject abruptly.*) You asked me why I quit the Movement. I had a lot of good reasons. One was myself, and another was my comrades, and the last was the breed of swine called men in general. For myself, I was forced to admit, at the end of thirty years' devotion to the Cause, that I was never made for it. I was born condemned to be one of those who has to see all sides of a question. When you're damned like that, the questions multiply for you until in the end it's all question and no answer. As history proves, to be a worldly success at anything, especially revolution, you have to wear blinders like a horse and see only straight in front of you. You have to see, too, that this is all black, and that is all white. As for my comrades in the Great Cause, I felt as Horace Walpole did about England, that he could love it if it weren't for the people in it. The material the ideal free society must be constructed from is men themselves and you can't build a marble temple out of a mixture of mud and manure. When man's soul isn't a sow's ear, it will be time enough to dream of silk purses. (*He chuckles sardonically—then irritably as if suddenly provoked at himself for talking so much*) Well, that's why I quit the Movement, if it leaves you any wiser. At any rate, you see it had nothing to do with your mother.

PARRITT—(*smiles almost mockingly*) Oh, sure, I see. But I'll bet Mother has always thought it was on her account. You know her, Larry. To hear her go on sometimes, you'd think she was the Movement.

LARRY—(*stares at him, puzzled and repelled—sharply*) That's a hell of a way for you to talk, after what happened to her!

PARRITT—(*at once confused and guilty*) Don't get me wrong. I wasn't sneering, Larry. Only kidding. I've said the same thing to her lots of times to kid her. But you're right. I know I shouldn't now. I keep forgetting she's in jail. It doesn't seem real. I can't believe it about her. She's always been so free. I— But I don't want to think of it. (*Larry is moved to a puzzled pity in spite of himself. Parritt changes the subject.*) What have you been doing all the years since you left—the Coast, Larry?

LARRY—(*sardonically*) Nothing I could help doing. If I don't believe in the Movement, I don't believe in anything else either, especially not the State. I've refused to become a useful member of its society. I've been a philosophical drunken bum, and proud of it. (*Abruptly his tone sharpens with resentful warning.*) Listen to me. I hope you've deduced that I've my own reason for answering the impertinent questions of a stranger, for that's all you are to me. I have a strong hunch you've come here expecting something of me. I'm warning you, at the start, so there'll be no misunderstanding, that I've nothing left to give, and I want to be left alone, and I'll thank you to keep your life to yourself. I feel you're looking for some answer to something. I have no answer to give anyone, not even myself. Unless you can call what Heine wrote in his poem to morphine an answer. (*He quotes a translation of the closing couplet sardonically.*)

> "Lo, sleep is good; better is death; in sooth,
> The best of all were never to be born."

PARRITT—(*shrinks a bit frightenedly*) That's the hell of an answer. (*then with a forced grin of bravado*) Still, you never know when it might come in handy. (*He looks away. Larry stares at him puzzledly, interested in spite of himself and at the same time vaguely uneasy.*)

LARRY—(*forcing a casual tone*) I don't suppose you've had much chance to hear news of your mother since she's been in jail?

PARRITT—No. No chance. (*He hesitates—then blurts out*) Anyway, I don't think she wants to hear from me. We had a fight just before that business happened. She bawled me out because I was going around with tarts. That got my goat, coming from her. I told her, "You've always acted the free woman, you've never let anything stop you from—" (*He checks himself—goes on hurriedly*) That made her sore. She said she wouldn't give a damn what I did except she'd begun to suspect I was too interested in outside things and losing interest in the Movement.

LARRY—(*stares at him*) And were you?

PARRITT—(*hesitates—then with intensity*) Sure I was! I'm no damned fool! I couldn't go on believing forever that gang was going to change the world by shooting off their loud traps on soapboxes and sneaking around blowing up a lousy building or a bridge! I got wise it was all a crazy pipe dream! (*appealingly*) The same as you did, Larry. That's why I came to you. I knew you'd understand. What finished me was this last business of someone selling out. How can you believe anything after a thing like that happens? It knocks you cold! You don't know what the hell is what! You're through! (*appealingly*) You know how I feel, don't you, Larry? (*Larry stares at him, moved by sympathy and pity in spite of himself, disturbed, and resentful at being disturbed, and puzzled by something he feels about Parritt that isn't right. But before he can reply, Hugo suddenly raises his head from his arms in a half-awake alcoholic daze and speaks.*)

HUGO—(*quotes aloud to himself in a guttural declamatory style*) "The days grow hot, O Babylon! 'Tis cool beneath thy villow trees!" (*Parritt turns startledly as Hugo peers muzzily without recognition at him. Hugo exclaims automatically in his tone of denunciation*) Gottammed stool pigeon!

PARRITT—(*shrinks away—stammers*) What? Who do you mean? (*then furiously*) You lousy bum, you can't call me that! (*He draws back his fist.*)

HUGO—(*ignores this—recognizing him now, bursts into his childish teasing giggle*) Hello, leedle Don! Leedle monkey-face. I did not recognize you. You have grown big boy. How is your mother? Where you come from? (*He breaks into his wheedling, bullying tone.*) Don't be a fool! Loan me a dollar! Buy me a trink! (*As if this exhausted him, he abruptly forgets it and plumps his head down on his arms again and is asleep.*)

PARRITT—(*with eager relief*) Sure, I'll buy you a drink, Hugo. I'm broke, but I can afford one for you. I'm sorry I got sore. I ought to have remembered when you're soused you call everyone a stool pigeon. But it's no damned joke right at this time. (*He turns to Larry, who is regarding him now fixedly with an uneasy expression as if he suddenly were afraid of his own thoughts—forcing a smile*) Gee, he's passed out again. (*He stiffens defensively.*) What are you giving me the hard look for? Oh, I know. You thought I was going to hit him? What do you think I am? I've always had a lot of respect for Hugo. I've always stood up for him when people in the Movement panned him for an old drunken has-been. He had the guts to serve ten years in the can in his own country and get his eyes ruined in solitary. I'd like to see some of them here stick that. Well, they'll get a chance now to show— (*hastily*) I don't mean— But let's forget that. Tell me some more about this dump. Who are all these tanks? Who's that guy trying to catch pneumonia? (*He indicates Lewis.*)

LARRY—(*stares at him almost frightenedly—then looks away and grasps eagerly this chance to change the subject. He begins to describe the sleepers with sardonic relish but at the same time showing his affection for them.*) That's Captain Lewis, a one-time hero of the British Army. He strips to display that scar on his back he got from a native spear whenever he's completely plastered. The bewhiskered bloke opposite him is General Wetjoen, who led a commando in the War. The two of them met when they came here to work in the Boer War spectacle at the St. Louis Fair and they've been bosom pals ever since. They dream the hours away in happy dispute over the brave days in South Africa when they tried to murder each other. The little guy between them was in it, too, as correspondent for some English paper. His nickname here is Jimmy Tomorrow. He's the leader of our Tomorrow Movement.

PARRITT—What do they do for a living?

LARRY—As little as possible. Once in a while one of them makes a successful touch somewhere, and some of them get a few dollars a month from connections at home who pay it on condition they never come back. For the rest, they live on free lunch and their old friend, Harry Hope, who doesn't give a damn what anyone does or doesn't do, as long as he likes you.

PARRITT—It must be a tough life.

LARRY—It's not. Don't waste your pity. They wouldn't thank you for it. They manage to get drunk, by hook or crook, and keep their pipe dreams, and that's all they ask of life. I've never known more contented men. It isn't often that men attain the true goal of their heart's desire. The same applies to Harry himself and his two cronies at the far table. He's so satisfied with life he's never set foot out of this place since his wife died twenty years ago. He has no need of the outside world at all. This place has a fine trade from the Market people across the street and the waterfront workers, so in spite of Harry's thirst and his generous heart, he comes out even. He never worries in hard times because there's always old friends from the days when he was a jitney Tammany politician, and a friendly brewery to tide him over. Don't ask me what his two pals work at because they don't. Except at being his lifetime guests. The one facing this way is his brother-in-law, Ed Mosher, who once worked for a circus in the ticket wagon. Pat McGloin, the other one, was a police lieutenant back in the flush times of graft when everything went. But he got too greedy and when the usual reform investigation came he was caught red-handed and thrown off the Force. (*He nods at Joe.*) Joe here has a yesterday in the same flush period. He ran a colored gambling house then and was a hell of a sport, so they say. Well, that's our whole family circle of inmates, except the two barkeeps and their girls, three ladies of the pavement that room on the third floor.

PARRITT—(*bitterly*) To hell with them! I never want to see a whore again! (*As Larry flashes him a puzzled glance, he adds confusedly*) I mean, they always get you in dutch. (*While he is speaking Willie Oban has opened his eyes. He leans toward them, drunk now from the effect of the huge drink he took, and speaks with a mocking suavity.*)

WILLIE—Why omit me from your Who's Who in Dypso-mania, Larry? An unpardonable slight, especially as I am the only inmate of royal blood. (*to Parritt—ramblingly*) Educated at Harvard, too. You must have noticed the atmosphere of culture here. My humble contribution. Yes, Generous Stranger—I trust you're generous—I was born in the purple, the son, but unfortunately not the heir, of the late world-famous Bill Oban, King of the Bucket Shops. A revolution deposed him, conducted by the District Attorney. He was sent into exile. In fact, not to mince matters, they locked him in the can and threw away the key. Alas, his was an adventur-ous spirit that pined in confinement. And so he died. Forgive these reminiscences. Undoubtedly all this is well known to you. Everyone in the world knows.

PARRITT—(*uncomfortably*) Tough luck. No, I never heard of him.

WILLIE—(*blinks at him incredulously*) Never heard? I thought everyone in the world— Why, even at Harvard I discovered my father was well known by reputation, although that was some time before the District Attorney gave him so much unwelcome publicity. Yes, even as a freshman I was no-torious. I was accepted socially with all the warm cordiality that Henry Wadsworth Longfellow would have shown a drunken Negress dancing the can can at high noon on Brattle Street. Harvard was my father's idea. He was an ambitious man. Dictatorial, too. Always knowing what was best for me. But I did make myself a brilliant student. A dirty trick on my classmates, inspired by revenge, I fear. (*He quotes*) "Dear col-lege days, with pleasure rife! The grandest gladdest days of life!" But, of course, that is a Yale hymn, and they're given to rah-rah exaggeration at New Haven. I was a brilliant student at Law School, too. My father wanted a lawyer in the family. He was a calculating man. A thorough knowledge of the law close at hand in the house to help him find fresh ways to evade it. But I discovered the loophole of whiskey and escaped his jurisdiction. (*abruptly to Parritt*) Speaking of whiskey, sir, reminds me—and, I hope, reminds you—that when meeting a Prince the customary salutation is "What'll you have?"

PARRITT—(*with defensive resentment*) Nix! All you guys seem to think I'm made of dough. Where would I get the coin to blow everyone?

WILLIE—(*sceptically*) Broke? You haven't the thirsty look of the impecunious. I'd judge you to be a plutocrat, your pockets stuffed with ill-gotten gains. Two or three dollars, at least. And don't think we will question how you got it. As Vespasian remarked, the smell of all whiskey is sweet.

PARRITT—What do you mean, how I got it? (*to Larry, forcing a laugh*) It's a laugh, calling me a plutocrat, isn't it, Larry, when I've been in the Movement all my life. (*Larry gives him an uneasy suspicious glance, then looks away, as if avoiding something he does not wish to see.*)

WILLIE—(*disgustedly*) Ah, one of those, eh? I believe you now, all right! Go away and blow yourself up, that's a good lad. Hugo is the only licensed preacher of that gospel here. A dangerous terrorist, Hugo! He would as soon blow the collar off a schooner of beer as look at you! (*to Larry*) Let us ignore this useless youth, Larry. Let us join in prayer that Hickey, the Great Salesman, will soon arrive bringing the blessed bourgeois long green! Would that Hickey or Death would come! Meanwhile, I will sing a song. A beautiful old New England folk ballad which I picked up at Harvard amid the debris of education. (*He sings in a boisterous baritone, rapping on the table with his knuckles at the indicated spots in the song.*)

    "Jack, oh, Jack, was a sailor lad
      And he came to a tavern for gin.
      He rapped and he rapped with a (*rap, rap, rap*)
      But never a soul seemed in."

(*The drunks at the tables stir. Rocky gets up from his chair in the bar and starts back for the entrance to the back room. Hope cocks one irritable eye over his specs. Joe Mott opens both of his and grins. Willie interposes some drunken whimsical exposition to Larry.*) The origin of this beautiful ditty is veiled in mystery, Larry. There was a legend bruited about in Cambridge lavatories that Waldo Emerson composed it during his uninformative period as a minister, while he was trying to write a sermon. But my own opinion is, it goes back much further, and Jonathan Edwards was the author of both words and music. (*He sings*)

"He rapped and rapped, and tapped and tapped
    Enough to wake the dead
    Till he heard a damsel (*rap, rap, rap*)
    On a window right over his head."

(*The drunks are blinking their eyes now, grumbling and cursing. Rocky appears from the bar at rear, right, yawning.*)

HOPE—(*with fuming irritation*) Rocky! Bejees, can't you keep that crazy bastard quiet? (*Rocky starts for Willie.*)

WILLIE—And now the influence of a good woman enters our mariner's life. Well, perhaps "good" isn't the word. But very, very kind. (*He sings*)

"Oh, come up," she cried, "my sailor lad,
    And you and I'll agree,
    And I'll show you the prettiest (*rap, rap, rap*)
    That ever you did see."

(*He speaks.*) You see, Larry? The lewd Puritan touch, obviously, and it grows more marked as we go on. (*He sings*)

"Oh, he put his arm around her waist,
    He gazed in her bright blue eyes
    And then he—"

(*But here Rocky shakes him roughly by the shoulder.*)

ROCKY—Piano! What d'yuh tink dis dump is, a dump?

HOPE—Give him the bum's rush upstairs! Lock him in his room!

ROCKY—(*yanks Willie by the arm*) Come on, Bum.

WILLIE—(*dissolves into pitiable terror*) No! Please, Rocky! I'll go crazy up in that room alone! It's haunted! I— (*He calls to Hope*) Please, Harry! Let me stay here! I'll be quiet!

HOPE—(*immediately relents—indignantly*) What the hell you doing to him, Rocky? I didn't tell you to beat up the poor guy. Leave him alone, long as he's quiet. (*Rocky lets go of Willie disgustedly and goes back to his chair in the bar.*)

WILLIE—(*huskily*) Thanks, Harry. You're a good scout. (*He closes his eyes and sinks back in his chair exhaustedly, twitching and quivering again.*)

HOPE—(*addressing McGloin and Mosher, who are sleepily awake—accusingly*) Always the way. Can't trust nobody. Leave it to that Dago to keep order and it's like bedlam in a cathouse, singing and everything. And you two big barflies are a hell of a help to me, ain't you? Eat and sleep and get drunk! All you're good for, bejees! Well, you can take that "I'll-have-the-same" look off your maps! There ain't going to be no more drinks on the house till hell freezes over! (*Neither of the two is impressed either by his insults or his threats. They grin hangover grins of tolerant affection at him and wink at each other. Harry fumes*) Yeah, grin! Wink, bejees! Fine pair of sons of bitches to have glued on me for life! (*But he can't get a rise out of them and he subsides into a fuming mumble. Meanwhile, at the middle table, Captain Lewis and General Wetjoen are as wide awake as heavy hangovers permit. Jimmy Tomorrow nods, his eyes blinking. Lewis is gazing across the table at Joe Mott, who is still chuckling to himself over Willie's song. The expression on Lewis's face is that of one who can't believe his eyes.*)

LEWIS—(*aloud to himself, with a muzzy wonder*) Good God! Have I been drinking at the same table with a bloody Kaffir?

JOE—(*grinning*) Hello, Captain. You comin' up for air? Kaffir? Who's he?

WETJOEN—(*blurrily*) Kaffir, dot's a nigger, Joe. (*Joe stiffens and his eyes narrow. Wetjoen goes on with heavy jocosity.*) Dot's joke on him, Joe. He don't know you. He's still plind drunk, the ploody Limey chentleman! A great mistake I missed him at the pattle of Modder River. Vit mine rifle I shoot damn fool Limey officers py the dozen, but him I miss. De pity of it! (*He chuckles and slaps Lewis on his bare shoulder.*) Hey, wake up, Cecil, you ploody fool! Don't you know your old friend, Joe? He's no damned Kaffir! He's white, Joe is!

LEWIS—(*light dawning—contritely*) My profound apologies, Joseph, old chum. Eyesight a trifle blurry, I'm afraid. Whitest colored man I ever knew. Proud to call you my friend. No hard feelings, what? (*He holds out his hand.*)

JOE—(*at once grins good-naturedly and shakes his hand*) No, Captain, I know it's mistake. Youse regular, if you is a Limey. (*then his face hardening*) But I don't stand for "nigger" from nobody. Never did. In de old days, people calls me "nigger" wakes up in de hospital. I was de leader ob de Dirty Half-Dozen Gang. All six of us colored boys, we was tough and I was de toughest.

WETJOEN—(*inspired to boastful reminiscence*) Me, in old days in Transvaal, I vas so tough and strong I grab axle of ox wagon mit full load and lift like feather.

LEWIS—(*smiling amiably*) As for you, my balmy Boer that walks like a man, I say again it was a grave error in our foreign policy ever to set you free, once we nabbed you and your commando with Cronje. We should have taken you to the London zoo and incarcerated you in the baboons' cage. With a sign: "Spectators may distinguish the true baboon by his blue behind."

WETJOEN—(*grins*) Gott! To dink, ten better Limey officers, at least, I shoot clean in the mittle of forehead at Spion Kopje, and you I miss! I neffer forgive myself! (*Jimmy Tomorrow blinks benignantly from one to the other with a gentle drunken smile.*)

JIMMY—(*sentimentally*) Now, come, Cecil, Piet! We must forget the War. Boer and Briton, each fought fairly and played the game till the better man won and then we shook hands. We are all brothers within the Empire united beneath the flag on which the sun never sets. (*Tears come to his eyes. He quotes with great sentiment, if with slight application*) "Ship me somewhere east of Suez—"

LARRY—(*breaks in sardonically*) Be God, you're there already, Jimmy. Worst is best here, and East is West, and tomorrow is yesterday. What more do you want?

JIMMY—(*with bleery benevolence, shaking his head in mild rebuke*) No, Larry, old friend, you can't deceive me. You pretend a bitter, cynic philosophy, but in your heart you are the kindest man among us.

LARRY—(*disconcerted—irritably*) The hell you say!

PARRITT—(*leans toward him—confidentially*) What a bunch of cuckoos!

JIMMY—(*as if reminded of something—with a pathetic at-

tempt at a brisk, no-more-nonsense air) Tomorrow, yes. It's high time I straightened out and got down to business again. (*He brushes his sleeve fastidiously.*) I must have this suit cleaned and pressed. I can't look like a tramp when I—

JOE—(*who has been brooding—interrupts*) Yes, suh, white folks always said I was white. In de days when I was flush, Joe Mott's de only colored man dey allows in de white gamblin' houses. "You're all right, Joe, you're white," dey says. (*He chuckles.*) Wouldn't let me play craps, dough. Dey know I could make dem dice behave. "Any odder game and any limit you like, Joe," dey says. Man, de money I lost! (*He chuckles—then with an underlying defensiveness*) Look at de Big Chief in dem days. He knew I was white. I'd saved my dough so I could start my own gamblin' house. Folks in de know tells me, see de man at de top, den you never has trouble. You git Harry Hope give you a letter to de Chief. And Harry does. Don't you, Harry?

HOPE—(*preoccupied with his own thoughts*) Eh? Sure. Big Bill was a good friend of mine. I had plenty of friends high up in those days. Still could have if I wanted to go out and see them. Sure, I gave you a letter. I said you was white. What the hell of it?

JOE—(*to Captain Lewis who has relapsed into a sleepy daze and is listening to him with an absurd strained attention without comprehending a word*) Dere. You see, Captain. I went to see de Chief, shakin' in my boots, and dere he is sittin' behind a big desk, lookin' as big as a freight train. He don't look up. He keeps me waitin' and waitin', and after 'bout an hour, seems like to me, he says slow and quiet like dere wasn't no harm in him, "You want to open a gamblin' joint, does you, Joe?" But he don't give me no time to answer. He jumps up, lookin' as big as two freight trains, and he pounds his fist like a ham on de desk, and he shouts, "You black son of a bitch, Harry says you're white and you better be white or dere's a little iron room up de river waitin' for you!" Den he sits down and says quiet again, "All right. You can open. Git de hell outa here!" So I opens, and he finds out I'se white, sure 'nuff, 'cause I run wide open for years and pays my sugar on de dot, and de cops and I is friends. (*He chuckles with pride.*) Dem old days! Many's de night I come in here. Dis was a first-class hangout for sports in dem days. Good whiskey, fifteen cents, two for two bits. I t'rows down a fifty-dollar bill like it was trash paper and says, "Drink it up, boys, I don't want no change." Ain't dat right, Harry?

HOPE—(*caustically*) Yes, and bejees, if I ever seen you throw fifty cents on the bar now, I'd know I had delirium tremens! You've told that story ten million times and if I have to hear it again, that'll give me D.T.s anyway!

JOE—(*chuckling*) Gittin' drunk every day for twenty years ain't give you de Brooklyn boys. You needn't be scared of me!

LEWIS—(*suddenly turns and beams on Hope*) Thank you, Harry, old chum. I will have a drink, now you mention it, seeing it's so near your birthday. (*The others laugh.*)

HOPE—(*puts his hand to his ear—angrily*) What's that? I can't hear you.

LEWIS—(*sadly*) No, I fancied you wouldn't.

HOPE—I don't have to hear, bejees! Booze is the only thing you ever talk about!

LEWIS—(*sadly*) True. Yet there was a time when my conversation was more comprehensive. But as I became burdened with years, it seemed rather pointless to discuss my other subject.

HOPE—You can't joke with me! How much room rent do you owe me, tell me that?

LEWIS—Sorry. Adding has always baffled me. Subtraction is my forte.

HOPE—(*snarling*) Arrh! Think you're funny! Captain, bejees! Showing off your wounds! Put on your clothes, for Christ's sake! This ain't no Turkish bath! Lousy Limey army! Took 'em years to lick a gang of Dutch hayseeds!

WETJOEN—Dot's right, Harry. Gif him hell!

HOPE—No lip out of you, neither, you Dutch spinach! General, hell! Salvation Army, that's what you'd ought t'been General in! Bragging what a shot you were, and, bejees, you missed him! And he missed you, that's just as bad! And now the two of you bum on me! (*threateningly*) But you've broke the camel's back this time, bejees! You pay up tomorrow or out you go!

LEWIS—(*earnestly*) My dear fellow, I give you my word

of honor as an officer and a gentleman, you shall be paid to-morrow.

WETJOEN—Ve swear it, Harry! Tomorrow vidout fail!

McGLOIN—(*a twinkle in his eye*) There you are, Harry. Sure, what could be fairer?

MOSHER—(*with a wink at McGloin*) Yes, you can't ask more than that, Harry. A promise is a promise—as I've often discovered.

HOPE—(*turns on them*) I mean the both of you, too! An old grafting flatfoot and a circus bunco steerer! Fine company for me, bejees! Couple of con men living in my flat since Christ knows when! Getting fat as hogs, too! And you ain't even got the decency to get me upstairs where I got a good bed! Let me sleep on a chair like a bum! Kept me down here waitin' for Hickey to show up, hoping I'd blow you to more drinks!

McGLOIN—Ed and I did our damnedest to get you up, didn't we, Ed?

MOSHER—We did. But you said you couldn't bear the flat because it was one of those nights when memory brought poor old Bessie back to you.

HOPE—(*his face instantly becoming long and sad and senti-mental—mournfully*) Yes, that's right, boys. I remember now. I could almost see her in every room just as she used to be—and it's twenty years since she— (*His throat and eyes fill up. A suitable sentimental hush falls on the room.*)

LARRY—(*in a sardonic whisper to Parritt*) Isn't a pipe dream of yesterday a touching thing? By all accounts, Bessie nagged the hell out of him.

JIMMY—(*who has been dreaming, a look of prim resolution on his face, speaks aloud to himself*) No more of this sitting around and loafing. Time I took hold of myself. I must have my shoes soled and heeled and shined first thing tomorrow morning. A general spruce-up. I want to have a well-groomed appearance when I— (*His voice fades out as he stares in front of him. No one pays any attention to him except Larry and Parritt.*)

LARRY—(*as before, in a sardonic aside to Parritt*) The to-morrow movement is a sad and beautiful thing, too!

McGLOIN—(*with a huge sentimental sigh—and a calcu-*

lating look at Hope) Poor old Bessie! You don't find her like in these days. A sweeter woman never drew breath.

MOSHER—(*in a similar calculating mood*) Good old Bess. A man couldn't want a better sister than she was to me.

HOPE—(*mournfully*) Twenty years, and I've never set foot out of this house since the day I buried her. Didn't have the heart. Once she'd gone, I didn't give a damn for anything. I lost all my ambition. Without her, nothing seemed worth the trouble. You remember, Ed, you, too, Mac—the boys was going to nominate me for Alderman. It was all fixed. Bessie wanted it and she was so proud. But when she was taken, I told them, "No, boys, I can't do it. I simply haven't the heart. I'm through." I would have won the election easy, too. (*He says this a bit defiantly.*) Oh, I know there was jealous wise guys said the boys was giving me the nomination because they knew they couldn't win that year in this ward. But that's a damned lie! I knew every man, woman and child in the ward, almost. Bessie made me make friends with everyone, helped me remember all their names. I'd have been elected easy.

McGLOIN—You would, Harry. It was a sure thing.

MOSHER—A dead cinch, Harry. Everyone knows that.

HOPE—Sure they do. But after Bessie died, I didn't have the heart. Still, I know while she'd appreciate my grief, she wouldn't want it to keep me cooped up in here all my life. So I've made up my mind I'll go out soon. Take a walk around the ward, see all the friends I used to know, get together with the boys and maybe tell 'em I'll let 'em deal me a hand in their game again. Yes, bejees, I'll do it. My birthday, tomorrow, that'd be the right time to turn over a new leaf. Sixty. That ain't too old.

McGLOIN—(*flatteringly*) It's the prime of life, Harry.

MOSHER—Wonderful thing about you, Harry, you keep young as you ever was.

JIMMY—(*dreaming aloud again*) Get my things from the laundry. They must still have them. Clean collar and shirt. If I wash the ones I've got on any more, they'll fall apart. Socks, too. I want to make a good appearance. I met Dick Trumbull on the street a year or two ago. He said, "Jimmy, the publicity department's never been the same since you

got—resigned. It's dead as hell." I said, "I know. I've heard
rumors the management were at their wits' end and would
be only too glad to have me run it for them again. I think
all I'd have to do would be go and see them and they'd
offer me the position. Don't you think so, Dick?" He said,
"Sure, they would, Jimmy. Only take my advice and wait a
while until business conditions are better. Then you can
strike them for a bigger salary than you got before, do you
see?" I said, "Yes, I do see, Dick, and many thanks for the
tip." Well, conditions must be better by this time. All I have
to do is get fixed up with a decent front tomorrow, and it's
as good as done.

HOPE—(*glances at Jimmy with a condescending affectionate
pity—in a hushed voice*) Poor Jimmy's off on his pipe dream
again. Bejees, he takes the cake! (*This is too much for Larry. He
cannot restrain a sardonic guffaw. But no one pays any attention
to him.*)

LEWIS—(*opens his eyes, which are drowsing again—dreamily
to Wetjoen*) I'm sorry we had to postpone our trip again this
April, Piet. I hoped the blasted old estate would be settled up
by then. The damned lawyers can't hold up the settlement
much longer. We'll make it next year, even if we have to work
and earn our passage money, eh? You'll stay with me at the
old place as long as you like, then you can take the *Union
Castle* from Southampton to Cape Town. (*sentimentally, with
real yearning*) England in April. I want you to see that, Piet.
The old veldt has its points, I'll admit, but it isn't home—
especially home in April.

WETJOEN—(*blinks drowsily at him—dreamily*) Ja, Cecil, I
know how beautiful it must be, from all you tell me many
times. I vill enjoy it. But I shall enjoy more ven I am home,
too. The veldt, ja! You could put England on it, and it
would look like a farmer's small garden. Py Gott, there is
space to be free, the air like vine is, you don't need booze to
be drunk! My relations vill so surprised be. They vill not
know me, it is so many years. Dey vill be so glad I haf come
home at last.

JOE—(*dreamily*) I'll make my stake and get my new gamblin' house open before you boys leave. You got to come to
de openin'. I'll treat you white. If you're broke, I'll stake you

to buck any game you chooses. If you wins, dat's velvet for you. If you loses, it don't count. Can't treat you no whiter dan dat, can I?

HOPE—(*again with condescending pity*) Bejees, Jimmy's started them off smoking the same hop. (*But the three are finished, their eyes closed again in sleep or a drowse.*)

LARRY—(*aloud to himself—in his comically tense, crazy whisper*) Be God, this bughouse will drive me stark, raving loony yet!

HOPE—(*turns on him with fuming suspicion*) What? What d'you say?

LARRY—(*placatingly*) Nothing, Harry. I had a crazy thought in my head.

HOPE—(*irascibly*) Crazy is right! Yah! The old wise guy! Wise, hell! A damned old fool Anarchist I-Won't-Worker! I'm sick of you and Hugo, too. Bejees, you'll pay up tomorrow, or I'll start a Harry Hope Revolution! I'll tie a dispossess bomb to your tails that'll blow you out in the street! Bejees, I'll make your Movement move! (*The witticism delights him and he bursts into a shrill cackle. At once McGloin and Mosher guffaw enthusiastically.*)

MOSHER—(*flatteringly*) Harry, you sure say the funniest things! (*He reaches on the table as if he expected a glass to be there—then starts with well-acted surprise.*) Hell, where's my drink? That Rocky is too damned fast cleaning tables. Why, I'd only taken one sip of it.

HOPE—(*his smiling face congealing*) No, you don't! (*acidly*) Any time you only take one sip of a drink, you'll have lockjaw and paralysis! Think you can kid me with those old circus con games?—me, that's known you since you was knee-high, and, bejees, you was a crook even then!

McGLOIN—(*grinning*) It's not like you to be so hard-hearted, Harry. Sure, it's hot, parching work laughing at your jokes so early in the morning on an empty stomach!

HOPE—Yah! You, Mac! Another crook! Who asked you to laugh? We was talking about poor old Bessie, and you and her no-good brother start to laugh! A hell of a thing! Talking mush about her, too! "Good old Bess." Bejees, she'd never forgive me if she knew I had you two bums living in her flat, throwing ashes and cigar butts on her carpet. You know her opinion of you, Mac. "That Pat McGloin is the biggest drunken grafter that ever disgraced the police force," she used to say to me. "I hope they send him to Sing Sing for life."

McGLOIN—(*unperturbed*) She didn't mean it. She was angry at me because you used to get me drunk. But Bess had a heart of gold underneath her sharpness. She knew I was innocent of all the charges.

WILLIE—(*jumps to his feet drunkenly and points a finger at McGloin—imitating the manner of a cross-examiner—coldly*) One moment, please. Lieutenant McGloin! Are you aware you are under oath? Do you realize what the penalty for perjury is? (*purringly*) Come now, Lieutenant, isn't it a fact that you're as guilty as hell? No, don't say, "How about your old man?" I am asking the questions. The fact that he was a crooked old bucket-shop bastard has no bearing on your case. (*with a change to maudlin joviality*) Gentlemen of the Jury, court will now recess while the D.A. sings out a little ditty he learned at Harvard. It was composed in a wanton moment by the Dean of the Divinity School on a moonlight night in July, 1776, while sobering up in a Turkish bath. (*He sings*)

"Oh, come up," she cried, "my sailor lad,
And you and I'll agree.
And I'll show you the prettiest (*rap, rap, rap on table*)
That ever you did see."

(*Suddenly he catches Hope's eyes fixed on him condemningly, and sees Rocky appearing from the bar. He collapses back on his chair, pleading miserably*) Please, Harry! I'll be quiet! Don't make Rocky bounce me upstairs! I'll go crazy alone! (*to McGloin*) I apologize, Mac. Don't get sore. I was only kidding you. (*Rocky, at a relenting glance from Hope, returns to the bar.*)

McGLOIN—(*good-naturedly*) Sure, kid all you like, Willie. I'm hardened to it. (*He pauses—seriously*) But I'm telling you some day before long I'm going to make them reopen my case. Everyone knows there was no real evidence against me, and I took the fall for the ones higher up. I'll be found innocent this time and reinstated. (*wistfully*) I'd like to have my old job on the Force back. The boys tell me there's fine pickings these days, and I'm not getting rich here, sitting with a parched throat waiting for Harry Hope to buy a drink. (*He glances reproachfully at Hope.*)

WILLIE—Of course, you'll be reinstated, Mac. All you need is a brilliant young attorney to handle your case. I'll be straightened out and on the wagon in a day or two. I've never practiced but I was one of the most brilliant students in Law School, and your case is just the opportunity I need to start. (*darkly*) Don't worry about my not forcing the D.A. to re-open your case. I went through my father's papers before the cops destroyed them, and I remember a lot of people, even if I can't prove— (*coaxingly*) You will let me take your case, won't you, Mac?

McGLOIN—(*soothingly*) Sure I will and it'll make your reputation, Willie. (*Mosher winks at Hope, shaking his head, and Hope answers with identical pantomime, as though to say, "Poor dopes, they're off again!"*)

LARRY—(*aloud to himself more than to Parritt—with irritable wonder*) Ah, be damned! Haven't I heard their visions a thousand times? Why should they get under my skin now? I've got the blues, I guess. I wish to hell Hickey'd turn up.

MOSHER—(*calculatingly solicitous—whispering to Hope*) Poor Willie needs a drink bad, Harry—and I think if we all joined him it'd make him feel he was among friends and cheer him up.

HOPE—More circus con tricks! (*scathingly*) You talking of your dear sister! Bessie had you sized up. She used to tell me, "I don't know what you can see in that worthless, drunken, petty-larceny brother of mine. If I had my way," she'd say, "he'd get booted out in the gutter on his fat behind." Sometimes she didn't say behind, either.

MOSHER—(*grins genially*) Yes, dear old Bess had a quick temper, but there was no real harm in her. (*He chuckles reminiscently.*) Remember the time she sent me down to the bar to change a ten-dollar bill for her?

HOPE—(*has to grin himself*) Bejees, do I! She coulda bit a piece out of a stove lid, after she found it out. (*He cackles appreciatively.*)

MOSHER—I was sure surprised when she gave me the ten spot. Bess usually had better sense, but she was in a hurry to go to church. I didn't really mean to do it, but you know how habit gets you. Besides, I still worked then, and the circus season was going to begin soon, and I needed a little practice to keep my hand in. Or, you never can tell, the first rube that came to my wagon for a ticket might have left with the right change and I'd be disgraced. (*He chuckles.*) I said, "I'm sorry, Bess, but I had to take it all in dimes. Here, hold out your hands and I'll count it out for you, so you won't kick afterwards I short-changed you." (*He begins a count which grows more rapid as he goes on.*) Ten, twenty, thirty, forty, fifty, sixty, seventy, eighty, ninety, a dollar. Ten, twenty, thirty, forty, fifty, sixty— You're counting with me, Bess, aren't you?—eighty, ninety, two dollars. Ten, twenty— Those are pretty shoes you got on, Bess—forty, fifty, seventy, eighty, ninety, three dollars. Ten, twenty, thirty— What's on at the church tonight, Bess?—fifty, sixty, seventy, ninety, four dollars. Ten, twenty, thirty, fifty, seventy, eighty, ninety— That's a swell new hat, Bess, looks very becoming—six dollars. (*He chuckles.*) And so on. I'm bum at it now for lack of practice, but in those days I could have short-changed the Keeper of the Mint.

HOPE—(*grinning*) Stung her for two dollars and a half, wasn't it, Ed?

MOSHER—Yes. A fine percentage, if I do say so, when you're dealing to someone who's sober and can count. I'm sorry to say she discovered my mistakes in arithmetic just after I beat it around the corner. She counted it over herself. Bess somehow never had the confidence in me a sister should. (*He sighs tenderly.*) Dear old Bess.

HOPE—(*indignant now*) You're a fine guy bragging how you short-changed your own sister! Bejees, if there was a war and you was in it, they'd have to padlock the pockets of the dead!

MOSHER—(*a bit hurt at this*) That's going pretty strong, Harry. I always gave a sucker some chance. There wouldn't be no fun robbing the dead. (*He becomes reminiscently melancholy.*) Gosh, thinking of the old ticket wagon brings those days back. The greatest life on earth with the greatest show on earth! The grandest crowd of regular guys ever gathered under one tent! I'd sure like to shake their hands again!

HOPE—(*acidly*) They'd have guns in theirs. They'd shoot you on sight. You've touched every damned one of them. Bejees, you've even borrowed fish from the trained seals and peanuts from every elephant that remembered you! (*This fancy tickles him and he gives a cackling laugh.*)

MOSHER—(*overlooking this—dreamily*) You know, Harry, I've made up my mind I'll see the boss in a couple of days and ask for my old job. I can get back my magic touch with change easy, and I can throw him a line of bull that'll kid him I won't be so unreasonable about sharing the profits next time. (*with insinuating complaint*) There's no percentage in hanging around this dive, taking care of you and shooing away your snakes, when I don't even get an eye-opener for my trouble.

HOPE—(*implacably*) No! (*Mosher sighs and gives up and closes his eyes. The others, except Larry and Parritt, are all dozing again now. Hope goes on grumbling.*) Go to hell or the circus, for all I care. Good riddance, bejees! I'm sick of you! (*then worriedly*) Say, Ed, what the hell you think's happened to Hickey? I hope he'll turn up. Always got a million funny stories. You and the other bums have begun to give me the graveyard fantods. I'd like a good laugh with old Hickey. (*He chuckles at a memory.*) Remember that gag he always pulls about his wife and the iceman? He'd make a cat laugh! (*Rocky appears from the bar. He comes front, behind Mosher's chair, and begins pushing the black curtain along the rod to the rear wall.*)

ROCKY—Openin' time, Boss. (*He presses a button at rear which switches off the lights. The back room becomes drabber and dingier than ever in the gray daylight that comes from the street windows, off right, and what light can penetrate the grime of the two backyard windows at left. Rocky turns back to Hope— grumpily*) Why don't you go up to bed, Boss? Hickey'd never turn up dis time of de mornin'!

HOPE—(*starts and listens*) Someone's coming now.

ROCKY—(*listens*) Aw, dat's on'y my two pigs. It's about time dey showed. (*He goes back toward the door at left of the bar.*)

HOPE—(*sourly disappointed*) You keep them dumb broads quiet. I don't want to go to bed. I'm going to catch a couple more winks here and I don't want no damn-fool laughing and screeching. (*He settles himself in his chair, grumbling*) Never thought I'd see the day when Harry Hope's would have tarts rooming in it. What'd Bessie think? But I don't let 'em use my rooms for business. And they're good kids. Good as anyone else. They got to make a living. Pay their rent, too, which is more than I can say for— (*He cocks an eye over his specs at Mosher and grins with satisfaction.*) Bejees, Ed, I'll bet Bessie is doing somersaults in her grave! (*He chuckles. But Mosher's eyes are closed, his head nodding, and he doesn't reply, so Hope closes his eyes. Rocky has opened the barroom door at rear and is standing in the hall beyond it, facing right. A girl's laugh is heard.*)

ROCKY—(*warningly*) Nix! Piano! (*He comes in, beckoning them to follow. He goes behind the bar and gets a whiskey bottle and glasses and chairs. Margie and Pearl follow him, casting a glance around. Everyone except Larry and Parritt is asleep or dozing. Even Parritt has his eyes closed. The two girls, neither much over twenty, are typical dollar street walkers, dressed in the usual tawdry get-up. Pearl is obviously Italian with black hair and eyes. Margie has brown hair and hazel eyes, a slum New Yorker of mixed blood. Both are plump and have a certain prettiness that shows even through their blobby make-up. Each retains a vestige of youthful freshness, although the game is beginning to get them and give them hard, worn expressions. Both are sentimental, feather-brained, giggly, lazy, good-natured and reasonably contented with life. Their attitude toward Rocky is much that of two maternal, affectionate sisters toward a bullying brother whom they like to tease and spoil. His attitude toward them is that of the owner of two performing pets he has trained to do a profitable act under his management. He feels a proud proprietor's affection for them, and is tolerantly lax in his discipline.*)

MARGIE—(*glancing around*) Jees, Poil, it's de Morgue wid all de stiffs on deck. (*She catches Larry's eye and smiles affectionately.*) Hello, Old Wise Guy, ain't you died yet?

LARRY—(*grinning*) Not yet, Margie. But I'm waiting impatiently for the end. (*Parritt opens his eyes to look at the two girls, but as soon as they glance at him he closes them again and turns his head away.*)

MARGIE—(*as she and Pearl come to the table at right, front, followed by Rocky*) Who's de new guy? Friend of yours, Larry? (*Automatically she smiles seductively at Parritt and addresses him in a professional chant.*) Wanta have a good time, kid?

PEARL—Aw, he's passed out. Hell wid him!

HOPE—(*cocks an eye over his specs at them—with drowsy*

irritation) You dumb broads cut the loud talk. (*He shuts his eye again.*)

ROCKY—(*admonishing them good-naturedly*) Sit down before I knock yuh down. (*Margie and Pearl sit at left, and rear, of table, Rocky at right of it. The girls pour drinks. Rocky begins in a brisk, business-like manner but in a lowered voice with an eye on Hope.*) Well, how'd you tramps do?

MARGIE—Pretty good. Didn't we, Poil?

PEARL—Sure. We nailed a coupla all-night guys.

MARGIE—On Sixth Avenoo. Boobs from de sticks.

PEARL—Stinko, de bot' of 'em.

MARGIE—We thought we was in luck. We steered dem to a real hotel. We figgered dey was too stinko to bother us much and we could cop a good sleep in beds that ain't got cobble stones in de mattress like de ones in dis dump.

PEARL—But we was outa luck. Dey didn't bother us much dat way, but dey wouldn't go to sleep either, see? Jees, I never hoid such gabby guys.

MARGIE—Dey got onta politics, drinkin' outa de bottle. Dey forgot we was around. "De Bull Moosers is de on'y reg'lar guys," one guy says. And de other guy says, "You're a God-damned liar! And I'm a Republican!" Den dey'd laugh.

PEARL—Den dey'd get mad and make a bluff dey was goin' to scrap, and den dey'd make up and cry and sing "School Days." Jees, imagine tryin' to sleep wid dat on de phonograph!

MARGIE—Maybe you tink we wasn't glad when de house dick come up and told us all to git dressed and take de air!

PEARL—We told de guys we'd wait for dem 'round de corner.

MARGIE—So here we are.

ROCKY—(*sententiously*) Yeah. I see you. But I don't see no dough yet.

PEARL—(*with a wink at Margie—teasingly*) Right on de job, ain't he, Margie?

MARGIE—Yeah, our little business man! Dat's him!

ROCKY—Come on! Dig! (*They both pull up their skirts to get the money from their stockings. Rocky watches this move carefully.*)

PEARL—(*amused*) Pipe him keepin' cases, Margie.

MARGIE—(*amused*) Scared we're holdin' out on him.

PEARL—Way he grabs, yuh'd tink it was him done de woik. (*She holds out a little roll of bills to Rocky.*) Here y'are, Grafter!

MARGIE—(*holding hers out*) We hope it chokes yuh. (*Rocky counts the money quickly and shoves it in his pocket.*)

ROCKY—(*genially*) You dumb baby dolls gimme a pain. What would you do wid money if I wasn't around? Give it all to some pimp.

PEARL—(*teasingly*) Jees, what's the difference—? (*hastily*) Aw, I don't mean dat, Rocky.

ROCKY—(*his eyes growing hard—slowly*) A lotta difference, get me?

PEARL—Don't get sore. Jees, can't yuh take a little kiddin'?

MARGIE—Sure, Rocky, Poil was on'y kiddin'. (*soothingly*) We know yuh got a reg'lar job. Dat's why we like yuh, see? Yuh don't live offa us. Yuh're a bartender.

ROCKY—(*genially again*) Sure, I'm a bartender. Everyone knows me knows dat. And I treat you goils right, don't I? Jees, I'm wise yuh hold out on me, but I know it ain't much, so what the hell, I let yuh get away wid it. I tink yuh're a coupla good kids. Yuh're aces wid me, see?

PEARL—You're aces wid us, too. Ain't he, Margie?

MARGIE—Sure, he's aces. (*Rocky beams complacently and takes the glasses back to the bar. Margie whispers*) Yuh sap, don't yuh know enough not to kid him on dat? Serve yuh right if he beat yuh up!

PEARL—(*admiringly*) Jees, I'll bet he'd give yuh an awful beatin', too, once he started. Ginnies got awful tempers.

MARGIE—Anyway, we wouldn't keep no pimp, like we was reg'lar old whores. We ain't dat bad.

PEARL—No. We're tarts, but dat's all.

ROCKY—(*rinsing glasses behind the bar*) Cora got back around three o'clock. She woke up Chuck and dragged him outa de hay to go to a chop suey joint. (*disgustedly*) Imagine him standin' for dat stuff!

MARGIE—(*disgustedly*) I'll bet dey been sittin' around kiddin' demselves wid dat old pipe dream about gettin' married and settlin' down on a farm. Jees, when Chuck's on de wagon, dey never lay off dat dope! Dey give yuh an earful every time yuh talk to 'em!

PEARL—Yeah. Chuck wid a silly grin on his ugly map, de big boob, and Cora gigglin' like she was in grammar school and some tough guy'd just told her babies wasn't brung down de chimney by a boid!

MARGIE—And her on de turf long before me and you was! And bot' of 'em arguin' all de time, Cora sayin' she's scared to marry him because he'll go on drunks again. Just as dough any drunk could scare Cora!

PEARL—And him swearin', de big liar, he'll never go on no more periodicals! An' den her pretendin'— But it gives me a pain to talk about it. We ought to phone de booby hatch to send round de wagon for 'em.

ROCKY—(*comes back to the table—disgustedly*) Yeah, of all de pipe dreams in dis dump, dey got de nuttiest! And nuttin' stops dem. Dey been dreamin' it for years, every time Chuck goes on de wagon. I never could figger it. What would gettin' married get dem? But de farm stuff is de sappiest part. When bot' of 'em was dragged up in dis ward and ain't never been nearer a farm dan Coney Island! Jees, dey'd think dey'd gone deef if dey didn't hear de El rattle! Dey'd get D.T.s if dey ever hoid a cricket choip! I hoid crickets once on my cousin's place in Joisey. I couldn't sleep a wink. Dey give me de heebie-jeebies. (*with deeper disgust*) Jees, can yuh picture a good bar-keep like Chuck diggin' spuds? And imagine a whore hustlin' de cows home! For Christ sake! Ain't dat a sweet picture!

MARGIE—(*rebukingly*) Yuh oughtn't to call Cora dat, Rocky. She's a good kid. She may be a tart, but—

ROCKY—(*considerately*) Sure, dat's all I meant, a tart.

PEARL—(*giggling*) But he's right about de damned cows, Margie. Jees, I bet Cora don't know which end of de cow has de horns! I'm goin' to ask her. (*There is the noise of a door opening in the hall and the sound of a man's and woman's arguing voices.*)

ROCKY—Here's your chance. Dat's dem two nuts now. (*Cora and Chuck look in from the hallway and then come in. Cora is a thin peroxide blonde, a few years older than Pearl and Margie, dressed in similar style, her round face showing more of the wear and tear of her trade than theirs, but still with traces of a doll-like prettiness. Chuck is a tough, thick-necked, barrel-chested Italian-American, with a fat, amiable, swarthy face. He has on a straw hat with a vivid band, a loud suit, tie and shirt, and yellow shoes. His eyes are clear and he looks healthy and strong as an ox.*)

CORA—(*gaily*) Hello, bums. (*She looks around.*) Jees, de Morgue on a rainy Sunday night! (*She waves to Larry— affectionately*) Hello, Old Wise Guy! Ain't you croaked yet?

LARRY—(*grins*) Not yet, Cora. It's damned tiring, this waiting for the end.

CORA—Aw, gwan, you'll never die! Yuh'll have to hire someone to croak yuh wid an axe.

HOPE—(*cocks one sleepy eye at her—irritably*) You dumb hookers, cut the loud noise! This ain't a cathouse!

CORA—(*teasingly*) My, Harry! Such language!

HOPE—(*closes his eyes—to himself with a gratified chuckle*) Bejees, I'll bet Bessie's turning over in her grave! (*Cora sits down between Margie and Pearl. Chuck takes an empty chair from Hope's table and puts it by hers and sits down. At Larry's table, Parritt is glaring resentfully toward the girls.*)

PARRITT—If I'd known this dump was a hooker hangout, I'd never have come here.

LARRY—(*watching him*) You seem down on the ladies.

PARRITT—(*vindictively*) I hate every bitch that ever lived! They're all alike! (*catching himself guiltily*) You can understand how I feel, can't you, when it was getting mixed up with a tart that made me have that fight with Mother? (*then with a resentful sneer*) But what the hell does it matter to you? You're in the grandstand. You're through with life.

LARRY—(*sharply*) I'm glad you remember it. I don't want to know a damned thing about your business. (*He closes his eyes and settles on his chair as if preparing for sleep. Parritt stares at him sneeringly. Then he looks away and his expression becomes furtive and frightened.*)

CORA—Who's de guy wid Larry?

ROCKY—A tightwad. To hell wid him.

PEARL—Say, Cora, wise me up. Which end of a cow is de horns on?

CORA—(*embarrassed*) Aw, don't bring dat up. I'm sick of hearin' about dat farm.

ROCKY—You got nuttin' on us!

CORA—(*ignoring this*) Me and dis overgrown tramp has been scrappin' about it. He says Joisey's de best place, and I says Long Island because we'll be near Coney. And I tells him, How do I know yuh're off of periodicals for life? I don't give a damn how drunk yuh get, the way we are, but I don't wanta be married to no soak.

CHUCK—And I tells her I'm off de stuff for life. Den she beefs we won't be married a month before I'll trow it in her face she was a tart. "Jees, Baby," I tells her. "Why should I? What de hell yuh tink I tink I'm marryin', a voigin? Why should I kick as long as yuh lay off it and don't do no cheatin' wid de iceman or nobody?" (*He gives her a rough hug.*) Dat's on de level, Baby. (*He kisses her.*)

CORA—(*kissing him*) Aw, yuh big tramp!

ROCKY—(*shakes his head with profound disgust*) Can yuh tie it? I'll buy a drink. I'll do anything. (*He gets up.*)

CORA—No, dis round's on me. I run into luck. Dat's why I dragged Chuck outa bed to celebrate. It was a sailor. I rolled him. (*She giggles.*) Listen, it was a scream. I've run into some nutty souses, but dis guy was de nuttiest. De booze dey dish out around de Brooklyn Navy Yard must be as turrible bug-juice as Harry's. My dogs was givin' out when I seen dis guy holdin' up a lamppost, so I hurried to get him before a cop did. I says, "Hello, Handsome, wanta have a good time?" Jees, he was paralyzed! One of dem polite jags. He tries to bow to me, imagine, and I had to prop him up or he'd fell on his nose. And what d'yuh tink he said? "Lady," he says, "can yuh kindly tell me de nearest way to de Museum of Natural History?" (*They all laugh.*) Can yuh imagine! At two A.M. As if I'd know where de dump was anyway. But I says, "Sure ting, Honey Boy, I'll be only too glad." So I steered him into a side street where it was dark and propped him against a wall and give him a frisk. (*She giggles.*) And what d'yuh tink he does? Jees, I ain't lyin', he begins to laugh, de big sap! He says, "Quit ticklin' me." While I was friskin' him for his roll! I near died! Den I toined him 'round and give him a push to start him. "Just keep goin'," I told him. "It's a big white building on your right. You can't miss it." He must be swimmin' in de North River yet! (*They all laugh.*)

CHUCK—Ain't Uncle Sam de sap to trust guys like dat wid dough!

CORA—(*with a business-like air*) I picked twelve bucks offa him. Come on, Rocky. Set 'em up. (*Rocky goes back to the bar. Cora looks around the room.*) Say, Chuck's kiddin' about de iceman a minute ago reminds me. Where de hell's Hickey?

ROCKY—Dat's what we're all wonderin'.

CORA—He oughta be here. Me and Chuck seen him.

ROCKY—(*excited, comes back from the bar, forgetting the drinks*) You seen Hickey? (*He nudges Hope.*) Hey, Boss, come to! Cora's seen Hickey. (*Hope is instantly wide awake and everyone in the place, except Hugo and Parritt, begins to rouse up hopefully, as if a mysterious wireless message had gone round.*)

HOPE—Where'd you see him, Cora?

CORA—Right on de next corner. He was standin' dere. We said, "Welcome to our city. De gang is expectin' yuh wid deir tongues hangin' out a yard long." And I kidded him, "How's de iceman, Hickey? How's he doin' at your house?" He laughs and says, "Fine." And he says, "Tell de gang I'll be along in a minute. I'm just finishin' figurin' out de best way to save dem and bring dem peace."

HOPE—(*chuckles*) Bejees, he's thought up a new gag! It's a wonder he didn't borry a Salvation Army uniform and show up in that! Go out and get him, Rocky. Tell him we're waitin' to be saved! (*Rocky goes out, grinning.*)

CORA—Yeah, Harry, he was only kiddin'. But he was funny, too, somehow. He was different, or somethin'.

CHUCK—Sure, he was sober, Baby. Dat's what made him different. We ain't never seen him when he wasn't on a drunk, or had de willies gettin' over it.

CORA—Sure! Gee, ain't I dumb?

HOPE—(*with conviction*) The dumbest broad I ever seen! (*then puzzledly*) Sober? That's funny. He's always lapped up a good starter on his way here. Well, bejees, he won't be sober long! He'll be good and ripe for my birthday party tonight at twelve. (*He chuckles with excited anticipation—addressing all of them*) Listen! He's fixed some new gag to pull on us. We'll pretend to let him kid us, see? And we'll kid the pants off him. (*They all say laughingly, "Sure, Harry," "Righto," "That's the stuff," "We'll fix him," etc., etc., their faces excited with the same eager anticipation. Rocky appears in the doorway at the end of the bar with Hickey, his arm around Hickey's shoulders.)*

ROCKY—(*with an affectionate grin*) Here's the old son of a bitch! (*They all stand up and greet him with affectionate acclaim, "Hello, Hickey!" etc. Even Hugo comes out of his coma to raise his head and blink through his thick spectacles with a welcoming giggle.*)

HICKEY—(*jovially*) Hello, Gang! (*He stands a moment, beaming around at all of them affectionately. He is about fifty, a little under medium height, with a stout, roly-poly figure. His face is round and smooth and big-boyish with bright blue eyes, a button nose, a small, pursed mouth. His head is bald except for a fringe of hair around his temples and the back of his head. His expression is fixed in a salesman's winning smile of self-confident affability and hearty good fellowship. His eyes have the twinkle of a humor which delights in kidding others but can also enjoy equally a joke on himself. He exudes a friendly, generous personality that makes everyone like him on sight. You get the impression, too, that he must have real ability in his line. There is an efficient, business-like approach in his manner, and his eyes can take you in shrewdly at a glance. He has the salesman's mannerisms of speech, an easy flow of glib, persuasive convincingness. His clothes are those of a successful drummer whose territory consists of minor cities and small towns—not flashy but conspicuously spic and span. He immediately puts on an entrance act, places a hand affectedly on his chest, throws back his head, and sings in a falsetto tenor*) "It's always fair weather, when good fellows get together!" (*changing to a comic bass and another tune*) "And another little drink won't do us any harm!" (*They all roar with laughter at this burlesque which his personality makes really funny. He waves his hand in a lordly manner to Rocky.*) Do your duty, Brother Rocky. Bring on the rat poison! (*Rocky grins and goes behind the bar to get drinks amid an approving cheer from the crowd. Hickey comes forward to shake hands with Hope—with affectionate heartiness*) How goes it, Governor?

HOPE—(*enthusiastically*) Bejees, Hickey, you old bastard, it's good to see you! (*Hickey shakes hands with Mosher and McGloin; leans right to shake hands with Margie and Pearl; moves to the middle table to shake hands with Lewis, Joe Mott,*

Wetjoen and Jimmy; waves to Willie, Larry and Hugo. He greets each by name with the same affectionate heartiness and there is an interchange of "How's the kid?" "How's the old scout?" "How's the boy?" "How's everything?" *etc., etc. Rocky begins setting out drinks, whiskey glasses with chasers, and a bottle for each table, starting with Larry's table. Hope says*) Sit down, Hickey. Sit down. (*Hickey takes the chair, facing front, at the front of the table in the second row which is half between Hope's table and the one where Jimmy Tomorrow is. Hope goes on with excited pleasure.*) Bejees, Hickey, it seems natural to see your ugly, grinning map. (*with a scornful nod to Cora*) This dumb broad was tryin' to tell us you'd changed, but you ain't a damned bit. Tell us about yourself. How've you been doin'? Bejees, you look like a million dollars.

ROCKY—(*coming to Hickey's table, puts a bottle of whiskey, a glass and a chaser on it—then hands Hickey a key*) Here's your key, Hickey. Same old room.

HICKEY—(*shoves the key in his pocket*) Thanks, Rocky. I'm going up in a little while and grab a snooze. Haven't been able to sleep lately and I'm tired as hell. A couple of hours good kip will fix me.

HOPE—(*as Rocky puts drinks on his table*) First time I ever heard you worry about sleep. Bejees, you never would go to bed. (*He raises his glass, and all the others except Parritt do likewise.*) Get a few slugs under your belt and you'll forget sleeping. Here's mud in your eye, Hickey. (*They all join in with the usual humorous toasts.*)

HICKEY—(*heartily*) Drink hearty, boys and girls! (*They all drink, but Hickey drinks only his chaser.*)

HOPE—Bejees, is that a new stunt, drinking your chaser first?

HICKEY—No, I forgot to tell Rocky— You'll have to excuse me, boys and girls, but I'm off the stuff. For keeps. (*They stare at him in amazed incredulity.*)

HOPE—What the hell— (*then with a wink at the others, kiddingly*) Sure! Joined the Salvation Army, ain't you? Been elected President of the W.C.T.U.? Take that bottle away from him, Rocky. We don't want to tempt him into sin. (*He chuckles and the others laugh.*)

HICKEY—(*earnestly*) No, honest, Harry. I know it's hard

to believe but— (*He pauses—then adds simply*) Cora was right, Harry. I have changed. I mean, about booze. I don't need it any more. (*They all stare, hoping it's a gag, but impressed and disappointed and made vaguely uneasy by the change they now sense in him.*)

HOPE—(*his kidding a bit forced*) Yeah, go ahead, kid the pants off us! Bejees, Cora said you was coming to save us! Well, go on. Get this joke off your chest! Start the service! Sing a God-damned hymn if you like. We'll all join in the chorus. "No drunkard can enter this beautiful home." That's a good one. (*He forces a cackle.*)

HICKEY—(*grinning*) Oh, hell, Governor! You don't think I'd come around here peddling some brand of temperance bunk, do you? You know me better than that! Just because I'm through with the stuff don't mean I'm going Prohibition. Hell, I'm not that ungrateful! It's given me too many good times. I feel exactly the same as I always did. If anyone wants to get drunk, if that's the only way they can be happy, and feel at peace with themselves, why the hell shouldn't they? They have my full and entire sympathy. I know all about that game from soup to nuts. I'm the guy that wrote the book. The only reason I've quit is— Well, I finally had the guts to face myself and throw overboard the damned lying pipe dream that'd been making me miserable, and do what I had to do for the happiness of all concerned—and then all at once I found I was at peace with myself and I didn't need booze any more. That's all there was to it. (*He pauses. They are staring at him, uneasy and beginning to feel defensive. Hickey looks round and grins affectionately—apologetically*) But what the hell! Don't let me be a wet blanket, making fool speeches about myself. Set 'em up again, Rocky. Here. (*He pulls a big roll from his pocket and peels off a ten-dollar bill. The faces of all brighten.*) Keep the balls coming until this is killed. Then ask for more.

ROCKY—Jees, a roll dat'd choke a hippopotamus! Fill up, youse guys. (*They all pour out drinks.*)

HOPE—That sounds more like you, Hickey. That water-wagon bull— Cut out the act and have a drink, for Christ's sake.

HICKEY—It's no act, Governor. But don't get me wrong.

That don't mean I'm a teetotal grouch and can't be in the party. Hell, why d'you suppose I'm here except to have a party, same as I've always done, and help celebrate your birthday tonight? You've all been good pals to me, the best friends I've ever had. I've been thinking about you ever since I left the house—all the time I was walking over here—

HOPE—Walking? Bejees, do you mean to say you walked?

HICKEY—I sure did. All the way from the wilds of darkest Astoria. Didn't mind it a bit, either. I seemed to get here before I knew it. I'm a bit tired and sleepy but otherwise I feel great. (*kiddingly*) That ought to encourage you, Governor—show you a little walk around the ward is nothing to be so scared about. (*He winks at the others. Hope stiffens resentfully for a second. Hickey goes on.*) I didn't make such bad time either for a fat guy, considering it's a hell of a ways, and I sat in the park a while thinking. It was going on twelve when I went in the bedroom to tell Evelyn I was leaving. Six hours, say. No, less than that. I'd been standing on the corner some time before Cora and Chuck came along, thinking about all of you. Of course, I was only kidding Cora with that stuff about saving you. (*then seriously*) No, I wasn't either. But I didn't mean booze. I meant save you from pipe dreams. I know now, from my experience, they're the things that really poison and ruin a guy's life and keep him from finding any peace. If you knew how free and contented I feel now. I'm like a new man. And the cure for them is so damned simple, once you have the nerve. Just the old dope of honesty is the best policy—honesty with yourself, I mean. Just stop lying about yourself and kidding yourself about tomorrows. (*He is staring ahead of him now as if he were talking aloud to himself as much as to them. Their eyes are fixed on him with uneasy resentment. His manner becomes apologetic again.*) Hell, this begins to sound like a damned sermon on the way to lead the good life. Forget that part of it. It's in my blood, I guess. My old man used to whale salvation into my heinie with a birch rod. He was a preacher in the sticks of Indiana, like I've told you. I got my knack of sales gab from him, too. He was the boy who could sell those Hoosier hayseeds building lots along the Golden Street! (*taking on a salesman's persuasiveness*) Now listen, boys and girls, don't look at me as if I was trying to sell you a goldbrick. Nothing up my sleeve, honest. Let's take an example. Any one of you. Take you, Governor. That walk around the ward you never take—

HOPE—(*defensively sharp*) What about it?

HICKEY—(*grinning affectionately*) Why, you know as well as I do, Harry. Everything about it.

HOPE—(*defiantly*) Bejees, I'm going to take it!

HICKEY—Sure, you're going to—this time. Because I'm going to help you. I know it's the thing you've got to do before you'll ever know what real peace means. (*He looks at Jimmy Tomorrow.*) Same thing with you, Jimmy. You've got to try and get your old job back. And no tomorrow about it! (*as Jimmy stiffens with a pathetic attempt at dignity—placatingly*) No, don't tell me, Jimmy. I know all about tomorrow. I'm the guy that wrote the book.

JIMMY—I don't understand you. I admit I've foolishly delayed, but as it happens, I'd just made up my mind that as soon as I could get straightened out—

HICKEY—Fine! That's the spirit! And I'm going to help you. You've been damned kind to me, Jimmy, and I want to prove how grateful I am. When it's all over and you don't have to nag at yourself any more, you'll be grateful to me, too! (*He looks around at the others.*) And all the rest of you, ladies included, are in the same boat, one way or another.

LARRY—(*who has been listening with sardonic appreciation—in his comically intense, crazy whisper*) Be God, you've hit the nail on the head, Hickey! This dump is the Palace of Pipe Dreams!

HICKEY—(*grins at him with affectionate kidding*) Well, well! The Old Grandstand Foolosopher speaks! You think you're the big exception, eh? Life doesn't mean a damn to you any more, does it? You're retired from the circus. You're just waiting impatiently for the end—the good old Long Sleep! (*He chuckles.*) Well, I think a lot of you, Larry, you old bastard. I'll try and make an honest man of you, too!

LARRY—(*stung*) What the devil are you hinting at, anyway?

HICKEY—You don't have to ask me, do you, a wise old guy like you? Just ask yourself. I'll bet you know.

PARRITT—(*is watching Larry's face with a curious sneering satisfaction*) He's got your number all right, Larry! (*He turns to Hickey.*) That's the stuff, Hickey. Show the old faker up! He's got no right to sneak out of everything.

HICKEY—(*regards him with surprise at first, then with a puzzled interest*) Hello. A stranger in our midst. I didn't notice you before, Brother.

PARRITT—(*embarrassed, his eyes shifting away*) My name's Parritt. I'm an old friend of Larry's. (*His eyes come back to Hickey to find him still sizing him up—defensively*) Well? What are you staring at?

HICKEY—(*continuing to stare—puzzledly*) No offense, Brother. I was trying to figure— Haven't we met before some place?

PARRITT—(*reassured*) No. First time I've ever been East.

HICKEY—No, you're right. I know that's not it. In my game, to be a shark at it, you teach yourself never to forget a name or a face. But still I know damned well I recognized something about you. We're members of the same lodge—in some way.

PARRITT—(*uneasy again*) What are you talking about? You're nuts.

HICKEY—(*dryly*) Don't try to kid me, Little Boy. I'm a good salesman—so damned good the firm was glad to take me back after every drunk—and what made me good was I could size up anyone. (*frowningly puzzled again*) But I don't see— (*suddenly breezily good-natured*) Never mind. I can tell you're having trouble with yourself and I'll be glad to do anything I can to help a friend of Larry's.

LARRY—Mind your own business, Hickey. He's nothing to you—or to me, either. (*Hickey gives him a keen inquisitive glance. Larry looks away and goes on sarcastically.*) You're keeping us all in suspense. Tell us more about how you're going to save us.

HICKEY—(*good-naturedly but seeming a little hurt*) Hell, don't get sore, Larry. Not at me. We've always been good pals, haven't we? I know I've always liked you a lot.

LARRY—(*a bit shamefaced*) Well, so have I liked you. Forget it, Hickey.

HICKEY—(*beaming*) Fine! That's the spirit! (*looking*

around at the others, who have forgotten their drinks) What's the matter, everybody? What is this, a funeral? Come on and drink up! A little action! (*They all drink.*) Have another. Hell, this is a celebration! Forget it, if anything I've said sounds too serious. I don't want to be a pain in the neck. Any time you think I'm talking out of turn, just tell me to go chase myself! (*He yawns with growing drowsiness and his voice grows a bit muffled.*) No, boys and girls, I'm not trying to put anything over on you. It's just that I know now from experience what a lying pipe dream can do to you—and how damned relieved and contented with yourself you feel when you're rid of it. (*He yawns again.*) God, I'm sleepy all of a sudden. That long walk is beginning to get me. I better go upstairs. Hell of a trick to go dead on you like this. (*He starts to get up but relaxes again. His eyes blink as he tries to keep them open.*) No, boys and girls, I've never known what real peace was until now. It's a grand feeling, like when you're sick and suffering like hell and the Doc gives you a shot in the arm, and the pain goes, and you drift off. (*His eyes close.*) You can let go of yourself at last. Let yourself sink down to the bottom of the sea. Rest in peace. There's no farther you have to go. Not a single damned hope or dream left to nag you. You'll all know what I mean after you— (*He pauses—mumbles*) Excuse— all in—got to grab forty winks— Drink up, everybody— on me— (*The sleep of complete exhaustion overpowers him. His chin sags to his chest. They stare at him with puzzled uneasy fascination.*)

HOPE—(*forcing a tone of irritation*) Bejees, that's a fine stunt, to go to sleep on us! (*then fumingly to the crowd*) Well, what the hell's the matter with you bums? Why don't you drink up? You're always crying for booze, and now you've got it under your nose, you sit like dummies! (*They start and gulp down their whiskies and pour another. Hope stares at Hickey.*) Bejees, I can't figure Hickey. I still say he's kidding us. Kid his own grandmother, Hickey would. What d'you think, Jimmy?

JIMMY—(*unconvincingly*) It must be another of his jokes, Harry, although— Well, he does appear changed. But he'll probably be his natural self again tomorrow— (*hastily*) I mean, when he wakes up.

LARRY—(*staring at Hickey frowningly—more aloud to him-self than to them*) You'll make a mistake if you think he's only kidding.

PARRITT—(*in a low confidential voice*) I don't like that guy, Larry. He's too damned nosy. I'm going to steer clear of him. (*Larry gives him a suspicious glance, then looks hastily away.*)

JIMMY—(*with an attempt at open-minded reasonableness*) Still, Harry, I have to admit there was some sense in his non-sense. It is time I got my job back—although I hardly need him to remind me.

HOPE—(*with an air of frankness*) Yes, and I ought to take a walk around the ward. But I don't need no Hickey to tell me, seeing I got it all set for my birthday tomorrow.

LARRY—(*sardonically*) Ha! (*then in his comically intense, crazy whisper*) Be God, it looks like he's going to make two sales of his peace at least! But you'd better make sure first it's the real McCoy and not poison.

HOPE—(*disturbed—angrily*) You bughouse I-Won't-Work harp, who asked you to shove in an oar? What the hell d'you mean, poison? Just because he has your number— (*He im-mediately feels ashamed of this taunt and adds apologetically*) Be-jees, Larry, you're always croaking about something to do with death. It gets my nanny. Come on, fellers, let's drink up. (*They drink. Hope's eyes are fixed on Hickey again.*) Stone cold sober and dead to the world! Spilling that business about pipe dreams! Bejees, I don't get it. (*He bursts out again in angry complaint*) He ain't like the old Hickey! He'll be a fine wet blanket to have around at my birthday party! I wish to hell he'd never turned up!

MOSHER—(*who has been the least impressed by Hickey's talk and is the first to recover and feel the effect of the drinks on top of his hangover—genially*) Give him time, Harry, and he'll come out of it. I've watched many cases of almost fatal teetotalism, but they all came out of it completely cured and as drunk as ever. My opinion is the poor sap is temporarily bughouse from overwork. (*musingly*) You can't be too careful about work. It's the deadliest habit known to science, a great phy-sician once told me. He practiced on street corners under a torchlight. He was positively the only doctor in the world who claimed that rattlesnake oil, rubbed on the prat, would cure heart failure in three days. I remember well his saying to me, "You are naturally delicate, Ed, but if you drink a pint of bad whiskey before breakfast every evening, and never work if you can help it, you may live to a ripe old age. It's staying sober and working that cuts men off in their prime." (*While he is talking, they turn to him with eager grins. They are longing to laugh, and as he finishes they roar. Even Parritt laughs. Hickey sleeps on like a dead man, but Hugo, who had passed into his customary coma again, head on table, looks up through his thick spectacles and giggles foolishly.*)

HUGO—(*blinking around at them. As the laughter dies he speaks in his giggling, wheedling manner, as if he were playfully teasing children.*) Laugh, leedle bourgeois monkey-faces! Laugh like fools, leedle stupid peoples! (*His tone suddenly changes to one of guttural soapbox denunciation and he pounds on the table with a small fist.*) I vill laugh, too! But I vill laugh last! I vill laugh at you! (*He declaims his favorite quotation.*) "The days grow hot, O Babylon! 'Tis cool beneath thy villow trees!" (*They all hoot him down in a chorus of amused jeering. Hugo is not offended. This is evidently their customary reaction. He giggles good-naturedly. Hickey sleeps on. They have all forgotten their uneasiness about him now and ignore him.*)

LEWIS—(*tipsily*) Well, now that our little Robespierre has got the daily bit of guillotining off his chest, tell me more about your doctor friend, Ed. He strikes me as the only bloody sensible medico I ever heard of. I think we should appoint him house physician here without a moment's delay. (*They all laughingly assent.*)

MOSHER—(*warming to his subject, shakes his head sadly*) Too late! The old Doc has passed on to his Maker. A victim of overwork, too. He didn't follow his own advice. Kept his nose to the grindstone and sold one bottle of snake oil too many. Only eighty years old when he was taken. The saddest part was that he knew he was doomed. The last time we got paralyzed together he told me: "This game will get me yet, Ed. You see before you a broken man, a martyr to medical science. If I had any nerves I'd have a nervous breakdown. You won't believe me, but this last year there was actually one night I had so many patients, I didn't even have time to get drunk. The shock to my system brought on a stroke which, as a doctor, I recognized was the beginning of the end." Poor old Doc! When he said this he started crying. "I hate to go before my task is completed, Ed," he sobbed. "I'd hoped I'd live to see the day when, thanks to my miraculous cure, there wouldn't be a single vacant cemetery lot left in this glorious country." (*There is a roar of laughter. He waits for it to die and then goes on sadly.*) I miss Doc. He was a gentleman of the old school. I'll bet he's standing on a street corner in hell right now, making suckers of the damned, telling them there's nothing like snake oil for a bad burn. (*There is another roar of laughter. This time it penetrates Hickey's exhausted slumber. He stirs on his chair, trying to wake up, managing to raise his head a little and force his eyes half open. He speaks with a drowsy, affectionately encouraging smile. At once the laughter stops abruptly and they turn to him startledly.*)

HICKEY—That's the spirit—don't let me be a wet blanket—all I want is to see you happy— (*He slips back into heavy sleep again. They all stare at him, their faces again puzzled, resentful and uneasy.*)

(*Curtain*)

ACT TWO

SCENE—*The back room only. The black curtain dividing it
from the bar is the right wall of the scene. It is getting on toward
midnight of the same day.*

*The back room has been prepared for a festivity. At center,
front, four of the circular tables are pushed together to form one
long table with an uneven line of chairs behind it, and chairs at
each end. This improvised banquet table is covered with old table
cloths, borrowed from a neighboring beanery, and is laid with
glasses, plates and cutlery before each of the seventeen chairs. Bottles of bar whiskey are placed at intervals within reach of any
sitter. An old upright piano and stool have been moved in and
stand against the wall at left, front. At right, front, is a table
without chairs. The other tables and chairs that had been in the
room have been moved out, leaving a clear floor space at rear for
dancing. The floor has been swept clean of sawdust and scrubbed.
Even the walls show evidence of having been washed, although
the result is only to heighten their splotchy leprous look. The electric
light brackets are adorned with festoons of red ribbon. In the
middle of the separate table at right, front, is a birthday cake
with six candles. Several packages, tied with ribbon, are also on the
table. There are two necktie boxes, two cigar boxes, a fifth containing a half dozen handkerchiefs, the sixth is a square jeweler's
watch box.*

*As the curtain rises, Cora, Chuck, Hugo, Larry, Margie, Pearl
and Rocky are discovered. Chuck, Rocky and the three girls have
dressed up for the occasion. Cora is arranging a bouquet of flowers
in a vase, the vase being a big schooner glass from the bar, on top
of the piano. Chuck sits in a chair at the foot (left) of the banquet
table. He has turned it so he can watch her. Near the middle of
the row of chairs behind the table, Larry sits, facing front, a drink
of whiskey before him. He is staring before him in frowning, disturbed meditation. Next to him, on his left, Hugo is in his habitual position, passed out, arms on table, head on arms, a full
whiskey glass by his head. By the separate table at right, front,
Margie and Pearl are arranging the cake and presents, and Rocky
stands by them. All of them, with the exception of Chuck and
Rocky, have had plenty to drink and show it, but no one, except
Hugo, seems to be drunk. They are trying to act up in the spirit*

*of the occasion but there is something forced about their manner,
an undercurrent of nervous irritation and preoccupation.*

CORA—(*standing back from the piano to regard the flower
effect*) How's dat, Kid?

CHUCK—(*grumpily*) What de hell do I know about
flowers?

CORA—Yuh can see dey're pretty, can't yuh, yuh big
dummy?

CHUCK—(*mollifyingly*) Yeah, Baby, sure. If yuh like 'em,
dey're aw right wid me. (*Cora goes back to give the schooner of
flowers a few more touches.*)

MARGIE—(*admiring the cake*) Some cake, huh, Poil?
Lookit! Six candles. Each for ten years.

PEARL—When do we light de candles, Rocky?

ROCKY—(*grumpily*) Ask dat bughouse Hickey. He's
elected himself boss of dis boithday racket. Just before Harry
comes down, he says. Den Harry blows dem out wid one
breath, for luck. Hickey was goin' to have sixty candles, but I
says, Jees, if de old guy took dat big a breath, he'd croak
himself.

MARGIE—(*challengingly*) Well, anyways, it's some cake,
ain't it?

ROCKY—(*without enthusiasm*) Sure, it's aw right by me.
But what de hell is Harry goin' to do wid a cake? If he ever
et a hunk, it'd croak him.

PEARL—Jees, yuh're a dope! Ain't he, Margie?

MARGIE—A dope is right!

ROCKY—(*stung*) You broads better watch your step or—

PEARL—(*defiantly*) Or what?

MARGIE—Yeah! Or what? (*They glare at him truculently.*)

ROCKY—Say, what de hell's got into youse? It'll be twelve
o'clock and Harry's boithday before long. I ain't lookin' for
no trouble.

PEARL—(*ashamed*) Aw, we ain't neider, Rocky. (*For the
moment this argument subsides.*)

CORA—(*over her shoulder to Chuck—acidly*) A guy what
can't see flowers is pretty must be some dumbbell.

CHUCK—Yeah? Well, if I was as dumb as you— (*then mollifyingly*) Jees, yuh got your scrappin' pants on, ain't yuh?

(*grins good-naturedly*) Hell, Baby, what's eatin' yuh? All I'm tinkin' is, flowers is dat louse Hickey's stunt. We never had no flowers for Harry's boithday before. What de hell can Harry do wid flowers? He don't know a cauliflower from a geranium.

ROCKY—Yeah, Chuck, it's like I'm tellin' dese broads about de cake. Dat's Hickey's wrinkle, too. (*bitterly*) Jees, ever since he woke up, yuh can't hold him. He's taken on de party like it was his boithday.

MARGIE—Well, he's payin' for everything, ain't he?

ROCKY—Aw, I don't mind de boithday stuff so much. What gets my goat is de way he's tryin' to run de whole dump and everyone in it. He's buttin' in all over de place, tellin' everybody where dey get off. On'y he don't really tell yuh. He just keeps hintin' around.

PEARL—Yeah. He was hintin' to me and Margie.

MARGIE—Yeah, de lousy drummer.

ROCKY—He just gives yuh an earful of dat line of bull about yuh got to be honest wid yourself and not kid yourself, and have de guts to be what yuh are. I got sore. I told him dat's aw right for de bums in his dump. I hope he makes dem wake up. I'm sick of listenin' to dem hop demselves up. But it don't go wid me, see? I don't kid myself wid no pipe dream. (*Pearl and Margie exchange a derisive look. He catches it and his eyes narrow.*) What are yuh grinnin' at?

PEARL—(*her face hard—scornfully*) Nuttin'.

MARGIE—Nuttin'.

ROCKY—It better be nuttin'! Don't let Hickey put no ideas in your nuts if you wanta stay healthy! (*then angrily*) I wish de louse never showed up! I hope he don't come back from de delicatessen. He's gettin' everyone nuts. He's ridin' someone every minute. He's got Harry and Jimmy Tomorrow run ragged, and de rest is hidin' in deir rooms so dey won't have to listen to him. Dey're all actin' cagey wid de booze, too, like dey was scared if dey get too drunk, dey might spill deir guts, or somethin'. And everybody's gettin' a prize grouch on.

CORA—Yeah, he's been hintin' round to me and Chuck, too. Yuh'd tink he suspected me and Chuck hadn't no real intention of gettin' married. Yuh'd tink he suspected Chuck wasn't goin' to lay off periodicals—or maybe even didn't want to.

CHUCK—He didn't say it right out or I'da socked him one. I told him, "I'm on de wagon for keeps and Cora knows it."

CORA—I told him, "Sure, I know it. And Chuck ain't never goin' to trow it in my face dat I was a tart, neider. And if yuh tink we're just kiddin' ourselves, we'll show yuh!"

CHUCK—We're goin' to show him!

CORA—We got it all fixed. We've decided Joisey is where we want de farm, and we'll get married dere, too, because yuh don't need no license. We're goin' to get married tomorrow. Ain't we, Honey?

CHUCK—You bet, Baby.

ROCKY—(*disgusted*) Christ, Chuck, are yuh lettin' dat bughouse louse Hickey kid yuh into—

CORA—(*turns on him angrily*) Nobody's kiddin' him into it, nor me neider! And Hickey's right. If dis big tramp's goin' to marry me, he ought to do it, and not just shoot off his old bazoo about it.

ROCKY—(*ignoring her*) Yuh can't be dat dumb, Chuck.

CORA—You keep outa dis! And don't start beefin' about crickets on de farm drivin' us nuts. You and your crickets! Yuh'd tink dey was elephants!

MARGIE—(*coming to Rocky's defense—sneeringly*) Don't notice dat broad, Rocky. Yuh heard her say "tomorrow," didn't yuh? It's de same old crap.

CORA—(*glares at her*) Is dat so?

PEARL—(*lines up with Margie—sneeringly*) Imagine Cora a bride! Dat's a hot one! Jees, Cora, if all de guys you've stayed wid was side by side, yuh could walk on 'em from here to Texas!

CORA—(*starts moving toward her threateningly*) Yuh can't talk like dat to me, yuh fat Dago hooker! I may be a tart, but I ain't a cheap old whore like you!

PEARL—(*furiously*) I'll show yuh who's a whore! (*They start to fly at each other, but Chuck and Rocky grab them from behind.*)

CHUCK—(*forcing Cora onto a chair*) Sit down and cool off, Baby.

ROCKY—(*doing the same to Pearl*) Nix on de rough stuff, Poil.

MARGIE—(*glaring at Cora*) Why don't you leave Poil alone, Rocky? She'll fix dat blonde's clock! Or if she don't, I will!

ROCKY—Shut up, you! (*disgustedly*) Jees, what dames! D'yuh wanta gum Harry's party?

PEARL—(*a bit shamefaced—sulkily*) Who wants to? But nobody can't call me a —.

ROCKY—(*exasperatedly*) Aw, bury it! What are you, a voigin? (*Pearl stares at him, her face growing hard and bitter. So does Margie.*)

PEARL—Yuh mean you tink I'm a whore, too, huh?

MARGIE—Yeah, and me?

ROCKY—Now don't start nuttin'!

PEARL—I suppose it'd tickle you if me and Margie did what dat louse, Hickey, was hintin' and come right out and admitted we was whores.

ROCKY—Aw right! What of it? It's de truth, ain't it?

CORA—(*lining up with Pearl and Margie—indignantly*) Jees, Rocky, dat's a fine hell of a ting to say to two goils dat's been as good to yuh as Poil and Margie! (*to Pearl*) I didn't mean to call yuh dat, Poil. I was on'y mad.

PEARL—(*accepts the apology gratefully*) Sure, I was mad, too, Cora. No hard feelin's.

ROCKY—(*relieved*) Dere. Dat fixes everything, don't it?

PEARL—(*turns on him—hard and bitter*) Aw right, Rocky. We're whores. You know what dat makes you, don't you?

ROCKY—(*angrily*) Look out, now!

MARGIE—A lousy little pimp, dat's what!

ROCKY—I'll loin yuh! (*He gives her a slap on the side of the face.*)

PEARL—A dirty little Ginny pimp, dat's what!

ROCKY—(*gives her a slap, too*) And dat'll loin you! (*But they only stare at him with hard sneering eyes.*)

MARGIE—He's provin' it to us, Poil.

PEARL—Yeah! Hickey's convoited him. He's give up his pipe dream!

ROCKY—(*furious and at the same time bewildered by their defiance*) Lay off me or I'll beat de hell—

CHUCK—(*growls*) Aw, lay off dem. Harry's party ain't no time to beat up your stable.

ROCKY—(*turns to him*) Whose stable? Who d'yuh tink yuh're talkin' to? I ain't never beat dem up! What d'yuh tink I am? I just give dem a slap, like any guy would his wife, if she got too gabby. Why don't yuh tell dem to lay off me? I don't want no trouble on Harry's boithday party.

MARGIE—(*a victorious gleam in her eye—tauntingly*) Aw right, den, yuh poor little Ginny. I'll lay off yuh till de party's over if Poil will.

PEARL—(*tauntingly*) Sure, I will. For Harry's sake, not yours, yuh little Wop!

ROCKY—(*stung*) Say, listen, youse! Don't get no wrong idea— (*But an interruption comes from Larry who bursts into a sardonic laugh. They all jump startledly and look at him with unanimous hostility. Rocky transfers his anger to him.*) Who de hell yuh laughin' at, yuh half-dead old stew bum?

CORA—(*sneeringly*) At himself, he ought to be! Jees, Hickey's sure got his number!

LARRY—(*ignoring them, turns to Hugo and shakes him by the shoulder—in his comically intense, crazy whisper*) Wake up, Comrade! Here's the Revolution starting on all sides of you and you're sleeping through it! Be God, it's not to Bakunin's ghost you ought to pray in your dreams, but to the great Nihilist, Hickey! He's started a movement that'll blow up the world!

HUGO—(*blinks at him through his thick spectacles—with guttural denunciation*) You, Larry! Renegade! Traitor! I vill have you shot! (*He giggles.*) Don't be a fool! Buy me a trink! (*He sees the drink in front of him, and gulps it down. He begins to sing the Carmagnole in a guttural basso, pounding on the table with his glass.*) "Dansons la Carmagnole! Vive le son! Vive le son! Dansons la Carmagnole! Vive le son des canons!"

ROCKY—Can dat noise!

HUGO—(*ignores this—to Larry, in a low tone of hatred*) That bourgeois svine, Hickey! He laughs like good fellow, he makes jokes, he dares make hints to me so I see what he dares to think. He thinks I am finish, it is too late, and so I do not vish the Day come because it vill not be my Day. Oh, I see what he thinks! He thinks lies even vorse, dat I— (*He stops abruptly with a guilty look, as if afraid he was letting something slip—then revengefully*) I vill have him hanged the first one of all on de first lamppost! (*He changes his mood abruptly and peers around at Rocky and the others—giggling again*) Vhy you so serious, leedle monkey-faces? It's all great joke, no? So ve get drunk, and ve laugh like hell, and den ve die, and de pipe dream vanish! (*A bitter mocking contempt creeps into his tone.*) But be of good cheer, leedle stupid peoples! "The days grow hot, O Babylon!" Soon, leedle proletarians, ve vill have free picnic in the cool shade, ve vill eat hot dogs and trink free beer beneath the villow trees! Like hogs, yes! Like beautiful leedle hogs! (*He stops startledly, as if confused and amazed at what he has heard himself say. He mutters with hatred*) Dot Gottamned liar, Hickey. It is he who makes me sneer. I want to sleep. (*He lets his head fall forward on his folded arms again and closes his eyes. Larry gives him a pitying look, then quickly drinks his drink.*)

CORA—(*uneasily*) Hickey ain't overlookin' no bets, is he? He's even give Hugo de woiks.

LARRY—I warned you this morning he wasn't kidding.

MARGIE—(*sneering*) De old wise guy!

PEARL—Yeah, still pretendin' he's de one exception, like Hickey told him. He don't do no pipe dreamin'! Oh, no!

LARRY—(*sharply resentful*) I—! (*Then abruptly he is drunkenly good-natured, and you feel this drunken manner is an evasive exaggeration.*) All right, take it out on me, if it makes you more content. Sure, I love every hair of your heads, my great big beautiful baby dolls, and there's nothing I wouldn't do for you!

PEARL—(*stiffly*) De old Irish bunk, huh? We ain't big. And we ain't your baby dolls! (*Suddenly she is mollified and smiles.*) But we admit we're beautiful. Huh, Margie?

MARGIE—(*smiling*) Sure ting! But what would he do wid beautiful dolls, even if he had de price, de old goat? (*She laughs teasingly—then pats Larry on the shoulder affectionately.*) Aw, yuh're aw right at dat, Larry, if yuh are full of bull!

PEARL—Sure. Yuh're aces wid us. We're noivous, dat's all. Dat lousy drummer—why can't he be like he's always been?

I never seen a guy change so. You pretend to be such a fox, Larry. What d'yuh tink's happened to him?

LARRY—I don't know. With all his gab I notice he's kept that to himself so far. Maybe he's saving the great revelation for Harry's party. (*then irritably*) To hell with him! I don't want to know. Let him mind his own business and I'll mind mine.

CHUCK—Yeah, dat's what I say.

CORA—Say, Larry, where's dat young friend of yours disappeared to?

LARRY—I don't care where he is, except I wish it was a thousand miles away! (*Then, as he sees they are surprised at his vehemence, he adds hastily*) He's a pest.

ROCKY—(*breaks in with his own preoccupation*) I don't give a damn what happened to Hickey, but I know what's gonna happen if he don't watch his step. I told him, "I'll take a lot from you, Hickey, like everyone else in dis dump, because yuh've always been a grand guy. But dere's tings I don't take from you nor nobody, see? Remember dat, or you'll wake up in a hospital—or maybe worse, wid your wife and de iceman walkin' slow behind yuh."

CORA—Aw, yuh shouldn't make dat iceman crack, Rocky. It's aw right for him to kid about it but—I notice Hickey ain't pulled dat old iceman gag dis time. (*excitedly*) D'yuh suppose dat he did catch his wife cheatin'? I don't mean wid no iceman, but wid some guy.

ROCKY—Aw, dat's de bunk. He ain't pulled dat gag or showed her photo around because he ain't drunk. And if he'd caught her cheatin' he'd be drunk, wouldn't he? He'd have beat her up and den gone on de woist drunk he'd ever staged. Like any other guy'd do. (*The girls nod, convinced by this reasoning.*)

CHUCK—Sure! Rocky's got de right dope, Baby. He'd be paralyzed. (*While he is speaking, the Negro, Joe, comes in from the hallway. There is a noticeable change in him. He walks with a tough, truculent swagger and his good-natured face is set in sullen suspicion.*)

JOE—(*to Rocky—defiantly*) I's stood tellin' people dis dump is closed for de night all I's goin' to. Let Harry hire a doorman, pay him wages, if he wants one.

ROCKY—(*scowling*) Yeah? Harry's pretty damned good to you.

JOE—(*shamefaced*) Sure he is. I don't mean dat. Anyways, it's all right. I told Schwartz, de cop, we's closed for de party. He'll keep folks away. (*aggressively again*) I want a big drink, dat's what!

CHUCK—Who's stoppin' yuh? Yuh can have all yuh want on Hickey.

JOE—(*has taken a glass from the table and has his hand on a bottle when Hickey's name is mentioned. He draws his hand back as if he were going to refuse—then grabs it defiantly and pours a big drink.*) All right, I's earned all de drinks on him I could drink in a year for listenin' to his crazy bull. And here's hopin' he gets de lockjaw! (*He drinks and pours out another.*) I drinks on him but I don't drink wid him. No, suh, never no more!

ROCKY—Aw, bull! Hickey's aw right. What's he done to you?

JOE—(*sullenly*) Dat's my business. I ain't buttin' in yours, is I? (*bitterly*) Sure, you think he's all right. He's a white man, ain't he? (*His tone becomes aggressive.*) Listen to me, you white boys! Don't you get it in your heads I's pretendin' to be what I ain't, or dat I ain't proud to be what I is, get me? Or you and me's goin' to have trouble! (*He picks up his drink and walks left as far away from them as he can get and slumps down on the piano stool.*)

MARGIE—(*in a low angry tone*) What a noive! Just because we act nice to him, he gets a swelled nut! If dat ain't a coon all over!

CHUCK—Talkin' fight talk, huh? I'll moider de nigger! (*He takes a threatening step toward Joe, who is staring before him guiltily now.*)

JOE—(*speaks up shamefacedly*) Listen, boys, I's sorry. I didn't mean dat. You been good friends to me. I's nuts, I guess. Dat Hickey, he gets my head all mixed up wit' craziness. (*Their faces at once clear of resentment against him.*)

CORA—Aw, dat's aw right, Joe. De boys wasn't takin' yuh serious. (*then to the others, forcing a laugh*) Jees, what'd I say, Hickey ain't overlookin' no bets. Even Joe. (*She pauses—then adds puzzledly*) De funny ting is, yuh can't stay sore at de bum when he's around. When he forgets de bughouse preachin', and quits tellin' yuh where yuh get off, he's de same old Hickey. Yuh can't help likin' de louse. And yuh got to admit he's got de right dope— (*She adds hastily*) I mean, on some of de bums here.

MARGIE—(*with a sneering look at Rocky*) Yeah, he's coitinly got one guy I know sized up right! Huh, Poil?

PEARL—He coitinly has!

ROCKY—Cut it out, I told yuh!

LARRY—(*is staring before him broodingly. He speaks more aloud to himself than to them.*) It's nothing to me what happened to him. But I have a feeling he's dying to tell us, inside him, and yet he's afraid. He's like that damned kid. It's strange the queer way he seemed to recognize him. If he's afraid, it explains why he's off booze. Like that damned kid again. Afraid if he got drunk, he'd tell— (*While he is speaking, Hickey comes in the doorway at rear. He looks the same as in the previous act, except that now his face beams with the excited expectation of a boy going to a party. His arms are piled with packages.*)

HICKEY—(*booms in imitation of a familiar Polo Grounds bleacherite cry—with rising volume*) Well! Well!! Well!!! (*They all jump startledly. He comes forward, grinning.*) Here I am in the nick of time. Give me a hand with these bundles, somebody. (*Margie and Pearl start taking them from his arms and putting them on the table. Now that he is present, all their attitudes show the reaction Cora has expressed. They can't help liking him and forgiving him.*)

MARGIE—Jees, Hickey, yuh scared me outa a year's growth, sneakin' in like dat.

HICKEY—Sneaking? Why, me and the taxi man made enough noise getting my big surprise in the hall to wake the dead. You were all so busy drinking in words of wisdom from the Old Wise Guy here, you couldn't hear anything else. (*He grins at Larry.*) From what I heard, Larry, you're not so good when you start playing Sherlock Holmes. You've got me all wrong. I'm not afraid of anything now—not even myself. You better stick to the part of Old Cemetery, the Barker for the Big Sleep—that is, if you can still let yourself get away with it! (*He chuckles and gives Larry a friendly slap on the back. Larry gives him a bitter angry look.*)

CORA—(*giggles*) Old Cemetery! That's him, Hickey. We'll have to call him dat.

HICKEY—(*watching Larry quizzically*) Beginning to do a lot of puzzling about me, aren't you, Larry? But that won't help you. You've got to think of yourself. I couldn't give you my peace. You've got to find your own. All I can do is help you, and the rest of the gang, by showing you the way to find it. (*He has said this with a simple persuasive earnestness. He pauses, and for a second they stare at him with fascinated resentful uneasiness.*)

ROCKY—(*breaks the spell*) Aw, hire a church!

HICKEY—(*placatingly*) All right! All right! Don't get sore, boys and girls. I guess that did sound too much like a lousy preacher. Let's forget it and get busy on the party. (*They look relieved.*)

CHUCK—Is dose bundles grub, Hickey? You bought enough already to feed an army.

HICKEY—(*with boyish excitement again*) Can't be too much! I want this to be the biggest birthday Harry's ever had. You and Rocky go in the hall and get the big surprise. My arms are busted lugging it. (*They catch his excitement. Chuck and Rocky go out, grinning expectantly. The three girls gather around Hickey, full of thrilled curiosity.*)

PEARL—Jees, yuh got us all het up! What is it, Hickey?

HICKEY—Wait and see. I got it as a treat for the three of you more than anyone. I thought to myself, I'll bet this is what will please those whores more than anything. (*They wince as if he had slapped them, but before they have a chance to be angry, he goes on affectionately.*) I said to myself, I don't care how much it costs, they're worth it. They're the best little scouts in the world, and they've been damned kind to me when I was down and out! Nothing is too good for them. (*earnestly*) I mean every word of that, too—and then some! (*then, as if he noticed the expression on their faces for the first time*) What's the matter? You look sore. What—? (*Then he chuckles.*) Oh, I see. But you know how I feel about that. You know I didn't say it to offend you. So don't be silly now.

MARGIE—(*lets out a tense breath*) Aw right, Hickey. Let it slide.

HICKEY—(*jubilantly, as Chuck and Rocky enter carrying a big wicker basket*) Look! There it comes! Unveil it, boys. (*They pull off a covering burlap bag. The basket is piled with quarts of champagne.*)

PEARL—(*with childish excitement*) It's champagne! Jees, Hickey, if you ain't a sport! (*She gives him a hug, forgetting all animosity, as do the other girls.*)

MARGIE—I never been soused on champagne. Let's get stinko, Poil.

PEARL—You betcha my life! De bot' of us! (*A holiday spirit of gay festivity has seized them all. Even Joe Mott is standing up to look at the wine with an admiring grin, and Hugo raises his head to blink at it.*)

JOE—You sure is hittin' de high spots, Hickey. (*boastfully*) Man, when I runs my gamblin' house, I drinks dat old bubbly water in steins! (*He stops guiltily and gives Hickey a look of defiance.*) I's goin' to drink it dat way again, too, soon's I make my stake! And dat ain't no pipe dream, neider! (*He sits down where he was, his back turned to them.*)

ROCKY—What'll we drink it outa, Hickey? Dere ain't no wine glasses.

HICKEY—(*enthusiastically*) Joe has the right idea! Schooners! That's the spirit for Harry's birthday! (*Rocky and Chuck carry the basket of wine into the bar. The three girls go back and stand around the entrance to the bar, chatting excitedly among themselves and to Chuck and Rocky in the bar.*)

HUGO—(*with his silly giggle*) Ve vill trink vine beneath the villow trees!

HICKEY—(*grins at him*) That's the spirit, Brother—and let the lousy slaves drink vinegar! (*Hugo blinks at him startledly, then looks away.*)

HUGO—(*mutters*) Gottamned liar! (*He puts his head back on his arms and closes his eyes, but this time his habitual pass-out has a quality of hiding.*)

LARRY—(*gives Hugo a pitying glance—in a low tone of anger*) Leave Hugo be! He rotted ten years in prison for his faith! He's earned his dream! Have you no decency or pity?

HICKEY—(*quizzically*) Hello, what's this? I thought you were in the grandstand. (*then with a simple earnestness, taking a chair by Larry, and putting a hand on his shoulder*) Listen,

Larry, you're getting me all wrong. Hell, you ought to know me better. I've always been the best-natured slob in the world. Of course, I have pity. But now I've seen the light, it isn't my old kind of pity—the kind yours is. It isn't the kind that lets itself off easy by encouraging some poor guy to go on kidding himself with a lie—the kind that leaves the poor slob worse off because it makes him feel guiltier than ever— the kind that makes his lying hopes nag at him and reproach him until he's a rotten skunk in his own eyes. I know all about that kind of pity. I've had a bellyful of it in my time, and it's all wrong! (*with a salesman's persuasiveness*) No, sir. The kind of pity I feel now is after final results that will really save the poor guy, and make him contented with what he is, and quit battling himself, and find peace for the rest of his life. Oh, I know how you resent the way I have to show you up to yourself. I don't blame you. I know from my own experience it's bitter medicine, facing yourself in the mirror with the old false whiskers off. But you forget that, once you're cured. You'll be grateful to me when all at once you find you're able to admit, without feeling ashamed, that all the grandstand foolosopher bunk and the waiting for the Big Sleep stuff is a pipe dream. You'll say to yourself, I'm just an old man who is scared of life, but even more scared of dying. So I'm keeping drunk and hanging on to life at any price, and what of it? Then you'll know what real peace means, Larry, because you won't be scared of either life or death any more. You simply won't give a damn! Any more than I do!

LARRY—(*has been staring into his eyes with a fascinated wondering dread*) Be God, if I'm not beginning to think you've gone mad! (*with a rush of anger*) You're a liar!

HICKEY—(*injuredly*) Now, listen, that's no way to talk to an old pal who's trying to help you. Hell, if you really wanted to die, you'd just take a hop off your fire escape, wouldn't you? And if you really were in the grandstand, you wouldn't be pitying everyone. Oh, I know the truth is tough at first. It was for me. All I ask is for you to suspend judgment and give it a chance. I'll absolutely guarantee— Hell, Larry, I'm no fool. Do you suppose I'd deliberately set out to get under everyone's skin and put myself in dutch with all my old pals, if I wasn't certain, from my own experience, that it means contentment in the end for all of you? (*Larry again is staring at him fascinatedly. Hickey grins.*) As for my being bughouse, you can't crawl out of it that way. Hell, I'm too damned sane. I can size up guys, and turn 'em inside out, better than I ever could. Even where they're strangers like that Parritt kid. He's licked, Larry. I think there is only one possible way out you can help him to take. That is, if you have the right kind of pity for him.

LARRY—(*uneasily*) What do you mean? (*attempting indifference*) I'm not advising him, except to leave me out of his troubles. He's nothing to me.

HICKEY—(*shakes his head*) You'll find he won't agree to that. He'll keep after you until he makes you help him. Because he has to be punished, so he can forgive himself. He's lost all his guts. He can't manage it alone, and you're the only one he can turn to.

LARRY—For the love of God, mind your own business! (*with forced scorn*) A lot you know about him! He's hardly spoken to you!

HICKEY—No, that's right. But I do know a lot about him just the same. I've had hell inside me. I can spot it in others. (*frowning*) Maybe that's what gives me the feeling there's something familiar about him, something between us. (*He shakes his head.*) No, it's more than that. I can't figure it. Tell me about him. For instance, I don't imagine he's married, is he?

LARRY—No.

HICKEY—Hasn't he been mixed up with some woman? I don't mean trollops. I mean the old real love stuff that crucifies you.

LARRY—(*with a calculating relieved look at him—encouraging him along this line*) Maybe you're right. I wouldn't be surprised.

HICKEY—(*grins at him quizzically*) I see. You think I'm on the wrong track and you're glad I am. Because then I won't suspect whatever he did about the Great Cause. That's another lie you tell yourself, Larry, that the good old Cause means nothing to you any more. (*Larry is about to burst out in denial but Hickey goes on.*) But you're all wrong about Parritt. That isn't what's got him stopped. It's what's behind that. And it's a woman. I recognize the symptoms.

LARRY—(*sneeringly*) And you're the boy who's never wrong! Don't be a damned fool. His trouble is he was brought up a devout believer in the Movement and now he's lost his faith. It's a shock, but he's young and he'll soon find another dream just as good. (*He adds sardonically*) Or as bad.

HICKEY—All right. I'll let it go at that, Larry. He's nothing to me except I'm glad he's here because he'll help me make you wake up to yourself. I don't even like the guy, or the feeling there's anything between us. But you'll find I'm right just the same, when you get to the final showdown with him.

LARRY—There'll be no showdown! I don't give a tinker's damn—

HICKEY—Sticking to the old grandstand, eh? Well, I knew you'd be the toughest to convince of all the gang, Larry. And, along with Harry and Jimmy Tomorrow, you're the one I want most to help. (*He puts an arm around Larry's shoulder and gives him an affectionate hug.*) I've always liked you a lot, you old bastard! (*He gets up and his manner changes to his bustling party excitement—glancing at his watch*) Well, well, not much time before twelve. Let's get busy, boys and girls. (*He looks over the table where the cake is.*) Cake all set. Good. And my presents, and yours, girls, and Chuck's, and Rocky's. Fine. Harry'll certainly be touched by your thought of him. (*He goes back to the girls.*) You go in the bar, Pearl and Margie, and get the grub ready so it can be brought right in. There'll be some drinking and toasts first, of course. My idea is to use the wine for that, so get it all set. I'll go upstairs now and root everyone out. Harry the last. I'll come back with him. Somebody light the candles on the cake when you hear us coming, and you start playing Harry's favorite tune, Cora. Hustle now, everybody. We want this to come off in style. (*He bustles into the hall. Margie and Pearl disappear in the bar. Cora goes to the piano. Joe gets off the stool sullenly to let her sit down.*)

CORA—I got to practice. I ain't laid my mits on a box in Gawd knows when. (*With the soft pedal down, she begins gropingly to pick out "The Sunshine of Paradise Alley."*) Is dat right, Joe? I've forgotten dat has-been tune. (*She picks out a few more notes.*) Come on, Joe, hum de tune so I can follow. (*Joe begins to hum and sing in a low voice and correct her. He forgets his sullenness and becomes his old self again.*)

LARRY—(*suddenly gives a laugh—in his comically intense, crazy tone*) Be God, it's a second feast of Belshazzar, with Hickey to do the writing on the wall!

CORA—Aw, shut up, Old Cemetery! Always beefin'! (*Willie comes in from the hall. He is in a pitiable state, his face pasty, haggard with sleeplessness and nerves, his eyes sick and haunted. He is sober. Cora greets him over her shoulder kiddingly*) If it ain't Prince Willie! (*then kindly*) Gee, kid, yuh look sick. Git a coupla shots in yuh.

WILLIE—(*tensely*) No, thanks. Not now. I'm tapering off. (*He sits down weakly on Larry's right.*)

CORA—(*astonished*) What d'yuh know? He means it!

WILLIE—(*leaning toward Larry confidentially—in a low shaken voice*) It's been hell up in that damned room, Larry! The things I've imagined! (*He shudders.*) I thought I'd go crazy. (*with pathetic boastful pride*) But I've got it beat now. By tomorrow morning I'll be on the wagon. I'll get back my clothes the first thing. Hickey's loaning me the money. I'm going to do what I've always said—go to the D.A.'s office. He was a good friend of my Old Man's. He was only assistant, then. He was in on the graft, but my Old Man never squealed on him. So he certainly owes it to me to give me a chance. And he knows that I really was a brilliant law student. (*self-reassuringly*) Oh, I know I can make good, now I'm getting off the booze forever. (*moved*) I owe a lot to Hickey. He's made me wake up to myself—see what a fool— It wasn't nice to face but— (*with bitter resentment*) It isn't what he says. It's what you feel behind—what he hints— Christ, you'd think all I really wanted to do with my life was sit here and stay drunk. (*with hatred*) I'll show him!

LARRY—(*masking pity behind a sardonic tone*) If you want my advice, you'll put the nearest bottle to your mouth until you don't give a damn for Hickey!

WILLIE—(*stares at a bottle greedily, tempted for a moment —then bitterly*) That's fine advice! I thought you were my friend! (*He gets up with a hurt glance at Larry, and moves away to take a chair in back of the left end of the table, where he sits in dejected, shaking misery, his chin on his chest.*)

JOE—(*to Cora*) No, like dis. (*He beats time with his finger and sings in a low voice*) "She is the sunshine of Paradise Alley." (*She plays.*) Dat's more like it. Try it again. (*She begins to play through the chorus again. Don Parritt enters from the hall. There is a frightened look on his face. He slinks in furtively, as if he were escaping from someone. He looks relieved when he sees Larry and comes and slips into the chair on his right. Larry pretends not to notice his coming, but he instinctively shrinks with repulsion. Parritt leans toward him and speaks ingratiatingly in a low secretive tone.*)

PARRITT—Gee, I'm glad you're here, Larry. That damned fool, Hickey, knocked on my door. I opened up because I thought it must be you, and he came busting in and made me come downstairs. I don't know what for. I don't belong in this birthday celebration. I don't know this gang and I don't want to be mixed up with them. All I came here for was to find you.

LARRY—(*tensely*) I've warned you—

PARRITT—(*goes on as if he hadn't heard*) Can't you make Hickey mind his own business? I don't like that guy, Larry. The way he acts, you'd think he had something on me. Why, just now he pats me on the shoulder, like he was sympathizing with me, and says, "I know how it is, Son, but you can't hide from yourself, not even here on the bottom of the sea. You've got to face the truth and then do what must be done for your own peace and the happiness of all concerned." What did he mean by that, Larry?

LARRY—How the hell would I know?

PARRITT—Then he grins and says, "Never mind, Larry's getting wise to himself. I think you can rely on his help in the end. He'll have to choose between living and dying, and he'll never choose to die while there is a breath left in the old bastard!" And then he laughs like it was a joke on you. (*He pauses. Larry is rigid on his chair, staring before him. Parritt asks him with a sudden taunt in his voice*) Well, what do you say to that, Larry?

LARRY—I've nothing to say. Except you're a bigger fool than he is to listen to him.

PARRITT—(*with a sneer*) Is that so? He's no fool where you're concerned. He's got your number, all right! (*Larry's face tightens but he keeps silent. Parritt changes to a contrite, appealing air.*) I don't mean that. But you keep acting as if you were sore at me, and that gets my goat. You know what I want most is to be friends with you, Larry. I haven't a single friend left in the world. I hoped you— (*bitterly*) And you could be, too, without it hurting you. You ought to, for Mother's sake. She really loved you. You loved her, too, didn't you?

LARRY—(*tensely*) Leave what's dead in its grave.

PARRITT—I suppose, because I was only a kid, you didn't think I was wise about you and her. Well, I was. I've been wise, ever since I can remember, to all the guys she's had, although she'd tried to kid me along it wasn't so. That was a silly stunt for a free Anarchist woman, wasn't it, being ashamed of being free?

LARRY—Shut your damned trap!

PARRITT—(*guiltily but with a strange undertone of satisfaction*) Yes, I know I shouldn't say that now. I keep forgetting she isn't free any more. (*He pauses.*) Do you know, Larry, you're the one of them all she cared most about? Anyone else who left the Movement would have been dead to her, but she couldn't forget you. She'd always make excuses for you. I used to try and get her goat about you. I'd say, "Larry's got brains and yet he thinks the Movement is just a crazy pipe dream." She'd blame it on booze getting you. She'd kid herself that you'd give up booze and come back to the Movement—tomorrow! She'd say, "Larry can't kill in himself a faith he's given his life to, not without killing himself." (*He grins sneeringly.*) How about it, Larry? Was she right? (*Larry remains silent. He goes on insistently.*) I suppose what she really meant was, come back to her. She was always getting the Movement mixed up with herself. But I'm sure she really must have loved you, Larry. As much as she could love anyone besides herself. But she wasn't faithful to you, even at that, was she? That's why you finally walked out on her, isn't it? I remember that last fight you had with her. I was listening. I was on your side, even if she was my mother, because I liked you so much; you'd been so good to me—like a father. I remember her putting on her high-and-mighty free-woman stuff, saying you were still a slave to bourgeois morality and jealousy and you thought a woman you loved was a piece of private property you owned. I remember that you got mad and you told her, "I don't like living with a whore, if that's what you mean!"

LARRY—(*bursts out*) You lie! I never called her that!

PARRITT—(*goes on as if Larry hadn't spoken*) I think that's why she still respects you, because it was you who left her. You were the only one to beat her to it. She got sick of the others before they did of her. I don't think she ever cared much about them, anyway. She just had to keep on having lovers to prove to herself how free she was. (*He pauses—then with a bitter repulsion*) It made home a lousy place. I felt like you did about it. I'd get feeling it was like living in a whorehouse—only worse, because she didn't have to make her living—

LARRY—You bastard! She's your mother! Have you no shame?

PARRITT—(*bitterly*) No! She brought me up to believe that family-respect stuff is all bourgeois, property-owning crap. Why should I be ashamed?

LARRY—(*making a move to get up*) I've had enough!

PARRITT—(*catches his arm—pleadingly*) No! Don't leave me! Please! I promise I won't mention her again! (*Larry sinks back in his chair.*) I only did it to make you understand better. I know this isn't the place to— Why didn't you come up to my room, like I asked you? I kept waiting. We could talk everything over there.

LARRY—There's nothing to talk over!

PARRITT—But I've got to talk to you. Or I'll talk to Hickey. He won't let me alone! I feel he knows, anyway! And I know he'd understand, all right—in his way. But I hate his guts! I don't want anything to do with him! I'm scared of him, honest. There's something not human behind his damned grinning and kidding.

LARRY—(*starts*) Ah! You feel that, too?

PARRITT—(*pleadingly*) But I can't go on like this. I've got to decide what I've got to do. I've got to tell you, Larry!

LARRY—(*again starts up*) I won't listen!

PARRITT—(*again holds him by the arm*) All right! I won't.

Don't go! (*Larry lets himself be pulled down on his chair. Parritt examines his face and becomes insultingly scornful.*) Who do you think you're kidding? I know damned well you've guessed—

LARRY—I've guessed nothing!

PARRITT—But I want you to guess now! I'm glad you have! I know now, since Hickey's been after me, that I meant you to guess right from the start. That's why I came to you. (*hurrying on with an attempt at a plausible frank air that makes what he says seem doubly false*) I want you to understand the reason. You see, I began studying American history. I got admiring Washington and Jefferson and Jackson and Lincoln. I began to feel patriotic and love this country. I saw it was the best government in the world, where everybody was equal and had a chance. I saw that all the ideas behind the Movement came from a lot of Russians like Bakunin and Kropotkin and were meant for Europe, but we didn't need them here in a democracy where we were free already. I didn't want this country to be destroyed for a damned foreign pipe dream. After all, I'm from old American pioneer stock. I began to feel I was a traitor for helping a lot of cranks and bums and free women plot to overthrow our government. And then I saw it was my duty to my country—

LARRY—(*nauseated—turns on him*) You stinking rotten liar! Do you think you can fool me with such hypocrite's cant! (*then turning away*) I don't give a damn what you did! It's on your head—whatever it was! I don't want to know— and I won't know!

PARRITT—(*as if Larry had never spoken—falteringly*) But I never thought Mother would be caught. Please believe that, Larry. You know I never would have—

LARRY—(*his face haggard, drawing a deep breath and closing his eyes—as if he were trying to hammer something into his own brain*) All I know is I'm sick of life! I'm through! I've forgotten myself! I'm drowned and contented on the bottom of a bottle. Honor or dishonor, faith or treachery are nothing to me but the opposites of the same stupidity which is ruler and king of life, and in the end they rot into dust in the same grave. All things are the same meaningless joke to me, for they grin at me from the one skull of death. So go away. You're wasting breath. I've forgotten your mother.

PARRITT—(*jeers angrily*) The old foolosopher, eh? (*He spits out contemptuously*) You lousy old faker!

LARRY—(*so distracted he pleads weakly*) For the love of God, leave me in peace the little time that's left to me!

PARRITT—Aw, don't pull that pitiful old-man junk on me! You old bastard, you'll never die as long as there's a free drink of whiskey left!

LARRY—(*stung—furiously*) Look out how you try to taunt me back into life, I warn you! I might remember the thing they call justice there, and the punishment for— (*He checks himself with an effort—then with a real indifference that comes from exhaustion*) I'm old and tired. To hell with you! You're as mad as Hickey, and as big a liar. I'd never let myself believe a word you told me.

PARRITT—(*threateningly*) The hell you won't! Wait till Hickey gets through with you! (*Pearl and Margie come in from the bar. At the sight of them, Parritt instantly subsides and becomes self-conscious and defensive, scowling at them and then quickly looking away.*)

MARGIE—(*eyes him jeeringly*) Why, hello, Tightwad Kid. Come to join de party? Gee, don't he act bashful, Poil?

PEARL—Yeah. Especially wid his dough. (*Parritt slinks to a chair at the left end of the table, pretending he hasn't heard them. Suddenly there is a noise of angry, cursing voices and a scuffle from the hall. Pearl yells*) Hey, Rocky! Fight in de hall! (*Rocky and Chuck run from behind the bar curtain and rush into the hall. Rocky's voice is heard in irritated astonishment,* "What de hell?" *and then the scuffle stops and Rocky appears holding Captain Lewis by the arm, followed by Chuck with a similar hold on General Wetjoen. Although these two have been drinking they are both sober, for them. Their faces are sullenly angry, their clothes disarranged from the tussle.*)

ROCKY—(*leading Lewis forward—astonished, amused and irritated*) Can yuh beat it? I've heard youse two call each odder every name yuh could think of but I never seen you— (*indignantly*) A swell time to stage your first bout, on Harry's boithday party! What started de scrap?

LEWIS—(*forcing a casual tone*) Nothing, old chap. Our business, you know. That bloody ass, Hickey, made some insinuation about me, and the boorish Boer had the impertinence to agree with him.

WETJOEN—Dot's a lie! Hickey made joke about me, and this Limey said yes, it was true!

ROCKY—Well, sit down, de bot' of yuh, and cut out de rough stuff. (*He and Chuck dump them down in adjoining chairs toward the left end of the table, where, like two sulky boys, they turn their backs on each other as far as possible in chairs which both face front.*)

MARGIE—(*laughs*) Jees, lookit de two bums! Like a coupla kids! Kiss and make up, for Gawd's sakes!

ROCKY—Yeah. Harry's party begins in a minute and we don't want no soreheads around.

LEWIS—(*stiffly*) Very well. In deference to the occasion, I apologize, General Wetjoen—provided that you do also.

WETJOEN—(*sulkily*) I apologize, Captain Lewis—because Harry is my goot friend.

ROCKY—Aw, hell! If yuh can't do better'n dat—! (*Mosher and McGloin enter together from the hall. Both have been drinking but are not drunk.*)

PEARL—Here's de star boarders. (*They advance, their heads together, so interested in a discussion they are oblivious to everyone.*)

McGLOIN—I'm telling you, Ed, it's serious this time. That bastard, Hickey, has got Harry on the hip. (*As he talks, Margie, Pearl, Rocky and Chuck prick up their ears and gather round. Cora, at the piano, keeps running through the tune, with soft pedal, and singing the chorus half under her breath, with Joe still correcting her mistakes. At the table, Larry, Parritt, Willie, Wetjoen and Lewis sit motionless, staring in front of them. Hugo seems asleep in his habitual position.*) And you know it isn't going to do us no good if he gets him to take that walk tomorrow.

MOSHER—You're damned right. Harry'll mosey around the ward, dropping in on everyone who knew him when. (*indignantly*) And they'll all give him a phony glad hand and a ton of good advice about what a sucker he is to stand for us.

McGLOIN—He's sure to call on Bessie's relations to do a

little cryin' over dear Bessie. And you know what that bitch and all her family thought of me.

MOSHER—(*with a flash of his usual humor*—*rebukingly*) Remember, Lieutenant, you are speaking of my sister! Dear Bessie wasn't a bitch. She was a God-damned bitch! But if you think my loving relatives will have time to discuss you, you don't know them. They'll be too busy telling Harry what a drunken crook I am and saying he ought to have me put in Sing Sing!

McGLOIN—(*dejectedly*) Yes, once Bessie's relations get their hooks in him, it'll be as tough for us as if she wasn't gone.

MOSHER—(*dejectedly*) Yes, Harry has always been weak and easily influenced, and now he's getting old he'll be an easy mark for those grafters. (*then with forced reassurance*) Oh, hell, Mac, we're saps to worry. We've heard Harry pull that bluff about taking a walk every birthday he's had for twenty years.

McGLOIN—(*doubtfully*) But Hickey wasn't sicking him on those times. Just the opposite. He was asking Harry what he wanted to go out for when there was plenty of whiskey here.

MOSHER—(*with a change to forced carelessness*) Well, after all, I don't care whether he goes out or not. I'm clearing out tomorrow morning anyway. I'm just sorry for you, Mac.

McGLOIN—(*resentfully*) You needn't be, then. Ain't I going myself? I was only feeling sorry for you.

MOSHER—Yes, my mind is made up. Hickey may be a lousy, interfering pest, now he's gone teetotal on us, but there's a lot of truth in some of his bull. Hanging around here getting plastered with you, Mac, is pleasant, I won't deny, but the old booze gets you in the end, if you keep lapping it up. It's time I quit for a while. (*with forced enthusiasm*) Besides, I feel the call of the old carefree circus life in my blood again. I'll see the boss tomorrow. It's late in the season but he'll be glad to take me on. And won't all the old gang be tickled to death when I show up on the lot!

McGLOIN—Maybe—if they've got a rope handy!

MOSHER—(*turns on him*—*angrily*) Listen! I'm damned sick of that kidding!

McGLOIN—You are, are you? Well, I'm sicker of your kidding me about getting reinstated on the Force. And whatever you'd like, I can't spend my life sitting here with you, ruining my stomach with rotgut. I'm tapering off, and in the morning I'll be fresh as a daisy. I'll go and have a private chin with the Commissioner. (*with forced enthusiasm*) Man alive, from what the boys tell me, there's sugar galore these days, and I'll soon be ridin' around in a big red automobile—

MOSHER—(*derisively—beckoning an imaginary Chinese*) Here, One Lung Hop! Put fresh peanut oil in the lamp and cook the Lieutenant another dozen pills! It's his gowed-up night!

McGLOIN—(*stung—pulls back a fist threateningly*) One more crack like that and I'll—!

MOSHER—(*putting up his fists*) Yes? Just start—! (*Chuck and Rocky jump between them.*)

ROCKY—Hey! Are you guys nuts? Jees, it's Harry's boithday party! (*They both look guilty.*) Sit down and behave.

MOSHER—(*grumpily*) All right. Only tell him to lay off me. (*He lets Rocky push him in a chair, at the right end of the table, rear.*)

McGLOIN—(*grumpily*) Tell him to lay off me. (*He lets Chuck push him into the chair on Mosher's left. At this moment Hickey bursts in from the hall, bustling and excited.*)

HICKEY—Everything all set? Fine! (*He glances at his watch.*) Half a minute to go. Harry's starting down with Jimmy. I had a hard time getting them to move! They'd rather stay hiding up there, kidding each other along. (*He chuckles.*) Harry don't even want to remember it's his birthday now! (*He hears a noise from the stairs.*) Here they come! (*urgently*) Light the candles! Get ready to play, Cora! Stand up, everybody! Get that wine ready, Chuck and Rocky! (*Margie and Pearl light the candles on the cake. Cora gets her hands set over the piano keys, watching over her shoulder. Rocky and Chuck go in the bar. Everybody at the table stands up mechanically. Hugo is the last, suddenly coming to and scrambling to his feet. Harry Hope and Jimmy Tomorrow appear in the hall outside the door. Hickey looks up from his watch.*) On the dot! It's twelve! (*like a cheer leader*) Come on now, everybody, with a Happy Birthday, Harry! (*With his voice leading they all shout "Happy Birthday, Harry!" in a spiritless chorus. Hickey signals to Cora, who starts playing and singing in a whiskey soprano "She's the Sunshine of Paradise Alley." Hope and Jimmy stand in the doorway. Both have been drinking heavily. In Hope the effect is apparent only in a bristling, touchy, pugnacious attitude. It is entirely different from the usual irascible beefing he delights in and which no one takes seriously. Now he really has a chip on his shoulder. Jimmy, on the other hand, is plainly drunk, but it has not had the desired effect, for beneath a pathetic assumption of gentlemanly poise, he is obviously frightened and shrinking back within himself. Hickey grabs Hope's hand and pumps it up and down. For a moment Hope appears unconscious of this handshake. Then he jerks his hand away angrily.)*

HOPE—Cut out the glad hand, Hickey. D'you think I'm a sucker? I know you, bejees, you sneaking, lying drummer! (*with rising anger, to the others*) And all you bums! What the hell you trying to do, yelling and raising the roof? Want the cops to close the joint and get my license taken away? (*He yells at Cora who has stopped singing but continues to play mechanically with many mistakes.*) Hey, you dumb tart, quit banging that box! Bejees, the least you could do is learn the tune!

CORA—(*stops—deeply hurt*) Aw, Harry! Jees, ain't I— (*Her eyes begin to fill.*)

HOPE—(*glaring at the other girls*) And you two hookers, screaming at the top of your lungs! What d'you think this is, a dollar cathouse? Bejees, that's where you belong!

PEARL—(*miserably*) Aw, Harry— (*She begins to cry.*)

MARGIE—Jees, Harry, I never thought you'd say that— like yuh meant it. (*She puts her arm around Pearl—on the verge of tears herself*) Aw, don't bawl, Poil. He don't mean it.

HICKEY—(*reproachfully*) Now, Harry! Don't take it out on the gang because you're upset about yourself. Anyway, I've promised you you'll come through all right, haven't I? So quit worrying. (*He slaps Hope on the back encouragingly. Hope flashes him a glance of hate.*) Be yourself, Governor. You don't want to bawl out the old gang just when they're congratulating you on your birthday, do you? Hell, that's no way!

HOPE—(*looking guilty and shamefaced now—forcing an unconvincing attempt at his natural tone*) Bejees, they ain't as dumb as you. They know I was only kidding them. They know I appreciate their congratulations. Don't you, fellers? (*There is a listless chorus of* "Sure, Harry," "Yes," "Of course we do," *etc. He comes forward to the two girls, with Jimmy and Hickey following him, and pats them clumsily.*) Bejees, I like you broads. You know I was only kidding. (*Instantly they forgive him and smile affectionately.*)

MARGIE—Sure we know, Harry.

PEARL—Sure.

HICKEY—(*grinning*) Sure. Harry's the greatest kidder in this dump and that's saying something! Look how he's kidded himself for twenty years! (*As Hope gives him a bitter, angry glance, he digs him in the ribs with his elbow playfully.*) Unless I'm wrong, Governor, and I'm betting I'm not. We'll soon know, eh? Tomorrow morning. No, by God, it's *this* morning now!

JIMMY—(*with a dazed dread*) *This* morning?

HICKEY—Yes, it's today at last, Jimmy. (*He pats him on the back.*) Don't be so scared! I've promised I'll help you.

JIMMY—(*trying to hide his dread behind an offended, drunken dignity*) I don't understand you. Kindly remember I'm fully capable of settling my own affairs!

HICKEY—(*earnestly*) Well, isn't that exactly what I want you to do, settle with yourself once and for all? (*He speaks in his ear in confidential warning.*) Only watch out on the booze, Jimmy. You know, not too much from now on. You've had a lot already, and you don't want to let yourself duck out of it by being too drunk to move—not this time! (*Jimmy gives him a guilty, stricken look and turns away and slumps into the chair on Mosher's right.*)

HOPE—(*to Margie—still guiltily*) Bejees, Margie, you know I didn't mean it. It's that lousy drummer riding me that's got my goat.

MARGIE—I know. (*She puts a protecting arm around Hope and turns him to face the table with the cake and presents.*) Come on. You ain't noticed your cake yet. Ain't it grand?

HOPE—(*trying to brighten up*) Say, that's pretty. Ain't ever had a cake since Bessie— Six candles. Each for ten years, eh? Bejees, that's thoughtful of you.

PEARL—It was Hickey got it.

HOPE—(*his tone forced*) Well, it was thoughtful of him. He means well, I guess. (*His eyes, fixed on the cake, harden angrily.*) To hell with his cake. (*He starts to turn away. Pearl grabs his arm.*)

PEARL—Wait, Harry. Yuh ain't seen de presents from Margie and me and Cora and Chuck and Rocky. And dere's a watch all engraved wid your name and de date from Hickey.

HOPE—To hell with it! Bejees, he can keep it! (*This time he does turn away.*)

PEARL—Jees, he ain't even goin' to look at our presents.

MARGIE—(*bitterly*) Dis is all wrong. We gotta put some life in dis party or I'll go nuts! Hey, Cora, what's de matter wid dat box? Can't yuh play for Harry? Yuh don't have to stop just because he kidded yuh!

HOPE—(*rouses himself—with forced heartiness*) Yes, come on, Cora. You was playing it fine. (*Cora begins to play half-heartedly. Hope suddenly becomes almost tearfully sentimental.*) It was Bessie's favorite tune. She was always singing it. It brings her back. I wish— (*He chokes up.*)

HICKEY—(*grins at him—amusedly*) Yes, we've all heard you tell us you thought the world of her, Governor.

HOPE—(*looks at him with frightened suspicion*) Well, so I did, bejees! Everyone knows I did! (*threateningly*) Bejees, if you say I didn't—

HICKEY—(*soothingly*) Now, Governor. I didn't say anything. You're the only one knows the truth about that. (*Hope stares at him confusedly. Cora continues to play. For a moment there is a pause, broken by Jimmy Tomorrow who speaks with muzzy, self-pitying melancholy out of a sentimental dream.*)

JIMMY—Marjorie's favorite song was "Loch Lomond." She was beautiful and she played the piano beautifully and she had a beautiful voice. (*with gentle sorrow*) You were lucky, Harry. Bessie died. But there are more bitter sorrows than losing the woman one loves by the hand of death—

HICKEY—(*with an amused wink at Hope*) Now, listen, Jimmy, you needn't go on. We've all heard that story about how you came back to Cape Town and found her in the hay with a staff officer. We know you like to believe that was what started you on the booze and ruined your life.

JIMMY—(*stammers*) I—I'm talking to Harry. Will you

kindly keep out of— (*with a pitiful defiance*) My life is not ruined!

HICKEY—(*ignoring this—with a kidding grin*) But I'll bet when you admit the truth to yourself, you'll confess you were pretty sick of her hating you for getting drunk. I'll bet you were really damned relieved when she gave you such a good excuse. (*Jimmy stares at him strickenly. Hickey pats him on the back again—with sincere sympathy*) I know how it is, Jimmy. I— (*He stops abruptly and for a second he seems to lose his self-assurance and become confused.*)

LARRY—(*seizing on this with vindictive relish*) Ha! So that's what happened to you, is it? Your iceman joke finally came home to roost, did it? (*He grins tauntingly.*) You should have remembered there's truth in the old superstition that you'd better look out what you call because in the end it comes to you!

HICKEY—(*himself again—grins to Larry kiddingly*) Is that a fact, Larry? Well, well! Then you'd better watch out how you keep calling for that old Big Sleep! (*Larry starts and for a second looks superstitiously frightened. Abruptly Hickey changes to his jovial, bustling, master-of-ceremonies manner.*) But what are we waiting for, boys and girls? Let's start the party rolling! (*He shouts to the bar*) Hey, Chuck and Rocky! Bring on the big surprise! Governor, you sit at the head of the table here. (*He makes Harry sit down on the chair at the end of the table, right. To Margie and Pearl*) Come on, girls, sit down. (*They sit side by side on Jimmy's right. Hickey bustles down to the left end of table.*) I'll sit here at the foot. (*He sits, with Cora on his left and Joe on her left. Rocky and Chuck appear from the bar, each bearing a big tray laden with schooners of champagne which they start shoving in front of each member of the party.*)

ROCKY—(*with forced cheeriness*) Real champagne, bums! Cheer up! What is dis, a funeral? Jees, mixin' champagne wid Harry's redeye will knock yuh paralyzed! Ain't yuh never satisfied? (*He and Chuck finish serving out the schooners, grab the last two themselves and sit down in the two vacant chairs remaining near the middle of the table. As they do so, Hickey rises, a schooner in his hand.*)

HICKEY—(*rapping on the table for order when there is nothing but a dead silence*) Order! Order, Ladies and Gents! (*He catches Larry's eyes on the glass in his hand.*) Yes, Larry, I'm going to drink with you this time. To prove I'm not teetotal because I'm afraid booze would make me spill my secrets, as you think. (*Larry looks sheepish. Hickey chuckles and goes on.*) No, I gave you the simple truth about that. I don't need booze or anything else any more. But I want to be sociable and propose a toast in honor of our old friend, Harry, and drink it with you. (*His eyes fix on Hugo, who is out again, his head on his plate—to Chuck, who is on Hugo's left*) Wake up our demon bomb-tosser, Chuck. We don't want corpses at this feast.

CHUCK—(*gives Hugo a shake*) Hey, Hugo, come up for air! Don't yuh see de champagne? (*Hugo blinks around and giggles foolishly.*)

HUGO—Ve will eat birthday cake and trink champagne beneath the villow tree! (*He grabs his schooner and takes a greedy gulp—then sets it back on the table with a grimace of distaste—in a strange, arrogantly disdainful tone, as if he were rebuking a butler*) Dis vine is unfit to trink. It has not properly been iced.

HICKEY—(*amusedly*) Always a high-toned swell at heart, eh, Hugo? God help us poor bums if you'd ever get to telling us where to get off! You'd have been drinking our blood beneath those willow trees! (*He chuckles. Hugo shrinks back in his chair, blinking at him, but Hickey is now looking up the table at Hope. He starts his toast, and as he goes on he becomes more moved and obviously sincere.*) Here's the toast, Ladies and Gents! Here's to Harry Hope, who's been a friend in need to every one of us! Here's to the old Governor, the best sport and the kindest, biggest-hearted guy in the world! Here's wishing you all the luck there is, Harry, and long life and happiness! Come on, everybody! To Harry! Bottoms up! (*They have all caught his sincerity with eager relief. They raise their schooners with an enthusiastic chorus of* "Here's how, Harry!" "Here's luck, Harry!" *etc., and gulp half the wine down, Hickey leading them in this.*)

HOPE—(*deeply moved—his voice husky*) Bejees, thanks, all of you. Bejees, Hickey, you old son of a bitch, that's white of you! Bejees, I know you meant it, too.

HICKEY—(*moved*) Of course I meant it, Harry, old friend!

And I mean it when I say I hope today will be the biggest day in your life, and in the lives of everyone here, the beginning of a new life of peace and contentment where no pipe dreams can ever nag at you again. Here's to that, Harry! (*He drains the remainder of his drink, but this time he drinks alone. In an instant the attitude of everyone has reverted to uneasy, suspicious defensiveness.*)

ROCKY—(*growls*) Aw, forget dat bughouse line of bull for a minute, can't yuh?

HICKEY—(*sitting down—good-naturedly*) You're right, Rocky, I'm talking too much. It's Harry we want to hear from. Come on, Harry! (*He pounds his schooner on the table.*) Speech! Speech! (*They try to recapture their momentary enthusiasm, rap their schooners on the table, call "Speech," but there is a hollow ring in it. Hope gets to his feet reluctantly, with a forced smile, a smoldering resentment beginning to show in his manner.*)

HOPE—(*lamely*) Bejees, I'm no good at speeches. All I can say is thanks to everybody again for remembering me on my birthday. (*bitterness coming out*) Only don't think because I'm sixty I'll be a bigger damned fool easy mark than ever! No, bejees! Like Hickey says, it's going to be a new day! This dump has got to be run like other dumps, so I can make some money and not just split even. People has got to pay what they owe me! I'm not running a damned orphan asylum for bums and crooks! Nor a God-damned hooker shanty, either! Nor an Old Men's Home for lousy Anarchist tramps that ought to be in jail! I'm sick of being played for a sucker! (*They stare at him with stunned, bewildered hurt. He goes on in a sort of furious desperation, as if he hated himself for every word he said, and yet couldn't stop.*) And don't think you're kidding me right now, either! I know damned well you're giving me the laugh behind my back, thinking to yourselves, The old, lying, pipe-dreaming faker, we've heard his bull about taking a walk around the ward for years, he'll never make it! He's yellow, he ain't got the guts, he's scared he'll find out— (*He glares around at them almost with hatred.*) But I'll show you, bejees! (*He glares at Hickey.*) I'll show you, too, you son of a bitch of a frying-pan-peddling bastard!

HICKEY—(*heartily encouraging*) That's the stuff, Harry! Of course you'll try to show me! That's what I want you to do!

(*Harry glances at him with helpless dread—then drops his eyes and looks furtively around the table. All at once he becomes miserably contrite.*)

HOPE—(*his voice catching*) Listen, all of you! Bejees, forgive me. I lost my temper! I ain't feeling well! I got a hell of a grouch on! Bejees, you know you're all as welcome here as the flowers in May! (*They look at him with eager forgiveness. Rocky is the first one who can voice it.*)

ROCKY—Aw, sure, Boss, you're always aces wid us, see?

HICKEY—(*rises to his feet again. He addresses them now with the simple, convincing sincerity of one making a confession of which he is genuinely ashamed.*) Listen, everybody! I know you are sick of my gabbing, but I think this is the spot where I owe it to you to do a little explaining and apologize for some of the rough stuff I've had to pull on you. I know how it must look to you. As if I was a damned busybody who was not only interfering in your private business, but even sicking some of you on to nag at each other. Well, I have to admit that's true, and I'm damned sorry about it. But it simply had to be done! You must believe that! You know old Hickey. I was never one to start trouble. But this time I had to—for your own good! I had to make you help me with each other. I saw I couldn't do what I was after alone. Not in the time at my disposal. I knew when I came here I wouldn't be able to stay with you long. I'm slated to leave on a trip. I saw I'd have to hustle and use every means I could. (*with a joking boastfulness*) Why, if I had enough time, I'd get a lot of sport out of selling my line of salvation to each of you all by my lonesome. Like it was fun in the old days, when I traveled house to house, to convince some dame, who was sicking the dog on me, her house wouldn't be properly furnished unless she bought another wash boiler. And I could do it with you, all right. I know every one of you, inside and out, by heart. I may have been drunk when I've been here before, but old Hickey could never be so drunk he didn't have to see through people. I mean, everyone except himself. And, finally, he had to see through himself, too. (*He pauses. They stare at him, bitter, uneasy and fascinated. His manner changes to deep earnestness.*) But here's the point to get. I swear I'd never act like I have if I wasn't absolutely sure it will be worth it to you in the end, after you're rid of the damned guilt that makes you lie to yourselves you're something you're not, and the remorse that nags at you and makes you hide behind lousy pipe dreams about tomorrow. You'll be in a today where there is no yesterday or tomorrow to worry you. You won't give a damn what you are any more. I wouldn't say this unless I knew, Brothers and Sisters. This peace is real! It's a fact! I know! Because I've got it! Here! Now! Right in front of you! You see the difference in me! You remember how I used to be! Even when I had two quarts of rotgut under my belt and joked and sang "Sweet Adeline," I still felt like a guilty skunk. But you can all see that I don't give a damn about anything now. And I promise you, by the time this day is over, I'll have every one of you feeling the same way! (*He pauses. They stare at him fascinatedly. He adds with a grin*) I guess that'll be about all from me, boys and girls—for the present. So let's get on with the party. (*He starts to sit down.*)

LARRY—(*sharply*) Wait! (*insistently—with a sneer*) I think it would help us poor pipe-dreaming sinners along the sawdust trail to salvation if you told us now what it was happened to you that converted you to this great peace you've found. (*more and more with a deliberate, provocative taunting*) I notice you didn't deny it when I asked you about the iceman. Did this great revelation of the evil habit of dreaming about tomorrow come to you after you found your wife was sick of you? (*While he is speaking the faces of the gang have lighted up vindictively, as if all at once they saw a chance to revenge themselves. As he finishes, a chorus of sneering taunts begins, punctuated by nasty, jeering laughter.*)

HOPE—Bejees, you've hit it, Larry! I've noticed he hasn't shown her picture around this time!

MOSHER—He hasn't got it! The iceman took it away from him!

MARGIE—Jees, look at him! Who could blame her?

PEARL—She must be hard up to fall for an iceman!

CORA—Imagine a sap like him advisin' me and Chuck to git married!

CHUCK—Yeah! He done so good wid it!

JIMMY—At least I can say Marjorie chose an officer and a gentleman.

LEWIS—Come to look at you, Hickey, old chap, you've sprouted horns like a bloody antelope!

WETJOEN—Pigger, py Gott! Like a water buffalo's!

WILLIE—(*sings to his Sailor Lad tune*)
          "Come up," she cried, "my iceman lad,
          And you and I'll agree—"
(*They all join in a jeering chorus, rapping with knuckles or glasses on the table at the indicated spot in the lyric.*)
          "And I'll show you the prettiest (*rap, rap, rap*)
          That ever you did see!"
(*A roar of derisive, dirty laughter. But Hickey has remained un-moved by all this taunting. He grins good-naturedly, as if he en-joyed the joke at his expense, and joins in the laughter.*)

HICKEY—Well, boys and girls, I'm glad to see you getting in good spirits for Harry's party, even if the joke is on me. I admit I asked for it by always pulling that iceman gag in the old days. So laugh all you like. (*He pauses. They do not laugh now. They are again staring at him with baffled uneasiness. He goes on thoughtfully.*) Well, this forces my hand, I guess, your bringing up the subject of Evelyn. I didn't want to tell you yet. It's hardly an appropriate time. I meant to wait until the party was over. But you're getting the wrong idea about poor Evelyn, and I've got to stop that. (*He pauses again. There is a tense stillness in the room. He bows his head a little and says qui-etly*) I'm sorry to tell you my dearly beloved wife is dead. (*A gasp comes from the stunned company. They look away from him, shocked and miserably ashamed of themselves, except Larry who continues to stare at him.*)

LARRY—(*aloud to himself with a superstitious shrinking*) Be God, I felt he'd brought the touch of death on him! (*Then suddenly he is even more ashamed of himself than the others and stammers*) Forgive me, Hickey! I'd like to cut my dirty tongue out! (*This releases a chorus of shamefaced mumbles from the crowd. "Sorry, Hickey." "I'm sorry, Hickey." "We're sorry, Hickey."*)

HICKEY—(*looking around at them—in a kindly, reassuring tone*) Now look here, everybody. You mustn't let this be a wet blanket on Harry's party. You're still getting me all wrong. There's no reason— You see, I don't feel any grief. (*They gaze at him startledly. He goes on with convincing sincerity.*) I've got to feel glad, for her sake. Because she's at peace. She's rid of me at last. Hell, I don't have to tell you—you all know what I was like. You can imagine what she went through, married to a no-good cheater and drunk like I was. And there was no way out of it for her. Because she loved me. But now she is at peace like she always longed to be. So why should I feel sad? She wouldn't want me to feel sad. Why, all that Evelyn ever wanted out of life was to make me happy. (*He stops, looking around at them with a simple, gentle frankness. They stare at him in bewildered, incredulous confusion.*)

(*Curtain*)

ACT THREE

SCENE—*Barroom of Harry Hope's, including a part of what had been the back room in Acts One and Two. In the right wall are two big windows, with the swinging doors to the street between them. The bar itself is at rear. Behind it is a mirror, covered with white mosquito netting to keep off the flies, and a shelf on which are barrels of cheap whiskey with spiggots and a small show case of bottled goods. At left of the bar is the doorway to the hall. There is a table at left, front, of barroom proper, with four chairs. At right, front, is a small free-lunch counter, facing left, with a space between it and the window for the dealer to stand when he dishes out soup at the noon hour. Over the mirror behind the bar are framed photographs of Richard Croker and Big Tim Sullivan, flanked by framed lithographs of John L. Sullivan and Gentleman Jim Corbett in ring costume.*

At left, in what had been the back room, with the dividing curtain drawn, the banquet table of Act Two has been broken up, and the tables are again in the crowded arrangement of Act One. Of these, we see one in the front row with five chairs at left of the barroom table, another with five chairs at left-rear of it, a third back by the rear wall with five chairs, and finally, at extreme left-front, one with four chairs, partly on and partly off stage, left.

It is around the middle of the morning of Hope's birthday, a hot summer day. There is sunlight in the street outside, but it does not hit the windows and the light in the back-room section is dim.

Joe Mott is moving around, a box of sawdust under his arm, strewing it over the floor. His manner is sullen, his face set in gloom. He ignores everyone. As the scene progresses, he finishes his sawdusting job, goes behind the lunch counter and cuts loaves of bread. Rocky is behind the bar, wiping it, washing glasses, etc. He wears his working clothes, sleeves rolled up. He looks sleepy, irritable and worried. At the barroom table, front, Larry sits in a chair, facing right-front. He has no drink in front of him. He stares ahead, deep in harried thought. On his right, in a chair facing right, Hugo sits sprawled forward, arms and head on the table as usual, a whiskey glass beside his limp hand. At rear of the front table at left of them, in a chair facing left, Parritt is sitting. He is staring in front of him in a tense, strained immobility.

As the curtain rises, Rocky finishes his work behind the bar. He comes forward and drops wearily in the chair at right of Larry's table, facing left.

Rocky—Nuttin' now till de noon rush from de Market. I'm goin' to rest my fanny. (*irritably*) If I ain't a sap to let Chuck kid me into workin' his time so's he can take de mornin' off. But I got sick of arguin' wid 'im. I says, "Aw right, git married! What's it to me?" Hickey's got de bot' of dem bugs. (*bitterly*) Some party last night, huh? Jees, what a funeral! It was jinxed from de start, but his tellin' about his wife croakin' put de K.O. on it.

Larry—Yes, it turned out it wasn't a birthday feast but a wake!

Rocky—Him promisin' he'd cut out de bughouse bull about peace—and den he went on talkin' and talkin' like he couldn't stop! And all de gang sneakin' upstairs, leavin' free booze and eats like dey was poison! It didn't do dem no good if dey thought dey'd shake him. He's been hoppin' from room to room all night. Yuh can't stop him. He's got his Reform Wave goin' strong dis mornin'! Did yuh notice him drag Jimmy out de foist ting to get his laundry and his clothes pressed so he wouldn't have no excuse? And he give Willie de dough to buy his stuff back from Solly's. And all de rest been brushin' and shavin' demselves wid de shakes—

Larry—(*defiantly*) He didn't come to my room! He's afraid I might ask him a few questions.

Rocky—(*scornfully*) Yeah? It don't look to me he's scared of yuh. I'd say you was scared of him.

Larry—(*stung*) You'd lie, then!

Parritt—(*jerks round to look at Larry—sneeringly*) Don't let him kid you, Rocky. He had his door locked. I couldn't get in, either.

Rocky—Yeah, who d'yuh tink yuh're kiddin', Larry? He's showed you up, aw right. Like he says, if yuh was so anxious to croak, why wouldn't yuh hop off your fire escape long ago?

Larry—(*defiantly*) Because it'd be a coward's quitting, that's why!

PARRITT—He's all quitter, Rocky. He's a yellow old faker!

LARRY—(*turns on him*) You lying punk! Remember what I warned you—!

ROCKY—(*scowls at Parritt*) Yeah, keep outta dis, you! Where d'yuh get a license to butt in? Shall I give him de bum's rush, Larry? If you don't want him around, nobody else don't.

LARRY—(*forcing an indifferent tone*) No. Let him stay. I don't mind him. He's nothing to me. (*Rocky shrugs his shoulders and yawns sleepily.*)

PARRITT—You're right, I have nowhere to go now. You're the only one in the world I can turn to.

ROCKY—(*drowsily*) Yuh're a soft old sap, Larry. He's a no-good louse like Hickey. He don't belong. (*He yawns.*) I'm all in. Not a wink of sleep. Can't keep my peepers open. (*His eyes close and his head nods. Parritt gives him a glance and then gets up and slinks over to slide into the chair on Larry's left, between him and Rocky. Larry shrinks away, but determinedly ignores him.*)

PARRITT—(*bending toward him—in a low, ingratiating, apologetic voice*) I'm sorry for riding you, Larry. But you get my goat when you act as if you didn't care a damn what happened to me, and keep your door locked so I can't talk to you. (*then hopefully*) But that was to keep Hickey out, wasn't it? I don't blame you. I'm getting to hate him. I'm getting more and more scared of him. Especially since he told us his wife was dead. It's that queer feeling he gives me that I'm mixed up with him some way. I don't know why, but it started me thinking about Mother—as if she was dead. (*with a strange undercurrent of something like satisfaction in his pitying tone*) I suppose she might as well be. Inside herself, I mean. It must kill her when she thinks of me—I know she doesn't want to, but she can't help it. After all, I'm her only kid. She used to spoil me and made a pet of me. Once in a great while, I mean. When she remembered me. As if she wanted to make up for something. As if she felt guilty. So she must have loved me a little, even if she never let it interfere with her freedom. (*with a strange pathetic wistfulness*) Do you know, Larry, I once had a sneaking suspicion that maybe, if the truth was known, you were my father.

LARRY—(*violently*) You damned fool! Who put that insane idea in your head? You know it's a lie! Anyone in the Coast crowd could tell you I never laid eyes on your mother till after you were born.

PARRITT—Well, I'd hardly ask them, would I? I know you're right, though, because I asked her. She brought me up to be frank and ask her anything, and she'd always tell me the truth. (*abruptly*) But I was talking about how she must feel now about me. My getting through with the Movement. She'll never forgive that. The Movement is her life. And it must be the final knockout for her if she knows I was the one who sold—

LARRY—Shut up, damn you!

PARRITT—It'll kill her. And I'm sure she knows it must have been me. (*suddenly with desperate urgency*) But I never thought the cops would get her! You've got to believe that! You've got to see what my only reason was! I'll admit what I told you last night was a lie—that bunk about getting patriotic and my duty to my country. But here's the true reason, Larry—the only reason! It was just for money! I got stuck on a whore and wanted dough to blow in on her and have a good time! That's all I did it for! Just money! Honest! (*He has the terrible grotesque air, in confessing his sordid baseness, of one who gives an excuse which exonerates him from any real guilt.*)

LARRY—(*grabs him by the shoulder and shakes him*) God damn you, shut up! What the hell is it to me? (*Rocky starts awake.*)

ROCKY—What's comin' off here?

LARRY—(*controlling himself*) Nothing. This gabby young punk was talking my ear off, that's all. He's a worse pest than Hickey.

ROCKY—(*drowsily*) Yeah, Hickey— Say, listen, what d'yuh mean about him bein' scared you'd ask him questions? What questions?

LARRY—Well, I feel he's hiding something. You notice he didn't say what his wife died of.

ROCKY—(*rebukingly*) Aw, lay off dat. De poor guy— What are yuh gettin' at, anyway? Yuh don't tink it's just a gag of his?

LARRY—I don't. I'm damned sure he's brought death here with him. I feel the cold touch of it on him.

ROCKY—Aw, bunk! You got croakin' on de brain, Old Cemetery. (*Suddenly Rocky's eyes widen.*) Say! D'yuh mean yuh tink she committed suicide, 'count of his cheatin' or someting?

LARRY—(*grimly*) It wouldn't surprise me. I'd be the last to blame her.

ROCKY—(*scornfully*) But dat's crazy! Jees, if she'd done dat, he wouldn't tell us he was glad about it, would he? He ain't dat big a bastard.

PARRITT—(*speaks up from his own preoccupation—strangely*) You know better than that, Larry. You know she'd never commit suicide. She's like you. She'll hang on to life even when there's nothing left but—

LARRY—(*stung—turns on him viciously*) And how about you? Be God, if you had any guts or decency—! (*He stops guiltily.*)

PARRITT—(*sneeringly*) I'd take that hop off your fire escape you're too yellow to take, I suppose?

LARRY—(*as if to himself*) No! Who am I to judge? I'm done with judging.

PARRITT—(*tauntingly*) Yes, I suppose you'd like that, wouldn't you?

ROCKY—(*irritably mystified*) What de hell's all dis about? (*to Parritt*) What d'you know about Hickey's wife? How d'yuh know she didn't—?

LARRY—(*with forced belittling casualness*) He doesn't. Hickey's addled the little brains he's got. Shove him back to his own table, Rocky. I'm sick of him.

ROCKY—(*to Parritt, threateningly*) Yuh heard Larry? I'd like an excuse to give yuh a good punch in de snoot. So move quick!

PARRITT—(*gets up—to Larry*) If you think moving to another table will get rid of me! (*He moves away—then adds with bitter reproach*) Gee, Larry, that's a hell of a way to treat me, when I've trusted you, and I need your help. (*He sits down in his old place and sinks into a wounded, self-pitying brooding.*)

ROCKY—(*going back to his train of thought*) Jees, if she

committed suicide, yuh got to feel sorry for Hickey, huh?
Yuh can understand how he'd go bughouse and not be responsible for all de crazy stunts he's stagin' here. (*then puzzledly*) But how can yuh be sorry for him when he says he's
glad she croaked, and yuh can tell he means it? (*with weary
exasperation*) Aw, nuts! I don't get nowhere tryin' to figger
his game. (*his face hardening*) But I know dis. He better lay
off me and my stable! (*He pauses—then sighs.*) Jees, Larry,
what a night dem two pigs give me! When de party went
dead, dey pinched a coupla bottles and brung dem up deir
room and got stinko. I don't get a wink of sleep, see? Just as
I'd drop off on a chair here, dey'd come down lookin' for
trouble. Or else dey'd raise hell upstairs, laughin' and
singin', so I'd get scared dey'd get de joint pinched and go
up to tell dem to can de noise. And every time dey'd crawl
my frame wid de same old argument. Dey'd say, "So yuh
agreed wid Hickey, do yuh, yuh dirty little Ginny? We're
whores, are we? Well, we agree wid Hickey about you, see!
Yuh're nuttin' but a lousy pimp!" Den I'd slap dem. Not
beat 'em up, like a pimp would. Just slap dem. But it don't
do no good. Dey'd keep at it over and over. Jees, I get de ear-
ache just thinkin' of it! "Listen," dey'd say, "if we're whores
we gotta right to have a reg'lar pimp and not stand for no
punk imitation! We're sick of wearin' out our dogs pound-
in' sidewalks for a double-crossin' bartender, when all de
thanks we get is he looks down on us. We'll find a guy who
really needs us to take care of him and ain't ashamed of it.
Don't expect us to work tonight, 'cause we won't, see? Not
if de streets was blocked wid sailors! We're goin' on strike
and yuh can like it or lump it!" (*He shakes his head.*) Whores
goin' on strike! Can yuh tie dat? (*going on with his story*)
Dey says, "We're takin' a holiday. We're goin' to beat it
down to Coney Island and shoot the chutes and maybe we'll
come back and maybe we won't. And you can go to hell!"
So dey put on deir lids and beat it, de bot' of dem stinko.
(*He sighs dejectedly. He seems grotesquely like a harried family
man, henpecked and browbeaten by a nagging wife. Larry is
deep in his own bitter preoccupation and hasn't listened to him.
Chuck enters from the hall at rear. He has his straw hat with
the gaudy band in his hand and wears a Sunday-best blue suit*

with a high stiff collar. He looks sleepy, hot, uncomfortable and grouchy.)

CHUCK—(*glumly*) Hey, Rocky. Cora wants a sherry flip. For her noives.

ROCKY—(*turns indignantly*) Sherry flip! Christ, she don't need nuttin' for her noive! What's she tink dis is, de Waldorf?

CHUCK—Yeah, I told her, what would we use for sherry, and dere wasn't no egg unless she laid one. She says, "Is dere a law yuh can't go out and buy de makings, yuh big tramp?" (*resentfully puts his straw hat on his head at a defiant tilt*) To hell wid her! She'll drink booze or nuttin'! (*He goes behind the bar to draw a glass of whiskey from a barrel.*)

ROCKY—(*sarcastically*) Jees, a guy oughta give his bride anything she wants on de weddin' day, I should tink! (*As Chuck comes from behind the bar, Rocky surveys him derisively.*) Pipe de bridegroom, Larry! All dolled up for de killin'! (*Larry pays no attention.*)

CHUCK—Aw, shut up!

ROCKY—One week on dat farm in Joisey, dat's what I give yuh! Yuh'll come runnin' in here some night yellin' for a shot of booze 'cause de crickets is after yuh! (*disgustedly*) Jees, Chuck, dat louse Hickey's coitinly made a prize coupla suckers outa youse.

CHUCK—(*unguardedly*) Yeah. I'd like to give him one sock in de puss—just one! (*then angrily*) Aw, can dat! What's he got to do wid it? Ain't we always said we was goin' to? So we're goin' to, see? And don't give me no argument! (*He stares at Rocky truculently. But Rocky only shrugs his shoulders with weary disgust and Chuck subsides into complaining gloom.*) If on'y Cora'd cut out de beefin'. She don't gimme a minute's rest all night. De same old stuff over and over! Do I really want to marry her? I says, "Sure, Baby, why not?" She says, "Yeah, but after a week yuh'll be tinkin' what a sap you was. Yuh'll make dat an excuse to go off on a periodical, and den I'll be tied for life to a no-good soak, and de foist ting I know yuh'll have me out hustlin' again, your own wife!" Den she'd bust out cryin', and I'd get sore. "Yuh're a liar," I'd say. "I ain't never taken your dough 'cept when I was drunk and not workin'!" "Yeah," she'd say, "and how long will yuh stay sober now? Don't tink yuh can kid me wid dat water-wagon bull! I've heard it too often." Dat'd make me sore and I'd say, "Don't call me a liar. But I wish I was drunk right now, because if I was, yuh wouldn't be keepin' me awake all night beefin'. If yuh opened your yap, I'd knock de stuffin' outa yuh!" Den she'd yell, "Dat's a sweet way to talk to de goil yuh're goin' to marry." (*He sighs explosively.*) Jees, she's got me hangin' on de ropes! (*He glances with vengeful yearning at the drink of whiskey in his hand.*) Jees, would I like to get a quart of dis redeye under my belt!

ROCKY—Well, why de hell don't yuh?

CHUCK—(*instantly suspicious and angry*) Sure! You'd like dat, wouldn't yuh? I'm wise to you! Yuh don't wanta see me get married and settle down like a reg'lar guy! Yuh'd like me to stay paralyzed all de time, so's I'd be like you, a lousy pimp!

ROCKY—(*springs to his feet, his face hardened viciously*) Listen! I don't take dat even from you, see!

CHUCK—(*puts his drink on the bar and clenches his fists*) Yeah? Wanta make sometin' of it? (*jeeringly*) Don't make me laugh! I can lick ten of youse wid one mit!

ROCKY—(*reaching for his hip pocket*) Not wid lead in your belly, yuh won't!

JOE—(*has stopped cutting when the quarrel started—expostulating*) Hey, you, Rocky and Chuck! Cut it out! You's ole friends! Don't let dat Hickey make you crazy!

CHUCK—(*turns on him*) Keep outa our business, yuh black bastard!

ROCKY—(*like Chuck, turns on Joe, as if their own quarrel was forgotten and they became natural allies against an alien*) Stay where yuh belong, yuh doity nigger!

JOE—(*snarling with rage, springs from behind the lunch counter with the bread knife in his hand*) You white sons of bitches! I'll rip your guts out! (*Chuck snatches a whiskey bottle from the bar and raises it above his head to hurl at Joe. Rocky jerks a short-barreled, nickel-plated revolver from his hip pocket. At this moment Larry pounds on the table with his fist and bursts into a sardonic laugh.*)

LARRY—That's it! Murder each other, you damned loons, with Hickey's blessing! Didn't I tell you he'd brought death with him? (*His interruption startles them. They pause to stare at him, their fighting fury suddenly dies out and they appear deflated and sheepish.*)

ROCKY—(*to Joe*) Aw right, you. Leggo dat shiv and I'll put dis gat away. (*Joe sullenly goes back behind the counter and slaps the knife on top of it. Rocky slips the revolver back in his pocket. Chuck lowers the bottle to the bar. Hugo, who has awakened and raised his head when Larry pounded on the table, now giggles foolishly.*)

HUGO—Hello, leedle peoples! Neffer mind! Soon you vill eat hot dogs beneath the villow trees and trink free vine— (*abruptly in a haughty fastidious tone*) The champagne vas not properly iced. (*with guttural anger*) Gottamned liar, Hickey! Does that prove I vant to be aristocrat? I love only the pro-letariat! I vill lead them! I vill be like a Gott to them! They vill be my slaves! (*He stops in bewildered self-amazement—to Larry appealingly*) I am very trunk, no, Larry? I talk foolish-ness. I am so trunk, Larry, old friend, am I not, I don't know vhat I say?

LARRY—(*pityingly*) You're raving drunk, Hugo. I've never seen you so paralyzed. Lay your head down now and sleep it off.

HUGO—(*gratefully*) Yes. I should sleep. I am too crazy trunk. (*He puts his head on his arms and closes his eyes.*)

JOE—(*behind the lunch counter—brooding superstitiously*) You's right, Larry. Bad luck come in de door when Hickey come. I's an ole gamblin' man and I knows bad luck when I feels it! (*then defiantly*) But it's white man's bad luck. He can't jinx me! (*He comes from behind the counter and goes to the bar— addressing Rocky stiffly*) De bread's cut and I's finished my job. Do I get de drink I's earned? (*Rocky gives him a hostile look but shoves a bottle and glass at him. Joe pours a brimful drink—sul-lenly*) I's finished wid dis dump for keeps. (*He takes a key from his pocket and slaps it on the bar.*) Here's de key to my room. I ain't comin' back. I's goin' to my own folks where I belong. I don't stay where I's not wanted. I's sick and tired of messin' round wid white men. (*He gulps down his drink—then looking around defiantly he deliberately throws his whiskey glass on the floor and smashes it.*)

ROCKY—Hey! What de hell—!

JOE—(*with a sneering dignity*) I's on'y savin' you de trouble,

White Boy. Now you don't have to break it, soon's my back's turned, so's no white man kick about drinkin' from de same glass. (*He walks stiffly to the street door—then turns for a parting shot—boastfully*) I's tired of loafin' 'round wid a lot of bums. I's a gamblin' man. I's gonna get in a big crap game and win me a big bankroll. Den I'll get de okay to open up my old gamblin' house for colored men. Den maybe I comes ·
back here sometime to see de bums. Maybe I throw a twenty-dollar bill on de bar and say, "Drink it up," and listen when dey all pat me on de back and say, "Joe, you sure is white." But I'll say, "No, I'm black and my dough is black man's dough, and you's proud to drink wid me or you don't get no drink!" Or maybe I just says, "You can all go to hell. I don't lower myself drinkin' wid no white trash!" (*He opens the door to go out—then turns again.*) And dat ain't no pipe dream! I'll git de money for my stake today, somehow, somewheres! If I has to borrow a gun and stick up some white man, I gets it! You wait and see! (*He swaggers out through the swinging doors.*)

CHUCK—(*angrily*) Can yuh beat de noive of dat dinge! Jees, if I wasn't dressed up, I'd go out and mop up de street wid him!

ROCKY—Aw, let him go, de poor old dope! Him and his gamblin' house! He'll be back tonight askin' Harry for his room and bummin' me for a ball. (*vengefully*) Den I'll be de one to smash de glass. I'll loin him his place! (*The swinging doors are pushed open and Willie Oban enters from the street. He is shaved and wears an expensive, well-cut suit, good shoes and clean linen. He is absolutely sober, but his face is sick, and his nerves in a shocking state of shakes.*)

CHUCK—Another guy all dolled up! Got your clothes from Solly's, huh, Willie? (*derisively*) Now yuh can sell dem back to him again tomorrow.

WILLIE—(*stiffly*) No, I—I'm through with that stuff. Never again. (*He comes to the bar.*)

ROCKY—(*sympathetically*) Yuh look sick, Willie. Take a ball to pick yuh up. (*He pushes a bottle toward him.*)

WILLIE—(*eyes the bottle yearningly but shakes his head—determinedly*) No, thanks. The only way to stop is to stop. I'd have no chance if I went to the D.A.'s office smelling of booze.

CHUCK—Yuh're really goin' dere?

WILLIE—(*stiffly*) I said I was, didn't I? I just came back here to rest a few minutes, not because I needed any booze. I'll show that cheap drummer I don't have to have any Dutch courage— (*guiltily*) But he's been very kind and generous staking me. He can't help his insulting manner, I suppose. (*He turns away from the bar.*) My legs are a bit shaky yet. I better sit down a while. (*He goes back and sits at the left of the second table, facing Parritt, who gives him a scowling, suspicious glance and then ignores him. Rocky looks at Chuck and taps his head disgustedly. Captain Lewis appears in the doorway from the hall.*)

CHUCK—(*mutters*) Here's anudder one. (*Lewis looks spruce and clean-shaven. His ancient tweed suit has been brushed and his frayed linen is clean. His manner is full of a forced, jaunty self-assurance. But he is sick and beset by katzenjammer.*)

LEWIS—Good morning, gentlemen all. (*He passes along the front of bar to look out in the street.*) A jolly fine morning, too. (*He turns back to the bar.*) An eye-opener? I think not. Not required, Rocky, old chum. Feel extremely fit, as a matter of fact. Though can't say I slept much, thanks to that interfering ass, Hickey, and that stupid bounder of a Boer. (*His face hardens.*) I've had about all I can take from that fellow. It's my own fault, of course, for allowing a brute of a Dutch farmer to become familiar. Well, it's come to a parting of the ways now, and good riddance. Which reminds me, here's my key. (*He puts it on the bar.*) I shan't be coming back. Sorry to be leaving good old Harry and the rest of you, of course, but I can't continue to live under the same roof with that fellow. (*He stops, stiffening into hostility as Wetjoen enters from the hall, and pointedly turns his back on him. Wetjoen glares at him sneeringly. He, too, has made an effort to spruce up his appearance, and his bearing has a forced swagger of conscious physical strength. Behind this, he is sick and feebly holding his booze-sodden body together.*)

ROCKY—(*to Lewis—disgustedly putting the key on the shelf in back of the bar*) So Hickey's kidded the pants offa you, too? Yuh tink yuh're leavin' here, huh?

WETJOEN—(*jeeringly*) Ja! Dot's vhat he kids himself.

LEWIS—(*ignores him—airily*) Yes, I'm leaving, Rocky. But

that ass, Hickey, has nothing to do with it. Been thinking things over. Time I turned over a new leaf, and all that.

WETJOEN—He's going to get a job! Dot's what he says!

ROCKY—What at, for Chris' sake?

LEWIS—(*keeping his airy manner*) Oh, anything. I mean, not manual labor, naturally, but anything that calls for a bit of brains and education. However humble. Beggars can't be choosers. I'll see a pal of mine at the Consulate. He promised any time I felt an energetic fit he'd get me a post with the Cunard—clark in the office or something of the kind.

WETJOEN—Ja! At Limey Consulate they promise anything to get rid of him vhen he comes there tronk! They're scared to call the police and have him pinched because it vould scandal in the papers make about a Limey officer and chentleman!

LEWIS—As a matter of fact, Rocky, I only wish a post temporarily. Means to an end, you know. Save up enough for a first-class passage home, that's the bright idea.

WETJOEN—He's sailing back to home, sveet home! Dot's biggest pipe dream of all. What leetle brain the poor Limey has left, dot isn't in whiskey pickled, Hickey has made crazy! (*Lewis' fists clench, but he manages to ignore this.*)

CHUCK—(*feels sorry for Lewis and turns on Wetjoen— sarcastically*) Hickey ain't made no sucker outa you, huh? You're too foxy, huh? But I'll bet you tink yuh're goin' out and land a job, too.

WETJOEN—(*bristles*) I am, ja. For me, it is easy. Because I put on no airs of chentleman. I am not ashamed to vork vith my hands. I vas a farmer before the war ven ploody Limey thieves steal my country. (*boastfully*) Anyone I ask for job can see vith one look I have the great strength to do work of ten ordinary mens.

LEWIS—(*sneeringly*) Yes, Chuck, you remember he gave a demonstration of his extraordinary muscles last night when he helped to move the piano.

CHUCK—Yuh couldn't even hold up your corner. It was your fault de damned box almost fell down de stairs.

WETJOEN—My hands vas sweaty! Could I help dot my hands slip? I could de whole veight of it lift! In old days in Transvaal, I lift loaded oxcart by the axle! So vhy shouldn't I get job? Dot longshoreman boss, Dan, he tell me any time I like, he take me on. And Benny from de Market he promise me same.

LEWIS—You remember, Rocky, it was one of those rare occasions when the Boer that walks like a man—spelled with a double o, by the way—was buying drinks and Dan and Benny were stony. They'd bloody well have promised him the moon.

ROCKY—Yeah, yuh big boob, dem boids was on'y kiddin' yuh.

WETJOEN—(*angrily*) Dot's lie! You vill see dis morning I get job! I'll show dot bloody Limey chentleman, and dot liar, Hickey! And I need vork only leetle vhile to save money for my passage home. I need not much money because I am not ashamed to travel steerage. I don't put on first-cabin airs! (*tauntingly*) Und *I can* go home to my country! Vhen I get there, they vill let *me* come in!

LEWIS—(*grows rigid—his voice trembling with repressed anger*) There was a rumor in South Africa, Rocky, that a certain Boer officer—if you call the leaders of a rabble of farmers officers —kept advising Cronje to retreat and not stand and fight—

WETJOEN—And I vas right! I vas right! He got surrounded at Poardeberg! He had to surrender!

LEWIS—(*ignoring him*) Good strategy, no doubt, but a suspicion grew afterwards into a conviction among the Boers that the officer's caution was prompted by a desire to make his personal escape. His countrymen felt extremely savage about it, and his family disowned him. So I imagine there would be no welcoming committee waiting on the dock, nor delighted relatives making the veldt ring with their happy cries—

WETJOEN—(*with guilty rage*) All lies! You Gottamned Limey— (*trying to control himself and copy Lewis' manner*) I also haf heard rumors of a Limey officer who, after the war, lost all his money gambling vhen he vas tronk. But they found out it vas regiment money, too, he lost—

LEWIS—(*loses his control and starts for him*) You bloody Dutch scum!

ROCKY—(*leans over the bar and stops Lewis with a straight-arm swipe on the chest*) Cut it out! (*At the same moment Chuck grabs Wetjoen and yanks him back.*)

WETJOEN—(*struggling*) Let him come! I saw them come before—at Modder River, Magersfontein, Spion Kopje—waving their silly swords, so afraid they couldn't show off how brave they vas!—and I kill them vith my rifle so easy! (*vindictively*) Listen to me, you Cecil! Often vhen I am tronk and kidding you I say I am sorry I missed you, but now, py Gott, I am sober, and I don't joke, and I say it!

LARRY—(*gives a sardonic guffaw—with his comically crazy, intense whisper*) Be God, you can't say Hickey hasn't the miraculous touch to raise the dead, when he can start the Boer War raging again! (*This interruption acts like a cold douche on Lewis and Wetjoen. They subside, and Rocky and Chuck let go of them. Lewis turns his back on the Boer.*)

LEWIS—(*attempting a return of his jaunty manner, as if nothing had happened*) Well, time I was on my merry way to see my chap at the Consulate. The early bird catches the job, what? Good-bye and good luck, Rocky, and everyone. (*He starts for the street door.*)

WETJOEN—Py Gott, if dot Limey can go, I can go! (*He hurries after Lewis. But Lewis, his hand about to push the swinging doors open, hesitates, as though struck by a sudden paralysis of the will, and Wetjoen has to jerk back to avoid bumping into him. For a second they stand there, one behind the other, staring over the swinging doors into the street.*)

ROCKY—Well, why don't yuh beat it?

LEWIS—(*guiltily casual*) Eh? Oh, just happened to think. Hardly the decent thing to pop off without saying good-bye to old Harry. One of the best, Harry. And good old Jimmy, too. They ought to be down any moment. (*He pretends to notice Wetjoen for the first time and steps away from the door—apologizing as to a stranger*) Sorry. I seem to be blocking your way out.

WETJOEN—(*stiffly*) No. I vait to say good-bye to Harry and Jimmy, too. (*He goes to right of door behind the lunch counter and looks through the window, his back to the room. Lewis takes up a similar stand at the window on the left of door.*)

CHUCK—Jees, can yuh beat dem simps! (*He picks up Cora's drink at the end of the bar.*) Hell, I'd forgot Cora. She'll be trowin' a fit. (*He goes into the hall with the drink.*)

ROCKY—(*looks after him disgustedly*) Dat's right, wait on her and spoil her, yuh poor sap! (*He shakes his head and begins to wipe the bar mechanically.*)

WILLIE—(*is regarding Parritt across the table from him with an eager, calculating eye. He leans over and speaks in a low confidential tone.*) Look here, Parritt. I'd like to have a talk with you.

PARRITT—(*starts—scowling defensively*) What about?

WILLIE—(*his manner becoming his idea of a crafty criminal lawyer's*) About the trouble you're in. Oh, I know. You don't admit it. You're quite right. That's my advice. Deny everything. Keep your mouth shut. Make no statements whatever without first consulting your attorney.

PARRITT—Say! What the hell—?

WILLIE—But you can trust me. I'm a lawyer, and it's just occurred to me you and I ought to co-operate. Of course I'm going to see the D.A. this morning about a job on his staff. But that may take time. There may not be an immediate opening. Meanwhile it would be a good idea for me to take a case or two, on my own, and prove my brilliant record in law school was no flash in the pan. So why not retain me as your attorney?

PARRITT—You're crazy! What do I want with a lawyer?

WILLIE—That's right. Don't admit anything. But you can trust me, so let's not beat about the bush. You got in trouble out on the Coast, eh? And now you're hiding out. Any fool can spot that. (*lowering his voice still more*) You feel safe here, and maybe you are, for a while. But remember, they get you in the end. I know from my father's experience. No one could have felt safer than he did. When anyone mentioned the law to him, he nearly died laughing. But—

PARRITT—You crazy mutt! (*turning to Larry with a strained laugh*) Did you get that, Larry? This damned fool thinks the cops are after me!

LARRY—(*bursts out with his true reaction before he thinks to ignore him*) I wish to God they were! And so should you, if you had the honor of a louse! (*Parritt stares into his eyes guiltily for a second. Then he smiles sneeringly.*)

PARRITT—And you're the guy who kids himself he's through with the Movement! You old lying faker, you're still in love with it! (*Larry ignores him again now.*)

WILLIE—(*disappointedly*) Then you're not in trouble, Parritt? I was hoping— But never mind. No offense meant. Forget it.

PARRITT—(*condescendingly—his eyes on Larry*) Sure. That's all right, Willie. I'm not sore at you. It's that damned old faker that gets my goat. (*He slips out of his chair and goes quietly over to sit in the chair beside Larry he had occupied before—in a low, insinuating, intimate tone*) I think I understand, Larry. It's really Mother you still love—isn't it?—in spite of the dirty deal she gave you. But hell, what did you expect? She was never true to anyone but herself and the Movement. But I understand how you can't help still feeling—because I still love her, too. (*pleading in a strained, desperate tone*) You know I do, don't you? You must! So you see I couldn't have expected they'd catch her! You've got to believe me that I sold them out just to get a few lousy dollars to blow in on a whore. No other reason, honest! There couldn't possibly be any other reason! (*Again he has a strange air of exonerating himself from guilt by this shameless confession.*)

LARRY—(*trying not to listen, has listened with increasing tension*) For the love of Christ will you leave me in peace! I've told you you can't make me judge you! But if you don't keep still, you'll be saying something soon that will make you vomit your own soul like a drink of nickel rotgut that won't stay down! (*He pushes back his chair and springs to his feet.*) To hell with you! (*He goes to the bar.*)

PARRITT—(*jumps up and starts to follow him—desperately*) Don't go, Larry! You've got to help me! (*But Larry is at the bar, back turned, and Rocky is scowling at him. He stops, shrinking back into himself helplessly, and turns away. He goes to the table where he had been before, and this time he takes the chair at rear facing directly front. He puts his elbows on the table, holding his head in his hands as if he had a splitting headache.*)

LARRY—Set 'em up, Rocky. I swore I'd have no more drinks on Hickey, if I died of drought, but I've changed my mind! Be God, he owes it to me, and I'd get blind to the world now if it was the Iceman of Death himself treating! (*He stops, startledly, a superstitious awe coming into his face.*) What made me say that, I wonder. (*with a sardonic laugh*) Well, be God, it fits, for Death was the Iceman Hickey called to his home!

ROCKY—Aw, forget dat iceman gag! De poor dame is dead. (*pushing a bottle and glass at Larry*) Gwan and get paralyzed! I'll be glad to see one bum in dis dump act natural. (*Larry downs a drink and pours another.*)

(*Ed Mosher appears in the doorway from the hall. The same change which is apparent in the manner and appearance of the others shows in him. He is sick, his nerves are shattered, his eyes are apprehensive, but he, too, puts on an exaggeratedly self-confident bearing. He saunters to the bar between Larry and the street entrance.*)

MOSHER—Morning, Rocky. Hello, Larry. Glad to see Brother Hickey hasn't corrupted you to temperance. I wouldn't mind a shot myself. (*As Rocky shoves a bottle toward him he shakes his head.*) But I remember the only breath-killer in this dump is coffee beans. The boss would never fall for that. No man can run a circus successfully who believes guys chew coffee beans because they like them. (*He pushes the bottle away.*) No, much as I need one after the hell of a night I've had— (*He scowls.*) That drummer son of a drummer! I had to lock him out. But I could hear him through the wall doing his spiel to someone all night long. Still at it with Jimmy and Harry when I came down just now. But the hardest to take was that flannel-mouth, flatfoot Mick trying to tell me where I got off! I had to lock him out, too. (*As he says this, McGloin comes in the doorway from the hall. The change in his appearance and manner is identical with that of Mosher and the others.*)

McGLOIN—He's a liar, Rocky! It was me locked him out! (*Mosher starts to flare up—then ignores him. They turn their backs on each other. McGloin starts into the back-room section.*)

WILLIE—Come and sit here, Mac. You're just the man I want to see. If I'm to take your case, we ought to have a talk before we leave.

McGLOIN—(*contemptuously*) We'll have no talk. You damned fool, do you think I'd have your father's son for my lawyer? They'd take one look at you and bounce us both out on our necks! (*Willie winces and shrinks down in his chair. McGloin goes to the first table beyond him and sits with his back to the bar.*) I don't need a lawyer, anyway. To hell with the law! All I've got to do is see the right ones and get them to pass the word. They will, too. They know I was framed. And once they've passed the word, it's as good as done, law or no law.

MOSHER—God, I'm glad I'm leaving this madhouse! (*He pulls his key from his pocket and slaps it on the bar.*) Here's my key, Rocky.

McGLOIN—(*pulls his from his pocket*) And here's mine. (*He tosses it to Rocky.*) I'd rather sleep in the gutter than pass another night under the same roof with that loon, Hickey, and a lying circus grifter! (*He adds darkly*) And if that hat fits anyone here, let him put it on! (*Mosher turns toward him furiously but Rocky leans over the bar and grabs his arm.*)

ROCKY—Nix! Take it easy! (*Mosher subsides. Rocky tosses the keys on the shelf—disgustedly*) You boids gimme a pain. It'd soive you right if I wouldn't give de keys back to yuh tonight. (*They both turn on him resentfully, but there is an interruption as Cora appears in the doorway from the hall with Chuck behind her. She is drunk, dressed in her gaudy best, her face plastered with rouge and mascara, her hair a bit disheveled, her hat on anyhow.*)

CORA—(*comes a few steps inside the bar—with a strained bright giggle*) Hello, everybody! Here we go! Hickey just told us, ain't it time we beat it, if we're really goin'. So we're showin' de bastard, ain't we, Honey? He's comin' right down wid Harry and Jimmy. Jees, dem two look like dey was goin' to de electric chair! (*with frightened anger*) If I had to listen to any more of Hickey's bunk, I'd brain him. (*She puts her hand on Chuck's arm.*) Come on, Honey. Let's get started before he comes down.

CHUCK—(*sullenly*) Sure, anyting yuh say, Baby.

CORA—(*turns on him truculently*) Yeah? Well, I say we stop at de foist reg'lar dump and yuh gotta blow me to a sherry flip—or four or five, if I want 'em!—or all bets is off!

CHUCK—Aw, yuh got a fine bun on now!

CORA—Cheap skate! I know what's eatin' you, Tightwad!

Well, use my dough, den, if yuh're so stingy. Yuh'll grab it all, anyway, right after de ceremony. I know you! (*She hikes her skirt up and reaches inside the top of her stocking.*) Here, yuh big tramp!

CHUCK—(*knocks her hand away—angrily*) Keep your lousy dough! And don't show off your legs to dese bums when yuh're goin' to be married, if yuh don't want a sock in de puss!

CORA—(*pleased—meekly*) Aw right, Honey. (*looking around with a foolish laugh*) Say, why don't all you barflies come to de weddin'? (*But they are all sunk in their own apprehensions and ignore her. She hesitates, miserably uncertain.*) Well, we're goin', guys. (*There is no comment. Her eyes fasten on Rocky—desperately*) Say, Rocky, yuh gone deaf? I said me and Chuck was goin' now.

ROCKY—(*wiping the bar—with elaborate indifference*) Well, good-bye. Give my love to Joisey.

CORA—(*tearfully indignant*) Ain't yuh goin' to wish us happiness, yuh doity little Ginny?

ROCKY—Sure. Here's hopin' yuh don't moider each odder before next week.

CHUCK—(*angrily*) Aw, Baby, what d'we care for dat pimp? (*Rocky turns on him threateningly, but Chuck hears someone upstairs in the hall and grabs Cora's arm.*) Here's Hickey comin'! Let's get outa here! (*They hurry into the hall. The street door is heard slamming behind them.*)

ROCKY—(*gloomily pronounces an obituary*) One regular guy and one all-right tart gone to hell! (*fiercely*) Dat louse Hickey oughta be croaked! (*There is a muttered growl of assent from most of the gathering. Then Harry Hope enters from the hall, followed by Jimmy Tomorrow, with Hickey on his heels. Hope and Jimmy are both putting up a front of self-assurance, but Cora's description of them was apt. There is a desperate bluff in their manner as they walk in, which suggests the last march of the condemned. Hope is dressed in an old black Sunday suit, black tie, shoes, socks, which give him the appearance of being in mourning. Jimmy's clothes are pressed, his shoes shined, his white linen immaculate. He has a hangover and his gently appealing dog's eyes have a boiled look. Hickey's face is a bit drawn from lack of sleep*) *and his voice is hoarse from continual talking, but his bustling energy appears nervously intensified, and his beaming expression is one of triumphant accomplishment.*)

HICKEY—Well, here we are! We've got this far, at least! (*He pats Jimmy on the back.*) Good work, Jimmy. I told you you weren't half as sick as you pretended. No excuse whatever for postponing—

JIMMY—I'll thank you to keep your hands off me! I merely mentioned I would feel more fit tomorrow. But it might as well be today, I suppose.

HICKEY—Finish it now, so it'll be dead forever, and you can be free! (*He passes him to clap Hope encouragingly on the shoulder.*) Cheer up, Harry. You found your rheumatism didn't bother you coming downstairs, didn't you? I told you it wouldn't. (*He winks around at the others. With the exception of Hugo and Parritt, all their eyes are fixed on him with bitter animosity. He gives Hope a playful nudge in the ribs.*) You're the damnedest one for alibis, Governor! As bad as Jimmy!

HOPE—(*putting on his deaf manner*) Eh? I can't hear— (*defiantly*) You're a liar! I've had rheumatism on and off for twenty years. Ever since Bessie died. Everybody knows that.

HICKEY—Yes, we know it's the kind of rheumatism you turn on and off! We're on to you, you old faker! (*He claps him on the shoulder again, chuckling.*)

HOPE—(*looks humiliated and guilty—by way of escape he glares around at the others.*) Bejees, what are all you bums hanging round staring at me for? Think you was watching a circus! Why don't you get the hell out of here and 'tend to your own business, like Hickey's told you? (*They look at him reproachfully, their eyes hurt. They fidget as if trying to move.*)

HICKEY—Yes, Harry, I certainly thought they'd have had the guts to be gone by this time. (*He grins.*) Or maybe I did have my doubts. (*Abruptly he becomes sincerely sympathetic and earnest.*) Because I know exactly what you're up against, boys. I know how damned yellow a man can be when it comes to making himself face the truth. I've been through the mill, and I had to face a worse bastard in myself than any of you will have to in yourselves. I know you become such a coward you'll grab at any lousy excuse to get out of killing your pipe dreams. And yet, as I've told you over and over, it's exactly those damned tomorrow dreams which keep you from making peace with yourself. So you've got to kill them like I did mine. (*He pauses. They glare at him with fear and hatred. They seem about to curse him, to spring at him. But they remain silent and motionless. His manner changes and he becomes kindly bullying.*) Come on, boys! Get moving! Who'll start the ball rolling? You, Captain, and you, General. You're nearest the door. And besides, you're old war heroes! You ought to lead the forlorn hope! Come on, now, show us a little of that good old battle of Modder River spirit we've heard so much about! You can't hang around all day looking as if you were scared the street outside would bite you!

LEWIS—(*turns with humiliated rage—with an attempt at jaunty casualness*) Right you are, Mister Bloody Nosey Parker! Time I pushed off. Was only waiting to say good-bye to you, Harry, old chum.

HOPE—(*dejectedly*) Good-bye, Captain. Hope you have luck.

LEWIS—Oh, I'm bound to, Old Chap, and the same to you. (*He pushes the swinging doors open and makes a brave exit, turning to his right and marching off outside the window at right of door.*)

WETJOEN—Py Gott, if dot Limey can, I can! (*He pushes the door open and lumbers through it like a bull charging an obstacle. He turns left and disappears off rear, outside the farthest window.*)

HICKEY—(*exhortingly*) Next? Come on, Ed. It's a fine summer's day and the call of the old circus lot must be in your blood! (*Mosher glares at him, then goes to the door. McGloin jumps up from his chair and starts moving toward the door. Hickey claps him on the back as he passes.*) That's the stuff, Mac.

MOSHER—Good-bye, Harry. (*He goes out, turning right outside.*)

McGLOIN—(*glowering after him*) If that crooked grifter has the guts— (*He goes out, turning left outside. Hickey glances at Willie who, before he can speak, jumps from his chair.*)

WILLIE—Good-bye, Harry, and thanks for all your kindness.

HICKEY—(*claps him on the back*) That's the way, Willie!

The D.A.'s a busy man. He can't wait all day for you, you know. (*Willie hurries to the door.*)

HOPE—(*dully*) Good luck, Willie. (*Willie goes out and turns right outside. While he is doing so, Jimmy, in a sick panic, sneaks to the bar and furtively reaches for Larry's glass of whiskey.*)

HICKEY—And now it's your turn, Jimmy, old pal. (*He sees what Jimmy is at and grabs his arm just as he is about to down the drink.*) Now, now, Jimmy! You can't do that to yourself. One drink on top of your hangover and an empty stomach and you'll be oreyeyed. Then you'll tell yourself you wouldn't stand a chance if you went up soused to get your old job back.

JIMMY—(*pleads objectly*) Tomorrow! I will tomorrow! I'll be in good shape tomorrow! (*abruptly getting control of himself—with shaken firmness*) All right. I'm going. Take your hands off me.

HICKEY—That's the ticket! You'll thank me when it's all over.

JIMMY—(*in a burst of futile fury*) You dirty swine! (*He tries to throw the drink in Hickey's face, but his aim is poor and it lands on Hickey's coat. Jimmy turns and dashes through the door, disappearing outside the window at right of door.*)

HICKEY—(*brushing the whiskey off his coat—humorously*) All set for an alcohol rub! But no hard feelings. I know how he feels. I wrote the book. I've seen the day when if anyone forced me to face the truth about my pipe dreams, I'd have shot them dead. (*He turns to Hope—encouragingly*) Well, Governor, Jimmy made the grade. It's up to you. If he's got the guts to go through with the test, then certainly you—

LARRY—(*bursts out*) Leave Harry alone, damn you!

HICKEY—(*grins at him*) I'd make up my mind about myself if I was you, Larry, and not bother over Harry. He'll come through all right. I've promised him that. He doesn't need anyone's bum pity. Do you, Governor?

HOPE—(*with a pathetic attempt at his old fuming assertiveness*) No, bejees! Keep your nose out of this, Larry. What's Hickey got to do with it? I've always been going to take this walk, ain't I? Bejees, you bums want to keep me locked up in here 's if I was in jail! I've stood it long enough! I'm free, white and twenty-one, and I'll do as I damned please, bejees!

You keep your nose out, too, Hickey! You'd think you was boss of this dump, not me. Sure, I'm all right! Why shouldn't I be? What the hell's to be scared of, just taking a stroll around my own ward? (*As he talks he has been moving toward the door. Now he reaches it.*) What's the weather like outside, Rocky?

ROCKY—Fine day, Boss.

HOPE—What's that? Can't hear you. Don't look fine to me. Looks 's if it'd pour down cats and dogs any minute. My rheumatism— (*He catches himself.*) No, must be my eyes. Half blind, bejees. Makes things look black. I see now it's a fine day. Too damned hot for a walk, though, if you ask me. Well, do me good to sweat the booze out of me. But I'll have to watch out for the damned automobiles. Wasn't none of them around the last time, twenty years ago. From what I've seen of 'em through the window, they'd run over you as soon as look at you. Not that I'm scared of 'em. I can take care of myself. (*He puts a reluctant hand on the swinging door.*) Well, so long— (*He stops and looks back—with frightened irascibility*) Bejees, where are you, Hickey? It's time we got started.

HICKEY—(*grins and shakes his head*) No, Harry. Can't be done. You've got to keep a date with yourself alone.

HOPE—(*with forced fuming*) Hell of a guy, you are! Thought you'd be willing to help me across the street, knowing I'm half blind. Half deaf, too. Can't bear those damned automobiles. Hell with you! Bejees, I've never needed no one's help and I don't now! (*egging himself on*) I'll take a good long walk now I've started. See all my old friends. Bejees, they must have given me up for dead. Twenty years is a long time. But they know it was grief over Bessie's death that made me— (*He puts his hand on the door.*) Well, the sooner I get started— (*Then he drops his hand—with sentimental melancholy*) You know, Hickey, that's what gets me. Can't help thinking the last time I went out was to Bessie's funeral. After she'd gone, I didn't feel life was worth living. Swore I'd never go out again. (*pathetically*) Somehow, I can't feel it's right for me to go, Hickey, even now. It's like I was doing wrong to her memory.

HICKEY—Now, Governor, you can't let yourself get away with that one any more!

HOPE—(*cupping his hand to his ear*) What's that? Can't hear you. (*sentimentally again but with desperation*) I remember now clear as day the last time before she— It was a fine Sunday morning. We went out to church together. (*His voice breaks on a sob.*)

HICKEY—(*amused*) It's a great act, Governor. But I know better, and so do you. You never did want to go to church or any place else with her. She was always on your neck, making you have ambition and go out and do things, when all you wanted was to get drunk in peace.

HOPE—(*falteringly*) Can't hear a word you're saying. You're a God-damned liar, anyway! (*then in a sudden fury, his voice trembling with hatred*) Bejees, you son of a bitch, if there was a mad dog outside I'd go and shake hands with it rather than stay here with you! (*The momentum of his fit of rage does it. He pushes the door open and strides blindly out into the street and as blindly past the window behind the free-lunch counter.*)

ROCKY—(*in amazement*) Jees, he made it! I'd a give yuh fifty to one he'd never— (*He goes to the end of the bar to look through the window—disgustedly*) Aw, he's stopped. I'll bet yuh he's comin' back.

HICKEY—Of course, he's coming back. So are all the others. By tonight they'll all be here again. You dumbbell, that's the whole point.

ROCKY—(*excitedly*) No, he ain't neider! He's gone to de coib. He's lookin' up and down. Scared stiff of automobiles. Jees, dey ain't more'n two an hour comes down dis street, de old boob! (*He watches excitedly, as if it were a race he had a bet on, oblivious to what happens in the bar.*)

LARRY—(*turns on Hickey with bitter defiance*) And now it's my turn, I suppose? What is it I'm to do to achieve this blessed peace of yours?

HICKEY—(*grins at him*) Why, we've discussed all that, Larry. Just stop lying to yourself—

LARRY—You think when I say I'm finished with life, and tired of watching the stupid greed of the human circus, and I'll welcome closing my eyes in the long sleep of death—you think that's a coward's lie?

HICKEY—(*chuckling*) Well, what do you think, Larry?

LARRY—(*with increasing bitter intensity, more as if he were fighting with himself than with Hickey*) I'm afraid to live, am I?—and even more afraid to die! So I sit here, with my pride drowned on the bottom of a bottle, keeping drunk so I won't see myself shaking in my britches with fright, or hear myself whining and praying: Beloved Christ, let me live a little longer at any price! If it's only for a few days more, or a few hours even, have mercy, Almighty God, and let me still clutch greedily to my yellow heart this sweet treasure, this jewel beyond price, the dirty, stinking bit of withered old flesh which is my beautiful little life! (*He laughs with a sneering, vindictive self-loathing, staring inward at himself with contempt and hatred. Then abruptly he makes Hickey again the antagonist.*) You think you'll make me admit that to myself?

HICKEY—(*chuckling*) But you just did admit it, didn't you?

PARRITT—(*lifts his head from his hands to glare at Larry— jeeringly*) That's the stuff, Hickey! Show the old yellow faker up! He can't play dead on me like this! He's got to help me!

HICKEY—Yes, Larry, you've got to settle with him. I'm leaving you entirely in his hands. He'll do as good a job as I could at making you give up that old grandstand bluff.

LARRY—(*angrily*) I'll see the two of you in hell first!

ROCKY—(*calls excitedly from the end of the bar*) Jees, Harry's startin' across de street! He's goin' to fool yuh, Hickey, yuh bastard! (*He pauses, watching—then worriedly*) What de hell's he stoppin' for? Right in de middle of de street! Yuh'd tink he was paralyzed or somethin'! (*disgustedly*) Aw, he's quittin'! He's turned back! Jees, look at de old bastard travel! Here he comes! (*Hope passes the window outside the free-lunch counter in a shambling, panic-stricken run. He comes lurching blindly through the swinging doors and stumbles to the bar at Larry's right.*)

HOPE—Bejees, give me a drink quick! Scared me out of a year's growth! Bejees, that guy ought to be pinched! Bejees, it ain't safe to walk in the streets! Bejees, that ends me! Never again! Give me that bottle! (*He slops a glass full and drains it and pours another—to Rocky, who is regarding him with scorn— appealingly*) You seen it, didn't you, Rocky?

ROCKY—Seen what?

HOPE—That automobile, you dumb Wop! Feller driving it must be drunk or crazy. He'd run right over me if I hadn't jumped. (*ingratiatingly*) Come on, Larry, have a drink. Everybody have a drink. Have a cigar, Rocky. I know you hardly ever touch it.

ROCKY—(*resentfully*) Well, dis is de time I do touch it! (*pouring a drink*) I'm goin' to get stinko, see! And if yuh don't like it, yuh know what yuh can do! I gotta good mind to chuck my job, anyways. (*disgustedly*) Jees, Harry, I thought yuh had some guts! I was bettin' yuh'd make it and show dat four-flusher up. (*He nods at Hickey—then snorts*) Automobile, hell! Who d'yuh tink yuh're kiddin'? Dey wasn' no automobile! Yuh just quit cold!

HOPE—(*feebly*) Guess I ought to know! Bejees, it almost killed me!

HICKEY—(*comes to the bar between him and Larry, and puts a hand on his shoulder—kindly*) Now, now, Governor. Don't be foolish. You've faced the test and come through. You're rid of all that nagging dream stuff now. You know you can't believe it any more.

HOPE—(*appeals pleadingly to Larry*) Larry, you saw it, didn't you? Drink up! Have another! Have all you want! Bejees, we'll go on a grand old souse together! You saw that automobile, didn't you?

LARRY—(*compassionately, avoiding his eyes*) Sure, I saw it, Harry. You had a narrow escape. Be God, I thought you were a goner!

HICKEY—(*turns on him with a flash of sincere indignation*) What the hell's the matter with you, Larry? You know what I told you about the wrong kind of pity. Leave Harry alone! You'd think I was trying to harm him, the fool way you act! My oldest friend! What kind of a louse do you think I am? There isn't anything I wouldn't do for Harry, and he knows it! All I've wanted to do is fix it so he'll be finally at peace with himself for the rest of his days! And if you'll only wait until the final returns are in, you'll find that's exactly what I've accomplished! (*He turns to Hope and pats his shoulder—coaxingly*) Come now, Governor. What's the use of being stubborn, now when it's all over and dead? Give up that ghost automobile.

HOPE—(*beginning to collapse within himself—dully*) Yes, what's the use—now? All a lie! No automobile. But, bejees, something ran over me! Must have been myself, I guess. (*He forces a feeble smile—then wearily*) Guess I'll sit down. Feel all in. Like a corpse, bejees. (*He picks a bottle and glass from the bar and walks to the first table and slumps down in the chair, facing left-front. His shaking hand misjudges the distance and he sets the bottle on the table with a jar that rouses Hugo, who lifts his head from his arms and blinks at him through his thick spectacles. Hope speaks to him in a flat, dead voice.*) Hello, Hugo. Coming up for air? Stay passed out, that's the right dope. There ain't any cool willow trees—except you grow your own in a bottle. (*He pours a drink and gulps it down.*)

HUGO—(*with his silly giggle*) Hello, Harry, stupid proletarian monkey-face! I vill trink champagne beneath the villow—(*with a change to aristocratic fastidiousness*) But the slaves must ice it properly! (*with guttural rage*) Gottamned Hickey! Peddler pimp for nouveau-riche capitalism! Vhen I lead the jackass mob to the sack of Babylon, I vill make them hang him to a lamppost the first one!

HOPE—(*spiritlessly*) Good work. I'll help pull on the rope. Have a drink, Hugo.

HUGO—(*frightenedly*) No, thank you. I am too trunk now. I hear myself say crazy things. Do not listen, please. Larry vill tell you I haf never been so crazy trunk. I must sleep it off. (*He starts to put his head on his arms but stops and stares at Hope with growing uneasiness.*) Vhat's matter, Harry? You look funny. You look dead. Vhat's happened? I don't know you. Listen, I feel I am dying, too. Because I am so crazy trunk! It is very necessary I sleep. But I can't sleep here vith you. You look dead. (*He scrambles to his feet in a confused panic, turns his back on Hope and settles into the chair at the next table which faces left. He thrusts his head down on his arms like an ostrich hiding its head in the sand. He does not notice Parritt, nor Parritt him.*)

LARRY—(*to Hickey with bitter condemnation*) Another one who's begun to enjoy your peace!

HICKEY—Oh, I know it's tough on him right now, the same as it is on Harry. But that's only the first shock. I promise you they'll both come through all right.

LARRY—And you believe that! I see you do! You mad fool!

HICKEY—Of course, I believe it! I tell you I know from my own experience!

HOPE—(*spiritlessly*) Close that big clam of yours, Hickey. Bejees, you're a worse gabber than that nagging bitch, Bessie, was. (*He drinks his drink mechanically and pours another.*)

ROCKY—(*in amazement*) Jees, did yuh hear dat?

HOPE—(*dully*) What's wrong with this booze? There's no kick in it.

ROCKY—(*worriedly*) Jees, Larry, Hugo had it right. He does look like he'd croaked.

HICKEY—(*annoyed*) Don't be a damned fool! Give him time. He's coming along all right. (*He calls to Hope with a first trace of underlying uneasiness.*) You're all right, aren't you, Harry?

HOPE—(*dully*) I want to pass out like Hugo.

LARRY—(*turns to Hickey—with bitter anger*) It's the peace of death you've brought him.

HICKEY—(*for the first time loses his temper*) That's a lie! (*But he controls this instantly and grins.*) Well, well, you did manage to get a rise out of me that time. I think such a hell of a lot of Harry— (*impatiently*) You know that's damned foolishness. Look at me. I've been through it. Do I look dead? Just leave Harry alone and wait until the shock wears off and you'll see. He'll be a new man. Like I am. (*He calls to Hope coaxingly*) How's it coming, Governor? Beginning to feel free, aren't you? Relieved and not guilty any more?

HOPE—(*grumbles spiritlessly*) Bejees, you must have been monkeying with the booze, too, you interfering bastard! There's no life in it now. I want to get drunk and pass out. Let's all pass out. Who the hell cares?

HICKEY—(*lowering his voice—worriedly to Larry*) I admit I didn't think he'd be hit so hard. He's always been a happy-go-lucky slob. Like I was. Of course, it hit me hard, too. But only for a minute. Then I felt as if a ton of guilt had been lifted off my mind. I saw what had happened was the only possible way for the peace of all concerned.

LARRY—(*sharply*) What was it happened? Tell us that! And don't try to get out of it! I want a straight answer! (*vindictively*) I think it was something you drove someone else to do!

HICKEY—(*puzzled*) Someone else?

LARRY—(*accusingly*) What did your wife die of? You've kept that a deep secret, I notice—for some reason!

HICKEY—(*reproachfully*) You're not very considerate, Larry. But, if you insist on knowing now, there's no reason you shouldn't. It was a bullet through the head that killed Evelyn. (*There is a second's tense silence.*)

HOPE—(*dully*) Who the hell cares? To hell with her and that nagging old hag, Bessie.

ROCKY—Christ. You had de right dope, Larry.

LARRY—(*revengefully*) You drove your poor wife to suicide? I knew it! Be God, I don't blame her! I'd almost do as much myself to be rid of you! It's what you'd like to drive us all to— (*Abruptly he is ashamed of himself and pitying.*) I'm sorry, Hickey. I'm a rotten louse to throw that in your face.

HICKEY—(*quietly*) Oh, that's all right, Larry. But don't jump at conclusions. I didn't say poor Evelyn committed suicide. It's the last thing she'd ever have done, as long as I was alive for her to take care of and forgive. If you'd known her at all, you'd never get such a crazy suspicion. (*He pauses— then slowly*) No, I'm sorry to have to tell you my poor wife was killed. (*Larry stares at him with growing horror and shrinks back along the bar away from him. Parritt jerks his head up from his hands and looks around frightenedly, not at Hickey, but at Larry. Rocky's round eyes are popping. Hope stares dully at the table top. Hugo, his head hidden in his arms, gives no sign of life.*)

LARRY—(*shakenly*) Then she—was murdered.

PARRITT—(*springs to his feet—stammers defensively*) You're a liar, Larry! You must be crazy to say that to me! You know she's still alive! (*But no one pays any attention to him.*)

ROCKY—(*blurts out*) Moidered? Who done it?

LARRY—(*his eyes fixed with fascinated horror on Hickey— frightenedly*) Don't ask questions, you dumb Wop! It's none of our damned business! Leave Hickey alone!

HICKEY—(*smiles at him with affectionate amusement*) Still the old grandstand bluff, Larry? Or is it some more bum pity? (*He turns to Rocky—matter-of-factly*) The police don't know who killed her yet, Rocky. But I expect they will before very long. (*As if that finished the subject, he comes forward to Hope and sits beside him, with an arm around his shoulder—affectionately coaxing*) Coming along fine now, aren't you, Governor?

Getting over the first shock? Beginning to feel free from guilt and lying hopes and at peace with yourself?

HOPE—(*with a dull callousness*) Somebody croaked your Evelyn, eh? Bejees, my bets are on the iceman! But who the hell cares? Let's get drunk and pass out. (*He tosses down his drink with a lifeless, automatic movement—complainingly*) Bejees, what did you do to the booze, Hickey? There's no damned life left in it.

PARRITT—(*stammers, his eyes on Larry, whose eyes in turn remain fixed on Hickey*) Don't look like that, Larry! You've got to believe what I told you! It had nothing to do with her! It was just to get a few lousy dollars!

HUGO—(*suddenly raises his head from his arms and, looking straight in front of him, pounds on the table frightenedly with his small fists*) Don't be a fool! Buy me a trink! But no more vine! It is not properly iced! (*with guttural rage*) Gottamned stupid proletarian slaves! Buy me a trink or I vill have you shot! (*He collapses into abject begging.*) Please, for Gott's sake! I am not trunk enough! I cannot sleep! Life is a crazy monkey-face! Always there is blood beneath the villow trees! I hate it and I am afraid! (*He hides his face on his arms, sobbing muffledly.*) Please, I am crazy trunk! I say crazy things! For Gott's sake, do not listen to me! (*But no one pays any attention to him. Larry stands shrunk back against the bar. Rocky is leaning over it. They stare at Hickey. Parritt stands looking pleadingly at Larry.*)

HICKEY—(*gazes with worried kindliness at Hope*) You're beginning to worry me, Governor. Something's holding you up somewhere. I don't see why— You've faced the truth about yourself. You've done what you had to do to kill your nagging pipe dreams. Oh, I know it knocks you cold. But only for a minute. Then you see it was the only possible way to peace. And you feel happy. Like I did. That's what worries me about you, Governor. It's time you began to feel happy—

(*Curtain*)

ACT FOUR

SCENE—*Same as Act One—the back room with the curtain separating it from the section of the barroom with its single table at right of curtain, front. It is around half past one in the morning of the following day.*

The tables in the back room have a new arrangement. The one at left, front, before the window to the yard, is in the same position. So is the one at the right, rear, of it in the second row. But this table now has only one chair. This chair is at right of it, facing directly front. The two tables on either side of the door at rear are unchanged. But the table which was at center, front, has been pushed toward right so that it and the table at right, rear, of it in the second row, and the last table at right in the front row, are now jammed so closely together that they form one group.

Larry, Hugo and Parritt are at the table at left, front. Larry is at left of it, beside the window, facing front. Hugo sits at rear, facing front, his head on his arms in his habitual position, but he is not asleep. On Hugo's left is Parritt, his chair facing left, front. At right of table, an empty chair, facing left. Larry's chin is on his chest, his eyes fixed on the floor. He will not look at Parritt, who keeps staring at him with a sneering, pleading challenge.

Two bottles of whiskey are on each table, whiskey and chaser glasses, a pitcher of water.

The one chair by the table at right, rear, of them is vacant.

At the first table at right of center, Cora sits at left, front, of it, facing front. Around the rear of this table are four empty chairs. Opposite Cora, in a sixth chair, is Captain Lewis, also facing front. On his left, McGloin is facing front in a chair before the middle table of his group. At right, rear, of him, also at this table, General Wetjoen sits facing front. In back of this table are three empty chairs.

At right, rear, of Wetjoen, but beside the last table of the group, sits Willie. On Willie's left, at rear of table, is Hope. On Hope's left, at right, rear, of table, is Mosher. Finally, at right of table is Jimmy Tomorrow. All of the four sit facing front.

There is an atmosphere of oppressive stagnation in the room, and a quality of insensibility about all the people in this group at right. They are like wax figures, set stiffly on their chairs, carrying out

*mechanically the motions of getting drunk but sunk in a numb
stupor which is impervious to stimulation.*

*In the bar section, Joe is sprawled in the chair at right of table,
facing left. His head rolls forward in a sodden slumber. Rocky is
standing behind his chair, regarding him with dull hostility.
Rocky's face is set in an expression of tired, callous toughness. He
looks now like a minor Wop gangster.*

ROCKY—(*shakes Joe by the shoulder*) Come on, yuh damned
nigger! Beat it in de back room! It's after hours. (*But Joe
remains inert. Rocky gives up.*) Aw, to hell wid it. Let de dump
get pinched. I'm through wid dis lousy job, anyway! (*He
hears someone at rear and calls*) Who's dat? (*Chuck appears from
rear. He has been drinking heavily, but there is no lift to his jag;
his manner is grouchy and sullen. He has evidently been brawling.
His knuckles are raw and there is a mouse under one eye. He has
lost his straw hat, his tie is awry, and his blue suit is dirty. Rocky
eyes him indifferently.*) Been scrappin', huh? Started off on
your periodical, ain't yuh? (*For a second there is a gleam of
satisfaction in his eyes.*)

CHUCK—Yeah, ain't yuh glad? (*truculently*) What's it to
yuh?

ROCKY—Not a damn ting. But dis is someting to me. I'm
out on my feet holdin' down your job. Yuh said if I'd take
your day, yuh'd relieve me at six, and here it's half past one
A.M. Well, yuh're takin' over now, get me, no matter how
plastered yuh are!

CHUCK—Plastered, hell! I wisht I was. I've lapped up a
gallon, but it don't hit me right. And to hell wid de job. I'm
goin' to tell Harry I'm quittin'.

ROCKY—Yeah? Well, I'm quittin', too.

CHUCK—I've played sucker for dat crummy blonde long
enough, lettin' her kid me into woikin'. From now on I take
it easy.

ROCKY—I'm glad yuh're gettin' some sense.

CHUCK—And I hope yuh're gettin' some. What a prize sap
you been, tendin' bar when yuh got two good hustlers in
your stable!

ROCKY—Yeah, but I ain't no sap now. I'll loin dem, when
dey get back from Coney. (*sneeringly*) Jees, dat Cora sure

played you for a dope, feedin' yuh dat marriage-on-de-farm hop!

CHUCK—(*dully*) Yeah. Hickey got it right. A lousy pipe dream. It was her pulling sherry flips on me woke me up. All de way walkin' to de ferry, every ginmill we come to she'd drag me in to blow her. I got tinkin', Christ, what won't she want when she gets de ring on her finger and I'm hooked? So I tells her at de ferry, "Kiddo, yuh can go to Joisey, or to hell, but count me out."

ROCKY—She says it was her told you to go to hell, because yuh'd started hittin' de booze.

CHUCK—(*ignoring this*) I got tinkin', too, Jees, won't I look sweet wid a wife dat if yuh put all de guys she's stayed wid side by side, dey'd reach to Chicago. (*He sighs gloomily.*) Dat kind of dame, yuh can't trust 'em. De minute your back is toined, dey're cheatin' wid de iceman or someone. Hickey done me a favor, makin' me wake up. (*He pauses—then adds pathetically*) On'y it was fun, kinda, me and Cora kiddin' our-selves— (*Suddenly his face hardens with hatred.*) Where is dat son of a bitch, Hickey? I want one good sock at day guy— just one!—and de next buttin' in he'll do will be in de morgue! I'll take a chance on goin' to de Chair—!

ROCKY—(*starts—in a low warning voice*) Piano! Keep away from him, Chuck! He ain't here now, anyway. He went out to phone, he said. He wouldn't call from here. I got a hunch he's beat it. But if he does come back, yuh don't know him, if anyone asks yuh, get me? (*As Chuck looks at him with dull surprise he lowers his voice to a whisper.*) De Chair, maybe dat's where he's goin'. I don't know nuttin', see, but it looks like he croaked his wife.

CHUCK—(*with a flash of interest*) Yuh mean she really was cheatin' on him? Den I don't blame de guy—

ROCKY—Who's blamin' him? When a dame asks for it— But I don't know nuttin' about it, see?

CHUCK—Is any of de gang wise?

ROCKY—Larry is. And de boss ought to be. I tried to wise de rest of dem up to stay clear of him, but dey're all so licked, I don't know if dey got it. (*He pauses—vindictively*) I don't give a damn what he done to his wife, but if he gets de Hot Seat I won't go into no mournin'!

CHUCK—Me, neider!

ROCKY—Not after his trowin' it in my face I'm a pimp. What if I am? Why de hell not? And what he's done to Harry. Jees, de poor old slob is so licked he can't even get drunk. And all de gang. Dey're all licked. I couldn't help feelin' sorry for de poor bums when dey showed up tonight, one by one, lookin' like pooches wid deir tails between deir legs, dat everyone'd been kickin' till dey was too punch-drunk to feel it no more. Jimmy Tomorrow was de last. Schwartz, de copper, brung him in. Seen him sittin' on de dock on West Street, lookin' at de water and cryin'! Schwartz thought he was drunk and I let him tink it. But he was cold sober. He was tryin' to jump in and didn't have de noive, I figgered it. Noive! Jees, dere ain't enough guts left in de whole gang to battle a mosquito!

CHUCK—Aw, to hell wid 'em! Who cares? Gimme a drink. (*Rocky pushes the bottle toward him apathetically.*) I see you been hittin' de redeye, too.

ROCKY—Yeah. But it don't do no good. I can't get drunk right. (*Chuck drinks. Joe mumbles in his sleep. Chuck regards him resentfully.*) Dis doity dinge was able to get his snootful and pass out. Jees, even Hickey can't faze a nigger! Yuh'd tink he was fazed if yuh'd seen him come in. Stinko, and he pulled a gat and said he'd plug Hickey for insultin' him. Den he dropped it and begun to cry and said he wasn't a gamblin' man or a tough guy no more; he was yellow. He'd borrowed de gat to stick up someone, and den didn't have de guts. He got drunk panhandlin' drinks in nigger joints, I s'pose. I guess dey felt sorry for him.

CHUCK—He ain't got no business in de bar after hours. Why don't yuh chuck him out?

ROCKY—(*apathetically*) Aw, to hell wid it. Who cares?

CHUCK—(*lapsing into the same mood*) Yeah. I don't.

JOE—(*suddenly lunges to his feet dazedly—mumbles in humbled apology*) Scuse me, White Boys. Scuse me for livin'. I don't want to be where I's not wanted. (*He makes his way swayingly to the opening in the curtain at rear and tacks down to the middle table of the three at right, front. He feels his way around it to the table at its left and gets to the chair in back of Captain Lewis.*)

CHUCK—(*gets up—in a callous, brutal tone*) My pig's in de back room, ain't she? I wanna collect de dough I wouldn't take dis mornin', like a sucker, before she blows it. (*He goes rear.*)

ROCKY—(*getting up*) I'm comin', too. I'm trough woikin'. I ain't no lousy bartender. (*Chuck comes through the curtain and looks for Cora as Joe flops down in the chair in back of Captain Lewis.*)

JOE—(*taps Lewis on the shoulder—servilely apologetic*) If you objects to my sittin' here, Captain, just tell me and I pulls my freight.

LEWIS—No apology required, old chap. Anybody could tell you I should feel honored a bloody Kaffir would lower himself to sit beside me. (*Joe stares at him with sodden perplexity—then closes his eyes. Chuck comes forward to take the chair behind Cora's, as Rocky enters the back room and starts over toward Larry's table.*)

CHUCK—(*his voice hard*) I'm waitin', Baby. Dig!

CORA—(*with apathetic obedience*) Sure. I been expectin' yuh. I got it all ready. Here. (*She passes a small roll of bills she has in her hand over her shoulder, without looking at him. He takes it, glances at it suspiciously, then shoves it in his pocket without a word of acknowledgment. Cora speaks with a tired wonder at herself rather than resentment toward him.*) Jees, imagine me kiddin' myself I wanted to marry a drunken pimp.

CHUCK—Dat's nuttin', Baby. Imagine de sap I'da been, when I can get your dough just as easy widout it!

ROCKY—(*takes the chair on Parritt's left, facing Larry—dully*) Hello, Old Cemetery. (*Larry doesn't seem to hear. To Parritt*) Hello, Tightwad. You still around?

PARRITT—(*keeps his eyes on Larry—in a jeeringly challenging tone*) Ask Larry! He knows I'm here, all right, although he's pretending not to! He'd like to forget I'm alive! He's trying to kid himself with that grandstand philosopher stuff! But he knows he can't get away with it now! He kept himself locked in his room until a while ago, alone with a bottle of booze, but he couldn't make it work! He couldn't even get drunk! He had to come out! There must have been something there he was even more scared to face than he is Hickey and me! I guess he got looking at the fire escape and thinking how

handy it was, if he was really sick of life and only had the
nerve to die! (*He pauses sneeringly. Larry's face has tautened,
but he pretends he doesn't hear. Rocky pays no attention. His head
has sunk forward, and he stares at the table top, sunk in the same
stupor as the other occupants of the room. Parritt goes on, his tone
becoming more insistent.*) He's been thinking of me, too,
Rocky. Trying to figure a way to get out of helping me! He
doesn't want to be bothered understanding. But he does understand all right! He used to love her, too. So he thinks I
ought to take a hop off the fire escape! (*He pauses. Larry's
hands on the table have clinched into fists, as his nails dig into his
palms, but he remains silent. Parritt breaks and starts pleading.*)
For God's sake, Larry, can't you say something? Hickey's got
me all balled up. Thinking of what he must have done has
got me so I don't know any more what I did or why. I can't
go on like this! I've got to know what I ought to do—

LARRY—(*in a stifled tone*) God damn you! Are you trying
to make me your executioner?

PARRITT—(*starts frightenedly*) Execution? Then you do
think—?

LARRY—I don't think anything!

PARRITT—(*with forced jeering*) I suppose you think I ought
to die because I sold out a lot of loud-mouthed fakers, who
were cheating suckers with a phony pipe dream, and put
them where they ought to be, in jail? (*He forces a laugh.*)
Don't make me laugh! I ought to get a medal! What a
damned old sap you are! You must still believe in the Movement! (*He nudges Rocky with his elbow.*) Hickey's right about
him, isn't he, Rocky? An old no-good drunken tramp, as
dumb as he is, ought to take a hop off the fire escape!

ROCKY—(*dully*) Sure. Why don't he? Or you? Or me?
What de hell's de difference? Who cares? (*There is a faint stir
from all the crowd, as if this sentiment struck a responsive chord in
their numbed minds. They mumble almost in chorus as one voice,
like sleepers talking out of a dully irritating dream,* "The hell
with it!" "Who cares?" *Then the sodden silence descends again
on the room. Rocky looks from Parritt to Larry puzzledly. He mutters*) What am I doin' here wid youse two? I remember I had
someting on my mind to tell yuh. What—? Oh, I got it now.
(*He looks from one to the other of their oblivious faces with a*

strange, sly, calculating look—ingratiatingly) I was tinking how
you was bot' reg'lar guys. I tinks, ain't two guys like dem
saps to be hangin' round like a coupla stew bums and wastin'
demselves. Not dat I blame yuh for not woikin'. On'y suckers
woik. But dere's no percentage in bein' broke when yuh can
grab good jack for yourself and make someone else woik for
yuh, is dere? I mean, like I do. So I tinks, Dey're my pals and
I ought to wise up two good guys like dem to play my system, and not be lousy barflies, no good to demselves or nobody else. (*He addresses Parritt now—persuasively*) What yuh
tink, Parritt? Ain't I right? Sure, I am. So don't be a sucker,
see? Yuh ain't a bad-lookin' guy. Yuh could easy make some
gal who's a good hustler, an' start a stable. I'd help yuh and
wise yuh up to de inside dope on de game. (*He pauses inquir-
ingly. Parritt gives no sign of having heard him. Rocky asks impatiently*) Well, what about it? What if dey do call yuh a
pimp? What de hell do you care—any more'n I do.

    PARRITT—(*without looking at him—vindictively*) I'm
through with whores. I wish they were all in jail—or dead!

    ROCKY—(*ignores this—disappointedly*) So yuh won't touch
it, huh? Aw right, stay a bum! (*He turns to Larry.*) Jees, Larry,
he's sure one dumb boob, ain't he? Dead from de neck up!
He don't know a good ting when he sees it. (*oily, even persuasive again*) But how about you, Larry? You ain't dumb. So
why not, huh? Sure, yuh're old, but dat don't matter. All de
hustlers tink yuh're aces. Dey fall for yuh like yuh was deir
uncle or old man or someting. Dey'd like takin' care of yuh.
And de cops 'round here, dey like yuh, too. It'd be a pipe for
yuh, 'specially wid me to help yuh and wise yuh up. Yuh
wouldn't have to worry where de next drink's comin' from,
or wear doity clothes. (*hopefully*) Well, don't it look good to
yuh?

    LARRY—(*glances at him—for a moment he is stirred to sar-
donic pity*) No, it doesn't look good, Rocky. I mean, the peace
Hickey's brought you. It isn't contented enough, if you have
to make everyone else a pimp, too.

    ROCKY—(*stares at him stupidly—then pushes his chair back
and gets up, grumbling*) I'm a sap to waste time on yuh. A
stew bum is a stew bum and yuh can't change him. (*He turns
away—then turns back for an afterthought.*) Like I was sayin'

to Chuck, yuh better keep away from Hickey. If anyone asks yuh, yuh don't know nuttin', get me? Yuh never even hoid he had a wife. (*His face hardens.*) Jees, we all ought to git drunk and stage a celebration when dat bastard goes to de Chair.

LARRY—(*vindictively*) Be God, I'll celebrate with you and drink long life to him in hell! (*then guiltily and pityingly*) No! The poor mad devil— (*then with angry self-contempt*) Ah, pity again! The wrong kind! He'll welcome the Chair!

PARRITT—(*contemptuously*) Yes, what are you so damned scared of death for? I don't want your lousy pity.

ROCKY—Christ, I hope he don't come back, Larry. We don't know nuttin' now. We're on'y guessin', see? But if de bastard keeps on talkin'—

LARRY—(*grimly*) He'll come back. He'll keep on talking. He's got to. He's lost his confidence that the peace he's sold us is the real McCoy, and it's made him uneasy about his own. He'll have to prove to us— (*As he is speaking Hickey appears silently in the doorway at rear. He has lost his beaming salesman's grin. His manner is no longer self-assured. His expression is uneasy, baffled and resentful. It has the stubborn set of an obsessed determination. His eyes are on Larry as he comes in. As he speaks, there is a start from all the crowd, a shrinking away from him.*)

HICKEY—(*angrily*) That's a damned lie, Larry! I haven't lost confidence a damned bit! Why should I? (*boastfully*) By God, whenever I made up my mind to sell someone something I knew they ought to want, I've sold 'em! (*He suddenly looks confused—haltingly*) I mean— It isn't kind of you, Larry, to make that kind of crack when I've been doing my best to help—

ROCKY—(*moving away from him toward right—sharply*) Keep away from me! I don't know nuttin' about yuh, see? (*His tone is threatening but his manner as he turns his back and ducks quickly across to the bar entrance is that of one in flight. In the bar he comes forward and slumps in a chair at the table, facing front.*)

HICKEY—(*comes to the table at right, rear, of Larry's table and sits in the one chair there, facing front. He looks over the crowd at right, hopefully and then disappointedly. He speaks with a strained attempt at his old affectionate jollying manner.*) Well,

well! How are you coming along, everybody? Sorry I had to leave you for a while, but there was something I had to get finally settled. It's all fixed now.

HOPE—(*in the voice of one reiterating mechanically a hopeless complaint*) When are you going to do something about this booze, Hickey? Bejees, we all know you did something to take the life out of it. It's like drinking dishwater! We can't pass out! And you promised us peace. (*His group all join in in a dull, complaining chorus,* "We can't pass out! You promised us peace!")

HICKEY—(*bursts into resentful exasperation*) For God's sake, Harry, are you still harping on that damned nonsense! You've kept it up all afternoon and night! And you've got everybody else singing the same crazy tune! I've had about all I can stand— That's why I phoned— (*He controls himself.*) Excuse me, boys and girls. I don't mean that. I'm just worried about you, when you play dead on me like this. I was hoping by the time I got back you'd be like you ought to be! I thought you were deliberately holding back, while I was around, because you didn't want to give me the satisfaction of showing me I'd had the right dope. And I did have! I know from my own experience. (*exasperatedly*) But I've explained that a million times! And you've all done what you needed to do! By rights you should be contented now, without a single damned hope or lying dream left to torment you! But here you are, acting like a lot of stiffs cheating the undertaker! (*He looks around accusingly.*) I can't figure it—unless it's just your damned pigheaded stubbornness! (*He breaks—miserably*) Hell, you oughtn't to act this way with me! You're my old pals, the only friends I've got. You know the one thing I want is to see you all happy before I go— (*rousing himself to his old brisk, master-of-ceremonies manner*) And there's damned little time left now. I've made a date for two o'clock. We've got to get busy right away and find out what's wrong. (*There is a sodden silence. He goes on exasperatedly.*) Can't you appreciate what you've got, for God's sake? Don't you know you're free now to be yourselves, without having to feel remorse or guilt, or lie to yourselves about reforming tomorrow? Can't you see there is no tomorrow now? You're rid of it forever! You've killed it! You don't have to care a damn about anything any more! You've finally got the game of life licked, don't you see that? (*angrily exhorting*) Then why the hell don't you get pie-eyed and celebrate? Why don't you laugh and sing "Sweet Adeline"? (*with bitterly hurt accusation*) The only reason I can think of is, you're putting on this rotten half-dead act just to get back at me! Because you hate my guts! (*He breaks again.*) God, don't do that, gang! It makes me feel like hell to think you hate me. It makes me feel you suspect I must have hated you. But that's a lie! Oh, I know I used to hate everyone in the world who wasn't as rotten a bastard as I was! But that was when I was still living in hell—before I faced the truth and saw the one possible way to free poor Evelyn and give her the peace she'd always dreamed about. (*He pauses. Everyone in the group stirs with awakening dread and they all begin to grow tense on their chairs.*)

CHUCK—(*without looking at Hickey—with dull, resentful viciousness*) Aw, put a bag over it! To hell wid Evelyn! What if she was cheatin'? And who cares what yuh did to her? Dat's your funeral. We don't give a damn, see? (*There is a dull, resentful chorus of assent,* "We don't give a damn." *Chuck adds dully*) All we want outa you is keep de hell away from us and give us a rest. (*a muttered chorus of assent*)

HICKEY—(*as if he hadn't heard this—an obsessed look on his face*) The one possible way to make up to her for all I'd made her go through, and get her rid of me so I couldn't make her suffer any more, and she wouldn't have to forgive me again! I saw I couldn't do it by killing myself, like I wanted to for a long time. That would have been the last straw for her. She'd have died of a broken heart to think I could do that to her. She'd have blamed herself for it, too. Or I couldn't just run away from her. She'd have died of grief and humiliation if I'd done that to her. She'd have thought I'd stopped loving her. (*He adds with a strange impressive simplicity*) You see, Evelyn loved me. And I loved her. That was the trouble. It would have been easy to find a way out if she hadn't loved me so much. Or if I hadn't loved her. But as it was, there was only one possible way. (*He pauses—then adds simply*) I had to kill her. (*There is a second's dead silence as he finishes—then a tense indrawn breath like a gasp from the crowd, and a general shrinking movement.*)

LARRY—(*bursts out*) You mad fool, can't you keep your mouth shut! We may hate you for what you've done here this time, but we remember the old times, too, when you brought kindness and laughter with you instead of death! We don't want to know things that will make us help send you to the Chair!

PARRITT—(*with angry scorn*) Ah, shut up, you yellow faker! Can't you face anything? Wouldn't I deserve the Chair, too, if I'd— It's worse if you kill someone and they have to go on living. I'd be glad of the Chair! It'd wipe it out! It'd square me with myself!

HICKEY—(*disturbed—with a movement of repulsion*) I wish you'd get rid of that bastard, Larry. I can't have him pretending there's something in common between him and me. It's what's in your heart that counts. There was love in my heart, not hate.

PARRITT—(*glares at him in angry terror*) You're a liar! I don't hate her! I couldn't! And it had nothing to do with her, anyway! You ask Larry!

LARRY—(*grabs his shoulder and shakes him furiously*) God damn you, stop shoving your rotten soul in my lap! (*Parritt subsides, hiding his face in his hands and shuddering.*)

HICKEY—(*goes on quietly now*) Don't worry about the Chair, Larry. I know it's still hard for you not to be terrified by death, but when you've made peace with yourself, like I have, you won't give a damn. (*He addresses the group at right again—earnestly*) Listen, everybody. I've made up my mind the only way I can clear things up for you, so you'll realize how contented and carefree you ought to feel, now I've made you get rid of your pipe dreams, is to show you what a pipe dream did to me and Evelyn. I'm certain if I tell you about it from the beginning, you'll appreciate what I've done for you and why I did it, and how damned grateful you ought to be—instead of hating me. (*He begins eagerly in a strange running narrative manner.*) You see, even when we were kids, Evelyn and me—

HOPE—(*bursts out, pounding with his glass on the table*) No! Who the hell cares? We don't want to hear it. All we want is to pass out and get drunk and a little peace! (*They are all, except Larry and Parritt, seized by the same fit and pound with their glasses, even Hugo, and Rocky in the bar, and shout in chorus,* "Who the hell cares? We want to pass out!")

HICKEY—(*with an expression of wounded hurt*) All right, if that's the way you feel. I don't want to cram it down your throats. I don't need to tell anyone. I don't feel guilty. I'm only worried about you.

HOPE—What did you do to this booze? That's what we'd like to hear. Bejees, you done something. There's no life or kick in it now. (*He appeals mechanically to Jimmy Tomorrow.*) Ain't that right, Jimmy?

JIMMY—(*More than any of them, his face has a wax-figure blankness that makes it look embalmed. He answers in a precise, completely lifeless voice, but his reply is not to Harry's question, and he does not look at him or anyone else.*) Yes. Quite right. It was all a stupid lie—my nonsense about tomorrow. Naturally, they would never give me my position back. I would never dream of asking them. It would be hopeless. I didn't resign. I was fired for drunkenness. And that was years ago. I'm much worse now. And it was absurd of me to excuse my drunkenness by pretending it was my wife's adultery that ruined my life. As Hickey guessed, I was a drunkard before that. Long before. I discovered early in life that living frightened me when I was sober. I have forgotten why I married Marjorie. I can't even remember now if she was pretty. She was a blonde, I think, but I couldn't swear to it. I had some idea of wanting a home, perhaps. But, of course, I much preferred the nearest pub. Why Marjorie married me, God knows. It's impossible to believe she loved me. She soon found I much preferred drinking all night with my pals to being in bed with her. So, naturally, she was unfaithful. I didn't blame her. I really didn't care. I was glad to be free— even grateful to her, I think, for giving me such a good tragic excuse to drink as much as I damned well pleased. (*He stops like a mechanical doll that has run down. No one gives any sign of having heard him. There is a heavy silence. Then Rocky, at the table in the bar, turns grouchily as he hears a noise behind him. Two men come quietly forward. One, Moran, is middle-aged. The other, Lieb, is in his twenties. They look ordinary in every way, without anything distinctive to indicate what they do for a living.*)

ROCKY—(*grumpily*) In de back room if yuh wanta drink. (*Moran makes a peremptory sign to be quiet. All of a sudden Rocky senses they are detectives and springs up to face them, his expression freezing into a wary blankness. Moran pulls back his coat to show his badge.*)

MORAN—(*in a low voice*) Guy named Hickman in the back room?

ROCKY—Tink I know de names of all de guys—?

MORAN—Listen, you! This is murder. And don't be a sap. It was Hickman himself phoned in and said we'd find him here around two.

ROCKY—(*dully*) So dat's who he phoned to. (*He shrugs his shoulders.*) Aw right, if he asked for it. He's de fat guy sittin' alone. (*He slumps down in his chair again.*) And if yuh want a confession all yuh got to do is listen. He'll be tellin' all about it soon. Yuh can't stop de bastard talkin'. (*Moran gives him a curious look, then whispers to Lieb, who disappears rear and a moment later appears in the hall doorway of the back room. He spots Hickey and slides into a chair at the left of the doorway, cutting off escape by the hall. Moran goes back and stands in the opening in the curtain leading to the back room. He sees Hickey and stands watching him and listening.*)

HICKEY—(*suddenly bursts out*) I've got to tell you! Your being the way you are now gets my goat! It's all wrong! It puts things in my mind—about myself. It makes me think, if I got balled up about you, how do I know I wasn't balled up about myself? And that's plain damned foolishness. When you know the story of me and Evelyn, you'll see there wasn't any other possible way out of it, for her sake. Only I've got to start way back at the beginning or you won't understand. (*He starts his story, his tone again becoming musingly reminiscent.*) You see, even as a kid I was always restless. I had to keep on the go. You've heard the old saying, "Ministers' sons are sons of guns." Well, that was me, and then some. Home was like a jail. I didn't fall for the religious bunk. Listening to my old man whooping up hell fire and scaring those Hoosier suckers into shelling out their dough only handed me a laugh, although I had to hand it to him, the way he sold them nothing for something. I guess I take after him, and that's what made me a good salesman. Well, anyway, as I said, home was like jail, and so was school, and so was that damned hick town. The only place I liked was the pool rooms, where I could smoke Sweet Caporals, and mop up a couple of beers, thinking I was a hell-on-wheels sport. We had one hooker shop in town, and, of course, I liked that, too. Not that I hardly ever had entrance money. My old man was a tight old bastard. But I liked to sit around in the parlor and joke with the girls, and they liked me because I could kid 'em along and make 'em laugh. Well, you know what a small town is. Everyone got wise to me. They all said I was a no-good tramp. I didn't give a damn what they said. I hated everybody in the place. That is, except Evelyn. I loved Evelyn. Even as a kid. And Evelyn loved me. (*He pauses. No one moves or gives any sign except by the dread in their eyes that they have heard him. Except Parritt, who takes his hands from his face to look at Larry pleadingly.*)

PARRITT—I loved Mother, Larry! No matter what she did! I still do! Even though I know she wishes now I was dead! You believe that, don't you? Christ, why can't you say something?

HICKEY—(*too absorbed in his story now to notice this—goes on in a tone of fond, sentimental reminiscence*) Yes, sir, as far back as I can remember, Evelyn and I loved each other. She always stuck up for me. She wouldn't believe the gossip—or she'd pretend she didn't. No one could convince her I was no good. Evelyn was stubborn as all hell once she'd made up her mind. Even when I'd admit things and ask her forgiveness, she'd make excuses for me and defend me against myself. She'd kiss me and say she knew I didn't mean it and I wouldn't do it again. So I'd promise I wouldn't. I'd have to promise, she was so sweet and good, though I knew darned well— (*A touch of strange bitterness comes into his voice for a moment.*) No, sir, you couldn't stop Evelyn. Nothing on earth could shake her faith in me. Even I couldn't. She was a sucker for a pipe dream. (*then quickly*) Well, naturally, her family forbid her seeing me. They were one of the town's best, rich for that hick burg, owned the trolley line and lumber company. Strict Methodists, too. They hated my guts. But they couldn't stop Evelyn. She'd sneak notes to me and meet me on the sly. I was getting more restless. The town was getting more like a jail. I made up my mind to beat it. I knew exactly what I wanted to be by that time. I'd met a lot of drummers around the hotel and liked 'em. They were always telling jokes. They were sports. They kept moving. I liked their life. And I knew I could kid people and sell things. The hitch was how to get the railroad fare to the Big Town. I told Mollie Arlington my trouble. She was the madame of the cathouse. She liked me. She laughed and said, "Hell, I'll stake you, Kid! I'll bet on you. With that grin of yours and that line of bull, you ought to be able to sell skunks for good ratters!" (*He chuckles.*) Mollie was all right. She gave me confidence in myself. I paid her back, the first money I earned. Wrote her a kidding letter, I remember, saying I was peddling baby carriages and she and the girls had better take advantage of our bargain offer. (*He chuckles.*) But that's ahead of my story. The night before I left town, I had a date with Evelyn. I got all worked up, she was so pretty and sweet and good. I told her straight, "You better forget me, Evelyn, for your own sake. I'm no good and never will be. I'm not worthy to wipe your shoes." I broke down and cried. She just said, looking white and scared, "Why, Teddy? Don't you still love me?" I said, "Love you? God, Evelyn, I love you more than anything in the world. And I always will!" She said, "Then nothing else matters, Teddy, because nothing but death could stop my loving you. So I'll wait, and when you're ready you send for me and we'll be married. I know I can make you happy, Teddy, and once you're happy you won't want to do any of the bad things you've done any more." And I said, "Of course, I won't, Evelyn!" I meant it, too. I believed it. I loved her so much she could make me believe anything. (*He sighs. There is a suspended, waiting silence. Even the two detectives are drawn into it. Then Hope breaks into dully exasperated, brutally callous protest.*)

HOPE—Get it over, you long-winded bastard! You married her, and you caught her cheating with the iceman, and you croaked her, and who the hell cares? What's she to us? All we want is to pass out in peace, bejees! (*A chorus of dull, resentful protest from all the group. They mumble, like sleepers who curse a person who keeps awakening them,* "What's it to us? We want to pass out in peace!" *Hope drinks and they mechanically follow his example. He pours another and they do the same. He complains with a stupid, nagging insistence*) No life in the booze! No kick! Dishwater. Bejees, I'll never pass out!

HICKEY—(*goes on as if there had been no interruption*) So I beat it to the Big Town. I got a job easy, and it was a cinch for me to make good. I had the knack. It was like a game, sizing people up quick, spotting what their pet pipe dreams were, and then kidding 'em along that line, pretending you believed what they wanted to believe about themselves. Then they liked you, they trusted you, they wanted to buy something to show their gratitude. It was fun. But still, all the while I felt guilty, as if I had no right to be having such a good time away from Evelyn. In each letter I'd tell her how I missed her, but I'd keep warning her, too. I'd tell her all my faults, how I liked my booze every once in a while, and so on. But there was no shaking Evelyn's belief in me, or her dreams about the future. After each letter of hers, I'd be as full of faith as she was. So as soon as I got enough saved to start us off, I sent for her and we got married. Christ, wasn't I happy for a while! And wasn't she happy! I don't care what anyone says, I'll bet there never was two people who loved each other more than me and Evelyn. Not only then but always after, in spite of everything I did— (*He pauses—then sadly*) Well, it's all there, at the start, everything that happened afterwards. I never could learn to handle temptation. I'd want to reform and mean it. I'd promise Evelyn, and I'd promise myself, and I'd believe it. I'd tell her, it's the last time. And she'd say, "I know it's the last time, Teddy. You'll never do it again." That's what made it so hard. That's what made me feel such a rotten skunk—her always forgiving me. My playing around with women, for instance. It was only a harmless good time to me. Didn't mean anything. But I'd know what it meant to Evelyn. So I'd say to myself, never again. But you know how it is, traveling around. The damned hotel rooms. I'd get seeing things in the wall paper. I'd get bored as hell. Lonely and homesick. But at the same time sick of home. I'd feel free and I'd want to celebrate a little. I never drank on the job, so it had to be dames. Any tart. What I'd want was some tramp I could be myself with without being ashamed—someone I could tell a dirty joke to and she'd laugh.

CORA—(*with a dull, weary bitterness*) Jees, all de lousy jokes I've had to listen to and pretend was funny!

HICKEY—(*goes on obliviously*) Sometimes I'd try some joke I thought was a corker on Evelyn. She'd always make herself laugh. But I could tell she thought it was dirty, not funny. And Evelyn always knew about the tarts I'd been with when I came home from a trip. She'd kiss me and look in my eyes, and she'd know. I'd see in her eyes how she was trying not to know, and then telling herself even if it was true, he couldn't help it, they tempt him, and he's lonely, he hasn't got me, it's only his body, anyway, he doesn't love them, I'm the only one he loves. She was right, too. I never loved anyone else. Couldn't if I wanted to. (*He pauses.*) She forgave me even when it all had to come out in the open. You know how it is when you keep taking chances. You may be lucky for a long time, but you get nicked in the end. I picked up a nail from some tart in Altoona.

CORA—(*dully, without resentment*) Yeah. And she picked it up from some guy. It's all in de game. What de hell of it?

HICKEY—I had to do a lot of lying and stalling when I got home. It didn't do any good. The quack I went to got all my dough and then told me I was cured and I took his word. But I wasn't, and poor Evelyn— But she did her best to make me believe she fell for my lie about how traveling men get things from drinking cups on trains. Anyway, she forgave me. The same way she forgave me every time I'd turn up after a periodical drunk. You all know what I'd be like at the end of one. You've seen me. Like something lying in the gutter that no alley cat would lower itself to drag in—something they threw out of the D.T. ward in Bellevue along with the garbage, something that ought to be dead and isn't! (*His face is convulsed with self-loathing.*) Evelyn wouldn't have heard from me in a month or more. She'd have been waiting there alone, with the neighbors shaking their heads and feeling sorry for her out loud. That was before she got me to move to the outskirts, where there weren't any next-door neighbors. And then the door would open and in I'd stumble—looking like what I've said—into her home, where she kept everything so spotless and clean. And I'd sworn it would never happen again, and now I'd have to start swearing again this was the last time. I could see disgust having a battle in her eyes with love. Love always won. She'd make herself kiss me, as if nothing had happened, as if I'd just come home from a business trip. She'd never complain or bawl me out. (*He bursts out in a tone of anguish that has anger and hatred beneath it*) Christ, can you imagine what a guilty skunk she made me feel! If she'd only admitted once she didn't believe any more in her pipe dream that some day I'd behave! But she never would. Evelyn was stubborn as hell. Once she'd set her heart on anything, you couldn't shake her faith that it had to come true—tomorrow! It was the same old story, over and over, for years and years. It kept piling up, inside her and inside me. God, can you picture all I made her suffer, and all the guilt she made me feel, and how I hated myself! If she only hadn't been so damned good—if she'd been the same kind of wife I was a husband. God, I used to pray sometimes she'd— I'd even say to her, "Go on, why don't you, Evelyn? It'd serve me right. I wouldn't mind. I'd forgive you." Of course, I'd pretend I was kidding—the same way I used to joke here about her being in the hay with the iceman. She'd have been so hurt if I'd said it seriously. She'd have thought I'd stopped loving her. (*He pauses—then looking around at them*) I suppose you think I'm a liar, that no woman could have stood all she stood and still loved me so much—that it isn't human for any woman to be so pitying and forgiving. Well, I'm not lying, and if you'd ever seen her, you'd realize I wasn't. It was written all over her face, sweetness and love and pity and forgiveness. (*He reaches mechanically for the inside pocket of his coat.*) Wait! I'll show you. I always carry her picture. (*Suddenly he looks startled. He stares before him, his hand falling back— quietly*) No, I'm forgetting I tore it up—afterwards. I didn't need it any more. (*He pauses. The silence is like that in the room of a dying man where people hold their breath, waiting for him to die.*)

CORA—(*with a muffled sob*) Jees, Hickey! Jees! (*She shivers and puts her hands over her face.*)

PARRITT—(*to Larry in a low insistent tone*) I burnt up Mother's picture, Larry. Her eyes followed me all the time. They seemed to be wishing I was dead!

HICKEY—It kept piling up, like I've said. I got so I

thought of it all the time. I hated myself more and more, thinking of all the wrong I'd done to the sweetest woman in the world who loved me so much. I got so I'd curse myself for a lousy bastard every time I saw myself in the mirror. I felt such pity for her it drove me crazy. You wouldn't believe a guy like me, that's knocked around so much, could feel such pity. It got so every night I'd wind up hiding my face in her lap, bawling and begging her forgiveness. And, of course, she'd always comfort me and say, "Never mind, Teddy, I know you won't ever again." Christ, I loved her so, but I began to hate that pipe dream! I began to be afraid I was going bughouse, because sometimes I couldn't forgive her for forgiving me. I even caught myself hating her for making me hate myself so much. There's a limit to the guilt you can feel and the forgiveness and the pity you can take! You have to begin blaming someone else, too. I got so sometimes when she'd kiss me it was like she did it on purpose to humiliate me, as if she'd spit in my face! But all the time I saw how crazy and rotten of me that was, and it made me hate myself all the more. You'd never believe I could hate so much, a good-natured, happy-go-lucky slob like me. And as the time got nearer to when I was due to come here for my drunk around Harry's birthday, I got nearly crazy. I kept swearing to her every night that this time I really wouldn't, until I'd made it a real final test to myself—and to her. And she kept encouraging me and saying, "I can see you really mean it now, Teddy. I know you'll conquer it this time, and we'll be so happy, dear." When she'd say that and kiss me, I'd believe it, too. Then she'd go to bed, and I'd stay up alone because I couldn't sleep and I didn't want to disturb her, tossing and rolling around. I'd get so damned lonely. I'd get thinking how peaceful it was here, sitting around with the old gang, getting drunk and forgetting love, joking and laughing and singing and swapping lies. And finally I knew I'd have to come. And I knew if I came this time, it was the finish. I'd never have the guts to go back and be forgiven again, and that would break Evelyn's heart because to her it would mean I didn't love her any more. (*He pauses.*) That last night I'd driven myself crazy trying to figure some way out for her. I went in the bedroom. I was going to tell her it was the end.

But I couldn't do that to her. She was sound asleep. I thought, God, if she'd only never wake up, she'd never know! And then it came to me—the only possible way out, for her sake. I remembered I'd given her a gun for protection while I was away and it was in the bureau drawer. She'd never feel any pain, never wake up from her dream. So I—

HOPE—(*tries to ward this off by pounding with his glass on the table—with brutal, callous exasperation*) Give us a rest, for the love of Christ! Who the hell cares? We want to pass out in peace! (*They all, except Parritt and Larry, pound with their glasses and grumble in chorus:* "Who the hell cares? We want to pass out in peace!" *Moran, the detective, moves quietly from the entrance in the curtain across the back of the room to the table where his companion, Lieb, is sitting. Rocky notices his leaving and gets up from the table in the rear and goes back to stand and watch in the entrance. Moran exchanges a glance with Lieb, motioning him to get up. The latter does so. No one notices them. The clamor of banging glasses dies out as abruptly as it started. Hickey hasn't appeared to hear it.*)

HICKEY—(*simply*) So I killed her. (*There is a moment of dead silence. Even the detectives are caught in it and stand motionless.*)

PARRITT—(*suddenly gives up and relaxes limply in his chair— in a low voice in which there is a strange exhausted relief*) I may as well confess, Larry. There's no use lying any more. You know, anyway. I didn't give a damn about the money. It was because I hated her.

HICKEY—(*obliviously*) And then I saw I'd always known that was the only possible way to give her peace and free her from the misery of loving me. I saw it meant peace for me, too, knowing she was at peace. I felt as though a ton of guilt was lifted off my mind. I remember I stood by the bed and suddenly I had to laugh. I couldn't help it, and I knew Evelyn would forgive me. I remember I heard myself speaking to her, as if it was something I'd always wanted to say: "Well, you know what you can do with your pipe dream now, you damned bitch!" (*He stops with a horrified start, as if shocked out of a nightmare, as if he couldn't believe he heard what he had just said. He stammers*) No! I never—!

PARRITT—(*to Larry—sneeringly*) Yes, that's it! Her and the damned old Movement pipe dream! Eh, Larry?

HICKEY—(*bursts into frantic denial*) No! That's a lie! I never said—! Good God, I couldn't have said that! If I did, I'd gone insane! Why, I loved Evelyn better than anything in life! (*He appeals brokenly to the crowd.*) Boys, you're all my old pals! You've known old Hickey for years! You know I'd never— (*His eyes fix on Hope.*) You've known me longer than anyone, Harry. You know I must have been insane, don't you, Governor?

HOPE—(*at first with the same defensive callousness—without looking at him*) Who the hell cares? (*Then suddenly he looks at Hickey and there is an extraordinary change in his expression. His face lights up, as if he were grasping at some dawning hope in his mind. He speaks with a groping eagerness.*) Insane? You mean— you went really insane? (*At the tone of his voice, all the group at the tables by him start and stare at him as if they caught his thought. Then they all look at Hickey eagerly, too.*)

HICKEY—Yes! Or I couldn't have laughed! I couldn't have said that to her! (*Moran walks up behind him on one side, while the second detective, Lieb, closes in on him from the other.*)

MORAN—(*taps Hickey on the shoulder*) That's enough, Hickman. You know who we are. You're under arrest. (*He nods to Lieb, who slips a pair of handcuffs on Hickey's wrists. Hickey stares at them with stupid incomprehension. Moran takes his arm.*) Come along and spill your guts where we can get it on paper.

HICKEY—No, wait, Officer! You owe me a break! I phoned and made it easy for you, didn't I? Just a few minutes! (*to Hope—pleadingly*) You know I couldn't say that to Evelyn, don't you, Harry—unless—

HOPE—(*eagerly*) And you've been crazy ever since? Everything you've said and done here—

HICKEY—(*for a moment forgets his own obsession and his face takes on its familiar expression of affectionate amusement and he chuckles.*) Now, Governor! Up to your old tricks, eh? I see what you're driving at, but I can't let you get away with— (*Then, as Hope's expression turns to resentful callousness again and he looks away, he adds hastily with pleading desperation*) Yes,

Harry, of course, I've been out of my mind ever since! All the time I've been here! You saw I was insane, didn't you?

MORAN—(*with cynical disgust*) Can it! I've had enough of your act. Save it for the jury. (*addressing the crowd, sharply*) Listen, you guys. Don't fall for his lies. He's starting to get foxy now and thinks he'll plead insanity. But he can't get away with it. (*The crowd at the grouped tables are grasping at hope now. They glare at him resentfully.*)

HOPE—(*begins to bristle in his old-time manner*) Bejees, you dumb dick, you've got a crust trying to tell us about Hickey! We've known him for years, and every one of us noticed he was nutty the minute he showed up here! Bejees, if you'd heard all the crazy bull he was pulling about bringing us peace—like a bughouse preacher escaped from an asylum! If you'd seen all the damned-fool things he made us do! We only did them because— (*He hesitates—then defiantly*) Because we hoped he'd come out of it if we kidded him along and humored him. (*He looks around at the others.*) Ain't that right, fellers? (*They burst into a chorus of eager assent: "Yes, Harry!" "That's it, Harry!" "That's why!" "We knew he was crazy!" "Just to humor him!"*)

MORAN—A fine bunch of rats! Covering up for a dirty, cold-blooded murderer.

HOPE—(*stung into recovering all his old fuming truculence*) Is that so? Bejees, you know the old story, when Saint Patrick drove the snakes out of Ireland they swam to New York and joined the police force! Ha! (*He cackles insultingly.*) Bejees, we can believe it now when we look at you, can't we, fellers? (*They all growl assent, glowering defiantly at Moran. Moran glares at them, looking as if he'd like to forget his prisoner and start cleaning out the place. Hope goes on pugnaciously.*) You stand up for your rights, bejees, Hickey! Don't let this smart-aleck dick get funny with you. If he pulls any rubber-hose tricks, you let me know! I've still got friends at the Hall! Bejees, I'll have him back in uniform pounding a beat where the only graft he'll get will be stealing tin cans from the goats!

MORAN—(*furiously*) Listen, you cockeyed old bum, for a plugged nickel I'd— (*controlling himself, turns to Hickey, who is oblivious to all this, and yanks his arm*) Come on, you!

HICKEY—(*with a strange mad earnestness*) Oh, I want to

go, Officer. I can hardly wait now. I should have phoned you from the house right afterwards. It was a waste of time coming here. I've got to explain to Evelyn. But I know she's forgiven me. She knows I was insane. You've got me all wrong, Officer. I want to go to the Chair.

MORAN—Crap!

HICKEY—(*exasperatedly*) God, you're a dumb dick! Do you suppose I give a damn about life now? Why, you bonehead, I haven't got a single damned lying hope or pipe dream left!

MORAN—(*jerks him around to face the door to the hall*) Get a move on!

HICKEY—(*as they start walking toward rear—insistently*) All I want you to see is I was out of my mind afterwards, when I laughed at her! I was a raving rotten lunatic or I couldn't have said— Why, Evelyn was the only thing on God's earth I ever loved! I'd have killed myself before I'd ever have hurt her! (*They disappear in the hall. Hickey's voice keeps on protesting.*)

HOPE—(*calls after him*) Don't worry, Hickey! They can't give you the Chair! We'll testify you was crazy! Won't we, fellers? (*They all assent. Two or three echo Hope's "Don't worry, Hickey." Then from the hall comes the slam of the street door. Hope's face falls—with genuine sorrow*) He's gone. Poor crazy son of a bitch! (*All the group around him are sad and sympathetic, too. Hope reaches for his drink.*) Bejees, I need a drink. (*They grab their glasses. Hope says hopefully*) Bejees, maybe it'll have the old kick, now he's gone. (*He drinks and they follow suit.*)

ROCKY—(*comes forward from where he has stood in the bar entrance—hopefully*) Yeah, Boss, maybe we can get drunk now. (*He sits in the chair by Chuck and pours a drink and tosses it down. Then they all sit still, waiting for the effect, as if this drink were a crucial test, so absorbed in hopeful expectancy that they remain oblivious to what happens at Larry's table.*)

LARRY—(*his eyes full of pain and pity—in a whisper, aloud to himself*) May the Chair bring him peace at last, the poor tortured bastard!

PARRITT—(*leans toward him—in a strange low insistent voice*) Yes, but he isn't the only one who needs peace, Larry.

I can't feel sorry for him. He's lucky. He's through, now. It's all decided for him. I wish it was decided for me. I've never been any good at deciding things. Even about selling out, it was the tart the detective agency got after me who put it in my mind. You remember what Mother's like, Larry. She makes all the decisions. She's always decided what I must do. She doesn't like anyone to be free but herself. (*He pauses, as if waiting for comment, but Larry ignores him.*) I suppose you think I ought to have made those dicks take me away with Hickey. But how could I prove it, Larry? They'd think I was nutty. Because she's still alive. You're the only one who can understand how guilty I am. Because you know her and what I've done to her. You know I'm really much guiltier than he is. You know what I did is a much worse murder. Because she is dead and yet she has to live. For a while. But she can't live long in jail. She loves freedom too much. And I can't kid myself like Hickey, that she's at peace. As long as she lives, she'll never be able to forget what I've done to her even in her sleep. She'll never have a second's peace. (*He pauses—then bursts out*) Jesus, Larry, can't you say something? (*Larry is at the breaking point. Parritt goes on.*) And I'm not putting up any bluff, either, that I was crazy afterwards when I laughed to myself and thought, "You know what you can do with your freedom pipe dream now, don't you, you damned old bitch!"

LARRY—(*snaps and turns on him, his face convulsed with detestation. His quivering voice has a condemning command in it.*) Go! Get the hell out of life, God damn you, before I choke it out of you! Go up—!

PARRITT—(*His manner is at once transformed. He seems suddenly at peace with himself. He speaks simply and gratefully.*) Thanks, Larry. I just wanted to be sure. I can see now it's the only possible way I can ever get free from her. I guess I've really known that all my life. (*He pauses—then with a derisive smile*) It ought to comfort Mother a little, too. It'll give her the chance to play the great incorruptible Mother of the Revolution, whose only child is the Proletariat. She'll be able to say: "Justice is done! So may all traitors die!" She'll be able to say: "I am glad he's dead! Long live the Revolution!" (*He adds with a final implacable jeer*) You know her, Larry! Always a ham!

LARRY—(*pleads distractedly*) Go, for the love of Christ, you mad tortured bastard, for your own sake! (*Hugo is roused by this. He lifts his head and peers uncomprehendingly at Larry. Neither Larry nor Parritt notices him.*)

PARRITT—(*stares at Larry. His face begins to crumble as if he were going to break down and sob. He turns his head away, but reaches out fumblingly and pats Larry's arm and stammers*) Jesus, Larry, thanks. That's kind. I knew you were the only one who could understand my side of it. (*He gets to his feet and turns toward the door.*)

HUGO—(*looks at Parritt and bursts into his silly giggle*) Hello, leedle Don, leedle monkey-face! Don't be a fool! Buy me a trink!

PARRITT—(*puts on an act of dramatic bravado—forcing a grin*) Sure, I will, Hugo! Tomorrow! Beneath the willow trees! (*He walks to the door with a careless swagger and disappears in the hall. From now on, Larry waits, listening for the sound he knows is coming from the backyard outside the window, but trying not to listen, in an agony of horror and cracking nerve.*)

HUGO—(*stares after Parritt stupidly*) Stupid fool! Hickey make you crazy, too. (*He turns to the oblivious Larry—with a timid eagerness*) I'm glad, Larry, they take that crazy Hickey avay to asylum. He makes me have bad dreams. He makes me tell lies about myself. He makes me want to spit on all I have ever dreamed. Yes, I am glad they take him to asylum. I don't feel I am dying now. He vas selling death to me, that crazy salesman. I think I have a trink now, Larry. (*He pours a drink and gulps it down.*)

HOPE—(*jubilantly*) Bejees, fellers, I'm feeling the old kick, or I'm a liar! It's putting life back in me! Bejees, if all I've lapped up begins to hit me, I'll be paralyzed before I know it! It was Hickey kept it from— Bejees, I know that sounds crazy, but he was crazy, and he'd got all of us as bughouse as he was. Bejees, it does queer things to you, having to listen day and night to a lunatic's pipe dreams—pretending you believe them, to kid him along and doing any crazy thing he wants to humor him. It's dangerous, too. Look at me pre-

tending to start for a walk just to keep him quiet. I knew
damned well it wasn't the right day for it. The sun was broil-
ing and the streets full of automobiles. Bejees, I could feel
myself getting sunstroke, and an automobile damn near ran
over me. (*He appeals to Rocky, afraid of the result, but daring
it.*) Ask Rocky. He was watching. Didn't it, Rocky?

ROCKY—(*a bit tipsily*) What's dat, Boss? Jees, all de booze
I've mopped up is beginning to get to me. (*earnestly*) De
automobile, Boss? Sure, I seen it! Just missed yuh! I thought
yuh was a goner. (*He pauses—then looks around at the others,
and assumes the old kidding tone of the inmates, but hesitantly,
as if still a little afraid.*) On de woid of a honest bartender!
(*He tries a wink at the others. They all respond with smiles that
are still a little forced and uneasy.*)

HOPE—(*flashes him a suspicious glance. Then he understands—with his natural testy manner*) You're a bartender, all
right. No one can say different. (*Rocky looks grateful.*) But,
bejees, don't pull that honest junk! You and Chuck ought to
have cards in the Burglars' Union! (*This time there is an eager
laugh from the group. Hope is delighted.*) Bejees, it's good to
hear someone laugh again! All the time that bas—poor old
Hickey was here, I didn't have the heart— Bejees, I'm getting drunk and glad of it! (*He cackles and reaches for the bottle.*) Come on, fellers. It's on the house. (*They pour drinks.
They begin rapidly to get drunk now. Hope becomes sentimental.*)
Poor old Hickey! We mustn't hold him responsible for anything he's done. We'll forget that and only remember him
the way we've always known him before—the kindest, biggest-hearted guy ever wore shoe leather. (*They all chorus
hearty sentimental assent:* "That's right, Harry!" "That's all!"
"Finest fellow!" "Best scout!" *etc. Hope goes on.*) Good luck
to him in Matteawan! Come on, bottoms up! (*They all
drink. At the table by the window Larry's hands grip the edge of
the table. Unconsciously his head is inclined toward the window
as he listens.*)

LARRY—(*cannot hold back an anguished exclamation*) Christ!
Why don't he—!

HUGO—(*beginning to be drunk again—peers at him*) Vhy
don't he what? Don't be a fool! Hickey's gone. He vas crazy.

Have a trink. (*then as he receives no reply—with vague uneasiness*) What's matter with you, Larry? You look funny. What you listen to out in backyard, Larry? (*Cora begins to talk in the group at right.*)

CORA—(*tipsily*) Well, I thank Gawd now me and Chuck did all we could to humor de poor nut. Jees, imagine us goin' off like we really meant to git married, when we ain't even picked out a farm yet!

CHUCK—(*eagerly*) Sure ting, Baby. We kidded him we was serious.

JIMMY—(*confidently—with a gentle, drunken unction*) I may as well say I detected his condition almost at once. All that talk of his about tomorrow, for example. He had the fixed idea of the insane. It only makes them worse to cross them.

WILLIE—(*eagerly*) Same with me, Jimmy. Only I spent the day in the park. I wasn't such a damned fool as to—

LEWIS—(*getting jauntily drunk*) Picture my predicament if I *had* gone to the Consulate. The pal of mine there is a humorous blighter. He would have got me a job out of pure spite. So I strolled about and finally came to roost in the park. (*He grins with affectionate kidding at Wetjoen.*) And lo and behold, who was on the neighboring bench but my old battlefield companion, the Boer that walks like a man—who, if the British Government had taken my advice, would have been removed from his fetid kraal on the veldt straight to the baboon's cage at the London Zoo, and little children would now be asking their nurses: "Tell me, Nana, is that the Boer General, the one with the blue behind?" (*They all laugh uproariously. Lewis leans over and slaps Wetjoen affectionately on the knee.*) No offense meant, Piet, old chap.

WETJOEN—(*beaming at him*) No offense taken, you tamned Limey! (*Wetjoen goes on—grinningly*) About a job, I felt the same as you, Cecil. (*At the table by the window Hugo speaks to Larry again.*)

HUGO—(*with uneasy insistence*) What's matter, Larry? You look scared. What you listen for out there? (*But Larry doesn't hear, and Joe begins talking in the group at right.*)

JOE—(*with drunken self-assurance*) No, suh, I wasn't fool enough to git in no crap game. Not while Hickey's around.

Crazy people puts a jinx on you. (*McGloin is now heard. He is leaning across in front of Wetjoen to talk to Ed Mosher on Hope's left.*)

MCGLOIN—(*with drunken earnestness*) I know you saw how it was, Ed. There was no good trying to explain to a crazy guy, but it ain't the right time. You know how getting reinstated is.

MOSHER—(*decidedly*) Sure, Mac. The same way with the circus. The boys tell me the rubes are wasting all their money buying food and times never was so hard. And I never was one to cheat for chicken feed.

HOPE—(*looks around him in an ecstasy of bleery sentimental content*) Bejees, I'm cockeyed! Bejees, you're all cockeyed! Bejees, we're all all right! Let's have another! (*They pour out drinks. At the table by the window Larry has unconsciously shut his eyes as he listens. Hugo is peering at him frightenedly now.*)

HUGO—(*reiterates stupidly*) What's matter, Larry? Why you keep eyes shut? You look dead. What you listen for in backyard? (*Then, as Larry doesn't open his eyes or answer, he gets up hastily and moves away from the table, mumbling with frightened anger*) Crazy fool! You vas crazy like Hickey! You give me bad dreams, too. (*He shrinks quickly past the table where Hickey had sat to the rear of the group at right.*)

ROCKY—(*greets him with boisterous affection*) Hello, dere, Hugo! Welcome to de party!

HOPE—Yes, bejees, Hugo! Sit down! Have a drink! Have ten drinks, bejees!

HUGO—(*forgetting Larry and bad dreams, gives his familiar giggle*) Hello, leedle Harry! Hello, nice, leedle, funny monkey-faces! (*warming up, changes abruptly to his usual declamatory denunciation*) Gottamned stupid bourgeois! Soon comes the Day of Judgment! (*They make derisive noises and tell him to sit down. He changes again, giggling good-naturedly, and sits at rear of the middle table.*) Give me ten trinks, Harry. Don't be a fool. (*They laugh. Rocky shoves a glass and bottle at him. The sound of Margie's and Pearl's voices is heard from the hall, drunkenly shrill. All of the group turn toward the door as the two appear. They are drunk and look blowsy and disheveled. Their manner as they enter hardens into a brazen defensive truculence.*)

MARGIE—(*stridently*) Gangway for two good whores!

PEARL—Yeah! And we want a drink quick!

MARGIE—(*glaring at Rocky*) Shake de lead outa your pants, Pimp! A little soivice!

ROCKY—(*his black bullet eyes sentimental, his round Wop face grinning welcome*) Well, look who's here! (*He goes to them unsteadily, opening his arms.*) Hello, dere, Sweethearts! Jees, I was beginnin' to worry about yuh, honest! (*He tries to embrace them. They push his arms away, regarding him with amazed suspicion.*)

PEARL—What kind of a gag is dis?

HOPE—(*calls to them effusively*) Come on and join the party, you broads! Bejees, I'm glad to see you! (*The girls exchange a bewildered glance, taking in the party and the changed atmosphere.*)

MARGIE—Jees, what's come off here?

PEARL—Where's dat louse, Hickey?

ROCKY—De cops got him. He'd gone crazy and croaked his wife. (*The girls exclaim, "Jees!" But there is more relief than horror in it. Rocky goes on.*) He'll get Matteawan. He ain't responsible. What he's pulled don't mean nuttin'. So forget dat whore stuff. I'll knock de block off anyone calls you whores! I'll fill de bastard full of lead! Yuh're tarts, and what de hell of it? Yuh're as good as anyone! So forget it, see? (*They let him get his arms around them now. He gives them a hug. All the truculence leaves their faces. They smile and exchange maternally amused glances.*)

MARGIE—(*with a wink*) Our little bartender, ain't he, Poil?

PEARL—Yeah, and a cute little Ginny at dat! (*They laugh.*)

MARGIE—And is he stinko!

PEARL—Stinko is right. But he ain't got nuttin' on us. Jees, Rocky, did we have a big time at Coney!

HOPE—Bejees, sit down, you dumb broads! Welcome home! Have a drink! Have ten drinks, bejees! (*They take the empty chairs on Chuck's left, warmly welcomed by all. Rocky stands in back of them, a hand on each of their shoulders, grinning with proud proprietorship. Hope beams over and under his crooked spectacles with the air of a host whose party is a huge success, and rambles on happily.*) Bejees, this is all right! We'll make this my birthday party, and forget the other. We'll get paralyzed! But who's missing? Where's the Old Wise Guy? Where's Larry?

ROCKY—Over by de window, Boss. Jees, he's got his eyes shut. De old bastard's asleep. (*They turn to look. Rocky dismisses him.*) Aw, to hell wid him. Let's have a drink. (*They turn away and forget him.*)

LARRY—(*torturedly arguing to himself in a shaken whisper*) It's the only way out for him! For the peace of all concerned, as Hickey said! (*snapping*) God damn his yellow soul, if he doesn't soon, I'll go up and throw him off!—like a dog with its guts ripped out you'd put out of misery! (*He half rises from his chair just as from outside the window comes the sound of something hurtling down, followed by a muffled, crunching thud. Larry gasps and drops back on his chair, shuddering, hiding his face in his hands. The group at right hear it but are too preoccupied with drinks to pay much attention.*)

HOPE—(*wonderingly*) What the hell was that?

ROCKY—Aw, nuttin'. Someting fell off de fire escape. A mattress, I'll bet. Some of dese bums been sleepin' on de fire escapes.

HOPE—(*his interest diverted by this excuse to beef—testily*) They've got to cut it out! Bejees, this ain't a fresh-air cure. Mattresses cost money.

MOSHER—Now don't start crabbing at the party, Harry. Let's drink up. (*Hope forgets it and grabs his glass, and they all drink.*)

LARRY—(*in a whisper of horrified pity*) Poor devil! (*A long-forgotten faith returns to him for a moment and he mumbles*) God rest his soul in peace. (*He opens his eyes—with a bitter self-derision*) Ah, the damned pity—the wrong kind, as Hickey said! Be God, there's no hope! I'll never be a success in the grandstand—or anywhere else! Life is too much for me! I'll be a weak fool looking with pity at the two sides of everything till the day I die! (*with an intense bitter sincerity*) May that day come soon! (*He pauses startledly, surprised at himself—then with a sardonic grin*) Be God, I'm the only real convert to death Hickey made here. From the bottom of my coward's heart I mean that now!

HOPE—(*calls effusively*) Hey there, Larry! Come over and get paralyzed! What the hell you doing, sitting there? (*Then as Larry doesn't reply he immediately forgets him and turns to the party. They are all very drunk now, just a few drinks ahead of the passing-out stage, and hilariously happy about it.*) Bejees, let's sing! Let's celebrate! It's my birthday party! Bejees, I'm oreyeyed! I want to sing! (*He starts the chorus of "She's the Sunshine of Paradise Alley," and instantly they all burst into song. But not the same song. Each starts the chorus of his or her choice. Jimmy Tomorrow's is "A Wee Dock and Doris"; Ed Mosher's, "Break the News to Mother"; Willie Oban's, the Sailor Lad ditty he sang in Act One; General Wetjoen's, "Waiting at the Church"; McGloin's, "Tammany"; Captain Lewis's, "The Old Kent Road"; Joe's, "All I Got Was Sympathy"; Pearl's and Margie's, "Everybody's Doing It"; Rocky's, "You Great Big Beautiful Doll"; Chuck's, "The Curse of an Aching Heart"; Cora's, "The Oceana Roll"; while Hugo jumps to his feet and, pounding on the table with his fist, bellows in his guttural basso the French Revolutionary "Carmagnole." A weird cacophony results from this mixture and they stop singing to roar with laughter. All but Hugo, who keeps on with drunken fervor.*)

HUGO—Dansons la Carmagnole!
　　　　　Vive le son! Vive le son!
　　　　　Dansons la Carmagnole!
　　　　　Vive le son des canons!

(*They all turn on him and howl him down with amused derision. He stops singing to denounce them in his most fiery style.*) Capitalist svine! Stupid bourgeois monkeys! (*He declaims*) "The days grow hot, O Babylon!" (*They all take it up and shout in enthusiastic jeering chorus*) " 'Tis cool beneath thy willow trees!" (*They pound their glasses on the table, roaring with laughter, and Hugo giggles with them. In his chair by the window, Larry stares in front of him, oblivious to their racket.*)

(*Curtain*)

LONG DAY'S JOURNEY
INTO NIGHT

For Carlotta, on our 12th Wedding Anniversary

*Dearest: I give you the original script of this play
of old sorrow, written in tears and blood. A sadly
inappropriate gift, it would seem, for a day
celebrating happiness. But you will understand. I
mean it as a tribute to your love and tenderness which
gave me the faith in love that enabled me to
face my dead at last and write this play—write it
with deep pity and understanding and forgiveness for
all the four haunted Tyrones.*

*These twelve years, Beloved One, have been a
Journey into Light—into love. You know my gratitude.
And my love!*

GENE

*Tao House
July 22, 1941.*

CHARACTERS

JAMES TYRONE

MARY CAVAN TYRONE, *his wife*

JAMES TYRONE, JR., *their elder son*

EDMUND TYRONE, *their younger son*

CATHLEEN, *second girl*

SCENES

ACT 1

Living room of the Tyrones' summer home 8:30 A.M. of a day in August, 1912

ACT 2

SCENE 1: The same, around 12:45
SCENE 2: The same, about a half hour later

ACT 3

The same, around 6:30 that evening

ACT 4

The same, around midnight

Long Day's Journey into Night

ACT ONE

Scene—*Living room of James Tyrone's summer home on a morning in August, 1912.*

At rear are two double doorways with portieres. The one at right leads into a front parlor with the formally arranged, set appearance of a room rarely occupied. The other opens on a dark, windowless back parlor, never used except as a passage from living room to dining room. Against the wall between the doorways is a small bookcase, with a picture of Shakespeare above it, containing novels by Balzac, Zola, Stendhal, philosophical and sociological works by Schopenhauer, Nietzsche, Marx, Engels, Kropotkin, Max Stirner, plays by Ibsen, Shaw, Strindberg, poetry by Swinburne, Rossetti, Wilde, Ernest Dowson, Kipling, etc.

In the right wall, rear, is a screen door leading out on the porch which extends halfway around the house. Farther forward, a series of three windows looks over the front lawn to the harbor and the avenue that runs along the water front. A small wicker table and an ordinary oak desk are against the wall, flanking the windows.

In the left wall, a similar series of windows looks out on the grounds in back of the house. Beneath them is a wicker couch with cushions, its head toward rear. Farther back is a large, glassed-in bookcase with sets of Dumas, Victor Hugo, Charles Lever, three sets of Shakespeare, The World's Best Literature in fifty large volumes, Hume's History of England, Thiers' History of the Consulate and Empire, Smollett's History of England, Gibbon's Roman Empire and miscellaneous volumes of old plays, poetry, and several histories of Ireland. The astonishing thing about these sets is that all the volumes have the look of having been read and reread.

The hardwood floor is nearly covered by a rug, inoffensive in design and color. At center is a round table with a green shaded reading lamp, the cord plugged in one of the four sockets in the chandelier above. Around the table within reading-light range are four chairs, three of them wicker armchairs, the fourth (at right front of table) a varnished oak rocker with leather bottom.

It is around 8.30. Sunshine comes through the windows at right. As the curtain rises, the family have just finished breakfast.

Mary Tyrone and her husband enter together from the back parlor, coming from the dining room.

Mary is fifty-four, about medium height. She still has a young, graceful figure, a trifle plump, but showing little evidence of middle-aged waist and hips, although she is not tightly corseted. Her face is distinctly Irish in type. It must once have been extremely pretty, and is still striking. It does not match her healthy figure but is thin and pale with the bone structure prominent. Her nose is long and straight, her mouth wide with full, sensitive lips. She uses no rouge or any sort of make-up. Her high forehead is framed by thick, pure white hair. Accentuated by her pallor and white hair, her dark brown eyes appear black. They are unusually large and beautiful, with black brows and long curling lashes.

What strikes one immediately is her extreme nervousness. Her hands are never still. They were once beautiful hands, with long, tapering fingers, but rheumatism has knotted the joints and warped the fingers, so that now they have an ugly crippled look. One avoids looking at them, the more so because one is conscious she is sensitive about their appearance and humiliated by her inability to control the nervousness which draws attention to them.

She is dressed simply but with a sure sense of what becomes her. Her hair is arranged with fastidious care. Her voice is soft and attractive. When she is merry, there is a touch of Irish lilt in it.

Her most appealing quality is the simple, unaffected charm of a shy convent-girl youthfulness she has never lost—an innate unworldly innocence.

James Tyrone is sixty-five but looks ten years younger. About five feet eight, broad-shouldered and deep-chested, he seems taller and slenderer because of his bearing, which has a soldierly quality of head up, chest out, stomach in, shoulders squared. His face has begun to break down but he is still remarkably good looking—a big, finely shaped head, a handsome profile, deep-set light-brown eyes. His grey hair is thin with a bald spot like a monk's tonsure.

The stamp of his profession is unmistakably on him. Not that he indulges in any of the deliberate temperamental posturings of the stage star. He is by nature and preference a simple, unpretentious man, whose inclinations are still close to his humble beginnings and his Irish farmer forebears. But the actor shows in all his unconscious habits of speech, movement and gesture. These have the quality of belonging to a studied technique. His voice is remarkably fine, resonant and flexible, and he takes great pride in it.

His clothes, assuredly, do not costume any romantic part. He wears a threadbare, ready-made, grey sack suit and shineless black shoes, a collar-less shirt with a thick white handkerchief knotted loosely around his throat. There is nothing picturesquely careless about this get-up. It is commonplace shabby. He believes in wearing his clothes to the limit of usefulness, is dressed now for gardening, and doesn't give a damn how he looks.

He has never been really sick a day in his life. He has no nerves. There is a lot of stolid, earthy peasant in him, mixed with streaks of sentimental melancholy and rare flashes of intuitive sensibility.

Tyrone's arm is around his wife's waist as they appear from the back parlor. Entering the living room he gives her a playful hug.

TYRONE—You're a fine armful now, Mary, with those twenty pounds you've gained.

MARY—(*smiles affectionately*) I've gotten too fat, you mean, dear. I really ought to reduce.

TYRONE—None of that, my lady! You're just right. We'll have no talk of reducing. Is that why you ate so little breakfast?

MARY—So little? I thought I ate a lot.

TYRONE—You didn't. Not as much as I'd like to see, anyway.

MARY—(*teasingly*) Oh you! You expect everyone to eat the enormous breakfast you do. No one else in the world could without dying of indigestion. (*She comes forward to stand by the right of table.*)

TYRONE—(*following her*) I hope I'm not as big a glutton as that sounds. (*with hearty satisfaction*) But thank God, I've kept my appetite and I've the digestion of a young man of twenty, if I am sixty-five.

MARY—You surely have, James. No one could deny that. (*She laughs and sits in the wicker armchair at right rear of table. He comes around in back of her and selects a cigar from a box on the table and cuts off the end with a little clipper. From the dining room Jamie's and Edmund's voices are heard. Mary turns her head that way.*) Why did the boys stay in the dining room, I wonder? Cathleen must be waiting to clear the table.

TYRONE—(*jokingly but with an undercurrent of resentment*) It's a secret confab they don't want me to hear, I suppose. I'll bet they're cooking up some new scheme to touch the Old Man. (*She is silent on this, keeping her head turned toward their voices. Her hands appear on the table top, moving restlessly. He lights his cigar and sits down in the rocker at right of table, which is his chair, and puffs contentedly.*) There's nothing like the first after-breakfast cigar, if it's a good one, and this new lot have the right mellow flavor. They're a great bargain, too. I got them dead cheap. It was McGuire put me on to them.

MARY—(*a trifle acidly*) I hope he didn't put you on to any new piece of property at the same time. His real estate bargains don't work out so well.

TYRONE—(*defensively*) I wouldn't say that, Mary. After all, he was the one who advised me to buy that place on Chestnut Street and I made a quick turnover on it for a fine profit.

MARY—(*smiles now with teasing affection*) I know. The famous one stroke of good luck. I'm sure McGuire never dreamed— (*Then she pats his hand.*) Never mind, James. I know it's a waste of breath trying to convince you you're not a cunning real estate speculator.

TYRONE—(*huffily*) I've no such idea. But land is land, and it's safer than the stocks and bonds of Wall Street swindlers. (*then placatingly*) But let's not argue about business this early in the morning. (*A pause. The boys' voices are again heard and one of them has a fit of coughing. Mary listens worriedly. Her fingers play nervously on the table top.*)

MARY—James, it's Edmund you ought to scold for not eating enough. He hardly touched anything except coffee. He needs to eat to keep up his strength. I keep telling him that but he says he simply has no appetite. Of course, there's nothing takes away your appetite like a bad summer cold.

TYRONE—Yes, it's only natural. So don't let yourself get worried—

MARY—(*quickly*) Oh, I'm not. I know he'll be all right in a few days if he takes care of himself. (*as if she wanted to dismiss the subject but can't*) But it does seem a shame he should have to be sick right now.

TYRONE—Yes, it is bad luck. (*He gives her a quick, worried look*.) But you mustn't let it upset you, Mary. Remember, you've got to take care of yourself, too.

MARY—(*quickly*) I'm not upset. There's nothing to be upset about. What makes you think I'm upset?

TYRONE—Why, nothing, except you've seemed a bit highstrung the past few days.

MARY—(*forcing a smile*) I have? Nonsense, dear. It's your imagination. (*with sudden tenseness*) You really must not watch me all the time, James. I mean, it makes me self-conscious.

TYRONE—(*putting a hand over one of her nervously playing ones*) Now, now, Mary. That's your imagination. If I've watched you it was to admire how fat and beautiful you looked. (*His voice is suddenly moved by deep feeling.*) I can't tell you the deep happiness it gives me, darling, to see you as you've been since you came back to us, your dear old self again. (*He leans over and kisses her cheek impulsively—then turning back adds with a constrained air*) So keep up the good work, Mary.

MARY—(*has turned her head away*) I will, dear. (*She gets up restlessly and goes to the windows at right.*) Thank heavens, the fog is gone. (*She turns back.*) I do feel out of sorts this morning. I wasn't able to get much sleep with that awful foghorn going all night long.

TYRONE—Yes, it's like having a sick whale in the back yard. It kept me awake, too.

MARY—(*affectionately amused*) Did it? You had a strange way of showing your restlessness. You were snoring so hard I couldn't tell which was the foghorn! (*She comes to him, laughing, and pats his cheek playfully.*) Ten foghorns couldn't disturb you. You haven't a nerve in you. You've never had.

TYRONE—(*his vanity piqued—testily*) Nonsense. You always exaggerate about my snoring.

MARY—I couldn't. If you could only hear yourself once— (*A burst of laughter comes from the dining room. She turns her head, smiling.*) What's the joke, I wonder?

TYRONE—(*grumpily*) It's on me. I'll bet that much. It's always on the Old Man.

MARY—(*teasingly*) Yes, it's terrible the way we all pick on you, isn't it? You're so abused! (*She laughs—then with a pleased, relieved air*) Well, no matter what the joke is about, it's a relief to hear Edmund laugh. He's been so down in the mouth lately.

TYRONE—(*ignoring this—resentfully*) Some joke of Jamie's, I'll wager. He's forever making sneering fun of somebody, that one.

MARY—Now don't start in on poor Jamie, dear. (*without conviction*) He'll turn out all right in the end, you wait and see.

TYRONE—He'd better start soon, then. He's nearly thirty-four.

MARY—(*ignoring this*) Good heavens, are they going to stay in the dining room all day? (*She goes to the back parlor doorway and calls*) Jamie! Edmund! Come in the living room and give Cathleen a chance to clear the table. (*Edmund calls back, "We're coming, Mama." She goes back to the table.*)

TYRONE—(*grumbling*) You'd find excuses for him no matter what he did.

MARY—(*sitting down beside him, pats his hand*) Shush. (*Their sons James, Jr., and Edmund enter together from the back parlor. They are both grinning, still chuckling over what had caused their laughter, and as they come forward they glance at their father and their grins grow broader.*)

(*Jamie, the elder, is thirty-three. He has his father's broad-shouldered, deep-chested physique, is an inch taller and weighs less, but appears shorter and stouter because he lacks Tyrone's bearing and graceful carriage. He also lacks his father's vitality. The signs of premature disintegration are on him. His face is still good look-ing, despite marks of dissipation, but it has never been handsome like Tyrone's, although Jamie resembles him rather than his mother. He has fine brown eyes, their color midway between his father's lighter and his mother's darker ones. His hair is thinning and already there is indication of a bald spot like Tyrone's. His nose is unlike that of any other member of the family, pronouncedly aquiline. Combined with his habitual expression of cynicism it gives his countenance a Mephistophelian cast. But on the rare oc-casions when he smiles without sneering, his personality possesses the remnant of a humorous, romantic, irresponsible Irish charm— that of the beguiling ne'er-do-well, with a strain of the sentimen-tally poetic, attractive to women and popular with men.*)

(*He is dressed in an old sack suit, not as shabby as Tyrone's,*) *and wears a collar and tie. His fair skin is sunburned a reddish, freckled tan.*

(Edmund is ten years younger than his brother, a couple of inches taller, thin and wiry. Where Jamie takes after his father, with little resemblance to his mother, Edmund looks like both his parents, but is more like his mother. Her big, dark eyes are the dominant feature in his long, narrow Irish face. His mouth has the same quality of hypersensitiveness hers possesses. His high forehead is hers accentuated, with dark brown hair, sunbleached to red at the ends, brushed straight back from it. But his nose is his father's and his face in profile recalls Tyrone's. Edmund's hands are noticeably like his mother's, with the same exceptionally long fingers. They even have to a minor degree the same nervousness. It is in the quality of extreme nervous sensibility that the likeness of Edmund to his mother is most marked.

(He is plainly in bad health. Much thinner than he should be, his eyes appear feverish and his cheeks are sunken. His skin, in spite of being sunburned a deep brown, has a parched sallowness. He wears a shirt, collar and tie, no coat, old flannel trousers, brown sneakers.)

MARY—*(turns smilingly to them, in a merry tone that is a bit forced)* I've been teasing your father about his snoring. *(to Tyrone)* I'll leave it to the boys, James. They must have heard you. No, not you, Jamie. I could hear you down the hall almost as bad as your father. You're like him. As soon as your head touches the pillow you're off and ten foghorns couldn't wake you. *(She stops abruptly, catching Jamie's eyes regarding her with an uneasy, probing look. Her smile vanishes and her manner becomes self-conscious.)* Why are you staring, Jamie? *(Her hands flutter up to her hair.)* Is my hair coming down? It's hard for me to do it up properly now. My eyes are getting so bad and I never can find my glasses.

JAMIE—*(looks away guiltily)* Your hair's all right, Mama. I was only thinking how well you look.

TYRONE—*(heartily)* Just what I've been telling her, Jamie. She's so fat and sassy, there'll soon be no holding her.

EDMUND—Yes, you certainly look grand, Mama. *(She is reassured and smiles at him lovingly. He winks with a kidding grin.)* I'll back you up about Papa's snoring. Gosh, what a racket!

JAMIE—I heard him, too. (*He quotes, putting on a ham-actor manner*) "The Moor, I know his trumpet." (*His mother and brother laugh.*)

TYRONE—(*scathingly*) If it takes my snoring to make you remember Shakespeare instead of the dope sheet on the ponies, I hope I'll keep on with it.

MARY—Now, James! You mustn't be so touchy. (*Jamie shrugs his shoulders and sits down in the chair on her right.*)

EDMUND—(*irritably*) Yes, for Pete's sake, Papa! The first thing after breakfast! Give it a rest, can't you? (*He slumps down in the chair at left of table next to his brother. His father ignores him.*)

MARY—(*reprovingly*) Your father wasn't finding fault with you. You don't have to always take Jamie's part. You'd think you were the one ten years older.

JAMIE—(*boredly*) What's all the fuss about? Let's forget it.

TYRONE—(*contemptuously*) Yes, forget! Forget everything and face nothing! It's a convenient philosophy if you've no ambition in life except to—

MARY—James, do be quiet. (*She puts an arm around his shoulder—coaxingly*) You must have gotten out of the wrong side of the bed this morning. (*to the boys, changing the subject*) What were you two grinning about like Cheshire cats when you came in? What was the joke?

TYRONE—(*with a painful effort to be a good sport*) Yes, let us in on it, lads. I told your mother I knew damned well it would be one on me, but never mind that, I'm used to it.

JAMIE—(*dryly*) Don't look at me. This is the Kid's story.

EDMUND—(*grins*) I meant to tell you last night, Papa, and forgot it. Yesterday when I went for a walk I dropped in at the Inn—

MARY—(*worriedly*) You shouldn't drink now, Edmund.

EDMUND—(*ignoring this*) And who do you think I met there, with a beautiful bun on, but Shaughnessy, the tenant on that farm of yours.

MARY—(*smiling*) That dreadful man! But he is funny.

TYRONE—(*scowling*) He's not so funny when you're his landlord. He's a wily Shanty Mick, that one. He could hide behind a corkscrew. What's he complaining about now, Edmund—for I'm damned sure he's complaining. I suppose he wants his rent lowered. I let him have the place for almost nothing, just to keep someone on it, and he never pays that till I threaten to evict him.

EDMUND—No, he didn't beef about anything. He was so pleased with life he even bought a drink, and that's practically unheard of. He was delighted because he'd had a fight with your friend, Harker, the Standard Oil millionaire, and won a glorious victory.

MARY—(*with amused dismay*) Oh, Lord! James, you'll really have to do something—

TYRONE—Bad luck to Shaughnessy, anyway!

JAMIE—(*maliciously*) I'll bet the next time you see Harker at the Club and give him the old respectful bow, he won't see you.

EDMUND—Yes. Harker will think you're no gentleman for harboring a tenant who isn't humble in the presence of a king of America.

TYRONE—Never mind the Socialist gabble. I don't care to listen—

MARY—(*tactfully*) Go on with your story, Edmund.

EDMUND—(*grins at his father provocatively*) Well, you remember, Papa, the ice pond on Harker's estate is right next to the farm, and you remember Shaughnessy keeps pigs. Well, it seems there's a break in the fence and the pigs have been bathing in the millionaire's ice pond, and Harker's foreman told him he was sure Shaughnessy had broken the fence on purpose to give his pigs a free wallow.

MARY—(*shocked and amused*) Good heavens!

TYRONE—(*sourly, but with a trace of admiration*) I'm sure he did, too, the dirty scallywag. It's like him.

EDMUND—So Harker came in person to rebuke Shaughnessy. (*He chuckles.*) A very bonehead play! If I needed any further proof that our ruling plutocrats, especially the ones who inherited their boodle, are not mental giants, that would clinch it.

TYRONE—(*with appreciation, before he thinks*) Yes, he'd be no match for Shaughnessy. (*Then he growls*) Keep your damned anarchist remarks to yourself. I won't have them in my house. (*But he is full of eager anticipation.*) What happened?

EDMUND—Harker had as much chance as I would with Jack Johnson. Shaughnessy got a few drinks under his belt and was waiting at the gate to welcome him. He told me he never gave Harker a chance to open his mouth. He began by shouting that he was no slave Standard Oil could trample on. He was a King of Ireland, if he had his rights, and scum was scum to him, no matter how much money it had stolen from the poor.

MARY—Oh, Lord! (*But she can't help laughing.*)

EDMUND—Then he accused Harker of making his foreman break down the fence to entice the pigs into the ice pond in order to destroy them. The poor pigs, Shaughnessy yelled, had caught their death of cold. Many of them were dying of pneumonia, and several others had been taken down with cholera from drinking the poisoned water. He told Harker he was hiring a lawyer to sue him for damages. And he wound up by saying that he had to put up with poison ivy, ticks, potato bugs, snakes and skunks on his farm, but he was an honest man who drew the line somewhere, and he'd be damned if he'd stand for a Standard Oil thief trespassing. So would Harker kindly remove his dirty feet from the premises before he sicked the dog on him. And Harker did! (*He and Jamie laugh.*)

MARY—(*shocked but giggling*) Heavens, what a terrible tongue that man has!

TYRONE—(*admiringly before he thinks*) The damned old scoundrel! By God, you can't beat him! (*He laughs—then stops abruptly and scowls.*) The dirty blackguard! He'll get me in serious trouble yet. I hope you told him I'd be mad as hell—

EDMUND—I told him you'd be tickled to death over the great Irish victory, and so you are. Stop faking, Papa.

TYRONE—Well, I'm not tickled to death.

MARY—(*teasingly*) You are, too, James. You're simply delighted!

TYRONE—No, Mary, a joke is a joke, but—

EDMUND—I told Shaughnessy he should have reminded Harker that a Standard Oil millionaire ought to welcome the flavor of hog in his ice water as an appropriate touch.

TYRONE—The devil you did! (*frowning*) Keep your damned Socialist anarchist sentiments out of my affairs!

EDMUND — Shaughnessy almost wept because he hadn't thought of that one, but he said he'd include it in a letter he's writing to Harker, along with a few other insults he'd overlooked. (*He and Jamie laugh.*)

TYRONE — What are you laughing at? There's nothing funny— A fine son you are to help that blackguard get me into a lawsuit!

MARY — Now, James, don't lose your temper.

TYRONE — (*turns on Jamie*) And you're worse than he is, encouraging him. I suppose you're regretting you weren't there to prompt Shaughnessy with a few nastier insults. You've a fine talent for that, if for nothing else.

MARY — James! There's no reason to scold Jamie. (*Jamie is about to make some sneering remark to his father, but he shrugs his shoulders.*)

EDMUND — (*with sudden nervous exasperation*) Oh, for God's sake, Papa! If you're starting that stuff again, I'll beat it. (*He jumps up.*) I left my book upstairs, anyway. (*He goes to the front parlor, saying disgustedly*) God, Papa, I should think you'd get sick of hearing yourself— (*He disappears. Tyrone looks after him angrily.*)

MARY — You mustn't mind Edmund, James. Remember he isn't well. (*Edmund can be heard coughing as he goes upstairs. She adds nervously*) A summer cold makes anyone irritable.

JAMIE — (*genuinely concerned*) It's not just a cold he's got. The Kid is damned sick. (*His father gives him a sharp warning look but he doesn't see it.*)

MARY — (*turns on him resentfully*) Why do you say that? It *is* just a cold! Anyone can tell that! You always imagine things!

TYRONE — (*with another warning glance at Jamie—easily*) All Jamie meant was Edmund might have a touch of something else, too, which makes his cold worse.

JAMIE — Sure, Mama. That's all I meant.

TYRONE — Doctor Hardy thinks it might be a bit of malarial fever he caught when he was in the tropics. If it is, quinine will soon cure it.

MARY — (*A look of contemptuous hostility flashes across her face.*) Doctor Hardy! I wouldn't believe a thing he said, if he swore on a stack of Bibles! I know what doctors are. They're all alike. Anything, they don't care what, to keep you coming to them. (*She stops short, overcome by a fit of acute self-consciousness as she catches their eyes fixed on her. Her hands jerk nervously to her hair. She forces a smile.*) What is it? What are you looking at? Is my hair—?

TYRONE—(*puts his arm around her—with guilty heartiness, giving her a playful hug*) There's nothing wrong with your hair. The healthier and fatter you get, the vainer you become. You'll soon spend half the day primping before the mirror.

MARY—(*half reassured*) I really should have new glasses. My eyes are so bad now.

TYRONE—(*with Irish blarney*) Your eyes are beautiful, and well you know it. (*He gives her a kiss. Her face lights up with a charming, shy embarrassment. Suddenly and startlingly one sees in her face the girl she had once been, not a ghost of the dead, but still a living part of her.*)

MARY—You mustn't be so silly, James. Right in front of Jamie!

TYRONE—Oh, he's on to you, too. He knows this fuss about eyes and hair is only fishing for compliments. Eh, Jamie?

JAMIE—(*His face has cleared, too, and there is an old boyish charm in his loving smile at his mother.*) Yes. You can't kid us, Mama.

MARY—(*laughs and an Irish lilt comes into her voice*) Go along with both of you! (*Then she speaks with a girlish gravity.*) But I did truly have beautiful hair once, didn't I, James?

TYRONE—The most beautiful in the world!

MARY—It was a rare shade of reddish brown and so long it came down below my knees. You ought to remember it, too, Jamie. It wasn't until after Edmund was born that I had a single grey hair. Then it began to turn white. (*The girlishness fades from her face.*)

TYRONE—(*quickly*) And that made it prettier than ever.

MARY—(*again embarrassed and pleased*) Will you listen to your father, Jamie—after thirty-five years of marriage! He isn't a great actor for nothing, is he? What's come over you, James? Are you pouring coals of fire on my head for teasing you about snoring? Well then, I take it all back. It must have been only the foghorn I heard. (*She laughs, and they laugh with her. Then she changes to a brisk businesslike air.*) But I can't stay with you any longer, even to hear compliments. I must see the cook about dinner and the day's marketing. (*She gets up and sighs with humorous exaggeration.*) Bridget is so lazy. And so sly. She begins telling me about her relatives so I can't get a word in edgeways and scold her. Well, I might as well get it over. (*She goes to the back-parlor doorway, then turns, her face worried again.*) You mustn't make Edmund work on the grounds with you, James, remember. (*again with the strange obstinate set to her face*) Not that he isn't strong enough, but he'd perspire and he might catch more cold. (*She disappears through the back parlor. Tyrone turns on Jamie condemningly.*)

TYRONE — You're a fine lunkhead! Haven't you any sense? The one thing to avoid is saying anything that would get her more upset over Edmund.

JAMIE — (*shrugging his shoulders*) All right. Have it your way. I think it's the wrong idea to let Mama go on kidding herself. It will only make the shock worse when she has to face it. Anyway, you can see she's deliberately fooling herself with that summer cold talk. She knows better.

TYRONE — Knows? Nobody knows yet.

JAMIE — Well, I do. I was with Edmund when he went to Doc Hardy on Monday. I heard him pull that touch of malaria stuff. He was stalling. That isn't what he thinks any more. You know it as well as I do. You talked to him when you went uptown yesterday, didn't you?

TYRONE — He couldn't say anything for sure yet. He's to phone me today before Edmund goes to him.

JAMIE — (*slowly*) He thinks it's consumption, doesn't he, Papa?

TYRONE — (*reluctantly*) He said it might be.

JAMIE — (*moved, his love for his brother coming out*) Poor kid! God damn it! (*He turns on his father accusingly.*) It might never have happened if you'd sent him to a real doctor when he first got sick.

TYRONE — What's the matter with Hardy? He's always been our doctor up here.

JAMIE — Everything's the matter with him! Even in this hick burg he's rated third class! He's a cheap old quack!

TYRONE — That's right! Run him down! Run down everybody! Everyone is a fake to you!

JAMIE—(*contemptuously*) Hardy only charges a dollar. That's what makes you think he's a fine doctor!

TYRONE—(*stung*) That's enough! You're not drunk now! There's no excuse— (*He controls himself—a bit defensively*) If you mean I can't afford one of the fine society doctors who prey on the rich summer people—

JAMIE—Can't afford? You're one of the biggest property owners around here.

TYRONE—That doesn't mean I'm rich. It's all mortgaged—

JAMIE—Because you always buy more instead of paying off mortgages. If Edmund was a lousy acre of land you wanted, the sky would be the limit!

TYRONE—That's a lie! And your sneers against Doctor Hardy are lies! He doesn't put on frills, or have an office in a fashionable location, or drive around in an expensive automobile. That's what you pay for with those other five-dollars-to-look-at-your-tongue fellows, not their skill.

JAMIE—(*with a scornful shrug of his shoulders*) Oh, all right. I'm a fool to argue. You can't change the leopard's spots.

TYRONE—(*with rising anger*) No, you can't. You've taught me that lesson only too well. I've lost all hope you will ever change yours. You dare tell me what I can afford? You've never known the value of a dollar and never will! You've never saved a dollar in your life! At the end of each season you're penniless! You've thrown your salary away every week on whores and whiskey!

JAMIE—My salary! Christ!

TYRONE—It's more than you're worth, and you couldn't get that if it wasn't for me. If you weren't my son, there isn't a manager in the business who would give you a part, your reputation stinks so. As it is, I have to humble my pride and beg for you, saying you've turned over a new leaf, although I know it's a lie!

JAMIE—I never wanted to be an actor. You forced me on the stage.

TYRONE—That's a lie! You made no effort to find anything else to do. You left it to me to get you a job and I have no influence except in the theater. Forced you! You never wanted to do anything except loaf in barrooms! You'd have been content to sit back like a lazy lunk and sponge on me for the rest of your life! After all the money I'd wasted on your education, and all you did was get fired in disgrace from every college you went to!

JAMIE—Oh, for God's sake, don't drag up that ancient history!

TYRONE—It's not ancient history that you have to come home every summer to live on me.

JAMIE—I earn my board and lodging working on the grounds. It saves you hiring a man.

TYRONE—Bah! You have to be driven to do even that much! (*His anger ebbs into a weary complaint.*) I wouldn't give a damn if you ever displayed the slightest sign of gratitude. The only thanks is to have you sneer at me for a dirty miser, sneer at my profession, sneer at every damned thing in the world—except yourself.

JAMIE—(*wryly*) That's not true, Papa. You can't hear me talking to myself, that's all.

TYRONE—(*stares at him puzzledly, then quotes mechanically*) "Ingratitude, the vilest weed that grows"!

JAMIE—I could see that line coming! God, how many thousand times—! (*He stops, bored with their quarrel, and shrugs his shoulders.*) All right, Papa. I'm a bum. Anything you like, so long as it stops the argument.

TYRONE—(*with indignant appeal now*) If you'd get ambition in your head instead of folly! You're young yet. You could still make your mark. You had the talent to become a fine actor! You have it still. You're my son—!

JAMIE—(*boredly*) Let's forget me. I'm not interested in the subject. Neither are you. (*Tyrone gives up. Jamie goes on casually.*) What started us on this? Oh, Doc Hardy. When is he going to call you up about Edmund?

TYRONE—Around lunch time. (*He pauses—then defensively*) I couldn't have sent Edmund to a better doctor. Hardy's treated him whenever he was sick up here, since he was knee high. He knows his constitution as no other doctor could. It's not a question of my being miserly, as you'd like to make out. (*bitterly*) And what could the finest specialist in America do for Edmund, after he's deliberately ruined his health by the mad life he's led ever since he was fired from college? Even before that when he was in prep school, he began dissipating and playing the Broadway sport to imitate you, when he's never had your constitution to stand it. You're a healthy hulk like me—or you were at his age—but he's always been a bundle of nerves like his mother. I've warned him for years his body couldn't stand it, but he wouldn't heed me, and now it's too late.

JAMIE—(*sharply*) What do you mean, too late? You talk as if you thought—

TYRONE—(*guiltily explosive*) Don't be a damned fool! I meant nothing but what's plain to anyone! His health has broken down and he may be an invalid for a long time.

JAMIE—(*stares at his father, ignoring his explanation*) I know it's an Irish peasant idea consumption is fatal. It probably is when you live in a hovel on a bog, but over here, with modern treatment—

TYRONE—Don't I know that! What are you gabbing about, anyway? And keep your dirty tongue off Ireland, with your sneers about peasants and bogs and hovels! (*accusingly*) The less you say about Edmund's sickness, the better for your conscience! You're more responsible than anyone!

JAMIE—(*stung*) That's a lie! I won't stand for that, Papa!

TYRONE—It's the truth! You've been the worst influence for him. He grew up admiring you as a hero! A fine example you set him! If you ever gave him advice except in the ways of rottenness, I've never heard of it! You made him old before his time, pumping him full of what you consider worldly wisdom, when he was too young to see that your mind was so poisoned by your own failure in life, you wanted to believe every man was a knave with his soul for sale, and every woman who wasn't a whore was a fool!

JAMIE—(*with a defensive air of weary indifference again*) All right. I did put Edmund wise to things, but not until I saw he'd started to raise hell, and knew he'd laugh at me if I tried the good advice, older brother stuff. All I did was make a pal of him and be absolutely frank so he'd learn from my mistakes that— (*He shrugs his shoulders—cynically*) Well, that if you can't be good you can at least be careful. (*His father snorts contemptuously. Suddenly Jamie becomes really moved.*) That's a rotten accusation, Papa. You know how much the Kid means

to me, and how close we've always been—not like the usual
brothers! I'd do anything for him.

TYRONE—(*impressed—mollifyingly*) I know you may have
thought it was for the best, Jamie. I didn't say you did it
deliberately to harm him.

JAMIE—Besides it's damned rot! I'd like to see anyone influence Edmund more than he wants to be. His quietness
fools people into thinking they can do what they like with
him. But he's stubborn as hell inside and what he does is
what he wants to do, and to hell with anyone else! What had
I to do with all the crazy stunts he's pulled in the last few
years—working his way all over the map as a sailor and all
that stuff. I thought that was a damned fool idea, and I told
him so. You can't imagine me getting fun out of being on the
beach in South America, or living in filthy dives, drinking
rotgut, can you? No, thanks! I'll stick to Broadway, and a
room with a bath, and bars that serve bonded Bourbon.

TYRONE—You and Broadway! It's made you what you
are! (*with a touch of pride*) Whatever Edmund's done, he's had
the guts to go off on his own, where he couldn't come whining to me the minute he was broke.

JAMIE—(*stung into sneering jealousy*) He's always come
home broke finally, hasn't he? And what did his going away
get him? Look at him now! (*He is suddenly shamefaced.*)
Christ! That's a lousy thing to say. I don't mean that.

TYRONE—(*decides to ignore this*) He's been doing well on
the paper. I was hoping he'd found the work he wants to do
at last.

JAMIE—(*sneering jealously again*) A hick town rag! Whatever bull they hand you, they tell me he's a pretty bum re-
porter. If he weren't your son— (*ashamed again*) No, that's
not true! They're glad to have him, but it's the special stuff
that gets him by. Some of the poems and parodies he's written are damned good. (*grudgingly again*) Not that they'd
ever get him anywhere on the big time. (*hastily*) But he's certainly made a damned good start.

TYRONE—Yes. He's made a start. You used to talk about
wanting to become a newspaper man but you were never
willing to start at the bottom. You expected—

JAMIE—Oh, for Christ's sake, Papa! Can't you lay off me!

TYRONE—(*stares at him—then looks away—after a pause*) It's damnable luck Edmund should be sick right now. It couldn't have come at a worse time for him. (*He adds, unable to conceal an almost furtive uneasiness*) Or for your mother. It's damnable she should have this to upset her, just when she needs peace and freedom from worry. She's been so well in the two months since she came home. (*His voice grows husky and trembles a little.*) It's been heaven to me. This home has been a home again. But I needn't tell you, Jamie. (*His son looks at him, for the first time with an understanding sympathy. It is as if suddenly a deep bond of common feeling existed between them in which their antagonisms could be forgotten.*)

JAMIE—(*almost gently*) I've felt the same way, Papa.

TYRONE—Yes, this time you can see how strong and sure of herself she is. She's a different woman entirely from the other times. She has control of her nerves—or she had until Edmund got sick. Now you can feel her growing tense and frightened underneath. I wish to God we could keep the truth from her, but we can't if he has to be sent to a sanatorium. What makes it worse is her father died of consumption. She worshiped him and she's never forgotten. Yes, it will be hard for her. But she can do it! She has the will power now! We must help her, Jamie, in every way we can!

JAMIE—(*moved*) Of course, Papa. (*hesitantly*) Outside of nerves, she seems perfectly all right this morning.

TYRONE—(*with hearty confidence now*) Never better. She's full of fun and mischief. (*Suddenly he frowns at Jamie suspiciously.*) Why do you say, seems? Why shouldn't she be all right? What the hell do you mean?

JAMIE—Don't start jumping down my throat! God, Papa, this ought to be one thing we can talk over frankly without a battle.

TYRONE—I'm sorry, Jamie. (*tensely*) But go on and tell me—

JAMIE—There's nothing to tell. I was all wrong. It's just that last night— Well, you know how it is, I can't forget the past. I can't help being suspicious. Any more than you can. (*bitterly*) That's the hell of it. And it makes it hell for Mama! She watches us watching her—

TYRONE—(*sadly*) I know. (*tensely*) Well, what was it? Can't you speak out?

JAMIE—Nothing, I tell you. Just my damned foolishness. Around three o'clock this morning, I woke up and heard her moving around in the spare room. Then she went to the bathroom. I pretended to be asleep. She stopped in the hall to listen, as if she wanted to make sure I was.

TYRONE—(*with forced scorn*) For God's sake, is that all? She told me herself the foghorn kept her awake all night, and every night since Edmund's been sick she's been up and down, going to his room to see how he was.

JAMIE—(*eagerly*) Yes, that's right, she did stop to listen outside his room. (*hesitantly again*) It was her being in the spare room that scared me. I couldn't help remembering that when she starts sleeping alone in there, it has always been a sign—

TYRONE—It isn't this time! It's easily explained. Where else could she go last night to get away from my snoring? (*He gives way to a burst of resentful anger.*) By God, how you can live with a mind that sees nothing but the worst motives behind everything is beyond me!

JAMIE—(*stung*) Don't pull that! I've just said I was all wrong. Don't you suppose I'm as glad of that as you are!

TYRONE—(*mollifyingly*) I'm sure you are, Jamie. (*A pause. His expression becomes somber. He speaks slowly with a superstitious dread.*) It would be like a curse she can't escape if worry over Edmund— It was in her long sickness after bringing him into the world that she first—

JAMIE—She didn't have anything to do with it!

TYRONE—I'm not blaming her.

JAMIE—(*bitingly*) Then who are you blaming? Edmund, for being born?

TYRONE—You damned fool! No one was to blame.

JAMIE—The bastard of a doctor was! From what Mama's said, he was another cheap quack like Hardy! You wouldn't pay for a first-rate—

TYRONE—That's a lie! (*furiously*) So I'm to blame! That's what you're driving at, is it? You evil-minded loafer!

JAMIE—(*warningly as he hears his mother in the dining room*) Ssh! (*Tyrone gets hastily to his feet and goes to look out the windows at right. Jamie speaks with a complete change of tone.*) Well, if we're going to cut the front hedge today, we'd better go to work. (*Mary comes in from the back parlor. She gives a quick, suspicious glance from one to the other, her manner nervously self-conscious.*)

TYRONE—(*turns from the window—with an actor's heartiness*) Yes, it's too fine a morning to waste indoors arguing. Take a look out the window, Mary. There's no fog in the harbor. I'm sure the spell of it we've had is over now.

MARY—(*going to him*) I hope so, dear. (*to Jamie, forcing a smile*) Did I actually hear you suggesting work on the front hedge, Jamie? Wonders will never cease! You must want pocket money badly.

JAMIE—(*kiddingly*) When don't I? (*He winks at her, with a derisive glance at his father.*) I expect a salary of at least one large iron man at the end of the week—to carouse on!

MARY—(*does not respond to his humor—her hands fluttering over the front of her dress*) What were you two arguing about?

JAMIE—(*shrugs his shoulders*) The same old stuff.

MARY—I heard you say something about a doctor, and your father accusing you of being evil-minded.

JAMIE—(*quickly*) Oh, that. I was saying again Doc Hardy isn't my idea of the world's greatest physician.

MARY—(*knows he is lying—vaguely*) Oh. No, I wouldn't say he was, either. (*changing the subject—forcing a smile*) That Bridget! I thought I'd never get away. She told me all about her second cousin on the police force in St. Louis. (*then with nervous irritation*) Well, if you're going to work on the hedge why don't you go? (*hastily*) I mean, take advantage of the sunshine before the fog comes back. (*strangely, as if talking aloud to herself*) Because I know it will. (*Suddenly she is self-consciously aware that they are both staring fixedly at her—flurriedly, raising her hands*) Or I should say, the rheumatism in my hands knows. It's a better weather prophet than you are, James. (*She stares at her hands with fascinated repulsion.*) Ugh! How ugly they are! Who'd ever believe they were once beautiful? (*They stare at her with a growing dread.*)

TYRONE—(*takes her hands and gently pushes them down*) Now, now, Mary. None of that foolishness. They're the sweetest hands in the world. (*She smiles, her face lighting up, and kisses him gratefully. He turns to his son.*) Come on Jamie.

Your mother's right to scold us. The way to start work is to start work. The hot sun will sweat some of that booze fat off your middle. (*He opens the screen door and goes out on the porch and disappears down a flight of steps leading to the ground. Jamie rises from his chair and, taking off his coat, goes to the door. At the door he turns back but avoids looking at her, and she does not look at him.*)

JAMIE—(*with an awkward, uneasy tenderness*) We're all so proud of you, Mama, so darned happy. (*She stiffens and stares at him with a frightened defiance. He flounders on.*) But you've still got to be careful. You mustn't worry so much about Edmund. He'll be all right.

MARY—(*with a stubborn, bitterly resentful look*) Of course, he'll be all right. And I don't know what you mean, warning me to be careful.

JAMIE—(*rebuffed and hurt, shrugs his shoulders*) All right, Mama. I'm sorry I spoke. (*He goes out on the porch. She waits rigidly until he disappears down the steps. Then she sinks down in the chair he had occupied, her face betraying a frightened, furtive desperation, her hands roving over the table top, aimlessly moving objects around. She hears Edmund descending the stairs in the front hall. As he nears the bottom he has a fit of coughing. She springs to her feet, as if she wanted to run away from the sound, and goes quickly to the windows at right. She is looking out, apparently calm, as he enters from the front parlor, a book in one hand. She turns to him, her lips set in a welcoming, motherly smile.*)

MARY—Here you are. I was just going upstairs to look for you.

EDMUND—I waited until they went out. I don't want to mix up in any arguments. I feel too rotten.

MARY—(*almost resentfully*) Oh, I'm sure you don't feel half as badly as you make out. You're such a baby. You like to get us worried so we'll make a fuss over you. (*hastily*) I'm only teasing, dear. I know how miserably uncomfortable you must be. But you feel better today, don't you? (*worriedly, taking his arm*) All the same, you've grown much too thin. You need to rest all you can. Sit down and I'll make you comfortable. (*He sits down in the rocking chair and she puts a pillow behind his back.*) There. How's that?

EDMUND—Grand. Thanks, Mama.

MARY—(*kisses him—tenderly*) All you need is your mother to nurse you. Big as you are, you're still the baby of the family to me, you know.

EDMUND—(*takes her hand—with deep seriousness*) Never mind me. You take care of yourself. That's all that counts.

MARY—(*evading his eyes*) But I am, dear. (*forcing a laugh*) Heavens, don't you see how fat I've grown! I'll have to have all my dresses let out. (*She turns away and goes to the windows at right. She attempts a light, amused tone.*) They've started clipping the hedge. Poor Jamie! How he hates working in front where everyone passing can see him. There go the Chatfields in their new Mercedes. It's a beautiful car, isn't it? Not like our secondhand Packard. Poor Jamie! He bent almost under the hedge so they wouldn't notice him. They bowed to your father and he bowed back as if he were taking a curtain call. In that filthy old suit I've tried to make him throw away. (*Her voice has grown bitter.*) Really, he ought to have more pride than to make such a show of himself.

EDMUND—He's right not to give a damn what anyone thinks. Jamie's a fool to care about the Chatfields. For Pete's sake, who ever heard of them outside this hick burg?

MARY—(*with satisfaction*) No one. You're quite right, Edmund. Big frogs in a small puddle. It is stupid of Jamie. (*She pauses, looking out the window—then with an undercurrent of lonely yearning*) Still, the Chatfields and people like them stand for something. I mean they have decent, presentable homes they don't have to be ashamed of. They have friends who entertain them and whom they entertain. They're not cut off from everyone. (*She turns back from the window.*) Not that I want anything to do with them. I've always hated this town and everyone in it. You know that. I never wanted to live here in the first place, but your father liked it and insisted on building this house, and I've had to come here every summer.

EDMUND—Well, it's better than spending the summer in a New York hotel, isn't it? And this town's not so bad. I like it well enough. I suppose because it's the only home we've had.

MARY—I've never felt it was my home. It was wrong from the start. Everything was done in the cheapest way. Your father would never spend the money to make it right. It's just as well we haven't any friends here. I'd be ashamed to have them step in the door. But he's never wanted family friends. He hates calling on people, or receiving them. All he likes is to hobnob with men at the Club or in a barroom. Jamie and you are the same way, but you're not to blame. You've never had a chance to meet decent people here. I know you both would have been so different if you'd been able to associate with nice girls instead of— You'd never have disgraced yourselves as you have, so that now no respectable parents will let their daughters be seen with you.

EDMUND—(*irritably*) Oh, Mama, forget it! Who cares? Jamie and I would be bored stiff. And about the Old Man, what's the use of talking? You can't change him.

MARY—(*mechanically rebuking*) Don't call your father the Old Man. You should have more respect. (*then dully*) I know it's useless to talk. But sometimes I feel so lonely. (*Her lips quiver and she keeps her head turned away.*)

EDMUND—Anyway, you've got to be fair, Mama. It may have been all his fault in the beginning, but you know that later on, even if he'd wanted to, we couldn't have had people here— (*He flounders guiltily.*) I mean, you wouldn't have wanted them.

MARY—(*wincing—her lips quivering pitifully*) Don't. I can't bear having you remind me.

EDMUND—Don't take it that way! Please, Mama! I'm trying to help. Because it's bad for you to forget. The right way is to remember. So you'll always be on your guard. You know what's happened before. (*miserably*) God, Mama, you know I hate to remind you. I'm doing it because it's been so wonderful having you home the way you've been, and it would be terrible—

MARY—(*strickenly*) Please, dear. I know you mean it for the best, but— (*A defensive uneasiness comes into her voice again.*) I don't understand why you should suddenly say such things. What put it in your mind this morning?

EDMUND—(*evasively*) Nothing. Just because I feel rotten and blue, I suppose.

MARY—Tell me the truth. Why are you so suspicious all of a sudden?

EDMUND—I'm not!

MARY—Oh, yes you are. I can feel it. Your father and Jamie, too—particularly Jamie.

EDMUND—Now don't start imagining things, Mama.

MARY—(*her hands fluttering*) It makes it so much harder, living in this atmosphere of constant suspicion, knowing everyone is spying on me, and none of you believe in me, or trust me.

EDMUND—That's crazy, Mama. We do trust you.

MARY—If there was only some place I could go to get away for a day, or even an afternoon, some woman friend I could talk to—not about anything serious, simply laugh and gossip and forget for a while—someone besides the servants—that stupid Cathleen!

EDMUND—(*gets up worriedly and puts his arm around her*) Stop it, Mama. You're getting yourself worked up over nothing.

MARY—Your father goes out. He meets his friends in barrooms or at the Club. You and Jamie have the boys you know. You go out. But I am alone. I've always been alone.

EDMUND—(*soothingly*) Come now! You know that's a fib. One of us always stays around to keep you company, or goes with you in the automobile when you take a drive.

MARY—(*bitterly*) Because you're afraid to trust me alone! (*She turns on him—sharply*) I insist you tell me why you act so differently this morning—why you felt you had to remind me—

EDMUND—(*hesitates—then blurts out guiltily*) It's stupid. It's just that I wasn't asleep when you came in my room last night. You didn't go back to your and Papa's room. You went in the spare room for the rest of the night.

MARY—Because your father's snoring was driving me crazy! For heaven's sake, haven't I often used the spare room as my bedroom? (*bitterly*) But I see what you thought. That was when—

EDMUND—(*too vehemently*) I didn't think anything!

MARY—So you pretended to be asleep in order to spy on me!

EDMUND—No! I did it because I knew if you found out I was feverish and couldn't sleep, it would upset you.

MARY—Jamie was pretending to be asleep, too, I'm sure, and I suppose your father—

EDMUND—Stop it, Mama!

MARY—Oh, I can't bear it, Edmund, when even you—! (*Her hands flutter up to pat her hair in their aimless, distracted way. Suddenly a strange undercurrent of revengefulness comes into her voice.*) It would serve all of you right if it was true!

EDMUND—Mama! Don't say that! That's the way you talk when—

MARY—Stop suspecting me! Please, dear! You hurt me! I couldn't sleep because I was thinking about you. That's the real reason! I've been so worried ever since you've been sick. (*She puts her arms around him and hugs him with a frightened, protective tenderness.*)

EDMUND—(*soothingly*) That's foolishness. You know it's only a bad cold.

MARY—Yes, of course, I know that!

EDMUND—But listen, Mama. I want you to promise me that even if it should turn out to be something worse, you'll know I'll soon be all right again, anyway, and you won't worry yourself sick, and you'll keep on taking care of yourself—

MARY—(*frightenedly*) I won't listen when you're so silly! There's absolutely no reason to talk as if you expected something dreadful! Of course, I promise you. I give you my sacred word of honor! (*then with a sad bitterness*) But I suppose you're remembering I've promised before on my word of honor.

EDMUND—No!

MARY—(*her bitterness receding into a resigned helplessness*) I'm not blaming you, dear. How can you help it? How can any one of us forget? (*strangely*) That's what makes it so hard—for all of us. We can't forget.

EDMUND—(*grabs her shoulder*) Mama! Stop it!

MARY—(*forcing a smile*) All right, dear. I didn't mean to be so gloomy. Don't mind me. Here. Let me feel your head. Why, it's nice and cool. You certainly haven't any fever now.

EDMUND—Forget! It's you—

MARY—But I'm quite all right, dear. (*with a quick, strange, calculating, almost sly glance at him*) Except I naturally feel tired and nervous this morning, after such a bad night. I really ought to go upstairs and lie down until lunch time and take a nap. (*He gives her an instinctive look of suspicion —then, ashamed of himself, looks quickly away. She hurries on nervously.*) What are you going to do? Read here? It would be much better for you to go out in the fresh air and sunshine. But don't get overheated, remember. Be sure and wear a hat. (*She stops, looking straight at him now. He avoids her eyes. There is a tense pause. Then she speaks jeeringly.*) Or are you afraid to trust me alone?

EDMUND—(*tormentedly*) No! Can't you stop talking like that! I think you ought to take a nap. (*He goes to the screen door —forcing a joking tone*) I'll go down and help Jamie bear up. I love to lie in the shade and watch him work. (*He forces a laugh in which she makes herself join. Then he goes out on the porch and disappears down the steps. Her first reaction is one of relief. She appears to relax. She sinks down in one of the wicker armchairs at rear of table and leans her head back, closing her eyes. But suddenly she grows terribly tense again. Her eyes open and she strains forward, seized by a fit of nervous panic. She begins a desperate battle with herself. Her long fingers, warped and knotted by rheumatism, drum on the arms of the chair, driven by an insistent life of their own, without her consent.*)

(*Curtain*)

ACT TWO
SCENE ONE

SCENE—*The same. It is around quarter to one. No sunlight comes into the room now through the windows at right. Outside the day is still fine but increasingly sultry, with a faint haziness in the air which softens the glare of the sun.*

Edmund sits in the armchair at left of table, reading a book. Or rather he is trying to concentrate on it but cannot. He seems to be listening for some sound from upstairs. His manner is nervously apprehensive and he looks more sickly than in the previous act.

The second girl, Cathleen, enters from the back parlor. She carries a tray on which is a bottle of bonded Bourbon, several whiskey glasses, and a pitcher of ice water. She is a buxom Irish peasant, in her early twenties, with a red-cheeked comely face, black hair and blue eyes—amiable, ignorant, clumsy, and possessed by a dense, well-meaning stupidity. She puts the tray on the table. Edmund pretends to be so absorbed in his book he does not notice her, but she ignores this.

CATHLEEN—(*with garrulous familiarity*) Here's the whiskey. It'll be lunch time soon. Will I call your father and Mister Jamie, or will you?

EDMUND—(*without looking up from his book*) You do it.

CATHLEEN—It's a wonder your father wouldn't look at his watch once in a while. He's a divil for making the meals late, and then Bridget curses me as if I was to blame. But he's a grand handsome man, if he is old. You'll never see the day you're as good looking—nor Mister Jamie, either. (*She chuckles.*) I'll wager Mister Jamie wouldn't miss the time to stop work and have his drop of whiskey if he had a watch to his name!

EDMUND—(*gives up trying to ignore her and grins*) You win that one.

CATHLEEN—And here's another I'd win, that you're making me call them so you can sneak a drink before they come.

EDMUND—Well, I hadn't thought of that—

CATHLEEN—Oh no, not you! Butter wouldn't melt in your mouth, I suppose.

743

EDMUND—But now you suggest it—

CATHLEEN—(*suddenly primly virtuous*) I'd never suggest a man or a woman touch drink, Mister Edmund. Sure, didn't it kill an uncle of mine in the old country. (*relenting*) Still, a drop now and then is no harm when you're in low spirits, or have a bad cold.

EDMUND—Thanks for handing me a good excuse. (*then with forced casualness*) You'd better call my mother, too.

CATHLEEN—What for? She's always on time without any calling. God bless her, she has some consideration for the help.

EDMUND—She's been taking a nap.

CATHLEEN—She wasn't asleep when I finished my work upstairs a while back. She was lying down in the spare room with her eyes wide open. She'd a terrible headache, she said.

EDMUND—(*his casualness more forced*) Oh well then, just call my father.

CATHLEEN—(*goes to the screen door, grumbling good-naturedly*) No wonder my feet kill me each night. I won't walk out in this heat and get sunstroke. I'll call from the porch. (*She goes out on the side porch, letting the screen door slam behind her, and disappears on her way to the front porch. A moment later she is heard shouting*) Mister Tyrone! Mister Jamie! It's time! (*Edmund, who has been staring frightenedly before him, forgetting his book, springs to his feet nervously.*)

EDMUND—God, what a wench! (*He grabs the bottle and pours a drink, adds ice water and drinks. As he does so, he hears someone coming in the front door. He puts the glass hastily on the tray and sits down again, opening his book. Jamie comes in from the front parlor, his coat over his arm. He has taken off collar and tie and carries them in his hand. He is wiping sweat from his forehead with a handkerchief. Edmund looks up as if his reading was interrupted. Jamie takes one look at the bottle and glasses and smiles cynically.*)

JAMIE—Sneaking one, eh? Cut out the bluff, Kid. You're a rottener actor than I am.

EDMUND—(*grins*) Yes, I grabbed one while the going was good.

JAMIE—(*puts a hand affectionately on his shoulder*) That's better. Why kid me? We're pals, aren't we?

EDMUND—I wasn't sure it was you coming.

JAMIE—I made the Old Man look at his watch. I was half-way up the walk when Cathleen burst into song. Our wild Irish lark! She ought to be a train announcer.

EDMUND—That's what drove me to drink. Why don't you sneak one while you've got a chance?

JAMIE—I was thinking of that little thing. (*He goes quickly to the window at right.*) The Old Man was talking to old Captain Turner. Yes, he's still at it. (*He comes back and takes a drink.*) And now to cover up from his eagle eye. He memorizes the level in the bottle after every drink. (*He measures two drinks of water and pours them in the whiskey bottle and shakes it up.*) There. That fixes it. (*He pours water in the glass and sets it on the table by Edmund.*) And here's the water you've been drinking.

EDMUND—Fine! You don't think it will fool him, do you?

JAMIE—Maybe not, but he can't prove it. (*putting on his collar and tie*) I hope he doesn't forget lunch listening to himself talk. I'm hungry. (*He sits across the table from Edmund—irritably*) That's what I hate about working down in front. He puts on an act for every damned fool that comes along.

EDMUND—(*gloomily*) You're in luck to be hungry. The way I feel I don't care if I ever eat again.

JAMIE—(*gives him a glance of concern*) Listen, Kid. You know me. I've never lectured you, but Doctor Hardy was right when he told you to cut out the redeye.

EDMUND—Oh, I'm going to after he hands me the bad news this afternoon. A few before then won't make any difference.

JAMIE—(*hesitates—then slowly*) I'm glad you've got your mind prepared for bad news. It won't be such a jolt. (*He catches Edmund staring at him.*) I mean, it's a cinch you're really sick, and it would be wrong dope to kid yourself.

EDMUND—(*disturbed*) I'm not. I know how rotten I feel, and the fever and chills I get at night are no joke. I think Doctor Hardy's last guess was right. It must be the damned malaria come back on me.

JAMIE—Maybe, but don't be too sure.

EDMUND—Why? What do you think it is?

JAMIE—Hell, how would I know? I'm no Doc. (*abruptly*) Where's Mama?

EDMUND—Upstairs.

JAMIE—(*looks at him sharply*) When did she go up?

EDMUND—Oh, about the time I came down to the hedge, I guess. She said she was going to take a nap.

JAMIE—You didn't tell me—

EDMUND—(*defensively*) Why should I? What about it? She was tired out. She didn't get much sleep last night.

JAMIE—I know she didn't. (*A pause. The brothers avoid looking at each other.*)

EDMUND—That damned foghorn kept me awake, too. (*another pause*)

JAMIE—She's been upstairs alone all morning, eh? You haven't seen her?

EDMUND—No. I've been reading here. I wanted to give her a chance to sleep.

JAMIE—Is she coming down to lunch?

EDMUND—Of course.

JAMIE—(*dryly*) No of course about it. She might not want any lunch. Or she might start having most of her meals alone upstairs. That's happened, hasn't it?

EDMUND—(*with frightened resentment*) Cut it out, Jamie! Can't you think anything but—? (*persuasively*) You're all wrong to suspect anything. Cathleen saw her not long ago. Mama didn't tell her she wouldn't be down to lunch.

JAMIE—Then she wasn't taking a nap?

EDMUND—Not right then, but she was lying down, Cathleen said.

JAMIE—In the spare room?

EDMUND—Yes. For Pete's sake, what of it?

JAMIE—(*bursts out*) You damned fool! Why did you leave her alone so long? Why didn't you stick around?

EDMUND—Because she accused me—and you and Papa— of spying on her all the time and not trusting her. She made me feel ashamed. I know how rotten it must be for her. And she promised on her sacred word of honor—

JAMIE—(*with a bitter weariness*) You ought to know that doesn't mean anything.

EDMUND—It does this time!

JAMIE—That's what we thought the other times. (*He leans over the table to give his brother's arm an affectionate grasp.*) Listen, Kid, I know you think I'm a cynical bastard, but remember I've seen a lot more of this game than you have. You never knew what was really wrong until you were in prep school. Papa and I kept it from you. But I was wise ten years or more before we had to tell you. I know the game backwards and I've been thinking all morning of the way she acted last night when she thought we were asleep. I haven't been able to think of anything else. And now you tell me she got you to leave her alone upstairs all morning.

EDMUND—She didn't! You're crazy!

JAMIE—(*placatingly*) All right, Kid. Don't start a battle with me. I hope as much as you do I'm crazy. I've been as happy as hell because I'd really begun to believe that this time— (*He stops—looking through the front parlor toward the hall—lowering his voice, hurriedly*) She's coming downstairs. You win on that. I guess I'm a damned suspicious louse. (*They grow tense with a hopeful, fearful expectancy. Jamie mutters*) Damn! I wish I'd grabbed another drink.

EDMUND—Me, too. (*He coughs nervously and this brings on a real fit of coughing. Jamie glances at him with worried pity. Mary enters from the front parlor. At first one notices no change except that she appears to be less nervous, to be more as she was when we first saw her after breakfast, but then one becomes aware that her eyes are brighter, and there is a peculiar detachment in her voice and manner, as if she were a little withdrawn from her words and actions.*)

MARY—(*goes worriedly to Edmund and puts her arm around him*) You mustn't cough like that. It's bad for your throat. You don't want to get a sore throat on top of your cold. (*She kisses him. He stops coughing and gives her a quick apprehensive glance, but if his suspicions are aroused her tenderness makes him renounce them and he believes what he wants to believe for the moment. On the other hand, Jamie knows after one probing look at her that his suspicions are justified. His eyes fall to stare at the floor, his face sets in an expression of embittered, defensive cynicism. Mary goes on, half sitting on the arm of Edmund's chair, her arm around him, so her face is above and behind his and he cannot look into her eyes.*) But I seem to be always picking on you, telling you don't do this and don't do that. Forgive me, dear. It's just that I want to take care of you.

EDMUND—I know, Mama. How about you? Do you feel rested?

MARY—Yes, ever so much better. I've been lying down ever since you went out. It's what I needed after such a restless night. I don't feel nervous now.

EDMUND—That's fine. (*He pats her hand on his shoulder. Jamie gives him a strange, almost contemptuous glance, wondering if his brother can really mean this. Edmund does not notice but his mother does.*)

MARY—(*in a forced teasing tone*) Good heavens, how down in the mouth you look, Jamie. What's the matter now?

JAMIE—(*without looking at her*) Nothing.

MARY—Oh, I'd forgotten you've been working on the front hedge. That accounts for your sinking into the dumps, doesn't it?

JAMIE—If you want to think so, Mama.

MARY—(*keeping her tone*) Well, that's the effect it always has, isn't it? What a big baby you are! Isn't he, Edmund?

EDMUND—He's certainly a fool to care what anyone thinks.

MARY—(*strangely*) Yes, the only way is to make yourself not care. (*She catches Jamie giving her a bitter glance and changes the subject.*) Where is your father? I heard Cathleen call him.

EDMUND—Gabbing with old Captain Turner, Jamie says. He'll be late, as usual. (*Jamie gets up and goes to the windows at right, glad of an excuse to turn his back.*)

MARY—I've told Cathleen time and again she must go wherever he is and tell him. The idea of screaming as if this were a cheap boardinghouse!

JAMIE—(*looking out the window*) She's down there now. (*sneeringly*) Interrupting the famous Beautiful Voice! She should have more respect.

MARY—(*sharply—letting her resentment toward him come out*) It's you who should have more respect! Stop sneering at your father! I won't have it! You ought to be proud you're his son! He may have his faults. Who hasn't? But he's worked hard all his life. He made his way up from ignorance and poverty to the top of his profession! Everyone else admires him and you should be the last one to sneer—you, who, thanks to him, have never had to work hard in your life! (*Stung, Jamie has turned to stare at her with accusing antagonism. Her eyes waver guiltily and she adds in a tone which begins to placate*) Remember your father is getting old, Jamie. You really ought to show more consideration.

JAMIE—*I* ought to?

EDMUND—(*uneasily*) Oh, dry up, Jamie! (*Jamie looks out the window again.*) And, for Pete's sake, Mama, why jump on Jamie all of a sudden?

MARY—(*bitterly*) Because he's always sneering at someone else, always looking for the worst weakness in everyone. (*then with a strange, abrupt change to a detached, impersonal tone*) But I suppose life has made him like that, and he can't help it. None of us can help the things life has done to us. They're done before you realize it, and once they're done they make you do other things until at last everything comes between you and what you'd like to be, and you've lost your true self forever. (*Edmund is made apprehensive by her strangeness. He tries to look up in her eyes but she keeps them averted. Jamie turns to her—then looks quickly out of the window again.*)

JAMIE—(*dully*) I'm hungry. I wish the Old Man would get a move on. It's a rotten trick the way he keeps meals waiting, and then beefs because they're spoiled.

MARY—(*with a resentment that has a quality of being automatic and on the surface while inwardly she is indifferent*) Yes, it's very trying, Jamie. You don't know how trying. You don't have to keep house with summer servants who don't care because they know it isn't a permanent position. The really good servants are all with people who have homes and not merely summer places. And your father won't even pay the wages the best summer help ask. So every year I have stupid, lazy greenhorns to deal with. But you've heard me say this a thousand times. So has he, but it goes in one ear and out the other. He thinks money spent on a home is money wasted. He's lived too much in hotels. Never the best hotels, of course. Second-rate hotels. He doesn't understand a home. He doesn't feel at home in it. And yet, he wants a home. He's even proud of having this shabby place. He loves it here. (*She laughs—a hopeless and yet amused laugh.*) It's really funny, when you come to think of it. He's a peculiar man.

EDMUND—(*again attempting uneasily to look up in her eyes*) What makes you ramble on like that, Mama?

MARY—(*quickly casual—patting his cheek*) Why, nothing in particular, dear. It *is* foolish. (*As she speaks, Cathleen enters from the back parlor.*)

CATHLEEN—(*volubly*) Lunch is ready, Ma'am, I went down to Mister Tyrone, like you ordered, and he said he'd come right away, but he kept on talking to that man, telling him of the time when—

MARY—(*indifferently*) All right, Cathleen. Tell Bridget I'm sorry but she'll have to wait a few minutes until Mister Tyrone is here. (*Cathleen mutters, "Yes, Ma'am," and goes off through the back parlor, grumbling to herself.*)

JAMIE—Damn it! Why don't you go ahead without him? He's told us to.

MARY—(*with a remote, amused smile*) He doesn't mean it. Don't you know your father yet? He'd be so terribly hurt.

EDMUND—(*jumps up—as if he was glad of an excuse to leave*) I'll make him get a move on. (*He goes out on the side porch. A moment later he is heard calling from the porch exasperatedly*) Hey! Papa! Come on! We can't wait all day! (*Mary has risen from the arm of the chair. Her hands play restlessly over the table top. She does not look at Jamie but she feels the cynically appraising glance he gives her face and hands.*)

MARY—(*tensely*) Why do you stare like that?

JAMIE—You know. (*He turns back to the window.*)

MARY—I don't know.

JAMIE—Oh, for God's sake, do you think you can fool me, Mama? I'm not blind.

MARY—(*looks directly at him now, her face set again in an expression of blank, stubborn denial*) I don't know what you're talking about.

JAMIE—No? Take a look at your eyes in the mirror!

EDMUND—(*coming in from the porch*) I got Papa moving. He'll be here in a minute. (*with a glance from one to the other, which his mother avoids—uneasily*) What's happened? What's the matter, Mama?

MARY—(*disturbed by his coming, gives way to a flurry of guilty, nervous excitement*) Your brother ought to be ashamed of himself. He's been insinuating I don't know what.

EDMUND—(*turns on Jamie*) God damn you! (*He takes a threatening step toward him. Jamie turns his back with a shrug and looks out the window.*)

MARY—(*more upset, grabs Edmund's arm—excitedly*) Stop this at once, do you hear me? How dare you use such language before me! (*Abruptly her tone and manner change to the strange detachment she has shown before.*) It's wrong to blame your brother. He can't help being what the past has made him. Any more than your father can. Or you. Or I.

EDMUND—(*frightenedly—with a desperate hoping against hope*) He's a liar! It's a lie, isn't it, Mama?

MARY—(*keeping her eyes averted*) What is a lie? Now you're talking in riddles like Jamie. (*Then her eyes meet his stricken, accusing look. She stammers*) Edmund! Don't! (*She looks away and her manner instantly regains the quality of strange detachment—calmly*) There's your father coming up the steps now. I must tell Bridget. (*She goes through the back parlor. Edmund moves slowly to his chair. He looks sick and hopeless.*)

JAMIE—(*from the window, without looking around*) Well?

EDMUND—(*refusing to admit anything to his brother yet— weakly defiant*) Well, what? You're a liar. (*Jamie again shrugs his shoulders. The screen door on the front porch is heard closing. Edmund says dully*) Here's Papa. I hope he loosens up with the old bottle. (*Tyrone comes in through the front parlor. He is putting on his coat.*)

TYRONE—Sorry I'm late. Captain Turner stopped to talk and once he starts gabbing you can't get away from him.

JAMIE—(*without turning—dryly*) You mean once he starts listening. (*His father regards him with dislike. He comes to the table with a quick measuring look at the bottle of whiskey. Without turning, Jamie senses this.*) It's all right. The level in the bottle hasn't changed.

TYRONE—I wasn't noticing that. (*He adds caustically*) As if it proved anything with you around. I'm on to your tricks.

EDMUND—(*dully*) Did I hear you say, let's all have a drink?

TYRONE—(*frowns at him*) Jamie is welcome after his hard morning's work, but I won't invite you. Doctor Hardy—

EDMUND—To hell with Doctor Hardy! One isn't going to kill me. I feel—all in, Papa.

TYRONE—(*with a worried look at him—putting on a fake heartiness*) Come along, then. It's before a meal and I've always found that good whiskey, taken in moderation as an appetizer, is the best of tonics. (*Edmund gets up as his father passes the bottle to him. He pours a big drink. Tyrone frowns admonishingly.*) I said, in moderation. (*He pours his own drink and passes the bottle to Jamie, grumbling*) It'd be a waste of breath mentioning moderation to you. (*Ignoring the hint, Jamie pours a big drink. His father scowls—then, giving it up, resumes his hearty air, raising his glass.*) Well, here's health and happiness! (*Edmund gives a bitter laugh.*)

EDMUND—That's a joke!

TYRONE—What is?

EDMUND—Nothing. Here's how. (*They drink.*)

TYRONE—(*becoming aware of the atmosphere*) What's the matter here? There's gloom in the air you could cut with a knife. (*turns on Jamie resentfully*) You got the drink you were after, didn't you? Why are you wearing that gloomy look on your mug?

JAMIE—(*shrugging his shoulders*) You won't be singing a song yourself soon.

EDMUND—Shut up, Jamie.

TYRONE—(*uneasy now—changing the subject*) I thought lunch was ready. I'm hungry as a hunter. Where is your mother?

MARY—(*returning through the back parlor, calls*) Here I am. (*She comes in. She is excited and self-conscious. As she talks, she glances everywhere except at any of their faces.*) I've had to calm down Bridget. She's in a tantrum over your being late again, and I don't blame her. If your lunch is dried up from waiting in the oven, she said it served you right, you could like it or leave it for all she cared. (*with increasing excitement*) Oh, I'm so sick and tired of pretending this is a home! You won't help me! You won't put yourself out the least bit! You don't know how to act in a home! You don't really want one! You never have wanted one—never since the day we were married! You should have remained a bachelor and lived in second-rate hotels and entertained your friends in barrooms! (*She adds strangely, as if she were now talking aloud to herself rather than to Tyrone*) Then nothing would ever have happened. (*They stare at her. Tyrone knows now. He suddenly looks a tired, bitterly sad old man. Edmund glances at his father and sees that he knows, but he still cannot help trying to warn his mother.*)

EDMUND—Mama! Stop talking. Why don't we go in to lunch.

MARY—(*starts and at once the quality of unnatural detachment settles on her face again. She even smiles with an ironical amusement to herself.*) Yes, it is inconsiderate of me to dig up the past, when I know your father and Jamie must be hungry. (*putting her arm around Edmund's shoulder—with a fond solicitude which is at the same time remote*) I do hope you have an appetite, dear. You really must eat more. (*Her eyes become fixed on the whiskey glass on the table beside him—sharply*) Why is that glass there? Did you take a drink? Oh, how can you be such a fool? Don't you know it's the worst thing? (*She turns on Tyrone.*) You're to blame, James. How could you let him? Do you want to kill him? Don't you remember my father? He wouldn't stop after he was stricken. He said doctors were fools! He thought, like you, that whiskey is a good tonic! (*A look of terror comes into her eyes and she stammers*) But, of course, there's no comparison at all. I don't know why I— Forgive me for scolding you, James. One small drink won't hurt Edmund. It might be good for him, if it gives him an appetite. (*She pats Edmund's cheek playfully, the strange detachment again in her manner. He jerks his head away. She seems not to notice, but she moves instinctively away.*)

JAMIE—(*roughly, to hide his tense nerves*) For God's sake, let's eat. I've been working in the damned dirt under the hedge all morning. I've earned my grub. (*He comes around in back of his father, not looking at his mother, and grabs Edmund's shoulder.*) Come on, Kid. Let's put on the feed bag. (*Edmund gets up, keeping his eyes averted from his mother. They pass her, heading for the back parlor.*)

TYRONE—(*dully*) Yes, you go in with your mother, lads. I'll join you in a second. (*But they keep on without waiting for her. She looks at their backs with a helpless hurt and, as they enter the back parlor, starts to follow them. Tyrone's eyes are on her, sad and condemning. She feels them and turns sharply without meeting his stare.)*

MARY—Why do you look at me like that? (*Her hands flutter up to pat her hair.*) Is it my hair coming down? I was so worn out from last night. I thought I'd better lie down this morning. I drowsed off and had a nice refreshing nap. But I'm sure I fixed my hair again when I woke up. (*forcing a laugh*) Although, as usual, I couldn't find my glasses. (*sharply*) Please stop staring! One would think you were accusing me— (*then pleadingly*) James! You don't understand!

TYRONE—(*with dull anger*) I understand that I've been a God-damned fool to believe in you! (*He walks away from her to pour himself a big drink.*)

MARY—(*Her face again sets in stubborn defiance.*) I don't know what you mean by "believing in me." All I've felt was distrust and spying and suspicion. (*then accusingly*) Why are you having another drink? You never have more than one before lunch. (*bitterly*) I know what to expect. You will be drunk tonight. Well, it won't be the first time, will it—or the thousandth? (*Again she bursts out pleadingly*) Oh, James, please! You don't understand! I'm so worried about Edmund! I'm so afraid he—

TYRONE—I don't want to listen to your excuses, Mary.

MARY—(*strickenly*) Excuses? You mean—? Oh, you can't believe that of me! You mustn't believe that, James! (*then slipping away into her strange detachment—quite casually*) Shall we not go into lunch, dear? I don't want anything but I know you're hungry. (*He walks slowly to where she stands in the doorway. He walks like an old man. As he reaches her she bursts out piteously*) James! I tried so hard! I tried so hard! Please believe—!

TYRONE—(*moved in spite of himself—helplessly*) I suppose you did, Mary. (*then grief-strickenly*) For the love of God, why couldn't you have the strength to keep on?

MARY—(*her face setting into that stubborn denial again*) I don't know what you're talking about. Have the strength to keep on what?

TYRONE—(*hopelessly*) Never mind. It's no use now. (*He*

*moves on and she keeps beside him as they disappear in the back
parlor.)*

(Curtain)

SCENE TWO

SCENE—*The same, about a half hour later. The tray with the
bottle of whiskey has been removed from the table. The family are
returning from lunch as the curtain rises. Mary is the first to enter
from the back parlor. Her husband follows. He is not with her as
he was in the similar entrance after breakfast at the opening of
Act One. He avoids touching her or looking at her. There is condemnation in his face, mingled now with the beginning of an old
weary, helpless resignation. Jamie and Edmund follow their father.
Jamie's face is hard with defensive cynicism. Edmund tries to copy
this defense but without success. He plainly shows he is heartsick as
well as physically ill.*

*Mary is terribly nervous again, as if the strain of sitting
through lunch with them had been too much for her. Yet at the
same time, in contrast to this, her expression shows more of that
strange aloofness which seems to stand apart from her nerves and
the anxieties which harry them.*

*She is talking as she enters—a stream of words that issues ca-
sually, in a routine of family conversation, from her mouth. She
appears indifferent to the fact that their thoughts are not on what
she is saying any more than her own are. As she talks, she comes
to the left of the table and stands, facing front, one hand fumbling
with the bosom of her dress, the other playing over the table top.
Tyrone lights a cigar and goes to the screen door, staring out.
Jamie fills a pipe from a jar on top of the bookcase at rear. He
lights it as he goes to look out the window at right. Edmund sits
in a chair by the table, turned half away from his mother so he
does not have to watch her.*

MARY—It's no use finding fault with Bridget. She doesn't
listen. I can't threaten her, or she'd threaten she'd leave. And
she does do her best at times. It's too bad they seem to be
just the times you're sure to be late, James. Well, there's this
consolation: it's difficult to tell from her cooking whether

she's doing her best or her worst. (*She gives a little laugh of detached amusement—indifferently*) Never mind. The summer will soon be over, thank goodness. Your season will open again and we can go back to second-rate hotels and trains. I hate them, too, but at least I don't expect them to be like a home, and there's no housekeeping to worry about. It's unreasonable to expect Bridget or Cathleen to act as if this was a home. They know it isn't as well as we know it. It never has been and it never will be.

TYRONE—(*bitterly without turning around*) No, it never can be now. But it was once, before you—

MARY—(*her face instantly set in blank denial*) Before I what? (*There is a dead silence. She goes on with a return of her detached air.*) No, no. Whatever you mean, it isn't true, dear. It was never a home. You've always preferred the Club or a barroom. And for me it's always been as lonely as a dirty room in a one-night stand hotel. In a real home one is never lonely. You forget I know from experience what a home is like. I gave up one to marry you—my father's home. (*At once, through an association of ideas she turns to Edmund. Her manner becomes tenderly solicitous, but there is the strange quality of detachment in it.*) I'm worried about you, Edmund. You hardly touched a thing at lunch. That's no way to take care of yourself. It's all right for me not to have an appetite. I've been growing too fat. But you must eat. (*coaxingly maternal*) Promise me you will, dear, for my sake.

EDMUND—(*dully*) Yes, Mama.

MARY—(*pats his cheek as he tries not to shrink away*) That's a good boy. (*There is another pause of dead silence. Then the telephone in the front hall rings and all of them stiffen startledly.*)

TYRONE—(*hastily*) I'll answer. McGuire said he'd call me. (*He goes out through the front parlor.*)

MARY—(*indifferently*) McGuire. He must have another piece of property on his list that no one would think of buying except your father. It doesn't matter any more, but it's always seemed to me your father could afford to keep on buying property but never to give me a home. (*She stops to listen as Tyrone's voice is heard from the hall.*)

TYRONE—Hello. (*with forced heartiness*) Oh, how are you, Doctor? (*Jamie turns from the window. Mary's fingers play more rapidly on the table top. Tyrone's voice, trying to conceal, reveals that he is hearing bad news.*) I see— (*hurriedly*) Well, you'll explain all about it when you see him this afternoon. Yes, he'll be in without fail. Four o'clock. I'll drop in myself and have a talk with you before that. I have to go uptown on business, anyway. Goodbye, Doctor.

EDMUND—(*dully*) That didn't sound like glad tidings. (*Jamie gives him a pitying glance—then looks out the window again. Mary's face is terrified and her hands flutter distractedly. Tyrone comes in. The strain is obvious in his casualness as he addresses Edmund.*)

TYRONE—It was Doctor Hardy. He wants you to be sure and see him at four.

EDMUND—(*dully*) What did he say? Not that I give a damn now.

MARY—(*bursts out excitedly*) I wouldn't believe him if he swore on a stack of Bibles. You mustn't pay attention to a word he says, Edmund.

TYRONE—(*sharply*) Mary!

MARY—(*more excitedly*) Oh, we all realize why you like him, James! Because he's cheap! But please don't try to tell me! I know all about Doctor Hardy. Heaven knows I ought to after all these years. He's an ignorant fool! There should be a law to keep men like him from practicing. He hasn't the slightest idea— When you're in agony and half insane, he sits and holds your hand and delivers sermons on will power! (*Her face is drawn in an expression of intense suffering by the memory. For the moment, she loses all caution. With bitter hatred*) He deliberately humiliates you! He makes you beg and plead! He treats you like a criminal! He understands nothing! And yet it was exactly the same type of cheap quack who first gave you the medicine—and you never knew what it was until too late! (*passionately*) I hate doctors! They'll do anything—anything to keep you coming to them. They'll sell their souls! What's worse, they'll sell yours, and you never know it till one day you find yourself in hell!

EDMUND—Mama! For God's sake, stop talking.

TYRONE—(*shakenly*) Yes, Mary, it's no time—

MARY—(*suddenly is overcome by guilty confusion—stammers*) I— Forgive me, dear. You're right. It's useless to be angry now. (*There is again a pause of dead silence. When she speaks again, her face has cleared and is calm, and the quality of uncanny detachment is in her voice and manner.*) I'm going upstairs for a moment, if you'll excuse me. I have to fix my hair. (*She adds smilingly*) That is if I can find my glasses. I'll be right down.

TYRONE—(*as she starts through the doorway—pleading and rebuking*) Mary!

MARY—(*turns to stare at him calmly*) Yes, dear? What is it?

TYRONE—(*helplessly*) Nothing.

MARY—(*with a strange derisive smile*) You're welcome to come up and watch me if you're so suspicious.

TYRONE—As if that could do any good! You'd only postpone it. And I'm not your jailor. This isn't a prison.

MARY—No. I know you can't help thinking it's a home. (*She adds quickly with a detached contrition*) I'm sorry, dear. I don't mean to be bitter. It's not your fault. (*She turns and disappears through the back parlor. The three in the room remain silent. It is as if they were waiting until she got upstairs before speaking.*)

JAMIE—(*cynically brutal*) Another shot in the arm!

EDMUND—(*angrily*) Cut out that kind of talk!

TYRONE—Yes! Hold your foul tongue and your rotten Broadway loafer's lingo! Have you no pity or decency? (*losing his temper*) You ought to be kicked out in the gutter! But if I did it, you know damned well who'd weep and plead for you, and excuse you and complain till I let you come back.

JAMIE—(*A spasm of pain crosses his face.*) Christ, don't I know that? No pity? I have all the pity in the world for her. I understand what a hard game to beat she's up against— which is more than you ever have! My lingo didn't mean I had no feeling. I was merely putting bluntly what we all know, and have to live with now, again. (*bitterly*) The cures are no damned good except for a while. The truth is there is no cure and we've been saps to hope— (*cynically*) They never come back!

EDMUND—(*scornfully parodying his brother's cynicism*) They never come back! Everything is in the bag! It's all a frame-up! We're all fall guys and suckers and we can't beat the game! (*disdainfully*) Christ, if I felt the way you do—!

JAMIE—(*stung for a moment—then shrugging his shoulders, dryly*) I thought you did. Your poetry isn't very cheery. Nor the stuff you read and claim you admire. (*He indicates the small bookcase at rear.*) Your pet with the unpronounceable name, for example.

EDMUND—Nietzsche. You don't know what you're talking about. You haven't read him.

JAMIE—Enough to know it's a lot of bunk!

TYRONE—Shut up, both of you! There's little choice between the philosophy you learned from Broadway loafers, and the one Edmund got from his books. They're both rotten to the core. You've both flouted the faith you were born and brought up in—the one true faith of the Catholic Church—and your denial has brought nothing but self-destruction! (*His two sons stare at him contemptuously. They forget their quarrel and are as one against him on this issue.*)

EDMUND—That's the bunk, Papa!

JAMIE—We don't pretend, at any rate. (*caustically*) I don't notice you've worn any holes in the knees of your pants going to Mass.

TYRONE—It's true I'm a bad Catholic in the observance, God forgive me. But I believe! (*angrily*) And you're a liar! I may not go to church but every night and morning of my life I get on my knees and pray!

EDMUND—(*bitingly*) Did you pray for Mama?

TYRONE—I did. I've prayed to God these many years for her.

EDMUND—Then Nietzsche must be right. (*He quotes from Thus Spake Zarathustra.*) "God is dead: of His pity for man hath God died."

TYRONE—(*ignores this*) If your mother had prayed, too— She hasn't denied her faith, but she's forgotten it, until now there's no strength of the spirit left in her to fight against her curse. (*then dully resigned*) But what's the good of talk? We've lived with this before and now we must again. There's no help for it. (*bitterly*) Only I wish she hadn't led me to hope this time. By God, I never will again!

EDMUND—That's a rotten thing to say, Papa! (*defiantly*) Well, I'll hope! She's just started. It can't have got a hold on her yet. She can still stop. I'm going to talk to her.

JAMIE—(*shrugs his shoulders*) You can't talk to her now.

She'll listen but she won't listen. She'll be here but she won't be here. You know the way she gets.

TYRONE—Yes, that's the way the poison acts on her always. Every day from now on, there'll be the same drifting away from us until by the end of each night—

EDMUND—(*miserably*) Cut it out, Papa! (*He jumps up from his chair.*) I'm going to get dressed. (*bitterly, as he goes*) I'll make so much noise she can't suspect I've come to spy on her. (*He disappears through the front parlor and can be heard stamping noisily upstairs.*)

JAMIE—(*after a pause*) What did Doc Hardy say about the Kid?

TYRONE—(*dully*) It's what you thought. He's got consumption.

JAMIE—God damn it!

TYRONE—There is no possible doubt, he said.

JAMIE—He'll have to go to a sanatorium.

TYRONE—Yes, and the sooner the better, Hardy said, for him and everyone around him. He claims that in six months to a year Edmund will be cured, if he obeys orders. (*He sighs—gloomily and resentfully*) I never thought a child of mine— It doesn't come from my side of the family. There wasn't one of us that didn't have lungs as strong as an ox.

JAMIE—Who gives a damn about that part of it! Where does Hardy want to send him?

TYRONE—That's what I'm to see him about.

JAMIE—Well, for God's sake, pick out a good place and not some cheap dump!

TYRONE—(*stung*) I'll send him wherever Hardy thinks best!

JAMIE—Well, don't give Hardy your old over-the-hills-to-the-poorhouse song about taxes and mortgages.

TYRONE—I'm no millionaire who can throw money away! Why shouldn't I tell Hardy the truth?

JAMIE—Because he'll think you want him to pick a cheap dump, and because he'll know it isn't the truth—especially if he hears afterwards you've seen McGuire and let that flannel-mouth, gold-brick merchant sting you with another piece of bum property!

TYRONE—(*furiously*) Keep your nose out of my business!

JAMIE—This is Edmund's business. What I'm afraid of is, with your Irish bog-trotter idea that consumption is fatal, you'll figure it would be a waste of money to spend any more than you can help.

TYRONE—You liar!

JAMIE—All right. Prove I'm a liar. That's what I want. That's why I brought it up.

TYRONE—(*his rage still smouldering*) I have every hope Edmund will be cured. And keep your dirty tongue off Ireland! You're a fine one to sneer, with the map of it on your face!

JAMIE—Not after I wash my face. (*Then before his father can react to this insult to the Old Sod, he adds dryly, shrugging his shoulders*) Well, I've said all I have to say. It's up to you. (*abruptly*) What do you want me to do this afternoon, now you're going uptown? I've done all I can do on the hedge until you cut more of it. You don't want me to go ahead with your clipping, I know that.

TYRONE—No. You'd get it crooked, as you get everything else.

JAMIE—Then I'd better go uptown with Edmund. The bad news coming on top of what's happened to Mama may hit him hard.

TYRONE—(*forgetting his quarrel*) Yes, go with him, Jamie. Keep up his spirits, if you can. (*He adds caustically*) If you can without making it an excuse to get drunk!

JAMIE—What would I use for money? The last I heard they were still selling booze, not giving it away. (*He starts for the front-parlor doorway.*) I'll get dressed. (*He stops in the doorway as he sees his mother approaching from the hall, and moves aside to let her come in. Her eyes look brighter, and her manner is more detached. This change becomes more marked as the scene goes on.*)

MARY—(*vaguely*) You haven't seen my glasses anywhere, have you, Jamie? (*She doesn't look at him. He glances away, ignoring her question but she doesn't seem to expect an answer. She comes forward, addressing her husband without looking at him.*) You haven't seen them, have you, James? (*Behind her Jamie disappears through the front parlor.*)

TYRONE—(*turns to look out the screen door*) No, Mary.

MARY—What's the matter with Jamie? Have you been

nagging at him again? You shouldn't treat him with such contempt all the time. He's not to blame. If he'd been brought up in a real home, I'm sure he would have been different. (*She comes to the windows at right—lightly*) You're not much of a weather prophet, dear. See how hazy it's getting. I can hardly see the other shore.

TYRONE—(*trying to speak naturally*) Yes, I spoke too soon. We're in for another night of fog, I'm afraid.

MARY—Oh, well, I won't mind it tonight.

TYRONE—No, I don't imagine you will, Mary.

MARY—(*flashes a glance at him—after a pause*) I don't see Jamie going down to the hedge. Where did he go?

TYRONE—He's going with Edmund to the Doctor's. He went up to change his clothes. (*then, glad of an excuse to leave her*) I'd better do the same or I'll be late for my appointment at the Club. (*He makes a move toward the front-parlor doorway, but with a swift impulsive movement she reaches out and clasps his arm.*)

MARY—(*a note of pleading in her voice*) Don't go yet, dear. I don't want to be alone. (*hastily*) I mean, you have plenty of time. You know you boast you can dress in one-tenth the time it takes the boys. (*vaguely*) There is something I wanted to say. What is it? I've forgotten. I'm glad Jamie is going uptown. You didn't give him any money, I hope.

TYRONE—I did not.

MARY—He'd only spend it on drink and you know what a vile, poisonous tongue he has when he's drunk. Not that I would mind anything he said tonight, but he always manages to drive you into a rage, especially if you're drunk, too, as you will be.

TYRONE—(*resentfully*) I won't. I never get drunk.

MARY—(*teasing indifferently*) Oh, I'm sure you'll hold it well. You always have. It's hard for a stranger to tell, but after thirty-five years of marriage—

TYRONE—I've never missed a performance in my life. That's the proof! (*then bitterly*) If I did get drunk it is not you who should blame me. No man has ever had a better reason.

MARY—Reason? What reason? You always drink too much when you go to the Club, don't you? Particularly when you meet McGuire. He sees to that. Don't think I'm finding fault, dear. You must do as you please. I won't mind.

TYRONE—I know you won't. (*He turns toward the front parlor, anxious to escape.*) I've got to get dressed.

MARY—(*Again she reaches out and grasps his arm—pleadingly*) No, please wait a little while, dear. At least, until one of the boys comes down. You will all be leaving me so soon.

TYRONE—(*with bitter sadness*) It's you who are leaving us, Mary.

MARY—I? That's a silly thing to say, James. How could I leave? There is nowhere I could go. Who would I go to see? I have no friends.

TYRONE—It's your own fault— (*He stops and sighs helplessly—persuasively*) There's surely one thing you can do this afternoon that will be good for you, Mary. Take a drive in the automobile. Get away from the house. Get a little sun and fresh air. (*injuredly*) I bought the automobile for you. You know I don't like the damned things. I'd rather walk any day, or take a trolley. (*with growing resentment*) I had it here waiting for you when you came back from the sanatorium. I hoped it would give you pleasure and distract your mind. You used to ride in it every day, but you've hardly used it at all lately. I paid a lot of money I couldn't afford, and there's the chauffeur I have to board and lodge and pay high wages whether he drives you or not. (*bitterly*) Waste! The same old waste that will land me in the poorhouse in my old age! What good did it do you? I might as well have thrown the money out the window.

MARY—(*with detached calm*) Yes, it was a waste of money, James. You shouldn't have bought a secondhand automobile. You were swindled again as you always are, because you insist on secondhand bargains in everything.

TYRONE—It's one of the best makes! Everyone says it's better than any of the new ones!

MARY—(*ignoring this*) It was another waste to hire Smythe, who was only a helper in a garage and had never been a chauffeur. Oh, I realize his wages are less than a real chauffeur's, but he more than makes up for that, I'm sure, by the graft he gets from the garage on repair bills. Something is always wrong. Smythe sees to that, I'm afraid.

TYRONE—I don't believe it! He may not be a fancy millionaire's flunky but he's honest! You're as bad as Jamie, suspecting everyone!

MARY—You mustn't be offended, dear. I wasn't offended when you gave me the automobile. I knew you didn't mean to humiliate me. I knew that was the way you had to do everything. I was grateful and touched. I knew buying the car was a hard thing for you to do, and it proved how much you loved me, in your way, especially when you couldn't really believe it would do me any good.

TYRONE—Mary! (*He suddenly hugs her to him—brokenly*) Dear Mary! For the love of God, for my sake and the boys' sake and your own, won't you stop now?

MARY—(*stammers in guilty confusion for a second*) I— James! Please! (*Her strange, stubborn defense comes back instantly.*) Stop what? What are you talking about? (*He lets his arm fall to his side brokenly. She impulsively puts her arm around him.*) James! We've loved each other! We always will! Let's remember only that, and not try to understand what we cannot understand, or help things that cannot be helped—the things life has done to us we cannot excuse or explain.

TYRONE—(*as if he hadn't heard—bitterly*) You won't even try?

MARY—(*Her arms drop hopelessly and she turns away—with detachment*) Try to go for a drive this afternoon, you mean? Why, yes, if you wish me to, although it makes me feel lonelier than if I stayed here. There is no one I can invite to drive with me, and I never know where to tell Smythe to go. If there was a friend's house where I could drop in and laugh and gossip awhile. But, of course, there isn't. There never has been. (*her manner becoming more and more remote*) At the Convent I had so many friends. Girls whose families lived in lovely homes. I used to visit them and they'd visit me in my father's home. But, naturally, after I married an actor—you know how actors were considered in those days—a lot of them gave me the cold shoulder. And then, right after we were married, there was the scandal of that woman who had been your mistress, suing you. From then on, all my old friends either pitied me or cut me dead. I hated the ones who cut me much less than the pitiers.

TYRONE—(*with guilty resentment*) For God's sake, don't dig up what's long forgotten. If you're that far gone in the past already, when it's only the beginning of the afternoon, what will you be tonight?

MARY—(*stares at him defiantly now*) Come to think of it, I do have to drive uptown. There's something I must get at the drugstore.

TYRONE—(*bitterly scornful*) Leave it to you to have some of the stuff hidden, and prescriptions for more! I hope you'll lay in a good stock ahead so we'll never have another night like the one when you screamed for it, and ran out of the house in your nightdress half crazy, to try and throw yourself off the dock!

MARY—(*tries to ignore this*) I have to get tooth powder and toilet soap and cold cream— (*She breaks down pitiably.*) James! You mustn't remember! You mustn't humiliate me so!

TYRONE—(*ashamed*) I'm sorry. Forgive me, Mary!

MARY—(*defensively detached again*) It doesn't matter. Nothing like that ever happened. You must have dreamed it. (*He stares at her hopelessly. Her voice seems to drift farther and farther away.*) I was so healthy before Edmund was born. You remember, James. There wasn't a nerve in my body. Even traveling with you season after season, with week after week of one-night stands, in trains without Pullmans, in dirty rooms of filthy hotels, eating bad food, bearing children in hotel rooms, I still kept healthy. But bearing Edmund was the last straw. I was so sick afterwards, and that ignorant quack of a cheap hotel doctor— All he knew was I was in pain. It was easy for him to stop the pain.

TYRONE—Mary! For God's sake, forget the past!

MARY—(*with strange objective calm*) Why? How can I? The past is the present, isn't it? It's the future, too. We all try to lie out of that but life won't let us. (*going on*) I blame only myself. I swore after Eugene died I would never have another baby. I was to blame for his death. If I hadn't left him with my mother to join you on the road, because you wrote telling me you missed me and were so lonely, Jamie would never have been allowed, when he still had measles, to go in the baby's room. (*her face hardening*) I've always believed Jamie did it on purpose. He was jealous of the baby. He hated him.

(*as Tyrone starts to protest*) Oh, I know Jamie was only seven, but he was never stupid. He'd been warned it might kill the baby. He knew. I've never been able to forgive him for that.

TYRONE—(*with bitter sadness*) Are you back with Eugene now? Can't you let our dead baby rest in peace?

MARY—(*as if she hadn't heard him*) It was my fault. I should have insisted on staying with Eugene and not have let you persuade me to join you, just because I loved you. Above all, I shouldn't have let you insist I have another baby to take Eugene's place, because you thought that would make me forget his death. I knew from experience by then that children should have homes to be born in, if they are to be good children, and women need homes, if they are to be good mothers. I was afraid all the time I carried Edmund. I knew something terrible would happen. I knew I'd proved by the way I'd left Eugene that I wasn't worthy to have another baby, and that God would punish me if I did. I never should have borne Edmund.

TYRONE—(*with an uneasy glance through the front parlor*) Mary! Be careful with your talk. If he heard you he might think you never wanted him. He's feeling bad enough already without—

MARY—(*violently*) It's a lie! I did want him! More than anything in the world! You don't understand! I meant, for his sake. He has never been happy. He never will be. Nor healthy. He was born nervous and too sensitive, and that's my fault. And now, ever since he's been so sick I've kept remembering Eugene and my father and I've been so frightened and guilty— (*then, catching herself, with an instant change to stubborn denial*) Oh, I know it's foolish to imagine dreadful things when there's no reason for it. After all, everyone has colds and gets over them. (*Tyrone stares at her and sighs helplessly. He turns away toward the front parlor and sees Edmund coming down the stairs in the hall.*)

TYRONE—(*sharply, in a low voice*) Here's Edmund. For God's sake try and be yourself—at least until he goes! You can do that much for him! (*He waits, forcing his face into a pleasantly paternal expression. She waits frightenedly, seized again by a nervous panic, her hands fluttering over the bosom of her dress, up to her throat and hair, with a distracted aimlessness.*

Then, as Edmund approaches the doorway, she cannot face him. She goes swiftly away to the windows at left and stares out with her back to the front parlor. Edmund enters. He has changed to a ready-made blue serge suit, high stiff collar and tie, black shoes. With an actor's heartiness) Well! You look spic and span. I'm on my way up to change, too. (*He starts to pass him.*)

EDMUND—(*dryly*) Wait a minute, Papa. I hate to bring up disagreeable topics, but there's the matter of carfare. I'm broke.

TYRONE—(*starts automatically on a customary lecture*) You'll always be broke until you learn the value— (*checks himself guiltily, looking at his son's sick face with worried pity*) But you've been learning, lad. You worked hard before you took ill. You've done splendidly. I'm proud of you. (*He pulls out a small roll of bills from his pants pocket and carefully selects one. Edmund takes it. He glances at it and his face expresses astonishment. His father again reacts customarily—sarcastically*) Thank you. (*He quotes*) "How sharper than a serpent's tooth it is—"

EDMUND—"To have a thankless child." I know. Give me a chance, Papa. I'm knocked speechless. This isn't a dollar. It's a ten spot.

TYRONE—(*embarrassed by his generosity*) Put it in your pocket. You'll probably meet some of your friends uptown and you can't hold your end up and be sociable with nothing in your jeans.

EDMUND—You meant it? Gosh, thank you, Papa. (*He is genuinely pleased and grateful for a moment—then he stares at his father's face with uneasy suspicion.*) But why all of a sudden—? (*cynically*) Did Doc Hardy tell you I was going to die? (*Then he sees his father is bitterly hurt.*) No! That's a rotten crack. I was only kidding, Papa. (*He puts an arm around his father impulsively and gives him an affectionate hug.*) I'm very grateful. Honest, Papa.

TYRONE—(*touched, returns his hug*) You're welcome, lad.

MARY—(*suddenly turns to them in a confused panic of frightened anger*) I won't have it! (*She stamps her foot.*) Do you hear, Edmund! Such morbid nonsense! Saying you're going to die! It's the books you read! Nothing but sadness and death! Your father shouldn't allow you to have them. And some of the

poems you've written yourself are even worse! You'd think
you didn't want to live! A boy of your age with everything
before him! It's just a pose you get out of books! You're not
really sick at all!

TYRONE—Mary! Hold your tongue!

MARY—(*instantly changing to a detached tone*) But, James,
it's absurd of Edmund to be so gloomy and make such a great
to-do about nothing. (*turning to Edmund but avoiding his
eyes—teasingly affectionate*) Never mind, dear. I'm on to you.
(*She comes to him.*) You want to be petted and spoiled and
made a fuss over, isn't that it? You're still such a baby. (*She
puts her arm around him and hugs him. He remains rigid and
unyielding. Her voice begins to tremble.*) But please don't carry
it too far, dear. Don't say horrible things. I know it's foolish
to take them seriously but I can't help it. You've got me—so
frightened. (*She breaks and hides her face on his shoulder, sobbing. Edmund is moved in spite of himself. He pats her shoulder
with an awkward tenderness.*)

EDMUND—Don't, Mother. (*His eyes meet his father's.*)

TYRONE—(*huskily—clutching at hopeless hope*) Maybe if you
asked your mother now what you said you were going to—
(*He fumbles with his watch.*) By God, look at the time! I'll have
to shake a leg. (*He hurries away through the front parlor. Mary
lifts her head. Her manner is again one of detached motherly solicitude. She seems to have forgotten the tears which are still in her
eyes.*)

MARY—How do you feel, dear? (*She feels his forehead.*)
Your head is a little hot, but that's just from going out in the
sun. You look ever so much better than you did this morning.
(*taking his hand*) Come and sit down. You mustn't stand on
your feet so much. You must learn to husband your strength.
(*She gets him to sit and she sits sideways on the arm of his chair,
an arm around his shoulder, so he cannot meet her eyes.*)

EDMUND—(*starts to blurt out the appeal he now feels is quite
hopeless*) Listen, Mama—

MARY—(*interrupting quickly*) Now, now! Don't talk. Lean
back and rest. (*persuasively*) You know, I think it would be
much better for you if you stayed home this afternoon and
let me take care of you. It's such a tiring trip uptown in the

dirty old trolley on a hot day like this. I'm sure you'd be much better off here with me.

EDMUND—(*dully*) You forget I have an appointment with Hardy. (*trying again to get his appeal started*) Listen, Mama—

MARY—(*quickly*) You can telephone and say you don't feel well enough. (*excitedly*) It's simply a waste of time and money seeing him. He'll only tell you some lie. He'll pretend he's found something serious the matter because that's his bread and butter. (*She gives a hard sneering little laugh.*) The old idiot! All he knows about medicine is to look solemn and preach will power!

EDMUND—(*trying to catch her eyes*) Mama! Please listen! I want to ask you something! You— You're only just started. You can still stop. You've got the will power! We'll all help you. I'll do anything! Won't you, Mama?

MARY—(*stammers pleadingly*) Please don't—talk about things you don't understand!

EDMUND—(*dully*) All right, I give up. I knew it was no use.

MARY—(*in blank denial now*) Anyway, I don't know what you're referring to. But I do know you should be the last one— Right after I returned from the sanatorium, you began to be ill. The doctor there had warned me I must have peace at home with nothing to upset me, and all I've done is worry about you. (*then distractedly*) But that's no excuse! I'm only trying to explain. It's not an excuse! (*She hugs him to her—pleadingly*) Promise me, dear, you won't believe I made you an excuse.

EDMUND—(*bitterly*) What else can I believe?

MARY—(*slowly takes her arm away—her manner remote and objective again*) Yes, I suppose you can't help suspecting that.

EDMUND—(*ashamed but still bitter*) What do you expect?

MARY—Nothing, I don't blame you. How could you believe me—when I can't believe myself? I've become such a liar. I never lied about anything once upon a time. Now I have to lie, especially to myself. But how can you understand, when I don't myself. I've never understood anything about it, except that one day long ago I found I could no longer call my soul my own. (*She pauses—then lowering her voice to a strange tone of whispered confidence*) But some day, dear, I will find it again—some day when you're all well, and I see you healthy and happy and successful, and I don't have to feel guilty any more—some day when the Blessed Virgin Mary forgives me and gives me back the faith in Her love and pity I used to have in my convent days, and I can pray to Her again—when She sees no one in the world can believe in me even for a moment any more, then She will believe in me, and with Her help it will be so easy. I will hear myself scream with agony, and at the same time I will laugh because I will be so sure of myself. (*Then as Edmund remains hopelessly silent, she adds sadly*) Of course, you can't believe that, either. (*She rises from the arm of his chair and goes to stare out the windows at right with her back to him—casually*) Now I think of it, you might as well go uptown. I forgot I'm taking a drive. I have to go to the drugstore. You would hardly want to go there with me. You'd be so ashamed.

EDMUND—(*brokenly*) Mama! Don't!

MARY—I suppose you'll divide that ten dollars your father gave you with Jamie. You always divide with each other, don't you? Like good sports. Well, I know what he'll do with his share. Get drunk someplace where he can be with the only kind of woman he understands or likes. (*She turns to him, pleading frightenedly*) Edmund! Promise me you won't drink! It's so dangerous! You know Doctor Hardy told you—

EDMUND—(*bitterly*) I thought he was an old idiot.

MARY—(*pitifully*) Edmund! (*Jamie's voice is heard from the front hall,* "Come on, Kid, let's beat it." *Mary's manner at once becomes detached again.*) Go on, Edmund. Jamie's waiting. (*She goes to the front-parlor doorway.*) There comes your father downstairs, too. (*Tyrone's voice calls,* "Come on, Edmund.")

MARY—(*kisses him with detached affection*) Goodbye, dear. If you're coming home for dinner, try not to be late. And tell your father. You know what Bridget is. (*He turns and hurries away. Tyrone calls from the hall,* "Goodbye, Mary," *and then Jamie,* "Goodbye, Mama." *She calls back*) Goodbye. (*The front screen door is heard closing after them. She comes and stands by the table, one hand drumming on it, the other fluttering up to pat her hair. She stares about the room with frightened, forsaken eyes and whispers to herself*) It's so lonely here. (*Then her face hardens into bitter self-contempt.*) You're lying to yourself again. You wanted to get rid of them. Their contempt and disgust aren't pleasant company. You're glad they're gone. (*She gives a little despairing laugh.*) Then Mother of God, why do I feel so lonely?

(*Curtain*)

ACT THREE

SCENE—*The same. It is around half past six in the evening. Dusk is gathering in the living room, an early dusk due to the fog which has rolled in from the Sound and is like a white curtain drawn down outside the windows. From a lighthouse beyond the harbor's mouth, a foghorn is heard at regular intervals, moaning like a mournful whale in labor, and from the harbor itself, intermittently, comes the warning ringing of bells on yachts at anchor.*

The tray with the bottle of whiskey, glasses, and pitcher of ice water is on the table, as it was in the pre-luncheon scene of the previous act.

Mary and the second girl, Cathleen, are discovered. The latter is standing at left of table. She holds an empty whiskey glass in her hand as if she'd forgotten she had it. She shows the effects of drink. Her stupid, good-humored face wears a pleased and flattered simper.

Mary is paler than before and her eyes shine with unnatural brilliance. The strange detachment in her manner has intensified. She has hidden deeper within herself and found refuge and release in a dream where present reality is but an appearance to be accepted and dismissed unfeelingly—even with a hard cynicism—or entirely ignored. There is at times an uncanny gay, free youthfulness in her manner, as if in spirit she were released to become again, simply and without self-consciousness, the naive, happy, chattering schoolgirl of her convent days. She wears the dress into which she had changed for her drive to town, a simple, fairly expensive affair, which would be extremely becoming if it were not for the careless, almost slovenly way she wears it. Her hair is no longer fastidiously in place. It has a slightly disheveled, lopsided look. She talks to Cathleen with a confiding familiarity, as if the second girl were an old, intimate friend. As the curtain rises, she is standing by the screen door looking out. A moan of the foghorn is heard.

MARY—(*amused—girlishly*) That foghorn! Isn't it awful, Cathleen?

CATHLEEN—(*talks more familiarly than usual but never with intentional impertinence because she sincerely likes her mistress*) It is indeed, Ma'am. It's like a banshee.

772

MARY—(*goes on as if she hadn't heard. In nearly all the following dialogue there is the feeling that she has Cathleen with her merely as an excuse to keep talking.*) I don't mind it tonight. Last night it drove me crazy. I lay awake worrying until I couldn't stand it any more.

CATHLEEN—Bad cess to it. I was scared out of my wits riding back from town. I thought that ugly monkey, Smythe, would drive us in a ditch or against a tree. You couldn't see your hand in front of you. I'm glad you had me sit in back with you, Ma'am. If I'd been in front with that monkey— He can't keep his dirty hands to himself. Give him half a chance and he's pinching me on the leg or you-know-where—asking your pardon, Ma'am, but it's true.

MARY—(*dreamily*) It wasn't the fog I minded, Cathleen. I really love fog.

CATHLEEN—They say it's good for the complexion.

MARY—It hides you from the world and the world from you. You feel that everything has changed, and nothing is what it seemed to be. No one can find or touch you any more.

CATHLEEN—I wouldn't care so much if Smythe was a fine, handsome man like some chauffeurs I've seen—I mean, if it was all in fun, for I'm a decent girl. But for a shriveled runt like Smythe—! I've told him, you must think I'm hard up that I'd notice a monkey like you. I've warned him, one day I'll give a clout that'll knock him into next week. And so I will!

MARY—It's the foghorn I hate. It won't let you alone. It keeps reminding you, and warning you, and calling you back. (*She smiles strangely.*) But it can't tonight. It's just an ugly sound. It doesn't remind me of anything. (*She gives a teasing, girlish laugh.*) Except, perhaps, Mr. Tyrone's snores. I've always had such fun teasing him about it. He has snored ever since I can remember, especially when he's had too much to drink, and yet he's like a child, he hates to admit it. (*She laughs, coming to the table.*) Well, I suppose I snore at times, too, and I don't like to admit it. So I have no right to make fun of him, have I? (*She sits in the rocker at right of table.*)

CATHLEEN—Ah, sure, everybody healthy snores. It's a sign of sanity, they say. (*then, worriedly*) What time is it,

Ma'am? I ought to go back in the kitchen. The damp is in Bridget's rheumatism and she's like a raging divil. She'll bite my head off. (*She puts her glass on the table and makes a movement toward the back parlor.*)

MARY—(*with a flash of apprehension*) No, don't go, Cathleen. I don't want to be alone, yet.

CATHLEEN—You won't be for long. The Master and the boys will be home soon.

MARY—I doubt if they'll come back for dinner. They have too good an excuse to remain in the barrooms where they feel at home. (*Cathleen stares at her, stupidly puzzled. Mary goes on smilingly.*) Don't worry about Bridget. I'll tell her I kept you with me, and you can take a big drink of whiskey to her when you go. She won't mind then.

CATHLEEN—(*grins—at her ease again*) No, Ma'am. That's the one thing can make her cheerful. She loves her drop.

MARY—Have another drink yourself, if you wish, Cathleen.

CATHLEEN—I don't know if I'd better, Ma'am. I can feel what I've had already. (*reaching for the bottle*) Well, maybe one more won't harm. (*She pours a drink.*) Here's your good health, Ma'am. (*She drinks without bothering about a chaser.*)

MARY—(*dreamily*) I really did have good health once, Cathleen. But that was long ago.

CATHLEEN—(*worried again*) The Master's sure to notice what's gone from the bottle. He has the eye of a hawk for that.

MARY—(*amusedly*) Oh, we'll play Jamie's trick on him. Just measure a few drinks of water and pour them in.

CATHLEEN—(*does this—with a silly giggle*) God save me, it'll be half water. He'll know by the taste.

MARY—(*indifferently*) No, by the time he comes home he'll be too drunk to tell the difference. He has such a good excuse, he believes, to drown his sorrows.

CATHLEEN—(*philosophically*) Well, it's a good man's failing. I wouldn't give a trauneen for a teetotaler. They've no high spirits. (*then, stupidly puzzled*) Good excuse? You mean

Master Edmund, Ma'am? I can tell the Master is worried about him.

MARY—(*stiffens defensively—but in a strange way the reaction has a mechanical quality, as if it did not penetrate to real emotion*) Don't be silly, Cathleen. Why should he be? A touch of grippe is nothing. And Mr. Tyrone never is worried about anything, except money and property and the fear he'll end his days in poverty. I mean, deeply worried. Because he cannot really understand anything else. (*She gives a little laugh of detached, affectionate amusement.*) My husband is a very peculiar man, Cathleen.

CATHLEEN—(*vaguely resentful*) Well, he's a fine, handsome, kind gentleman just the same, Ma'am. Never mind his weakness.

MARY—Oh, I don't mind. I've loved him dearly for thirty-six years. That proves I know he's lovable at heart and can't help being what he is, doesn't it?

CATHLEEN—(*hazily reassured*) That's right, Ma'am. Love him dearly, for any fool can see he worships the ground you walk on. (*fighting the effect of her last drink and trying to be soberly conversational*) Speaking of acting, Ma'am, how is it you never went on the stage?

MARY—(*resentfully*) I? What put that absurd notion in your head? I was brought up in a respectable home and educated in the best convent in the Middle West. Before I met Mr. Tyrone I hardly knew there was such a thing as a theater. I was a very pious girl. I even dreamed of becoming a nun. I've never had the slightest desire to be an actress.

CATHLEEN—(*bluntly*) Well, I can't imagine you a holy nun, Ma'am. Sure, you never darken the door of a church, God forgive you.

MARY—(*ignores this*) I've never felt at home in the theater. Even though Mr. Tyrone has made me go with him on all his tours, I've had little to do with the people in his company, or with anyone on the stage. Not that I have anything against them. They have always been kind to me, and I to them. But I've never felt at home with them. Their life is not my life. It has always stood between me and— (*She gets up—abruptly*) But let's not talk of old things that couldn't be helped. (*She goes to the porch door and stares out.*) How thick the fog is. I can't see the road. All the people in the world could pass by and I would never know. I wish it was always that way. It's getting dark already. It will soon be night, thank goodness. (*She turns back—vaguely*) It was kind of you to keep me company this afternoon, Cathleen. I would have been lonely driving uptown alone.

CATHLEEN—Sure, wouldn't I rather ride in a fine automobile than stay here and listen to Bridget's lies about her relations? It was like a vacation, Ma'am. (*She pauses—then stupidly*) There was only one thing I didn't like.

MARY—(*vaguely*) What was that, Cathleen?

CATHLEEN—The way the man in the drugstore acted when I took in the prescription for you. (*indignantly*) The impidence of him!

MARY—(*with stubborn blankness*) What are you talking about? What drugstore? What prescription? (*then hastily, as Cathleen stares in stupid amazement*) Oh, of course, I'd forgotten. The medicine for the rheumatism in my hands. What did the man say? (*then with indifference*) Not that it matters, as long as he filled the prescription.

CATHLEEN—It mattered to me, then! I'm not used to being treated like a thief. He gave me a long look and says insultingly, "Where did you get hold of this?" and I says, "It's none of your damned business, but if you must know, it's for the lady I work for, Mrs. Tyrone, who's sitting out in the automobile." That shut him up quick. He gave a look out at you and said, "Oh," and went to get the medicine.

MARY—(*vaguely*) Yes, he knows me. (*She sits in the armchair at right rear of table. She adds in a calm, detached voice*) I have to take it because there is no other that can stop the pain—*all* the pain—I mean, in my hands. (*She raises her hands and regards them with melancholy sympathy. There is no tremor in them now.*) Poor hands! You'd never believe it, but they were once one of my good points, along with my hair and eyes, and I had a fine figure, too. (*Her tone has become more and more far-off and dreamy.*) They were a musician's hands. I used to love the piano. I worked so hard at my music in the Convent—if you can call it work when you do something you love. Mother Elizabeth and my music teacher both said I had more talent than any student they remembered. My father paid for special lessons. He spoiled me. He would do anything I asked. He would have sent me to Europe to study after I graduated from the Convent. I might have gone—if I hadn't fallen in love with Mr. Tyrone. Or I might have become a nun. I had two dreams. To be a nun, that was the more beautiful one. To become a concert pianist, that was the other. (*She pauses, regarding her hands fixedly. Cathleen blinks her eyes to fight off drowsiness and a tipsy feeling.*) I haven't touched a piano in so many years. I couldn't play with such crippled fingers, even if I wanted to. For a time after my marriage I tried to keep up my music. But it was hopeless. One-night stands, cheap hotels, dirty trains, leaving children, never having a home— (*She stares at her hands with fascinated disgust.*) See, Cathleen, how ugly they are! So maimed and crippled! You would think they'd been through some horrible accident! (*She gives a strange little laugh.*) So they have, come to think of it. (*She suddenly thrusts her hands behind her back.*) I won't look at them. They're worse than the foghorn for reminding me— (*then with defiant self-assurance*) But even they can't touch me now. (*She brings her hands from behind her back and deliberately stares at them—calmly*) They're far away. I see them, but the pain has gone.

CATHLEEN—(*stupidly puzzled*) You've taken some of the medicine? It made you act funny, Ma'am. If I didn't know better, I'd think you'd a drop taken.

MARY—(*dreamily*) It kills the pain. You go back until at last you are beyond its reach. Only the past when you were happy is real. (*She pauses—then as if her words had been an evocation which called back happiness she changes in her whole manner and facial expression. She looks younger. There is a quality of an innocent convent girl about her, and she smiles shyly.*) If you think Mr. Tyrone is handsome now, Cathleen, you should have seen him when I first met him. He had the reputation of being one of the best looking men in the country. The girls in the Convent who had seen him act, or seen his photographs, used to rave about him. He was a great matinee idol then, you know. Women used to wait at the stage door just to see him come out. You can imagine how excited I was when my father wrote me he and James Tyrone had become friends, and that I was to meet him when I came home for Easter vacation. I showed the letter to all the girls, and how envious they were! My father took me to see him act first. It was a play about the French Revolution and the leading part was a nobleman. I couldn't take my eyes off him. I wept when he was thrown in prison—and then was so mad at myself because I was afraid my eyes and nose would be red. My father had said we'd go backstage to his dressing room right after the play, and so we did. (*She gives a little excited, shy laugh.*) I was so bashful all I could do was stammer and blush like a little fool. But he didn't seem to think I was a fool. I know he liked me the first moment we were introduced. (*coquettishly*) I guess my eyes and nose couldn't have been red, after all. I was really very pretty then, Cathleen. And he was handsomer than my wildest dream, in his make-up and his nobleman's costume that was so becoming to him. He was different from all ordinary men, like someone from another world. At the same time he was simple, and kind, and unassuming, not a bit stuck-up or vain. I fell in love right then. So did he, he told me afterwards. I forgot all about becoming a nun or a concert pianist. All I wanted was to be his wife. (*She pauses, staring before her with unnaturally bright, dreamy eyes, and a rapt, tender, girlish smile.*) Thirty-six years ago, but I can see it as clearly as if it were tonight! We've loved each other ever since. And in all those thirty-six years, there has never been a breath of scandal about him. I mean, with any other woman. Never since he met me. That has made me very happy, Cathleen. It has made me forgive so many other things.

CATHLEEN—(*fighting tipsy drowsiness—sentimentally*) He's a fine gentleman and you're a lucky woman. (*then, fidgeting*) Can I take the drink to Bridget, Ma'am? It must be near dinnertime and I ought to be in the kitchen helping her. If she don't get something to quiet her temper, she'll be after me with the cleaver.

MARY—(*with a vague exasperation at being brought back from her dream*) Yes, yes, go. I don't need you now.

CATHLEEN—(*with relief*) Thank you, Ma'am. (*She pours out a big drink and starts for the back parlor with it.*) You won't be alone long. The Master and the boys—

MARY — (*impatiently*) No, no, they won't come. Tell Bridget I won't wait. You can serve dinner promptly at half past six. I'm not hungry but I'll sit at the table and we'll get it over with.

CATHLEEN — You ought to eat something, Ma'am. It's a queer medicine if it takes away your appetite.

MARY — (*has begun to drift into dreams again — reacts mechanically*) What medicine? I don't know what you mean. (*in dismissal*) You better take the drink to Bridget.

CATHLEEN — Yes, Ma'am. (*She disappears through the back parlor. Mary waits until she hears the pantry door close behind her. Then she settles back in relaxed dreaminess, staring fixedly at nothing. Her arms rest limply along the arms of the chair, her hands with long, warped, swollen-knuckled, sensitive fingers drooping in complete calm. It is growing dark in the room. There is a pause of dead quiet. Then from the world outside comes the melancholy moan of the foghorn, followed by a chorus of bells, muffled by the fog, from the anchored craft in the harbor. Mary's face gives no sign she has heard, but her hands jerk and the fingers automatically play for a moment on the air. She frowns and shakes her head mechanically as if a fly had walked across her mind. She suddenly loses all the girlish quality and is an aging, cynically sad, embittered woman.*)

MARY — (*bitterly*) You're a sentimental fool. What is so wonderful about that first meeting between a silly romantic schoolgirl and a matinee idol? You were much happier before you knew he existed, in the Convent when you used to pray to the Blessed Virgin. (*longingly*) If I could only find the faith I lost, so I could pray again! (*She pauses — then begins to recite the Hail Mary in a flat, empty tone.*) "Hail, Mary, full of grace! The Lord is with Thee; blessed art Thou among women." (*sneeringly*) You expect the Blessed Virgin to be fooled by a lying dope fiend reciting words! You can't hide from her! (*She springs to her feet. Her hands fly up to pat her hair distractedly.*) I must go upstairs. I haven't taken enough. When you start again you never know exactly how much you need. (*She goes toward the front parlor — then stops in the doorway as she hears the sound of voices from the front path. She starts guiltily.*) That must be them — (*She hurries back to sit down. Her face sets in stubborn defensiveness — resentfully*) Why are they coming back?

They don't want to. And I'd much rather be alone. (*Suddenly her whole manner changes. She becomes pathetically relieved and eager.*) Oh, I'm so glad they've come! I've been so horribly lonely! (*The front door is heard closing and Tyrone calls uneasily from the hall*)

TYRONE—Are you there, Mary? (*The light in the hall is turned on and shines through the front parlor to fall on Mary.*)

MARY—(*rises from her chair, her face lighting up lovingly—with excited eagerness*) I'm here, dear. In the living room. I've been waiting for you. (*Tyrone comes in through the front parlor. Edmund is behind him. Tyrone has had a lot to drink but beyond a slightly glazed look in his eyes and a trace of blur in his speech, he does not show it. Edmund has also had more than a few drinks without much apparent effect, except that his sunken cheeks are flushed and his eyes look bright and feverish. They stop in the doorway to stare appraisingly at her. What they see fulfills their worst expectations. But for the moment Mary is unconscious of their condemning eyes. She kisses her husband and then Edmund. Her manner is unnaturally effusive. They submit shrinkingly. She talks excitedly.*) I'm so happy you've come. I had given up hope. I was afraid you wouldn't come home. It's such a dismal, foggy evening. It must be much more cheerful in the barrooms uptown, where there are people you can talk and joke with. No, don't deny it. I know how you feel. I don't blame you a bit. I'm all the more grateful to you for coming home. I was sitting here so lonely and blue. Come and sit down. (*She sits at left rear of table, Edmund at left of table, and Tyrone in the rocker at right of it.*) Dinner won't be ready for a minute. You're actually a little early. Will wonders never cease. Here's the whiskey, dear. Shall I pour a drink for you? (*Without waiting for a reply she does so.*) And you, Edmund? I don't want to encourage you, but one before dinner, as an appetizer, can't do any harm. (*She pours a drink for him. They make no move to take the drinks. She talks on as if unaware of their silence.*) Where's Jamie? But, of course, he'll never come home so long as he has the price of a drink left. (*She reaches out and clasps her husband's hand—sadly*) I'm afraid Jamie has been lost to us for a long time, dear. (*Her face hardens.*) But we mustn't allow him to drag Edmund down with him, as he's like to do. He's jealous because Edmund has always been the baby—just as he used to be of Eugene. He'll never be content until he makes Edmund as hopeless a failure as he is.

EDMUND—(*miserably*) Stop talking, Mama.

TYRONE—(*dully*) Yes, Mary, the less you say now— (*then to Edmund, a bit tipsily*) All the same there's truth in your mother's warning. Beware of that brother of yours, or he'll poison life for you with his damned sneering serpent's tongue!

EDMUND—(*as before*) Oh, cut it out, Papa.

MARY—(*goes on as if nothing had been said*) It's hard to believe, seeing Jamie as he is now, that he was ever my baby. Do you remember what a healthy, happy baby he was, James? The one-night stands and filthy trains and cheap hotels and bad food never made him cross or sick. He was always smiling or laughing. He hardly ever cried. Eugene was the same, too, happy and healthy, during the two years he lived before I let him die through my neglect.

TYRONE—Oh, for the love of God! I'm a fool for coming home!

EDMUND—Papa! Shut up!

MARY—(*smiles with detached tenderness at Edmund*) It was Edmund who was the crosspatch when he was little, always getting upset and frightened about nothing at all. (*She pats his hand—teasingly*) Everyone used to say, dear, you'd cry at the drop of a hat.

EDMUND—(*cannot control his bitterness*) Maybe I guessed there was a good reason not to laugh.

TYRONE—(*reproving and pitying*) Now, now, lad. You know better than to pay attention—

MARY—(*as if she hadn't heard—sadly again*) Who would have thought Jamie would grow up to disgrace us. You remember, James, for years after he went to boarding school, we received such glowing reports. Everyone liked him. All his teachers told us what a find brain he had, and how easily he learned his lessons. Even after he began to drink and they had to expel him, they wrote us how sorry they were, because he was so likable and such a brilliant student. They predicted a wonderful future for him if he would only learn to take life seriously. (*She pauses—then adds with a strange, sad detach-*

ment) It's such a pity. Poor Jamie! It's hard to understand— (*Abruptly a change comes over her. Her face hardens and she stares at her husband with accusing hostility.*) No, it isn't at all. You brought him up to be a boozer. Since he first opened his eyes, he's seen you drinking. Always a bottle on the bureau in the cheap hotel rooms! And if he had a nightmare when he was little, or a stomach-ache, your remedy was to give him a teaspoonful of whiskey to quiet him.

TYRONE—(*stung*) So I'm to blame because that lazy hulk has made a drunken loafer of himself? Is that what I came home to listen to? I might have known! When you have the poison in you, you want to blame everyone but yourself!

EDMUND—Papa! You told me not to pay attention. (*then, resentfully*) Anyway it's true. You did the same thing with me. I can remember that teaspoonful of booze every time I woke up with a nightmare.

MARY—(*in a detached reminiscent tone*) Yes, you were continually having nightmares as a child. You were born afraid. Because I was so afraid to bring you into the world. (*She pauses—then goes on with the same detachment.*) Please don't think I blame your father, Edmund. He didn't know any better. He never went to school after he was ten. His people were the most ignorant kind of poverty-stricken Irish. I'm sure they honestly believed whiskey is the healthiest medicine for a child who is sick or frightened. (*Tyrone is about to burst out in angry defense of his family but Edmund intervenes.*)

EDMUND—(*sharply*) Papa! (*changing the subject*) Are we going to have this drink, or aren't we?

TYRONE—(*controlling himself—dully*) You're right. I'm a fool to take notice. (*He picks up his glass listlessly.*) Drink hearty, lad. (*Edmund drinks but Tyrone remains staring at the glass in his hand. Edmund at once realizes how much the whiskey has been watered. He frowns, glancing from the bottle to his mother—starts to say something but stops.*)

MARY—(*in a changed tone—repentantly*) I'm sorry if I sounded bitter, James. I'm not. It's all so far away. But I did feel a little hurt when you wished you hadn't come home. I was so relieved and happy when you came, and grateful to you. It's very dreary and sad to be here alone in the fog with night falling.

TYRONE—(*moved*) I'm glad I came, Mary, when you act like your real self.

MARY—I was so lonesome I kept Cathleen with me just to have someone to talk to. (*Her manner and quality drift back to the shy convent girl again.*) Do you know what I was telling her, dear? About the night my father took me to your dressing room and I first fell in love with you. Do you remember?

TYRONE—(*deeply moved—his voice husky*) Can you think I'd ever forget, Mary? (*Edmund looks away from them, sad and embarrassed.*)

MARY—(*tenderly*) No. I know you still love me, James, in spite of everything.

TYRONE—(*His face works and he blinks back tears—with quiet intensity*) Yes! As God is my judge! Always and forever, Mary!

MARY—And I love you, dear, in spite of everything. (*There is a pause in which Edmund moves embarrassedly. The strange detachment comes over her manner again as if she were speaking impersonally of people seen from a distance.*) But I must confess, James, although I couldn't help loving you, I would never have married you if I'd known you drank so much. I remember the first night your barroom friends had to help you up to the door of our hotel room, and knocked and then ran away before I came to the door. We were still on our honeymoon, do you remember?

TYRONE—(*with guilty vehemence*) I don't remember! It wasn't on our honeymoon! And I never in my life had to be helped to bed, or missed a performance!

MARY—(*as though he hadn't spoken*) I had waited in that ugly hotel room hour after hour. I kept making excuses for you. I told myself it must be some business connected with the theater. I knew so little about the theater. Then I became terrified. I imagined all sorts of horrible accidents. I got on my knees and prayed that nothing had happened to you—and then they brought you up and left you outside the door. (*She gives a little, sad sigh.*) I didn't know how often that was to happen in the years to come, how many times I was to wait in ugly hotel rooms. I became quite used to it.

EDMUND—(*bursts out with a look of accusing hate at his*

father) Christ! No wonder—! (*He controls himself—gruffly*) When is dinner, Mama? It must be time.

TYRONE—(*overwhelmed by shame which he tries to hide, fumbles with his watch*) Yes. It must be. Let's see. (*He stares at his watch without seeing it. Pleadingly*) Mary! Can't you forget—?

MARY—(*with detached pity*) No, dear. But I forgive. I always forgive you. So don't look so guilty. I'm sorry I remembered out loud. I don't want to be sad, or to make you sad. I want to remember only the happy part of the past. (*Her manner drifts back to the shy, gay convent girl.*) Do you remember our wedding, dear? I'm sure you've completely forgotten what my wedding gown looked like. Men don't notice such things. They don't think they're important. But it was important to me, I can tell you! How I fussed and worried! I was so excited and happy! My father told me to buy anything I wanted and never mind what it cost. The best is none too good, he said. I'm afraid he spoiled me dreadfully. My mother didn't. She was very pious and strict. I think she was a little jealous. She didn't approve of my marrying—especially an actor. I think she hoped I would become a nun. She used to scold my father. She'd grumble, "You never tell me, never mind what it costs, when I buy anything! You've spoiled that girl so, I pity her husband if she ever marries. She'll expect him to give her the moon. She'll never make a good wife." (*She laughs affectionately.*) Poor mother! (*She smiles at Tyrone with a strange, incongruous coquetry.*) But she was mistaken, wasn't she, James? I haven't been such a bad wife, have I?

TYRONE—(*huskily, trying to force a smile*) I'm not complaining, Mary.

MARY—(*A shadow of vague guilt crosses her face.*) At least, I've loved you dearly, and done the best I could—under the circumstances. (*The shadow vanishes and her shy, girlish expression returns.*) That wedding gown was nearly the death of me and the dressmaker, too! (*She laughs.*) I was so particular. It was never quite good enough. At last she said she refused to touch it any more or she might spoil it, and I made her leave so I could be alone to examine myself in the mirror. I was so pleased and vain. I thought to myself, "Even if your nose and mouth and ears are a trifle too large, your eyes and hair and figure, and your hands, make up for it. You're just as pretty

as any actress he's ever met, and you don't have to use paint."
(*She pauses, wrinkling her brow in an effort of memory.*) Where
is my wedding gown now, I wonder? I kept it wrapped up in
tissue paper in my trunk. I used to hope I would have a
daughter and when it came time for her to marry— She
couldn't have bought a lovelier gown, and I knew, James,
you'd never tell her, never mind the cost. You'd want her to
pick up something at a bargain. It was made of soft, shim-
mering satin, trimmed with wonderful old duchesse lace, in
tiny ruffles around the neck and sleeves, and worked in with
the folds that were draped round in a bustle effect at the back.
The basque was boned and very tight. I remember I held my
breath when it was fitted, so my waist would be as small as
possible. My father even let me have duchesse lace on my
white satin slippers, and lace with the orange blossoms in my
veil. Oh, how I loved that gown! It was so beautiful! Where
is it now, I wonder? I used to take it out from time to time
when I was lonely, but it always made me cry, so finally a
long while ago— (*She wrinkles her forehead again.*) I wonder
where I hid it? Probably in one of the old trunks in the attic.
Some day I'll have to look. (*She stops, staring before her. Tyrone sighs, shaking his head hopelessly, and attempts to catch his
son's eye, looking for sympathy, but Edmund is staring at the
floor.*)

TYRONE—(*forces a casual tone*) Isn't it dinner time, dear?
(*with a feeble attempt at teasing*) You're forever scolding me
for being late, but now I'm on time for once, it's dinner
that's late. (*She doesn't appear to hear him. He adds, still pleasantly*) Well, if I can't eat yet, I can drink. I'd forgotten I had
this. (*He drinks his drink. Edmund watches him. Tyrone scowls
and looks at his wife with sharp suspicion—roughly*) Who's been
tampering with my whiskey? The damned stuff is half water!
Jamie's been away and he wouldn't overdo his trick like this,
anyway. Any fool could tell— Mary, answer me! (*with angry
disgust*) I hope to God you haven't taken to drink on
top of—

EDMUND—Shut up, Papa! (*to his mother, without looking at
her*) You treated Cathleen and Bridget, isn't that it, Mama?

MARY—(*with indifferent casualness*) Yes, of course. They
work hard for poor wages. And I'm the housekeeper, I have

to keep them from leaving. Besides, I wanted to treat Cathleen because I had her drive uptown with me, and sent her to get my prescription filled.

EDMUND—For God's sake, Mama! You can't trust her! Do you want everyone on earth to know?

MARY—(*her face hardening stubbornly*) Know what? That I suffer from rheumatism in my hands and have to take medicine to kill the pain? Why should I be ashamed of that? (*turns on Edmund with a hard, accusing antagonism—almost a revengeful enmity*) I never knew what rheumatism was before you were born! Ask your father! (*Edmund looks away, shrinking into himself.*)

TYRONE—Don't mind her, lad. It doesn't mean anything. When she gets to the stage where she gives the old crazy excuse about her hands she's gone far away from us.

MARY—(*turns on him—with a strangely triumphant, taunting smile*) I'm glad you realize that, James! Now perhaps you'll give up trying to remind me, you and Edmund! (*abruptly, in a detached, matter-of-fact tone*) Why don't you light the light, James? It's getting dark. I know you hate to, but Edmund has proved to you that one bulb burning doesn't cost much. There's no sense letting your fear of the poorhouse make you too stingy.

TYRONE—(*reacts mechanically*) I never claimed one bulb cost much! It's having them on, one here and one there, that makes the Electric Light Company rich. (*He gets up and turns on the reading lamp—roughly*) But I'm a fool to talk reason to you. (*to Edmund*) I'll get a fresh bottle of whiskey, lad, and we'll have a real drink. (*He goes through the back parlor.*)

MARY—(*with detached amusement*) He'll sneak around to the outside cellar door so the servants won't see him. He's really ashamed of keeping his whiskey padlocked in the cellar. Your father is a strange man, Edmund. It took many years before I understood him. You must try to understand and forgive him, too, and not feel contempt because he's close-fisted. His father deserted his mother and their six children a year or so after they came to America. He told them he had a premonition he would die soon, and he was homesick for Ireland, and wanted to go back there to die. So he went and he did die. He must have been a peculiar man, too. Your father had to go to work in a machine shop when he was only ten years old.

EDMUND—(*protests dully*) Oh, for Pete's sake, Mama. I've heard Papa tell that machine shop story ten thousand times.

MARY—Yes, dear, you've had to listen, but I don't think you've ever tried to understand.

EDMUND—(*ignoring this—miserably*) Listen, Mama! You're not so far gone yet you've forgotten everything. You haven't asked me what I found out this afternoon. Don't you care a damn?

MARY—(*shakenly*) Don't say that! You hurt me, dear!

EDMUND—What I've got is serious, Mama. Doc Hardy knows for sure now.

MARY—(*stiffens into scornful, defensive stubbornness*) That lying old quack! I warned you he'd invent—!

EDMUND—(*miserably dogged*) He called in a specialist to examine me, so he'd be absolutely sure.

MARY—(*ignoring this*) Don't tell me about Hardy! If you heard what the doctor at the sanatorium, who really knows something, said about how he'd treated me! He said he ought to be locked up! He said it was a wonder I hadn't gone mad! I told him I had once, that time I ran down in my nightdress to throw myself off the dock. You remember that, don't you? And yet you want me to pay attention to what Doctor Hardy says. Oh, no!

EDMUND—(*bitterly*) I remember, all right. It was right after that Papa and Jamie decided they couldn't hide it from me any more. Jamie told me. I called him a liar! I tried to punch him in the nose. But I knew he wasn't lying. (*His voice trembles, his eyes begin to fill with tears.*) God, it made everything in life seem rotten!

MARY—(*pitiably*) Oh, don't. My baby! You hurt me so dreadfully!

EDMUND—(*dully*) I'm sorry, Mama. It was you who brought it up. (*then with a bitter, stubborn persistence*) Listen, Mama. I'm going to tell you whether you want to hear or not. I've got to go to a sanatorium.

MARY—(*dazedly, as if this was something that had never occurred to her*) Go away? (*violently*) No! I won't have it! How dare Doctor Hardy advise such a thing without consulting me! How dare your father allow him! What right has he? You are my baby! Let him attend to Jamie! (*more and more excited and bitter*) I know why he wants you sent to a sanatorium. To take you from me! He's always tried to do that. He's been jealous of every one of my babies! He kept finding ways to make me leave them. That's what caused Eugene's death. He's been jealous of you most of all. He knew I loved you most because—

EDMUND—(*miserably*) Oh, stop talking crazy, can't you, Mama! Stop trying to blame him. And why are you so against my going away now? I've been away a lot, and I've never noticed it broke your heart!

MARY—(*bitterly*) I'm afraid you're not very sensitive, after all. (*sadly*) You might have guessed, dear, that after I knew you knew—about me—I had to be glad whenever you were where you couldn't see me.

EDMUND—(*brokenly*) Mama! Don't! (*He reaches out blindly and takes her hand—but he drops it immediately, overcome by bitterness again.*) All this talk about loving me—and you won't even listen when I try to tell you how sick—

MARY—(*with an abrupt transformation into a detached bullying motherliness*) Now, now. That's enough! I don't care to hear because I know it's nothing but Hardy's ignorant lies. (*He shrinks back into himself. She keeps on in a forced, teasing tone but with an increasing undercurrent of resentment.*) You're so like your father, dear. You love to make a scene out of nothing so you can be dramatic and tragic. (*with a belittling laugh*) If I gave you the slightest encouragement, you'd tell me next you were going to die—

EDMUND—People do die of it. Your own father—

MARY—(*sharply*) Why do you mention him? There's no comparison at all with you. He had consumption. (*angrily*) I hate you when you become gloomy and morbid! I forbid you to remind me of my father's death, do you hear me?

EDMUND—(*his face hard—grimly*) Yes, I hear you, Mama. I wish to God I didn't! (*He gets up from his chair and stands staring condemningly at her—bitterly*) It's pretty hard to take at times, having a dope fiend for a mother! (*She winces—all life seeming to drain from her face, leaving it with the appearance of a plaster cast. Instantly Edmund wishes he could take back what he has said. He stammers miserably*) Forgive me, Mama. I was angry. You hurt me. (*There is a pause in which the foghorn and the ships' bells are heard.*)

MARY—(*goes slowly to the windows at right like an automaton—looking out, a blank, far-off quality in her voice*) Just listen to that awful foghorn. And the bells. Why is it fog makes everything sound so sad and lost, I wonder?

EDMUND—(*brokenly*) I—I can't stay here. I don't want any dinner. (*He hurries away through the front parlor. She keeps staring out the window until she hears the front door close behind him. Then she comes back and sits in her chair, the same blank look on her face.*)

MARY—(*vaguely*) I must go upstairs. I haven't taken enough. (*She pauses—then longingly*) I hope, sometime, without meaning it, I will take an overdose. I never could do it deliberately. The Blessed Virgin would never forgive me, then. (*She hears Tyrone returning and turns as he comes in, through the back parlor, with a bottle of whiskey he has just uncorked. He is fuming.*)

TYRONE—(*wrathfully*) The padlock is all scratched. That drunken loafer has tried to pick the lock with a piece of wire, the way he's done before. (*with satisfaction, as if this was a perpetual battle of wits with his elder son*) But I've fooled him this time. It's a special padlock a professional burglar couldn't pick. (*He puts the bottle on the tray and suddenly is aware of Edmund's absence.*) Where's Edmund?

MARY—(*with a vague far-away air*) He went out. Perhaps he's going uptown again to find Jamie. He still has some money left, I suppose, and it's burning a hole in his pocket. He said he didn't want any dinner. He doesn't seem to have any appetite these days. (*then stubbornly*) But it's just a summer cold. (*Tyrone stares at her and shakes his head helplessly and pours himself a big drink and drinks it. Suddenly it is too much for her and she breaks out and sobs*) Oh, James, I'm so frightened! (*She gets up and throws her arms around him and hides her face on his shoulder—sobbingly*) I know he's going to die!

TYRONE—Don't say that! It's not true! They promised me in six months he'd be cured.

MARY—You don't believe that! I can tell when you're acting! And it will be my fault. I should never have borne him.
It would have been better for his sake. I could never hurt him
then. He wouldn't have had to know his mother was a dope
fiend—and hate her!

TYRONE—(*his voice quivering*) Hush, Mary, for the love of
God! He loves you. He knows it was a curse put on you
without your knowing or willing it. He's proud you're his
mother! (*abruptly as he hears the pantry door opening*) Hush,
now! Here comes Cathleen. You don't want her to see you
crying. (*She turns quickly away from him to the windows at right,
hastily wiping her eyes. A moment later Cathleen appears in the
back-parlor doorway. She is uncertain in her walk and grinning
woozily.*)

CATHLEEN—(*starts guiltily when she sees Tyrone—with
dignity*) Dinner is served, Sir. (*raising her voice unnecessarily*)
Dinner is served, Ma'am. (*She forgets her dignity and addresses
Tyrone with good-natured familiarity.*) So you're here, are you?
Well, well. Won't Bridget be in a rage! I told her the Madame
said you wouldn't be home. (*then reading accusation in his eye*)
Don't be looking at me that way. If I've a drop taken, I didn't
steal it. I was invited. (*She turns with huffy dignity and disappears through the back parlor.*)

TYRONE—(*sighs—then summoning his actor's heartiness*)
Come along, dear. Let's have our dinner. I'm hungry as a
hunter.

MARY—(*comes to him—her face is composed in plaster again
and her tone is remote*) I'm afraid you'll have to excuse me,
James. I couldn't possibly eat anything. My hands pain me
dreadfully. I think the best thing for me is to go to bed and
rest. Good night, dear. (*She kisses him mechanically and turns
toward the front parlor.*)

TYRONE—(*harshly*) Up to take more of that God-damned
poison, is that it? You'll be like a mad ghost before the night's
over!

MARY—(*starts to walk away—blankly*) I don't know what
you're talking about, James. You say such mean, bitter things
when you've drunk too much. You're as bad as Jamie or Edmund. (*She moves off through the front parlor. He stands a second*

as if not knowing what to do. He is a sad, bewildered, broken old man. He walks wearily off through the back parlor toward the dining room.)

(*Curtain*)

ACT FOUR

SCENE—*The same. It is around midnight. The lamp in the front hall has been turned out, so that now no light shines through the front parlor. In the living room only the reading lamp on the table is lighted. Outside the windows the wall of fog appears denser than ever. As the curtain rises, the foghorn is heard, followed by the ships' bells from the harbor.*

Tyrone is seated at the table. He wears his pince-nez, and is playing solitaire. He has taken off his coat and has on an old brown dressing gown. The whiskey bottle on the tray is three-quarters empty. There is a fresh full bottle on the table, which he has brought from the cellar so there will be an ample reserve at hand. He is drunk and shows it by the owlish, deliberate manner in which he peers at each card to make certain of its identity, and then plays it as if he wasn't certain of his aim. His eyes have a misted, oily look and his mouth is slack. But despite all the whiskey in him, he has not escaped, and he looks as he appeared at the close of the preceding act, a sad, defeated old man, possessed by hopeless resignation.

As the curtain rises, he finishes a game and sweeps the cards together. He shuffles them clumsily, dropping a couple on the floor. He retrieves them with difficulty, and starts to shuffle again, when he hears someone entering the front door. He peers over his pince-nez through the front parlor.

TYRONE—(*his voice thick*) Who's that? Is it you, Edmund? (*Edmund's voice answers curtly, "Yes." Then he evidently collides with something in the dark hall and can be heard cursing. A moment later the hall lamp is turned on. Tyrone frowns and calls*) Turn that light out before you come in. (*But Edmund doesn't. He comes in through the front parlor. He is drunk now, too, but like his father he carries it well, and gives little physical sign of it except in his eyes and a chip-on-the-shoulder aggressiveness in his manner. Tyrone speaks, at first with a warm, relieved welcome.*) I'm glad you've come, lad. I've been damned lonely. (*then resentfully*) You're a fine one to run away and leave me to sit alone here all night when you know— (*with sharp irritation*) I told you to turn out that light! We're not giving a ball.

There's no reason to have the house ablaze with electricity at this time of night, burning up money!

EDMUND—(*angrily*) Ablaze with electricity! One bulb! Hell, everyone keeps a light on in the front hall until they go to bed. (*He rubs his knee.*) I damned near busted my knee on the hat stand.

TYRONE—The light from here shows in the hall. You could see your way well enough if you were sober.

EDMUND—If *I* was sober? I like that!

TYRONE—I don't give a damn what other people do. If they want to be wasteful fools, for the sake of show, let them be!

EDMUND—One bulb! Christ, don't be such a cheap skate! I've proved by figures if you left the light bulb on all night it wouldn't be as much as one drink!

TYRONE—To hell with your figures! The proof is in the bills I have to pay!

EDMUND—(*sits down opposite his father—contemptuously*) Yes, facts don't mean a thing, do they? What you want to believe, that's the only truth! (*derisively*) Shakespeare was an Irish Catholic, for example.

TYRONE—(*stubbornly*) So he was. The proof is in his plays.

EDMUND—Well he wasn't, and there's no proof of it in his plays, except to you! (*jeeringly*) The Duke of Wellington, there was another good Irish Catholic!

TYRONE—I never said he was a good one. He was a renegade but a Catholic just the same.

EDMUND—Well, he wasn't. You just want to believe no one but an Irish Catholic general could beat Napoleon.

TYRONE—I'm not going to argue with you. I asked you to turn out that light in the hall.

EDMUND—I heard you, and as far as I'm concerned it stays on.

TYRONE—None of your damned insolence! Are you going to obey me or not?

EDMUND—Not! If you want to be a crazy miser put it out yourself!

TYRONE—(*with threatening anger*) Listen to me! I've put up with a lot from you because from the mad things you've done at times I've thought you weren't quite right in your head. I've excused you and never lifted my hand to you. But there's a straw that breaks the camel's back. You'll obey me and put out that light or, big as you are, I'll give you a thrashing that'll teach you—! (*Suddenly he remembers Edmund's illness and instantly becomes guilty and shamefaced.*) Forgive me, lad. I forgot— You shouldn't goad me into losing my temper.

EDMUND—(*ashamed himself now*) Forget it, Papa. I apologize, too. I had no right being nasty about nothing. I am a bit soused, I guess. I'll put out the damned light. (*He starts to get up.*)

TYRONE—No, stay where you are. Let it burn. (*He stands up abruptly—and a bit drunkenly—and begins turning on the three bulbs in the chandelier, with a childish, bitterly dramatic self-pity.*) We'll have them all on! Let them burn! To hell with them! The poorhouse is the end of the road, and it might as well be sooner as later! (*He finishes turning on the lights.*)

EDMUND—(*has watched this proceeding with an awakened sense of humor—now he grins, teasing affectionately*) That's a grand curtain. (*He laughs.*) You're a wonder, Papa.

TYRONE—(*sits down sheepishly—grumbles pathetically*) That's right, laugh at the old fool! The poor old ham! But the final curtain will be in the poorhouse just the same, and that's not comedy! (*Then as Edmund is still grinning, he changes the subject.*) Well, well, let's not argue. You've got brains in that head of yours, though you do your best to deny them. You'll live to learn the value of a dollar. You're not like your damned tramp of a brother. I've given up hope he'll ever get sense. Where is he, by the way?

EDMUND—How would I know?

TYRONE—I thought you'd gone back uptown to meet him.

EDMUND—No. I walked out to the beach. I haven't seen him since this afternoon.

TYRONE—Well, if you split the money I gave you with him, like a fool—

EDMUND—Sure I did. He's always staked me when he had anything.

TYRONE—Then it doesn't take a soothsayer to tell he's probably in the whorehouse.

EDMUND—What of it if he is? Why not?

TYRONE—(*contemptuously*) Why not, indeed. It's the fit place for him. If he's ever had a loftier dream than whores and whiskey, he's never shown it.

EDMUND—Oh, for Pete's sake, Papa! If you're going to start that stuff, I'll beat it. (*He starts to get up.*)

TYRONE—(*placatingly*) All right, all right, I'll stop. God knows, I don't like the subject either. Will you join me in a drink?

EDMUND—Ah! Now you're talking!

TYRONE—(*passes the bottle to him—mechanically*) I'm wrong to treat you. You've had enough already.

EDMUND—(*pouring a big drink—a bit drunkenly*) Enough is *not* as good as a feast. (*He hands back the bottle.*)

TYRONE—It's too much in your condition.

EDMUND—Forget my condition! (*He raises his glass.*) Here's how.

TYRONE—Drink hearty. (*They drink.*) If you walked all the way to the beach you must be damp and chilled.

EDMUND—Oh, I dropped in at the Inn on the way out and back.

TYRONE—It's not a night I'd pick for a long walk.

EDMUND—I loved the fog. It was what I needed. (*He sounds more tipsy and looks it.*)

TYRONE—You should have more sense than to risk—

EDMUND—To hell with sense! We're all crazy. What do we want with sense? (*He quotes from Dowson sardonically.*)

"They are not long, the weeping and the laughter,
    Love and desire and hate:
    I think they have no portion in us after
    We pass the gate.

They are not long, the days of wine and roses:
    Out of a misty dream
    Our path emerges for a while, then closes
    Within a dream."

(*staring before him*) The fog was where I wanted to be. Halfway down the path you can't see this house. You'd never know it was here. Or any of the other places down the avenue. I couldn't see but a few feet ahead. I didn't meet a soul. Everything looked and sounded unreal. Nothing was what it

is. That's what I wanted—to be alone with myself in another
world where truth is untrue and life can hide from itself. Out
beyond the harbor, where the road runs along the beach, I
even lost the feeling of being on land. The fog and the sea
seemed part of each other. It was like walking on the bottom
of the sea. As if I had drowned long ago. As if I was a ghost
belonging to the fog, and the fog was the ghost of the sea. It
felt damned peaceful to be nothing more than a ghost within
a ghost. (*He sees his father staring at him with mingled worry
and irritated disapproval. He grins mockingly.*) Don't look at me
as if I'd gone nutty. I'm talking sense. Who wants to see life
as it is, if they can help it? It's the three Gorgons in one. You
look in their faces and turn to stone. Or it's Pan. You see him
and you die—that is, inside you—and have to go on living
as a ghost.

TYRONE—(*impressed and at the same time revolted*) You
have a poet in you but it's a damned morbid one! (*forcing a
smile*) Devil take your pessimism. I feel low-spirited enough.
(*He sighs.*) Why can't you remember your Shakespeare and
forget the third-raters. You'll find what you're trying to say in
him—as you'll find everything else worth saying. (*He quotes,
using his fine voice*) "We are such stuff as dreams are made on,
and our little life is rounded with a sleep."

EDMUND—(*ironically*) Fine! That's beautiful. But I wasn't
trying to say that. We are such stuff as manure is made on, so
let's drink up and forget it. That's more my idea.

TYRONE—(*disgustedly*) Ach! Keep such sentiments to yourself. I shouldn't have given you that drink.

EDMUND—It did pack a wallop, all right. On you, too.
(*He grins with affectionate teasing.*) Even if you've never
missed a performance! (*aggressively*) Well, what's wrong with
being drunk? It's what we're after, isn't it? Let's not kid
each other, Papa. Not tonight. We know what we're trying to
forget. (*hurriedly*) But let's not talk about it. It's no use now.

TYRONE—(*dully*) No. All we can do is try to be resigned
—again.

EDMUND—Or be so drunk you can forget. (*He recites,
and recites well, with bitter, ironical passion, the Symons' translation of Baudelaire's prose poem.*)

"Be always drunken. Nothing else matters: that is the only question. If you would not feel the horrible burden of Time weighing on your shoulders and crushing you to the earth, be drunken continually.

Drunken with what? With wine, with poetry, or with virtue, as you will. But be drunken.

And if sometimes, on the stairs of a palace, or on the green side of a ditch, or in the dreary solitude of your own room, you should awaken and the drunkenness be half or wholly slipped away from you, ask of the wind, or of the wave, or of the star, or of the bird, or of the clock, of whatever flies, or sighs, or rocks, or sings, or speaks, ask what hour it is; and the wind, wave, star, bird, clock, will answer you: 'It is the hour to be drunken! Be drunken, if you would not be martyred slaves of Time; be drunken continually! With wine, with poetry, or with virtue, as you will.' "
(*He grins at his father provocatively.*)

TYRONE—(*thickly humorous*) I wouldn't worry about the virtue part of it, if I were you. (*then disgustedly*) Pah! It's morbid nonsense! What little truth is in it you'll find nobly said in Shakespeare. (*then appreciatively*) But you recited it well, lad. Who wrote it?

EDMUND—Baudelaire.

TYRONE—Never heard of him.

EDMUND—(*grins provocatively*) He also wrote a poem about Jamie and the Great White Way.

TYRONE—That loafer! I hope to God he misses the last car and has to stay uptown!

EDMUND—(*goes on, ignoring this*) Although he was French and never saw Broadway and died before Jamie was born. He knew him and Little Old New York just the same. (*He recites the Symons' translation of Baudelaire's "Epilogue."*)

"With heart at rest I climbed the citadel's
    Steep height, and saw the city as from a tower,
    Hospital, brothel, prison, and such hells,

Where evil comes up softly like a flower.
    Thou knowest, O Satan, patron of my pain,
    Not for vain tears I went up at that hour;

But like an old sad faithful lecher, fain
To drink delight of that enormous trull
Whose hellish beauty makes me young again.

Whether thou sleep, with heavy vapours full,
Sodden with day, or, new apparelled, stand
In gold-laced veils of evening beautiful,

I love thee, infamous city! Harlots and
Hunted have pleasures of their own to give,
The vulgar herd can never understand."

TYRONE—(*with irritable disgust*) Morbid filth! Where the hell do you get your taste in literature? Filth and despair and pessimism! Another atheist, I suppose. When you deny God, you deny hope. That's the trouble with you. If you'd get down on your knees—

EDMUND—(*as if he hadn't heard—sardonically*) It's a good likeness of Jamie, don't you think, hunted by himself and whiskey, hiding in a Broadway hotel room with some fat tart—he likes them fat—reciting Dowson's Cynara to her. (*He recites derisively, but with deep feeling.*)

"All night upon mine heart I felt her warm heart beat,
Night-long within mine arms in love and sleep she lay;
Surely the kisses of her bought red mouth were sweet;
But I was desolate and sick of an old passion,
When I awoke and found the dawn was gray:
I have been faithful to thee, Cynara! in my fashion."

(*jeeringly*) And the poor fat burlesque queen doesn't get a word of it, but suspects she's being insulted! And Jamie never loved any Cynara, and was never faithful to a woman in his life, even in his fashion! But he lies there, kidding himself he is superior and enjoys pleasures "the vulgar herd can never understand"! (*He laughs.*) It's nuts—completely nuts!

TYRONE—(*vaguely—his voice thick*) It's madness, yes. If you'd get on your knees and pray. When you deny God, you deny sanity.

EDMUND—(*ignoring this*) But who am I to feel superior? I've done the same damned thing. And it's no more crazy than Dowson himself, inspired by an absinthe hangover, writing it to a dumb barmaid, who thought he was a poor crazy souse, and gave him the gate to marry a waiter! (*He laughs—*

then soberly, with genuine sympathy) Poor Dowson. Booze and consumption got him. (*He starts and for a second looks miserable and frightened. Then with defensive irony*) Perhaps it would be tactful of me to change the subject.

TYRONE—(*thickly*) Where you get your taste in authors— That damned library of yours! (*He indicates the small bookcase at rear.*) Voltaire, Rousseau, Schopenhauer, Nietzsche, Ibsen! Atheists, fools, and madmen! And your poets! This Dowson, and this Baudelaire, and Swinburne and Oscar Wilde, and Whitman and Poe! Whoremongers and degenerates! Pah! When I've three good sets of Shakespeare there (*he nods at the large bookcase*) you could read.

EDMUND—(*provocatively*) They say he was a souse, too.

TYRONE—They lie! I don't doubt he liked his glass— it's a good man's failing—but he knew how to drink so it didn't poison his brain with morbidness and filth. Don't compare him with the pack you've got in there. (*He indicates the small bookcase again.*) Your dirty Zola! And your Dante Gabriel Rossetti who was a dope fiend! (*He starts and looks guilty.*)

EDMUND—(*with defensive dryness*) Perhaps it would be wise to change the subject. (*a pause*) You can't accuse me of not knowing Shakespeare. Didn't I win five dollars from you once when you bet me I couldn't learn a leading part of his in a week, as you used to do in stock in the old days. I learned Macbeth and recited it letter perfect, with you giving me the cues.

TYRONE—(*approvingly*) That's true. So you did. (*He smiles teasingly and sighs.*) It was a terrible ordeal, I remember, hearing you murder the lines. I kept wishing I'd paid over the bet without making you prove it. (*He chuckles and Edmund grins. Then he starts as he hears a sound from upstairs—with dread*) Did you hear? She's moving around. I was hoping she'd gone to sleep.

EDMUND—Forget it! How about another drink? (*He reaches out and gets the bottle, pours a drink and hands it back. Then with a strained casualness, as his father pours a drink*) When did Mama go to bed?

TYRONE—Right after you left. She wouldn't eat any dinner. What made you run away?

EDMUND—Nothing. (*abruptly raising his glass*) Well, here's how.

TYRONE—(*mechanically*) Drink hearty, lad. (*They drink. Tyrone again listens to sounds upstairs—with dread*) She's moving around a lot. I hope to God she doesn't come down.

EDMUND—(*dully*) Yes. She'll be nothing but a ghost haunting the past by this time. (*He pauses—then miserably*) Back before I was born—

TYRONE—Doesn't she do the same with me? Back before she ever knew me. You'd think the only happy days she's ever known were in her father's home, or at the Convent, praying and playing the piano. (*jealous resentment in his bitterness*) As I've told you before, you must take her memories with a grain of salt. Her wonderful home was ordinary enough. Her father wasn't the great, generous, noble Irish gentleman she makes out. He was a nice enough man, good company and a good talker. I liked him and he liked me. He was prosperous enough, too, in his wholesale grocery business, an able man. But he had his weakness. She condemns my drinking but she forgets his. It's true he never touched a drop till he was forty, but after that he made up for lost time. He became a steady champagne drinker, the worst kind. That was his grand pose, to drink only champagne. Well, it finished him quick—that and the consumption— (*He stops with a guilty glance at his son.*)

EDMUND—(*sardonically*) We don't seem able to avoid unpleasant topics, do we?

TYRONE—(*sighs sadly*) No. (*then with a pathetic attempt at heartiness*) What do you say to a game or two of Casino, lad?

EDMUND—All right.

TYRONE—(*shuffling the cards clumsily*) We can't lock up and go to bed till Jamie comes on the last trolley—which I hope he won't—and I don't want to go upstairs, anyway, till she's asleep.

EDMUND—Neither do I.

TYRONE—(*keeps shuffling the cards fumblingly, forgetting to deal them*) As I was saying, you must take her tales of the past with a grain of salt. The piano playing and her dream of becoming a concert pianist. That was put in her head by the nuns flattering her. She was their pet. They loved her for being so devout. They're innocent women, anyway, when it comes to the world. They don't know that not one in a million who shows promise ever rises to concert playing. Not that your mother didn't play well for a schoolgirl, but that's no reason to take it for granted she could have—

EDMUND—(*sharply*) Why don't you deal, if we're going to play.

TYRONE—Eh? I am. (*dealing with very uncertain judgment of distance*) And the idea she might have become a nun. That's the worst. Your mother was one of the most beautiful girls you could ever see. She knew it, too. She was a bit of a rogue and a coquette, God bless her, behind all her shyness and blushes. She was never made to renounce the world. She was bursting with health and high spirits and the love of loving.

EDMUND—For God's sake, Papa! Why don't you pick up your hand?

TYRONE—(*picks it up—dully*) Yes, let's see what I have here. (*They both stare at their cards unseeingly. Then they both start. Tyrone whispers*) Listen!

EDMUND—She's coming downstairs.

TYRONE—(*hurriedly*) We'll play our game. Pretend not to notice and she'll soon go up again.

EDMUND—(*staring through the front parlor—with relief*) I don't see her. She must have started down and then turned back.

TYRONE—Thank God.

EDMUND—Yes. It's pretty horrible to see her the way she must be now. (*with bitter misery*) The hardest thing to take is the blank wall she builds around her. Or it's more like a bank of fog in which she hides and loses herself. Deliberately, that's the hell of it! You know something in her does it deliberately—to get beyond our reach, to be rid of us, to forget we're alive! It's as if, in spite of loving us, she hated us!

TYRONE—(*remonstrates gently*) Now, now, lad. It's not her. It's the damned poison.

EDMUND—(*bitterly*) She takes it to get that effect. At least, I know she did this time! (*abruptly*) My play, isn't it? Here. (*He plays a card.*)

TYRONE—(*plays mechanically—gently reproachful*) She's been terribly frightened about your illness, for all her pretending. Don't be too hard on her, lad. Remember she's not responsible. Once that cursed poison gets a hold on anyone—

EDMUND—(*His face grows hard and he stares at his father with bitter accusation.*) It never should have gotten a hold on her! I know damned well she's not to blame! And I know who is! You are! Your damned stinginess! If you'd spent money for a decent doctor when she was so sick after I was born, she'd never have known morphine existed! Instead you put her in the hands of a hotel quack who wouldn't admit his ignorance and took the easiest way out, not giving a damn what happened to her afterwards! All because his fee was cheap! Another one of your bargains!

TYRONE—(*stung—angrily*) Be quiet! How dare you talk of something you know nothing about! (*trying to control his temper*) You must try to see my side of it, too, lad. How was I to know he was that kind of a doctor? He had a good reputation—

EDMUND—Among the souses in the hotel bar, I suppose!

TYRONE—That's a lie! I asked the hotel proprietor to recommend the best—

EDMUND—Yes! At the same time crying poorhouse and making it plain you wanted a cheap one! I know your system! By God, I ought to after this afternoon!

TYRONE—(*guiltily defensive*) What about this afternoon?

EDMUND—Never mind now. We're talking about Mama! I'm saying no matter how you excuse yourself you know damned well your stinginess is to blame—

TYRONE—And I say you're a liar! Shut your mouth right now, or—

EDMUND—(*ignoring this*) After you found out she'd been made a morphine addict, why didn't you send her to a cure then, at the start, while she still had a chance? No, that would have meant spending some money! I'll bet you told her all she had to do was use a little will power! That's what you still believe in your heart, in spite of what doctors, who really know something about it, have told you!

TYRONE—You lie again! I know better than that now! But how was I to know then? What did I know of morphine? It was years before I discovered what was wrong. I thought she'd never got over her sickness, that's all. Why didn't I send her to a cure, you say? (*bitterly*) Haven't I? I've spent thousands upon thousands in cures! A waste. What good have they done her? She always started again.

EDMUND — Because you've never given her anything that would help her want to stay off it! No home except this summer dump in a place she hates and you've refused even to spend money to make this look decent, while you keep buying more property, and playing sucker for every con man with a gold mine, or a silver mine, or any kind of get-rich-quick swindle! You've dragged her around on the road, season after season, on one-night stands, with no one she could talk to, waiting night after night in dirty hotel rooms for you to come back with a bun on after the bars closed! Christ, is it any wonder she didn't want to be cured. Jesus, when I think of it I hate your guts!

TYRONE — (*strickenly*) Edmund! (*then in a rage*) How dare you talk to your father like that, you insolent young cub! After all I've done for you.

EDMUND — We'll come to that, what you're doing for me!

TYRONE — (*looking guilty again — ignores this*) Will you stop repeating your mother's crazy accusations, which she never makes unless it's the poison talking? I never dragged her on the road against her will. Naturally, I wanted her with me. I loved her. And she came because she loved me and wanted to be with me. That's the truth, no matter what she says when she's not herself. And she needn't have been lonely. There was always the members of my company to talk to, if she'd wanted. She had her children, too, and I insisted, in spite of the expense, on having a nurse to travel with her.

EDMUND — (*bitterly*) Yes, your one generosity, and that because you were jealous of her paying too much attention to us, and wanted us out of your way! It was another mistake, too! If she'd had to take care of me all by herself, and had that to occupy her mind, maybe she'd have been able —

TYRONE — (*goaded into vindictiveness*) Or for that matter, if you insist on judging things by what she says when she's not in her right mind, if you hadn't been born she'd never — (*He stops ashamed.*)

EDMUND — (*suddenly spent and miserable*) Sure. I know that's what she feels, Papa.

TYRONE—(*protests penitently*) She doesn't! She loves you
as dearly as ever mother loved a son! I only said that because
you put me in such a God-damned rage, raking up the past,
and saying you hate me—

EDMUND—(*dully*) I didn't mean it, Papa. (*He suddenly
smiles—kidding a bit drunkenly*) I'm like Mama, I can't help
liking you, in spite of everything.

TYRONE—(*grins a bit drunkenly in return*) I might say the
same of you. You're no great shakes as a son. It's a case of
"A poor thing but mine own." (*They both chuckle with real,
if alcoholic, affection. Tyrone changes the subject.*) What's happened to our game? Whose play is it?

EDMUND—Yours, I guess. (*Tyrone plays a card which
Edmund takes and the game gets forgotten again.*)

TYRONE—You mustn't let yourself be too downhearted,
lad, by the bad news you had today. Both the doctors promised me, if you obey orders at this place you're going, you'll
be cured in six months, or a year at most.

EDMUND—(*his face hard again*) Don't kid me. You don't
believe that.

TYRONE—(*too vehemently*) Of course I believe it! Why
shouldn't I believe it when both Hardy and the specialist—?

EDMUND—You think I'm going to die.

TYRONE—That's a lie! You're crazy!

EDMUND—(*more bitterly*) So why waste money? That's
why you're sending me to a state farm—

TYRONE—(*in guilty confusion*) What state farm? It's the
Hilltown Sanatorium, that's all I know, and both doctors said
it was the best place for you.

EDMUND—(*scathingly*) For the money! That is, for nothing,
or practically nothing. Don't lie, Papa! You know damned
well Hilltown Sanatorium is a state institution! Jamie suspected you'd cry poorhouse to Hardy and he wormed the truth
out of him.

TYRONE—(*furiously*) That drunken loafer! I'll kick him out
in the gutter! He's poisoned your mind against me ever since
you were old enough to listen!

EDMUND—You can't deny it's the truth about the state
farm, can you?

TYRONE—It's not true the way you look at it! What if it

is run by the state? That's nothing against it. The state has the money to make a better place than any private sanatorium. And why shouldn't I take advantage of it? It's my right—and yours. We're residents. I'm a property owner. I help to support it. I'm taxed to death—

EDMUND—(*with bitter irony*) Yes, on property valued at a quarter of a million.

TYRONE—Lies! It's all mortgaged!

EDMUND—Hardy and the specialist know what you're worth. I wonder what they thought of you when they heard you moaning poorhouse and showing you wanted to wish me on charity!

TYRONE—It's a lie! All I told them was I couldn't afford any millionaire's sanatorium because I was land poor. That's the truth!

EDMUND—And then you went to the Club to meet McGuire and let him stick you with another bum piece of property! (*as Tyrone starts to deny*) Don't lie about it! We met McGuire in the hotel bar after he left you. Jamie kidded him about hooking you, and he winked and laughed!

TYRONE—(*lying feebly*) He's a liar if he said—

EDMUND—Don't lie about it! (*with gathering intensity*) God, Papa, ever since I went to sea and was on my own, and found out what hard work for little pay was, and what it felt like to be broke, and starve, and camp on park benches because I had no place to sleep, I've tried to be fair to you because I knew what you'd been up against as a kid. I've tried to make allowances. Christ, you have to make allowances in this damned family or go nuts! I have tried to make allowances for myself when I remember all the rotten stuff I've pulled! I've tried to feel like Mama that you can't help being what you are where money is concerned. But God Almighty, this last stunt of yours is too much! It makes me want to puke! Not because of the rotten way you're treating me. To hell with that! I've treated you rottenly, in my way, more than once. But to think when it's a question of your son having consumption, you can show yourself up before the whole town as such a stinking old tightwad! Don't you know Hardy will talk and the whole damned town will know! Jesus, Papa, haven't you any pride or shame? (*bursting with rage*) And

don't think I'll let you get away with it! I won't go to any
damned state farm just to save you a few lousy dollars to buy
more bum property with! You stinking old miser—! (*He
chokes huskily, his voice trembling with rage, and then is shaken
by a fit of coughing.*)

TYRONE—(*has shrunk back in his chair under this attack, his
guilty contrition greater than his anger. He stammers*) Be quiet!
Don't say that to me! You're drunk! I won't mind you. Stop
coughing, lad. You've got yourself worked up over nothing.
Who said you had to go to this Hilltown place? You can go
anywhere you like. I don't give a damn what it costs. All I
care about is to have you get well. Don't call me a stinking
miser, just because I don't want doctors to think I'm a millionaire they can swindle. (*Edmund has stopped coughing. He
looks sick and weak. His father stares at him frightenedly.*) You
look weak, lad. You'd better take a bracer.

EDMUND—(*grabs the bottle and pours his glass brimfull—
weakly*) Thanks. (*He gulps down the whiskey.*)

TYRONE—(*pours himself a big drink, which empties the bottle,
and drinks it. His head bows and he stares dully at the cards on
the table—vaguely*) Whose play is it? (*He goes on dully, without
resentment.*) A stinking old miser. Well, maybe you're right.
Maybe I can't help being, although all my life since I had
anything I've thrown money over the bar to buy drinks for
everyone in the house, or loaned money to sponges I knew
would never pay it back— (*with a loose-mouthed sneer of self-
contempt*) But, of course, that was in barrooms, when I was
full of whiskey. I can't feel that way about it when I'm sober
in my home. It was at home I first learned the value of a
dollar and the fear of the poorhouse. I've never been able to
believe in my luck since. I've always feared it would change
and everything I had would be taken away. But still, the more
property you own, the safer you think you are. That may not
be logical, but it's the way I have to feel. Banks fail, and your
money's gone, but you think you can keep land beneath your
feet. (*Abruptly his tone becomes scornfully superior.*) You said you
realized what I'd been up against as a boy. The hell you do!
How could you? You've had everything—nurses, schools,
college, though you didn't stay there. You've had food, clothing. Oh, I know you had a fling of hard work with your back

and hands, a bit of being homeless and penniless in a foreign land, and I respect you for it. But it was a game of romance and adventure to you. It was play.

EDMUND—(*dully sarcastic*) Yes, particularly the time I tried to commit suicide at Jimmie the Priest's, and almost did.

TYRONE—You weren't in your right mind. No son of mine would ever— You were drunk.

EDMUND—I was stone cold sober. That was the trouble. I'd stopped to think too long.

TYRONE—(*with drunken peevishness*) Don't start your damned atheist morbidness again! I don't care to listen. I was trying to make plain to you— (*scornfully*) What do you know of the value of a dollar? When I was ten my father deserted my mother and went back to Ireland to die. Which he did soon enough, and deserved to, and I hope he's roasting in hell. He mistook rat poison for flour, or sugar, or something. There was gossip it wasn't by mistake but that's a lie. No one in my family ever—

EDMUND—My bet is, it wasn't by mistake.

TYRONE—More morbidness! Your brother put that in your head. The worst he can suspect is the only truth for him. But never mind. My mother was left, a stranger in a strange land, with four small children, me and a sister a little older and two younger than me. My two older brothers had moved to other parts. They couldn't help. They were hard put to it to keep themselves alive. There was no damned romance in our poverty. Twice we were evicted from the miserable hovel we called home, with my mother's few sticks of furniture thrown out in the street, and my mother and sisters crying. I cried, too, though I tried hard not to, because I was the man of the family. At ten years old! There was no more school for me. I worked twelve hours a day in a machine shop, learning to make files. A dirty barn of a place where rain dripped through the roof, where you roasted in summer, and there was no stove in winter, and your hands got numb with cold, where the only light came through two small filthy windows, so on grey days I'd have to sit bent over with my eyes almost touching the files in order to see! You talk of work! And what do you think I got for it? Fifty cents a week! It's the truth! Fifty cents a week! And my poor mother washed and scrubbed for the Yanks by the day, and my older sister sewed, and my two younger stayed at home to keep the house. We never had clothes enough to wear, nor enough food to eat. Well I remember one Thanksgiving, or maybe it was Christmas, when some Yank in whose house mother had been scrubbing gave her a dollar extra for a present, and on the way home she spent it all on food. I can remember her hugging and kissing us and saying with tears of joy running down her tired face: "Glory be to God, for once in our lives we'll have enough for each of us!" (*He wipes tears from his eyes.*) A fine, brave, sweet woman. There never was a braver or finer.

EDMUND—(*moved*) Yes, she must have been.

TYRONE—Her one fear was she'd get old and sick and have to die in the poorhouse. (*He pauses—then adds with grim humor*) It was in those days I learned to be a miser. A dollar was worth so much then. And once you've learned a lesson, it's hard to unlearn it. You have to look for bargains. If I took this state farm sanatorium for a good bargain, you'll have to forgive me. The doctors did tell me it's a good place. You must believe that, Edmund. And I swear I never meant you to go there if you didn't want to. (*vehemently*) You can choose any place you like! Never mind what it costs! Any place I can afford. Any place you like—within reason. (*At this qualification, a grin twitches Edmund's lips. His resentment has gone. His father goes on with an elaborately offhand, casual air.*) There was another sanatorium the specialist recommended. He said it had a record as good as any place in the country. It's endowed by a group of millionaire factory owners, for the benefit of their workers principally, but you're eligible to go there because you're a resident. There's such a pile of money behind it, they don't have to charge much. It's only seven dollars a week but you get ten times that value. (*hastily*) I don't want to persuade you to anything, understand. I'm simply repeating what I was told.

EDMUND—(*concealing his smile—casually*) Oh, I know that. It sounds like a good bargain to me. I'd like to go there. So that settles that. (*Abruptly he is miserably desperate again—dully*) It doesn't matter a damn now, anyway. Let's forget it! (*changing the subject*) How about our game? Whose play is it?

TYRONE—(*mechanically*) I don't know. Mine, I guess. No, it's yours. (*Edmund plays a card. His father takes it. Then about to play from his hand, he again forgets the game.*) Yes, maybe life overdid the lesson for me, and made a dollar worth too much, and the time came when that mistake ruined my career as a fine actor. (*sadly*) I've never admitted this to anyone before, lad, but tonight I'm so heartsick I feel at the end of everything, and what's the use of fake pride and pretense. That God-damned play I bought for a song and made such a great success in—a great money success—it ruined me with its promise of an easy fortune. I didn't want to do anything else, and by the time I woke up to the fact I'd become a slave to the damned thing and did try other plays, it was too late. They had identified me with that one part, and didn't want me in anything else. They were right, too. I'd lost the great talent I once had through years of easy repetition, never learning a new part, never really working hard. Thirty-five to forty thousand dollars net profit a season like snapping your fingers! It was too great a temptation. Yet before I bought the damned thing I was considered one of the three or four young actors with the greatest artistic promise in America. I'd worked like hell. I'd left a good job as a machinist to take supers' parts because I loved the theater. I was wild with ambition. I read all the plays ever written. I studied Shakespeare as you'd study the Bible. I educated myself. I got rid of an Irish brogue you could cut with a knife. I loved Shakespeare. I would have acted in any of his plays for nothing, for the joy of being alive in his great poetry. And I acted well in him. I felt inspired by him. I could have been a great Shakespearean actor, if I'd kept on. I know that! In 1874 when Edwin Booth came to the theater in Chicago where I was leading man, I played Cassius to his Brutus one night, Brutus to his Cassius the next, Othello to his Iago, and so on. The first night I played Othello, he said to our manager, "That young man is playing Othello better than I ever did!" (*proudly*) That from Booth, the greatest actor of his day or any other! And it was true! And I was only twenty-seven years old! As I look back on it now, that night was the high spot in my career. I had life where I wanted it! And for a time after that I kept on upward with ambition high. Married your mother. Ask her what I was like in those days. Her love was an added incentive to ambition. But a few years later my good bad luck made me find the big money-maker. It wasn't that in my eyes at first. It was a great romantic part I knew I could play better than anyone. But it was a great box office success from the start—and then life had me where it wanted me—at from thirty-five to forty thousand net profit a season! A fortune in those days—or even in these. (*bitterly*) What the hell was it I wanted to buy, I wonder, that was worth— Well, no matter. It's a late day for regrets. (*He glances vaguely at his cards.*) My play, isn't it?

EDMUND—(*moved, stares at his father with understanding— slowly*) I'm glad you've told me this, Papa. I know you a lot better now.

TYRONE—(*with a loose, twisted smile*) Maybe I shouldn't have told you. Maybe you'll only feel more contempt for me. And it's a poor way to convince you of the value of a dollar. (*Then as if this phrase automatically aroused an habitual association in his mind, he glances up at the chandelier disapprovingly.*) The glare from those extra lights hurts my eyes. You don't mind if I turn them out, do you? We don't need them, and there's no use making the Electric Company rich.

EDMUND—(*controlling a wild impulse to laugh—agreeably*) No, sure not. Turn them out.

TYRONE—(*gets heavily and a bit waveringly to his feet and gropes uncertainly for the lights—his mind going back to its line of thought*) No, I don't know what the hell it was I wanted to buy. (*He clicks out one bulb.*) On my solemn oath, Edmund, I'd gladly face not having an acre of land to call my own, nor a penny in the bank— (*He clicks out another bulb.*) I'd be willing to have no home but the poorhouse in my old age if I could look back now on having been the fine artist I might have been. (*He turns out the third bulb, so only the reading lamp is on, and sits down again heavily. Edmund suddenly cannot hold back a burst of strained, ironical laughter. Tyrone is hurt.*) What the devil are you laughing at?

EDMUND—Not at you, Papa. At life. It's so damned crazy.

TYRONE—(*growls*) More of your morbidness! There's nothing wrong with life. It's we who— (*He quotes*) "The fault, dear Brutus, is not in our stars, but in ourselves that we are underlings." (*He pauses—then sadly*) The praise Edwin Booth gave my Othello. I made the manager put down his exact words in writing. I kept it in my wallet for years. I used to read it every once in a while until finally it made me feel so bad I didn't want to face it any more. Where is it now, I wonder? Somewhere in this house. I remember I put it away carefully—

EDMUND—(*with a wry ironical sadness*) It might be in an old trunk in the attic, along with Mama's wedding dress. (*Then as his father stares at him, he adds quickly*) For Pete's sake, if we're going to play cards, let's play. (*He takes the card his father had played and leads. For a moment, they play the game, like mechanical chess players. Then Tyrone stops, listening to a sound upstairs.*)

TYRONE—She's still moving around. God knows when she'll go to sleep.

EDMUND—(*pleads tensely*) For Christ's sake, Papa, forget it! (*He reaches out and pours a drink. Tyrone starts to protest, then gives it up. Edmund drinks. He puts down the glass. His expression changes. When he speaks it is as if he were deliberately giving way to drunkenness and seeking to hide behind a maudlin manner.*) Yes, she moves above and beyond us, a ghost haunting the past, and here we sit pretending to forget, but straining our ears listening for the slightest sound, hearing the fog drip from the eaves like the uneven tick of a rundown, crazy clock—or like the dreary tears of a trollop spattering in a puddle of stale beer on a honky-tonk table top! (*He laughs with maudlin appreciation.*) Not so bad, that last, eh? Original, not Baudelaire. Give me credit! (*then with alcoholic talkativeness*) You've just told me some high spots in your memories. Want to hear mine? They're all connected with the sea. Here's one. When I was on the Squarehead square rigger, bound for Buenos Aires. Full moon in the Trades. The old hooker driving fourteen knots. I lay on the bowsprit, facing astern, with the water foaming into spume under me, the masts with every sail white in the moonlight, towering high above me. I became drunk with the beauty and singing rhythm of it, and for a moment I lost myself—actually lost my life. I was set free! I dissolved in the sea, became white sails and flying spray, became beauty and rhythm, became moonlight and the ship

and the high dim-starred sky! I belonged, without past or
future, within peace and unity and a wild joy, within something greater than my own life, or the life of Man, to Life
itself! To God, if you want to put it that way. Then another
time, on the American Line, when I was lookout on the
crow's nest in the dawn watch. A calm sea, that time. Only a
lazy ground swell and a slow drowsy roll of the ship. The
passengers asleep and none of the crew in sight. No sound of
man. Black smoke pouring from the funnels behind and beneath me. Dreaming, not keeping lookout, feeling alone, and
above, and apart, watching the dawn creep like a painted
dream over the sky and sea which slept together. Then the
moment of ecstatic freedom came. The peace, the end of the
quest, the last harbor, the joy of belonging to a fulfillment
beyond men's lousy, pitiful, greedy fears and hopes and
dreams! And several other times in my life, when I was swimming far out, or lying alone on a beach, I have had the same
experience. Became the sun, the hot sand, green seaweed anchored to a rock, swaying in the tide. Like a saint's vision of
beatitude. Like the veil of things as they seem drawn back by
an unseen hand. For a second you see—and seeing the secret,
are the secret. For a second there is meaning! Then the hand
lets the veil fall and you are alone, lost in the fog again, and
you stumble on toward nowhere, for no good reason! (*He
grins wryly.*) It was a great mistake, my being born a man, I
would have been much more successful as a sea gull or a fish.
As it is, I will always be a stranger who never feels at home,
who does not really want and is not really wanted, who can
never belong, who must always be a little in love with death!

TYRONE—(*stares at him—impressed*) Yes, there's the makings of a poet in you all right. (*then protesting uneasily*) But
that's morbid craziness about not being wanted and loving
death.

EDMUND—(*sardonically*) The *makings* of a poet. No, I'm
afraid I'm like the guy who is always panhandling for a
smoke. He hasn't even got the makings. He's got only the
habit. I couldn't touch what I tried to tell you just now. I just
stammered. That's the best I'll ever do. I mean, if I live. Well,
it will be faithful realism, at least. Stammering is the native

eloquence of us fog people. (*A pause. Then they both jump startledly as there is a noise from outside the house, as if someone had stumbled and fallen on the front steps. Edmund grins.*) Well, that sounds like the absent brother. He must have a peach of a bun on.

TYRONE—(*scowling*) That loafer! He caught the last car, bad luck to it. (*He gets to his feet.*) Get him to bed, Edmund. I'll go out on the porch. He has a tongue like an adder when he's drunk. I'd only lose my temper. (*He goes out the door to the side porch as the front door in the hall bangs shut behind Jamie. Edmund watches with amusement Jamie's wavering progress through the front parlor. Jamie comes in. He is very drunk and woozy on his legs. His eyes are glassy, his face bloated, his speech blurred, his mouth slack like his father's, a leer on his lips.*)

JAMIE—(*swaying and blinking in the doorway—in a loud voice*) What ho! What ho!

EDMUND—(*sharply*) Nix on the loud noise!

JAMIE—(*blinks at him*) Oh, hello, Kid. (*with great seriousness*) I'm as drunk as a fiddler's bitch.

EDMUND—(*dryly*) Thanks for telling me your great secret.

JAMIE—(*grins foolishly*) Yes. Unneshesary information Number One, eh? (*He bends and slaps at the knees of his trousers.*) Had serious accident. The fron steps tried to trample on me. Took advantage of fog to waylay me. Ought to be a lighthouse out there. Dark in here, too. (*scowling*) What the hell is this, the morgue? Lesh have some light on sibject. (*He sways forward to the table, reciting Kipling.*)

"Ford, ford, ford o' Kabul river,
  Ford o' Kabul river in the dark!
  Keep the crossing-stakes beside you, an' they will surely
      guide you
  'Cross the ford o' Kabul river in the dark."

(*He fumbles at the chandelier and manages to turn on the three bulbs.*) Thash more like it. To hell with old Gaspard. Where is the old tightwad?

EDMUND—Out on the porch.

JAMIE—Can't expect us to live in the Black Hole of Calcutta. (*His eyes fix on the full bottle of whiskey.*) Say! Have I got the d.t.'s? (*He reaches out fumblingly and grabs it.*) By God, it's real. What's matter with the Old Man tonight? Must be ossified to forget he left this out. Grab opportunity by the forelock. Key to my success. (*He slops a big drink into a glass.*)

EDMUND—You're stinking now. That will knock you stiff.

JAMIE—Wisdom from the mouth of babes. Can the wise stuff, Kid. You're still wet behind the ears. (*He lowers himself into a chair, holding the drink carefully aloft.*)

EDMUND—All right. Pass out if you want to.

JAMIE—Can't, that's trouble. Had enough to sink a ship, but can't sink. Well, here's hoping. (*He drinks.*)

EDMUND—Shove over the bottle. I'll have one, too.

JAMIE—(*with sudden, big-brotherly solicitude, grabbing the bottle*) No, you don't. Not while I'm around. Remember doctor's orders. Maybe no one else gives a damn if you die, but I do. My kid brother. I love your guts, Kid. Everything else is gone. You're all I've got left. (*pulling bottle closer to him*) So no booze for you, if I can help it. (*Beneath his drunken sentimentality there is a genuine sincerity.*)

EDMUND—(*irritably*) Oh, lay off it.

JAMIE—(*is hurt and his face hardens*) You don't believe I care, eh? Just drunken bull. (*He shoves the bottle over.*) All right. Go ahead and kill yourself.

EDMUND—(*seeing he is hurt—affectionately*) Sure I know you care, Jamie, and I'm going on the wagon. But tonight doesn't count. Too many damned things have happened to-day. (*He pours a drink.*) Here's how. (*He drinks.*)

JAMIE—(*sobers up momentarily and with a pitying look*) I know, Kid. It's been a lousy day for you. (*then with sneering cynicism*) I'll bet old Gaspard hasn't tried to keep you off booze. Probably give you a case to take with you to the state farm for pauper patients. The sooner you kick the bucket, the less expense. (*with contemptuous hatred*) What a bastard to have for a father! Christ, if you put him in a book, no one would believe it!

EDMUND—(*defensively*) Oh, Papa's all right, if you try to understand him—and keep your sense of humor.

JAMIE—(*cynically*) He's been putting on the old sob act for you, eh? He can always kid you. But not me. Never again. (*then slowly*) Although, in a way, I do feel sorry for him about one thing. But he has even that coming to him. He's to blame. (*hurriedly*) But to hell with that. (*He grabs the bottle and pours another drink, appearing very drunk again.*) That lash drink's getting me. This one ought to put the lights out. Did you tell Gaspard I got it out of Doc Hardy this sanatorium is a charity dump?

EDMUND—(*reluctantly*) Yes. I told him I wouldn't go there. It's all settled now. He said I can go anywhere I want. (*He adds, smiling without resentment*) Within reason, of course.

JAMIE—(*drunkenly imitating his father*) Of course, lad. Anything within reason. (*sneering*) That means another cheap dump. Old Gaspard, the miser in "The Bells," that's a part he can play without make-up.

EDMUND—(*irritably*) Oh, shut up, will you. I've heard that Gaspard stuff a million times.

JAMIE—(*shrugs his shoulders—thickly*) Aw right, if you're shatisfied—let him get away with it. It's your funeral—I mean, I hope it won't be.

EDMUND—(*changing the subject*) What did you do uptown tonight? Go to Mamie Burns?

JAMIE—(*very drunk, his head nodding*) Sure thing. Where else could I find suitable feminine companionship? And love. Don't forget love. What is a man without a good woman's love? A God-damned hollow shell.

EDMUND—(*chuckles tipsily, letting himself go now and be drunk*) You're a nut.

JAMIE—(*quotes with gusto from Oscar Wilde's "The Harlot's House"*)

> "Then, turning to my love, I said,
> 'The dead are dancing with the dead,
> The dust is whirling with the dust.'
>
> But she—she heard the violin,
> And left my side and entered in:
> Love passed into the house of lust.
>
> Then suddenly the tune went false,
> The dancers wearied of the waltz . . ."

(*He breaks off, thickly*) Not strictly accurate. If my love was with me, I didn't notice it. She must have been a ghost. (*He pauses.*) Guess which one of Mamie's charmers I picked to bless me with her woman's love. It'll hand you a laugh, Kid. I picked Fat Violet.

EDMUND—(*laughs drunkenly*) No, honest? Some pick! God, she weighs a ton. What the hell for, a joke?

JAMIE—No joke. Very serious. By the time I hit Mamie's dump I felt very sad about myself and all the other poor bums in the world. Ready for a weep on any old womanly bosom. You know how you get when John Barleycorn turns on the soft music inside you. Then, soon as I got in the door, Mamie began telling me all her troubles. Beefed how rotten business was, and she was going to give Fat Violet the gate. Customers didn't fall for Vi. Only reason she'd kept her was she could play the piano. Lately Vi's gone on drunks and been too boiled to play, and was eating her out of house and home, and although Vi was a goodhearted dumbbell, and she felt sorry for her because she didn't know how the hell she'd make a living, still business was business, and she couldn't afford to run a home for fat tarts. Well, that made me feel sorry for Fat Violet, so I squandered two bucks of your dough to escort her upstairs. With no dishonorable intentions whatever. I like them fat, but not that fat. All I wanted was a little heart-to-heart talk concerning the infinite sorrow of life.

EDMUND—(*chuckles drunkenly*) Poor Vi! I'll bet you recited Kipling and Swinburne and Dowson and gave her "I have been faithful to thee, Cynara, in my fashion."

JAMIE—(*grins loosely*) Sure—with the Old Master, John Barleycorn, playing soft music. She stood it for a while. Then she got good and sore. Got the idea I took her upstairs for a joke. Gave me a grand bawling out. Said she was better than a drunken bum who recited poetry. Then she began to cry. So I had to say I loved her because she was fat, and she wanted to believe that, and I stayed with her to prove it, and that cheered her up, and she kissed me when I left, and said she'd fallen hard for me, and we both cried a little more in the hallway, and everything was fine, except Mamie Burns thought I'd gone bughouse.

EDMUND—(*quotes derisively*)

"Harlots and
Hunted have pleasures of their own to give,
The vulgar herd can never understand."

JAMIE—(*nods his head drunkenly*) Egzactly! Hell of a good time, at that. You should have stuck around with me, Kid. Mamie Burns inquired after you. Sorry to hear you were sick. She meant it, too. (*He pauses—then with maudlin humor, in a ham-actor tone*) This night has opened my eyes to a great career in store for me, my boy! I shall give the art of acting back to the performing seals, which is its most perfect expression. By applying my natural God-given talents in their proper sphere, I shall attain the pinnacle of success! I'll be the lover of the fat woman in Barnum and Bailey's circus! (*Edmund laughs. Jamie's mood changes to arrogant disdain.*) Pah! Imagine me sunk to the fat girl in a hick town hooker shop! Me! Who have made some of the best-lookers on Broadway sit up and beg! (*He quotes from Kipling's "Sestina of the Tramp-Royal."*)

"Speakin' in general, I 'ave tried 'em all,
The 'appy roads that take you o'er the world."

(*with sodden melancholy*) Not so apt. Happy roads is bunk. Weary roads is right. Get you nowhere fast. That's where I've got—nowhere. Where everyone lands in the end, even if most of the suckers won't admit it.

EDMUND—(*derisively*) Can it! You'll be crying in a minute.

JAMIE—(*starts and stares at his brother for a second with bitter hostility—thickly*) Don't get—too damned fresh. (*then abruptly*) But you're right. To hell with repining! Fat Violet's a good kid. Glad I stayed with her. Christian act. Cured her blues. Hell of a good time. You should have stuck with me, Kid. Taken your mind off your troubles. What's the use coming home to get the blues over what can't be helped. All over—finished now—not a hope! (*He stops, his head nodding drunkenly, his eyes closing—then suddenly he looks up, his face hard, and quotes jeeringly*)

"If I were hanged on the highest hill,
Mother o' mine, O mother o' mine!
I know whose love would follow me still . . ."

EDMUND—(*violently*) Shut up!

JAMIE—(*in a cruel, sneering tone with hatred in it*) Where's the hophead? Gone to sleep? (*Edmund jerks as if he'd been struck. There is a tense silence. Edmund's face looks stricken and sick. Then in a burst of rage he springs from his chair.*)

EDMUND—You dirty bastard! (*He punches his brother in the face, a blow that glances off the cheekbone. For a second Jamie reacts pugnaciously and half rises from his chair to do battle, but suddenly he seems to sober up to a shocked realization of what he has said and he sinks back limply.*)

JAMIE—(*miserably*) Thanks, Kid. I certainly had that coming. Don't know what made me—booze talking— You know me, Kid.

EDMUND—(*his anger ebbing*) I know you'd never say that unless— But God, Jamie, no matter how drunk you are, it's no excuse! (*He pauses—miserably*) I'm sorry I hit you. You and I never scrap—that bad. (*He sinks back on his chair.*)

JAMIE—(*huskily*) It's all right. Glad you did. My dirty tongue. Like to cut it out. (*He hides his face in his hands—dully*) I suppose it's because I feel so damned sunk. Because this time Mama had me fooled. I really believed she had it licked. She thinks I always believe the worst, but this time I believed the best. (*His voice flutters.*) I suppose I can't forgive her—yet. It meant so much. I'd begun to hope, if she'd beaten the game, I could, too. (*He begins to sob, and the horrible part of his weeping is that it appears sober, not the maudlin tears of drunkenness.*)

EDMUND—(*blinking back tears himself*) God, don't I know how you feel! Stop it, Jamie!

JAMIE—(*trying to control his sobs*) I've known about Mama so much longer than you. Never forget the first time I got wise. Caught her in the act with a hypo. Christ, I'd never dreamed before that any women but whores took dope! (*He pauses.*) And then this stuff of you getting consumption. It's got me licked. We've been more than brothers. You're the only pal I've ever had. I love your guts. I'd do anything for you.

EDMUND—(*reaches out and pats his arm*) I know that, Jamie.

JAMIE—(*his crying over—drops his hands from his face—with a strange bitterness*) Yet I'll bet you've heard Mama and old Gaspard spill so much bunk about my hoping for the worst, you suspect right now I'm thinking to myself that Papa is old and can't last much longer, and if you were to die, Mama and I would get all he's got, and so I'm probably hoping—

EDMUND—(*indignantly*) Shut up, you damned fool! What the hell put that in your nut? (*He stares at his brother accusingly.*) Yes, that's what I'd like to know. What put that in your mind?

JAMIE—(*confusedly—appearing drunk again*) Don't be a dumbbell! What I said! Always suspected of hoping for the worst. I've got so I can't help— (*then drunkenly resentful*) What are you trying to do, accuse me? Don't play the wise guy with me! I've learned more of life than you'll ever know! Just because you've read a lot of highbrow junk, don't think you can fool me! You're only an overgrown kid! Mama's baby and Papa's pet! The family White Hope! You've been getting a swelled head lately. About nothing! About a few poems in a hick town newspaper! Hell, I used to write better stuff for the Lit magazine in college! You better wake up! You're setting no rivers on fire! You let hick town boobs flatter you with bunk about your future— (*Abruptly his tone changes to disgusted contrition. Edmund has looked away from him, trying to ignore this tirade.*) Hell, Kid, forget it. That goes for Sweeny. You know I don't mean it. No one is prouder you've started to make good. (*drunkenly assertive*) Why shouldn't I be proud? Hell, it's purely selfish. You reflect credit on me. I've had more to do with bringing you up than anyone. I wised you up about women, so you'd never be a fall guy, or make any mistakes you didn't want to make! And who steered you on to reading poetry first? Swinburne, for example? I did! And because I once wanted to write, I planted it in your mind that someday you'd write! Hell, you're more than my brother. I made you! You're my Frankenstein! (*He has risen to a note of drunken arrogance. Edmund is grinning with amusement now.*)

EDMUND—All right, I'm your Frankenstein. So let's have a drink. (*He laughs.*) You crazy nut!

JAMIE—(*thickly*) I'll have a drink. Not you. Got to take care of you. (*He reaches out with a foolish grin of doting affection and grabs his brother's hand.*) Don't be scared of this sanatorium business. Hell, you can beat that standing on your head.

Six months and you'll be in the pink. Probably haven't got consumption at all. Doctors lot of fakers. Told me years ago to cut out booze or I'd soon be dead—and here I am. They're all con men. Anything to grab your dough. I'll bet this state farm stuff is political graft game. Doctors get a cut for every patient they send.

EDMUND—(*disgustedly amused*) You're the limit! At the Last Judgment, you'll be around telling everyone it's in the bag.

JAMIE—And I'll be right. Slip a piece of change to the Judge and be saved, but if you're broke you can go to hell! (*He grins at this blasphemy and Edmund has to laugh. Jamie goes on.*) "Therefore put money in thy purse." That's the only dope. (*mockingly*) The secret of my success! Look what it's got me! (*He lets Edmund's hand go to pour a big drink, and gulps it down. He stares at his brother with bleary affection— takes his hand again and begins to talk thickly but with a strange, convincing sincerity.*) Listen, Kid, you'll be going away. May not get another chance to talk. Or might not be drunk enough to tell you truth. So got to tell you now. Something I ought to have told you long ago—for your own good. (*He pauses—struggling with himself. Edmund stares, impressed and uneasy. Jamie blurts out*) Not drunken bull, but "in vino veritas" stuff. You better take it seriously. Want to warn you— against me. Mama and Papa are right. I've been rotten bad influence. And worst of it is, I did it on purpose.

EDMUND—(*uneasily*) Shut up! I don't want to hear—

JAMIE—Nix, Kid! You listen! Did it on purpose to make a bum of you. Or part of me did. A big part. That part that's been dead so long. That hates life. My putting you wise so you'd learn from my mistakes. Believed that myself at times, but it's a fake. Made my mistakes look good. Made getting drunk romantic. Made whores fascinating vampires instead of poor, stupid, diseased slobs they really are. Made fun of work as sucker's game. Never wanted you succeed and make me look even worse by comparison. Wanted you to fail. Always jealous of you. Mama's baby, Papa's pet! (*He stares at Edmund with increasing enmity.*) And it was your being born that started Mama on dope. I know that's not your fault, but all the same, God damn you, I can't help hating your guts—!

EDMUND—(*almost frightenedly*) Jamie! Cut it out! You're crazy!

JAMIE—But don't get wrong idea, Kid. I love you more than I hate you. My saying what I'm telling you now proves it. I run the risk you'll hate me—and you're all I've got left. But I didn't mean to tell you that last stuff—go that far back. Don't know what made me. What I wanted to say is, I'd like to see you become the greatest success in the world. But you'd better be on your guard. Because I'll do my damnedest to make you fail. Can't help it. I hate myself. Got to take revenge. On everyone else. Especially you. Oscar Wilde's "Reading Gaol" has the dope twisted. The man was dead and so he had to kill the thing he loved. That's what it ought to be. The dead part of me hopes you won't get well. Maybe he's even glad the game has got Mama again! He wants company, he doesn't want to be the only corpse around the house! (*He gives a hard, tortured laugh.*)

EDMUND—Jesus, Jamie! You really have gone crazy!

JAMIE—Think it over and you'll see I'm right. Think it over when you're away from me in the sanatorium. Make up your mind you've got to tie a can to me—get me out of your life—think of me as dead—tell people, "I had a brother, but he's dead." And when you come back, look out for me. I'll be waiting to welcome you with that "my old pal" stuff, and give you the glad hand, and at the first good chance I get stab you in the back.

EDMUND—Shut up! I'll be God-damned if I'll listen to you any more—

JAMIE—(*as if he hadn't heard*) Only don't forget me. Remember I warned you—for your sake. Give me credit. Greater love hath no man than this, that he saveth his brother from himself. (*very drunkenly, his head bobbing*) That's all. Feel better now. Gone to confession. Know you absolve me, don't you, Kid? You understand. You're a damned fine kid. Ought to be. I made you. So go and get well. Don't die on me. You're all I've got left. God bless you, Kid. (*His eyes close. He mumbles*) That last drink—the old K. O. (*He falls into a drunken doze, not completely asleep. Edmund buries his face in his hands miserably. Tyrone comes in quietly through the screen door from the porch, his dressing gown wet with fog, the collar turned up around his throat. His face is stern and disgusted but at the same time pitying. Edmund does not notice his entrance.*)

TYRONE—(*in a low voice*) Thank God he's asleep. (*Edmund looks up with a start.*) I thought he'd never stop talking. (*He turns down the collar of his dressing gown.*) We'd better let him stay where he is and sleep it off. (*Edmund remains silent. Tyrone regards him—then goes on.*) I heard the last part of his talk. It's what I've warned you. I hope you'll heed the warning, now it comes from his own mouth. (*Edmund gives no sign of having heard. Tyrone adds pityingly*) But don't take it too much to heart, lad. He loves to exaggerate the worst of himself when he's drunk. He's devoted to you. It's the one good thing left in him. (*He looks down on Jamie with a bitter sadness.*) A sweet spectacle for me! My first-born, who I hoped would bear my name in honor and dignity, who showed such brilliant promise!

EDMUND—(*miserably*) Keep quiet, can't you, Papa?

TYRONE—(*pours a drink*) A waste! A wreck, a drunken hulk, done with and finished! (*He drinks. Jamie has become restless, sensing his father's presence, struggling up from his stupor. Now he gets his eyes open to blink up at Tyrone. The latter moves back a step defensively, his face growing hard.*)

JAMIE—(*suddenly points a finger at him and recites with dramatic emphasis*)

"Clarence is come, false, fleeting, perjured Clarence,
   That stabbed me in the field by Tewksbury.
   Seize on him, Furies, take him into torment."

(*then resentfully*) What the hell are you staring at? (*He recites sardonically from Rossetti.*)

"Look in my face. My name is Might-Have-Been;
   I am also called No More, Too Late, Farewell."

TYRONE—I'm well aware of that, and God knows I don't want to look at it.

EDMUND—Papa! Quit it!

JAMIE—(*derisively*) Got a great idea for you, Papa. Put on revival of "The Bells" this season. Great part in it you can play without make-up. Old Gaspard, the miser! (*Tyrone turns away, trying to control his temper.*)

EDMUND—Shut up, Jamie!

JAMIE—(*jeeringly*) I claim Edwin Booth never saw the day

when he could give as good a performance as a trained seal. Seals are intelligent and honest. They don't put up any bluffs about the Art of Acting. They admit they're just hams earning their daily fish.

TYRONE—(*stung, turns on him in a rage*) You loafer!

EDMUND—Papa! Do you want to start a row that will bring Mama down? Jamie, go back to sleep! You've shot off your mouth too much already. (*Tyrone turns away.*)

JAMIE—(*thickly*) All right, Kid. Not looking for argument. Too damned sleepy. (*He closes his eyes, his head nodding. Tyrone comes to the table and sits down, turning his chair so he won't look at Jamie. At once he becomes sleepy, too.*)

TYRONE—(*heavily*) I wish to God she'd go to bed so that I could, too. (*drowsily*) I'm dog tired. I can't stay up all night like I used to. Getting old—old and finished. (*with a bone-cracking yawn*) Can't keep my eyes open. I think I'll catch a few winks. Why don't you do the same, Edmund? It'll pass the time until she— (*His voice trails off. His eyes close, his chin sags, and he begins to breathe heavily through his mouth. Edmund sits tensely. He hears something and jerks nervously forward in his chair, staring through the front parlor into the hall. He jumps up with a hunted, distracted expression. It seems for a second he is going to hide in the back parlor. Then he sits down again and waits, his eyes averted, his hands gripping the arms of his chair. Suddenly all five bulbs of the chandelier in the front parlor are turned on from a wall switch, and a moment later someone starts playing the piano in there—the opening of one of Chopin's simpler waltzes, done with a forgetful, stiff-fingered groping, as if an awkward schoolgirl were practicing it for the first time. Tyrone starts to wide-awakeness and sober dread, and Jamie's head jerks back and his eyes open. For a moment they listen frozenly. The playing stops as abruptly as it began, and Mary appears in the doorway. She wears a sky-blue dressing gown over her nightdress, dainty slippers with pompons on her bare feet. Her face is paler than ever. Her eyes look enormous. They glisten like polished black jewels. The uncanny thing is that her face now appears so youthful. Experience seems ironed out of it. It is a marble mask of girlish innocence, the mouth caught in a shy smile. Her white hair is braided in two pigtails which hang over her breast. Over one arm, carried neglectfully, trailing on the floor, as if she had forgotten she held it, is an*

*old-fashioned white satin wedding gown, trimmed with duchesse
lace. She hesitates in the doorway, glancing round the room, her
forehead puckered puzzledly, like someone who has come to a room
to get something but has become absent-minded on the way and
forgotten what it was. They stare at her. She seems aware of them
merely as she is aware of other objects in the room, the furniture,
the windows, familiar things she accepts automatically as naturally
belonging there but which she is too preoccupied to notice.*)

JAMIE—(*breaks the cracking silence—bitterly, self-defensively
sardonic*) The Mad Scene. Enter Ophelia! (*His father and
brother both turn on him fiercely. Edmund is quicker. He slaps
Jamie across the mouth with the back of his hand.*)

TYRONE—(*his voice trembling with suppressed fury*) Good
boy, Edmund. The dirty blackguard! His own mother!

JAMIE—(*mumbles guiltily, without resentment*) All right,
Kid. Had it coming. But I told you how much I'd hoped—
(*He puts his hands over his face and begins to sob.*)

TYRONE—I'll kick you out in the gutter tomorrow, so help
me God. (*But Jamie's sobbing breaks his anger, and he turns and
shakes his shoulder, pleading*) Jamie, for the love of God, stop
it! (*Then Mary speaks, and they freeze into silence again, staring
at her. She has paid no attention whatever to the incident. It is
simply a part of the familiar atmosphere of the room, a background
which does not touch her preoccupation; and she speaks aloud to
herself, not to them.*)

MARY—I play so badly now. I'm all out of practice. Sister
Theresa will give me a dreadful scolding. She'll tell me it
isn't fair to my father when he spends so much money for
extra lessons. She's quite right, it isn't fair, when he's so
good and generous, and so proud of me. I'll practice every
day from now on. But something horrible has happened to
my hands. The fingers have gotten so stiff— (*She lifts her
hands to examine them with a frightened puzzlement.*) The
knuckles are all swollen. They're so ugly. I'll have to go to
the Infirmary and show Sister Martha. (*with a sweet smile of
affectionate trust*) She's old and a little cranky, but I love her
just the same, and she has things in her medicine chest
that'll cure anything. She'll give me something to rub on my
hands, and tell me to pray to the Blessed Virgin, and they'll
be well again in no time. (*She forgets her hands and comes*

into the room, the wedding gown trailing on the floor. She glances around vaguely, her forehead puckered again.) Let me see. What did I come here to find? It's terrible, how absent-minded I've become. I'm always dreaming and forgetting.

TYRONE—(*in a stifled voice*) What's that she's carrying, Edmund?

EDMUND—(*dully*) Her wedding gown, I suppose.

TYRONE—Christ! (*He gets to his feet and stands directly in her path—in anguish*) Mary! Isn't it bad enough—? (*controlling himself—gently persuasive*) Here, let me take it, dear. You'll only step on it and tear it and get it dirty dragging it on the floor. Then you'd be sorry afterwards. (*She lets him take it, regarding him from somewhere far away within herself, without recognition, without either affection or animosity.*)

MARY—(*with the shy politeness of a well-bred young girl toward an elderly gentleman who relieves her of a bundle*) Thank you. You are very kind. (*She regards the wedding gown with a puzzled interest.*) It's a wedding gown. It's very lovely, isn't it? (*A shadow crosses her face and she looks vaguely uneasy.*) I remember now. I found it in the attic hidden in a trunk. But I don't know what I wanted it for. I'm going to be a nun—that is, if I can only find— (*She looks around the room, her forehead puckered again.*) What is it I'm looking for? I know it's something I lost. (*She moves back from Tyrone, aware of him now only as some obstacle in her path.*)

TYRONE—(*in hopeless appeal*) Mary! (*But it cannot penetrate her preoccupation. She doesn't seem to hear him. He gives up helplessly, shrinking into himself, even his defensive drunkenness taken from him, leaving him sick and sober. He sinks back on his chair, holding the wedding gown in his arms with an unconscious clumsy, protective gentleness.*)

JAMIE—(*drops his hand from his face, his eyes on the table top. He has suddenly sobered up, too—dully*) It's no good, Papa. (*He recites from Swinburne's "A Leave-taking" and does it well, simply but with a bitter sadness.*)

"Let us rise up and part; she will not know.
Let us go seaward as the great winds go,
Full of blown sand and foam; what help is here?
There is no help, for all these things are so,
And all the world is bitter as a tear.

And how these things are, though ye strove to show,
She would not know."

MARY—(*looking around her*) Something I miss terribly. It can't be altogether lost. (*She starts to move around in back of Jamie's chair.*)

JAMIE—(*turns to look up into her face—and cannot help appealing pleadingly in his turn*) Mama! (*She does not seem to hear. He looks away hopelessly.*) Hell! What's the use? It's no good. (*He recites from "A Leave-taking" again with increased bitterness.*)

> "Let us go hence, my songs; she will not hear.
> Let us go hence together without fear;
> Keep silence now, for singing-time is over,
> And over all old things and all things dear.
> She loves not you nor me as all we love her.
> Yea, though we sang as angels in her ear,
> She would not hear."

MARY—(*looking around her*) Something I need terribly. I remember when I had it I was never lonely nor afraid. I can't have lost it forever, I would die if I thought that. Because then there would be no hope. (*She moves like a sleepwalker, around the back of Jamie's chair, then forward toward left front, passing behind Edmund.*)

EDMUND—(*turns impulsively and grabs her arm. As he pleads he has the quality of a bewilderedly hurt little boy.*) Mama! It isn't a summer cold! I've got consumption!

MARY—(*For a second he seems to have broken through to her. She trembles and her expression becomes terrified. She calls distractedly, as if giving a command to herself*) No! (*And instantly she is far away again. She murmurs gently but impersonally*) You must not try to touch me. You must not try to hold me. It isn't right, when I am hoping to be a nun. (*He lets his hand drop from her arm. She moves left to the front end of the sofa beneath the windows and sits down, facing front, her hands folded in her lap, in a demure schoolgirlish pose.*)

JAMIE—(*gives Edmund a strange look of mingled pity and jealous gloating*) You damned fool. It's no good. (*He recites again from the Swinburne poem.*)

> "Let us go hence, go hence; she will not see.
> Sing all once more together; surely she,

She too, remembering days and words that were,
Will turn a little toward us, sighing; but we,
We are hence, we are gone, as though we had not been there.
Nay, and though all men seeing had pity on me,
She would not see."

TYRONE—(*trying to shake off his hopeless stupor*) Oh, we're fools to pay any attention. It's the damned poison. But I've never known her to drown herself in it as deep as this. (*gruffly*) Pass me that bottle, Jamie. And stop reciting that damned morbid poetry. I won't have it in my house! (*Jamie pushes the bottle toward him. He pours a drink without disarranging the wedding gown he holds carefully over his other arm and on his lap, and shoves the bottle back. Jamie pours his and passes the bottle to Edmund, who, in turn, pours one. Tyrone lifts his glass and his sons follow suit mechanically, but before they can drink Mary speaks and they slowly lower their drinks to the table, forgetting them.*)

MARY—(*staring dreamily before her. Her face looks extraordinarily youthful and innocent. The shyly eager, trusting smile is on her lips as she talks aloud to herself.*) I had a talk with Mother Elizabeth. She is so sweet and good. A saint on earth. I love her dearly. It may be sinful of me but I love her better than my own mother. Because she always understands, even before you say a word. Her kind blue eyes look right into your heart. You can't keep any secrets from her. You couldn't deceive her, even if you were mean enough to want to. (*She gives a little rebellious toss of her head—with girlish pique*) All the same, I don't think she was so understanding this time. I told her I wanted to be a nun. I explained how sure I was of my vocation, that I had prayed to the Blessed Virgin to make me sure, and to find me worthy. I told Mother I had had a true vision when I was praying in the shrine of Our Lady of Lourdes, on the little island in the lake. I said I knew, as surely as I knew I was kneeling there, that the Blessed Virgin had smiled and blessed me with her consent. But Mother Elizabeth told me I must be more sure than that, even, that I must prove it wasn't simply my imagination. She said, if I was so sure, then I wouldn't mind putting myself to a test by going home after I graduated, and living as other girls lived, going out to parties and dances and enjoying myself; and then if after a year or two I still felt sure, I could come back to see her and we would talk it over again. (*She tosses her head—indignantly*) I never dreamed Holy Mother would give me such advice! I was really shocked. I said, of course, I would do anything she suggested, but I knew it was simply a waste of time. After I left her, I felt all mixed up, so I went to the shrine and prayed to the Blessed Virgin and found peace again because I knew she heard my prayer and would always love me and see no harm ever came to me so long as I never lost my faith in her. (*She pauses and a look of growing uneasiness comes over her face. She passes a hand over her forehead as if brushing cobwebs from her brain—vaguely*) That was in the winter of senior year. Then in the spring something happened to me. Yes, I remember. I fell in love with James Tyrone and was so happy for a time. (*She stares before her in a sad dream. Tyrone stirs in his chair. Edmund and Jamie remain motionless.*)

(*Curtain*)

HUGHIE

CHARACTERS

Hughie

SCENE—*The desk and a section of lobby of a small hotel on a West Side street in midtown New York. It is between 3 and 4 A.M. of a day in the summer of 1928.*

It is one of those hotels, built in the decade 1900–10 on the side streets of the Great White Way sector, which began as respectable second class but soon were forced to deteriorate in order to survive. Following the First World War and Prohibition, it had given up all pretense of respectability, and now is anything a paying guest wants it to be, a third class dump, catering to the catch-as-catch-can trade. But still it does not prosper. It has not shared in the Great Hollow Boom of the twenties. The Everlasting Opulence of the New Economic Law has overlooked it. It manages to keep running by cutting the overhead for service, repairs, and cleanliness to a minimum.

The desk faces left along a section of seedy lobby with shabby chairs. The street entrance is off-stage, left. Behind the desk are a telephone switchboard and the operator's stool. At right, the usual numbered tiers of mailboxes, and above them a clock.

The Night Clerk sits on the stool, facing front, his back to the switchboard. There is nothing to do. He is not thinking. He is not sleepy. He simply droops and stares acquiescently at nothing. It would be discouraging to glance at the clock. He knows there are several hours to go before his shift is over. Anyway, he does not need to look at clocks. He has been a night clerk in New York hotels so long he can tell time by sounds in the street.

He is in his early forties. Tall, thin, with a scrawny neck and jutting Adam's apple. His face is long and narrow, greasy with perspiration, sallow, studded with pimples from ingrowing hairs. His nose is large and without character. So is his mouth. So are his ears. So is his thinning brown hair, powdered with dandruff. Behind horn-rimmed spectacles, his blank brown eyes contain no discernible expression. One would say they had even forgotten how it feels to be bored. He wears an ill-fitting blue serge suit, white shirt and collar, a blue tie. The suit is old and shines at the elbows as if it had been waxed and polished.

Footsteps echo in the deserted lobby as someone comes in from the street. The Night Clerk rises wearily. His eyes remain empty but his gummy lips part automatically in a welcoming The-Patron-Is-Always-Right grimace, intended as a smile. His big uneven teeth are in bad condition.

Erie Smith enters and approaches the desk. He is about the same age as the Clerk and has the same pasty, perspiry, night-life complexion. There the resemblance ends. Erie is around medium height but appears shorter because he is stout and his fat legs are too short for his body. So are his fat arms. His big head squats on a neck which seems part of his beefy shoulders. His face is round, his snub nose flattened at the tip. His blue eyes have drooping lids and puffy pouches under them. His sandy hair is falling out and the top of his head is bald. He walks to the desk with a breezy, familiar air, his gait a bit waddling because of his short legs. He carries a Panama hat and mops his face with a red and blue silk handkerchief. He wears a light grey suit cut in the extreme, tight-waisted, Broadway mode, the coat open to reveal an old and faded but expensive silk shirt in a shade of blue that sets teeth on edge, and a gay red and blue foulard tie, its knot stained by perspiration. His trousers are held up by a braided brown leather belt with a brass buckle. His shoes are tan and white, his socks white silk.

In manner, he is consciously a Broadway sport and a Wise Guy—the type of small fry gambler and horse player, living hand to mouth on the fringe of the rackets. Infesting corners, doorways, cheap restaurants, the bars of minor speakeasies, he and his kind imagine they are in the Real Know, cynical oracles of the One True Grapevine.

Erie usually speaks in a low, guarded tone, his droop-lidded eyes suspiciously wary of nonexistent eavesdroppers. His face is set in the prescribed pattern of gambler's dead pan. His small, pursy mouth is always crooked in the cynical leer of one who possesses superior, inside information, and his shifty once-over glances never miss the price tags he detects on everything and everybody. Yet there is something phoney about his characterization of himself, some sentimental softness behind it which doesn't belong in the hard-boiled picture.

Erie avoids looking at the Night Clerk, as if he resented him.

ERIE—(*peremptorily*) Key. (*then as the Night Clerk gropes with his memory—grudgingly*) Forgot you ain't seen me before. Erie Smith's the name. I'm an old timer in this fleabag. 492.

NIGHT CLERK—(*in a tone of one who is wearily relieved when he does not have to remember anything—he plucks out the key*) 492. Yes, sir.

ERIE—(*taking the key, gives the Clerk the once-over. He appears not unfavorably impressed but his tone still holds resentment.*) How long you been on the job? Four, five days, huh? I been off on a drunk. Come to now, though. Tapering off. Well, I'm glad they fired that young squirt they took on when Hughie got sick. One of them fresh wise punks. Couldn't tell him nothing. Pleased to meet you, Pal. Hope you stick around. (*He shoves out his hand. The Night Clerk takes it obediently.*)

NIGHT CLERK—(*with a compliant, uninterested smile*) Glad to know you, Mr. Smith.

ERIE—What's your name?

NIGHT CLERK—(*as if he had half forgotten because what did it matter, anyway?*) Hughes. Charlie Hughes.

ERIE—(*starts*) Huh? Hughes? Say, is that on the level?

NIGHT CLERK—Charlie Hughes.

ERIE—Well, I be damned! What the hell d'you know about that! (*warming toward the Clerk*) Say, now I notice, you don't look like Hughie, but you remind me of him somehow. You ain't by any chance related?

NIGHT CLERK—You mean to the Hughes who had this job so long and died recently? No, sir. No relation.

ERIE—(*gloomily*) No, that's right. Hughie told me he didn't have no relations left—except his wife and kids, of course. (*He pauses—more gloomily*) Yeah. The poor guy croaked last week. His funeral was what started me off on a bat. (*then boastfully, as if defending himself against gloom*) Some drunk! I don't go on one often. It's bum dope in my book. A guy gets careless and gabs about things he knows and when he comes to he's liable to find there's guys who'd feel easier if he wasn't around no more. That's the trouble with knowing things. Take my tip, Pal. Don't never know nothin'. Be a sap and stay healthy. (*His manner has become secretive, with sinister undertones. But the Night Clerk doesn't notice this. Long experience with guests who stop at his desk in the small hours to talk about themselves has given him a foolproof technique of self-defense. He appears to listen with agreeable submissiveness and be im-*

pressed, but his mind is blank and he doesn't hear unless a direct question is put to him, and sometimes not even then. Erie thinks he is impressed.) But hell, I always keep my noggin working, booze or no booze. I'm no sucker. What was I sayin'? Oh, some drunk. I sure hit the high spots. You shoulda seen the doll I made night before last. And did she take me to the cleaners! I'm a sucker for blondes. (*He pauses—giving the Night Clerk a cynical, contemptuous glance*) You're married, ain't you?

NIGHT CLERK—(*Long ago he gave up caring whether questions were personal or not.*) Yes, sir.

ERIE—Yeah, I'd'a laid ten to one on it. You got that old look. Like Hughie had. Maybe that's the resemblance. (*He chuckles contemptuously.*) Kids, too, I bet?

NIGHT CLERK—Yes, sir. Three.

ERIE—You're worse off than Hughie was. He only had two. Three, huh? Well, that's what comes of being careless! (*He laughs. The Night Clerk smiles at a guest. He had been a little offended when a guest first made that crack—must have been ten years ago—yes, Eddie, the oldest, is eleven now—or is it twelve? Erie goes on with good-natured tolerance.*) Well, I suppose marriage ain't such a bum racket, if you're made for it. Hughie didn't seem to mind it much, although if you want my low-down, his wife is a bum—in spades! Oh, I don't mean cheatin'. With her puss and figure, she'd never make no one except she raided a blind asylum. (*The Night Clerk feels that he has been standing a long time and his feet are beginning to ache and he wishes 492 would stop talking and go to bed so he can sit down again and listen to the noises in the street and think about nothing. Erie gives him an amused, condescending glance.*) How old are you? Wait! Let me guess. You look fifty or over but I'll lay ten to one you're forty-three or maybe forty-four.

NIGHT CLERK—I'm forty-three. (*He adds vaguely*) Or maybe it is forty-four.

ERIE—(*elated*) I win, huh? I sure can call the turn on ages, Buddy. You ought to see the dolls get sored up when I work it on them! You're like Hughie. He looked like he'd never see fifty again and he was only forty-three. Me, I'm forty-five. Never think it, would you? Most of the dames don't think I've hit forty yet. (*The Night Clerk shifts his position so he can lean more on the desk. Maybe those shoes he sees advertised for fallen arches— But they cost eight dollars, so that's out— Get a pair when he goes to heaven. Erie is sizing him up with another cynical, friendly glance.*) I make another bet about you. Born and raised in the sticks, wasn't you?

NIGHT CLERK—(*faintly aroused and defensive*) I come originally from Saginaw, Michigan, but I've lived here in the Big Town so long I consider myself a New Yorker now. (*This is a long speech for him and he wonders sadly why he took the trouble to make it.*)

ERIE—I don't deserve no medal for picking that one. Nearly every guy I know on the Big Stem—and I know most of 'em—hails from the sticks. Take me. You'd never guess it but I was dragged up in Erie, P-a. Ain't that a knockout! Erie, P-a! That's how I got my moniker. No one calls me nothing but Erie. You better call me Erie, too, Pal, or I won't know when you're talkin' to me.

NIGHT CLERK—All right, Erie.

ERIE—Atta Boy. (*He chuckles.*) Here's another knockout. Smith is my real name. A Broadway guy like me named Smith and it's my real name! Ain't that a knockout! (*He explains carefully so there will be no misunderstanding.*) I don't remember nothing much about Erie, P-a, you understand—or want to. Some punk burg! After grammar school, my Old Man put me to work in his store, dealing out groceries. Some punk job! I stuck it till I was eighteen before I took a run-out powder. (*The Night Clerk seems turned into a drooping waxwork, draped along the desk. This is what he used to dread before he perfected his technique of not listening: The Guest's Story of His Life. He fixes his mind on his aching feet. Erie chuckles.*) Speaking of marriage, that was the big reason I ducked. A doll nearly had me hooked for the old shotgun ceremony. Closest I ever come to being played for a sucker. This doll in Erie— Daisy's her name—was one of them dumb wide-open dolls. All the guys give her a play. Then one day she wakes up and finds she's going to have a kid. I never figured she meant to frame me in particular. Way I always figured, she didn't have no idea who, so she holds a lottery all by herself. Put about a thousand guys' names in a hat—all she could remember— and drew one out and I was it. Then she told her Ma, and

her Ma told her Pa, and her Pa come round looking for me.
But I was no fall guy even in them days. I took it on the lam.
For Saratoga, to look the bangtails over. I'd started to be a
horse player in Erie, though I'd never seen a track. I been one
ever since. (*with a touch of bravado*) And I ain't done so bad,
Pal. I've made some killings in my time the gang still gab
about. I've been in the big bucks. More'n once, and I will be
again. I've had tough breaks too, but what the hell, I always
get by. When the horses won't run for me, there's draw or
stud. When they're bad, there's a crap game. And when
they're all bad, there's always bucks to pick up for little
errands I ain't talkin' about, which they give a guy who can
keep his clam shut. Oh, I get along, Buddy. I get along fine.
(*He waits for approving assent from the Night Clerk, but the
latter is not hearing so intently he misses his cue until the expec-
tant silence crashes his ears.*)

    NIGHT CLERK—(*hastily, gambling on "yes"*) Yes, Sir.

    ERIE—(*bitingly*) Sorry if I'm keeping you up, Sport. (*with
an aggrieved air*) Hughie was a wide-awake guy. He was always waiting for me to roll in. He'd say, "Hello, Erie, how'd
the bangtails treat you?" Or, "How's luck?" Or, "Did you
make the old bones behave?" Then I'd tell him how I'd done.
He'd ask, "What's new along the Big Stem?" and I'd tell him
the latest off the grapevine. (*He grins with affectionate condescension.*) It used to hand me a laugh to hear old Hughie
crackin' like a sport. In all the years I knew him, he never bet
a buck on nothin'. (*excusingly*) But it ain't his fault. He'd have
took a chance, but how could he with his wife keepin' cases
on every nickel of his salary? I showed him lots of ways
he could cross her up, but he was too scared. (*He chuckles.*)
The biggest knockout was when he'd kid me about dames.
He'd crack, "What? No blonde to-night, Erie? You must be
slippin'." Jeez, you never see a guy more bashful with a doll
around than Hughie was. I used to introduce him to the
tramps I'd drag home with me. I'd wise them up to kid him
along and pretend they'd fell for him. In two minutes, they'd
have him hanging on the ropes. His face'd be red and he'd
look like he wanted to crawl under the desk and hide. Some
of them dolls was raw babies. They'd make him pretty raw
propositions. He'd stutter like he was paralyzed. But he ate it

up, just the same. He was tickled pink. I used to hope maybe I could nerve him up to do a little cheatin'. I'd offer to fix it for him with one of my dolls. Hell, I got plenty, I wouldn't have minded. I'd tell him, "Just let that wife of yours know you're cheatin', and she'll have some respect for you." But he was too scared. (*He pauses—boastfully*) Some queens I've brought here in my time, Brother—frails from the Follies, or the Scandals, or the Frolics, that'd knock your eye out! And I still can make 'em. You watch. I ain't slippin'. (*He looks at the Night Clerk expecting reassurance, but the Clerk's mind has slipped away to the clanging bounce of garbage cans in the outer night. He is thinking: "A job I'd like. I'd bang those cans louder than they do! I'd wake up the whole damned city!" Erie mutters disgustedly to himself*) Jesus, what a dummy! (*He makes a move in the direction of the elevator, off right front—gloomily*) Might as well hit the hay, I guess.

NIGHT CLERK—(*comes to—with the nearest approach to feeling he has shown in many a long night—approvingly*) Good night, Mr. Smith. I hope you have a good rest. (*But Erie stops, glancing around the deserted lobby with forlorn distaste, jiggling the room key in his hand.*)

ERIE—What a crummy dump! What did I come back for? I shoulda stayed on a drunk. You'd never guess it, Buddy, but when I first come here this was a classy hotel—and clean, can you believe it? (*He scowls.*) I've been campin' here, off and on, fifteen years, but I've got a good notion to move out. It ain't the same place since Hughie was took to the hospital. (*gloomily*) Hell with going to bed! I'll just lie there worrying— (*He turns back to the desk. The Clerk's face would express despair, but the last time he was able to feel despair was back around World War days when the cost of living got so high and he was out of a job for three months. Erie leans on the desk—in a dejected, confidential tone*) Believe me, Brother, I never been a guy to worry, but this time I'm on a spot where I got to, if I ain't a sap.

NIGHT CLERK—(*in the vague tone of a corpse which admits it once overheard a favorable rumor about life*) That's too bad, Mr. Smith. But they say most of the things we worry about never happen. (*His mind escapes to the street again to play bouncing cans with the garbage men.*)

ERIE—(*grimly*) This thing happens, Pal. I ain't won a bet at nothin' since Hughie was took to the hospital. I'm jinxed. And that ain't all— But to hell with it! You're right, at that. Something always turns up for me. I was born lucky. I ain't worried. Just moaning low. Hell, who don't when they're getting over a drunk? You know how it is. The Brooklyn Boys march over the bridge with bloodhounds to hunt you down. And I'm still carrying the torch for Hughie. His checking out was a real K.O. for me. Damn if I know why. Lots of guys I've been pals with, in a way, croaked from booze or something, or got rubbed out, but I always took it as part of the game. Hell, we all gotta croak. Here today, gone tomorrow, so what's the good of beefin'? When a guy's dead, he's dead. He don't give a damn, so why should anybody else? (*But this fatalistic philosophy is no comfort and Erie sighs.*) I miss Hughie, I guess. I guess I'd got to like him a lot. (*Again he explains carefully so there will be no misunderstanding.*) Not that I was ever real pals with him, you understand. He didn't run in my class. He didn't know none of the answers. He was just a sucker. (*He sighs again.*) But I sure am sorry he's gone. You missed a lot not knowing Hughie, Pal. He sure was one grand little guy. (*He stares at the lobby floor. The Night Clerk regards him with vacant, bulging eyes full of a vague envy for the blind. The garbage men have gone their predestined way. Time is that much older. The Clerk's mind remains in the street to greet the noise of a far-off El train. Its approach is pleasantly like a memory of hope; then it roars and rocks and rattles past the nearby corner, and the noise pleasantly deafens memory; then it recedes and dies, and there is something melancholy about that. But there is hope. Only so many El trains pass in one night, and each one passing leaves one less to pass, so the night recedes, too, until at last it must die and join all the other long nights in Nirvana, the Big Night of Nights. And that's life. "What I always tell Jess when she nags me to worry about something: That's life, isn't it? What can you do about it?" Erie sighs again —then turns to the Clerk, his foolishly wary, wise-guy eyes defenseless, his poker face as self-betraying as a hurt dog's —appealingly*) Say, you do remind me of Hughie somehow, Pal. You got the same look on your map. (*But the Clerk's mind is far away attending the obsequies of night, and it takes it some time to get back. Erie is hurt —con-*

temptuously) But I guess it's only that old night clerk look! There's one of 'em born every minute!

NIGHT CLERK—(*His mind arrives just in time to catch this last—with a bright grimace*) Yes, Mr. Smith. That's what Barnum said, and it's certainly true, isn't it?

ERIE—(*grateful even for this sign of companionship, growls*) Nix on the Mr. Smith stuff, Charlie. There's ten of *them* born every minute. Call me Erie, like I told you.

NIGHT CLERK—(*automatically, as his mind tiptoes into the night again*) All right, Erie.

ERIE—(*encouraged, leans on the desk, clacking his room key like a castanet*) Yeah. Hughie was one grand little guy. All the same, like I said, he wasn't the kind of guy you'd ever figger a guy like me would take to. Because he was a sucker, see— the kind of sap you'd take to the cleaners a million times and he'd never wise up he was took. Why, night after night, just for a gag, I'd get him to shoot crap with me here on the desk. With *my* dice. And he'd never ask to give 'em the once-over. Can you beat that! (*He chuckles—then earnestly*) Not that I'd ever ring in no phoneys on a pal. I'm no heel. (*He chuckles again.*) And anyway, I didn't need none to take Hughie be- cause he never even made me knock 'em against nothing. Just a roll on the desk here. Boy, if they'd ever let me throw 'em that way in a real game, I'd be worth ten million dollars. (*He laughs.*) You'da thought Hughie woulda got wise something was out of order when, no matter how much he'd win on a run of luck like suckers have sometimes, I'd always take him to the cleaners in the end. But he never suspicioned nothing. All he'd say was "Gosh, Erie, no wonder you took up gam- bling. You sure were born lucky." (*He chuckles.*) Can you beat that? (*He hastens to explain earnestly*) Of course, like I said, it was only a gag. We'd play with real jack, just to make it look real, but it was all my jack. He never had no jack. His wife dealt him four bits a day for spending money. So I'd stake him at the start to half of what I got—in chicken feed, I mean. We'd pretend a cent was a buck, and a nickel was a fin and so on. Some big game! He got a big kick out of it. He'd get all het up. It give me a kick, too—especially when he'd say, "Gosh, Erie, I don't wonder you never worry about money, with your luck." (*He laughs.*) That guy would believe anything! Of course, I'd stall him off when he'd want to shoot nights when I didn't have a goddamned nickel. (*He chuckles.*) What laughs he used to hand me! He'd always call horses "the bangtails," like he'd known 'em all his life—and he'd never seen a race horse, not till I kidnaped him one day and took him down to Belmont. What a kick he got out of that! I got scared he'd pass out with excitement. And he wasn't doing no betting either. All he had was four bits. It was just the track, and the crowd, and the horses got him. Mostly the horses. (*with a surprised, reflective air*) Y'know, it's funny how a dumb, simple guy like Hughie will all of a sudden get something right. He says, "They're the most beautiful things in the world, I think." And he wins! I tell you, Pal, I'd rather sleep in the same stall with old Man o' War than make the whole damn Follies. What do you think?

NIGHT CLERK—(*His mind darts back from a cruising taxi and blinks bewilderedly in the light: "Say yes."*) Yes, I agree with you, Mr.—I mean, Erie.

ERIE—(*with good-natured contempt*) Yeah? I bet you never seen one, except back at the old Fair Grounds in the sticks. I don't mean them kind of turtles. I mean a real horse. (*The Clerk wonders what horses have to do with anything—or for that matter, what anything has to do with anything—then gives it up. Erie takes up his tale.*) And what d'you think happened the next night? Damned if Hughie didn't dig two bucks out of his pants and try to slip 'em to me. "Let this ride on the nose of whatever horse you're betting on tomorrow," he told me. I got sore. "Nix," I told him, "if you're going to start playin' sucker and bettin' on horse races, you don't get no assist from me." (*He grins wryly.*) Was that a laugh! Me advising a sucker not to bet when I've spent a lot of my life tellin' saps a story to make 'em bet! I said, "Where'd you grab this dough? Outa the Little Woman's purse, huh? What tale you going to give her when you lose it? She'll start breaking up the furniture with you!" "No," he says, "she'll just cry." "That's worse," I said, "no guy can beat that racket. I had a doll cry on me once in a restaurant full of people till I had to promise her a diamond engagement ring to sober her up." Well, anyway, Hughie sneaked the two bucks back in the Little Woman's purse when he went home that morning, and that was the end of that. (*cynically*) Boy Scouts got nothin' on me, Pal, when it comes to good deeds. That was one I done. It's too bad I can't remember no others. (*He is well wound up now and goes on without noticing that the Night Clerk's mind has left the premises in his sole custody.*) Y'know I had Hughie sized up for a sap the first time I see him. I'd just rolled in from Tia Juana. I'd made a big killing down there and I was lousy with jack. Came all the way in a drawing room, and I wasn't lonely in it neither. There was a blonde movie doll on the train—and I was lucky in them days. Used to follow the horses South every winter. I don't no more. Sick of traveling. And I ain't as lucky as I was— (*hastily*) Anyway, this time I'm talkin' about, soon as I hit this lobby I see there's a new night clerk, and while I'm signing up for the bridal suite I make a bet with myself he's never been nothin' but a night clerk. And I win. At first, he wouldn't open up. Not that he was cagey about gabbin' too much. But like he couldn't think of nothin' about himself worth saying. But after he'd seen me roll in here the last one every night, and I'd stop to kid him along and tell him the tale of what I'd win that day, he got friendly and talked. He'd come from a hick burg upstate. Graduated from high school, and had a shot at different jobs in the old home town but couldn't make the grade until he was took on as night clerk in the hotel there. Then he made good. But he wasn't satisfied. Didn't like being only a night clerk where everybody knew him. He'd read somewhere—in the Suckers' Almanac, I guess—that all a guy had to do was come to the Big Town and Old Man Success would be waitin' at the Grand Central to give him the key to the city. What a gag that is! Even I believed that once, and no one could ever call me a sap. Well, anyway, he made the break and come here and the only job he could get was night clerk. Then he fell in love—or kidded himself he was—and got married. Met her on a subway train. It stopped sudden and she was jerked into him, and he put his arms around her, and they started talking, and the poor boob never stood a chance. She was a sales girl in some punk department store, and she was sick of standing on her dogs all day, and all the way home to Brooklyn, too. So, the way I figger it, knowing Hughie and dames, she proposed and said "yes" for him, and married him, and after that, of course, he never dared stop being a night clerk, even if he could. (*He pauses.*) Maybe you think I ain't giving her a square shake. Well, maybe I ain't. She never give me one. She put me down as a bad influence, and let her chips ride. And maybe Hughie couldn't have done no better. Dolls didn't call him no riot. Hughie and her seemed happy enough the time he had me out to dinner in their flat. Well, not happy. Maybe contented. No, that's boosting it, too. Resigned comes nearer, as if each was givin' the other a break by thinking, "Well, what more could I expect?" (*Abruptly he addresses the Night Clerk with contemptuous good nature.*) How d'you and your Little Woman hit it off, Brother?

NIGHT CLERK—(*His mind has been counting the footfalls of the cop on the beat as they recede, sauntering longingly toward the dawn's release. "If he'd only shoot it out with a gunman some night! Nothing exciting has happened in any night I've ever lived through!" He stammers gropingly among the echoes of Erie's last words*) Oh—you mean *my* wife? Why, we get along all right, I guess.

ERIE—(*disgustedly*) Better lay off them headache pills, Pal. First thing you know, some guy is going to call you a dope. (*But the Night Clerk cannot take this seriously. It is years since he cared what anyone called him. So many guests have called him so many things. The Little Woman has, too. And, of course, he has, himself. But that's all past. Is daybreak coming now? No, too early yet. He can tell by the sound of that surface car. It is still lost in the night. Flat wheeled and tired. Distant the carbarn, and far away the sleep. Erie, having soothed resentment with his wisecrack, goes on with a friendly grin.*) Well, keep hoping, Pal. Hughie was as big a dope as you until I give him some interest in life. (*slipping back into narrative*) That time he took me home to dinner. Was that a knockout! It took him a hell of a while to get up nerve to ask me. "Sure, Hughie," I told him, "I'll be tickled to death." I was thinking, I'd rather be shot. For one thing, he lived in Brooklyn, and I'd sooner take a trip to China. Another thing, I'm a guy that likes to eat what I order and not what somebody deals me. And he had kids and a wife, and the family racket is out of my line. But Hughie looked so tickled I couldn't welsh on him. And it didn't work out so bad. Of course, what he called home was only a dump

of a cheap flat. Still, it wasn't so bad for a change. His wife
had done a lot of stuff to doll it up. Nothin' with no class,
you understand. Just cheap stuff to make it comfortable. And
his kids wasn't the gorillas I'd expected, neither. No throwin'
spitballs in my soup or them kind of gags. They was quiet
like Hughie. I kinda liked 'em. After dinner I started tellin'
'em a story about a race horse a guy I know owned once. I
thought it was up to me to put out something, and kids like
animal stories, and this one was true, at that. This old turtle
never wins a race, but he was as foxy as ten guys, a natural
born crook, the goddamnedest thief, he'd steal anything in
reach that wasn't nailed down— Well, I didn't get far.
Hughie's wife butt in and stopped me cold. Told the kids it
was bedtime and hustled 'em off like I was giving 'em measles. It got my goat, kinda. I coulda liked her—a little—if
she'd give me a chance. Not that she was nothin' Ziegfeld
would want to glorify. When you call her plain, you give her
all the breaks. (*resentfully*) Well, to hell with it. She had me
tagged for a bum, and seein' me made her sure she was right.
You can bet she told Hughie never invite me again, and he
never did. He tried to apologize, but I shut him up quick.
He says, "Irma was brought up strict. She can't help being
narrow-minded about gamblers." I said, "What's it to me? I
don't want to hear your dame troubles. I got plenty of my
own. Remember that doll I brung home night before last?
She gives me an argument I promised her ten bucks. I told
her, 'Listen, Baby, I got an impediment in my speech. Maybe
it sounded like ten, but it was two, and that's all you get.
Hell, I don't want to buy your soul! What would I do with
it?' Now she's peddling the news along Broadway I'm a rat
and a chiseler, and of course all the rats and chiselers believe
her. Before she's through, I won't have a friend left." (*He
pauses—confidentially*) I switched the subject on Hughie, see,
on purpose. He never did beef to me about his wife again.
(*He gives a forced chuckle.*) Believe me, Pal, I can stop guys
that start telling me their family troubles!

NIGHT CLERK—(*His mind has hopped an ambulance clanging down Sixth, and is asking without curiosity: "Will he die,
Doctor, or isn't he lucky?" "I'm afraid not, but he'll have to be
absolutely quiet for months and months." "With a pretty nurse*

*taking care of him?" "Probably not pretty." "Well, anyway, I
claim he's lucky. And now I must get back to the hotel. 492 won't
go to bed and insists on telling me jokes. It must have been a joke
because he's chuckling." He laughs with a heartiness which has
forgotten that heart is more than a word used in "Have a heart,"
an old slang expression.)* Ha— Ha! That's a good one, Erie.
That's the best I've heard in a long time!

ERIE—*(For a moment is so hurt and depressed he hasn't the
spirit to make a sarcastic crack. He stares at the floor, twirling his
room key—to himself)* Jesus, this sure is a dead dump. About
as homey as the Morgue. *(He glances up at the clock.)* Gettin'
late. Better beat it up to my cell and grab some shut eye. *(He
makes a move to detach himself from the desk but fails and remains wearily glued to it. His eyes prowl the lobby and finally come
to rest on the Clerk's glistening, sallow face. He summons up
strength for a withering crack.)* Why didn't you tell me you was
deaf, Buddy? I know guys is sensitive about them little afflic-
tions, but I'll keep it confidential. *(But the Clerk's mind has
rushed out to follow the siren wail of a fire engine. "A fireman's
life must be exciting." His mind rides the engine, and asks a fireman with disinterested eagerness: "Where's the fire? Is it a real
good one this time? Has it a good start? Will it be big enough, do
you think?" Erie examines his face—bitingly)* Take my tip, Pal,
and don't never try to buy from a dope peddler. He'll tell you
you had enough already. *(The Clerk's mind continues its dialogue with the fireman: "I mean, big enough to burn down the
whole damn city?" "Sorry, Brother, but there's no chance. There's
too much stone and steel. There'd always be something left." "Yes,
I guess you're right. There's too much stone and steel. I wasn't
really hoping, anyway. It really doesn't matter to me." Erie gives
him up and again attempts to pry himself from the desk, twirling
his key frantically as if it were a fetish which might set him free.)*
Well, me for the hay. *(But he can't dislodge himself—dully)*
Christ, it's lonely. I wish Hughie was here. By God, if he
was, I'd tell him a tale that'd make his eyes pop! The bigger
the story the harder he'd fall. He was that kind of sap. He
thought gambling was romantic. I guess he saw me like a sort
of dream guy, the sort of guy he'd like to be if he could take
a chance. I guess he lived a sort of double life listening to me
gabbin' about hittin' the high spots. Come to figger it, I'll bet

he even cheated on his wife that way, using me and my dolls.
(*He chuckles.*) No wonder he liked me, huh? And the bigger I
made myself the more he lapped it up. I went easy on him at
first. I didn't lie—not any more'n a guy naturally does when
he gabs about the bets he wins and the dolls he's made. But
I soon see he was cryin' for more, and when a sucker cries for
more, you're a dope if you don't let him have it. Every tramp
I made got to be a Follies' doll. Hughie liked 'em to be Follies' dolls. Or in the Scandals or Frolics. He wanted me to be
the Sheik of Araby, or something that any blonde 'd go
round-heeled about. Well, I give him plenty of that. And I
give him plenty of gambling tales. I explained my campin' in
this dump was because I don't want to waste jack on nothin'
but gambling. It was like dope to me, I told him. I couldn't
quit. He lapped that up. He liked to kid himself I'm mixed
up in the racket. He thought gangsters was romantic. So I
fed him some baloney about highjacking I'd done once. I told
him I knew all the Big Shots. Well, so I do, most of 'em, to
say hello, and sometimes they hello back. Who wouldn't
know 'em that hangs around Broadway and the joints? I run
errands for 'em sometimes, because there's dough in it, but
I'm cagey about gettin' in where it ain't healthy. Hughie
wanted to think me and Legs Diamond was old pals. So I
give him that too. I give him anything he cried for. (*earnestly*)
Don't get the wrong idea, Pal. What I fed Hughie wasn't all
lies. The tales about gambling wasn't. They was stories of big
games and killings that really happened since I've been
hangin' round. Only I wasn't in on 'em like I made out—
except one or two from way back when I had a run of big
luck and was in the bucks for a while until I was took to the
cleaners. (*He stops to pay tribute of a sigh to the memory of brave
days that were and that never were—then meditatively*) Yeah,
Hughie lapped up my stories like they was duck soup, or a
beakful of heroin. I sure took him around with me in tales
and showed him one hell of a time. (*He chuckles—then seriously*) And, d'you know, it done me good, too, in a way. Sure.
I'd get to seein' myself like he seen me. Some nights I'd come
back here without a buck, feeling lower than a snake's belly,
and first thing you know I'd be lousy with jack, bettin' a
grand a race. Oh, I was wise I was kiddin' myself. I ain't a

sap. But what the hell, Hughie loved it, and it didn't cost nobody nothin', and if every guy along Broadway who kids himself was to drop dead there wouldn't be nobody left. Ain't it the truth, Charlie? (*He again stares at the Night Clerk appealingly, forgetting past rebuffs. The Clerk's face is taut with vacancy. His mind has been trying to fasten itself to some noise in the night, but a rare and threatening pause of silence has fallen on the city, and here he is, chained behind a hotel desk forever, awake when everyone else in the world is asleep, except Room 492, and he won't go to bed, he's still talking, and there is no escape.*)

NIGHT CLERK—(*His glassy eyes stare through Erie's face. He stammers deferentially*) Truth? I'm afraid I didn't get— What's the truth?

ERIE—(*hopelessly*) Nothing, Pal. Not a thing. (*His eyes fall to the floor. For a while he is too defeated even to twirl his room key. The Clerk's mind still cannot make a getaway because the city remains silent, and the night vaguely reminds him of death, and he is vaguely frightened, and now that he remembers, his feet are giving him hell, but that's no excuse not to act as if the Guest is always right: "I should have paid 492 more attention. After all, he is company. He is awake and alive. I should use him to help me live through the night. What's he been talking about? I must have caught some of it without meaning to." The Night Clerk's forehead puckers perspiringly as he tries to remember. Erie begins talking again but this time it is obviously aloud to himself, without hope of a listener.*) I could tell by Hughie's face before he went to the hospital, he was through. I've seen the same look on guys' faces when they knew they was on the spot, just before guys caught up with them. I went to see him twice in the hospital. The first time, his wife was there and give me a dirty look, but he cooked up a smile and said, "Hello, Erie, how're the bangtails treating you?" I see he wants a big story to cheer him, but his wife butts in and says he's weak and he mustn't get excited. I felt like crackin', "Well, the Docs in this dump got the right dope. Just leave you with him and he'll never get excited." The second time I went, they wouldn't let me see him. That was near the end. I went to his funeral, too. There wasn't nobody but a coupla his wife's relations. I had to feel sorry for her. She looked like she ought to be parked in a coffin, too. The kids was bawlin'. There wasn't no flowers but a coupla lousy wreaths. It woulda been a punk showing for poor old Hughie, if it hadn't been for my flower piece. (*He swells with pride.*) That was some display, Pal. It'd knock your eye out! Set me back a hundred bucks, and no kiddin'! A big horseshoe of red roses! I knew Hughie'd want a horse-shoe because that made it look like he'd been a horse player. And around the top printed in forget-me-nots was "Good-by, Old Pal." Hughie liked to kid himself he was my pal. (*He adds sadly*) And so he was, at that—even if he was a sucker. (*He pauses, his false poker face as nakedly forlorn as an organ grinder's monkey's. Outside, the spell of abnormal quiet presses suffocatingly upon the street, enters the deserted, dirty lobby. The Night Clerk's mind cowers away from it. He cringes behind the desk, his feet aching like hell. There is only one possible escape. If his mind could only fasten onto something 492 has said. "What's he been talking about? A clerk should always be attentive. You even are duty bound to laugh at a guest's smutty jokes, no matter how often you've heard them. That's the policy of the hotel. 492 has been gassing for hours. What's he been telling me? I must be slipping. Always before this I've been able to hear without bothering to lis-ten, but now when I need company— Ah! I've got it! Gambling! He said a lot about gambling. That's something I've always wanted to know more about, too. Maybe he's a professional gam-bler. Like Arnold Rothstein."*)

NIGHT CLERK—(*blurts out with an uncanny, almost lifelike eagerness*) I beg your pardon, Mr.—Erie—but did I under-stand you to say you are a gambler by profession? Do you, by any chance, know the Big Shot, Arnold Rothstein? (*But this time it is Erie who doesn't hear him. And the Clerk's mind is now suddenly impervious to the threat of Night and Silence as it pursues an ideal of fame and glory within itself called Arnold Rothstein.*)

ERIE—(*with mournful longing*) Christ, I wish Hughie was alive and kickin'. I'd tell him I win ten grand from the book-ies, and ten grand at stud, and ten grand in a crap game! I'd tell him I bought one of those Mercedes sport roadsters with nickel pipes sticking out of the hood! I'd tell him I lay three babes from the Follies—two blondes and one brunette! (*The Night Clerk dreams, a rapt hero worship transfiguring his pimply face: "Arnold Rothstein! He must be some guy! I read a story* *about him. He'll gamble for any limit on anything, and always wins. The story said he wouldn't bother playing in a poker game unless the smallest bet you could make—one white chip!—was a hundred dollars. Christ, that's going some! I'd like to have the dough to get in a game with him once! The last pot everyone would drop out but him and me. I'd say, 'Okay, Arnold, the sky's the limit,' and I'd raise him five grand, and he'd call, and I'd have a royal flush to his four aces. Then I'd say, 'Okay, Arnold, I'm a good sport, I'll give you a break. I'll cut you double or nothing. Just one cut. I want quick action for my dough.' And I'd cut the ace of spades and win again."* Beatific vision swoons on the empty pools of the Night Clerk's eyes. He resembles a holy saint, recently elected to Paradise. Erie breaks the silence—bitterly resigned)* But Hughie's better off, at that, being dead. He's got all the luck. He needn't do no worryin' now. He's out of the racket. I mean, the whole goddamned racket. I mean life.

NIGHT CLERK—(*kicked out of his dream—with detached, pleasant acquiescence*) Yes, it is a goddamned racket when you stop to think, isn't it, 492? But we might as well make the best of it, because— Well, you can't burn it all down, can you? There's too much steel and stone. There'd always be something left to start it going again.

ERIE—(*scowls bewilderedly*) Say, what is this? What the hell you talkin' about?

NIGHT CLERK—(*at a loss—in much confusion*) Why, to be frank, I really don't— Just something that came into my head.

ERIE—(*bitingly, but showing he is comforted at having made some sort of contact*) Get it out of your head quick, Charlie, or some guys in uniform will walk in here with a butterfly net and catch you. (*He changes the subject—earnestly*) Listen, Pal, maybe you guess I was kiddin' about that flower piece for Hughie costing a hundred bucks? Well, I ain't! I didn't give a damn what it cost. It was up to me to give Hughie a big-time send-off, because I knew nobody else would.

NIGHT CLERK—Oh, I'm not doubting your word, Erie. You won the money gambling, I suppose— I mean, I beg your pardon if I'm mistaken, but you are a gambler, aren't you?

ERIE—(*preoccupied*) Yeah, sure, when I got scratch to put up. What of it? But I don't win that hundred bucks. I don't win a bet since Hughie was took to the hospital. I had to get down on my knees and beg every guy I know for a sawbuck here and a sawbuck there until I raised it.

NIGHT CLERK—(*his mind concentrated on the Big Ideal—insistently*) Do you by any chance know—Arnold Rothstein?

ERIE—(*his train of thought interrupted—irritably*) Arnold? What's he got to do with it? He wouldn't loan a guy like me a nickel to save my grandmother from streetwalking.

NIGHT CLERK—(*with humble awe*) Then you do know him!

ERIE—Sure I know the bastard. Who don't on Broadway? And he knows me—when he wants to. He uses me to run errands when there ain't no one else handy. But he ain't my trouble, Pal. My trouble is, some of these guys I put the bite on is dead wrong G's, and they expect to be paid back next Tuesday, or else I'm outa luck and have to take it on the lam, or I'll get beat up and maybe sent to a hospital. (*He suddenly rouses himself and there is something pathetically but genuinely gallant about him.*) But what the hell. I was wise I was takin' a chance. I've always took a chance, and if I lose I pay, and no welshing! It sure was worth it to give Hughie the big send-off. (*He pauses. The Night Clerk hasn't paid any attention except to his own dream. A question is trembling on his parted lips, but before he can get it out Erie goes on gloomily.*) But even that ain't my big worry, Charlie. My big worry is the run of bad luck I've had since Hughie got took to the hospital. Not a win. That ain't natural. I've always been a lucky guy—lucky enough to get by and pay up, I mean. I wouldn't never worry about owing guys, like I owe them guys. I'd always know I'd make a win that'd fix it. But now I got a lousy hunch when I lost Hughie I lost my luck—I mean, I've lost the old confidence. He used to give me confidence. (*He turns away from the desk.*) No use gabbin' here all night. You can't do me no good. (*He starts toward the elevator.*)

NIGHT CLERK—(*pleadingly*) Just a minute, Erie, if you don't mind. (*with awe*) So you're an old friend of Arnold Rothstein! Would you mind telling me if it's really true when Arnold Rothstein plays poker, one white chip is—a hundred dollars?

ERIE—(*dully exasperated*) Say, for Christ's sake, what's it to you—? (*He stops abruptly, staring probingly at the Clerk. There is a pause. Suddenly his face lights up with a saving revelation. He grins warmly and saunters confidently back to the desk.*) Say, Charlie, why didn't you put me wise before, you was interested in gambling? Hell, I got you all wrong, Pal. I been tellin' myself, this guy ain't like old Hughie. He ain't got no sportin' blood. He's just a dope. (*generously*) Now I see you're a right guy. Shake. (*He shoves out his hand which the Clerk clasps with a limp pleasure. Erie goes on with gathering warmth and self-assurance.*) That's the stuff. You and me'll get along. I'll give you all the breaks, like I give Hughie.

NIGHT CLERK—(*gratefully*) Thank you, Erie. (*then insistently*) Is it true when Arnold Rothstein plays poker, one white chip—

ERIE—(*with magnificent carelessness*) Sets you back a hundred bucks? Sure. Why not? Arnold's in the bucks, ain't he? And when you're in the bucks, a C note is chicken feed. I ought to know, Pal. I was in the bucks when Arnold was a piker. Why, one time down in New Orleans I lit a cigar with a C note, just for a gag, y'understand. I was with a bunch of high class dolls and I wanted to see their eyes pop out—and believe me, they sure popped! After that, I coulda made 'em one at a time or all together! Hell, I once win twenty grand on a single race. That's action! A good crap game is action, too. Hell, I've been in games where there was a hundred grand in real folding money lying around the floor. That's travelin'! (*He darts a quick glance at the Clerk's face and begins to hedge warily. But he needn't. The Clerk sees him now as the Gambler in 492, the Friend of Arnold Rothstein—and nothing is incredible. Erie goes on.*) Of course, I wouldn't kid you. I'm not in the bucks now—not right this moment. You know how it is, Charlie. Down today and up tomorrow. I got some dough ridin' on the nose of a turtle in the 4th at Saratoga. I hear a story he'll be so full of hop, if the joc can keep him from jumpin' over the grandstand, he'll win by a mile. So if I roll in here with a blonde that'll knock your eyes out, don't be surprised. (*He winks and chuckles.*)

NIGHT CLERK—(*ingratiatingly pally, smiling*) Oh, you can't surprise me that way. I've been a night clerk in New

York all my life, almost. (*He tries out a wink himself.*) I'll forget the house rules, Erie.

ERIE—(*dryly*) Yeah. The manager wouldn't like you to remember something he ain't heard of yet. (*then slyly feeling his way*) How about shootin' a little crap, Charlie? I mean just in fun, like I used to with Hughie. I know you can't afford takin' no chances. I'll stake you, see? I got a coupla bucks. We gotta use real jack or it don't look real. It's all my jack, get it? You can't lose. I just want to show you how I'll take you to the cleaners. It'll give me confidence. (*He has taken two one-dollar bills and some change from his pocket. He pushes most of it across to the Clerk.*) Here y'are. (*He produces a pair of dice—carelessly*) Want to give these dice the once-over before we start?

NIGHT CLERK—(*earnestly*) What do you think I am? I know I can trust you.

ERIE—(*smiles*) You remind me a lot of Hughie, Pal. He always trusted me. Well, don't blame me if I'm lucky. (*He clicks the dice in his hand—thoughtfully*) Y'know, it's time I quit carryin' the torch for Hughie. Hell, what's the use? It don't do him no good. He's gone. Like we all gotta go. Him yesterday, me or you tomorrow, and who cares, and what's the difference? It's all in the racket, huh? (*His soul is purged of grief, his confidence restored.*) I shoot two bits.

NIGHT CLERK—(*manfully, with an excited dead-pan expression he hopes resembles Arnold Rothstein's*) I fade you.

ERIE—(*throws the dice*) Four's my point. (*gathers them up swiftly and throws them again*) Four it is. (*He takes the money.*) Easy when you got my luck—and know how. Huh, Charlie? (*He chuckles, giving the Night Clerk the slyly amused, contemptuous, affectionate wink with which a Wise Guy regales a Sucker.*)

(*Curtain*)

A MOON
FOR THE MISBEGOTTEN

A Moon for the Misbegotten is published herewith with no revisions or deletions. It is an exact reproduction of the original manuscript which I delivered to Random House, Inc., on completing the play in 1943.

It has never been presented on the New York stage nor are there outstanding rights or plans for its production. Since I cannot presently give it the attention required for appropriate presentation, I have decided to make it available in book form.

April, 1952   E. O'N.

CHARACTERS

Josie Hogan
Phil Hogan, *her father*
Mike Hogan, *her brother*
James Tyrone, Jr.
T. Stedman Harder

SCENES

Act One
The farmhouse. Around noon. Early September, 1923.

Act Two
The same, but with the interior of sitting room revealed—
11 o'clock that night.

Act Three
The same as Act One. No time elapses between Acts Two
and Three.

Act Four
The same—Dawn of the following morning.

SCENE OF THE PLAY

The play takes place in Connecticut at the home of tenant farmer, Phil Hogan, between the hours of noon on a day in early September, 1923, and sunrise of the following day.

The house is not, to speak mildly, a fine example of New England architecture, placed so perfectly in its setting that it appears a harmonious part of the landscape, rooted in the earth. It has been moved to its present site, and looks it. An old boxlike, clapboarded affair, with a shingled roof and brick chimney, it is propped up about two feet above ground by layers of timber blocks. There are two windows on the lower floor of this side of the house which faces front, and one window on the floor above. These windows have no shutters, curtains or shades. Each has at least one pane missing, a square of cardboard taking its place. The house had once been painted a repulsive yellow with brown trim, but the walls now are a blackened and weathered gray, flaked with streaks and splotches of dim lemon. Just around the left corner of the house, a flight of steps leads to the front door.

To make matters worse, a one-story, one-room addition has been tacked on at right. About twelve feet long by six high, this room, which is Josie Hogan's bedroom, is evidently homemade. Its walls and sloping roof are covered with tar paper, faded to dark gray. Close to where it joins the house, there is a door with a flight of three unpainted steps leading to the ground. At right of door is a small window.

From these steps there is a footpath going around an old pear tree, at right-rear, through a field of hay stubble to a patch of woods. The same path also extends left to join a dirt road which leads up from the county highway (about a hundred yards off left) to the front door of the house, and thence back through a scraggly orchard of apple trees to the barn. Close to the house, under the window next to Josie's bedroom, there is a big boulder with a flat-top.

A Moon for the Misbegotten

ACT ONE

SCENE—*As described. It is just before noon. The day is clear and hot.*

The door of Josie's bedroom opens and she comes out on the steps, bending to avoid bumping her head.

Josie is twenty-eight. She is so oversize for a woman that she is almost a freak—five feet eleven in her stockings and weighs around one hundred and eighty. Her sloping shoulders are broad, her chest deep with large, firm breasts, her waist wide but slender by contrast with her hips and thighs. She has long smooth arms, immensely strong, although no muscles show. The same is true of her legs.

She is more powerful than any but an exceptionally strong man, able to do the manual labor of two ordinary men. But there is no mannish quality about her. She is all woman.

The map of Ireland is stamped on her face, with its long upper lip and small nose, thick black eyebrows, black hair as coarse as a horse's mane, freckled, sunburned fair skin, high cheekbones and heavy jaw. It is not a pretty face, but her large dark-blue eyes give it a note of beauty, and her smile, revealing even white teeth, gives it charm.

She wears a cheap, sleeveless, blue cotton dress. Her feet are bare, the soles earth-stained and tough as leather.

She comes down the steps and goes left to the corner of the house and peers around it toward the barn. Then she moves swiftly to the right of the house and looks back.

JOSIE—Ah, thank God. (*She goes back toward the steps as her brother, Mike, appears hurrying up from right-rear.*)

(*Mike Hogan is twenty, about four inches shorter than his sister. He is sturdily built, but seems almost puny compared to her. He has a common Irish face, its expression sullen, or slyly cunning, or primly self-righteous. He never forgets that he is a good Catholic, faithful to all the observances, and so is one of the élite of Almighty God in a world of damned sinners composed of Protestants and bad Catholics. In brief, Mike is a New England Irish Catholic Puritan, Grade B, and an extremely irritating youth to have around.*)

(*Mike wears dirty overalls, a sweat-stained brown shirt. He carries a pitchfork.*)

JOSIE—Bad luck to you for a slowpoke. Didn't I tell you half-past eleven?

MIKE—How could I sneak here sooner with him peeking round the corner of the barn to catch me if I took a minute's rest, the way he always does? I had to wait till he went to the pig pen. (*He adds viciously*) Where he belongs, the old hog! (*Josie's right arm strikes with surprising swiftness and her big hand lands on the side of his jaw. She means it to be only a slap, but his head jerks back and he stumbles, dropping the pitchfork, and pleads cringingly*) Don't hit me, Josie! Don't, now!

JOSIE—(*quietly*) Then keep your tongue off him. He's my father, too, and I like him, if you don't.

MIKE—(*out of her reach—sullenly*) You're two of a kind, and a bad kind.

JOSIE—(*good-naturedly*) I'm proud of it. And I didn't hit you, or you'd be flat on the ground. It was only a love tap to waken your wits, so you'll use them. If he catches you running away, he'll beat you half to death. Get your bag now. I've packed it. It's inside the door of my room with your coat laid over it. Hurry now, while I see what he's doing. (*She moves quickly to peer around the corner of the house at left. He goes up the steps into her room and returns carrying an old coat and a cheap bulging satchel. She comes back.*) There's no sight of him. (*Mike drops the satchel on the ground while he puts on the coat.*) I put everything in the bag. You can change to your Sunday suit in the can at the station or in the train, and don't forget to wash your face. I know you want to look your best when our brother, Thomas, sees you on his doorstep. (*Her tone becomes derisively amused.*) And him way up in the world, a noble sergeant of the Bridgeport police. Maybe he'll get you on the force. It'd suit you. I can see you leading drunks to the lockup while you give them a lecture on temperance. Or if Thomas can't get you a job, he'll pass you along to our brother, John, the noble barkeep in Meriden. He'll teach you the trade. You'll make a nice one, who'll never steal from the till, or drink, and who'll tell customers they've had enough and better go home just when they're beginning to feel happy. (*She sighs regretfully.*) Ah, well, Mike, you was born a priest's pet, and there's no help for it.

MIKE—That's right! Make fun of me again, because I want to be decent.

JOSIE—You're worse than decent. You're virtuous.

MIKE—Well, that's a thing nobody can say about— (*He stops, a bit ashamed, but mostly afraid to finish.*)

JOSIE—(*amused*) About me? No, and what's more, they don't. (*She smiles mockingly.*) I know what a trial it's been to you, Mike, having a sister who's the scandal of the neighborhood.

MIKE—It's you that's saying it, not me. I don't want to part with hard feelings. And I'll keep on praying for you.

JOSIE—(*roughly*) Och! To hell with your prayers!

MIKE—(*stiffly*) I'm going. (*He picks up his bag.*)

JOSIE—(*her manner softening*) Wait. (*She comes to him.*) Don't mind my rough tongue, Mike. I'm sorry to see you go, but it's the best thing for you. That's why I'm helping you, the same as I helped Thomas and John. You can't stand up to the Old Man any more than Thomas or John could, and the old divil would always keep you a slave. I wish you all the luck in the world, Mike. I know you'll get on—and God bless you. (*Her voice has softened, and she blinks back tears. She kisses him—then fumbling in the pocket of her dress, pulls out a little roll of one-dollar bills and presses it in his hand.*) Here's a little present over your fare. I took it from his little green bag, and won't he be wild when he finds out! But I can handle him.

MIKE—(*enviously*) You can. You're the only one. (*gratefully moved for a second*) Thank you, Josie. You've a kind heart. (*then virtuously*) But I don't like taking stolen money.

JOSIE—Don't be a bigger jackass than you are already. Tell your conscience it's a bit of the wages he's never given you.

MIKE—That's true, Josie. It's rightfully mine. (*He shoves the money into his pocket.*)

JOSIE—Get along now, so you won't miss the trolley. And don't forget to get off the train at Bridgeport. Give my love to Thomas and John. No, never mind. They've not written me in years. Give them a boot in the tail for me.

MIKE—That's nice talk for a woman. You've a tongue as dirty as the Old Man's.

JOSIE—(*impatiently*) Don't start preaching, like you love to, or you'll never go.

MIKE—You're as bad as he is, almost. It's his influence made you what you are, and him always scheming how he'll cheat people, selling them a broken-down nag or a sick cow or pig that he's doctored up to look good for a day or two. It's no better than stealing, and you help him.

JOSIE—I do. Sure, it's grand fun.

MIKE—You ought to marry and have a home of your own away from this shanty and stop your shameless ways with men. (*He adds, not without moral satisfaction*) Though it'd be hard to find a decent man who'd have you now.

JOSIE—I don't want a decent man, thank you. They're no fun. They're all sticks like you. And I wouldn't marry the best man on earth and be tied down to him alone.

MIKE—(*with a cunning leer*) Not even Jim Tyrone, I suppose? (*She stares at him.*) You'd like being tied to money, I know that, and he'll be rich when his mother's estate is settled. (*sarcastically*) I suppose you've never thought of that? Don't tell me! I've watched you making sheep's eyes at him.

JOSIE—(*contemptuously*) So I'm leading Jim on to propose, am I?

MIKE—I know it's crazy, but maybe you're hoping if you got hold of him alone when he's mad drunk— Anyway, talk all you please to put me off, I'll bet my last penny you've cooked up some scheme to hook him, and the Old Man put you up to it. Maybe he thinks if he caught you with Jim and had witnesses to prove it, and his shotgun to scare him—

JOSIE—(*controlling her anger*) You're full of bright thoughts. I wouldn't strain my brains any more, if I was you.

MIKE—Well, I wouldn't put it past the Old Man to try any trick. And I wouldn't put it past you, God forgive you. You've never cared about your virtue, or what man you went out with. You've always been brazen as brass and proud of your disgrace. You can't deny that, Josie.

JOSIE—I don't. (*then ominously*) You'd better shut up now.

I've been holding my temper, because we're saying good-bye. (*She stands up.*) But I'm losing patience.

MIKE—(*hastily*) Wait till I finish and you won't be mad at me. I was going to say I wish you luck with your scheming, for once. I hate Jim Tyrone's guts, with his quotin' Latin and his high-toned Jesuit College education, putting on airs as if he was too good to wipe his shoes on me, when he's nothing but a drunken bum who never done a tap of work in his life, except acting on the stage while his father was alive to get him the jobs. (*vindictively*) I'll pray you'll find a way to nab him, Josie, and skin him out of his last nickel!

JOSIE—(*makes a threatening move toward him*) One more word out of you— (*then contemptuously*) You're a dirty tick and it'd serve you right if I let you stay gabbing until Father came and beat you to a jelly, but I won't. I'm too anxious to be rid of you. (*roughly*) Get out of here, now! Do you think he'll stay all day with the pigs, you gabbing fool? (*She goes left to peer around the corner of the house—with real alarm*) There he is, coming up to the barn. (*Mike grabs the satchel, terrified. He slinks swiftly around the corner and disappears along the path to the woods, right-rear. She keeps watching her father and does not notice Mike's departure.*) He's looking toward the meadow. He sees you're not working. He's running down there. He'll come here next. You'd better run for your life! (*She turns and sees he's gone—contemptuously*) I might have known. I'll bet you're a mile away by now, you rabbit! (*She peeks around the corner again—with amused admiration*) Look at my poor old father pelt. He's as spry on his stumpy legs as a yearling—and as full of rage as a nest of wasps! (*She laughs and comes back to look along the path to the woods.*) Well, that's the last of you, Mike, and good riddance. It was the little boy you used to be that I had to mother, and not you, I stole the money for. (*This dismisses him. She sighs.*) Well, himself will be here in a minute. I'd better be ready. (*She reaches in her bedroom corner by the door and takes out a sawed-off broom handle.*) Not that I need it, but it saves his pride. (*She sits on the steps with the broom handle propped against the steps near her right hand. A moment later, her father, Phil Hogan, comes running up from left-rear and charges around the corner of the house, his*

*arms pumping up and down, his fists clenched, his face full of
fighting fury.*)

(*Hogan is fifty-five, about five feet six. He has a thick neck,
lumpy, sloping shoulders, a barrel-like trunk, stumpy legs, and big
feet. His arms are short and muscular, with large hairy hands.
His head is round with thinning sandy hair. His face is fat with
a snub nose, long upper lip, big mouth, and little blue eyes with
bleached lashes and eyebrows that remind one of a white pig's. He
wears heavy brogans, filthy overalls, and a dirty short-sleeved
undershirt. Arms and face are sunburned and freckled. On his
head is an old wide-brimmed hat of coarse straw that would look
more becoming on a horse. His voice is high-pitched with a pronounced brogue.*)

HOGAN—(*stops as he turns the corner and sees her—
furiously*) Where is he? Is he hiding in the house? I'll wipe the
floors with him, the lazy bastard! (*turning his anger against
her*) Haven't you a tongue in your head, you great slut you?

JOSIE—(*with provoking calm*) Don't be calling me names,
you bad-tempered old hornet, or maybe I'll lose my temper,
too.

HOGAN—To hell with your temper, you overgrown cow!

JOSIE—I'd rather be a cow than an ugly little buck goat.
You'd better sit down and cool off. Old men shouldn't run
around raging in the noon sun. You'll get sunstroke.

HOGAN—To hell with sunstroke! Have you seen him?

JOSIE—Have I seen who?

HOGAN—Mike! Who else would I be after, the Pope? He
was in the meadow, but the minute I turned my back he
sneaked off. (*He sees the pitchfork.*) There's his pitchfork! Will
you stop your lying!

JOSIE—I haven't said I didn't see him.

HOGAN—Then don't try to help him hide from me, or—
Where is he?

JOSIE—Where you'll never find him.

HOGAN—We'll soon see! I'll bet he's in your room under
the bed, the cowardly lump! (*He moves toward the steps.*)

JOSIE—He's not. He's gone like Thomas and John before
him to escape your slave-driving.

HOGAN—(*stares at her incredulously*) You mean he's run off
to make his own way in the world?

JOSIE—He has. So make up your mind to it, and sit down.

HOGAN—(*baffled, sits on the boulder and takes off his hat to scratch his head—with a faint trace of grudging respect*) I'd never dream he had that much spunk. (*his temper rising again*) And I know damned well he hadn't, not without you to give him the guts and help him, like the great soft fool you are!

JOSIE—Now don't start raging again, Father.

HOGAN—(*seething*) You've stolen my satchel to give him, I suppose, like you did before for Thomas and John?

JOSIE—It was my satchel, too. Didn't I help you in the trade for the horse, when you got the Crowleys to throw in the satchel for good measure? I was up all night fixing that nag's forelegs so his knees wouldn't buckle together till after the Crowleys had him a day or two.

HOGAN—(*forgets his anger to grin reminiscently*) You've a wonderful way with animals, God bless you. And do you remember the two Crowleys came back to give me a beating, and I licked them both?

JOSIE—(*with calculating flattery*) You did. You're a wonderful fighter. Sure, you could give Jack Dempsey himself a run for his money.

HOGAN—(*with sharp suspicion*) I could, but don't try to change the subject and fill me with blarney.

JOSIE—All right. I'll tell the truth then. They were getting the best of you till I ran out and knocked one of them tail over tin cup against the pigpen.

HOGAN—(*outraged*) You're a liar! They was begging for mercy before you came. (*furiously*) You thief, you! You stole my fine satchel for that lump! And I'll bet that's not all. I'll bet, like when Thomas and John sneaked off, you— (*He rises from the boulder threateningly.*) Listen, Josie, if you found where I hid my little green bag, and stole my money to give to that lousy altar boy, I'll—

JOSIE—(*rises from the steps with the broom handle in her right hand*) Well, I did. So now what'll you do? Don't be threatening me. You know I'll beat better sense in your skull if you lay a finger on me.

HOGAN—I never yet laid hands on a woman—not when I was sober—but if it wasn't for that club— (*bitterly*) A fine curse God put on me when he gave me a daughter as big and strong as a bull, and as vicious and disrespectful. (*Suddenly his eyes twinkle and he grins admiringly*.) Be God, look at you standing there with the club! If you ain't the damnedest daughter in Connecticut, who is? (*He chuckles and sits on the boulder again.*)

JOSIE—(*laughs and sits on the steps, putting the club away*) And if you ain't the damnedest father in Connecticut, who is?

HOGAN—(*takes a clay pipe and plug of tobacco and knife from his pocket. He cuts the plug and stuffs his pipe—without rancor*) How much did you steal, Josie?

JOSIE—Six dollars only.

HOGAN—*Only!* Well, God grant someone with wits will see that dopey gander at the depot and sell him the railroad for the six. (*grumbling*) It isn't the money I mind, Josie—

JOSIE—I know. Sure, what do you care for money? You'd give your last penny to the first beggar you met—if he had a shotgun pointed at your heart!

HOGAN—Don't be teasing. You know what I mean. It's the thought of that pious lump having my money that maddens me. I wouldn't put it past him to drop it in the collection plate next Sunday, he's that big a jackass.

JOSIE—I knew when you'd calmed down you'd think it worth six dollars to see the last of him.

HOGAN—(*finishes filling his pipe*) Well, maybe I do. To tell the truth, I never liked him. (*He strikes a match on the seat of his overalls and lights his pipe.*) And I never liked Thomas and John, either.

JOSIE—(*amused*) You've the same bad luck in sons I have in brothers.

HOGAN—(*puffs ruminatively*) They all take after your mother's family. She was the only one in it had spirit, God rest her soul. The rest of them was a pious lousy lot. They wouldn't dare put food in their mouths before they said grace for it. They was too busy preaching temperance to have time for a drink. They spent so much time confessing their sins, they had no chance to do any sinning. (*He spits disgustedly.*) The scum of the earth! Thank God, you're like me and your mother.

JOSIE—I don't know if I should thank God for being like

you. Sure, everyone says you're a wicked old tick, as crooked as a corkscrew.

HOGAN—I know. They're an envious lot, God forgive them. (*They both chuckle. He pulls on his pipe reflectively.*) You didn't get much thanks from Mike, I'll wager, for your help.

JOSIE—Oh, he thanked me kindly. And then he started to preach about my sins—and yours.

HOGAN—Oho, did he? (*exploding*) For the love of God, why didn't you hold him till I could give him one good kick for a father's parting blessing!

JOSIE—I near gave him one myself.

HOGAN—When I think your poor mother was killed bringing that crummy calf into life! (*vindictively*) I've never set foot in a church since, and never will. (*A pause. He speaks with a surprising sad gentleness.*) A sweet woman. Do you remember her, Josie? You were only a little thing when she died.

JOSIE—I remember her well. (*with a teasing smile which is half sad*) She was the one could put you in your place when you'd come home drunk and want to tear down the house for the fun of it.

HOGAN—(*with admiring appreciation*) Yes, she could do it, God bless her. I only raised my hand to her once—just a slap because she told me to stop singing, it was after daylight. The next moment I was on the floor thinking a mule had kicked me. (*He chuckles.*) Since you've grown up, I've had the same trouble. There's no liberty in my own home.

JOSIE—That's lucky—or there wouldn't be any home.

HOGAN—(*after a pause of puffing on his pipe*) What did that donkey, Mike, preach to you about?

JOSIE—Oh, the same as ever—that I'm the scandal of the countryside, carrying on with men without a marriage license.

HOGAN—(*gives her a strange, embarrassed glance and then looks away. He does not look at her during the following dialogue. His manner is casual.*) Hell roast his soul for saying it. But it's true enough.

JOSIE—(*defiantly*) It is, and what of it? I don't care a damn for the scandal.

HOGAN—No. You do as you please and to hell with everyone.

you. Sure, everyone says you're a wicked old tick, as crooked as a corkscrew.

HOGAN—I know. They're an envious lot, God forgive them. (*They both chuckle. He pulls on his pipe reflectively.*) You didn't get much thanks from Mike, I'll wager, for your help.

JOSIE—Oh, he thanked me kindly. And then he started to preach about my sins—and yours.

HOGAN—Oho, did he? (*exploding*) For the love of God, why didn't you hold him till I could give him one good kick for a father's parting blessing!

JOSIE—I near gave him one myself.

HOGAN—When I think your poor mother was killed bringing that crummy calf into life! (*vindictively*) I've never set foot in a church since, and never will. (*A pause. He speaks with a surprising sad gentleness.*) A sweet woman. Do you remember her, Josie? You were only a little thing when she died.

JOSIE—I remember her well. (*with a teasing smile which is half sad*) She was the one could put you in your place when you'd come home drunk and want to tear down the house for the fun of it.

HOGAN—(*with admiring appreciation*) Yes, she could do it, God bless her. I only raised my hand to her once—just a slap because she told me to stop singing, it was after daylight. The next moment I was on the floor thinking a mule had kicked me. (*He chuckles.*) Since you've grown up, I've had the same trouble. There's no liberty in my own home.

JOSIE—That's lucky—or there wouldn't be any home.

HOGAN—(*after a pause of puffing on his pipe*) What did that donkey, Mike, preach to you about?

JOSIE—Oh, the same as ever—that I'm the scandal of the countryside, carrying on with men without a marriage license.

HOGAN—(*gives her a strange, embarrassed glance and then looks away. He does not look at her during the following dialogue. His manner is casual.*) Hell roast his soul for saying it. But it's true enough.

JOSIE—(*defiantly*) It is, and what of it? I don't care a damn for the scandal.

HOGAN—No. You do as you please and to hell with everyone.

JOSIE—Yes, and that goes for you, too, if you are my father. So don't you start preaching too.

HOGAN—Me, preach? Sure, the divil would die laughing. Don't bring me into it. I learned long since to let you go your own way because there's no controlling you.

JOSIE—I do my work and I earn my keep and I've a right to be free.

HOGAN—You have. I've never denied it.

JOSIE—No. You've never. I've often wondered why a man that likes fights as much as you didn't grab at the excuse of my disgrace to beat the lights out of the men.

HOGAN—Wouldn't I look a great fool, when everyone knows any man who tried to make free with you, and you not willing, would be carried off to the hospital? Anyway, I wouldn't want to fight an army. You've had too many sweethearts.

JOSIE—(*with a proud toss of her head—boastfully*) That's because I soon get tired of any man and give him his walking papers.

HOGAN—I'm afraid you were born to be a terrible wanton woman. But to tell the truth, I'm well satisfied you're what you are, though I shouldn't say it, because if you was the decent kind, you'd have married some fool long ago, and I'd have lost your company and your help on the farm.

JOSIE—(*with a trace of bitterness*) Leave it to you to think of your own interest.

HOGAN—(*puffs on his pipe*) What else did my beautiful son, Mike, say to you?

JOSIE—Oh, he was full of stupid gab, as usual. He gave me good advice—

HOGAN—(*grimly*) That was kind of him. It must have been good—

JOSIE—I ought to marry and settle down—if I could find a decent man who'd have me, which he was sure I couldn't.

HOGAN—(*beginning to boil*) I tell you, Josie, it's going to be the saddest memory of my life I didn't get one last swipe at him!

JOSIE—So the only hope, he thought, was for me to catch some indecent man, who'd have money coming to him I could steal.

HOGAN—(*gives her a quick, probing side glance—casually*) He meant Jim Tyrone?

JOSIE—He did. And the dirty tick accused you and me of making up a foxy scheme to trap Jim. I'm to get him alone when he's crazy drunk and lead him on to marry me. (*She adds in a hard, scornful tone*) As if that would ever work. Sure, all the pretty little tarts on Broadway, New York, must have had a try at that, and much good it did them.

HOGAN—(*again with a quick side glance—casually*) They must have, surely. But that's in the city where he's suspicious. You never can tell what he mightn't do here in the country, where he's innocent, with a moon in the sky to fill him with poetry and a quart of bad hootch inside of him.

JOSIE—(*turns on him angrily*) Are you taking Mike's scheme seriously, you old goat?

HOGAN—I'm not. I only thought you wanted my opinion. (*She regards him suspiciously, but his face is blank, as if he hadn't a thought beyond enjoying his pipe.*)

JOSIE—(*turning away*) And if that didn't work, Mike said maybe we had a scheme that I'd get Jim in bed with me and you'd come with witnesses and a shotgun, and catch him there.

HOGAN—Faith, me darlin' son never learnt that from his prayer book! He must have improved his mind on the sly.

JOSIE—The dirty tick!

HOGAN—Don't call him a tick. I don't like ticks but I'll say this for them, I never picked one off me yet was a hypocrite.

JOSIE—Him daring to accuse us of planning a rotten trick like that on Jim!

HOGAN—(*as if he misunderstood her meaning*) Yes, it's as old as the hills. Everyone's heard of it. But it still works now and again, I'm told, and sometimes an old trick is best because it's so ancient no one would suspect you'd try it.

JOSIE—(*staring at him resentfully*) That's enough out of you, Father. I never can tell to this day, when you put that dead mug on you, whether you're joking or not, but I don't want to hear any more—

HOGAN—(*mildly*) I thought you wanted my honest opinion on the merits of Mike's suggestion.

JOSIE—Och, shut up, will you? I know you're only trying to make game of me. You like Jim and you'd never play a dirty trick on him, not even if I was willing.

HOGAN—No—not unless I found he was playing one on me.

JOSIE—Which he'd never.

HOGAN—No, I wouldn't think it, but my motto in life is never trust anyone too far, not even myself.

JOSIE—You've reason for the last. I've often suspected you sneak out of bed in the night to pick your own pockets.

HOGAN—I wouldn't call it a dirty trick on him to get you for a wife.

JOSIE—(*exasperatedly*) God save us, are you off on that again?

HOGAN—Well, you've put marriage in my head and I can't help considering the merits of the case, as they say. Sure, you're two of a kind, both great disgraces. That would help make a happy marriage because neither of you could look down on the other.

JOSIE—Jim mightn't think so.

HOGAN—You mean he'd think he was marrying beneath his station? He'd be a damned fool if he had that notion, for his Old Man who'd worked up from nothing to be rich and famous didn't give a damn about station. Didn't I often see him working on his grounds in clothes I wouldn't put on a scarecrow, not caring who saw him? (*with admiring affection*) God rest him, he was a true Irish gentleman.

JOSIE—He was, and didn't you swindle him, and make me help you at it? I remember when I was a slip of a girl, and you'd get a letter saying his agent told him you were a year behind in the rent, and he'd be damned if he'd stand for it, and he was coming here to settle the matter. You'd make me dress up, with my hair brushed and a ribbon in it, and leave me to soften his heart before he saw you. So I'd skip down the path to meet him, and make him a courtesy, and hold on to his hand, and bat my eyes at him and lead him in the house, and offer him a drink of the good whiskey you didn't keep for company, and gape at him and tell him he was the handsomest man in the world, and the fierce expression he'd put on for you would go away.

HOGAN—(*chuckles*) You did it wonderful. You should have gone on the stage.

JOSIE—(*dryly*) Yes, that's what he'd tell me, and he'd reach in his pocket and take out a half dollar, and ask me if you hadn't put me up to it. So I'd say yes, you had.

HOGAN—(*sadly*) I never knew you were such a black traitor, and you only a child.

JOSIE—And then you'd come and before he could get a word out of him, you'd tell him you'd vacate the premises unless he lowered the rent and painted the house.

HOGAN—Be God, that used to stop him in his tracks.

JOSIE—It didn't stop him from saying you were the damnedest crook ever came out of Ireland.

HOGAN—He said it with admiration. And we'd start drinking and telling stories, and singing songs, and by the time he left we were both too busy cursing England to worry over the rent. (*He grins affectionately.*) Oh, he was a great man entirely.

JOSIE—He was. He always saw through your tricks.

HOGAN—Didn't I know he would? Sure, all I wanted was to give him the fun of seeing through them so he couldn't be hard-hearted. That was the real trick.

JOSIE—(*stares at him*) You old divil, you've always a trick hidden behind your tricks, so no one can tell at times what you're after.

HOGAN—Don't be so suspicious. Sure, I'd never try to fool you. You know me too well. But we've gone off the track. It's Jim we're discussing, not his father. I was telling you I could see the merit in your marrying him.

JOSIE—(*exasperatedly*) Och, a cow must have kicked you in the head this morning.

HOGAN—I'd never give it a thought if I didn't know you had a soft spot in your heart for him.

JOSIE—(*resentfully*) Well, I haven't! I like him, if that's what you mean, but it's only to talk to, because he's educated and quiet-spoken and has politeness even when he's drunkest, and doesn't roar around cursing and singing, like some I could name.

HOGAN—If you could see the light in your eyes when he blarneys you—

JOSIE—(*roughly*) The light in me foot! (*scornfully*) I'm in love with him, you'll be saying next!

HOGAN—(*ignores this*) And another merit of the case is, he likes you.

JOSIE—Because he keeps dropping in here lately? Sure, it's only when he gets sick of the drunks at the Inn, and it's more to joke with you than see me.

HOGAN—It's your happiness I'm considering when I recommend your using your wits to catch him, if you can.

JOSIE—(*jeeringly*) If!

HOGAN—Who knows? With all the sweethearts you've had, you must have a catching way with men.

JOSIE—(*boastfully*) Maybe I have. But that doesn't mean—

HOGAN—If you got him alone tonight—there'll be a beautiful moon to fill him with poetry and loneliness, and—

JOSIE—That's one of Mike's dirty schemes.

HOGAN—Mike be damned! Sure, that's every woman's scheme since the world was created. Without it there'd be no population. (*persuasively*) There'd be no harm trying it, anyway.

JOSIE—And no use, either. (*bitterly*) Och, Father, don't play the jackass with me. You know, and I know, I'm an ugly overgrown lump of a woman, and the men that want me are no better than stupid bulls. Jim can have all the pretty, painted little Broadway girls he wants—and dancers on the stage, too—when he comes into his estate. That's the kind he likes.

HOGAN—I notice he's never married one. Maybe he'd like a fine strong handsome figure of a woman for a change, with beautiful eyes and hair and teeth and a smile.

JOSIE—(*pleased, but jeering*) Thank you kindly for your compliments. Now I know a cow kicked you in the head.

HOGAN—If you think Jim hasn't been taking in your fine points, you're a fool.

JOSIE—You mean you've noticed him? (*suddenly furious*) Stop your lying!

HOGAN—Don't fly in a temper. All I'm saying is, there may be a chance in it to better yourself.

JOSIE—(*scornfully*) Better myself by being tied down to a man who's drunk every night of his life? No, thank you!

HOGAN—Sure, you're strong enough to reform him. A taste of that club you've got, when he came home to you paralyzed, and in a few weeks you'd have him a dirty prohibitionist.

JOSIE—(*seriously*) It's true, if I was his wife, I'd cure him of drinking himself to death, if I had to kill him. (*then angrily*) Och, I'm sick of your crazy gab, Father! Leave me alone!

HOGAN—Well, let's put it another way. Don't tell me you couldn't learn to love the estate he'll come into.

JOSIE—(*resentfully*) Ah, I've been waiting for that. That's what Mike said, again. Now we've come to the truth behind all your blather of my liking him or him liking me. (*her manner changing—defiantly*) All right, then. Of course I'd love the money. Who wouldn't? And why shouldn't I get my hands on it, if I could? He's bound to be swindled out of it, anyway. He'll go back to the Broadway he thinks is heaven, and by the time the pretty little tarts, and the barroom sponges and racetrack touts and gamblers are through with him he'll be picked clean. I'm no saint, God knows, but I'm decent and deserving compared to those scum.

HOGAN—(*eagerly*) Be God, now you're using your wits. And where there's a will there's a way. You and me have never been beat when we put our brains together. I'll keep thinking it over, and you do the same.

JOSIE—(*with illogical anger*) Well, I won't! And you keep your mad scheming to yourself. I won't listen to it.

HOGAN—(*as if he were angry, too*) All right. The divil take you. It's all you'll hear from me. (*He pauses—then with great seriousness, turning toward her*) Except one thing— (*as she starts to shut him up—sharply*) I'm serious, and you'd better listen, because it's about this farm, which is home to us.

JOSIE—(*surprised, stares at him*) What about the farm?

HOGAN—Don't forget, if we have lived on it twenty years, we're only tenants and we could be thrown out on our necks any time. (*quickly*) Mind you, I don't say Jim would ever do it, rent or no rent, or let the executors do it, even if they wanted, which they don't, knowing they'd never find another tenant.

JOSIE—What's worrying you, then?

HOGAN—This. I've been afraid lately the minute the estate is out of probate, Jim will sell the farm.

JOSIE—(*exasperatedly*) Of course he will! Hasn't he told us and promised you can buy it on easy time payments at the small price you offered?

HOGAN—Jim promises whatever you like when he's full of whiskey. He might forget a promise as easy when he's drunk enough.

JOSIE—(*indignantly*) He'd never! And who'd want it except us? No one ever has in all the years—

HOGAN—Someone has lately. The agent got an offer last month, Jim told me, bigger than mine.

JOSIE—Och, Jim loves to try and get your goat. He was kidding you.

HOGAN—He wasn't. I can tell. He said he told the agent to tell whoever it was the place wasn't for sale.

JOSIE—Of course he did. Did he say who'd made the offer?

HOGAN—He didn't know. It came through a real-estate man who wouldn't tell who his client was. I've been trying to guess, but I can't think of anyone crazy enough unless it'd be some damn fool of a millionaire buying up land to make a great estate for himself, like our beautiful neighbor, Harder, the Standard Oil thief, did years ago. (*He adds with bitter fervency*) May he roast in hell and his Limey superintendent with him!

JOSIE—Amen to that. (*then scornfully*) This land for an estate? And if there was an offer, Jim's refused it, and that ends it. He wouldn't listen to any offer, after he's given his word to us.

HOGAN—Did I say he would—when he's in his right mind? What I'm afraid of is, he might be led into it sometime when he has one of his sneering bitter drunks on and talks like a Broadway crook himself, saying money is the only thing in the world, and everything and anyone can be bought if the price is big enough. You've heard him.

JOSIE—I have. But he doesn't fool me at all. He only acts like he's hard and shameless to get back at life when it's tormenting him—and who doesn't? (*He gives her a quick, curious side glance which she doesn't notice.*)

HOGAN—Or take the other kind of queer drunk he gets on sometimes when, without any reason you can see, he'll suddenly turn strange, and look sad, and stare at nothing as if he was mourning over some ghost inside him, and—

JOSIE—I think I know what comes over him when he's like that. It's the memory of his mother comes back and his grief for her death. (*pityingly*) Poor Jim.

HOGAN—(*ignoring this*) And whiskey seems to have no effect on him, like water off a duck's back. He'll keep acting natural enough, and you'd swear he wasn't bad at all, but the next day you find his brain was so paralyzed he don't remember a thing until you remind him. He's done a lot of mad things, when he was that way, he was sorry for after.

JOSIE—(*scornfully*) What drunk hasn't? But he'd never— (*resentfully*) I won't have you suspecting Jim without any cause, d'you hear me!

HOGAN—I don't suspect him. All I've said is, when a man gets as queer drunk as Jim, he doesn't know himself what he mightn't do, and we'd be damned fools if we didn't fear the possibility, however small it is, and do all we can to guard against it.

JOSIE—There's no possibility! And how could we guard against it, if there was?

HOGAN—Well, you can put yourself out to be extra nice to him, for one thing.

JOSIE—How nice is extra nice?

HOGAN—You ought to know. But here's one tip. I've noticed when you talk rough and brazen like you do to other men, he may grin like they do, as if he enjoyed it, but he don't. So watch your tongue.

JOSIE—(*with a defiant toss of her head*) I'll talk as I please, and if he don't like it he can lump it! (*scornfully*) I'm to pretend I'm a pure virgin, I suppose? That would fool him, wouldn't it, and him hearing all about me from the men at the Inn? (*She gets to her feet, abruptly changing the subject.*) We're wasting the day, blathering. (*then her face hardening*) If he ever went back on his word, no matter how drunk he was, I'd be with you in any scheme you made against him, no matter how dirty. (*hastily*) But it's all your nonsense. I'd never believe it. (*She comes and picks up the pitchfork.*) I'll go to the meadow and finish Mike's work. You needn't fear you'll miss his help on the farm.

HOGAN—A hell of a help! A weak lazy back and the appetite of a drove of starving pigs! (*as she turns to go—suddenly bellicose*) Leaving me, are you? When it's dinner time? Where's my dinner, you lazy cow?

JOSIE—There's stew on the stove, you bad-tempered runt. Go in and help yourself. I'm not hungry. Your gab has bothered my mind. I need hard work in the sun to clear it. (*She starts to go off toward rear-right.*)

HOGAN—(*glancing down the road, off left-front*) You'd better wait. There's a caller coming to the gate—and if I'm not mistaken, it's the light of your eyes himself.

JOSIE—(*angrily*) Shut up! (*She stares off—her face softens and grows pitying.*) Look at him when he thinks no one is watching, with his eyes on the ground. Like a dead man walking slow behind his own coffin. (*then roughly*) Faith, he must have a hangover. He sees us now. Look at the bluff he puts up, straightening himself and grinning. (*resentfully*) I don't want to meet him. Let him make jokes with you and play the old game about a drink you both think is such fun. That's all he comes for, anyway. (*She starts off again.*)

HOGAN—Are you running away from him? Sure, you must be afraid you're in love. (*Josie halts instantly and turns back defiantly. He goes on.*) Go in the house now, and wash your face, and tidy your dress, and give a touch to your hair. You want to look decent for him.

JOSIE—(*angrily*) I'll go in the house, but only to see the stew ain't burned, for I suppose you'll have the foxiness to ask him to have a bite to eat to keep in his good graces.

HOGAN—Why shouldn't I ask him? I know damned well he has no appetite this early in the day, but only a thirst.

JOSIE—Och, you make me sick, you sly miser! (*She goes in through her bedroom, slamming the door behind her. Hogan refills his pipe, pretending he doesn't notice Tyrone approaching, his eyes bright with droll expectation. Jim Tyrone enters along the road from the highway, left.*)

(*Tyrone is in his early forties, around five feet nine, broad-shouldered and deep-chested. His naturally fine physique has become soft and soggy from dissipation, but his face is still good-looking despite its unhealthy puffiness and the bags under the eyes. He has thinning dark hair, parted and brushed back to cover a bald spot. His eyes are brown, the whites congested and yellowish. His nose, big and aquiline, gives his face a certain Mephistophelian quality which is accentuated by his habitually cynical expression. But when he smiles without sneering, he still has the ghost of a former youthful, irresponsible Irish charm—that of the beguiling ne'er-do-well, sentimental and romantic. It is his humor and charm which have kept him attractive to women, and popular with men as a drinking companion. He is dressed in an expensive dark-brown suit, tight-fitting and drawn in at the waist, dark-brown made-to-order shoes and silk socks, a white silk shirt, silk handkerchief in breast pocket, a dark tie. This get-up suggests that he follows a style set by well-groomed Broadway gamblers who would like to be mistaken for Wall Street brokers.*

(He has had enough pick-me-ups to recover from morning-after nausea and steady his nerves. During the following dialogue, he and Hogan are like players at an old familiar game where each knows the other's moves, but which still amuses them.)

TYRONE—*(approaches and stands regarding Hogan with sardonic relish. Hogan scratches a match on the seat of his overalls and lights his pipe, pretending not to see him. Tyrone recites with feeling)*

"Fortunate senex, ergo tua rura manebunt,
  et tibi magna satis, quamvis lapis omnia nudus."

HOGAN—*(mutters)* It's the landlord again, and my shotgun not handy. *(He looks up at Tyrone.)* Is it Mass you're saying, Jim? That was Latin. I know it by ear. What the hell—insult does it mean?

TYRONE—Translated very freely into Irish English, something like this. *(He imitates Hogan's brogue.)* "Ain't you the lucky old bastard to have this beautiful farm, if it is full of nude rocks."

HOGAN—I like that part about the rocks. If cows could eat them this place would make a grand dairy farm. *(He spits.)* It's easy to see you've a fine college education. It must be a big help to you, conversing with whores and barkeeps.

TYRONE—Yes, a very valuable worldly asset. I was once offered a job as office boy—until they discovered I wasn't qualified because I had no Bachelor of Arts diploma. There had been a slight misunderstanding just before I was to graduate.

HOGAN—Between you and the Fathers? I'll wager!

TYRONE—I made a bet with another Senior I could get a tart from the Haymarket to visit me, introduce her to the Jebs as my sister—and get away with it.

HOGAN—But you didn't?

TYRONE—Almost. It was a memorable day in the halls of learning. All the students were wise and I had them rolling in the aisles as I showed Sister around the grounds, accompanied by one of the Jebs. He was a bit suspicious at first, but Dutch Maisie—her professional name—had no make-up on, and was dressed in black, and had eaten a pound of Sen-Sen to kill the gin on her breath, and seemed such a devout girl that he forgot his suspicions. (*He pauses.*) Yes, all would have been well, but she was a mischievous minx, and had her own ideas of improving on my joke. When she was saying good-bye to Father Fuller, she added innocently: "Christ, Father, it's nice and quiet out here away from the damned Sixth Avenue El. I wish to hell I could stay here!" (*dryly*) But she didn't, and neither did I.

HOGAN—(*chuckles delightedly*) I'll bet you didn't! God bless Dutch Maisie! I'd like to have known her.

TYRONE—(*sits down on the steps—with a change of manner*) Well, how's the Duke of Donegal this fine day?

HOGAN—Never better.

TYRONE—Slaving and toiling as usual, I see.

HOGAN—Hasn't a poor man a right to his noon rest without being sneered at by his rich landlord?

TYRONE—"Rich" is good. I would be, if you'd pay up your back rent.

HOGAN—You ought to pay me, instead, for occupying this rockpile, miscalled a farm. (*his eyes twinkling*) But I have fine reports to give you of a promising harvest. The milkweed and the thistles is in thriving condition, and I never saw the poison ivy so bounteous and beautiful. (*Tyrone laughs. Without their noticing, Josie appears in the doorway behind Tyrone. She has tidied up and arranged her hair. She smiles down at Jim, her face softening, pleased to hear him laugh.*)

TYRONE—You win. Where did Josie go, Phil? I saw her here—

HOGAN—She ran in the house to make herself beautiful for you.

JOSIE—(*breaks in roughly*) You're a liar. (*to Tyrone, her manner one of bold, free-and-easy familiarity*) Hello, Jim.

TYRONE—(*starts to stand up*) Hello, Josie.

JOSIE—(*puts a hand on his shoulder and pushes him down*) Don't get up. Sure, you know I'm no lady. (*She sits on the top step—banteringly*) How's my fine Jim this beautiful day? You don't look so bad. You must have stopped at the Inn for an eye-opener—or ten of them.

TYRONE—I've felt worse. (*He looks up at her sardonically.*) And how's my Virgin Queen of Ireland?

JOSIE—Yours, is it? Since when? And don't be miscalling me a virgin. You'll ruin my reputation, if you spread that lie about me. (*She laughs. Tyrone is staring at her. She goes on quickly.*) How is it you're around so early? I thought you never got up till afternoon.

TYRONE—Couldn't sleep. One of those heebie-jeebie nights when the booze keeps you awake instead of— (*He catches her giving him a pitying look—irritably*) But what of it!

JOSIE—Maybe you had no woman in bed with you, for a change. It's a terrible thing to break the habit of years.

TYRONE—(*shrugs his shoulders*) Maybe.

JOSIE—What's the matter with the tarts in town, they let you do it? I'll bet the ones you know on Broadway, New York, wouldn't neglect their business.

TYRONE—(*pretends to yawn boredly*) Maybe not. (*then irritably*) Cut out the kidding, Josie. It's too early.

HOGAN—(*who has been taking everything in without seeming to*) I told you not to annoy the gentleman with your rough tongue.

JOSIE—Sure I thought I was doing my duty as hostess making him feel at home.

TYRONE—(*stares at her again*) Why all the interest lately in the ladies of the profession, Josie?

JOSIE—Oh, I've been considering joining their union. It's easier living than farming, I'm sure. (*then resentfully*) You think I'd starve at it, don't you, because your fancy is for dainty dolls of women? But other men like—

TYRONE—(*with sudden revulsion*) For God's sake, cut out that kind of talk, Josie! It sounds like hell.

JOSIE—(*stares at him startledly—then resentfully*) Oh, it does, does it? (*forcing a scornful smile*) I'm shocking you, I suppose? (*Hogan is watching them both, not missing anything in their faces, while he seems intent on his pipe.*)

TYRONE—(*looking a bit sheepish and annoyed at himself for his interest—shrugs his shoulders*) No. Hardly. Forget it. (*He smiles kiddingly.*) Anyway, who told you I fall for the dainty dolls? That's all a thing of the past. I like them tall and strong and voluptuous, now, with beautiful big breasts. (*She blushes and looks confused and is furious with herself for doing so.*)

HOGAN—There you are, Josie, darlin'. Sure he couldn't speak fairer than that.

JOSIE—(*recovers herself*) He couldn't, indeed. (*She pats Tyrone's head—playfully*) You're a terrible blarneying liar, Jim, but thank you just the same. (*Tyrone turns his attention to Hogan. He winks at Josie and begins in an exaggeratedly casual manner.*)

TYRONE—I don't blame you, Mr. Hogan, for taking it easy on such a blazing hot day.

HOGAN—(*doesn't look at him. His eyes twinkle.*) Hot, did you say? I find it cool, meself. Take off your coat if you're hot, Mister Tyrone.

TYRONE—One of the most stifling days I've ever known. Isn't it, Josie?

JOSIE—(*smiling*) Terrible. I know you must be perishing.

HOGAN—I wouldn't call it a damned bit stifling.

TYRONE—It parches the membranes in your throat.

HOGAN—The what? Never mind. I can't have them, for my throat isn't parched at all. If yours is, Mister Tyrone, there's a well full of water at the back.

TYRONE—Water? That's something people wash with, isn't it? I mean, some people.

HOGAN—So I've heard. But, like you, I find it hard to believe. It's a dirty habit. They must be foreigners.

TYRONE—As I was saying, my throat is parched after the

long dusty walk I took just for the pleasure of being your guest.

HOGAN—I don't remember inviting you, and the road is hard macadam with divil a spec of dust, and it's less than a quarter mile from the Inn here.

TYRONE—I didn't have a drink at the Inn. I was waiting until I arrived here, knowing that you—

HOGAN—Knowing I'd what?

TYRONE—Your reputation as a generous host—

HOGAN—The world must be full of liars. So you didn't have a drink at the Inn? Then it must be the air itself smells of whiskey today, although I didn't notice it before you came. You've gone on the water-wagon, I suppose? Well, that's fine, and I ask pardon for misjudging you.

TYRONE—I've wanted to go on the wagon for the past twenty-five years, but the doctors have strictly forbidden it. It would be fatal—with my weak heart.

HOGAN—So you've a weak heart? Well, well, and me thinking all along it was your head. I'm glad you told me. I was just going to offer you a drink, but whiskey is the worst thing—

TYRONE—The Docs say it's a matter of life and death. I must have a stimulant—one big drink, at least, whenever I strain my heart walking in the hot sun.

HOGAN—Walk back to the Inn, then, and give it a good strain, so you can buy yourself two big drinks.

JOSIE—(laughing) Ain't you the fools, playing that old game between you, and both of you pleased as punch!

TYRONE—(gives up with a laugh) Hasn't he ever been known to loosen up, Josie?

JOSIE—You ought to know. If you need a drink you'll have to buy it from him or die of thirst.

TYRONE—Well, I'll bet this is one time he's going to treat.

HOGAN—Be God, I'll take that bet!

TYRONE—After you've heard the news I've got for you, you'll be so delighted you won't be able to drag out the old bottle quick enough.

HOGAN—I'll have to be insanely delighted.

JOSIE—(full of curiosity) Shut up, Father. What news, Jim?

TYRONE—I have it off the grapevine that a certain exalted personage will drop in on you before long.

HOGAN—It's the sheriff again. I know by the pleased look on your mug.

TYRONE—Not this time. (*He pauses tantalizingly.*)

JOSIE—Bad luck to you, can't you tell us who?

TYRONE—A more eminent grafter than the sheriff— (*sneeringly*) A leading aristocrat in our Land of the Free and Get-Rich-Quick, whose boots are licked by one and all—one of the Kings of our Republic by Divine Right of Inherited Swag. In short, I refer to your good neighbor, T. Stedman Harder, Standard Oil's sappiest child, whom I know you both love so dearly. (*There is a pause after this announcement. Hogan and Josie stiffen, and their eyes begin to glitter. But they can't believe their luck at first.*)

HOGAN—(*in an ominous whisper*) Did you say Harder is coming to call on us, Jim?

JOSIE—It's too good to be true.

TYRONE—(*watching them with amusement*) No kidding. The great Mr. Harder intends to stop here on his way back to lunch from a horseback ride.

JOSIE—How do you know?

TYRONE—Simpson told me. I ran into him at the Inn.

HOGAN—That English scum of a superintendent!

TYRONE—He was laughing himself sick. He said he suggested the idea to Harder—told him you'd be overwhelmed with awe if he deigned to interview you in person.

HOGAN—Overwhelmed isn't the word. Is it, Josie?

JOSIE—It isn't indeed, Father.

TYRONE—For once in his life, Simpson is cheering for you. He doesn't like his boss. In fact, he asked me to tell you he hopes you kill him.

HOGAN—(*disdainfully*) To hell with the Limey's good wishes. I'd like both of them to call together.

JOSIE—Ah, well, we can't have everything. (*to Tyrone*) What's the reason Mr. Harder decided to notice poor, humble scum the like of us?

TYRONE—(*grinning*) That's right, Josie. Be humble. He'll expect you to know your place.

HOGAN—Will he now? Well, well. (*with a great happy sigh*) This is going to be a beautiful day entirely.

JOSIE—But what's Harder's reason, Jim?

TYRONE—Well, it seems he has an ice pond on his estate.

HOGAN—Oho! So that's it!

TYRONE—Yes. That's it. Harder likes to keep up the good old manorial customs. He clings to his ice pond. And your pigpen isn't far from his ice pond.

HOGAN—A nice little stroll for the pigs, that's all.

TYRONE—And somehow Harder's fence in that vicinity has a habit of breaking down.

HOGAN—Fences are queer things. You can't depend on them.

TYRONE—Simpson says he's had it repaired a dozen times, but each time on the following night it gets broken down again.

JOSIE—What a strange thing! It must be the bad fairies. I can't imagine who else could have done it. Can you, Father?

HOGAN—I can't, surely.

TYRONE—Well, Simpson can. He knows you did it and he told his master so.

HOGAN—(*disdainfully*) Master is the word. Sure, the English can't live unless they have a lord's backside to kiss, the dirty slaves.

TYRONE—The result of those breaks in the fence is that your pigs stroll—as you so gracefully put it—stroll through to wallow happily along the shores of the ice pond.

HOGAN—Well, why not? Sure, they're fine ambitious American-born pigs and they don't miss any opportunities. They're like Harder's father who made the money for him.

TYRONE—I agree, but for some strange reason Harder doesn't look forward to the taste of pig in next summer's ice water.

HOGAN—He must be delicate. Remember he's delicate, Josie, and leave your club in the house. (*He bursts into joyful menacing laughter.*) Oh, be God and be Christ in the mountains! I've pined to have a quiet word with Mr. Harder for years, watching him ride past in his big shiny automobile with his snoot in the air, and being tormented always by the complaints of his Limey superintendent. Oh, won't I welcome him!

JOSIE—Won't *we*, you mean. Sure, I love him as much as you.

HOGAN—I'd kiss you, Jim, for this beautiful news, if you wasn't so damned ugly. Maybe Josie'll do it for me. She has a stronger stomach.

JOSIE—I will! He's earned it. (*She pulls Tyrone's head back and laughingly kisses him on the lips. Her expression changes. She looks startled and confused, stirred and at the same time frightened. She forces a scornful laugh.*) Och, there's no spirit in you! It's like kissing a corpse.

TYRONE—(*gives her a strange surprised look—mockingly*) Yes? (*turning to Hogan*) Well, how about that drink, Phil? I'll leave it to Josie if drinks aren't on the house.

HOGAN—*I* won't leave it to Josie. She's prejudiced, being in love.

JOSIE—(*angrily*) Shut up, you old liar! (*then guiltily, forcing a laugh*) Don't talk nonsense to sneak out of treating Jim.

HOGAN—(*sighing*) All right, Josie. Go get the bottle and one small glass, or he'll never stop nagging me. I can turn my back, so the sight of him drinking free won't break my heart. (*Josie gets up, laughing, and goes in the house. Hogan peers at the road off left.*) On his way back to lunch, you said? Then it's time— (*fervently*) O Holy Joseph, don't let the bastard change his mind!

TYRONE—(*beginning to have qualms*) Listen, Phil. Don't get too enthusiastic. He has a big drag around here, and he'll have you pinched, sure as hell, if you beat him up.

HOGAN—Och, I'm no fool. (*Josie comes out with a bottle and a tumbler.*) Will you listen to this, Josie. He's warning me not to give Harder a beating—as if I'd dirty my hands on the scum.

JOSIE—As if we'd need to. Sure, all we want is a quiet chat with him.

HOGAN—That's all. As neighbor to neighbor.

JOSIE—(*hands Tyrone the bottle and tumbler*) Here you are, Jim. Don't stint yourself.

HOGAN—(*mournfully*) A fine daughter! I tell you a small

glass and you give him a bucket! (*As Tyrone pours a big drink, grinning at him, he turns away with a comic shudder.*) That's a fifty-dollar drink, at least.

TYRONE—Here's luck, Phil.

HOGAN—I hope you drown. (*Tyrone drinks and makes a wry face.*)

TYRONE—The best chicken medicine I've ever tasted.

HOGAN—That's gratitude for you! Here, pass me the bottle. A drink will warm up my welcome for His Majesty. (*He takes an enormous swig from the bottle.*)

JOSIE—(*looking off left*) There's two horseback riders on the county road now.

HOGAN—Praise be to God! It's him and a groom. (*He sets the bottle on top of the boulder.*)

JOSIE—That's McCabe. An old sweetheart of mine. (*She glances at Tyrone provokingly—then suddenly worried and protective*) You get in the house, Jim. If Harder sees you here, he'll lay the whole blame on you.

TYRONE—Nix, Josie. You don't think I'm going to miss this, do you?

JOSIE—You can sit inside by my window and take in everything. Come on, now, don't be stubborn with me. (*She puts her hands under his arms and lifts him to his feet as easily as if he was a child—banteringly*) Go into my beautiful bedroom. It's a nice place for you.

TYRONE—(*kiddingly*) Just what I've been thinking for some time, Josie.

JOSIE—(*boldly*) Sure, you've never given me a sign of it. Come up tonight and we'll spoon in the moonlight and you can tell me your thoughts.

TYRONE—That's a date. Remember, now.

JOSIE—It's you who'll forget. Get inside now, before it's too late. (*She gives him a shove inside and closes the door.*)

HOGAN—(*has been watching the visitor approach*) He's dismounting—as graceful as a scarecrow, and his poor horse longing to give him a kick. Look at Mac grinning at us. Sit down, Josie. (*She sits on the steps, he on the boulder.*) Pretend you don't notice him. (*T. Stedman Harder appears at left. They act as if they didn't see him. Hogan knocks out his pipe on the palm of his hand.*)

(*Harder is in his late thirties but looks younger because his face is unmarked by worry, ambition, or any of the common hazards of life. No matter how long he lives, his four undergraduate years will always be for him the most significant in his life, and the moment of his highest achievement the time he was tapped for an exclusive Senior Society at the Ivy university to which his father had given millions. Since that day he has felt no need for further aspiring, no urge to do anything except settle down on his estate and live the life of a country gentleman, mildly interested in saddle horses and sport models of foreign automobiles. He is not the blatantly silly, playboy heir to millions whose antics make newspaper headlines. He doesn't drink much except when he attends his class reunion every spring—the most exciting episode of each year for him. He doesn't give wild parties, doesn't chase after musical-comedy cuties, is a mildly contented husband and father of three children. A not unpleasant man, affable, good-looking in an ordinary way, sunburnt and healthy, beginning to take on fat, he is simply immature, naturally lethargic, a bit stupid. Coddled from birth, everything arranged and made easy for him, deferred to because of his wealth, he usually has the self-confident attitude of acknowledged superiority, but assumes a supercilious, insecure air when dealing with people beyond his ken. He is dressed in a beautifully tailored English tweed coat and whipcord riding breeches, immaculately polished English riding boots with spurs, and carries a riding crop in his hand.*

(*It would be hard to find anyone more ill-equipped for combat with the Hogans. He has never come in contact with anyone like them. To make matters easier for them he is deliberate in his speech, slow on the uptake, and has no sense of humor. The experienced strategy of the Hogans in verbal battle is to take the offensive at once and never let an opponent get set to hit back. Also, they use a beautifully co-ordinated, bewildering change of pace, switching suddenly from jarring shouts to low, confidential vituperation. And they exaggerate their Irish brogues to confuse an enemy still further.*)

HARDER—(*walks toward Hogan—stiffly*) Good morning. I want to see the man who runs this farm.

HOGAN—(*surveys him deliberately, his little pig eyes gleaming with malice*) You do, do you? Well, you've seen him. So run along now and play with your horse, and don't bother me.

(*He turns to Josie, who is staring at Harder, much to his discom-fiture, as if she had discovered a cockroach in her soup.*) D'you see what I see, Josie? Be God, you'll have to give that damned cat of yours a spanking for bringing it to our doorstep.

HARDER— (*determined to be authoritative and command re-spect—curtly*) Are you Hogan?

HOGAN— (*insultingly*) I am *Mister* Philip Hogan—to a gentleman.

JOSIE— (*glares at Harder*) Where's your manners, you spindle-shanked jockey? Were you brought up in a stable?

HARDER— (*does not fight with ladies, and especially not with this lady—ignoring her*) My name is Harder. (*He obviously ex-pects them to be immediately impressed and apologetic.*)

HOGAN— (*contemptuously*) Who asked you your name, me little man?

JOSIE—Sure, who in the world cares who the hell you are?

HOGAN—But if you want to play politeness, we'll play with you. Let me introduce you to my daughter, Harder— Miss Josephine Hogan.

JOSIE— (*petulantly*) I don't want to meet him, Father. I don't like his silly sheep's face, and I've no use for jockeys, anyway. I'll wager he's no damned good to a woman. (*From inside her bedroom comes a burst of laughter. This revelation of an unseen audience startles Harder. He begins to look extremely un-sure of himself.*)

HOGAN—I don't think he's a jockey. It's only the funny pants he's wearing. I'll bet if you asked his horse, you'd find he's no cowboy either. (*to Harder, jeeringly*) Come, tell us the truth, me honey. Don't you kiss your horse each time you mount and beg him, please don't throw me today, darlin', and I'll give you an extra bucket of oats. (*He bursts into an extravagant roar of laughter, slapping his thigh, and Josie guffaws with him, while they watch the disconcerting effect of this theatri-cal mirth on Harder.*)

HARDER— (*beginning to lose his temper*) Listen to me, Ho-gan! I didn't come here— (*He is going to add "to listen to your damned jokes" or something like that, but Hogan silences him.*)

HOGAN— (*shouts*) What? What's that you said? (*He stares at the dumbfounded Harder with droll amazement, as if he couldn't believe his ears.*) You didn't come here? (*He turns to*

Josie—in a whisper) Did you hear that, Josie? (*He takes off his hat and scratches his head in comic bewilderment.*) Well, that's a puzzle, surely. How d'you suppose he got here?

JOSIE—Maybe the stork brought him, bad luck to it for a dirty bird. (*Again Tyrone's laughter is heard from the bedroom.*)

HARDER—(*so off balance now he can only repeat angrily*) I said I didn't come here—

HOGAN—(*shouts*) Wait! Wait, now! (*threateningly*) We've had enough of that. Say it a third time and I'll send my daughter to telephone the asylum.

HARDER—(*forgetting he's a gentleman*) Damn you, I'm the one who's had enough—!

JOSIE—(*shouts*) Hold your dirty tongue! I'll have no foul language in my presence.

HOGAN—Och, don't mind him, Josie. He's said he isn't here, anyway, so we won't talk to him behind his back. (*He regards Harder with pitying contempt.*) Sure, ain't you the poor crazy creature? Do you want us to believe you're your own ghost?

HARDER—(*notices the bottle on the boulder for the first time—tries to be contemptuously tolerant and even to smile with condescending disdain*) Ah! I understand now. You're drunk. I'll come back sometime when you're sober—or send Simpson— (*He turns away, glad of an excuse to escape.*)

JOSIE—(*jumps up and advances on him menacingly*) No, you don't! You'll apologize first for insulting a lady—insinuating I'm drunk this early in the day—or I'll knock some good breeding in you!

HARDER—(*actually frightened now*) I—I said nothing about you—

HOGAN—(*gets up to come between them*) Aisy now, Josie. He didn't mean it. He don't know what he means, the poor loon. (*to Harder—pityingly*) Run home, that's a good lad, before your keeper misses you.

HARDER—(*hastily*) Good day. (*He turns eagerly toward left but suddenly Hogan grabs his shoulder and spins him around—then shifts his grip to the lapel of Harder's coat.*)

HOGAN—(*grimly*) Wait now, me Honey Boy. I'll have a word with you, if you plaze. I'm beginning to read some sense into this. You mentioned that English bastard, Simpson. I know who you are now.

HARDER — (*outraged*) Take your hands off me, you drunken fool. (*He raises his riding crop.*)

JOSIE — (*grabs it and tears it from his hand with one powerful twist — fiercely*) Would you strike my poor infirm old father, you coward, you!

HARDER — (*calling for help*) McCabe!

HOGAN — Don't think McCabe will hear you, if you blew Gabriel's horn. He knows I or Josie can lick him with one hand. (*sharply*) Josie! Stand between us and the gate. (*Josie takes her stand where the path meets the road. She turns her back for a moment, shaking with suppressed laughter, and waves her hand at McCabe and turns back. Hogan releases his hold on Harder's coat.*) There now. Don't try running away or my daughter will knock you senseless. (*He goes on grimly before Harder can speak.*) You're the blackguard of a millionaire that owns the estate next to ours, ain't you? I've been meaning to call on you, for I've a bone to pick with you, you bloody tyrant! But I couldn't bring myself to set foot on land bought with Standard Oil money that was stolen from the poor it ground in the dust beneath its dirty heel — land that's watered with the tears of starving widows and orphans — (*He abruptly switches from this eloquence to a matter-of-fact tone.*) But never mind that, now. I won't waste words trying to reform a born crook. (*fiercely, shoving his dirty unshaven face almost into Harder's*) What I want to know is, what the hell d'you mean by your contemptible trick of breaking down your fence to entice my poor pigs to take their death in your ice pond? (*There is a shout of laughter from Josie's bedroom, and Josie doubles up and holds her sides. Harder is so flabbergasted by this mad accusation he cannot even sputter. But Hogan acts as if he'd denied it — savagely*) Don't lie, now! None of your damned Standard Oil excuses, or be Jaysus, I'll break you in half! Haven't I mended that fence morning after morning, and seen the footprints where you had sneaked up in the night to pull it down again. How many times have I mended that fence, Josie?

JOSIE — If it's once, it's a hundred, Father.

HOGAN — Listen, me little millionaire! I'm a peaceful, mild man that believes in live and let live, and as long as the neighboring scum leave me alone, I'll let them alone, but when it comes to standing by and seeing my poor pigs murthered one by one—! Josie! How many pigs is it caught their death of cold in his damned ice pond and died of pneumonia?

JOSIE—Ten of them, Father. And ten more died of cholera after drinking the dirty water in it.

HOGAN—All prize pigs, too! I was offered two hundred dollars apiece for them. Twenty pigs at two hundred, that's four thousand. And a thousand to cure the sick and cover funeral expenses for the dead. Call it four thousand you owe me. (*furiously*) And you'll pay it, or I'll sue you, so help me Christ! I'll drag you in every court in the land! I'll paste your ugly mug on the front page of every newspaper as a pig-murdering tyrant! Before I'm through with you, you'll think you're the King of England at an Irish wake! (*with a quick change of pace to a wheedling confidential tone*) Tell me now, if it isn't a secret, whatever made you take such a savage grudge against pigs? Sure, it isn't reasonable for a Standard Oil man to hate hogs.

HARDER—(*manages to get in three sputtering words*) I've had enough—!

HOGAN—(*with a grin*) Be God, I believe you! (*switching to fierceness and grabbing his lapel again*) Look out, now! Keep your place and be soft-spoken to your betters! You're not in your shiny automobile now with your funny nose cocked so you won't smell the poor people. (*He gives him a shake.*) And let me warn you! I have to put up with a lot of pests on this heap of boulders some joker once called a farm. There's a cruel skinflint of a landlord who swindles me out of my last drop of whiskey, and there's poison ivy, and ticks and potato bugs, and there's snakes and skunks! But, be God, I draw the line somewhere, and I'll be damned if I'll stand for a Standard Oil man trespassing! So will you kindly get the hell out of here before I plant a kick on your backside that'll land you in the Atlantic Ocean! (*He gives Harder a shove.*) Beat it now! (*Harder tries to make some sort of disdainfully dignified exit. But he has to get by Josie.*)

JOSIE—(*leers at him idiotically*) Sure, you wouldn't go without a word of good-bye to me, would you, darlin'? Don't scorn me just because you have on your jockey's pants. (*in a hoarse whisper*) Meet me tonight, as usual, down by the pig-pen. (*Harder's retreat becomes a rout. He disappears on left, but a second later his voice, trembling with anger, is heard calling back threateningly.*)

HARDER—If you dare touch that fence again, I'll put this matter in the hands of the police!

HOGAN—(*shouts derisively*) And I'll put it in my lawyer's hands and in the newspapers! (*He doubles up with glee.*) Look at him fling himself on his nag and spur the poor beast! And look at McCabe behind him! He can hardly stay in the saddle for laughing! (*He slaps his thigh.*) O Jaysus, this is a great day for the poor and oppressed! I'll do no more work! I'll go down to the Inn and spend money and get drunk as Moses!

JOSIE—Small blame to you. You deserve it. But you'll have your dinner first, to give you a foundation. Come on, now. (*They turn back toward the house. From inside another burst of laughter from Tyrone is heard. Josie smiles.*) Listen to Jim still in stitches. It's good to hear him laugh as if he meant it. (*Tyrone appears in the doorway of her bedroom.*)

TYRONE—O God, my sides are sore. (*They all laugh together. He joins them at the left corner of the house.*)

JOSIE—It's dinner time. Will you have a bit to eat with us, Jim? I'll boil you some eggs.

HOGAN—Och, why do you have to mention eggs? Don't you know it's the one thing he might eat? Well, no matter. Anything goes today. (*He gets the bottle of whiskey.*) Come in, Jim. We'll have a drink while Josie's fixing the grub. (*They start to go in the front door, Hogan in the lead.*)

TYRONE—(*suddenly—with sardonic amusement*) Wait a minute. Let us pause to take a look at this very valuable property. Don't you notice the change, Phil? Every boulder on the place has turned to solid gold.

HOGAN—What the hell—? You didn't get the D.T.'s from my whiskey, I know that.

TYRONE—No D.T.'s about it. This farm has suddenly become a gold mine. You know that offer I told you about? Well, the agent did a little detective work and he discovered it came from Harder. He doesn't want the damned place but he dislikes you as a neighbor and he thinks the best way to get rid of you would be to become your landlord.

HOGAN—The sneaking skunk! I'm sorry I didn't give him that kick.

TYRONE—Yes. So am I. That would have made the place even more valuable. But as it is, you did nobly. I expect him to double or triple his first offer. In fact, I'll bet the sky is the limit now.

HOGAN—(*gives Josie a meaningful look*) I see your point! But we're not worrying you'd ever forget your promise to us for any price.

TYRONE—Promise? What promise? You know what Kipling wrote: (*paraphrasing the "Rhyme of the Three Sealers"*) There's never a promise of God or man goes north of ten thousand bucks.

HOGAN—D'you hear him, Josie? We can't trust him.

JOSIE—Och, you know he's kidding.

HOGAN—I don't! I'm becoming suspicious.

TYRONE—(*a trace of bitterness beneath his amused tone*) That's wise dope, Phil. Trust and be a sucker. If I were you, I'd be seriously worried. I've always wanted to own a gold mine—so I could sell it.

JOSIE—(*bursts out*) Will you shut up your rotten Broadway blather!

TYRONE—(*stares at her in surprise*) Why so serious and indignant, Josie? You just told your unworthy Old Man I was kidding. (*to Hogan*) At last, I've got you by the ears, Phil. We must have a serious chat about when you're going to pay that back rent.

HOGAN—(*groans*) A landlord who's a blackmailer! Holy God, what next! (*Josie is smiling with relief now.*)

TYRONE—And you, Josie, please remember when I keep that moonlight date tonight I expect you to be very sweet to me.

JOSIE—(*with a bold air*) Sure, you don't have to blackmail me. I'd be that to you, anyway.

HOGAN—Are you laying plots in my presence to seduce my only daughter? (*then philosophically*) Well, what can I do? I'll be drunk at the Inn, so how could I prevent it? (*He goes up the steps.*) Let's eat, for the love of God. I'm starving. (*He disappears inside the house.*)

JOSIE—(*with an awkward playful gesture, takes Tyrone by the hand*) Come along, Jim.

TYRONE—(*smiles kiddingly*) Afraid you'll lose me? Swell chance! (*His eyes fix on her breasts—with genuine feeling*) You have the most beautiful breasts in the world, do you know it, Josie?

JOSIE—(*pleased—shyly*) I don't—but I'm happy if you think— (*then quickly*) But I've no time now to listen to your kidding, with my mad old father waiting for his dinner. So come on. (*She tugs at his hand and he follows her up the steps. Her manner changes to worried solicitude.*) Promise me you'll eat something, Jim. You've got to eat. You can't go on the way you are, drinking and never eating, hardly. You're killing yourself.

TYRONE—(*sardonically*) That's right. Mother me, Josie, I love it.

JOSIE—(*bullyingly*) I will, then. You need one to take care of you. (*They disappear inside the house.*)

(*Curtain*)

ACT TWO

SCENE—*The same, with the wall of the living room removed. It is a clear warm moonlight night, around eleven o'clock.*

Josie is sitting on the steps before the front door. She has changed to her Sunday best, a cheap dark-blue dress, black stockings and shoes. Her hair is carefully arranged, and by way of adornment a white flower is pinned on her bosom. She is hunched up, elbows on knees, her chin in her hands. There is an expression on her face we have not seen before, a look of sadness and loneliness and humiliation.

She sighs and gets slowly to her feet, her body stiff from sitting long in the same position. She goes into the living room, fumbles around for the box of matches, and lights a kerosene lamp on the table.

The living room is small, low-ceilinged, with faded, fly-specked wallpaper, a floor of bare boards. It is cluttered up with furniture that looks as if it had been picked up at a fire sale. There is a table at center, a disreputable old Morris chair beside it; two ugly side-boards, one at left, the other at right-rear; a porch rocking-chair, painted green, with a hole in its cane bottom; a bureau against the rear wall, with two chairs on either side of a door to the kitchen. On the bureau is an alarm clock which shows the time to be five past eleven. At right-front is the door to Josie's bedroom.

JOSIE—(*looks at the clock—dully*) Five past eleven, and he said he'd be here around nine. (*Suddenly in a burst of humiliated anger, she tears off the flower pinned to her bosom and throws it in the corner.*) To hell with you, Jim Tyrone! (*From down the road, the quiet of the night is shattered by a burst of melancholy song. It is unmistakably Hogan's voice wailing an old Irish lament at the top of his lungs. Josie starts—then frowns irritably.*) What's bringing him home an hour before the Inn closes? He must be more paralyzed than ever I've known him. (*She listens to the singing—grimly*) Ah, here you come, do you, as full as a tick! I'll give you a welcome, if you start cutting up! I'm in no mood to put up with you. (*She goes into her bedroom and returns with her broomstick club. Outside the singing grows louder as Hogan approaches the house. He only remembers one verse of the song and he has been repeating it.*)

HOGAN—Oh the praties they grow small
        Over here, over here,
        Oh, the praties they grow small
        Over here.
        Oh the praties they grow small
        And we dig them in the fall
        And we eat them skins and all
        Over here, over here.

(*He enters left-front, weaving and lurching a bit. But he is not as drunk as he appears. Or rather, he is one of those people who can drink an enormous amount and be absolutely plastered when they want to be for their own pleasure, but at the same time are able to pull themselves together when they wish and be cunningly clear-headed. Just now, he is letting himself go and getting great satisfaction from it. He pauses and bellows belligerently at the house*) Hurroo! Down with all tyrants, male and female! To hell with England, and God damn Standard Oil!

JOSIE—(*shouts back*) Shut up your noise, you crazy old billy goat!

HOGAN—(*hurt and mournful*) A sweet daughter and a sweet welcome home in the dead of night. (*beginning to boil*) Old goat! There's respect for you! (*angrily—starting for the front door*) Crazy billy goat, is it? Be God, I'll learn you manners! (*He pounds on the door with his fist.*) Open the door! Open this door, I'm saying, before I drive a fist through it, or kick it into flinders! (*He gives it a kick.*)

JOSIE—It's not locked, you drunken old loon! Open it yourself!

HOGAN—(*turns the knob and stamps in*) Drunken old loon, am I? Is that the way to address your father?

JOSIE—No. It's too damned good for him.

HOGAN—It's time I taught you a lesson. Be Jaysus, I'll take you over my knee and spank your tail, if you are as big as a cow! (*He makes a lunge to grab her.*)

JOSIE—Would you, though! Take that, then! (*She raps him smartly, but lightly, on his bald spot with the end of her broom handle.*)

HOGAN—(*with an exaggerated howl of pain*) Ow! (*His anger evaporates and he rubs the top of his head ruefully—with bitter complaint*) God forgive you, it's a great shame to me I've raised a daughter so cowardly she has to use a club.

JOSIE—(*puts her club on the table—grimly*) Now I've no club.

HOGAN—(*evades the challenge*) I never thought I'd see the day when a daughter of mine would be such a coward as to threaten her old father when he's helpless drunk and can't hit back. (*He slumps down on the Morris chair.*)

JOSIE—Ah, that's better. Now that little game is over. (*then angrily*) Listen to me, Father. I have no patience left, so get up from that chair, and go in your room, and go to bed, or I'll take you by the scruff of your neck and the seat of your pants and throw you in and lock the door on you! I mean it, now! (*on the verge of angry tears*) I've had all I can bear this night, and I want some peace and sleep, and not to listen to an old lush!

HOGAN—(*appears drunker, his head wagging, his voice thick, his talk rambling*) That's right. Fight with me. My own daughter has no feelings or sympathy. As if I hadn't enough after what's happened tonight.

JOSIE—(*with angry disgust*) Och, don't try— (*then curiously*) What's happened? I thought something must be queer, you coming home before the Inn closed, but then I thought maybe for once you'd drunk all you could hold. (*scathingly*) And, God pity you, if you ain't that full, you're damned close to it.

HOGAN—Go on. Make fun of me. Old lush! You wouldn't feel so comical, if— (*He stops, mumbling to himself.*)

JOSIE—If what?

HOGAN—Never mind. Never mind. I didn't come home to fight, but seek comfort in your company. And if I was singing coming along the road, it was only because there's times you have to sing to keep from crying.

JOSIE—I can see you crying!

HOGAN—You will. And you'll see yourself crying, too, when— (*He stops again and mumbles to himself.*)

JOSIE—When what? (*exasperatedly*) Will you stop your whiskey drooling and talk plain?

HOGAN—(*thickly*) No matter. No matter. Leave me alone.

JOSIE—(*angrily*) That's good advice. To hell with you! I

know your game. Nothing at all has happened. All you want is to keep me up listening to your guff. Go to your room, I'm saying, before—

HOGAN—I won't. I couldn't sleep with my thoughts tormented the way they are. I'll stay here in this chair, and you go to your room and let me be.

JOSIE—(*snorts*) And have you singing again in a minute and smashing the furniture—

HOGAN—Sing, is it? Are you making fun again? I'd give a keen of sorrow or howl at the moon like an old mangy hound in his sadness if I knew how, but I don't. So rest aisy. You won't hear a sound from me. Go on and snore like a pig to your heart's content. (*He mourns drunkenly*) A fine daughter! I'd get more comfort from strangers.

JOSIE—Och, for God's sake, dry up! You'll sit in the dark then. I won't leave the lamp lit for you to tip over and burn down the house. (*She reaches out to turn down the lamp.*)

HOGAN—(*thickly*) Let it burn to the ground. A hell of a lot I care if it burns.

JOSIE—(*in the act of turning down the lamp, stops and stares at him, puzzled and uneasy*) I never heard you talk that way before, no matter how drunk you were. (*He mumbles. Her tone becomes persuasive.*) What's happened to you, Father?

HOGAN—(*bitterly*) Ah it's "Father" now, is it, not old billy goat? Well, thank God for small favors. (*with heavy sarcasm*) Oh, nothing's happened to me at all, at all. A trifle, only. I wouldn't waste your time mentioning it, or keep you up when you want sleep so bad.

JOSIE—(*angrily*) Och, you old loon, I'm sick of you. Sleep it off till you get some sense. (*She reaches for the lamp again.*)

HOGAN—Sleep it off? We'll see if you'll sleep it off when you know— (*He lapses into drunken mumbling.*)

JOSIE—(*again stares at him*) Know what, Father?

HOGAN—(*mumbles*) The son of a bitch!

JOSIE—(*trying a light tone*) Sure, there's a lot of those in the neighborhood. Which one do you mean? Is Harder on your mind again?

HOGAN—(*thickly*) He's one and a prize one, but I don't mean him. I'll say this for Harder, you know what to expect from him. He's no wolf in sheep's clothing, nor a treacherous snake in the grass who stabs you in the back with a knife—

JOSIE—(*apprehensive now—forces a joke*) Sure, if you've found a snake who can stab you with a knife, you'd better join the circus with him and make a pile of money.

HOGAN—(*bitterly*) Make jokes, God forgive you! You'll soon laugh from the wrong end of your mouth! (*He mumbles*) Pretending he's our friend! The lying bastard!

JOSIE—(*bristles resentfully*) Is it Jim Tyrone you're calling hard names?

HOGAN—That's right. Defend him, you big soft fool! Faith, you're a prize dunce! You've had a good taste of believing his word, waiting hours for him dressed up in your best like a poor sheep without pride or spirit—

JOSIE—(*stung*) Shut up! I was calling him a lying bastard myself before you came, and saying I'd never speak to him again. And I knew all along he'd never remember to keep his date after he got drunk.

HOGAN—He's not so drunk he forgot to attend to business.

JOSIE—(*as if she hadn't heard—defiantly*) I'd have stayed up anyway a beautiful night like this to enjoy the moonlight, if there wasn't a Jim Tyrone in the world.

HOGAN—(*with heavy sarcasm*) In your best shoes and stockings? Well, well. Sure, the moon must feel flattered by your attentions.

JOSIE—(*furiously*) You won't feel flattered if I knock you tail over tincup out of that chair! And stop your whiskey gabble about Jim. I see what you're driving at with your dark hints and curses, and if you think I'll believe— (*with forced assurance*) Sure, I know what's happened as well as if I'd been there. Jim saw you'd got drunker than usual and you were an easy mark for a joke, and he's made a goat of you!

HOGAN—(*bitterly*) Goat, again! (*He struggles from his chair and stands swaying unsteadily—with offended dignity*) All right, I won't say another word. There's no use telling the truth to a bad-tempered woman in love.

JOSIE—Love be damned! I hate him now!

HOGAN—Be Christ, you have me stumped. A great proud slut who's played games with half the men around here, and now you act like a numbskull virgin that can't believe a man would tell her a lie!

JOSIE—(*threateningly*) If you're going to your room, you'd better go quick!

HOGAN—(*fixes his eyes on the door at rear—with dignity*) That's where I'm going, yes—to talk to meself so I'll know someone with brains is listening. Good night to you, Miss Hogan. (*He starts—swerves left—tries to correct this and lurches right and bumps against her, clutching the supporting arm she stretches out.*)

JOSIE—God help you, if you try to go upstairs now, you'll end up in the cellar.

HOGAN—(*hanging on to her arm and shoulder—maudlinly affectionate now*) You're right. Don't listen to me. I'm wrong to bother you. You've had sorrow enough this night. Have a good sleep, while you can, Josie, darlin'—and good night and God bless you. (*He tries to kiss her, but she wards him off and steers him back to the chair.*)

JOSIE—Sit down before you split in pieces on the floor and I have to get the wheelbarrow to collect you. (*She dumps him in the chair where he sprawls limply, his chin on his chest.*)

HOGAN—(*mumbles dully*) It's too late. It's all settled. We're helpless, entirely.

JOSIE—(*really worried now*) How is it all settled? If you're helpless, I'm not. (*then as he doesn't reply—scornfully*) It's the first time I ever heard you admit you were licked. And it's the first time I ever saw you so paralyzed you couldn't shake the whiskey from your brains and get your head clear when you wanted. Sure, that's always been your pride—and now look at you, the stupid object you are, mumbling and drooling!

HOGAN—(*struggles up in his chair—angrily*) Shut up your insults! Be God, I can get my head clear if I like! (*He shakes his head violently.*) There! It's clear. I can tell you each thing that happened tonight as clear as if I'd not taken a drop, if you'll listen and not keep calling me a liar.

JOSIE—I'll listen, now I see you have hold of your wits.

HOGAN—All right, then. I'll begin at the beginning when him and me left here, and you gave him a sweet smile, and rolled your big beautiful cow's eyes at him, and wiggled your backside, and stuck out your beautiful breasts you know he admires, and said in a sick sheep's voice: "Don't forget our moonlight date, Jim."

JOSIE—(*with suppressed fury*) You're a—! I never—! You old—!

HOGAN—And he said: "You bet I won't forget, Josie."

JOSIE—The lying crook!

HOGAN—(*His voice begins to sink into a dejected monotone.*) We went to the Inn and started drinking whiskey. And I got drunk.

JOSIE—(*exasperatedly*) I guessed that! And Jim got drunk, too. And then what?

HOGAN—(*dully*) Who knows how drunk he got? He had one of his queer fits when you can't tell. He's the way I told you about this morning, when he talks like a Broadway crook, who'd sell his soul for a price, and there's a sneering divil in him, and he loves to pick out the weakness in people and say cruel, funny things that flay the hide off them, or play cruel jokes on them. (*with sudden rage*) God's curse on him, I'll wager he's laughing to himself this minute, thinking it's the cutest joke in the world, the fools he's made of us. You in particular. Be God, I had my suspicions, at least, but your head was stuffed with mush and love, and you wouldn't—

JOSIE—(*furiously*) You'll tell that lie about my love once too often! And I'll play a joke on him yet that'll make him sorry he—

HOGAN—(*sunk in drunken defeatism again*) It's too late. You shouldn't have let him get away from you to the Inn. You should have kept him here. Then maybe, if you'd got him drunk enough you could have— (*his head nodding, his eyes blinking—thickly*) But it's no good talking now—no good at all—no good—

JOSIE—(*gives him a shake*) Keep hold of your wits or I'll give you a cuff on both ears! Will you stop blathering like an old woman and tell me plainly what he's done!

HOGAN—He's agreed to sell the farm, that's what! Simpson came to the Inn to see him with a new offer from Harder. Ten thousand, cash.

JOSIE—(*overwhelmed*) Ten thousand! Sure, three is all it's

worth at most. And two was what you offered that Jim promised—

HOGAN—What's money to Harder? After what we did to him, all he wants is revenge. And here's where he's foxy. Simpson must have put him up to it knowing how Jim hates it here living on a small allowance, and he longs to go back to Broadway and his whores. Jim won't have to wait for his half of the cash till the estate's settled. Harder offers to give him five thousand cash as a loan against the estate the second the sale is made. Jim can take the next train to New York.

JOSIE—(*tensely, on the verge of tears*) And Jim accepted? I don't believe it!

HOGAN—Don't then. Be God, you'll believe it tomorrow! Harder proposed that he meet with Jim and the executors in the morning and settle it, and Jim promised Simpson he would.

JOSIE—(*desperately*) Maybe he'll get so drunk he'll never remember—

HOGAN—He won't. Harder's coming in his automobile to pick him up and make sure of him. Anyway don't think because he forgot you were waiting—in the moonlight, eating your heart out, that he'd ever miss a date with five thousand dollars, and all the pretty whores of Broadway he can buy with it.

JOSIE—(*distractedly*) Will you shut up! (*angrily*) And where were you when all this happened? Couldn't you do anything to stop it, you old loon?

HOGAN—I couldn't. Simpson came and sat at the table with us—

JOSIE—And you let him!

HOGAN—Jim invited him. Anyway, I wanted to find out what trick he had up his sleeve, and what Jim would do. When it was all over, I got up and took a swipe at Simpson, but I missed him. (*with drunken sadness*) I was too drunk— too drunk—too drunk— I missed him, God forgive me! (*His chin sinks on his chest and his eyes shut.*)

JOSIE—(*shakes him*) If you don't keep awake, be God, I won't miss you!

HOGAN—I was going to take a swipe at Jim, too, but I couldn't do it. My heart was too broken with sorrow. I'd come

to love him like a son—a real son of my heart!—to take
the place of that jackass, Mike, and me two other jackasses.

JOSIE—(*her face hard and bitter*) I think now Mike was the
only one in this house with sense.

HOGAN—I was too drowned in sorrow by his betraying
me—and you he'd pretended to like so much. So I only
called him a dirty lying skunk of a treacherous bastard, and I
turned my back on him and left the Inn, and I made myself
sing on the road so he'd hear, and they'd all hear in the Inn,
to show them I didn't care a damn.

JOSIE—(*scathingly*) Sure, wasn't you the hero! A hell of a
lot of good—

HOGAN—Ah, well, I suppose the temptation was too
great. He's weak, with one foot in the grave from whiskey.
Maybe we shouldn't blame him.

JOSIE—(*her eyes flashing*) Not blame him? Well, I blame
him, God damn him! Are you making excuses for him, you
old fool!

HOGAN—I'm not. He's a dirty snake! But I was thinking
how do I know what I wouldn't do for five thousand cash,
and how do you know what you wouldn't do?

JOSIE—Nothing could make me betray him! (*Her face
grows hard and bitter.*) Or it couldn't before. There's nothing
I wouldn't do now. (*Hogan suddenly begins to chuckle.*) Do you
think I'm lying? Just give me a chance—

HOGAN—I remembered something. (*He laughs drunkenly.*)
Be Christ, Josie, for all his Broadway wisdom about women,
you've made a prize damned fool of him and that's some
satisfaction!

JOSIE—(*bewildered*) How'd you mean?

HOGAN—You'll never believe it. Neither did I, but he kept
on until, be God, I saw he really meant it.

JOSIE—Meant what?

HOGAN—It was after he'd turned queer—early in the night
before Simpson came. He started talking about you, as if you
was on his mind, worrying him—and before he finished I
take my oath I began to hope you could really work Mike's
first scheme on him, if you got him alone in the moonlight,
because all his gab was about his great admiration for you.

JOSIE—Och! The liar!

HOGAN—He said you had great beauty in you that no one appreciated but him.

JOSIE—(*shakenly*) You're lying.

HOGAN—Great strength you had, and great pride, he said—and great goodness, no less! But here's where you've made a prize jackass of him, like I said. (*with a drunken leer*) Listen now, darlin', and don't drop dead with amazement. (*He leans toward her and whispers*) He believes you're a virgin! (*Josie stiffens as if she'd been insulted. Hogan goes on.*) He does, so help me! He means it, the poor dunce! He thinks you're a poor innocent virgin! He thinks it's all boasting and pretending you've done about being a slut. (*He chuckles.*) A virgin, no less! You!

JOSIE—(*furiously*) Stop saying it! Boasting and pretending, am I? The dirty liar!

HOGAN—Faith, you don't have to tell me. (*Then he looks at her in drunken surprise—thickly*) Are you taking it as an insult? Why the hell don't you laugh? Be God, you ought to see what a stupid sheep that makes him.

JOSIE—(*forces a laugh*) I do see it.

HOGAN—(*chuckling drunkenly*) Oh, be God, I've just remembered another thing, Josie. I know why he didn't keep his date with you. It wasn't that he'd forgot. He remembered well enough, for he talked about it—

JOSIE—You mean he deliberately, knowing I'd be waiting— (*fiercely*) God damn him!

HOGAN—He as much as told me his reason, though he wouldn't come out with it plain, me being your father. His conscience was tormenting him. He's going to leave you alone and not see you again—for your sake, because he loves you! (*He chuckles.*)

JOSIE—(*looks stricken and bewildered—her voice trembling*) Loves me? You're making it up.

HOGAN—I'm not. I know it sounds crazy but—

JOSIE—What did he mean, for my sake?

HOGAN—Can't you see? You're a pure virgin to him, but all the same there's things besides your beautiful soul he feels drawn to, like your beautiful hair and eyes, and—

JOSIE—(*strickenly*) Och, don't, Father! You know I'm only a big—

HOGAN—(*as if she hadn't spoken*) So he'll keep away from temptation because he can't trust himself, and it'd be a sin on his conscience if he was to seduce you. (*He laughs drunkenly.*) Oh, be God! If that ain't rich!

JOSIE—(*Her voice trembles.*) So that was his reason— (*then angrily*) So he thinks all he has to do is crook a finger and I'll fall for him, does he, the vain Broadway crook!

HOGAN—(*chuckling*) Be Jaysus, it was the maddest thing in the world, him gabbing like a soft loon about you—and there at the bar in plain sight was two of the men you've been out with, the gardener at Smith's and Regan, the chauffeur for Driggs, having a drink together!

JOSIE—(*with a twitching smile*) It must have been mad, surely. I wish I'd been there to laugh up my sleeve. (*angry*) But what's all his crazy lying blather got to do with him betraying us and selling the place?

HOGAN—(*at once hopelessly dejected again*) Nothing at all. I only thought you'd like to know you'd had that much revenge.

JOSIE—A hell of a revenge! I'll have a better one than that on him—or I'll try to! I'm not like you, owning up I'm beaten and crying wurra-wurra like a coward and getting hopeless drunk! (*She gives him a shake.*) Get your wits about you and answer me this: Did Simpson get him to sign a paper?

HOGAN—No, but what good is that? In the morning he'll sign all they shove in front of him.

JOSIE—It's this good. It means we still have a chance. Or I have.

HOGAN—What chance? Are you going to beg him to take pity on us?

JOSIE—I'll see him in hell first! There's another chance, and a good one. But I'll need your help— (*angrily*) And look at you, your brains drowned in whiskey, so I can't depend on you!

HOGAN—(*rousing himself*) You can, if there's any chance. Be God, I'll make myself as sober as a judge for you in the wink of an eye! (*then dejectedly*) But what can you do now, darlin'? You haven't even got him here. He's down at the Inn sitting alone, drinking and dreaming of the little whores he'll be with tomorrow night on Broadway.

JOSIE—I'll get him here! I'll humble my pride and go down to the Inn for him! And if he doesn't want to come I've a way to make him. I'll raise a scene and pretend I'm in a rage because he forgot his date. I'll disgrace him till he'll be glad to come with me to shut me up. I know his weakness, and it's his vanity about his women. If I was a dainty, pretty tart he'd be proud I'd raise a rumpus about him. But when it's a big, ugly hulk like me— (*She falters and forces herself to go on.*) If he ever was tempted to want me, he'd be ashamed of it. That's the truth behind the lies he told you of his conscience and his fear he might ruin me, God damn him!

HOGAN—No, he meant it, Josie. But never mind that now. Let's say you've got him here. Then what will you do?

JOSIE—I told you this morning if he ever broke his promise to us I'd do anything and not mind how crooked it was. And I will! Your part in it is to come at sunrise with witnesses and catch us in— (*She falters.*)

HOGAN—In bed, is it? Then it's Mike's second scheme you're thinking about?

JOSIE—I told you I didn't care how dirty a trick— (*with a hard bitter laugh*) The dirtier the better now!

HOGAN—But how'll you get him in bed, with all his honorable scruples, thinking you're a virgin? But I'm forgetting he stayed away because he was afraid he'd be tempted. So maybe—

JOSIE—(*tensely*) For the love of God, don't harp on his lies. He won't be tempted at all. But I'll get him so drunk he'll fall asleep and I'll carry him in and put him in bed—

HOGAN—Be God, that's the way! But you'll have to get a pile of whiskey down him. You'll never do it unless you're more sociable and stop looking at him, the way you do, whenever he takes a drink, as if you was praying Almighty God to forgive a poor drunkard. You've got to encourage him. The best way would be for you to drink with him. It would put him at his ease and unsuspecting, and it'd give you courage, too, so you'd act bold for a change instead of giving him brazen talk he's tired of hearing, while you act shy as a mouse.

JOSIE—(*gives her father a bitter, resentful look*) You're full of sly advice all of a sudden, ain't you? You dirty little tick!

HOGAN—(*angrily*) Didn't you tell me to get hold of my wits? Be God, if you want me drunk, I've only to let go. That'd suit me. I want to forget my sorrow, and I've no faith in your scheme because you'll be too full of scruples. Like the drinking. You're such a virtuous teetotaller—

JOSIE—I've told you I'd do anything now! (*then confusedly*) All I meant was, it's not right, a father to tell his daughter how to— (*then angrily*) I don't need your advice. Haven't I had every man I want around here?

HOGAN—Ah, thank God, that sounds natural! Be God, I thought you'd started playing virgin with me just because that Broadway sucker thinks you're one.

JOSIE—(*furiously*) Shut up! I'm not playing anything. And don't worry I can't do my part of the trick.

HOGAN—That's the talk! But let me get it all clear. I come at sunrise with my witnesses, and you've forgot to lock your door, and we walk in, and there's the two of you in bed, and I raise the roof and threaten him if he don't marry you—

JOSIE—Marry him? After what he's done to us? I wouldn't marry him now if he was the last man on earth! All we want is a paper signed by him with witnesses that he'll sell the farm to you for the price you offered, and not to Harder.

HOGAN—Well, that's justice, but that's all it is. I thought you wanted to make him pay for his black treachery against us, the dirty bastard!

JOSIE—I do want! (*She again gives him a bitter resentful glance.*) It's the estate money you're thinking of, isn't it? Leave it to you! (*hastily*) Well, so am I! I'd like to get my hooks on it! (*with a hard, brazen air*) Be God, if I'm to play whore, I deserve my pay! We'll make him sign a paper he owes me ten thousand dollars the minute the estate is settled. (*She laughs.*) How's that? I'll bet none of his tarts on Broadway ever got a thousandth part of that out of him, no matter how dainty and pretty! (*laughing again*) And here's what'll be the greatest joke to teach him a lesson. He'll pay it for nothing! I'll get him in bed but I'll never let him—

HOGAN—(*with delighted admiration*) Och, by Jaysus, Josie, that's the best yet! (*He slaps his thigh enthusiastically.*) Oh, that'll teach him to double-cross his friends! That'll show him two can play at tricks! And him believing you so innocent!

Be God, you'll make him the prize sucker of the world! Won't I roar inside me when I see his face in the morning! (*He bursts into coarse laughter.*)

JOSIE — (*again with illogical resentment*) Stop laughing! You're letting yourself be drunk again. (*then with a hard, business-like air*) We've done enough talking. Let's start—

HOGAN — Wait, now. There's another thing. Just what do you want me to threaten him with when I catch you? That we'll sue him for outraging your virtue? Sure, his lawyer would have all your old flames in the witness box, till the jury would think you'd been faithful to the male inhabitants of America. So what threat—I can't think of any he wouldn't laugh at.

JOSIE — (*tensely*) Well, I can! Do I have to tell you his weakness again? It's his vanity about women, and his Broadway pride he's so wise no woman could fool him. It's the disgrace to his vanity—being caught with the likes of me— (*falteringly, but forcing herself to go on*) My mug beside his in all the newspapers—the New York papers, too—he'll see the whole of Broadway splitting their sides laughing at him—and he'll give anything to keep us quiet, I tell you. He will! I know him! So don't worry— (*She ends up on the verge of bitter humiliated tears.*)

HOGAN — (*without looking at her—enthusiastic again*) Be God, you're right!

JOSIE — (*gives him a bitter glance—fiercely*) Then get the hell out of that chair and let's start it! (*He gets up. She surveys him resentfully.*) You're steady on your pins, ain't you, you scheming old thief, now there's the smell of money around! (*quickly*) Well, I'm glad. I know I can depend on you now. You'll walk down to the Inn with me and hide outside until you see me come out with him. Then you can sneak in the Inn yourself and pick the witnesses to stay up with you. But mind you don't get drunk again, and let them get too drunk.

HOGAN — I won't, I take my oath! (*He pats her on the shoulder approvingly.*) Be God, you've got the proud, fighting spirit in you that never says die, and you make me ashamed of my weakness. You're that eager now, be damned if I don't almost think you're glad of the excuse!

JOSIE — (*stiffens*) Excuse for what, you old—

HOGAN—To show him no man can get the best of you—what else?—like you showed all the others.

JOSIE—I'll show him to his sorrow! (*then abruptly, starting for the screen door at left*) Come on. We've no time to waste. (*But when she gets to the door, she appears suddenly hesitant and timid—hurriedly*) Wait. I'd better give a look at myself in the mirror. (*in a brazen tone*) Sure, those in my trade have to look their best! (*She hurries back across the room into her bedroom and closes the door. Hogan stares after her. Abruptly he ceases to look like a drunk who, by an effort, is keeping himself half-sober. He is a man who has been drinking a lot but is still clear-headed and has complete control of himself.*)

HOGAN—(*watches the crack under Josie's door and speaks half-aloud to himself, shaking his head pityingly*) A look in the mirror and she's forgot to light her lamp! (*remorsefully*) God forgive me, it's bitter medicine. But it's the only way I can see that has a chance now. (*Josie's door opens. At once, he is as he was. She comes out, a fixed smile on her lips, her head high, her face set defiantly. But she has evidently been crying.*)

JOSIE—(*brazenly*) There, now. Don't I look ten thousand dollars' worth to any drunk?

HOGAN—You look a million, darlin'!

JOSIE—(*goes to the screen door and pushes it open with the manner of one who has burned all bridges*) Come along, then. (*She goes out. He follows close on her heels. She stops abruptly on the first step—startledly*) Look! There's someone on the road—

HOGAN—(*pushes past her down the steps—peering off left-front—as if aloud to himself, in dismay*) Be God, it's him! I never thought—

JOSIE—(*as if aloud to herself*) So he didn't forget—

HOGAN—(*quickly*) Well, it proves he can't keep away from you, and that'll make it easier for you— (*then furiously*) Oh, the dirty, double-crossing bastard! The nerve of him! Coming to call on you, after making you wait for hours, thinking you don't know what he's done to us this night, and it'll be a fine cruel joke to blarney you in the moonlight, and you trusting him like a poor sheep, and never suspecting—

JOSIE—(*stung*) Shut up! I'll teach him who's the joker! I'll let him go on as if you hadn't told me what he's done—

HOGAN—Yes, don't let him suspect it, or you wouldn't fool him. He'd know you were after revenge. But he can see me here now. I can't sneak away or he'd be suspicious. We've got to think of a new scheme quick to get me away—

JOSIE—(*quickly*) I know how. Pretend you're as drunk as when you came. Make him believe you're so drunk you don't remember what he's done, so he can't suspect you told me.

HOGAN—I will. Be God, Josie, damned if I don't think he's so queer drunk himself he don't remember, or he'd never come here.

JOSIE—The drunker he is the better! (*lowering her voice— quickly*) He's turned in the gate where he can hear us. Pretend we're fighting and I'm driving you off till you're sober. Say you won't be back tonight. It'll make him sure he'll have the night alone with me. You start the fight.

HOGAN—(*becomes at once very drunk. He shouts*) Put me out of my own home, will you, you undutiful slut!

JOSIE—Celebration or not, I'll have no drunks cursing and singing all night. Go back to the Inn.

HOGAN—I will! I'll get a room and two bottles and stay drunk as long as I please!

JOSIE—Don't come back till you've slept it off, or I'll wipe the floor with you! (*Tyrone enters, left-front. He does not appear to be drunk—that is, he shows none of the usual symptoms. He seems much the same as in Act One. The only perceptible change is that his eyes have a peculiar fixed, glazed look, and there is a certain vague quality in his manner and speech, as if he were a bit hazy and absent-minded.*)

TYRONE—(*dryly*) Just in time for the Big Bout. Or is this the final round?

HOGAN—(*whirls on him unsteadily*) Who the hell— (*peering at him*) Oh, it's you, is it?

TYRONE—What was the big idea, Phil, leaving me flat?

HOGAN—Leave you flat? Be Jaysus, that reminds me I owe you a swipe on the jaw for something. What was it? Be God, I'm too drunk to remember. But here it is, anyway. (*He turns loose a round-house swing that misses Tyrone by a couple of feet, and reels away. Tyrone regards him with vague surprise.*)

JOSIE—Stop it, you damned old fool, and get out of here!

HOGAN—Taking his side against your poor old father, are you? A hell of a daughter! (*He draws himself up with drunken dignity.*) Don't expect me home tonight, Miss Hogan, or tomorrow either, maybe. You can take your bad temper out on your sweetheart here. (*He starts off down the road, left-front, with a last word over his shoulder.*) Bad luck to you both. (*He disappears. A moment later he begins to bawl his mournful Irish song.*) "Oh, the praties they grow small, Over here, over here," etc. (*During a part of the following scene the song continues to be heard at intervals, receding as he gets farther off on his way to the Inn.*)

JOSIE—Well, thank God. That's good riddance. (*She comes to Tyrone, who stands staring after Hogan with a puzzled look.*)

TYRONE—I've never seen him that stinko before. Must have got him all of a sudden. He didn't seem so lit up at the Inn, but I guess I wasn't paying much attention.

JOSIE—(*forcing a playful air*) I should think, if you were a real gentleman, you'd be apologizing to me, not thinking of him. Don't you know you're two hours and a half late? I oughtn't to speak to you, if I had any pride.

TYRONE—(*stares at her curiously*) You've got too damn much pride, Josie. That's the trouble.

JOSIE—And just what do you mean by that, Jim?

TYRONE—(*shrugs his shoulders*) Nothing. Forget it. I do apologize, Josie. I'm damned sorry. Haven't any excuse. Can't think up a lie. (*staring at her curiously again*) Or, now I think of it, I had a damned good honorable excuse, but— (*He shrugs.*) Nuts. Forget it.

JOSIE—Holy Joseph, you're full of riddles tonight. Well, I don't need excuses. I forgive you, anyway, now you're here. (*She takes his hand—playfully*) Come on now and we'll sit on my bedroom steps and be romantic in the moonlight, like we planned to. (*She leads him there. He goes along in an automatic way, as if only half-conscious of what he is doing. She sits on the top step and pulls him down on the step beneath her. A pause. He stares vaguely at nothing. She bends to give him an uneasy appraising glance.*)

TYRONE—(*suddenly, begins to talk mechanically*) Had to get out of the damned Inn. I was going batty alone there. The old heebie-jeebies. So I came to you. (*He pauses—then adds with strange, wondering sincerity*) I've really begun to love you a lot, Josie.

JOSIE — (*blurts out bitterly*) Yes, you've proved that tonight, haven't you? (*hurriedly regaining her playful tone*) But never mind. I said I'd forgive you for being so late. So go on about love. I'm all ears.

TYRONE — (*as if he hadn't listened*) I thought you'd have given me up and gone to bed. I remember I had some nutty idea I'd get in bed with you—just to lie with my head on your breast.

JOSIE — (*moved in spite of herself—but keeps her bold, playful tone*) Well, maybe I'll let you— (*hurriedly*) Later on, I mean. The night's young yet, and we'll have it all to ourselves. (*boldly again*) But here's for a starter. (*She puts her arms around him and draws him back till his head is on her breast.*) There, now.

TYRONE — (*relaxes—simply and gratefully*) Thanks, Josie. (*He closes his eyes. For a moment, she forgets everything and stares down at his face with a passionate, possessive tenderness. A pause. From far-off on the road to the Inn, Hogan's mournful song drifts back through the moonlight quiet:* "Oh, the praties they grow small, Over here, over here." *Tyrone rouses himself and straightens up. He acts embarrassed, as if he felt he'd been making a fool of himself—mockingly*) Hark, Hark, the Donegal lark! "Thou wast not born for death, immortal bird." Can't Phil sing anything but that damned dirge, Josie? (*She doesn't reply. He goes on hazily.*) Still, it seems to belong tonight—in the moonlight—or in my mind— (*He quotes*)

"Now more than ever seems it rich to die,
   To cease upon the midnight with no pain,
   In such an ecstasy!"

(*He has recited this with deep feeling. Now he sneers*) Good God! Ode to Phil the Irish Nightingale! I must have the D.T.'s.

JOSIE — (*her face grown bitter*) Maybe it's only your bad conscience.

TYRONE — (*starts guiltily and turns to stare into her face—suspiciously*) What put that in your head? Conscience about what?

JOSIE — (*quickly*) How would I know, if you don't? (*forcing a playful tone*) For the sin of wanting to be in bed with me. Maybe that's it.

TYRONE—(*with strange relief*) Oh. (*a bit shamefacedly*) Forget that stuff, Josie. I was half nutty.

JOSIE—(*bitterly*) Och, for the love of God, don't apologize as if you was ashamed of— (*She catches herself.*)

TYRONE—(*with a quick glance at her face*) All right. I certainly won't apologize—if you're not kicking. I was afraid I might have shocked your modesty.

JOSIE—(*roughly*) *My* modesty? Be God, I didn't know I had any left.

TYRONE—(*draws away from her—irritably*) Nix, Josie. Lay off that line, for tonight at least. (*He adds slowly*) I'd like tonight to be different.

JOSIE—Different from what? (*He doesn't answer. She forces a light tone.*) All right. I'll be as different as you please.

TYRONE—(*simply*) Thanks, Josie. Just be yourself. (*again as if he were ashamed, or afraid he had revealed some weakness— off-handedly*) This being out in the moonlight instead of the lousy Inn isn't a bad bet, at that. I don't know why I hang out in that dump, except I'm even more bored in the so-called good hotels in this hick town.

JOSIE—(*trying to examine his face without his knowing*) Well, you'll be back on Broadway soon now, won't you?

TYRONE—I hope so.

JOSIE—Then you'll have all the pretty little tarts to comfort you when you get your sorrowful spell on.

TYRONE—Oh, to hell with the rough stuff, Josie! You promised you'd can it tonight.

JOSIE—(*tensely*) You're a fine one to talk of promises!

TYRONE—(*vaguely surprised by her tone*) What's the matter? Still sore at me for being late?

JOSIE—(*quickly*) I'm not. I was teasing you. To prove there's no hard feelings, how would you like a drink? But I needn't ask. (*She gets up.*) I'll get a bottle of his best.

TYRONE—(*mechanically*) Fine. Maybe that will have some kick. The booze at the Inn didn't work tonight.

JOSIE—Well, this'll work. (*She starts to go into her bedroom. He sits hunched up on the step, staring at nothing. She pauses in the doorway to glance back. The hard, calculating expression on her face softens. For a second she stares at him, bewildered by her conflicting feelings. Then she goes inside, leaving the door open. She opens the door from her room to the lighted living room, and is seen going to the kitchen on the way to the cellar. She has left the door from the living room to her bedroom open and the light reveals a section of the bedroom framed in the doorway behind Tyrone. The foot of the bed which occupies most of the room can be seen, and that is all except that the walls are unpainted pine boards. Tyrone continues to stare at nothing, but becomes restless. His hands and mouth twitch.*)

TYRONE — (*suddenly, with intense hatred*) You rotten bastard! (*He springs to his feet — fumbles in his pockets for cigarettes — strikes a match which lights up his face, on which there is now an expression of miserable guilt. His hand is trembling so violently he cannot light the cigarette.*)

(*Curtain*)

ACT THREE

SCENE—*The living-room wall has been replaced and all we see now of its lighted interior is through the two windows. Otherwise, everything is the same, and this Act follows the preceding without any lapse of time. Tyrone is still trying with shaking hands to get his cigarette lighted. Finally he succeeds, and takes a deep inhale, and starts pacing back and forth a few steps, as if in a cell of his own thought. He swears defensively)* God damn it. You'll be crying in your beer in a minute. (*He begins to sing sneeringly half under his breath a snatch from an old sob song, popular in the Nineties.*)

> "And baby's cries can't waken her
> In the baggage coach ahead."

(*His sneer changes to a look of stricken guilt and grief.*) Christ! (*He seems about to break down and sob but he fights this back.*) Cut it out, you drunken fool! (*Josie can be seen through the windows, returning from the kitchen. He turns with a look of relief and escape.*) Thank God! (*He sits on the boulder and waits. Josie stops by the table in the living room to turn down the lamp until only a dim light remains. She has a quart of whiskey under her arm, two tumblers, and a pitcher of water. She goes through her bedroom and appears in the outer doorway. Tyrone gets up.*) Ah! At last the old booze! (*He relieves her of the pitcher and tumblers as she comes down the steps.*)

JOSIE—(*with a fixed smile*) You'd think I'd been gone years. You didn't seem so perishing for a drink.

TYRONE—(*in his usual, easy, kidding way*) It's you I was perishing for. I've been dying of loneliness—

JOSIE—You'll die of lying some day. But I'm glad you're alive again. I thought when I left you really were dying on me.

TYRONE—No such luck.

JOSIE—Och, don't talk like that. Come have a drink. We'll use the boulder for a table and I'll be barkeep. (*He puts the pitcher and tumblers on the boulder and she uncorks the bottle. She takes a quick glance at his face—startledly*) What's come over you, Jim? You look as if you've seen a ghost.

TYRONE—(*looks away—dryly*) I have. My own. He's punk company.

912

JOSIE—Yes, it's the worst ghost of all, your own. Don't I know? But this will keep it in its place. (*She pours a tumbler half full of whiskey and hands it to him.*) Here. But wait till I join you. (*She pours the other tumbler half full.*)

TYRONE—(*surprised*) Hello! I thought you never touched it.

JOSIE—(*glibly*) I have on occasion. And this is one. I don't want to be left out altogether from celebrating our victory over Harder. (*She gives him a sharp bitter glance. Meeting his eyes, which are regarding her with puzzled wonder, she forces a laugh.*) Don't look at me as if I was up to some game. A drink or two will make me better company, and help me enjoy the moon and the night with you. Here's luck. (*She touches his glass with hers.*)

TYRONE—(*shrugs his shoulders*) All right. Here's luck. (*They drink. She gags and sputters. He pours water in her glass. She drinks it. He puts his glass and the pitcher back on the boulder. He keeps staring at her with a puzzled frown.*)

JOSIE—Some of it went down the wrong way.

TYRONE—So I see. That'll teach you to pour out baths instead of drinks.

JOSIE—It's the first time I ever heard you complain a drink was too big.

TYRONE—Yours was too big.

JOSIE—I'm my father's daughter. I've a strong head. So don't worry I'll pass out and you'll have to put me to bed. (*She gives a little bold laugh.*) Sure, that's a beautiful notion. I'll have to pretend I'm—

TYRONE—(*irritably*) Nix on the raw stuff, Josie. Remember you said—

JOSIE—(*resentment in her kidding*) I'd be different? That's right. I'm forgetting it's your pleasure to have me pretend I'm an innocent virgin tonight.

TYRONE—(*in a strange tone that is almost threatening*) If you don't look out, I'll call you on that bluff, Josie. (*He stares at her with a deliberate sensualist's look that undresses her.*) I'd like to. You know that, don't you?

JOSIE—(*boldly*) I don't at all. You're the one who's bluffing.

TYRONE—(*grabs her in his arms—with genuine passion*) Josie! (*Then as suddenly he lets her go.*) Nix. Let's cut it out.

(*He turns away. Her face betrays the confused conflict within her of fright, passion, happiness, and bitter resentment. He goes on with an abrupt change of tone.*) How about another drink? That's honest-to-God old bonded Bourbon. How the devil did Phil get hold of it?

JOSIE—Tom Lombardo, the bootlegger, gave him a case for letting him hide a truckload in our barn when the agents were after him. He stole it from a warehouse on faked permits. (*She pours out drinks as she speaks, a half tumblerful for him, a small one for herself.*) Here you are. (*She gives him his drink—smiles at him coquettishly, beginning to show the effect of her big drink by her increasingly bold manner.*) Let's sit down where the moon will be in our eyes and we'll see romance. (*She takes his arm and leads him to her bedroom steps. She sits on the top step, pulling him down beside her but on the one below. She raises her glass.*) Here's hoping before the night's out you'll have more courage and kiss me at least.

TYRONE—(*frowns—then kiddingly*) That's a promise. Here's how. (*He drains his tumbler. She drinks half of hers. He puts his glass on the ground beside him. A pause. She tries to read his face without his noticing. He seems to be lapsing again into vague preoccupation.*)

JOSIE—Now don't sink back half-dead-and-alive in dreams the way you were before.

TYRONE—(*quickly*) I'm not. I had a good final dose of heebie-jeebies when you were in the house. That's all for tonight. (*He adds a bit maudlinly, his two big drinks beginning to affect him*) Let the dead past bury its dead.

JOSIE—That's the talk. There's only tonight, and the moon, and us—and the bonded Bourbon. Have another drink, and don't wait for me.

TYRONE—Not now, thanks. They're coming too fast. (*He gives her a curious, cynically amused look.*) Trying to get me soused, Josie?

JOSIE—(*starts—quickly*) I'm not. Only to get you feeling happy, so you'll forget all sadness.

TYRONE—(*kiddingly*) I might forget all my honorable intentions, too. So look out.

JOSIE—I'll look forward to it—and I hope that's another promise, like the kiss you owe me. If you're suspicious I'm trying to get you soused—well, here goes. (*She drinks what is left in her glass.*) There, now. I must be scheming to get myself soused, too.

TYRONE—Maybe you are.

JOSIE—(*resentfully*) If I was, it'd be to make you feel at home. Don't all the pretty little Broadway tarts get soused with you?

TYRONE—(*irritably*) There you go again with that old line!

JOSIE—All right, I won't! (*forcing a laugh*) I must be eaten up with jealousy for them, that's it.

TYRONE—You needn't be. They don't belong.

JOSIE—And I do?

TYRONE—Yes. You do.

JOSIE—For tonight only, you mean?

TYRONE—We've agreed there is only tonight—and it's to be different from any past night—for both of us.

JOSIE—(*in a forced, kidding tone*) I hope it will be. I'll try to control my envy for your Broadway flames. I suppose it's because I have a picture of them in my mind as small and dainty and pretty—

TYRONE—They're just gold-digging tramps.

JOSIE—(*as if he hadn't spoken*) While I'm only a big, rough, ugly cow of a woman.

TYRONE—Shut up! You're beautiful.

JOSIE—(*jeeringly, but her voice trembles*) God pity the blind!

TYRONE—You're beautiful to me.

JOSIE—It must be the Bourbon—

TYRONE—You're real and healthy and clean and fine and warm and strong and kind—

JOSIE—I have a beautiful soul, you mean?

TYRONE—Well, I don't know much about ladies' souls— (*He takes her hand.*) But I do know you're beautiful. (*He kisses her hand.*) And I love you a lot—in my fashion.

JOSIE—(*stammers*) Jim— (*hastily forcing her playful tone*) Sure, you're full of fine compliments all of a sudden, and I ought to show you how pleased I am. (*She pulls his head back and kisses him on the lips—a quick, shy kiss.*) That's for my beautiful soul.

TYRONE—(*The kiss arouses his physical desire. He pulls her head down and stares into her eyes.*) You have a beautiful strong body, too, Josie—and beautiful eyes and hair, and a beautiful smile and beautiful warm breasts. (*He kisses her on the lips. She pulls back frightenedly for a second—then returns his kiss. Suddenly he breaks away—in a tone of guilty irritation*) Nix! Nix! Don't be a fool, Josie. Don't let me pull that stuff.

JOSIE—(*triumphant for a second*) You meant it! I know you meant it! (*then with resentful bitterness—roughly*) Be God, you're right I'm a damned fool to let you make me forget you're the greatest liar in the world! (*quickly*) I mean, the greatest kidder. And now, how about another drink?

TYRONE—(*staring at nothing—vaguely*) You don't get me, Josie. You don't know—and I hope you never will know—

JOSIE—(*blurts out bitterly*) Maybe I know more than you think.

TYRONE—(*as if she hadn't spoken*) There's always the aftermath that poisons you. I don't want you to be poisoned—

JOSIE—Maybe you know what you're talking about—

TYRONE—And I don't want to be poisoned myself—not again—not with you. (*He pauses—slowly*) There have been too many nights—and dawns. This must be different. I want— (*His voice trails off into silence.*)

JOSIE—(*trying to read his face—uneasily*) Don't get in one of your queer spells, now. (*She gives his shoulder a shake—forcing a light tone*) Sure, I don't think you know what you want. Except another drink. I'm sure you want that. And I want one, too.

TYRONE—(*recovering himself*) Fine! Grand idea. (*He gets up and brings the bottle from the boulder. He picks up his tumbler and pours a big drink. She is holding out her tumbler but he ignores it.*)

JOSIE—You're not polite, pouring your own first.

TYRONE—I said a drink was a grand idea—for me. Not for you. You skip this one.

JOSIE—(*resentfully*) Oh, I do, do I? Are you giving me orders?

TYRONE—Yes. Take a big drink of moonlight instead.

JOSIE—(*angrily*) You'll pour me a drink, if you please, Jim Tyrone, or—

TYRONE—(*stares at her—then shrugs his shoulders*) All right, if you want to take it that way, Josie. It's your funeral. (*He pours a drink into her tumbler.*)

JOSIE—(*ashamed but defiant—stiffly*) Thank you kindly. (*She raises her glass—mockingly*) Here's to tonight. (*Tyrone is staring at her, a strange bitter disgust in his eyes. Suddenly he slaps at her hand, knocking the glass to the ground.*)

TYRONE—(*his voice hard with repulsion*) I've slept with drunken tramps on too many nights!

JOSIE—(*stares at him, too startled and bewildered to be angry. Her voice trembles with surprising meekness.*) All right, Jim, if you don't want me to—

TYRONE—(*now looks as bewildered by his action as she does*) I'm sorry, Josie. Don't know what the drink got into me. (*He picks up her glass.*) Here. I'll pour you another.

JOSIE—(*still meek*) No, thank you. I'll skip this one. (*She puts the glass on the ground.*) But you drink up.

TYRONE—Thanks. (*He gulps down his drink. Mechanically, as if he didn't know what he was doing, he pours another. Suddenly he blurts out with guilty loathing*) That fat blonde pig on the train—I got her drunk! That's why— (*He stops guiltily.*)

JOSIE—(*uneasily*) What are you talking about? What train?

TYRONE—No train. Don't mind me. (*He gulps down the drink and pours another with the same strange air of acting unconsciously.*) Maybe I'll tell you—later, when I'm— That'll cure you—for all time! (*Abruptly he realizes what he is saying. He gives the characteristic shrug of shoulders—cynically*) Nuts! The Brooklyn boys are talking again. I guess I'm more stewed than I thought—in the center of the old bean, at least. (*dully*) I better beat it back to the Inn and go to bed and stop bothering you, Josie.

JOSIE—(*bullyingly—and pityingly*) Well, you won't, not if I have to hold you. Come on now, bring your drink and sit down like you were before. (*He does so. She pats his cheek—forcing a playful air*) That's a good boy. And I won't take any more whiskey. I've all the effect from it I want already. Everything is far away and doesn't matter—except the moon and its dreams, and I'm part of the dreams—and you are, too. (*She adds with a rueful little laugh*) I keep forgetting the thing

I've got to remember. I keep hoping it's a lie, even though I know I'm a damned fool.

TYRONE—(*hazily*) Damned fool about what?

JOSIE—Never mind. (*forcing a laugh*) I've just had a thought. If my poor old father had seen you knocking his prize whiskey on the ground—Holy Joseph, he'd have had three paralytic strokes!

TYRONE—(*grins*) Yes, I can picture him. (*He pauses—with amused affection*) But that's all a fake. He loves to play tightwad, but the people he likes know better. He'd give them his shirt. He's a grand old scout, Josie. (*a bit maudlin*) The only real friend I've got left—except you. I love his guts.

JOSIE—(*tensely—sickened by his hypocrisy*) Och, for the love of God—!

TYRONE—(*shrugs his shoulders*) Yes, I suppose that does sound like moaning-at-the-bar stuff. But I mean it.

JOSIE—Do you? Well, I know my father's virtues without you telling me.

TYRONE—You ought to appreciate him because he worships the ground you walk on—and he knows you a lot better than you think. (*He turns to smile at her teasingly.*) As well as I do—almost.

JOSIE—(*defensively*) That's not saying much. Maybe I can guess what you think you know— (*forcing a contemptuous laugh*) If it's that, God pity you, you're a terrible fool.

TYRONE—(*teasingly*) If it's what? I haven't said anything.

JOSIE—You'd better not, or I'll die laughing at you. (*She changes the subject abruptly.*) Why don't you drink up? It makes me nervous watching you hold it as if you didn't know it was there.

TYRONE—I didn't, at that. (*He drinks.*)

JOSIE—And have another.

TYRONE—(*a bit drunkenly*) Will a whore go to a picnic? Real bonded Bourbon. That's my dish. (*He goes to the boulder for the bottle. He is as steady on his feet as if he were completely sober.*)

JOSIE—(*in a light tone*) Bring the bottle back so it'll be handy and you won't have to leave me. I miss you.

TYRONE—(*comes back with the bottle. He smiles at her cynically.*) Still trying to get me soused, Josie?

JOSIE—I'm not such a fool—with your capacity.

TYRONE—You better watch your step. It might work—
and then think of how disgusted you'd feel, with me lying
beside you, probably snoring, as you watched the dawn
come. You don't know—

JOSIE—(*defiantly*) The hell I don't! Isn't that the way I've
felt with every one of them, after?

TYRONE—(*as if he hadn't heard—bitterly*) But take it from
me, I know. I've seen too God-damned many dawns creeping
grayly over too many dirty windows.

JOSIE—(*ignores this—boldly*) But it might be different with
you. Love could make it different. And I've been head over
heels in love ever since you said you loved my beautiful soul.
(*Again he doesn't seem to have heard—resentfully*) Don't stand
there like a loon, mourning over the past. Why don't you
pour yourself a drink and sit down?

TYRONE—(*looks at the bottle and tumbler in his hands, as if
he'd forgotten them—mechanically*) Sure thing. Real bonded
Bourbon. I ought to know. If I had a dollar for every drink
of it I had before Prohibition, I'd hire our dear bully, Harder,
for a valet. (*Josie stiffens and her face hardens. Tyrone pours a
drink and sets the bottle on the ground. He looks up suddenly into
her eyes—warningly*) You'd better remember I said you had
beautiful eyes and hair—and breasts.

JOSIE—I remember you did. (*She tries to be calculatingly
enticing.*) So sit down and I'll let you lay your head—

TYRONE—No. If you won't watch your step, I've got to.
(*He sits down but doesn't lean back.*) And don't let me get away
with pretending I'm so soused I don't know what I'm doing.
I always know. Or part of me does. That's the trouble. (*He
pauses—then bursts out in a strange threatening tone*) You better look out, Josie. She was tickled to death to get me pie-
eyed. Had an idea she could roll me, I guess. She wasn't so
tickled about it—later on.

JOSIE—What she? (*He doesn't reply. She forces a light tone.*)
I hope you don't think I'm scheming to roll you.

TYRONE—(*vaguely*) What? (*coming to—indignantly*) Of
course not. What are you talking about? For God's sake,
you're not a tart.

JOSIE—(*roughly*) No, I'm a fool. I'm always giving it away.

TYRONE—(*angrily*) That lousy bluff again, eh? You're a liar! For Christ sake, quit the smut stuff, can't you!

JOSIE—(*stung*) Listen to me, Jim! Drunk or not, don't you talk that way to me or—

TYRONE—How about your not talking the old smut stuff to me? You promised you'd be yourself. (*pauses—vaguely*) You don't get it, Josie. You see, she was one of the smuttiest talking pigs I've ever listened to.

JOSIE—What she? Do you mean the blonde on the train?

TYRONE—(*starts—sharply*) Train? Who told you—? (*quickly*) Oh—that's right—I did say— (*vaguely*) What blonde? What's the difference? Coming back from the Coast. It was long ago. But it seems like tonight. There is no present or future—only the past happening over and over again—now. You can't get away from it. (*abruptly*) Nuts! To hell with that crap.

JOSIE—You came back from the Coast about a year ago after— (*She checks herself.*)

TYRONE—(*dully*) Yes. After Mama's death. (*quickly*) But I've been to the Coast a lot of times during my career as a third-rate ham. I don't remember which time—or anything much—except I was pie-eyed in a drawing room the whole four days. (*abruptly*) What were we talking about before? What a grand guy Phil is. You ought to be glad you've got him for a father. Mine was an old bastard.

JOSIE—He wasn't! He was one of the finest, kindest gentlemen ever lived.

TYRONE—(*sneeringly*) Outside the family, sure. Inside, he was a lousy tightwad bastard.

JOSIE—(*repelled*) You ought to be ashamed!

TYRONE—To speak ill of the dead? Nuts! He can't hear, and he knows I hated him, anyway—as much as he hated me. I'm glad he's dead. So is he. Or he ought to be. Everyone ought to be, if they have any sense. Out of a bum racket. At peace. (*He shrugs his shoulders.*) Nuts! What of it?

JOSIE—(*tensely*) Don't Jim. I hate you when you talk like that. (*forcing a light tone*) Do you want to spoil our beautiful moonlight night? And don't be telling me of your old flames, on trains or not. I'm too jealous.

TYRONE—(*with a shudder of disgust*) Of that pig? (*He drinks his whiskey as if to wash a bad taste from his mouth—then takes one of her hands in both of his—simply*) You're a fool to be jealous of anyone. You're the only woman I care a damn about.

JOSIE—(*deeply stirred, in spite of herself—her voice trembling*) Jim, don't— (*forcing a tense little laugh*) All right, I'll try and believe that—for tonight.

TYRONE—(*simply*) Thanks, Josie. (*A pause. He speaks in a tone of random curiosity.*) Why did you say a while ago I'd be leaving for New York soon?

JOSIE—(*stiffens—her face hardening*) Well, I was right, wasn't I? (*Unconsciously she tries to pull her hand away.*)

TYRONE—Why are you pulling your hand away?

JOSIE—(*stops*) Was I? (*forcing a smile*) I suppose because it seems crazy for you to hold my big ugly paw so tenderly. But you're welcome to it, if you like.

TYRONE—I do like. It's strong and kind and warm—like you. (*He kisses it.*)

JOSIE—(*tensely*) Och, for the love of God—! (*She jerks her hand away—then hastily forces a joking tone.*) Wasting kisses on my hand! Sure, even the moon is laughing at us.

TYRONE—Nuts for the moon! I'd rather have one light on Broadway than all the moons since Rameses was a pup. (*He takes cigarettes from his pocket and lights one.*)

JOSIE—(*her eyes searching his face, lighted up by the match*) You'll be taking a train back to your dear old Broadway tomorrow night, won't you?

TYRONE—(*still holding the burning match, stares at her in surprise*) Tomorrow night? Where did you get that?

JOSIE—A little bird told me.

TYRONE—(*blows out the match in a cloud of smoke*) You'd better give that bird the bird. By the end of the week, is the right dope. Phil got his dates mixed.

JOSIE—(*quickly*) He didn't tell me. He was too drunk to remember anything.

TYRONE—He was sober when I told him. I called up the executors when we reached the Inn after leaving here. They said the estate would be out of probate within a few days. I told Phil the glad tidings and bought drinks for all and

sundry. There was quite a celebration. Funny, Phil wouldn't
remember that.

JOSIE—(*bewildered—not knowing what to believe*) It is—
funny.

TYRONE—(*shrugs his shoulders*) Well, he's stewed to the
ears. That always explains anything. (*then strangely*) Only
sometimes it doesn't.

JOSIE—No—sometimes it doesn't.

TYRONE—(*goes on without real interest, talking to keep from
thinking*) Phil certainly has a prize bun on tonight. He never
took a punch at me before. And that drivel he talked about
owing me one— What got into his head, I wonder.

JOSIE—(*tensely*) How would I know, if you don't?

TYRONE—Well, I don't. Not unless— I remember I did
try to get his goat. Simpson sat down with us. Harder sent
him to see me. You remember after Harder left here I said
the joke was on you, that you'd made this place a gold mine.
I was kidding, but I had the right dope. What do you think
he told Simpson to offer? Ten grand! On the level, Josie.

JOSIE—(*tense*) So you accepted?

TYRONE—I told Simpson to tell Harder I did. I decided
the best way to fix him was to let him think he'd got away
with it, and then when he comes tomorrow morning to drive
me to the executor's office, I'll tell him what he can do with
himself, his bankroll, and tin oil tanks.

JOSIE—(*knows he is telling the truth—so relieved she can only
stammer stupidly*) So that's—the truth of it.

TYRONE—(*smiles*) Of course, I did it to kid Phil, too. He
was right there, listening. But I know I didn't fool him.

JOSIE—(*weakly*) Maybe you did fool him, for once. But I
don't know.

TYRONE—And that's why he took a swing at me? (*He
laughs, but there is a forced note to it.*) Well, if so, it's one hell
of a joke on him. (*His tone becomes hurt and bitter.*) All the
same, I'll be good and sore, Josie. I promised this place
wouldn't be sold except to him. What the hell does he think
I am? He ought to know I wouldn't double-cross you and
him for ten million!

JOSIE—(*giving away at last to her relief and joy*) Don't I
know! Oh, Jim, darling! (*She hugs him passionately and kisses*

him on the lips.) I knew you'd never—I told him— (*She kisses him again.*) Oh, Jim, I love you.

TYRONE—(*again with a strange, simple gratitude*) Thanks, Josie. I mean, for not believing I'm a rotten louse. Everyone else believes it—including myself—for a damned good reason. (*abruptly changing the subject*) I'm a fool to let this stuff about Phil get under my skin, but— Why, I remember telling him tonight I'd even written my brother and got his okay on selling the farm to him. And Phil thanked me. He seemed touched and grateful. You wouldn't think he'd forget that.

JOSIE—(*her face hard and bitter*) I wouldn't, indeed. There's a lot of things he'll have to explain when he comes at sun— (*hastily*) When he comes back. (*She pauses—then bursts out*) The damned old schemer, I'll teach him to—(*again checking herself*) to act like a fool.

TYRONE—(*smiles*) You'll get out the old club, eh? What a bluff you are, Josie. (*teasingly*) You and your lovers, Messalina—when you've never—

JOSIE—(*with a faint spark of her old defiance*) You're a liar.

TYRONE—"Pride is the sin by which the angels fell." Are you going to keep that up—with me?

JOSIE—(*feebly*) You think I've never because no one would—because I'm a great ugly cow—

TYRONE—(*gently*) Nuts! You could have had any one of them. You kidded them till you were sure they wanted you. That was all you wanted. And then you slapped them groggy when they tried for more. But you had to keep convincing yourself—

JOSIE—(*tormentedly*) Don't, Jim.

TYRONE—You can take the truth, Josie—from me. Because you and I belong to the same club. We can kid the world but we can't fool ourselves, like most people, no matter what we do—nor escape ourselves no matter where we run away. Whether it's the bottom of a bottle, or a South Sea Island, we'd find our own ghosts there waiting to greet us— "sleepless with pale commemorative eyes," as Rossetti wrote. (*He sneers to himself*) The old poetic bull, eh? Crap! (*reverting to a teasing tone*) You don't ask how I saw through your bluff, Josie. You pretend too much. And so do the guys. I've listened to them at the Inn. They all lie to each other. No one wants to admit all he got was a slap in the puss, when he thinks a lot of other guys made it. You can't blame them. And they know you don't give a damn how they lie. So—

JOSIE—For the love of God, Jim! Don't!

TYRONE—Phil is wise to you, of course, but although he knew I knew, he would never admit it until tonight.

JOSIE—(*startled—vindictively*) So he admitted it, did he? Wait till I get hold of him!

TYRONE—He'll never admit it to you. He's afraid of hurting you.

JOSIE—He is, is he? Well— (*almost hysterically*) For the love of God, can't you shut up about him!

TYRONE—(*glances up at her, surprised—then shrugs his shoulders*) Oh, all right. I wanted to clear things up, that's all—for Phil's sake as well as yours. You have a hell of a license to be sore. He's the one who ought to be. Don't you realize what a lousy position you've put him in with your brazen-trollop act?

JOSIE—(*tensely*) No. He doesn't care, except to use me in his scheming. He—

TYRONE—Don't be a damned fool. Of course he cares. And so do I. (*He turns and pulls her head down and kisses her on the lips.*) I care, Josie. I love you.

JOSIE—(*with pitiful longing*) Do you, Jim? Do you? (*She forces a trembling smile—faintly*) Then I'll confess the truth to you. I've been a crazy fool. I am a virgin. (*She begins to sob with a strange forlorn shame and humiliation.*) And now you'll never—and I want you to—now more than ever—because I love you more than ever, after what's happened— (*Suddenly she kisses him with fierce passion.*) But you will! I'll make you! To hell with your honorable scruples! I know you want me! I couldn't believe that until tonight—but now I know. It's in your kisses! (*She kisses him again—with passionate tenderness*) Oh, you great fool! As if I gave a damn what happened after! I'll have had tonight and your love to remember for the rest of my days! (*She kisses him again.*) Oh, Jim darling, haven't you said yourself there's only tonight? (*She whispers tenderly*) Come. Come with me. (*She gets to her feet, pulling at his arm—with a little self-mocking laugh*) But I'll have to make you leave before sunrise. I mustn't forget that.

TYRONE—(*A strange change has come over his face. He looks her over now with a sneering cynical lust. He speaks thickly as if he was suddenly very drunk.*) Sure thing, Kiddo. What the hell else do you suppose I came for? I've been kidding myself. (*He steps up beside her and puts his arm around her and presses his body to hers.*) You're the goods, Kid. I've wanted you all along. Love, nuts! I'll show you what love is. I know what you want, Bright Eyes. (*She is staring at him now with a look of frightened horror. He kisses her roughly.*) Come on, Baby Doll, let's hit the hay. (*He pushes her back in the doorway.*)

JOSIE—(*strickenly*) Jim! Don't! (*She pulls his arms away so violently that he staggers back and would fall down the steps if she didn't grab his arm in time. As it is he goes down on one knee. She is on the verge of collapse herself—brokenly*) Jim! I'm not a whore.

TYRONE—(*remains on one knee—confusedly, as if he didn't know what had happened*) What the hell? Was I trying to rape you, Josie? Forget it. I'm drunk—not responsible. (*He gets to his feet, staggering a bit, and steps down to the ground.*)

JOSIE—(*covering her face with her hands*) Oh, Jim! (*She sobs.*)

TYRONE—(*with vague pity*) Don't cry. No harm done. You stopped me, didn't you? (*She continues to sob. He mutters vaguely, as if talking to himself*) Must have drawn a blank for a while. Nuts! Cut out the faking. I knew what I was doing. (*slowly, staring before him*) But it's funny. I *was* seeing things. That's the truth, Josie. For a moment I thought you were that blonde pig— (*hastily*) The old heebie-jeebies. Hair of the dog. (*He gropes around for the bottle and his glass.*) I'll have another shot—

JOSIE—(*takes her hands from her face—fiercely*) Pour the whole bottle down your throat, if you like! Only stop talking! (*She covers her face with her hands and sobs again.*)

TYRONE—(*stares at her with a hurt and sad expression—dully*) Can't forgive me, eh? You ought to. You ought to thank me for letting you see— (*He pauses, as if waiting for her to say something but she remains silent. He shrugs his shoulders, pours out a big drink mechanically.*) Well, here's how. (*He drinks and puts the bottle and glass on the ground—dully*) That

was a nightcap. Our moonlight romance seems to be a flop,
Josie. I guess I'd better go.

JOSIE—(*dully*) Yes. You'd better go. Good night.

TYRONE—Not good night. Good-bye.

JOSIE—(*lifts her head*) Good-bye?

TYRONE—Yes. I won't see you again before I leave for
New York. I was a damned fool to come tonight. I hoped—
But you don't get it. How could you? So what's the good—
(*He shrugs his shoulders hopelessly and turns toward the road.*)

JOSIE—Jim!

TYRONE—(*turning back—bitter accusation in his tone now*)
Whore? Who said you were a whore? But I warned you,
didn't I, if you kept on— Why did you have to act like one,
asking me to come to bed? That wasn't what I came here for.
And you promised tonight would be different. Why the hell
did you promise that, if all you wanted was what all the others want, if that's all love means to you? (*then guiltily*) Oh,
Christ, I don't mean that, Josie. I know how you feel, and if
I could give you happiness— But it wouldn't work. You
don't know me. I'd poison it for myself and for you. I've
poisoned it already, haven't I, but it would be a million times
worse after— No matter how I tried not to, I'd make it like
all the other nights—for you, too. You'd lie awake and watch
the dawn come with disgust, with nausea retching your
memory, and the wine of passion poets blab about, a sour
aftertaste in your mouth of Dago red ink! (*He gives a
sneering laugh.*)

JOSIE—(*distractedly*) Oh, Jim, don't! Please don't!

TYRONE—You'd hate me and yourself—not for a day or
two but for the rest of your life. (*with a perverse, jeering note
of vindictive boastfulness in his tone*) Believe me, Kid, when I
poison them, they stay poisoned!

JOSIE—(*with dull bitterness*) Good-bye, Jim.

TYRONE—(*miserably hurt and sad for a second—appealingly*)
Josie— (*gives the characteristic shrug of his shoulders—simply*)
Good-bye. (*He turns toward the road—bitterly*) I'll find it hard
to forgive, too. I came here asking for love—just for this one
night, because I thought you loved me. (*dully*) Nuts. To hell
with it. (*He starts away.*)

JOSIE—(*watches him for a second, fighting the love that, in spite of her, responds to his appeal—then she springs up and runs to him—with fierce, possessive, maternal tenderness*) Come here to me, you great fool, and stop your silly blather. There's nothing to hate you for. There's nothing to forgive. Sure, I was only trying to give you happiness, because I love you. I'm sorry I was so stupid and didn't see— But I see now, and you'll find I have all the love you need. (*She gives him a hug and kisses him. There is passion in her kiss but it is a tender, protective maternal passion, which he responds to with an instant grateful yielding.*)

TYRONE—(*simply*) Thanks, Josie. You're beautiful. I love you. I knew you'd understand.

JOSIE—Of course I do. Come, now. (*She leads him back, her arm around his waist.*)

TYRONE—I didn't want to leave you. You know that.

JOSIE—Indeed I know it. Come now. We'll sit down. (*She sits on the top step and pulls him down on the step below her.*) That's it—with my arm around you. Now lay your head on my breast—the way you said you wanted to do— (*He lets his head fall back on her breast. She hugs him—gently*) There, now. Forget all about my being a fool and forgive— (*Her voice trembles—but she goes on determinedly.*) Forgive my selfishness, thinking only of myself. Sure, if there's one thing I owe you tonight, after all my lying and scheming, it's to give you the love you need, and it'll be my pride and my joy— (*forcing a trembling echo of her playful tone*) It's easy enough, too, for I have all kinds of love for you—and maybe this is the greatest of all—because it costs so much. (*She pauses, looking down at his face. He has closed his eyes and his haggard, dissipated face looks like a pale mask in the moonlight—at peace as a death mask is at peace. She becomes frightened.*) Jim! Don't look like that!

TYRONE—(*opens his eyes—vaguely*) Like what?

JOSIE—(*quickly*) It's the moonlight. It makes you look so pale, and with your eyes closed—

TYRONE—(*simply*) You mean I looked dead?

JOSIE—No! As if you'd fallen asleep.

TYRONE—(*speaks in a tired, empty tone, as if he felt he ought to explain something to her—something which no longer interests him*) Listen, and I'll tell you a little story, Josie. All my life I had just one dream. From the time I was a kid, I loved racehorses. I thought they were the most beautiful things in the world. I liked to gamble, too. So the big dream was that some day I'd have enough dough to play a cagey system of betting on favorites, and follow the horses south in the winter, and come back north with them in the spring, and be at the track every day. It seemed that would be the ideal life— for me. (*He pauses.*)

JOSIE—Well, you'll be able to do it.

TYRONE—No. I won't be able to do it, Josie. That's the joke. I gave it a try-out before I came up here. I borrowed some money on my share of the estate, and started going to tracks. But it didn't work. I played my system, but I found I didn't care if I won or lost. The horses were beautiful, but I found myself saying to myself, what of it? Their beauty didn't mean anything. I found that every day I was glad when the last race was over, and I could go back to the hotel—and the bottle in my room. (*He pauses, staring into the moonlight with vacant eyes.*)

JOSIE—(*uneasily*) Why did you tell me this?

TYRONE—(*in the same listless monotone*) You said I looked dead. Well, I am.

JOSIE—You're not! (*She hugs him protectively.*) Don't talk like that!

TYRONE—Ever since Mama died.

JOSIE—(*deeply moved—pityingly*) I know. I've felt all along it was that sorrow was making you— (*She pauses—gently*) Maybe if you talked about your grief for her, it would help you. I think it must be all choked up inside you, killing you.

TYRONE—(*in a strange warning tone*) You'd better look out, Josie.

JOSIE—Why?

TYRONE—(*quickly, forcing his cynical smile*) I might develop a crying jag, and sob on your beautiful breast.

JOSIE—(*gently*) You can sob all you like.

TYRONE—Don't encourage me. You'd be sorry. (*A deep conflict shows in his expression and tone. He is driven to go on in spite of himself.*) But if you're such a glutton for punishment— After all, I said I'd tell you later, didn't I?

JOSIE—(*puzzled*) You said you'd tell me about the blonde on the train.

TYRONE—She's part of it. I lied about that. (*He pauses—then blurts out sneeringly*) You won't believe it could have happened. Or if you did believe, you couldn't understand or forgive— (*quickly*) But you might. You're the one person who might. Because you really love me. And because you're the only woman I've ever met who understands the lousy rotten things a man can do when he's crazy drunk, and draws a blank—especially when he's nutty with grief to start with.

JOSIE—(*hugging him tenderly*) Of course I'll understand, Jim, darling.

TYRONE—(*stares into the moonlight—hauntedly*) But I didn't draw a blank. I tried to. I drank enough to knock out ten men. But it didn't work. I knew what I was doing. (*He pauses—dully*) No, I can't tell you, Josie. You'd loathe my guts, and I couldn't blame you.

JOSIE—No! I'll love you no matter what—

TYRONE—(*with strange triumphant harshness*) All right! Remember that's a promise! (*He pauses—starts to speak—pauses again.*)

JOSIE—(*pityingly*) Maybe you'd better not—if it will make you suffer.

TYRONE—Trying to welch now, eh? It's too late. You've got me started. Suffer? Christ, I ought to suffer! (*He pauses. Then he closes his eyes. It is as if he had to hide from sight before he can begin. He makes his face expressionless. His voice becomes impersonal and objective, as though what he told concerned some man he had known, but had nothing to do with him. This is the only way he can start telling the story.*) When Mama died, I'd been on the wagon for nearly two years. Not even a glass of beer. Honestly. And I know I would have stayed on. For her sake. She had no one but me. The Old Man was dead. My brother had married—had a kid—had his own life to live. She'd lost him. She had only me to attend to things for her and take care of her. She'd always hated my drinking. So I quit. It made me happy to do it. For her. Because she was all I had, all I cared about. Because I loved her. (*He pauses.*) No one would believe that now, who knew— But I did.

JOSIE—(*gently*) I know how much you loved her.

TYRONE—We went out to the Coast to see about selling a

piece of property the Old Man had bought there years ago. And one day she suddenly became ill. Got rapidly worse. Went into a coma. Brain tumor. The docs said, no hope. Might never come out of coma. I went crazy. Couldn't face losing her. The old booze yen got me. I got drunk and stayed drunk. And I began hoping she'd never come out of the coma, and see I was drinking again. That was my excuse, too—that she'd never know. And she never did. (*He pauses— then sneeringly*) Nix! Kidding myself again. I know damned well just before she died she recognized me. She saw I was drunk. Then she closed her eyes so she couldn't see, and was glad to die! (*He opens his eyes and stares into the moonlight as if he saw this deathbed scene before him.*)

JOSIE—(*soothingly*) Ssshh. You only imagine that because you feel guilty about drinking.

TYRONE—(*as if he hadn't heard, closes his eyes again*) After that, I kept so drunk I did draw a blank most of the time, but I went through the necessary motions and no one guessed how drunk— (*He pauses.*) But there are things I can never forget—the undertakers, and her body in a coffin with her face made up. I couldn't hardly recognize her. She looked young and pretty like someone I remembered meeting long ago. Practically a stranger. To whom I was a stranger. Cold and indifferent. Not worried about me any more. Free at last. Free from worry. From pain. From me. I stood looking down at her, and something happened to me. I found I couldn't feel anything. I knew I ought to be heartbroken but I couldn't feel anything. I seemed dead, too. I knew I ought to cry. Even a crying jag would look better than just standing there. But I couldn't cry. I cursed to myself, "You dirty bastard, it's Mama. You loved her, and now she's dead. She's gone away from you forever. Never, never again—" But it had no effect. All I did was try to explain to myself, "She's dead. What does she care now if I cry or not, or what I do? It doesn't matter a damn to her. She's happy to be where I can't hurt her ever again. She's rid of me at last. For God's sake, can't you leave her alone even now? For God's sake, can't you let her rest in peace?" (*He pauses—then sneeringly*) But there were several people around and I knew they expected me to show something. Once a ham, always a ham!

So I put on an act. I flopped on my knees and hid my face in my hands and faked some sobs and cried, "Mama! Mama! My dear mother!" But all the time I kept saying to myself, "You lousy ham! You God-damned lousy ham! Christ, in a minute you'll start singing 'Mother Macree'!" (*He opens his eyes and gives a tortured, sneering laugh, staring into the moonlight.*)

JOSIE — (*horrified, but still deeply pitying*) Jim! Don't! It's past. You've punished yourself. And you were drunk. You didn't mean—

TYRONE — (*again closes his eyes*) I had to bring her body East to be buried beside the Old Man. I took a drawing room and hid in it with a case of booze. She was in her coffin in the baggage car. No matter how drunk I got, I couldn't forget that for a minute. I found I couldn't stay alone in the drawing room. It became haunted. I was going crazy. I had to go out and wander up and down the train looking for company. I made such a public nuisance of myself that the conductor threatened if I didn't quit, he'd keep me locked in the drawing room. But I'd spotted one passenger who was used to drunks and could pretend to like them, if there was enough dough in it. She had parlor house written all over her—a blonde pig who looked more like a whore than twenty-five whores, with a face like an overgrown doll's and a come-on smile as cold as a polar bear's feet. I bribed the porter to take a message to her and that night she sneaked into my drawing room. She was bound for New York, too. So every night—for fifty bucks a night— (*He opens his eyes and now he stares torturedly through the moonlight into the drawing room.*)

JOSIE — (*her face full of revulsion—stammers*) Oh, how could you! (*Instinctively she draws away, taking her arms from around him.*)

TYRONE — How could I? I don't know. But I did. I suppose I had some mad idea she could make me forget—what was in the baggage car ahead.

JOSIE — Don't. (*She draws back again so he has to raise his head from her breast. He doesn't seem to notice this.*)

TYRONE — No, it couldn't have been that. Because I didn't seem to want to forget. It was like some plot I had to carry out. The blonde—she didn't matter. She was only something that belonged in the plot. It was as if I wanted revenge—because I'd been left alone—because I knew I was lost, without any hope left—that all I could do would be drink myself to death, because no one was left who could help me. (*His face hardens and a look of cruel vindictiveness comes into it—with a strange horrible satisfaction in his tone*) No, I didn't forget even in that pig's arms! I remembered the last two lines of a lousy tear-jerker song I'd heard when I was a kid kept singing over and over in my brain.

> "And baby's cries can't waken her
> In the baggage coach ahead."

JOSIE—(*distractedly*) Jim!

TYRONE—I couldn't stop it singing. I didn't want to stop it!

JOSIE—Jim! For the love of God. I don't want to hear!

TYRONE—(*after a pause—dully*) Well, that's all—except I was too drunk to go to her funeral.

JOSIE—Oh! (*She has drawn away from him as far as she can without getting up. He becomes aware of this for the first time and turns slowly to stare at her.*)

TYRONE—(*dully*) Don't want to touch me now, eh? (*He shrugs his shoulders mechanically.*) Sorry. I'm a damned fool. I shouldn't have told you.

JOSIE—(*her horror ebbing as her love and protective compassion returns—moves nearer him—haltingly*) Don't, Jim. Don't say—I don't want to touch you. It's—a lie. (*She puts a hand on his shoulder.*)

TYRONE—(*as if she hadn't spoken—with hopeless longing*) Wish I could believe in the spiritualists' bunk. If I could tell her it was because I missed her so much and couldn't forgive her for leaving me—

JOSIE—Jim! For the love of God—!

TYRONE—(*unheeding*) She'd understand and forgive me, don't you think? She always did. She was simple and kind and pure of heart. She was beautiful. You're like her deep in your heart. That's why I told you. I thought— (*Abruptly his expression becomes sneering and cynical—harshly*) My mistake. Nuts! Forget it. Time I got a move on. I don't like your damned moon, Josie. It's an ad for the past. (*He recites mockingly*)

"It is the very error of the moon:
She comes more nearer earth than she was wont,
And makes men mad."

(*He moves.*) I'll grab the last trolley for town. There'll be a speak open, and some drunk laughing. I need a laugh. (*He starts to get up.*)

JOSIE—(*throws her arms around him and pulls him back—tensely*) No! You won't go! I won't let you! (*She hugs him close—gently*) I understand now, Jim, darling, and I'm proud you came to me as the one in the world you know loves you enough to understand and forgive—and I do forgive!

TYRONE—(*lets his head fall back on her breast—simply*) Thanks, Josie. I knew you—

JOSIE—As *she* forgives, do you hear me! As *she* loves and understands and forgives!

TYRONE—(*simply*) Yes, I know she— (*His voice breaks.*)

JOSIE—(*bends over him with a brooding maternal tenderness*) That's right. Do what you came for, my darling. It isn't drunken laughter in a speakeasy you want to hear at all, but the sound of yourself crying your heart's repentance against her breast. (*His face is convulsed. He hides it on her breast and sobs rackingly. She hugs him more tightly and speaks softly, staring into the moonlight.*) She hears. I feel her in the moonlight, her soul wrapped in it like a silver mantle, and I know she understands and forgives me, too, and her blessing lies on me. (*A pause. His sobs begin to stop exhaustedly. She looks down at him again and speaks soothingly as she would to a child.*) There. There, now. (*He stops. She goes on in a gentle, bullying tone.*) You're a fine one, wanting to leave me when the night I promised I'd give you has just begun, our night that'll be different from all the others, with a dawn that won't creep over dirty windowpanes but will wake in the sky like a promise of God's peace in the soul's dark sadness. (*She smiles a little amused smile.*) Will you listen to me, Jim! I must be a poet. Who would have guessed it? Sure, love is a wonderful mad inspiration! (*A pause. She looks down. His eyes are closed. His face against her breast looks pale and haggard in the moonlight. Calm with the drained, exhausted peace of death. For a second she is frightened. Then she realizes and whispers softly*) Asleep. (*in a tender crooning tone like a lullaby*) That's right. Sleep in peace, my darling. (*then with sudden anguished longing*) Oh, Jim, Jim, maybe my love could still save you, if you could want it enough! (*She shakes her head.*) No. That can never be. (*Her eyes leave his face to stare up at the sky. She looks weary and stricken and sad. She forces a defensive, self-derisive smile.*) God forgive me, it's a fine end to all my scheming, to sit here with the dead hugged to my breast, and the silly mug of the moon grinning down, enjoying the joke!

(*Curtain*)

ACT FOUR

Scene—*Same as Act Three. It is dawn. The first faint streaks of color, heralding the sunrise, appear in the eastern sky at left.*

Josie sits in the same position on the steps, as if she had not moved, her arms around Tyrone. He is still asleep, his head on her breast. His face has the same exhausted, death-like repose. Josie's face is set in an expression of numbed, resigned sadness. Her body sags tiredly. In spite of her strength, holding herself like this for hours, for fear of waking him, is becoming too much for her.

The two make a strangely tragic picture in the wan dawn light—this big sorrowful woman hugging a haggard-faced, middle-aged drunkard against her breast, as if he were a sick child.

Hogan appears at left-rear, coming from the barn. He approaches the corner of the house stealthily on tiptoe. Wisps of hay stick to his clothes and his face is swollen and sleepy, but his little pig's eyes are sharply wide awake and sober. He peeks around the corner, and takes in the two on the steps. His eyes fix on Josie's face in a long, probing stare.

Josie—(*speaks in a low grim tone*) Stop hiding, Father. I heard you sneak up. (*He comes guiltily around the corner. She keeps her voice low, but her tone is commanding.*) Come here, and be quiet about it. (*He obeys meekly, coming as far as the boulder silently, his eyes searching her face, his expression becoming guilty and miserable at what he sees. She goes on in the same tone, without looking at him.*) Talk low, now. I don't want him wakened— (*She adds strangely*) Not until the dawn has beauty in it.

Hogan—(*worriedly*) What? (*He decides it's better for the present to ask no questions. His eyes fall on Tyrone's face. In spite of himself, he is startled—in an awed, almost frightened whisper*) Be God, he looks dead!

Josie—(*strangely*) Why wouldn't he? He is.

Hogan—Is?

Josie—Don't be a fool. Can't you see him breathing? Dead asleep, I mean. Don't stand there gawking. Sit down. (*He sits meekly on the boulder. His face betrays a guilty dread of what is coming. There is a pause in which she doesn't look at him, but he keeps glancing at her, growing visibly more uneasy. She speaks bitterly.*) Where's your witnesses?

HOGAN—(*guiltily*) Witnesses? (*then forcing an amused grin*) Oh, be God, if that ain't a joke on me! Sure, I got so blind drunk at the Inn I forgot all about our scheme and came home and went to sleep in the hayloft.

JOSIE—(*her expression harder and more bitter*) You're a liar.

HOGAN—I'm not. I just woke up. Look at the hay sticking to me. That's proof.

JOSIE—I'm not thinking of that, and well you know it. (*with bitter voice*) So you just woke up—did you?—and then came sneaking here to see if the scheme behind your scheme had worked!

HOGAN—(*guiltily*) I don't know what you mean.

JOSIE—Don't lie any more, Father. This time, you've told one too many. (*He starts to defend himself but the look on her face makes him think better of it and he remains uneasily silent. A pause.*)

HOGAN—(*finally has to blurt out*) Sure, if I'd brought the witnesses, there's nothing for them to witness that—

JOSIE—No. You're right, there. There's nothing. Nothing at all. (*She smiles strangely.*) Except a great miracle they'd never believe, or you either.

HOGAN—What miracle?

JOSIE—A virgin who bears a dead child in the night, and the dawn finds her still a virgin. If that isn't a miracle, what is?

HOGAN—(*uneasily*) Stop talking so queer. You give me the shivers. (*He attempts a joking tone.*) Is it you who's the virgin? Faith, that *would* be a miracle, no less! (*He forces a chuckle.*)

JOSIE—I told you to stop lying, Father.

HOGAN—What lie? (*He stops and watches her face worriedly. She is silent, as if she were not aware of him now. Her eyes are fixed on the wanton sky.*)

JOSIE—(*as if to herself*) It'll be beautiful soon, and I can wake him.

HOGAN—(*can't retain his anxiety any longer*) Josie, darlin'! For the love of God, can't you tell me what happened to you?

JOSIE—(*her face hard and bitter again*) I've told you once. Nothing.

HOGAN—Nothing? If you could see the sadness in your face—

JOSIE—What woman doesn't sorrow for the man she loved who has died? But there's pride in my heart, too.

HOGAN—(*tormentedly*) Will you stop talking as if you'd gone mad in the night! (*raising his voice—with revengeful anger*) Listen to me! If Jim Tyrone has done anything to bring you sorrow— (*Tyrone stirs in his sleep and moans, pressing his face against her breast as if for protection. She looks down at him and hugs him close.*)

JOSIE—(*croons softly*) There, there, my darling. Rest in peace a while longer. (*turns on her father angrily and whispers*) Didn't I tell you to speak low and not wake him! (*She pauses—then quietly*) He did nothing to bring me sorrow. It was my mistake. I thought there was still hope. I didn't know he'd died already—that it was a damned soul coming to me in the moonlight, to confess and be forgiven and find peace for a night—

HOGAN—Josie! Will you stop!

JOSIE—(*after a pause—dully*) He'd never do anything to hurt me. You know it. (*self-mockingly*) Sure, hasn't he told me I'm beautiful to him and he loves me—in his fashion. (*then matter-of-factly*) All that happened was that he got drunk and he had one of his crazy notions he wanted to sleep the way he is, and I let him sleep. (*with forced roughness*) And, be God, the night's over. I'm half dead with tiredness and sleepiness. It's that you see in my face, not sorrow.

HOGAN—Don't try to fool me, Josie. I—

JOSIE—(*her face hard and bitter—grimly*) Fool you, is it? It's you who made a fool of me with your lies, thinking you'd use me to get your dirty greasy paws on the money he'll have!

HOGAN—No! I swear by all the saints—

JOSIE—You'd swear on a Bible while you were stealing it! (*grimly*) Listen to me, Father. I didn't call you here to answer questions about what's none of your business. I called you here to tell you I've seen through all the lies you told last night to get me to— (*as he starts to speak*) Shut up! I'll do the talking now. You weren't drunk. You were only putting it on as part of your scheme—

HOGAN—(*quietly*) I wasn't drunk, no. I admit that, Josie.

But I'd had slews of drinks and they were in my head or I'd
never have the crazy dreams—

JOSIE—(*with biting scorn*) Dreams, is it? The only dream
you've ever had, or will have, is of yourself counting a fistful
of dirty money, and divil a care how you got it, or who you
robbed or made suffer!

HOGAN—(*winces—pleadingly*) Josie!

JOSIE—Shut up. (*scathingly*) I'm sure you've made up a
whole new set of lies and excuses. You're that cunning and
clever, but you can save your breath. They wouldn't fool me
now. I've been fooled once too often. (*He gives her a frightened look, as if something he had dreaded has happened. She goes
on, grimly accusing.*) You lied about Jim selling the farm. You
knew he was kidding. You knew the estate would be out of
probate in a few days, and he'd go back to Broadway, and
you had to do something quick or you'd lose the last chance
of getting your greedy hooks on his money.

HOGAN—(*miserably*) No. It wasn't that, Josie.

JOSIE—You saw how hurt and angry I was because he'd
kept me waiting here, and you used that. You knew I loved
him and wanted him and you used that. You used all you
knew about me— Oh, you did it clever! You ought to be
proud! You worked it so it was me who did all the dirty
scheming— You knew I'd find out from Jim you'd lied
about the farm, but not before your lie had done its work—
made me go after him, get him drunk, get drunk myself so I
could be shameless—and when the truth did come out,
wouldn't it make me love him all the more and be more
shameless and willing? Don't tell me you didn't count on
that, and you such a clever schemer! And if he once had me,
knowing I was a virgin, didn't you count on his honor and
remorse, and his loving me in his fashion, to make him offer
to marry me? Sure, why wouldn't he, you thought. It
wouldn't hold him. He'd go back to Broadway just the same
and never see me again. But there'd be money in it, and
when he'd finished killing himself, I'd be his legal widow
and get what's left.

HOGAN—(*miserably*) No! It wasn't that.

JOSIE—But what's the good of talking? It's all over. I've
only one more word for you, Father, and it's this: I'm leaving

you today, like my brothers left. You can live alone and work alone your cunning schemes on yourself.

HOGAN—(*after a pause—slowly*) I knew you'd be bitter against me, Josie, but I took the chance you'd be so happy you wouldn't care how—

JOSIE—(*as if she hadn't heard, looking at the eastern sky which is now glowing with color*) Thank God, it's beautiful. It's time. (*to Hogan*) Go in the house and stay there till he's gone. I don't want you around to start some new scheme. (*He looks miserable, starts to speak, thinks better of it, and meekly tiptoes past her up the steps and goes in, closing the door quietly after him. She looks down at Tyrone. Her face softens with a maternal tenderness—sadly*) I hate to bring you back to life, Jim, darling. If you could have died in your sleep, that's what you would have liked, isn't it? (*She gives him a gentle shake.*) Wake up, Jim. (*He moans in his sleep and presses more closely against her. She stares at his face.*) Dear God, let him remember that one thing and forget the rest. That will be enough for me. (*She gives him a more vigorous shake.*) Jim! Wake up, do you hear? It's time.

TYRONE—(*half wakens without opening his eyes—mutters*) What the hell? (*dimly conscious of a woman's body—cynically*) Again, eh? Same old stuff. Who the hell are you, sweetheart? (*irritably*) What's the big idea, waking me up? What time is it?

JOSIE—It's dawn.

TYRONE—(*still without opening his eyes*) Dawn? (*He quotes drowsily*)

"But I was desolate and sick of an old passion,
    When I awoke and found the dawn was gray."

(*then with a sneer*) They're all gray. Go to sleep, Kid—and let me sleep. (*He falls asleep again.*)

JOSIE—(*tensely*) This one isn't gray, Jim. It's different from all the others— (*She sees he is asleep—bitterly*) He'll have forgotten. He'll never notice. And I'm the whore on the train to him now, not— (*Suddenly she pushes him away from her and shakes him roughly.*) Will you wake up, for God's sake! I've had all I can bear—

TYRONE—(*still half asleep*) Hey! Cut out the rough stuff, Kid. What? (*awake now, blinking his eyes—with dazed surprise*) Josie.

JOSIE—(*still bitter*) That's who, and none of your damned tarts! (*She pushes him.*) Get up now, so you won't fall asleep again. (*He does so with difficulty, still in a sleepy daze, his body stiff and cramped. She conquers her bitter resentment and puts on her old free-and-easy kidding tone with him, but all the time waiting to see how much he will remember.*) You're stiff and cramped, and no wonder. I'm worse from holding you, if that's any comfort. (*She stretches and rubs her numbed arms, groaning comically.*) Holy Joseph, I'm a wreck entirely. I'll never be the same. (*giving him a quick glance*) You look as if you'd drawn a blank and were wondering how you got here. I'll bet you don't remember a thing.

TYRONE—(*moving his arms and legs gingerly—sleepily*) I don't know. Wait till I'm sure I'm still alive.

JOSIE—You need an eye-opener. (*She picks up the bottle and glass and pours him a drink.*) Here you are.

TYRONE—(*takes the glass mechanically*) Thanks, Josie. (*He goes and sits on the boulder, holding the drink as if he had no interest in it.*)

JOSIE—(*watching him*) Drink up or you'll be asleep again.

TYRONE—No, I'm awake now, Josie. Funny. Don't seem to want a drink. Oh, I've got a head all right. But no heebie-jeebies—yet.

JOSIE—That's fine. It must be a pleasant change—

TYRONE—It is. I've got a nice, dreamy peaceful hangover for once—as if I'd had a sound sleep without nightmares.

JOSIE—So you did. Divil a nightmare. I ought to know. Wasn't I holding you and keeping them away?

TYRONE—You mean you— (*suddenly*) Wait a minute. I remember now I was sitting alone at a table in the Inn, and I suddenly had a crazy notion I'd come up here and sleep with my head on your— So that's why I woke up in your arms. (*shamefacedly*) And you let me get away with it. You're a nut, Josie.

JOSIE—Oh, I didn't mind.

TYRONE—You must have seen how blotto I was, didn't you?

JOSIE—I did. You were as full as a tick.

TYRONE—Then why didn't you give me the bum's rush?

JOSIE—Why would I? I was glad to humor you.

TYRONE—For God's sake, how long was I cramped on you like that?

JOSIE—Oh, a few hours, only.

TYRONE—God, I'm sorry Josie, but it's your own fault for letting me—

JOSIE—Och, don't be apologizing. I was glad of the excuse to stay awake and enjoy the beauty of the moon.

TYRONE—Yes, I can remember what a beautiful night it was.

JOSIE—Can you? I'm glad of that, Jim. You seemed to enjoy it the while we were sitting here together before you fell asleep.

TYRONE—How long a while was that?

JOSIE—Not long. Less than an hour, anyway.

TYRONE—I suppose I bored the hell out of you with a lot of drunken drivel.

JOSIE—Not a lot, no. But some. You were full of blarney, saying how beautiful I was to you.

TYRONE—(*earnestly*) That wasn't drivel, Josie. You were. You are. You always will be.

JOSIE—You're a wonder, Jim. Nothing can stop you, can it? Even me in the light of dawn, looking like something you'd put in the field to scare the crows from the corn. You'll kid at the Day of Judgment.

TYRONE—(*impatiently*) You know damned well it isn't kidding. You're not a fool. You can tell.

JOSIE—(*kiddingly*) All right, then, I'm beautiful and you love me—in your fashion.

TYRONE—"In my fashion," eh? Was I reciting poetry to you? That must have been hard to take.

JOSIE—It wasn't. I liked it. It was all about beautiful nights and the romance of the moon.

TYRONE—Well, there was some excuse for that, anyway. It sure was a beautiful night. I'll never forget it.

JOSIE—I'm glad, Jim.

TYRONE—What other bunk did I pull on you—or I mean, did old John Barleycorn pull?

JOSIE—Not much. You were mostly quiet and sad—in a kind of daze, as if the moon was in your wits as well as whiskey.

TYRONE—I remember I was having a grand time at the Inn, celebrating with Phil, and then suddenly, for no reason, all the fun went out of it, and I was more melancholy than ten Hamlets. (*He pauses.*) Hope I didn't tell you the sad story of my life and weep on your bosom, Josie.

JOSIE—You didn't. The one thing you talked a lot about was that you wanted the night with me to be different from all the other nights you'd spent with women.

TYRONE—(*with revulsion*) God, don't make me think of those tramps now! (*then with deep, grateful feeling*) It sure was different, Josie. I may not remember much, but I know how different it was from the way I feel now. None of my usual morning-after stuff—the damned sick remorse that makes you wish you'd died in your sleep so you wouldn't have to face the rotten things you're afraid you said and did the night before, when you were so drunk you didn't know what you were doing.

JOSIE—There's nothing you said or did last night for you to regret. You can take my word for it.

TYRONE—(*as if he hadn't heard—slowly*) It's hard to describe how I feel. It's a new one on me. Sort of at peace with myself and this lousy life—as if all my sins had been forgiven— (*He becomes self-conscious—cynically*) Nuts with that sin bunk, but you know what I mean.

JOSIE—(*tensely*) I do, and I'm happy you feel that way, Jim. (*A pause. She goes on.*) You talked about how you'd watched too many dawns come creeping grayly over dirty windowpanes, with some tart snoring beside you—

TYRONE—(*winces*) Have a heart. Don't remind me of that now, Josie. Don't spoil this dawn! (*A pause. She watches him tensely. He turns slowly to face the east, where the sky is now glowing with all the colors of an exceptionally beautiful sunrise. He stares, drawing a deep breath. He is profoundly moved but immediately becomes self-conscious and tries to sneer it off—cynically*) God seems to be putting on quite a display. I like Belasco better. Rise of curtain, Act-Four stuff. (*Her face has fallen into lines of bitter hurt, but he adds quickly and angrily*) God damn it! Why do I have to pull that lousy stuff? (*with genuine deep feeling*) God, it's beautiful, Josie! I—I'll never forget it—here with you.

JOSIE—(*her face clearing—simply*) I'm glad, Jim. I was hoping you'd feel beauty in it—by way of a token.

TYRONE—(*watching the sunrise—mechanically*) Token of what?

JOSIE—Oh, I don't know. Token to me that—never mind. I forget what I meant. (*abruptly changing the subject*) Don't think I woke you just to admire the sunrise. You're on a farm, not Broadway, and it's time for me to start work, not go to bed. (*She gets to her feet and stretches. There is a growing strain behind her free-and-easy manner.*) And that's a hint, Jim. I can't stay entertaining you. So go back to the Inn, that's a good boy. I know you'll understand the reason, and not think I'm tired of your company. (*She forces a smile.*)

TYRONE—(*gets up*) Of course, I understand. (*He pauses— then blurts out guiltily*) One more question. You're sure I didn't get out of order last night—and try to make you, or anything like that.

JOSIE—You didn't. You kidded back when I kidded you, the way we always do. That's all.

TYRONE—Thank God for that. I'd never forgive myself if—I wouldn't have asked you except I've pulled some pretty rotten stuff when I was drawing a blank. (*He becomes conscious of the forgotten drink he has in his hand.*) Well, I might as well drink this. The bar at the Inn won't be open for hours. (*He drinks—then looks pleasantly surprised.*) I'll be damned! That isn't Phil's rotgut. That's real, honest-to-God bonded Bourbon. Where— (*This clicks in his mind and suddenly he remembers everything and Josie sees that he does. The look of guilt and shame and anguish settles over his face. Instinctively he throws the glass away, his first reaction one of loathing for the drink which brought back memory. He feels Josie staring at him and fights desperately to control his voice and expression.*) Real Bourbon. I remember now you said a bootlegger gave it to Phil. Well, I'll run along and let you do your work. See you later, Josie. (*He turns toward the road.*)

JOSIE—(*strickenly*) No! Don't, Jim! Don't go like that! You won't see me later. You'll never see me again now, and I know that's best for us both, but I can't bear to have you ashamed you wanted my love to comfort your sorrow—when I'm so proud I could give it. (*pleadingly*) I hoped, for your sake, you wouldn't remember, but now you do, I want you to remember my love for you gave you peace for a while.

TYRONE—(*stares at her, fighting with himself. He stammers defensively*) I don't know what you're talking about. I don't remember—

JOSIE—(*sadly*) All right, Jim. Neither do I then. Good-bye, and God bless you. (*She turns as if to go up the steps into the house.*)

TYRONE—(*stammers*) Wait, Josie! (*coming to her*) I'm a liar! I'm a louse! Forgive me, Josie. I do remember! I'm glad I remember! I'll never forget your love! (*He kisses her on the lips.*) Never! (*kissing her again*) Never, do you hear! I'll always love you, Josie. (*He kisses her again.*) Good-bye—and God bless you! (*He turns away and walks quickly down the road off left without looking back. She stands, watching him go, for a moment, then she puts her hands over her face, her head bent, and sobs. Hogan comes out of her room and stands on top of the steps. He looks after Tyrone and his face is hard with bitter anger.*)

JOSIE—(*sensing his presence, stops crying and lifts her head—dully*) I'll get your breakfast in a minute, Father.

HOGAN—To hell with my breakfast! I'm not a pig that has no other thought but eating! (*then pleadingly*) Listen, darlin'. All you said about my lying and scheming, and what I hoped would happen, is true. But it wasn't his money, Josie. I did see it was the last chance—the only one left to bring the two of you to stop your damned pretending, and face the truth that you loved each other. I wanted you to find happiness— by hook or crook, one way or another, what did I care how? I wanted to save him, and I hoped he'd see that only your love could— It was his talk of the beauty he saw in you that made me hope— And I knew he'd never go to bed with you even if you'd let him unless he married you. And if I gave a thought to his money at all, that was the least of it, and why shouldn't I want to have you live in ease and comfort for a change, like you deserve, instead of in this shanty on a lousy farm, slaving for me? (*He pauses—miserably*) Can't you believe that's the truth, Josie, and not feel so bitter against me?

JOSIE—(*her eyes still following Tyrone—gently*) I know it's the truth, Father. I'm not bitter now. Don't be afraid I'm going to leave you. I only said it to punish you for a while.

HOGAN—(*with humble gratitude*) Thank God for that, darlin'.

JOSIE—(*forces a teasing smile and a little of her old manner*) A ginger-haired, crooked old goat like you to be playing Cupid!

HOGAN—(*His face lights up joyfully. He is almost himself again—ruefully*) You had me punished, that's sure. I was thinking after you'd gone I'd drown myself in Harder's ice pond. There was this consolation in it, I knew that the bastard would never look at a piece of ice again without remembering me. (*She doesn't hear this. Her thoughts are on the receding figure of Tyrone again. Hogan looks at her sad face worriedly—gently*) Don't, darlin'. Don't be hurting yourself. (*Then as she still doesn't hear, he puts on his old, fuming irascible tone.*) Are you going to moon at the sunrise forever, and me with the sides of my stomach knocking together?

JOSIE—(*gently*) Don't worry about me, Father. It's over now. I'm not hurt. I'm only sad for him.

HOGAN—For him? (*He bursts out in a fit of smoldering rage.*) May the blackest curse from the pit of hell—

JOSIE—(*with an anguished cry*) Don't, Father! I love him!

HOGAN—(*subsides, but his face looks sorrowful and old—dully*) I didn't mean it. I know whatever happened he meant no harm to you. It was life I was cursing— (*with a trace of his natural manner*) And, be God, that's a waste of breath, if it does deserve it. (*then as she remains silent—miserably*) Or maybe I was cursing myself for a damned old scheming fool, like I ought to.

JOSIE—(*turns to him, forcing a teasing smile*) Look out. I might say Amen to that. (*gently*) Don't be sad, Father. I'm all right—and I'm well content here with you. (*forcing her teasing manner again*) Sure, living with you has spoilt me for any other man, anyway. There'd never be the same fun or excitement.

HOGAN—(*plays up to this—in his fuming manner*) There'll be excitement if I don't get my breakfast soon, but it won't be fun, I'm warning you!

JOSIE—(*forcing her usual reaction to his threats*) Och, don't be threatening me, you bad-tempered old tick. Let's go in the house and I'll get your damned breakfast.

HOGAN—Now you're talking. (*He goes in the house through her room. She follows him as far as the door—then turns for a last look down the road.*)

JOSIE—(*her face sad, tender and pitying—gently*) May you have your wish and die in your sleep soon, Jim, darling. May you rest forever in forgiveness and peace. (*She turns slowly and goes into the house.*)

(*Curtain*)

Tomorrow

IT WAS back in my sailor days, in the winter of my great down-and-outness, that all this happened. In those years of wandering, to be broke and "on the beach" in some seaport or other of the world was no new experience; but this had been an unusually long period of inaction even for me. Six months before I had landed in New York after a voyage from Buenos Aires as able seaman on a British tramp. Since that time I had loafed around the water front, eking out an existence on a small allowance from my family, too lazy of body and mind, too indifferent to things in general, to ship to sea again or do anything else. I shared a small rear room with another "gentleman-ranker," Jimmy Anderson, an old friend of mine, over an all-night dive near South street known as Tommy the Priest's.

This is the story of Jimmy, my roommate, and it begins on a cold night in the early part of March. I had waited in Tommy the Priest's, hunched up on a chair near the stove in the back room, all the late afternoon until long after dark. My nerves were on edge as a result of a two days' carouse ensuing on the receipt of my weekly allowance. Now all that money was gone—over the bar—and the next few days gloomed up as a dreary, sober and hungry ordeal which must, barring miracles, be endured patiently or otherwise. Three or four others of the crowd I knew were sitting near me, equally sick and penniless. We stared gloomily before us, in listless attitudes, spitting dejectedly at the glowing paunch of the stove. Every now and then someone would come in bringing with him a chill of the freezing wind outside. We would all look up hopefully. No, only a stranger. Nothing in the way of hospitality to be expected from him. "Close that damned door!" we would growl in chorus and huddle closer to the stove, shivering, muttering disappointed curses. In mocking contrast the crowd at the bar were drinking, singing, arguing in each other's ears with loud, care-free voices. None of them noticed our existence.

Surely a bad night for Good Samaritans, I thought, and reflected with bitterness that I counted several in that jubilant throng who had eagerly accepted my favors of the two nights previous. Now they saw me and nodded—but that was all. Suddenly sick with human ingratitude, I got out of my chair and, grumbling a surly "good-night, all" to the others, went out the side door and up the rickety stairs to our room— Jimmy's and mine.

The thought of spending a long evening alone in the room seemed intolerable to me. I lit the lamp and glanced around angrily. A fine hole! The two beds took up nearly all the space but Jimmy had managed to cram in, in front of the window, a small table on which stood his dilapidated typewriter. The typewriter, of course, was broken and wouldn't work. Jimmy was always going to have it fixed—tomorrow. But then Jimmy lived in a dream of tomorrows; and nothing he was ever associated with ever worked.

The lamp on the table threw a stream of light through the dirty window, revealing the fire-escape outside. Inside, on a shelf along the windowsill, a dyspeptic geranium plant sulked in a small red pot. This plant was Jimmy's garden and his joy. Even when he was too sick to wash his own face he never forgot to water it the first thing after getting up. It goes without saying, the silly thing never bloomed. Nothing that Jimmy loved ever bloomed; but he always hoped, in fact he was quite sure, it would eventually blossom out—in the dawn of some vague tomorrow.

For me it had value only as a symbol of Jimmy's everlasting futility, of his irritating inefficiency. However, at that period in my life, all flowers were yellow primroses and nothing more, and Jimmy's pet was out of place, I thought, and in the way.

Books were piled on the floor against the walls—and what books! Where Jimmy got them and what for, God only knows. He never read them, except a few pages at haphazard to put him to sleep. Yet there must have been fifty at least cluttering up the room—books about history, about journalism, about economics—books of impossible poetry and incredible prose, written by unknown authors and published by firms one had never heard of. He had a craze for buying them and never failed, on the days he was paid for the odd bits of work he did as occasional stenographer for a theatrical booking firm, to stagger weakly into Tommy's, very drunk, with two or three of these unreadable volumes clutched to his breast—books with titles like: "A Commentary on the Bulls of Pope Leo XIII," or "God and the Darwinian Theory" by John Jones, or "Sunflowers and Other Verses" by Lydia Smith. Think of it!

I used to grow wild with rage as I watched him showing them to Tommy, or Big John, if he was on, or to anyone else who would look and listen, with all the besotted pride in the world. I would think of the drinks and the food—kippered herring and bread and good Italian cheese—he might have purchased for the price of these dull works; and I would swear to myself to thrash him good and hard if he even dared to speak to me.

And then—Jimmy would come and lay his idiotic books on my table and I would look up at him furiously; and there he would stand, wavering a bit, smiling his sweet, good-natured smile, trying to force half his remaining change into my hand, his lonely, wistful eyes watching me with the appealing look of a lost dog hungry for an affectionate pat. What could I do but laugh and love him and show him I did by a slap on the back or in some small way or another? It was worth while forgetting all the injuries in the world just to see the light of gratitude shine up in his eyes.

This night I am speaking of I picked up one of the books in desperation and lay down to read with the lamp at the head of the bed; but I couldn't concentrate. I was too sick in body, brain, and soul to follow even the words.

I threw the book aside and lay on my back staring gloomily at the ceiling. The inmate of the next room, a broken-down telegrapher—"the Lunger" we used to call him—had a violent attack of coughing which seemed to be tearing his chest to pieces. I shuddered. He used to spit blood in the back room below. In fact, when drunk, he was quite proud of this achievement, but grew terrified at all allusions to consumption and wildly insisted that he only had "bloody bronchitis," and that he was getting better every day. He died soon after in that same room next to ours. Perhaps his treatment was at fault. A quart and a half of five-cent whiskey a day and only a plate of free soup at noon to eat is hardly a diet conducive to the cure of any disease—not even "bloody bronchitis."

He coughed and coughed until, in a frenzy of tortured nerves, I yelled to him: "For God's sake, shut up!" Then he subsided into a series of groans and querulous, choking complaints. I thought of consumption, the danger of contagion, and remembered that the window ought to be open. But it was too cold. Besides, what was the difference? "Con" or something else, today or tomorrow, it was all the same—the end. What did I care? I had failed—or rather I had never cared enough about it all to want to succeed.

I must have dozed for I came to with a nervous jump to find the lamp sputtering and smoking and the light growing dimmer every minute. No oil! That fool Jimmy had promised to brink back some. I had given him my last twenty cents and he had taken the can with him. He was sober, had been for almost a week, was suffering from one of his infrequent and brief efforts at reformation. No, there was no excuse. I cursed him viciously for the greatest imbecile on earth. The lamp was going out. I would have to lie in darkness or return to the misery of the back room downstairs.

Just then I recognized his step on the stairs and a moment later he came in, bringing the oil. I glared at him. "Where've you been?" I shouted. "Look at that lamp, you idiot! I'd have been in the dark in another second."

Jimmy came forward shrinkingly, a look of deep hurt in his faded blue eyes. He murmured something about "office" and stooped down to fill the lamp.

"Office!" I taunted scornfully, "what office? What do you take me for? I've heard that bunk of yours a million times."

Jimmy finished filling the lamp and sat down on the side of his bed opposite me. He didn't answer; only stared at me with an irritating sort of compassionate pity. How prim he was sitting there is his black suit, wispy, grey hair combed over his bald spot, his jowly face scraped close and chalky with too much cheap powder, the vile odor of which filled the room. I noticed for the first time his clean collar, his fresh shirt. He must have been to the Chinaman's and retrieved part of his laundry. This was what he usually did when he had a windfall of a dollar or so from some unexpected source. Never took out all his laundry. That would have been too expensive. Just called at the Chink's and changed his shirt and collar. His other articles of clothing he washed himself at the sink in the hallway.

I eyed him up and down resentfully. Here was a man who ought always to remain drunk. Sober, he was a respectable nuisance. And his shoes were shined!

"Why the profound meditation?" I asked. "You'd think, to look at you, you were sitting up with my corpse. Cheer up! I feel bad enough without your adding to the gloom."

"That's just it, Art," he began in slow, doleful tones. "I hate to see you in this condition. You wouldn't ever feel this way if you'd—only—only—" he hesitated as he saw my sneer.

"Only what?" I urged.

"Only stop your hard drinking," he mumbled, avoiding my eyes.

"This is almost too much, Jimmy. The water wagon is fatal to your sense of humor. After a week's ride you've accumulated more cheap moralizing than any anchorite in all his years of fasting."

"I'm your friend," he blundered on, "and you know it, Art—or I wouldn't say it."

"And it hurts you more than it does me, I'll bet!"

Jimmy had the piqued air of the rebuffed but well-intentioned. "If that's the way you want to take it—" he was staring unhappily at the floor. We were silent for a time. Then he continued with the obstinacy of the reformed turned reformer: "I'm your friend, the best friend you've got." His eyes looked up into mine and his glance was timidly questioning. "You know that, don't you, Art?"

All my peevishness vanished in a flash before his woeful sincerity. I reached over and grabbed his hand—his white, pudgy little hand so in keeping with the rest of him—warm and soft. "Of course I know it, Jimmy. Don't be foolish and take what I've said seriously. I've got a full-sized grouch against everything tonight."

Jimmy brightened up and cleared his throat. He evidently

thought my remarks an expression of willingness to serve as audience for his temperance lecture. Still he hesitated politely. "I know you don't want to listen—"

I laughed shortly. "Go ahead. Shoot. I'm all ears."

Then he began. You know the sort of drool—introduced by a sage wag of the head and the inevitable remark: "I've been through it all myself, and I know." I won't bore you with it. Coming from Jimmy it was the last word in absurdity.

I tried not to listen, concentrating my mind on the man himself, my nerves soothed by the monotonous flow of his soft-voiced syllables. Yes, he'd been through it all, there was no doubt of that, from soup to nuts. What he didn't realize was that none of it had ever touched him deeply. Forgetful of the last kick his eyes had always looked up at life again with the same appealing, timid uncertainty, pleading for a caress, fearful of a blow. And life had never failed to deal him the expected kick, never a vicious one, more of a shove to get him out of the way of a spirited boot at someone who really mattered. Spurned, Jimmy had always returned, affectionate, uncomprehending, wagging his tail ingratiatingly, so to speak. The longed-for caress would come, he was sure of it, if not today, then tomorrow. Ah, tomorrow!

I looked searchingly at his face—the squat nose, the wistful eyes, the fleshy cheeks hanging down like dewlaps on either side of his weak mouth with its pale, thick lips. The usual marks of dissipation were there but none of the scars of intense suffering. The whole effect was characterless, unfinished; as if some sculptor at the last moment had suddenly lost interest in his clay model of a face and abandoned his work in disgust. I wondered what Jimmy would do if he ever saw that face in the clear, cruel mirror of Truth. Straggle on in the same lost way, no doubt, and cease to have faith in mirrors.

Although most of his lecture was being lost on me I couldn't prevent a chance word now and then from seeping into my consciousness. "Wasted youth—your education—ability—a shame—lost opportunity—drink—some nice girl"— these words my ears retained against my will, and each word had a sting to it. Gradually my feeling of kindliness toward

Jimmy petered out. I began to hate him for a pestiferous little crank. What right had he to meddle with my sins? Some of the things he was saying were true; and truth—that kind of truth—should be seen and not heard.

I was becoming angry enough to shrivel him up with some contemptuous remark about his hypocrisy and the doubtful duration of time he would stay on the wagon when he suddenly disgressed from my misdeeds and began virtuously holding himself up as a horrible example.

He began at the beginning, and, even though I welcomed the change of subject, I swore inwardly at the prospect of hearing the history of his life all over again. He had told me this tale at least fifty times while in all stages of maudlin drunkenness. Usually he wept—which was sometimes funny and sometimes not, depending on my own condition. At all events it would be a novelty to hear his sober version. I might get at some facts this time.

To my surprise this story seemed to be identical with the others I had been lulled to sleep by on so many nights. Making allowances for the natural exaggeration of one in liquor, there was but little difference. It started with the Anderson estate in Scotland where Jimmy had spent his boyhood. This estate of the family extended over the greater part of a Scotch county, so Jimmy claimed, and he was touchy when anyone seemed skeptical regarding its existence.

He loved to dilate on the beauty of the country, the old manor house, the farms, the game park, and all the rest of it. All this was heavily mortgaged, he admitted; and he was not in good standing with most of his relatives on the other side; but he declared that there was one aunt, far gone in years and hoarded wealth, who still treasured his memory, and he promised all the gang in the back room a rare blowout should the old lady pass away in the proper frame of mind. To all of this the crowd would listen with an amiable pretence of belief. For, after all, he was Jimmy and they all swore by him, and a fairy tale like that is no great matter to hold against a man.

But here he was spinning the same yarn in all its details! I looked at him suspiciously. No, he was certainly stone sober. Could there be any truth in it then? Impossible. I finally concluded that Jimmy, after the fashion of liars, had ended by mistaking his own fabrications for fact.

He continued on through his years in Edinburgh University, his graduation with honors, his going into journalism first in Scotland, then in England, afterwards as a correspondent on the Continent, and finally his work in South Africa during the Boer War as representative of some news service.

I had never been able to verify any of this except that relating to the Boer War. An old friend of his had once told me that Jimmy did hold a responsible position in South Africa during the war and had received a large salary. Then the old friend, old-friendlike, shook his head gravely and muttered: "Too bad! Too bad! Drink!" Whether the rest of Jimmy's life, as related by him, had ever been lived or not hardly mattered, I thought. Undoubtedly he had been well educated and what is called a gentleman over there. Of course the Anderson estate was a work of fiction, or, at best, a glorified country house.

"And mind you, Art, up to that time," Jimmy's story had reached the point where he was at the front in South Africa for the news service company, "I had never touched a drop except a glass of wine with dinner now and again. That was ten years ago and I was thirty-five. Then—something happened. Ten years," he repeated sadly, "and now look where I am!" He stared despondently before him for a moment, then brightened up and squared his bent shoulders. "But that's all past and gone now, and I'm through with this kind of life for good and all."

"There's always tomorrow," I ventured ironically.

"Yes, and I'm going to make the most of it." His eyes were bright with the dream of a new hope; or rather, the old hope eternally redreamed. He glanced at the table. "I'll have to have that typewriter fixed up."

"Tomorrow?"

"Yes, tomorrow, if I can spare the time." He hadn't noticed my sarcasm.

"Why, is your day all taken up?" I asked, marvelling at his imagination.

"Pretty well so." He put on an air of importance. "I saw Edwards today"—Edwards was a friend of his who had risen to be an editor on one of the big morning papers—"and he's found an opening for me—a real opening which will give me an opportunity to show them all I'm still in the race."

"And you start in tomorrow?" I was dumbfounded.

"Yes, in the afternoon." His face was alive with energy. "Oh, I'll show them all, Art, that I'm still one of the best when I want to be. They've sneered at me long enough."

"Then you really are about to become a wage slave?" I simply couldn't believe it.

"Honestly, Art. Tomorrow. Do you think I'm spoofing you about it?"

"I must admit you seem to be confessing the shameless truth. Well, at any rate, you seem to be pleased, so—" here I jumped up and pumped his hand up and down—"a million congratulations, Jimmy, old scout!" Jimmy's joy was good to see. There were tears in his eyes as he thanked me. Good old Jimmy! It took him quite a while to get over his emotion. Then, as if he had suddenly remembered something, he began hurriedly fumbling through all his pockets.

"I must have lost it," he said finally, giving up the search. "I wanted to show it to you."

"What?"

"A letter I received today from Aunt Mary." Aunt Mary was the elderly relative in whose will Jimmy hoped to be remembered. "She complains of having felt very feeble for the past half year. She appears to be entirely ignorant of my present condition, thank God. Writes that I'm to come and pay her a long visit should I decide to take a trip abroad this Spring. Fancy!"

"And you've lost the letter?" I asked, trying to hide my skepticism.

"Yes—was showing it to Edwards—must have dropped on the floor—or else he—" Jimmy stopped abruptly. I think he must have sensed my amused incredulity, for he seemed very put out at something and didn't look at me. "I do hope the poor old lady isn't seriously ill," he murmured after a pause.

"What!" I laughed. "Have you the face to tell me that, when you know you've been looking forward to her timely taking off ever since I've known you?"

Jimmy's face grew red and he stammered confusedly. He

knew he'd said things which might have sounded that way when he'd been drinking. It was whiskey talking and he didn't mean it. Really he liked her a lot. He remembered she'd been very kind to him when he was a lad. Had hardly seen her since then—twenty-five years ago. No, money or no money, he wanted her to live to be a hundred.

"But you've told me she's almost ninety now! Isn't she?"

"Yes, eighty-six, I think."

"Then," I said with finality, "she's overlingered her welcome, and you're a simpleton to be wasting your crocodile tears—in advance, at that. Besides, I've never noticed her sending you any of her vast fortune. She might at least have made you a present once in a while if she cared to earn any regrets over her demise."

"I've never written her about my hard luck. I hardly ever wrote to her," Jimmy said slowly. His tones were ridiculously dismal, and he sat holding his face in his hands in the woebegone attitude of a mourner.

"Well, you should have written." A sudden thought made me smile. "What will the bunch in the back room say when they hear this? You may give them that long-promised blow-out—tomorrow," I added maliciously.

Jimmy stirred uneasily and turned on me a glance full of dim suspicion. "Why do you keep repeating that word tomorrow? You've said it now a dozen times."

"Because tomorrow is your day, Jimmy," I answered carelessly. "Doesn't your career as a sober, industrious citizen begin then?"

"Oh," he sighed with relief, "I thought—" he walked up and down in the narrow space between the beds, his hands deep in his pockets. Finally he stopped and stood beside me. There was an exultant ring to his voice. "Ah, I tell you, Art, it's great to feel like a man again, to know you're done for good and all with that mess downstairs." After a pause he went on in a coaxing, motherly tone. "Don't you think you ought to go to work and do something? I hate to see you— like this. You know what a pal I am, Art. You can listen to me. It's a shame for you to let yourself go to seed this way. Really, Art, I mean it."

"Now, Jimmy," I got up and put my hands on his shoulders. "I say it without any hard feeling, but I've had about enough of your reform movement for one night. It'll be more truly charitable of you to offer me the price of a drink—if you have it. Your day of reformation is none so remote you can't realize from experience how rotten I feel. I can hear polar bears baying at the Northern Lights."

Jimmy sighed disconsolately and dug some small change out of his pocket. "I borrowed a dollar from Edwards," he explained. "I'll pay him back out of my first salary." The self-sufficient pride he put into that word salary!

But his financial aid proved to be unnecessary. As I was about to take half of his change, there was a great trampling from the stairs outside. Our door was kicked open with a bang and Lyons, the stoker, and Paddy Mehan, the old deep-water sailor, came crowding into the room. Lyons was in the first jovial frenzy of drink but poor Paddy was already awash and rapidly sinking. They had been paid off that afternoon after a trip across on the American liner St. Paul.

"Hello, Lyons! Hello, Paddy!" Jimmy and I hailed them in pleased chorus.

"Hello, yourself!" Lyons crushed Jimmy's hand in one huge paw and patted me affectionately on the back with the other. The jar of it nearly knocked me off my feet but I managed to smile. Lyons and I were old pals. I had once made a trip as sailor on the Philadelphia when he was in her stokehold, and we had become great friends through a chance adventure together ashore in Southampton—which is another story. He stood grinning, swaying a bit in the lamp-light, a great, hard bulk of a man, dwarfing the proportions of our little room. Paddy lurched over to one of the beds and fell on it. "Thick weather! Thick weather!" he groaned to himself, and started to sing an old chanty in a thin, quavering, nasal whine.

> "A-roving, a-roving
>   Since roving's been my ru-i-in,
>   No more I'll go a-ro-o-ving with you, fair maid."

"Shut up!" roared Lyons and turned again to me. "Art, how are ye?" I dodged an attempt at another love-tap and replied that I was well but thirsty.

"Thirsty, is ut? D'ye hear that, Paddy, ye slimy Corkonian? Here's a mate complainin' av thirst and we wid a full pay day in our pockets." He pulled out a roll of bills and flaunted them before me with a splendid, spendthrift gesture.

"Oh, whiskey killed my poor old dad! Whiskey! O Johnny!" carolled Paddy dolorously.

"Listen to 'im!" Lyons reached over and shook him vigorously. "That's the throuble wid all thim lazy, deck-scrubbers the loike av 'im. They can't stand up to their dhrink loike men. Wake up, Paddy! We'll be goin' below." He hauled Paddy to his feet and held him there. Come on, Art. There's some av the boys ye know below waitin'. Ye'll have all the dhrink ye can pour down your throat, and welcome; and anything more you're wishful for ye've but to name. Come on, Jimmy, you're wan av us."

"I've got something to do before I go down. I'll join you in a few minutes," Jimmy replied, wisely evading a direct refusal.

"See that ye do, me sonny boy," warned Lyons, pushing Paddy to the door. I turned to Jimmy as I was going out. "Well, good luck till tomorrow, Jimmy, if I don't see you before then."

"Thank you, Art," he murmured huskily and shook my hand. I started down. From the bottom of the flight below I heard Lyons' rough curses and Paddy wailing lugubriously: "Old Joe is dead, and gone to hell, poor old Joe!"

"Ye'll be in hell yourself if ye fall in this black hole," Lyons cautioned, steering him to the top of the second flight as I caught up with them.

The fiesta which began with our arrival in the bar didn't break up until long after daylight the next morning. It was one of the old, lusty debauches of my sailor days—songs of the sea and yarns about ships punctuated by rounds of drinks.

The last I remember was Lyons bawling out for someone to come down to the docks and strip to him and see which was the better man. "Have a bit av fun wid 'im" was the way he put it. I believe I was Dutch-courageous enough to accept his challenge but he pushed me back in my chair with a warning to be "a good bye" or I'd get a spanking. So the party had no fatal ending.

As you can well imagine I slept like a corpse all the next day and didn't witness Jimmy's departure for his long hard climb back to respectability and the man who was. When he came home that night he appeared very elated, full of the dignity of labor, tremendously conscious of his position in life, provokingly solicitous concerning my welfare. It would have been insufferable in anyone else; but Jimmy—well, Jimmy was Jimmy, and the most lovable chap on earth. You couldn't stay mad at him more than a minute, if you had the slightest sense of humor.

Had he toiled and spun much on his first day, I asked him. No, he admitted after a moment's hesitation, he had spent the time mostly in feeling about, getting the hang of his work. Now tomorrow he'd get the typewriter fixed so he could do Sunday special stuff in his spare moments—stories of what he'd seen in South Africa and things of that kind. Wasn't that a bully idea? I agreed that it was, and retreated to the gang below who were still celebrating, leaving Jimmy with pencil poised over a blank sheet of paper determined to map out one of his stories then and there.

I didn't see him the next day or the day after. I was touring the water front with Lyons and Paddy and never returned to the room. The fourth day of his job I ran into him for a second in the hallway. He said hello in a hurried tone and brushed past me. For my part I was glad he didn't stop. I felt he'd immediately start on a heart-to-heart talk which I was in no mood to hear. Later on I remembered his manner had been strange and that he looked drawn and fagged out.

The fifth day Paddy and Lyons were both broke, but I collected my puny allowance and we sat at a table in the back room squandering it lingeringly on enormous scoops of lager and porter which were filling and lasted a long time. We were still sitting there talking when Jimmy came back from work. He looked in from the hallway, saw us and nodded, but went on upstairs without speaking.

"What's the matther wid Jimmy?" grumbled Lyons. "Can't he speak to a man?"

"He looks like he was sick," said Paddy. "Go up, Art, that's a good lad, and ask him if he won't take a bit of a drink, maybe."

"I'll go," I said, getting up, "but he won't drink anything. Jimmy's strictly temperance these days. He's more likely to give us all a sermon on our sins."

"Divil take him, then," growled Lyons, "but run and get him all the same. He looks loike he'd been drawn through a crack in the wall."

I ran quickly up the stairs and opened the door of our room. Jimmy was sitting on the side of his bed, his head in his hands. I glanced at the typewriter. The keys were still grey with a layer of long-accumulated dust. Then he hadn't had it fixed. The same old tomorrow, I thought to myself.

"Jimmy," I called to him. He jumped to his feet with a frightened start. When he saw who it was a flush of anger came over his face.

"Why don't you scare the life out of a man!" he said irritably. I was astonished. I'd never known him to flare up like this over a trifle.

"Come down and join us for a while. You don't have to drink, you know. You look done-up. What's the trouble— been working too hard?"

He winced at this last remark as if I'd shaken my fist in his face. Then he made a frantic gesture with his arms as though he were pushing me out of the room. "Go! Go back!" His voice was unnaturally shrill. "Leave me alone. I want to be alone."

"Jimmy!" I went to him in genuine alarm. "What's the matter? Anything wrong?"

He pressed my hand and tried a feeble attempt at a smile. There were dark rings under his eyes, and, somehow, in some indefinable manner, he seemed years older, a broken old man.

"No, Art, I'm all right. Don't mind me. I've a splitting headache—"

"Don't be a fool and let them work you to death." He raised his hands as if he were going to clap them over his ears to shut out my words.

"Leave me alone, Art, will you? I'm going to bed," he stammered.

"Right-o, that's the stuff. Get a good sleep and you'll be O. K." I went downstairs slowly, vaguely worried about him, wondering what the trouble could be. In the end I laid his peculiar actions to a struggle he was having with his craving for drink. Paddy and Lyons agreed with this opinion and called him a "game little swine" for sticking to his guns. And as such we toasted him in our lager and porter.

When I went up to the room to turn in he was asleep, or pretending to be, and I was careful not to disturb him. The next morning I heard him moving about, but as soon as he saw I was awake, he appeared in a nervous flurry to get away, and we didn't speak more than a few words to each other. That night he never came home at all. I went to bed early—everyone was broke and there was nothing else to do—and when I was roused out of my slumber by the sun shining on my face through the dirty window, I saw that his bed hadn't been touched. A somber presentiment of evil seemed to hover around that bed. The white spread, threadbare and full of holes, which he had tucked in with such precise neatness, had the suggestion of a shroud about it—a shroud symbolically woven for one whose life had been threadbare and full of holes.

I tried to laugh at such grim imaginings. Jimmy had stayed with Edwards or someone else from his paper. What was strange in that? This wasn't the first time he'd remained away all night, was it? If I was to give way to such worries I might just as well put on skirts and be done with it.

But my phantoms, however foolish, refused to be laid. I got dressed in a hurry, anxious to escape from this room, bright with sunlight, dark with uncanny threat. Before I went down, struck by a sentimental mood, I got some water from the sink in the hallway and poured it on his ridiculous geranium plant.

After a breakfast of free soup, I walked with Paddy and Lyons down to the Battery. We spent the afternoon there, lounging on one of the benches. It was as warm as a day in Spring and we sat blinking in the sunshine drowsily listening to each other's yarns about the sea and lazily watching the passing ships.

When the sun went down we returned to Tommy the Priest's. On the way back I remembered this was Jimmy's pay day and wondered if he would show up. He owed me some money which I hoped would be forthcoming. Otherwise the night was liable to prove an uneventful one. And a farewell bust-up was imperative because Paddy and Lyons would have to go on board ship the following day if they wanted to make the next trip.

The evening didn't pass off as dully as we had feared. Old McDonald, the printer, was in a festive mood and invited us to join him. Two of the telegraph operators, out of a job at that time, had borrowed some money somewhere and were anxious to return the many treats they had received from us in the past. So the time whiled away very pleasantly.

It was shortly after midnight when Jimmy came in. As soon as I saw his face I knew that something had happened to him, something very serious. He was incredibly haggard and pale, and there were deep lines of suffering about his mouth and eyes. His eyes—I can't describe them. There was nothing behind them. He nodded and took his place at the bar beside us. Then he spoke, asked us what we'd have, in a strained, forced voice as though it cost him a tremendous effort to talk. He took whiskey himself, poured out a glass brim full, and downed it straight. Big John changed a bill for him, and without looking at me, he held out the couple of dollars he owed me. I put them in my pocket. Jimmy motioned to Big John and called for another round. A spell of silence was on the whole barroom. Everyone there knew him well. They had all joked with him during the week about his being on the wagon, but they had secretly admired his firmness of will. Now they stared at him with genuine regret that he should have fallen. Their faces grew sad. They had done the same thing themselves so many times. They understood.

"Jimmy!" He caught the reproach in my voice and turned to me with a twisted smile. "It doesn't matter," he said. "Nothing matters." His voice became harsh. "Don't forget what you said about my lectures and start in yourself." He immediately felt sorry for having said this. "No, Art, I don't mean that. Never mind what I say. I'm upset—about something."

"Tell me what it is, Jimmy. Maybe I can help."

"Help?" He laughed hysterically. "No, no help please. After all, why shouldn't I tell you now? You're bound to find out sooner or later. They'll all know it." He indicated the others who, feeling that Jimmy wanted to be alone with me, had taken their drinks to a table in the rear and were sitting around talking in low, constrained voices. Jimmy blurted out: "My job, Art, is gone to hell!"

"What!" I pretended more astonishment than I felt. I had guessed what the trouble was.

"Yes, they asked me to quit—politely requested. Edwards was very nice about it—very kind—very charitable." He put all the bitterness of his heart into these last words.

"The rotten swine!"

"Oh no, Art, it wasn't his fault. If they hadn't—fired me—I'd have had to resign anyway. I—I couldn't do the work."

"That's all nonsense, Jimmy. Well, cheer up. All said and done, it's only a job the less. You can always get another for the asking."

He looked at me with a sort of wild scorn in his eyes. "Can't you understand any better than that? What do I care for the job itself? It isn't that. I tell you I couldn't do the work! I tried and tried. What I wrote was rot. I couldn't get any news. No initiative—no imagination—no character—no courage! All gone. Nothing left—not even cleverness. No memory even!" He stopped, breathing hard, the perspiration glistening on his forehead. "It came to me gradually—the realization. I couldn't believe it. I had been so sure of myself all these years. All I needed was a chance. It had been so easy for me in the past—long ago. These last few days I've guessed the truth. I've been going crazy. Last night I walked—walked and walked—thinking—and finally—I knew!" He paused, choking back a sob, his face twitching convulsively with the effort he made to control himself. Then he uttered a cracked sound intended for a laugh. "I'm done—burnt out—wasted! It's time to dump the garbage. Nothing here." He tapped his head with a silly gesture and laughed again. I began to be afraid he really was going mad. "No, Art, it isn't the job that's lost. I'm lost!"

"Now you're talking like a fool!" I spoke roughly, trying to shake him out of this mood.

"I won't talk any more," he said quite calmly. "Don't worry. I'm all shot to pieces—no sleep." He broke down suddenly and turned away from me. "But it's hell, Art, to realize all at once—you're dead!"

I put my arm around his shoulders. "Have a drink, Jimmy. Hey you, John, a little service!" What else was there to do? Life had jammed the clear, cruel mirror in front of his eyes and he had recognized himself—in that pitiful thing he saw. "Have a drink, Jimmy, and forget it. Take a real drink!" I urged. What else was there to do?

After we had had a couple at the bar, Jimmy filling his glass to the brim each time, I led him in back and we sat down at the table with the crowd. More drinks were immediately forthcoming, and it wasn't long before Jimmy became very drunk. He didn't say anything but his eyes glazed, his lips drooped loosely, his head wagged uncertainly from side to side. I saw he'd had enough and I hoped his tired brain had been numbed to a forgetful oblivion.

"Come on to bed, Jimmy," I shook him by the arm.

He stared at me vacantly. "Bed—yes—sleep! sleep!" he mumbled, and came with me willingly enough. I helped him up the stairs to the room and lit the lamp. He sat on the side of the bed, swaying, unlacing his shoes with difficulty. Presently he began to weep softly to himself. "It's you, Alice— cause of all this—damn you—no—didn't mean that—beg pardon," he muttered. He lifted his head and saw me sitting on the other bed. "One word advice, Art—never get married—all rotten, all of 'em—"

This was something new. "What do you know about marriage?" I asked curiously. "Nothing from experience, surely."

He winked at me with drunken cunning. "Don't I, though! Not half! Never told you that, what? Never told you what happened—Cape Town?"

"No, you never did. What was it?"

"Might s'well tell Art—best friend—tell you everything to-night—all over. Yes—married in England—English girl, pretty's picture—big blue eyes—just before war—took her South Africa with me, 'n left her in Cape Town when I went to front. I was called back to Cape Town s'denly—found her with staff officer—dirty swine! No chance for doubt—didn't expect me to turn up—saw them with my own eyes—*flagrante delictu*, you know—dirty swine of a staff officer! Good bye, Jimmy Anderson! All over! Drink! Drink! Forget!" He blubbered to himself, his face a grotesque masque of tragedy.

In a flash it came back to me how he'd always stopped in the stories of his life at the point where he'd commenced drinking. Even at his drunkest he'd always ended the history there by saying abruptly: "and then—something happened." I'd never attached much importance to it—thought he merely wanted to suggest a mysterious reason as an excuse for his tobogganing. Now, I knew. Who could doubt the truth of his statements, knowing all he had been through that day? He was in a mood for truth. So this was the something which happened! Here was real tragedy.

Real tragedy! And there he was sobbing, hiccuping, rolling his eyes stupidly, scratching with limp fingers at the tears which ran down and tickled the sides of his nose. I felt a mad desire to laugh.

"I suppose you and she were divorced?" I asked after a pause.

"No—I couldn't—no proof—no money. Besides, what'd I care about divorce? Never want to marry again—never love anyone else." He wept more violently than ever.

"But didn't she get a divorce?"

"No, she's too cute for that—thinks Aunt Mary'll leave me money—and I'll drink myself to death. No," he interrupted himself hastily, "can't be that—not s'bad s' that—not Alice— no, no, mustn't say that—not right for me to say that—don't know her reason—never can tell—about women. Damn shoes!" He gave up the attempt to get his shoes off and flung himself on the bed, fully dressed. In a minute he was dead to the world and snoring. I left him and went downstairs.

Most of the people in the back room were asleep, but Paddy and Lyons and the operators were still drinking at one table, and I sat down with them. I talked at random on every subject that came up, seeking to forget Jimmy and his woes, for a time at least. His two confessions that night had got on my nerves.

Later on I must have dozed, for I was jolted out of a half dream by a sharp cracking smash in the back yard. Everyone was awake and cursing in an instant. Big John appeared from behind the curtain, grumbling: "Dot's right! Leave bottle on the fire escape, you fellers! Dot's right! Und I have to sweep up."

We heard someone racing down the stairs and Jimmy burst into the room. His face was livid, his eyes popping out of his head. He rushed to the chair beside me and sat down, shaking, his teeth chattering as if he had a chill. I told Big John to bring him a drink.

"What's the trouble now, Jimmy?" I asked him when he'd calmed down a little. He appeared to be quite sober after his sleep.

"The geranium—" he began, his lips trembling, his eyes filling up.

"So that's what fell down just now, is it?"

"Yes, I woke up, and I remembered I'd forgotten to water it. I got up and went to get the water. The window was open. I must have stumbled over something. I put out my hand to steady myself. It was so dark I couldn't see. I knocked it out on the fire escape. Then I heard it crash in the yard." He put his hands over his face and cried heart-brokenly like a sick child whose only remaining toy has been smashed. Not drunken tears this time, but real tears which made all of us at the table blink our eyes and swear fiercely at nothing.

After a while he grew quiet again, attempted a smile, asked our pardons for having created a foolish scene. He stared at his drink standing untouched on the table in front of him; but never made any motion to take it, didn't seem to realize what it was. For fully fifteen minutes he sat and stared, as still as stone, never moving his eyes, never even seeming to breathe. Then he got up from his chair and walked slowly to the door like a man in a trance. As he was going out he turned to me and said: "I'm tired, Art. I think I'll go to sleep," and something like a wan smile trembled on his pale lips. He left the door open behind him and I heard him climbing the stairs, and the slam of our door as he closed it behind him.

A buzz of conversation broke out as if his going had lifted a weight of silence off the roomful of men. Then it happened—a swish, a sickish thud as of a heavy rock dropping into thick mud. We looked wildly at one another. We knew. We rushed into the hall and out to the yard. There it was—a motionless, dark huddle of clothes, a splintered, protruding bone or two, a widening pool of blood black against the grey flags—Jimmy!

The sky was pale with the light of dawn. Tomorrow had come.

Chronology

1888 Born October 16 at the Barrett House, West 43rd Street and Broadway, New York City, third son of Mary Ellen "Ella" Quinlan (O'Neill) and James O'Neill, and christened November 1 as Eugene Gladstone O'Neill. (Father, born 1846 in Kilkenny, Ireland, came to America with his family in 1855, experienced extreme childhood poverty, and began acting by 1866. After succeeding in Shakespearean roles, he first starred in the Charles Fechter adaptation of Alexandre Dumas' *The Count of Monte Cristo* in 1883 and purchased the lucrative rights to the Fechter dramatization in 1885. Mother, daughter of Irish immigrants, was born 1857 in New Haven, Connecticut, and soon moved with her family to Cleveland, Ohio, where her father became a successful storeowner. She attended St. Mary's Academy, convent school in Notre Dame, Indiana, studied piano, and married James O'Neill in 1877. Their first son, James "Jamie" O'Neill, Jr., was born in 1878, their second, Edmund Burke O'Neill, in 1883. Edmund died in 1885 of measles contracted from Jamie.) Mother is given morphine for pain during and after O'Neill's birth and becomes addicted.

1889–94 Travels with parents (brother is at boarding school) across United States for up to nine months a year as father tours in *Monte Cristo*. Family spends summers at "Monte Cristo" cottage at 325 Pequot Avenue, New London, Connecticut. Becomes close to his Cornish nurse, Sarah Jane Bucknell Sandy, who tells him ghost and murder stories. Father attempts to play new roles during 1890 season, but is rejected by public and soon returns to the financially successful *Monte Cristo* (will perform role about 4,000 times through 1912).

1895–99 October 1895, enrolls at St. Aloysius, boarding school taught by Sisters of Charity on campus of Academy of Mount St. Vincent, Riverdale, New York. Serves as altar boy at Sunday Mass. Reads Kipling (especially enjoys *Captains Courageous* and *The Jungle Book*), the elder Dumas, Victor Hugo, and Shakespeare. Becomes strong swimmer during summers in New London.

1900   Makes First Communion on May 25. Autumn, enters
        De La Salle Institute in New York City, taught by Chris-
        tian Brothers; lives in family's hotel apartment on West
        68th Street near Central Park West.

1901   Becomes boarding student at De La Salle Institute in fall,
        living at school on West 58th Street near Sixth Avenue.
        Does well in history, English, and religion and poorly in
        mathematics.

1902   Fall, enters Betts Academy, non-sectarian boarding school
        in Stamford, Connecticut. Takes long walks in surround-
        ing countryside, enjoys rowing, but does not participate
        in team sports.

1903–05 Summer 1903, learns that mother is morphine addict when
        she attempts to throw herself into Thames River outside
        cottage while undergoing withdrawal. Renounces reli-
        gious faith and refuses to attend Mass with father. Re-
        turns to Betts and explores theaters, restaurants, saloons,
        and brothels of New York City with brother Jamie (now
        acting with father's company). Begins drinking. Patron-
        izes Unique Book Shop in New York, owned by anarchist
        journalist Benjamin Tucker, and reads radical political
        tracts, including those of Emma Goldman, as well as
        works by Shaw, Ibsen, Nietzsche, Baudelaire, Wilde,
        Swinburne, Ernest Dowson, and Edward FitzGerald.
        Corresponds with New London friend Marion Welch
        about school life and his enjoyment of musicals (*The Rog-
        ers Brothers in Ireland*, *Pearl and Pumpkin*) and popular
        novels (including works by Thomas Dixon, Henry Har-
        land, George Barr McCutcheon, and Harold McGrath).

1906   Passes entrance examinations for Princeton University
        in spring and enters college in fall. Frequents bars and
        brothels of Trenton and explores Hell's Kitchen and Green-
        wich Village sections of New York City. Reads *Thus Spake
        Zarathustra* by Nietzsche, *The Ego and His Own* by Max
        Stirner, Tolstoy, Dostoyevsky, and Maxim Gorky.

1907   Sees Alla Nazimova in Ibsen's *Hedda Gabler* ten times.
        Suspended at end of second semester for "poor scholastic
        standing" after failing to take any final examinations.

Takes secretarial job father finds him with mail-order firm, the New York–Chicago Supply Company, for $25 a week. Lives in parents' apartment in Hotel Lucerne on Amsterdam Avenue and 79th Street. Explores saloons and brothels of Tenderloin district. Becomes friends with Greenwich Village restaurant owner Polly Holladay and her brother Louis, painters Edward Keefe and George Bellows, and theater publicist James Findlater Byth. Reads Schopenhauer.

1908   Leaves job and begins receiving $7 a week allowance from parents. Stays with friends as relationship with father becomes increasingly strained.

1909   Spends January with Keefe and Bellows on farm owned by father in Zion, New Jersey, writing sonnets while they paint (later describes poems as "bad imitations of Dante Gabriel Rossetti"). Returns to New York and becomes romantically involved with twenty-year-old Kathleen Jenkins, daughter of prosperous middle-class family. Agrees when father, who disapproves of her Episcopalian background, proposes that he accompany mining engineer Fred C. Stevens on gold prospecting trip to Honduras. Marries Kathleen Jenkins in Hoboken, New Jersey, October 2; ceremony is kept secret from both families. Reads Jack London and Joseph Conrad before leaving for San Francisco in early October. Sails with Stevens and his wife, Ann, to Amapala, Honduras, travels on muleback to Tegucigalpa, and begins prospecting along Rio Seale without success in mid-November. Dislikes Honduran food and is plagued by insect bites.

1910   Contracts malaria and spends three weeks ill with fever in Tegucigalpa before returning to New York in March. Takes job as assistant stage manager with father's company, now touring with play *The White Sister*. Son Eugene Gladstone O'Neill, Jr., born May 4; O'Neill does not see him or Kathleen. Sails from Boston on Norwegian steel barque *Charles Racine* June 4, and arrives in Buenos Aires August 4. Works at Singer sewing machine factory, Swift meat packing plant, and on docks loading ships. Lives in cheap hotels and onboard moored *Charles Racine*, and frequents brothels and rough waterfront bars.

1911   Leaves Buenos Aires March 21 as ordinary seaman on Brit-
        ish freighter *Ikala*, arriving in New York April 15. Calls
        once on Kathleen and sees his son, but does not return
        and never sees her again. Moves to waterfront saloon and
        flophouse run by James "Jimmy the Priest" Condon at 252
        Fulton Street, where he stays for $3 a month. Sails for
        Southampton, England, July 22 as ordinary seaman on
        liner *New York* and returns August 26 as able-bodied sea-
        man on liner *Philadelphia*. Visits New London, but re-
        turns by mid-September to Jimmy the Priest's saloon.
        December, Kathleen requests divorce without asking for
        alimony or child support. O'Neill arranges to substantiate
        adultery charges by being discovered in hotel room with
        prostitute. Sees all of the plays performed by Abbey Play-
        ers from Dublin during six-week New York engagement,
        including T. C. Murray's *Birthright* and J. M. Synge's
        Riders to the Sea and *The Playboy of the Western World*.

1912   Attempts suicide with overdose of sleeping drug Veronal
        at Jimmy the Priest's in early January, but is saved by
        roommate James Byth (Byth will commit suicide at flop-
        house in 1913). Joins family on western vaudeville circuit,
        where father is touring in abridged version of *Monte
        Cristo*, and plays roles of courier and jailer of the Château
        d'If. Returns to New York in March and goes to New
        London in April. Divorce from Kathleen becomes final in
        July. Joins staff of *New London Telegraph* in August, covers
        local events and writes poetry for the paper, and becomes
        friends with editor Frederick Latimer. Falls in love with
        Maibelle Scott, eighteen-year-old neighbor; both families
        disapprove of romance. Develops persistent cough in
        October, and is diagnosed as having tuberculosis in No-
        vember. Resigns newspaper job and enters Fairfield
        County State Sanatorium in Shelton, Connecticut, De-
        cember 9, but leaves after two days. December 24, enters
        Gaylord Farm, private sanatorium in Wallingford, Con-
        necticut.

1913   Has brief romance with fellow patient Catherine MacKay.
        Reads plays of Synge, Eugène Brieux, Gerhart Haupt-
        mann, and August Strindberg. June 3, leaves Gaylord
        Farm with tuberculosis arrested and returns to New Lon-
        don. Writes vaudeville sketch, *A Wife for a Life*, and four
        one-act plays, *The Web*, *Thirst*, *Recklessness*, and *Warnings*.

Moves in autumn into boarding house run by Rippin family near Monte Cristo cottage. Resumes romance with Maibelle Scott. Writes film scenarios to make money, but none are accepted.

1914   Mother overcomes morphine addiction during stay at convent. Romance with Maibelle Scott ends and O'Neill begins to see Beatrice Ashe, eighteen-year-old daughter of New London trolley-car superintendent. Completes two full-length plays, *Bread and Butter* and *Servitude*, and four one-act plays, *Fog*, *Bound East for Cardiff* (then titled *Children of the Sea*), *Abortion*, and *The Movie Man*. First book, *Thirst and Other One Act Plays*, containing *Thirst*, *The Web*, *Warnings*, *Fog*, and *Recklessness*, published by Gorham Press of Boston in August (father pays printing costs). Fall, enrolls as special student in English 47 play-writing workshop at Harvard University, taught by Professor George Pierce Baker. Lives in boarding house at 1105 Massachusetts Avenue. Learns from Baker practice of writing detailed scenario of play before working on the dialogue (will follow this procedure for remainder of career). Writes one-act play "The Dear Doctor" (later destroyed) and full-length play "Belshazzar" (later destroyed), a collaboration with classmate Colin Ford. Studies French and German on his own.

1915   Completes one-act play *The Sniper* and full-length play *The Personal Equation* for course. Spends summer in New London. Father becomes increasingly concerned about financial situation after his producers declare bankruptcy, and O'Neill is unable to study further with Baker. Goes to New York in fall and lives at the Garden Hotel, Madison Avenue and 27th Street. Drinks heavily in hotel saloon and at The Golden Swan (known to patrons as the "Hell Hole") at Sixth Avenue and 4th Street. Becomes friendly at the Hell Hole with the "Hudson Dusters," Irish-American street gang, and Terry Carlin, an anarchistic, alcoholic drifter deeply influenced by Nietzsche. Writes poetry intermittently.

1916   Sees production of Hauptmann's *The Weavers* six times. Watches six-day bicycle races at Madison Square Garden (event becomes a favorite New York pastime of O'Neill's). Goes with Carlin to Provincetown, Massachusetts, in

June. Meets summer colony of writers, including George Cram Cook, his wife, Susan Glaspell, radical journalist John Reed, Louise Bryant, Hutchins and Neith Boyce Hapgood, and Wilbur Daniel Steele, who had started amateur theater in Provincetown wharf shed the previous year. Led by Cook, group stages series of original one-act plays, including *Bound East for Cardiff* on July 28 and *Thirst* in August; O'Neill appears in both plays. Completes one-act plays *Before Breakfast* and "The G.A.N." (later destroyed), three-act *Now I Ask You*, and short story "Tomorrow." Forms friendship with medical student Saxe Commins. Begins affair with Louise Bryant. September, joins others in organizing The Provincetown Players: The Playwrights' Theatre, dedicated to the production of new American plays. Group moves to New York in fall and opens 140-seat theater, The Provincetown Playhouse, at 139 Macdougal Street in Greenwich Village. Provincetown Players stage *Bound East for Cardiff*, November 3, and *Before Breakfast*, December 1. Affair with Louise Bryant continues after she marries John Reed in November.

1917 Provincetown Players stage *Fog*, January 5, and *The Sniper*, February 16. Goes to Provincetown in March. Writes four one-act plays, *In the Zone*, *Ile*, *The Long Voyage Home*, and *The Moon of the Caribbees*, and short story "The Hairy Ape" (later destroyed). "Tomorrow" published in *Seven Arts* magazine, June, earning O'Neill $50. Louise Bryant and John Reed leave for Russia. O'Neill returns to New York in fall and becomes friends with journalist Dorothy Day. October, *The Long Voyage Home* appears in *The Smart Set*. The Washington Square Players stage *In the Zone*, October 31, and Provincetown Players stage *The Long Voyage Home*, November 2, and *Ile*, November 30. Introduced to Agnes Boulton, twenty-four-year-old writer of magazine stories and novelettes, at the Hell Hole in late autumn.

1918 Shaken by death of Louis Holladay from heroin overdose, January. Goes to Provincetown with Agnes Boulton in late winter. Ends affair with Louise Bryant after her return from Russia. Marries Agnes, April 12. Earns money from vaudeville production of *In the Zone*. Completes *Beyond the Horizon* and "Till We Meet" (later destroyed) and four one-act plays, *The Rope* (staged by Provincetown Players

April 26), *Shell Shock*, *Where the Cross Is Made*, and *The Dreamy Kid*. Broadway producer J. D. Williams options *Beyond the Horizon* for $500. Reads *Dubliners* and *A Portrait of the Artist as a Young Man* by James Joyce. Moves in autumn to house owned by Agnes in West Point Pleasant, New Jersey. Provincetown Players stage *Where the Cross Is Made*, November 22, and *The Moon of the Caribbees*, December 20, at their new location, 133 Macdougal Street.

1919   Engages Richard Madden of the American Play Company as literary agent and Harry Weinberger as his attorney; both become trusted friends. *The Moon of the Caribbees and Six Other Plays of the Sea*, published by Boni & Liveright, Inc., receives good reviews (Boni & Liveright will continue to publish his plays, generally coinciding with their first production). Begins long friendship with drama critic George Jean Nathan. Grows closer to father and spends time playing cards with him. Returns to Provincetown in late May and moves to Peaked Hill Bar on eastern side of Cape Cod, living in former Coast Guard station bought for him by father as wedding present (purchase includes furnishings of previous occupant, Mabel Dodge). Becomes enthusiastic kayaker. Completes *The Straw*, *Chris Christophersen*, and three one-act plays, "Exorcism," "Honor Among the Bradleys," and "The Trumpet" (all later destroyed). Broadway producer George C. Tyler options *Chris Christophersen*. Rents cottage in Provincetown at end of summer. Second son, Shane Rudraighe O'Neill, born October 30. Provincetown Players stage *The Dreamy Kid*, October 31, with all-black cast (one of the first productions by a white theater company to cast black actors in black roles).

1920   Goes to New York in early January for rehearsals of *Beyond the Horizon*, which begins series of matinees on February 3. Play is critically praised and runs for 144 evening performances, earning O'Neill $5,264. Father is deeply gratified by play's success, but soon has stroke and is discovered to have intestinal cancer. Production of *Chris Christophersen* is not brought to New York after performances in Atlantic City and Philadelphia. Provincetown Players stage "Exorcism" (O'Neill later recalls and destroys all copies of play, which depicts young man's suicide attempt). Returns to Provincetown in early March and completes *Gold*, longer version of *Where the Cross Is Made*. *Beyond the Horizon* receives Pulitzer Prize for drama in June. Goes to New London in late July and is at father's bedside when he slips into coma. Father dies of cancer, August 10. Jamie stops drinking and stays with mother, who proves capable of managing father's complex estate. Returns to Peaked Hill Bar, completes *"Anna Christie"* (revised version of *Chris Christophersen*), and writes *The Emperor Jones* and *Diff'rent*. *The Emperor Jones*, staged by Provincetown Players, November 1, is widely acclaimed and later moves to Broadway under commercial management, running for 204 performances. *Diff'rent*, produced by Provincetown Players, opens December 27 and runs for 100 performances in Village and on Broadway.

1921   Becomes friends with theatrical critic Kenneth Macgowan and stage designer Robert Edmond Jones. Writes draft of *The First Man* in March. Joins successful protest against New York Drama League's decision not to invite black actor Charles Gilpin, lead player in *The Emperor Jones*, to its annual awards dinner. Has teeth worked on by Saxe Commins, now practicing dentistry in Rochester, New York (O'Neill will continue to have serious dental problems for remainder of his life). *Gold* opens on Broadway June 1 and closes after 13 performances. Finishes draft of *The Fountain* in late August. Agrees to pay child support when Kathleen Jenkins, now married to George Pitt-Smith, contacts him through her lawyer. Goes to New York for rehearsals in October. Meets Eugene, Jr., who had been given name of Richard Pitt-Smith, now attending military school; O'Neill and son both enjoy visit. *"Anna Christie"* opens on Broadway November 2 and runs for 177 performances. *The Straw* opens November 10 at Greenwich Village Theatre and closes after 20 performances. Impressed by German film *The Cabinet of Dr. Caligari*. Returns to Provincetown. Writes *The Hairy Ape* in December.

1922   January, attends rehearsals in New York. Mother dies in Los Angeles after series of strokes, February 28. *The First Man* opens March 4 and closes after 27 performances. March 9, Provincetown Players staging of *The Hairy Ape* opens on same evening that mother's body arrives in New

York, accompanied by Jamie, who has suffered severe alcoholic relapse. O'Neill does not attend opening and remains at his hotel, sending family friend to meet train. *The Hairy Ape* moves to Broadway in April and runs for 120 performances. Returns to Provincetown and completes *The Fountain*. *"Anna Christie"* wins Pulitzer Prize. Visited by Eugene, Jr., and by Jamie, who is drinking heavily. Begins *Welded* in September. Buys Brook Farm, thirty-acre estate with fifteen-room house in Ridgefield, Connecticut, for $32,500, and moves there in autumn. Earns $44,000 during year.

1923   Awarded gold medal by National Institute of Arts and Letters. Successful production of *"Anna Christie"* in London helps establish European reputation. Finishes *Welded* in spring. Lives at Peaked Hill Bar for summer and begins *Marco Millions*. Jamie is committed to sanatorium in June after suffering acute alcoholic breakdown. O'Neill joins Kenneth Macgowan and Robert Edmond Jones in assuming control of Provincetown Players, who have become inactive due to financial difficulties and artistic differences (later adopt name of The Experimental Theatre, Inc., for their productions). Begins *All God's Chillun Got Wings* in September and finishes it after returning to Brook Farm in fall. Visited by Hart Crane and Malcolm Cowley in early November. Jamie dies in Paterson, New Jersey, sanatorium, November 8. O'Neill, recovering from severe drinking episode, does not attend service or burial.

1924   Begins *Desire Under the Elms* in January. Saddened by death in Greece of George Cram Cook. Rehearsals for *All God's Chillun Got Wings* begin in February amid newspaper controversy over play's depiction of interracial marriage, centering on scene in which white actress Mary Blair kisses black actor Paul Robeson's hand. O'Neill, Blair, and Robeson receive hate mail and death threats from Ku Klux Klan and others. *Welded*, produced by O'Neill, Macgowan, Jones, and Edgar Selwyn, opens March 17 and runs for 24 performances. *The Ancient Mariner*, O'Neill's dramatic arrangement of Coleridge's poem, opens April 6 at Provincetown Playhouse and closes after 33 performances. *All God's Chillun Got Wings* opens at Provincetown Playhouse May 15 and runs for 100 performances; first scene is read aloud by director James Light after city refuses to issue permits needed by child actors appearing in production. Finishes *Desire Under the Elms* in June. Resumes work on *Marco Millions* at Peaked Hill Bar in July. Revises and corrects previously published plays for *The Complete Works of Eugene O'Neill*, two-volume limited edition published by Boni & Liveright. Goes to New York in October for rehearsals. *Desire Under the Elms* opens November 11 at Greenwich Village Theatre. O'Neill is dissatisfied with stage set (which is based on his own sketches) but pleased by Walter Huston's performance (tells interviewer for 1948 profile that Huston, Charles Gilpin in *The Emperor Jones*, and Louis Wolheim in *The Hairy Ape* were the only actors in his plays who "lived up to the conceptions I had as I wrote"). Sails to Bermuda November 29 and rents cottage in Paget Parish on south shore.

1925   January, condenses *Marco Millions* from original eight-act length and begins *The Great God Brown*. *Desire Under the Elms* moves to Broadway and is threatened with prosecution for indecency by Manhattan district attorney Joab Banton until panel of citizens serving as "play-jury" clears it; production runs for 208 performances. (Play is later banned in Boston and England.) Finishes *The Great God Brown* in late March. Reads Nietzsche (*The Birth of Tragedy*, *Joyful Wisdom*) and Freud (*Beyond the Pleasure Principle*, *Group Psychology and the Analysis of the Ego*). Begins extended period of heavy drinking in April. Daughter Oona born, May 14. Goes to Nantucket in late July and writes scenarios for *Lazarus Laughed* and *Strange Interlude*. Returns to Ridgefield in October and works on *Lazarus Laughed* for remainder of year. *The Fountain*, produced by Macgowan, Jones, and O'Neill, opens at the Greenwich Village Theatre on December 10 and runs for 24 performances. Continues to drink heavily; Macgowan arranges for him to see psychoanalyst Dr. G. V. Hamilton.

1926   Participates in Hamilton's survey of marital sexual behavior and psychological attitudes (published in 1929 as *A Research in Marriage*) and undergoes six weeks of psychoanalytic treatment with him. Stops drinking (except for intense, short episodes, will abstain for remainder of life). *The Great God Brown*, produced by Macgowan, Jones, and O'Neill, opens on January 23 and runs for 278 performances. Returns to Bermuda in late February and moves to Bellevue, rented estate in Paget Parish. Works on *Lazarus Laughed* and finishes first draft in May. Reads Joyce's *Ulysses*. Buys Spithead, 200-year-old house on Little Turtle Bay, for $17,500. Begins writing *Strange Interlude* in late May. Receives D. Litt. degree from Yale University, June 23, and sees George Pierce Baker, now teaching at Yale. Visits New London before spending summer in Belgrade Lakes, Maine, where he works steadily on *Strange Interlude*. Visited by Eugene, Jr., and Barbara Boulton, Agnes's eleven-year-old daughter by earlier marriage (Barbara lives with her grandparents). Meets again actress Carlotta Monterey (born Hazel Neilson Tharsing, 1888), who had played Mildred in *The Hairy Ape* on Broadway. Interviewed by journalist Elizabeth Shepley Sergeant for profile in *The New Republic*, beginning friendship. Goes to New York in October, sees Carlotta Monterey frequently, and writes film scenarios for *The Hairy Ape* and *Desire Under the Elms* (neither of his scenarios are ever produced). Returns to Bermuda in November and moves into guest cottage at Spithead while main house is renovated. Revises *Marco Millions* for publication by Boni & Liveright in hopes of encouraging its production (appears April 1927).

1927   Finishes first draft of *Strange Interlude* in February. Visited in March by Lawrence Langner, a director of the Theatre Guild, New York producers' organization, who reads first six acts of *Strange Interlude*. April, Theatre Guild board accepts *Marco Millions* for production and options *Strange Interlude*. Revises *Lazarus Laughed* (published in November by Boni & Liveright) and *Strange Interlude* during summer before going to New York at end of August. Suffers from depression and extreme nervousness; consults doctors and is diagnosed as having prostate condition and thyroid deficiency (weighs 137 pounds at height of five feet eleven inches). Eugene, Jr., enters Yale. O'Neill goes to Bermuda in late October before returning to New York in November for rehearsals. Writes increasingly angry letters to Agnes as affair with Carlotta Monterey intensifies.

1928   *Marco Millions* opens January 9 and runs for 92 performances. *Strange Interlude* opens January 30 and runs for 426 performances (published version sells over 100,000 copies by 1931, and O'Neill eventually earns $275,000 from play). Leaves with Carlotta Monterey for Europe on February 10. Goes to London and Paris before renting villa at Guéthary in southern France, March. Keeps whereabouts secret from Agnes and most friends. Begins writing *Dynamo*, first in planned trilogy "Myths for the God-forsaken," to be completed by *Days Without End* (originally titled *Without Endings of Days*) and "It Cannot Be Mad." *Lazarus Laughed* staged by Pasadena Community Playhouse, April 9, and runs for 28 performances. Receives Pulitzer Prize for *Strange Interlude*. Becomes enraged by Agnes's demands in divorce settlement negotiations and by newspaper interview she gives, discussing separation. Finishes draft of *Dynamo* in August and sends it to Saxe Commins, who is living in Paris, to be typed. Leaves with Carlotta Monterey for China, October 5. Becomes ill with influenza during brief stay in Saigon. Arrives in Shanghai, November 9. Drinks heavily and is briefly separated from Carlotta before being hospitalized. Leaves for Manila under assumed name to avoid newspaper reporters, December 12. Resumes drinking onboard ship bound for Singapore.

1929   Carlotta leaves him in Colombo, Ceylon, January 1, but they are reunited in Port Said, Egypt, January 15. Rents villa in late January at Cap d'Ail, on French Riviera near Monte Carlo. Works on scenario for "It Cannot Be Mad." Theatre Guild production of *Dynamo* opens February 11 and receives harsh reviews; runs for 50 performances, mostly to Guild subscribers. O'Neill regrets having had play produced in his absence and makes extensive changes in text while reviewing proofs of published version. Sets trilogy aside in May and begins writing scenarios for *Mourning Becomes Electra*. Sued for $1,250,000 by Gladys Lewis, who claims that *Strange Interlude* was plagiarized from her privately published novel *The Temple of Pallas-Athenæ*, written under name of Georges Lewys. Moves in early June to Château Le Plessis in St. Antoine-du-Rocher, near Tours. Agnes is granted divorce on grounds of desertion in Reno, Nevada, July 2; settlement gives her life interest in Spithead and $6,000–$10,000 per year alimony, depending on O'Neill's income. Marries Carlotta in Paris, July 22. Finishes scenarios for *Mourning Becomes Electra* in early August. Visited by Eugene, Jr. Fall, buys

Bugatti sports car, which he enjoys driving at high speed, and Silverdene Emblem ("Blemie"), prize Dalmatian (dog becomes O'Neill's favorite of several he has owned).

1930   Completes first draft of *Mourning Becomes Electra* in late February. Visits Paris and tours France before beginning second draft at end of March. Film version of *"Anna Christie,"* directed by Clarence Brown and starring Greta Garbo in her first talking role, is popular success (earlier silent version, released in 1923, had starred Blanche Sweet). May, sees *All God's Chillun Got Wings* and *Desire Under the Elms* performed in Russian by Kamerny, experimental Soviet theater company that uses music, dance, and stylized decor in its stagings. Meets its founder, Aleksandr Tairov, and writes letter praising productions. Finishes third draft of *Mourning Becomes Electra* in September and fourth draft in October. Travels in Spain and Morocco. Returns in November and begins fifth draft.

1931   Completes fifth draft in February. Writes sixth draft at Las Palmas in the Canary Islands in March before mailing typescript to Theatre Guild from Paris, April 7. Federal district judge John W. Woolsey rules for defendants in plagiarism case and awards O'Neill $7,500 costs (is unable to collect from bankrupt plaintiff). Resolution of suit allows sale of film rights to *Strange Interlude*, from which O'Neill receives $37,500 (released in 1932, film stars Norma Shearer, Clark Gable, Frank Morgan, and Robert Young, and is directed by Robert Z. Leonard). Returns to United States with Carlotta to prepare for production of *Mourning Becomes Electra*, May 17. Artist Ralph Barton, Carlotta's third husband, commits suicide May 19, leaving note declaring love for her; O'Neills are upset by resulting publicity. Rents house in Northport, Long Island, in June. Takes pride in Eugene, Jr., who recently has won Yale prize for his scholarship in classics. Visited for two weeks in August by Shane, who is entering Lawrenceville School in New Jersey. Works on proofs for published version of *Mourning Becomes Electra* with Saxe Commins, now editor at Horace Liveright, Inc. (formerly Boni & Liveright). Takes duplex apartment at 1095 Park Avenue when rehearsals begin in early September. *Mourning Becomes Electra* opens October 26 to wide critical acclaim and runs for 150 performances. O'Neill is "overjoyed" the following day, but soon writes in work diary: "Reaction—sunk—worn out—depressed—sad that the Mannons exist no more—for me!" November, goes with Carlotta to Sea Island, Georgia, where they decide to build house. Returns to New York in December and meets Mexican artist and writer Miguel Covarrubias.

1932   January, meets Nellie Tharsing, Carlotta's mother, and Cynthia Chapman, Carlotta's fourteen-year-old daughter by her second husband. Sees Oona and Shane. Begins work in February on scenario for *Days Without End*. Sees George Jean Nathan, actress Lillian Gish, Saxe and Dorothy Commins, and James Speyer, wealthy banker and former lover of Carlotta's, who had established trust fund that pays her $14,000 a year. (O'Neill is unaware of Speyer's affair with Carlotta and believes aunt in California is source of her annuity.) Meets German playwright Gerhart Hauptmann. Goes with Carlotta to Sea Island in May, staying in cottage while house is finished. Begins writing *Days Without End*, but work is difficult and he makes little progress. Twenty-room house, costing $100,000 (including land), is finished in late June; O'Neills name it Casa Genotta (name derived from "Eugene" and "Carlotta"). Enjoys swimming and surf fishing. Becomes associate editor of new literary journal *The American Spectator*, edited by George Jean Nathan, and contributes "Memoranda on Masks," "Second Thoughts," and "A Dramatist's Notebook," essays on use of masks in contemporary theater (series appears November 1932–January 1933). Writes in "Memoranda on Masks": "One's outer life passes in a solitude haunted by the masks of others; one's inner life passes in a solitude hounded by the masks of oneself." Resumes work on *Days Without End*, but sets it aside on morning of September 1 to begin *Ah, Wilderness!* (writes in work diary: "Awoke with idea for this 'Nostalgic Comedy' & worked out tentative outline—seems fully formed & ready to write"). Completes first draft by end of September. Returns to *Days Without End* and with difficulty finishes third draft by end of year.

1933   Works on "The Life of Bessie Bowen" (formerly "It Cannot Be Mad") in January, then returns to *Days Without End* in early February and finishes fifth draft by end of March. Sale of film rights to *The Emperor Jones* for $30,000 lessens worries over continuing expenses, which include financial support for Terry Carlin and other friends. (Film, released later in year, is directed by Dudley Murphy and stars Paul Robeson and Dudley Digges.) Saxe Commins secures royalties owed O'Neill by Liveright, Inc., before firm declares bankruptcy in May. O'Neill signs with Bennett Cerf, co-founder of Random House, on condition that Cerf hire Commins as editor (Commins later becomes editor-in-chief of Random House). Contract provides for 20 percent royalty rate and $10,000 advance. Revises *Ah, Wilderness!* in June before beginning sixth draft of *Days Without End*. August, vacations at Big Wolf Lake in Adirondack Mountains. Attends rehearsals of *Ah, Wilderness!* and becomes friends with Russel Crouse, publicist for the Theatre Guild. Play opens in New York, October 2, and runs for 289 performances. Returns to Sea Island in mid-October and revises *Days Without End*. Enjoys player piano "Rosie" given him by Carlotta. Receives $37,500 for screen rights to *Ah, Wilderness!* (film, directed by Clarence Brown and starring Lionel Barrymore, Wallace Beery, and Mickey Rooney, is released in 1935; a musical version, *Summer Holiday*, is released in 1948). Goes to New York in late November for rehearsals.

1934   Theatre Guild production of *Days Without End* opens in New York January 8 and runs for 57 performances; O'Neill is angered by "very prejudiced" reviews. (Play is well received in Ireland when Abbey Theatre stages it later in the year.) Returns to Sea Island at end of January and suffers from severe nervousness and digestive troubles. Told by doctor during visit to New York in March that he must rest for six months to avoid nervous breakdown. Begins taking insulin to gain weight and buys kayak. Has several ship models made for his use in planning "The Calms of Capricorn," play set aboard clipper ship rounding Cape Horn. Goes to Big Wolf Lake in early August and stays until end of September. October, meets Irish playwright Sean O'Casey in New York. Works on notes and outlines for several plays at Sea Island during fall. Visited in December by Shane, now student at Florida Military Academy after doing poorly at Lawrenceville.

1935   January, begins planning cycle of seven plays, incorporating "The Life of Bessie Bowen" and "The Calms of

Capricorn," examining American life since the early nineteenth century through several generations of the Harford family (will eventually adopt title "A Tale of Possessors Self-Dispossessed" for cycle). Writes scenarios for first two plays, *A Touch of the Poet* (originally titled *The Hair of the Dog*) and *More Stately Mansions*, February–April. Visited by Sherwood Anderson and by Eugene, Jr., now graduate student in classics. Works on notes and outlines for scenario through summer and fall despite episodes of nervousness and depression and series of minor ailments. Begins writing draft of *A Touch of the Poet* in November. Visited by Somerset Maugham in December.

1936   Hospitalized with gastritis during visit to New York in February. Suffers from depression, extreme nervousness, and continuing stomach pains after returning to Sea Island. Leaves draft of *A Touch of the Poet* unfinished to work on other plays in cycle. Expands plan to include nine plays, beginning in late eighteenth century. Blames poor health on hot Sea Island climate. Goes to New York in October for medical treatment and is told to rest. November, moves with Carlotta to Seattle at invitation of friend Sophus Keith Winther, professor at University of Washington and author of study of O'Neill's work, who finds house they rent at 4701 West Ruffner Street, overlooking Puget Sound. Awarded Nobel Prize for Literature, November 12. Writes acceptance letter acknowledging influence of Strindberg. Moves with Carlotta to San Francisco in December. Enters Merritt Hospital in Oakland, suffering from abdominal pain and prostate trouble, on December 26, and has appendix removed December 29.

1937   Nearly dies from infection in mid-January, then begins slow recovery. Sells Casa Genotta for $75,000. Leaves hospital in early March but continues to suffer from prostate and stomach ailments. April, moves from San Francisco hotel to house at 2909 Avalon Avenue in Berkeley. Buys 160 acres of land for new home in Las Trampas Hills near Danville, California. Rents house in nearby Lafayette while Danville house is being built, June. Resumes work despite poor health. Writes draft of new first play in cycle that is longer than nine-act *Strange Interlude*, but is uncertain about cutting it. Develops painful neuritis in arm,

November. Moves to Tao House, new Danville home, at end of year.

1938 Neuritis prevents work until late March. Begins draft of *More Stately Mansions*, April. Visited by Shane, now attending ranch school in Colorado. Finishes draft in September and begins rewriting. Disturbed when he learns that Shane is returning to Lawrenceville School, but feels powerless to intervene in his education.

1939 Completes and revises second draft of *More Stately Mansions* in January. Begins rewriting *A Touch of the Poet*, now third play in cycle. Suffers from neuritis, melancholia, low blood pressure, and anxiety over eye operation Carlotta must undergo (surgery is successful). Finishes third draft of *A Touch of the Poet* in mid-May. Decides June 5 to set cycle aside and work on plays outside it. Reviews notes on June 6 and chooses two autobiographical ideas to develop. Finishes outline of first, *The Iceman Cometh*, in late June and of the second, *The Long Day's Journey* (later retitled *Long Day's Journey into Night*), in early July. Visited by Eugene, Jr., now teaching classics at Yale, in July and by Oona in August ("really a charming girl, both in looks and manner—And she has intelligence, too"). Follows outbreak of World War II; writes in diary, "Spengler was right." Finishes first draft of *The Iceman Cometh* in mid-October. Tremor in hands, present intermittently since childhood, becomes more pronounced. Completes third draft of *The Iceman Cometh* in mid-December and considers play to be essentially finished.

1940 Exhaustion prevents steady work on cycle. February, meets director John Ford and screenwriter Dudley Nichols to discuss their plans for filming S. S. *Glencairn* plays (*Bound East for Cardiff*, *The Moon of the Caribbees*, *In the Zone*, and *The Long Voyage Home*) under title *The Long Voyage Home* (O'Neill will see film, which stars John Wayne, Thomas Mitchell, and Barry Fitzgerald, in July and praise it as the best screen adaptation of his work). Begins draft of *Long Day's Journey into Night* in late March, but writes slowly due to continued poor health. Injures back at end of April. Develops "war obsession" after German invasion of France and the Low Countries, May 10, closely following news and doing no writing. Resumes work on *Long Day's Journey into Night* June 26 and finishes first draft in late September. Writes second draft before returning to cycle in late October. Decides to divide first two plays into four, creating eleven-play cycle. November, plans "By Way of Obit.", series of one-act monologue plays. Dalmatian "Blemie" dies December 17. O'Neill and Carlotta are deeply grieved; O'Neill writes "The Last Will and Testament of Silverdene Emblem O'Neill" as tribute.

1941   Ill with prostate and digestive disorders and bronchitis. Begins notes in February for non-cycle play "The Thirteenth Apostle." Works on *Long Day's Journey into Night* in March (writes that play "does most with the least—a quiet play!—and a great one, I believe"). Writes draft of *Hughie*, one-act play in "By Way of Obit." series, April. Has increasing difficulty controlling pencil as hand tremor worsens. Tremor diagnosed as Parkinson's disease; receives vitamin shots that prove ineffective and doubts that he will be able to complete cycle. Visited by Oona in July. Eugene, Jr., is deeply moved by reading *Long Day's Journey into Night* and *The Iceman Cometh* during visit in September, which pleases O'Neill. Makes notes at end of October for *A Moon for the Misbegotten*. Works on draft for remainder of year. Preoccupation with war grows after Japanese attack on Pearl Harbor, December 7. Shane joins merchant marine.

1942   Finishes first draft of *A Moon for the Misbegotten* in January. Able to work only sporadically on *A Touch of the Poet*, "The Thirteenth Apostle," and *Hughie* as tremor, prostate, and other health problems worsen. Carlotta develops serious back problem. O'Neill is intensely angered by news in April that Oona has been chosen "Debutante No. 1" at the Stork Club in New York, considering distinction frivolous and inappropriate during wartime. Eugene, Jr., leaves Yale faculty to do war work (rejected for intelligence and military service, will work in cable factory and begin drinking heavily). Sends manuscripts, typescripts, and other materials to Princeton and Yale libraries for safekeeping. Finishes revising *Hughie* in June. Suffers from effects of drugs taken to control Parkinson's (writes in diary in late July: "Tough game—take sedatives and feel a dull dope—don't take, and feel as if maggots were crawling all over inside your skin"). Finishes revision of *A Touch of the Poet* in mid-November. Refuses to see Oona when she comes to California to pursue a screen career and writes letter threatening permanent break in relations. Works on "The Last Conquest" (formerly "The Thirteenth Apostle"). Departure of servants for war work, gasoline rationing, and O'Neills' inability to drive leaves them increasingly isolated at Tao House.

1943   Begins second draft of *A Moon for the Misbegotten* in January and finishes in May, working three hours a day despite worsening tremor. Destroys notes for seven plays he no longer expects to write. Tries to begin play "Blind Alley Guy" in June but is forced to stop, no longer capable of controlling pencil and unable to compose on typewriter or dictate. Oona attempts reconciliation with O'Neill after her marriage to Charlie Chaplin on June 16, but he does not respond (will not reply to several other letters from her and never sees any of the five children she will have in his lifetime). Financial worries reduced by sale of film rights to *The Hairy Ape* for $30,000 (film, directed by Alfred Santell and starring William Bendix and Susan Heyward, is released in 1944). Shane suffers nervous collapse after extensive service in North Atlantic and is hospitalized.

1944   Sells Tao House in February and moves to Huntington Hotel in San Francisco. Burns manuscripts of two unfinished cycle plays. Carlotta dangerously ill from kidney infection. Saddened by death of friend and attorney Harry Weinberger. Hires Jane Caldwell, daughter of Carlotta's school friend Myrtle Caldwell, as typist. Revises *A Moon for the Misbegotten* and *A Touch of the Poet*. Meets with Lawrence Langner during summer to discuss production of completed plays, recommending that *The Iceman Cometh* be staged after anticipated mood of post-war optimism recedes. Tremor causes occasional shaking of entire body.

1945   O'Neill's minor flirtation with Jane Caldwell leads to exchange of bitter accusations between him and Carlotta. Moves with Carlotta to New York in October, taking suite at Hotel Barclay. Goes to jazz clubs and sporting events with George Jean Nathan and new attorney, Winfield Aronberg. Sees Eugene, Jr., now pursuing erratic teaching and radio broadcasting career in New York, and Shane, who is drinking heavily, drifting between jobs, and has twice attempted suicide. Grandson Eugene O'Neill III born to Shane and his wife, Catherine Givens, November 19 (O'Neill never sees child, who dies in crib February 10, 1946). Deposits sealed copy of *Long Day's Journey into Night* in Random House safe, November 29, with instructions that it not be published until twenty-five years after his death and never be staged (Carlotta, his literary executor, has play published and produced in 1956; it wins Pulitzer Prize).

1946   Sees Shane and Catherine before they go to Spithead to recover from death of their son. Continuing tension with Carlotta eased when they move in spring into six-room penthouse apartment at 35 East 84th Street. Sees Dudley Nichols about his screen adaptation of *Mourning Becomes Electra* (film, directed by Nichols and starring Rosalind Russell, Michael Redgrave, and Katina Paxinou, is released following year). Works on design and casting of Theatre Guild production of *The Iceman Cometh* and with Saxe Commins on published version. Attends afternoon rehearsals, beginning in early September. Play opens to mixed reviews October 9 and runs for 136 performances.

1947   Attends rehearsals for Theatre Guild staging of *A Moon for the Misbegotten*. Becomes dissatisfied with production, which the Guild decides to try out on tour. Play opens in Columbus, Ohio, February 20 and is performed in Pittsburgh, Detroit, and St. Louis, where it closes March 29. O'Neill does not press for another production and asks Guild to postpone planned staging of *A Touch of the Poet*. Settles remaining alimony claims with Agnes for $17,000. Relationship with Carlotta becomes increasingly strained during fall.

1948   Carlotta leaves after quarrel, January 18. O'Neill drinks, stumbles, and breaks left arm, January 27. Considers leaving Carlotta while in hospital (tells friends that he has learned of her true relationship with James Speyer), but they are reconciled in March. Moves with Carlotta to Boston in April, where they buy shorefront cottage on Point O'Rocks Lane in nearby Marblehead Neck. Purchase and renovation ultimately cost about $85,000 (half coming from Carlotta's savings). Shane is arrested for possession of three vials of heroin, August 10. O'Neill refuses to send $500 bail and breaks off relations (Shane spends four months in federal hospital in Lexington, Kentucky, but is not cured of his addiction). Tremor worsens in legs, making walking difficult, but lessens in hands; O'Neill expresses hope that he may begin writing again. Moves into cottage in fall.

1949   Worsening tremor in hands makes resumption of writing impossible, though O'Neill's desk remains arranged for work. Listens to large collection of jazz and blues records and occasionally visits Boston.

1950   Eugene, Jr., after years of heavy drinking and failed attempt at television career, commits suicide in Woodstock, New York, September 25.

1951   Leaves house, thinly dressed and without cane, after quarrel with Carlotta on night of February 5. Trips over rock beneath snow in garden and breaks right leg at knee. Lies outside for nearly an hour before family doctor arrives and takes him to Salem Hospital (O'Neill later tells friends that Carlotta had tauntingly refused to assist him). Carlotta, severely disoriented, is hospitalized as psychiatric patient February 6, suffering effects of bromide poisoning caused by over-medication (remains in hospital until March 29). O'Neill is visited by New York friends, including Commins, Aronberg, and Langner, who try to arrange permanent separation from Carlotta. Signs petition alleging that Carlotta is insane and incapable, March 23, and enters Doctors' Hospital in New York, March 31. Weighs less than 100 pounds and occasionally hallucinates (is diagnosed as having bromide poisoning less severe than Carlotta's). Develops pneumonia in early April, but responds to penicillin treatment. Declines offer from Saxe and Dorothy Commins to live with them in Princeton. Withdraws petition, April 23. Rejoins Carlotta in Boston on May 17, moving into Suite 401 of Shelton Hotel at 91 Bay State Road (will not leave suite, except for medical reasons, for remainder of his life). Marblehead Neck cottage is sold; O'Neill donates large archive of literary material to Yale, including typescript of *More Stately Mansions*. Visited by Russel Crouse, his only friend still on good terms with Carlotta. Reads mysteries, listens to baseball games on the radio, and takes increasing amounts of sedatives.

1952   Makes Carlotta sole literary executor of his published and unpublished writings. Destroys drafts and scenarios of unfinished cycle plays. *A Moon for the Misbegotten*, published by Random House, receives mixed reviews and sells poorly.

1953   Health deteriorates until he is confined to bed in September. Dies of pneumonia at the Shelton at 4:37 P.M., November 27. Post-mortem examination reveals rare degenerative disease of the cerebellum, possibly inherited and superficially resembling Parkinson's, as primary cause of tremor. Buried at Forest Hills Cemetery in Boston, December 2.

Note on the Texts

This volume includes the seven plays that Eugene O'Neill completed between 1932 and 1943, as well as one play he left incomplete. O'Neill's health declined during these years, and the tremor in his hands, present intermittently since childhood, worsened. Writing with a pencil, the method he had always used to compose his plays, became increasingly difficult and finally, in 1943, impossible. He tried other means— an electric typewriter and dictation both to a secretary and to a recording machine—but none proved successful. Only four of the plays in this volume were produced and published during O'Neill's lifetime. The plays are arranged according to the years O'Neill did most of the writing on them rather than the years he last revised them.

O'Neill began writing *Ah, Wilderness!* early in September 1932 and finished the first draft a month later. He had recently finished a first draft of the play that would become *Days Without End* but was not satisfied with it; and, as he explained to his friend Saxe Commins on January 3, 1933, when he sent him the manuscript of *Ah, Wilderness!* to be typed, he had laid it aside "and started writing this. It simply gushed out of me. Wrote the whole damned thing in the month of Sept." O'Neill revised *Ah, Wilderness!* in June 1933 and submitted it to the Theatre Guild for production on August 1. He attended all the rehearsals in New York from August 30 through September 23, making revisions and cuts, some of which he incorporated into the text of the book version he prepared for his new publisher, Random House (Horace Liveright, Inc., having gone bankrupt earlier in the year). O'Neill made further cuts in the play to shorten the running time after attending a tryout performance in Pittsburgh. An acting version, published by Samuel French, Inc. (ca. 1933) as *Ah, Wilderness!: A Comedy of Recollections in Three Acts*, contains the cuts and stage directions made for the staged version, including those that were not retained by O'Neill in the Random House edition. The staged play was made into three acts by combining Acts One and Two into Act One, Scenes One and Two. O'Neill decided against calling the play a comedy and asked that the Theatre Guild, in their official announcement, substitute "An American Folk Play" for the earlier subtitle. The Random House edition was published on October 2, 1933, the same day the play opened in New York. O'Neill made no revisions in later editions. The text of the first printing of the Random House edition is printed here.

O'Neill had begun writing the scenario for *Days Without End* in February 1932. In September, after finishing one draft of the play and having difficulty with the next, he set it aside to write *Ah, Wilderness!* Only after completing the fifth draft of the play on April 12, 1933, did he feel sure enough about his course to send it off to be typed. He continued work on *Days Without End* (titled at different times "Without Endings of Days," "Endings of Days," "Without End of Days," and "An End of Days"), selecting the final title on May 30, 1933, and finishing a sixth draft somewhat later. After working on the production of *Ah, Wilderness!*, he finished the seventh and last draft on November 12, 1933, shortly before the Theatre Guild began rehearsing the play in New York. O'Neill attended almost all the rehearsals and continued to make cuts and revisions. The play was tried out in Boston on December 27, and it opened in New York on January 8, 1934. He prepared the script for publication and in late December and early January corrected and revised the proofs. *Days Without End: A Modern Miracle Play* was published by Random House on January 17, 1934. O'Neill's subtitle was not printed on the title page but appeared on the original dust jacket. He took no part in the preparation of later editions; the text of the first printing of the first edition is printed here.

From January 1935 to June 1939, when he recorded in his diary that he was going to lay it "on shelf" and "forget it for awhile," O'Neill worked on what eventually was intended to be an eleven-play cycle, "A Tale of Possessors Self-Dispossessed." The total number of plays grew gradually through the years, and the overall title of the cycle and names of individual plays changed as well. His earliest plan was to have four plays in the cycle, but by the time he had finished writing the first series of scenarios for the plays, in November 1935, there were eight projected plays. Since the plays were interrelated, decisions made during the writing of one often led to revisions in other previously written plays and scenarios. O'Neill finished only one play in the cycle, *A Touch of the Poet*; another, *More Stately Mansions*, was left in a revised type-script among his papers. The drafts for other plays of the cycle were destroyed.

O'Neill began writing *A Touch of the Poet* (then placed second in the cycle and titled "The Hair of the Dog") on November 25, 1935, and completed the first draft on March 18, 1936. After expanding the cycle to nine plays, making "Hair of the Dog" the third play, he worked on the second draft from June 28 to August 21, 1936. On August 9, 1937, he changed the title of the play to *A Touch of the Poet*, which he had previously been using as a title for the cycle as a whole, and named the full cycle "Lament for Possessors Self-Dispossessed." After finishing three drafts of *More Stately Mansions*, the fourth play in the cycle, O'Neill revised *A Touch of the Poet* in January 1939, to bring Deborah, a major character in *More Stately Mansions*, more fully into this play. Working steadily, he completed two more drafts by May 19, 1939. In February 1942, as the tremor in his hands worsened and his health declined, O'Neill resumed work on *A Touch of the Poet*, now the fifth play in an eleven-play cycle, hoping, as he noted in his work diary on February 16, 1942, "to get at least one play of Cycle definitely & finally finished." He completed this last revision on November 13, 1942. The play was not produced or published in O'Neill's lifetime. The text of the first edition of *A Touch of the Poet* (New Haven: Yale University Press, 1957) is printed here.

O'Neill began writing *More Stately Mansions* (he had earlier briefly considered calling it "Oh, Sour-apple Tree") in September 1936, but the work was interrupted by illness and travel after he had completed only a draft of Act One, Scene One. He resumed work on the play in late March 1938 and on January 20, 1939, recorded in his diary that he had completed the third draft of what had become the fourth play in a nine-play cycle. In October 1940, O'Neill decided to lengthen the cycle to eleven plays by making the first two plays, which he considered to be "too complicated" and too long, into four plays. He then drew up outlines for rewriting parts of *A*

Touch of the Poet and *More Stately Mansions* in order to incorporate into them the three sisters who are important figures in the first four plays. The three sisters were brought into *A Touch of the Poet* (see Deborah's speech to Sara in Act Two), but he never included them in *More Stately Mansions*. Although O'Neill made further notes to himself about the play, and in a few instances crossed out the name "Abigail" and replaced it with "Deborah," there is no record that he ever made further revisions in the play later than January 1939. He destroyed the earlier drafts but kept the third-draft typescript which includes numerous holograph revisions in the first three acts. O'Neill also added a page on which he wrote: "Unfinished Work. This script to be destroyed in case of my death!" This typescript, however, was inadvertently given to Yale University Library with other O'Neill papers in 1951. In 1957, his widow and literary executor, Carlotta Monterey O'Neill, gave Karl Ragnar Gierow, Director of the Royal Dramatic Theatre in Stockholm, permission to translate and shorten the play for production in Sweden. The Swedish version opened in Stockholm on November 9, 1962. In 1964, Yale University Press published a shortened, restructured version of *More Stately Mansions*, edited by Donald Gallup and based on the Swedish acting script prepared by Gierow, which is less than half of the original typescript. A new edition, *More Stately Mansions: The Unexpurgated Edition*, edited by Martha Bower (New York: Oxford University Press, 1988), presents the text of the entire typescript; that edition is printed here.

In early June 1939 O'Neill, feeling "stale" after working for so long on the cycle plays, decided to write one or two plays outside the cycle. By July 3, he had completed outlines for both *The Iceman Cometh* and *Long Day's Journey into Night*. Choosing to write *The Iceman Cometh* first, he began work on the play in July and by January 3, 1940, had finished it. Saxe Commins typed the final version when he visited O'Neill at Tao House in California in January. O'Neill copyrighted the play as an unpublished work on February 12, 1940, but postponed production and publication until after the war. He was at that time living in New York and was able to attend rehearsals before the play opened on October 9, 1946, in a

Theatre Guild production. By then O'Neill's tremor was so severe that he could not mark revisions and corrections on the proofs for the published version himself, so Saxe Commins inserted them for him. O'Neill made no revisions in later editions. The text of the first edition of *The Iceman Cometh*, published by Random House on October 10, 1946, is printed in this volume.

O'Neill worked on *Long Day's Journey into Night* in March and April 1940, but after completing a first draft of Act One he was forced to stop because of illness and his "obsession with the war." In late June he resumed work on the play and wrote fairly steadily until October 16, 1940, when he noted in his diary that he had completed the second draft. In March 1941, he cut and revised the typescript, stating on March 30 that this would be the last draft. He completed work on it on April 2, 1941. Saxe Commins typed the play when he visited O'Neill at Tao House in January 1942, making four copies, one of which he took with him when he returned to New York. O'Neill did not want the play published or produced until twenty-five years after his death. On his return to New York in 1945 a formal agreement to this effect was drawn up and signed by Bennett Cerf of Random House and O'Neill; the sealed play was deposited in the vault at Random House. In 1955, two years after O'Neill's death, Carlotta Monterey O'Neill requested that Random House publish the book, but Bennett Cerf felt he had to honor the agreement he had made with O'Neill and refused. Mrs. O'Neill then gave the rights to Yale University Library and *Long Day's Journey into Night* was published by Yale University Press on February 20, 1956. A line was dropped in the first printing of the first edition (821.36–37, Kid . . . old) and not corrected until the fifth printing. This volume prints the text of the fifth printing of the first edition.

Hughie, O'Neill's only one-act play after *Where the Cross Is Made* (1918), was originally to be part of a series of eight short monologue plays under the general title "By Way of Obit." No other plays in this projected series were ever completed. O'Neill began writing the play in April 1941 and by May 19 had completed the second draft. He made his last revisions in

June 22–23, 1942. The play was not produced or published in his lifetime. This volume prints the text of the first edition of *Hughie* (New Haven: Yale University Press, 1959).

O'Neill began the outline of *A Moon for the Misbegotten*, his last completed play, in late October 1941. On January 20, 1942, he recorded in his work diary that he had finished a first draft of the play, but he then added: "had to drag myself through it since Pearl Harbor and it needs revision—wanders all over place." In January 1943 he resumed work on the play, but writing had become almost impossible for him, and on April 10, 1943, he wrote in his diary that his "only complaint is takes so long—work so slowly now, no matter how interested." According to his own notation on the holograph manuscript of Act Four, O'Neill apparently completed the second draft on May 17, 1943. A typed copy was made from this second draft with additional corrections and revisions. The play was copyrighted first as an unpublished work in 1945. O'Neill helped with the casting of the Theatre Guild production of the play and attended a few rehearsals in New York, but he did not make any revisions. The play was tried out in Columbus, Ohio, opening there on February 20, 1947, and later performed in Pittsburgh, Detroit, and St. Louis, but it never opened in New York. The play was first published by Random House on June 30, 1952. Proofs for this edition were set from a clean typed copy of the 1943 revised typescript and sent to O'Neill, but by this time he was very weak, and according to the note he prefaced to the first edition he made no revisions or corrections (see page 854 in this volume). The text of the first edition of *A Moon for the Misbegotten* (1952) is printed here.

This volume presents the texts of the editions chosen for inclusion here. It does not attempt to reproduce features of the physical layout or design of these documents, such as the typography of speech headings and stage directions. The texts are reproduced without change, except for the correction of errors in the lists of characters and typographical errors. Spelling, punctuation, and capitalization are often expressive features, and they are not altered, even when inconsistent or irregular. The following is a list of the typographical errors corrected, cited by page and line number: 72.8, automobiles;

123.3, perigrinations; 211.24, *the the*; 567.5, *hand*; 605.12, no-body?; 633.33, you; 635.11, was; 640.28, its; 702.20, That's; 710.2, asleep; 768.19, mother; 782.35, *repentently*; 822.25, Clarence; 882.23, heart; 898.3, voice.; 935.38−936.1, *him but,*; 961.14, presentment.

Notes

In the notes below, the reference numbers denote page and line of the present volume (the line count includes act and scene headings). No note is made for material included in a standard desk-reference book. Quotations from Shakespeare are keyed to *The Riverside Shakespeare*, edited by G. Blakemore Evans (Boston: Houghton Mifflin, 1974). For more detailed notes, references to other studies, and further biographical background, see: *The Unknown O'Neill*, edited by Travis Bogard (New Haven: Yale University Press, 1988); *Selected Letters of Eugene O'Neill*, edited by Travis Bogard and Jackson R. Bryer (New Haven: Yale University Press, 1988); *"Love and Admiration and Respect": The O'Neill-Commins Correspondence*, edited by Dorothy Commins (Durham: Duke University Press, 1986); *"As Ever, Gene": The Letters of Eugene O'Neill to George Jean Nathan*, edited by Nancy L. Roberts and Arthur W. Roberts (Rutherford, New Jersey: Farleigh Dickinson University Press, 1987); *"The Theatre We Worked For": The Letters of Eugene O'Neill to Kenneth Macgowan*, edited by Jackson R. Bryer, introductions by Travis Bogard (New Haven: Yale University Press, 1982); *Eugene O'Neill Work Diary 1924–1943*, preliminary edition, edited by Donald Gallup (2 vols.; New Haven: Yale University Library, 1981); Jennifer McCabe Atkinson, *Eugene O'Neill: A Descriptive Bibliography* (Pittsburgh: University of Pittsburgh Press, 1974); Travis Bogard, *Contour in Time: The Plays of Eugene O'Neill*, revised edition (New York: Oxford University Press, 1987); Arthur and Barbara Gelb, *O'Neill*, enlarged edition (New York: Harper & Row, 1973); Jordan Y. Miller, *Playwright's Progress: O'Neill and the Critics* (Chicago: Scott, Foresman and Company, 1965); Margaret Loftus Ranald, *The Eugene O'Neill Companion* (Westport, Connecticut: Greenwood Press, 1984); Louis Sheaffer, *O'Neill: Son and Playwright* (Boston: Little, Brown and Company, 1968) and *O'Neill: Son and Artist* (Boston: Little, Brown and Company, 1973).

The cast lists of the first American productions are supplied below from the opening-night playbills and do not always correspond exactly with the character lists in the texts of the plays.

Contrary to current practice, O'Neill described stage settings from the point of view of the audience rather than the actors.

AH, WILDERNESS!

First produced by The Theatre Guild, September 25, 1933, at the Nixon Theatre, Pittsburgh; opened October 2 at The Guild Theatre, New York City.

Direction: Philip Moeller	*Sid Davis:* Gene Lockhart
Design: Robert Edmond Jones	*Lily Miller:* Eda Heinemann
	David McComber: Richard Sterling
Nat Miller: George M. Cohan	*Muriel McComber:* Ruth Gilbert
Essie: Marjorie Marquis	*Wint Selby:* John Wynne
Arthur: William Post, Jr.	*Belle:* Ruth Holden
Richard: Elisha Cook, Jr.	*Norah:* Ruth Chorpenning
Mildred: Adelaide Bean	*Bartender:* Donald McClelland
Tommy: Walter Vonnegut, Jr.	*Salesman:* John Butler

2.1   GEORGE JEAN NATHAN]   Drama critic, editor, and essayist (1882–1958); long-time friend and supporter of O'Neill's.

8.27–28   "Dunno . . . Rose—velt."]   Cf. "Mighty lak' a Rose," popular song by Frank L. Stanton and Ethelbert Nevin.

14.21–22   "The days . . . trees!"]   Cf. "The day grows hot, O Babylon!" in Ferdinand Freiligrath (1810–76), "Die Revolution," translated by Ernest Jones, in *Mother Earth*, March 1910.

33.25–26   "They . . . heart."]   Cf. George Bernard Shaw, *Candida*, Act III.

40.15–16   "We'll . . . dies."]   "The Revel," by Bartholomew Dowling (1823–63).

40.38   Sandow Exerciser]   Eugene Sandow (1867–1925) was a professional strongman and propagandist for physical culture.

49.30–31   "Drink! . . . where!"]   Edward FitzGerald, *The Rubáiyát of Omar Khayyám*, Stanza 74 (1879 edition).

54.19   Sweet]   A Caporal cigarette.

58.34–35   "But . . . her."]   Cf. Rudyard Kipling, "The Ladies" (1895).

59.14–15   "For . . . smoke."]   Rudyard Kipling, "The Betrothed" (1885).

59.21–60.2   "Yet . . . Shame!"]   Richard is quoting from Oscar Wilde, *The Ballad of Reading Gaol* (1898).

60.16   Eilert Lovborg]   Character in Henrik Ibsen's *Hedda Gabler* (1890).

61.20   a Mary Ann]   A fist, in Cockney or Australian slang.

71.33   Vesta Victoria]   English comedienne and variety artist (1873–1951).

73.17–19   "Yesterday . . . for—"]   Edward FitzGerald, *The Rubáiyát of Omar Khayyám*, Stanza 74 (1879 edition).

73.30–31   "And then . . . hair!"]   Cf. Henrik Ibsen, *Hedda Gabler*, Act II.

73.37   "Fancy that, Hedda!"]   A phrase often repeated by Hedda Gabler's husband, George Tesman.

82.18–19   General Gabler's pistols]   Hedda Gabler's inheritance, one of which she uses to commit suicide.

85.4–5   "Women . . . act."]   Cf. Oscar Wilde, *The Picture of Dorian Gray*, Chapter 8: "But women never know when the curtain has fallen. They always want a sixth act, and as soon as the interest in the play is entirely over they propose to continue it."

87.22–25   "Nay, . . . summernight—"]   Oscar Wilde, "Panthea," in *Poems* (1881).

88.5–7   "And lo . . . her—"]   Algernon Charles Swinburne, "Laus Veneris," *Poems and Ballads*, first series (1866).

89.29–30   "Something . . . Hope!"]   Oscar Wilde, *The Ballad of Reading Gaol* (1898).

97.24–26   Somewhere . . . China!]   Cf. "The Long Trail" and "Mandalay."

DAYS WITHOUT END

First produced by The Theatre Guild, December 27, 1933, at the Plymouth Theatre, Boston; opened January 8, 1934, at the Henry Miller Theatre, New York City.

Direction: Philip Moeller
Design: Lee Simonson

John: Earle Larimore
Loving: Stanley Ridges
William Eliot: Richard Barbee
Father Matthew Baird: Robert Loraine

Elsa: Serena Royle
Margaret: Caroline Newcombe
Lucy Hillman: Ilka Chase
Dr. Herbert Stillwell: Frederick Forrester
Nurse: Margaret Swope

A TOUCH OF THE POET

The world premiere was March 29, 1957, by Dramaten, Kungliga Dramatiska Teatern, Stockholm, Sweden. First produced in the United States by Robert Whitehead Productions, September 6, 1958, at the Shubert Theater, New

Haven, and September 15 at the Colonial Theatre, Boston; opened October 2, 1958, at the Helen Hayes Theatre, New York City.

Direction: Harold Clurman
Design: Ben Edwards

Mickey Maloy: Tom Clancy
Jamie Cregan: Curt Conway
Sara Melody: Kim Stanley
Nora Melody: Helen Hayes

Cornelius Melody: Eric Portman
Deborah: Betty Field
Dan Roche: John Call
Paddy O'Dowd: Art Smith
Patch Riley: Farrell Pelly
Nicholas Gadsby: Luis Van Rooten

184.32–34   Salamanca . . . Talavera]   Sites of British victories over French forces in Spain during the Peninsular War (1808–14).

199.12–13   rock of Cashel]   Monumental cliff in Tipperary, Republic of Ireland.

199.34–35   "There . . . fool!"]   Cf. Lord Byron, *Childe Harold's Pilgrimage*, Canto I, Stanza 42.

203.7–13   "I have . . . them . . . "]   *Childe Harold's Pilgrimage*, Canto III, Stanza 113.

205.10–12   "But . . . fall . . . "]   *Don Juan* (1818), Canto I, Stanza 127.

224.29   daughters-in-law]   A common 19th-century variant of step-daughters.

235.20–28   "But midst . . . Solitude!"]   *Childe Harold's Pilgrimage*, Canto II, Stanza 27.

267.14   square]   Military formation in the shape of a hollow square used by infantry to repel cavalry.

MORE STATELY MANSIONS

The world premiere was September 11, 1962, by Dramaten, Kungliga Dramatiska Teatern, Stockholm, Sweden. First American production by Elliot Martin, September 12, 1967, at the Ahmanson Theatre, Los Angeles, California. The play in both productions was extensively abridged.

Direction: José Quintero
Design: Ben Edwards
Lighting: John Harvey
Costumes: Jane Greenwood

Jamie Cregan: Barry Macollum
Mickey Maloy: Vincent Dowling
Nora Melody: Helen Craig

Sara: Colleen Dewhurst
Simon Harford: Arthur Hill
Joel Harford: Lawrence Linville
Deborah: Ingrid Bergman
Nicholas Gadsby: Fred Stewart
Cato: John Marriott
Benjamin Tenard: Kermit Murdock

284.8   DEBORAH]   When O'Neill was writing *More Stately Mansions*, Mrs. Harford was called "Abigail." In *A Touch of the Poet*, he changed her name to

"Deborah," and penciled emendations in the *More Stately Mansions* typescript indicate he intended to make the change consistent throughout the "Cycle," a series of eleven projected plays of which only *A Touch of the Poet* and *More Stately Mansions* are extant.

294.11–13   (*At . . . find.*)]   Incomplete revision by O'Neill.

301.27   [. . . . .]]   A leaf of typescript is missing at this point.

304.20–34   farm . . . other]   In early drafts of *A Touch of the Poet*, several scenes were laid in the cabin and Simon appeared as a character; but in the final revision the cabin scenes were eliminated, leaving this minor inconsistency. The farm was also the setting for the first scene in the next play in the cycle, *The Calms of Capricorn*, and was to recur as a significant location throughout all the plays.

325.27   *Moniteur*]   *Le Moniteur Patriote, ou Nouvelles de France et de Brabant* (published 1789–90), falsely attributed to Jean Paul Marat.

327.33–39   I have . . . them—]   *Childe Harold's Pilgrimage*, Canto III, Stanza 113.

328.2–3   "But . . . hell."]   *Childe Harold's Pilgrimage*, Canto III, Stanza 42.

357.17   Garrison's *Liberator*]   Abolitionist journal published by William Lloyd Garrison (1805–79).

404.24–27   "This . . . fool."]   *Childe Harold's Pilgrimage*, Canto III, Stanza 48.

418.30–419.18   But . . . ingloriously.]   *Childe Harold's Pilgrimage*, Canto III, Stanzas 42–44.

422.1–18   There . . . unknown.]   *Childe Harold's Pilgrimage*, Canto IV, Stanzas 178 and 179.

422.27   "And . . . Ocean."]   *Childe Harold's Pilgrimage*, Canto IV, Stanza 184.

488.38–39   poem . . . Holmes]   Oliver Wendell Holmes' "The Chambered Nautilus" was published in 1858.

540.8   [   ]]   Word(s) missing in typescript.

THE ICEMAN COMETH

First produced by The Theatre Guild, October 9, 1946, at the Martin Beck Theatre, New York City.

Direction: Eddie Dowling
Design and Lighting: Robert Edmond Jones

Harry Hope: Dudley Digges
Ed Mosher: Morton L. Stevens
Pat McGloin: Al McGranery
Willie Oban: E. G. Marshall
Joe Mott: John Marriott
Piet Wetjoen: Frank Tweddell
Cecil Lewis: Nicholas Joy
James Cameron: Russell Collins

Hugo Kalmar: Leo Chalzel
Larry Slade: Carl Benton Reid
Rocky Pioggi: Tom Pedi
Don Parritt: Paul Crabtree
Pearl: Ruth Gilbert
Margie: Jeanne Cagney
Cora: Marcella Markham
Chuck Morello: Joe Marr
Theodore Hickman: James E. Barton
Moran: Michael Wyler
Lieb: Charles Hart

561.1   THE ICEMAN COMETH]   Cf. Matthew 25:6: "And at midnight there was a cry made, "Behold, the bridegroom cometh; go ye out to meet him." The Biblical allusion is conflated with a bawdy story in which a husband, returning home early, calls to his wife upstairs, "Has the iceman come yet?" The wife's reply: "No, but he's breathing hard." In a letter to George Jean Nathan, February 8, 1940, O'Neill wrote: "Well, I hope you like *The Iceman Cometh*. Including the title, which I love, because it characteristically expresses so much of the outer and the inner spirit of the play."

563.13   Raines-Law hotel]   The Raines Law was named for New York state senator John Raines (1840–1909).

570.38   Malatesta]   Enrico Malatesta (1850–1932), Italian anarchist.

571.17   de Island]   Blackwells Island, then a city prison site; later Welfare, now Roosevelt Island in the East River, New York City.

573.3   De Brooklyn boys]   Menacing pursuers imagined during the course of delerium tremens.

579.12   Burns]   William J. Burns International Detective Agency.

582.1–2   Heine . . . morphine]   German poet Heinrich Heine (1797–1856), "Morphia" from *Romancero*, (1851).

584.4   St. Louis Fair]   St. Louis World Exposition, St. Louis, Missouri, 1904.

585.35–36   Brattle Street]   One of the streets that runs into Harvard Square in Cambridge, Massachusetts; Longfellow's home was on Brattle Street.

588.32   Modder River]   In the Orange Free State, South Africa; crossed by British forces after their defeat of the Boers under Cronjé in November 1899.

589.19–20   Spion Kopje]   Spion Kop, hill in Natal, South Africa; site of a British defeat by the Boers in January 1900.

589.28–29   "Ship . . . Suez—"]   Rudyard Kipling, "Mandalay."

595.15   I-Won't-Worker]   Member of the radical Industrial Workers of the World (I.W.W.).

610.9   Astoria]   A residential neighborhood in the borough of Queens, New York, across the East River from Manhattan.

632.4–5   feast . . . wall!]   Cf. Daniel 5.

663.22   Poardeberg]   Paardeberg, a battlefield on the Modder River in the West Orange Free State, South Africa; scene of General Cronjé's surrender to the British in February 1900.

664.2   Magersfontein]   A battlefield in the West Orange Free State where Cronjé checked the advance of British forces in December 1899.

697.30   Bellevue]   New York City hospital.

706.32   Matteawan]   New York state hospital for the criminally insane.

LONG DAY'S JOURNEY INTO NIGHT

World premiere February 10, 1956, by Dramaten, Kungliga Dramatiska Teatern, Stockholm, Sweden. First produced in the United States by Leigh Connell, Theodore Mann, and José Quintero, October 22, 1956, at the Wilbur Theatre, Boston; opened November 7 at the Helen Hayes Theatre, New York City.

Direction: José Quintero
Lighting: Tharon Musser
Design: David Hays
Costumes: Motley

James Tyrone: Frederic March
Mary Cavan Tyrone: Florence Eldridge
James Tyrone, Jr.: Jason Robards, Jr.
Edmund Tyrone: Bradford Dillman
Cathleen: Katherine Ross

724.2   "The Moor . . . trumpet."]   *Othello*, II, i, 178.

736.15   iron man]   Silver dollar.

759.27–29   Nietzsche . . . died."]   *Thus Spake Zarathustra*, Part II, Chapter 3.

767.18–20   "How . . . child."]   *King Lear*, I, iv, 288–89.

795.27–34   "They . . . dream."]   Ernest Dowson, (1867–1900), *Vita Summa Brevis Spem Nos Vetat Incohare Longam* (1896).

796.22–23   "We . . . sleep."]   *The Tempest*, IV, i, 156–158.

796.39   *Baudelaire's prose poem*]   "Envirez-vous," *Petits Poèmes en Prose* (1869), translated by Arthur Symons.

798.18   Dowson's Cynara] Ernest Dowson, "Non Sum Qualis Eram Bonae Sub Regno Cynarae" (1891).

804.10   "A poor . . . own."] Cf. *As You Like It*, V, iv, 57–58.

809.9–11   That . . . fortune.] In 1883, James O'Neill bought the rights to Charles Fechter's dramatic adaptation (1868) of Alexandre Dumas' novel *The Count of Monte Cristo*; he starred in it for decades.

810.39–811.1   "The fault . . . underlings."] *Julius Caesar*, I, ii, 140–41.

813.28–32   "Ford . . . dark."] "Ford o' Kabul River" (1898).

815.13   Old Gaspard . . . Bells,"] Gaspard was a character in the light opera *The Bells of Corneville* (1877), also known as *The Chimes of Normandy*, by Robert Planquette, rather than *The Bells*, Leopold Lewis's adaptation of *Le Juif polonaise* by Émile Erckman and Louis-Alexandre Chatrian.

817.1–3   "Harlots . . . understand."] Cf. Baudelaire, "Épilogue," *Petits Poèmes en Prose*.

817.36–38   "If . . . still . . . "] Rudyard Kipling, "Mother o' Mine," Dedication to *The Light that Failed*.

819.22   Sweeny] A naif who would believe anything.

820.13   "Therefore . . . purse."] *Othello*, I, iii, 352.

822.25–27   "Clarence . . . torment."] *Richard III*, I, iv, 55–57.

822.30–31   "Look . . . Farewell."] Dante Gabriel Rossetti, *The House of Life*, Sonnet 97, "A Superscription" (1870).

824.10   The Mad Scene.] Cf. *Hamlet*, IV, v.

825.34   "*A Leave-taking*"] From *Poems and Ballads*, first series (1866).

HUGHIE

World premiere September 18, 1958, by Dramaten, Kungliga Dramatiska Teatern, Stockholm, Sweden. First produced in the United States by Theodore Mann and Joseph Levine in association with Katzka-Berne, December 22, 1964, at the Royale Theatre, New York City.

Direction: José Quintero	*"Erie" Smith:* Jason Robards, Jr.
Design: David Hays	*A Night Clerk (Charlie Hughes):*
Setting: Noel Taylor	Jack Dodson

837.7–8   Follies, . . . Frolics,] Musical revues: the Ziegfeld Follies and Frolics, the George White Scandals.

838.6–7   The Brooklyn Boys] See note to 573.3.

840.14   Man o' War] Famous American thoroughbred, won 20 of 21 races in 1919–20, setting five world records.

845.10 Sheik of Araby] Title of a popular song with an allusion to the romantic figure cut by Rudolph Valentino in the films *The Sheik* (1921) and *Son of the Sheik* (1926).

845.23 Legs Diamond] Alias of John T. Noland (1896–1931), gambler and racketeer.

847.24 *Arnold Rothstein*] A professional gambler and gambling-house operator, Rothstein (1883–1928) was popularly believed to have master-minded many gambling scandals, including the 1919 World Series "Black Sox" scandal.

A MOON FOR THE MISBEGOTTEN

First produced by The Theatre Guild, February 20, 1947, at The Hartman Theater, Columbus, Ohio. The play closed in out-of-town tryouts; it was not presented in New York City until May 2, 1957.

Direction: Arthur Shields
Design and Lighting: Robert Edmond Jones

Josie Hogan: Mary Welch
Phil Hogan: J. M. Kerrigan
Mike Hogan: J. Joseph O'Donnelly
James Tyrone, Jr.: James Dunn
T. Stedman Harder: Lex Lindsay

863.21 Jack Dempsey] William Harrison Dempsey (1895–1983), American heavyweight boxing champion (1919–26).

875.25–26 "Fortunate . . . nudus."] Virgil, *Eclogues* 1:46: "Happy old man! So these lands will still be yours, and large enough for you, though bare stones cover all . . . "

909.24–31 "Thou . . . ecstasy!"] John Keats (1795–1821), "Ode to a Nightingale" (1819).

917.29 The Brooklyn boys] See note to 573.3.

923.36 "sleepless . . . eyes,"] Cf. Dante Gabriel Rossetti, *The House of Life*, Sonnet 97, "A Superscription": "Sleepless with cold commemorative eyes."

933.1–3 "It . . . mad."] *Othello*, V, ii, 109–11.

939.28–29 "But . . . gray."] Ernest Dowson, "Non Sum Qualis Eram Bonae Sub Regno Cynarae" (1891).

941.29 "In my fashion,"] Ernest Dowson, "Non Sum Qualis Eram Bonae Sub Regno Cynarae."

942.35 Belasco] David Belasco (1845–1921), American theatrical producer known for his sky-lighting effects.

TOMORROW

"Tomorrow," O'Neill's only published short story, was written in 1916 as one of a projected series of tales concerning the inhabitants of "Tommy the Priest's" saloon. *The Hairy Ape* was first conceived as one of the same series. "Tomorrow" is based on an actual suicide in the saloon of Jimmy the Priest where O'Neill lived in 1911. The character of Jimmy Tomorrow in *The Iceman Cometh* was based on the same figure. "Tomorrow" was first published in *The Smart Set*, June 1917.

CATALOGING INFORMATION

O'Neill, Eugene Gladstone, 1888–1953.
  Complete plays 1932–1943.

  (The Library of America ; 42)
  Edited by Travis Bogard.
  Contents (v.3): Ah, wilderness!—Days without end—A touch
of the poet—More stately mansions—The iceman cometh—Long
day's journey into night—Hughie—A moon for the misbegotten—Appendix: Tomorrow.
  1. Theater—American—20th century. I. Title. II. Series.
PS3529.N5 1988   812'52   88–50687
ISBN 0–940450–50–X (v.3)

*This book is set in 10 point Linotron Galliard,
a face designed for photocomposition by Matthew Carter
and based on the sixteenth-century face Granjon. The paper
is acid-free Ecusta Nyalite and meets the requirements for permanence of the American National Standards Institute. The binding
material is Brillianta, a 100% woven rayon cloth made by
Van Heek-Scholco Textielfabrieken, Holland. The composition is by Haddon Craftsmen, Inc., and The
Clarinda Company. Printing and binding
by R. R. Donnelley & Sons Company.
Designed by Bruce Campbell.*